Die If You Must

JOHN HEMMING was Director of the Royal Geographical Society in London from 1975 to 1996. He has been on several surveying and environmental-research expeditions to unexplored parts of Amazonia, and has probably visited more Indian tribes than any other non-Brazilian. For this work he has been awarded the Brazilian Order of the Southern Cross and the Peruvian Order of Merit for contributions to their countries. He is the author of several books including the prize-winning *The Conquest of the Incas*.

John Hemming

DIE IF YOU MUST

Brazilian Indians in the Twentieth Century

PAN BOOKS

First published 2003 by Macmillan

This edition published 2004 by Pan Books
an imprint of Pan Macmillan Ltd
Pan Macmillan, 20 New Wharf Road, London N1 9RR
Basingstoke and Oxford
Associated companies throughout the world
www.panmacmillan.com

ISBN 0 330 49371 X

Map artwork by Raymond Turvey

Typeset by SetSystems Ltd, Saffron Walden, Essex
Printed and bound in Great Britain by
Mackays of Chatham plc, Chatham, Kent

All Pan Macmillan titles are available from
www.panmacmillan.com
or from Bookpost by telephoning 01624 677237

FOR SUKIE

'Die if you must, but never kill'

This was Colonel Rondon's instruction to his new Indian Protection Service in 1910, and it became the Service's motto. When contacting tribes, his men might fire into the air but must never shoot back at the Indians.

Acknowledgements

This book, *Die If You Must*, is the third volume of my history of Brazilian indigenous peoples since the arrival of the first Europeans. In the previous volumes, *Red Gold* (which covered the period 1500 to 1760) and *Amazon Frontier* (roughly 1760 to 1910), I acknowledged help given to my first contacts with Brazilian Indians and Indianists. These started during the Iriri River Expedition of 1961 (when Richard Mason was killed by the Panará), and continued with my own visits to many tribes in 1971–2 and as part of the team sent by the Aborigines Protection Society (part of the Anti-Slavery Society) in 1972. I was one of the founders of Survival International, with my friend Robin Hanbury-Tenison and others, in 1968, and that non-government organization continues to do excellent work for indigenous peoples' rights.

I first met Orlando Villas Boas in 1961 and have observed with admiration the achievements of him and his brothers in the Xingu. Professor Robert Baruzzi of the São Paulo Medical School has been a close friend ever since we met on an expedition with Cláudio Villas Boas in 1971, and it was he who took me and my son to meet the Panará and attend the funerary Quarup ceremony in honour of Cláudio in 1998.

I warmly thank the many people who have lent photographs, given permission for quotations, or commented on parts of this manuscript. These include Orlando Villas Boas, Sydney Possuelo, Cláudia Andujar, Betty Mindlin and Mauro Leonel, Adrian Cowell, Darrell Posey, Howard Reid, Jesco von Puttkamer's estate, and many others. Beto Ricardo and his colleagues in ISA (Instituto Socioambiental) have been particularly generous and helpful, and the Institute's publications during the past twenty years must be the finest record of indigenous peoples anywhere in the world. Fiona Watson, Survival's Brazilian campaigner who knows more about indigenous politics in that country than anyone else in Europe, has made very helpful comments on much of this book, as have Tanya Stobbs, Nicholas Blake, and other editors at Macmillan. I also thank the staff of the Museu do Índio in Rio de Janeiro, and those of other libraries that I have used in Brazil, England and other countries.

Permissions Acknowledgements

Grateful acknowledgement is given for permission to quote excerpts from the following copyright material:

William Balée, *Footprints in the Forest* (Columbia University Press, New York, 1994), reprinted by permission of the publisher.

Dennison Berwick, *Savages. The Life and Killing of the Yanomani* and article in the *Sunday Times Magazine* by permission of the author.

Kenneth Brecher editor and translator, Orlando and Cláudio Villas Boas, *Xingu: the Indians, their Myths* (Farrar, Straus and Giroux, New York, 1973) by permission of Souvenir Press Ltd.

Alan Campbell, *Getting to Know Waiwai* (Routledge, London and New York, 1995), by permission of Taylor & Francis Ltd.

Gerard Colby and Charlotte Dennett, *Thy Will be Done* (HarperCollins, New York, 1995), Gerard Colby Zilg, c/o RLR Associates Ltd., New York.

Adrian Cowell, *The Heart of the Forest* (Victor Gollancz, 1960) and *The Decade of Destruction* (Headway, Hodder & Stoughton, 1990) by permission of the author; *The Tribe that Hides from Man* (Bodley Head, 1973) by permission of The Random House Group.

John Early and John Peters, *The Xilixana Yanomami of the Amazon* (Gainesville, 2000) by permission of the University Press of Florida.

Brian Fawcett, *Exploration Fawcett* (Hutchinson, 1953) by permission of The Random House Group.

Iara Ferraz, *O Partakatêgê das Matas do Tocantins: a epopéia de um líder timbira (EdUSP, São Paulo, 1983) by permission of the Editora da Universidade de São Paulo.*

Seth Garfield, ' "The roots of a plant that today is Brazil" ', *Journal of Latin American Studies*, 1997, by permission of the Journal's editors and Cambridge University Press.

Mercio Gomes, *The Indians and Brazil* (translated by John Moon, 2000) with permission of the University of Florida Press.

Nicholas Guppy, *Wai-Wai* (John Murray, 1958) by permission of John Murray (Publishers) ltd.

Instituto Socioambiental (ISA, formerly CEDI (Centro Ecuménico da Documentação Indígena)), São Paulo, permission for quotations from Carlos A. Ricardo, ed., série *Povos Indígenas no Brasil* (3 vols., 1981–83); série *Aconteceu Especial. Povos Indígenas no Brasil* (8 vols., 1981–2000); and Ricardo Arnt, Lúcio Flávio Pinto, and Raimundo Pinto, *Panará. A volta dos 'Indios Gigantes'* (1998).

Claude Lévi-Strauss, *Tristes Tropiques* (Librairie Plon, Paris, 1955) by permission of the publisher.

Norman Lewis, *The Missionaries* (Secker & Warburg, 1988) the author, via Richard Scott Simon Ltd., c/o Sheil Land Associates Ltd., London.

David Maybury-Lewis, *The Savage and the Innocent* (Evans Brothers, 1965) by permission of the author.

Curt Nimuendajú, 'Os Gorotire', *Revista do Museu Paulista*, 1952, by permission of Museu Paulista, Universidade de São Paulo; 'Os índios Parintintin do rio Madeira' (1924) and 'Reconhecimento dos rios Içana, Ayarí e Uaupés' (1950) by permission of *Journal des Américanistes*, Paris (translations by John Hemming).

João Pacheco di Oliveira, editor, *Indigenismo e territorialização* (1998) and *A Viagem da Volta* (1999), by permission of Contra Capa Livraria, Rio de Janeiro.

David Price, *Before the Bulldozer* (1989) Seven Locks Press, Cabin John, Maryland.

Darcy Ribeiro, *Os índios e a Civilização* (Civilização Brasiliera, 1970), by permission of the Fundação Darcy Ribeiro, Rio de Janeiro.

Jan Rocha, *Murder in the Rainforest* (Latin American Bureau, London, 1999) by permission of the author.

Stephan Schwartzman, *Os Panará do Peixoto de Azevedo e Cabeceiras do Iriri* (Environmental Defense Fund, Washington, DC, 1992) and passages in Ricardo Arnt et al., *Panará. A volta dos índios gigantes* (Instituto Socioambiental, São Paulo, 1998) by permission of the author.

Greg Urban, 'Interpretations of inter-cultural contact: the Shokleng and Brazilian national society, 1914–1916', *Ethnohistory* (1985) by permission of the author.

Gustaaf Verswijver, *The Club-Fighters of the Amazon* (Uitgeverij Universa, Gent, 1992) by permission of the Universiteit Gent, Belgium.

Orlando Villas Boas, *A Marcha Para o Oeste* (Editôra Globo S/A, São Paulo, 1994) by permission of the publisher and author.

Charles Wagley, *Welcome of Tears* (Oxford University Press, New York, 1977) by permission of the publisher.

Robin M. Wright, editor, *Transformando os Deuses. Os múltiplos sentidos da conversão entre os povos indígenas no Brasil* (Editora da Unicamp, Campinas, SP, 1999) by permission of the publisher.

Contents

List of Illustrations

Section One

1. The Tiriyó gave a warm welcome to General Rondon during his frontier inspection in 1928. Upper Paru river, near Suriname.
2. A group of Xokleng captured by a professional Indian hunter. Santa Catarina, early twentieth century. Contact with the Xokleng was an early success of the Indian Protection Service.
3. Ex-President Theodore Roosevelt and Colonel Rondon in front of the Rio da Dúvida (later renamed Roosevelt), with peccary and a brocket deer, shot for the pot, at their feet.
4. Parintintin archers used powerful bows to rain arrows at Curt Nimuendajú, 1922.
5. Cooking at the Franciscans' Mundurukú mission, Cururu river, upper Tapajós.
6. First contact with the Xavante in 1946. A warrior warns Francisco Meirelles' men to keep their distance.
7. Francisco 'Chico' Mierelles with a Xavante in 1946.
8. Xikrin Kayapó women groom one another and regularly renew black genipap body-paint.
9. Orlando Villas Boas, aged thirty-one, with Kalapalo soon after reaching the Xingu in 1946.
10. Mentuktire Kayapó, the most feared warriors in the Xingu before the arrival of the Villas Boas brothers brought inter-tribal peace to the region.
11. Mentuktire Kayapó sing their thanks to Dr Roberto Baruzzi's team from the Paulista Medical School. Jarina river, Xingu.
12. Kretire was the most belligerent chief of the Mentuktire Kayapó.
13. The three Villas Boas brothers, Cláudio, Orlando and Leonardo, with the great Kalapalo chief Izarari, shortly before he died of disease in January 1947.
14. Cláudio Villas Boas with the Mentuktire Raoni, Prepori of the Kayabi and the Kayabi patriarch.

Section Two

Section Three

Section Four

the forests of Maranhão. Sydney Possuelo contacted one group in 1978.

Acknowledgements

1: Museu do Indio, Rio de Janeiro. 2: Copyright © Royal Geographical Society. 3: Copyright © American Museum of Natural History Library. 4, 6, 7, 27: author's collection. 5, 8, 10, 11, 12, 15, 16, 17, 21, 22, 23, 24, 28, 29, 30, 31, 32, 33, 34, 35, 36, 37, 38, 39, 40, 41, 42, 43, 44, 45, 46, 47, 48, 49, 51, 52, 53, 54, 55, 56, 57, 58, 59, 60, 62, 63, 70, 73, 76, 77, 78, 79, 81, 82: Copyright © John Hemming. 9, 13, 14, 18, 19, 20, 64, 65, 66: Copyright © Orlando Villas Boas. 25, 61, 83, 86: Copyright © Sydney Possuelo. 50, 75: Copyright © Cláudia Andujar. 67: Copyright © Marina Helena Brancher/ Arquivo Cimi. 68: Copyright © Sue Cunningham. 69, 80: Copyright © Beto Ricardo/ ISA. 71, 72: Copyright © Gilberto Pinto, author's collection. 74: Copyright © Edson Silva/ Arquivo Cimi. 84: Copyright © Julian Burger, Survival International. 85: Copyright © Jesco von Puttkamer, IGPA/ UCG.

Maps

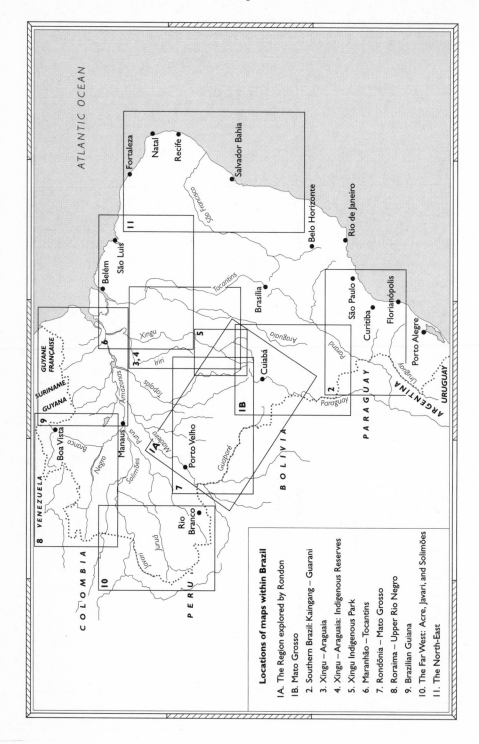

Locations of maps within Brazil

IA. The Region explored by Rondon
IB. Mato Grosso
2. Southern Brazil: Kaingang – Guarani
3. Xingu – Araguaia
4. Xingu – Araguaia: Indigenous Reserves
5. Xingu Indigenous Park
6. Maranhão – Tocantins
7. Rondônia – Mato Grosso
8. Roraima – Upper Rio Negro
9. Brazilian Guiana
10. The Far West: Acre, Javari, and Solimões
11. The North-East

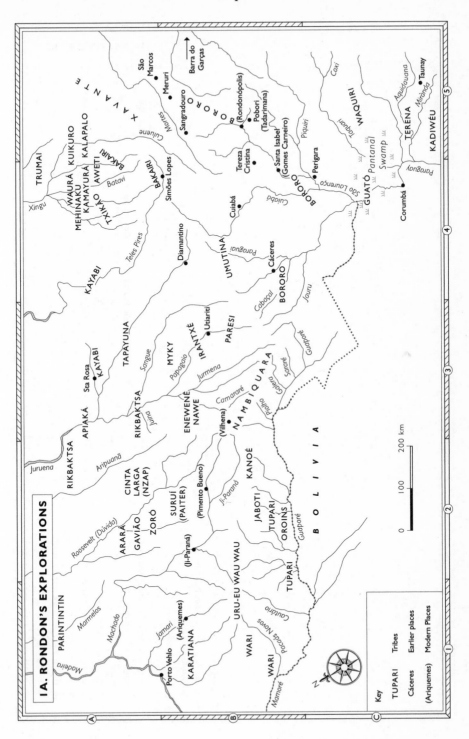

IA. RONDON'S EXPLORATIONS

Key

TUPARI   Tribes
Cáceres   Earlier places
(Ariquemes) Modern Places

0   100   200 km

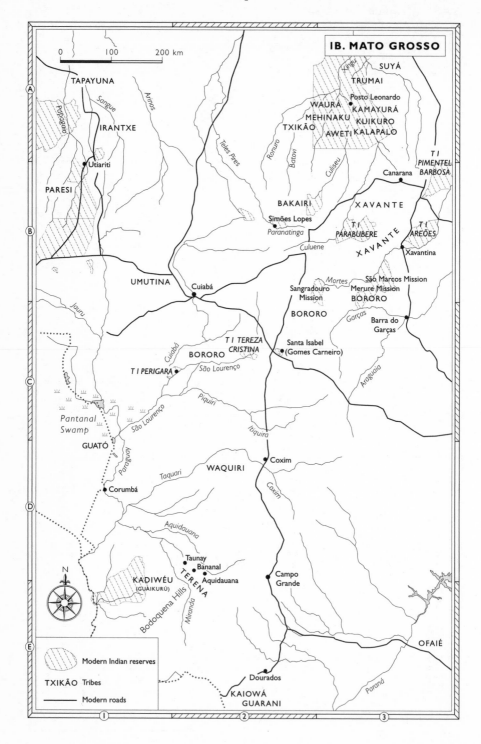

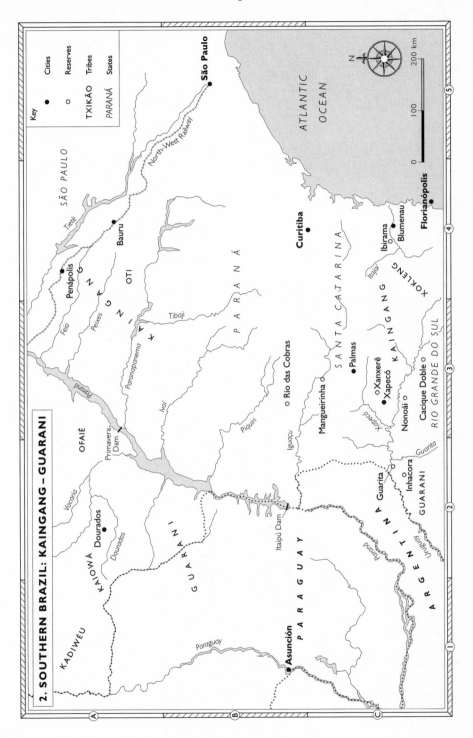

2. SOUTHERN BRAZIL: KAINGANG–GUARANI

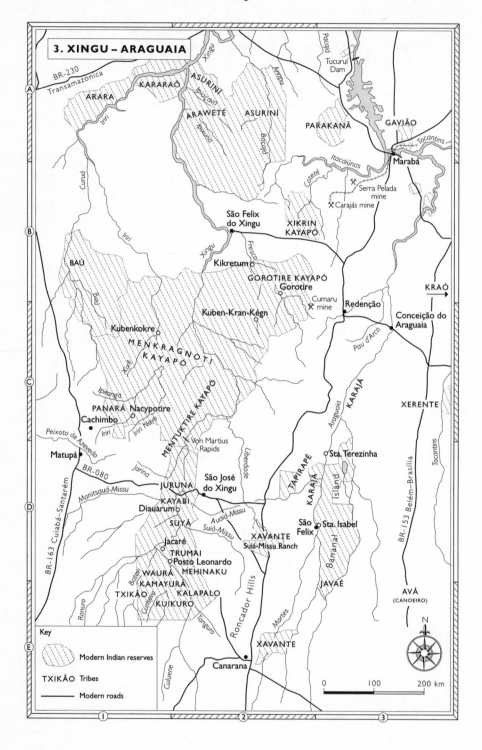

3. XINGU – ARAGUAIA

BR-230
Transamazonica

ARARA
KARARAÓ
ASURINÍ
Ipiaçava
Ipixuna
ARAWETÉ
ASURINÍ
Bacajá
Pacajá
Tucuruí Dam
PARAKANÃ
GAVIÃO
Tocantins
Itacaiúnas
Marabá
Serra Pelada mine
Carajás mine

São Felix do Xingu
XIKRIN KAYAPÓ
Kikretum
Fresco
GOROTIRE KAYAPÓ
Gorotire
Cumaru mine
Redenção
KRAÓ
Conceição do Araguaia
Kuben-Kran-Kégn
Pau d'Arco
Kubenkokre
MENKRAGNOTI KAYAPÓ
Xingu
BAÚ
Iriri
Bau
Curuá
Iriri
Ipiranga
Xé
KARAJÁ
XERENTE
PANARÁ Nacypotire
Cachimbo
Iriri Novo
Iriri
MENTUKTIRE KAYAPÓ
Von Martius Rapids
Peixoto de Azevedo
Matupá
BR-080
Jarina
Liberdade
Sta. Terezinha
São José do Xingu
JURUNA
KAYABI
Diauarumo
Manitsauá-Missu
SUYÁ
Aualá-Missu
Suiá-Missu
TAPIRAPÉ
KARAJÁ
Bananal Island
São Felix
Sta. Isabel
XAVANTE
Suiá-Missu Ranch
Jacaré
TRUMAI
Posto Leonardo
MEHINAKU
WAURÁ
KAMAYURÁ
TXIKÃO
KALAPALO
KUIKURO
Batovi
Curisevo
Ronuro
Tanguro
Roncador Hills
Mortes
JAVAÉ
AVÁ (CANOEIRO)
BR-163 Cuiabá–Santarém
Araguaia
Tocantins
BR-153 Belém–Brasilia
XAVANTE
Canarana
Culuene

Key

Modern Indian reserves

TXIKÃO   Tribes

Modern roads

0   100   200 km

N

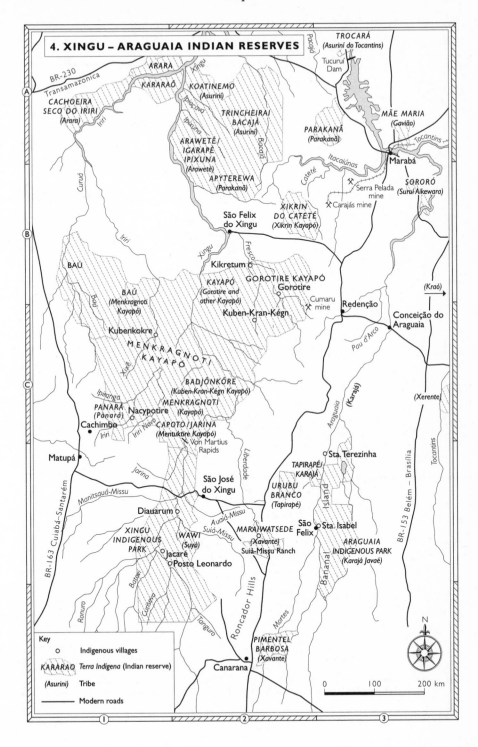

4. XINGU – ARAGUAIA INDIAN RESERVES

TROCARÁ
(Asuriní do Tocantins)

Tucuruí Dam

BR-230
Transamazonica

ARARA

KARARAÔ

Xingu

KOATINEMO
(Asuriní)

MÃE MARIA
(Gavião)

CACHOEIRA
SECO DO IRIRI
(Arara)

TRINCHEIRAI
BACAJÁ
(Asuriní)

PARAKANÃ
(Parakanã)

Marabá

Tocantins

ARAWETÉ/
IGARAPÉ
IPIXUNA
(Araweté)

Itacaiúnas

SORORÓ
(Suruí Aikewara)

APYTEREWA
(Parakanã)

Cateté

Serra Pelada
mine

Carajás mine

XIKRIN
DO CATETÉ
(Xikrin Kayapó)

São Felix
do Xingu

BAÚ

Iriri

Xingu

Kikretum

Fresco

(Kraó)

BAÚ
(Menkragnoti
Kayapó)

KAYAPÓ
(Gorotire and
other Kayapó)

GOROTIRE KAYAPÓ
Gorotire

Cumaru
mine

Redenção

Conceição do
Araguaia

Kuben-Kran-Kégn

Kubenkokre

M E N K R A G N O T I
K A Y A P Ó

Xingu

Xé

Pau d'Arco

Ipiranga

BADJÔNKÔRE
(Kuben-Kran-Kégn Kayapó)

Araguaia

(Karajá)

(Xerente)

PANARÁ
(Pànará)

Nacypotire

MENKRAGNOTI
(Kayapó)

Cachimbo

Irin Novo

Iriri

CAPOTO/JARINA
(Mentuktire Kayapó)

Von Martius
Rapids

Liberdade

Matupá

Jarina

Sta. Terezinha

TAPIRAPÉ/
KARAJÁ

BR-163 Cuiabá-Santarém

Manitsauá-Missu

São José
do Xingu

URUBU
BRANCO
(Tapirapé)

Island

BR-153 Belém – Brasília

Tocantins

Diauarum

Auaiá-Missu

Suiá-Missu

MARAIWATSEDE
(Xavante)

São
Felix

Sta. Isabel

XINGU
INDIGENOUS
PARK

WAWI
(Suyá)

Suiá-Missu Ranch

ARAGUAIA
INDIGENOUS PARK
(Karajá Javaé)

Jacaré

Posto Leonardo

Batovi

Bananal

Curuseú

Ronuro

Tanguro

Roncador Hills

Mortes

N

PIMENTEL
BARBOSA
(Xavante)

Canarana

Key

○   Indigenous villages

⬡ KARARAÔ   *Terra Indígena (Indian reserve)*

(Asuriní)   Tribe

——   Modern roads

0   100   200 km

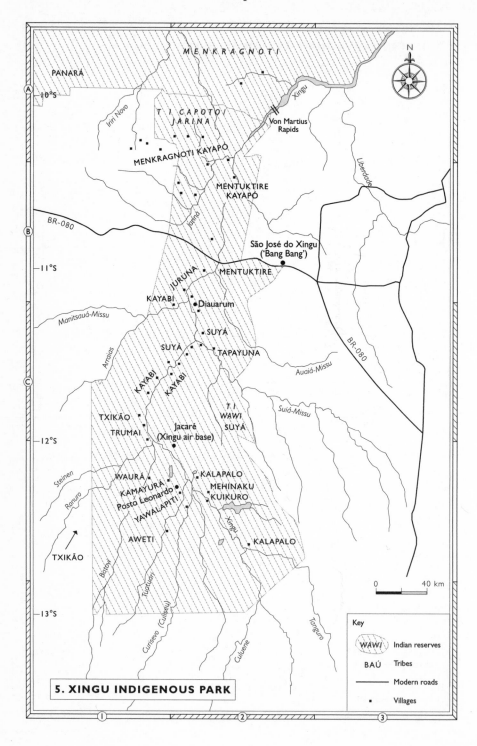

5. XINGU INDIGENOUS PARK

Key

WAWI   Indian reserves

BAÚ   Tribes

——   Modern roads

▪   Villages

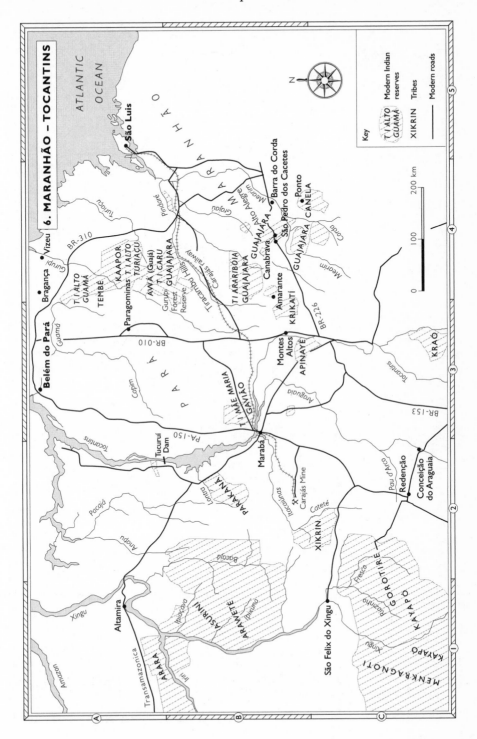

6. MARANHÃO – TOCANTINS

Key

Modern Indian reserves — T I ALTO GUAMÁ

Tribes — XIKRIN

Modern roads

0   100   200 km

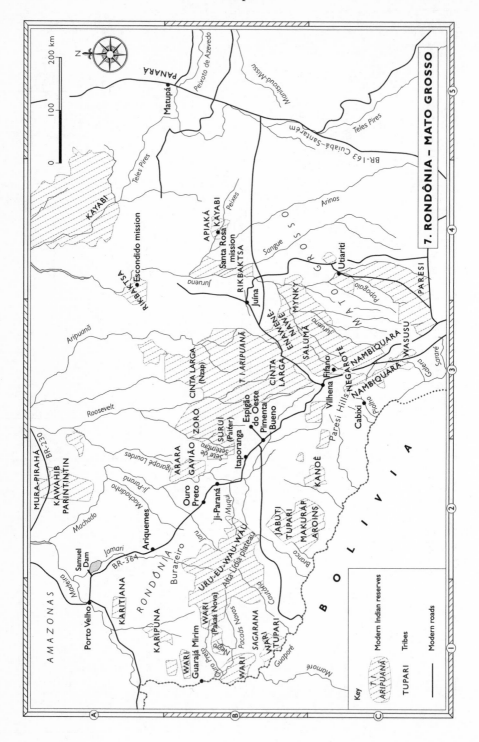

7. RONDÔNIA – MATO GROSSO

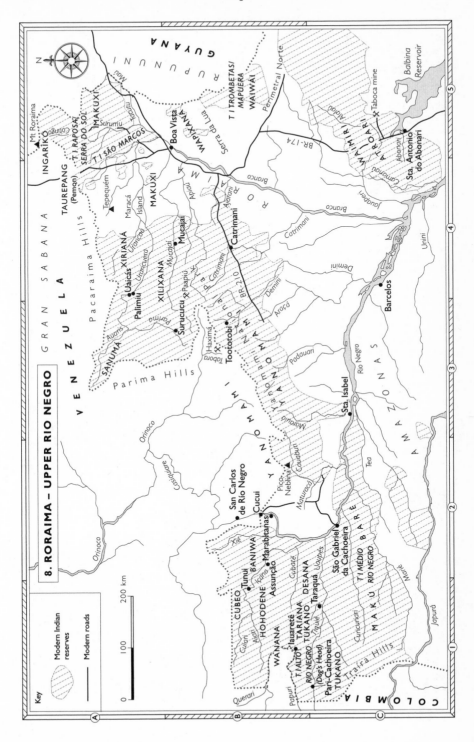

8. RORAIMA – UPPER RIO NEGRO

Key

Modern Indian
reserves

Modern roads

0   100   200 km

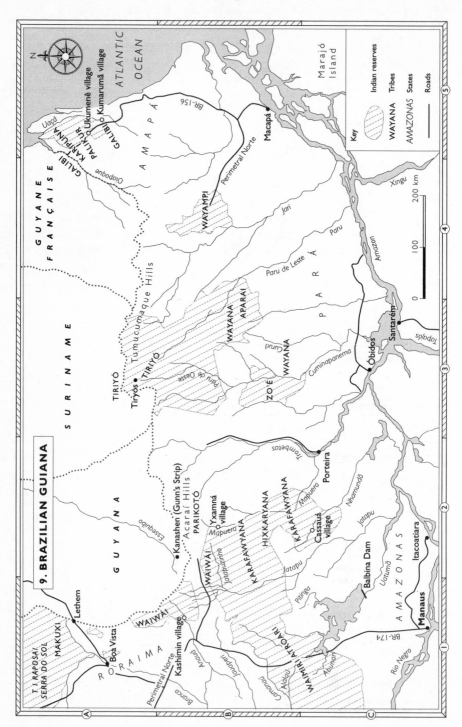

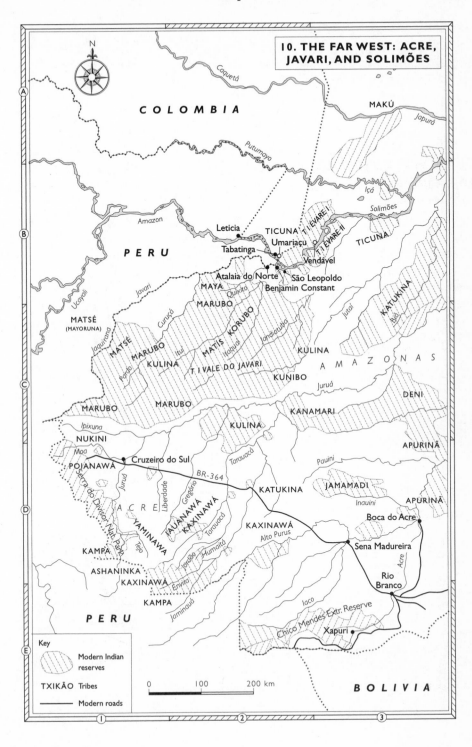

10. THE FAR WEST: ACRE, JAVARI, AND SOLIMÕES

COLOMBIA

MAKÚ

Caquetá

Japurá

Putumayo

Içá

Solimões

PERU

Amazon

Leticia

TICUNA T.I. ÉVARE I

Umariaçu   T.I. ÉVARE II

Tabatinga   TICUNA

Vendável

Atalaia do Norte

São Leopoldo

Benjamin Constant

MAYA

Javari

Quixito

MARUBO

Curuçá

KATUKINA

Jutaí

Içó

MATSÉ
(MAYORUNA)

Ucayali

Jaquirana

MATSÉ

MARUBO

Pardo

Itui

KULINA

MATIS KORUBO

Ituí

Itaquaí

Jandiatuba

T.I. VALE DO JAVARI

KULINA

AMAZONAS

KUNIBO

Juruá

DENI

MARUBO

MARUBO

KANAMARI

KULINA

Ipixuna

NUKINI

Moa

Cruzeiro do Sul

APURINÃ

Tarauacá

BR-364

KATUKINA

Pauini

JAMAMADI

APURINÃ

POIANAWÁ

Juruá

Gregório

Liberdade

TAUANAWÁ KAXINAWÁ

Tarauacá

Boca do Acre

Sierra do Divisor Nat. Park

ACRE

YAMINAWA

KAXINAWÁ

Inauini

Alto Purus

Sena Madureira

Acre

KAMPA

Tejo

Jordão

Humaitá

KAXINAWÁ

Rio
Branco

ASHANINKA

KAXINAWÁ

Envira

KAMPA

Iaco

Chico Mendes Extr. Reserve

Xapuri

PERU

Jaminaud

Key

Modern Indian
reserves

TXIKÃO   Tribes

Modern roads

0   100   200 km

BOLIVIA

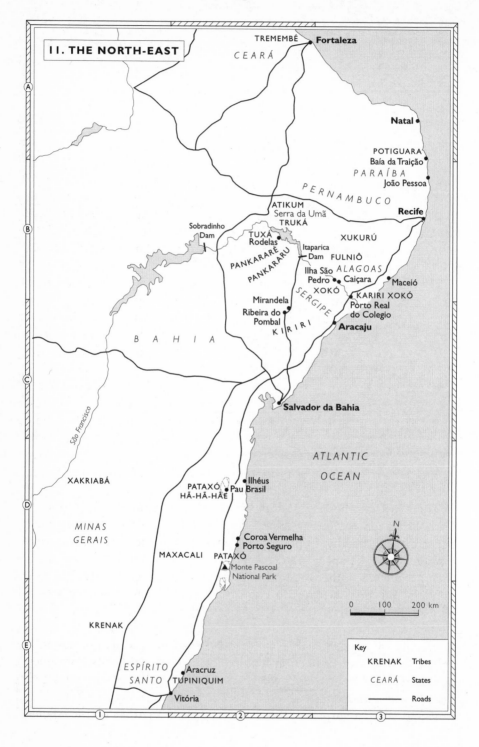

II. THE NORTH-EAST

TREMEMBÉ ● **Fortaleza**

CEARÁ

Natal ●

POTIGUARA
Baía da Traição ●
PARAÍBA
João Pessoa ●

PERNAMBUCO

Recife

ATIKUM
Serra da Umã
TRUKÁ

Sobradinho
Dam

TUXÁ
Rodelas
XUKURÚ

Itaparica
Dam   FULNIÔ

PANKARARÉ

PANKARARU

Ilha São   *ALAGOAS*
Pedro ● ● Caiçara   ● Maceió
XOKÓ
Mirandela   ● **KARIRI XOKÓ**
Porto Real
Ribeira do   do Colegio
Pombal   *SERGIPE*

B A H I A   *K I R I R I*   **Aracaju**

São Francisco

● **Salvador da Bahia**

ATLANTIC

OCEAN

XAKRIABÁ

● Ilhéus
PATAXÓ ● ● Pau Brasil
HÃ-HÃ-HÃE

MINAS
GERAIS

● Coroa Vermelha
MAXACALI   ● Porto Seguro
PATAXÓ
▲ Monte Pascoal
National Park

N

KRENAK

0   100   200 km

ESPÍRITO   ● Aracruz
SANTO   TUPINIQUIM

● Vitória

Key

KRENAK   Tribes

CEARÁ   States

———   Roads

1. Rondon

On 7 September 1910, the tribal Indians of Brazil were offered new hope. An Indian Protection Service was inaugurated, with a revolutionary philosophy governing relations between Brazil's indigenous peoples and the European immigrants who were occupying most of their land. After four centuries of conflict, brutality, exploitation, and mistrust, the Indians were to be respected and treated with kindness.

The new Service's charter defined its mission: 'to provide protection and assistance to the Indians of Brazil, guaranteeing the natives' lives, liberty and property, defending them from extermination, rescuing them from oppression and exploitation, and sheltering them from misery – whether they live settled in villages, united in tribes, or intermingled with *civilizados* [neo-Brazilians or colonists]'.

The new legislation contained many sensible clauses. It guaranteed to the Indians the effective possession of the land they inhabited, because land tenure was 'an indispensable and basic precondition for their tranquillity and future development'. Indian lands were defined as areas on which a tribe lived now or on which it had lived originally; and it was to include all territory 'necessary for their way of life . . . for hunting, fishing, extractive industries, agriculture or stock breeding.'

There was to be no attempt to convert the indigenous people to Catholicism or any other creed. The new Service was a government department staffed by disinterested laymen, from which missionaries were excluded. Protection and assistance were to be taken to the Indians in their homelands, rather than relocating them for the convenience of their minders. Far from seeking to convert Indians, the new Service was to 'ensure that the tribes' internal organization, customs and institutions are respected' – although it added slightly ominously: 'intervening to alter them only when unavoidable, and then with gentleness and persuasion'.

The new Indian Protection Service (always known by its Portuguese initials SPI) was to provide medical care for Indians. It was also to remedy 'dietary deficiencies' – even though tribal people's diets and physical fitness usually far surpassed those of neighbouring settlers on the colonial frontier. SPI officials were to protect their charges from exploitation or cheating by neo-Brazilians. They were to prosecute the latter for crimes against indigenous peoples.

The law establishing the Indian Protection Service was remarkably enlightened for its age. But there were massive potential problems. Other clauses in the legislation were more colonialist, less respectful of Indian culture and customs. This new law might read inspiringly on paper; but its enforcement in the remote and lawless backlands of Amazonia or in the labyrinth of the Brazilian legal and political systems was another matter altogether. The new Service depended on the altruism of its lay officials; and, in the event, its fifty-seven-year history was to prove decidedly chequered. However, the legislation of 1910 appeared as an inspiring new dawn for the survivors of Brazil's original inhabitants. It remained to be seen whether it would be another cruel deception, a repeat of broken promises in earlier pro-Indian laws during the four centuries since the first Europeans landed on Brazil's Atlantic shores.

The creation of the SPI was the achievement of a small group of liberal activists, inspired by a remarkable man: Cândido Mariano da Silva Rondon. This forty-five-year-old Lieutenant-Colonel of Army Engineers was invited to be the first head of the new Service, and he personally wrote much of its constitution. It is fascinating to see how Rondon had evolved into Brazil's greatest champion of the Indians. And it is equally instructive to learn how the machinations of a few Indian sympathizers achieved such favourable legislation.

Cândido Rondon was born in a modest house in Mimoso, a dusty hamlet in the heart of Brazil. The year was 1865, one of the bloodiest in Brazilian history, when the army of a megalomaniac dictator of Paraguay had invaded Mato Grosso. Rondon's father had died of smallpox just before his birth; the Paraguayans drove Rondon's mother to flee from Mimoso, and she died of the same disease in a refugee camp two years later. The boy was brought up by his grandparents, one of whom had some Indian blood. His childhood was that of a true backwoodsman, learning the language of the Bororo people as well as Portuguese and playing happily in the forests and savannahs surrounding his grandparents' ranch. At the age of seven, the boy was moved to live with a widowed uncle in the gold-mining town of Cuiabá.

Despite his humble origins, Rondon excelled at school sufficiently to gain entry to the prestigious military academy in the capital, Rio de Janeiro. Short, weakened by a childhood illness, poor, earnest, and timid, Rondon was a country bumpkin at a social disadvantage to the other more sophisticated officer cadets. But he was good at work and at games (swimming and climbing Rio's famous rocky outcrops). Above all, Rondon was disciplined and fanatically hard-working, so that he excelled in the engineering, mathematics, and sciences taught at the academy. He passed out top of his class.

Rondon graduated in 1888 to a newly created Escola Superior de Guerra (Senior War College). At both the academy and college, the cadet was deeply influenced by his mathematics teacher, Benjamin Constant Botelho de Magalhães. The charismatic Benjamin Constant was also tutor to the children of the Emperor Dom Pedro II, who had ruled Brazil benignly for most of the period since the nation's independence from Portugal in 1822. Despite his affection for the Emperor, Benjamin Constant was a passionate republican. He was also an ardent member of the new Positivist cult, a creed that enjoined its followers to be morally upright and that preached human progression towards social perfection.

Rondon acknowledged Benjamin Constant as an inspiration. In his dictated memoirs he called him 'my beloved master, who made a deep impression on everyone through his great intellectual powers, his crystalline integrity of character and the purity of his heart.' (Rondon remained a fanatical Positivist and republican throughout his long life. He even played a minor role in the revolution that created the Brazilian republic. In 1888 the much-loved old Emperor Dom Pedro abdicated in favour of his daughter Isabela, resigning so that a 'golden law' could be introduced to free Brazil's remaining slaves. On 14 November 1889, the monarchy was overthrown, bloodlessly and almost by accident. Cadet Rondon was present when his mentor Benjamin Constant persuaded the navy to join the insurrection and expel the ministers of the former government from their offices.)

It was geographical politics that in 1890 took the young Rondon back to the frontier in his native state of Mato Grosso. Brazilian defeats at the start of the war against Paraguay – in the year of Rondon's birth – had shown how precarious communications were with the outlying parts of that gigantic country. It took many weeks to get messages to Brazil's frontier regions. The answer seemed to be to build lines of telegraph wires, the only way (before the invention of wireless radio) to communicate quickly over long distances. A strategic telegraph line had been built as far as the Araguaia river, which then formed the frontier between colonized or 'civilized' Brazil and the Indian lands of the Amazon forests to the west. The telegraph now had to cut through the territory of the hostile eastern Bororo tribe, between the Araguaia and Cuiabá. This task was given to an enlightened army engineer, Major Ernesto Gomes Carneiro. He chose the twenty-five-year-old Lieutenant Cândido Rondon as his adjutant.

The Bororo were a proud nation who had been in contact with the gold-prospecting frontiersmen and ranchers of Mato Grosso for two centuries. The parts of this people that lived south and west of Cuiabá had long since come to terms with the intruders. Many of these 'plains' Bororo worked for settlers as cowhands, casual labourers, or domestic servants; and a Bororo woman was Rondon's maternal great-grandmother. This part of the tribe was disappearing, extinguished by alien diseases and social disruption, but the eastern Bororo to the north-east of Cuiabá fought back. Their warriors were magnificent men, tall, handsome, with their long hair piled on the tops of their heads amid dazzling ornaments of featherwork, and their lips adorned with mother-of-pearl labrets. As with most Indians, they were awesomely fit, consummate woodsmen, and deadly archers. Their hostility was defensive, protecting their lands from invasion and retaliating against decades of treachery and slaughter at the hands of white settlers.

The telegraph team led by Major Gomes Carneiro pushed eastwards from Cuiabá into this dangerous territory. At times its men were reopening an old trail abandoned because of Bororo attack. At other times they cut into virgin forest and dense thorny *campo cerrado*, often with Gomes Carneiro and Rondon leading the reconnaissance team. They rode their mules hard, from morning until late afternoon, and kept the animals haltered at night for quick escape. The young Rondon worshipped his commander, who taught him much about natural history as well as respect for the indigenous peoples whose land they were invading. Gomes Carneiro fixed notices to his telegraph poles, forbidding anyone to try to kill or evict the Bororo. He declared that 'no one should ever shoot *at* Indians, even to frighten them'. This was a revolutionary concept for its day, and it made a profound influence on Rondon.

It was a tough expedition, hacking through dense vegetation, often short of food and sometimes of water, or drenched by tropical rains and electric storms. As it approached the Araguaia, there were increasing signs of Indian presence – twigs broken in an unnatural way, remains of branch-covered hunting shelters and campfires. The surveyors' camp was guarded by sentries and dogs. One night Major Gomes Carneiro woke Lieutenant Rondon and whispered to him.

'Cândido, are you listening?' The forest was becoming animated. At some distance around our campsite apes yelled and howler-monkeys roared, *prego* macaques were whistling, *jáos* [large game birds] and partridges were chirping . . . It was as if all the wildlife around us was conversing. 'I can hear the chirps of partridges – but they do not chirp at night like jáos. Apart from that, it is unnatural for all this animal life to decide to converse at this hour of the night.' 'What do you think, then?' 'That these are Indians communicating with one another at a distance.' Gomes Carneiro got up. 'I am determined never to fight Indians. Besides being unjust, it would prejudice the results of our expedition. We therefore have only one option: to strike camp and leave. In this way we can give the Bororo a victory. For they are planning to avenge on us the armed attacks of which they have been victims.'

So the explorers extinguished their fires and moved off in darkness before the Indians could launch a dawn attack.

Years later, Rondon paid tribute to Gomes Carneiro. He called him the master of the *sertão* – the wilderness, backlands, or bush that are ever present in Brazilian frontier history. 'There you taught me to be a soldier . . . It was with you that I learned to love Indians, partly by pondering the orders you enforced to defend and protect them, along that telegraph line through Bororo country, but also by your thrilling example of yielding in the face of the warnings that Indians nobly gave invaders of their lands, before teaching them violently that their presence was unwelcome.'

Gomes Carneiro was transferred to other duties in 1892, and died heroically quelling a rebellion in southern Brazil. But Rondon continued rebuilding and improving the Cuiabá–Araguaia telegraph line during most of the next eight years. He became a seasoned woodsman. Conditions were very hard, with long periods when supply lines failed and the men were literally barefoot, reduced to eating snakes and monkeys or even black vultures. Rondon was a good hunter who often bagged forest game birds – partridge-like *jacu* or big black *mutum* (curassow, or wild turkey). Such shooting is for the pot, not for sport: you stalk the birds and try to hit them as they peck amid the dead leaves of the forest floor – once they fly into the canopy, they are gone. But the main staples were palm-hearts and perfumed wild honey. As Rondon knew: 'The forest I learned to love would never let us die of starvation.'

There were successive desertions and mutinies among soldiers forced to camp for months on end in the sunless gloom and rotting damp of the rainforests, racked by malaria and seriously undernourished. Rondon was ruthless in crushing unrest. Some drunken mutineers were ceremonially flogged; another ringleader was tied to a flagpole for a week, howling.

Rondon had to face a military inquiry in Rio de Janeiro for such draconian punishments.

The next phase of telegraph-line construction was south from Cuiabá to frontier forts on the Paraguay river. Rondon was in command and work started in 1900. This was through very difficult country, skirting the world's largest swampy wetland, called the Pantanal. The Bororo in this southern part of Mato Grosso were at peace with the whites. Because Rondon had learned (or revived) his spoken Bororo, and because he knew how to treat the tribe with courtesy, the Indians willingly helped the telegraph-cutting expedition. A Bororo chief assigned teams of men to work with the Brazilian soldiers, in return only for food for them and their families. These Indian volunteers cheerfully adapted to the military routine, provided that they were led by their own chiefs and by the 'big chief' Rondon. The Bororo worked with Rondon's team for a year. Relations between the two races were harmonious, even though many Bororo were killed in a measles epidemic that struck the village of Coxim. When a telegraph substation was inaugurated at Itiquira, in April 1901, the tribe organized a formidable *bacororo* festival, with its warriors decked in jaguar-skin regalia. The expedition pushed southwards throughout the next two years. The Indians often helped. A canoe capsized crossing the Piquiri river and Bororo divers 'promptly went into action and succeeded in recovering rolls of wire, cases of insulators and brackets, and sacks of provisions from the bottom of the river'. Indians gave invaluable help in carrying supplies across the marshy headwaters of another river. 'They alone could have . . . transported such heavy material across an immense swamp, partly because they alone knew it intimately.' It was often necessary to explore ahead, to discover the best route for the line. On one such exploration, two Bororo and a Guaikurú Indian guided Rondon through difficult forest and *cerrado* or *campo cerrado*, natural savannah with patches of thorny bush, gnarled trees, or stands of buriti palms. The Indians kept the party fed by hunting jaguar and peccary (akin to wild boars).

In January 1904, after four years' labour, the telegraph line reached Corumbá on the Paraguay river and was formally opened. It was the product of some of the toughest exploration of its era. Among Rondon's group of forest veterans were two brilliant brothers called Horta Barbosa – both top cadets from the Military Academy, as Rondon himself had been. Shortly before the inaugural ceremony at Corumbá, one of these brothers, Francisco, was exploring a flooded part of the Pantanal. His drenched men were having difficulty finding dry land on which to camp and Lieutenant Horta Barbosa offered to swim to investigate a possible site. But halfway across, blood from his wounded mule attracted piranhas and the young officer was killed in their frenzied attack: when his skeleton was found, 'all but his feet inside his boots had been devoured by the piranhas'. On another exploration, Rondon and the other brother, Officer-Cadet Nicolau Horta Barbosa, made contact with the reclusive Wachiri tribe.

All these tribes had had little contact with Brazilians. The eastern Bororo were still hostile or justifiably wary of so-called civilizados; and the southern Bororo who helped Rondon build the telegraph line south from Cuiabá were still proudly independent, magnificent warriors who worked out of friendship and disdained monetary reward.

Rondon then met a fully acculturated people. The Terena of the Aquidauana river, near the terminus of the southern telegraph line, had been coexisting with the colonial frontier for at least 150 years. Rondon was appalled to see the problems of this tribe, who had always coopera-ted with the settlers. The Terena (and the related Kinikinao and Guaná) were a docile, industrious and prolific people. A provincial President described them as 'Indians of excellent disposition who now provide various services for society. They work as labourers on farms or cattle ranches, and they paddle canoes that navigate between ports of the lower Paraguay river and [Cuiabá].' Another President thought that future generations of Terena 'will be even more useful, and it will not be long before they melt into the mass of our population'. This Aruak-speaking tribe had extensive plantations of corn, manioc, celery, sugar cane, cot-ton, and tobacco. Its fine cotton blankets and hammocks were in demand in frontier society, and its belts, saddles, and fish sold as far away as Cuiabá. But the amiable Terena shocked one French traveller by the behaviour of their beautiful and pale-skinned women. These 'are totally unbridled – the more so because their husbands are devoid of jealousy and offer them to strangers with the greatest facility in return for some money or pieces of cloth.'

The Terena had been victims of the bloody war between Brazil and Paraguay in the 1860s. Both armies pressed these compliant Indians into service or stole their food; many died of the measles and smallpox epidemics that had also killed Rondon's parents; and a wave of frontier settlement in the war's aftermath invaded Terena lands. When Rondon met them forty years later, they were converted to Christianity by missionaries, wore clothing, and no longer used bows and arrows. 'Besides being excellent cowhands, they were farmers and therefore sedentary. Often procured by *fazendeiros* [ranchers], they were content with little remuneration and were generally exploited.' Slavery of Indians had long been outlawed in Brazil; but it continued unabated, as debt-bondage. 'It was rare to meet a Terena who did not owe the hair on his head to a fazendeiro. His work was not paid what it was worth; and he was wretchedly robbed in purchases from his boss. This was a new form of slavery. No casual labourer could leave one employer without his new one becoming responsible for his debts. And if he was brave enough to flee, he ran the greatest risk of being persecuted and even killed. For in the towns and settlements the police were always controlled by the landowners.'

Rondon was disgusted by what he saw. At the big Ipegue *fazenda*, he persuaded twenty Terena to return to their chief and village to 'resume their ancient way of life'. The nearby Guarani, 'hard-working and peaceful people', were losing their precious land to revolutionaries who had been expelled from the south of Brazil. Major Rondon persuaded the President of the state of Mato Grosso to recognize these Guaranis' land rights. In gratitude, the Indians came one by one to offer Rondon their most precious possessions. He did not accept, but was moved by this 'gesture of rare nobility'.

At the largest Terena village, Rondon found that settlers had moved boundary markers to the Indians' detriment. He resolved the dispute in a series of meetings, and spent a week with his soldiers fixing new markers of stone and wood. This was disinterested work, done because 'we [Brazilians] had contracted a great moral debt to the Indians, from the time of our ancestors who invaded their territories, destroyed their game and stole their honey – not to mention far worse crimes.' This action helped to save the Terena. When the author visited them half a century after Rondon, a two-room primary school in the Terena village of Bananal proudly bore the date 1910 and was named after Colonel Rondon.

No sooner was this arduous line completed than Rondon was given an even greater challenge. Early in 1907 he was summoned by President Afonso Pena to discuss the feasibility of pushing another strategic tele-graph line north-*westwards* from Cuiabá, across 1,000 kilometres (620 miles) of unexplored country towards the rubber-rich state of Acre. Rondon said that it could be done, even though the line would be cut across a watershed plateau whereas earlier explorations had often followed rivers. He was put in command.

Rondon divided his men into three teams. The greatest hardship and excitement awaited the group exploring the route for the main line. Rondon characteristically chose to lead this team. The other groups actually built the two main trunk lines: one north-west towards the Madeira river, and another due west from Cuiabá to the upper Paraguay river. By September 1907, Rondon's team was north of Cuiabá amid the Paresi (or Parecis) tribe. This large and peaceful Aruak-speaking people had been horribly persecuted in the early eighteenth century by slave raiders who carried off thousands of men and women to forced labour near São Paulo. The remnants of the Paresi retreated into ravines and hidden valleys of their territory; and, in the 1870s, the related Cabixi (pronounced Kabishi) avenged ill-treatment by raiding isolated farms and destroying abandoned gold-mining settlements of western Mato Grosso. Rondon's expedition was welcomed by the Paresi, and it responded by distributing presents. He was delighted by the exquisite architecture of Paresi huts, with thatches of palm leaves woven onto an elaborate wooden trellis. He was also impressed by these Indians' tenderness towards their children – a characteristic of all Brazilian tribes – and by their hospitality, with a pot of stew constantly ready in each hut. The tribe used to collect and trade the medicinal root ipecac, and it now tapped rubber, to be exchanged for guns and a few other manufactured goods.

After visiting several Paresi villages, Rondon's team went on to contact the tribe's most isolated group, called Irantxe (Iranches). Rondon was appalled to learn of an atrocity against these Indians. He was shown where the peaceful Irantxe Paresi had recently been attacked by the *seringueiro* (rubber-tapper) Domingos Antônio Pinto, who was invading their forests. Pinto's men, armed with carbines, crept up during the night to surround a village in the rubber-rich forest of Corece-Inazá. 'At dawn, when the wretched people were about to begin their daily labour, the men hidden in ambush opened fire, hitting the first to emerge into the open from their huts. Those who were not killed immediately retreated into their houses in the vain hope of finding shelter from the fury of their barbaric and unprovoked enemies . . . One seringueiro decided to clamber onto the roof of a hut. He tore an opening in it, pushed the barrel of his rifle through, and aimed at and shot the people inside, one by one without distinction of age or sex.' The Indians fired a single arrow in retaliation, hitting this murderer in the throat and killing him. But the other seringueiros systematically burned the village's entire population alive in its huts. Rondon later described this genocidal attack in a lecture in São Paulo. He told his distinguished audience to 'tremble with indignation and shame' at this slaughter of innocent people whose only crime was to defend their forest home against unprovoked invasion.

Beyond the Paresi, Rondon's exploratory party entered unknown lands, the territory of the large but scattered Nambiquara (Nambikwara) peoples. At times he was pushing through tall rainforests or crossing low, drier campo cerrado. It was often possible to ride across this open country, with a scout blazing trees and signalling with a trumpet. Behind came an adjutant, calculating distances with a horse of measured gait; after him the axe- and machete-men opening a trail two metres (six feet) wide; behind them came the camp and cooking service; and then the wagon train bringing supplies.

As the explorers advanced, there were increasing signs of Nambiquara activity. One day, Rondon and a companion stood motionless and watched a lone Nambiquara gathering wild honey. He skilfully opened a hole in a tree containing the hive, and extracted handfuls of honey without disturbing the bees. 'Then he heard the noise of the axes and machetes of the sappers who were approaching, opening the path. He looked towards us. And, showing no fear, he slowly withdrew.'

In late October 1907 the team crossed the Juruena, a large headwater of one of the Amazon's mightiest southern tributaries, the Tapajós. Beyond the Juruena, Rondon and three companions decided to follow an increasing network of trails to visit a Nambiquara village. They were unaware that many of this tribe had recently been slaughtered by the carbines of a rubber-tapper called Pedro Vigné. Suddenly, Rondon recalled, 'I felt a puff of wind on my face and glimpsed something like a small bird crossing my path, at eye level and very close. I turned to my right to watch it, and only then understood: the shaft of an arrow was vibrating with its point buried in the sandy soil. A second deadly messenger passed close to the nape of my neck, grazing my sun helmet. In front of me, some twelve paces away, two Nambiquara warriors were drawing their bowstrings.' The two Nambiquara were powerful men, 'with broad chests, large heads and salient brows and cheekbones. They stood firmly with their bodies bent almost horizontally, their bows drawn ready to fire more arrows. Both had their eyes fixed on mine, hard, penetrating and as implacable as the points of their silent arrows.' 'I snatched the shotgun from my shoulder and fired one shot to the left and another to the right . . . A third arrow broke when it stuck my shotgun. . . . It all took place so quickly that it was over before my companions realized what was happening.' Examining the area, the explorers found other spent arrows and traces of an ambush by three groups of Nambiquara. Rondon had to pull rank to prevent his men from pursuing and shooting at the Indians. He decided to withdraw altogether rather than risk a conflict.

A ninety-kilometre (fifty-five-mile) detour took the expedition around the headwaters of one river; and at another, the commander spent a day swimming to pull his supplies and sick men across in a makeshift coracle. The upper Juruena was thus explored, with the loss of most of the animals in the baggage train but of none of the emaciated and exhausted men.

Only later did Rondon's team find the site of the battle between the Nambiquara and Vigné's rubber-tappers. 'The ground was covered in spent cartridges. We thus had before our eyes proof of the furious violence of the attack and could hardly believe how men armed only with bows and arrows could overcome the dense hail of bullets that must have fallen on them.' But the Nambiquara had prevented Vigné's seringueiros from reaching the rich rubber forests of the upper Tapajós.

In July 1908, a second expedition set out, 'with a hundred and twenty-seven men, ninety-six pack oxen, fifty-eight pack mules, thirty saddle mules, six horses for the cattle service, and twenty oxen for slaughter'. The guide was a Paresi shaman, Toloiri. Rondon's men cut their way through cerrado and dense forest, into stream valleys and out beyond. They protected their camps with barriers of packing cases and saddles and posted sentries at night. The reveille trumpet sounded at four in the morning. In addition to the scouting and cutting parties, there was a band of hunters with dogs who sought deer, jaguar, or game birds. These brought in much meat; but not as much as Toloiri and his expert Paresi would have killed, for they could climb a tree, spot a deer up to two kilometres (2,200 yards) away, stalk it swiftly and silently, and shoot it with gun or bow, never missing.

Approaching the site of the previous year's crossing of the Juruena, the expedition visited two recently abandoned Nambiquara villages. They admired the cleanliness of these settlements, with their refuse of nut shells and bones neatly deposited in waste tips, and the efficiency of plantations of manioc in nearby forest clearings. But the Nambiquara were less sophisticated than other Brazilian tribes. They slept on the ashes of their fires rather than in hammocks or on cane mats, and gathered wild produce more than they hunted.

The huge expedition advanced slowly and was extremely vigilant. But Rondon ordered that, even if men were wounded by Indian attack, there must be no reprisals. This was the crucial policy of non-retaliation that he had learned from Major Gomes Carneiro. He explained to his men: 'They are defending their lands and families, within their just rights.' Rondon's fifteen years of exploration had brought him into contact with a series of tribes at different stages of acculturation. These experiences had transformed the unthinkingly disciplined young army engineer. The humanitarian attitudes of his mentor Major Gomes Carneiro evolved in him into the conviction of a crusade. He expressed this creed in the order to his men: 'Die if you must, but never kill.'

At the Juruena itself, there was near-panic when arrows were fired at the Brazilians' rearguard and Indians were seen on the far bank massed to resist any attempt at crossing. Rondon desisted. Instead, he visited other empty Nambiquara villages, invariably leaving presents as a sign of friendship. The river was crossed later, and the explorers charted new lands and rivers. In the distance they saw a line of hills 'hitherto totally unknown except from Indian reports'.

The explorations resumed in the following year, 1909. Rondon led a team of forty-two men, including some of his veteran officers, a medical doctor, a geologist, a botanist, a zoologist, and a chemist. The telegraph commission was developing into a multi-disciplinary enterprise that involved ethnography, exploratory surveying and other scientific discovery. But there were hardships and disease. Rondon himself suffered from a serious attack of malaria 'which disdained the various preparations of quinine recommended by modern medicine'. The admirable Paresi guide and hunter Toloiri died from double pneumonia, one of the many imported diseases against which Brazilian Indians have no inherited immunity. He was replaced by another Paresi headman, Libânio Colui-Zorocô.

The Nambiquara were leaving ominous signs. They had burned a hut built by the previous year's expedition. At one river crossing Rondon had left bizarre presents of fireworks and tins of Knorr food; but the natives were frightened by the exploding fireworks and ignored the tins – perhaps for want of tin-openers or metal knives. A Brazilian flag had been toppled.

As Rondon's team were advancing through a tall forest, they suddenly came face to face with ten Nambiquara. 'They stopped and, after some instants of hesitation, entered a bamboo thicket and walked away from us at a calm pace.' As they advanced into uncharted territory, Lieutenant Lyra did most of the exploring into difficult hilly country, the eroded edge of an ancient plateau. Men died of beriberi, a scourge of Amazonian explorers until it was found to be caused by vitamin B deficiency. There were many sightings of Indians and their trails, and one man was seriously wounded by an arrow in his chest.

When Rondon finally recovered from his malaria, he hurried forward to join the exploration team. It was moving with great difficulty through superb hyleian rainforests: colossal 50 metre (165 foot) trees whose trunks rose for 18 metres (60 feet) before spreading the first branches of their canopies. The men were depressed by weeks without seeing the sun, cutting through the cathedral-like gloom of the forest on a never-ending mat of roots and decaying leaf litter. Great tracts of forest and many rivers were put on the map. Lieutenant Lyra called one river Dúvida (Doubt) because he was unsure where it emerged. This was pure exploration of the most exciting kind, one of the greatest bursts of discovery of the twentieth century. Rondon had trained a skilled and dedicated team. He often sent parties off down unknown rivers while others cut *picada* trails overland, trying to advance along fixed compass bearings. There were many hardships on such expeditions: torrential tropical rains, dense undergrowth, thundering rapids, and omnipresent insects. Hunger was a constant threat: supply lines failed when pack animals died, and the emaciated explorers barely survived by finding wild honey and palm hearts. There were more contacts with native tribes, groups of Nambiquara and Tupi-speaking tribes in the forests to the north-west of them.

On one exploration, Rondon suddenly came upon a large group of indigenous people. Before he could restrain his dogs they rushed, barking, at the terrified Indians, who rapidly disappeared. Rondon was just able to rescue a seven-year-old boy who had been knocked down by the dogs and was being savaged by them. 'I took him in my lap and smothered him with caresses, trying in every way to . . . calm him. But he did not appear unduly frightened. He did not cry, but started to talk very volubly, often repeating the same words.' The explorers left the child where they had found him, surrounded by presents. They later found that the boy had gone, but not their presents.

The early years of the twentieth century were a time of heroic exploration. Britain was sending Scott and Shackleton to Antarctica; the Americans Peary and Cook reached the North Pole; Norway took justifiable pride in the achievements of Nansen and Amundsen. The African explorers Livingstone, Burton, Stanley, Brazza, and others from many European nations had made themselves popular idols. Brazilians were understandably thrilled by the exploits of Rondon and his team, who were among the world's toughest and most successful explorers, yet seemed motivated by military duty and scientific curiosity more than by personal glory. On the rare occasions when Rondon returned to the cities of the Atlantic coast, his lectures attracted huge audiences, from the President of the Republic down. He was later able to put this fame and prestige to the service of the Indians through the creation of the SPI.

The short but ramrod-stiff Rondon had amazing stamina. On one expedition, his men were exhausted and Rondon himself had malaria with a fever of 41°C (106°F) – the author has had such a malarial fever and I can attest that it annihilated me. The expedition's doctor advised that Rondon might die if he did not go back to recuperate. He refused. He said that any *men* found to be ill might return, but that he as leader could never do so. The doctor insisted that Rondon at least ride, on one of the pack oxen that had been trained to take riders. But after 500 metres (550 yards), Rondon dismounted, ordered that the animal return to the baggage train, and 'proceeded on foot as always, resisting the agonies of his feverish condition and physical exhaustion until the end of the long march, which lasted for eight months.' When the 1907 expedition encountered an unexpected powerful river, the men wearily collapsed on its banks, tired and hopeless. But their leader quickly organized an ox-skin coracle and swam across, pulling one or two companions in this improvised craft. Rondon continued to swim for six consecutive hours across the swift Papagaio tributary of the Juruena. 'Inspired by his edifying example' the men rallied from their depression and helped him complete the crossing. His companion Captain Botelho de Magalhães was amazed by Rondon's toughness. 'Apart from being satisfied with minimal portions of food, the thing that I admired most about Rondon . . . was the few hours with which he satisfied his need for sleep. He was the last to retire in the camp and the first to get up. Sometimes, if I rose before the dawn call at 4 a.m., when daylight came, I would confirm that he had already written dozens of service telegrams and the long daily letters that he wrote to his beloved family, all by the dim light of a single candle at his camp table. He was already in his khaki uniform, had shaved with a razor (which he did in the dark without a mirror, pacing from side to side), and would even earlier have taken his habitual dawn bath in the river or stream nearest the camp.' He even mastered the knack of sleeping in the saddle when it was necessary to ride into the night.

An English traveller called McDermott met Rondon in 1931. He was in his usual khaki drill tunic and breeches, with a Sam Browne belt and (by then) a general's gold-braided cap. Although quite small, Rondon 'commanded instant attention – an atmosphere of conscious dignity and power that immediately singled him out . . . His courtesy was innate. His friendliness was the spontaneity of one who lives . . . in close touch with nature in all her moods. Before that dazzling smile and the honest friendliness of those keen eyes, the hostility of even the most savage of living mankind has melted.'

Cândido Rondon was a product of his age: morally upright, a dedicated army officer inflexible in discipline, convinced of his Positivist religious beliefs, fervently nationalistic, but sometimes sanctimonious and pompous in the manner of his era. His patriotism was demonstrated by a daily ceremony of raising and lowering Brazil's green, yellow, and blue flag. Whenever possible, the expedition celebrated the national day, 7 September, with speeches, parades, and fireworks. At the camp on the Juruena, Rondon entertained the Indians with a recording on a wind-up gramophone of Enrico Caruso singing the national anthem.

Rondon's strength was sustained by his passionate and lifelong belief in

Positivism. This creed was devised by Auguste Comte and Benjamin Constant in France in the early nineteenth century and was introduced to Brazil in the 1850s. Positivism preached human progress and perfectibility through social order. Its motto 'Order and Progress' was emblazoned on Brazil's republican flag. It was based on sociology, which was thought to be an exact science founded on natural laws. Positivists were not anti-Christian; but they argued that Positivism should eventually replace Catholicism, since monotheism was only a phase in mankind's spiritual evolution.

Benjamin Constant Botelho de Megalhães, the professor in the Escola Militar in the 1880s, had been the fervent Positivist who exerted great influence on Rondon and other young officers such as the Horta Barboza brothers, Alípio Bandeira and Manuel Rabelo, all of whom later worked with Rondon. Some Positivists thought that their ideals would best be achieved under a monarchy, but this Benjamin Constant and others were republicans. Botelho de Megalhães became Minister of War in the Republic's first government and he helped to promulgate a decree separating Church and state. Positivist power declined thereafter, although its adherents influenced educational reforms that removed the religious content from the school curriculum.

The Positivist creed was generally favourable to the Brazilian Indians. Positivists thought that indigenous people were at what they called 'the first religious phase', fetishism, and should progress to polytheism, then to monotheism (Christianity), and finally to rationalism. In a draft constitution in 1890, the Positivists Miguel Lemos and R. Teixeira Mendes argued that the 'fetichist hordes' of tribal peoples should be protected by the federal government in their own 'American-Brazilian states'. Such political autonomy would have been a breathtakingly revolutionary concept. This draft constitution was not adopted; but the many Positivists in the new Republic fought for their view of native rights. In 1893 the Positivist Mariano de Oliveira argued that the federal government must guarantee the protection of Indian lives, property, and land, demarcate their territory, and punish crimes against them. These admirable ideas were to be repeated in Indian policy throughout the twentieth century. But when Oliveira proposed them, they were far ahead of their time. And they were all too often ignored or flouted.

The new Republic of 1889 was dominated by powerful landowners and businessmen, and they prevailed over the more idealistic and eccentric Positivists. The Republic's constitution mentioned Indians only once. In article 12 of Decree 7, state governments were bidden to 'promote the . . . catechism and civilization of Indians and the establishment of colonies'. In this context, 'catechism' meant conversion to Catholicism and the suppression of tribal cultures. 'Civilization' was pacification (cessation of self-defence) and integration into neo-Brazilian society. 'Colonies' were attempts to turn tribal Indians into agricultural labourers – a concept that continued in the legislation of 1910 that established the Indian Protection Service. The involvement of state governments was disastrous for indigenous peoples. As a rule, attitudes to Indians harden with proximity. Frontiersmen, who were influential in state governments, feared and despised the tribes on their colonization frontier, whereas the federal government in the distant capital city could afford to be more detached and liberal. In 1906 a new Ministry of Agriculture was created, with Indian affairs under its control. This meant that indigenous people were moved from state to more benign federal government; but the new Ministry was still given the task of 'catechism and civilization' of Indians.

The first decade of the twentieth century witnessed a brilliant campaign by Indian sympathizers, which culminated in the Indian Protection Service legislation of 1910. In 1903 a remarkable woman called Leolinda Daltro founded the Association for the Protection and Assistance of the Natives of Brazil. She was joined in this by officials of the National Museum, which had a flourishing ethnography department, and by the distinguished Brazilian Historical and Geographical Institute. Leolinda Daltro had abandoned a teaching career to spend five years living among tribes of the Tocantins and Araguaia rivers. She shared the Positivist belief that only laymen should have contact with tribal people. This attitude led to a clash with missionaries, who forced her out of the region. She brought five Indians from different tribes back with her, and had them educated in Rio de Janeiro. Her Association did not prosper; but Daltro herself gained prestige from her adventures among the 'forest dwellers'.

The pro-Indian movement developed in learned societies, both within Brazil and internationally. In 1908 the Congress of Americanists (scholars who study Latin American anthropology, society, and history) met in Vienna and a Czech anthropologist, Vojtech Frič, described appalling atrocities that he had seen in the southern Brazilian states of Santa Catarina and Rio Grande do Sul. He told of massacres, enslavement, and degradation of Kaingang and Xokleng Indians. Many settlers in this southern region were of German origin. They had employed professional Indian hunters to exterminate tribes that occupied lands they coveted. Brazilian diplomats and German newspapers dismissed Frič's revelations as exaggerations inspired by his Czech origin.

The Indian sympathizers then had a stoke of luck, finding a convenient whipping-boy. Dr Hermann von Ihering, the scientific director of the São

Paulo Museum, wrote an article for the Saint Louis Exposition of 1904, in which he argued that the only possible end for the Brazilian Indians was extinction. This paper was made even more terrible when translated into Portuguese by his own Museum's *Review*, in 1908. In this version, von Ihering wrote that 'the present-day Indians of the State of São Paulo are an element that contributes neither to labour nor to progress. Because no serious or sustained labour can be expected from the Indians of this or any other state of Brazil, and because savage Kaingang are an impediment to the colonisation of the wild regions they inhabit, it seems that we have no alternative but to exterminate them.'

Von Ihering's article was immediately attacked by the Positivist Sílvio de Almeida, who contrasted German ruthlessness and efficiency with Brazilian warmth and generosity. A month later another Positivist, Luis Horta Barboza, urged patriotic Brazilians to condemn 'this ruthless and barbaric theory of a scientist alien to our sentiments and best instincts'. Horta Barboza knew far more about Indians than did the museum curator von Ihering. He reminded his readers that Indians *did* work hard and effectively to feed their families and on some tasks for the government – such as helping Rondon's telegraph commission. He told Brazilians that they had a moral duty to protect Indians, who were the country's original and rightful inhabitants and who had suffered centuries of appalling oppression.

Hermann von Ihering tried to defend himself by championing frontier settlers against the natives they were supplanting. 'The life of a woodsman and colonist is certainly worth more to us than the life of a savage. The fate of the Indians is certain. Many of them will accept our culture. The remainder will continue to be our enemies and as such will gradually disappear.'

Von Ihering thought that this Nietzschean call for genocide in the name of progress would appeal to modern Brazilians. He was wrong. His clumsy pragmatism handed a moral advantage to the Indianists among Brazilian intellectuals. This was a time of anti-German feeling. A German politician had been carried away in a nationalistic speech and included the settlers of Germanic origin in southern Brazil in a listing of his country's overseas empire. The champions of Indians cleverly manipulated the resulting xenophobia. They recalled romantic writings of nineteenth-century Brazilians who depicted Indians as heroic and noble savages in the Hiawatha mould. The head of the Positivist Church wrote to the President of Brazil to warn him that von Ihering had preached 'the extermination of Brazil's natives. This means that he dares to recommend the murder of thousands of innocent people.' The staff of the National Museum in Rio

de Janeiro signed a petition condemning the genocide apparently advocated by the scientific director of the rival museum in São Paulo. They
declared: 'We protest [against this attempt] to encourage violence in the
interests of colonial expansion. We are, however, certain that the public
will not permit the victory of this criminal idea.' There were debates in
newspapers and lectures to learned societies. Leolinda Daltro knew, from
personal experience, that Indians were 'intelligent, kind, grateful, obedient
and thirsty for instruction. They respect justice and derive pleasure from
manual labour.' Rondon telegraphed his support, 'from the midst of
Brazil's [unexplored] north-west, where the [Indians], legitimate sons of
the fatherland, . . . have taken refuge to escape captivity and extermination by the von Iherings of all times. I can demonstrate that Indians are as
susceptible as the most sensitive westerner to love and goodness, not to
mention their intelligence . . .' Teixeira Mendes said simply: 'Extermination of neither Indians nor of woodsmen; humanity and justice for all.'

  Throughout 1909, the debate turned to implementation of a new
Indian policy. There were three main issues: the protection of Indian lands
and persons; whether Indian affairs should be in the hands of missionaries
or laymen; and the degree to which Indians should be trained for
agricultural labour. The learned society of Campinas created a Commission to Promote the Defence of the Indians and this demanded that native
lands must be protected. Only with their lands secure could tribal people
be incorporated into Brazilian society. A large Brazilian Geographical
Congress in September 1909 was attended by Nilo Peçanha, the dynamic
young President of Brazil. At its opening, a journalist called Nelson de
Senna argued eloquently for redress of atrocities committed against Indians and for a new federal government policy of kindness towards them.

  The role of missionaries was more difficult, since these ecclesiastics had
been concerned with the Indians ever since the mid-sixteenth century.
Positivists and Freemasons called for the removal of clerics from native
affairs. One Positivist told the Geographical Congress that foreign missionaries were 'groups of veritable exploiters of ignorance and poverty'. Others
defended missionaries as being the only people sufficiently dedicated to
devote their lives to Indian protection. The Geographical Congress heard
praise of French Dominicans among tribes of the Araguaia, of Belgian
Benedictines with the Makuxi and Wapixana of the northern Rio Branco
region (Roraima), of Italian Salesians among the Bororo, and of the Jesuits
expelled from Brazil in 1760. This argument split some learned societies
and caused the collapse of Leolinda Daltro's Association for the Protection
of the Natives. But that campaigner persuaded the Congress to adopt a

resolution calling on the civil authorities 'to establish a programme of *secular* education of Indians with help from the Republican government,' since such instruction is the only one compatible with its Constitution'.

President Nilo Peçanha now appointed a rich and able young politician as Minister of Agriculture, which meant that he controlled Indian affairs. Rodolfo Nogueira da Rocha Miranda personally managed vast estates that he had inherited in the interior of the State of São Paulo, and he turned them into some of the country's finest coffee plantations. In January 1910 this powerful and popular minister visited the National Museum and paid particular attention to its fine collections of Indian ethnography. He declared that he wanted to mobilize the skills and energies of these native Brazilians. He would protect their lands and grant them the same incentives as offered to foreign immigrants. But no attempt should be made to change native cultures or religions.

Two weeks later, on 6 February, Colonel Cândido Rondon sailed into Rio de Janeiro from the Amazon. Brazilians had been following press reports of his daring explorations. Rondon was given a hero's welcome. Four launches filled with generals, cabinet ministers, senators, congressmen and academics went out to greet his ship. As Rondon landed, a military band played, schoolgirls threw petals in the national colours, and the ubiquitous Leolinda Daltro made a speech. All this was reported extensively in the press. After recovering from a bout of malaria, Rondon went to call on the President. He took his Paresi guide Libânio, whom he had made an honorary major in the Brazilian army.

Later that month, Rondon visited Rocha Miranda and the minister asked him to organize a new Indian Service. This was confirmed in a letter of 2 March. Rocha Miranda stressed that the new Service would be manned by professionals. He wrote that 'it is the government's duty . . . to establish a new basis for catechism of Indians, without preoccupation for religious proselytizing. It would take the form of a special Service, based on this capital city but radiating out into the states wherever its action is needed, patiently and without slackening its efforts.' This letter confirmed that the minister felt that missionary efforts were useless and misguided, that the service must be a federal one, and that it should follow republican ideals. Rondon wrote his acceptance a week later. He welcomed the initiative and agreed to lead the Indian Protection Service. He opposed missionary conversion, partly because he was a Positivist but also because the multiplicity of religious sects confused converts. Also, the state was supposed to have separated itself from the Church and to support no single creed.

Rondon therefore accepted, on six conditions:

1. Indians would not be forced into rapid acceptance of Christian doctrine or white civilization.

2. The attempt to incorporate Indians into national society should not be based on religious indoctrination or any other metaphysical or scientific system.

3. The new Service would take the form of an inspectorate that supervised public or private initiatives.

4. Protection of Indian lands would be the main responsibility of the Service. Territory stolen from tribes should either be returned to them or they should be given compensation of equivalent areas nearby.

5. Indians would be encouraged to change to a more settled way of life and given cattle and farm implements to this end. However, white officials must be sparing and sensitive when advising Indians. They must ensure that any assistance was practical and did not conflict with native traditions.

6. Officers of the service would contact nomadic tribes, in order to prevent frontier or inter-tribal warfare. These officers must be selfless and devoted to the Indians' welfare. Such disinterestedness was essential – more important even than the methods used.

In his letter, Rondon argued that Indian tribes must be treated as if they were powerful foreign nations. Any changes should be introduced to them only prudently and gradually, respecting the native peoples' social organization. The Minister wrote back: 'I agree without qualification to the measures you suggest, all of which will lead to the protection, defence and care of the Indians, without forcing them to accept our habits or religion.'

By modern standards, there was only one controversial element in all this. The Positivist Teixeira Mendes had argued that, alongside respect for Indian culture, there should be 'progress' in the form of clothing, housing, and a new economic order. Rondon also accepted this contradiction. Thus, the new department was called the Service for Indian Protection and Localization of National Labourers (Serviço de Proteção aos Indios e Localização de Trabalhadores Nacionais), or SPILTN for short. The 'national labourers' in its title were freed black or mestizo slaves who were supposed to form communities to work for the powerful landowners who dominated Brazilian politics. The hope was that pacified Indians would mingle with these free workers in new frontier settlements – even though it was well known that Indians and blacks did not respect or like one another. At that time, Rondon believed that Indians could be fully assimilated into Brazilian society, given time and sensitive guidance by SPI officials. The prevailing view was that Indians could gradually evolve towards a 'superior' culture – but not as autonomous entities. The anthropologist Mércio Gomes later commented that 'the SPI worked on the expectation that the Indian would one day become a full-fledged Brazilian'.

Implementation of the new Service went smoothly and very fast. Minister Rocha Miranda wrote to state governors, praising the Indians for resisting barbarous captivity. He said that support for his new Service was 'so universal and unequivocal that I am convinced that . . . it represents a lofty national aspiration.' He asked the states to give Indians 'the protection they deserve as human beings and the benevolent assistance they merit as helpless rustics.' All the governors replied enthusiastically, promising land and education to their Indians. In reality, their support may have had less lofty motives than Rocha Miranda imagined. Many of them welcomed the new Service as a federal attempt to pacify hostile tribes and turn them into much-needed agricultural workers. Since the abolition of slavery in 1888, there had been a serious labour shortage on the large fazendas.

Rocha Miranda and his supporters had to move rapidly. There was no time to be lost, for a conservative reaction was gathering momentum against the lay nature of the new Service. The Church realized what was afoot and protested against 'an infernal plan, forged in the depths of Masonic lodges'. Debate raged in the learned societies and in press editorials. In a speech to the Historical and Geographical Institute of São Paulo, Brasilio Machado argued that the new system would never work. 'It lacks the vital breath of sacrifice and abnegation, which the love of God alone has succeeded in inspiring.' This was a valid point. No one questioned Rondon's integrity and dedication; but many doubted whether he could find other officers or lay civil servants prepared to make equal sacrifices.

The Church mounted a propaganda campaign to remind people of the imagined success of past missionary efforts. Many Brazilian towns had started as missions – mostly as Jesuit aldeias (villages) before the black-robed fathers were expelled in 1760. (The transformation of missions into settler towns was, of course, nothing to boast about: it meant that the Indian inhabitants had perished from disease, abuse, overwork, and despair, and that their lands had been stolen from them.) Monsignor Armando Bahlman made a speech praising the 'order and obedience' of Indians managed by missionaries in three parts of Brazil. The government would do better to support missionaries than to try to establish a lay service. It was the Church's duty to civilize Indians and 'infuse in them sentiments of justice, love of work, morality, and love of God. For to be good citizens, they must first be made good Christians.' The ecclesiastical authorities were alarmed at the prospect of losing their power over Indian catechism – and the government subsidies that went with it.

The Minister of Agriculture, Rocha Miranda, came under heavy pressure from Catholic journalists. He stressed that missionaries would continue to care for Indians' religious conversion alongside officials of his new lay protection service – but the latter would have the ultimate power in indigenous affairs. Father Antonio Malan, head of the vigorous Salesian missionaries working among some Bororo of Mato Grosso, asked for a renewal of government funding but was told that grants would be made only after he had submitted accounts to show how the money was spent. Also, in future, his mission would be inspected by officials from the Ministry of Agriculture.

The influential newspaper *Jornal do Commércio* joined the Catholic side. It accused Positivists of wanting to supplant missionaries in their fine work among Indians. It argued that the best instrument of catechism was the locomotive, on new railway lines driven into Indian territory! Some anthropologists supported von Ihering in arguing that Indians should be granted their lands, but that conversion by the Church was preferable to government inspection. Other so-called scientists spouted pseudo-Darwinian cant: 'The progress of races, the victory of the strongest and natural annihilation of the weak, the fusion of one with the other, are virtually biological phenomena that cannot be modified by government plans.' Subsidies to either missionary or lay help for Indians were pointless, since these people were doomed to extinction. Miranda's new Service was 'a fine but futile dream'.

The pro-missionary reaction was too late. The new regulations for the SPI were drafted in May 1910, submitted to President Nilo Peçanha in early June, and approved as Decree no. 8,072 on 20 June. In explaining the decree of June 1910 that created the SPI, Minister Rocha Miranda condemned the Indian policy of the nineteenth-century Brazilian Empire as contradictory and ineffective. 'The Republic cannot continue such inaction. [By doing nothing] it connives in the massacre of Indians or in their subjection to regimes of labour akin to slavery. On the contrary, it behoves [the Republic] to protect them and guide them prudently, without violence. If they are weak and inferior, the greater is our duty to defend them against the privileged and powerful.' A favourable editorial in O *Paíz* said that the new Service would prevent the extermination of Indians or their subordination to stultifying missionary discipline. Rocha Miranda was 'an illustrious republican with the courage to affirm officially that Indians are men. They have the same rights as other men in the country of their birth.'

So, on Brazil's Independence Day, 7 September 1910, the new Indian Protection Service was inaugurated amid flowery speeches. Its head, Colonel Cândido Rondon, described it as a triumph of Positivist doctrine. But he stressed that it was 'not a risky experiment, neither in the methods that will be put into practice nor in the officials entrusted in so doing. On the contrary, both have been put to the test on more than one occasion and in very difficult circumstances.' The lay SPI seemed to herald the dawn of a new age for Brazil's beleaguered indigenous peoples.

2. First Contacts:
Kaingang, Xokleng, and Nambiquara

Rondon organized the Indian Protection Service at different levels. Exciting contacts with isolated peoples were done by attraction teams led by a handful of qualified *sertanistas*. Sertanista was a high rank in the SPI, an elite of expert backwoodsmen who led contact expeditions. Tribes were invariably won over by presents and kindness that contrasted with the previous bloody hostility of the colonial frontier. The 'attraction post' from which they received their presents generally became their Indian post, named either after the tribe or after a hero of Brazilian Indianist history.

Once contacted (or 'pacified', in the parlance of that period), an indigenous people (then called a tribe) embarked on an uncertain path towards what was then known as 'acculturation', with a view to ultimate 'assimilation' into the melting-pot of national society. Being intelligent human beings, with distinct cultures, living in a wide range of habitats, and dealing with contrasting elements of white society (from well-intentioned to hostile, from Indian Service officials and missionaries to land-grabbers and adventurers), every tribe reacted differently. Each was a separate case study. This book therefore deals with different regions and peoples, and seeks to tell how each dealt with the changes inflicted on it.

The newly created Indian Service had to impress politicians and confound its critics with a successful 'pacification'. In the words of its report for 1911: 'The SPI had to start work in [the interior of] São Paulo in a difficult atmosphere [of reciprocal hatred between Indians and colonists]. It was acting in full view of spectators, nearby and distant, who were highly sceptical about the efficacy of its methods.'

At the start of the twentieth century, Brazil enjoyed great wealth from exports of two raw materials: rubber, in which the Amazon basin then enjoyed a world monopoly, and coffee, which grew superbly in the interior of São Paulo state. Westwards from the city of São Paulo stretches a plateau at an altitude of 500–900 metres (1,640–2,950 feet), where coffee plants grow on a violet-coloured *terra roxa* soil formed of decomposing basalt. Local coffee barons dominated the politics of the young

Brazilian Republic. They wanted to improve the marketing of their precious crop by extending a railway north-westwards from their city to the coffee-growing plateau in the interior. The problem was that this North-West Railroad (Estrada de Ferro do Noroeste) was pushing into the territory of the fiercely independent Kaingang Indians.

The Kaingang of São Paulo were the northernmost group of a great family of Jê-speaking Indians who had survived centuries of contact with white invaders. They lived in a 600-kilometre (370-mile) arc, east of the Paraná river in the states of São Paulo, Paraná, Santa Catarina and Rio Grande do Sul. In the sixteenth and seventeenth centuries, the Kaingang had resisted the attentions of Spanish Jesuits from Paraguay and slave raiders from São Paulo. Tough warriors, semi-nomadic, and agile woodsmen, they suffered far less than the more populous and sedentary Tupi-Guarani tribes. Repeated deceptions and delusions in their dealings with whites left the Kaingang hostile and shrewdly suspicious of all frontier settlers. Their bellicose reputation and harassment of travellers had earned the Kaingang a special mention in a royal decree of 1808 that 'launched war against these barbaric Indians'. That was the last official war proclaimed against a Brazilian tribe.

Franz Keller, a German settler in the 1860s, marvelled at the toughness of the Kaingang. 'They are an eminently warlike people. If they have no one to fight, they use hunting as an outlet to demonstrate their strength and cunning. It must be acknowledged that they achieve rare perfection in hunting tapirs and peccaries. The weapons they use in these pursuits are finished with extraordinary skill. Their long bows are veneered with bark of *imbé* lianas and their arrows are made of a wood of great elasticity, so well worked that they appear to be machine-made.' Their games were very violent. Kaingang from rival villages confronted one another with piles of short heavy cudgels, sharpened at both ends. They hurled these at their opponents with such force that they often inflicted serious wounds.

The southern groups of Kaingang had frequently clashed with colonists, many of whom were immigrants from Germany. At times the settlers incited Kaingang chiefs to fight one another; and they herded some groups into dusty villages deprived of land for hunting. Those who resisted were mercilessly ambushed, gunned down, or enslaved by *bugreiros* ('savage-hunters'), professional Indian killers employed by the settlers' colonies.

In the north, there had been fighting between ranchers and coffee-planters and Indians since the 1850s. Gustav von Koenigswald wrote that 'the whites greatly fear the Coroados ['Crowned' Indians or Kaingang] and people on the frontier are never safe from their attack ... They strike sporadically, plundering and killing on isolated farmsteads before disappearing back into the forest.' The settlers responded by *batidas*, genocidal raids on native villages. 'In 1888 the bugreiro Joaquim Bueno poisoned the pools of water of a Kaingang village in the Paranapanema forests with strychnine, killing some 2,000 Indians of all ages. Bueno himself reported this; but he remained unpunished.'

At the end of the nineteenth century, a cleric called Father Claro Monteiro do Amaral founded the Society for Ethnography and the Civilization of Indians. This group sought to justify the Church's control of Indian affairs. But it hoped to operate without gathering the tribal people into mission villages, where they would become detribalized forced-labourers for surrounding farmers. In 1901 Father Claro decided to descend the unexplored Feio ('Ugly') river in order to contact and convert the northern Kaingang. He made the fatal error of taking Guarani Indians from near Bauru who had previously guided a bugreiro posse that slaughtered a Kaingang village. The expedition turned back after twenty-four days, but it was ambushed on 9 May: Father Claro and the two Guarani were killed and their bodies hidden on a forested riverbank. Those who escaped spread anti-Indian fear and hatred. Another missionary, Father Bernardino de Lavalle, tried again in 1902, but also without success. And in 1905–6 a geographical and geological commission explored into Kaingang territory.

After 1905 the North-West Railroad advanced beyond Bauru, and its construction teams fought Indians. No quarter was given by either side. Once, in 1907, a train came along the new line 'carrying the bodies of five men who had been decapitated by the Indians. Needless to say, all the workers downed tools and disbanded. On another occasion two groups of sleeping men were massacred.'

Reprisals were swift and brutal. The newspaper *Correio da Manhã* wrote on 16 October 1908: 'It is horrible what the workers of the North-West Railroad are doing to the unfortunate [Kaingang] Indians of the region between Bauru and Avanhandava. Massacring them is a kind of sport: a highly entertaining form of game-hunting'. We have an eyewitness account of one such atrocity by a perpetrator called João Pedro. The raiding party consisted of thirty-one men, heavily armed with Winchester .44-calibre carbines, shotguns, and machetes. After four days' advance, they silently approached a Kaingang village as night was falling. The Indians were celebrating around a fire in the middle of their village. The attackers deduced that this was a marriage ceremony 'because one girl appeared to be the centre of attention and was more adorned than the others. The Indians danced and sang happily, entirely unaware of the terrible catastrophe that awaited them.' Those in ambush were impressed by the cleanliness of the village and the good order of its finely thatched huts. 'They were particularly surprised by the constant friendliness maintained throughout the festival, with open laughter and playfulness between the Indians.' The different characters of individuals was observed, some more extrovert, others withdrawn. The black bugreiro João Pedro told Lieutenant Pedro Dantas of the Commission of Inquiry: 'They seemed almost like real people, Lieutenant.' The celebration lasted most of the night.

The bugreiros launched their attack in darkness, just before dawn. Lieutenant Dantas reported: 'They fired the first general volley. One may appreciate its murderous effect when you know what good marksmen these people are, and consider how long they had to take aim at leisure, each selecting one victim so that the killing would not strike only random targets. Other volleys were fired in addition to that one. The poor Indians did not have a chance. They awoke under attack and were completely disorganized by that cowardly and unprovoked aggression. Some claim that over a hundred lives were sacrificed there: for the opening volleys were followed by a machete attack that spared nobody.' The leaders of this illegal raid tried to conceal it; but junior members boasted of their 'clean sweep' of the sleeping village 'and even proved their achievement by exhibiting ears cut from their victims! . . . They spared only one young girl whom they abused in a most barbarous fashion before proceeding to ransack the encampment.'

Rondon later recalled meeting a businessman called Castilho whose men had raped a Kaingang girl on his estate at Avanhandava. Castilho and his family did not await the tribe's revenge, but fled at once. At Platina, near the Paranapanema river in the south-west of the State of São Paulo lived 'Colonel' Sanches, one of the most odious bugreiros. In 1911, Inspector Manuel Rabelo of the SPI freed three male Kaingang slaves and Indian women concubines from Sanches' house, and managed to stop a state subsidy for 'Indian catechism' to some Franciscan friars who were in league with him. But Rabelo was too late to prevent Sanches from exterminating the last of the inoffensive and peaceful Oti Indians. The Oti were simple hunter-gatherers who had the misfortune of living on open campo country, sleeping in lines of rough shelters along watercourses. Their homeland was a fertile plain that was discovered by the colonization frontier in the late nineteenth century, so that the Oti were victims of a brutal massacre in the 1870s. Fifty-seven gunmen surrounded their camp and shot them down as they awoke. A young German immigrant who was to become an outstanding anthropologist, Curt (Unkel) Nimuendajú, wrote that 'they were all killed without exception of age or sex, until [the attackers] verified only two or three children, who were taken as living trophies . . . José Paiva, who had participated in the group of attackers, told me that the dead were lying in heaps on the ground.' Some fifty remnants of the Oti went into hiding and survived precariously for forty years. One Brazilian, Verissimo de Goes, tried to befriend them; but others were gunned down because they raided settlers' cattle or were mistaken for feared Kaingang. Nimuendajú in 1908 tracked down the last three Oti: two women married to *caboclo* (mestizo peasants), and a man. 'When I finally found him, the malaria virus already had him on the verge of the grave and he was soon resting with his brothers. With José Chavantes, the last male of the Oti tribe died.'

Such was the climate of hatred in which the new SPI started its pacification. As already noted, the attraction of the implacable Kaingang was the new Service's first major challenge. Colonel Rondon had already laid down the instruction that was to become the SPI's proud motto: 'Die if you must, but never kill.' This meant that, at the first face-to-face contact with a tribe, there must be no retaliation, even if the Indians killed members of the attraction team.

Rondon studied the Kaingang problem and left Lieutenant Manoel Rabelo and two other officers in charge. They started with four months of trail-cutting from the railway to the Feio river, then built a thatched hut in a clearing in the 'mysterious forest' that extended uninterrupted for hundreds of kilometres to the Paraná river. Six hectares (fifteen acres) of this ancient forest were felled, to create plantations of corn and beans and to attract the attention of the Kaingang. A trail was cut for eighteen kilometres (eleven miles) beyond the attraction post. An Indian hut was discovered, but its inhabitants had disappeared. The teams cutting these trails frequently sounded horns as a sign of friendship and left presents of machetes and other gifts. At first the Kaingang refused these; but then some were removed.

One day, the SPI sub-director Manuel Miranda was ambushed when riding along the new trail. 'He escaped death only by a miracle. An arrow struck his animal's saddle, and his pacified Indian [interpreter] received a wound through his hand.' The sub-director 'forbade any act of reprisal, but ordered his interpreters to explain the expedition's presence there. This was done. After a long silence, a powerful voice replied from within the forest. It declared, in the name of them all, that they had not known that the expedition consisted of those friends who had for so long been leaving presents along the trails. Instead, they had been taken for enemies.' Despite this amicable dialogue shouted through the forest vegetation, the Kaingang refused to accept face-to-face contact.

The Indians shot and killed a soldier in the nearby camp and burned the attraction hut. Lieutenant Rabelo and other soldiers were withdrawn. Trail-cutting resumed after the rains, in March 1912, and the camp was rebuilt. The Indians 'surrounded the camp by night and day, sometimes sounding lugubrious roars on their horns – which signified war and extermination – or smashing their terrible clubs against trees, breaking the silence of the night with fearful banging. All this left us transfixed with fear, recalling that no single victim of these formidable warriors had ever survived attack by similar war clubs.' The clearing around the attraction post was protected by a barrier of felled trees and a barbed-wire fence. At night, this perimeter was lit by paraffin lamps. In its midst were huts to house the attraction team – never more than twelve people. The frightened group 'kept talking and singing to show that they were vigilant and not afraid . . . They kept a gramophone playing, with records that gave the impression of many people laughing and celebrating.'

The SPI had with them some married couples of pacified Kaingang from the Paraná part of the tribe, including an old woman called Vanuire who had recently been captured by bugreiros in this northern region. These intermediaries issued 'words of peace and festive songs by the incomparable Vanuire, with cheerful sounds of benevolent goodwill spread out over the gloomy forest on horns blown by our Kaingang interpreters from Paraná, all from a platform erected high in a tree . . . For six months no single shot was fired, not even to kill the splendid game birds that flew past almost within arm's reach.' Lieutenant Horta Barboza reduced the panic among his people 'with gramophone music, with the peace songs of Vanuire, and sometimes the interpreters calling to the terrifying visitors to enter our camp to receive axes, blankets and beads.'

The first contact finally happened on 19 March 1912. 'Twelve Indians appeared at the edge of the trail, completely naked and unarmed. There were seven men and five women. These were received with much goodwill and were immediately dressed. They remained for five days [at the attraction post] and were invariably orderly, affectionate and grateful.' When these twelve Indians returned to their people, they asked that SPI personnel should accompany them. Three Brazilian employees and four Paraná Kaingang interpreters went, and were festively received by over a hundred Kaingang. Other members of the tribe returned, and 'Since that time, relations have continued in a spirit of intimate camaraderie.'

In the early stages of such a contact, the two sides appear equal: the Indians are powerful and the whites not yet numerous. During the first two years after contact, the Kaingang were sure that it was *they* who had tamed the civilizados. Chief Vauhim used to embrace Horta Barboza and reassure him, 'Do not be afraid, we will protect you,' against the still-uncontacted parts of the tribe. At this stage, Vauhim saw the whites as allies to help him dominate other Indians and the tools they gave him as tribute. But he later admitted how concerned his people had been by the seemingly endless numbers of intruders. Whenever the Indians killed white men, they had removed their hair and genitals to prevent them from procreating after death.

The new Indian Service had achieved its first success. The SPI boasted that it had 'put a stop to attacks by savages on civilizados . . . and gained their confidence to such an extent . . . that [the railway men] may now penetrate with impunity into their remotest dominions . . . Such a conquest is all the more remarkable, given the bad reputation of the Kaingang, and all the former opposition to the Service's methods.' So the real winners were the coffee planters, who profited at the Indians' expense.

The consequences were predictable and tragic. Within five years, Lieutenant Horta Barboza wrote that a horde of colonists had poured into Kaingang territory since the tribe's pacification. The SPI finally persuaded the Indians of Chief Vauhim to come to a 'land demarcation'. Fraternization went so well that 'the former suspicion has turned into blind trust'. The Kaingang brought their families to the railway engineers' camp and even to the town of Penápolis. Inspector Horta Barboza feared that alcoholism and prostitution were afflicting these Indians thrust into the midst of frontier society. In March 1916 these newly contacted people were struck by influenza, against which they had no inherited immunity. And by the end of the year they were decimated 'by an even more terrible epidemic, of measles' – the greatest and most persistent killer of Brazilian Indians. The well-intentioned officer blamed the Indians for refusing to accept Western medicine – although we now know that there were then no cures for either influenza or measles. Horta Barboza said that dying Kaingang used to accept the SPI's remedies only after they had exhausted all their tribal shaman's rituals. 'We can achieve no precautions. A sick Indian starts by spending the night in the open outside his hut. When he feels fever, his only concern is to go and bathe in the nearest river or stream at any hour of day or night.'

The SPI inspector drew up a balance sheet of the first four years since the Kaingang accepted contact. There had been no live births among this entire tribal population: only three babies were born and all had died. The Indians' diet had 'improved' to the extent of containing salt and fat and 'constant use of new foods like black beans, rice and sugar'. The indigenous people now slept on beds rather than mattresses of leaves, and they no longer had to make long hunting expeditions. However, the bewildered official admitted that 'it appears incontestable that they have suffered a great shock to their morale. This trauma arises from the indefinable disruption caused by the simple fact of being placed in contact with us.' Horta Barboza stressed that the Kaingang suffered cultural disruption despite being left 'absolutely free to continue to practise their customs and to live in accordance with their traditions. We have not consciously interfered with or even disparaged any single one of their usages. On the contrary, we have always done our utmost to show respect and consideration for all their customs. For we know that the greatest harm to any human society is to destroy its foundations, even when others are substituted for them.'

The Indians were further demoralized by their changing perception of the neo-Brazilians. At first, the Kaingang thought that they must pacify the murderous invaders of their territory: hence their early euphoria when they found some members of this curious new tribe to be friendly. In 1914 a group of Kaingang men and women was taken down the new railway to São Paulo. As they saw the wealth and size of each successive town and city, they realized that, far from a peace between tribes of roughly equal stature, it was they who had been conquered by the immensely powerful Brazilians. Once in the State capital, São Paulo, the Kaingang were dignified in the face of the crowd's curiosity and effusive generosity; but when they saw the Tietê river they asked for canoes so that they could paddle home. Disillusioned and humiliated, they lost pride in their dances, beliefs, and customs. The tragedy of decimation by diseases that seemed to attack only Indians heightened this despair.

The officials of the new Indian Protection Service were active with other groups of Kaingang. There had originally been six nomadic groups of northern Kaingang, and they were often at war with one another. When Vauhim's 200 people joined the Brazilians, the other groups thought that he had done it in order to obtain weapons and allies with which to fight them. They therefore fled deeper into the forest. This did not save them from diseases against which they had no immunity. The terrible flu epidemic of March–April 1913 halved the number of Kaingang. Chief Congue-Hui's group was totally exterminated by it. When SPI agents hurried to that village, they found nothing but heaps of bones lying on the ground. Measles struck soon after. Horta Barboza wrote that it was impossible to describe the horror of this epidemic. 'The mortality among the sick reached enormous proportions, and the tribe was reduced to a miserable remnant of what it had been.' So each in turn emerged to accept peaceful contact: the Kaingang of chiefs Iacry, Careg, Rugre, Congue-Hui, and finally in 1915 of Charin.

The Kaingang who had surrendered near the railway received inadequate parcels of their own territory. Chief Vauhim's group originally settled at the attraction post on the Ribeirão dos Patos ('Duck Bank'). But when farmers pressed for this camp to be removed so that they could occupy its fine lands, the SPI agreed. In 1916, sixty-four surviving Indians of this group were relocated in a new Indian post called Icatu, but it was at the edge of the Penápolis–Aguapei road, close to the new railway and quite far from their homeland on the Feio river. Other chiefs requested land and were granted a small reserve on the site of Chief Iacry's village, now named Vanuire.

The opening of the railway and pacification of the Kaingang increased the value of land fifteen-fold between 1912 and 1915. Senator Luis Piza claimed title to much of the tribe's territories, and made a fortune selling plots to large and small farmers. The Senator refused to grant anything to the indigenous inhabitants. Two SPI officials finally persuaded him to give them two small parcels of land as a reward for the pacification, and they registered these as tribal reserves. The tribe was thus abruptly reduced from hunting over a vast region to confinement in twenty-five square kilometres (less than ten square miles). Spanish immigrants who settled in the Aguapei valley brought the epidemic of measles, from which the doughty chief Vauhim and many of his people perished. During those years of property boom, the population of the northern Kaingang fell from 700 to 200 and most of the tribe's women and children died.

When the Kaingang were flourishing and uncontacted, they observed a strict marriage code. Couples were prohibited, on pain of death or banishment, from marrying within their own moiety (half) of the village. This custom prevented inbreeding. But when the Kaingang were decimated, it became almost impossible for couples to find mates according to tribal custom. Dr Horta Barboza persuaded a few couples who wanted to marry within their moiety to flee to sanctuary with other Indian groups. His successor, Eurico Sampaio, who was in charge of the Kaingang post for over twenty years, also tried to stop this practice that was accelerating the tribe's numerical decline. He finally succeeded, by himself marrying a first cousin. The Kaingang loved and admired Sampaio. So when they saw him marrying a close relative, they were finally persuaded that this was acceptable. But by the 1950s the once-feared northern Kaingang were reduced to sixty-five people. This was despite the efforts of dedicated SPI officials to save the tribe whose pacification had been such a triumph of their fledgeling Service.

*

Far to the south, at the western end of the State of Santa Catarina, lived the Xokleng (pronounced Shock-leng), a tribe closely related to the Kaingang linguistically and ethnographically but often at war with them. The Xokleng were divided into three groups, each of some 500 people, and they were semi-nomadic hunter-gatherers. They hunted, chiefly peccary and tapir, and gathered wild fruits and nuts such as the nutritious kernels of the magnificent araucaria pines that covered this more temperate part of Brazil.

German colonists, introduced to Santa Catarina in 1850 by one Dr Blumenau, clashed with the Xokleng when they expanded into the interior. The Indians previously practised simple agriculture, but they found it easier to raid the settlers' farms for crops and animals. To these hunters the sight of large docile cattle was irresistible. The Xokleng often approached colonists' farms in search of food or metal for their arrowheads. Their hunting lands were all being occupied, so that they suffered periods of deprivation and attacked farms out of hunger. Others simply wanted to observe the strange white invaders and mix with them. The immigrant settlers responded by establishing a militia. One provincial president declared that: 'These barbarians, who think only of robbing us or attacking us in ambush, can never be treated with kindness or consideration . . . I am increasingly convinced that it is practical, even necessary, to snatch these savages by force from the forests and place them somewhere whence they cannot escape. We could thus protect our farmers from these murderers, and we might even make useful citizens of the barbarians' children.' His solution was to turn to bugreiro Indian-hunters. A cycle of bloody vendettas ensued. Bugreiros avenged Indian raids with murderous campaigns of extermination, or attacked Xokleng villages in order to gain government bounties. In the sixty years prior to 1914, sixty-one attacks by Indians were recorded in the valley of the Itajaí, resulting in the deaths of forty-one settlers and wounding of a further twenty-two. We have no records of Xokleng mortality; but it was known to have far exceeded that among their oppressors.

The new SPI established an inspectorate to try to contact the Xokleng. Its inspector, Dr Raul Abbot, went to the Itajaí do Norte, surveyed the area, started to locate the Indians, and persuaded the colonization company to allocate 30,000 hectares (120 square miles) to house them after pacification. There was no success at first. The colonists' German-language newspaper *Der Urwaldsbote* commented scathingly, in November 1913, that 'With the exception of a few individuals who profit from Indian protection or who show signs of mental aberration, all Blumenau is convinced that the catechism of Indians is not only useless but actually produces bad effects.' Dr Abbot resigned, for lack of funds or support from the SPI.

The delicate task of attraction was left to a young man from Rio de Janeiro, Eduardo de Lima e Silva Hoerhan, who had joined the SPI in a burst of enthusiasm for the indigenous cause. Hoerhan made his first contact with the Xokleng, on the banks of the Plate tributary of the Itajaí do Norte. The Indians attacked and destroyed his attraction post. Hoerhan arrived by river on the following day, 22 September 1914, and when he and his interpreter landed they bravely left their carbines in their canoe. *Der Urwaldsbote* reported:

> While they walked among the still-smoking ashes of the destroyed huts, the interpreter called out in a loud voice to the attackers, who were presumed to be hidden in the forest and the nearby clearings. This supposition was soon confirmed by an infernal clamour from behind the wall of vegetation, from whence some men emerged, with the arrows in their bows ready to fire. Eduardo bravely redoubled his efforts to make those men understand his intentions and desire. The Indians appeared to be moved by the young man's attitude. But they hesitated and withdrew with each step that he took towards them. Eduardo had an intuition. It was natural that they should suspect that all this was all a trap, intended to catch them off guard and punish them for the previous day's depredation. He had to prove to them that he was approaching them without any ulterior motive. He therefore removed everything that he had on him and, arms uplifted, walked resolutely towards the Indians who were in front of him ready to fire a fatal shot. The interpreter accompanied him, imitating everything he did and constantly repeating appeals to friendship and fraternisation in their barbarous language.

One nervous Indian fired two arrows, one of which grazed Hoerhan's Indian companion. 'Seeing this action by their companion, the other Indians became angry, grabbed him, and then threw his weapon to the ground.' The Xokleng hesitated, but lowered their weapons and accepted Hoerhan and his interpreter as their brothers. They accepted the presents 'although continuing to show themselves very mistrustful'.

We should try to see this dramatic contact from the native point of view. Brazilian Indians have an effective system of government, in which the adult men of the tribe discuss its affairs each evening. This is the democracy of a Rousseauan city-state. Decisions are reached by consensus, although based on tribal custom and with added weight given to the views of chiefs, elders, and shamans. Once the situation is fully understood, tribes tend to take sensible decisions. However, with first contacts there is no precedent and the origin, strength, motives, and behaviour of the invaders are bewilderingly unpredictable.

We normally hear the history of Brazilian tribes only from the European side. In the case of the Xokleng contact, there is an Indian's version. The narrator was Wânpô, son of Kamren, one of the tribe's two main chiefs at the time of contact. Wânpô was about sixteen in 1915, and he told his life story to the American anthropologist Greg Urban sixty years later. He recalled that at a site south of the attraction post,

> we found a path and when we arrived in the village there were knives, cups, shirts, blankets and axes. The white men had already captured [three Indians]. [Chief] Gakrā thought that it was they who had put the things there because they wanted us to meet the white men. We took everything and returned to the village, where we brewed mead [honey-spirit – i.e. they held a celebration]. After this, we moved camp to Deneke because we wanted to kill cattle. There was a farm there. We killed some cattle and ate its meat. Then we returned here [the Indian post on the site of the first contact], where Eduardo [Hoerhan] had already made a farm . . . [The group then divided and migrated for several months.] When they returned and came down the mountain here, Eduardo was already there. They wanted to kill him, so they left the women above while the men descended. There were five tents, and the one closest to the river was filled with things such as knives and axes. Womle and Kowi came and took everything. They knew that these were presents. And they knew that Eduardo was watching . . .
>
> Next day, Eduardo was farming on the far side of the river. Wâneki, Womle, Paci, everyone came. Kowi wanted to kill Eduardo so he fired a shot, but his arrow missed the mark. The white men quickly crossed back over the river, shouting, in their canoe. Then Eduardo showed them clothes and things, saying 'Come and get these clothes. My relatives, I will give you red clothes, and white clothes. Also knives.' So Womle said 'Bring the clothes here'. He put them in a sack and carried them away . . . Womle then went alone with Eduardo, who asked 'Do you want to eat beef?' Womle said yes and Eduardo invited him to come and kill a bull. So everyone came. They killed the bull and took its meat away. Then Eduardo said 'Do you want to eat manioc flour?' They killed two bulls and eight pigs. They then reassured one another that there would be no attack or killing on either side. So the Indians disappeared into the woods.

Eduardo Hoerhan sent downriver for two canoeloads of food. The Xokleng who had been with him reported back to the rest of the tribe:

'Everyone was saying "Can they really make contact?" Nil then returned and said "It is true: we have discovered the white man".'

Wâñpô's memories of the contact revolved around presents of animals, manioc, clothing, machetes, and axes from Hoerhan. The chiefs used to divide these gifts and the meat among the tribe's families. When there were plenty of slaughtered pigs and bulls, the Xokleng could hold their traditional celebrations, on one occasion to entertain a group of visiting Kaingang. At another time, some Indians went into a settlers' village in search of Eduardo. Hoerhan mentioned this incident in his official report for the year 1915. 'The Indians appeared half an hour's distance from the settlement of Scharlack, in the middle of the road, shouting and letting it be known that they desired to know where our personnel were, because they wanted to be given food, clothes, and blankets ... It required considerable effort to prevent the settlers, agitated by the sight of Indians killing their cattle, from shooting the Indians. Day after day, more Indians arrived and, day after day, the exodus of settlers continued.' Frightened families abandoned their frontier farms. Eduardo Hoerhan meanwhile had to pay compensation for every animal killed by the Xokleng. He realized that this was the only way to prevent violence. The Indians could not be stopped from hunting cattle; and the colonists would have shot the natives had there been no government recompense.

Hoerhan saw his work as heroic and altruistic. He was often in danger, since at times over a hundred Xokleng would arrive at his isolated post seeking food and presents. By December 1915, Hoerhan reported that they were 'in numbers immeasurably superior to our own group and became extremely insolent, incessantly attempting to disrupt the established order. The Xokleng are of an extremely treacherous character, and the more friendly they appear, the more precautions one must take.' A Xokleng woman married to an SPI interpreter warned that 'her brothers fully intended to murder all the personnel and principally the post's chief [Hoerhan], who was dozens of times in imminent danger'.

The Indians had accepted peaceful contact, but they were in no sense militarily defeated or cowed. Their only concern was presents, at first cutting tools and clothes, then meat, manioc, beans, and rice. It is remarkable that Wâñpô many years later recalled exactly how many animals or sacks of food were given at each encounter. But the Indians could not appreciate that the SPI's policy was to seduce tribes with presents and then, once they were pacified, to stop the supply of free tools and produce. Hoerhan, for his part, was struggling to survive with erratic and dwindling funds from the SPI and nothing from the settlers whose lands he was protecting. Perhaps misguidedly, he hoped to turn the nomadic, hunting Xokleng into settled agriculturalists. He wrote: '[I] made the greatest efforts to get the Xokleng to begin to work on the farms. Some Xokleng already work in the fields, but only when they are summoned and without the slightest persistence. Even so, when they do work, they carry out their tasks. They are exceedingly lazy and do not like to exert themselves, even when they greatly desire the promised reward. Not liking work, they nevertheless do not fail to enjoy feasts and dances, for which they prepare a drink from honey, water, and other ingredients that is strongly alcoholic.' Ever since the first Europeans reached Brazil in 1500, efforts to instil a Western work-ethic into Indians had generally failed. Hunter-gatherers were highly skilled at feeding themselves from the surrounding forests and rivers. They practised environmentally sensible slash-and-burn farming in forest clearings that were exploited for only a few years. Plantations were on a small scale and it seemed pointless to produce a surplus to immediate requirements, in a land of evergreen vegetation and abundant game.

Alien diseases now struck the newly contacted Xokleng. This was another tragic constant in the history of every Brazilian tribe. In Wâñpô's words: 'It was at this point that the Indians began to get sick. First Zeca died. Everyone began to get flu. They decided to divide up because of the sickness. This was the first time disease had come, and many died. . . . Those who had gone into the forest tried to administer their medicines, but nothing worked. Many people died.' Wâñpô named twenty-four men and women, including his own father, who perished from imported diseases against which they had no inherited immunity. 'And this was only among the adults. Many, many more children died. So my group went to live south of here, on the reserve. Then Eduardo saw our smoke, so he called to us with his [hunting] horn.' Contacts were intermittent during those early months, and the Xokleng memories concentrated on how many animals were given to them. 'We Indians liked beef, and at first we liked Eduardo too, because he gave us everything. We never lacked anything. It was only later that he refused to give us medicines.'

The confusion of contacts, presents, and disease and death was so traumatic that tribal customs were disrupted. For a time, initiations, seclusions, and mourning rituals were not properly observed. Then the tribe decided to hold its greatest festival, called *aygin*, and invited Eduardo. 'He gave two pigs and a cow. He also gave presents to all the widows.' Later came an *âgran* initiation ceremony, the first to be held at the attraction post. The Indians brewed five vats of mead; Eduardo gave two bulls and two pigs as well as clothing and blankets – particularly to the widows of men killed by disease. The chief even suggested that the

SPI official should bring his camera to take pictures of the occasion. 'At that time, Eduardo was good for the Indians . . . We always used to work together with Eduardo at that time . . . At first, Eduardo had given us meat to eat. He had given us everything. But later all of this stopped. When we had all the workers together, we would plant three sacks of corn and two sacks of beans with no trouble at all. When all the corn and beans were ready, the Indians got some to eat. But it turned out not to be worth it because we got so little. The children went hungry and starved.'

An SPI Indian post was run either by a salaried *encarregado* ('entrusted person', agent, or manager) or by a *delegado*, an unpaid individual expected to find his own resources and work on behalf of the Service. Thus, Eduardo Hoerhan, as delegado of the Xoklengs' Duque de Caxias reserve (later renamed Ibirama), was constantly short of funds from SPI central resources. He made his Indians work collectively on such tasks as gathering erva maté for the herbal tea so popular with gaúcho cattlemen. Hoerhan traded on behalf of his tribe and supplied its few needs for outside products. But as the Xokleng became more sophisticated about the market economy, they misunderstood this system. One elderly Indian later complained that 'in that [early] period we worked, and Eduardo kept everything. When we needed something, we had to implore him.'

There were times when Eduardo Hoerhan became equally bitter towards the tribe he had approached with youthful idealism. He condemned the Xokleng character in his official report: 'They are ungrateful, not recognizing the good that has been done to them. They are cruel and implacable, even among themselves in the bosom of their own families. They are treacherous and cowardly, always attacking by ambush. They are gluttonous and insatiable. Nothing is enough for them: they want everything.' When the Xokleng came to Hoerhan's post to obtain presents, they often remained there and had to be fed. Hoerhan's funds were exhausted and he almost abandoned the effort; but he persevered and his attraction huts became the SPI Indian post Duque de Caxias.

The colonists were sceptical about the young official's claim to have pacified the dreaded Xokleng and sent a commission of inquiry. But when the pacification was verified, the Companhia Hanseática reneged on most of its promised 30,000 hectare (120 square mile) concession. Once the warlike tribe laid down its arms, its lands could be invaded with impunity. The Indians were awarded only a small area at the furthest end of their traditional homelands. This remains theirs – a pocket of forest and fields surrounded by open farmland. It was a cruel and disgraceful deception.

As proof that his pacification had succeeded, Hoerhan in 1919 took a hundred Xokleng to Blumenau. Years later, he told the anthropologist

Darcy Ribeiro about a pathetic episode that occurred during this visit. A local doctor, Hugo Gensch, had adopted a ten-year-old Xokleng girl called Korikrã whom he renamed Maria and was raising as a young Brazilian woman, in a strange social experiment. The girl's father and relatives were in the group brought by Hoerhan. The father was angry that Maria refused to recognize him. He made her remove her blouse and hat and undid her hairdo. Then he berated her:

'I see that you are ashamed of me, ashamed of all your people.' He showed his enormous hands and said: 'These hands carried you many times. These hands lifted your body up into the pine trees to pick the pine seeds you ate. These hands of mine raised me into many trees to gather honey for you to eat. Honey, you understand, honey! honey! which went down in your throat, here' – and he ran his hand violently down Maria's neck, to her disgust. The old man then took Maria's aunt and held one of her breasts in his hands and said: 'Look, these breasts fed you, these arms cradled you.' The old man was filled with hatred and disgust. He went up to his daughter and pushed her away violently. Turning to Eduardo [Hoerhan] he said: 'She is of no further use to us, but she could still serve you. Take her and bring her to your white house [on the post] and impregnate her many times. She can no longer perform for us, but she still could for you.'

Poor Maria. Her adoptive father Dr Gensh loved her and taught her German and French. He even took her to Paris and Buenos Aires. But the local colonists would have nothing to do with her, and Maria Gensch died a spinster at forty-two.

Despite occasional disillusion on both sides, Eduardo Hoerhan ran his post among the Xokleng for forty years until 1954. At first, Duque de Caxias could be reached only by river. But this isolation did not prevent the Xokleng being struck by successive epidemics: of flu, measles, and smallpox. Hoerhan tried to restrict movement to and from the reserve; but in 1918 he made the mistake of taking most of his Indians to Ibirama to impress a visiting state governor. The presentation never took place; but during their stay in the town, many Xokleng caught smallpox and died. The Xokleng of Santa Catarina were in 1918 ravaged by whooping cough that 'shook adults and children in convulsions of coughing that exhausted them and eventually killed many.' In the following year came the worldwide epidemic of Spanish flu. 'The mortality was so great that they did not even bother to bury the dead: bodies were left unburied, as fodder for the village dogs.' The first attack of measles struck the tribe in 1927, followed by mumps, which prostrated many. In 1939 an Indian woman who had mixed with labourers outside the reserve contaminated the Xokleng with gonorrhoea that left Indians sterile, blind, or dead. At the time of contact in 1914, this part of the tribe numbered between three and four hundred; but when the American anthropologist Jules Henry was with them twenty years later, they were reduced by two-thirds.

One Indian reproached Hoerhan: 'You made us come down here, close to you, only to kill us with so many diseases.' To which he answered: 'Had I foreseen that you were going to die so wretchedly, I would have left you in the forest. There you would at least have died happier, defending yourselves against the attacks of bugreiros with weapons in your hands.' Years later, Hoerhan blamed lack of support by the SPI as 'the major reason behind my lack of success in achieving my original objectives. I do not feel that my work has been completely useless, but I never imagined that the Indians would arrive at this state of degeneration.' The author visited the Xokleng in the 1970s and I found them living in considerable squalor. Although completely acculturated in clothing and housing, they did still retain some of their independent pride.

Another group of Xokleng frequented one of the SPI's earliest posts, Rincão do Tigre in the Palmas region on the Santa Catarina–Paraná border. The official in charge was a good man called Fioravante Esperança. One day in 1915 Esperança entertained to lunch two passing fazendeiros, unaware that one of them, Cândido Mendes, had previously participated in an Indian slaughter. Among the Xokleng, people eat only with close friends. The Indians therefore assumed that Esperança was in league with the killers. They removed the visitors' weapons on the pretext of examining them, and then attacked all the post's staff and its two visitors. Esperança defended himself with his fists, trying to reason with the Indians. His body was found near the post's flagpole, with his revolver still in his belt and no shots fired from it. 'He fell faithful to the Service's device: "Die if you must; but never kill".' The dead farmers had powerful friends who wanted revenge; but the SPI managed to prevent this and re-established contact with this branch of the tribe.

The new SPI started with a brave and dedicated group of army officers, most of whom had been trained on Rondon's strategic telegraph expeditions. In its early years, it achieved well-publicized 'successes' in pacifying the hitherto hostile Kaingang and Xokleng. These contacts were the pinnacles of the Service's ambitions – but there were actually very few of them. With hindsight, 'pacifications' are seen to contain elements of hypocrisy and duplicity. Presents of irresistible metal blades and other goods soon dried up. Axes and machetes exerted a fatal fascination for isolated tribes. It was fatal because, all too often, medical back-up for contacts was criminally inadequate, so that Indians were decimated before they could enjoy their new peace with the colonization frontier. And as soon as a tribe had ceased to be a military threat, its lands were exposed to invasion, exploitation, or theft.

The southern Kaingang fared no better than their Xokleng relatives. A concentration of over 1,400 Kaingang at Nonoái in Rio Grande do Sul had been in peaceful contact for several decades. The SPI initially hoped to congregate them 'into agricultural centres, in order to transform them into national workers'. This attempt was a total failure. (Indeed, after a few years, the Indian Protection Service dropped the second half of its original title referring to 'localization of national workers'.) The state government later demarcated an area of 34,908 hectares (135 square miles) at Nonoái and congregated Kaingang within it. But in March 1941 a corrupt temporary state governor used an executive decree to reduce Nonoái to 14,910 hectares (58 square miles) before handing it over to the SPI. The rest of Nonoái became a 'state forest reserve', and the SPI did nothing to stop this illegal action. The pillage of this reserve proceeded when, in 1958, the state government deceived its Assembly into granting permission to sell off the land taken from the Indians in 1941. Four years later, a corrupt governor of Rio Grande do Sul authorized the sale of this land in plots to so-called 'landless farmers'; but it soon passed into the hands of land-development companies with links to the Governor.

The last autonomous groups of Kaingang in northern Paraná were engulfed by settlers, many from an English land-colonization scheme in the 1930s. At that time, no one realized that the soil under cleared rainforest was almost useless for farming, so the first action by immigrants was to fell forests. Carlos Moreira commented that 'the total destruction of the original animal and vegetable resources was completed when the land was divided up into small holdings for planting coffee.' Scattered groups of Kaingang in the Tibaji and Ivaí valleys either perished or were distributed with tiny landholdings on the settlement frontier.

It became SPI policy to try to earn income from indigenous areas. This *renda indígena* or 'Indian yield' was an invitation to corruption by the poorly paid agents who administered it. The SPI sold a concession to log valuable araucaria pines on the Kaingang's Mangueirinha reserve. The resulting deforestation was an irreversible environmental disaster, and the removal of the pine trees deprived the Indians of nutritious pine kernels that fed them through much of the year. So their beautiful forests were turned into secondary growth and weedy fields, and they themselves became dependent on imported food.

Colonel Cândido Rondon was the full-time Director of the Indian Protection Service for only seven months in 1910–11. Thereafter until 1930 he became 'Effective Director' with the executive work done by others such as José Bezerra Cavalcanti. Beneath them, the SPI was divided into a few regional inspectorates, which contained the posts run either by encarregado agents or unpaid delegados.

At the end of 1911, the fledgeling Service suffered a devastating blow: the Ministry of War requested the return of its officers to regular army service. Bezerra Cavalcanti argued that the SPI desperately needed officers as its regional inspectors. This was because such officials had to have 'an element of war' (the courage to confront hostile Indians and not fire back) and 'an element of civilization' (the moral rectitude that came from military discipline). Although Brazil had fought no war since that against Paraguay half a century previously, the army was highly regarded and the SPI needed the prestige of its uniforms. Director Bezerra Cavalcanti pointed out that the new Indian Service was 'an excellent and incomparable training ground for our worthy military men, who dedicate themselves sincerely to a perfect understanding of our fatherland, in order better to serve and defend it.' Most of Rondon's team were Positivists, and it was a basic tenet of that creed that the army should be a force of order and patriotic service. The Indian Service could give soldiers jungle training and enable the army to 'conquer' the interior of its country.

Rondon's excellent officers were on the army's payroll: without them, the SPI's meagre finances would be strained and it might have to return to supposedly disinterested missionaries. This was precisely the objective of the pro-Church reactionaries. It was they who inspired the government of the new President, Hermes da Fonseca, to cut the Ministry of Agriculture's budget by a third in 1912 in order to stifle the new SPI, and to recall the army officers. The Minister of War duly removed four of the best sertanistas: Alípio Bandeira, the inspector in Amazonas, Viana Estigarribia, in Espírito Santo, Pedro Dantas, in Maranhão, and Manuel Rabelo, from the Kaingang pacification in São Paulo. The *Estado de São Paulo* newspaper predicted that Lieutenant Rabelo's withdrawal 'may mean the failure of his mission and the loss of all the work that had started so well. But those who created every form of obstruction to him will certainly now be satisfied.' Some of Rondon's dedicated team chose to resign from the army in order to remain with the Indian Service.

In October 1912, the Positivist Teixeira Mendes published a pamphlet revealing that the government was once again subsidizing missionaries to convert Indians. He reminded his readers that Indian protection was supposed to be the work of *lay* government officials, one of whose tasks was to prevent interference by religious sects. Indigenous people were meant to enjoy full freedom – personal, domestic, civic, and *religious*.

In the following month, Rondon accompanied the head of the Salesian missionaries in Mato Grosso, Father Antonio Malan, on a tour of inspection of his mission villages. Rondon's resulting report was published in the press. He noted various irregularities and demanded their correction. The Salesians had hired out Bororo Indians to work for fazendeiros, separated mothers from children, gave Indians insufficient food, charged too much for goods sold to them, and demanded that Indians attend mass. One missionary kicked his Indians and supervised their plantation labour with a gun in his hand. Rondon asked Father Malan to grant the mission Indians their own lands, and he was angry when they were awarded trivial plots of only 150 square metres (179 square yards). He insisted that the SPI was supposed to protect all Indians, including those on long-established missions.

The intolerant Salesian missionaries were intent on total conversion of the 'cruel and barbaric' Bororo. They saw their mission station as 'the most advanced outpost of civilization', themselves as 'bandeirantes of Christ, a vanguard in the immense wastes of an endless hinterland', and their task as civilizing, with contemporary European modernity but steeped in Christian values. Their first act of vandalism was to destroy the men's huts at the heart of each circular village, since these were the central institution of Bororo society and religious ceremonial. Rituals are constant in Bororo life, with celebrations of all rites of passage (particularly naming ceremonies, coming of age, and funerals) and seasons, and these festivities revolve around the men's meeting-place *baito* and the *bororo* courtyard in front of it. So the Salesians told their congregations: 'If you really want the Devil to cease to reign among you, go and get axes and picks, demolish that centre of all evil, and set fire to it'.

Some newspapers criticized Rondon as 'a secular who abuses his office to persecute Catholicism'. But the great Indianist fought back, in a letter to the press on 10 November 1912. He denied that he was a Freemason or that he sequestered large sums intended for the missionaries. He reminded his readers that the SPI had to protect its charges from the imposition of any alien creed, and to guarantee them the freedom and respect enjoyed by all Brazilians.

*

In 1913, Colonel Rondon was back in the territory of the Nambiquara (often spelled Nambikwara), in what is now called in his honour the State of Rondônia. He sought to gain the friendship of Indian groups near a new post called Vilhena, and he trained other tribes to maintain the telegraph lines. Two Paresi Indians were sent to learn Morse code and telegraphy, so that they could take charge of telegraph posts.

Towards the end of that year, a remarkable personage entered this remote part of Brazil: Theodore Roosevelt, the hugely popular twenty-sixth President of the United States from 1901 to 1908. The ex-President was now fifty-five, overweight but vigorous, and keen to repeat in the Americas his African big-game-hunting exploits. The Brazilian Foreign Minister turned to Rondon, his country's leading explorer, to provide adventure for this visiting grandee. Rondon agreed, on condition that their expedition's objectives should be scientific rather than slaughtering animals for trophies – although Roosevelt's son Kermit was to be allowed to take some stuffed specimens of Brazilian fauna back to the New York Museum of Natural History.

Colonel Rondon joined ex-President Roosevelt when his ship sailed up the Paraguay river into Brazilian waters. The two men got on well. Roosevelt later wrote that 'Colonel Rondon immediately showed that he was all, and more than all, that could be desired. It was evident that he knew his business thoroughly, and it was equally evident that he would be a pleasant companion.' He was 'neat, trim, alert and soldierly'. The Brazilian explorer regaled his visitor with stories of piranhas: how Lieutenant Pyrineus de Souza lost half his tongue and much blood to a bite from this fish; Rondon himself lost a toe; and in 1903 Ensign Francisco Bueno Horta Barboza had been killed by piranha during the construction of the telegraph line around the Pantanal. It was agreed, however, that the greatest danger would come from insects and the diseases they transmitted, from dysentery and starvation, and from accidents in rapids, rather than from snakes, jaguars, or caimans.

Roosevelt was equally impressed when the expedition visited the Paresi. 'In dealing with the wild, naked savages [Rondon] showed a combination of fearlessness, wariness, good judgement, and resolute patience and kindliness.' Rondon was pleased that 'the Paresi received me as a friend and a beloved and respected chief . . . I had been introducing the benefits of civilization among them gradually, which is the only way to make their progress permanent. Mr Roosevelt was delighted by the process and by the results obtained.' Neither man questioned the wisdom or ethics of imposing this 'civilization' and 'progress'. At that time Americans were as convinced as Brazilian Positivists of their superiority.

The former President admired the Paresis' gentleness towards their children, and the latter's obedience. 'In each house there were several families, and life went on with no privacy but with good humour, consideration, and fundamentally good manners . . . The children played together, or lay in little hammocks, or tagged round after their mothers . . . They were friendly little souls, and accustomed to good treatment.' Meanwhile, the Paresi men played a wild game of headball, with a hollow rubber ball that was touched only with the top of the head. 'It is hard to decided whether to wonder most at the dexterity and strength with which it is hit or butted with the head, as it comes down through the air, or at the reckless speed and skill with which the players throw themselves headlong on the ground to return the ball if it comes low down. Why they do not grind off their noses I cannot imagine . . . Looking at the strong supple bodies of the players, and at the number of children roundabout, it seemed as if the tribe must be in vigorous health; yet the Paresis have decreased in numbers, for measles and smallpox have been fatal to them.'

Moving north-westwards beyond the Juruena, the expedition met recently contacted Nambiquara. They were 'very friendly and sociable, and very glad to see Colonel Rondon . . . Their confidence and bold friendliness showed how well they had been treated.' One of Rondon's officers recalled the scene: 'The arrival of the Nambiquara Indians at our camps is an unforgettable spectacle. They march behind one another in an interminable file, completely naked, with the women carrying the small infants and all the baggage, while the men carry only their bows and arrows. When they come to find us, they leave these weapons hidden in the forest as a gesture of friendship.' President Roosevelt loved this handsome tribe. 'They were a laughing, easy-tempered crew, and the women were as well-fed as the men, and were obviously well-treated, from the savage standpoint; there was no male brutality.' Nambiquara men secured their penises with a string, but the women wore neither 'a string, or a bead, or even an ornament in their hair. They were all . . . as entirely at ease and unconscious as so many friendly animals . . . They flocked into the house, and when I sat down to write surrounded me so closely that I had to push them gently away . . . It seemed like a contradiction in terms, but it is nevertheless a fact that the behaviour of these completely naked women and men was entirely modest. There was never an indecent look or a consciously indecent gesture.' Rondon told his visitor that the Nambiquara used no blanket or covering by day or night. If it was cold, they slept in the ashes alongside their fires. As hunter-gatherers frequently in open savannah country, the Nambiquara are a dark-skinned people; but their bodies are often covered in a ghostly powdering of ash from this method of sleeping. At a meeting with another group of this indigenous nation, the warriors showed Roosevelt their skill as archers, firing arrows high into the air so that they fell in a straight line.

Like some extraordinary adventure-travel agent, Rondon offered Roosevelt a choice of four unexplored north-flowing rivers to tackle. The macho President chose the most difficult, a river called Dúvida (Doubt) because its course towards the main Amazon was unknown. It proved to be more formidable even than Rondon had imagined: totally unknown for 750 kilometres (470 miles) before it joined the lower Aripuanã and thence flowed into the Madeira and Amazon. The Dúvida was full of rapids, and for week after week the team had to manhandle boats and supplies down raging falls and races, through gorges, and between mazes of rock outcrops. On one occasion, Kermit Roosevelt insisted on inspecting a rapid too closely despite the rowers' warnings. A canoe was swept down and overturned by a whirlpool, a Brazilian rower was sucked under and killed, and Kermit was 'very nearly drowned, with his [pith-]helmet pushed down over his face by the current'. When a canoe was lost in another rapid, the party split, with eighteen men cutting a trail through the forest while new dugout canoes were built. In all, five of the expedition's original seven boats were lost and had to be replaced.

Unknown Indians (perhaps Suruí or Cinta Larga) shot Rondon's favourite dog, Lobo ('Wolf'), with an arrow. Rondon was heartbroken 'when I contemplated my dead companion . . . [but I followed] my habitual rule of conduct towards Indians, and left them presents as proof that we who were passing were friends.' In another incident, one of the men murdered his sergeant and ran off into the forest. He was briefly sighted, gesticulating from the bank downriver. Roosevelt was for pressing on and abandoning the killer; but Rondon's moral rectitude insisted that he be found and brought to justice. Rondon also made the expedition carry out a full survey of the river, even when Roosevelt wanted to move rapidly on a mere reconnaissance.

Rondon named one tributary the Kermit and then surprised the ex-President by a ceremony, authorized by the Brazilian government, to change the main river's name to Roosevelt. In the latter's words: 'This was a complete surprise to me . . . [Kermit and I] felt that the "River of Doubt" was an unusually good name; and it is always well to keep a name of this character. But my kind friends insisted otherwise, and it would have been churlish of me to object longer. I was most touched by their action, and by the ceremony itself.'

Kermit suffered malarial fever, as did many of the men; Lieutenant

Lyra and the American George Cherrie had dysentery; and Roosevelt hurt his foot badly while pushing a canoe. His leg was abscessed. 'I could hardly hobble, and was pretty well laid up.' Rondon recalled that 'This was not all. He was overcome by a tremendous attack of fever and it was necessary to interrupt the journey. Roosevelt was delirious. He called me and said: "The expedition cannot stop. On the other hand, I cannot continue. Leave without me!"' Rondon could hardly abandon his illustrious companion, so they pressed on with the ex-President being nursed in a covered canoe. Roosevelt's malaria 'gave rise to such extreme bodily weakness that his back became covered with boils and he was forced to lie face downwards in the canoe to avoid excruciating agony.'

'The days became repetitive ... We descended a meter for every kilometre we advanced, and our morale ... – it also descended.' Finally, on 15 April 1914, after six punishing weeks of exploration, the expedition met the first rubber-tapper's hut and then made its way more peacefully down to the Aripuanã, Madeira, and main Amazon rivers. Another team was sent to meet the explorers and its leader, Leo Miller, found Roosevelt 'wasted to a mere shadow of his former self; but his unbounded enthusiasm remained undiminished.' Rondon accompanied the Americans down to the mouth of the Amazon at Belém do Pará. Roosevelt said goodbye 'with real friendship and regret ... They were a fine set, brave, patient, obedient and enduring ... Together with my admiration for their hardihood, courage, and resolution, I had grown to feel a strong and affectionate friendship for them ... I was glad to feel that I had been their companion in the performance of a feat which possessed a certain lasting importance.' The expedition had covered over 1,000 kilometres (620 miles), most of which were unexplored. It was extremely arduous and it lasted for five months.

The Roosevelt Expedition enhanced Rondon's already massive reputation, but he needed all his prestige to save the fledgeling SPI. The status of Indians was discussed in 1915 during a debate on a new civil code. Rondon made a moving appeal to members of Congress, reminding them of the pressures suffered by the Indian Service and begging them not to let it fail for lack of resources. When a new Civil Code was published in January 1916, Article 6 said that 'native Indians will remain subject to the protective regime established by special laws and regulations. This will cease when they become adapted to the national civilization.' Legally, Indians were classed in the same category as minors and married women. This was not altogether bad for them: it meant that they could not be punished for acts sanctioned by tribal custom – even ritual killing – that would be criminal offences if committed by non-Indians.

What of the Nambiquara and Rondon's telegraph line? The great French anthropologist Claude Lévi-Strauss said that the Nambiquara's relations with the whites had gradually deteriorated until, in 1925, seven workers whom they invited to their village were never seen again. After that, the Nambiquara and the telegraph operatives avoided one another. In 1931, seventeen years after the Roosevelt–Rondon expedition, the telegraph post of Parecis, 300 kilometres (190 miles) north of Cuiabá, was attacked and destroyed by unknown Indians. This feared tribe was known only as Beiço de Pau (Wooden Beaks) because they wore round lip discs in their lower lips – a clear sign that they were a Jê-speaking group (now known to be Tapayuna).

In 1933 an American Protestant mission settled near the Juruena telegraph post. Friendly relations with the Nambiquara deteriorated when the Indians were dissatisfied by the paucity of presents given them by the missionaries as reward for helping them build a house and plant a garden. Then a Nambiquara with fever went to the mission for treatment. Although probably suffering from tuberculosis, he was simply given two aspirins, in full view of the other Indians. The sick man then bathed in the river, developed lung congestion, and died. The Nambiquara concluded that their relative had been poisoned. So they attacked the mission and killed six people, including an infant. After this and other incidents, Lévi-Strauss found a state of apprehension all along the telegraph line. If the Nambiquara did not appear as usual, it was assumed they had reverted to their usual belligerence. In 1938, three 'picturesque' Jesuit fathers started a mission close to the Juruena post. 'There were three of them: a Dutchman who prayed to God, a Brazilian who was hoping to civilize the Indians, and a Hungarian, a former aristocrat and a great shot whose role was to supply the mission with game.'

The telegraph line itself was not a success. It was manned by about a hundred people, some of whom were Paresi Indians trained by Rondon. For a few minutes each day they tapped messages to one another, mostly ominous news about the Nambiquara, about whom the telegraph workers were morbidly fascinated. They were feared as a potential threat; but, on the other hand, visits by their nomadic bands provide a distraction from the isolation and tedium as well as an opportunity for human contact. Lévi-Strauss lived with the Nambiquara near the telegraph post of Utiarity on the Papagaio ('Parrot') tributary of the Arinos headwater of the Tapajós. The plateau to the west was a barren place of sandy savannah and clumps of low forest. The anthropologist was depressed by this lunar landscape, in which the rough track alongside the telegraph line was the only landmark for 700 kilometres (435 miles). The strategic telegraph line, built with such effort, was almost obsolete. It was superseded by the invention of wireless telegraphy and there was no threat from Paraguay or Bolivia on this sleepy frontier. So its wires sagged, and posts were abandoned when toppled by termites or Indians – who mistook the hum of the telegraph wire for the buzzing of bees and thought that there might be some of their beloved wild honey.

Claude Lévi-Strauss's time with the twenty Nambiquara near Utiarity was the turning point in his formation as an anthropological philosopher. At first, he was appalled by the contrast between them and the far more sophisticated Bororo and Kadiwéu. 'The Nambiquara take an observer back to what he might readily, but wrongly, take to be a human childhood . . . The destitution in which the Nambiquara live seems barely credible. Neither sex wears any clothing, and they differ from neighbouring tribes in both their physical type and the poverty of their culture.' Of small stature, their relatively dark skins and abundant but 'gently curly' hair made some observers wonder whether they had intermarried with runaway black slaves; but Lévi-Strauss showed that their blood groups proved that this was not so. 'The women's attire was reduced to a thin string of mollusc beads, either knotted round their waists or as a form of necklace or bandolier. Their earrings were of mother-of-pearl or feathers and bracelets were carved from giant-armadillo shells . . . Masculine dress was even scantier, apart from an occasional straw pompom fastened to a belt above their sexual parts.'

For the seven months of the dry season, small bands of Nambiquara roam the savannah gathering any small animal or edible insect that 'will prevent them dying of hunger'. They live in crude shelters of palm thatch on a circle of sticks, and all their time is spent searching for food. Women use digging sticks to extract roots or club small animals. Men are skilled and avid hunters, with long bows and different arrow-heads appropriate to the type of game being stalked. As nomadic bands walk in single file across the barren campo, each woman is bent beneath a long urn-shaped open-weave basket that carries the family's possessions. The Nambiquara hod contains potentially useful materials, such as wood for making fire by twirling, lumps of wax or resin, vegetable fibres, animal bones, teeth and claws, scraps of fur, feathers, porcupine quills, shells of nuts or freshwater molluscs, stones, cotton or seeds. When Lévi-Strauss examined such a load, he despaired of its value to an ethnographic collector: it looked like the foraging of a race of giant ants. During the rainy months, from October to March, the Nambiquara settle by a stream near rainforest. They burn a clearing, a *roça*, and grow a crop of manioc, maize, beans, and peanuts.

As Lévi-Strauss came to know his group of Indians better, to understand their language and grasp their tribal customs, he grew to love these
delightful people. Their family life was almost carefree, and relations with
children were wonderfully harmonious and affectionate. The French
anthropologist took lyrical photographs of men and women laughing and
playing together in innocent abandon. These are one of the glories of his
famous book *Tristes Tropiques*. The Nambiquara have never adopted
hammocks, but sleep on the ground in the ashes of their fires. Lévi-Strauss
recorded one scene in his notebook:

> On the dark savannah, the camp-fires twinkle. Near these hearths that
> are the only protection against the descending cold [of night], behind
> frail windbreaks of palm-leaves and branches hastily pushed into the
> ground on the side from which wind or rain are feared, beside basket-
> hods filled with the pathetic objects that constitute their entire temporal
> wealth, lying on the bare earth stretching away in all directions, haunted
> by other equally hostile and fearful bands, married couples lie closely
> intertwined. They see themselves as one another's support and comfort,
> the sole protection against daily difficulties and the dreamlike melan-
> choly that sometimes engulfs Nambiquara souls.

As he picked his way through the scrub in the darkness, trying not to step
on naked limbs of Indians barely visible in the glow of their fires, Lévi-
Strauss felt pity for a people so totally bereft. But he then heard that

> this misery is animated by whispering and laughter. The couples
> embrace as if nostalgic for a lost unity, and their caresses are not
> interrupted by [my] passage. [I sense] in all of them an immense
> kindness, a profoundly carefree, naive and charming animal satisfaction.
> These varied sentiments are gathered together in something that resem-
> bles the most moving and genuine expression of human tenderness.

This mutual affection was no protection against the forces of cultural
change. When Claude Lévi-Strauss was with the Nambiquara they had
already been decimated by imported diseases, but their way of life was
unaltered. Ten years later, in 1948, the anthropologist Kalervo Oberg
found the group near Utiarity to be the most miserable Indians he saw in
all Mato Grosso. Two missions were concerned with them – the Jesuits
and a return of the American Protestant mission – and the group was
reduced to eighteen individuals. 'Of the eight men, one had syphilis,
another had some kind of infection in his side, another had an injured
foot, another was covered with some kind of scaly disease from head
to foot [presumably leishmaniasis], and another was deaf and dumb.' The

women were unaccustomed to washing, so that their skins and the clothes that the missionaries liked them to wear smelled terribly of dust and ash and decayed food. They had swollen bellies, from bad infestation by intestinal parasites, and they often had to break wind. When they crowded into his work space, the fastidious Swedish anthropologist had to stop and air the room. The carefree people who had enchanted Lévi-Strauss (and influenced his anthropological theories) had become surly, rude, and demanding when they wanted something from the missionaries or academics. Oberg was depressed by the Nambiquara's latent hatred, mistrust, and despair, but he understood that they were the product of cultural shock and mishandled contact.

3. Parintintin and Munduruku

As Rondon and Roosevelt finished their dangerous descent of the Dúvida (Roosevelt) river, their first contact with 'civilization' was with huts of rubber-tappers. During the final decades of the nineteenth century and in the early twentieth, the Amazon basin enjoyed a monopoly of the world's rubber. It alone contained the giant *Hevea brasiliensis* trees that produced this versatile latex. With the inventions by Charles Macintosh (to apply rubber to cloth), by Charles Goodyear (of vulcanization, to prevent rubber from melting or freezing), and by John Dunlop (of pneumatic tyres for bicycles and then motor cars), demand for rubber increased insatiably. Tens of thousands of seringueiro rubber-tappers poured into the upper Amazon from other parts of Brazil and occasionally from Europe or America. Many headed for rivers such as the Juruá, Purus, and Acre in western Brazil that were rich in *Hevea* trees. Their bosses lived in ostentatious luxury in Manaus and other wild cities of the rubber boom.

A few Indian tribes tapped rubber commercially – notably the Munduruku and Apiaká on the Tapajós – but most fled deeper into the forests to escape the guns, oppression, disease, and slavery brought by the seringueiros. Outside Brazil, in the lawless no man's land of the Putumayo river between Peru and Colombia, horrible atrocities were committed on the Witoto and Bora Indians by a British-registered Peruvian rubber company.

Rubber extraction in Amazonia always consisted of tapping the milk from isolated wild *Hevea* trees. Any rainforest contains dozens of different tree species, naturally scattered to avoid the onslaughts of insect predators, parasites, and diseases. The *Heveas* were no exception. They had to remain in the wild: all attempts to grow them in plantations eventually failed from attack by one of their natural enemies. However, those parasites did not exist in south-east Asia. When British agents removed rubber seeds from Amazonia in the 1870s, the trees flourished in carefully tended plantations in Malaya, Ceylon (Sri Lanka), and Java. The Asian rubber plantations had plentiful local labour and were close to ocean transport. The first Asian-grown rubber reached London in 1900. A decade later it had destroyed the Amazonian monopoly, and from then onwards the cumbersome tapping of the original *Hevea* trees accounted for a diminishing fraction of the world supply. Curiously, rubber production in Amazonia was greater in 1917 than in 1911; but during those years the world price dropped dramatically. Businesses went bankrupt at every level of the industry, from tapper to trader. For a time, there was a move away from rubber-tapping to the collection of Brazil nuts. But by the 1920s it was all over. The Amazon rubber boom collapsed, dramatically and irreversibly.

This was good news for the native tribes of Amazonia. Rubber-tappers were largely immigrants from other parts of Brazil, and these tough backwoodsmen were no friends to the Indians. Ignorant and frightened, they tended to shoot any Indian on sight. In 1920 there were over 92,000 civilizados in the relatively small territory of Acre alone; but with the depression in the rubber industry, most of these drifted back to Ceará and other parts of Brazil. However, the English missionary Kenneth Grubb, who was there in 1920, wrote that the region's commercial development had caused the complete disintegration and disappearance of many Indian tribes. All the main rivers of western Brazil, from the Negro to the Solimões–Amazon and the Juruá and Purus, were denuded. 'These rivers are silent today, except for the lap of the waters along some deserted beach, the hoarse cry of the parrots or the call of the *inambu*. The past has gone, with its peoples, in central Amazonia, leaving only a bitter sense of impotence.' Grubb gave three main reasons for the decline. One was the disappearance of game. 'The [guns] of the Christian were destructive and his capacity for slaughter unlimited. Wherever he went . . . he massacred the beasts and destroyed the turtle by thousands.' Another reason was disease. Measles killed unknown thousands of natives. 'Consumption [tuberculosis] seems to be found even among the remotest tribes. The influenza epidemic of 1918–19 ravaged the whole area from Bolivia to Venezuela.' Malaria was also a terrible scourge. In an analysis of mortality in Manaus in 1910, *half* the deaths were from malaria, with the next killer (digestive and intestinal attacks) accounting for only 8.5 per cent.

Faced with such calamities, Indians could lose the will to live. 'He succumbs to dark forebodings, a silent melancholy, a consonance of spirit with the damp forest around. The end comes clothed in spectral despair, destitute of a single ray of hope. "It is better to fall", they say, "into the power of our spirits than into the hands of the Christians".'

A third reason was outright killing. We shall never know how many massacres or battles were launched against Indians in remote forests of western Amazonia. Such attacks were known as *correrias* (hunts). Kenneth Grubb saw how

> the leading *patrões* or employers assemble from all the district and a count is made of how many hands may be available. The men bring their rifles and are handed out ammunition. They then proceed by arrangement to occupy positions around the given Indian village or communal place. They close in on this at a predetermined time and fall on the defenceless Indians, preferably surprising them. The *correria* 'comes out well' if they are able to annexe the men without bloodshed and carry them off, but if much bloodshed takes place it is 'an ugly thing', but apparently a necessary one . . . The Indians are beasts and must be treated as such. Society . . . is divided into two strata, Christians and *bichos da matta* or beasts of the forest. Christians are, of course, disciples of Christ, characterised by a boundless mercilessness . . . 'Bichos' comprehend the tribal Indians without exception.

Kenneth Grubb liked the simple, hard-working caboclos of Amazonia. But they lived in a lawless society. They told him: 'We do not respect the Constitution here. We have our own constitution with one article in it – Article 44 of the Winchester constitution.' The lethal Winchester .44 carbine was the settlers' favourite weapon.

Rondon was appalled by the cruelty that had occurred during the rubber boom. 'What innumerable atrocities! Raids were the rule, bringing death to all the *malocas* [communal dwellings], all the *papiris* [thatched huts], all the *igarapés* [forest creeks] where the persecuted took refuge. And when the onslaught had passed, the women knew nothing of the whereabouts of their children. Wandering, helpless tribes could scarcely recognize the site of their former dwellings, such was the devastation!' To Darcy Ribeiro, a post-war anthropologist and politician, seringueiros denied Indians everything that they needed for survival. They occupied their lands, disrupted their tribal cohesion, dispersed the men, and seized the women. 'In short, they subjected Indians to a regime of exploitation, which no society could survive.' Lonely rubber-tappers spent months on end in their isolated huts and were desperate for women. The easiest way to solve this problem was to raid Indian malocas.

Racial prejudice against Indians pervaded all strata of Amazonian society. The French geographer Paul Le Cointe published a two-volume study of Brazilian Amazonia in 1922 that echoed contemporary racism. He wrote that isolated tribes in the rubber-bearing forests fought one another and regarded whites as hereditary enemies. 'They generally live miserably and their numbers are declining. With very few exceptions, it is very difficult to enter into relations with these tribes. Some are openly aggressive. For these, their disappearance – which is only a question of time – can alone put an end to the atrocities that they commit on any unfortunate civilized person who falls into their power.' (The fact that there were no recorded examples of such atrocities did not prevent the perception that they might occur.) 'When we seek to civilize a savage people, we only give them new vices that lead to their gradual disappearance: they can never be assimilated. We can easily succeed in accustoming Indians to drinking alcohol and smoking. But we cannot suddenly enlarge their brains, so that their intelligence can become capable of appreciating our moral theories or following scientific arguments.' A Colonel Themístocles also despised these Indians, and wrote similar ugly nonsense. 'They produce nothing, not even enough for their own comfort, are nomadic, obey no laws and have no knowledge of them, . . . their brains are only partly evolved . . . and cannot fully assimilate the education and other demands of our civilization.'

Every Indian tribe has its own history of contact with Brazilian national society. Each reacts differently to the traumas of attraction, acculturation, and possible assimilation into that society. The variations are the result of geographical factors (the tribe's remoteness from the frontier or its type of environmental habitat), the nature of the contact (whether by SPI agents, missionaries, or potentially malevolent prospectors or frontiersmen), and above all the tribe's own reactions (which depend on its traditions, its nature, and often on the attitudes of individual leaders). In the following chapters, we shall examine case studies of tribes' contacts during the early decades of the SPI, moving from west to east along the great southern tributaries of the Amazon. The more western of these rivers lie within the great mass of Amazonian rainforests, so that contacts were with the extractive rubber frontier; but east of the Araguaia–Tocantins the terrain is often more open, so that there has been a longer history of a cattle-ranching and farming frontier.

Far to the west, the Javari river has been the boundary between Brazil and Peru since the mid-eighteenth century. This area is still densely forested and contains tribes that have had little or no contact with the outside world. A few glimpses of life in this remote region were revealed during the decades of the 1920s and 1930s, when seringueiros were trickling away or were turning from tapping rubber and caucho latex to timber-logging. Some of these frontiersmen became 'bosses' with paternalistic control over Indians. One such was known as Inglês. He lived on a tributary of the Curuçá and gathered latex with the help of some Maya Indians. Inglês's trading hut was close to a maloca of Panoan-speaking

Marubo, who in turn answered to an old black from north-east Brazil called Antonio Rosa. (A maloca is a large communal hut that houses a number of families; but the term maloca can apply to any small tribal community or village.) Inglês, Rosa, and other outsiders had themselves been controlled by bosses in the rubber hierarchy; but almost all the higher traders had failed commercially and disappeared. The Marubo, Maya, and other Indians occasionally fought one another, often incited by their bosses. On one occasion, the Marubo seized Inglês's Maya Indians and some of his women; at another time, a boss called Chapiama tried to get the Marubo to kill Inglês, but they failed. An outsider called Vargas married a Marubo and lived for years in her tribe's maloca until he was killed, either by Brazilians or by the Indians because he had failed to deliver trade goods promised in return for his wife. Chapiama was also accused of arranging the murder of a jovial Peruvian who was trading successfully with these Marubo. The Indians retreated deeper into the forests to avoid being indicted for the crime.

Another band of eighty Marubo moved to work on one Luzeiro's rubber forest at the mouth of the Batã river on the upper Javari, but fifty of these died in the terrible influenza epidemic of 1921. An Indian woman recalled that three or four of her people were dying every day. At that time, a group of Matsé (Mayoruna) lost their chief in a battle with skin trappers. A tribal meeting decided to send forty warriors to explore along the Pardo tributary of the Curuçá to seek a safer home. After four months they succeeded in finding a place that was free of whites and full of game, so that the entire village made a long migration to this new hunting ground. They lived there for forty years, disturbed only by occasional fights with Marubo or raids to steal tools or utensils from distant huts of civilizados.

A doctor called João Braulino de Carvalho was on the Javari in 1926, and his descriptions of its Kapanáwa, Matsé (Mayoruna), Nukini, and Marubo Indians show how much these peoples had moved – and declined in numbers – during the ensuing decades. Meanwhile, the collapse of the rubber boom continued. A few tappers tried to turn to logging. In 1921 the first big raft of timber logs was floated down the Jaquirana (headwater of the Javari), accompanied by 300 seringueiro families leaving the region. But 'it was in 1928 that the withdrawal of settlers from those rivers really started and in 1932 rubber hit its lowest market price.' In 1938 'everything failed'. Darcy Ribeiro felt that the collapse of the extractive economy was the salvation of the surviving Indians. One more decade of intense rubber boom would have extinguished them.

Other tribes of these western forests remained isolated, and came into contact only during the latter part of the twentieth century. Such were the Maya and Matís of the Ituí–Quixito, and bands of Marubo, Korubo, and Kanamari of the Jutaí and other rivers in this vast, flat rainforest. There were still a score of uncontacted groups (in the Javari Valley indigenous territory and on the Brazilian–Peruvian border in south-western Acre) at the start of the new millennium.

The Amazon's two largest tributaries in this region, the meandering Juruá and Purus, rise amid the richest stands of *Hevea brasiliensis* rubber trees. This became the Territory (later State) of Acre, which Brazil acquired from Bolivia at the start of the twentieth century. These water-ways had therefore suffered the greatest influx of seringueiros. By 1920 their headwaters contained a civilized population of over 90,000 and a number of towns had sprung up on their banks. Any remaining native population was either decimated or coerced into rubber gathering.

The first pro-Indian inspectors entered this wild frontier in 1911. On the Inauini headwater of the Purus, an inspector found a camp of Peruvian latex-gatherers with sixty Jamamadi as their forced labourers. A ring of armed guards surrounded these slaves. 'They had been captured in their maloca, many leagues from there, and had been taken to the latex forest with every sort of violence. This included starvation, for they received no food whatever during the entire journey. Some died during the march, others when they reached the camp.'

The nearby Apurinã fought back against their oppressors. Two serin-gueiros tried to seize an Indian couple, but there was a fierce physical struggle in which the man was killed and his wife fled. Two days later the Apurinã under Chief João Grande drove off a band of nine seringueiros, leaving six dead. Reprisals came ten days after that. A troop of fifty heavily armed rubber men 'made a surprise attack on a maloca, wreaking a veritable slaughter. All the malocas then united and armed themselves. Terrified by the attitude of the Indians, the seringueiros fled precipitously from the banks of the Purus, often abandoning all their possessions.' But such a native counter-attack was unusual, and it was short-lived.

When the seringueiros encountered weaker Indians, they killed piti-lessly, stole women and children, destroyed roça plantations, and set fire to malocas. A seringueiro called José Marques de Oliveira snatched two children and raised them despite pleas from their parents for their return. One night, the Indians rescued the children. The seringueiro's revenge was the usual cowardly dawn ambush of the native village, during which four women were killed. 'Two children who failed to escape were thrown into a stream and there killed with rifle shots. Not satisfied with this, the attackers sacked the maloca, destroying everything they found, from the plantations to the houses and utensils, leaving these people in complete misery.' The French ethnographer Father Constant Tastevin was on the Liberdade and Gregório headwaters of the Juruá in the decades after 1918. He witnessed atrocities as well as more gradual acculturation. In one incident, Peruvian *caucheros* (latex-gatherers) were using sixty Panoan-speaking Yaminawa as slave-labourers alongside acculturated Indians. After a few months, the Yaminawa tried to escape to their forests, but were recaptured and shut in a hut for several days under heavily armed guard. Some 'civilized' Kaxinawá were then given carbines and told to pick off the Yaminawa as they tried to run from the hut to their canoes. 'Apart from young women, who were kept for the so-called civilized Indians, only one man managed to escape.' Tastevin also described a massacre by Peruvians of a hut full of neighbouring Nehanawa. However, some Kaxinawá resisted. Their famous chief Teskon 'boasted of having personally killed twenty-two civilizados and having pillaged an incalculable number of rubber stores.'

In a survey in 1927, Kenneth Grubb reported that many groups, such as the Kulina of the lower Javari and Jutaí, the Arawak-speaking Korubo of the upper Jutaí, or the Marawa of the lower Juruá were 'almost entirely incorporated into the civilized population' or survived in seriously reduced conditions. Many tribes or clans had been extinguished or were 'doomed to an apparently inevitable disappearance'. The Kanamari and related Katukina, for instance, had once been numerous nations with groups on various tributaries of the Tefé and Juruá. By the 1920s, these were diminishing catastrophically. One of Rondon's officers lamented that the Kulina of the Santa Rosa tributary of the Purus were 'contaminated by the civilizados . . . [they suffered] enormous mortality, and until now the remedies taken to reduce this are non-existent'.

Some Panoan-speaking tribes, already much divided into clans, suffered social disintegration with the onslaught of the rubber-tappers. An exception occurred in a pocket of land between the Tarauacá and Envira headwaters of the Juruá. This was 'a locality destitute of rubber trees, and as a consequence the remnants of several tribes [Kaxinawá, Kontanawa, Mainawa, and Yaminawa] have made it a refuge. These tribes are constantly at war with the Brazilians and Peruvians.'

The young SPI made some efforts in this immense and fragmented region. They had a post for the Kaxinawá on the Gregório and another on the Tarauacá some miles to the east. SPI agents made contact with some Kuya Indians near the Moa, at the western end of Acre Territory, but nearby 'wander the miserable remnants of the Nukini. The Nawa, who formerly occupied the picturesque hills where now stands the township of Cruzeiro do Sul, have only one survivor.' Further east, the Indian Service was doing 'remarkable educative work' among some 2,000 very assimilated Apurinã (Ipurinã or Kangite) on the upper Purus.

Some 600 kilometres (370 miles) south-east of Acre, the Tupi-speaking Tupari were also coming to terms with the rubber frontier. At the height of the rubber boom, seringueiros sought rubber trees in the forests of this tribe's homeland, a stream called rio Branco that flows into the middle Guaporé river. The Tupari chief Vaitó in 1948 told a Swiss ethnographer, Franz Caspar, how his people had met the first Brazilians. In the early decades of the twentieth century, the Tupari were on friendly relations with neighbouring Tupi-Mondé-speaking tribes – the Makuráp, Wayoró, Aruá, and Jabuti – all of whom were drawn into the world of the seringueiros. They occasionally gathered rubber or went to work at the barracão, the depot or trading post that the rubber men established at a place they called São Luis, near where the Branco joins the Guaporé. These tribes told the Tupari about the strangers, some with white skins and others black, who wore clothes and 'moved about on the river in big boats driven by a monster which made a great noise. They did not hunt with bow and arrow but fired with a tube from which small hard grains went into the animals' bodies with a big bang . . . They built their houses on the riverbank and looked for the [rubber] trees which we call *herub* and from the sap of which we make balls for games . . . They fetched the Makuráp men and gave them knives and axes and also shirts and trousers, hammocks and mosquito nets. In return the Makuráp had to help them fell trees and cut paths through the woods.' The Tupari were just as amazed by the cutting power of metal blades as all other Indians before and after them. 'These axes were much harder than the stone axes with which we chopped wood and they did not break. The strangers' knives, too, were much better than the bamboo knives and the blades of grass with which we cut meat and feathers for our arrows. We also wanted to have axes and knives like that, but we were afraid of the strangers.' Tribal elders said that the intruders were *tarupa*, evil spirits who bring death.

The price paid for the civilizados' wonderful metal tools was the usual tragedy of imported disease. The Tupari were dazzled by the goods their neighbours had received from the whites, 'but we also saw that many Makuráp were coughing and dying. It was the motors from the strangers' village which brought this cough up here. All the Makuráp were coughing and many, very many, died. The tarupa [whites] also went to the Jabuti, Wayoró, Aruá, and Arikapú and took them to work in their plantations [of maize and manioc] and to the rubber forests. They too received axes and knives, shirts and trousers. But they too began to cough, got headaches and fever and very many of them died. Soon only a few were left alive.'

Eventually, in 1927, a friendly Indian guided two white men to the Tupari village. 'We had never yet seen a tarupa and were very frightened. We rushed out of the hut with bows and arrows, and our wives and children howled and hid in the hut or fled into the forest.' But the strangers brought many presents, and also distributed sugar and salt. They easily persuaded some Tupari to accompany them to work at the barracão rubber depot, in return for more machetes and knives. 'But when the white man Cravo was with us, he coughed a great deal and much slime came from his nose. And our men and women and many children began to cough too, slime flowed from their noses and they had bad pains in the head and chest. Many Tupari died. Many a chief and magician also died. So we were afraid and no longer wanted to go to the white men. But we very much wanted to have more axes and knives.'

In 1934 the distinguished German anthropologist Dr Heinrich Snethlage visited the Tupari. He arrived with Indians from other tribes and three Brazilians, including a black called Nicolau. 'The *toto alemão* ['German doctor'] brought many gifts: knives, axes, mirrors, combs, necklaces, clothes and many other things besides. He was a very good man and he was very tall, much taller than you or I and all the rest of us. The black Nicolau laughed a great deal and danced much with our wives and he gave us many beads. But the *toto alemão* was ill and coughed much. Our wives and children and the men too began coughing again. And many died.'

Franz Caspar reckoned that there were 3,000 Tupari at the time of their first contact. Although feared warriors, they were at peace with neighbouring tribes. They seem to have been contented, 'with secure and tranquil attitudes, little aggressiveness, a communicative spirit, open enjoyment of innocent fun, great love of children, etc.'. All this was destroyed by the imported viral disease, which seems to have transformed itself into a mixture of pneumonia and acute bronchitis, from which many died. By the time of Snethlage's visit, the tribe was decimated, reduced to 250 people in only three huts.

The introduction of the coveted tools had unexpected effects on Tupari life. Metal axes and machetes greatly reduced the annual labour of clearing forest. They thus increased the food supply and lessened periods of near-starvation – in the past, the Tupari had even been forced to eat people for food. Now the survivors could open large farm clearings, they had plenty to eat and drink and they could enjoy more festivals. There was less reliance on hunting and fishing or the collection of wild fruit and insects. But the labour-saving went almost too far. The men now had nothing to do during the rainy season. 'They are bored and spend weeks and months in their hammocks, scarcely emerging except for occasional hunting. During such periods, the young men often expressed a desire to return to São Luis to be alongside the seringueiros, where there was always some activity.' Although naturally conservative about food, the Indians readily adopted chickens and ducks and even liked condensed milk. The Tupari got no artistic, intellectual, or spiritual inspiration from the whites, apart from enjoying civilizado dancing when they were at the barracão. By 1955 all the tribe wore clothing, partly as protection against insects, but 'the essential function of clothing appeared to the Tupari to be the transformation of naked and savage Indians into civilized caboclos participating in the world of white men.' To Caspar, there was nothing ridiculous about such aspirations, and there was no pressure on the Indians to clothe themselves. Indeed, many women still went naked except when they wanted to integrate with frontier society: they did not associate clothes with modesty.

Caspar found that the seringueiros were generally not too brutal and were friendly enough to the Indians, whose help they wanted. The rubber-tappers were also from the lowest stratum of Brazilian society, themselves subject to the bosses in the barracão. Chief Vaitó described some seringueiros as 'very good men' who gave them ample presents. This atmosphere changed in the mid-1930s. An official of the SPI took a number of Indians from São Luis and nearby tribes, against their will, to work in a labour colony at the town of Guajará-Mirim far down the Guaporé and Mamoré rivers. This same man later left the Service and bought large stands of rubber forests on the middle Guaporé. He installed a Bolivian overseer who instituted a reign of terror at the barracão at São Luis. Each morning the Indians who had gone to live there were paraded and allotted crushing tasks. 'In the evening anyone who had not fulfilled his quota or who had not conducted himself satisfactorily in some other way was bound, locked up, and flogged without mercy. The Bolivian made free with their wives and daughters.' The Indians endured these torments uncomplainingly, because the whites were so obviously powerful, with all their possessions and their armed henchmen known as *capangas*.

Finally, in 1937, there was a reaction. André, the son of a Makuráp chief, fell foul of the overseer Severino and was bound and beaten; but he and his fellow Makuráp then escaped back to their village. Severino was furious and sent his Indian foreman Alfredo and four capangas with orders to 'Bring me this bandit, dead or alive. If he won't come of his own free will, then shoot him and bring me his head!' The posse reached André's village and, at gunpoint, bound his hands and those of the other men behind their backs. They appeared to submit tamely. The capangas went in search of other fugitives, leaving one man to guard the prisoners. But André whispered to a woman, who got a boy to creep up behind him and cut his bonds. 'André seized an old axe which lay on the ground and split the capanga's skull. He slumped in the hammock without a sound. André then snatched up the shotgun and a Winchester which were standing near the hammock. He was about to go after the other two, but at that moment one of them came in through the door of the hut. He saw his companion lying dead in the hammock, and then André fired a charge of shot in his face and followed it with a bullet from the Winchester.' Another capanga ran up, was shot and wounded, grappled with André but was overpowered and killed. A fourth capanga was hit as he ran back into the village; he fired wildly at the maloca; but André finished him with two shots in the chest. Alfredo, who later told this to Franz Caspar, found his kinsman André with the dead capangas. They walked to a nearby maloca to consult Chief Mutum, and determined to attack São Luis itself. The women prepared drink for a war party of the village's young men. These approached São Luis by night and alerted the Indians there. At dawn next morning, the hated Severino emerged from his hut to visit his outhouse. André shot him in the chest. 'Severino realized at once what was happening. "Don't do it, André!" he screamed, and ran towards the mango tree where André was hidden. Then he collapsed, dead.' The Indians went on to kill nine people, including two women and a child.

When news of the massacre reached Guajará-Mirim, there was the usual outcry against Rondon and the SPI. Hotheads clamoured for revenge: 'Low, treacherous beasts, these savages. There's only one argument to be used – bullets!' But no one was keen to approach São Luis with its armed Indians, and it was clear that these had been cruelly provoked. So the authorities found Regino, a seringueiro who had been a friend of the tribes of the rio Branco (a tributary of the Guaporé). He went alone to São Luis and made peace with its Indians, on condition that there were no punishments for what had happened.

During the War, with south-east-Asian plantation rubber in Japanese hands, the Brazilian government mobilized a 'rubber army' to try to revive Amazonian rubber tapping. Only about a hundred of these seringueiros reached this region, but they were enough to upset relations with its tribes. 'For the Indians, the most violent result of this influx was an almost general promiscuity of Indian women with the strangers . . . The frequency of such relations and the facility with which the native women consented soon became known throughout the Guaporé territory [Rondônia]. As payment, the Indian women received bars of soap, perfume, cloth, and similar things . . . There were also cases of rape of Indian women. During this period only one Indian man in the barracão reacted violently against the situation, killing his wife's seducer with three arrows.'

The atmosphere improved after the war, and with the advent of a Catholic mission at São Luis in 1952. But in that year emissaries from the barracão persuaded what was left of the Tupari tribe to migrate down to it. Two years later, a seringueiro suffering from measles reached the rio Branco. Within a few weeks over half the Indians at São Luis were dead. The shattered remnant of the Tupari fled back to their maloca, but more died during the journey. Franz Caspar returned to the tribe in 1955 and was devastated by what he saw. 'Of the two hundred Tupari with whom I had lived in 1948 I found only sixty-seven survivors. Two-thirds had succumbed to the epidemic, and the remainder had fallen victims to civilization. They had all been given shirts, trousers, and dresses and would not now be parted from them. Even at this moment they were flirting with the idea of returning to the rubber gatherers . . . There could be no doubt about it: the impact of civilization had finally broken the Tupari, more quickly than I would have believed possible. It will be only a matter of a year or two before the last members of the tribe will have been submerged among the rubber gatherers. And then the memory of the Tupari, once a mighty and dreaded people, will live only in the showcases of ethnographic museums and in a few dusty volumes.'

One tribe defended its independence and territory with admirable tenacity for two centuries. The Tupi-speaking Kawahib occupied a great stretch of forest along the east bank of the middle Madeira river (between its tributaries the Ji-Paraná (Machado) and the Roosevelt–Aripuanã descended by Roosevelt and Rondon in 1914). The Kawahib were known as Parintintin, a derogatory name given them by their enemies the Munduruku and the Mura-Pirahá. Rubber-tappers and travellers on the Madeira river were all terrified of the Parintintin, who were ruthless and formidable warriors.

The first anthropologist to study the Parintintin described them as

a warlike tribe which lived in conflict with everyone without exception who was not part of it. They had not the slightest respect for the lives or property of others. For the Parintintin, war is not a tough and deplorable necessity: it forms the preferred sport of boys from the age of twelve onwards . . . Attacks by the Parintintin on neo-Brazilians are made at any time of year and at any hour of day or night. Attacks are more frequent in the summer, when the *igapós* [seasonally flooded woods] are dry and the paths good, facilitating excursions. However, since these Indians have canoes hidden all over their territory, they are capable of penetrating, via lakes and floodlands, to their enemies' establishments even at the height of the rainy season.

Hundreds of people, both Brazilians and Indians of neighbouring tribes, had been killed in surprise attacks by the Parintintin.

Retaliation by the rubber-tappers was equally brutal. In the early years of the twentieth century there were large and bloody raids on the Parintintin. A Peruvian called Benjamin Maya led a horde of seringueiros on one such attack. Firing their rifles from a river boat, these killed native women in a village and their men when they shot arrows at the boat. The Parintintin were forced to flee, taking their dead. The raiders burned their huts and destroyed their plantations.

It would be a tremendous achievement for the new SPI to pacify this formidable tribe. Rondon sent a dedicated agent called João Portatil to attempt a peaceful contact. Although he spent weeks on end in the forests, Portatil met no Parintintin. 'In the end, the poor man fell into a pitfall trap at the entrance to an abandoned maloca, hurt himself seriously, and only regained the banks of the Madeira carried by his companions who, from then onwards, refused to accompany him.' In 1919 Bento Lemos, the SPI Inspector in Manaus, sent an explorer/surveyor, Captain E. S. Amarante, to try to make contact with the Parintintin. Amarante started by establishing a post among the nearby Mura-Pirahá. Although isolated, this tribe was pacific; but its people were mortal enemies of the Parintintin, so that there was no hope of success from an expedition based among the Mura-Pirahá.

In September 1921 Inspector Lemos asked the thirty-eight-year-old German anthropologist Curt Nimuendajú to attempt the pacification. This seasoned sertanista had already worked among Brazilian Indians for sixteen years. He spoke excellent Tupi-Guarani, and the Apapokuva Guarani of western São Paulo had formally adopted him into their tribe with the sonorous name Nimuendajú, 'He who lives among us'. He ended his description of his night-long naming ceremony: 'When the sun rose behind the forest, its rays illuminated a new companion of the Guarani tribe who, despite his pale skin, faithfully shared with them for two years the misery of a moribund people.' When he adopted Brazilian nationality in 1922, he made this his surname. But Nimuendajú was no romantic who 'went native'. Life in an Indian village was no picnic. In one depressed moment, he wrote that 'the life of south-Brazilian forest Indians is incredibly miserable, full of penury and privations, of persecutions and danger. Prolonged habitation with the puerile, fearful and obstinate savages is so insufferable that even a fugitive criminal would be mad to submit to all this.'

A tireless field-worker and meticulous scholar, Nimuendajú was to become the outstanding anthropologist of early-twentieth-century Brazil. He made almost continuous expeditions every single year for four decades until his death in 1945. He explained that he lived among Indians because 'it is necessary to feel in your own flesh the problems of the group as if they were your own – to fear the same threats, raise the same hopes, grow angry at the same injustices and oppressions.' Nimuendajú was the first anthropologist to be concerned as much with shattered, semi-acculturated tribes as with glamorous newly contacted peoples. And he was one of the first to campaign for their rights. The distinguished ethnologist Herbert Baldus wrote that 'throughout his life, this honourable man fought in defence of the Indians against representatives of our civilization that was invading the sertão with the power of superior arms. He thus gained the love of the persecuted and became one of them. Like them, he suffered the hatred of colonizers, for whom "Indians are not real people".' But it was not only peaceful natives, already disarmed and humiliated, whom Nimuendajú defended. Ignoring dangers and hardships, he made contact with some of the most feared tribes, to put an end to reciprocal killings between valiant warriors and their white neighbours.

Curt Nimuendajú pondered why his predecessors had failed with the Parintintin. He learned that Portatil had been told a common fallacy: that the best means to contact a hostile tribe was to make a peaceful expedition to its villages. An intractable people like the Parintintin could never be approached so easily. 'The pacifier must make a permanent establishment in its territory and thus oblige it gradually to reach an understanding with him, after convincing it that his position is impregnable and of the advantages that his presence brings to the tribe.' This attraction post must be clearly separated from the tribe's enemies, the settlers. It must be in the tribe's territory, but not too close to their villages to make them fear an ambush. It should be accessible to its lines of communication, prefer- ably all year long.

Nimuendajú chose to locate his base near a rubber plantation burned by the Parintintin. In March 1922 he started unloading supplies to build this attraction post. The Parintintin made their first attack on his tempor- ary camp 'with a great war cry'. One worker was almost hit by an arrow, but no one fired back. Curt Nimuendajú gathered up the arrows and left them on the Indians' trail, with a present tied to each shaft.

The builders left, and Nimuendajú remained in his attraction post with six men. It was a riverbank clearing, surrounded by barbed wire but with a gate always open. The house was near the river, roofed in corrugated iron, and with three rooms, kitchen, and veranda. The metal roof eaves came down low on the side facing the forest. There was a second attack on 28 April and a third on 4 May but the arrows always hit the metal roof, and no one reacted. On 15 May the Parintintin attacked in the open for the first time. Nimuendajú watched them break out of the forest into his clearing

horribly painted in black, with beautiful headdresses of yellow and red feathers on their heads and macaw tail-feathers hanging down their backs. Their arrows crackled against the wall plates like a fusillade. Uttering furious cries, they advanced along the perimeter towards the gate. This was exactly what I wanted. I immediately called out to them in the *lingua geral* [Tupi], inviting them to enter. From their military experience, the last thing they must have expected at that moment was an invitation and, perplexed, they appeared to pay attention to me for a moment. But they then redoubled their savage shouting and, brandishing their weapons, disappeared down the trail from which they had emerged.

The decisive encounter occurred on the 28th May. At 10.30 am the Parintintin ran in through the gate to attack me, amid their war cries and a hail of arrows. They scarcely gave me time to escape by the veranda. At the moment that I shielded my body behind a corner of the house, arrows struck beside me. In an instant the veranda was riddled with them and the yard was strewn with others that fragmented when they hit the walls. Over the top of the wall I could see a group of attackers advancing against the house, continually shouting and shooting, while others were cutting the perimeter wire on both sides of the gate, carrying off the pieces into the forest. I called to them, but they shouted so frenetically that I could hardly hear my own voice. I threatened them with a rifle, but even this produced no effect. I then ordered the men to prepare to fire a volley above their heads. But while I was hesitating to give the order 'fire' for fear of putting them to flight, they suddenly yielded and started to retreat towards the gate. I immediately exchanged my gun for an axe and a machete, which I showed and offered to them; and indeed some who were already near the exit stopped. I then quickly jumped down to the yard and, showing them some strands of beads, approached them. However, they were very

excited and suspicious and recoiled before me, so that I had to follow
them outside the perimeter where, since they asked me to, I laid the
beads on the ground and then withdrew a little so that they could come
to pick them up. I immediately ordered other presents to be brought
up, and they gathered these from within the perimeter.

Some twenty minutes later, they attacked again from the other bank
of the stream. I again emerged onto the yard and offered them presents,
and a band of them then swam across the Maicy-Mirim river and came
to take up a position on the left bank, right in front of the post's house.
From there they again fired a few arrows at us, but they then started to
ask for beads, offering their feather headdresses in exchange and inviting
me to go and trade with them where they were. I did not go, but after
twice giving them beads, etc., which I placed in a bowl that I pushed
along the current of the river for them to swim out and take, one of
them finally crossed to our bank and took some strands of beads that, at
his request, I had placed on the riverbank outside the perimeter fence
. . . Then, furiously beating their clubs against a little wrought-iron
shelter . . . they withdrew amid war cries. [Four other Parintintin swam
across the river and] approached the fence, completely unarmed. I
emerged to meet them and offered them more beads. They stopped at
a distance of fifteen paces and, not allowing me to approach closer,
asked me to throw the present to them. When this was done, one of
them tied a headdress to a piece of wood and, throwing this present at
my feet, said, '*Erohó!*' – 'Take it!'.

I asked what they wanted and they promptly answered that they
wanted axes, machetes, and knives. While I ordered these goods brought
from the house, they sought information: Whether we had come from
up or down the river; where was our home and what the river there
was called; whether the men of the garrison were my relatives; whether
I had a wife and children and what size were the latter, etc. They gave
me another headdress and received from us clothing, fishing line, a
grinding stone, in short a little of everything we had in the post. I then
asked whether they were hungry and when they answered that they
were, I gave them three bowls of manioc, tapioca, and sugar. This was
the first gift that they resolved to receive directly from my hands. They
withdrew to a small clearing, some twenty paces away, placed the bowls
on the ground, danced for an instant around them, and squatted to eat
a little. They then came back close to me, asked for more of this and
that, and finally at 3.30 p.m. withdrew peacefully, taking the presents.

The great miracle had happened. The 'indomitable wild beasts, the
man-eaters with whom one could talk only through the mouth of a rifle'
had conversed peacefully with me and exchanged presents during

almost three hours! Even the men of the post kept saying that there was absolutely nothing brutal or ferocious in their appearance or behaviour while they were there conversing with me. That which the population of the Madeira had all judged to be an absurd aspiration had been done. However many more arrows the Parintintin might decide to fire at the post, I was fully convinced that, little by little, the friendly relations would improve, until a complete pacification [was achieved].

The hoped-for 'pacification' brought little benefit to the Parintintin. Tragically, in ensuing months the tribe suffered terribly from its surrender, decimated by diseases and with its lands invaded. Nimuendajú's friend Herbert Baldus wrote that he soon 'deplored his own heroic act, realizing that the happiest Indians are those who keep themselves independent by their fighting valour and by intransigent hostility to any usurper of their lands.' By 1970 the head of the Indian service admitted that they 'live in extreme misery, exploited by regatões [riverine traders] and rubber-tappers with whom they have coexisted for a long time'. In the following decade the lands of 114 members of the tribe were finally delimited, and many Parintintin were converted by Protestant missionaries.

'Parintintin' means 'enemy' in the language of the Kawahib's inveterate opponents, the fearsome Munduruku. That great warrior tribe lived on the Tapajós, the next large southern tributary of the Amazon to the east of the Madeira. The Munduruku had once been an aggressive, militaristic people, whose warriors festooned their huts and their own bodies with the mummified heads of enemies they had killed. In the eighteenth century Brazilian settlers had been terrified of the Munduruku. But in 1795 this numerous tribe abruptly and unexpectedly decided to accept peace overtures from the whites; and the Munduruku remained surprisingly faithful to the colonists from that time onwards. For several decades, until reduced by disease, they were the bulwark that defended the settlers against other indigenous enemies.

In the later nineteenth century the Munduruku were also remarkable for the enthusiasm with which they took up rubber-tapping. They suffered the same commercial exploitation as did non-Indian seringueiros; but their cohesion and bellicose reputation saved them from the oppression that devastated other tribes during the rubber boom. The American Herbert Smith reported that the Munduruku 'gather [rubber] gum in immense quantities, and sell it to the traders or bring it [downriver] . . . Of course, the Indians are kept in debt to the merchant, and the merchant to the exporter; an inverted pyramid, all resting on the Indian workman.'

The racist French explorer Henri Coudreau in 1897 wrote, almost triumphantly, that 'the Munduruku are in total decadence, from the social,
moral and economic points of view. They are no longer "the terrible
Mundurukus" . . . In its decline, the horde is no longer an object of terror
to anyone, not even small neighbouring tribes . . . Their plains and forests
would lend themselves perfectly to European colonization, and even more
so to local colonization. I would offer a large bet that it will be only a few
years before one sees the last Munduruku sorcerer dry his last human
head.'

Fortunately for the Munduruku, Coudreau would have lost his bet
concerning their survival. By 1914 the rubber of the upper Tapajós was
controlled by a rubber baron called Raymundo Pereira Brazil. But even he
accepted that the Cururu tributary of the upper Tapajós was 'the exclusive domain of 400 tame Munduruku Indians'. The American William
Farabee described them in that year as 'honest, upright, good laborers
[who] with careful treatment will become of inestimable value to the
region.' He was impressed by how well they had adapted to the daily
routine of rubber-tapping.

There was little missionary activity in the lawless Amazonia of the
rubber boom. However, in 1911 two German Franciscans, Friars Ludwig
(Luis) Wand and Hugo Mense, paddled up the Cururu. They saw a
Munduruku in the distance, stood up in their canoe, and spoke to him
in the Tupi lingua geral, which they knew that the tribe understood.
'Suddenly Friar Luis put his hand into the bag he always wore and pulled
out a flute, which he started to play. Friar Hugo accompanied him with a
religious canticle. Then the savage approached and expressed his satisfac-
tion, but abruptly broke into a run and disappeared. Hours later, the two
missionaries found themselves surrounded by dozens of Indians who
examined them, felt them and smelled their habits. They then said the
word "*Anilcatcat, anilcatcat* (man)".'

The Franciscan mission grew slowly but steadily, and it has survived to
the present day. One of Rondon's exploratory expeditions visited the new
mission in 1911 and was welcomed by the Munduruku chief. The
explorers found that a few huts and a provisional chapel roofed in palm-
leaf thatch had already been built. By 1914 the mission's two priests and
three nuns were catechizing several hundred adults and had twenty-six
children in their school. Two years later, another missionary called Plácido
Toelle arrived and he soon moved the village to a better location across
the Cururu, 200 kilometres (125 miles) up the river at a boundary
between forest and savannah. Half-timbered houses with high-pitched
roofs were built in the German manner.

In 1895, settlers had employed the Munduruku to attack the dreaded Parintintin. Sixty warriors and forty women went on this raid; but it was a tragic disaster, for virulent malaria wiped out most of the Munduruku before they reached their traditional enemies. The advent of the Franciscans, together with depopulation, the absence of nearby enemy tribes, and the demands of rubber gathering put an end to warfare. The American anthropologist Robert Murphy saw this as 'a severe blow to the native culture, for one of its central foci had now disappeared; the primary interest of the Munduruku male had been valor, trophy-head and captive taking, and the great ceremonies centering on the heads. It is a loss still felt today [the 1950s] by the older Munduruku men, who now look skeptically at the future and nostalgically at the past.'

The same powerful forces that ended Munduruku bellicosity also transformed the tribe's social life. Large villages, with huts arranged in a circle and the inhabitants grouped in exogamous clans and divided into moieties, gave way to smaller units. Villages ceased to be political entities, the men's hut lost its significance, and houses were built more like those of local Brazilian frontiersmen. At first, villages along the Cururu turned from hunting and warfare to growing manioc for export. This activity was women's work, so that clans became matrilocal; but the trade was controlled by chiefs. But when the tribe changed to rubber production, it split up, individuals dealt directly with rubber companies, and chiefs lost their authority. Both the missions and the SPI were unable to revive the power of the ancient chiefs.

Outside pressures caused the Munduruku to divide into three groupings: some lived scattered among rubber men on the main Tapajós river; others were on the forested lower Cururu tributary, increasingly influenced by the Franciscan mission; others continued a more traditional life on the savannahs of the upper Cururu. Rubber-tapping is lonely work, with each seringueiro tapping trees along a fixed trail. Thus, family units gained greater importance than villages among some Munduruku, and along the Tapajós families lived isolated from the rest of tribal society.

In the 1920s, the remote backwater of the Tapajós was suddenly invaded by international big business. British and Dutch growers of plantation rubber in south-east Asia had formed a cartel that limited production and forced up prices fourfold. This angered Henry Ford, the world's largest automobile manufacturer, and he decided to smash the cartel by growing his own rubber. He bought a 2.5 million hectare (9,650 square mile) concession on the middle Tapajós, close to the place where Henry Wickham had collected his rubber seeds half a century earlier. Shiploads of equipment were sent to the Tapajós, to create what became known to Brazilians as Fordlândia. Despite the millions of dollars pumped into it, the venture was dogged by problems and incompetence. Its land was poor. Tree-planting proceeded painfully slowly and it was years before Ford hired qualified tropical botanists, who introduced techniques that had long been successful in Africa and Asia. In 1935 disaster struck: the canopies of the trees growing at Fordlândia were closing, and the dreaded South American leaf blight (*Microcyclos*) became virulent. Within a year it had devastated most of Fordlândia's plantations, killing millions of trees. The Americans obtained another tract downriver at Belterra, only fifty kilometres (thirty miles) from Santarém, and a further five million seeds were sowed. A town was laid out for the rubber workers, complete with cinema, golf course, swimming pools, and soccer fields. Experiments in grafting techniques, in importing other strains of rubber tree, and in introducing foreign labour, did not solve the problems. Some 2,500 workers were employed at the two Ford estates. These were mostly Brazilian north-easterners, not Indians; and unrest among them contributed to the venture's failure. By 1940, after the planting of 3.65 million rubber seedlings, there was not a single tree ready to tap! Once the trees were large enough to lose their leaves, they too fell victim to a devastating epidemic. Henry Ford finally gave up: he had invested $20 million but had no rubber to show for it. This was the greatest failure of his career.

The collapse of the rubber boom in general, and of the Ford plantations in particular, brought a slight respite to the Munduruku's acculturation process. There were fewer Brazilian seringueiros and traders, and less demand for Indian labour or produce. But, as Murphy observed, 'the Mundurukú had already become completely dependent on manufactured goods and continued to tap rubber, although on a reduced scale'.

The mission on the Cururu also drew Indians towards its part of the river. The German missionaries gained kudos by acting as middlemen in the rubber process: for although the Indians understood little of prices or weights, they learned that they received more for their rubber or manioc from the Franciscans than from traders. During the 1920s, even the more isolated Munduruku of the savannahs came downriver to tap rubber during the season. Gradually permanent native villages grew along the Cururu. In 1939 the Brazilian government designated the entire region as a reserve for the Munduruku and in 1941 the SPI established a post on the Cururu. But the nearby mission continued to be the main magnet. This was no accident: the German Franciscans 'were deliberately attempting to attract the population and modify their culture. The missionaries achieved little success during their first ten to fifteen years of activity and attracted large numbers of Indians only after . . . they offered high rubber prices and low-cost merchandise, and thereby accelerated the migration process.' The third group, of traditional villages near the source of the Cururu, also dwindled. In 1938 Rondon reported that 'twenty-five malocas of these Indians dominate the area from the eastern bank of the Cururu to the general plains, an immense savannah at the headwaters of that river, formed naturally within the dense Amazonian forests. Each maloca consists of eight great huts, four of which are the exclusive residence of the women and the other four in which only men live. The women's are situated on the banks of the Cururu; the men's quarters in the plain, a certain distance inland.' There were only seven of these 'traditional' malocas in the 1950s and none by the end of the century. Population shifted to the banks of the Cururu, but in frontier-style villages without the traditional circle of huts or central men's house.

The long-bearded Friar Hugo Mense worked at the Munduruku mission for thirty years before retiring to a monastery in Rio de Janeiro. But when the author visited the Cururu in 1972, the equally long-bearded Friar Plácido was still there, like a benign Methuselah. He presided over a clean and efficient mission, but one of stultifying regimentation and sanctity. Boys and girls were strictly segregated in their highly disciplined school. They received a good but conservative primary education of little relevance to their lives in the heart of Brazil. The place was a tiny German hamlet, devoid of any trace of Indian heritage. Even ideology and folklore changed as a result of such powerful external pressures. Murphy found legends that were based on African mythology, on the German Hansel and Gretel story, and one on the Crucifixion – with the resurrected hero descending the Tapajós towards promised lands in Germany or North America. In the 1950s, the once-mighty Munduruku were reduced to 360 people living in the savannahs, 700 on the Cururu, and perhaps as many again scattered along the Tapajós but no longer living in tribal communities. By the 1980s there were reckoned to be 1,400–1,600 of this tribe, mostly in ten aldeias along the Cururu.

4. The Xingu

By the end of the nineteenth century most of the mighty southern tributaries of the Amazon had been thoroughly explored, and the main rivers were long since denuded of their original indigenous peoples. There was one great exception: the Xingu. The mouth of this magnificent river had been colonized since the early seventeenth century. Several hundred kilometres of the lower river were exploited and its tribes enslaved or killed by disease. But the upper Xingu, above the formidable Von Martius rapids, remained inviolate, a sanctuary for a dozen tribes speaking most of the main native languages of Brazil.

This isolation was broken only in 1884, when the German anthropologist Karl von den Steinen reached the upper river overland across northern Mato Grosso, contacted some of its tribes, and continued downriver in the first descent of the Xingu by a European. Fortunately for the Xingu Indians, von den Steinen was one of the most sympathetic anthropologists ever to work with indigenous Brazilians. He was the first person to write about them as real human beings, with individual characters, qualities, and defects. Von den Steinen returned to the Xingu in 1887 with another great anthropologist, Paul Ehrenreich; and during the ensuing decades a number of other German and Brazilian scientists reached the river and admired its handsome peoples. So there was a succession of visitors to the upper Xingu in the early years of the twentieth century.

The main Xingu river is formed by a fan of headwaters, delightful rivers and streams that flow across a flat land of savannahs and low forests. This upper Xingu was a haven for nine tribes, some of whom had lived there for centuries, others who had fled from persecution by colonial settlers or other Indians. Although each tribe retained its language and social structure, the Xingu Indians had grown uncannily similar. The great Brazilian anthropologist Eduardo Galvão called this process 'cultural compression' and felt that it was intensified by the proximity of the pioneer frontier. He also referred to this unique assemblage of peoples as the 'Uluri culture area' because its women all wear a tiny bark-cloth triangle called *uluri* tied in their vaginas; others call them Xinguanos.

Anthropologists are baffled by this cohesion and homogeneity of distinct tribes, who speak radically different languages but live at peace with one another. No one knows how or when the confederation occurred. Mércio Gomes described it as 'a singular political experiment' and 'a very rare social phenomenon'.

Xinguanos still live in identical villages formed of a circle of mighty oblong thatched huts, each housing thirty to forty people, built in the same elegant architectural style with double-arched roofs and thatch descending to the ground on all sides. From a distance they look like the upturned hulls of wooden ships. The body paint, hairstyles, feather ornaments, even the physiques and facial expressions of both men and women are virtually identical. Years of proximity and some intermarriage have given these tribes common diets, agriculture, religious beliefs, and social customs. Orlando and Cláudio Villas Boas, who later spent a lifetime among the Xinguanos, wrote that 'they are gentle and hospitable, doing everything possible to be agreeable. At times *we* tactfully rejected some of their food; but they, out of politeness, never refused what we offered them. Their children are docile and affectionate. We never witnessed an argument or saw a brusque gesture that might betray disagreement. They live an enviable social life.'

Each tribe is governed democratically. With populations rarely exceed-ing 500 people, villages are miniature city-states in which the adult men meet every night to discuss tribal affairs. The initiated males sit on log benches in the centre of the village plaza, passing cheroots of tobacco-like grasses to one another. This group meets at sundown and for hours every evening the men talk, argue, and smoke convivially. Their conversation might be about past warfare, neighbouring tribes, hunting or fishing expeditions, journeys to other tribes to trade, or sex. Chiefs have little authority over other heads of household, but they make speeches to the nightly gathering, just as the village shamans use it to practise their art. At times, the men find emotional release through angry speeches. A Trumai, Maibu, once suggested to the anthropologist Buell Quain that they have a mock argument. 'Facing each other in the centre of the village, the two men hurled epithets and insults at each other at the tops of their voices. When Quain was at a loss for something to say, Maibu suggested that he repeat a speech he had made about the theft of his supplies.'

The savannah grasslands of the upper Xingu are too weak to sustain intensive agriculture, but the Indians grow enough manioc, beans, and sweet potatoes on slash-and-burn clearings in the forests. Unlike other Indians, Xinguanos use hand-presses rather than *tipiti* basketry tubes to squeeze prussic acid out of bitter manioc; and they consume it as tapioca *beiju* cakes rather than roasted flour. There is wild honey in the forests, and delicious fruit from the wild pequi (or piquí; *Caryocar villosum*) trees or from bananas or pineapple grown in the clearings. The main source of protein for the upper-Xingu tribes is the fish and turtles that abound in their rivers and lakes. They also hunt some species of game birds, monkeys, and land tortoises – but have a curious taboo against eating peccary, tapir, or any other meat. Xingu Indians shoot fish with bow and arrow, standing motionless in a gliding bark canoe, and they rarely miss. They also use basket fish traps, or they dam a stream and stun its fish with *timbó* poison beaten out of creepers.

Xingu Indians instinctively keep their populations stable, so that villages never outgrow the surrounding natural resources. This stability is achieved by infanticide of any baby born with a defect, late marriages, and years of breast-feeding that inhibit further conception.

The dozen villages of the upper-Xingu peoples are only a few days' walk apart. Tribes sometimes used to fight one another, but there was also friendly commerce between them. They congregate for an annual *moitará*, a bartering session held each year in a different village. Although the tribes look so very similar, and their huts, villages, and customs are almost identical, each group has developed a distinct manufacturing skill. The value of an object is based on the time taken to make it. The Carib-speaking Kuikuro, Kalapalo, and Nahukwá are masters of necklaces of shells (*uruca*) and of molluscs (*urapeí*) – the former worn on men's waists and women's necks, the latter around the necks of all men and most boys. Both types of necklace are laborious to make, taking not less than six or eight months. The Tupi-speaking Kamayurá and Aweti carve lovely bows from a dark wood such as *ipe*. Trumai Indians manufacture stone axes. Aruak women (Waurá and Mehinaku) are skilled potters, producing medium-sized pots (*mulatai*), huge basin-like *camalupe* pans that are used to roast manioc, and charming small vessels in the shapes of animals. This pottery is essential for cooking the Xingu Indians' favourite manioc and fish dishes. It is almost the only basic possession that depends on manufacturing skill and is not found in the forests. Brilliantly coloured bird feathers, bark canoes, hammocks (compact-weave for men, fine texture for women), and large baskets are also traded. The moitará has evolved into a ceremonial ritual, despite the lack of a common language, and there is minimal bargaining. When a woman occasionally leaves a village to marry into another, she takes her traditional skill with her.

The Villas Boas brothers once witnessed a barter ceremony between the Trumai, whose crops had failed and who were starving, and the

Kamayurá, who had plenty of food. The impoverished Trumai offered a tiny, symbolic piece of pequi-fruit paste. The Kamayurá gave in return immense baskets of manioc loaves, hundreds of kilos of it. 'We had watched a beautiful demonstration of solidarity – and it is worth recalling that for years these two tribes had been bitter enemies.'

Wrestling remains the favourite sport of the tribes of the upper Xingu. It helps give warriors their splendid physiques, and a strong and successful wrestler gains prestige in his tribe. Almost every evening, men grapple on the sand of the village plaza in a few minutes of fast and fierce, but ritualized wrestling called *huka-huka*. Opponents crouch against one another, seeking to force the other man's arm or torso onto the ground. 'Each wrestler tried for a grip by grabbing at the body of the other. A variant of the half-Nelson was frequently attempted. The match could be terminated by mutual consent and without the need for either contestant to concede defeat. The wrestlers were often pushed around considerably, but except for grunts of effort, there were no expressions of pain or anger.' There are matches between tribes, at which 'competitive spirits run high, but the onlookers make every effort to conceal latent intertribal hostility. They are always friendly to each other, and at the end of the match they exchange a friendly embrace.'

Rondon's telegraph commission sent several teams to explore the region west of the Xingu and converse with its tribes. The SPI continued such expeditions. In 1915 the Bakairi helped Lieutenant Antonio Pyrineus de Souza survey long stretches of the upper Paranatinga and Teles Pires headwaters of the Tapajós. It was only when Pyrineus de Souza's men were over 600 kilometres (375 miles) downriver that they made contact with the formidable Tupi-speaking Kayabi. The first encounter was with a canoe-load of frightened Indians, but these were appeased by presents of axes, knives, and beads. When more Kayabi appeared, arrows were fired from the forest and the Brazilians withdrew to an island. Indians were observed on the bank 'all dragging great bundles of arrows', so the surveyors tried a show of strength by exploding dynamite. This served only to anger the Kayabi. A strapping chief 'entered the water up to his waist, carrying a large bow and a bundle of arrows, and began to talk energetically. He threatened us with his bow drawn and making the gesture of firing an arrow, and called out in a fine, vibrant voice. He then pounded his imposing chest, indicating by significant gestures on all sides that he was the owner of all this. Meanwhile all the Indians in the forest on both banks imitated jaguars, wolves, coatis, and various birds. It was an imposing spectacle . . . We prepared our defence, now that we could not avoid an attack.' For a time Pyrineus' men waited behind a barrier of tree trunks, but they then slipped off downriver in their canoes and passed a wretched night crouching in the boats and devoured by mosquitoes. The surveyors continued their work for three more days; but they were shadowed by Kayabi on the riverbanks and in canoes. The contact ended with an amicable encounter with seventeen Kayabi men and two attractive girls in a pair of canoes. Matches and beads were traded for Brazil nuts and a duck.

These same Kayabi used to raid eastwards to attack the tribes of the upper Xingu. Rondon also wanted to map some of the dozen rivers that converge fan-like to form the main Xingu river, and to re-establish contact with the many tribes in this idyllic land. Captain Ramiro Noronha led one such expedition in 1920, exploring and mapping the Culuene, the largest of the Xingu's headwaters. He returned up the Culiseu, making a traverse (rough survey) of this stream, which contains a cluster of tribes. His contacts with the Indians were friendly, thanks to generous distribution of presents, and Noronha was thus able to assemble vocabularies of its Tupi-, Aruak-, and Carib-speaking peoples. He also established an Indian post called Simões Lopes for the Bakairi of the Paranatinga river. This was linked to Cuiabá by a rough road and became the starting point for all later expeditions to the Xingu, particularly since the Bakairi tribe was divided, with a more acculturated group at Simões Lopes who acted as intermediaries to their cousins on a Xingu headwater to the north-east.

Four years later two more of Rondon's officers, Captains Vicente de Paula Vasconcellos and Thomaz Reis, entered the Xingu with a Swiss scientific mission headed by a Dr Hintermann. The explorers mapped the Ronuro and Jatobá, two large western headwaters, and returned up the Culuene, Culiseu, and Arame headwaters. They visited the villages of tribes first contacted by Von den Steinen forty years previously: the Aweti, Kamayurá, Mehinaku, Suyá, Trumai, Yawalipiti, and Waurá. At each maloca, Vasconcellos generously distributed tools, which were the products of neo-Brazilian society most coveted by these Indians. He even gave a Yawalipiti chief a Winchester carbine. All the tribes were friendly, apart from the Nahukwá chief Aloique, who was initially hostile because one of his people had been killed by the Bakairi – who were the expedition's boatmen.

The Carib-speaking Kuikuro have a tradition of reciting tribal history through speeches sung by their chiefs. In these, they recalled their first contacts with the whites, at a time when they had lived on savannahs south of the Xingu headwaters. In their legends, the Kuikuro told how *they* had pacified the white men, turning their previous violence into benign present-giving. They recalled that 'to make a roça clearing they first had to cut the small saplings and then fell big trees with [axes tipped] with the teeth of red piranha. They lit large fires in their roças, and next day they would continue the felling . . . That's what it was like in the past. Then came sharp knives. Some axes appeared, with which they started to open the roças. They became the owners of these things.' Karl von den Steinen, the first European to visit the upper Xingu, described the magical impact of those first metal blades. Indians who received them danced through the forest, slicing at saplings with delirious abandon. The Kuikuro chants recalled that 'the *caraíbas* [white men] gradually arrived and the knives accumulated: there were small knives for everyone.' The women got lovely beads. But there was a terrible price for these presents. 'Afterwards the deaths started. Illnesses and sorcery arrived. We became few. When the white men came, they brought the illnesses.' One Kuikuro went to visit the Bakairi and brought back 'knives, axes and scissors – but also coughing.'

The tranquillity of the upper Xingu was now disturbed by an eccentric foreigner. Colonel Percy Fawcett was a British artillery officer who had in 1906 done survey work on the frontier between Brazilian Acre and Bolivian Beni, and in 1908 and 1909 on the frontier that runs along the Verde tributary of the Guaporé in western Mato Grosso. Fawcett had returned in 1914, to visit groups of Indians in the Paresi Hills.

During these expeditions, Percy Fawcett developed ugly racist notions about the native Americans. He wrote that 'there are three kinds of Indians. The first are docile and miserable people, easily tamed; the second, dangerous, repulsive cannibals very rarely seen; the third, a robust and fair people, who must have a civilized origin'. He described the Pacaragua of the Bolivian Beni as 'degenerate indigenes – a small, dark people'. The Maricoxi group of Nambiquara were 'large, hairy men, with exceptionally long arms, and with foreheads sloping back from pro- nounced eye ridges – men of a very primitive kind . . . villainous savages . . . great ape-like brutes who looked as if they had scarcely evolved beyond the level of beasts'. These 'Neanderthals' were in fact a sub-tribe of the handsome Nambiquara that had so impressed President Roosevelt in 1913. By contrast, Fawcett admired the Maxubi Paresi. One of their boys was 'red-haired with blue eyes' and the Nietzschean explorer con- cluded: 'I believe that these people are the descendants of a higher civilization . . . [The Maxubi had fallen] from a state high in man's development rather than [being] a people evolving from savagery.'

In addition to this eugenic gibberish, Colonel Fawcett was obsessed with the exotic and occult. In a lecture to the Royal Geographical Society in London in 1910, he had spoken of 'rumours of old ruins . . . hidden in the forests of the Amazon basin'. He was told about a huge ruined city said to have been seen by Portuguese bandeirante raider-explorers north of Minas Gerais in 1743. But he reckoned its location to be near the middle São Francisco river in the state of Bahia – in long-colonized country, 1,200 kilometres (745 miles) east of the Xingu! After service in France during the First World War, the colonel returned to Brazil in 1920 to seek his legendary lost cities. He went from Cuiabá by road to the recently designated Indian post of the Bakairi on the Paranatinga. Fawcett then marched north-eastwards across the campo savannah, but had to turn back after a few days when his horse died.

In 1925, Colonel Fawcett, now aged fifty-eight, decided to make another attempt to reach the mysterious city in the state of Bahia – but again by starting from the Xingu. He wrote that 'it is certain that amazing ruins of ancient cities – ruins incomparably older than those in Egypt – exist in the interior of Matto Grosso'. Fawcett took with him his son Jack, who was 'big, very powerful physically, and absolutely virgin in mind and body. He neither smokes nor drinks.' The third member of the tiny expedition was Jack's friend Raleigh Rimell. Neither young man had any experience of the 'supreme endurance test' that awaited them. The trio took twelve pack animals and retraced Fawcett's earlier route from Cuiabá to the ranch of his friend Hermenegildo Galvão and thence to the Bakairi post on the Paranatinga. While they were there, in May 1925, a group of Mehinaku arrived from the Xingu: in a letter home, Fawcett described these Xinguanos as 'of the brown or Polynesian type, and it is the fair or red type I associate with [lost] cities'. The explorers then rode their mules across the open savannah to the headwaters of the Xingu. At the place where Fawcett's horse had died five years previously, they sent their men back, taking Fawcett's final letter, dated 29 May 1925. The three pressed on with eight mules, expecting to reach the river in a week. Colonel Fawcett hoped to see a mushroom-shaped monument and 'a sort of fat tower of stone. [The Indians] are thoroughly scared of it because they say at night a light shines from door and windows! . . . I expect to be in touch with the old civilisation within a month, and to be at the main objective in August.' This was the last heard from the quixotic English colonel.

Fawcett had a dangerous attitude to the Indians. He wrote that his expedition 'will be no pampered exploration party, with an army of bearers, guides and cargo animals. . . . Where the real wilds start . . . it is a matter of cutting equipment to the absolute minimum, carrying it all oneself, and trusting that one will be able to exist by making friends with the various tribes one meets.' Brazilian Indians *are* hospitable and gener-ous, but they expect visitors to be equally liberal. Previous expeditions to the Xingu had brought quantities of presents. So the tribes of the upper river must have been offended by the three strangers who arrived in their midst expecting to be fed and helped for no reward.

The disappearance of a British army colonel, on a quest for lost civilizations in the midst of Amazon rainforests, caused a sensation. This was not long after the discovery of the Inca 'lost city' of Machu Picchu in the Peruvian Amazon, or of the treasures of Tutankhamun in Egypt. The world's press seized on the Fawcett story – and the weird adventure continues to generate interest to this day.

So what did happen to Colonel Percy Fawcett and his two young companions? Expeditions soon set off for the Xingu to search for them. One was Commander George Dyott's large and well-equipped venture in 1928. Commander Dyott was guided by a Bakairi Indian called Bernardino who had accompanied the Englishmen to the sources of the Xingu three years previously. Bernardino told Dyott that Colonel Fawcett had broken an unwritten rule of forest travel: he had seen two canoes moored on a tributary of the Culiseu and had simply commandeered them. The canoes belonged to Carib-speaking Nahukwá who were hunting in nearby forest. These Indians were understandably angry when they learned that their boats had been stolen by visitors who later went to their village expecting to be welcomed. Dyott had long conversations in sign language with the Nahukwá chief, Aloique. He saw objects – a tin trunk, and a metal label with the name of an English company in an Indian's necklace – which could have come from Fawcett's or from one of the many earlier expeditions. Chief Aloique told how three white men had stayed with the Nahukwá, then travelled on across cerrado and forest towards the village of the neighbouring and related Kalapalo tribe. Dyott's team also moved on to the Kalapalo and were delighted by its friendly people and elegant thatched huts.

All the upper-Xingu tribes were at war with the fierce and formidable Suyá, one of the Jê-speaking tribes living downriver to their north. On one occasion Chief Aloique gave Dyott a graphic description of how, five days' travel beyond the Culiseu, the Suyá had appeared to offer the three white strangers food, but had treacherously hidden their heavy wooden war clubs. Aloique's acted narrative reached its climax: 'In the most dramatic manner imaginable he yelled at the top of his lungs: "Suyás! Bung-bung-bung!" at the same time hitting himself three violent blows on the back of the neck with the edge of his flattened hand. "Caraíba [white man]," he gasped, and collapsed in a senseless heap on the ground as if he himself had been killed.' The Kalapalo gave a similar version of Fawcett's fate, except that they (and Dyott) suspected his killers to have been the

Nahukwá themselves. Commander Dyott had planned to find the English-men's bones. But he had exhausted his supply of gifts – knives and cheap jewellery – and his party found themselves surrounded by increasingly importunate and hostile Indians demanding more. They panicked and decided to flee downriver, slipping away by night and descending the entire length of the Xingu.

In 1932 came a sighting by a Swiss woodsman, Stefan Rattin, of 'an old man clad in skins, with a long yellowish-white beard and long hair' who was an unwilling prisoner in a village of a tribe called Morcegos ('bats' in Portuguese). The old captive obligingly said, 'I am an English colonel,' but neglected to give his name or write a message. This Methuselah was seen near the Morena Hills, on a western tributary of the São Manoel river some 800 difficult kilometres (500 miles) from the Xingu. Various authorities believed Rattin's story; but others, including General Rondon and Fawcett's surviving son Brian, did not. There were rumours of strange white men in other parts of Brazil, and other Fawcett-search expeditions; but none carried credibility.

The next stage in the Fawcett drama came in 1946. The Brazilian government had sent a massive expedition that spent a year cutting a trail from the Araguaia north-westwards to the upper Xingu. This Roncador–Xingu Expedition was led by three young brothers from São Paolo called Villas Boas, who were to become Rondon's successors as the most famous champions of the Brazilian Indians. The explorers reached the Culuene at the beginning of 1946 and soon established good relations with the many tribes of the Xingu headwaters. They saw much of Chief Kamalive of the Nahukwá who had, as a boy, accompanied Chief Aloique when he guided Fawcett's expedition from the Culiseu river to the Kalapalo village.

The Villas Boas also became close friends of the great Chief Izarari of the Kalapalo. Chief Izarari died tragically of influenza on 1 January 1947. But during his illness he told the Brazilian brothers that it was his own Kalapalo people who had killed Fawcett twenty-two years previously. A Kalapalo called Comatsi later gave Orlando Villas Boas a detailed description of the expedition's fate. The English author and film-maker Adrian Cowell recorded this version: 'The three caraíba [white men] were one old and two young men. They carried things on their backs, had guns, and one was lame. They came from the west with Aloique, chief of the Nahukwá, and his son, who brought them from their village on the Culiseu river. At that time, all the Kalapalo were in their fishing village, to the east beyond the Culuene, apart from Cavuquire and his son who were in the main village [which was then far up the Culuene]. These two agreed to guide the Englishmen to the fishing settlement, so that they

could pass beyond it into the country to the east.' The two Nahukwá
were also with them, making a party of seven. After walking for a day and
a half, Fawcett shot a duck. Cavuquire ran to pick it up and was examining
the bird when Fawcett snatched it from him as though he was about to
steal it; the English colonel cut the bird up that evening, and brusquely
pushed aside the Indian boy when he played with the knife; Fawcett
also tried to have only his trio eat the duck. These seem trivial offences.
But striking an Indian in anger is a deep insult. The Xingu Indians are
infuriated by any aggression against a child, since they are deeply affectionate parents, protective of their young whom they *never* reprimand.
And native hunters invariably share out their game, eating none themselves. Cavuquiri had heard the rattle of beads in the Englishmen's packs
and thought that he would be rewarded; but when the village gathered to
say goodbye to the disagreeable strangers, no presents were given. Fawcett
clearly planned to take his trade goods on towards his 'lost city' rather
than distribute them among his current hosts.

According to the version that Orlando Villas Boas told Cowell, Cavuquiri demanded death and obtained the agreement of his chief, Caiabi, on
condition that it be done beyond the small Lake Verde so that the
Nahukwá should not see. So Cavuquiri and Kululi went ahead and hid in
ambush, and the boy Tuendi ferried the Englishmen across the lake. On
the far bank was a small but steep cliff, which Fawcett climbed first,
leaving his companions to bring up their luggage. 'As he got to his feet,
he turned to look down at the young men below. Cavuquiri emerged
from behind his tree with a club he had cut from a sapling. He struck his
blow on the back of the neck. The old one cried out, wheeled, clutched a
tree, and started to fall swivelling round it. Cavuquiri hit again on the
right shoulder and the body collapsed, doubled up on the ground. At the
cry, the young Englishmen dropped their baggage and started to climb
the cliff. Immediately the two Kalapalo [Araco and Cululi] hidden in the
bushes at the bottom leapt out and struck upwards at their necks and
heads. The bodies toppled back into the water.'

Orlando Villas Boas later told a journalist that the entire village was
watching the lake crossing, and saw the killing of Colonel Fawcett. 'Chief
Caiabi was taken by surprise, while the rest of the Indians ran back to the
village, shouting. The two last victims were still alive, but were pushed
under the waters of the lake with the same club that had smashed them.
When the massacre was over, Chief Caiabi was very angry with Cululi,
Araco, and Cavuquiri – the latter was the oldest and most responsible for
the deaths of the white men. The chief said: "Now the civilizados will
come here to punish and kill us. The Bakairi will tell that these men had

been here. We will be given no respite. So go now and hide their remains. Bury the one on the bank and make sure that the other two, who must be floating on the lake, are secured on its bottom."' All this was done. Adrian Cowell recorded many more details of the burials of the three unfortunate explorers.

The Director of the SPI lamented that 'Colonel Fawcett . . . was deaf to all advice. He went ahead, accompanied by the young men one of whom was his son, without reaching an understanding with the SPI, which at that time could fully have guaranteed [their safety] with all the tribes of the sources of the Xingu.' The Villas Boas commented that 'Fawcett was the victim, as anyone else would have been, of the harshness and lack of tact that all recognized in him'.

Protestant missionaries who were on the Xingu in the 1930s were sure that the adventurers had been killed by the Kalapalo. The Villas Boas were given their detailed account in 1946 by the Kalapalo chiefs Izarari and Komatsi, who told it in a three-hour discourse in front of many of their tribesmen, in the forest close to Lake Verde, where some bones were later disinterred. This version was later challenged. Ellen Basso, an American anthropologist who worked among the Kalapalo in 1968, wrote that 'modern Kalapalo emphatically deny any knowledge of [the Fawcett] incident and judge it to be the slander of other Indians who wished to provide overanxious information-seekers with anything deemed worthy of payment'. They told her that the Englishmen journeyed onwards and then disappeared, either killed by another tribe or more probably dead from hunger and exposure. This was the view of the distinguished German anthropologist Max Schmidt, who was in the Xingu only two years after the tragedy: 'Fawcett and his two companions probably fell, exhausted and without food, in some place in the campo or forest and not necessarily killed by the violence of an Indian enemy'.

In 1950 the Villas Boas brothers organized a search of Lake Verde by more than forty Kalapalo, but their diving failed to find the remains of the two young men in the mud of its bed. The bones of one skeleton were, however, exhumed from the bank. These were brought to London in a diplomatic bag in 1951. The Brazilian Ambassador at the time was a flamboyant publisher called Assis Chateaubriand, who fully appreciated the publicity value of Fawcett's bones. The Ambassador hosted a lavish reception at Claridge's Hotel and revealed the relics, arranged on a salver flanked by candelabra on a black-draped table. But this party was spoiled when the explorer's son Brian refused to accept that the skull and bones belonged to his father. The remains were therefore sent to the Royal Anthropological Institute for expert examination. Although the skeleton was that of a middle-aged man, the teeth in the jaw did not appear to correspond to Fawcett's (who wore dentures) and the leg bones seemed too short for a man of his height. The controversial relics were returned to Brazil, where they lay in museum storerooms. Orlando Villas Boas told this author that he remained convinced that they were those of the English explorer.

The Fawcett saga is irrelevant to the plight of the Brazilian Indians. However, the tragedy of the three misguided English adventurers caught the imagination of the European and American press. It was the first – and only – story that many readers in those countries heard about the indigenous peoples of Brazil.

5. Araguaia, Xavante

One of the many expeditions searching for Colonel Fawcett never got closer to the Xingu than the Araguaia, the next great southern tributary of the Amazon, 300 kilometres (190 miles) east of the region where the eccentric explorer disappeared. This was a British venture and it spawned Peter Fleming's *Brazilian Adventure*, a bestseller that was the first book to make fun of the heroics of exploring. It all started with a small advertisement in *The Times* for 'Two more guns' on an 'exploring and sporting expedition . . . to explore rivers Central Brazil, if possible ascertain fate Colonel Fawcett; abundance game, big and small; exceptional fishing.' Fleming was a witty young Etonian who saw through the sham of the bombastic incompetents leading this ridiculous expedition. He rapidly realized that 'adventure is really a soft option . . . It requires far less courage to be an explorer than to be a chartered accountant'. Fleming and his two equally irreverent and insubordinate friends saw the humorous side of everything and, not surprisingly, fell out with the venture's leaders.

Peter Fleming concluded that 'most of the terrors of the Central Brazilian jungle had a way of paling into rather ludicrous insignificance when looked at closely. In the dry season, Mato Grosso is more of a health resort than a White Man's Grave.' They debunked aggressive piranha fish which they had been warned 'would tear the flesh from your bones before you could scramble ashore'. So when they waded up a shallow river past 'man-eating shoals [of piranha] . . . a few feet from our unprotected thighs', Fleming 'could not but admire the rigid self-control with which they ruled their blood-lust. We noted the ascetic, indeed the almost apprehensive glances which they cast at our tempting calves. Sometimes, if we stood still, a small shoal, a kind of deputation, would approach and hang diffidently suspended in the translucent water, staring at our thighs with a wistful, perhaps a slightly covetous awe: as shop-girls gaze at the sentries outside Buckingham Palace.'

The most useful product of Fleming's expedition was a foray up the Tapirapé tributary of the Araguaia to visit the Tupi-speaking Tapirapé tribe. Tupi-Gurarani was the language spoken by tribes all along the

Atlantic seaboard of Brazil, so that it was the first native tongue encountered by sixteenth-century European explorers and became the lingua geral, the 'general language' of missionaries, caboclo settlers, and many tribes throughout Brazil. But the Tapirapé were geographically isolated, far from other Tupi speakers, evidently a remnant of an earlier migration westwards from a coastal homeland.

The young Englishmen liked the Tapirapé very much. They were a warm-hearted, merry people with a good sense of humour and – to Fleming's delight – a keen sense of the ridiculous. They were obviously fascinated by the foreigners' belongings and baffled by their gaucheness in tackling the local environment. Peter Fleming saw the Tapirapé as naturally remote, but 'like elves, capriciously aloof, their native bliss unqualified by envy. They were curious, but not covetous.' The Tapirapé made an equally amiable impression on a French couple who visited them three years later. This gentle, recently contacted tribe struck observers as inhabiting an earthly paradise – just as Amerigo Vespucci and others had described the first Brazilian Indians four centuries earlier, which had in turn inspired Rousseau's philosophical notion of the noble savage.

> In the Tapirapé village people live completely naked and with all their body hair removed. This means that they are free from any concerns about modesty. They live with free bodies and souls equally free, apparently without shame or malice. They live joyously: the Tapirapé are cheerful . . . As in the garden of Eden, the Tapirapé know nothing about money . . . They have established their habitat in a marvellous climate in the midst of abundant vegetation. A lovely river that crosses the village furnishes their fish, and the forest their game. Good farmers, they have clearings of cereals and vegetables. The earth is fine and fertile, true agricultural land that yields effortlessly.

Another brilliant and irreverent English writer was in Brazil in that same year, 1932. Evelyn Waugh entered the northern tip of Brazil on a journey inland from British Guiana (modern Guyana). Waugh saw the Makuxi, shyer and more reserved than the ebullient Tapirapé, and paid them the ultimate compliment of comparing them to his own race. 'The more I saw of Indians the greater I was struck by their similarity to the English. They like living with their own families at great distances from their neighbours; they regard strangers with suspicion and despair; they are unprogressive and unambitious, fond of pets, hunting and fishing; they are undemonstrative in love, unwarlike, morbidly modest; their chief aim seems to be on all occasions to render themselves inconspicuous.'

At the start of the twentieth century, the Tapirapé had numbered between 1,000 and 1,500 people, living in five villages. They occupied a vast swathe of land, mostly forests, to the west of the middle Araguaia. But this relatively gentle people was often at war with powerful neighbours: a series of tough, Jê-speaking Kayapó tribes to the north; even fiercer Jê-speaking Xavante to the south-west; and, to the east, the riverine Karajá who navigated hundreds of kilometres of the broad, smooth Araguaia. Repeated raids by Kayapó caused the northernmost Tapirapé village to be abandoned. Then, in 1911, a group of Brazilian north-easterners in search of rubber trees paddled up the Tapirapé river and made the first contact with three of the tribe's villages. It was an amiable meeting, for the Brazilians gave the Indians plenty of trade goods. The whites' leader, Alfredo Olimpio de Oliveira, took three Indians back to see the mission village of Conceição do Araguaia. An inspector of the newly created SPI went to the Tapirapé in 1912 and occasionally there-after; a Karajá called Valdarão arrived with one of the civilizado expeditions and he remained, to exert a powerful influence over the tribe; and in 1914 came the first of many visits by French Dominican mission-aries from Conceição.

All these encounters were friendly and peaceful, and they brought machetes, axes, and other useful tools. But contacts with the outside world unwittingly introduced alien diseases. In two decades there was appalling mortality. Tribal tradition reported that half one village died of 'fevers' – evidently malaria transmitted by mosquitoes from infected Karajá. Soon after the early contacts came influenza, possibly the virulent strain that swept the world after the First World War, and the common cold, which could be equally lethal to Indians with no inherited immunity. By the time of Fleming's visit, the Tapirapé were reduced to one village large enough to function according to tribal custom. This tragedy was a repeat of the decimation that struck almost every tribe throughout Brazil. Indians who were physically very fit and admirably nourished could easily die of respiratory infections that developed into pneumonia. They also died of measles, smallpox, and, more rarely, yellow fever. These lethal epidemics could rage from tribe to tribe, striking isolated people before direct contact with colonists.

Although the SPI was a lay service independent of established Churches, missionaries were increasingly active in many frontier regions. Protestant missionaries were now permitted, and they often competed with the long-established Catholics – such as the French Dominicans on the Araguaia, German Franciscans among the Munduruku on the Tapajós, or Italian Salesians with the Bororo in Mato Grosso and on the Rio Negro in north-western Brazil. The two branches of Christianity disliked one another. Peter Fleming met a young English Protestant missionary who 'spoke with some bitterness of evangelistic claim-jumping, and of the base tricks employed by the rival missions in the race for converts.'

After their first visit in 1914, the Dominicans returned often. They built a hut at a place they called Porto São Domingos, far up the Tapirapé river and close to the tribe's southernmost (and last surviving) village, Tampiitawa. This hut became a depot for trade goods and the location of baptisms and masses by the missionaries. But the Dominicans' brief annual visits did not disturb the native culture. Then, in 1932, the Scottish missionary Frederick S. Kegel of the Evangelical Union of South America went and lived for some months with the Tapirapé. He returned for long periods in the dry seasons of the ensuing three years. The American anthropologist Charles Wagley never met Kegel, but he learned that

> Frederico was loved by the Tapirapé of Tampiitawa – and sometimes just a little feared, for he became angry when men beat their wives . . . The Tapirapé had many stories to tell of Frederico. He went hunting with them, he danced with them, and he told them stories about Papai Grande (the Christian God in the sky). Above all, he could sing. He learned their songs and taught them new ones, and he would sit on a tree trunk and sing Tapirapé songs and hymns. The Tapirapé learned several hymns in Portuguese and even in English, which they called *pederico monika* (Frederico's songs). His repertoire was not limited to hymns, for in addition to 'When the Roll is Called up Yonder' one Tapirapé man sang 'Loch Lomond' to me in understandable English in 1939.

As a sensitive, rather than an aggressively fundamentalist, missionary, Frederick Kegel respected Tapirapé custom and did not try to modify it. 'He did leave an indelible mark on their memory as a man they loved, and he must have loved them also.'

All these contacts brought the seemingly inevitable diseases. During the three years he visited Tampiitawa village, Kegel witnessed fifty to sixty deaths. By 1939, when Charles Wagley was with the Tapirapé, there were 147 people in that village, and these were joined by forty remnants from the tribe's only other community. Thus, the six villages and 1,000 to 1,500 Tapirapé at the start of the century were reduced in forty years to fewer than 190 in one village. Worse was to follow. When Herbert Baldus saw them in 1947, they were under a hundred. One problem was that in its heyday this tribe – like most in Brazil – had instinctively kept its population low. (This was done by traditional practices of late marriage, lengthy breast-feeding of children which inhibited further pregnancies, marriage only across village moieties, and infanticide if there were any physical or spiritual blemishes on an infant.) Before the impact of alien diseases, the vast territories and hunting–farming skills of the Tapirapé could have supported far more people. But they chose not to breed faster. The tragedy was that, when demographic catastrophe struck them, the Tapirapé could not quickly change their customs that guaranteed zero population growth.

Late in 1947 there was another disaster, when a group of warlike Gorotiré Kayapó attacked Tampiitawa village. They charged in early one morning when many Tapirapé men were away hunting or clearing forest roças. The battle was brief and one-sided. The attackers burned three longhouses and the men's hut, carried off some women and girls, and looted everything portable. The survivors abandoned the village.

For three years the tribe almost disintegrated. Forty fled eastwards, taking refuge either with a Brazilian rancher, Lúcio da Luz, or at an SPI post at the mouth of their river which was run by a remarkable friend of the Tapirapé called Valentim Gomes. But twenty people, led by a tough warrior called Kamairá, trekked deeper into the forest. These refugees thought that they were the last of the Tapirapé. They made a settlement and struggled to survive by hunting and gathering until they could grow a few crops. They had a hard time, with years of drought or seasons when their crops failed. 'Snakebite killed one of the valuable young warriors. Babies were born, but died of malnutrition, malaria and other sicknesses. Older members of the group died from the privations. The women grew too old to have babies, and finally there was only one young woman to keep the group alive, a beautiful young maiden. Before she could marry, a jaguar attacked her in the forest. Other members of the group killed the animal, but it was too late. The young girl died.' When this remnant was discovered by a Brazilian hunter, in 1971, it was reduced to Kamairá, his wife, and their son. The three were persuaded to travel down to the mouth of the Tapirapé river, where the remainder of their people had established a thriving new village. When the survivors rejoined their kindred after twenty-five years in the wilderness, there was a stunned silence followed by cries of recognition by the tribal elders. There were tears of joy, and a mighty celebration of singing and dancing. Kamairá died soon after; but his wife settled happily amid her people, as did their strapping son after a period of confusion and introversion at the shock of the reunion.

The Tapirapés' survival during those terrible years was remarkable, a testimony of their resilience and social cohesion. As Charles Wagley wrote, 'they could easily have joined the long list of extinct tribes of

Brazil. Perhaps it is due to one man that they did not. It seems unbeliev-able that Valentim Gomes, as a lowly agent of the SPI, was able to gather the Tapirapé Indians into a single, new village established near the Indian post. It is equally admirable that Valentim was able to help them survive until their gardens were growing and there was enough to eat.' Wagley learned about Valentim's hardships during the first two years, when he was starved of funds and salary by the regional office of the SPI in Goiânia. 'He told me that he personally went into debt to buy manioc flour and other necessities for the Indians. He made several long and laborious trips upriver to Goiânia (it took ten days by riverboat and two by truck) to beg his superiors for help before he finally secured funds to repay his debts.'

When Wagley visited the tribe's New Village in 1953, it was reduced to fifty-three people. Brazilian settlers were establishing farms along the Tapirapé river, and the nearby village of Santa Terezinha was rapidly growing into a town with an airstrip. Tapirapé women now wore skirts, mainly 'because of the Brazilians gaping at nude women', and the men had shorts for when they visited civilizado settlements. Wagley credited ecclesiastics with the tribe's further salvation. The Indians 'could easily have been swallowed up by the expanding frontier, as ranch hands or as miserable loafers in Santa Terezinha. In my opinion, it was the arrival of the Little Sisters of Jesus and of Padre François Jentel and their residence in New Village that saved the Tapirapé from total disorganization and, probably, extinction.' The missionary sisters brought some medicines and they tried to dissuade the Tapirapé from infanticide. Wagley was impressed by their otherwise gentle approach.

> Both the padre and the nuns tried to intervene as little as possible in Tapirapé life. Never did I hear these missionaries attempt religious proselytism . . . They hope to influence 'by living example', and not by persuasion . . . Several times in the 1960s Padre François travelled to Brasília, where he lobbied with the SPI for lands for the Tapirapé. The Little Sisters and Padre François were able to persuade the Tapirapé to continue their subsistence activities; they sometimes supervised barter transactions with itinerant Brazilian traders who came to the village seeking animal skins and 'Indian' artefacts; they urged the Tapirapé not to travel to 'see the city'; and, above all, they gave them pride in their own customs and ceremonials.

Thus the now tiny tribe revived. By 1965 it had 80 people and a decade later there were 130.

*

The only neighbours with whom the Tapirapé had friendly contact were the Karajá to the east. This independent and distinctive people had endured two centuries of contact with the Brazilian colonial frontier. The Karajás' world was the Araguaia river, a mighty waterway that flows northwards for 1,000 kilometres (620 miles), to join the Tocantins and then the mouth of the Amazon itself. The river is immensely broad and, during the dry season, flanked by wide swathes of smooth and inviting sandbanks. The Araguaia is generally placid, except when it cascades over rapids, and a visionary Brazilian governor in the 1880s tried to establish a regular steamship service along this great artery. The venture failed because there was no demand for traffic along such a remote stretch of the then colonial frontier. The Araguaia never became a Mississippi. But the steamship company briefly established outposts and logwood stations among the Karajá, and there was a short-lived college to educate Indian boys and girls in Brazilian culture.

At the end of the nineteenth century, French Dominicans established their mission at Conceição do Araguaia at the northern limit of the hundreds of kilometres of river plied by the Karajá. Later came a Protestant mission at the tribe's heartland on Bananal Island, 350 kilometres (220 miles) long and probably the world's largest riverine island.

The Karajá were largely impervious to these outside influences. Although they enjoyed trading for a few manufactured goods, their lives continued – and still continue to this day – to revolve around the river and its fishing. Karajá men were consummate fishermen, shooting fish with bows and arrows with devastating accuracy, stunning them with poison from the timbó liana, or harpooning huge *pirarucu* that swim on the riverbed. Tall men, they have fine physiques with shoulders broadened by constant paddling. Throughout the dry season, the Karajá leave their few villages and camp on the Araguaia's beaches, in low barrel-vaulted shelters of palm-frond matting.

To casual observers, the Karajá are distinctive in several ways. Their language is 'isolated', differing from any of the main linguistic trunks of Brazilian Indians. They are famous for making exquisite feather ornaments, with headdresses and coronets of baroque inventiveness, and doll-like pottery figurines reminiscent of early Greek Cycladean art or prehistoric fertility fetishes. These creations did deteriorate after contact. Herbert Baldus noted that by the late 1930s, Karajá clay pottery had adapted for sale to passing tourists: instead of strict standards and uniform design, artists indulged in saleable fantasies and the dolls' bodies ceased to have the exaggerated hips and bottoms of original patterns. One aspect of Karajá religion is a mask cult, in which shamans dance completely covered in conical straw capes surmounted by tall wooden diadems. Another striking feature peculiar to the Karajá is a tribal tattoo, of a black circle on each cheek just below the eye, worn by both sexes.

Young Karajá women 'are permitted to behave with perfect freedom, whereas men behave with a shy and deferential modesty resembling that of the Victorian maiden', and some travellers disliked the Karajá because of this etiquette. They saw them as aloof, ungrateful, and dour, in contrast to the naively cheerful Tapirapé. The Karajá were by nature dignified and independent; and many years of deceptions had taught them to be wary of civilizado visitors. They had learned to demand good prices for their food or their services as boatmen. Unlike other travellers, Peter Fleming found that 'it was always fun calling on the Karajás. The women and the pot-bellied children would come crowding round as the nose of the leading canoe grated on the sand.' He noticed the difference between a man's formal, courtly manner of speech and a woman's 'hurried, plaintive sing-song. Until you get used to it you think that she is going to break at any moment into rather angry tears. The voices of the men are by contrast dignified and deliberate.' In 1932, at the time of Fleming's visit, the Karajá were starting to wear clothing, to accommodate the increasing number of outsiders along their river. 'In their natural state the men go naked, and the women wear only a kind of fibre apron. But contact with the forces of enlightenment, and increased opportunities for acquiring what they regard as finery, have in a few cases resulted in the appearance of skirts and trousers. The condition of these garments is usually an offence against hygiene, and their wearing an entirely unnecessary prop to the natural modesty of the Indians.' Disease was taking a toll of this tribe, just as it decimated every other indigenous group after contact. Later that decade, the anthropologist William Lipkind counted just over 1,500 Karajá – a terrible contrast to the German Fritz Krause's estimate of 10,000 thirty years previously, and the French Comte Francis de Castelnau's rather wild guess of 100,000 in the 1840s.

Fleming's expedition visited the Karajás' main village, Santa Isabel on the west shore of Bananal Island. It was here that the SPI had established a post in 1927. An experienced and energetic official, Manuel Sylvino Bandeira de Mello, set about creating a model post, complete with a museum, football field, and workshops. The Bishop of Conceição do Araguaia, Bishop Sebastião Thomaz (Sebastien Thomas), was highly impressed by the efficiency of the post, particularly its farming: 'Here reign order, discipline, work and peace. The Indians are healthy and satisfied, considering their directors as true fathers.' The Protestant pastor Archie MacIntyre also noted the 'confidence and esteem' shown by the

Karajá to their SPI staff, and how the latter protected the Indians from exploitation by passing *garimpeiros* (prospectors). But by 1932 the government presence was gone. Fleming heard that

> Good work was done while the funds lasted; but when we arrived there were only the labels left to show how zeal had been expended. The 'School of Sewing' was tenanted by two parakeets, who sat, solemnly regarding each other, on top of the blackboard; from time to time they defaced it with an air of distraction. . . . Then your eye was caught by a large notice in green and yellow (the national colours of Brazil) prohibiting the import into Santa Isabel of alcoholic liquors, and you saw over the doors of half a dozen white-walled huts similar notices, announcing the purposes of enlightenment to which these buildings were variously devoted. But they were all, like the School of Sewing, empty. The outposts of culture had been evacuated. Only the brave green and yellow notices remained.
>
> The wheel had come full circle. The Indians . . . were not so naked now, and not nearly so numerous; they had picked up a few of the white man's bad habits and some of his diseases, and the clothes which he insisted on their wearing had made them more susceptible to the cold at night, and so to fever. They were dying out, but they were still there.

When the son of the SPI agent Bandeira de Mello returned in 1937 to his father's 'model' post on Bananal, he was appalled. 'My God, what desolation! Everything, everything on the adorable island had a melancholy air of misery and abandonment! Harmful vegetation covered almost the entire area. As for the Indians, my admirable friends and companions, they were wandering on the beaches in a state of mendicancy. [Many were dead.] The great and extraordinary tribe was entering a gradual and cruel extinction.' Nothing had changed when an English broadcaster visited Santa Isabel in 1955. All that he saw was an abandoned radio transmitter and 'a derelict school, all that was left of some reformer's dream of conferring letters as well as fig-leafs on the Karajá.' The only modern presence was an efficient Dutch nurse, who had vaccinated all the Indians.

In fact, the Karajá had survived the short-lived attempt to turn them into industrious citizens: they continue until the present day with their riverine way of life reasonably intact. But conditions at Santa Isabel continued to be wretched. The SPI rashly took a group of senators there in 1960 and they found only dust, heat, and flies. 'Some huts shelter a few sick Indians, attacked by tuberculosis, dysentery, pneumonia, and influenza. Miserable and ill, the Indians live from trading in figurines, bows, arrows, and clubs. The arrival of a guest does not succeed in rousing them from their torpor.' Eleven years later, the British champion of indigenous peoples, Robin Hanbury-Tenison, found the post surrounded by ranchers who occupied most of Bananal Island. The Karajá were 'in a thoroughly depressed state due to their enforced settlement, the poverty of the soil, and continuous contact with a competing and growing population of settlers. They are . . . in danger of losing their tribal skills and pride.' Three hours' boat-ride down the Araguaia was another Karajá village, Fontoura, where a Seventh-Day Adventist mission had operated since 1934. The Indians were demoralized, dirty, and lethargic. 'Barbed wire was much in evidence and the scene resembled pictures of nineteenth-century slave settlements.' In the 1960s, the SPI built a hospital at Santa Isabel intended to treat Indians from all over central Brazil. After initial success, this also decayed. By 1972, this author found it infested with vermin, the ceiling flaking onto the unusable operating theatre, and the resident doctor without any pharmaceuticals. The Karajá lost their pride. A decade later, the Brazilian anthropologist Alcida Ramos cited them as 'a pathetic example of social and physical deterioration due to disruptive contact with the national society'. They had been swamped by settlers and tourism. 'The Karajá are now [1983] notorious for their drunkenness, dirtiness and defeatism. Even their crafts, once highly regarded for their aesthetic expression, are no longer of artistic value.'

The Tupi-speaking Tapirapé and the riverine Karajá were surrounded by Jê-speaking tribes. Morally and physically tough and very belligerent, the warriors of these Jê peoples terrorized their neighbours. They preferred to attack from ambush or in surprise raids on unsuspecting Indian villages or white colonists' homesteads. Fine hunters and archers, the Jê (as they are known generically) excelled as runners and their most fearsome weapon was a heavy club longer than a baseball bat. They could move so fast across open savannah that they ran down game animals and clubbed them to death.

The amiable and relatively gentle Tapirapé lived in dread of a cluster of Jê-speaking Kayapó tribes to their north, and of the Xavante nation to the south-west. To the east, along the Tocantins and in the mesopotamia between it and the Araguaia, were more peaceful Jê: the Xerente, Krahó to their north, and downriver of them the Apinayé. Below the junction of the Araguaia and Tocantins lay the territory of the fierce Gavião. The Tapirapés' main defence lay in distance: there was so much land and, after

1. The Tiriyó gave a warm welcome to General Rondon during his frontier inspection in 1928. Upper Paru river, near Suriname.

2. A group of Xokleng captured by a professional Indian hunter. Santa Catarina, early twentieth century. Contact with the Xokleng was an early success of the Indian Protection Service.

3. Ex-President Theodore Roosevelt and Colonel Rondon in front of the Rio da Dúvida (later renamed Roosevelt) with peccary and a brocket deer, shot for the pot, at their feet. 1914.

4. Parintintin archers used powerful bows to rain arrows at Curt Nimuendajú, 1922.

5. Cooking at the Franciscans' Munduruku mission, Cururu river, upper Tapajós.

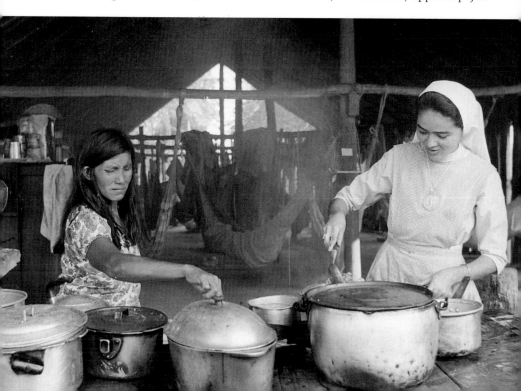

6. First contact with the Xavante in 1946. A warrior warns Francisco Meirelles' men to keep their distance.

7. Francisco 'Chico' Mierelles with a Xavante in 1946.

8. Xikrin Kayapó women groom one another and regularly renew black genipap body-paint.

9. Orlando Villas Boas, aged thirty-one, with Kalapalo soon after reaching the Xingu in 1946. (*Orlando Villas Boas*)

10. Mentuktire Kayapó, the most feared warriors in the Xingu before the arrival of the Villas Boas brothers brought inter-tribal peace to the region.

11. Mentuktire Kayapó sing their thanks to Dr Roberto Baruzzi's team from the Paulista Medical School. Jarina river, Xingu.

12. Kretire was the most belligerent chief of the Mentuktire Kayapó.

13. The three Villas Boas brothers, Cláudio, Orlando, and Leonardo, with the great Kalapalo Chief Izarari, shortly before he died of disease in January 1947. (*Orlando Villas Boas*)

14. Cláudio Villas Boas with the Mentuktire Raoni, Prepori of the Kayabi, and the Kayabi patriarch. (*Orlando Villas Boas*)

15. Cláudio Villas Boas liked to lie in his hammock for hours, talking to Indians. Here he is with Mentuktire Kayapó. Jarina river, Xingu.

16. Volunteer doctors from the São Paulo Medical School gave excellent medical treatment to Xingu Indians. Preparing a health survey of the Mentuktire, 1971.

17. Orlando Villas Boas giving presents to apprehensive Txikão at the moment of contact. Ronuro river, upper Xingu, 1964.

18. Orlando Villas Boas and a feared Txikão on the day of first contact.
(*Orlando Villas Boas*)

the ravages of imported diseases, the Indians were so few in number that there was little motive for inter-tribal warfare.

The Xavante (previously written Chavante, and pronounced Shavante) had a history unique among Brazilian tribes. In 1788 over 2,000 of the feared Xavante had accepted peaceful settlement among Portuguese colonists. They were lodged in purpose-built villages north of the old city of Goiás, between the Araguaia and Tocantins rivers some 300 kilometres (190 miles) south of Bananal Island. Most Xavante adults accepted Christianity in ceremonies of mass baptism. But their taste of 'civilization' went badly wrong. The Xavante were hit by a devastating epidemic of measles, which was made more lethal by the Indians being closely congregated in the new 'model villages'. In one settlement, the Xavante were mixed with 1,000 of their traditional enemies the Javaé subgroup of Karajá, as well as some Kayapó. Although Xavante men worked hard at agriculture, their farming near the villages was not a success, and they were not allowed to hunt extensively in the surrounding savannahs. Worst of all, the model aldeias were run by brutal soldiers who tried to impose strict discipline, corporal punishment, and work levies. Within a few years, the proud Xavante realized that they had been duped. They abandoned the government villages and migrated westwards. Thus, although depleted in numbers, they escaped from the lion's jaw of colonial assimilation with their culture and tribal identity intact. A contemporary German traveller wrote that 'from that time onwards [the Xavante] no longer trusted any white man but fled whenever possible. They are impetuous, vengeful, and with an excellent memory for insults and humiliations ... These abused people have therefore changed from compatriots into the most dangerous and determined enemies. They generally kill anyone they can easily catch; but it is also admitted that, in cruel reprisal, if they meet whites they can expect only death. A form of war of extermination is being waged; and it offers a truly sad spectacle.' One Xavante tactic was to set fire to the thatched roofs of isolated settlers' huts. Another was for lithe and beautiful Xavante women to lure men into an embrace, so that warriors could club them to death.

After they wisely abandoned the Goiás aldeias, the Xavante migrated westwards and were unmolested for almost 150 years. Although not a riverine people, they managed to cross the upper Araguaia and then its tributary the Mortes ('Deaths'). By the 1930s several thousand Xavante were established in villages on the campo savannahs and forests northwest of the Mortes, towards the low Roncador ('Snorer') Hills and the sources of the Xingu. The migration was not a single, well-planned movement. It was a gradual affair, involving only one part of the Xavante, the A'uwe or Akwê group. There were battles against other tribes as the Xavante crossed their territory, notably the Karajá and possibly the Bororo.

The Xavantes' isolation was broken in the 1920s. Settlers arriving in the area between the Araguaia and Mortes were often attacked, as were missionized Bororo south of the Mortes. Even the Karajá were reluctant to camp on the west bank of the Araguaia south of Bananal: five of them were killed by Xavante in 1930–31. In 1932 four mineral prospectors were killed on the Garças river, as were a woodsman and his family. In that same year a Swiss Salesian missionary, Father Johannes Baptist Fuchs, founded a post called Santa Teresinha about 160 kilometres (100 miles) up the rio das Mortes. Father Fuchs took his Karajá and Bororo Indians on annual journeys up the Mortes, leaving presents on its north bank in the hope of attracting the Xavante. There was no contact. Then, on 1 November 1934, Fuchs and Father Pietro Sacilotti noticed some Indians on the shore. They landed, followed tracks, and came upon some 'naked, barbarous and wild' Xavante. Sacilotti was carrying presents, and Fuchs a cross. The two missionaries plunged into the midst of a large group of Indians, about 1,200 metres (1,310 yards) from the river, and tried to talk to them in the Karajá language. The presents were soon exhausted and Sacilotti called to his companions to bring more. But as the men went to fetch them, they heard a cry, ' "The Xavante are attacking us!", followed by the horrible din of Xavante war cries and the crash of their clubs. The others ran headlong to the boat, grabbed guns and returned to help the missionaries. They . . . found nothing. They shouted for the padres; but there was no reply.' Night fell. Next day, the boatmen returned and found the missionaries' bodies, with their bones broken but little blood spilled. 'It was some time before their friends dared to return and collect up the bodies, which had literally been battered to pieces, for burial. They erected a cross which the Xavante later came and knocked down. It was re-erected once but the Xavante threw it down again, so the local travellers gave up the struggle.'

Two years later, a colonist's child was killed near Merure, a Salesian mission well to the west of the killing of the two missionaries. The child's father, Bento Costa, obtained permission to mount a heavily armed reprisal raid. This posse found a Xavante village occupied only by women and children. The whites on the raid claimed to have murdered only one child; but Bororo Indians who accompanied them reported that the leader saw his child's hammock and went berserk, shooting some thirty unarmed Indians. Xavante men returned and attacked the raiders as they withdrew.

The Xavante had long memories of their disastrous encounter with Portuguese colonial society in the eighteenth century. They now felt threatened by the advance of cattlemen, missionaries, and garimpeiros towards their area. There were brushes with adventurers from São Paulo in 1937 and 1938. Then, in 1941, the SPI decided to make its own attempt at peaceful contact. This was led by Dr Genésio Pimentel Barbosa, and established a base at the Salesian hut at São Domingos. Moving along the river, Dr Pimentel Barbosa's men met a band of Xavante, who received them exceedingly cautiously. They camped a few kilometres from Arobonipó, the village of Chief Apowe or Apewen, later known to Brazilians as Apoena. The leader decided to disarm his nervous men to prevent a chance shot provoking hostility. One expeditioner was sent off on reconnaissance with three Xerente Indians who formed part of the attraction team. This man reported, in an official despatch, that 'when they returned at nightfall they found the camp destroyed and four naked corpses. Beneath each body they found a club, and behind the cookhouse, which was destroyed, a great heap of clubs as a final warning to the survivors.' Later, two other members of the party who had been gathering fuel wood reappeared. 'They witnessed the danteesque and profoundly moving scene of those four heroic victims . . . There was a smile on the face of their leader's body . . . and he was still holding in his two rigid hands a set of presents that he was clearly trying to offer to the attackers.' Seventeen years later, an anthropologist noted 'a line of rusting guns hanging in the storeroom [at São Domingos] . . . They were the guns which Pimentel Barbosa's men took with them on their expedition – and had kept locked away. It was not in the tradition of the Indian Protection Service that they should fire on Indians, however hostile.'

Colonel Vasconcellos, Director of the SPI, ordered that the attraction campaign must continue. The base at São Domingos was re-established seventy-two kilometres (forty-five miles) away from where Pimentel Barbosa had died. Another expedition under Luiz Acioly Lopes left presents near the area, but was careful not to approach too close to the Xavante village. 'He visited this place every fortnight, leaving presents. At first the Indians did not take these, although they were evidently nearby. Then they started to take them; and later they left things in return. They kept the hut where the presents were left cleanly swept. Eventually they removed the presents almost within sight of our men.'

In 1943 Getúlio Vargas's government decided that, as a nation of 43 million people, Brazil could not continue to have large parts of its national territory unexplored. Until then, Amazonia was known only from its multitude of rivers – and movement along these was often blocked by rapids. A Central Brazilian Foundation (Fundação Brasil Central or FBC) was created, to open the hinterland. It was thought that aviation could end the region's isolation. If airstrips could be built in Brazil's remote interior, the Dakotas that were helping to win the war could bring civilization to the wilderness and its native peoples. So in 1943 the federal government launched the Expedição Roncador–Xingu, a massive expedition to cut trails and build a line of airstrips from the Roncador Hills beyond the rio das Mortes diagonally north-westwards towards the headwaters of the Xingu. The Expedition's mission was 'to explore and penetrate areas that appear as blanks on the map'.

Three brothers in their twenties from São Paulo, recently orphaned sons of a failed coffee planter, decided to enlist on this exciting new venture. These were Orlando, Cláudio, and Leonardo Villas Bôas, aged respectively twenty-seven, twenty-five, and twenty-three. The brothers' first application was turned down because the expedition was recruiting only backwoodsmen, so they travelled to Mato Grosso to enlist at the project's base at Aragarças. They were taken on and, when it emerged that they were educated and enterprising, they soon became its junior officers. Their lifelong devotion to exploration – and eventually to protecting Indians – started when the expedition paddled across the rio das Mortes, with sixteen men, on 12 June 1945. This crossing was well to the west of the site of Pimentel Barbosa's death, but it was into the territory of another group of Xavante. The Roncador–Xingu Expedition started opening a trail that was eventually to run for many hundreds of kilometres, initially across open campo and cerrado savannah, then through swamps, over streams lined with riverine forest, and then into unbroken high rainforest.

After ten days, the Xavante became evident. Bird calls sounded during the night, fleeting figures were glimpsed on the trail, and stones landed beside the hammocks of the sleeping men. The Xavante then became bolder, prowling around the intruders' camp, sometimes shouting. The expedition's sentries found tortoise shells and snake skins at a place where the Indians had camped. Smoke from fires was visible across the plain. Then, on 25 July 1945, the trail-cutters were surrounded by a fearful shouting that continued interminably. They quickly assembled in one place. The Villas Boas suspected that the noise was a diversion from the main attack. One brother climbed onto a termite hill. 'From the top of this little mound, we saw a group of twenty or thirty Indians running forward through the cerrado undergrowth. They were coming towards us, in the opposite direction to the shouting. We alerted the men from the top of the termite hill, while the attackers approached swiftly. There was no way to stop their advance other than, quickly, to fire some shots into the air. We decided to do this. The men immediately raised their guns and fired simultaneously. As if by magic, the shouting and the advance ceased. Had it not been for the termite hill, there would today have been one more to add to the chronicle of massacres!' The Xavante had every right to resist the expedition invading their land. But they also had painful memories of the lethal power of guns.

The Roncador–Xingu Expedition saw more signs of Xavante during the ensuing weeks, but there were no further attacks. Weeks were spent in the punishing, hot work of trail-cutting. Food was always a problem. In the early stages, the twenty men of the cutting party were supplied by ox and mule trains along the path they had cut. Later, the trail was too broken for draft animals and the weary explorers were fed only by occasional bundles of dried meat and food thrown from low-flying aircraft. They suffered terribly from hunger and frequent illness. Some were prostrate from malarial fever, so weak that they had to be carried from their hammocks to defecate. By September the team had cut over fifty kilometres (thirty miles) of picada, to reach the Xingu's Ronuro head-water on the far side of the low watershed of the Roncador Hills. It had crossed the territory of the Xavante.

When awarded the Royal Geographical Society's gold medal, some thirty years later, Orlando Villas Boas wrote that 'the Xavante were not as terrible and ferocious as the chroniclers said. It is true that they tried to surround the troop of donkeys on four or five occasions, and they once made a huge mixture of all the cargo, putting into a single pile the rice, beans, sugar, salt, lard, and all the rest. . . . Then old Rondon, fearing that something might happen to the Indians – for the expedition was under the command of a truculent and anti-Indian colonel [Flaviano Vanique] – decided to name [the Villas Boas] as officials of the [Indian Protection] Council.'

The Brazilian press was already excited by the presence of the fierce Xavante tribe on its western colonization frontier. In June 1944 a popular journalist, David Nasser, flew a plane at only thirty feet above the arc of huts of a large Xavante village. He took vivid pictures of tall warriors defiantly shooting arrows and hurling clubs at the intruding plane. Amid all this bravado about fierce savages, the anthropologist Herbert Baldus dared to ask 'Are the Xavante bellicose?' He argued that they were simply acting in legitimate self-defence.

The pacification of the Xavante was then entrusted to the SPI Inspector Francisco ('Chico') Furtado Soares de Meirelles. A Pernambucan from north-east Brazil, Meirelles entered the SPI with a vocation to help Indians. Thin, taciturn, and tough, Meirelles was by now a thirty-eight-year-old veteran of many expeditions. He had learned about attracting tribes from Dr Pimentel Barbosa, and had just completed the difficult three-year contact with the Pakaá Nova tribe south of the Parintintin near the upper Madeira. Meirelles established an attraction post with an infrastructure that included farming and cattle ranching, at São Domingos on the Mortes. On one expedition in early 1946, Meirelles rode inland to the place where Pimentel Barbosa had been killed. Raymond Maufrais, a young Frenchman who was with him, recalled that

> we dismounted and walked forward slowly, discovering at each step some fresh reminder of those unfortunate explorers. A rusty tin of meat and a spear with a horn point. A torn prospectus praising the quality of a certain make of ammunition. Strips of material, a piece of newspaper in shreds, a faggot of wood . . . and then, what had once been Barbosa's camp. A sort of open maquis surrounding a clearing hacked out with machetes, a little brook fringed with luxuriant vegetation, a dilapidated blackened hut, a circle of beaten earth on which were scattered pieces of worn leather and the batteries of a portable wireless set . . . On the scene of the massacre we found several Indian *bordunas*, the bludgeons which had served to kill our friends.

The expedition left machetes in the clearing, and these were removed by unseen Indians. Two days later, after more presents had been left and removed, the camp's watchman saw about twenty Xavante. 'We could see them slipping from thicket to thicket, armed with bows and arrows, in an encircling movement worthy of any general.' After leaving some necklaces, the expedition struck camp, loaded its horses and rode off. But Meirelles decided to approach the village.

> We rode slowly in close single file. '*Cuidado aos peles!* [Watch your skins!]' cried Manoel, turning towards Meirelles. I turned my head just in time to see an arrow land five inches away from my horse's rear hoof. A second fell close to Guardino, who with an ashen face cried: 'They're attacking. For God's sake, let's run for it or we're done for!' Our horses forged ahead, but a volley of arrows quelled any desire on our part to continue . . . Meirelles rode on ahead. He was brandishing his necklaces and gleaming brand-new machetes, shouting at the top of his voice, 'Xavantes, Oh ho! Xavantes!', roaring words of welcome and peace in an Indian dialect. The next moment Alfredo had tumbled from his horse, killed outright by an arrow in his neck.

The expedition turned and rode for the river, weakened by fatigue, by dysentery from having drunk at a water-hole, and in Meirelles's case shivering from an attack of malaria.

Later that year an old Xavante approached the attraction post, saying that he was hungry and ill. He said that his companions were camped nearby and wished to parlay with Meirelles. Next day, four more Indians appeared. They carried arrows without heads, and they wore white cord necklaces from which hung tufts of cotton – both pacific gestures. They invited Meirelles to meet their Chief Apewen.

Then, on 6 August 1946, came the breakthrough, the moment of peaceful contact. Meirelles again led his men to the site of Pimentel Barbosa's death. 'On the platform in the hut, he found an arrow with its point cut: a clear signal of peace. The Indians immediately started to give signs of their presence around the hut. Inspector Meirelles then organized his men, leaving part on one side of the hut's square clearing, and advanced towards the hut with the most courageous, calm, and confident men . . . He started to speak, facing the forest, using words and gestures to invite the Indians to approach.'

'Before long, a group of six or eight Xavante emerged from a part of the forest, preceded by their chief and their shaman. The latter was sprinkling handfuls of bark fragments and leaves over his people – clearly to immunise them against sorcery or treachery by our men. These Indians were unarmed.' '[Paumecedi] the Paramount Chief of the tribe walked alongside the shaman, a powerful great man about 1.80 metres [5ft 11in] tall. This cacique stopped close to Meirelles and delivered an oration in a tone of voice that could be heard clearly for a long distance . . . But none of our people understood, not even the Indian interpreters on the pacification party. Meirelles attracted [the Xavante] with two fine aluminium cooking pots that shone in the sun, and showed them machetes with scabbards, axes, hoes, beads, mirrors, etc. At length the chief approached, somewhat nervously, extended his arm towards the Inspector and his assistants and gave them arrows with the heads broken as a sign of peace, and clubs that were offered in a friendly manner.'

'Next, at a summons from him, Indians emerged from all sides, completely surrounding our people. The Inspector reckoned that there were 400. They came cheerfully, smiling, and carrying only arrows with the heads broken and no bows. They brought a few clubs, but then presented these weapons to our people, and accepted the gifts that were offered, in a spirit of open fraternization. They were without women or children. When the presents were finished, our men tried to withdraw. Inspector Meirelles first explained to the Xavante chief by sign language that he would return within a certain time [with a new load of presents], and would announce this with a smoke signal.'

It was later learned that there had been long and reasoned debate among the Xavante. Some, including the powerful old chief Paumecedi, opposed contact because they feared white men's military power, treachery, and the force of their diseases that tribal shamans could not cure. Paumecedi's son Apewen (Apoena) was the leader of the band that killed Dr Pimentel Barbosa. 'It was also Apewen who had fought off the whites for years and incited his men to reject the presents that were offered to them. Brazilians would time and again cross the rio das Mortes and leave such things as knives and salt and metal pans on trails which were evidently in use. And time and again they had returned to find the salt bags burst open and their contents scattered on the ground, the knives even flung carelessly into the undergrowth.' But Apewen had changed his mind: he now favoured an alliance with the strangers. This discussion continued in front of Meirelles's expedition. After receiving sufficient assurances, those in favour of peaceful contact prevailed. It is important to realize that it was the Xavante who took the initiative in accepting this contact – it was not a triumphant 'pacification', as depicted in the contemporary press. Unlike many uncontacted tribes, the Xavante knew much about their opponents. Tribal legend recalled the bruising experience of the eighteenth-century aldeias. So the decision to seek accommodation was not a surrender. It came after careful evaluation of all the options and of the precarious condition in which these people found themselves.

Meirelles proceeded tactfully during the ensuing months. He maintained friendly relations and exchanged presents with two Xavante groups who were hostile to one another. But it was not until 1950 that the sertanista accepted an invitation to enter the Xavante aldeia. By then, Meirelles was considered as an *imuman*, a father-chief of the tribe; and he named his only son Apoena. A fine orator, Apewen came to be Paramount Chief of all the eastern Xavante. David Maybury-Lewis, the first anthropologist to live with these Akwê Xavante, felt that this chief's 'aquiline features and the greying shoulder-length hair . . . would not have looked out of place as a doge of Venice'. This author was with Apewen (Apoena) fourteen years later, and found him to be an old man of great dignity and powerful charisma.

The peaceful contact in August 1946 was the start of some years of attraction of other groups of Xavante. There was another contact in 1947, with a group near the junction of the Mortes and Araguaia, but those north-eastern Xavante continued to raid nearby settlers, taking what they needed from colonists' homes and leaving bows and arrows as payment. In September 1953, the peace process was jeopardized by the treacherous folly of some settlers. A group of Xavante from the village of Apewen's brother, Chief Suretçuna, went to collect presents from an SPI post at the Lago de Bois ('Ox Lake') in north-eastern Xavante country. As they were returning to their village on the rio Solidão, they were ambushed by settlers from São Felix on the Araguaia. 'The men who killed Suretçuna and his twenty-one companions hid where the Xavantes were sure to pass and opened fire when the Indians had no chance of defending themselves.' Meirelles was appalled, fearing revenge: 'The Indians now have reason to repent having put faith in the whites. The same thing had happened with the Bororo, the Nambiquara, Kaingang, and so on. At great pains, we had convinced the principal chiefs of the Xavante that we were there to guarantee their lands and their lives . . . It will only be a matter of time before they pay back the massacre of São Felix.' Edward Weyer, an American anthropologist who was in Brazil at the time, commented that Suretçuna and his brother Apewen had been won over by Meirelles's promises that the 'civilized people' would not take the Xavantes' lands from them. Suretçuna was killed by civilizados trying to do just that. Amazingly, the SPI managed to prevent a bloody vendetta and the Xavante showed remarkable restraint. The local SPI official took the names of eight perpetrators of the massacre to Rio de Janeiro; but they were not brought to justice.

Chico Meirelles went on to make contacts with other tribes. He took a hard line on assimilation, regarding tribal isolation as folly. He did not agree with those who considered the Indian way of life as superior to that of civilizados, because all the tribes he contacted expressed a desire to 'live like us'. Meirelles therefore felt that 'we should intelligently help them in this reasonable desire and fraternally help them achieve it. For if we do not do so, we are being inhuman and practising blatant racial discrimination.' Not content with advocating the gradual suffocation of tribal society, he even condoned the occupation of native lands. 'The Indians cannot remain in their habitats indefinitely, because the frontier of civilization will eventually advance irresistibly on top of them.' Meirelles argued that it was dangerously misguided to fail to prepare them for life on the frontier. 'The solution lies in integration, not only of the Indians but of all the poor population of the Brazilian interior, into the development process. The confinement of Indians [in reserves] or resistance to progress will inevitably lead to their marginalization and, consequently, their destruction.'

Once contacted, the Xavante proved to be a typical Jê-speaking people: warlike, virile, and with customs and beliefs different to those of Tupi-speaking tribes. Xavante men keep superbly fit, for they maintain the ancient ritual sport of log-racing. Each village is divided into moieties, and the races are between the young men of the two halves. The race starts some kilometres away from the village and ends with the two teams pounding around the semicircle of its huts. The runners move very fast, barefoot of course on the sandy soil of their cerrado plains. What makes the race so demanding is that each team carries an extremely heavy section of palm-tree trunk on its shoulders. From time to time one runner rolls this relay burden onto the shoulder of another of his team. When the race ends, in a cloud of dust, the winning team casually drops its log and walks away unconcernedly with no hint of triumph.

Xavante men and women wear their gleaming black hair in a fringe across their foreheads but hanging down the backs of their necks in a handsome mane. Both sexes are naked, apart from minuscule straw penis sheaths and pencil-shaped plugs in the ear lobes of the men, and simple necklaces. The warriors' lean, muscular bodies are painted with quarter-ings of red and black dyes for special occasions and they then wear beautiful headdresses of feathers fanning out from a woven straw circlet. But their ornaments are modest by the standards of other tribes. A hallmark of the Xavante is their warrior pride. The men like to stand to attention, gazing ahead in a fierce unswerving stare. This self-assurance combined with strong tribal loyalty gives the Xavante resilience in the face of the traumas of contact. These people also demonstrate an engaging curiosity and eagerness to learn. The Xavante are not interested in alcoholic drink or hallucinogenic plants, so that, after contact with neo-Brazilian society, they avoid the cachaça rum that has turned some other Indians into alcoholics.

A Xavante village is an arc of evenly spaced huts, each housing only one or two families. These huts are conical, beehive-shaped, and made of shaggy grey thatch over a simple frame of sapling logs. In the centre of the village oval are two circular patches of bare ground, the meeting places of the two moieties. A web of paths links the houses to one another and to the central focus, like spokes on an elliptical and incomplete wheel.

As soon as the dreaded Xavante laid down their arms in 1946, squatters and colonists flooded into their territory. The President of Brazil in 1952 sent a bill to Congress to create a huge million-hectare (3,860 square mile) Indian reserve area north-west of the Mortes and embracing the upper Xingu. This was never passed. The Director of the SPI wrote despairingly that his Service had spent over five million cruzeiros and lost lives in the pacification of the Xavante. The result of this sacrifice was a property boom. Land along the Pindaiba tributary of the Mortes that was worthless in 1940 sold for about 1 cruzeiro a hectare in 1943, and for a hundred times that ten years later. 'The Xavante are being gunned down by land-speculators and property agents, who call themselves pioneers of our wilderness, with the connivance of the Mato Grosso police.' Since they had been contacted by Meirelles, a sertanista who favoured integration, the Xavante had no one to fight for their territorial rights. The main villain was the government of the local State of Mato Grosso. As Maybury-Lewis wrote at that time, 'land speculation is the major economic activity of the state' and its authorities were 'selling off tracts of territory which had been earmarked for the Indians' long before the President's bill had been rejected by Congress.

In 1956 the Mato Grosso legislature awarded the SPI a stretch of land for the Xavante beyond the rio das Mortes. But there was a proviso that, if this land were not demarcated within two years, it would revert to the state. The SPI had neither funds nor surveyors and therefore did nothing. So the land was duly lost – as the state legislators had expected: they had already sold parts of it to private buyers. The great Xavante nation was thus reduced to a few isolated reserves on its former vast savannahs. By the 1960s, small homesteaders were settled all along the Mortes above a new town ironically called Xavantina (the former base of the FBC), and below it large developers were clearing ranches. 'The powerful Xavante bands that had previously managed to keep settlers off these reaches had been reduced to enclaves. For the first time, they became aware of their impotence in the face of encroachments.'

The Xavante people were rarely united: there was constant fragmentation and feuding between villages or followers of different chiefs. This disruption was aggravated by the trauma of accommodation with the whites. The Xavante who had crossed the Araguaia in the nineteenth century split into three main groups. One settled near São Domingos (later renamed Pimentel Barbosa) on the lower Mortes: these were the people contacted by Chico Mierelles. Another group continued for 250 kilometres (160 miles) to the south-west, to the Batovi, a source of the Xingu near Colonel Fawcett's route from Cuiabá to that river. The third migration was to Parabubure, the plain between the Couto de Magalhães and Culuene, two other headwaters of the Xingu roughly between the Batovi and the upper rio das Mortes. Meanwhile, other groups of Xavante were at Areões, on the upper Mortes not far from Xavantina; and another village was far to the north, near São Felix on the Araguaia.

The Xavante at Parabubure subdivided further in the mid-twentieth century. Their complicated migrations are worth repeating, since they illustrate the pressures that shattered tribes after contact. The first village on the Couto de Magalhães lasted for two years. Its inhabitants moved to one they called Wedetede; but it was struck by an epidemic that took several lives. It split, with some Indians making a new village on the Couto de Magalhães and others on the Culuene. There were further scissions, with some Xavante dividing themselves among local settlers. The new village of Parabubure on the Couto de Magalhães was attacked by civilizados in 1951, forcing a move to a previously occupied site. A further split next year sent one faction back to the rio das Mortes, to settle at Areões. Those left behind were in 1956 stricken by disease. It was even said that this epidemic was inflicted deliberately – caught from clothing and presents infected with measles and influenza that were thrown onto their village from planes. The survivors moved to the Noidore river, a tributary of the Mortes south (upriver) of Xavantina. These migrants from Parabubure then went south, crossed the rio das Mortes, and took refuge in the old missions that the Salesians were operating for the Bororo – traditional enemies of the Xavante. These last refugees were ill and harassed by settlers when they arrived at the missions of Sangradouro and Meruri. They were joined in the Salesian establish-ments by Xavante from Oniudu village on the Batovi. Others from Oniudu moved west to the Paranatinga and were welcomed in 1954–55 by Pedro Vani de Oliveira, the SPI official in charge of the Simões Lopes (now Bakairi) post, on the tributary of that name on the upper Teles Pires–Tapajós river.

These bewildering moves may have been a strategy by the Xavante to avoid attacks by frontier settlers and the diseases they brought with them. The smaller groups may have sought peace with the whites in order to learn their customs and language, and to get medicines against the terrible new scourges. But the Xavante also feared one another. When David Maybury-Lewis was with them in 1958, he went on a long hunting expedition onto the low plateau known as the Serra do Roncador. His group was constantly wary of the tracks and distant fires of other Xavante. Maybury-Lewis was with Chief Apewen's people, who lived in a trad-itional village of twenty beehive-shaped thatch huts ranged in a long oval, near the SPI post of São Domingos, but Apewen's community was on bad terms with the 'wild' uncontacted Xavante away to the north-east at a place the Indians called Maraiwatsede. There were rumours that the latter, who had suffered the murderous ambush five years previously, 'had come out on the river [Mortes] and killed many white people'. The Brazilian press was full of stories that the Indians were on the warpath, although there was no more than one skirmish. Meanwhile, to the south, 'Apewen's Xavante were on bad terms with the Xavante upriver who had established their base camp near the Catholic mission station of Santa Teresinha.' The leader of that group, the 'bad' Chief Eribewen, had been killed when he visited another Xavante village. A scout who witnessed all this reported to his village: 'War parties had been out – here he gave an account of the killed and wounded, showing where the clubs had struck and exactly where the arrows had gone in. The white men were also angry, he went on. Xavante had attacked the mission and the white men had sent aeroplanes to take away the wounded.'

The movements of the Xavante became even more turbulent in the late 1950s and early '60s. The bewildered Indians were constantly migrating and making contact with different elements of Brazilian frontier society. A group led by Chief Öribiwe emerged at the town of Xavantina and decided to settle nearby. This alarmed the townspeople, most of whom were functionaries of the FBC; they appealed to the SPI, which in 1955 created a post called Capitariquara for this group. Meanwhile, fundamentalist American Protestants started a mission nearby and persuaded some Xavante to move to it. But conflicts between Indians in the SPI post and those in the mission caused the closure of the latter in 1958. Its people were moved downriver to the Salesian mission Santa Teresinha, which had been created in 1954 for two other groups from the Serra do Roncador and from the Culuene. Confusingly, in that same year 1958, half the community from Santa Teresinha and all the people from Areões (the former American mission) went to Capitariquara post; then some moved on to the Salesian reserve São Marcos and others went back to a village called Isôrepré. In 1961 the Salesians closed Santa Teresinha, which had been abandoned by its Indians. The SPI moved its post to Areões, which eventually became a permanent Indian area.

Orlando Villas Boas exploded, in an interview in 1961,

The Xavante, exploited from all sides and in all ways by settlers and missions . . . have ended by being split into groups. The final phase that carries a tribe to extinction has started: internal fighting. Brazilians have succeeded in undermining what is most pure – tribal identity. Over a hundred Xavante now live from alms in the vicinity of Xavantina. They are in rags, for people insisted that they be clothed but did not provide clothing; starving, because people demonstrated that their farming methods were primitive, but did not furnish them with instruction, seeds, or tools. Abandoned to their fate, infected with diseases that cause them irreparable damage, the Xavante are on the road to extinction. They were undoubtedly the tribe that inspired most respect in the Brazilian interior. Their exploits, their courage, their refusal to maintain contact with [white] men in this century . . . became legendary. Today, they are nothing more than pariahs, with a standard of subsistence lower than the caboclos' – which is worse than miserable.

North-west of Pimentel Barbosa, at the edge of the Serra do Roncador, the Suiá-Missu river flows northwards towards the Xingu. A gigantic territory on the upper part of this river was granted to a firm of Italian-Brazilians to create the 695,800 hectare (2,690 square mile) Suiá-Missu ranch. For a time, a group of 263 Xavante continued to live on this ranch in their village Maraiwatsede, initially unaware that their lands had been sold – the concept of 'legal' ownership of land was, of course, incomprehensible to them. The ranch owner, Orlando Ometto, used to show off his group of tame Xavante to his guests. Then, in 1966, he decided to get rid of them. He organized their airlift by the Brazilian air force (FAB) to the Salesian mission of São Marcos, far to the south. The local press said, approvingly, that 'the Ometto family like Indians . . . So after the deportation they donated a tractor to the mission, with a sum equivalent to $100 a month for one year to help support these Indians.' These Xavante were sick and undernourished when they reached São Marcos. Very soon after arrival they were struck by a terrible measles epidemic and eighty-three people, almost a third of the group, died.

The anthropologist-historian Aracy Lopes da Silva summarized the

> constants imposed on the Xavante: reduction in the limits of their territory; loss of areas rich in produce for gathering or hunting; demographic imbalance; daily contact with non-Indians; ever-increasing settlement of a people that had been semi-nomadic; steady replacement of traditional activities (hunting, gathering, and basic farming) with increasing agricultural labour – with a consequent deterioration in diet and less protein; fewer ritual activities; control or suppression of some rituals, particularly cosmological ones and those considered reprehensible by non-Indians; exposure to Christian ceremonial and beliefs; exposure to towns and cities; experience of selling their physical labour. These were all trends that started in the first years of permanent contact between the Xavante and regional society. With the passage of time, all these pressures intensified.

The Xavante eventually came to terms with contact, but terrible epidemics cost many lives. In 1957 Darcy Ribeiro guessed that there were 2,000–3,000 Xavante, whereas a decade later, Dale Kietzman reckoned only 1,660 in the five main villages. But the Xavante are robust people and their populations were soon expanding, with births exceeding deaths. They were robbed of most of the territory they had defended so valiantly and that had been promised to them so insistently and persuasively. The group who had migrated furthest west, to Simões Lopes post, abandoned it to the Bakairi Indians and returned to the Couto de Magalhães river region. So, in the end, the Xavante were left with six official reserves, pockets of land isolated from one another. These reserves add up to a total of 1,160,000 hectares (4,500 square miles). This sounds extensive, but in the vast open spaces and weak soils of Mato Grosso it was not. Also, two of the fragmented areas were Salesian missions for the Bororo south of the rio das Mortes. The Xavante had to wage a bitter and protracted campaign to recover their lost territory.

6. The Kayapó

Five hundred kilometres (310 miles) north of the Xavante is the territory of another warlike Jê-speaking people, the Kayapó. There are many similarities between the two nations. The Kayapó look quite like the Xavante, although with subtle differences in ornament, body paint, and hair style. Their villages are perfect circles, with thatched houses evenly spaced around the circumference, each connected to the central men's hut by a straight path. This elegant plan looks from the air like a gigantic cartwheel.

All these peoples refer to themselves and their language as Mebengokré, meaning 'people of the large water', because they had lived near (and migrated across) the mighty Tocantins–Araguaia rivers. As so often in Brazilian history, the Kayapó are known by a pejorative name from another language. 'Kayapó' is thought to come from the Karajá words for 'looking like' and 'monkey'; but it has been applied to these northern Jê-speaking tribes since the eighteenth century, and they have come to accept it.

Both sexes have always been physically and mentally tough. They shun all alcohol or hallucinogens and do not indulge in messianic visions. Boys undergo hard initiation rites, which include invading a wasp nest that symbolizes an enemy village, duels with heavy clubs (the favourite Kayapó weapon), races and competitions, and skin scarification. Adult men wear wooden discs in holes in their lower lips, to make themselves look fiercer. This effect is certainly achieved, but the lip-discs make eating awkward – a man often has to use his fingers to push food into his mouth – and they flap up and down when they talk. But lips are also pierced to emphasize the power of speech, for oratory is highly prized among the Kayapó. A man is admired for the passion of his speeches in the village plaza. And we shall see how skilfully the Kayapó came to use this eloquence when they entered the arena of Brazilian politics. Ear lobes are also pierced, to take ear-discs, and this is because hearing is associated with learning and knowledge.

It is a Kayapó custom to shave the front of children's heads up to the crown, leaving the remaining hair hanging down the sides and back. Attractive children look curiously like ageing monks as a result. Adolescents and grown men are shaved in this way only on ritual occasions. Hair lengths and other details of head ornament vary according to a person's age and marital status, or they may signify mourning. The Kayapó create dramatic ornaments – mussel-shell necklaces and dazzling feather headdresses – and they constantly decorate their lean bodies with geometric designs, usually in black genipap dye. Before contact, the warlike Kayapó lacked the pottery, hammocks, and canoes of some non-Jê-speaking peoples, and their basketry and architecture seemed less skilled. But the Kayapó were quick learners, open-minded about adopting or imitating ideas from other indigenous peoples and frontiersmen.

The American anthropologist Darrell Posey and others marvelled at Kayapó knowledge of their natural environment. It ensured that villages were near a variety of ecological zones, each associated with specific plants and animals. 'The distinct advantage is that Kayapó villages are in the midst of maximum species diversity, because each zone provides natural products and attracts different game species during different seasons.' When Posey went on hunting trips with the Gorotire Kayapó he noticed that they carried little food: whenever they stopped to camp or take rare rests, they always seemed to have the produce they wanted in the surrounding forest. Posey realized that this was no accident. The Kayapó manipulate and manage apparently pristine forest by planting desired species at strategic places. When they hunt, they carry useful seeds and fertilize them with their own excrement. They also create *apetê* 'resource islands' in clearings that arise either from a large tree falling or by their cutting one down. The sudden opening of the forest floor to sunlight and direct rainfall allows the proliferation of small plants, which in turn provide food for a myriad of birds and animals hunted by the Indians. The Kayapó love honey and know a great deal about husbanding fifty-four species of stingless bees and two types of stinging bee. So they usually fell trees that contain bees' nests. 'This provides a double bonus for the Kayapó: bees' honey and wax for food and artefacts, and the legacy of an area that will not only provide a variety of useful plants, but will also stimulate game populations.'

Fields near villages are tended by women. To a tidy Western farmer, these plantations appear chaotic – a tangle of felled trees, half-burned vegetation, and a mixture of useful plants and rampant weeds. There is, however, considerable method in this agricultural mayhem. Trees are cut to produce 'planting corridors between masses of debris', fragile soils are exposed to direct sunlight for the shortest possible time, burning is controlled so that is does not destroy developing cultigens, and dozens of plant species are exploited. Discarded banana leaves are piled to rot and attract scarab and other beetles whose eggs grow into tasty and nutritious grubs. Roça clearings are abandoned after a few years; but the Indians return to them for decades to continue harvesting trees and plants with longer lifespans. Posey gradually learned that the Kayapó 'practice long-term "nomadic agriculture" that includes the management of forest openings, trail-sides and rock outcroppings': both the 'forest islands' and 'sophisticated management of disturbed ecological zones and secondary forests emerging from such agricultural plots . . . The genius of Kayapó cultural landscapes' is in its flexibility, catering to tribal needs in times of peace and war, drought, and rain.

Some Kayapó terrain is scrub savannah, and they manage this harsh environment just as skilfully as they do the forest. Like the Xavante, the Kayapó regularly burned this campo cerrado, to herd its animals for hunting, and for regeneration of an ecosystem that can withstand burning and even thrive on it. But Kayapó manipulation of savannahs went far beyond burning. The Gorotire Kayapó told Anthony Anderson and Darrell Posey that they actively enhanced clumps of woody vegetation by transferring litter fertilizer and termite and ant nests to them. The ethnobotanists found that the Gorotire obtained a remarkable 120 species of plants from such savannah 'garden islands'. They used every species, 'with major use categories including medicines (72%), game attractants (40%), foods (25%), firewoods (12%), fertilizers (8%), shade (3%) and other uses (30%).'

Like the Xavante, the Kayapó had migrated westwards across the Araguaia river to escape the advancing colonial frontier. They also divided and subdivided repeatedly and became more bellicose towards one another, partly as a reaction to the civilizado threat. Once across the Araguaia, some 4,000 Kayapó divided into four main groups. This migration brought the Kayapó into the edge of the great mass of Amazon rainforests. They then learned to adapt from cerrado and *caatinga* ecosystems – open scrub vegetation interspersed with forest along river courses – to living in dense canopy forest.

One group of some 1,500 Kayapó, the Irã-Amrayre, decided to accommodate with the whites. It settled on the Pau d'Arco ('Bow-wood') river not far up the Araguaia from the French Dominican mission (and present-day city) of Conceição do Araguaia. Their reward for this collaboration was to obtain guns by trading with settlers, and they used these weapons against rival Kayapó groups, the Gorotire and Xikrin. It is an unfortunate constant of the Kayapó during the twentieth century that much of their warfare was internecine: they tended to attack frontiersmen largely to obtain firearms for use against Kayapó and other tribes.

The Pau d'Arco group paid a heavy price for relations with its real enemy, white men. This tribe was extinguished in only half a century – from the inevitable diseases and from attrition or intermarriage with settlers. By living near the accessible Araguaia river, these Irã-Amrayre Kayapó lost their land, their cultural identity, and their lives. When first contacted in 1892 they occupied four villages; these were later amalgamated by the missionaries into two aldeias; but with criminal lack of medical help, by 1920 these two villages were reduced to one. When Nimuendajú saw the Pau d'Arco Kayapó in 1940, they were down to six people; and the last old woman died in 1960. The Belgian anthropologist Gustaaf Verswijver commented, bitterly: 'This once numerous and important Kayapó group thus became extinct because of a basic lack of interest on the part of the missionaries. Once this group had arrived at a "good" relationship with the members of Western society, some two thousand (or more?) Indians died due to insufficient assistance, in the space of less than fifty years.'

Another group of some 1,500 Kayapó, the Gorotire, fared better. These Indians settled in lovely low hills, forests, and savannahs on the upper part of the Fresco affluent of the Xingu and its tributary the Riozinho ('Little River'), some 250 kilometres (150 miles) west of Conceição do Araguaia. In the early twentieth century, most northern Kayapó lived in one ancestral village, Pyka-tô-ti, the 'Great' or 'Beautiful Village', with three concentric rows of huts and in the centre two men's huts facing east and west. 'Although Pyka-tô-ti was permanently inhabited, trekking groups would leave for trips that ranged from a few weeks to several months. The travellers would return to the village with captives, valuable feathers, ritual items, booty, and abundant meat for the festivals and ceremonies that inevitably followed (and often prompted) such treks. Pyka-tô-ti would swell with inhabitants during these ceremonial periods.' But the Beautiful Village disintegrated in about 1919, torn apart by feuds and migrations. Some of these schisms were the result of epidemics that led to accusations of *udgy* – sorcery. Those suspected of causing illness had to flee or be killed, and they established new villages with their clans.

The Gorotire had to escape the attentions of rubber-tappers, who searched for *Hevea* trees on the Fresco in the final decade of the rubber boom. Peaceful relations ended when seringueiros led by Antonio Firmino twice attacked the Gorotire. The first raid failed; but the second destroyed a village and its stock of food. The Indians retaliated with bloody raids on settlers, on the lower Fresco and the Xingu; and they ranged far to the west, into the forests of the Iriri and Curuá rivers.

Missionaries of the two branches of Christianity then sought to convert the Gorotire. During the early 1930s Bishop Sebastião Tomas of Conceição made three journeys to the tribe. Then in 1935, to the alarm of the Bishop's Dominicans, three English Protestants of the Unevangelized Fields Mission also tried to change the tribe's faith. All the English missionaries were named Fred, so that they are always known as the Three Freds. In the words of their Catholic rival: 'Robust young men, they had come to seek the Gorotire to tame them and teach them to work. . . . They wanted to do this by themselves, with no interpreter or guides, dispensing even with presents, and with only a vocabulary of the Kayapó language . . . They wanted to hold the Indians in esteem, to enter their main aldeia, and to spend months or even years with them there.' The Three Freds themselves were fired only by missionary zeal. They wrote: 'We are fully aware that, humanly speaking, we are already as good as dead . . . We are beyond criticism as we go forward in the name of the Lord and under His command.' They got seringueiros from the lower Fresco to wheel their heavy motor boat around some rapids. These eager but innocent laymen were never seen alive again. The Gorotire killed them, near the Fumaça ('Smoke') waterfall on the Riozinho near their village, Krã-abom.

The Dominican fathers did not make the mistake of approaching Indians empty-handed. On their expedition in 1935 they took '100 heavy machetes, 50 cowling axes, . . . over 200 good-quality American knives and almost 300 large pairs of scissors, fish-hooks and line, numerous necklaces of beautiful white and blue beads, bracelets, cloths of bright colours, combs, mirrors, a great many sack-purses . . . and hundreds of boxes of wooden matches.' They walked across the watershed towards the Xingu and then took a boat up the Fresco and Riozinho. After eight days, they re-established contact with the Gorotire whom they had met in earlier years. The tribe was assembled at its main village below the lovely Fumaça waterfall and the presents were distributed. In return, the Dominicans wanted children, to be taken back to the mission for indoctrination. They asked, through an interpreter: 'Prepare some children to deliver to us tomorrow. We want to take them to Conceição to teach them, to load them with presents, and bring them back to the aldeia. Do not fear, they will be well treated and will return grown and in good health.' Five reluctant boys and girls were finally assembled and left with the missionaries. But on the first night of the return march, all suddenly fled. A Dominican wrote: 'Our smiling hopes for the conversion of the Gorotire tribe, which were starting so auspiciously, have gone!' He consoled himself that a similar flight had occurred with the Tapirapé nine years before, but 'today that tribe is all tame and half its members are baptized.'

In 1936 the Gorotire split. Schisms were commonplace among the Kayapó: disputes within a tribe – often over women – could be settled either by a ritual club fight or by a chief taking his followers off to found a new village. Such moves were easy for a people as self-sufficient as the Kayapó, hunters and raiders who were constantly travelling and knew vast areas of forests. A group known as Kuben-Kran-Kégn ('People with Shaved Heads') remained near the Fumaça Falls on the upper Riozinho. Chief Kapaíre took another group, first to attack the inoffensive and charming Tupi-speaking Asuriní to the north, and then returned – with prisoners – to settle on the upper Fresco. Then, in March 1937, 800 of these under Chiefs Takoére and Vicente (a settler's child captured as an infant) went to live at Nova Olinda, a former Kayapó village and rubber outpost where the Riozinho joins the Fresco. This horde had good relations with the seringueiros and wanted access to their trade goods. But the move was a disaster. 'A quarter of them soon died of flu. Contact with alcohol and prostitution began. All the efforts of the civilizados were aimed at dissolving or destroying the band as quickly as possible . . . The excessive arrogance of the civilizados, their hatred and contempt for the *bichos* [beasts], all cloaked in shameful insincerity, made any true feeling of friendship or unity impossible.' The SPI appointed a superintendent called Pedro Silva, and he did his utmost to protect these Gorotire against 'the mortal hatred of almost all the civilizados on the Xingu'. Silva had some gifts and supplies for the Indians. But they coveted only guns and ammunition, for which they traded anything they could offer. The tragedy was that they wanted these to attack the Kuben-Kran-Kégn, their own tribespeople from whom they had parted only a few months earlier. 'By early 1938 the situation [at Nova Olinda] had become untenable. Mutual aversion [between Indians and settlers] reached a peak. Filth and misery, sickness and famine reigned in the camp at the mouth of the Riozinho. The Gorotire abandoned the place: only a small number stayed with Pedro Silva.'

Missionaries come in all guises. Some lack sympathy or understanding of the people they come to convert, because they are either rigid fundamentalists or conservative traditionalists, but a few are remarkably sensitive to the Indians' society and dedicated to their welfare. The Unevangelized Fields Mission now sent one such to investigate the fate of the Three Freds: a cheerful and energetic Englishman called Horace Banner. He arrived in 1938 and rapidly went up the Riozinho to discover the Freds' sunken launch and learn their sad end. He then established a house and maize plantation a few kilometres up the Riozinho from Nova Olinda. The stern and highly professional German anthropologist Curt Nimuendajú was impressed. Banner's 'friendliness, invariably calm and genuine, his readiness to help any in need, and his manner of treating Indians with the same consideration as civilizados delighted the Gorotire. His conduct contrasted so markedly from that of other civilizados that the Indians decided that he must have descended from the world they believe exists above the sky. In one year, he learned Kayapó fluently.' By 1939 most of the Gorotire were with Horace Banner. He lived in a simple house, unfortified, and with some 400 Indians in huts round about his. Banner did not shower them with presents, and if they wanted something he asked them to do some work to earn it. He lived modestly, without any servant. He never gave orders to the Indians, but often explained and reasoned with them. Banner spent hours every day visiting the Gorotire huts, to talk and heal the sick. They liked this so much that they would complain if he neglected someone. 'The Gorotires' confidence in Horace was limitless. One could see that they were convinced that he was acting in their interest and did not exploit them . . . His calm and amiability never altered. Even when he had to reprove them, he did it with a serious countenance but not angrily. They remained silent and after a while came to ask if he was still annoyed with them.' Banner himself described these visits. He might begin by asking 'What have you eaten today?' and, if the answer was negative, would produce some simple local food. 'If [the Indian] is full, he may take the opportunity of rising to his feet to tell an elaborate story of the tapir or peccary he killed, both being first-class game and excellent material for story-telling. Then, by way of a change, one can ask about children, sisters, brothers or parents. Wives are better left unmentioned, for separations and changes are common and references may cause embarrassment . . . Another valuable aid to friendship is a song. Sing a song to an Indian and irrespective of theme, tune, or talent, the singer is assured of a sympathetic hearing. All Kayapó love singing.'

Banner recorded a Gorotire legend about the arrival of white men. When the Kayapó used to live on the Araguaia–Tocantins, some of their young men were attacked by sorcerer-termites from a gigantic termite mound. 'Some time later the termites returned, but in the form of white men, in boats moved by sails, an evolution of the wings that termites possess when they emerge from the earth at the first rains. Among them were soldiers (*krã-kam-ngoira*) and padres (*ôaiangára*).' The name they gave to the white soldiers meant 'pan on the head'. 'As proof of the humble origin of the white race – in contrast with the Men of Heaven, who are the Indians – they point out the houses of red mud, full of compartments, which the civilizados of the interior still build, and which they built on a smaller scale when they lived in the ground as termites.' Anthropologists have recorded other Kayapó legends about the origins of white men. In one such myth, there is a hated shaman called Angme kapran who is repeatedly killed by the Indians but resurrects as a white man. This sorcerer made guns from his shin bones, powder from the ashes of his burned body, cattle from his ankle bones, and European maize from his teeth. The shaman 'scared away the Indians with gunshots. They were terrified and never more returned to him.' Another legend had a snake show the Indian Iprere how to make a gun and ammunition. This same snake gave Indians arrows with which to hunt; but he told Iprere to give the white men guns.

The negative side to Horace Banner was that he was primarily there for missionary work, for his own salvation and that of the Indians. So Banner made his part of the tribe live in rows of rectangular huts, an arrangement that totally undermined the many customs that depend on a circular plan for the aldeia revolving around the men's hut. He also persuaded the Indians to exchange their feather headdresses for what Nimuendajú described as 'ludicrous caps of the type worn by English carol singers'. But Nimuendajú felt that the SPI official Pedro Silva was wrong to oppose Banner, since both men were working for the good of the Gorotire. The German-Brazilian anthropologist praised Silva for being a convinced friend of the Indians, who spoke their language and struggled to defend them, but chided him for claiming credit for pacifying the Gorotire, since this was 'the work of the Indians themselves, who had first sent their prisoners of war as their spokesmen'.

Horace Banner left to return to England, and some of his group of Gorotire dispersed. In 1939 an important contingent, under Chief Bepmaiti, roamed the open country between the Fresco and Araguaia. There, Brazilians killed an Indian woman in her garden clearing; three Brazilians were killed in revenge; and there was savage reprisal by a posse of fifty armed men. In three raids, these frontiersmen killed some seventy Kayapó, including Bepmaiti. Then a group of forty went off under another chief and disappeared into the western forests. Some 200 survivors returned to the post at Nova Olinda, bringing its population back to over 400, but poor hygiene and inadequate medical resources had devastating consequences.

The SPI created Gorotire post with the remnant of Banner's Indians.

An enlightened official called Cícero Cavalcanti, a fluent Jê-speaker, took charge of this post in 1945. He was dismayed to find only 150 Indians in it; and by 1947 these were reduced to 89 individuals. Cavalcanti moved this group upriver to an attractive location called Sobreiro, where the Gorotire settled for many years. An epidemic of flu and measles in 1959 killed a further twenty Gorotire. Carlos Moreira commented that these diseases 'should have been benign among them, after over twenty years' contact with neo-Brazilian populations', but the deaths occurred because of the SPI's shameful lack of medical care. The demographic catastrophe, with the population reduced by 90 per cent in a few years, shattered the Gorotires' social structure. Edson Diniz said that marriages took place that violated tribal norms and would previously have been considered incestuous, and the group was forced to cooperate with the settlers' frontier. By 1960 it had entered the local economy more than any other Kayapó group. Brazil nuts were gathered and tonka beans (cumarú) were grown for export, pigs and chickens were farmed, and animals hunted for their skins. All this activity was run by the Indian agency; but a local businessman duped the encarregado, paying too little and charging too much, and transportation of the produce was beyond the impoverished SPI's resources.

In 1953, after a year of 'wooing', Cícero Cavalcanti made a peaceful contact with the Kuben-Kran-Kégn – the group whom Banner referred to as the KKK, who had remained near the Fumaça falls, and who had killed the Three Freds. Cavalcanti loved the Kayapó, but he explained why Tupi-speaking peoples looked down on these warlike tribes. 'These Indians did not know the art of ceramics, and could not weave hammocks. They were semi-nomadic and [often] lived in temporary huts. Married couples slept on mats on the ground, while single men slept on platforms with a fire below.' There were about 300 Kuben-Kran-Kégn when Cavalcanti contacted them. This became yet another tragically bungled 'pacification'. As usual, the SPI did not have adequate medical back-up. In 1958 there was a calamitous measles epidemic that killed a fifth of the tribe before missionaries arrived with medical aid. In the following year, a chief was taken to Belém but died there. His successor as chief accused some southern Menkragnoti, other Kayapó who were living with the Kuben-Kran-Kégn, of killing him through sorcery. There was a slaughter of the immigrant Menkragnoti from which few escaped.

During these years, the Kayapó were probing westwards to the lower Xingu and across it, sometimes trading with the settlers, at other times fighting them. The Xingu had too few *Hevea* trees to have been at the heart of the rubber frenzy; but the boom's collapse had still transformed this region. Nimuendajú recalled that in 1915 there had been several thousand seringueiros controlled by bosses known as 'colonels', who had private armies of ruthless mulattos called cabras. 'Conscious of their power and certain of immunity – for in those days they had money, or were thought to, even though the rubber crisis had started – these [colonels] committed violence and killings compared to which the Kayapó attacks were child's play. Today [1940], the [civilizado] population is reduced to a few hundred people who live by extracting [Brazil] nuts and rubber. The old bosses have died, except for two or three . . . who are still intoxicated with narrating their old exploits, although poverty has made them so wretched, stingy and cowardly that I could hardly recognize them.'

The rubber man who lived furthest up the Xingu was Constantino Viana. He fancied himself as a pacifier of bichos and had had intermittent contact with the Tupi-speaking Juruna, a much-reduced tribe that had gradually been forced up the Xingu ever since its first contacts with European colonists in the seventeenth century. Viana equipped a large boat with fifteen Juruna and had them paddle it down to Altamira, where in 1915 Curt Nimuendajú saw thirteen of them die wretchedly from disease. When the rest of the Juruna at Viana's camp heard about this, they took one of his canoes and fled upriver. 'He pursued the fugitives, caught them, and massacred them. He himself told me this exploit amid the guffaws of his cabras.' The Juruna were ravaged by disease at Viana's outpost, Pedra Seca. Decades later, Chief Bibina said that so many had died that 'it seemed almost like witchcraft'. It was 'because of diseases' that the surviving Juruna finally migrated upriver, south of the great Von Martius rapids. It was a move that saved what remained of the tribe.

Years later, the Juruna, armed with rifles, tried to rob women and children from the Suyá – a bellicose Jê-speaking people who frightened the tribes of the upper Xingu. The Juruna raid failed – they themselves lost people to the Suyá – so they turned to Viana for help. Constantino Viana therefore 'armed his gang of half-castes, went up the Xingu [above the Von Martius rapids], surrounded the Suyá aldeia, . . . set fire to its fifteen large houses, and shot those who fled from the flames. On his return, he even attacked a peaceful group of Kamayurá and Waurá, who live on the headwaters of the Xingu, stealing their women and children. The return of this expedition with its canoes loaded with spoil and prisoners was the greatest moment of glory in Constantino's life.' In September 1939 some 400 Kuben-Kran-Kégn appeared at the house of this same Viana, and camped in his clearings until they had consumed his manioc.

Meanwhile, another small group of Gorotire had made its way across hundreds of kilometres of forests and rivers to emerge at Porto do Moz, a former Jesuit mission near the mouth of the Xingu. An SPI officer settled these Kayapó near the town, but 'the result was disgracefully similar to that of Nova Olinda'. Some of the Indians rapidly succumbed to disease: Nimuendajú saw pictures of their dead bodies thrown alongside their living relatives on the floor of a house that was their dwelling. The town of Altamira and impoverished outposts along the lower Xingu were abuzz with exaggerated tales of Kayapó 'attacks'. Nimuendajú gradually discovered the reality. One small group of Indians had settled far down the Xingu, where passing boats had friendly contact with them. But when some of these appeared at the town of Vitória (below Altamira) asking for transportation across a river, they were lodged in a room; during the night, armed men appeared at the doors and slaughtered nine sleeping men and women.

At the end of 1939, the people of Altamira were rejoicing at reports that one Jacinto Mota had taken his cabras to inflict a series of defeats on the Kayapó of the plains towards the Araguaia. The true story was told to Nimuendajú by one of the participants. Mota had pretended to want peaceful relations with the Kayapó. He invited them to a celebration at a house near Arraias, and 'ordered an ox to be killed and gave them a banquet. That night, when they were sleeping on the floor of the house, he attacked them with the rifle fire of some fifty cabras. [A later witness] at the scene of this massacre counted the putrefying bodies of sixteen men, women and children. . . . and a further two bodies some distance away.' Nimuendajú was dismayed by how trusting the Indians were. He saw some of them visit Constantino Viana. They came unarmed and calmly went to sleep on sacks of nuts. Viana's son and his cabras planned to murder the sleeping Kayapó and were stopped only by the old seringueiro himself. The anthropologist later saw some Gorotire who had escaped from Mota's massacre, and was equally amazed by their indifference to their injuries.

An eight-year-old girl had been shot through both her buttocks, but the wound had now completely formed a scar. One woman was shot in the hand. Another called Bubu had a shot go through her right thigh and then deeply scar the skin of the left thigh. The hole soon healed, but the scratch became a deep suppurating wound as wide as the palm of a hand. It is incredible how she can have endured a [long] march in this state . . . The Indians made remarkably little of the attack they had suffered. One woman told me how she escaped by dragging herself along the ground with her children while bullets passed over her. Even among themselves they rarely talked about this event, which was already almost forgotten. The Gorotire are not impressed by death – either of themselves or of others.

Early in the twentieth century, an important group of Gorotire crossed the mighty Xingu river and moved into the forests and occasional cerrado to the west. This group was named after its men's house: Menkragnoti. The Kayapó like to locate their villages in areas of open cerrado, close to high forest for hunting. The Menkragnoti found such a site between the Jarina (a western tributary of the middle Xingu) and the upper Iriri, a large river that joins the Xingu far downstream near the town of Altamira. Soon after reaching this rich region, the Menkragnoti in 1921 attacked another Jê-speaking tribe living to the west near the source of the Iriri. This was the Panará (a tribe then known as Kren Akróre – 'Kren' is pronounced Crane and means 'people'). But the belligerent Kayapó had met their match. Verswijver described this raid as 'a significant landmark in Menkragnoti history: the assaulted tribe took revenge and the Menkragnoti were attacked in their own village by a non-Kayapó group. This had never happened before in their history.' For the next twenty years, Menkragnoti history was dominated by conflict with this adversary, and the tribe frequently moved its village for fear of Panará reprisals.

By interrogating aged Indians and from occasional data from the settlers' side, Gustaaf Verswijver pieced together a history of Menkragnoti movements in the dry and rainy seasons of every year during four decades prior to their contact in the 1950s. An amazing picture of restless, warlike hyperactivity emerges. In a ten-year period, some Kayapó moved their villages half a dozen times, often migrating for well over 100 kilometres (62 miles). We have to remind ourselves how self-sufficient these people are: every household makes all its own belongings, and building a new village is easy for a community in which every member has the requisite skills and the forest provides all construction materials. Also, Kayapó hunters range over large areas of forest and savannah, so that they know all the good locations for villages within a radius of perhaps 200 kilometres. During the period of his study, Verswijver noted eighty-two relocations of villages by the Menkragnoti groups. In those same years, he recorded equally frenzied military activity. The three groups of Menkragnoti Kayapó, most of whom had crossed to the west of the Xingu, made ninety-two fighting expeditions in some forty-five years. Sixty of these were against non-Indian Brazilians, twenty-two against other Kayapó, four attacked the Panará, and six were raids on non-Jê-speaking tribes such as the Tapirapé or Asuriní. The American anthropologist Terence Turner quoted Chief Raoni of the southern Menkragnoti, who boasted that 'we Kayapó dived into our territory and swam through our lands'. Other Kayapó were equally belligerent during the period of their first contacts with settlers. In the eight years from 1942 to 1950, the Kuben-Kran-Kégn undertook seventeen raids.

The warlike Kayapó used bows and arrows and sometimes lances. But, as Verswijver wrote, 'Whether during attacks, while hunting certain animals, or during duels, the Kayapó seem to prefer hand-to-hand fights. For this purpose, clubs are by far the most favoured of all weapons: they are handled with extreme ability.' The standard club, *kô*, is a long, round, hardwood weapon that thickens towards its end like a baseball bat. But the Kayapó use a variety of clubs for different fighting purposes. All are well over a metre long, but one of the most formidable ends in a sharply pointed flat spearhead. These *kop* are used in stylized duels during arguments within the village. 'Armed with the heavy spatulate clubs, the men stand in pairs and take turns in striking each other at a point between the shoulder and the elbow. The striking is done with the sharp sides of the *kop* club until one of the combatants is unable to continue (e.g. from having broken his arm) or until some kinsmen intervene to stop the fight.'

Such warriors were naturally thrilled by the power of guns. 'Through the acquisition of firearms, the Kayapó were able to overcome their initial military disadvantage in relation to the local Brazilians: they were able to match them on equal terms. More importantly . . . such weapons [helped them] defend their villages against Indian enemies who also owned firearms.' Of course, guns and ammunition could be manufactured only by whites, so that the Kayapó's ever-increasing demand for them resulted in heavy dependence on contact with Brazilians. The Indians could get firearms by raiding settlements. But they preferred to acquire them peacefully. On one occasion, in 1942, Chief Tapyet of the Menkragnoti and his men 'tried to "pacify" the Brazilians: the Indians hoped to enter into friendly relations with the inhabitants of a small settlement on the Jamanxim river in order to obtain more firearms and ammunition while taking fewer risks.' But the attempt failed, and the Indians could see no alternative to resumed raiding of Brazilian settlements, to satisfy their needs.

When they raided frontiersmen, the Kayapó ensured that they greatly outnumbered their prey: between ten and thirty warriors attacking the huts of one or two families. Scouts went ahead to watch the number and movements of the Brazilians. A magic mixture of plants and centipedes was thrown towards the huts, to weaken and perhaps remove the inhabitants. Fearing Kayapó attack, settlers tended to go to their plantations with their wives and families. The Indians might therefore find empty huts to pillage during daylight hours. But if they encountered people, they killed adults and sometimes took children as captives. When there was a battle, it could be a bloody affair. The Kayapó therefore tried to avoid confrontation, not because they were afraid, but because their motive was booty rather than destroying white colonists. They raided as far west as the Tapajós river, which had once been a centre of the rubber trade. Roberto Décio de Las Casas interviewed rubber-tappers who had suffered Kayapó raids during the fifteen years prior to 1956. Although the stories differed,

> there was great similarity in details: destruction of the hut and all possessions; deaths generally from club blows; body full of arrow wounds; all the seringueiros fled . . . The Indians always appeared as exceptionally strong and absolute masters of the forest . . . They robbed and 'spared no one when it came to killing' . . . The Kayapó arrived as invaders. If they found manioc flour, ammunition, etc., they appropriated it purely and simply . . . In battles, the Indians had the upper hand. The seringueiros had no way of confronting them: they feared them above all else . . . They all viewed the Kayapó as savages, non-Christians, more or less beasts of the forest. Killing them would not be a crime, but rather a mixture of self-defence and hunting.

Most isolated rubber-tappers were restrained by fear of the Kayapó, by the difficulty of finding them in their forests, and above all by a conviction that the Indians were implacable in hunting down and killing any who harmed them. However, in July 1956 the Kayapó made a raid on an unguarded storehouse of the Alto Tapajós rubber company that was too successful. They took 4,000 cartridges, 80 kilos (176 pounds) of shot for making cartridges, and quantities of tools, fishing line, manioc, and tobacco. The company decided on savage retaliation. Twelve heavily armed seringueiros and two Munduruku guides set out under a leader known as Paxiúba. After five days' tracking, they spotted a campfire and laid an ambush. 'All lying on the ground . . . at 5 a.m. on 13 July, the seringueiros were all ready with their guns aimed. One of the Indians, presumed to be the chief, arose and shouted the signal for the others to get up for their journey. At this moment the attack was launched, with a volley aimed at the Indians who were taken by surprise.' Twenty men were killed instantly and others ran off wounded and bleeding. 'As proof of their victory, the criminal seringueiros pulled the wooden discs from the lower lips of several Indians and brought these back together with clubs and utensils such as gourds used to store feathers for ornaments.' There was an official inquiry, but 'the SPI took no action to bring the authors of this crime to justice. Powerful pressures had been brought to bear', so that the company's owners were certain that no criminal proceedings would be instigated against them. The SPI sertanista Cícero Cavalcanti commented, bitterly, that 'there is no report of anyone in Brazil having been convicted for killing Indians'.

Attacks on other Indians were different. With non-Jê-speaking tribes – such as the Juruna on the Xingu, the Asuriní north-west of the Xikrin, or the Tapirapé to the south – there would often be two attacks: a preliminary exploratory skirmish followed by a later onslaught by many warriors. A favourite tactic was for the less experienced or older fighters to advance directly against a village, shouting, while one or two groups of the best warriors moved round the flanks to catch the enemy as they fled. The Juruna were often attacked when they were in their garden clearings, because the Kayapó wanted to capture women who were tending the crops. With the Tapirapé, there would be a direct attack on a large village, which could yield ceramics and other useful plunder.

Fighting against other Kayapó also involved surrounding a village in a dawn attack. But the motive now was revenge in an internecine vendetta. So, although firearms might be used during the initial charge, the main struggle took place in the village's central plaza, with the rival Kayapó fighting hand-to-hand with their clubs. The attackers wanted to demonstrate their courage, strength, agility, and martial prowess. Kayapó games, initiation ceremonies, and oratory were all designed to train and toughen the warriors and make them impervious to pain.

During the 1950s, teams from the SPI made a series of peaceful contacts with Kayapó groups. Their successes were due to guns. During the period from 1950 to 1957, the Kokraimoro launched thirteen raids. This group, led by Chief Kokraimor, lived at the headwaters of a stream that flowed into the west of the middle Xingu. Francisco Meirelles – the pacifier of the Xavante – wrote that 'they became the most rancorous enemies of the seringueiros and settlers of the Xingu and its tributaries. They brought death and terror to the regions of the middle Xingu, lower Iriri, rio Novo, Igarapé Preto, etc.' But Meirelles had no difficulty in 'pacifying' the Kokraimoro, in April 1957. He took a large expedition that included a dozen Kayapó. He was pushing on an open door: the Indians were clearly keen on peaceful contact with the whites. Meirelles said that he was also able to reconcile a split between two factions of this group, and to settle 160 of them at a new post called Kokraimoro, on an island where their stream joins the Xingu. This was a disaster. Carlos Moreira described the place in 1958: 'The conditions of hygiene and health were appalling. The lack of space, absence of plantations or adequate boats, lack of equipment for hunting or fishing – all these factors had reduced the Kokraimoro to a serious deficiency of food. Most were ill.' Exposed to passing rubber-gatherers on the main Xingu, the tribe soon caught flu, and half died.

Meanwhile, another Kayapó group called Kararaô 'spontaneously attempted a peaceful contact with the town of Porto de Vitoria (48 kilometres [30 miles] upstream of Altamira and linked to it by road). They were pitilessly machine-gunned by perverse elements of that locality. Those who escaped the massacre were settled at the head of the Limão stream, a tributary of the Curuá.' In 1957, the Kararaô killed more seringueiros on the lower Curuá and even fortified one dead rubber man's hut: 'they cut embrasures in the walls through which to fire their guns and bows. They had also placed themselves strategically in various places on the riverbank, and scattered hidden paxiuba palm spines on all the access paths.' But when Meirelles found the Kararaô village, the Kayapó in his attraction party rapidly made peace with these Indians.

Thanks to presents of guns, the Kararaô chief guided Meirelles for twelve hours up the Limão river and then through the forests to the village of the Kayapó. It was a splendid place. 'The main path from the landing stage was well tended and led to the maloca: it had bridges over the various streams. There were other improvements such as great plantations of manioc, maize, sweet potatoes and extensive banana groves extending as far as the eye could see, demonstrating that a great redoubt of Indians lived here.' Meirelles sent for reinforcements and returned with thirty-five men, fifteen of whom were Indians. These Kayapó were sent ahead to parlay. An hour later, they came to tell the whites to leave their weapons and advance into the village. Meirelles accepted and went with ten unarmed volunteers to talk to old Chief Angme'ê in the men's hut. He explained that the expedition was well intentioned and he promised many presents, including guns and ammunition. This did the trick. The Chief accepted peace and even agreed to help Meirelles 'pacify' other Kayapó groups. The visitors were given a feast of bananas, beiju (manioc bread), yams, and roast game meat, 'in a clear demonstration of the plentiful and happy life they led until then.' This group was later moved to a post on the Baú tributary of the Curuá, where they were united with the Kararaô to form a village of 200 people. But they no longer lived a plentiful or happy life. As one head of the SPI wrote: 'Yet again, these Indians [of Limão] paid a tribute, a rather expensive one, for the disgraceful methods of "attraction".' Soon after their transfer, an epidemic of influenza ravaged these communities: eighty per cent died and only forty Indians survived. (Another group of eighty-two Kararaô were contacted in 1965; but within seven years all but three were dead from disease.)

In the following dry season, June 1958, Meirelles had further 'success' – based entirely on presents of guns. There had been raids and killings on the Iriri (which the Curuá joins shortly before it flows into the lower Xingu). 'It was a situation of panic. There was talk that all the settlers and seringueiros of this river – reckoned to be about 500 people, including children – were going to abandon the river and make for Altamira, terrified by successive attacks by the Indians on seringueiros, fishermen, farmers in roças [clearings], etc.' Meirelles reassured the terrified colonists and then took his expedition up the Iriri for twenty-one days – a voyage made more difficult because the river was so low. His Indians advised that *they* should proceed without the whites: otherwise the Mekragnotire of the Iriri might think that it was a punitive raid to avenge the recent killings. They were gone for thirty-eight days, because those Mekragnotire had moved to a more distant village. But, once again, the Kayapó were eager for peaceful relations with the whites if this meant regular trading. Chief Airuté came to meet Meirelles, who recalled: 'When we arrived there we found the forest all cleared and carpeted with *açaí* palm leaves, and the Indians all painted and adorned with their ornaments as though it were a festival.' The Chief declared his intention to live peacefully henceforth. 'I answered . . . that we were satisfied by his proposals and [wanted them] to possess guns for their defence and hunting, so that they would not need to kill anyone else. Passing from words to action, I distributed among them thirty shotguns and a .44-calibre rifle for each chief.'

Verswijver noted that 'much to the Brazilians' surprise, the "pacification" of the warlike Kayapó groups went extremely placidly; and when the SPI almost immediately after "pacification" insisted that the Indians collect rubber and Brazil nuts in exchange for more commodities, the Indians willingly did so.' Carlos Moreira, a distinguished historian of the Brazilian Indians, was furious about the SPI's bungled attraction campaigns. Although he acknowledged the bravery and endurance of Meirelles' men, 'the SPI attraction teams were so badly equipped that they ran out of supplies before even contacting the Indians'. They failed to mobilize air transport or medical supplies to check the almost-inevitable flu epidemics. They also connived with the rubber companies. 'Rubber-tappers and nut extractors attach themselves to the actual pacification teams, and immediately occupy any areas that become accessible through the pacification of hostile groups.' Nothing was done to protect tribal lands. Writing in 1959, Moreira said that almost 'no Indian group in [the State of] Pará possesses territory with definitive title deed.' And the SPI still practised the fatal policy of moving tribes, after contact, to more accessible locations. This removed Indians from their plantations and hunting grounds, and it exposed them to the dangers of association with Brazilian colonists. It was contrary to the stark lesson of the history of Brazilian Indians, 'the leitmotiv of Indian depopulation: that cohabitation means contamination'.

The tough Panará (Kren Akróre) lived south-west of these western groups of Kayapó. We now know that this tribe is a remnant of the southern Kayapó, who once lived south of Goiás and in southern Mato Grosso but were thought to have become extinct during the nineteenth century. The Panará had worsted the Menkragnoti in battle, and were the only Indians who had had the audacity to counter-attack a Kayapó village. So, after their contact by Meirelles, the northern Menkragnoti in 1968 used guns and ammunition (obtained from him and from a missionary) for a murderous ambush on the Panará. 'The Menkragnoti party surrounded the village before dawn and attacked by firing guns into the houses. The [Panará] were taken totally unaware . . . Resistance was brief in the face of the gunfire, with most of the inhabitants fleeing into the forest.' Many Panará were slaughtered.

The third group of Kayapó to migrate across the Araguaia in the nineteenth century were some 2,000 Indians who settled in the forests of the upper Itacaiúnas, a western tributary of the Tocantins. This northern section of the Kayapó consisted of 1,500 Putkarôt, who later adopted the name Xikrin (given to them by other Kayapó, and pronounced Sheekreen) and 500 Djoré. There was the usual myopic hatred between these northernmost Kayapó and their kindred living to the south and southwest. When Bishop Sebastião Tomás visited the Gorotire in 1935, their Chief Kukungrati had just returned from attacking the Djoré, some 150 kilometres (95 miles) to the north-east. The Djoré and Xikrin were 'pitiless enemies of both Christians and of their own Kayapó relatives' and they had acquired rifles. So they had ambushed the Gorotires' camp, killing many.

The northern groups also suffered at the hands of civilizados and from their diseases. It was not long before the Djoré were decimated by an epidemic, and the survivors took refuge and merged with the rest of the Xikrin. There had been sporadic clashes with rubber-tappers early in the twentieth century. The end of the rubber boom brought two decades of peace, but this was broken when nut-gatherers (*castanheiros*) started to push up the Itacaiúnas in search of Brazil-nut trees. The world price of these luxury nuts peaked in 1930 so that castanheiros became very active. But two of them were killed by the Xikrin. In 1931 the Indians 'launched repeated attacks against settlers on the Vermelho [tributary of the Itacaiúnas]. One of these, of calamitous proportions, occurred in the Brazil-nut forest of Boca do Cardoso, where twelve people including two little girls were barbarously slaughtered by warriors of the [Xikrin] tribe.' The colonists abandoned a dozen farms on these rivers and fled to the town of Marabá on the Tocantins.

The inevitable retaliation ensued: one António Pires Leal took sixty armed men on a surprise raid on a Xikrin village. 'Half its population, probably 180 people, were killed that day. They spared no one, not even children.' This traumatic attack, coupled with fear of Gorotire Kayapó enemies from the south-west, caused the Xikrin to divide and flee. Some went north-westwards to the upper Bacajá (a river that flows into the Xingu below Altamira), others to the headwaters of their Itacaiúnas river. A journalist reported the tragic incomprehension and hostilities between castanheiros and Indians. The nut- and rubber-gatherers lived in absolute poverty, in shelters roofed in buriti-palm thatch, eating only manioc flour, and perpetually in debt to bosses who took their produce and sold them their few necessities at exorbitant prices. These seringueiros and castanheiros shot Indians on sight. The latter felt that they must acquire guns and ammunition – to defend themselves, to retaliate, and to get the better of other Kayapó. So they raided isolated huts to get these weapons. 'The Kayapó could not distinguish between good and bad whites, so they shot or clubbed many innocent victims.' But one castanheiro said that 'between the Indians and my boss, I prefer the former. The Indians come and kill us instantly. The boss liquidates us little by little, gradually sucking our blood, and abandons us only when we are old, tired, or sick.'

After a lull, hostilities between the Xikrin and castanheiros flared again. There were also skirmishes with rubber-tappers, who reappeared when prices for wild rubber rose during the Second World War. A newspaper in Belém summed up the tit-for-tat fighting: 'The Kayapó nation wished to oppose this new incursion by its old enemies, and new battles took place. Surprise attacks by the warriors of the forest. Bloody revenge by the rubber men. And, as a result, a renewed desire for vengeance by the savages.' Unusually for indigenous people, the tribe decided on concerted retaliation. On one day in 1952 they killed ten civilizados, in different locations. The SPI tried to respond to the resulting clamour. An SPI inspector, Dorival Pamplona, penetrated the upper Itacaiúnas and became convinced that these Indians wanted peace but were victimized by the castanheiros because they had stolen some of their few possessions.

Also in 1952, Leonardo Villas Boas (the third of the three famous brothers, who was to die young) contacted some Xikrin on the savannah behind Conceição do Araguaia. In that year, there was a quarrel in the Xikrin's Kokorekre village – caused by jealousy of some Indian girls of a young white girl who had been captured from settlers and raised by the Kayapó. This led to the death of the white captive, and her protector Bemoti took a dozen of his friends to settle at the SPI's Las Casas post on the lower Itacaiúnas. Then, in August 1952, Bemoti's father Chief Bep-Karoti followed, with 180 warriors. 'They all burst, unexpected, into Las Casas in a truly impressive spectacle: singing battle songs, painted, menacingly clutching the clubs of which they are masterful users.'

In the following year, Hilmar Kluck of the SPI visited a number of Xikrin villages and confirmed that they were pacific. Then Plinio Pinheiro led an approximation team to the Cateté headwater of the Itacaiúnas. His men cut a sixty-kilometre (thirty-seven-mile) picada wide enough for mule transport, and a contact was achieved next year. Hilmar Kluck took the Xikrin who had appeared at Las Casas in a slow, four-month migration, to Kokorekre, a former Djoré village, and then on to Motikre village on the Cateté. They remained there, contentedly enough; but Bemoti ruefully told the anthropologist Lux Vidal: 'Before that [move] we were fierce and warlike, but now we are peaceful'.

The Xikrin who had moved north-westwards to the Bacajá had skirmishes with its settlers, and the Mayor of Altamira threatened to arm a posse against them. So in 1959–60 Francisco Meirelles led a tough three-month expedition towards the Tocantins, and some of his men made peaceful contact with the Bacajá Xikrin. Meirelles ordered that the group be moved to an abandoned post near Altamira. He reported, next year, that 'the remainder of these Indians are settled there – but they were almost totally decimated by the famous strain of influenza known as 204.' Meirelles had a terrible record of making newsworthy contacts but failing to follow them with medical provision.

In 1962, 164 people of the eastern Xikrin returned to their old territory on the Cateté. But in 1963 a third of that village died in a polio epidemic. Perhaps shattered by this catastrophe, in that same year the younger, more aggressive part of the Xikrin tried a bold approximation to Brazilian frontier society. Led by Bemoti – who was always fascinated by the colonists' way of life – they moved downstream to settle where their river joins the larger Itacaiúnas. Everything changed for this group. They built shacks in a straight line rather than the traditional circle, and they abandoned their festivals and other customs. There were no more speeches, which occur every evening in the centre of Kayapó villages and are such an important element in their democratic governance. They had no men's hut, so that the young men soon preferred to sleep in the house of the anthropologist Protásio Frikel (himself a bachelor) in order to escape from family houses full of women. All this was done in order to obtain trade goods, particularly guns and ammunition.

This Xikrin village, called Aldeia da Boca, became a form of trading post. Each castanheiro would stop there on his way upriver, to get Brazil nuts and skins from the Indians – and 'to get to know the village women' who prostituted themselves in return for knives, manioc flour, and other basic necessities. The village became 'a hotel and a brothel' for passing castanheiros. The Xikrin lost heavily in this attempt at peaceful integration. In the first year alone, sixteen people died of influenza and other diseases; and venereal disease was soon rampant. Unable to read and ignorant of commercial values, they were flagrantly cheated in the amount paid for their produce and the charges for trade goods. The Indians realized that they were being robbed and threatened to retaliate with their newly acquired guns; but civilizados told the Dominican Father Raymond Caron that 'they would know how to resolve this' – by massacring the Xikrin. A third of the tribe died as a result of the disastrous move to the village at the mouth of their river.

During the first half of the twentieth century, the various Kayapó groups reacted to the advancing frontier differently to any other Brazilian Indians. They became far more warlike – but their aggression was largely directed against other Kayapó. They also became more volatile. Terence Turner noted that those decades of tension were marked by the continual fragmentation of larger communities into smaller and mutually hostile ones. There was constant movement, either of entire communities, or of groups of people between many scattered village sites. At first, warfare was waged to obtain weapons and as a response to attacks by Brazilians. 'It degenerated into inter-tribal attacks to get guns, and by those with guns destroying those without. War parties also captured other manufactured goods: metal tools, beads, cloth, and hammocks. By the 1940s, pillage was for some groups their main means of obtaining manufactured goods.' The militarization of Kayapó society was the result of the advancing Brazilian frontier. But this was because Brazilians were seen as a source of guns and manufactured goods, whereas fighting against other Kayapó groups was for vengeance and military glory.

Although the Kayapó were inveterate warriors, they readily accepted peaceful contacts with attraction teams. This was because they were pragmatic. They saw contact with the whites not as surrender but simply as an easier way to obtain goods for which they had acquired an appetite. Their need for arms and ammunition became a spiralling necessity.

The turbulent years during which the Kayapó came to terms with the Brazilian frontier had a devastating effect on tribal society. The intense military activity was related to accelerated splits in Kayapó villages. For instance, Verswijver showed that the Menkragnoti he studied had a period of military 'hyperactivity', during which there were twenty-one splits and forty-five internal conflicts. He defined a split as the hostile fission of a village that lasted for at least a year. An internal conflict was a battle or formalized club duel that caused deaths or serious wounds. Chief Kokrai-mor's group of some 200 northern Menkragnoti made more military raids and also suffered most ruptures and internal strife. During the sixteen years before their pacification, the Kokraimoro launched thirty-seven attacks, and they suffered six splits and fourteen serious internal fights.

Terence Turner wrote that 'the Kayapó have a Homeric theory that all ruptures of the peace are caused by a woman. This is an exaggeration; but it is true that much tension between men's societies [which are the focal points of Kayapó villages] is linked to sexual and family disputes. Many important ruptures in the history of the Gorotire and Menkragnoti were caused by cases of adultery or sexual rivalries.' All too often, one side in a quarrel left to follow its leader to form a new village.

Warfare further disrupted the formerly large Kayapó villages. Rather than uniting the tribe, the fighting undermined traditional chiefs by raising charismatic warriors as the new leaders. When such men took groups away from the main village, it meant that the remnant was too small to support a full moiety system, which involved two men's huts and elabor-ate rules about cross-moiety marriage. The disappearance of the moiety system coincided with the advance of the Brazilian frontier. For the Pau d'Arco and Xikrin groups it came at the end of the nineteenth century; for the Gorotire in the 1930s; and with the Menkragnoti in the early 1950s.

Once a Kayapó group accepted 'pacification' and intensive contact with Brazilian society, the old tribal customs were further undermined. Large communities continued to fragment into smaller ones – and these could no longer maintain moieties. Groups became less mobile after contact. They often found that they were hemmed in by the colonization frontier, so that there were fewer village sites and the hunting grounds available to them were restricted. The accumulation of manufactured goods and private property diluted the tribe's communal spirit. Family and domestic ties became more important for Kayapó men, with consequent weakening of their bonds to masculine societies. The extended matrilocal family structure was eroded. Turner noticed that this centrifugal tendency – away from the central men's hut – was counterbalanced by a trend to community-wide ritual.

Darrell Posey wrote that 'the Kayapó have an elaborate and complex ceremonial repertoire. Ceremony is a *raison d'être* for the Kayapó, for they believe that without the performance of the prescribed rituals, the world would collapse: crops would not grow, children would not be born, the sun and moon would cease to travel across the sky.' A crucial element of ceremonies is dancing, always accompanied by singing. 'Men are the principal dancers and singers. They dance in pairs, following a circular path around the village plaza, or arm-in-arm swaying back and forth in circular or semicircular lines. The dance steps are simple and the music monotonous and repetitive to the Western ear, yet harmonious and vaguely melodic. Singing and dancing often begin at sundown and continue until sunrise, sometimes extending for seven or more consecutive nights. The combination of little sleep, and the methodical, repetitious meter and tone of the music leads the participants into altered states of consciousness.' With increased contact, new ceremonies evolved, and they acquired social significance. Above all, pacification meant an end to warfare and raiding, so that fighting leaders lost their appeal and there were fewer reasons for migrations. Men and women started to adopt clothing, with the resulting modesty and shame over nakedness, and a range of new needs for clothing, cloth, thread and needles, and soap.

7. The Villas Boas' Xingu

In November 1945 the Villas Boas brothers saw their first headwater of the Xingu river. They and their team of trail-cutters of the Roncador–Xingu Expedition had crossed most of the territory of the Xavante and were now 200 kilometres (125 miles) from their starting place on the rio das Mortes. Although the men were weak from hunger, sick, exhausted, plagued by mosquitoes, and suffering from the heat and humidity, they cleared a 610 metre (670 yard) airstrip on a patch of savannah near the Tanguro stream, which flows into the Xingu's easternmost headwater, the Culuene. The Xavante lit fires around the intruders' camp, made noises, and left signs of their proximity, but did not attack.

The Central Brazil Foundation had originally intended to plant towns in the remote interior. But when it was realized that such settlement was not yet appropriate, 'the Roncador–Xingu Expedition would have had no objective. So [two generals] decided that it should undertake "a more important mission", the opening of airstrips for the safety of aviation.' Its leaders were told to create a line of landing places to support short-range Dakotas, or larger planes flying from Rio de Janeiro to Miami, and thus to 'open up' central Brazil. Such airstrips would also become weather stations and radio transmitters. Contact with Indians was coincidental.

The airstrip on the Tanguro was finished by the end of March 1946; supplies were flown into the hungry team; two boats and a dugout canoe were built; and at the end of September the explorers set off down a stream they called Sete de Setembro, towards the Tanguro and Culuene. One of their men wrote: 'We were going to descend a completely unknown river, through eighty kilometres [fifty miles] of virgin forest. No white man had previously dared to penetrate it.' The river was full of fish, particularly voracious white and red piranha, and the forests abounded in game, with gigantic anacondas and cayman.

On 6 October 1946 came the first meeting with Xingu Indians. The riverine expedition surprised a small group. One lad remained motionless and the Villas Boas went up to him. 'He was rather agitated, talking a lot in a language we could not understand, apart from the word Kalapalo, which he kept repeating. We drew closer to him until we could place a hand on his shoulder, and we said a few words, interjecting "caraíba" [white man] and "Kalapalo" to indicate that we were friends.' Within a few days, most of the Kalapalo tribe, 150 people led by Chief Izarari, had come to inspect the expedition's camp.

In mid-November, the Villas Boas were guests in the Kalapalo village and had their first sight of some of the ceremonial that absorbs the lives of the upper-Xingu tribes. They recorded in their journals that 'the men were painting themselves and the women made stripes of [black] genipap along their thighs which were already all red from urucum. There were frequent sharp whoops by some men, to which all responded.' Then came a visit by the nearby Kuikuro – another Carib-speaking tribe – under their Chief Afukaká. After formal speeches of welcome, there were huka-huka wrestling matches in the village's circular plaza. These bouts followed careful rules, 'disciplined and sporting at all times. The victor never despises the vanquished. There is never a false movement or a harsh word.' Then came the *atangá*, when two warriors, wearing superb head-dresses of macaw, mutum (curassow or wild turkey), and other plumages, ran around the huts of the village in a special tripping gait, playing long three-metre (ten-foot) flutes, and each with a girl trotting behind with one arm on the man's shoulder and the other swinging rhythmically across her chest as they ran. At night, three men emerged from the men's hut, magnificently painted in red urucum with arabesques of black charcoal and genipap oil, each playing a metre-long *carrutu* flute – a sacred instrument that may be heard but never seen by the women. The men hold these flutes down the fronts of their bodies, stamp their feet and play music 'without melody but with extraordinary rhythm, their regular movements accompanied by shaking of rattles and by the cadenced beating of their feet and entire bodies. It is a severe ritual, of impressive gravity.'

The expedition cleared another airstrip near the Kalapalo village, and when the first plane arrived 'there was true delirium among the Indians'. A pilot took five chiefs up for a short flight, which delighted them – 'there was no sign of unease or fright: they boarded and left the plane with equal tranquillity'.

The Villas Boas brothers gradually came to know all the peaceful tribes of this magically beautiful region – people who had welcomed a number of white expeditions during the previous sixty years, and who had killed Colonel Fawcett's sad incursion two decades earlier. They were able to help the Kalapalo overcome a shortage of food, caused by unusually heavy rains and too many peccary raiding their plantations. Such was the shortage of fish and manioc that 'the tribe's food is becoming grasshoppers, which they catch daily in great quantities. Grasshoppers are the shrimps of the cerrado. Stripped of wings and heads, they are roasted on hot plates and are very edible.'

Tragically, the explorers brought the scourge of outside diseases. Both camp and village were soon wracked by colds and flu. Already by December 1946, the situation was becoming critical, and the three brothers had exhausted their supplies of penicillin and sulpha drugs. 'On reaching the Kalapalo village we witnessed a desolate scene. Nine recent burials indicated the tribe's anxious situation. Their Paramount Chief Izarari was almost dead. Desolation and hunger pervaded the village. We tried to treat Izarari with the penicillin we had brought. We had too little medicine to treat the innumerable cases we encountered; so we helped those who seemed to us to be most critical.' A gruelling day's march across hot savannah and swampy forest brought the Villas Boas to the Kuikuro village where 'we saw eight graves dug on the central plaza, a clear sign of the gravity of the situation.'

The revered Chief Izarari expired from influenza on 1 January 1947. 'Although strong and corpulent, he died rapidly. The shaman's smoke incantations and our own remedies were not enough to save him. The chief's funeral was most moving. From the moment of his death, the village lost its tranquil air. Some cried, others gesticulated, giving vent to their grief at this irreparable loss. We noticed that only one Indian remained indifferent: Maiuri, the village shaman. Izarari was buried with all his personal possessions, from the most simple: a toy tin airplane, a necklace of jaguar claws, his machete, his basket full of feather ornaments – all that belonged to him.' His body was wrapped in a Brazilian flag that the Villas Boas had given him and which he occasionally flew over his village. 'The death of the great chief profoundly depressed the Kalapalo . . . At the moment in which Izarari's body was placed in his grave, the lamentation was deafening. The tomb consisted of two holes, each eight spans [five feet] deep and 1.5 metres [five feet] apart. Below, a tunnel was dug linking the two holes. A tree trunk was erected in each hole and the hammock containing the unfortunate chief was slung in the tunnel. Thus, the earth thrown into the holes did not reach the dead man's body. No great chief, when buried, should have earth on his body or face.' A few days later, the tribe exacted vengeance on the unsuccessful shaman, Maiuri. He was summoned from his hut, late one night. 'Maiuri certainly realized that his end was close, but this did not make him hesitate or recoil. As soon as he reached the centre of the village, he was brusquely struck down and prostrated by a violent blow from a club. He died without a groan or any defensive gesture. His burial was rapid and simple.'

Luckily for the Villas Boas, they did not suffer similar punishment for their equally ineffective Western medicines or for the fact that Izarari had died of a disease brought by their team. The brothers appreciated that it was the Roncador–Xingu Expedition that had introduced the devastating influenza epidemic. They appealed for penicillin but were told by the FBC that its own staff were also ill, so that there were no antibiotics to spare for mere Indians. A journalist reported this callous reply, and the bad publicity achieved a medical improvement.

When General Cândido Rondon heard about the Villas Boas' concern for the Xinguanos, late in 1947, he enlisted them as the SPI's representatives in the Xingu. The brothers were delighted by this recognition from the great champion of the Indians. Orlando later wrote: 'One of the greatest humanists we have ever had, Rondon was a beacon. Before him, Indians were regarded as beasts. If an Indian was encountered in the forest, he was killed like a pig. It was Rondon who gave a conscience to our laws and turned Indians into respected figures . . . During most of his life, Rondon defended the need to bring Indians towards civilization, to create the conditions for them to become "civilizados". It was only at the end of his life that he recognized that the only way to save Indians was to preserve them in their habitat, living in their own culture.'

Some doctors came to the region, but there was never enough medicine. At the beginning, a Dr Estilac examined the Indians and found some cases of advanced malaria and of intestinal worms. When a potent shaman, Chief Petalacinho of the Matipuí, came to the camp, the two medical men conversed: the shaman told Estilac, by sign language, that his people were suffering from malaria, worms, and diarrhoea. Then came the rotund, ebullient Dr Noel Nutels, a malaria expert and a spellbinding raconteur, 'a fabulous companion' who was to become Orlando's closest friend. 'The Kuikuro are impressed and amazed by "civilizado" medicine. Dr Vahia examined their appendixes; Dr Estilac looked at their eyelids and tongues and listened to their chests; and Dr Noel [Nutels] felt their spleens, laid down and turned over his patients.' Nutels later recalled that 'The first time I used penicillin was in '46, when the Roncador Expedition had its first contact with the Kalapalo Indians. As the Expedition's doctor I had to play a role in consolidating relations between civilizados and Indians . . . The first contact always leaves a residue of great anxiety, of inhibition on both sides, of respect and fear.' Other scientists present soon after the expedition reached the Xingu included the ornithologist Helmut

Sick and the talented anthropologists Eduardo Galvão, Mário Simões, and Pedro Lima. Dr Lima worked with the Waurá, but also reported on tension among all the Xingu tribes and on their blood groups.

Although some twenty expeditions had previously penetrated the rivers of the upper Xingu, the Villas Boas were the first strangers to take up permanent residence among its peoples. So, in later years, 'the first appearance of Orlando' became a semi-legend recounted by tribal elders, as was the landing of the first aircraft and the decision of some curious men to go to visit the intruders' camp. Bruna Franchetto, who studied the Kuikuro, said that one of those who went to the camp on the Culuene was an Indian who had learned Portuguese at the Bakairi post Simões Lopes. It was he who guided the Villas Boas to his village, 'and he became an honoured intermediary with the caraíba [white men], a powerful and envied figure, and a new type of "chief".'

The Villas Boas brothers spent much of 1947 exploring the Xingu headwaters. They took their canoes down the Culuene and entered the village of the Tupi-speaking Kamayurá. It is built in the classic upper-Xingu model: a circular sandy plaza surrounded by half a dozen superb huts, great lozenge-shaped structures on a frame of mighty beams, some of which are diagonal braces against the thrust of the heavy thatched roof. The three brothers and their Indian companions entered the Kamayurá village, which had seen few strangers. Young men ran into their huts and emerged menacingly with bows and arrows, while their women disappeared into the forest. The tension was calmed by shouted greetings. The Villas Boas had heard about two important Kamayurá: Maricá and Tamacu. 'Here were the two of them in the centre of the village. It was they, with the Chief Tamapu and the very old and agreeable Karatsipá, who had calmed the young men and women.' Maricá immediately joined the brothers in their journey downriver. The Kamayurá were to become one of the Villas Boas' favourite tribes, close allies in dealing with other Indians.

The other 'trusted' tribe was the Yawalipiti, Aruak-speakers who had been reduced to some fifty people dispersed in other villages. The Villas Boas encouraged the Yawalipiti 'to rebuild a village that had disintegrated twenty years ago, with the death of old Chief Aritana. All that had been left were young people and children with no elders, so they were taken in by other tribes, chiefly the Kuikuro. Now grown up, twenty years later, it was easy to persuade them to erect their own village – against the wishes of their former hosts.' The Villas Boas paid for the tools and food while the Yawalipiti reconstituted their home. Their chief was also called Aritana, a handsome, powerful, and serious young man who was to become, by the end of the century, Paramount Chief of all the upper-Xingu tribes.

East of the Kamayurá, on the far side of the Culuene, the Villas Boas met the Trumai, a small tribe that was currently at loggerheads with the Kamayurá because these suspected them of witchcraft in the death of a young man in the larger village. The expedition spent some weeks clearing a small airstrip at the Trumai village, Jacaré ('Cayman'), which was later to become an important base of the Brazilian air force. Jacaré had splendid groves of mango trees that the Trumai and Kamayurá had planted there. Moving onto the main Xingu river and down it for a hundred kilometres (sixty miles), the explorers saw a lovely village location on its right bank. This was Diauarum, 'Place of the Black Jaguar' in Tupi.

Further down the Xingu, near the mouth of its Manitsauá-Missu tributary, the Villas Boas saw the canoes and village of an unknown group. But when they overtook an Indian canoe, its three crew dived into the river, swam ashore, and disappeared into the forest. Artefacts were taken from a deserted hut – with a manufactured present, usually a knife or machete, left in the place of each item removed. Back at Jacaré, the aged Kamayurá Karatsipá was consulted about the artefacts. 'Karatsipá is the oldest Indian in the Xingu and is therefore listened to and respected by all. He must be about ninety, which is very rare among Indians. Old Karatsipá called us his sons and favoured us very much. He would wake us up late at night to tell stories about the Xingu. When he arrives, he is our guest and as such comes to our hut.' The old man insisted that the objects from the tribe downriver were Juruna. He recalled the arrival of the first white man, Dr Carl von den Steinen, in the 1880s, and 'used to tell in great detail of battles between his tribe and the Juruna, Suyá and Trumai.' In the following year, 1948, Karatsipá arrived 'with uncontrollable dysentery'. The Villas Boas slung his hammock between theirs and tried to cure him – following instructions radioed in by Dr Nutels – but it was in vain. The old man returned to his village, but he had decided that his time had come. The Villas Boas 'once found old Karatsipá taking advantage of a fierce storm to remain in the midst of the rain, dancing and singing. We called his son, and explained that at his age and in that rain he could fall ill and die. The son's reply was definitive: "Leave him alone, he wants to die".' Which he did, in June 1948.

Early that year, the Villas Boas went up the Batovi headwater of the Xingu and met the Aruak-speaking Waurá, another peaceful, traditional upper-Xingu tribe. In August they returned downriver to the Manitsauá-Missu and again saw huts on a sandbank island, with 'innumerable canoes' being paddled down the river. They were frightened that these might be fierce Mentuktire Kayapó or the Suyá who had terrorized so many upper-Xingu tribes. The brothers waded ashore towards a group of Indians. 'Their shouts seemed to be warning us not to approach further', and a volley of arrows followed. But the Villas Boas continued, waist-high in water and getting cold. 'We were advancing with great caution. One man on the bank was still suspicious, holding a clutch of arrows in his right hand, and signalling that we should not advance another step.' Then Tamacu, the former Juruna who was with the brothers, realized that the Indians were indeed Juruna, and called out his name in their language. Most of the group had run off into the forest and only the one man remained. 'We took advantage of his moment of amazement, climbed the bank and remained three metres [ten feet] from that stupendous Juruna figure. Broad-shouldered, strong, with a waving mass of hair descending to the middle of his back, rigid as a statue, clutching an enormous bunch of arrows, the Indian gave us a hard look. We, quaking with cold, each holding two machetes, stopped for a moment in silence before that extraordinary person who had been keeping us at a distance with his bow.' Orlando went towards him, offering a necklace; and the Indian responded by removing his feather headdress and holding it out towards them. It was later learned that this had been the first contact with a hitherto hostile group of Juruna. 'Only the old people had known civilizados [far down the Xingu], and they regarded them as enemies. The younger ones, of the age of the one with the headdress, had never seen a white man.'

In October 1948, the Villas Boas started clearing an airstrip at the place called Diauarum. This activity had become the main mission of the Central Brazil Foundation, and its leading engineer noted that 'Orlando Villas Boas and his brothers were extremely valuable because they had a natural gift for cordial relations so that, far from being attacked, they gained precious advice from the Indians about places where airstrips could be located.' The bluff of Diauarum on the right bank of the Xingu had been the site of Indian villages since time immemorial. Successive occupants had planted pequi trees (*Caryocar villosum*) on the level ground above the river. The pequi is a tree of the cerrado savannah, and the clearing at Diauarum is its northernmost limit. 'It had been brought there by the Indians, in their proverbial love of transplanting. The species that they like is big and fleshy, yellow or white . . . Pequi is very good in rice; and when there is mutum it becomes a banquet.' It was at Diauarum in 1884 that the German anthropologist Karl von den Steinen – the first white man to descend the Xingu – had a dramatic meeting with the Suyá. That tribe later reverted to hostility with indigenous peoples and whites in the upper Xingu.

Tamacu, the aged Juruna on the expedition, told his own adventures at Diauarum. In the anarchy of inter-tribal warfare, the young Tamacu had been seized from his people by the Jê-speaking Suyá, then from them by the Trumai, then by the Tupi-speaking Kamayurá. While he was at Diauarum with the Suyá, decades earlier, he had witnessed a terrible attack by the Mentuktire, a group of the Menkragnoti Kayapó who had crossed to the west of the Xingu. The Suyá were a bellicose tribe who had annihilated surrounding groups of Indians. But they were no match for the Mentuktire. One day the Suyá found their village surrounded by these hostile Indians, who had approached from the north up the rio da Liberdade. 'The women and children wept at the surprise. The men, seeing the attackers' superiority, retreated into the huts.' One old man, Cocoró, remained in the centre of the village, dancing and chanting defiance; but the Mentuktire advanced and felled him with a blow from a stone axe. 'This was the signal for the attack. Wave after wave of Indians came out of the woods screaming. They invaded the village, storming the huts and attacking the people inside.' 'A battle took place. The Suyá admitted the superiority of the enemy: many of them ran for their canoes and crossed the river. From the far bank, they witnessed throughout the night the macabre dance of their enemies around their slaughtered brothers.' Having no weapons, they could not fight back. For three days, 'the invaders stayed in the destroyed village, spending most of their time playing their flutes and dancing among the corpses. When the strangers finally left, the Suyá hurried across the river to see what was left. There was nobody alive in what had once been their village. In the clearing, now encircled by ashes, the corpses were laid out in a row. The women, whom they thought would have been spared, lay face up, their lifeless bodies in an advanced state of putrefaction, their legs spread apart by wooden struts forced between the knees.' From then onwards Diauarum was abandoned. The Suyá went up the Suiá-Missu river and built a new village far from its mouth. The Mentuktire onslaught was followed by a later raid that captured many Suyá women, and the Trumai from the upper Xingu also harassed the Suyá. The latter solved their tragic loss by themselves capturing wives from the Aruak-speaking Waurá. These new spouses were doubly precious, for they were the region's expert potters. They brought the secrets of their craft, and they gradually taught the Suyá how to make ceramic manioc pans. Although Jê speakers, possibly survivors of the southern Kayapó, the Suyá had lived in the Xingu region for many decades. The anthropologist Vanessa Lea points out that they have 'as many Jê cultural traces as they do indelible marks from more than a century of upper-Xingu influence.' Their women wear uluris – tiny bark-cloth triangles tied over their vaginas; the people eat beiju manioc pancakes; and they keep a harpy eagle in a wooden cage in the midst of their village.

By the end of 1948, after two months' tough work, the airstrip of Diauarum was ready. Throughout that time, Indians – presumably Suyá – prowled round the camp and even entered by night to gather pequi fruit. In 1952, the brothers built a small post at Diauarum. It was later to develop into their northern base in the Xingu region.

The explorers spent four weeks investigating the Manitsauá-Missu, a secluded tributary of the Xingu whose waters mirror banks of luxuriant rainforest. It was a difficult journey, beset by rapids and rains, and there was nowhere in the dense vegetation suitable for an airstrip. The brothers decided to desist, for the Manitsauá river 'was hostile to us. It was an Indian river and wanted nothing to do with "civilizados". On reflection, it was right. We were going to cut down trees and open airstrips that would be wounds in its dense forests; we would make noise, agitate and finally break its millennial tranquillity. It prefers to live roughly, as wild as when it was born. Let those with machines go and descend other valleys; not here. Here its own noises are sufficient: the rustling of trees blown by the wind and the rush of waters splashing over rocks. The river was expelling us.'

Despite their hesitation born of respect for its isolation, the Villas Boas brothers did ascend the Manitsauá-Missu in the following year, 1949. They were pursuing the Central Brazil Foundation's mission to push a trail and open airstrips in a diagonal line across this part of the country. Having cut from the rio das Mortes to the Xingu, they now wanted to continue westwards to the next great southern tributary of the Amazon, the Tapajós. The expedition started by ascending the river for a week. The Villas Boas later recalled the excitement of pure exploration.

> The river is monotonous. No clearings, no beaches. The same forest along the banks, the same curves, the same dark water flowing rapidly . . . Nothing beyond the sensation of navigating up a totally unknown river. At times, on a sharp bend, we surprised bands of curious monkeys who came to watch us from the bank . . . and then disappeared into the forest chattering and whistling . . . The river continued to have an average width of a hundred metres. The riverine vegetation now changed slightly with an abundance of wild banana trees, which give

the forest a more sombre appearance. There are high crowns of gigantic kapoks on the banks of the river. Here and there we could see most beautiful and luxuriant mimosas, shading lesser trees. The austerity of the Manitsauá is obvious: there are no signs – recent or ancient – of Indians in these parts.

(This author can attest that, at the start of the new millennium, the Manitsauá-Missu is still pristine. Its headwaters have been ravaged for cattle pasture; but for most of its length the river flows between virgin forests that are protected thanks to the Villas Boas brothers.) Early in 1950, the expedition left the river and had to cut overland to the west. This punishing work lasted for three months, to open 150 kilometres (93 miles) of trails. Since it was *terra firme* upland forest, during the dry season there was often nothing to drink apart from the liquid found in the occasional water-bearing creeper. There was plenty of game in those forests, but the men were plagued by mosquitoes, sweat bees, and poisonous snakes, and some grew depressed, with feverish colds. After three months they finally reached the Teles Pires headwater of the Tapajós, and the team celebrated by swimming in its waters; but they then had to return to bring up supplies, in a gruelling six-day march, with each man carrying thirty kilos (sixty-six pounds) and donkeys loaded with almost three times that amount.

The Teles Pires was home to the Kayabi, 'restless and unpredictable Indians' and with a warlike reputation. The explorers were on guard. 'This vigilance was because, on the previous night . . . we heard jaguar growling, monkey howls, bird calls, even the grunting of peccary. It was evident – from their insistence and by the simultaneous manifestations of animals that do not go well together, such as jaguar with peccary, monkey with curassow, monkey near jacamim – that all this was imitations by Indians.' Knowing that the Kayabi speak Tupi, the brothers shouted some words in that language. 'The imitations ceased, as if by magic.' There were answering cries from the forest across the broad river. 'We clearly heard "Aiôt" ("Come here").' The Villas Boas embarked in a small canoe and eventually met two Kayabi Indians on the far bank. 'They were nervous and agitated, moving from side to side, but they did not flee on our arrival. Looking intently at us, they beat their chests and said in a perturbed manner: "Kayabi! Kayabi! Kayabi!". We slowly climbed the bank and each held out a machete, deliberately saying, in the Tupi of the Kamayurá, "Icatu ié" ("We are friends"). With the most expressive gestures that occurred to us, and using some Kamayurá expressions, we managed to instil confidence in the two Indians, eventually convincing them to accompany us to our camp on the far side of the river.' The Indians were sent home with more presents. Soon, large groups of Kayabi visited the Villas Boas' camp, always bringing very welcome presents of food – fish, game, and palm-hearts.

The Kayabi were almost pathetically eager to make friends with these well-intentioned whites, because the tribe had suffered terribly. Although their forests along the Teles Pires river were very remote, they lay at the edge of an area of rubber trees, and the revival of Amazon rubber-tapping during the Second World War meant that seringueiros pushed up the Arinos and Teles Pires headwaters of the Tapajós. Quite a few Kayabi worked for the rubber company Erion during the 1940s. The situation worsened. The Kayabi felt threatened in their homeland, the rio das Peixes tributary of the Arinos. When some Indians appeared at this river's mouth, in 1953, they were mistaken for fierce Rikbaktsa 'canoers' and fired at by rubber-tappers.

The SPI had had a presence in the region for many years. This started with Posto Pedro Dantas on the rio Verde, from 1922 until the Kayabi destroyed it two years later. It was then moved to the Teles Pires; but in 1927 the Indians killed first the SPI's agent and then three more Brazilians, so it was closed in 1929. In 1941 the Service opened Posto Caiabi lower down the river and a few Kayabi moved there; but its chief told a Jesuit missionary that its forty-three people had little food and no clothes, and that the agent shouted at them. The SPI later founded Posto José Bezerra on the upper Teles Pires. But this was also a wretched place, alongside a seringueiros' depot that had a bad influence on the Indians, and hopelessly devoid of resources. When the Jesuit missionary Father João Evangelista Dornstauder visited Bezerra in 1955 he found nothing there, not even beds or hammocks. Meanwhile, the Kayabi were further threatened by a colonization company called Conomali that was bringing settlers from southern Brazil and aggressively deforesting the region. The anthropologist Bruna Franchetto wrote that 'the SPI was impotent to resist this often-violent invasion. It may even have connived in it.'

In 1945 some clothing brought to the SPI post proved to be infected with measles. During a terrible two weeks 198 Indians died, leaving only forty survivors. There were flu epidemics in 1955 and 1956, followed in 1964–65 by another outbreak of measles that killed ten people. A Kayabi called Aturi later remembered experiencing the first catastrophe when he was a small boy. 'The measles killed many Kayabi. A group came from downriver and brought the disease to our village. Everyone there caught this disease, measles. At that time there was no doctor nor health monitor, nothing. That epidemic finished off four Kayabi villages. Everyone died. How could they save themselves? From that disease I lost my mother, my brother.' He knew that life had once been far better. 'In the past there were no caraíbas. We did not know the whites because they lived far away. We thought that the whites would never encounter our people. But the whites increased in numbers until they reached the Indians' lands. Then the whites destroyed the life of the Indians. In the past there was no disease, no malaria, measles, flu, coughing, whooping cough, nothing. After the whites came, the Indians caught their diseases. The white men's diseases were killing our people. We were very weak, so any disease killed us.' Ranchers and rubber-tappers took advantage of the Kayabis' misfortune. 'The whites started to abuse us Indians. They started to invade our lands, to fell the forest, to seize our land. All my people's land was taken.' Another Kayabi, Yawet, was told by his father: 'They abused us more whenever they wanted an Indian woman. [The woman's] husband, brother or relative would tell the seringueiro that he could not molest her. But when they spoke thus, the woodsmen would answer only with revolvers. They not only abused us with revolvers, they also harmed us with whips.'

So when the Villas Boas arrived in 1952, three of the beleaguered Kayabi from the Peixoto de Azevedo tributary of the Tapajós followed them back along their long picada to the Xingu. Two of these, Canísio and Mairawé, later recalled how 'one family came to see whether they were interested in staying in the Xingu.' They visited the Juruna and other tribes, then returned to their home on the Teles Pires. 'They told their relatives stories about the Xingu, saying that there were many other Indians there.' The first Kayabi to move east in 1952 included a remarkable leader called Iperuri, who was known as Prepori on the Xingu and became one of its outstanding figures. The son of a rubber-tapper and a Kayabi woman, Prepori could be violent and treacherous; but he was a forceful leader and pragmatic manager who learned the ways of the whites' world.

Forty more Kayabi moved to the Xingu in 1955. They were encouraged to migrate by the charismatic personalities of Prepori and of Cláudio Villas Boas. This group settled first on the upper Arraias, a large western tributary that joins the Xingu downstream of Diauarum; but they soon moved down to the main river and built villages near the Diauarum base. They also planted gardens, for this tribe are fine farmers who introduced crops such as large peanuts to the Xingu. It was they who supplied Diauarum with food over the ensuing years – bananas, peanuts, manioc flour, and corn – without which the administrators there would have starved.

A decade later, these Kayabi remembered their kinsmen still living on the rio das Peixes. With the sertanista Olimpio Serra, they walked for many days to the village of Chief Temeoni. His people had endured further sufferings: from a gold rush in 1963 that brought 6,000 prospectors to the Paranatinga tributary of the Teles Pires; and from the measles epidemic of 1965. Listening to the emissaries, the Chief said: 'We will come to seek you, because we now have very little land. The caraíbas will finish our land ... So we will go, to live better.' Chief Temeoni took thirty people to the Xingu, in 1966, and this was the last migration in the diaspora known as 'Operation Kayabi'.

Cláudio Villas Boas justified this exodus because the Kayabi of the Peixes seemed to have lost their homeland for ever to the seringueiros. But in an interview in *Realidade* magazine he also criticized the missionaries for destroying indigenous culture. The Jesuits saw it differently. Their Father Dornstauder had been active with the Kayabi since 1953. He knew that many wanted to remain in their homelands despite the pressure from settlers and rubber men. A chief confirmed that 'Our land is right here; our ancestors died here; so we shall stay near the burial place of our ancestors.' The missionaries felt it their duty to prepare the Indians for good relations with the colonists – which they seemed to want. They sought to alleviate cultural shock, so that the tribe could preserve some social and economic autonomy. In 1957 the Kayabi helped Dornstauder contact the Rikbaktsa (then known as Erigpactsa), the 'canoers' who terrified seringueiros. In the following year, with the local rubber boom finished, the missionary took over the seringueiros' depot alongside a village called Tatuí. He renamed it Posto Santa Rosa and resided there for many years.

The Kayabi who chose to remain on the Arinos-Peixes became very acculturated, from their Christian conversion and from close contact with the settlers who occupied most of their land. Those who had migrated to the Xingu prospered and retained much of their cultural heritage. But they remained nostalgic about the richer forests they had abandoned, and their Chief Canísio often returned. He was heartbroken by what he saw.

Every time, I see that prospectors are invading more, and loggers are finishing everything. [They are] destroying the trees, the forest ... I see sad things and I think: 'Will they leave us anything? We will have nothing for the future, no clean water ... no more game, no more monkeys, curassows, or above all fish ... [There is] effluent of sawdust that the sawmill makes and throws into the water. Since we live

downstream, we will have to drink that dirty water.' Also the ranchers
. . . Where we Kayabi used to live on the rio das Peixes, there were
once two thousand Indians in the old village . . . Now you see only
cattle. Once there was a big Indian village, now there's only a ranch.

The situation improved somewhat. In 1968, prompted by the Jesuits,
Funai achieved the creation of a small Apiaká-Kayabi reserve on the rio
das Peixes; and territories have since been added, for other Kayabi and
Rikbaktsa, where the Peixes joins the Juruena. But this is rich farming
country. During the 1970s, colonization schemes bought settlers flooding
into the area and new towns sprung up around the reserve. A Jesuit wrote
that relations between Indians and farmers were good. 'In general, the
Kayabi are received in a friendly way, although they do encounter
exploitation when they work as labourers or sell and trade their produce,
and this provokes resentment among them . . . In their [brief] contacts
with the evolving society, the Kayabi are sociable and easily establish
friendly relations . . . Their seeking contact [in this way] may prove to be
a threat to their ethnic identity. And their lands are always coveted.'

Back on the Xingu, there was still the problem of contacting the Mentuktire, the Kayapó whom the Juruna knew as Txukarramãe and who
terrorized them and the Suyá. The Villas Boas learned that 'they were
greatly superior [to the Juruna] in numbers and in fighting tactics, with
their ambushes and surprise attacks. Shortly before our arrival at Jacaré,
our second post along the Culuene, the [Mentuktire] had made an
incursion into that region, killing a Kamayurá chief during a brief battle.'
A group of them was sighted in 1949 on a sandbank near the Auaiá-
Missu, an eastern tributary of the Xingu north of Diauarum. They fled
when approached; but they later removed presents left for them. In the
following year, the Juruna were alarmed to see smoke from extensive fires
downriver and a newly built trail near their village. Going to investigate,
the Villas Boas bravely followed a trail – which had been opened by hand
without cutting tools – and entered a hunting camp that had just been
vacated. It had eighty banana-leaf mattresses in a dozen rough shelters.
They left more presents. The Mentuktire were being seduced by the
magical power of metal blades.

The Villas Boas decided to use the Juruna as their intermediaries in
pursuing this contact and, despite the previous hostility between the
two tribes, this worked remarkably well. In 1952 some Mentuktire
appeared at a Juruna village, bringing large bundles of arrows and feather
headdresses. 'They then asked for machetes and axes. The Juruna made

sure that the [Mentuktire] should understand that the machetes and axes they were receiving came from caraíba who lived very far away. The visitors then withdrew, but said that they would return at a later date.' The Mentuktire Bebcuche later recalled this exchange: 'We gave arrows and the Juruna gave us knives, beads for our ears, and water from their canoe.' This 'water' was the mildly alcoholic cashiri, which the Juruna brew in vats made from dugout canoes inside their huts. It was too strong for the teetotal Mentuktire, who were 'sick for many days' from it.

Early in 1953, the Villas Boas saw signs of Indians at Piá, a former Juruna village near the Von Martius rapids that the Mentuktire had totally destroyed. When their calls were answered, they re-entered their boats and called again. A group of Indians emerged from the trees, all painted in black genipap dye – a sign that they were ready for battle. The Villas Boas brothers paddled slowly towards them. It was a very tense moment. Cláudio later told Adrian Cowell: 'As I stepped out of the canoe, I unbuckled my belt so that the revolver dropped into the water.' In his journal, he wrote: 'They appeared very agitated, confused, making sweeping gestures and talking ceaselessly . . . There were over forty there, most of them young men.' 'They asked, with gestures, for machetes, axes and other things . . . Rather anxious, and immediately seeking to hide in the forest, the Indians gathered up the presents that were offered to them. We saw no women or children, doubtless because this was a hunting party. This direct contact with the Txukarramãe [Mentuktire] proved to us that they were definitely Jê Indians, with the same characteristics of the other hordes generally called Kayapó. They almost all had their lower lips exaggeratedly deformed with enormous wooden discs, their heads shaven above their foreheads, and their ears pierced.'

Returning in August of that year, 1953, the Villas Boas had a more friendly encounter with a large group, at the mouth of the Jarina tributary. Although there were too few presents for so many Indians, they seemed content. The brothers met the important Chief Kremor (or Kremuro) and persuaded him and six of his men to accompany them for ten days' voyage up the Xingu to their base Posto Capitão Vasconcelos. The arrival of these feared 'Men without bows' caused a sensation among the upper-Xingu tribes. 'These were terrified, confused and nervous when confronted with what they had regarded as impossible'; but they soon welcomed the awesome strangers.

Two half-brothers, Bebcuche and Raoni, remained for some months at the post. They were later to be important players in Xingu politics. Adrian Cowell recalled the very different brothers.

Raoni was the younger, about eighteen, with broad shoulders and standing some 5 ft. 9 in. [1.75 metres] in height. His long tresses hung back over his shoulders, bead necklaces dangled from his ear lobes, and ever since childhood his lower lip had been extended by bigger and bigger pieces of wood [lip discs]. He was quick to learn, jovial, keen to talk once some friendship had been established, and very much a back-slapping sort of person. He was, however, basically unreliable, selfish and shameless as he used his charm to extract presents from visiting pilots and air-crews. Bebcuche, on the other hand, was seven or eight years older and the reverse of almost every trait to be found in his half-brother. Where Raoni's face was smooth and comparatively handsome, his seemed beaten, anthropoid and rather menacing in its structure. And where Raoni had a lip disc, he just had a hole under his mouth where his lower lip had burst. Bebcuche spoke only a few guttural words of Portuguese, was slow to learn, and had none of the jovial inquisitiveness that made Raoni such an amusing companion. He stood aloof; he looked ugly and sombre; he seldom talked to anyone who was not already a friend. But . . . he was loyal, unselfish, gentle by nature, and thoughtful in the interests of the Villas Boas . . . He was neither a clever nor an amusing man, but an Indian of immense dignity.

All that remained was for the Villas Boas brothers to enter a Mentuktire village. They obtained large quantities of presents from the SPI and returned to the Von Martius rapids in November 1953. Summoned by Chief Kremor, groups of Indians appeared and eventually over 300 were at the expedition's camp. These included Kretire, a chief whom Kremor had described as the most aggressive raider of settlers' outposts and leader of war-parties. 'Painted black, highly agitated, they beat their chests as they spoke and did not stay in one place for a second. They seemed to be walking on a hot plate . . . Next day, in the best order possible, we distributed the presents. We were pleased to see that they were highly satisfied and, to demonstrate this, they sang almost all that night and the following day.' The contact group – Orlando and Cláudio Villas Boas, two journalists and the two Juruna, Pauaide (the powerful warrior whom they had encountered in 1949) and Dudica – was then taken along a forest trail for an entire ten-hour day, walking westwards up and down hills towards the Indians' village, Roikore on the Jarina river. The visitors were apprehensive, in the midst of a long file of hundreds of excitable warriors. During the journey, they noticed Indians scooping up handfuls of termite earth to devour the protein-rich insects – this confirmed a report that this tribe ate earth. Although the chiefs had told the village of their approach, 'our arrival caused confusion. Men beat their chests and said that they were our brothers; women hastily hid behind trees or buried themselves in the forest; boys and girls ran about. Infants cried.' Chief Kretire gradually restored calm.

During two days in the village, the Villas Boas noted that these Kayapó had very few utensils – none of the pottery, tipiti manioc-presses, graters or hammocks of the upper-Xingu tribes. They were starting to grow plantations of manioc, maize, and yams, a sign of transition from being nomadic hunter-gatherers to more settled farmers. Bananas were their favourite food, which they ate at all times, from breakfast to last meal at night. But they also consumed every form of meat and fish, including sting-rays, jaguars, and hawks; and 'from their big game nothing was wasted, not even tripe.' The Mentuktire were clearly learning agriculture, the use of bows and arrows, and other practices from decades of contact with the more acculturated Juruna. And, like other Kayapó, they immediately developed an appetite for metal blades. This was why the contact with this warlike tribe had been so easy.

The Mentuktire escorted the explorers back to their camp on the Xingu. More Indians appeared during the following days and were given more presents. One night, twenty warriors swam across to the expedition's camp with their clubs tied to their backs, and urgently demanded that the Villas Boas immediately accompany them. They explained that their women were frightened and angry that there had been no presents for them. It was a stormy night, and they marched into the forest to the light of burning grass torches. Each of the four – two Villas Boas and two Juruna – found warriors tightly holding both his arms as they moved through the darkness. At the forest camp, they were greeted by some 400 agitated warriors, painted in black genipap dye. The Mentuktire women, as tough as their men, remained hidden in the surrounding forest, but one man called out, in Jê: 'Kill! Kill! The white men are worthless.' There were more calls for their deaths; the aggressive warrior advanced and kicked out the fire, plunging the camp into darkness; Cláudio had to restrain the Juruna Pauaide from trying to grab a club and fight his way out. Then the Villas Boas saw one woman's face appear from the darkness and approach the campfire. 'She was an aged woman who was chewing something, which she deposited in her hand and rubbed on our faces. We easily led her close to the fire and asked her to summon the women. She understood and did so. Soon after, over 200 women, dozens of them with children on their backs, emerged with enormous loads. They were angry and did not speak to the men, but merely demanded pacova (banana leaves). A dozen men went into the forest and soon returned loaded with banana leaves. A platform was made with the leaves, on which the women deposited the reserves of food.' They had been keeping the tribe's food out of the rain. Although the men were hungry, 'they gave us some beijus; but what was left over they put on the ground and trod on it, giving not a scrap to the men.' The brothers explained that they would bring many presents for the women on their next visit. The hostility was relieved, and the visitors were allowed to return to the river, accompanied by two young women as their sureties. 'This reminded us of the importance of women, particularly of old women, in Mentuktire communities.' In their preliminary notes, they wrote that these women are 'generally tall, enjoy excellent health and are strong. It is they who carry almost all the loads during marches. A married woman is rarely without a baby suspended in a shoulder band. They paint themselves with [black] genipap, in broad stripes and highly varied designs. They are completely naked, do not pluck their body hair, pierce their ears, and cut their hair in the same way as men – namely in a wide crescent above their foreheads.'

In periodical subsequent visits, including a two-month stay in a village, the Villas Boas won the friendship of these groups of Menkragnoti Kayapó. Unknown to them, this was a turbulent period in the tribe's history. Verswijver found that in 1952 'a fire broke out in the village, burning down nearly all the houses. Tension was high and a collective club-fight [over a case of adultery] followed.' This resulted in a split: Chief Kremor left with his people to settle near the Von Martius rapids; Chiefs Kretire and Bepgogoti remained with their groups in the traditional site. The Villas Boas briefly persuaded two bands of Mentuktire, who had split over the quarrel in the previous year, to reunite in a single village called Rõtinõr (at the source of the Iriri Novo, a short distance west of the Xingu), which had been occupied on-and-off by the tribe for many years. But epidemics of influenza struck both this village and another group of Mentuktire who settled on the main Xingu, close to the Von Martius rapids. So in 1956, different groups, led by Chiefs Kretire, Kremor and Bepgogoti, moved far to the north-west to Piydyam village on the Xixê tributary of the Iriri. For a few years this became the largest of all Kayapó villages, with 400 inhabitants. After Francisco Meirelles contacted the people of Piydiãm in 1958, the SPI called it Posto Indígena Menkragnoti.

The only Mentuktire to remain in the south, in the Villas Boas' region, were the disease-stricken group who in 1956 moved from the Von Martius rapids to the mouth of the Liberdade. Orlando and Cláudio visited this village in 1958, guided by Bebcuche. Adrian Cowell was also there and recalled their dramatic entry, at night, marching by the light of flaming grass torches. The village's fires were all stoked so that they flared up as the strangers entered. 'These fires cast a red and roaring light over a scene that, in its confusion, can only be compared to a dervish dance in a foundry blast furnace. Tribespeople shouted and whirled about. A score of dogs lunged yapping at our legs. Women and children pawed at our clothes. There was a wailing generated by some emotion beyond all civilizado understanding. Primitive faces rattling lip-discs peered into mine, and then whirled away. We had leapt, quite suddenly, from the peaceful night into the noise and glare of one of the most primitive societies on earth. That society had gone berserk at our coming.' The village proved to have only a dozen small huts and some fifty people. The welcoming dance soon gave way to a song by three attractive girls, a gourd of wild honey brought by an old woman, and each man coming forward to greet the Villas Boas.

In the ensuing days, Cowell observed the subtle process whereby the Villas Boas introduced the Mentuktire to useful new products. The tribe was eager to learn; but the process of acculturation must be gradual. Some Mentuktire already knew how to build and paddle dugout canoes 'which the Juruna under the Villas Boas' protection had shown them how to make; a small patch of rice was growing at one of the abandoned villages; Bebcuche owned two pigs; tomorrow, pots, knives, hooks, and bullets would be handed out at the boat.'

'Above all, the Villas Boas had once again been accepted as guests by a people which previously had friendly relations with no one.' This peaceful contact was a notable triumph. Other tribes had told of their dread of the Mentuktire. After contact, these Indians revealed how warlike they had been, and how little they thought of killing. The otherwise gentle Bebcuche told Adrian Cowell how a group of them had raided westwards towards the Curuá. '"We kill all seringueiros in hut. Then we take clothes and rifle and knife . . . We slaughter everyone, man and woman too."' Cowell asked why they had not kept the settlers' women. '"[Mentuktire] only keep children. Much time before, we have three girls from over there. They all finished now, but axe and gun and line for fish still good."' Just before their contact, they had also plundered the colonial frontier far to the east on the Araguaia. '"Raoni go and bring back rifle, machete, knife, and clothes. He go with Mengire and Krumare, who already kill two. Mengire long ago go to the green forest and see women working clothes in water near man with carbine. Man runs and has much fear. Krumare comes near man . . . . . ."' Bebcuche imitated a terror-stricken settler, crouching and making croaking noises, with his arms sheltering his head. '"Krumare beat man with war-club. Dead. Mengire slaughter women. They carry [back to Mentuktire] carbine, knife, machete, and much clothes."' On their return, the raiding party met a group of six Xavante women with their children. Bebcuche killed a woman and dashed the brains of two children. Cowell asked him: '"Did you take many guns or clothes from them?" "No, only one knife." "Then why did you kill?" "We don't know them. First time we see."' With the Panará (Kren Akróre) to the west it was a matter of vengeance rather than mere unfamiliarity. Bebcuche recalled a Panará attack that had killed his grandmother and other relatives. Later, when he was a grown man, a large group of Mentuktire had made a very long journey westwards against that formidable tribe. Bebcuche's hands demonstrated how they advanced in a crescent formation. '"We come like this and all the Panará tribe asleep. We work medicine, and then when morning come we work arrow and rifle. Fire. Fire. Fire. Bang. Bang. Panará do arrow, arrow, too. Then Chief of Panará, string of bow breaks. He runs. Others run. Three dead. Then much time more and we see Chief of Panará passing in forest. We kill Chief and take son."'

The years after the first contacts in 1953 were a period of disease and repeated separations and reunions by the various groups of Mentuktire, the southernmost of the Menkragnoti Kayapó who had crossed to the west of the Xingu. Some remained on the Jarina, in what was to become the Xingu Indian park, and others near the Von Martius rapids, but most migrated north-westwards to the upper Iriri Novo, Iriri and Curuá rivers, where they were contacted by Francisco Meirelles during the late 1950s. An important village was Piydyam on the Xixê tributary of the upper Iriri, under Chiefs Kretire and Bepgogoti, both of whom had migrated there to escape epidemics. The Menkragnoti seem to have realized that the diseases that ravaged them had come from the white men and could be cured best by their medicines. Gustaaf Verswijver learned that in the decade between 1958 and 1968 the Menkragnoti were constantly searching for efficient medical assistance. 'The number of victims of diseases such as measles, whooping cough, influenza and common colds was extremely high.' Dennis Werner reckoned that 99 of the 214 deaths among these groups during those years were due to contact diseases; Verswijver felt that the number of disease fatalities was far greater.

Tragically, the migrations away from epidemics on the Xingu proved futile, because of the SPI's policy of creating posts and permitting settlement near the tribes contacted by Meirelles. 'After "pacification" along the Jarina river in 1953, the central Menkragnoti moved to the Iriri-Curuá river area, where on three occasions the government Indian agency tried to settle these Indians near newly established posts. In vain, however, since the Indians always retreated to their former habitat. Whenever discussing these movements . . . they insisted over and over again that many had died (especially children and older people) near each of these posts. It is therefore rather ironic that the central Menkragnoti, who departed from the traditional Jarina river area to flee from diseases and from the "inadequate" medical assistance, suffered more from contact diseases that the southern Menkragnoti [Mentuktire] who remained in the Jarina area.' The latter's 'less dramatic death rate was partly due to the better medical assistance provided by the Villas Boas brothers, and partly due to the fact that no post was erected near [their] village during those critical years. Contact with outsiders was thus limited to the very minimum.' This contrasted with the lack of medicines or doctors, and the proximity of colonists, at the SPI posts to the north-west.

Death from imported diseases was a constant threat during the Villas Boas' first decades on the Xingu. In 1946–47 there were the epidemics among the Kalapalo and Kuikuro. Then in 1948 many Kamayurá caught influenza. Leonardo Villas Boas hurried to their village with the medical doctors Kalervo Oberg and Altenfelder. They returned next day with twenty-five sick people, and back in the village a hundred more were treated with 'large quantities of medicine: penicillin, flu injections, sulpha drugs, bronco-pneumonia syrup'. On that occasion, none died; but other tribes were less fortunate. A decade later, Adrian Cowell was with Cláudio Villas Boas on the Manitsauá-Missu when there was a serious epidemic of influenza among the Juruna, and then among some of the Kayabi who had come from the Tapajós to find sanctuary at Diauarum on the Xingu. Cowell recalled that 'the Kayabi lay in filthy hammocks in filthy clothes, sick and showing that they knew they were sick; all the animal vitality that usually made them such noble beings had utterly gone. Bows, firewood, pans, odd bits of food were scattered amongst the dirt on the floor.' Although the Indians appreciated that the white men were trying to help them, they understandably blamed them for the disease. Cláudio told Cowell that 'epidemics were unusually destructive in Xingu because the civilizado had to work against the patient. Without supervision the sick took no rest, ate no food and spat out medicine as soon as the doctor's back was turned. Only injections – painful and involving a fussy process of sterilization and manipulation – were appreciated, as a magic that was both interesting and powerful. As it was, all of us could feel the resentment creeping across the hut's filthy floor, licking over boxes, sliding round hammocks, and curling about our part of the building.' Cláudio's ministrations saved the Kayabis' lives, but it was a hollow victory. Cowell recalled this admirable man, 'so plump and dirty, with clothes hanging about him, so unimpressive in the squalor, hopeless, knowing in despair that if he saved a life now it would probably, in a few years' time, be lost for some [other] reason . . . For the Indian it was different. Previously he had been proud as the king of his forest; now he owed his life to a stranger. It was a bitter thing to swallow.'

Some observers felt that Indians could 'give up the ghost', losing the will to live and causing themselves to die. But the Villas Boas did not agree that there was any collective despair. They wrote that

> it is an error to think that Indians are indifferent or fatalistic [about the disappearance of their race]. Like all other creatures, they are vibrant beings who think of the future and lament the magnificent past of their nation. For these tribes who now inhabit the upper Xingu were powerful nations some decades ago. Each tribe used to occupy an enormous area and possessed various densely populated villages. The 'great wars' between different groups were responsible for the disappearance of some tribes, of whom only the names now remain . . . But it was not wars that were the principal cause of the diminution and disappearance of the region's native groups. The greatest destroyer of lives among them was the epidemics that rage in the region almost every year. Important tribes, such as the Naruvoto, Custenaú, or Tsuva, are no more: they were destroyed by strains of influenza and their complications. Infant mortality is appalling. Of eight infants whom we had seen born, only two are living. We attribute this to their mothers' precarious health. Malaria is another scourge of the new-born.

The upper Xingu had suffered catastrophic depopulation ever since the first imported diseases struck its peoples. When the first white man, Carl von den Steinen, was there in the 1890s, he estimated its population at 3,000 in thirty-nine villages. The epidemic of Spanish flu that swept the world after the First World War reached Brazil in 1918 and somehow penetrated the Xingu, with fatal effects. In 1952 the anthropologists Eduardo Galvão and Mário Simões calculated that only 652 people remained, in ten villages – a decline of 80 per cent in six decades. The two anthropologists ascribed this tragic depopulation to diseases, to high infant mortality, to the tribes' voluntary birth control through late marriage and infanticide from social taboos, and to inter-tribal fighting.

Worse was to follow. An SPI doctor, João Leão da Mota, described a devastating sickness in 1954. 'From mid-June to early October, the region of the Xingu headwaters was ravaged by a tremendous epidemic of measles. Its inhabitants paid the high tribute of 114 lives in that short interval of time.' That loss represented almost a fifth of the area's meagre total. Dr Leão da Mota told how the disease was introduced by the son of the Kamayurá Chief Tamapu, who had been taken to the town of Xavantina and caught measles there. The epidemic spread from the Kamayurá and Trumai to the Aweti, then to the Yawalipiti and to the Kalapalo. The doctors felt that as many deaths were caused by complications (dysentery or gastro-enteritis and pneumonia) as by the measles itself, and that these afflictions were exacerbated by poor nutrition. 'We believe that alimentary deficiency was the main cause of the high mortality among Indians struck by epidemics on the Xingu.' The disease raged at the height of the dry season, when no forest fruits were available to the Indians. Aritana, a handsome young Yawalipiti whom the Villas Boas groomed to become the eventual paramount chief of the upper Xingu, recalled seeing the epidemic when he was a boy. 'At the Kalapalo village now called Jakui there were many dead but no one to bury them. A white man was there and he buried the dead, but not in [the traditional] grave in a round hole: he made a long burial pit and threw the Indians into it. The ugliest was in the Kalapalo village . . . Then it passed from there to the Kuikuro, the Kamayurá where it killed more Indians, then more strongly to the Mehinaku . . . To this day I cannot forget it. It was horrible.'

In all, 393 Indians were treated, and there would have been more deaths but for the SPI's medical help. Dr Leão da Mota praised the great work of his colleague Dr Serôa da Mota, also Orlando Villas Boas, and Cláudio who had 'an undoubted medical vocation and a polymorphic talent, and who showed extreme dedication to the natives, in exhausting and monotonous tasks, from the first patient to the last, both at the post and in their villages.' Cláudio Villas Boas lamented: 'The Tsuva tribe has already vanished from the Xingu. The Nahukwá and Matipuhy are almost gone. The Aweti have one hut, no dances, no chief. The Trumai and Yawalipiti are down to twenty. The Kamayurá had twelve huts when I first came; now they have five.' When Galvão and Simões returned in 1963, they recorded only 623 inhabitants of the upper Xingu. That was the nadir: since then, the tribes' populations have risen steadily, thanks to better medical attention, improved natal care, and revived morale. When Ellen Basso was with the Kalapalo in 1968, she was shown the graves of those who had died in the measles epidemic fourteen years earlier. It had produced many orphans who were a constant reminder of 'the life which they led in the old villages, a subject of frequent reminiscences'. The Indians' better health was due to the São Paulo Medical School. From 1965 to the present, teams of volunteer doctors came every year, led by the admirable Dr Roberto Baruzzi. They provided every Xingu Indian man and woman with a complete personal medical record.

One important Kayabi to enter the Xingu in 1952 was Sabino, who had once worked as a builder on an SPI post. The Villas Boas used him to help construct a base they were creating in the upper Xingu, which was opened in 1954 as Posto Capitão Vasconcellos (renamed Posto Leonardo in 1961, after the Villas Boas brother who died of disease). Sabino spoke some Portuguese and, like most Kayabi, was diligent and intelligent; so he became Cláudio's right-hand man at Diauarum and then Orlando's at Posto Leonardo.

Vasconcellos/Leonardo was not a glamorous place. Built in a dusty clearing surrounded by charred felled logs, it had a large central shed that the English author Adrian Cowell described as nothing more than a log palisade with a matted palm thatch, surrounded by a few storage huts roofed in corrugated iron. Fifteen years later, in the early 1970s, there had been some improvements. Leonardo is on a bluff overlooking the small Tuatuari stream, with an open floodplain studded by campo trees stretching beyond. Inland are low woods, broken by paths leading to the nearest villages, of the Yawalipiti, Trumai, and Txikão. Each more distant upper-Xingu tribe now had a hut at the post, a form of embassy at which visiting Indians might camp. A huge drawing of the dead brother, Leonardo – bearded and in a battle cap, looking like Che Guevara – dominated the kitchen–dining hut. Cooking was done by young Mentuktire, big lads with flowing black hair, wearing check sports shirts issued by the post and bits of air force uniforms. There was now a visitors' bungalow, of rough board walls and a corrugated-iron roof around a courtyard. Orlando had built himself a small house, painted ox-red. He slept in his hammock slung across its door, snoring prodigiously. All this became more hospitable after 1969, when he married a delightful nurse called Marina Lopes de Lima: they had two boys, and built a two-storey house overlooking the river. The most efficient place at Posto Leonardo was the medical dispensary, clean and functional, but always short of medicine.

Whenever this author went there in the 1970s, I could see that the entire post existed for the Indians. There was a constant traffic of indigenous visitors, most in drab clothes but some men naked and splendid in urucum body paint, with their bowl of hair thickly lacquered in red and black dyes. Women were always clothed in simple dresses at the post, but naked in their villages when there were no strangers present. There was a cheerful atmosphere with much laughter and horseplay. The Indians were under no pressure to do anything, but many chose to work

– particularly the industrious Kayabi, who farmed rice on the floodplain. The Indians were kings. Conversations ceased when they wandered up, to be greeted warmly, with light-hearted banter for all but the most important. They liked to sit on beds or hammocks, seeking entertainment or asking for presents, which visitors were expected to give generously since they had come from the outside world that produces fishhooks and line, mirrors, shirts, knives, soap, and beads. Everyone was happy if there were *caramelo* sweets for the children. Dogs, pigs, and chickens wandered about Leonardo and there was one sheep. There was also an unrideable horse and a donkey. The latter caused a sensation when it arrived, for Indians are consummate hunters who thought that they knew every animal in creation. They were baffled by a new one, that stood still, that carried small loads, and that was inedible and not immediately killed by Indian arrows.

Diauarum is far lovelier than Leonardo, with elegant rectangular thatched huts spread out on a grassy bank overlooking a magnificent sweep of the Xingu. This northern post is well shaded with mango and pequi trees, and the surrounding forest is taller than the drier woods at Leonardo.

During the early years on the Xingu, the Villas Boas brothers developed an instinctive empathy to the Indians, and evolved their unique approach to treatment of indigenous people. Kenneth Brecher, himself a charismatic anthropologist who worked among the Waurá, knew and admired these Indianists. The Waurá chief told Brecher:

'The brothers appeared to be chiefs who for some unknown reason had left their own tribesmen, their lands, their women, and their way of life, to live among the tribes of the Xingu.' How long they would stay, no one knew, but it became obvious to the perceptive Indian observers that the oldest brother (Orlando) seemed instinctively to know their secrets without even speaking their language; the youngest brother (Leonardo) seemed more at ease squatting with the men in the village plaza, or lying in a palm-fibre hammock in the house of the chief of the Kamayurá, than sitting on the canvas stool or resting on the hard wooden bed of his own tribesmen; while the middle brother (Cláudio) was unlike either of them. He carried books with him at all times and spent entire days staring at the mysterious paper. He spoke very quietly and seemed happiest when among the tribes of the north [around Diauarum] . . . All three of the brothers were remarkable in that they went alone among those unnamed tribes whom the rest of the Xinguanos dismissed as too wild, and too dangerous, to be considered men.

Indians are acute observers who rapidly pass judgement on any stranger
– sometimes humorously, usually critically, and, if the intruder's behaviour is too disgraceful, fatally. They noticed that the brothers became
quite skilled at moving silently through the forests and had no difficulty
with the hardships of the rainy season. The Villas Boas were clearly
disinterested. Generous with presents, they expected nothing in return.
They were affectionate with Indians of all ages, always embracing their
friends, whose names they remembered unerringly. But there were no
sexual overtones to this physical warmth: they promptly expelled anyone,
even close friends, who broke such codes of conduct. They provided
powerful medicines and desirable trade goods, but never competed with
shamans or belittled any tribal custom.

Missionaries were rigorously excluded from the Xingu, for fear that
they might try to convert its peoples. Brecher noted that the Villas Boas
were 'spiritual men who have fought for more than two decades to keep
missionaries of all religions away from the tribes; revolutionaries whose
cause finds little support among the intelligentsia of Brazil and none at all
among the masses.' Cláudio once explained to the author the distinction
between magic in the Indians' world and religion. Fearless about death,
Indians do not need the 'selfish solace of belief in the after-life'; but those
left behind deeply mourn the dead. Many anthropologists worked among
the Xingu tribes, but Cláudio was scathing about those who could only
translate Indian life into detailed terminology based on their own society,
failing to appreciate the grandeur or clarity of Indian thinking. Orlando
accepted that religious conversion might have a place at a later stage of
Indians' acculturation. 'But why this preoccupation with Indians?' he
asked. 'Why not catechise the caboclos of Amazonia, who are many times
less fortunate? The Indians have a rich religion. Converting them to
Christianity would be madness: it would mean the overthrow of their
cultural values. With what object?'

Another admirer was the English writer and film-maker Adrian Cowell.
He first met the Villas Boas in 1958, when they were in their early forties,
had been in the wilds for fifteen years, and were already becoming famous
throughout Brazil. The legendary explorer Orlando proved to be 'a little
man, 5 ft. 6 in. [1.68 metres], bare-footed, barebacked and with a pot
belly lipping over his bottle-green pants. He might have been an attendant
in a Turkish bath or a musician in a Paris salon. The only remarkable
feature was a most powerful bearded and hawk-like face with many lines
of hardship across it. It could have been a pirate's face, or perhaps even
the face of a saint who had spent years in mortification.' All who met
Orlando Villas Boas were impressed, even awed, by the force of his

personality. He could be an exuberant extrovert, and he was a spellbinding raconteur. The author was once with Orlando and a group of friends in a São Paulo restaurant. When he started telling stories about the Xingu, the entire restaurant fell silent and the kitchen staff crept out to listen. And the proprietor would accept no payment from any of us, since it was such an honour to have Orlando Villas Boas in his establishment.

Cláudio Villas Boas was utterly different. Although one of the twentieth century's greatest explorers, who could walk through the Amazon forests for weeks on end with only a .22 rifle, he was short, stooped, and pallid. He peered at the world through round spectacles or dark glasses. By the late 1960s his straggling black hair and beard were streaked with white. His clothes were even more haphazard than Orlando's: a nondescript shirt with one tail hanging loose, baggy old denims or jeans cut into shorts, and the regulation flip-flop sandals that everyone wears in Xingu villages. Cowell noted that 'where Orlando was a baked Indian brown, Cláudio's pale complexion had the green tinge of a forest shadow. Where Orlando had a sharp bold face, he was chubby, wore glasses and had the mild demeanour of a country grocer.' To Kenneth Brecher, the brothers were 'a fat man and a thin man, who have the faces of El Greco saints yet own one hundred firearms between them.'

The Villas Boas' reading matter also mirrored their different characters: Cláudio's bookshelves were filled with well-thumbed works of philosophers from Russell to Marx, economists, and anthropologists, whereas Orlando liked crime thrillers and had comics flown in with his monthly post. Cláudio 'is a kind and unpretentious man, and the visitor who has time to penetrate his reserve will listen all night as he talks with passion, speed and excitement about Kant, economics and his Indian theories.' He spoke eloquently, quietly and quickly, as though enunciating poetry but with sudden stresses on certain words and using his hands expressively. It was not always easy to follow the rambling discourses. At Diauarum, his bedroom was cluttered with shelves of dusty boxes and cardboard suitcases. A constant press of Indians, particularly women, thronged round his iron bedstead or the hammock on which he liked to recline, talking incessantly, in expedition camps. 'By contrast, the visitor at Posto Leonardo is met by Orlando's Rabelaisian humour and magnificent cooking, and plays rummy till midnight.' When the American anthropologist Anthony Seeger arrived in the Xingu and Orlando found that he and his wife were accomplished folk-singers, he organized almost-nightly concerts in the dimly lit big central building at Leonardo, with the Seegers singing beautifully to their guitars surrounded by an audience of silent, slightly bemused Indians. Orlando's favourite was 'Guantanamera', the anthem of the Cuban revolution. Cowell said that 'in many ways, one brother is the stereotype fat man, extrovert, company-loving and witty. The other is almost the typical thin man, shy, thoughtful and retiring. It is very probably these differences in character that have made the Villas Boas brothers such an effective unit. Orlando handles all the administration and is a publicist of flair and skill . . . Cláudio on the other hand feels most at home in the Indian villages, and it is his gentle touch that has softened the shock of civilisation for the tribes. His lonely thoughts originate many of Xingu's policies, and he now [1971] handles most of the expeditions and difficult journeys.' He was affectionate and dignified to the Indians, although he sometimes joked or indulged in horseplay with them. Quietly firm in command and immensely experienced, Cláudio Villas Boas received complete obedience from Indians and Brazilians alike.

The philosophy that the brothers evolved was that acculturation and assimilation into Brazilian society were inevitable, but they must be gradual. Change should be at whatever speed the Indians wanted, not imposed violently from outside. Orlando's friend Dr Noel Nutels said: 'I think that the policy of integration is correct – although it has not yet been proven historically. But I am against haste. If it is done too fast, the result is disintegration. Indians are self-sufficient, perfectly attuned to their surroundings, and without economic problems. Rapid acculturation kills them, more than bullets. Indians can and should be integrated, but in a slow process that is scientifically planned. Our civilization should be administered to them in small doses.' Indian children receive an intense education in their own crafts and the lore of their forest habitat. They therefore had no immediate need of education in the Brazilian curriculum – that could come later. To permit choice in the speed of assimilation, it was essential to protect the Indians' lands and their physical health. Therefore, after the disasters of the early epidemics of influenza and measles, the brothers ensured regular medical attention for the tribes and built airstrips alongside most villages, for medical emergencies.

Two warrior tribes in the upper Xingu remained to be contacted and pacified: the Suyá and Txikão. We have seen how the once-feared Suyá had been mauled by the Juruna helped by seringueiro rifles, and had then watched their village at Diauarum shattered by the Mentuktire Kayapó (then known as Txukarramãe). They fled up a river, named Suiá-Missu after them, taking captured Waurá women. But Eduardo Galvão wrote that these kidnappings 'were avenged by an expedition in which Waurá, Mehinaku, Trumai, and Kamayurá participated, constituting a flotilla of over twenty canoes. The Suyá village was attacked by surprise and burned.

The Kamayurá said that the Waurá grabbed Suyá infants, abandoned by their parents, to throw them into the burning huts . . . [In 1948] both among the Kamayurá as among the Trumai, there were continual rumours that the Suyá were present nearby, the result of which was a constant fear of attack.'

When the Villas Boas established their northern post at Diauarum, they were often aware of Indians prowling in the surrounding forests and even entering the clearing to gather pequi fruit. 'One morning [in 1959], two Juruna came to tell us that there were Suyá canoes nearby, at the mouth of the Suiá-Missu.' The brothers rushed for their boat and took it for some ninety minutes up the Suyás' river, then pursued the Indians for over an hour up a narrow stream clogged with sunken logs.

We emerged onto a broader stretch of the creek and saw a high bank with two canoes drawn up at it. We arrived there. One Indian was on the bank, with his arrow at the ready and an unwelcoming expression: he gestured that we should stay where we were. We obeyed; but we behaved as casually as possible regarding his presence, turning our backs on him. The number of Indians on the bank increased. They were gesticulating violently that we should go away. We pretended to be unconcerned and started to converse, pretending to ignore their presence. They had no alternative but to lower their bows and continue to stare at us. As naturally as possible, we brought a box of presents out of the boat – mirrors, necklaces, knives, machetes, and axes – and placed them at the foot of the bank. We gestured that they should come and gather them. They were perplexed, immobile. One of them, bolder than the rest, descended the bank and approached the box to take it . . . Before he could do so, we advanced and opened it. We gave him a knife, a machete, and an axe. We called to the others. They came. We asked them to bring their women. They ran off and went to some houses nearby. They reappeared on the bank soon after, each bringing his wife, or rather dragging her. We went there and each of us took care of one woman, removing her from her husband's hands and decorating her with an attractive necklace. The mirrors were also a success with them. Some shouts, and more women appeared. They were suspicious, but curious about the mirrors and necklaces. The fraternization was complete. They laughed, but both men and women avoided looking at the two Juruna who had remained seated in the boat.

The anthropologist Harald Schultz said that in the following year, 1960, the Suyá appeared at Diauarum 'making unequivocal signs of their peaceful intentions'. He therefore went to visit them in their hunting village, up the Suiá-Missu and the narrow stream. Peccary had destroyed most of the group's plantations, so it existed on a diet of inajá-nut meal, fish, wild honey, and occasional monkeys, currassow, or other game. The men of this Jê-speaking tribe wore large lip-discs in their lower lips. 'Their lip muscles are well developed by practice, so that a man can easily move his disc in all directions. When raised over the nose, this means "anger" or "shyness", but it is normally horizontal.' Discs make it impossible to drink by sucking: the liquid has to be poured in over the wooden plate. The discs also press lower teeth inwards. 'Married men remove their lip discs daily and wash the orifices carefully.'

Once again, a seemingly hostile tribe had been won over by presents of metal tools. Or rather, the Suyá may well have felt that it was they who had pacified the strange intruders and thus ensured a regular flow of their coveted trade goods. The Villas Boas persuaded the tribe to move down their river to the hunting village where they had been contacted, Soconi ('Heron') not far from Diauarum. 'To consolidate the harmony of the region, we brought the Suyá together with their enemies the Juruna, just as we had done with the Juruna and the "Men Without Bows" [Mentuk-tire].' Such pacifications, between tribes as well as between hostile groups and the white frontier, were one of the brothers' greatest achievements. Amazingly, they have endured: there have been tensions, but no inter-tribal fighting since then.

The attraction of the Txikão was far more difficult. This mysterious group's name (pronounced roughly Shikown in English) meant 'hostile people' in Tupi: they would prefer to be called Ikpeng ('we, people'), but the earlier name has stuck. They lived in the south-western part of the fan of rivers that form the Xingu's headwaters, and they frequently attacked its tribes. There were records of them killing a dozen Nahukwá in 1942, and a further four men in 1944; attacking the Waurá in 1945 and burning a hut (although these retaliated by burning a Txikão village); harassing the SPI's Culiseu post on the Batovi in 1946; burning the Mehinaku village in 1950, but being repulsed by the chief armed with a gun when they tried another such attack two years later. Orlando Villas Boas recalled how Chief Kamalive of the Nahukwá, a tall, thin, brave man, once ran to him in a state of agitation, pointing to the west and crying out: '"The Txikão are fierce. The Txikão attacked my village and stole my baby daughter." . . . He told us a long and dramatic history. We learned that the Txikão gave no rest to his peaceful and good-natured people. Every year, during the dry season, they appeared, shooting their arrows, setting fire to huts, seizing children. In the latest attack, Kamalive said that twelve Nahukwá were killed, three children kidnapped, and the village reduced to a heap of ash.' The Nahukwá moved their village, and the Txikão turned their attention to the Mehinaku. They eventually attacked the latter's village, in a hail of arrows, and burned its six great huts. The Mehinaku twice moved their village to more defensible locations; but another attack by the Txikão wounded their Chief Aiuruá. 'He staggered in, covered in blood with an arrow buried in his ribs. Immediately brought to our post on the Culuene, Aiuruá was operated on and saved.'

In the wet season of 1952, there was a battle between the Txikão and Waurá, and the Waurá were organizing a massive reprisal by many of the upper-Xingu tribes. The Villas Boas decided to attempt a contact. Not knowing what language the Txikão spoke, they took chosen Indians speaking five different languages. After twelve days' march south-westwards, their expert guides found a Txikão trail leading from the river into the forest and a recently occupied camp. The expedition returned to the Batovi river and hid its boat among the vegetation.

Next day, they advanced cautiously along the trail, pausing frequently to listen. After three hours,

> we heard the chatter of men, women and children. Treading gently, we advanced a few paces until, peering through the foliage, we could see the Txikão camp. There were over a hundred people gathered unconcernedly. Between their hammocks, various curassows, parrots, and macaws wandered tranquilly. Here and there were half-lit small fires: you could see that these were alight only by wisps of blue smoke that rose from them. The sun was at its zenith. It was the hour of general quiet, when, in the solitude of the forest, you have the impression that at this time of day nature rests. The leaves of the trees grow silent, and the wind stops blowing . . . The birds do not fly, terrestrial animals do not walk; all nature sleeps for an instant; and the Indians rest.

Although they appreciated that it was a difficult moment to make contact, the Villas Boas

> resolved to go on to attempt the impossible. Then, accompanied by two Kayabi Indians called Acuchim and Coá, we entered the camp. An old man was drowsing, half seated, in a hammock. The people he saw when he opened his eyes did not cause him shock; he was distracted, dreamy; but his distraction lasted for only two or three seconds. He confronted us. We took a step forward and held out a fine machete with a red handle. Standing and straightening his body, the old man started to shout. As if shaken by thunder, they all rose and the camp then plunged

into tremendous confusion. Women cried out and ran to hustle their children into the forest; men, bellowing incomprehensible words, seized their weapons, and the sound of clustered arrows reached our ears. Although we felt that it was useless, we resolved to persist in our demonstrations of friendship for a little longer. All in vain. When the arrows started to whistle [towards us], we managed to take refuge behind a thick tree that grew at the edge of the camp. There, making a rapid assessment, we concluded that simple flight was no longer possible. This was because there was the open area of the camp to be traversed before reaching our return path. In that case, none of us would escape the arrows. Realizing that it was a difficult situation, we sought an exit. Only one was possible: to put the Txikão to flight by means of some shots into the air. Having no other remedy, we fired; and they fled into the forest.

The expedition left presents and then raced back to their boat before the Txikão could cut them off. They left a further four boxes of axes, one of scythes, and four dozen knives on the riverbank, and departed downstream.

In 1960 a dozen Waurá, armed with guns obtained from a Brazilian adventurer, attacked the Txikão village. They hoped to recapture two Waurá girls kidnapped by the hostile tribe, and their raid killed twelve Txikão. That tribe was also struck by influenza that halved its small population. The Txikão retreated to the lower Jatobá river, a tributary of the Ronuro that lies south-west of the Xingu reserve area.

More time elapsed until 1964 when first the Aweti and then the Yawalipiti reported that Txikão were prowling around their small villages, which were close to the administration post Leonardo. There happened to be two small planes in the Xingu, and these managed to find the Txikão village, forty minutes' flight west of Leonardo. Next day, the planes buzzed the village and dropped presents on it. Indians were seen, hiding in the undergrowth with their bows and arrows ready to shoot. The pilots succeeded in landing on a dry floodplain. The attraction team – Orlando and Cláudio Villas Boas, the anthropologist Eduardo Galvão, the film-maker Jesco von Puttkamer, and the Kayabi Piunin – moved from the planes towards a group of Txikão. More Indians emerged.

Gesticulating nervously, shouting, all talking at once in a strange language, they gave the impression that they were sending us away. With our arms raised, also saying whatever occurred to us at that moment, we continued to advance across the floodplain towards them. Some – doubtless the boldest – held their ground; others fled. However, even the bravest almost jumped backwards when we attempted to touch them. At one moment, we had the impression that the contact had failed: they all beat a retreat and disappeared from our view. But their absence did not last long. They returned, shouting and gesticulating, a minute later. Suddenly, twenty or thirty Indians, arranged in a line, energetically brandishing their bows and arrows, came running to our side. They stopped a short distance away but did not remain in one place: they started walking agitatedly from side to side as if they were treading on a brazier, but their sharp eyes did not miss any of our movements. Step by step, we walked towards the group. We felt that this was the decisive moment: if they withdrew, it would be necessary to start everything again. But the Txikão did not withdraw. Talking incessantly, gesticulating, dancing, they held their bows and arrows out towards us or simply threw them at our feet. We could not have hoped for a more obvious demonstration of peace.

Orlando later learned that 'one of them was ready to strike me with a club at any moment. I did not see this, and it helped. The Indian was impressed by my involuntary demonstration of courage – which came from being unaware of the threat from the club.'

Presents were available, but the Villas Boas wanted to give the women theirs in person. The shock of contact was a traumatic experience for them.

> The women were arriving, almost dragged by their husbands and relatives. They were trembling so much and their babies were crying so loudly that we had difficulty in calming them. If one of us approached, a mother and child would retreat, trembling. We finally started distributing the presents . . . The first tools we handed over were immediately hidden in the thickets and the recipients came back for more. Axes and machetes, because of their extraordinary utility, provoked exclamations of joy. Matches caused laughter and amazement: such an easy fire, for people who had to struggle so hard to light one. Aluminium pots were also distributed; they would replace gourds and segments of *taquaruçu* bamboo. . . . The women, who had been reserved at first, revealed themselves as more brazen than the men. They seemed almost possessed. Talking, pulling at our clothes, they tried to obtain more objects than they could carry in their hands.

This contact involved only thirty men and eight women.

A few months later, the Villas Boas returned to the Txikão by boat – a five-day journey down the Tuatuari and Culuene and then up the Ronuro and lower Jatobá. The Indians were still suspicious at this second contact, but were won over by more presents during a three-day visit. A new threat now emerged. The Txikão were aware of strangers near their village, and these proved to be garimpeiro mineral prospectors. They brought a scourge of diseases, so that the once-fierce Indians looked like skeletons, covered in ulcers and racked by fevers.

The Villas Boas decided that they must bring the weakened Txikão within the boundaries of the Xingu park. Although aggressive warriors, the Txikão are very short in stature, almost pygmies. Some 500 upper-Xingu warriors, painted, adorned with brilliant feather ornaments, singing and dancing, had assembled to welcome the strangers. 'Suddenly from the side of the post's administration building came a loud, high shout. All were paralysed, and then . . . as if following a drill order over a hundred small and rickety Indians emerged. Some people shouted "It is the Txikão!" The atmosphere became tense. Once the initial impact was over, this small group moved against the other far more numerous group composed of taller and stronger men, in a clear demonstration of people about to kill or die. Another loud shout came from Orlando Villas Boas and the two groups stopped, but maintaining a hostile glare.' But fighting was avoided, despite the legacy of past aggressions. The animosity and fear of the Waurá and Mehinaku – both of whom had suffered so much from the Txikão – was finally overcome, and some eighty of the once-feared tribe moved to a site on a deep stretch of the Tuatuari river, only half a kilometre from Posto Leonardo. The Villas Boas thought that they would be safer from reprisals this close to the base.

The Txikão proved to be Carib-speaking Arara, who had migrated into the region from the upper Tapajós and Iriri during the nineteenth century. They had had to resist larger and more warlike tribes, particularly Panará and Kayabi and to a lesser extent the Bakairi. It was learned that they greatly feared malign magic, and would kill their own members who were suspected of such evil. Patrick Menget, a French anthropologist who studied the tribe, wrote that 'hostile witchcraft directly provokes deaths among the Txikão, and they take captives to substitute for the deceased'. The Txikão gradually adopted only some of their new neighbours' common traits. The huts in their village, the hammocks within them, and the caged harpy eagle were identical to those of other tribes; their women adopted the uluri vagina-guard; they came to use the lighter but less durable Xingu tipiti for leaching manioc. But they retained their more elaborate feather ornaments, basketry, and textiles, and they continued to be more diligent farmers and eat more game animals than the nearby peoples.

*

As the years passed, the Villas Boas came to know the individual Xingu Indians. They observed their daily lives – how the women worked with manioc, tending it in the forest clearings, then peeling off the bark with a shell, grating the pulpy tuber, and washing it repeatedly to leach out the poisonous prussic acid found in bitter manioc. The Indians invented the tipiti to accelerate this leaching. This is a sausage-shaped tube of basketry, the size of a man, that expands when filled with a mass of wet manioc and gradually contracts, from the weight of a stone at one end, so that the poisoned liquid is squeezed out through the woven sides. The women then roast the cleansed manioc on broad pans, and shape it into beiju pancakes or brew it into *cauim* beer. Manioc is the Xingu Indians' basic food and nourishment. Most meats are taboo, but they supplement their diet with quantities of fish from their broad lakes and rivers. The men are constantly fishing, gliding across the water in bark canoes, one man standing motionless in the bow while the other paddles. The standing Indian shoots swimming fish with his bow and arrows. Visitors are amazed by the skill with which archers can see a fish underwater, instantly calculate the angle of refraction and speed of movement, and hit it with uncanny accuracy. Suddenly, an arrow attached to a line is wildly bobbing in the water from the thrashing of the fish it has hit. In the dry season, when the streams are drying up, the Xingu Indians dam a stretch of water and poison it with the sap of the timbó liana. All the fish in that stream are stunned by the timbó and float to the surface, to be caught by an eager crowd of Indians of both sexes.

The Villas Boas also came to understand the annual moitará bartering fair between the Xingu tribes. Each tribe has its own speciality. Cláudio Villas Boas developed a theory about the Waurás' control of pottery: it made them wealthy and powerful, and they used this influence to 'act as mediating diplomats throughout Xingu ... Their pacifications had brought the Trumai under their protection, halted the Kamayurá war against [the Trumai], and drawn this last of the eight tribes into the group.' Carib-speaking tribes spent months making necklaces of mollusc shells. 'In the barter, a necklace is worth a canoe or a large pan. Feathers of fine birds are also traded, as are large baskets (*tuavi*) which have many uses in the villages.' This trading formed a bond between the tribes of the upper river, a 'common market' that reduced inter-tribal tensions. In later years, the Villas Boas sought to restrict entry to the Xingu of manufactured goods that would undermine a tribe by competing with its speciality.

The brothers never saw themselves as agents of the Brazilian government or colonial administrators, but rather as friends and helpers of the tribes among which they chose to live. They had the patience that appealed to Indians, and they learned to be open and generous with their time, their belongings, and even their privacy. They described a typical day, in their journal: 'There are over a hundred Indians on our patch. Noise, shouting, chatter, and laughter all day long. Children running, babies crying, and men shouting. No movement by us goes unobserved by them. There are never fewer than three leaning against the wattle wall of our hut, spying on us inside. The door may be shut, but they prefer to watch through the cracks. They spend hours in that position. Their attention doubles and their eyes shine if someone inside opens a suitcase.'

The Xingu Indians have learned to offset this communal living by creating artificial privacy and seclusion. Thomas Gregor, an American anthropologist who worked with the Mehinaku during the 1960s, noticed that there were times of day when Indians ignored one another, to respect the other person's privacy. He also recorded the elaborate codes of seclusion that are common to all upper-Xingu tribes. A father and mother remain secluded in a partitioned part of the communal hut for up to a year after the birth of their first child; for later children, only the mother disappears for a few weeks. But the new infant remains hidden for some eighteen months, until a godfather cuts its hair and gives it a new name. Every boy goes into seclusion when his ears are first pierced, at the age of nine or ten. For a chief's son, this could last for two years, followed by six months' freedom and a further year's seclusion. During these long periods of isolation, boys are brought down to bathe in the river three or four times a day, but the rest of the time they gaze out between the bamboo walls of their quarters. They urinate into a tube pushed through the wall, and defecate after dark. These boys are supposed to refrain from rough play, shouting, or other emotions, and they observe elaborate food taboos, violent fasting, and even drinking and vomiting poisons to prove their courage. A youth described these ordeals and the boredom. 'Look at how I live. I sit on my bench all day, working . . . Little boys tease me from outside. But I can't leave the house: witches would shoot me with magic arrows if I did. I must stay in seclusion. This is the way to become a man.' Girls are also secluded for a year after their first menstruation, but it is less rigid than for boys. Another, very rigorous, seclusion occurs for up to a year after the death of a person's spouse: no one but immediate family may see a widow or widower during this period. All these rules mean that 10 per cent or more of a small tribe could be hidden away, incommunicado, at any time.

*

Three years after the Txikão were moved into the security of the upper Xingu, in 1968 the Villas Boas made another rescue. The American anthropologist Anthony Seeger had been studying the Suyá and dis- covered that this Jê-speaking tribe had another branch still living far to the west. This remote group of Suyá were the Tapayuna, also known as Beiço de Pau ('Wooden Beaks') because of the discs in their warriors' lower lips.

The Tapayuna lived on the Arinos, a headwater of the Juruena–Tapajós 400 kilometres (250 miles) west of the Xingu. That region was rapidly developing as a settlement frontier. The first farmers from southern Brazil had moved down the Arinos in 1955 and in the following decade the aggressive Conamali property company started selling tracts of what was clearly Indian land. The Tapayuna often shot arrows at colonists' boats, so they suffered persecution and even genocide, with those who coveted their lands burning their villages and trying to kill them with poisoned tapir meat or sugar laced with arsenic.

The Tapayuna also had brushes with the Jesuit 'Anchieta Mission' and in May 1967 almost massacred an expedition led by Father Antonio Iasi (later a leading missionary champion of Indians). Iasi was building a hut on the bank of the river when the attack occurred. It lasted for eighteen hours, with the missionaries and an Irantxe Indian cowering in a shelter pounded by arrows – they later recovered fifty of these – and then fleeing downriver. Iasi later made contact with the Tapayuna and drew up a brief vocabulary of their Jê-related language.

The Indian agency Funai (successor to the SPI) engaged a sertanista called João Peret to contact the tribe, which he did in 1969. This was another tragic disaster. The new Indian Foundation was avid for publicity, so Peret invited a team of journalists to be the first to visit a Tapayuna village. One reporter had Hong Kong flu and the disease struck the tribe with devastating force. Two Indians were taken to Rio de Janeiro and São Paulo to appear on television (the same programme that showed the Americans' moon landing); but both died during this public-relations exploitation. When Peret returned to the village, he found bodies scat- tered on the ground and the rest of the tribe hiding in the forest; and when the Jesuits went there a few days after Peret, they counted 73 unburied bodies with further dead nearby. Of the original 200 Tapayuna, they could assemble only 40 people.

Funai had had a reserve 'interdicted' for the tribe in 1968, but the situation seemed so desperate that it was felt that the only hope was to transfer the surviving Tapayuna to a sanctuary. Since Anthony Seeger had

shown the link between these people and the Suyá in the Xingu, even
Father Iasi recommended that the remnant be taken there – despite the
Villas Boas' prohibition of missionary activity in the park. The air force
performed the evacuation, from the Arinos river in 1968 and the Sangue
river in 1969. It was not a success. Some Tapayuna fled during the exodus,
others died soon after reaching the Xingu, and the rest were almost
absorbed into the Suyá village near Diauarum. The tribe gradually recovered its identity, morale, and numbers. But its homeland on the Arinos
was lost for ever to frontier settlers.

A few years after their arrival in the Xingu, the Villas Boas brothers and
their friends started to plan the protection of this beautiful world of
pristine forests and rivers. On 27 April 1952 a Draft Project for legislation
governing an Indian reserve around the Xingu was presented to the
federal government by four pioneers: the former explorer Brigadier
Raimundo Vasconcelos, the formidable anthropologist Heloisa Alberto
Torres, another anthropologist (and future minister) Darcy Ribeiro, and
Orlando Villas Boas. They reminded the government that the Xingu
Indians' lands enjoyed a general protection under Article 216 of the
Brazilian Constitution, which assured indigenous peoples 'the possession
of lands where they find themselves permanently located'. In a Justification accompanying this draft, the authors proposed a radical new concept
of reserve, a national park that would protect flora and fauna as well as
indigenous people. It would be a base for scientific research, and possibly
a refuge for persecuted tribes from other areas. The proposed park was
also seen as 'a kind of greenhouse in which the region's groups could
gradually become acculturated'. The Xingu tribes would be protected
from disease and also from 'the threat of compulsory enlistment into an
economic system which can offer them only a situation beneath that
enjoyed by the lowest classes of our caboclo population.' Therefore, the
park would prepare its Indians 'biologically and culturally to face contact
with our society.' It would assist their cultural development, 'cushioning
them from [outside] attrition and pressure, so that their economic evolution may be allowed to develop at a natural rhythm.' There would even
be an environmental bonus: the 'priceless heritage' of the tribes' ancient
system of ecological adaptation would be preserved.
    The initial project was to protect a vast swathe of forests, the size of
Belgium, stretching from the Peixoto de Azevedo tributary of the Tapajós
east to the Xingu valley. It would thus embrace the lands of the Panará
and of some Kayabi. It included the cerrado and savannah around the
sources of all the Xingu's headwaters and tributaries. This land – as large

as all the property in England – was to be inalienable and only for the hereditary communal use of the tribes. Vice-President Café Filho accepted the draft project in principle.

Not surprisingly, so enlightened a law was not easy to pass. The head of the SPI wrote that the main problem was land. 'Property companies are organized with the connivance of some in authority. Indian lands are invaded, divided up and sold, under the well-known pretext of "colonization" – a pretext that conceals simple profiteering.' The State of Mato Grosso, which contained all the land in the proposed Xingu Indian park (PIX), was selling almost all of it to property speculators. The ethnographer Roberto Cardoso de Oliveira, head of the SPI's research department, published in 1953 a devastating report on the extent of these sales of Indian lands. He noted that the legislation for the PIX had been proceeding normally 'when we learned that the state – on a claim to be colonizing the wilderness of Mato Grosso – was delivering enormous areas to speculative companies, not only throughout the state but, particularly, within the limits of the Xingu Indian park.' Oliveira pointed out that the Xingu lands were far too remote to be of any commercial value for several decades. He found that 'the alienation of Indian lands by the state government has taken place in two ways: a) vast areas are reserved for colonizing purposes, then conceded to private companies for them to divide up into plots and start selling, obtaining a fabulous profit; b) selling directly to petitioners areas that do not exceed 10,000 hectares [24,710 acres], but which, by contiguity, end up forming very extensive areas controlled by a single person or firm.' Oliveira then listed in detail the concessions awarded to eighteen companies – all in 1953, just after the launch of the bid to create the PIX. He argued that all this was undesirable or illegal. It violated the Indians' rights under Article 216 of the Constitution; it prejudiced the hopes of genuine settlers by making land impossibly expensive; and it even affected national security, because some of the property companies planned to sell most of their concessions to foreigners such as Japanese. Unfortunately, the logic of such arguments was denied by interested politicians. And the Speaker of the National Assembly was from Mato Grosso. Orlando Villas Boas later commented that 'a thousand people emerged to claim lands, but in the Xingu itself we never saw the slightest process or threat of land surveying.'

After nine years of lobbying and political manoeuvring, and with the election of the reforming President Jânio Quadros, the Indian-sympathizers won. On 14 April 1961, Decree 50,455 formally created the Xingu Indian park. All the principles of its architects were respected and, even though it lay within the State of Mato Grosso, the new entity came directly under the federal government. The only drawback was that the park's boundaries fell far short of the original proposal. They omitted all the western forests, of the Kayabi and then-unknown Panará, and they failed to include the sources of any headwaters or tributaries of the Xingu. Nevertheless, this national park covered 22,000 square kilometres (8,500 square miles) – an immense area larger than Wales; and it fulfilled Orlando Villas Boas' vision of part of Amazonia reserved for its indigenous peoples, flora, and fauna.

Orlando Villas Boas instinctively appreciated the importance of public relations in protecting the Xingu Indians. He cultivated successive journalists, and the media adored the glamour and exoticism of this idyllic enclave in the midst of rapidly modernizing Brazil. So the Villas Boas generally got an excellent press. They were equally astute and assiduous in welcoming politicians of any persuasion; and they always kept on good terms with the military, particularly with the air force, which provided regular supply flights. Ellen Basso studied the Kalapalo in 1968, and praised the success of the Villas Boas' policies as being unique 'in allowing indigenous people the free pursuit of their own traditionally defined goals ... Their policy has been one of non-intervention, provision of medical treatment, and the deliberate maintenance of the population's isolation from national society. The result of this policy has been the cultural vitality of a basically healthy population, in many important respects unchanged from the time Von den Steinen first visited them.'

There were enemies. Missionaries, frustrated at being excluded from this rich spiritual pasture, accused the brothers of operating a 'human zoo'. They claimed that the Xingu Indians were kept retarded for the delectation of visiting dignitaries, journalists, and camera crews, and for laboratory study by anthropologists. Official visits of inspection put the lie to this: three separate missions by foreign observers in the early 1970s found that the Xingu Indians enjoyed more self-government and were often more skilled in non-Indian ways than any other tribes in Brazil, whether the latter were under government or missionary tutelage. Robin Hanbury-Tenison, for Survival International, said that the Xingu Indians were 'the healthiest in mind and body of those we saw in Brazil, ... better able to cope with their present problems and with a better chance of eventually adapting to the 20th century as useful citizens'. The Aborigines Protection Society team in 1972 (of which the author was a member) was impressed by 'the self-confidence of the [Xingu] Indians and their lack of that inferiority complex which characterises other tribes with long contact. Much of this is undoubtedly due to the steady integration which has taken place among the various tribes, and the political experience they have gained from it.'

Frontier settlers and prospectors, who coveted the lands of the Xingu, spread rumours that the brothers were living in dissolute luxury in their Eden. But anyone who saw the reality of their spartan existence was easily able to refute that calumny. The Villas Boas did not hesitate to attack those whom they felt had failed the Indians. In 1960 Orlando poured scorn on the SPI as 'non-existent, a ghostly entity, stripped of resources or serious men'. He accused its head, Colonel Guedes, of gradually removing any dedicated or honest workers. Guedes counter-attacked pathetically by claiming that, in his years in the Xingu, 'Mr Villas Boas . . . has left no achievement of value, despite receiving substantial funds during the period he has been there.' He also accused Orlando of stealing a 5hp outboard motor from 'the national patrimony', to repay an alleged debt.

Some Brazilian anthropologists were less impressed by the Xingu formula than their foreign counterparts. Bruna Franchetto aptly described it as 'a synthesis of isolationist conservation, of effective protection with gradual and controlled integration of the Indians, [and] the maintenance of an area that had been Indian since time immemorial.' She was unhappy about migration of tribes such as the Kayabi, Txikão, and later the Panará into this area that 'had been appropriated by the state as a reserve, for both its original inhabitants but also for other groups who "took refuge" there when their own lands were released for colonization.' There was an aura of ethnic cleansing about these rescues; but the brothers should not be blamed for the invasions and oppressions that had necessitated the emergency moves. Franchetto also regretted the way in which many tribes relocated their villages to be close to Posto Leonardo. It became the 'symbol of the Brazilian state in the Xingu Indian territory'. Posto Leonardo was the source of medicine and manufactured goods, 'the main props of the regime of tutelage and of dependence on white imports'. This is hardly fair criticism. Without the 'prop' of medicine, there would now be no Xingu Indians; and, far from creating a regime of tutelage, the Villas Boas have also been accused of being too cautious in introducing manufactured goods into the Xingu. Antonio de Souza Lima liked the way in which scientists were able to dictate the creation of the Xingu park as a haven for all types of research. But he worried that this reserve gave other tribes and Indianists unattainable aspirations for similarly vast protected territories. He praised the Villas Boas for helping to reverse the expansionist rhetoric of the Vargas era, with its 'March to the West' imitating the aggressively anti-Indian pioneers of the American frontier – even though the brothers had started their careers in 1944 as part of that very movement. It did not take long for the Villas Boas to devote their lives to the Xingu Indians. Their profound, almost instinctive understanding of indigenous thinking led them to evolve their formula of change at whatever speed the tribes themselves desired. The great natural sanctuary of the Xingu is their legacy. So also is the physical, social, and mental well-being of its peoples.

8. Tocantins–Maranhão

Between the Araguaia and the Atlantic seaboard, Brazil is more open, with far more campo, cerrado, and dry caatinga woods. There are patches of tropical forest, in secluded valleys or along river courses, but most of the land has long since been divided into ranches and farms. Most indigenous peoples in this vast area were extinguished during the centuries of colonial rule. The few surviving tribes have been in contact with national or frontier society for decades or centuries; some are almost fully acculturated, others cling to a precarious tribal identity in pockets of land surrounded by cattle ranches or perilously close to settlers' towns.

By the twentieth century, Jê-speaking tribes occupied a 1,500 kilometre (930 mile) crescent of the central-Brazilian plateau, from the states of Mato Grosso in the south-west to Goiás, Tocantins, and Maranhão towards the north-east. We have considered the more warlike and independent Jê who crossed the Araguaia and Xingu to escape the advancing settlement frontier – the Xavante, various Kayapó groups, and the still-uncontacted Panará. North-east of them lay the Jê-speakers who stayed behind. These were the Xerente and the various Timbira tribes: the Krahó on the upper Tocantins, the Apinayé and Gavião near the junction of the Tocantins and Araguaia, and the Canela (Ramkókamekra) to the north-east of the latter. These tribes suffered because of their failure to migrate westwards or to resist. Each reacted differently to the baffling problem of survival in the midst of aggressive colonists.

Curt Nimuendajú painted a deeply depressed picture of the Xerente, a tribe that had once been proud cousins of the Xavante, warriors who marauded far eastwards towards Bahia. But that had been in the eighteenth century. From the mid-nineteenth century, the Xerente (pronounced Sher-ent-eh) had to live on uneasy terms with colonists' farms that surrounded them. Their last circular village with a central men's hut disintegrated shortly after 1900. From then on, the tribe has lived in hamlets averaging eight scattered huts. Nimuendajú saw nine such aldeias in 1930, and seven a few years later.

In the beginning of the twentieth century the Xerente became demoralized by Neo-Brazilian contacts, and in 1937 I found the aboriginal culture in a state of collapse. Economically and socially ruined, hemmed in by Neo-Brazilian settlers, the people were on the verge of complete subjection to these influences. Once more the leap from primitive collectivism to individualism has failed: I know no single Indian in even fairly satisfactory circumstances under the new regime. Hence a Xerente prefers loafing, begging, and stealing among Neo-Brazilians to providing for his needs. His native village has turned into a place of scarcity; tribal influence steadily wanes as the settlers' increases; miscegenation extends, altering the tribal character.

The Xerente had received the attentions of benign Italian missionaries throughout the second half of the nineteenth century; but when the fathers left, their religion went with them. Nimuendajú found that the Xerente liked having their children baptized – but only in order to acquire a generous godfather – and they regarded a church in the town of Piabanha as belonging to them. 'However, they do not dream of ever attending a service there. To be sure, they never play truant at Neo-Brazilian neighbours' saints-day feasts, but their usually undesired attendance is due solely to the prospect of sharing in the food.' The only legacy of all the missionary proselytizing seemed to be negative: it had weakened their original spiritual coherence. 'The bulk of their ancient faith has dropped out of the memory of the present generation. It is hardly worth while discussing such matters with them: they neither know nor want to know anything.'

One surprising attribute of the demoralized Xerente was that their mythology identified them with other *Indians*. Nimuendajú said that: 'Of all the tribes I have known, the Xerente are the only one with some sense of racial solidarity, transcending linguistic differences and tribal wars.' Their sun god identified the Xerente alongside even traditionally hostile tribes as having common cause against the mutual enemy: the white men. Nimuendajú was right to notice this. Until very recently, indigenous peoples have been hopelessly divided. For almost five centuries they were defeated piecemeal, too isolated or too unaware of the magnitude of the threat to unite with other tribes against the European invaders.

Eighteen years later, in 1955, the British anthropologist David Maybury-Lewis chose to study the Xerente to prepare himself for fieldwork with the fiercer Xavante. The latter had long ago migrated away from the white frontier, disgusted by a brief experience of settlement in government 'model villages' in the late eighteenth century. Most were now hostile, living 500 kilometres (300 miles) to the south-west beyond the Tocantins and Araguaia rivers. Maybury-Lewis arrived at Tocantinia, the SPI's Indian post for the Xerente. It proved to be a mud hut above a slippery riverbank, its only equipment a small boat rotting at its moorings, its only furniture a table. Even by SPI standards, this was a miserable post, remote and forgotten, with no airstrip because it was not on an exciting contact frontier. The agent was a young mulatto with a family of a wife and three tattered children. The Xerente found the land near the post too weak, so had moved twenty-five kilometres (sixteen miles) inland. Maybury-Lewis was told that 'they were bad Xerente at that village – idle, treacherous, always involved in fights with their neighbours and with the settlers. Worst of all, their chief, Pedro, claimed to be paramount chief of all the Xerente and yet he was the worst Indian of them all.' Other 'difficult' Indians lived to the south on the Tocantins; another hamlet of industrious farmers lay downriver to the north; and the rest were far away to the east on the Sono (Balsas) river. The SPI authorities preferred to forget about Tocantinia. Everyone ignored the Xerente, 'except for the local settlers who lived in a perpetual state of anti-Xerente indignation and the Indian agent who got no thanks from either side. [The agent] incurred the enmity of all the influential people in the miserable hamlet of Tocantinia and in return he drew a salary of about four pounds a month. It was his favourite, one might say his only, topic of conversation.' This poor man was supposed to raise cattle around the post, but was not allowed to eat its meat. He complained to his visitors that there was no grass for any healthy animals, and if the SPI ever sent a truckload of salt or tools, the Indians claimed these as belonging to them.

When Maybury-Lewis visited the farming Xerente on the Gurgulho stream, the clothes of both sexes 'were the same as those of any back-woodsman, but tattered and indescribably filthy. They wore their hair short. Only their markedly mongoloid features and the nasal bumble of their speech served to distinguish them from the settlers.' During the ensuing months, the anthropologist was able to observe the vestiges of tribal custom among these Xerente. They told him how they longed to recover the broad territory awarded to them by the nineteenth-century Emperor but long since occupied by frontier towns and farms. The men hunted far into the surrounding countryside, but returned empty-handed or with only one or two small animals; the women foraged for wild fruits. They sometimes removed their clothes for a festive dance, shamans performed ancient rituals to heal the sick, people suspected of witchcraft were killed, young men on rare occasions ran the log race, and there were remnants of traditional ceremonies for puberty and children's naming.

Maybury-Lewis 'noticed that they fought sickness without medicines, that they hunted without powder and shot, that they cleared their gardens without proper tools.' He and his wife grew disenchanted with the Xerentes' constant intrigue and malice, their wheedling and their feckless-ness. But he concluded that they should not be blamed 'for their begging and their truculence, for their hypocrisy and their deceit. They were fighting for their lives in a way which people who have never faced the total obliteration of their own society cannot understand. And everything was against them.'

Travelling eastwards towards the Sono, he entered an unprepossessing patch of forest known as the Basin. This was the cause of a passionate dispute between Indians and settlers, typical of similar incidents all over Brazil. The cattlemen claimed the Basin and grazed their cattle there; but the Indians possessed it and maintained that it had always been theirs. The ranchers complained to the state authorities that the Xerente had killed their cattle; an attempt to occupy the forest was met by armed Indians; a posse of adventurers burned a native encampment; and the SPI agent summoned an inspector, who managed to get compensation paid to the wronged Xerente.

An old man told the anthropologist of the times when 'the first missionaries had been carried into Goiás on the backs of friendly Indians and had terrified the children with their cavernous sunken eyes and bushy beards' and of relations between the Xerente and 'the tough and impov-erished settlers'. He said that the whites cheated the Indians and worked against them; but the Xerente made matters worse by disunity and constant intrigue and quarrelling. He recalled the days when 'all the Xerente had their hair long like the [neighbouring tribe of] Krahó, and in the villages the women wore no clothes . . . But then the young men used to be separated from the rest. We had to live in a separate hut until our hair grew long and we were old enough to get married.'

Some 200 kilometres (120 miles) down the Tocantins, north of the Xerente, live their erstwhile enemies, the Krahó. This tribe has fared better than the unfortunate Xerente, perhaps because of its greater cohesion and moral toughness. The Jê-speaking Krahó are one of a group of peoples known as Timbira, all of whom are survivors of a century or more of conflict and contact with the unruly colonists of the Tocantins valley and the interior of Maranhão. When Curt Nimuendajú was with the Krahó in 1930, he found some 400 of them in two groups. The southern group, furthest from the Tocantins, had recently split because of 'pressure of the near-by fazendeiros . . . A friend of the Indians long resident in their vicinity, Santo Moreira, tried hard to prop up the tottering community and to defend the last bit of Indian land against the intruding stockbreeders. But the wiles and calumny of his opponents, with whom the despicable Chief Secundo was in league, thwarted all his efforts.'

Matters came to a head in 1940, when thirty-eight gunmen, armed with Winchester .44-calibre carbines, attacked the Krahó village and murdered many Indians. For once, the frontiersmen had gone too far. A Protestant missionary, Francisco Colares, alerted the SPI; the Indian agency's Council protested to the Ministry of Agriculture; General Rondon had a meeting with President Vargas (who had just had his first sight of Indians: the Karajá of Bananal Island not far to the west of the Krahó); and the Minister of Justice sent army and police officers to investigate. Even with such powerful intervention, it was almost impossible to obtain justice for crimes against Indians on the Brazilian frontier. The trial of 'sixty-one men indicted for the horrible massacre of twenty-six Krahó Indians and the wounding of six others took place in the city of Pedro Afonso, where they live and have influence, instead of in a neighbouring district as had been agreed.' After a six-day trial, the jury acquitted all the accused. However, the state prosecutor launched an appeal. This was heard in the state capital and led to seven years' imprisonment for each of the eleven leaders of the murderous raid.

The outcome of the atrocity was that the Brazilian government in 1944 made the State of Goiás grant the tribe a large reserve, of 320 square kilometres (124 square miles). It has weak soil, looking like an arid version of Scottish heath, and described by one team of visitors as poor, dry, savannah-type land. But it gave the tribe the essential cushion for cultural survival. The SPI also established an Indian post for the Krahó, but it was on the edge of their territory and had little effect on their way of life. Government agents did not interfere with young Indians' love of travel – they often hitched rides to Brazil's large cities, out of curiosity and to beg for presents from the authorities – nor did they 'impose their preferred chiefs on aldeias, as happened with other Indian groups'. Darcy Ribeiro later noted that the Krahó were shrewd about their use of this land: they allowed settlers to farm part of it – but only in return for rent expressed in cattle, produce, money, or hunting rights outside the reserve. 'Here, the SPI's intervention has permitted the tribe to be preserved, and to coexist with the whites without being dependent on them.' Julio Cesar Melatti, who studied the Krahó in the mid-1960s, observed that they were able to conserve many tribal customs because the surrounding cattle ranches did not need them as labourers. Thus disputes were about land, but not people. The SPI's commercial policy also caused trouble. By 1970, the Indian agency was raising 300 head of cattle on the Krahó reserve. 'The Indians, however, are not allowed to eat meat from this cattle. If they want any, they have to buy it from the neighbouring fazendeiro in this so-called reserve.'

In Nimuendajú's day, the northern group of Krahó was fifty kilometres (thirty miles) away from the southern, living in two close-knit villages, each of some sixteen huts arranged in the traditional cartwheel pattern that is so typical of Timbira tribes. This beautifully symmetrical plan has survived to the present; but the houses around its perimeter are now strongly influenced by those of surrounding civilizados – rectangular, with pitched roofs of palm thatch, and walls of vertical laths coated in mud or thatch.

When Curt Nimuendajú was with the Krahó in 1930 he felt that missionaries posed a considerable threat. Brazilian Baptists 'are exerting themselves to break up the old organization. They wish to settle the Indians according to the missionaries' notions of a colony, with abolition of log racing, etc.' Nimuendajú hoped that the tribe would survive this cultural dislocation, since the missionaries' influence seemed slight; and he was proved right. When Melatti was with the Krahó from 1962 onwards, he found that the tribe classified civilizados as either Catholic or Protestant, with the former 'drinking cachaça rum, carrying guns, using swear words, smoking and cheating on their wives' and the latter committing none of these sins. 'Although the Krahó practise neither of these religions, they do try to maintain good relations with missionaries of each. It is their custom to have their children baptized, with the sole objective of gaining a civilizado godfather who might give them some assistance.'

Proximity to the settlement frontier bred frustration and insecurity, which inspired 'a messianic movement, a form of "cargo cult".' This was led by Ropkur Txortxó Kraté (also known as José Nogueira), an Indian in his thirties who had lost two relatives in the massacre of 1940, and was a fine orator with leadership qualities. His movement was preached in great secrecy, in 1950–51. It was based on the apparition of a bearded man known as Rain who symbolized all manifestations of rainfall, from clouds and lightning to the downpour itself. The cult sought to punish 'Christians' for the massacre and for invading Indian land, but it also aimed to turn the Krahó into civilizados. Ropkur had his followers build a large hut for Western-style dancing, which was performed in couples as settlers did. He enforced his doctrine with a loaded shotgun. Melatti wrote that 'the visionary had many followers among the young and middle-aged, who wanted to be transformed into civilizados. Only the old were disgusted at having to abandon customs inherited from their ancestors.' The Krahó who travelled to Brazilian cities had noticed prejudice against blacks, which the Indians shared. So Ropkur threatened any who did not obey him that they would turn black. But the movement was short-lived. It collapsed when predictions of dramatic change did not happen.

Despite the failure of this cult, the Krahó continued to seek a compromise between their culture and surrounding Brazilian society. Melatti observed them practising a wealth of festivals to mark every stage of their people's life cycles. Alongside such traditional ceremonies there were Brazilian-style parties, night-long affairs with national dancing and food (pork with rice and manioc) and the Indians wearing clothes. Some settlers were invited as guests – on condition that they surrender their guns and machetes, in case they became violent from the cachaça rum they brought with them.

Manuela Carneiro da Cunha noted that Krahó culture remained strong in the early 1970s precisely because the tribe was at the margin of the local ranching and farming economy. She wrote that

> a group's traditionalism cannot be measured by the vigour of its ancient artefacts, nor of its farming techniques or houses, but rather by what use it makes of old norms as the organizing principles of its current way of life . . . The conservation of language seems to be of utmost importance . . . Well, the Krahó maintain their language, so that only the men and some adolescents speak Portuguese . . . I think that the principal disruptive elements were the suppression of warlike expeditions and the introduction of manufactured goods that could no longer be made by the tribe. It was possibly the first of these that caused the disappearance of age groups, and the second modified the system of inheritance.

Downriver from the Krahó, in the mesopotamia where the great rivers Tocantins and Araguaia join, lives another Timbira tribe, the Apinayé. Like their compatriots, the Apinayé were survivors of two centuries of contact with the white frontier and a spell of missionary activity. They had been decimated by disease, including the Spanish flu that swept the world in 1918. When Nimuendajú reached them in 1928, he found that 'economically and socially there was manifest decadence . . . Of its ancient territory hardly any part is still in the possession of the tribe, for Neo-Brazilian settlers are sprinkled all over its hereditary habitat . . . Until about twenty years ago it never occurred to the Apinayé to suspect that this [immigration] posed any danger to their own future. On the contrary, they good-naturedly accepted at face value the intruders' professions of friendship, and when their eyes were opened it was too late: . . . [almost] their entire country now has alien masters with legal title.' Of the tribe's four villages, two disappeared, engulfed by surrounding ranchers who took their land and intermarried with their few survivors. Another village, Gato Preto ('Black Cat'), had been attacked and pillaged in 1923 by the Krahó, who suspected its people of evil sorcery. By 1935 Nimuendajú found this village with seventy people, but its chief was 'addicted to [locally distilled] whisky and grows brutal and quarrelsome when under the influence'.

The fourth Apinayé village, Bacaba, very nearly disappeared because settlers invaded its territory, behaving 'like overlords by mendaciously telling the Indians that they had bought the land from the government.' A tenacious chief, Matuk, went to all the relevant cities to try to substantiate his people's land title, and the SPI finally give him some support. On his return, Matuk organized a great party for all the settlers 'with much guzzling of gin and dancing to the tune of guitars'. He hoped that his people might survive by aping the frontiersmen; but it was a forlorn hope. When Nimuendajú was there in 1928, 'Bacaba presented a sorry picture, with five wretched huts ranged round a plaza overgrown with rank weeds. The boisterous vivacity typical of Timbira settlements had disappeared.' But the admirable anthropologist managed to start a revival in Apinayé morale. By 1930 there were two more huts and the village was tidier; on later visits he found that ancient festivals and puberty initiations had been revived. 'Even considering the remarkable conserva-tism of all Timbira peoples, the tenacity with which this miserable remnant of a once-numerous tribe clings to its traditions is truly amazing.' The greatest problem in reviving tribal custom lay in the decimated population: by 1940 only 150 Apinayé remained in their two villages. Unlike the Xerente or Krahó, the Apinayé were 'very peaceable and honest folk', too gentle to stand up to the settlers' aggressions. And they were too few to restore all their traditional way of life.

Soon after the creation of the SPI, Curt Nimuendajú witnessed the destruction of other Timbira groups. The Krikatí (the name means 'big village') had often featured in the history of the region during the previous century. A census of 1919 said that they had two villages totalling over 270 people. But when Nimuendajú saw the Krikatí in the following year, 'I found only a remnant of eight souls . . . living impoverished and in a very sad plight from the pressure of nearby fazendeiros, who had usurped the whole tribal domain leaving the aborigines the choice between abandonment of their last settlement and being massacred. In the previous year, owing to a conflict with the wealthiest and greediest fazendeiro, one Salomão Barros, the villagers of the other two aldeias had scattered . . .' The SPI agent Marcellino Miranda averted a general massacre planned by the ranchers. But when he suggested that the Krikatí move to a safer location, they obstinately refused to leave their tribal lands. They argued, reasonably, that it was the colonial farmers who should depart if they objected to the proximity of Indians. 'In 1930 the situation came to a head. Pressed by the fazendeiros, the President of [the State of] Maranhão informed the SPI agent that unless the Krikatí consented to depart he would have them forcibly removed by the constabulary.' The agent tried in vain to find a safe haven for these Indians with another tribe. So 'the Krikatí scattered in all directions. I do not know where the survivors may be hidden nowadays, but probably they have ceased to exist as a distinct tribe.' We shall see that this dire prediction proved wrong.

Well to the east of the Krikatí was another group of 150 Timbira called Kenkateyé. In 1913 these Indians 'were wiped out by the fazendeiro Raymundo Arruda. With a company of fifty followers and a barrel of gin he entered the aldeia to the music of an accordion, got the men drunk, put them in irons, tied them to one another, dragged them outside the village, and had his troop shoot down some fifty males. Several women were also massacred with firearms and machetes . . . The SPI inspector of Maranhão had the murderers put on trial, but the jury in Barra do Corda [in the interior of Maranhão] unanimously acquitted them, and even today [1946] the residents proudly point out the members of Arruda's troop who began the massacre.' Silvio Fróes Abreu wrote that over a hundred people were murdered. He condemned the slaughter as 'an act of barbarity motivated by the loss of cattle that strangers had come to raise on lands that the Indians already occupied.' The shattered remnants of the Kenkateyé fled to the Krahó and other groups; and the evil rancher got their land.

East of the shattered Krikatí and Kenkateyé live the closely related Canela, another Timbira tribe that has managed to maintain much of its traditional society in the midst of cattle ranches. The name Canela, meaning 'shinbone' or 'cinnamon' in Portuguese, has stuck to the Ramkókamekra and remnants of other Timbira who congregated with them. They live in a beautiful circular village called Ponto, eighty kilometres (fifty miles) south of the town of Barra do Corda. Survivors of over a century of skirmishes with surrounding ranchers and some violent epidemics, the Canela are amazingly resilient. Curt Nimuendajú spent many months with this

attractive tribe, on six field seasons between 1929 and 1936. He proudly
wrote that he was adopted by the son of a Canela chief and 'I bear his
Indian name'.

In 1941 the SPI established a post alongside the Canela, with mixed
results for the Indians. The Service's main role was to protect them from
surrounding cattle men. The American anthropologist William Crocker
regarded this as 'a service of inestimable importance' without which the
tribe would have been dispersed or destroyed. Darcy Ribeiro reported
that there was a profound gulf between the Canela and local cowhands,
even though they greeted one another with mock friendliness. 'Probably
nowhere else in Brazil is there such deep animosity as in this cattle
country. The cattlemen accuse the Indians of every fault: they are lazy,
treacherous brigands, stupid, dissolute, cowardly, etc.' Indians were widely
regarded as subhuman animals who could be used for only the crudest
work, and then only by punishment or the stimulus of cachaça. All
Timbira had suffered from disease and constant persecution, driven from
every parcel of land to which they retreated. Those accused of cattle-
raiding were hunted down and often slaughtered. Ribeiro refuted the
notion that cattle country suited Indians. They gained nothing from it.
The Indians lost their ancestral territory to ranchers, were driven to the
edges of fazendas, and forced onto the weakest soils. The cowboys did not
even covet Indian women – despite the beauty of Timbira girls. They
regarded Indians simply as nuisances to be cleared from the land.

Crocker also praised SPI agents because, 'in keeping with the national
policy, they have . . . encouraged the maintenance of aboriginal practices.'
Many cultural traits persisted among these naturally conservative people.
Both sexes still wore their hair hanging long, but with a horizontal parting
around their heads to produce a bonnet-like crown of hair. They preferred
to go naked, but the men finally adopted shorts and the women skirts but
no tops. The Canela liked to paint their bodies and wear straw and feather
ornaments, and the men pierced their ears to insert wooden discs. Their
complex society was and is based on moieties in the circular village, with
log races between the black and red teams, and matrilineal descent with a
newly married couple moving into the wife's family house. These divisions
and hierarchies are based on kinship clans, age groups, and economic or
ritual skills. Although there is competition between them, they help to
maintain social harmony.

The strain of survival in the midst of a hostile ranching frontier proved
too unsettling. In 1963 the Canela were seduced by a messianic message,
just as the Krahó had been a decade earlier. A prophetess called Kee-
khwei predicted a reversal in roles between Indians and civilizados. The

natives would take over the cities, planes, and buses, while the whites would be banished to hunting in the woods. 'Disillusioned with civilizado support and with faith in their ancestral ways all but lost, the Canela fabricated a sequel to [their origin] myth to express their wished-for remodelling of the world, with themselves using civilizado equipment, and their aboriginal way of life completely abandoned.' The shaman made a triumphal entry into the village of Ponto, and for a time the Indians obeyed her injunction to dance in their manner during the week and in the Brazilian style at weekends. They celebrated frantically, for 'he who danced the most would be the richest when the great day came'. The faithful were also forced to give Kee-khwei presents, for which they sold shotguns, machetes, and cooking pots. William Crocker noticed a change in the tribe's thinking: for the first time its elders predicted that young Indians would adopt civilizado ways, and that these were better than Canela traditions.

The prophetess preached a dangerous doctrine: that it was permissible to kill and eat ranchers' cattle, and that Indians who did so would have magical protection against retaliation. Forty or fifty head of cattle were taken – which was far more than the previous average of six a year, which the fazendeiros could overlook. The backwoodsmen duly retaliated, first by burning houses in another village, where they killed one man and wounded others, then launching a massive dawn onslaught on Ponto village. Luckily, the Canela had anticipated this and prepared effective defensive traps. Some Indians fought back, but most had prudently hidden in the woods, so that the murderous attackers killed only three more Canela, wounded eight, and burned the village. Crocker arrived at this tense juncture, and wrote that 'when the attack finally occurred in July [1963], a number of bullets actually hit their targets, and with the harsh evidence of dead relatives lying on the ground, the Canela soon considered the [messianic] movement to have been a deception and Kee-khwei a liar.' An SPI agent and the local mayor tried to talk the ranchers' posse out of its aggression. They moved the Canela from their village to sanctuary in the Sardinha village of the Tupi-speaking and forest-dwelling Guajajara. More Canela refugees died after the exodus, of diseases such as typhoid and malaria, and because they could not survive in a forest environment.

Carlos Moreira blamed the invading cattlemen for this atrocity. 'The Indians were continually humiliated and exploited. The ranchers let their cattle loose in the [Indians'] farms, got the police and administrative authorities to persecute them, and accused them of theft, alcoholism, and vagrancy.' Since the SPI seemed unable to guarantee the Canelas' minimal security, the desperate Indians sought salvation in Kee-khwei's promised land. Another anthropologist saw the messianic movement as a parallel to the Canelas' legend of their founder Auké. This mythical creator had bestowed manufactured goods on the whites; and the new cult promised a return to balance in attitudes and wealth between settlers and Indians.

After two years' exile, the Canela filtered back to create a new village near Ponto. But a terrible epidemic of smallpox and flu at this time killed about sixty more of the unfortunate tribe. Despite these afflictions, the Canela revived with remarkable resilience. By the 1970s their population increased rapidly, most customs (such as the log race) were fully observed, and morale was high. When I saw them at that time their elegant circular village was functioning smoothly. The messianic movement, the ranchers' attack, and the period of exile seemed almost forgotten. The tribe's main problems were the weak soil of its village and the lack of game to be hunted in the surrounding cerrado. Today, the Canela Rankokamekra are the only tribe to live entirely in one village; and with a population of 900, Ponto is probably the largest indigenous village in Brazil.

The Guajajara, part of a cluster of tribes known as Tenetehara, were more acculturated than the nearby Canela. And yet in 1901 even this peaceful group had rebelled against Capuchin missionaries who had arrived from Italy four years earlier. The friars had beaten an Indian called João Caboré for refusing to give up one of his two wives. He went around the Guajajara villages to complain of this savage punishment, and found deep resentment about the foreign missionaries' stern zealotry. Among other wrongs, they had removed infants from their parents and shut them away in convent boarding schools. Then, in 1900, a terrible measles epidemic killed thirty Indian children. Caboré soon assembled a war party. But this was no spontaneous outburst: Caboré and his men carefully reconnoitred the mission station at Alto Alegre. An Indian woman repeatedly warned the friars of the danger, but they ignored her. 'Then', as a farmer told the British anthropologist Francis Huxley, 'one day when they were all in the church celebrating mass, the Indians fell on the place and killed every one, all the friars, all the people.' The uprising continued from March until June 1901. Mércio Gomes wrote that 'the Tenetehara waged a true war, perhaps the last of its kind in Brazil, whose sole objective was the total expulsion of the whites from their region, and above all of the missionary regime.' They killed all non-Indians at Alto Alegre, including four Franciscan friars, one monastic brother, seven teaching sisters, twenty white parents of children at the school, and settlers who worked in a sugar mill and in agriculture, and attacked cowboys in surrounding fazendas and travellers. The settlers' response was a posse of police and volunteers; but it could not break the Indians' defences. After several defeats, the authorities recruited forty-two Canela – traditional enemies of the Guajajara – and launched an attack by 140 well-armed men. The tribe's trenches were overrun; many Indians fled into the forests; hundreds died of starvation or were killed; and in September forty Guajajara leaders were taken to the town for trial. Their leader, João Caboré, died in prison in suspicious circumstances. 'Regional folklore has terrible stories of murders and brutality, both by the Indians and by the whites.'

The situation was slightly better among the Guajajara-Tenetehara elsewhere in Maranhão. On the Grajaú and Pindaré the pressure came from copaíba-oil extraction, and on the upper Mearim, where there was plenty of available land, from farming and ranching. Many Guajajara lived in dense rainforests rich in hardwoods, copaíba trees, palms such as the babassú whose leaves and nuts were economically important to the Indians, and some rubber trees. Numbers fell from perhaps 5,000 to little over 2,000 in the four decades between 1900 and 1940.

Two anthropologists, Charles Wagley and Eduardo Galvão, in 1949 made a remarkable study of the Guajajara – the Tenetehara in Maranhão. This was ground-breaking because it was an optimistic study of a people undergoing rapid acculturation. The authors felt that the Guajajara owed their relative demographic survival to shrewd adaptation to the frontier economy. Missionaries and then the civil authorities suppressed inter-tribal fighting and encouraged large families. 'The Tenetehara learned that children might be useful in collecting babassú nuts for sale to Luso-Brazilians. Steel instruments and new plants (such as rice, bananas, lemons, etc.) made agriculture more productive. The sale of babassú nuts, copaíba oil, and other forest products brought the Tenetehara imported products. Although Tenetehara culture and society were modified, the aboriginal and the borrowed elements slowly combined to form a new culture and a new social system which at least met the minimum requirements for survival.' Wagley and Galvão were pleased that the Guajajara did not cling 'unhealthily' to tribal custom and isolation. But they felt that the tribe was close to cultural 'saturation' and predicted – wrongly – that future assimilation into Brazilian society would be rapid.

These Guajajara had suffered the usual epidemics of alien diseases; but by the twentieth century had developed inherited immunity to some of them. Fortunately, they had few practices designed to keep their popula-tions low and stable – such as late marriage or infanticide for spiritual reasons. Many tribes practised these curbs, almost instinctively, so that they could live sustainably from the surrounding forests and rivers. But when such tribes were decimated by diseases, they could not quickly change ancient customs to a system that produced more babies. By contrast, the Guajajara had a more adaptable social structure. They were organized by family and kin groups. Wagley saw that their men were proud of having several children and women were eager to give birth. 'Cooperation of large extended families in gardening and in collecting babassú nuts and copaíba oil is still the general pattern among the Tenetehara.' Ever adaptable, the Guajajara later collected leaves of the jaburandi bush, which contained an essential oil for perfumery.

By the 1930s the Guajajara had reoccupied most of the land from which they fled after the 1901 uprising. The Capuchins returned in 1931 and tried to claim the lands that they had bought when they came from Italy in 1896, but their legal action dragged on and they failed. Instead, the state government in 1936 decreed that almost all the Guajajara lands south-west of Barra do Corda should become three reserves, administered for them by the SPI.

With the collapse of the Amazon rubber boom, poor peasants driven from north-east Brazil by droughts or unemployment could no longer find work as seringueiros. Instead, such migrants started to seek a frontier in the border region between Maranhão and Pará. They were moving into a vast forested triangle, ten million hectares (38,600 square miles) devoid of Brazilian inhabitants. 'The mass of pioneers moved towards the north-west, on the road to Belém. Their progression was rapid: [by] 1940 to Pedreiras, 1950 Bacabal, 1960 Alto Turi . . . It was, however, in these regions of the middle and upper valleys of the Pindaré and Gurupi, where the forest is most dense, that Tupi-speaking tribes [Tenetehara and Kaapor] had installed their final refuge.' A bloody clash seemed inevitable.

Charles Wagley and Eduardo Galvão predicted that within one or two generations this indigenous people would be totally assimilated into the regional caboclo population. In the event, they were wrong. The Guajajara were sufficiently self-assured and proud of their ethnicity to survive as a tribe. During the next three decades, the populations of the Tenetehara within these reserves tripled – in contrast to the decimation among those on the Pindaré and in other unprotected areas. As Gomes commented, this growth came 'despite all the SPI's institutionalized paternalism, its appalling medical assistance, and the exploitative regime adopted by the local small farmers and traders. [The increase came because] of the assurance throughout this period that their lands were protected.'

To the north-west, in the State of Pará, the Tembé-Tenetehara suffered more from their contacts with that state's settlement frontier. Throughout the nineteenth century, the Tembé had been engaged in collecting copaíba oil, constantly in debt to traders and harassed by *regatões* (itinerant riverine pedlars). Copaíba trees are scarce and scattered, and they cannot be milked of their oil in successive seasons; so the Tembé dispersed, in their extended families, living in tiny shifting settlements above the annual flood line. In the early days of the SPI, small groups of Tembé were on the Capim river, selling manioc flour and tobacco to regatões to buy trade goods 'at exorbitant prices . . . They are not very fond of work, but despite this they are exploited over the little they do produce.' The regatões paid only a tenth of the market value for Tembé raw materials, so that the Indians sank into debt bondage.

At that time, the Tembé were the main paddlers of canoes on the Gurupi, of which they knew every stone and rapid. Ribeiro said that 'As rowers, the Tembé work for ten to fourteen hours at a stretch, with only brief rest periods too short for nourishing food. They rely on stimulants – pinga rum and marijuana, which every canoe carries. The work is so exhausting that only men under thirty do it, with a few of the older men as helmsmen.' These Indians also worked at felling forest timber. But their population was too reduced for the hard labour of cutting the trees and clearing paths to drag them to the river. If they brought their wives, these became the victims of passing caboclos or of the timber boss.

The Tembé were terribly reduced, from 6,000 in the 1870s, to 1,091 in 1920, to 150 by 1940 – a decline of 97 per cent in sixty-seven years. There was a boom in balsam from the copaíba trees that abound on their lands. Copaíba extractors and their network of dealers, middle-men, and regatão itinerant traders destroyed the Tembé physically and culturally. As usual, disease was the main killer: a terrible measles epidemic that in 1949 decimated the Kaapor to the east also struck them. An old woman later told the American anthropologist William Balée that so many people perished in her village that they could not bury the dead: vultures descended to feed on the corpses. Very few Tembé survived. Darcy Ribeiro in 1950 encountered the depot of one of the last regatão traders, Luis Tavares, on the Gurupi river. 'We saw two young Tembé girls who were his concubines. In that year, out of a Tembé population of 120, there were scarcely nineteen people of marriageable age. There were only four women, in addition to Tavares's two, for fifteen men.'

By now all Tembé had Christian names, they spoke Portuguese, and the old system of extended matrilocal families with polygynous marriages had given way to independent monogamous families. The men retained some skills in hunting and fishing, although they preferred guns to bows and arrows; but the women had abandoned making traditional ceramics.

The group no longer practised shamanism, ceremonies related to the life cycle, or body painting and scarring. It was a classic case of acculturation, with the Indians drifting to the lowest stratum of frontier society. Their independence was maintained only by the SPI reserve and by the many rapids that hindered movement up the Gurupi and Guamá rivers. 'In general, the components of the tribe survived only in a most precarious existence, from the little they produced through basic subsistence activities or the minute wages they got – after long delays – for labour for timber companies or ranchers.'

In March 1945 the SPI got the State of Pará to award a 278,000 hectare (1,070 square mile) reserve for the Tembé and other native groups. At first, the Service hoped to attract the Indians to 'regular' paid employment; but it also sought to cover its own costs from the profit from native labour. All Tembé men were put to work building a rough road between the Guamá and Gurupi rivers. They were also expected to continue collecting lucrative copaíba oil and other extracted produce, with the SPI selling these and most of their farmed crops at Belém and other markets. When the SPI was desperate to increase income from the *renda indígena* it encouraged the Tembé to sell jaguar skins, vast quantities of (now endangered) river turtles, birds, and resins. Later, the main product sold to regatões and in nearby towns was timber. Far from being idle, the Tembé also marketed surplus rice, bananas, manioc flour, and emollient mallow leaves. The Service kept a store full of goods that the Indians now needed, and it 'sold' these against extractive income. 'Any surplus production went to the upkeep of the post itself. This system, which aimed at the production of saleable surpluses, and which placed the post at the centre of the Indians' economic activity, remained invariable until the SPI itself was extinguished.' Although it paid somewhat better than copaíba traders did, the SPI effectively replaced them as exploiters of the Tembé. It built a school, but this never attracted more than a dozen Indian children and its teaching was sporadic.

In the 1960s the SPI agent tried to generate income by admitting more settlers into the reserve. As a result, interethnic marriages were more common and Portuguese became the official language. But the Indian Service collapsed here as elsewhere in Brazil. By 1970 'none of the old projects subsisted, the Indian post of the Alto Rio Guamá was in almost total abandon, and the Tembé reverted to planting their own gardens in an area that was largely deforested.' In that year General Bandeira de Mello, who was in charge of the SPI's successor Funai, illegally conceded a 11,000 hectare (27,000 acre) part of the reserve to a big meat company, on the grounds that this benefited the state's development and that Indians had ceased to live in that area. At that time, many industrious Tembé men were taken off to work on the Transamazonica highway and other grandiose schemes. The result was a shortage of hunted meat and fish, and further decline in tribal traditions.

It is instructive to examine the fate of the Timbira tribe of Gavião ('Hawks'). Part of this nation fought the frontiersmen, while part succumbed like the docile Apinayé or the collaborating Krahó. The Gavião call themselves Parketeyê, 'the Downstream People', and other names, but the tag Gavião has clung to them for almost 200 years. It inspired terror during the first half of the twentieth century. This was a period when the region was transformed by extractive products: latex, copaíba oil, and, in the 1920s, sought-after Brazil nuts whose trees abound in the tribe's territory.

Gavião oral tradition recalls that relations with the *kupen*, white men, started reasonably amicably. The Indians tolerated Brazil-nut gatherers, castanheiros, entering their forests; and they received some coveted knives and axes in return for supplying food. But in 1937 there were violent clashes, with a chief killed on the Tauri river. The Gavião retaliated by killing three castanheiros and burning their huts. Relations between Indians and whites degenerated into vendetta. Throughout the 1940s the town of Marabá (formerly Itacaiúnas) was growing rich from Brazil nuts; but its people clamoured for the extermination of the Gavião. Local politicians and Brazil-nut traders organized armed expeditions to slaughter these 'perpetrators of great barbarities'.

Although the SPI had fallen on hard times by the late 1930s, it tried to make contact with this feared tribe. The Service had a few Gavião at a post on the lower Tocantins during the 1940s, under José Maria da Gama Malcher who was later to be one of the SPI's finest directors. But there were constant clashes by settlers invading this post for its Brazil nuts. In 1937 another attraction post was established on the Ipixuna river near Marabá, and on a dozen occasions Indians came to collect presents. But they were furious when they came again and found the post devoid of either tools or manioc flour. They lured a worker to the riverbank, killed him, and never returned. The SPI tried again in 1945, with an attraction post at a place called Ambauá on the Tucuruí river. The agent was a settler called Aurélio dos Santos, who had made friendly contact with the Indians. But six months later they killed Aurélio and wounded two other SPI men, probably because these had sold the crop from a manioc clearing, thinking that the Indians would not return. In 1946 sixty Gavião, including some women and children, appeared at the post and sacked its storage shed; they were back two months later but, disappointed by the tools they were offered, they hid the post's guns and clubbed two workmen to death.

In 1951 the popular magazine O *Cruzeiro* carried lurid pictures of woodsmen shot by arrows. 'The Gavião are absolutely savage Indians. They dominate the right bank of the Tocantins for a distance of some 500 kilometres [300 miles] . . . They have shown themselves to be so consummately perverse in their killings that panic now grips the inhabitants of small communities of the Tocantins.' One town's population was halved in a few years. 'In this climate of insecurity, the more enlightened people of the Tocantins villages are asking ironically that the Indian Protection Service be replaced by a Civilizados Protection Service.' Various people had been shot by the Gavião – one woodsman was 'transformed into a veritable human pin-cushion' with sixty-eight arrows in him. A train on the local railway was riddled with arrows, as in a Western movie; but when railway workers encountered Indians they repelled them with a barrage of gunfire.

The Gavião response was to fight back. They later told the anthropologist Expedito Arnaud that their natural inclination was to resolve conflicts by violence, both within the tribe and externally. Their legend about white men, kupen, was that these were descended from part of the tribe that had left to follow another deity, who transformed them, made them very numerous, and taught them to make guns from the shells of açaí palms and bullets from their seed kernels. 'Fathers sought to transmit their aversion of the kupen to their sons at an early age. They were reluctant to take boys on expeditions, because the kupen were not only bad but also ugly and should not be seen.'

Chief Krohokrenhum later told the anthropologist Iara Ferraz that the tribe reacted to the threat from the settlement frontier by fragmentation and internecine warfare. 'At that time it was fighting . . . Wretched people, we seemed like forest peccaries. We fought, wretchedly . . . We ran, alone, through the forests, without plantations or anything . . . We migrated all round here, on the run, only on the run, eating nothing but palm-hearts, nothing else. We looked like animals, with no territory and starving.'

Contact came in 1956. The Dominican friar Gil Gomes Leitão and Hilmar Kluck, an army lieutenant working for the SPI, organized an expedition to reach this group. They had to move fast, before punitive raids that were being armed by local politicians who wanted the Brazil-nut forests occupied by the Gavião. The once-warlike Gavião, disunited, scattered, and destitute, readily accepted peaceful contact with the well-meaning expedition.

After contact, this group spent some months at the town of Itupiranga, downstream of Marabá. The Indians eked out a living by fetching water or firewood or giving displays of their brilliant archery. Already under-nourished, these Gavião succumbed to Western diseases. Krohokrenhum recalled it as a terrible time. 'We arrived all emaciated. . . . There no one took medicine. It was dying, dying, dying, dying . . . I remember death. At one moment two died, at another three, one day four died. My mother died, my sister died, so I remained alone: I had nothing. My wife died, so I remained nothing and I thought "Ah, I will give all away." [In despair, he surrendered his beloved child.] I said [to the civilizado]: "You can look after it and raise it, I shall remain alone, because I know that I shall die!"'

This desperate band was saved in 1958 by Friar Gil Gomes. He brought food – 'coffee, sugar, manioc flour – ah! plenty of flour' – and sent four men to create a plantation of manioc and bananas. This raised the Indians' morale sufficiently for them to start their own farming. 'Now, we our-selves, how we worked! We made another clearing and planted it. Now our farm grew and went on growing. Friar Gil helped us for four years.' The Dominican handed over to the SPI, who brought medicines and more goods, but who left after a mere four months. The trouble was that the forests where the group took refuge were claimed by a state deputy called Benedito. He tolerated the Indians' presence; but it was a precarious arrangement.

Krohokrenhum's Gavião adversaries, who had driven them out of the tribal village on the Moju, appeared in 1958 at the Ambauá post: seventy people with their children, who remained for forty days. But soon afterwards a group of twelve warriors came, intent on revenge for past murders and for a lethal influenza epidemic that they considered (with some reason) to be due to white men's sorcery. Expedito Arnaud was present and saw that 'on the day of their arrival they appeared cheerful: they sang, danced and exchanged presents with the post's employees. But on the second day they began to adopt a more hostile attitude. They constantly challenged the staff to wrestling matches, spat in their faces, snatched plates of food from their hands, etc. On the third day, when those workers returned to work, they failed to ambush them, but fired many arrows at them from a distance, destroyed a barbed-wire fence, killed various pack animals, and disappeared into the forest.' The larger group returned to Ambauá on the Tucuruí three years later in 1961, to settle near the post. Disease had more than halved their numbers, to a mere thirty-one; and they feared extermination by Krohokrenhum's rival group who had by now acquired guns.

Different circumstances of contact rapidly changed the three parts of the Gavião tribe. Krohokrenhum's band found that, in their new forests, they were able to hunt jaguars and other animals for their skins and to collect Brazil nuts. Friar Gil Gomes and the SPI official Jaime Pimentel helped them sell this produce; but they soon grasped the use of money, learned Portuguese, and reckoned that they could do better by trading directly with frontiersmen. They shrewdly used force or the threat of force to evict nut collectors or land claimants from these forests; but there was constant friction.

Meanwhile, the group that took refuge at Ambauá post came to terms with life under SPI protection. In the first year they consumed a nine hectare (twenty-two acre) farm of maize and manioc; they took what they needed from the post and from surrounding settlers' houses (much to the latter's dismay); and the women even burned all the timbers of a hut before collecting firewood in the forest. The SPI agent persuaded them that they must earn money by selling animal skins and Brazil nuts, in order to buy the goods they now needed. They preferred to deal directly with settlers, except in selling Brazil nuts that the SPI had to transport to Belém. They became convinced that the Service was cheating them over the nuts, keeping the profit to pay for the upkeep of the post itself. The Gavião grew some of their traditional crops, but they refused to labour alongside the post's one or two workmen in growing the bulk of their food requirement. They argued that the SPI must continue to provide this support, as it had done at first contact.

Roberto da Matta in 1962 saw how quickly, and ruinously, the tribe sought to enter the market economy. Traditional barter and subsistence activities collapsed. 'Today, the life of the Gavião can be summarized as a constant struggle to produce a surplus in order to get a few cruzeiros with which to buy the objects that, to the Gavião, define the white way of life: toothbrushes, soap, towels, trousers, perfume, wallets, etc. . . . Things have reached the absurdity of seeing Indians who have some money, but who go hungry in their village because all their productive activity is directed toward the regional market of Itupiranga. Their objective is to buy things that could make them seem like Brazilians.' Some Indians despised old customs, and communal labour gave way to individual collecting from privately owned Brazil-nut trees. The nuts were of no value to the Gavião, except as a means of entering frontier society. And, of course, the Indians were cheated by merchants and insulted when they entered settlements.

Ever since 1943 the SPI had earmarked a reserve for the Gavião in an expanse of forest across the Tocantins from Marabá; but the Indians had not settled there. By 1966 this reserve, called Mãe Maria ('Mother Mary'), was about to be cut by a new road linking Marabá to the Belém–Brasília highway, and pressure from squatters was intensifying. The SPI worried that they would lose Mãe Maria if the Gavião did not occupy it. Jaime Pimentel of the SPI took Chief Krohokrenhum to inspect this land, promising him a life of plenty from its abundant Brazil-nut trees. Meanwhile Antonio Cotrim, one of the most idealistic and effective of the SPI's young sertanistas, persuaded another group of Gavião who were settled at Itupiranga to join their compatriots at Mãe Maria. The tribe built a row of huts, rectangular with pitched thatch roofs like those of the regional settlers. Carlos Moreira criticized the SPI's move of these Indians into Mãe Maria. He felt that they suffered disease 'as a result of the arbitrary and unjustifiable transfer of these Gavião onto the bank of the Tocantins, in a place open to the curiosity and constant visits of inhabitants of the region.'

The Mãe Maria reserve had been invaded by squatters. Prompted by the SPI, young warriors painted themselves in red urucum and went by night, talking loudly and firing their shotguns, to frighten off a group of these interlopers. Krohokrenhum recalled this psychological victory: 'They all left by night, abandoning their planting, abandoning everything! Off they went . . . We chucked out six chaps who lived there.'

Chief Krohokrenhum played a decisive role in the Gavião decision to come to terms with the whites. Born in about 1930, he was a natural leader whose prestige was enhanced by his ability as a singer and supreme skill as an archer. It was he who decided that the tribe had fallen so low that it could survive only by accommodation with frontier society. He also led the move to commercial gathering of Brazil nuts. Slim and ruggedly handsome, Krohokrenhum wore his hair in the traditional Timbira manner of a fringe across the forehead and hanging to his shoulders at the sides and back. He was a staunch upholder of tribal tradition, taking a lead in log races and other ceremonials. Iara Ferraz knew him well. 'The guardian of the integrity of the tribe's territory, . . . Krohokrenhum knows that dealings with the civilizados consist of "struggle, struggle, struggle . . . it never ends. The *kupen* think nothing of us . . . We are not real people to them, we might as well be beasts or dogs."'

As the turbulent years of contact elapsed, Krohokrenhum got the measure of his adversaries and proved a tough, astute negotiator over everything from pay for Brazil nuts to obtaining government subsidies. His firm leadership enhanced his prestige as the chief of all the Gavião.

His reward was an income from the tribe's Brazil-nut trade, and wealth by frontier standards. By 1972 he had a white-plastered three-room bungalow, with a couple of electric light bulbs, a butane-gas stove, sewing machine, bathroom, and $150-worth of plastic furniture. Chief Krohok-renhum's new lifestyle was complemented by an attractive young wife and children.

Missionaries also participated in the transformation of the Gavião. After Friar Gil's departure, there were sporadic contacts with the parish priests of Tucuruí, largely for baptisms. For five years, from 1965 to 1970, a Protestant of the New Tribes Mission vigorously taught basic schooling and, of course, Christianity. But when this missionary left, the Indians' enthusiasm for the new religion soon waned. For the young, a more powerful influence was weekly visits to the growing frontier town of Marabá, a few kilometres downriver of Mãe Maria on the far side of the Tocantins. Young men told the author that they had many friends there. They acquired smart clothes, most had Western haircuts (two with fashionably full heads of hair), and they survived this rapid change without resorting to drink as some other Indians did. But with no formal education they could not rise above the lowest level of frontier society, and they risked losing their indigenous heritage.

While the Gavião at Mãe Maria and at Ambauá were rapidly becoming acculturated, a third part of the tribe was uncontacted and uncontam-inated, living in forests far to the east, in the state of Maranhão not far from the city of Imperatriz. The Indian agency organized an attraction team under Antonio Cotrim Soares. With the few people at his disposal, Cotrim planned to make a rapid survey of the tribal area. 'Feeling that we had been discovered [by the Indians], I could do nothing but attempt a contact.' The Indians wanted peace and Cotrim handled the contact with sensitivity.

The spur road had duly been cut through Mãe Maria, and it led to invasions by log-cutters and settlers awarded illegal land titles. The Gavião tribal council complained repeatedly to the Indian agency. 'Cotrim made various promises to the Gavião that were guaranteed by Funai. For example, he said that white colonists would no longer approach the area. However, none of the promises was kept. The Gavião prepared for war . . . They started to attack and kill settlers.' In July 1969 Indians killed three whites in separate attacks on new farms, but they then behaved with restraint. There was panic in this frontier society, so that the local government moved fast, forbidding entry to the area and asking the police to remove settlers. Chief Korroty promised Cotrim that they would cease hostilities if he received a solid guarantee of their land.

Later in 1969 the SPI's successor Funai acted to prevent a supposed revenge massacre by the frontiersmen. It transferred the newly contacted Indians into the interior of the Mãe Maria reserve. This was a classic move, one repeated at other times in other parts of Brazil. It appeared as an emergency rescue mission; but its outcome was the violation of the Indians' constitutional right to lands on which they lived or hunted. The forests from which the Maranhão Gavião were moved were sold by the SPI to a property company: they were eventually occupied by some 15,000 families of settlers in dozens of hamlets. Even the local Mayor of Imperatriz condemned the property company for flagrant invasion of indigenous lands – 'the work of unscrupulous politicians, economic groups of the same ilk, and representatives of an inhuman power'. But the territory of the 'Maranhão' Gavião was lost.

The idealistic Antonio Cotrim resigned from the Indian Service soon after this, disgusted that the tribe had been cheated. He felt ashamed about his contact. 'In our approximation campaign, the Indians are steadily subjected to economic pressures and made dependent. For we create new needs for them, generally unnecessary goods such as clothing, mirrors, beads, or firearms. Our offers of peace are a decoy. In the first year, everything is given as a present. But in the second, they are invited to earn these same goods through the market economy, by organizing labour for which they have no preparation. Our society's experience of work has evolved over millennia: it cannot be instantly transmitted. Hence the Indians' reputation for laziness.' The more cynical SPI agent at Mãe Maria commented to the author: 'Ah, you have to promise things that you know cannot be granted. Pacification is a difficult business.'

The forest Gavião relocated into Mãe Maria, were initially housed at a place liable to flooding and riddled with malaria. Seeing them at that time, it was hard to appreciate that the tribe had fragmented little more than a decade earlier. The newcomers were in a pristine state, naked hunter-gatherers who maintained all the Timbira tribal customs and who contrasted dramatically to their acculturated and almost urbanized cousins. But within a few years, these 'Maranhão' Gavião acquired the trappings of frontier society – Western haircuts (but still with the trad-itional straw head-band), and shabby shorts for the men and dresses for the women. Most lived alongside the more civilizado branch of the tribe in the village above the Marabá–Belém road, crowded into three open-sided thatched shelters crammed with hammocks, fires, baskets, arrows, feather ornaments, gourds, and other artefacts of their customary society hanging from beams or stored on shelves. António Cotrim saw that their entire society was being shattered – their communal approach to work was replaced by materialistic individualism, beliefs were undermined, and family bonds, tribal solidarity, and personal relationships all suffered. When they complained to him, he had no answer to give them. He felt that he had unwittingly lured them into a trap.

The third fragment of the Gavião was still living far down the Tocantins at Ambaué, half an hour by boat from the town and rapids of Tucuruí. This was precisely the location of one of the Brazilian government's 'great projects', the construction of one of the world's largest hydroelectric dams. The Indian settlement would eventually be drowned beneath the gigantic reservoir above the Tucuruí dam. So, from 1971 onwards the Indian agency sought to move these Gavião into Mãe Maria, despite their reluctance to leave their homes or to mix with their former enemies of Krohokrenhum's group. Work on the dam started in 1974; but one family stubbornly remained at Ambaué under the formidable matriarch Rõnõre, known as Big Mamma. Her group was finally moved to Mãe Maria in 1977. They received derisory compensation – a few tools and boards with which to build themselves houses.

The Gavião were increasingly exasperated by having to sell their hard-won Brazil nuts through Funai. In 1975–76 the Indian Foundation made an enlightened move by engaging a young anthropologist, Iara Ferraz, to organize a community-development project for the Indians themselves to transport and market their nut harvest. Ferraz had little difficulty in empowering the astute Gavião, and her project 'eliminated the paternalistic nature of relations between Funai and the Indians'. Ferraz herself was dismissed at the end of 1976 for 'indiscipline', but the Brazil-nut scheme was too successful to be reversed. In 1977 the tribe obtained a bank loan to improve its commercial operation; it soon had twenty Brazilian employees, and it expelled its Funai agent when he tried to intervene. But trading income was handled collectively and used to reinforce tribal traditions and control of what remained of its land. Alcida Ramos saw the Gavião case as 'a most clear-cut instance of economic integration of an Indian community into the national economy – via one of its regional markets – without a loss of ethnic identity'.

When the SPI was created in 1910, it hoped to achieve the pacification of a mysterious people that lived in the forests of the upper Gurupi and Turiaçu rivers, near the boundary between the states of Pará and Maranhão. These people were known to other Tupi-speakers as the Urubu ('Vultures'), but they refer to themselves as Kaapor (pronounced Ka'apor, with a glottal stop, and meaning 'Forest people' or literally 'Footprints of the forest'). A naturalist wrote at that time that 'the upper Turiaçu is a mystery. The denseness of the forests, the problems of navigation, and hostility of the Indians have impeded not only colonization but even simple exploration. To the north, the great forest is cut by a road [the Belém–São Luís, now called BR-316] and a telegraph line ... Tragic incidents between savages and civilizados mark the history of this road.'

For sixteen years to 1928, the SPI agent Lieutenant Pedro Dantas tried the traditional method of leaving presents – metal tools, cloth, beads – on sandbanks and other places frequented by the Kaapor. His efforts started well. But the attraction was frustrated by lack of continuity, the legacy of three centuries of violence (the first attempt to wipe out these Tupi-speakers had occurred when the Portuguese first entered this region in the early seventeenth century), and the usual hostility of frontiersmen. A local newspaper reported that a manager of the telegraph line, João Grande, organized atrocious raids against the Kaapor and stuck the heads of his victims on telegraph poles to deter any interference with his installations. An old settler woman told the American anthropologist-naturalist William Balée that she recalled several posses against the tribe in the 1920s. Women and children were killed in these attacks. On one occasion Indians fired at an SPI team, wounding a young worker. They were retaliating for a 'famous massacre of the Indians of the Alto Turi, planned and executed by so-called civilizados who invited them to lunch and then cowardly pounced on them while the trusting Indians were peacefully eating.'

The vendetta raged. Year after year, SPI reports told of Kaapor attacks on outposts of collectors of forest products, mining prospectors, and timber men, as well as on boats moving along the rivers. Kaapor raids were to obtain machetes and manufactured goods, particularly since the tribe now made metal arrowheads. One such attack was on the Gonçalves Dias Indian post on the Pindaré, inhabited by peaceful Guajajara. As the Kaapor emerged from the forest, the Guajajara asked them, in Tupi, what they wanted. 'In response, they received a volley of arrows.' The raiders started to ransack the post's huts; the Guajajara fired guns, first into the air and then directly at the Kaapor, wounding one Indian. The SPI agent ran up in time to hear 'a loud shouting and [see] a troop of many people spread out running along the riverbank, among them the wounded man, who even thus did not abandon the objects taken from a sacked house.'

Such operations were so efficient and covered so wide an area that settlers imagined either that they were planned by an escaped convict, or that a nebulous figure called Jorge Cochrane Amir was provoking Indian hostility so that he could control rich gold deposits in those forested hills, or that the Kaapor were mixed with descendants of runaway black slaves.

Punitive raids were organized. In 1922 the police chief of Peralva took fifty-six heavily armed men into the upper Turi. After six days' march, they attacked a Kaapor village but killed only two men before the rest escaped. The Indians returned next morning and fired many arrows at the assailants, who eventually withdrew after setting fire to the village and destroying its plantations.

Pacification work was resumed in 1927. Miguel Silva of the SPI knew the region and decided to found an attraction post, named after his predecessor Pedro Dantas, on an island where the Kaapor used to cross the Gurupi. Trails were cut into the forest and shelters filled with presents. But the Indians destroyed the shelters and all the presents apart from some metal medallions, which they presumably used for arrowheads. A Tembé who worked for the post was killed by an arrow while paddling its boat; and soon afterwards another worker was hit in the jaw. The acculturated Tembé became 'the principal intermediaries between the "Christians" and the Kaapor. They served the SPI as guides, paddlers, and labourers in the roça gardens and manioc-flour houses – for manioc flour was an important element in attracting the Kaapor.' The new campaign started to work. On four occasions presents were removed, and in December 1927 some Kaapor appeared on a riverbank and accepted gifts directly from the crew of a boat sent across to them. In 1928 the Kaapor kept the post under observation and accepted more presents. There were shouted exchanges between forest Indians and the SPI's Tembé. 'Some [Kaapor] made signals . . . and left wooden models of machetes and knives to make it known that they needed these objects; with which we complied.' The first women visited the post in July – elderly women, trembling with fear. One old lady crossed the river with her son. 'She came with a heavy catarrh and, as she entered the hut, spat out phlegm that she caught in her hand and used to anoint her hair. This old woman was offered a cup of coffee, which she took as a form of medicine. It was the first food accepted [directly] by them, and from then onwards they started to accept coffee as a remedy, sugar, salt, and tobacco.' In November some Indians 'at great cost allowed themselves to be photographed'; eight people came on the 5th and 'danced and sang as thanks for the presents they had received'. By the end of 1928 large groups of up to eighty men visited Pedro Dantas post. Vast quantities of presents – axes, machetes, knives, pans, beads, and many other objects – were taken upriver and given to an estimated 2,000 Indians.

The attraction was going so well that the SPI regional head, Soera Mesquita (whom Darcy Ribeiro described as cowardly, ineffectual, and drunken), decided to flaunt his success by taking five Indians first to the town of Vizeu and then to the city of Belém. On the return journey these 'trophies' succumbed to influenza. Two died during the river trip and the other three were gravely ill when the agent Benedito Araújo (a competent and good man) brought them back to their lands. Another group of twenty-five Indians who had visited a local town in a gesture of friendship also caught flu and contaminated their village. There was then an outbreak of malaria throughout the Gurupi valley, which struck Indians and frontiersmen alike. Darcy Ribeiro, who studied the Kaapor in the 1950s, reckoned that half their entire population died in the terrible epidemics of 1929.

The son of Chief Arara died at the post, after taking medicine from Araújo. An Indian called Oropok, who had lost two wives, decided to make a desperate act of revenge for these tragedies. He appeared alone at the post and, contrary to its rules, was allowed to enter with his bow and arrows. He went up to the main hut and called for Araújo. 'This man, with his customary benevolence and blind trust, offered the Indian a bench to sit on, and started to ask him questions. The Indian then showed the agent a very broad-headed arrow, saying that it was for hunting tapir. He fixed that arrow into his bow, aimed it towards the garden, and said "Araú[jo] is a tapir". Drawing the bow with all his strength, he suddenly turned his aim and fired the arrow at Araújo's chest. He fell dead without a murmur.' The distraught Indian went on to wound the Timbira Marcolino who had been Araújo's interpreter, before vanishing into the forest. Obeying Rondon's general instruction to die if you must but never kill, no one on the post fired at Oropok. He lived on in an isolated village in the upper Turiaçu, never again came to an SPI post, and refused a visit by Darcy Ribeiro two decades later.

While the SPI was claiming a successful pacification on the Gurupi, other Kaapor also achieved a ceasefire with settlers at the town of Alto Turi. Several Indians appeared at the edge of the nearby forest and, as William Balée later learned, 'the men turned the points of their arrows to the ground, symbolizing their friendly intent. They shouted "*Katu kamarar, Katu kamarar!*" ("Greetings comrades, Greetings comrades!"). "*Yane katu apo*" ("We are now peaceful"). A few of these Kaapor men spent the night in the town, amid the *karaí* [whites]. The "time of rage" (*parahi-wa-rahã*) had ended. Although the Kaapor were said to be "pacified", in Kaapor lore it was a *Pa'i* (priest), one of their own, who "pacified" (*mukatu*) the savage non-Indians.'

When they accepted the presents and friendship of SPI agents, the Kaapor could scarcely appreciate that they were crossing a rubicon in their tribe's history. As Balée observed, the year 1928 marked an irrevocable break with the past in Kaapor history . . . First, the Kaapor raiding complex abruptly ended, bringing relief to the settlers and many Kaapor (the women especially were said to be, by one elderly female informant, *huri-riki* ('very happy') with the end of hostilities). Second, the cessation of hostilities was perceived by many Kaapor to bring new economic opportunities. Instead of risking their lives to obtain steel tools, the Kaapor now received them free of charge . . . In 1928 the Kaapor surely had no idea that accepting gifts from SPI agents would constitute the end of their socio-political auton-omy. And they could not anticipate the massive depopulation they would suffer from introduced diseases. Finally, they could not then have predicted that activities of the Luso-Brazilian frontier, so long held in check by the uncompromising hostility of their ancestors, would expand into their eastern and southern border lands during the 1960s and throughout the 1980s. A new and fearful order had come into being, and the earlier inbuilt defenses of the indigenous society would be worn away.

The first shock was the ending of free gifts. Once a newly contacted tribe was reckoned to be 'tame', government largesse was no longer necessary. The Indians had acquired an appetite for axes, machetes, and other manufactured goods. But these were no longer given to them: they would henceforth have to earn them. 'They were told that they must pay in labor, native crafts, game meat, agricultural produce, or anything else that had a commercial value.' In 1943 some priests from Bragança visited the Kaapor post Felipe Camarão and were full of admiration for the way in which its SPI agent Miguel Pereira da Silva, who had worked there for over thirty years, patiently 'instilled a love of work in the Indians and counselled them with fatherly affection'.

Next came the trauma of depopulation. Estimates of Kaapor numbers at the time of contact varied between 2,000 and 5,000. Fifteen years later in 1943, a detailed SPI census showed that they were down to 1,095. In 1949 a group went to trade in the town of Bragança and brought back measles. Darcy Ribeiro witnessed the impact of this new disease.

The epidemic . . . spread rapidly. The first aldeia we reached was deserted. All its inhabitants had fled, imagining that the disease was a supernatural being that had attacked the village and could be avoided if they escaped far away. We went to meet them camped in the forest, fleeing the disease but still being attacked by it. When they arrived there, some Indians still had the strength to erect palm-leaf shelters above their hammocks; but the majority were prostrated by the illness and lay in the open, burning with fever under the rain. Ravaged by the measles and complications such as eye sores and lung and intestinal disorders, they were reduced to such a pitch of organic impoverishment that they no longer had the energy to reach the extensive plantations they had left at their village, in order to fetch food; and they could not even find water. They were dying of hunger and thirst as well as from the disease. Sick children rolled on the ground trying to stoke the fires from which they warmed themselves in the rain. Their parents were consumed with fever and could do nothing. Mothers, scarcely conscious, repelled their infants when they sought to be suckled.

Ribeiro wrote to his wife:

I have never seen anything more horrible. They have nothing to eat, because no one can go to the roça to harvest manioc and grate it, nor hunt, nor fish, nor gather fruit or anything. None can even fetch water . . . The saddest is José. The strongest Indian in all the Jararaca villages, famous for his gigantic body, with a round face framed in a mane of hair, whom everyone wanted to watch dancing to a tambourine, he was now moribund and weighed barely forty kilos [88 pounds] . . . This giant's little wife was coiled around what was left of him, crying at hurting him.

This epidemic killed 170 people, almost a quarter of the reduced Kaapor population.

More horrors were to follow. William Balée studied the reports of João Carvalho, a legendary SPI agent at Canindé post, and read that he constantly begged for more medical supplies to help his charges. Respiratory diseases (influenza, pneumonia, and tuberculosis) were always a serious threat. In January 1954, Carvalho reported that 'malaria is spreading, both at the post and in the villages, and we do not have enough medicine'. Four years later came a form of flu whose symptoms were fever, chest pain, excruciating headache, bleeding at the nose and mouth, and then pus from the lungs. Healthy Indians were killed in a couple of days. All these afflictions halved the group's population between 1955 and 1975, from 912 to 488 people.

Unfortunately, Kaapor custom tended to keep the population low to achieve ecological equilibrium. Mothers wanted to look after only one child at a time, and they carried infants with them even when farming in the plantations, drawing water or travelling with their men. So the Kaapor spaced pregnancies by four or five years, by contraception using coitus interruptus, abortion from herbal drinks or chewing toxic roots, and years of breastfeeding. The tribe could not quickly change such practices to rebuild its numbers after the catastrophic depopulation from disease.

The British anthropologist Francis Huxley was with the Kaapor at this time. It took him ten days by boat to go up the Gurupi to Canindé. He found the post 'a handsome place. The bank has been cleared of its jungle and planted with palm trees, with guava trees and a lone jack tree . . . There is a large barn with a corrugated iron roof and no sides, where manioc flour is prepared' on a clay and copper oven. The post's other machinery was a sugar mill and a steam-driven rice husker. The main building was 'a large wooden house with a tiled roof, a wooden plank floor and a spacious veranda. Here João Carvalho lives with his family.' Behind was a row of palm-thatched huts for the workers and their families. 'In the middle is the earth-closet, a fine building usually occupied by goats.' Huxley and Ribeiro both admired João Carvalho. He was a good example of an SPI official: fond of the Indians with whom he had lived for so many years, plying the river to take their produce to market, disinterested in his dealings with them, and officiating at ceremonies such as baptisms.

Contact with Brazilians brought social upheaval. Kaapor society had been based on the glories of fighting. A great warrior was supreme. Francis Huxley found that the tribe spoke constantly of 'hardening' men and women by often painful rituals, or harking back to the glorious days of warfare. When hostilities (against either Brazilian settlers or enfeebled neighbouring tribes) ceased, young men could no longer prove themselves in battle and trophies ceased. So young Kaapor would walk for vast distances to visit Brazilian cities, as a way of proving their manhood. Others wanted to be farm labourers, partly because they were bored with inactivity in their peaceful village, but they soon became disillusioned by the drudgery of such labour.

The SPI introduced the tribe to trade, but at first the Indians were grossly cheated by the settlers. They would trade arrows, which were now superfluous for warfare, for a few fish-hooks or old clothes. The Kaapor are famous for making the most beautiful feather ornaments of any Brazilian tribe – delicate, jewellery-like creations often of tiny iridescent feathers. Darcy Ribeiro wrote that 'all people here use ornaments: bead necklaces, bracelets, fillets [hair bands], anklets of feathers, even combs decorated with plumes and beautiful hummingbird ear-pendants. Even the dogs wear collars of pieces of wood interlaced with bones. Pets are innumerable. Every couple has some – mutum [curassow, or wild turkey], monkeys, various species of parrot, macaw, and parakeet, trumpeter birds – all with human names, treated with much affection, and they too wearing ornaments.' But these treasures were only for ceremonies or personal use, and were then cast off or traded for trivial sums. Perhaps rightly, the Kaapor could never be persuaded to make their most dazzling confections purely for sale.

William Balée made a famous study of Kaapor farming, which showed them to be brilliant horticulturalists. The Kaapor know the plants of their forests intimately and they waste nothing. Balée identified tribal names for a remarkable eighty-three cultivated or domesticated plants. He divided their farming into four types of plot: 'house gardens', in which 93 per cent of plant species are managed; 'young swidden' (newly opened slash-and-burn clearings), of which half was managed; 'old swidden', with only a quarter managed; and 'fallow', where no plants are managed but the sites are periodically revisited and harvested. In the roças that Balée called 'young swiddens' there was an apparently haphazard jumble, with half the species planted and the rest spontaneous herbs, shrubs, and vines. But of fifty-six common plant species collected in such a clearing, the Kaapor had a use for every single one – either as human food, game fodder, a technological use such as making rope or fish poison, personal adornment, magic and medicine, and (recently) rice for sale to outsiders.

When this tribe foraged in apparently virgin forest, it was in fact exploiting an ecosystem that had been altered by them over many centuries. 'Forest management entails a broad spectrum of activities; the Ka'apor manipulate animals as well as plants in this process. Ka'apor forest management involves neither destruction of the forest nor the complete avoidance of the forest. Ka'apor forest management is, rather, a clear example of "intermediate disturbance" which evidently makes possible the sustainable use of vegetational zones in different phases of recovery.' As time goes by, these Indians change the forests near their villages to make them more productive. They create dense patches of useful plants, which in turn attract desirable animals; and they evolve vegetation zones in which such plants and animals thrive. Their artificial biotic niches have, over the centuries, become what he calls 'anthropogenic forests'. Evidence of such manipulation is in a layer of ash or even potsherds on the floor of apparently pristine forest, and an unnatural abundance of palms, lianas, and fruit trees.

Individual Kaapor reacted differently to the trauma of contact. A chief called Uirá went to the city of São Luis do Maranhão to seek the tribe's legendary creator Maíra, because he had lost a child. Uirá was arrested on the city's streets, imprisoned, and beaten because of his nudity. Back at the SPI post, he handed his chief's regalia to his son, with the words: '"My son, a chief is not thrashed. You return with your mother; your father cannot go on living after being beaten by the whites."' Chief Uirá then committed suicide by jumping into a river filled with piranha. Another Kaapor called Kosó, whom Ribeiro knew well, lost his wife and children in an epidemic and had a vision of his dead father. The anguish of these deaths made Kosó 'retire to his hammock and, in one day, give up the ghost, even though he was young and vigorous'.

9. The Rise and Fall of the Indian Protection Service

The youthful enthusiasm of the Indian Protection Service soon evaporated. This was partly due to the dispersal of Cândido Rondon's team of idealistic volunteers, most of them elite army officers, but the main causes were political and financial. By 1923, Major Alípio Bandeira had to write a passionate defence of the SPI against a deputy who accused the Service of being a 'scandalous bluff' that consumed 'sumptuous funds' on useless Indians. Bandeira showed that the SPI cost only 0.1 per cent of the Brazilian federal budget. Its turnover of some US $130,000 compared dramatically with that of the United States, which spent thirty-three times that amount on only 200,000 indigenous people. On this tiny allowance, the SPI was maintaining thirty-one posts and four Indian settlements, as well as conducting several attraction campaigns. It was active in exploring new areas, surveying and demarcating the impossibly remote boundaries of its reserves, training Indians in agricultural techniques, and providing basic education. Helped by this counter-attack, the Service's funding improved during the later 1920s.

Alípio Bandeira was co-author of a memorial that argued for a different legal status for Indians. Instead of the SPI's original concept of indigenous people being in a state of transition between primitive wildness and full citizenship, the authors wanted the state to acknowledge tutelage over Indians as separate communities within the Brazilian nation. The relative civil capacity of each tribe differed according to its degree of 'civilization'. To a large extent, this new status was recognized in a Law of 27 June 1928. Tribes were divided into four stages: nomadic; settled in villages or malocas; protected in SPI Indian posts; and integrated among civilizados. The word 'Indian' acquired legal meaning and tribal custom took precedence over national law. Thus, a tribe was allowed to practise infanticide or even ritual execution of members deemed spiritually dangerous. The price for such exemption was that individuals in tribal communities became legal minors, without the rights or obligations of Brazilian citizens. The federal SPI – rather than missionaries or other authorities – was given full power over them. However, indigenous territories were considered as

terras devolutas or unoccupied lands and therefore came under the control
of states rather than the federal government. The SPI therefore had to beg
each state for the territory that rightfully belonged to its Indians.

The Service was bedevilled by contradictions. It justified contacts with
isolated tribes in order to save them from the advance of the colonization
frontier. But success in 'pacifying' hostile groups meant that Indians
were unable to defend themselves against invasion by settlers. The SPI's
'triumphs of pacification' removed the threat from tribal warriors – but
this meant that politicians and business lobbies lost interest in its work.
Immediately after contact, the SPI continued to give Indians the goods
that had helped to pacify them; but this produced an attitude of perpetual
dependence, and it was too expensive. So the flow of presents abruptly
ceased.

At its foundation, one of the Service's missions was to turn Indians into
productive citizens. But this meant persuading self-sufficient and skilled
hunter-gatherers to become labourers at the base of a capitalist economy.
Indians were shrewd enough to appreciate that they lost heavily in this
process, and most had no desire to abandon proven customs.

Darcy Ribeiro (who rose to a senior position in the SPI and then
became Minister of Education) commented that in theory 'the economy
of an Indian post is primarily a means of organizing Indian production,
with the purpose of assuring them a higher standard of living.' Of course
it did not work like that. Contacted Indians acquired desires for some
basic commodities: metal tools, fats and salt, clothes and soap, guns and
ammunition, and medicine. 'The price of satisfying these new wants that
we create for the Indians is their final submission to our system of
production. This almost always means their enslavement, their subjection
under extortionate conditions, the disintegration of tribal life, demoralization, and disappearance.'

Starved of resources, SPI posts were supposed to pay their own way
from a profit generated by their charges. The Indian Service was always
open to the accusation of exploiting the natives and trafficking in their
produce – just as Jesuit missionaries had done two centuries earlier. 'The
most serious problem of Indian protection was to reconcile a collective
tribal economy with a system of private enterprise.' According to their
terrain, Indians were encouraged either to raise cattle, to gather forest
produce like Brazil nuts and rubber, or to farm. Not surprisingly, tribes
changing to settler-style agriculture (even with help from some machinery) usually produced less than they had before contact. This was because
the group lost its collective spirit of organization and mutual help; hunting
skills were ignored; women, children, and hunters worked less; and the

fragile tropical soil of a settled tribe became exhausted. Ribeiro concluded: 'I know of no single Indian post or religious mission that has satisfactorily responded to this challenge.'

Recruitment to the SPI was always a problem. Rondon had sought to imbue the Service with his love of Indians and respect for their way of life. His followers from the telegraph commission were dedicated officers concerned to preserve native beliefs and customs. But such conservation was a delicate and difficult task, and later SPI officials failed to appreciate its importance.

During its first twenty years the SPI struggled on, 'alternately elevated and depressed in the results and efficiency of its posts . . . due to fluctuations in the funds voted each year for the Service.' A later head of the Service recalled its chaotic finances: 'In 1913, for instance, its funds were 2,200 *contos* [2.2 million cruzeiros], only to fall brusquely to a mere 800 *contos* in 1914. In 1930 its grant was 3,880 *contos*, which was reduced to 1,560 the following year!'

A further blow was the removal of General Rondon from his Indian Service. In 1923 there was a rebellion in Brazil's southernmost states, and in the following year the rebels briefly occupied the city of São Paulo. A force of 12,000 troops loyal to the President of Brazil was sent to attack them in their southern strongholds, and this was led by General Rondon. He described this assignment as 'the most difficult undertaking of my entire life'. As a devoted army officer, Rondon hated having his men fight their 'brothers' in Brazilian army uniform, but he succeeded in crushing the last rebel redoubt. A force of rebels escaped and went on the five-year 'long march' of the 'Coluna Prestes', a column led by the charismatic Captain Luis Carlos Prestes that inspired the poor of the Brazilian interior and became a legend in Brazilian revolutionary history.

In 1927 the sixty-two-year-old Rondon received orders to 'proceed with a detailed inspection of the frontiers of our country, to study the conditions for their settlement and security'. The General accepted with enthusiasm, reassembled some of his original team of expeditionary officers, and embarked for the remotest fastnesses of Amazonia. He divided Brazil's immense and often unexplored frontiers between teams, and he himself led the northernmost group on the frontiers of Venezuela and British Guiana. The seven years of this frontier inspection brought Rondon back into direct contact with Indians. He was greeted as a revered protector by tribe after tribe. Rondon organized assemblies of chiefs of semi-acculturated groups such as the Wapixana and Makuxi of Roraima (then called Rio Branco) and was often able to redress their grievances or prevent oppression by local officials or frontiersmen. The tough old general climbed Mount Roraima, an ancient 2,810 metre (9,220 foot) sandstone table mountain at Brazil's northern extremity. He ascended many rapids on the Uraricoera river to carve his name in a rock at the foot of the Purumame waterfall, in uninhabited forests at the western end of Maracá island. He then moved eastwards, to visit the Purukotó, Tiriyó, and other groups near the frontiers with Dutch Suriname and French Guyana. All welcomed him warmly. Rondon repeated his calls for good treatment of the Indians: 'expelled from the land of which they were legitimate owners by invaders who came with signs of peace, only to bring blood, ruin, destruction. These people are the most deserving of our benevolence.'

As part of his frontier inspection, Rondon also travelled to the border with Uruguay at the southernmost extremity of Brazil. By bad luck, this brought him into the midst of the 'Liberal Revolution' of 1930. The revolutionaries, led by Getúlio Vargas, captured Rondon and briefly held him prisoner in the capital of Rio Grande do Sul. Vargas triumphed, went on to be elected President for successive terms, and became virtual dictator of Brazil until 1945. This brought the urban-industrial bourgeoisie to power, replacing the feudal barons of the states. Identified with the old order and opposed to Vargas's new politics, Rondon wanted to retire from active service. He tried to remain neutral, feeling that Brazil's problems were moral rather than political. Rondon himself was accused of irregularities. He asked to be allowed to clear his name, but Vargas refused and ordered the General to continue his frontier inspection.

The SPI's budget, halved in 1931, then dropped steadily until 1939. Throughout that decade the Service suffered 'a decline, a veritable collapse of its vitality, which had been becoming so exuberant and promising.' The SPI's internal bulletin later described this as 'the phase of absolute misery of the SPI' when it operated 'without organization or funds'. Pity the SPI, the unloved Indian Protection Service. It withered into near-terminal decline because its founder and mentor, Rondon, had fallen foul of President Vargas.

An official wrote later: 'We can still sadly recall the collapse into which the Service fell between 1930 and 1939, and the sad consequences for the Brazilian Indians entrusted to it.' Rondon lamented that the SPI 'preserved only a few of the sixty Indian posts' originally founded throughout Brazil. The posts that survived did so because they had been 'prepared for self-sufficiency by the foresight and capability of an individual inspector or agent. Such a man succeeded in getting the Indians to give the cooperation that was essential for our work to continue throughout the crisis.' Officials struggled on in their posts, 'isolated, lacking resources, sharing the discomfort and privation of their Indians.'

The impoverished Service became a political football. For a time it came under the Ministry of Trade and Employment; and in 1934 it was transferred to the Ministry of War as a department of the Frontier Inspectorate. It was felt that Indians might be enlisted to protect Brazil's remote forested frontiers. Rondon argued that 'the army will find in them the best elements to serve the nation where it needs them most: to guard the frontiers.' 'Because of their moral qualities, physical robustness and adaptability to environment, it would be advantageous to use and educate [Indians] by suitable methods, attracting them to our nation before neighbouring countries attract them to theirs.'

Catholic and Protestant missionaries exploited the SPI's weakness during the 1930s. 'In some Indian villages, foreign [religious] organizations illegally erected buildings for worship, without licence or authorization – which, in any case, no SPI servant could grant . . . There were posts in which a missionary or priest resided permanently in the administration house and used its buildings for his preaching or cult. In others, the [SPI's] own agent takes the initiative and . . . *invites* the Indians to attend the respective ceremonies.' Rondon, as a Positivist, opposed such missionary opportunism. Curtailment of proselytizing 'will give Indians the capacity to make the best use of their race's natural endowments in basic qualities of character.'

Rondon started to mend his differences with President Vargas. In 1934 he was appointed to oversee the arbitration, for the League of Nations, of a boundary dispute between Peru and Colombia. Four years later, he was officially praised for his diplomatic success, which resulted in Colombia's panhandle to Leticia on the Amazon river.

Surprisingly, a new Constitution in 1934 was the first to contain policy about Indian territory that was based on SPI ideals. Article 129 respected tribal right to land on which it was permanently located and made such control inalienable. Indian affairs were also removed from Brazil's states and made a purely federal concern. These pro-Indian clauses were repeated in another Constitution in 1937 and in the liberal-democratic Constitution of 1946. All subsequent national codes of law have contained clauses to protect indigenous lands, and this has been of fundamental importance to Indian sympathizers in fighting for their rights. However, there were flaws in these constitutions. Land was held by the SPI as protector of tribes – it did not actually belong to the Indians themselves, nor was it held collectively by them. And most SPI reserves were ill-defined, did not have demarcated boundaries, and were not entered in land registries. A great many tribes had no legal definition to their territories, and scores were still uncontacted.

A decree of 6 April 1936 gave new regulations to the SPI. Its duty to protect and help the Indians was reiterated. But damaging new measures were proposed 'to nationalize the Indians, with a view to incorporating them into Brazilian society'. This was to be achieved by teaching indigenous people basic civic duties, symbolized by the cult of the flag, singing the national anthem, and other patriotic rituals that Rondon had emphasized since the start of the SPI. Primary education was intended to undermine native cultures. When a senior SPI official visited a post in southern Brazil in 1941, he was delighted by what he saw in its school. 'All the benches were filled. One saw tiny Indians, who would have been in a kindergarten had they lived in a city, alongside almost adult Indians. They received us cheerfully. They sang the national anthem, the prayer to the flag, and a school song "I Am a Brazilian" in as correct a manner as I have seen in few schools in big cities. During the hour I attended the class, there was an excellent demonstration of progress in reading, language, writing, geography, rudiments of national history, arithmetic, and civic education.' Perhaps fortunately for indigenous cultures, such 'model' schools were rare and short-lived.

The Regulation of 1936 said that tribal lands could be occupied 'in the national interest'. However, it also sensibly insisted that 'protection, assistance, defence, or aid' should be given to Indians in the lands they inhabit, and the SPI should prevent them from drifting into colonial frontier towns as 'urban nomads'.

President Getúlio Vargas was impressed by the rise of the fascist dictatorships in Europe. In 1937 he dismissed Congress, disbanded political parties, and formed the Estado Novo ('New State'), which sought to create a more independent and unified Brazil. In that same year, he proclaimed a 'March to the West' to open Brazil's great hinterland. This was launched amid maximum publicity, with its own Carnival samba and music by Hector Villa-Lobos. A new Department of Press and Propaganda stressed the national identity. This included rediscovery of the Indians, who were projected as romantic figures, the true roots of 'Brazilianness'.

General Rondon was back in favour after his success in the arbitration between Peru and Colombia and returned to the public eye, making powerful speeches. In August 1938 he demanded that indigenous Brazilians should enjoy the same rights as foreign immigrants, 'namely respect for property, sanctity of the home, enjoyment of paternal power, and the guarantee of personal freedom including liberty of conscience.' In

September of the following year, Rondon lamented the eclipse of the SPI after the revolution of 1930. He mentioned in particular how the thriving post among the Karajá on Bananal had been abandoned – the decay witnessed by Peter Fleming. Rondon begged the government to reorganize and revitalize the Service.

There was a surge of pro-Indian sentiment throughout the Americas at this time, and Brazil was considered to be a model of good treatment of its native peoples. President Vargas started to change his mind about Indians. He saw them as the romantic embodiment of the Brazilian national identity he was seeking to inculcate. A decree of 3 November 1939 again placed the SPI under the Ministry of Agriculture, because Indians were still regarded as potential agricultural colonists in the country's 'March to the West'. This decree said that 'the problem of protection of Indians is intimately linked to colonization, for in a material sense it involves orienting and interesting the Indians in cultivation of the soil, so that they will become useful to the nation and can collaborate with the civilized populations involved in farming.' This was a return to discredited notions at the start of the Indian Service.

However, the government also created a National Council for the Protection of Indians (CNPI). Rondon was promoted to Marshal and named as President of this new think-tank, which was intended to be the intellectual guide for indigenous policy. It contained some of the country's most enlightened anthropologists and champions of native Brazilians. In his first speech as President of the CNPI, Marshal Rondon described its mission to study 'material forms of Indian life – habits, customs and language, social and political organization, commerce, industry and other development, the arts – in short, all manifestations of Indian intelligence'. In addition, the CNPI would be the link between the SPI and government policy. All this represented a sensible shift in official attitudes. It was tacitly admitted that Indians might never 'progress' smoothly to full Brazilian citizenship. Ethnographic study of the finer points of tribal societies raised their prestige. In the useful Portuguese word, native customs were '*valorizado*' – their true value was appreciated. It was also important for the SPI to catch up with advances in anthropology, since for its first thirty years it had adhered too rigidly to Positivist principles. John Collier, who ran the US Bureau of Indian Affairs, unreservedly praised the SPI at this time because of its protection of indigenous cultures and lands and its humanitarian philosophy.

In the following year, Marshal Rondon outlined his approach to treatment of Indians. This was a mixture of enlightenment and the old aspirations to turn natives into successful farmers or farm labourers.

Rondon insisted that Indian lands should be demarcated, in accordance with Article 154 of the Constitution, and that people must be left in their habitats. But he then laid down six 'norms' for 'making the most' of Indians. These included such dubious notions as: 'Create new needs among the Indians . . . [and then] induce [them] to work that suits them and that yields resources to buy the articles that fulfil their needs.' Rondon went on to recommend that lands be 'prepared for labour' and was confident that 'their output should naturally increase, because of [agricultural] training, the help given by tools, and to meet the growing needs of the Indians [for items such as] cloth, weapons, decorations and dresses for the women, etc.'. Their trade should then be organized, in such a way as 'to avoid the introduction of alcohol or cheating by civilizados . . . Only in these ways will the Indians come to us; and it will not take long.'

In later years, as he grew old, Rondon admitted that the SPI's early attempts to train Indians to evolve into 'civilized' Brazilians were flawed. He acknowledged that the indigenous way of life was often far superior to the brutal attitudes of the colonization frontier and that Indians who left their tribes sacrificed a more genuine (and environmentally better) existence but gained nothing.

The year 1939 also saw the first chair of Brazilian Ethnology created at a college in São Paulo. Herbert Baldus, who taught in this school, argued that by studying native society ethnologists could propose appropriate policy and legislation. The role of ethnology was 'to cushion the shock caused by the encounter of such different groups of human beings'. By protecting Indians' health and respecting tribal customs, they could be shielded from the dangers and excesses of frontier society.

In 1940 Vargas became the first Brazilian President to see an Indian village. He was on his way to a fishing safari on the Araguaia river, during which he was filmed flying over a village of 'extremely ferocious Xavante' before landing at the Karajá post on Bananal Island. The Indians performed ritual dances, and sang the national anthem in front of a Brazilian flag. The President was charmed by the Karajá. His propaganda department issued a picture of the paunchy President, in a white shirt and a solar topee, holding a cigar in one hand and smiling down at a chubby, naked, glowering Karajá baby in the other.

The American anthropologist Seth Garfield has chronicled an extraordinary propaganda campaign involving Indians. 'In a veritable blitz, the state organized museum exhibitions, radio programmes, speeches and films about the Indians . . . During the Estado Novo, the state orchestrated or promoted an Indian discourse that resonated with all the issues abuzz in world politics at the time: racism, xenophobia and chauvinism.'

Rondon entered into the spirit of this campaign. In September 1940 he made a speech about the March to the West and the Indians' contribution to the greatness of Brazil. Warming to this theme, he praised the 'resistance, bravery, generosity, and modesty brought by the Indians to the formation of our people'. Other intellectuals joined in. The great sociologist Gilberto Freyre listed the many ways in which Indians had influenced modern Brazilians – innumerable place names, foods, hammocks, even carrying a comb for frequent grooming. Angyone Costa urged his readers to value the Indians because they loved the land of which they were the first lords. Affonso Arinos de Mello Franco showed how early Europeans imagined Brazilian Indians as noble savages living in an earthly utopia apparently devoid of kings, laws, or clergy – a subversive message that influenced philosophers right up to the French Revolution and Karl Marx. The SPI claimed that the Indian soul was 'superior to the European in temperament, in patient energy, and even, in truth, in justice and charity'. Indian cleanliness and physiques were praised as 'comparable to masculine beauty of the Greeks of the Olympics'. After the War, native warriors were seen as 'sentinels' to protect Brazilian frontiers against hordes of starving refugees from Europe.

In 1943 Vargas declared 19 April as 'The Day of the Indian'. Rondon gave fulsome praise to the President. He declared that, after a decade of neglect of the SPI, 'Dr Getúlio Vargas recognized, after long and reflective observation, the injustice of the calumnious imputations launched against the Service by clerics, and decided to give it decisive support. He created the CNPI. He decided to go in person to visit the secular village of the Karajá and Javaé Indians on Bananal Island in the Araguaia river. Since then the SPI has had his patriotic support, and he has become the greatest friend of the Indians of all heads of state there have ever been in Brazil.' So the dictatorial president became a champion of Indian rights. By 1945, the rejuvenated SPI was running 106 posts, which included seventy-two schools, twenty infirmaries, and many cattle ranches and farms.

Of course, all the glorification of indigenous people was a sham: the authorities were determined to change Indians towards being more like 'superior' whites. Garfield found a letter that a Tembé Indian, Lírio do Valle, wrote to President Vargas in 1945, asking for a job as an Inspector in the SPI. Valle assured Vargas that 'we Indians are the roots of a plant that today is Brazil'. But he complained that 'the SPI lately is not interested in Indians, because only whites work there and whites are not interested in Indians'. The letter went unanswered, and Valle never got his job.

Valle's case was typical of detribalized Indians. Individuals who tried to

enter the tough frontier economy lacked the necessary basic education
and competitive will, so they sank to a standard of living lower than that
of the poorest caboclos. Their problems were exacerbated by the traumatic collapse of tribal culture, beliefs, and values when confronted by
successful materialistic society. Their customs were extinguished and
mocked. Outside the shelter of a tribal village Indians lost their self-
respect. Darcy Ribeiro admitted that 'We all know that the classic picture
of an acculturated Indian – as lazy, addicted to cachaça rum, and abnormal
– is dramatically true.' Semi-acculturated tribes 'which had survived . . .
as islands in the midst of the national populace . . . were an unwanted
minority, restricted to segments of the lands they had formerly held or
cast out of territory rightly theirs and forced to roam from place to place.'
Groups that lost communal cohesion were headed for disintegration.

The Indian Protection Service had two periods of revival, before lapsing
into terminal decay. A government report in 1940 admitted that 'because
of lack of resources and disorganization suffered by the SPI since 1931, it
has succeeded in doing little since then of direct benefit to the Indians.
But it is now going to be provided with somewhat larger funds, which
will permit a start on its reorganization and [initiate] prompt, efficient
action.' The Indian Service's budget increased five-fold in four years. It
embarked on a period of great activity, with many posts reopened. By
1943, the SPI's Bulletin reported that it 'is currently undergoing one of
the most favourable phases of its existence, for it enjoys the goodwill
of the public powers.'

The Service was run by Colonel Vasconcellos, an officer who had long
served under Rondon. He saw the priority as the protection of Indian
lands. Then the main efforts were medical (a dream of providing hospitals
and dispensaries at each post), teaching literacy, and economic self-
sufficiency (a euphemism for making Indians work to pay for their posts).
There was also a revival of operations to contact isolated tribes.

The burst of activity of the early 1940s was eventually stifled by red
tape and central control. Darcy Ribeiro experienced this management
crisis: 'Within a few years the Service was invaded – not in the posts in
the interior, but in the cities – by bureaucrats incapable of understanding
or identifying ideologically with the work to which it was dedicated. In
these conditions, the posts were entrusted to agents recruited at random,
entirely unprepared for the duties they were called upon to fulfil. [These
agents were] managed by functionaries in the cities, who understood even
less of the Indian problem and were concerned only with formal bureaucratic norms that were often irrelevant to such a singular activity as

protecting Indians.' A restructuring in 1947 created many new jobs at headquarters, but drastically cut the number of agents in the field. 'In compensation we have a pilot (although we have no plane), a cameraman and a chauffeur.' Positions were found for people 'who had no intention of leaving the asphalt'. An incoming Director wrote that 'the SPI can be compared to a child with glandular deficiency – long arms and legs, a disproportionate head and thin body. Its creators hoped for an Apollo, but they produced someone atrophied due to irregular nourishment and continued "changes of air" and, worst of all, with an inferiority complex, reluctance to tell the truth, and fear of the powers that be.' Of ninety-seven Indian posts, seven were closed for lack of funds, half the remainder were run by non-salaried persons, and only forty-six had SPI agents in charge.

A second revival came with the appointment of a lover of Indians, José Maria da Gama Malcher, as Director of the SPI in 1950. He wrote at the time that SPI staff must be given training and 'no longer recruited haphazardly and paid derisory salaries which are commonly incredibly in arrears.' Malcher got out into the field to tackle the problems of the posts. He tried to weed out incompetents, moonlighters, and the corrupt. But by 1953, the thirteen enquiries into misconduct that he instituted were all bogged down in bureaucracy. Malcher made strenuous efforts to improve medical assistance, particularly against the worst scourges: respiratory diseases such as influenza, tuberculosis, pneumonia, and whooping cough. He was helped in this by outstanding doctors like Orlando Villas Boas' friends Noel Nutels and Leão da Motta. (Paradoxically, this period of excellence in the SPI coincided with the population nadir for the tribes themselves: their numbers probably fell to little more than 100,000; but have risen steadily ever since.) Gama Malcher also tried to make the education taught in the SPI's sixty-six schools more relevant to tribal life. But it proved almost impossible to recruit good teachers, because of the poor pay and the difficult conditions in remote aldeias.

Darcy Ribeiro wrote a report on the SPI for UNESCO, in which he argued that, although intent on educating tribes for integration, it was also keen not to interfere violently with their way of life, beliefs, or customs. The problem was that it rarely used anthropologists but relied on trial and error. So there was a gulf between 'pragmatic' (or lazy and corrupt) SPI officials and academic theorists. Malcher tried to change this. His greatest legacy was to base the SPI's work on ethnographic research. He put Brazil's most dynamic anthropologists – Darcy Ribeiro, Eduardo Galvão, Carlos Moreira Neto, Roberto Cardoso de Oliveira, and Mário

Simões – in charge of a new research department. He also corresponded with Curt Nimuendajú, Herbert Baldus, and other anthropologists of the previous generation, and he listened to their advice.

Gama Malcher later wrote: 'I understood that the assistance we must give the Indians (to prepare them for an [often] fatal assimilation, which has to be long-term) should be based on a tripod: anthropologist, medical doctor, and agronomist.' He insisted that Indians must live in protected reserves so that they could maintain their customs. They could assimilate Brazilian culture if they wished, but at their initiative. 'Unless we make contact with isolated groups in a slow, sure, and humane manner – without shocks – we will have led the entire indigenous population to extinction in the worst form of genocide . . . Attempts at rapid integration have always been a disaster.' It was during his directorship that the Museum of the Indian was founded in Rio de Janeiro, an excellent institution 'dedicated to fight against prejudice' that flourishes to this day.

The SPI thus started to acknowledge a revolution in anthropological thinking. For a brief moment, it abandoned Rondon's Positivist ideal of incorporating Indians into Brazilian society and sought to use culturalist anthropology (in vogue at that time) as a guide to its practical fieldwork. Studies of many tribal societies had shown that they were far more varied and complex than had been thought. They were also complete in themselves. The modern anthropologist Mércio Gomes wrote that 'they must be explained in their own terms and not in comparison with other cultures: thus there are no superior or inferior cultures. Indian cultures, then, were raised to equal standing with any other, including that of Brazil.' This put an end to cultural evolution, the Positivist theory that tribes became acculturated and progressed through stages of development. Individuals in so-called primitive societies are just as intelligent as other human beings, even if they lack advanced material possessions or intellectual theories.

Malcher appreciated the work being done by the Villas Boas brothers in the Xingu as 'a matter of pride for all of us, known and respected throughout the world . . . From long experience, I can affirm that what the Villas Boas have been achieving for many years is possibly the only truly valid activity . . . We cannot in all honesty present anything better.' Malcher's modern scientific approach was successful. The Service flourished: by 1955 it had 106 posts throughout Brazil.

In the late 1950s, Darcy Ribeiro published a detailed estimate of tribal populations. He concluded that during the first half of the twentieth century tribal Indians fell by a catastrophic 80 per cent, from about 1,000,000 to 200,000. For 1900 he listed 230 tribes, of which 105 were still isolated, 57 in intermittent contact, 39 in permanent contact, and 29 fully integrated. Almost sixty years later, the first two categories had dropped drastically: to a total of only 56 – 33 isolated and 23 in intermittent contact. But the most chilling finding was that 'of the 230 tribes reported, 87 or 37.8 per cent have disappeared': Ribeiro listed them in a column headed 'extinct'. Many of these vanished peoples were hit by the cattle-ranching frontier; but most were in forested areas, the 'extractive frontier' of rubber and nut gatherers or gold and diamond prospectors. (A few groups on Ribeiro's 'extinct' list had in fact survived – their shattered remnants later resurfaced and, in some cases, have revived as cultural entities.)

Had it not been for the SPI, the situation would have been even worse. After its first five decades, the Service's main achievement was 'to assure for the Indians the minimal conditions that were essential for their survival as independent ethnic groups, as peoples. Dozens of groups that would otherwise have been destroyed are there to bear witness. The SPI guaranteed them the lands that were being plundered, the right to live according to their customs, and it gave them some assistance against illness and misery.' Equally importantly, the SPI had done much to persuade academic and public opinion to 'respect the persons of the Indians'. Mércio Gomes acknowledged that, for all its faults, the SPI *did* persuade Brazilians that Indians deserve a place of their own within the nation and that their culture is a unique element of Brazilianness. 'It also instituted the concept of Indian parks, thus bringing two powerful ideas together: the defence of cultures and the defence of the environment.' The Service tried to execute a policy of 'indigenism' based on respect for Indians as people, with the state assuming responsibility for the destiny of descendants of its original inhabitants. It also instilled an altruistic attitude in the best of its field personnel.

However, tribes contacted in the SPI's early 'successes' had suffered appallingly. In the words of Shelton Davis, author of the powerful polemic book *Victims of the Miracle*: 'The Kaingang of São Paulo were reduced from 1200 persons at the time of their pacification in 1912 to a mere 87 ragged and starving individuals in 1957. The Xokleng of Santa Catarina were reduced from over 800 to less than 190. The Nambiquara of Mato Grosso were reduced from an estimated 10,000 to less than 1000' – and there was similar decline among other groups who had once resisted the invading colonists. Imported diseases accounted for most of this demographic catastrophe. But social disruption and demoralization, caused by loss of land and undermining of tribal culture, was an important factor: it lowered life expectancy, reduced the birth rate, and sometimes led to starvation. Commenting on the extinction of so many tribes, José de Queiros Campos (a future head of the Indian service) savagely attacked the SPI at an international congress in 1968. 'Indians who maintain effective contact with Brazilian society have been exterminated thanks to methods used by white men, both those of the SPI and some missionaries and adventurers. All are responsible for the crime, either by action or omission.'

The fate of newly contacted tribes was particularly disgraceful. Carlos Moreira in 1958 condemned contact expeditions that were launched with hopelessly inadequate medical or financial back-up. This was later repeated by Queiros Campos: 'We must stop launching pacifying expeditions without thinking of the [Indians'] subsequent destiny. This was the crass error of the SPI. It pacified tribes criminally, for it made no plan for their protection – either from a medical point of view, or the defence of the tribal economy, or respect for their traditions, or prohibition of intrusion by alien elements.'

Malcher ran the SPI for only four years. He was replaced in July 1955 to make way for a presidential crony, in what the press described as 'one of the most monstrous and notorious injustices'. Another interpretation was that Malcher was forced to resign because he 'lost the battle' against economic forces with whom he was not prepared to bargain or compromise – timber companies in south Brazil and land speculators in Mato Grosso. Brazil then elected the extrovert President Juscelino Kubitschek, who launched a programme of development that included the building of the new capital, Brasília. Such expansion was a threat to the Indians. With the change of government the SPI became a pawn in party politics, and it suffered a new collapse. Competent anthropologists gradually left, and their innovations (such as a post-graduate course in applied anthropology) ceased. There was some protest about this, and in 1957 the SPI was removed from the political arena. But it now became 'an organ of military influence' entrusted to a succession of senior officers who had none of the dedication of Rondon's original military team. Its next two directors were 'anonymous, inexpressive and lustreless, with none of what is needed by a department as serious as the SPI should be'. The Service fell to the lowest ebb in its history. 'In some regions, it descended to the degrading condition of being an agent for the despoilers and murderers of Indians.'

After two able directors, the SPI was entrusted to a series of military men with little sense of mission. In 1961 one of these urged that foreign visitors should be excluded from Indian posts because 'in their present condition these constitute a sad spectacle . . . and are a very bad recommendation for the Service and for Brazil.' The next Director was equally scathing. 'With a few honourable exceptions ... the posts are in a lamentable state, unassisted, deficient in everything, lacking inspections. The Indians are left to their own devices, and Indian lands are at the mercy of greedy outsiders or, all too often, to clandestine exploitation by the agents themselves or other functionaries. Laziness, irresponsibility, and outrages against the public patrimony are rife. The Regional Inspectorates, which should be vigorous and active entities, are simply bureaucratic and sedentary departments because of total lack of funds (above all for rapid travel) and having no control or stimulus.'

The new managers of the SPI disbanded the Section for Anthropological Studies created by Darcy Ribeiro in the early 1950s. Field agents were urged to make their Indian charges productive, so that income from the Indians would pay for the running of the Service. Several Indian posts were put under missionary control. Some authorities sounded alarms. In 1960 the former Director José Maria da Gama Malcher condemned the Service's excessive bureaucracy, its lack of trained staff, and its powerlessness. 'As if this were not enough, immunity of delinquents, recruitment of incompetents, and laziness complete the sad picture. The SPI is increasingly distanced from its objectives, a completely demoralized service.' The sacked anthropologist Roberto Cardoso de Oliveira denounced most SPI officials as 'unqualified for any duty of protection or assistance, ... revealing no quality that could identify them as Indianists. There are of course exceptions, but they are not in the offices – in the headquarters, Federal District, inspectorates or state capitals – but in a few Indian posts, in the forests or the pacification groups.' Carlos Moreira said that the leaders of the SPI lacked any vision about its purposes. He watched in horror as 'functionaries with absolutely no training or sensibility towards Indians or their problems and needs were promoted to run the SPI, with tragic results for the prestige and efficiency of the organization'. The Service was 'marked by every sort of violence, illegality, and betrayal of the most elementary rights of the Indians'.

Cardoso de Oliveira went on to condemn the SPI's mercenary attitude. 'The inherent concept is that Indians can be "civilized" only by work – but not work to which they are culturally conditioned, but rather induced work that they are taught by civilizados.' Indian posts became businesses, expected to earn a surplus towards the upkeep of the Service. Indigenous workers did not benefit directly from their labours. Any profit went to the renda indígena (the Indian yield) to pay for office overheads or costs of attraction teams. Managers with this business mentality 'want the cost of assistance and protection to be paid by the very victims of Brazilian society as it expands and occupies their tribal territories.' Shelton Davis later concluded: 'In simplest terms, during this period economic rather than humanitarian considerations began to form the basis of Indian policy in Brazil.'

Two outstanding men dominated the treatment of Indians during the first half of the twentieth century: Curt Nimuendajú, who died in 1945, and Cândido Rondon, who died thirteen years later in 1958. Curt (Unkel) Nimuendajú was once asked for autobiographical notes and he answered: 'My life is very simple: I was born in Jena in 1883, had no university education of any sort, and I came to Brazil in 1903. Until 1913 my permanent residence was in São Paulo and after that in Belém, but all the rest until now [1939] was an almost uninterrupted series of explorations . . . I have no photograph of myself.' Curt Unkel reached Brazil as a young emigrant, and two years after arrival chose to live among the Guarani Indians of western São Paulo state. The tribe loved the quiet German and he developed an empathy for indigenous thinking that has never been matched by any other anthropologist. In 1907 the Apapokuva (Ñandeva) Guarani formally admitted him to their tribe in an elaborate ceremony. They gave him the name Nimuendajú ('He who resides with us') which he adopted with pride; and in 1922 he took Brazilian citizenship with this as his surname.

Slight and slim, reserved and precise, with a neat moustache that he shaved daily, Curt Nimuendajú looked like a stern bank manager; but his affinity for Indians became innate and lifelong. He understood Indian philosophy and society profoundly and intimately because he spent so much time with indigenous people. During the four decades from 1905 to his death in 1945, Curt Nimuendajú was on an expedition to a tribe, or living with Indians, or on an archaeological excavation almost every single year. This was a staggering achievement, at a time when there were no roads or vehicles in the Brazilian interior, no outboard motors, and no planes, so that every expedition involved months of arduous travel. He once complained that 'the life of south-Brazilian forest Indians is incredibly miserable, full of penury and privations, of persecutions and dangers', and he often suffered from malaria or malnutrition. (On one occasion his life was saved by the ministrations of a shaman, and writing in an academic German journal he emphasized that he was cured by native medicine.) But Nimuendajú explained that he lived among Indians because 'it is necessary to feel in your own flesh the problems of the group as if they were your own – to fear the same threats, raise the same hopes, grow angry at the same injustices and oppressions'.

Although Nimuendajú made the first contact with the Parintintin (Tupi-Kawahib) and saw other groups with their cultures intact, he was one of the first anthropologists to be concerned with tribes who had been in contact for centuries and were struggling at the base of frontier society. He wrote major studies of the Xerente and Apinayé, once powerful tribes that were reduced to demoralized remnants – and he was proud of his role in restoring morale among the Apinayé and Ticuna. He was the first to study poor and shattered tribes in north-east Brazil, at the northern tip of Amapá, and among the Salesian missionaries of the Upper Rio Negro; and he tracked down the last survivors of three tribes at the moment of extinction – the Pau d'Arco Kayapó on the Araguaia, the Oti in western São Paulo, and the Ofaié in southern Mato Grosso.

Although self-taught, Nimuendajú was a natural scholar and meticulous observer. From his very first book, he 'used simple and pure language: far from being academic, Nimuendajú's form of expression is full of the spirit of Guarani thinking.' His accounts of forty-five different tribes in all parts of Brazil are classics of anthropological writing. He left a posthumously published *Ethno-Historical Map* that is a monument of research, showing the geographical movements and linguistic affiliations of every Brazilian tribe during four centuries, and is accompanied by comprehensive lists of historical sources. I cannot imagine how he found the time, between his arduous fieldwork, for the months of historical research involved in that great opus. The modest and unorthodox German scholar was acclaimed during his lifetime, with his work published by leading institutions in Germany, France, and the United States. After his death one Brazilian anthropologist considered him 'without any doubt the principal figure of Brazilian ethnology' in the first half of the twentieth century; and Darcy Ribeiro wrote to the equally distinguished Roberto da Matta that Nimuendajú's 'classics of anthropology . . . are worth more than the entire output of Brazilian ethnologists' – which included their own considerable literature.

Most importantly, Curt Nimuendajú was the first anthropologist to become an *active champion* of indigenous rights. Herbert Baldus wrote that 'throughout his life this honourable man fought in defence of the Indians, against representatives of our civilization who were invading the wilderness with the power of superior weapons. He thus gained the love of the persecuted, becoming one of them and, like them, came to suffer the hatred of the colonizers, for whom "Indians are not people".' In this he was the precursor and, to some extent, inspiration of the modern generation of Brazilian anthropologist-activists. Nimuendajú died aged sixty-two, appropriately among the downtrodden Ticuna of the Solimões. His health was bad, but he defied doctor's orders to return to another field trip.

By this time Cândido Rondon was already eighty, but destined to live to the venerable age of ninety-two. He died in 1958, just after he had been nominated for the Nobel Peace Prize. We have seen how Rondon had initial triumphs as an explorer with the strategic telegraph lines but gained fame as a humanitarian with the formation of the SPI in 1910. Then came the expedition with Theodore Roosevelt, in 1927 the inspection of Brazil's northern frontiers, and further military duties. After a period of eclipse in the early 1930s, Rondon was rehabilitated by President Vargas after his successful boundary arbitration. In 1939, when seventy-four, he was named President of the new National Council for the Protection of Indians (CNPI) and also promoted to Marshal. In 1956 the vast Guaporé Territory, home of the Nambiquara, was renamed Rondônia in honour of the champion of the Indians – it was elevated to statehood long after his death. Rondon received medals and awards from many countries; and when Brazil created an internal voluntary youth-service organization it called it Projeto Rondon.

Towards the end of his life, Rondon changed his mind about the SPI's early policy of trying to transform Indians into frontier farmers and ranchers. In 1949 he wrote that 'the present tendency is to isolate Indians wherever possible from pernicious contact with whites. We no longer subscribe to the erroneous idea that Indians should be incorporated into our civilization.' In conversation with Egon Schaden, he admitted that Indians who left their tribes and tried to enter national society became impoverished and sacrificed their more genuine way of life. He decided that tribes were better off when left to decide their own destinies and to change only at a speed they themselves wanted. Orlando Villas Boas was delighted that his mentor Rondon, whom he admired so much, had had this change of heart.

Edilberto Coutinho, a reporter who interviewed the nonagenarian Marshal Rondon, found him surrounded by birds, plants, and Indian relics in his apartment in Copacabana, Rio de Janeiro. The old explorer was extraordinarily lucid. 'He relived his forest experiences in amazing detail, citing names and dates, telling anecdotes or recalling companions.' On his last visit to the forests Rondon had visited the old Bororo Chief Cadete, who had often helped him during his expeditions and who considered him as a brother. The aged Indian invited Rondon to come to die among the Bororo, since his tribe (to which Rondon was related through one great-grandmother) alone knew how to give him a sufficiently elaborate funerary ceremony. In the event, Rondon was buried in Rio de Janeiro amid national mourning and with full military honours. He might have preferred the Bororo funeral.

In 1961 Brazil was thrown into political turmoil by the sudden (and never fully explained) resignation of its popular President Jânio Quadros, the man who had finally legalized the Xingu Indian park. Under the Constitution at that time, the President and Vice-President were each elected in their own right. When the supposedly right-of-centre Quadros abruptly withdrew, his Vice-President was the hard-left João Goulart – who was visiting Communist China at the time. A civil war was narrowly averted and Goulart was allowed to return and take office. But the military were increasingly dissatisfied by his erratic administration, and in 1964, encouraged by the United States, the armed forces overthrew the socialistic government and Brazil embarked on almost a quarter-century of military rule, with successive army marshals assuming the presidency.

These political upheavals were eventually to change the treatment of Indians. President Goulart had in November 1963 appointed the ebullient and able doctor Noel Nutels as head of the SPI, but it was too late for him to revive the Service before the coup in the following April. The new military government started by appointing an obscure officer, Air Force Major Luis Vinhas Neves, as director of the demoralized Indian Protection Service. He complained bitterly about lack of funding. 'Brazilian Indians are relegated to abandonment for lack of funds for the SPI . . . I found the organization enfeebled and mismanaged, and it continues with insufficient resources to fulfil the objectives for which it was created.' Neves was determined to maximize the *renda indígena*, to make the SPI as profitable as possible. The Service's internal Bulletin is full of homilies, for instance to tighten budgeting procedures after 'all our administrative units have, through traditional carelessness, been living without discipline . . . with incomprehension, even absurd interpretation, in their application.' Efforts were made to expel invaders from Indian lands and to recover territory that had been removed from reserves. But it was done to protect the SPI's revenue rather than for the indigenous communities.

The Bulletin quoted admiringly a nineteenth-century declaration that 'we must seek to create among Indians the needs of civilized men, not solely for our convenience but also for theirs.' The inspectorate in Paraná, which used to support the SPI with a 'fabulous output', had been failing; but it should now improve. Posts were praised for getting Indians to work with frontier settlers. 'This succeeds in embedding in the Indians' spirit a clear impression of [civilizado] knowledge and human comprehension.

Settlers adapt Indians to varied and useful work, both in farm labour and in other services such as extractive industries in wood, sawmills, rubber-tapping, and others appropriate to the habitat where the new pioneers of modern Brazil toil and struggle.'

José Maria da Gama Malcher, who had been such a fine director of the SPI in the early 1950s, wrote that 'Air Force Major Vinhas Neves surrounded himself with a veritable "gang" and, with his connivance and even participation, the SPI suffered the greatest spoliation, the greatest dilapidation of the Indian patrimony in the fifty years since its creation.' A parliamentary inquiry a few years later said that 'during the Vinhas Neves administration . . . the devastation of the Indian patrimony was something fantastic. It is impossible to evaluate the damage done to the Indians. But if we speak in terms of half a trillion cruzeiros, or perhaps even a trillion, it would be no exaggeration.' In the Curitiba inspectorate, quantities of land, Indian produce, and splendid Paraná-pine trees were sold – the trees in lots of 500,000 at a time. Further west, the lands of the Kadiwéu were rented off, with payment in cattle which was later sold to ranchers at absurdly low prices. Gama Malcher summed up this system as: 'the produce of the "protected" is used to meet the expenditure of the "protector".'

There had been half-hearted inquiries into mismanagement and fraud in the SPI, in 1956 and more seriously in 1963 when a parliamentary commission found 'theft and misapplication of funds, irregular transactions with cattle . . . and crimes against the national patrimony'. But these reports did not mention abuse of Indians. After the military coup that overthrew Goulart's chaotic (and anti-Indian) government in 1964, protests about the state of the SPI reached a peak. The respected academic Paulo Duarte said that 'the SPI has no moral authority or material resources to make pacifications'. He stressed the need to protect Indians' health and land, but he condemned attempts to change indigenous societies. 'This business of integrating Indians is an idiotic phrase, only capable of making an impression in a country whose people are 60 per cent illiterate.' Gama Malcher lamented that with 'all these pressures from all sides, innumerable persecutions, planned massacres, and forced miscegenation, we can say with certainty that Brazilian natives are today a faceless race . . . We know that there are honest servants in the organs for assistance. But that is not enough . . . It is imperative to punish the dishonest. The SPI does not need a great number of bureaucrats living in the big and comfortable cities with no bond to the Indians – either of culture or affection.'

The corruption went too far. In 1967 the powerful Minister of the

Interior, General Afonso Augusto de Albuquerque Lima, appointed the Procurator-General Jader Figueiredo Correia to head a parliamentary inquiry into irregularities of the SPI. The Commission went to work with enthusiasm. In the fourteen months from April 1967 to June 1968 it travelled in eighteen states and territories, heard 130 witnesses, and managed to substantiate a large part of their accusations. The Commission produced a massive report, of 5,115 pages in twenty-one volumes weighing forty-eight kilos (106 pounds).

(This investigation was completed despite a mysterious fire that in June 1967 destroyed the records of the SPI on the seventh floor of a new office building in Brasília. Everyone assumed that this was arson to eliminate incriminating evidence. It was a tragedy for historians since it destroyed unique films, photographs, and recordings, and quantities of unpublished reports.)

The inquiry's evidence was explosive. Jader Figueiredo divulged its most sensational findings in a series of broadcasts and press interviews that culminated in an international press conference. In October 1967 he said that his investigation had already uncovered atrocities against Indians and gigantic losses to the Indian patrimony. The President of Brazil announced that the SPI would be abolished, with its work (and that of the hitherto independent Xingu park) taken on by a new National Indian Foundation, always known by its acronym Funai.

Procurator Jader Figueiredo was deeply distressed by what he found, and he fuelled the outcry by emotional language. After describing the financial losses, he said that 'more shameful than the corruption is the fact that the Indians have suffered tortures similar to those of the [Nazi concentration] camps of Treblinka and Dachau.'

The crimes against Indians were indeed terrible. In 1963 there was an attempt at genocide of villages of the Cinta Larga ('Broad Belt') tribe of Rondônia, carefully planned by Chico Luis de Brito, the brutal overseer of the rubber company Arruda e Junqueira. A former Inspector of the SPI in Cuiabá accused Brito of renting a Cessna and getting the pilot to bomb a village with sticks of dynamite. The attack was timed to coincide with a festival when the village was full of Indians. 'On the first run packets of sugar were dropped to calm the fears of those who had scattered and run for shelter at the sight of the plane. They had opened the packets and were tasting the sugar ten minutes later when it returned to carry out the attack. No one has ever been able to find out how many Indians were killed, because the bodies were buried in the bank of the river and the village deserted.'

This bombing was followed by a land raid to exterminate another Cinta

Larga village. One gunman, Ataíde Pereira, was bitter because he was not
paid his promised $15 fee for the raid. He confessed to the Jesuit
missionary Father Edgard Schmidt, who tape-recorded the chilling testimony and gave it to the SPI. Ataíde said that six men led by a psychopath
called Chico Luis had gone up the Juruena for many days before striking
inland. They got lost, were found by the Cessna which threw them some
food, and dug up manioc at a village 'that had been wiped out by a
gunman called Tenente'. Five days later, the killers saw Indian smoke. As
Ataíde boasted, 'We were hand-picked for the job, as quiet as any Indian
party when it came to slipping between the trees. When we reached
Cinta Larga country there were no more fires and no talking.' They
camped near a village and, before dawn, crept towards it through the
undergrowth. Chico told Ataíde to kill the chief and to leave the rest to
him – since he enjoyed killing. The Indians emerged and started to build
some shelters. Ataíde decided which was the chief and

> I got him in the chest with the first shot . . . Although I have only an
> ancient shotgun I can safely say that I never miss. Chico gave the chief
> a burst with his tommy gun to make sure, and after that he let the rest
> of them have it . . . All the other fellows had to do was to finish off
> anyone who showed signs of life . . . There was a young Indian girl they
> didn't shoot, with a kid of about five in one hand, yelling his head
> off. . . . Chico shot the kid through the head with his .45 and then
> grabbed hold of the woman – who by the way was very pretty. 'Be
> reasonable,' I said. 'Why do you have to kill her?' In my view, apart
> from anything else, it was a waste. 'What's wrong with giving her to the
> boys? They haven't set eyes on a woman for six weeks. Or . . . we could
> take her back as a present to de Brito.'

But Chico was crazed with blood-lust.

> He tied the Indian girl up and hung her head-downwards from a tree,
> legs apart, and chopped her in half right down the middle with his
> machete. Almost with a single stroke I'd say. The village was like a
> slaughter-house. He calmed down after he'd cut the woman up, and
> told us to burn down all the huts and throw the bodies into the
> [Aripuanã] river.

An SPI official commented that 'no Indian had time to use his weapons,
bows and arrows; and only two or three managed to escape by plunging
into the forest.' The prosecutor Jader Figueiredo later told the Brazilian
Chamber of Deputies that the Indian mother had been 'cut open alive
from her pubis to her head. This was not done by employees of the SPI;

but the Service sinned by omission, as did other entities. We ourselves found this legal action buried in one of the Criminal Jurisdictions of Cuiabá.'

Sebastião Arruda and Antonio Junqueira, the two principals of the rubber firm of Arruda e Junqueira, were accused of ordering these murders. Another priest, Father Valdemar Veber, said that 'this is not the first time that the firm of Arruda and Junqueira has committed crimes against the Indians. A number of expeditions have been organized in the past. This firm acts as a cover for other undertakings that are interested in acquiring land or that plan to exploit the rich mineral deposits that exist in this area.' Inspector Salgado of the Cuiabá police investigated the case, but was thwarted by the disappearance of most of the six men on the raid. However, after three years he completed the police case against Arruda and Junqueira. Three further years of legal wrangling then ensued. But when, in late 1967, an indictment was finally issued against the surviving murderers of the Cinta Larga, the names of the two principals were initially omitted 'as their assent to the massacre of the Indians has never been established'.

Another crime was committed against the Tapayuna or Beiço de Pau ('Wooden Beaks' – a tribe later moved into the Xingu park to be alongside their relatives the Suyá) of the Arinos headwater of the Tapajós. In 1957 an expedition of rubber-tappers went up the river to contact the Tapayuna but used up most of the supplies intended for the Indians. All that was left was a sack of sugar. 'The seringueiros added arsenic and ant-killer to this sugar and distributed it to the Indians. By the following morning many Indians were dead, and the seringueiros spread the news that a great epidemic was raging in the area.'

The Figueiredo Commission also reported massacres of Indians on the Tocantins–Maranhão frontier: the killing of Canela and burning of their village in July 1963, in retaliation for their taking cattle; and the slaughter of twenty-six Krahó by ranchers' gunmen in 1940. In fact, local SPI agents had acted reasonably effectively over both those atrocities. Two of the surviving tribes of north-eastern Brazil, the Maxacali of Minas Gerais and the Pataxó of Bahia, were also cited as victims of horrible crimes. Corrupt SPI agents had stolen the Maxacalis' cattle and land; the Indians retaliated by attacking nearby fazendas; and the farmers responded by plying the tribe with alcohol and then hiring gunmen to shoot them down. In the case of the Maxacali, a local police officer had by 1967 restored much of the tribe's property and had cracked down on its oppressors. The nearby Pataxó, living north-east of the Maxacali near the Atlantic seaboard, had had two villages exterminated by being given smallpox injections or presents of contaminated clothing. Jader Figueiredo said the SPI officials watched Pataxó die one by one, and did it so that 'big-shots in Bahia state government' could acquire coveted Indian lands.

The Figueiredo report also recorded sexual crimes on Indian women. In March 1968 the military commander of Tabatinga, the frontier fort on the main Amazon (or Solimões) river where Brazil joins Peru and Colombia, investigated allegations of torture of the Ticuna – the last tribe still living on the banks of the Amazon itself. Major Leal dos Santos said that 'what revolted me most was the testimonies of young Indian girls, who were violated by the son of the owner of their village'. These acculturated Ticuna cling to one ancient ceremony marking the coming of age of their virgins. At this festival so much cachaça was consumed that the Indians fell into a drunken stupor. 'Leandro Aires de Almeida, aged twenty-three, son of [the local landowner], would then choose his prey, generally the youngest Indian girl of all . . . The youth Leandro filled the village with terror.' A police investigation revealed that the proprietor, Jordão Aires de Almeida, 'kept his own "police" of seven caboclos to maintain discipline. When Indians disobeyed, he said that they were chained to a pepper-tree post on the veranda of his house.' A Ticuna called Verissimo complained that 'he had been chained there for seven days without food or drink, with his hands and feet chained, satisfying his physical needs standing up. His body was bitten all over by mosquitoes.' Verissimo went to report this, but when he returned to his village he was flogged with a whip of manatee hide, and he later fled.

Similar abuse occurred at Teresa Cristina, a former Salesian mission for the Bororo in Mato Grosso. The reserve had been sold off by the state government. A Bororo girl testified that the agent of Posto Fraternidade Indígena, Flávio de Abreu, and his wife Teresinha 'prostituted Indian girls . . . One day the SPI agent [Abreu] called an old carpenter to make an oven for his farmhouse. When the carpenter had finished, the agent asked him how much he wanted for doing the job. The carpenter said he wanted an Indian girl, and the agent took him to the school and told him to choose one. [He took an eleven-year-old called Rosa.] No one saw any more of her.' The witness said that she herself was taken from her mother and forced to work as a slave, subjected to rawhide whipping if she failed in her labour. 'There was a mill for crushing sugar cane, and to spare the horses they used Indian children to turn the mill . . . They forced the Indian Octaviano to beat his own mother . . . Indians were used for target practice.' Abreu and two other agents in the southern Mato Grosso inspectorate were 'famous for the cruelty with which they "protected" Indians.'

At Nonoái post in Rio Grande do Sul the Commission found a dark prison cell measuring 1 x 1.30 metres (3ft 4ins by 4ft 4ins). 'At Cacique Doble they held Indians naked at a time when it was snowing. There were crucifixions of Indians, and some were suspended by their wrists. They even used the log torture.' In this, the victim's ankles were fastened to logs that were forced apart until, on occasion, the ankle bones broke. All this was done to enforce policy and discipline on posts run by dictatorial agents.

Such were the violent and sordid crimes exposed by the Figueiredo Commission. Most had been committed by frontiersmen rather than by SPI officials. However, the majority of the inquiry's findings were cases of financial fraud and corruption perpetrated by SPI staff. Jader Figueiredo noted that 'it is sufficient to say that the SPI had in its ranks no doctor, no agronomist, no nurse and no midwife. Of its 700 former employees, 500 are suspected of calculated irregularities.' The crimes ranged from large-scale theft of Indian lands or timber to pettier larceny of SPI property or funds. On the grand scale, there was the case of the Kadiwéu, who had been given a fine tract of land by the Emperor Pedro II in gratitude for their help in the war against Paraguay. Deputy Celso Amaral (who had conducted an earlier inquiry, in 1963) said in a parliamentary debate that of the Kadiwéu's 700,000 hectares (2,700 square miles) 'half was leased out for money and half for cattle. I saw nothing of the cattle. It was all sold without authorization.' The consortium of ranchers who leased the land grazed 500,000 head of cattle on it, but paid only 6 per cent of the correct value. Far away in northern Brazil, the huge São Marcos ranch in Roraima (the home of Makuxi and some Wapixana Indians) had 20,000 head of cattle in its inventory; but the investigator counted only 1,800 – he was told that 'many cattle die up there'.

A typical entry in the pages of indictments was that of Flávio de Abreu – the criminal who paid for his oven with an Indian girl. 'He was indicted for various crimes against the persons of Indians, including mistreatment, keeping a private prison, expulsion, and enslavement, as well as damaging the Indian patrimony by removal of cattle, stealing farm produce and destroying improvements. He said nothing in his defence.' But he was punished only by dismissal.

A far more important accused was Inspector Francisco Meirelles, the man who had led the attraction of the Xavante and the tragically bungled contacts with various Kayapó groups. Meirelles was accused of irregularities in presenting his accounts and of issuing promissory notes in his own name to finance agricultural production by Indians in his care. Charges against him involved sales of Brazil nuts and cattle, and the cutting of

2,000 hardwood logs. Meirelles was also accused of transforming Munduruku and Kayabi posts into 'veritable branches of his friends [the rubber-trading firm] Arruda, Pinto & Cia.' He was said to have concealed a massacre of Menkragnoti Kayapó on the Jamanchim tributary of the Iriri by employees of this same company. And he was alleged to have acted criminally towards the Pakaá Nova (Wari) during their contact. Francisco Meirelles gave detailed and fairly convincing denials to all nineteen charges, in a signed statement on 6 May 1968; and he was let off with twenty days' suspension.

The most prominent officials indicted by the Figueiredo Commission were three former directors of the SPI: Lieutenant Colonel (now promoted to General) Moacyr Ribeiro Coelho, Police Colonel Hamilton de Oliveira Castro, and Air Force Major Luís Vinhas Neves. Each was accused of serious financial irregularities, including illegal transactions, taking bribes, buying supplies from cronies at exorbitant prices, unauthorized loans and expenditure, and deals that diminished the Indian patrimony and (in the case of Neves) the national patrimony. In a broadcast in April 1968, Procurator Figueiredo blamed Neves for 'appalling dilapidation of the Indian patrimony through three Internal Service Orders to all SPI inspectorates and the São Paulo agency to a) sell cattle, b) sell timber, and c) rent out lands.' By that date, the Procurator could boast that his Commission had removed 200 SPI employees and accused 134 others. Of the latter, 'seventeen have already suffered administrative imprisonment and thirty-eight were given dishonourable discharge from the public service.' The Brazilian press published the names of all the accused and listed their alleged crimes. Two years later, José Maria da Gama Malcher wrote that the rigorous inquiry had led to the sacking of a hundred employees, some of whom had done little wrong but others 'composed of the most sordidly corrupt also fell. However, those most strongly indicted – known embezzlers, veritable despoilers – remained out of it or suffered light penalties. These continue to act today as they did in the past, as if nothing abnormal had happened . . . In short, this "rigorous enquiry" was partial, badly planned, and badly conducted.' It investigated only some of the SPI's inspectorates and thus missed some guilty parties. Major 'Vinhas Neves and [his crony] José Fernando Cruz, two of the principal indicted, suffered nothing, or rather escaped prison which was their rightful destination. The first was promoted [within the air force]; and Cruz is now working for a company in Rondônia.' Gilberto Pinto, Inspector for the Manaus region and one of the SPI's most dedicated sertanistas, told the author how bitter he was that the 'notorious crook' Neves emerged unscathed, whereas he himself was arrested, held for a month without charge, and then released without explanation or apology. Apart from Hélio Bucker who had a military background, *all* those arrested were civilians. But the inquiry had been instigated by a military regime.

It is difficult to understand why Minister Albuquerque Lima instituted the inquiry and then gave so much publicity to its findings. The Minister was clearly shocked by what he had heard about the Indian Protection Service. Most of its crimes (apart from those under Major Neves) had been committed during the democratic period before the military coup of 1964. So General Albuquerque Lima may have seen the inquiry as a means of discrediting his civilian predecessors. If that was his intention, this public-relations exercise was a total fiasco, a disastrous own goal. A UN Conference on Human Rights happened to be taking place in 1967 and it promptly accused Brazil of permitting the massacre of Indians. The world's press was eager to attack a regime that had driven many liberal or left-leaning Brazilians into exile, and editors were not concerned whether atrocities against Indians were done before or after the military coup. So the Figueiredo report became a stick with which to beat Brazil's military rulers.

By far the most powerful denunciation was by the distinguished writer Norman Lewis, who was sent to investigate by the *Sunday Times* of London. Lewis did not meet any Indians, but he used the dreadful evidence of the Figueiredo report to write a long, eloquent, and passionate condemnation of Brazil's treatment of its indigenous peoples. His article was called: 'Genocide. From fire and sword to arsenic and bullets – civilisation has sent six million Indians to extinction'. Norman Lewis opened his essay with an unashamed return to the vision of the noble savage. 'By the descriptions of all who had seen them, there were no more inoffensive and charming human beings on the planet than the forest Indians of Brazil, and brusquely we were told that they had been rushed to the verge of extinction.' Lewis told of the atrocities against the Cinta Larga, Ticuna, and other tribes. He ended with Darcy Ribeiro's prediction that there would not be a single Indian left by 1980. 'What a tragedy, what a reproach it will be for the human race if this is allowed to happen!' Norman Lewis's article was reprinted all over the world, and it caused a sensation.

The Brazilian authorities were totally unprepared for this international outcry. The Figueiredo report was hastily withdrawn from public circulation. But it was too late. Even the pro-Indian Gama Malcher later deplored 'the frivolous idea, that came from the ministerial cabinet itself, of assembling the press and denouncing, as a form of promotion, "genocide".' An aggrieved Procurator Figueiredo (whose vivid language had fuelled the uproar) said: 'It is lamentable that some newspapers have abused the desire of the Brazilian Government to cleanse the public service ... They have used this to cause a scandal and blacken the good name of Brazil abroad.'

In London, the Lewis article led a group of sympathizers (including this author) to found Survival International, a charity to protect indigenous peoples' rights throughout the world. Similar non-government organizations were started in other countries. In Brazil activists launched a number of pro-Indian movements during the ensuing decades; Indians themselves learned how to influence political opinion and manipulate the press; and the treatment of Indians entered a new era.

10. Missionaries

In 1942 the SPI's internal Bulletin reminded its staff that the Service had been established as a lay one. For centuries, missionaries had had a monopoly of treatment and protection of Brazilian Indians. Under the SPI's revised legislation of 1936, its officials were forbidden to indulge in any religious propaganda or teaching. The Indians were free to practise their traditional beliefs. However, priests and preachers *were* allowed to teach or conduct services on posts, provided that it cost nothing to public funds and neither disturbed nor coerced the Indians.

These norms were being abused by both Catholic and Protestant missionaries. 'There are posts where a missionary or priest is permanently resident at the seat of the post and uses its building for his preaching or cult. In others, it is the agent himself who takes the initiative ... He *invites* the Indians to attend the respective ceremonies; and, given the position of the agent, such an invitation is in practice coercion ... Agents must on no account interfere in the Indians' way of thinking about religious matters.' During the bad period in the 1930s, foreign missionaries had illegally built churches on SPI posts.

Some missionaries had always continued to operate outside the SPI, although if they established permanent missions among Indians they theoretically acted as agents of the government Service. French Dominicans at Conceição do Araguaia were active with the Kayapó and Tapirapé, and German Franciscans ran villages of Munduruku on the Cururu tributary of the Tapajós. The most active Catholics were the Salesians, a missionary order founded in Italy in 1859 and invited to take over some Bororo villages in Mato Grosso in 1895. After a shaky start, and a brief period of removal from Indian catechism, the Italian Salesians returned in 1910 and rapidly expanded their domain to include all the former territories of the Bororo between Cuiabá and the upper Araguaia. They acquired a former military-run post called Tereza Cristina, but the Bororo disliked the missionaries and left. The Salesians then managed to attract many Indians to a mission near Rondon's old telegraph line called Sagrada Coração ('Sacred Heart'), which later reverted to its indigenous name, Meruri.

The Salesians instituted stern discipline and violent proselytizing. Circular villages with a central men's hut were changed into a grid plan, to the Bororos' continued distress. Families were forced to live in rectangular wattle-and-daub houses that were manifestly inferior to their previous communal huts. Children were isolated from their parents and given intensive religious training in boarding schools. There was heavy emphasis on work. An English traveller at that time was impressed by the 'useful trades' taught to the mission Indians: weaving and spinning, farming, metalworking, and carpentry. 'What pleased me most of all was to notice how devoted to the Salesians the Indians were, and how happy and well cared-for they seemed to be.' Cândido Rondon also visited these missions in 1911, but was less impressed. He complained to the Salesian Inspector General, Father Antonio Malan, about Bororo being forced into an alien way of life. In a newspaper article, Rondon wrote that he had protested about the hiring-out of Indians to work for nearby farmers. 'I also objected to the Indians being given such meagre and poor food, when the Fathers enjoyed such vast wealth – much of it arising from Indian labour.' He had heard that one Father Salveto 'treated the Indians with reprehensible violence, to the point of punishing them with kicks and driving them to work in their roça clearings at gunpoint.' Father Malan replied that Salveto was 'good at heart' and an excellent agronomist who could not be spared. Life on the Salesian missions settled into a regimented rhythm. Father Antonio Colbacchini in 1926 published a fine anthropological study of the eastern Bororo, describing the tribal customs that his colleagues were seeking to eradicate. He reckoned that the Salesians had 500 Indians in their four mission villages, but that there were a further 1,037 Bororo living beyond missionary rule.

One Bororo custom that continued throughout the twentieth century was mobility. To the missionaries' dismay, the Bororo love to move between villages. This continual flux, *maguru*, was either for trade – with villages exchanging tobacco, cotton, or gourds for arrows and other artefacts – or because of quarrels, deaths, or a simple love of travel. During the dry season, a large part of each village would set off on long maguru trips. The anthropologist Irmhild Wüst found that almost a third of the people in the village she studied, Tadarimana, changed their residence in the course of a year. The Bororo are a homogeneous people with fixed villages, so that migrants who arrived with their domestic animals and household possessions could settle into another community. This author once drove three Bororo chiefs on a tour of visits to their friends in other places and I saw the warm welcomes they received, with ritual greetings using gourd rattles and blankets. Some small bands were constantly on the move, trekking between temporary campsites. Boys reaching puberty were expected to travel for up to two years, so that they learned the geography of the Bororo homeland in the campo cerrado, forests and dramatic cliffs and table mountains of Mato Grosso. They then took their places in the *baito* men's huts at the heart of each circular village. 'In the men's clubhouse, men conduct ceremonial activities, make wooden and bone artefacts, and spin cotton, which among the Bororo are exclusively male tasks.' They also make the ornaments that are the glory of handsome Bororo warriors: headdresses with visors of yellow *japú* weaver-bird feathers beneath a towering diadem of blue and red macaw feathers, labrets of mother-of-pearl and bone suspended from lower lips, a mass of eagle feathers gummed to their elegantly painted bodies, and feathers of the harpy eagle projecting horizontally from their nose septums.

The Bororo are also famous for their elaborate funerals, which last for six weeks or more. The missionary-anthropologist Guilherme (Wilhelm) Saake described the first night of one. 'I encountered an unforgettable scene: naked Indians, decorated with multicoloured feathers and painted with [red] urucum, were dancing bathed in sweat to the rhythm of a monotonous mortuary chant and the sound of rattles ... The flames of the fire illuminated this expressive scene ... It was a very well rehearsed theatrical production and an act of profound religious conviction.' Each new participant was led up to the body, laid out on a platform. 'The chants and dances were long and exhausting,' joined at a later stage by the women, whose monotone refrain was equally impressive. A month later came the ceremony of decorating the dead man's bones with feathers and red dye, amid further chanting, invocations of the spirits, and 'an unforgettable dance by the [feather-decked] spirits, accompanied by four warriors, to the light of the setting sun, in front of the tomb.' There were further days of ceremonial before the bones were formally interred.

The modern expert on the Bororo, Sylvia Caiuby Novaes, comments that

> it may sound paradoxical, but it is precisely through funerals that Bororo society reaffirms the vitality of its cultural life. This is a special moment for the socialising of the young, not only because it is through participation in the collective chants, dances, and hunting and fishing trips performed on such occasions that they have a chance to learn and appreciate how rich their culture is. But why should a time of loss, someone's death, be a moment of cultural reaffirmation and even recreation of life? For the Bororo, death results from actions of the *bope*,

a supernatural entity involved in every process of creation and transformation, such as birth, puberty, and death. When a person dies his or her soul, which the Bororo call *aroe*, moves into the body of certain animals such as jaguars or jaguatiricas [smaller felines].

Although now largely assimilated into frontier society, the Bororo continue to celebrate traditional funerals. Novaes feels that this is deliberate resistance to the old SPI dream of 'harmonious integration into national society.'

By the 1930s some Bororo were undergoing intensive indoctrination by the missionaries. Herbert Baldus reported that the Indians dressed and had their hair cut in the European manner. 'During weekdays, boys and girls worked alternately in school or in the fields. They learned Christian prayers and stories by heart, by repeating them in unison innumerable times. They lived as boarders and could visit their parents' huts only from eleven to half-past one . . . Their parents took them to church every morning and evening, and adults educated in the missions went to mass every Sunday and holiday.' Despite all this, the Bororo retained a surprising amount of traditional culture, wearing penis-sheaths or the women's bark aprons beneath their Western clothing, and still hunting between their agricultural labours. Claude Lévi-Strauss told the story of a Bororo boy who did so well in his studies that the missionaries took him to Rome, where he met the Pope. However, when the Salesians attempted to marry him in the Christian manner, contrary to tribal custom, he suffered a spiritual crisis and reverted to the old Bororo ideals. The French anthropologist met him back in his village in 1935, where 'for fifteen years he had led an exemplary life as a savage: completely naked, painted red, his nose and lower lip pierced by a septum ornament and labret, adorned with feathers, the "Pope's Indian" proved to be a marvellous teacher of Bororo sociology.' This man's village, Kejara on the rio Vermelho, had escaped Salesian control thanks to the presence of a 'haughty and enigmatic chief'. Lévi-Strauss praised the way in which the Salesians and SPI had brought peace between settlers and Indians, and the excellence of the missionaries' ethnographic enquiries. But he deplored their 'methodical operation to eradicate native culture'.

A Decree of 16 October 1942 gave the SPI more control over missions. The Service's internal Bulletin attacked the disgraceful behaviour of some missionaries. 'Our Indians have been . . . victims of exploitation and the greed of non-Brazilian individuals on the pretext of catechism and assistance. The general result has been on the one hand the debasing and extinction of the natives, and on the other the enrichment and power of their pseudo-protectors.' Missions were accused of obtaining Indian lands, which they registered in the name of their order, creating fazendas and commercial operations, and exploiting the natives as their private work-force. But Bororo who lived outside the missions fared even worse. Decimated by disease and demoralized by contact, most of their villages disappeared. The survivors became casual labourers on settlers' farms, living in clusters of a few huts, and paid for their work only in handouts of cloth, tobacco, or alcohol. By the 1940s these scattered, miserable bands had almost abandoned agriculture and were in physical and cultural decline.

The SPI instituted reserves outside Salesian missionary control, and many Bororo returned to their traditional village areas. But they had suffered such depopulation and crushing change that they continued for many years to be depressed and disoriented. In their despair, some groups resorted to infanticide. I saw this at Barbosa de Farias (former Pobori) in the 1970s, where over thirty adults had only five children among them. They told me that this was deliberate: they were too sad to want children, and did not wish to raise young Bororo into the hostile and insulting world of the ranches that surrounded them. These people told me that they preferred the spiritual release of getting drunk on cachaça rum to rearing children. By contrast the village of Gomes Carneiro, on a hill above a beautiful curve of the São Lourenço river, was thriving. With over a hundred inhabitants, living in a tight circle of traditional thatched huts, there was an atmosphere of cheerful, scruffy vitality. The huts were sparsely furnished, but full of food, with arrows and baskets of headdresses and other ornaments on shelves or hanging from the beams. Chubby children and emaciated dogs were everywhere. The chief told me of the Bororos' love of Marshal Rondon, but also praised the Funai official Hélio Bucker who had personally revived Bororo self-esteem, pride in traditional customs, and morale.

The only Salesian mission that flourished and survived was Sangra-douro, which later extended to one called São Marcos on the south bank of the rio das Mortes. It was here that a group of Xavante took refuge after their contact in 1946 and later eviction from homelands north of the river. When the author visited it in 1972, the Bororo were living in rows of boxlike houses like clean frontiersmen but were still downcast by the eradication of their tribal culture. They desperately wanted a circular village with a central men's hut. The nearby Xavante, by contrast, were in buoyant spirits, keen to learn mechanized agriculture and other skills, and with a booming infant population. By the 1970s, the Salesians of Mato Grosso had learned to temper their missionary zeal and were permitting the Xavante to continue at least some of their traditional way of life. And later in the century, they even allowed the Bororo to rebuild a central men's hut, seeing it as a manifestation of spirituality that did not conflict with Christianity.

The Salesians developed another theocratic realm, far away in north-western Brazil. The tribes of the upper Negro and its great tributaries, the Uaupés, Tiquié, and Içana, were badly in need of help. These people had survived centuries of contact with frontier society – seized by slave-raiders, regimented in an eighteenth-century missionary empire under the Carmel-ites, decimated by appalling epidemics of smallpox, abused by lay 'direct-ors' in the nineteenth century, and subjected to a bizarre missionary experiment by Italian Capuchins in the 1870s. When the great German anthropologist Theodor Koch-Grünberg went up the Uaupés in 1904, he found its various Baniwa tribes living in dread of rubber collectors who crossed the frontier from Colombia and terrorized them. Rubber trees were not plentiful in this part of Brazil, but they and balata latex trees grew further upstream where the rivers rose inside Colombia. Armed Colombi-ans stole food, boys, and women from the defenceless Brazilian Indians.

At the extreme north-west of Brazil, other Indians fled across inter-national frontiers to escape the murderous empires of the Venezuelan rubber baron Tomás Funes or the Colombian Don Germano Garrido y Otero. Garrido later moved to the Içana in Brazil, where he controlled hundreds of Baniwa absolutely until his death in 1921. This feudal overlord cleverly manipulated his charges, by placing his sons as overseers in strategic villages, arranging god-parentage or marriages, and regularly supplying trade goods. So the Baniwa remembered Garrido as their most powerful master; but they had greater fear of the soldiers of Fort Cucuí (on the Rio Negro at the Venezuelan frontier). The American explorer Dr Alexander Hamilton Rice admired the tribes of the upper Içana. But he found that, as so often on the Brazilian frontier, 'lower down [the river], where Indians and whites do occasionally meet, petty theft and ill manners commence, and increase in proportion to the frequency of association . . . The Uaupés people have been made extremely treacherous by the unscrupulous acts of the "blancos".'

A few families of Portuguese traders, often married to native women, dominated the Middle Rio Negro. Alexander Hamilton Rice in 1917 saw how these all-powerful and intermarried families 'maintained a condition of Indian vassalage . . . almost feudal, not only in the number of retainers and servants, but in the large area of territory that a single individual controls and works.' At that time the Rio Negro was divided into four departments governed by superintendents who 'exercised authority over all Indians in their particular domain, or over as many as could be apprehended. [Indians were] a lucrative prerogative for [officials] engaged in commercial as well as political life.' Many Indians fled into the forests to escape such persecutors and also three great epidemics that decimated their population.

Far up the Uaupés, Curt Nimuendajú in 1927 met the notorious Brazilian Antonio Maia, who acted as agent for the Peruvian criminal Julio Cesar Barreto. Maia's men 'were constantly on the move to extort from Indian malocas the payment of "debts" for Barreto and to pile new burdens on the backs of these wretched people in order to force them to work for his boss ... Maia personally used the same system at Yutica, helped by a certain João Lima, whom the Indians indicated to me as one of the worst rapists of girls who plagued their malocas.' Nimuendajú met a boatload of heavily armed Colombian latex-tappers who had come to 'grab Indians' inside Brazil. These drank cachaça rum all night and 'when drunk they would combine to seize the village's women by force'. An American traveller called Gordon MacCreagh heard how Maia 'would arrive at an Indian village and demand food; and if it were not forthcoming on the instant, he would cut down the man with a machete. He would force the Indians to work for him and would pay them nothing; and if one had the temerity to ask for the promised payment, he would laugh and would shoot him with a big pistol.' MacCreagh found Maia on his island base, lying in 'a most gorgeous grass hammock decorated with humming-bird's feathers ... a gross, ponderous person, dressed in dingy white-duck trousers and an open coat displaying a corpulent expanse of black hairy chest and stomach.' From the hammock hung a holster with a sawed-off double-barrelled shotgun, and nearby stood a Winchester .45 rifle. This villain was of course affable to his American guests, lodging them in a 'palace' full of decaying furniture, a broken music-box, glass chandeliers and peeling frescoes of 'lewd figures'.

Curt Nimuendajú was profoundly depressed by what he saw on the Uaupés and Içana rivers. He found these Indians fearful, truculent, and deeply suspicious of all whites. Many ran off as soon as they saw him. Relations between indigenous people and civilizados were irreparably damaged, worse than he had seen anywhere else in Brazil. An abyss had opened between the two races. This experienced anthropologist found it impossible to gain the confidence of these Indians or to penetrate their psyches. 'For me personally, accustomed to intimate converse with Indians of very different tribes and regions, my stay among those of the Içana and Uaupés was a veritable martyrdom, seeing myself treated naturally as a criminal, perverse brute.' Women and children fled from him and Indian leaders treated him with hatred or disdain. This was clearly the fault of other whites; for those same Indians welcomed Nimuendajú's rowers with every hospitality. He also learned that, on the Rio Negro, 'civilizado' travellers took food for themselves but nothing for their rowers – these had to scrounge food from relatives, or starve.

Nimuendajú deplored the prevailing regime of forced labour, imposed in the name of progress and public need. To him, the only true wealth and stability of the region lay not in rubber or latex but in the Indians themselves. But he also blamed these tribes for being too docile. 'These men, who possess terrible weapons like their *curabis* [blowgun darts] poisoned with curare, never rise against the abuses committed by a small number of "whites" in their midst.' So 'civilizados' felt that they could commit any outrages with impunity.

The SPI was little help. Reports by its office in Manaus in the 1920s and 1930s were full of atrocities against the Indians of the Upper Rio Negro. It was well aware of the slavery of those forced to work for Colombians. But the SPI had minimal presence in north-west Brazil, and it appointed a drunken rascal called Manduca, of the powerful Albuquer-que family that controlled the Uaupés, as the local Director of Indians. This Manduca was notorious as one of the worst abusers of indigenous people, responsible for several deaths and much cruelty. He forced Indians to produce rubber and manioc for him, and to paddle on innumerable canoe journeys. Manduca later died of a mysterious disease, having been cursed by a Desana shaman on the Tiquié river.

To compound their misery, the indigenous peoples of the Upper Rio Negro also suffered terribly from diseases. The famous Brazilian doctor Oswaldo Cruz was sent to visit the region in 1913. He was appalled by the high incidence of malaria, introduced by the rubber- and latex-tappers, writing that malaria was responsible for 'the almost complete extermination of its inhabitants'. Then, in 1919, the global pandemic of Spanish influenza struck the lower Rio Negro, and it spread upriver during the next three years. The Indians learned that it was spread by whites who had colds, and they feared that merchandise could also carry the lethal germs. On one occasion they refused to paddle canoes full of cargo that they feared was infected. A Salesian wrote that an evil Colombian threatened them: 'Either you carry the merchandise [around the rapids] for us, or I shall immediately open all the crates and spread catarrh through every corner of your villages, and you will die!' The reluctant Indians moved the sealed boxes.

Nimuendajú reckoned that half the people of the Içana perished during the first quarter of the twentieth century. Indians tried in vain to understand the spread and nature of diseases, just as Europeans had agonized about them before modern medical discoveries. Dominique Buchillet learned how shamans developed rituals to combat the white men's dreadful scourges. The Desana associated influenza with a benign ailment of theirs that was thought to derive from ancestors' belongings. So their incantations mentioned any object that could cause pain to the head – Christ's crown of thorns, white women's hair clips, spectacle frames, etc. With measles (and before it, smallpox) it was obvious that Indians sickened and died more readily than whites – who had acquired some immunity from centuries of exposure to these diseases. So the Tukano identified the spots of measles with glass beads brought by the newcomers. Desana mythology also sought to explain the third great killer, malaria. They noticed that both Indians and non-Indians caught this disease, so in one myth it was vomited over the world by an evil spirit. In another legend it came from the oily fruit *umari* (just as some Americans used to think that it was caught by eating watermelons). A third myth considered malaria to be a poison like curare, since its victims became lethargic like animals hit by curare strychnine. They noticed that malaria was worse during the rainy season, which is when its vector the *Anopheles* mosquito breeds. So they regard pools in rapids as 'jars of malaria' that exude the disease as they evaporate. The nineteenth-century scientists Bates and Wallace had also noticed that rapids seemed to be related to malaria, while others believed that it came from tropical vapours, the 'bad air' (*mal aria*) of its name – all before the research that discovered that malaria is caused by the *Plasmodium* protozoon and is transmitted from one victim to another by the bite of a female mosquito.

The Hohodene Baniwa, further north on the Içana, developed their own mythology to explain the terrible scourges that were destroying them. The American anthropologist Robin Wright found that they blamed the diseases on a smoke produced by factories of a creator woman called Amaru. In one of their complex creation myths, Indian women were punished for robbing Amaru's son Kuwai. These women were dispersed to the four quarters, where they made factories. 'In these factories they had jars of metal (gold, silver, iron, steel, etc.) and these jars exuded the "smoke" that planes, boats and cars bring back (namely, pollution) together with manufactured goods to the "centre of the world" where the Baniwa live. It is this smoke that causes the whites' diseases, which are principally characterized by fever and dysentery.'

When a Bishop of Manaus visited the blighted Upper Rio Negro in 1908, the Indians at Taraquá begged him: 'Help us or these men are going to put an end to us!' The Bishop therefore arranged for Pope Pius X to confer the apostolic prelacy of the Rio Negro on the Salesian missionary order. The first Salesians, led by Fathers Lourenço Giordano and João Balzola, in 1914 reached São Gabriel da Cachoeira, a former mission village alongside sixty kilometres (thirty-seven miles) of rapids on the Middle Rio Negro. They came full of zeal, and the Indians looked to them as protectors, almost saviours. But the Salesians on the Rio Negro were to prove even more conservative and authoritarian than their brethren in Mato Grosso.

The Salesian fathers brought security from the rubber raiders, as well as some medicines and trade goods. As the anthropologist Janet Chernela said, 'their bases became religious, educational and mercantile centres'. But it was at a cost. The missionaries soon determined to abolish the magnificent multi-family malocas, elaborate thatched dwellings that Koch-Grünberg described as 'beautiful and spacious . . . painted with bright designs on the bark that covers the front wall'. These houses were rectangular, with triangular facades and mighty pitched roofs sloping down to the ground on either side of the central gable. One measured by the German anthropologist was 29 metres long by 21 wide and 10 high (95 by 69 by 33 feet).

Ignorant Italian missionaries had a ludicrous, ugly prejudice against these communal dwellings. Father Brüzzi da Silva wrote that 'these Indians may still live completely naked, dirty, fetid, promiscuously congregated in infected malocas, with their poor belongings confusedly scattered on the flea-ridden ground, including even their food – fruit, dried fish, beiju, etc . . . It is a standard of living that grieves our hearts, without any doubt unworthy of human beings.' Monsignor Pedro Massa wrote a horrifying account of his destruction of the 'great and old maloca' at Taraquá, which measured 20 by 40 metres (66 by 132 feet).

> You should know that for the Indians the maloca is their kitchen, dormitory, refectory, workshop, meeting place during the rainy season, and place for dancing during great ceremonies. It is where the Indians are born, live, and die: it is their world. However, the maloca is also – as the zealous Dom [Bishop] Balzola used to say – 'the house of the Devil', for it is there that they hold their infernal orgies and plot the most atrocious vengeance against the whites and other Indians. In the maloca, vices are transmitted from parents to children. Very well. This world of the Indians, this house of the Devil, no longer exists at Taraquá. We dismantled it and substituted a discreet number of small houses covered in palm thatch and with mud walls. So the maloca of the Tucanos is gone!

Curt Nimuendajú had a very different view of such vandalism. He praised the malocas as proof against the strongest tropical rains, dry and spotlessly clean, shady and agreeably cool – unlike the hot little boxes that replaced them. Far from being dens of promiscuity, 'because of rigorous exogamy, amorous relationships between children of the same maloca do not exist'. Nimuendajú was deeply moved when he watched the Tariana of Urubuquara on the Uaupés celebrate their final dance before the demolition of their beautiful hut. Because the Salesians had denounced such dances as sinful, the anthropologist tried to explain that such rituals were entirely legal in Brazil and that

> I personally found their dance ornaments most lovely and that their superb maloca was far better than the civilizados' cages . . . The men danced in headdresses. Young men and girls dedicated themselves with ardour to their favourite dance, to the sound of pan-pipes. Free of ridiculous civilized clothing, superb in their nakedness enhanced by feather ornaments and body-paint, these Indians looked extremely handsome and picturesque. I could not fail to be indignant at the thought that this could be the last festival of this nature. But I was leaving next day, whereas Father João [Balzola, who had ordered the destruction] remained.

Nimuendajú knew that 'the principal reason for the missionaries' aversion to collective habitations is . . . that they see in them – with every reason – the symbol, the veritable bulwark of the former organization and tradition of the pagan culture that is so contrary to their plans for conversion, for spiritual and social domination.' The entire community participated in building one of these architectural masterpieces, so that all shared in its ownership. Inside, the maloca was divided into areas for families and for ceremonies and rituals that were the basis of tribal society. 'The Indians' own culture is condensed in the malocas: everything in them breathes tradition and independence. This is why they have to fall.'

Dr Hamilton Rice approved of such order and progress. 'São Gabriel today [1920] with its clean, nicely dressed, courteous schoolchildren, neatly fenced gardens, cleared spaces, and atmosphere of order and industry, is in striking contrast to the squalid little village of naked little savages, neglected purlieus, and lack of municipal control and mission influence that prevailed up to three years ago.' But the indigenous inhabitants were less enchanted. They tried to modify the rectilinear village plan. Janet Chernela noted, upriver, that 'the Indians sought to retain some features of the old malocas . . . – with houses that replicated where families would have been in the maloca, or with houses extended to accommodate up to fifteen people.'

In their determination to smash tribal beliefs, the Salesians concentrated on the young – just as all missionaries had done ever since the first Jesuits arrived in Brazil in the sixteenth century. But Hamilton Rice was appalled by their impractical curriculum. 'Until the Roman Catholic missionaries . . . recognize the necessity for education of more practical value than mere theology, the results cannot be but disappointing.' The Indians needed to learn self-respect, some Portuguese, 'and a little elementary education beyond theological dogma'. The missionaries eventually founded three boarding schools and sixty day-schools in their vast apostolic province. The children in these schools suffered stultifying discipline – in contrast to the carefree training in tribal skills of young Indians running freely about their villages. A rigid timetable had to be obeyed, and it of course included much religious worship and instruction. The sexes were strictly separated at all times. Children were even forbidden to glance sideways at the opposite sex when entering church, and they had to look only at the priest during mass. One German missionary at Pari-Cachoeira even stopped early-morning bathing in the river, which is an essential and agreeable part of tribal routine. All these rules were enforced by beatings and other punishments. Ettore Biocca, an Italian medical doctor who admired the Salesians' boarding schools, admitted in 1963 that 'the way of life of the young Indians changes abruptly: they pass from a free existence in the forests to strict cohabitation.' Aloísio Cabalzar concluded that it was 'an environment completely alien to local reality, one in which notions of sin, indecency, and disobedience were applied to the most simple acts.' The author visited the seminary-like school at São Gabriel in the 1970s. At that time, there were fourteen white-robed missionary fathers and sisters teaching 316 boarders aged from ten upwards. Girls dressed in bright velveteen frocks lined up to sing 'Frère Jacques' in French. It was charming, but hopelessly irrelevant to the tough Brazilian society in their town, or to the forests and river beyond it.

Gordon MacCreagh reported ironically how two priests at São Gabriel

struggle against overwhelming odds to persuade the heathen that their God is better than the medicine-man . . . They taught their converts to labor for the betterment of their own condition. They cleared the jungle and showed the naked savages how to plant beans and potatoes and sugar cane . . . Then [after a few years] the sauba [leaf-cutter] ants came out of the jungle. And now they have eaten every last vestige of all that planting, and their tunnels and underground caverns infest the whole of the twenty hard-won acres [eight hectares]. Why? The patient priests cross themselves and say it was the will of their God, and they look hopelessly upon the ruin of the labor of years. The Indians say it all happened because the great spirit of the rapids was scorned.

Aloísio Cabalzar, an expert on the Upper Rio Negro tribes, summed up the early years: 'Salesian activity was based on truculence and perseverance. Their truculence, on arrival, was to characterize Indians as degenerate and ignorant beings and to be bent on baptizing them and destroying all signs of difference. Perseverance was in erecting missionary centres and the effort to remove children from their homes to be educated as boarders in the mission schools.' A leader of the tribes of the Middle Rio Negro looked back at the work of the missionaries, and concluded that they had done more damage than good.

At first they wanted to settle Indians in villages, in order to liberate them from the clutches of bosses, and they obliged them to believe in God through Catholic evangelization. This onslaught was worse than any physical suffering, because it forced the Indians to abandon many cultural practices – such as shamanistic cures, *dabacuri* festivals [an exchange of goods, such as food or handicrafts, between groups], puberty rites, and their ways of worshipping and thanking the great creator of the universe. All these practices were condemned as diabolical by the missionaries.

The white-robed fathers gradually extended their network of missions in the Upper Rio Negro. They started at Uaupés, the seat of their bishopric of São Gabriel da Cachoeira, established in 1921. In 1923 they founded Taraquá on the Uaupés close to the mouth of the Tiquié; in 1929 Iauareté where the Uaupés and Papuri join and there is a fine waterfall at the Colombian frontier; in 1940 Pari-Cachoeira, at a rapids on the upper Tiquié; in 1942 Tapuruquara at Santa Isabel on the Rio Negro downstream of São Gabriel; and in 1952 Assunção on the Içana. Curt Nimuendajú described Taraquá in 1927, four years after its foundation: 'At first sight you realize that you are dealing with an enterprise that has sufficient resources to establish itself permanently. The church is surely the best in all the Upper Rio Negro. Beside it rises the solid and spacious mission building with various out-buildings. On a hill behind you can see a meteorological station. The shacks of the Indians contrast somewhat with these very modern constructions. There are seven huts, located on the riverbank, and seeming to me far inferior to their primitive malocas.'

Ettore Biocca wrote in 1963 that 'the merit of the Salesian missions consists in their creating the only hospitals that exist on the Rio Negro'. They treat both Indians and settlers. 'Unfortunately, . . . the hospitals house moribund patients suffering from tuberculosis alongside those with malaria and other non-contagious diseases. The hospitals thus become the most dangerous centres for the diffusion of tuberculosis.' All these patients shared the same kitchens, laundry, and accommodation unprotected from insects. 'Male and female missionaries, who are heroically dedicated, are among the first victims.' Despite his admiration for the Salesians, Dr Biocca was appalled by their destruction of the airy great communal malocas, so clean and hygienic, in order to house Indians in dangerously unhealthy houses of mud or concrete. Biocca also praised the Indians' former nakedness, which was utterly modest and appropriate in the equatorial climate, and which had none of the hygienic problems of clothing. However, he acknowledged that nudity was associated in our culture with moral lassitude. 'Missionaries generally consider nudity of Indian women as sinful and seek to eliminate it.' Also, of course, Indians had to wear clothing to blend in to the world of the frontier. Diet also deteriorated with acculturation. Indians stopped eating nutritious insects, reptiles, and other forest foods in favour of 'the irrational diet of the civilizados', which reduced their organic resistance and thus favoured the spread of disease.

Curt Nimuendajú saw that these poor Indians suffered from four 'calamities': Colombian rubber men, Brazilian traders, selfish officials, and intolerant missionaries. Of these, the last were the most bearable. For, unlike the other oppressors, the Salesians never used violence against Indians, they freed many from servitude, and they always paid for labour or goods. The trouble was that 'Indians are harmed by missionaries because of their inability to comprehend . . . any culture other than their Christian one. The intolerance inherent in their calling, which obliges them to see every Indian as an object for religious conversion, is incompatible with the duty of protecting native individuality.' Nimuendajú was amazed by the laughable howlers in a book that one Salesian wrote about tribal cultures, and he mocked another who was frightened to sleep in a village with these peaceful people or, after his canoe capsized, felt he was 'brave' to eat their 'nauseating' food from a common vessel.

Even today [1927], the ideal of all of these 'civilizers of Indians' is a large Indian town of modern appearance, with a vast boarding school for the Indians' children, all located at a place that guarantees rapid commercial and industrial development. Then, after a generation has elapsed, they can demonstrate, by a deserted settlement and a replete cemetery, that their mission has fulfilled at least its final objective: for the [natives] all died as good Catholics, confessing and receiving extreme unction. The Indians of the Uaupés ... possess a fairly advanced culture, to the point where they would need very little from modern civilization apart from tools. Were they not robbed at every instant, they would live not only in plenty but would even export food ... What these Indians need with the greatest urgency is moral regeneration, to restore their individual and racial esteem – sentiments that were scorned by the civilizados until their last vestiges were extinguished. The missions' tutelage will never produce any such effect; but rather the contrary.

The anthropologist Adélia de Oliveira interviewed aged Baniwa on the Içana and found that the Salesians did little to protect Indians on that remote river. Her witnesses confirmed that, from the 1930s onwards, they were exploited by bosses who used their dependence on trade goods to keep them in debt-bondage. Some employers were in league with military and government authorities, so that Indians fled to Venezuela and Colombia where pay was better. Despite these hardships, some Baniwa started to work on their own account and even competed against the *regatão* riverine traders.

The great Colombian anthropologist Gerardo Reichel-Dolmatoff made a damning assessment of the Salesians' work. 'Fifty years of missionizing produced a population of demoralized, almost cultureless, socially incongruous individuals, the result of constant pressure by nuns and priests to change and "civilize" Indians' customs.' A visitor to Pari-Cachoeira on the upper Tiquié in 1966 reported that 'segregation of the sexes is complete. The church has two entrances, one for the priests and boys and the other for the women. Inside the church, too, they each keep to their own part. The same applies to all secular activities.' In the refectory, food was passed through a hatch so that the sexes could not glimpse one another. 'The Roman Catholic system of indoctrination is centred on the schools' where strict supervision ensures that 'religious duties and obligations are scrupulously observed ... Direct contact between persons of opposite sexes, whether priests, nuns, lay helpers or school children, is something that practically never happens.'

I visited Iauareté, a big mission for the Tariana, Tukano, and other groups at a great waterfall on the Uaupés that marks the frontier with Colombia. The boarding school housed over 300 children from the age of ten upwards. It was well equipped, with sports grounds, a carpentry shop for the boys and sewing and basketry workshops for girls. There was an impressive pharmacy and dispensary, run by missionary sisters, but visited regularly by an air force doctor who transported all medicines free of charge. A large, multicoloured wooden church with a spire dominated the school's quadrangles and dormitories, and there were religious icons everywhere – shrines, statues, devotional pictures, messages, and grottoes – and most children wore medallions. An old frontiersman told me that he deplored the way in which the missionaries had robbed the Indians of their former culture, pride, and self-sufficiency. They had become humble and sheepish, with a cloistered view of Christian civilization.

The peoples of the Upper Rio Negro are proficient at making all their basic necessities. However, they have an almost mythical tradition that each tribe has a craft speciality that it trades with others – as the peoples of the upper Xingu do. The Baniwa have an absolute monopoly in making manioc graters, elegant concave wooden slabs studded with rows of sharp quartz that occurs only at a rapids on the middle Içana river. Since manioc and its roasted farinha flour are staples of this region, these Baniwa graters are essential possessions. Tukano groups specialize in carved stools decorated with symbolic paintings. The Cubeo and Wanana produce red dyes for body paint, and the Tukano, Desana, and Barasana make magnificent great wooden drums used for sending messages over long distances. The Baniwa are superb potters, and they in turn get gourds from the Wanana, their neighbours on the upper Uaupés. The Tuyuka make highly prized canoes. But the craft for which all these tribes are famous is basketry. Men make all sizes of baskets, adorned with delicate geometric designs in dark and pale straw. In recent years the Salesian missionaries have helped to stimulate this Indian skill, supported by the air force (which transports the baskets to markets downriver) and by government subsidies. The anthropologist Berta Ribeiro (wife of Darcy Ribeiro) wrote that 'in exchange for their handicrafts and manioc farinha, rowan sorbs, and *titica* lianas, the missions offer the Indians of the Içana and Uaupés medical and sanitary assistance, education, and reasonably priced industrial goods.'

In the forests between the rivers are nomadic groups known collectively as Makú, hunter-gatherers who do not depend on farming. Because of their mobility, the Makú have a less sophisticated material culture than the large tribes of the Uaupés and its tributaries. However, the Makú also have a trading speciality: elegant carrying baskets made from tough imbé lianas. These baskets are used primarily for carrying bitter manioc from gardens to houses, and they do not rot when wet.

The British anthropologists Peter Silverwood-Cope and Howard Reid worked during the 1960s and 1970s with the Bará and Hupdu groups of

Makú, and learned about their deep understanding of their forest environment and their rich mythology and culture. 'They live in small family groups, prefer the deep forest to the rivers, and are constantly on the move. In fact, they never stay in one place for more than a few days. As they are so mobile it means that they can have few possessions, and what they have must be easily portable. At a minute's notice, therefore, they can wrap up their fibre-string hammocks (which are their only real furniture), put their pots and few remaining items in home-made rucksacks, and move on.' Consummate hunters with blowguns and curare-tipped darts, 'the Makú eat fish, game, turtles, fruit, vegetables, nuts, insects and honey. Indeed, it is hard to think of a healthier or more balanced diet.'

For centuries, these forest nomads were encountered as servants among the Tukano, Desana, and other large tribes. Travellers and anthropologists, who visited only the riverine tribes, thought that the Makú were being exploited as virtual slaves. Silverwood-Cope and Reid learned more about the curious symbiotic relationship between the two groups. The nomadic and settled Indians frequently visit one another, and the Makú occasionally toil in the plantations of the riverine tribes for derisory reward or small amounts of coca or tobacco that they can steal. The river tribes are arrogant and demanding towards the naked Makú. But they are also impressed by the latter's ceremonials, and they ask them back to their own festivals – provided that the Makú bring quantities of forest produce. Several times a year the Tukano hold great *dabucuri* rituals for exchange of goods. The Makú are invited, greeted with formal dances, and share in the copious drinking and feasting, but there is always a sense of superiority among the settled tribes. Reid observed that 'the unequal status relations between the two groups exist mainly at a putative, symbolic level. True, the Hupdu [Makú] have to tolerate the jokes and arrogance of the Tukanoans, but the criteria which mark the Hupdu as inferior are derived directly from the Tukanoan world view and not from that of the Hupdu.' The Makú take their shabbiest belongings when visiting river villages, in order to scrounge better goods; but this apparent poverty fooled anthropologists who had never reached their comfortable forest abodes. The relationship between Tukano and Makú was a patron–client system, based on perceived mutual benefits and tradition rather than force.

Having detribalized and acculturated the larger tribes of the Upper Rio Negro, the Salesians turned their attention to the nomadic Makú. The missionaries travelled only along the navigable rivers, but they started to visit Makú settlements that were within easy reach. During the 1940s they launched their first campaign to change the tribe's nomadic lifestyle.

They Salesians made every mistake. They exhorted the Indians to farm in large gardens on cleared forest, to settle in single-hearth rectangular houses of wattle and daub, and to open broad trails to the nearest large river so that priests could easily visit them. They also removed Makú children to their boarding schools – although most were so unhappy there that they soon ran home. The Salesians knew very little about the Makú, whom they regarded as melancholic, primitive, and in need of 'rehabilitation and civilization'.

The first attempt to convert the Makú came to nothing, but in 1968 a priest from Iauareté persuaded six groups to congregate in a settlement on a stream called the Japu, off the upper Uaupés. A church and large garden were built; but there was a fight between the groups of Makú; the priest died; and the concentration dispersed. In the early 1970s a Spanish missionary, Father Alfonso Casanova, tried again, with a village of twenty houses for some 160 Makú, a church, and a house for himself. The site was six hours' walk from the large Iauareté mission, and was called Serra dos Porcos ('Pigs' Hill') because it was a foraging place for peccary. Despite gifts of tools and manioc flour, the village was not a success. The Salesians tried to stop 'sinful' practices. One Hupdu Makú complained to Howard Reid: 'The priests come here and tell us to stop chewing coca and drinking beer. They tell us we shouldn't dance and play pan-pipes or *jurupari* trumpets. This is like a man coming to our village and taking away all our food. What should we do? Without food, without music, there is no movement in the world and the people are sad, become sick and die.' There were serious fights between the settlement's inhabitants in both 1971 and 1974, with subsequent dispersals; and the Indians so disliked the missionary that they gradually poisoned his food.

Father Casanova devised an even more grotesque experiment for the Makú. He revived an abandoned mission called Fátima on the bank of the main Tiquié river, a wretched place with a concrete house surrounded by barbed wire on pointed stakes. Three groups of Hupdu Makú were moved 200 kilometres (125 miles) to this totally inappropriate settlement; and three other clans were brought from forests to the south. A Spanish couple was contracted to teach and administer medicines to the Makú at Fátima. The forest nomads were totally dependent on food from the missionary, and became understandably miserable. In 1974 there was a fight between Hupdu and Yuhup Makú, and the groups burned huts and returned to their forests. It took the Indians from near Iauareté several months to walk back to their homelands.

An energetic Austrian missionary now attempted an even nastier 'model' village for the Makú. His Cucura on the Tiquié consisted of thirty-seven 3 by 5 metre (10 by 16 feet) huts plus the usual mission buildings, in straight lines around a totally deforested parade ground. The Salesians gave the Makú plenty of free food and medicines, but this did not compensate for the damage done by congregating nomads. 'The most striking and alarming result was the collapse of health and nutrition.' Small roving bands of Makú could escape epidemics, but the concentration at Cucura was vulnerable to successive diseases. One group lost a quarter of its population in a single outbreak of measles. The accumulation of people in one village caused problems of refuse and pollution of the stream in which they washed, drank, and drained their effluents. The presence of many superb hunters denuded surrounding forests of game, so that children suffered protein deficiency. The Salesians' answer was to introduce cattle; but although the Makú toiled to clear patches of weedy grazing land, only six animals were brought and the yield of milk was too little for the groups' children. Various Makú customs, such as sharing game or coca among the entire community and ritual festivals, did not work in the larger village of regimented huts. One benefit of life with the missionaries was a supply of trade goods at less cost than that demanded by the Tukano and Desana. 'Trading . . . escalated to include such items as shotguns and ammunition, mirrors, toys, even transistor radios. The standard of material wealth grew rapidly in the years following the opening of mission villages.' But when the Makú started to use their newly acquired guns and cartridges in inter-tribal feuds, the Salesians stopped supplying ammunition. 'Hupdu [Makú] who had traded ten blowpipes for one shotgun found themselves with useless new weapons.' And the demands of the arrogant river tribes did not diminish.

Howard Reid wondered why 260 Hupdu Makú chose to remain in the two mission villages throughout the 1970s. He concluded that access to manufactured goods – hammocks, cooking pots, machetes, and axes – was a powerful lure. Also, the nomads were in awe of the Salesians. 'The Hupdu were prepared to tolerate a great deal of unintelligible and often irrational behaviour by the missionaries rather than offend them and risk incurring their "anger" and thus inciting revenge sorcery from them.' Thirdly, some Makú wanted their children to be educated and learn Portuguese, so that they could become as sophisticated as the larger settled tribes. 'They wanted this advantage for their children, and the Salesians offered them the opportunity.'

Reid also wondered why the priests tried to impose such abrupt and profound change on the nomadic Makú. The missionaries saw themselves as motivated on humanitarian and religious grounds. But they failed to understand that the Makú were admirably nourished in their small hunting bands. They also had a misguided notion of making the Makú 'progress' towards integration into Brazilian national society. However, the Salesian concept of progress involved abandonment of traditional ways and indoctrination of children in mission schools. And the rarified, regimented, and pious world of missions like Iauareté bore no relation to the real world of the Brazilian interior. Conversion to Christianity was the ultimate objective of missionaries at that time, but the British anthropologists found that the Hupdu deeply deplored the abandonment of their beliefs and rituals.

Two other agencies began to challenge the Salesians in the late 1970s. Protestants of the Summer Institute of Linguistics wanted to translate the Bible into Makú languages, and approached nomadic groups from both Brazil (despite opposition from Catholic missionaries) and from nearby Colombia. Funai also started to penetrate the Salesians' theocracy of the Upper Rio Negro. They engaged Peter Silverwood-Cope (who was then with the University of Brasília) to implement a programme of medical assistance to the Makú, in their forest refuges. But Silverwood-Cope fell foul of politics within Funai. His punishment for criticizing the Salesians was expulsion from Brazil, in 1976. The Makú became disillusioned with all forms of missionary interference: they returned to the satisfying and sustainable life in the forests.

Although often suffocating and ethnocidal, missionary tutelage did at least protect the lives of most tribes of the Upper Rio Negro. Having fallen in numbers because of disease and abuse, their populations started to increase. By the late 1970s there were some 10,000 within the Prelacy of the Rio Negro, but over 2,000 of these were Protestant.

As we have seen, Catholic missionaries were also active in other parts of Brazil. French Dominicans had long been established on the Araguaia, with some Kayapó, Karajá, and Tapirapé. German Franciscans were with the Munduruku on the Tapajós-Cururu and later with the Tiriyó in northern Pará. Higher up the Tapajós, the Jesuits in mid-century established the Missão Anchieta for the Kayabi and other tribes. Italian Capuchins had a chequered history with the Guajajara in Maranhão. Non-monastic diocesan priests worked with Indian communities in southern Brazil and along the Atlantic seaboard, among the Terena of South Mato Grosso, with one village of Wari (Pakaá Nova) on the Guaporé, Ticuna, and others on the Solimões, and in northern Amapá. The Italian Consolata mission succeeded the Benedictines among tribes of Roraima.

*

In contrast to the long-established Catholics, Protestant missionaries moved into Brazil only gradually; but they eventually came to dominate entire tribes. Individuals such as Frederick Glass of the British and Foreign Bible Society roamed about Brazil dispensing Bibles: he saw the Bororo early in the century, and was impressed by the cleanliness and manliness of the Karajá in the 1920s. Kenneth Grubb worked with tribes of the rubber forests in western Brazil and later joined the SPI. In 1925, the American Presbyterian Revd L. L. Legters made a survey of the Amazon basin for the Inland South American Missionary Union and reported that 'there must be Indian tribes all over the [vast] area.' A few years later one of Legters' colleagues, who was pursuing this survey in what is now Rondônia, was killed by Nambiquara Indians.

The Worldwide Evangelization Crusade started work among the Guajajara of Maranhão in 1923 and eventually converted many of these people and the nearby Canela Timbira to its wholesome brand of Christianity. Horace Banner and the Three Freds of the Unevangelized Fields Mission (which evolved from the Crusade) worked among the Gorotire Kayapó in the late 1930s, and other Protestants were active with the nearby Tapirapé and Karajá at that time. The SPI praised the work of the missionaries Mr and Mrs Thomas Young and their nurse, Marjorie Clarke, in combating a malaria epidemic among the Bakairi at Simões Lopes later that decade. These Protestants started to investigate the tempting tribes of the upper Xingu, just before the arrival of the Villas Boas brothers (who eventually excluded all missionaries from that region). The Director of the SPI, Colonel Vasconcellos, wrote to their head in 1943 politely warning them to desist. 'The SPI and everyone who lives with Indians know the apathy and indifference of catechized Indians . . . The first drawback we observe after the entry of missionaries into an Indian tribe is the breakdown of tribal fraternity. Indians who become Catholic or Protestant form hostile groups and lose interest in their tribe . . . We see no advantage in the religious instruction of the Indians. We even feel that it is preferable that no such instruction ever take place.'

The SPI's new Regimento of October 1942 gave the Service more control over missions, particularly those receiving government help. Its staff were told that 'our Indians have been victims of exploitation and greed by non-Brazilian individuals on the pretext of catechism and aid' – to the detriment of the Indians and enrichment of their 'pseudo-protectors'. Vasconcellos expelled missionaries from all SPI posts (but not from established missions), a ban that lasted for twelve years from 1943 to 1955. The zealous Protestants remained active among ordinary Brazilians. So when their expulsion from Indian posts ended in 1955 the Unevangelized Fields Mission resumed activity in three regions: among the Kayapó (Banner's Gorotire, Kuben-Kran-Kégn, and Kokraimoro); in three villages of Guajajara and nearby Canela in Maranhão, where its proselytizers had been active since the 1920s; and among the Wapixana and Makuxi in Roraima, where by 1962 they maintained four posts serving some 2,500 Indians. Fifteen years later, the Unevangelized Fields Mission had over 140 adults working in Brazil. Many of these were married couples, and the Mission maintained schools for their children at Belém and Manaus. Its head, the Reverend McAlistair, told the author that his Mission disagreed with Funai about not interfering with native beliefs. 'From a religious point of view, Indians are bound by superstition. We try to stop that. We don't change any Indian custom that we feel is not harmful. But once we start preaching, we find that the Indians themselves tell us what is detrimental, what in their dances and culture belongs to the evil spirit world – things that we might not recognize as evil . . . Our main purpose is religious conversion; but we also do much social work – medical and teaching.' He felt that the Christian faith (preferably Protestant) prepared Indians for inevitable contact with unscrupulous civilizados.

In 1945 Sophie Muller, an American missionary who later joined the New Tribes Mission, started evangelizing among the Kuripako in southeast Colombia. 'She had a pioneering spirit, was brave and endowed with clear messianic tendencies.' In 1948 she moved down the Aiari river to the Içana in Brazil, where she worked with the Baniwa and later with Cubeo on the Querari – oppressed peoples who had turned to the Salesians for protection. Muller's teaching had a thunderous impact. Robin Wright noted that 'by sheer stroke of luck, she fell upon a people who would accept her and her message with open arms. As she relates in her diary, [published as] *Beyond Civilization* (1952), she was looked upon as a messiah. The Indians flocked to hear her preach the gospel; flotillas of canoes followed her from one village to the next. Indians constructed lodgings for her in eighteen settlements. They asked her to bring trousers from heaven, make their gardens grow, protect them from illness, and chase away evil spirits.' Aloísio Cabalzar wrote that 'Her conversion of the Baniwa to Protestant evangelism had all the signs of a messianic movement. With her anti-Catholic messages, and preaching redemption and an end to suffering, she converted various indigenous groups of the Içana. Many Baniwa considered Muller as a messiah. They came from all sides to hear her preaching and to adhere to the new faith.'

During her years with Indians in Colombia, Sophie Muller had protected them against ranchers and other white oppressors. She taught them pride in their indigenous independence. But she totally obliterated her Indians' spiritual heritage. When David Stoll, who investigated the various Protestant missionary sects, asked Muller whether she had destroyed native culture, 'she exclaimed "I should hope so – drunkenness and wild dancing, you know dancing leads to immorality. The idiots had all this witchcraft. The men would drink and dance all night, then go off into the woods with girls and (pause) do their immorality."' She was obsessed with evil demons and saw the hand of Satan in every aspect of tribal dancing and ritual. For her, the Baniwa's mythological heroes Inyaime and Kuwai were the Devil, and she was determined to eradicate them.

Muller was very energetic and a fine linguist, so that she translated the four gospels and many epistles into the Baniwas' Aruak language. She then taught many Indians to read, and they regarded her as someone sent by God. Protestant churches were built in every village, where 'for long hours of night and morning all the Indians gathered to sing and read in their own language'. A Salesian father who met Sophie Muller in 1953 described her as 'a lady little over thirty years of age, well educated, who spoke German, but was a tremendous fanatic'.

This branch of Christianity was seen as a form of resistance to white oppression and domination. The Baniwa and related tribes had a history of messianic movements, so they eagerly adopted this new one. As the years went by, the New Tribes Mission organized a system of native elders and deacons; there were monthly Holy Suppers for each riverine community; and the congregations met in six-monthly Conferences. The Mission's own radio station broadcast weekly religious programmes in the Baniwa language. A missionary pastor wrote that 'these peoples were quite civilized at the time. A literacy program was launched with extraordinary success. More than 75 per cent of them learned to read in a short period of time. They were given portions of God's Holy Word in their own tongue. The impact of the teachings of Scriptures had a positive effect on them. It transformed them from being the most depraved, useless and thievish people of the area to being the most productive and trustworthy.' By 1957 the Brazilian anthropologist Eduardo Galvão observed 'the routine observance of religious services conducted in Baniwa, with no assistance whatever from the Protestant missionary who lived many kilometres upriver. These meetings consisted of readings of passages from the Bible and singing of hymns.' Two New Tribes missionaries, Keith and Myrtle Wardlaw, told the author about those glorious years on the Içana, when native beliefs were constantly 'breaking' and everyone was accepting 'the message of Jesus Christ'. One of Muller's idiosyncrasies was to destroy fruit trees because Adam had been tempted by fruit. She also forbade her people to buy civilizado food, because all needs should come from heaven: she thus weakened their dependence on traders. Unlike other missionaries, she did not used trade goods as a weapon of conversion.

Sophie Muller was strongly anti-Catholic. Images of Catholic saints were broken and thrown into the river, and Sophie (as the Indians called her) tore medallions of the Virgin off people's necks and hung them on dogs' collars. The Catholic Salesians were outraged and alarmed. They sent the veteran missionary José Schneider to found a mission called Assunção at the mouth of the Içana; but it was too late to impress the tribes upriver. The SPI was also worried that this movement would undermine its policies of frontier settlement and turning Indians into patriotic Brazilians. So in June 1953, under strong pressure from the Salesians, an SPI official went up the Içana to summon Sophie Muller downriver for police questioning about her unauthorized teaching and proselytizing. The two met at a village near the Tunui rapids and Sophie pretended to obey the order. But, instead, she fled upriver during the night in a canoe with five paddlers, then changed canoes above the waterfalls, ascended the Cuiari, and returned to Colombia in another boat. This dramatic escape entered Baniwa mythology, and is retold to this day alongside the adventures of the tribe's legendary hero Kamiko. Sophie Muller never returned to Brazil, but she continued to work among Colombian Indians for many years, almost until her death in the 1990s.

The Catholics launched a propaganda war to try to win back the Baniwa. They played the nationalism card for all it was worth, persuading the government and military that fundamentalist Protestant Indians in the north-west corner of Brazil threatened the nation's security. Finally, in 1961, soldiers from the Cucui garrison expelled Pastor Henry Loewen (later head of the New Tribes Mission in Brazil) from the Içana. The Salesians crowed in their journal that 'Divine providence appears to want to facilitate the conversion of these people of the Içana, corrupted by heresy.' They founded a boarding school on that river and built more missions in Protestant villages. But the attempt to win the Baniwa back to Catholicism failed. Few Indians attended mass and children ran away from the strict school. By the 1970s the Salesian mission in this region was almost finished, with leaf-cutter ants eating its plantations and the Indians reverting either to their shamanism or Protestantism. The New Tribes Mission's influence among the Baniwa also waned. Many crentes (believers) admitted that some of them were now 'half-crentes' who occasionally indulged in smoking, drinking beer, or dancing, had resumed their interest in tribal mythology and shamanism and attended fewer services.

Sophie Muller's New Tribes Mission was founded in California in 1950 and swept into Brazil a few years later as the Missão Novas Tribos do Brasil (MNTB). This movement was aggressively determined to make converts. Its own literature said: 'The New Tribes Mission is a fundamental, non-denominational-faith missionary society, composed of born-again believers, and dedicated to the evangelization of unreached tribal peoples; in their own tongue the translation of Scripture; and the planting of indigenous New Testament churches.' By 1960 it had twenty-eight families operating among ten tribes in different parts of Brazil. The MNTB preferred to send married couples where both husband and wife were activists, often with children. Its missionaries went into the field straight from their American churches, clean-living and God-fearing, fanatics armed only with frightening conviction in the rectitude of their cause. Even Jim Wilson, head of the Brazilian operation of the Summer Institute of Linguistics, admitted to the author that 'the New Tribes Mission suffered from lack of training and preparation. It sent in people quite unprepared to deal with cultures different to their own. They had no sympathy with Indian outlooks, and were overeager for rapid change.'

The head of the SPI in 1962, Lieutenant Colonel Moacyr Ribeiro Coelho, had no such qualms. Coelho was deeply impressed by this Mission, 'which possesses great resources, such as planes, boats, and a considerable number of missionaries with their respective families in various parts of the globe.' At that time the MNTB, in addition to its successes on the Içana, was active among tribes of the Tocantins-Araguaia – the Karajá of Bananal Island, Xerente, Apinayé, and Gavião – with the Kaingang in the extreme south of Brazil, the Yanomami of the Demini river in the north, and the Marubo of the Javari and Ituí in the west. Colonel Coelho assured his Minister that these missionaries were neither American spies nor mineral prospectors and that they included many Brazilians. 'The work of the missionaries is scientific, disinterested, honest, and above all of the greatest value to the SPI and its wards, the Indians ... Their ultimate goal ... is the diffusion of Bible-teaching among the natives, for which they must enter the forest and live with them and learn their languages.' This was a far cry from Rondon's lay Service, pledged not to interfere with indigenous beliefs. Coelho had no concept of the ideals of the Service he was leading. Instead, he advocated an accelerated campaign of contacting remote tribes and 'acculturating those already pacified. This would achieve a double objective: to facilitate the civilizados' destiny of penetrating the forests; and to enable the use of Indian labour, above all in the extractive industries. This would rapidly enable the aborigines to collaborate with civilizados without fighting them or being attacked or exploited by them.'

Unlike some military men running Funai, Brazilian anthropologists were appalled by the damage done by the New Tribes Mission, which regarded itself as an 'Army of Angels'. It grew rapidly: to 198 missionaries in twenty-eight tribes in 1975; and to 337 in thirty-seven tribes by 1981, a year in which its budget was $9 million. Mauro Leonel wrote that '"linguistics" is the main camouflage of this organization for the demoralization of tribal culture. In fact, its source of recruitment is the unemployed of the US and Europe. Of the New Tribes' 110 missionaries and linguists, only 15 have had a form of university-level training. 27 are manual labourers (factory workers and farm hands) and 72 from the service sector (clerks, domestics, housewives, and students). The training of the New Tribes "linguists" lasts for only two months, with some refresher courses.' The sect was like a medieval crusade, inspiring its workers for a war against unbelievers. 'Their ethnocentrism is accompanied by open racism – in minutes of conversations there is prejudice against Indians, blacks, and Jews. As with all fanatical groupings, they are extremely closed and hostile to non-believers. Their contribution to linguistics is nil.' Totally ignorant of indigenous culture, they contributed nothing whatever to anthropology in Brazil.

Of all the Protestant missions, the best-endowed, most intelligent, and most politically adept was the Summer Institute of Linguistics (SIL), now renamed Field International. This somewhat sinister organization was the creation of William Cameron Townsend, later known as Cam or 'Uncle Cam' because of his work in spreading the geopolitical gospel of Uncle Sam. In 1930 Cam Townsend, who had worked for years as a missionary in Central America, announced his intention of starting a movement of fundamentalist proselytizers who would be presented as 'linguistic investigators' rather than missionaries. They were to study every known language, in order to translate the New Testament into each one. From the outset, the SIL was funded by affluent Baptist organizations backed by the Rockefeller family, whose Standard Oil gained much of its vast wealth from wells in American Indian lands. SIL's parallel, but more openly evangelistic, mission is the Wycliffe Bible Translators; and it gains academic respectability by association with the University of Oklahoma at Norman. The SIL expanded gradually southwards, from Mexico and Central America to Ecuador and Peru. In the Peruvian Amazon, the SIL developed a headquarters at Yarinacocha off the Ucayali, a sprawling and spotless garden city of bungalows resembling an army camp or college campus. In 1946 it started a Jungle Aviation and Radio Service whose small planes, skilled bush pilots, and network of airstrips could carry the word of the Lord to the most isolated tribe.

The idea that the Amazon basin was a cornucopia had a long history. The first European explorers were seduced by the lush tropical vegetation, and in the nineteenth century American and European geographers enthused about its potential. The dream persisted into the twentieth century. The American Earl Hanson in 1932 visited Manaus – by then in full decay – and wrote: 'I find myself confronted at every turn by the romantic argument that the conquest of South America's wilderness would do for the Western Hemisphere what the conquest of the West did for the United States at a critical time.'

In 1941 President Franklin Roosevelt appointed the rich and dynamic Nelson Rockefeller to a new post of Coordinator of Inter-American Affairs and he soon employed Hanson to develop a strategy for exploiting the Amazon. A Brazilian official wrote to Rockefeller's man in Brazil with a mouth-watering list of Amazonia's riches: petroleum, rubber, gold, fibres, coal, aluminium, and many natural foods, 'meat of every sort to be obtained from the transformation of the forests of the low Amazon into evergreen pastures . . . The wealth of an immense empire is kept intact . . . and clamors desperately for American action.' We now know that most of this was unrealizable fantasy. But at the time it made a deep impression – despite the total failure of Henry Ford's rubber plantations at Fordlândia and Belterra a few years previously.

Rockefeller sent a businessman, J. C. King, to assess the region's prospects. King was dismayed by the apathy of its inhabitants, the horrors of rubber-tapping, and the squalor of the few towns; but he made an optimistic report. 'The Amazon basin . . . offers our greatest challenge and hope.' King spoke to the head of the SPI in Pará and told Rockefeller that the Indians' 'hostile attitude is justified because of ill-treatment from whites . . . Before the Indian can be civilized the white settler must be. The present white habits of drink and transmission of venereal disease are serious.'

In 1953 Nelson Rockefeller and his brothers bought a half-interest in the vast 417,000 hectare (1,600 square mile) Bodoquena ranch in southern Mato Grosso, on what had once been the lands of the Kadiwéu Indians and their Terena vassals. The Summer Institute of Linguistics finally expanded from Spanish-speaking countries into Brazil in 1956. One of the first teams – led by Dale Kietzman, a future head of the SIL in Brazil – went to study the language of (and convert) the Terena, just as Rockefellers' ranching experts were moving into the Bodoquena fazenda on their homelands. Gerard Colby and Charlotte Dennett commented:

'No American would have more influence over the conquest of the Amazon than would Nelson Rockefeller. No American missionary would have more influence on the Brazilian tribes affected by that conquest than would Kietzman as SIL's first Brazil branch director. Ironically, both Rockefeller and Kietzman started their operations in the Brazilian Indian frontier in the same year, and in the same location, the land of the Terena Indians.' Of all tribes in Brazil, the Terena were perhaps the most eager to imitate the white way of life and merge into the rural community. Populous, hard-working, gentle and sober people, the Terena were perfect converts to Christianity. But they were equally enthusiastic about Catholic and Protestant teaching, so that their communities were often woefully divided between the two faiths.

Surprisingly, the man who invited the Summer Institute of Linguistics into Brazil was the anthropologist Darcy Ribeiro. Ribeiro met the SIL linguist Kenneth Pike at a Congress of Americanists held in Rio de Janeiro in 1954. Pike offered help in classifying the languages of Brazil's tribes, a task dear to Darcy Ribeiro's heart. So the liberal head of the SPI's study section wrote in 1956 to invite the American missionary-linguists. He hoped that the SIL's people would be more dedicated and better financed than the employees of his own demoralized Service. He probably wanted to counterbalance the disastrous series of ex-army officers put in charge of the SPI. In 1961 President Jânio Quadros suddenly resigned and was replaced by his leftist Vice-President João Goulart. Goulart made Darcy Ribeiro the Rector of the new University of Brasília and, as such, Ribeiro asked the SIL to help him establish a department of linguistics and to provide linguistically trained anthropologists to help the SPI in the field. This new union was sealed at a ceremony in Brasília in May 1963, filmed by the US Information Agency. The SIL donated a Helio Courier plane that was perfect for surveying rainforests; and Rector Ribeiro was seen putting his arm round the SIL's Cam Townsend. Colby and Dennett pointed out that 'What Ribeiro did not know was that SIL had ties to the American right wing. Nor could he have known of SIL's history of moving within a course set by even more powerful forces: the Rockefellers, US intelligence agencies, and, ironically, the US military. At the very time Ribeiro was looking to the missionaries as innocent protectors of Brazil's embattled tribes, SIL was reinforcing its ties with these more powerful forces in the Amazon region of Brazil's western neighbour, Ecuador.'

Jim Wilson, a later head of the Summer Institute of Linguistics in Brazil, told the author: 'From the time we arrived in 1956 we watched the old SPI go steadily downhill. It became the dregs of the civil service. It was refreshing to see it collapse. Since the foundation of Funai [in

1968] the road has definitely been going upwards.' By 1959 the SIL had eleven teams in Brazil, always working closely with the SPI and sometimes even resident in its posts – in direct contradiction to Rondon's original vision and later regulations. The mission's activities were defined under an agreement dated 20 November 1958. Its linguists worked under the Head of the Ethnology Section of the National Museum, Professor Roberto Cardoso de Oliveira, and its chief linguist, Professor J. Mattoso Câmara. The first teams were in the south, with the Terena, Kadiwéu, and nearby Guarani-speaking Kaiowá. Others worked with the Kaingang in southern Brazil and in an arc northwards among the Bororo, Apinayé, Karajá, and Guajajara, as well as with the Fulniô near the Atlantic coast. On the Amazon itself, the SIL studied the Tupi language of the Sateré-Mawé, downriver from Manaus, who were heavily influenced by Seventh-Day Adventists; and it was with the Hixkaryana (Purukotó) north-west of the city. A decade later, the SIL had expanded to thirty-five locations.

In 1964 the Brazilian military, with covert political and financial help from the United States, overthrew the communistic President João Goulart. With armies advancing against him, the embattled President fled from Brasília on 18 June 1964. He left his chief domestic adviser, Darcy Ribeiro, in charge. The ex-anthropologist closed the airport, organized a university rally in support of Goulart, tried to call a general strike, and broadcast a call to arms. Ribeiro's last-ditch efforts were swept aside by the military, and he was later stripped of his citizen's rights.

The Summer Institute of Linguistics was by now seen as an indispensable component of the Cold War, so that it was well received by the new military regime. Late in 1964 its head Cam Townsend asked Dale Kietzman (by now local director for Brazil) to investigate the tribes of Acre and the upper Juruá and Purus valleys in the far west of Brazil. Kietzman's survey team pushed up the two big rivers and crossed the territory of Acre as far as the Peruvian border. He reported eagerly that this remote region had 'the heaviest concentration' of tribes not yet reached by American fundamentalist missionaries. The area had been heavily hit by the rubber boom, so that the surviving tribes were 'badly fragmented and scattered. Villages are small and quite frequently one section of a tribe is not aware of the continuing existence of other sections of the tribe.' Kietzman listed seventeen tribal groups, mostly speaking Aruak or Panoan. They were in very different stages of acculturation. 'Tribes located along the mainstreams are generally well integrated into the local economy, while those on headwaters are often very isolated and even out of contact with Brazilians.' Cam Townsend duly ordered that considerable resources be shifted there from the SIL's big base in the

Peruvian Amazon. This included a Catalina flying boat, which was named 'Marshal Rondon' and ceremonially donated to the SPI.

In 1968 Cameron Townsend met the first head of the SPI's successor Funai, the well-meaning former journalist José de Queiros Campos, at the Sixth Inter-American Indian Congress in Mexico. After lobbying the Brazilian Ambassador in Washington for an accord between SIL and Funai, Townsend flew to Brazil to cement the relationship in a series of public-relations events. There was a reception in the Museum of the Indian in Rio de Janeiro (founded by the now-disgraced Darcy Ribeiro); and meetings in Brasília with the military President of Brazil and his Minister of the Interior, General Albuquerque Lima, to negotiate an agreement whereby SIL's linguists would resume work among Indians. The Minister was uneasy about this licence for foreign missionary pilots to fly uncontrolled over distant parts of his country's forests. But Albuquerque Lima, the instigator of the Figueiredo Commission that led to abolition of the SPI, was losing favour – partly because his pro-Indian sympathies ran counter to his Ministry's mission to open up the interior of Brazil. He was dismissed a few months later; and the SIL then got its licence. So the Summer Institute moved into Acre and western Amazonas, its well-educated linguist-missionaries started work among the tribes, and its jungle pilots flew again. Seeing the SIL's efficient and securely guarded installations, and the obvious wealth behind its flying service, I recall that local Brazilians assumed that the CIA must be financing the venture. But they were at a loss to explain why the Intelligence Agency would want to know what was happening in such a remote and thinly populated part of Brazil's Amazon forests.

By 1970 the SIL had fifty-six missionaries working with thirty-seven tribes in nine states of Brazil. The Institute defined its mission as: 'God loves everyone, including the Indians who have a right to know God and to live better'. The definition of 'living better' was made by the operatives, most of whom arrived from the United States with no anthropological training or experience. They reckoned to spend two years learning a tribe's language, one year to transcribe it and teach the Indians to read, and eight to fifteen years to complete their mission of conversion. This was done by giving the Indians the New Testament, in their language, in twenty-seven booklets.

Protestant missionaries also made inroads into tribes all along Brazil's northern frontiers. They often came from bases in neighbouring countries such as Colombia, Venezuela, Guyana, or Suriname, and they exploited the vacuum left by the SPI's and Funai's inactivity in this inaccessible region so far from Brasília. In other chapters we see how missionaries tried to convert Yanomami at Surucucu and Toototobi, Seventh-Day Adventists dominated the Taurepang of northern Roraima from the 1960s onwards, evangelical Baptists from Kanashen in Guyana won over the Waiwái in southern Roraima and on the Mapuera in Pará, American Protestants from Suriname converted some Tiriyó alongside the Franciscans and the Baptist SIL is with the Wayana to the south of them, the New Tribes Mission converted the Wayampi east of there in Amapá and made first contact with the related Zo'é, and Pentecostalists converted the Palikur of northern Amapá.

Despite its academic cover, the SIL's Bible-translators were just as intent on religious conversion as were the other Protestant fundamentalists. The Figueiredo report mentioned this. Norman Lewis, the British writer who powerfully reported the collapse of the SPI and who came to despise and mistrust missionaries, regarded the SIL as Janus-faced because its missionaries pretended to be 'linguistic investigators, wholly absorbed in scientific studies of language'. The SIL's founder Townsend defended this deception by comparing it to God's sending his son Jesus into the world disguised as a carpenter. Individual SIL operatives came across as fine people who were not intent on religious or ethnographic vandalism. They dispensed many medicines – which had for centuries been missionaries' main weapon in influencing Indians. William Merrifield, an SIL anthropologist, explained his work: 'I and many other members are not ordained and we concentrate on the specific task of Bible translation . . . We specifically refrain from regularly leading religious services. We do, of course, share our faith on a personal level.' But Norman Lewis regarded this as duplicitous. 'Despite the use of linguistics as a scientific front for less-than-scientific activities, a huge amount of biblical translation goes on . . . In reality, those in command of these Indian Protection posts are North American missionaries – they are in all the posts – and they disfigure the original Indian culture and enforce the acceptance of Protestantism.' These missionaries preferred the Old Testament to Christ's teaching about the blessedness of the poor. Their manuals told simple biblical stories in a local idiom, with each page facing an illustration of Indian village life and Amazonian flora and fauna. It came as a shock to turn from a picture of jaguars and tapirs to one of the crucified Christ.

The French anthropologist Dominique Gallois watched in dismay as New Tribes missionaries dominated the Wayampi and newly contacted Zo'é. She learned from the NTM's literature how keen it was to capture the 'blank slate' of uncontacted tribes – just as the Jesuits had been since their arrival in Brazil in 1549. The missionaries were determined to eliminate 'savage' or 'negative' customs and replace them with Christian practices. An internal teaching manual was called *Are the Heathen Really Happy? Fear, Superstition, Witchcraft, Infanticide*, and its cover carried a lurid drawing of a bestial Indian woman killing her twin infants. 'The coercive nature of this strategy is evident in the technical instrument that evangelical missionaries prefer: language. All alien values that are to be introduced are translated into the native language and idiom . . . in order that they will be readily appropriated. Apparent respect for their language and culture is, in fact, only a process aimed at the complete assimilation of Indians into the Christian-civilized world.' The internal bulletin, teaching manuals, and self-congratulatory books about the New Tribes Mission continue to be full of doctrinaire jargon about bringing the good news of Christ to the unenlightened, about victories in this struggle, sacrifices by heroic missionaries, reaping the fruits of tribes' conversion, and breaking sinful customs and beliefs. The Bible *is* the Word of God, and translating it into indigenous languages, although very difficult, is the most rewarding task on earth.

When Norman Lewis was in Brazil in 1968, his photographer Donald McCullin went into the interior to photograph some Indians. Ironically, the Brazilian authorities sent him to the Kadiwéu – part of whose land was occupied by the Rockefeller ranch, and who had been among the first Brazilian Indians tackled by the SIL. The only Indians seen by the photographer were 'a few sick and starving women and children who rode their skeletal horses each morning down to the mission house to beg for scraps. The missionary seemed indifferent to their plight. He was lost in a single all-absorbing task: the translation of the Epistle of [St Paul to] the Galatians into Kadiwéu.' He admitted that all the Indians might have died before he completed this work.

In January 1971 the World Council of Churches organized a meeting in Barbados of anthropologists and activists to discuss the terrible problems of indigenous peoples of the Americas. This conference's final Declaration condemned the military governments of many South American countries whose 'official "Indian policies" . . . are explicitly directed toward the destruction of aboriginal culture.' It blamed missionaries of all persuasions for being accessories to this ethnocide, and even for 'connivance with genocide'. 'The missionary presence has always implied the imposition of criteria and patterns of thought and behavior alien to the colonized Indian societies. A religious pretext has too often justified the economic and human exploitation of the aboriginal population.'

Although organized by the World Council of Churches, this Barbados gathering was scathing in its criticism of many Christian field workers. It insisted that missionaries cease to regard Indian beliefs as pagan and heretical. 'True respect for Indian culture' must replace 'the long and shameful history of despotism and intolerance characteristic of missionary work, which rarely manifests sensitivity to aboriginal religious sentiments and values.' There must be an end to 'the theft of Indian property by religious missionaries who appropriate labor, lands and natural resources as their own', and missionaries must fight harder against such fraud by others. The Conference condemned Indian boarding schools, such as those operated for half a century by the Salesians on the Rio Negro. These filled their pupils with alien values and, in the name of evangelization, caused 'an increase in morbidity, mortality, and family disorganisation among Indian communities.' Missionaries must stop competing with one another for 'Indian souls'. And they should 'abandon those blackmail procedures implicit in offering goods and services to Indian society in return for total submission.' In fact, it would be best if all missionary activity were suspended, 'for the good of Indian society and for the moral integrity of the churches involved'.

The Barbados Declaration was even more critical of anthropologists than of missionaries. These social scientists were accused of rationalizing 'in scientific language the domination of some people by others. The discipline has continued to supply information and methods of action useful in maintaining, reaffirming and disguising social relations of a colonial nature.' Of course, as Colby and Dennett pointed out, 'many of Latin America's anthropologists had only themselves to blame for being passive bystanders. Most of them lived in comfortable academic surround-ings . . . They were simply unwilling to endure the hardships of the jungle the way the missionaries were.' These academics must stop patronizing indigenous peoples by viewing them only from a Western perspective. Indians should be allowed to command their own destinies. And anthro-pologists must become more active in supporting political action by oppressed minorities. They needed to shed the clinical detachment whereby they continued to take notes as the last member of a tribe perished.

The Summer Institute of Linguistics was condemned as being both anthropological and missionary. Its workers were doubtless sincere and dedicated to their work. But by translating tribal languages and 'reducing' them to writing, they broke down an important bulwark of that group's identity and seclusion. They did not do this to give a tribe the ability to communicate in order to protect its way of life. It was done 'to destroy the culture's core belief system, its pre-Christian religion, and replace it with an American version of Fundamentalist Protestantism'. All this opened the way to a tribe's invasion by frontier settlement and its absorption into the national state. The Declaration noted that the SIL was widely spread, with 2,200 missionaries in twenty-two countries around the world, 1,500 of them in Latin America. It was involved with Indians who were being oppressed in many countries. One signatory of the Barbados Declaration was Darcy Ribeiro, the recent friend of the SIL.

There was a violent backlash from religious organizations, particularly American Protestant Churches. The Barbados Declaration was condemned as a 'highly biased and inaccurate' promoter of 'neo-racism similar to "Black Power"', and 'not a scientific document, but a radical opinion statement'. The Seventh Inter-American Indian Congress was held in Brasília in 1972. The Brazilian authorities sought to impress its delegates with Funai's successes in tackling 'the delicate and complex problem of forest Indians'. The visitors were taken on excursions to the Villas Boas' admirable Xingu park (which owed almost nothing to Funai or the SPI) and on a (disastrous) visit to the wretched Karajá on Bananal Island. It was argued – not wholly without reason – that the outburst in the international press about the Figueiredo Commission into the SPI had been exaggerated. And the Congress officially honoured the aged 'Uncle Cam' Townsend of the SIL as 'Benefactor of the Linguistically-Isolated Human Groups of the Americas'.

It is easy to criticize missionaries of both Christian faiths. They did great harm in undermining tribal beliefs and self-esteem. But they also did good, in protecting Indians' lands, persons, and health. They gave religious solace to those detribalized Indians who abandoned traditional customs and adopted Christianity. I have seen many missionaries in the field, and they of course varied widely in their attitudes to indigenous cultures and in their acceptance by the tribal community in which they worked. This often came down to the personalities of individual missionaries. In a sense, they proved the claim by critics of Rondon in 1910, that his new Indian Protection Service could never maintain the self-sacrifice and devotion to duty of the religiously inspired missionaries. It is difficult for people who do not devote their lives to living among tribal people to condemn the missionaries who do.

The Barbados Declaration recognized that radical elements within the Churches were starting to re-evaluate the evangelical process. By the 1970s, missionaries were often better motivated, more disinterested, and more richly endowed than their lay counterparts in the civil service. Reform movements were underway in both Catholic and Protestant faiths. These were to transform the behaviour of missionaries during the final decades of the twentieth century. One positive outcome was greater cooperation between organizations representing the two branches of Christianity among Indians. In parts of Brazil, such as the Javari valley, partnerships of Catholics and Protestants replaced the myopic rivalries that had confused and divided indigenous communities.

The Summer Institute of Linguistics' licence to work in Brazil expired at the end of 1976. Before this could be renewed, the SIL's former partner the National Museum was asked to assess the effectiveness of its methods. The Museum's report was negative. So the SIL's agreement was not renewed, and in November 1977 it was asked to leave Brazil altogether. The reason given was not to protect indigenous cultures from destructive Christianity, nor because of nationalistic rumours that these missionaries were prospecting for minerals and 'threatening national security'. It was claimed to be to give Brazilian linguists a fairer crack at studying their own tribes' languages. The missionary-linguists of the SIL soon reversed this expulsion. By 1980 the Institute had forty-four linguistic projects in Brazil and published an eighty-four-page bibliography of its work in that country. Even Father José Vicente César of CIMI (Conselho Indigenista Missionário) praised its work as valuable anthropologically and, above all, linguistically. The SIL continued to work with many tribes in the 1990s, and thereafter as Field International.

At the end of the century, missionaries were more active than ever throughout Brazil. Robin Wright, an anthropologist at Campinas University, surveyed the entire missionary effort with indigenous peoples. Catholic organizations still respected the general guidelines laid down by CNBB (the Conference of Brazilian Bishops) and coordinated by CIMI, while non-missionary ordinary priests treated Indians in the same way as their other parishioners.

In addition, the former liberation-theology radicals of CIMI maintain its tremendous fight for indigenous rights – almost forty years after Vatican II. CIMI operated with 400 missionaries in 112 teams. These were less concerned with proselytizing than with indigenous politics and some health, education, and legal assistance. During the 1990s, the Catholic Church developed 'Anas' – national associations for self-support by Indians. Missionaries, non-government sympathizers, and the indigenous peoples themselves developed community enterprises. The emphasis was on communal effort and benefit, but not profit; and they sought to work with tribal hierarchies rather than undermining them. Not surprisingly, some succeed while others fail.

The most active Catholic missionary orders were still the Salesians on the Rio Negro and in Mato Grosso (represented in thirty villages by male fathers and in twelve by female auxiliaries), and the Consolata in Roraima (eleven male and eleven female). These two largest missionary orders also dominated the two most committed dioceses: the Salesians in that of São Gabriel on the Rio Negro (sixteen missionaries) and Consolata in Boa Vista, Roraima (twenty-nine) who worked closely with the CIR (Indigenous Council of Roraima). Other active dioceses were that of the upper Solimões (twenty-five), Macapá with tribes of Amapá (ten) and the largely Jesuit Diamantino in Mato Grosso (nine). Dominicans were still with the Tapirapé, Xikrin, and others on the Araguaia; and Franciscans worked with the Munduruku and Tiriyó.

Protestants were far more diverse. Robin Wright divided them into four main groupings. The Lutheran, Anglican, and Methodist Churches 'are committed to a more "erudite", "liberal" and "modernising" interpretation of the Bible. They seek "to adjust religious teachings to knowledge" and participate in the liberal position that abandons the proselytizing vision and recognizes that "divine revelation can also be expressed in non-Christian religions"'. Among these first two groups of milder Protestant missionaries, Wright noted that twenty-one indigenous communities had Lutherans, twenty-six had various Baptist Churches, seven Methodist, and seven the different Presbyterian missions. There are two umbrella organizations: Comin (Indigenous Peoples' Missionary Council) and GTME (Evangelical Missionary Work Group). Although committed to evangelization, these Protestants also emphasized education, health (the traditional justification for missionary presence), and fostering native-Brazilian movements. They often cooperated with Catholics and NGOs in advancing the indigenous cause – notably in the great demonstration against the 500th Anniversary celebration in 2000.

By contrast, there were the 'missions of faith'. These used strict ecclesiastical terms to rationalize their beliefs, regarded the Bible as holy writ, and saw indigenous tribes as victims of isolation that deprived them of access to the Christian faith. These missionaries sought to preach the Gospel to peoples who had not heard the Word of God, and they did so through assistance under the umbrella of official indigenist policy. The 'missions of faith' were very active. The MNTB (New Tribes Mission of Brazil) worked in fifty-two posts; and it increased the numbers of missionaries in these tribes and its Brazilian offices from 437 in 1989 to almost 500 by the end of the century. The Summer Institute of Linguistics was in forty-four villages, the Evangelical Mission of Amazonia in fourteen, and there were various others.

Lastly, there were the Pentecostalists of the Assembly of God, active with fifteen peoples, and the Seventh-Day Adventists with eight. There were other sects, such as the messianic Santa Cruz Brotherhood in twenty mostly Ticuna villages, and the Bahai in the north-east.

Rondon would have been surprised and disappointed that missionaries would be so nearly omnipresent among Indians, ninety years after the foundation of his secular Indian Protection Service. But most modern missionaries have changed radically from the authoritarian bigots of Rondon's day. Recent political successes are the result of cooperation between missions, indigenous peoples' organizations, lay activists, anthropologists, and Funai.

11. Generals and Highways

By the end of the 1960s – when the SPI was disgraced, and the military were enjoying power in Brazil – the vast expanse of the Amazon rainforest was still largely intact. The Amazon basin and the adjacent Orinoco contain the majority of the world's tropical forests, and these in turn are the world's richest ecosystem. Their vegetation is as exuberant as it is beautiful, and they contain perhaps half the species with which we share this planet. Seeing such biodiversity, foreigners imagined prodigious wealth in Amazonia. But their visions of industrial progress in Amazonia were illusory.

By the twentieth century, man had scarcely damaged this environmental treasure-house. Indians had always manipulated the forest, planting useful trees around their villages, in their forest clearings, and at convenient places on their hunting routes. Some tribes also burned savannahs to round up game. But such impacts were trivial in comparison to the seemingly endless expanses of the forests. During the colonial period and the Brazilian empire, there was organized collection of medicinal plants from the forests and some cacao or palm-oil plantations; but the environmental damage was negligible. An exception was the wanton destruction of freshwater turtles, both for food and for the oil from millions of their eggs. The nineteenth-century rubber boom was extractive and therefore sustainable, since the *Hevea* trees were bled of their latex but not destroyed. Rubber brought tens of thousands of seringueiros into Amazonia, particularly to western Brazil; but many of these immigrants drifted away when the boom burst. The immigrants of course moved along the river system and planted a few settlements along its banks, but the human imprint was very small.

All this changed in the second half of the twentieth century. The Central Brazil Foundation in the 1940s sent teams of trail-cutters into the forest to open airstrips (which brought the Villas Boas brothers into the Xingu). This introduced a means of communication beyond the rivers, but the damage to the rainforests was still slight. Then in 1953 the Brazilian government set up a Superintendency to develop the Amazon, known by its initials, SPVEA. This provided finance for development of the region and it defined the largely forested part of Brazil as 'Amazonia Legal'. The city of Manaus was declared a free port, to which Brazilians could fly to buy imported goods free of the country's high tariffs and where manufacturers enjoyed tax concessions. But SPVEA was corrupt and ineffectual. Its main legacy was to have had a hand in construction of the 'Road of the Jaguar', the 1,900 kilometre (1,180 mile) BR-010 and BR-153 linking Belém at the mouth of the Amazon with the new federal capital Brasília. Built between 1958 and 1960 (and later paved by 1973) this Belém–Brasília highway ran north–south through the mesopotamia between the Tocantins and Araguaia rivers, thus skirting the eastern edge of the Amazon rainforests. Because it was generally in open campo and savannah grasslands, the new road was a planners' triumph – if success is measured in inwards migration and farming development. By the end of its first decade, the Belém–Brasília had helped the area's population increase twenty-fold to 2,000,000, its towns from 10 to 120, its cattle from almost none to 5,000,000 head, and its farms to yield impressive harvests of black beans, rice, and maize. The road meant that farmers could transport their beef or crops to market, which they had hardly been able to do by river or air.

The next move was to push a road along the southern edge of the forest mass. In 1967–68 the BR-364, which started at the old gold-mining town of Cuiabá in Mato Grosso, was extended north-westwards to Porto Velho on the Madeira river. This was the route followed by Rondon's strategic telegraph line sixty years earlier. It ran across the lands of the Nambiquara and then close to the Cinta Larga (the victims of the massacre in 1963) and other Tupi-speaking peoples. When it remained on the watershed plateau of the geologically ancient Central Brazilian Shield, this road was often on open scrub or grasslands, but it cut through virgin forests as it approached Porto Velho. In later decades it was destined to attract millions of settlers, transmigrants from other parts of Brazil. The BR-364 was thus to become notorious as the greatest destroyer of Amazonian rainforests.

The generals who ruled Brazil after 1964 were even more beguiled by the supposed wealth of Amazonia than their democratic predecessors had been. The leading historian of the Amazon in 1968 wrote a widely read book arguing that Amazonia would attract foreign envy. So the authorities were determined to exploit this El Dorado before greedy foreigners could occupy the vacuum. An influential military strategist, General Golbery do Couto e Silva (a senior figure in the General Staff and military intelligence, and adviser to successive presidents), stressed the need to open up 'the vast hinterlands waiting and hoping to be aroused to life and to fulfil their historic destiny'. Brazil could then 'inundate the Amazon forest with civilization'. SPVEA was abolished and replaced by a more efficient Superintendency known as SUDAM. The first military President, Marshal Humberto de Castello Branco, took businessmen and legislators on a voyage up the Amazon and offered amazing tax incentives to any enterprise that would invest there. In 1969 Eliseu Resende, the director of the national highways department and the main architect of the Belém–Brasília highway, published an article calling for a 'penetration road' right across the Amazon rainforests. He called his vision the Transamazonica and imagined it running parallel to and several hundred kilometres south of the Amazon river. It would join up the towns at the rapids where each north-flowing tributary dropped off the Central Brazilian Shield towards the main river: Marabá on the Tocantins-Araguaia, Altamira on the Xingu, Itaituba and Jacareacanga on the Tapajós, Humaitá on the Madeira, and thence westwards towards the Peruvian frontier.

In June 1970 the third military President, General Emílio Garrastazú Médici, visited the arid and impoverished north-east, which had been hit by one of the most terrible droughts in its history. Deeply moved, he declared that such suffering must end; and only ten days later he announced the Programme for National Integration (PIN) and the construction of a Transamazonica highway and a network of lateral roads. This would open 'a land without people for a people without land'. The federal government reserved to itself the land for a hundred kilometres (sixty miles) on either side of the new roads. The idea was that this roadside land should be awarded in small holdings to poor settlers from the north-east (whose 28 million people had an income of only half the national average) and the shanty favelas of the big cities. A rural-colonization agency called Incra was established, to oversee this settlement programme. It was hoped that the penetration road would initially accommodate 500,000 government-sponsored settlers plus a further 500,000 spontaneous migrants, and that this number would have doubled by 1980. All this was presented in fashionable planners' jargon. Susanna Hecht and Alexander Cockburn summed it up: 'To an optimist the blueprint for what blithe planners in Brasília described as the *faixas*, swaths of "social occupation" connecting "dynamic growth poles", must have seemed compelling.'

The Transamazonica highway had not appeared in any plans for Amazonian development. It was announced on the spur of the moment, and its route (and even its name) were remarkably faithful to Resende's vision of the previous year. The government moved fast: tenders for the long stretches of the Transamazonica and a north–south road from Cuiabá to Santarém on the Amazon were invited in mid-June 1970; contracts awarded to the country's eight largest civil-engineering contractors; and work started in September.

The engineering specification was for a pioneer road: a swathe of cleared forest seventy metres (230 feet) wide, a nine metre (thirty foot) roadway with a gravelled surface along its central seven metres, wooden bridges over the many creeks and ravines and ferries on larger rivers, and gradients of not more than a steep 9 per cent. Construction was an amazing feat, one that few other countries could have accomplished. Teams of rugged woodsmen cut trails towards one another for hundreds of kilometres from the terminal towns on the main rivers. They lived rough and were supplied and guided by air. Other workers with chainsaws then opened the clearing in the forest, sufficiently for the big yellow earth-movers to grade the highway. The surface coating was aggregate crushed from occasional rock outcrops, and the trellis bridges were of course built from local trees. This author saw the arduous construction effort on the ground and, from the air, the road slicing straight to the horizon through the unbroken carpet of the forest canopy. From Estreito on the Tocantins to Humaitá on the Madeira, the Transamazonica penetrated an incredible 2,232 kilometres (1,386 miles) of mostly pristine forest. It was completed in 1974 at a cost, well over budget, of some $120 million. The road itself, and subsequent clearing on either side, caused the destruction of millions of hectares of tropical rainforest.

The Transamazonica connected no major centres, as the Belém–Brasília had done, so it carried minimal traffic. From a settlement point of view, the highway was also a disaster. The first colonists planted along the road by Incra were given small wooden houses in 100-hectare (247-acre) plots of which the front part was cleared of trees. They soon found that the laterite soils under cleared rainforest are desperately weak (because the evergreen forest system recycles all nutrients into the growing vegetation), erosion from tropical rains removes any veneer of exposed topsoil, the fierce equatorial sun bakes the surface into what one ecologist called 'a pink parking lot', and such crops as do grow are consumed by the world's most abundant and voracious insects. Added to these miseries, basic commodities, from tools to fuel oil, were many times more expensive than in the coastal cities; and the price of taking surplus produce or animals to market was prohibitive. The Transamazonica itself could not withstand the Amazon's rains. Trucks slithered and submerged in the deep mud. The road became impassable for much of the rainy season from October to March and deeply rutted during the dry months.

Word rapidly spread that settlement along the Transamazonica was a waste of effort. Already in 1970 Brazilian journalists dubbed it the Transmiseriana. In a powerful polemic five years later, Robert Goodland and Howard Irwin of the World Bank commented that 'integration of the poor and populous Northeast with the poor and almost unpopulated Amazonia becomes feasible only if the immigrants can sustain themselves. It was tacitly assumed that the Northeasterner would be more self-sufficient in Amazonia than in the north-east. If a peasant cannot sustain himself in the land of his forefathers, he is unlikely to achieve much success in the harsh and constraining environment of Amazonia, different in almost every way.' These authors then demolished other arguments for building the highway: it was useless for the military to defend Brazil's frontiers; and it was most unlikely to stumble across mineral deposits which, even if found, would best be removed by river.

The government soon stopped sponsoring immigration by poor colonists to the new forest highway. Instead, in 1973 it invited Brazilian and multinational companies to create large cattle ranches there. Some responded, because of the tempting tax incentives, because land seemed a good financial hedge at a time of high inflation, and to please the government. Large tracts of forest were cleared and burned over. White zebu cattle were installed on the pasture that grew on the ash of the destroyed vegetation. It looked good in publicity photographs; but it did not last. The ranches soon decayed, choked by weeds, the fragile soil was trampled hard or eroded away, and the emaciated and tick-infested animals were hardly worth transporting to distant slaughterhouses.

The Transamazon and other penetration highways were a costly fiasco that helped plunge Brazil into foreign debt. They were also disastrous for the Indians along their routes. Goodland and Irwin made a careful list of 171 tribal groups in Brazil in 1974. They then calculated that 96 – over half – of these would have their territories violated by the network of planned highways. Even more alarmingly, 'most of the affected tribes remain isolated or have experienced only intermittent contact. These will suffer far more from the highway program' than more acculturated groups would have. Forty-five of the threatened tribes were virtually uncontacted. Funai did almost nothing to protect them. Its President, General Oscar Bandeira de Mello, a former head of the national security service, blithely said that the Foundation 'hoped to encounter' 10,000 Indians along the new roads, 3,500 of whom were still isolated. The Indian agency regarded the government's road programme as all-important. 'Funai has now allowed itself to degenerate into acting as a buffer between highway crews and the Indians whose lands they are penetrating.' Funai requested a paltry $10,000 as additional funds to cope with all work caused by the Transamazonica. It also signed an agreement with SUDAM for the latter to finance its attraction teams. It never once suggested that a road be diverted to avoid indigenous territory. There was no time to train more sertanistas in the delicate skills of contacting new tribes. 'Funai workers are under such pressure that they frequently manage to keep only a few kilometres ahead of the bulldozers. Each highway crew is supposed to be accompanied by a Funai employee who, more often than not, considers himself fortunate if he has contact with the Indians a few hours in advance of the construction crew.' Missionaries sometimes joined the contact teams, something that had rarely happened with the discredited SPI. 'Inadequately trained [Funai] employees, including missionaries and pros-elytes of assorted biases and persuasions, are often forced to depend for food and, more significantly, for transport, on the construction crews – the very people whose activities are most threatening the Indians.'

The first tribe to be hit by the Transamazonica was the Parakanã. This elegant Tupi-speaking people had come into occasional contact with an old railway, started in 1895 to bypass the rapids on the lower Tocantins. Local settlers blamed the Parakanã (or the nearby Asurini of the Tocantins) for raids that killed railway workers and Brazil-nut gatherers. An engineer led a reprisal in 1928 that killed eight Asurini, and a punitive expedition in 1930 resulted in more deaths. The tribes fought back. A police team on a railway car was wiped out in 1933 and there were further raids by both sides. Despite this, Indians started to appear at the SPI's Tocantins post in the decade after it was founded in 1927. In 1931, 115 Parakanã, including women and children, visited the post. They may then have been victims of a measles epidemic that raged through the region in 1938, for they then appeared less frequently.

In 1945 the Central Brazil Foundation (FBC) took charge of the Tocantins Railway, and installed as its director an engineer called Carlos Teles, who was also the local chief of police. This man blamed the Parakanã for attacks on his trains. The anthropologist Curt Nimuendajú was there at the time and learned that Teles made a brutal speech to his staff: 'From today onwards, when you see Indians on the line, no one should investigate whether or not they are coming with peaceful inten-tions. You must open fire on them, and you should not shoot into the air or the ground, but aim to kill!' Teles then sent a murderous raid against the tribe – thirty men led by a killer known as Pá-torta ('Hothead') who boasted of bashing Indian babies' heads against tree trunks during the massacre in 1930. Nimuendajú was appalled to see that the punitive raid was armed with grenades and gas bombs belonging to the Central-Brazilian Foundation! The anthropologist promptly wrote to complain to the relevant Minister, and resigned from his contract with the National Museum in collaboration with the Central Brazil Foundation. Luckily that raid caught no Indians, although it destroyed some of their houses and plantations. Four years later in 1949 the Asuriní killed people at different places along the line; small farmers abandoned their holdings, and railway-maintenance teams were protected by armed guards.

After 1953, large groups of Indians would appear at the SPI post to receive presents. (It is unclear whether these were Parakanã or Asuriní fleeing from Parakanã attack.) During 1964 these people took '50 machetes, 24 axes, 40 hammocks, 30 pairs of shorts, 30 trousers, 1 kilo of beads, 150 60-kilo sacks of manioc flour, 20 of maize' as well as tobacco, sweet potatoes, and bananas. They also loved to be given dogs. The SPI agent was worried that their interest in such goods might lead them to clashes with the growing settler population, with the consequent risk of disease. He was right. The Parakanã (or Asuriní) did catch influenza; over fifty Indians died; and the survivors fled into the forest and sensibly shunned further contact with Brazilian society.

All that was known about this elusive tribe was that its men wore small cylindrical plugs in their lower lips (like the first Tupi-speakers encountered by sixteenth-century voyagers) but no ear-discs or penis-guards, and that both sexes shaved their heads either completely or keeping only a small circle of short hair like a skull cap. It was later learned that the Parakanã are skilled and artistic makers of bows, ceramics, and other artefacts, and build fine houses. One attractive custom is 'formal friendship', whereby an individual adopts a friend of the same sex in another part of the tribe. This starts at an elaborate ceremony at puberty, and continues with exchanges of presents, of goods and hunted or farmed food. The bonded friends smoke or dance together throughout their lives.

The Parakanã were Funai's first target, since they lived on the direct route of the Transamazonica a short distance west of Marabá. Two attraction teams set out towards their known campsites. The Parakanã seemed to have no fear of whites, only a strong desire for their goods. The first attraction team was therefore surprised by seventy Indian men, completely unarmed, who sacked their camp and then disappeared into the forest. The other team soon found native camps and a large maloca full of hammocks, ceramics, necklaces, and a headdress. On 30 November 1970 this group met some Parakanã gathering honey. Its leader, João Carvalho, wrote: 'We advanced side by side so that we could all shout at once. When we did so, the Indians fell silent . . . Then they replied angrily and gave war cries, running towards us with arrows in their bows, ordering us to withdraw or they would kill us all . . . They stayed twenty metres away, shouting and talking.' Carvalho answered, speaking for over five minutes. The Indians 'lowered their arrows and came to meet us. We distributed the presents, and they gave us three jabuti [land tortoises] and a baby agouti.' Two months later, the team was surprised by the arrival of a hundred Parakanã men and women, who danced with Funai men, took whatever they wanted, and left. 'We danced a lot with the men, at least twenty times, and they rubbed their foreheads against ours . . . The women are very pretty and they have attractive children. There are also handsome men, some quite white, but all without exception with shaven heads.' The Parakanã loved the Brazilians to sing for them. On one occasion they grabbed Carvalho, held him in the air, and said that he was light. They also insisted that the Funai men remove their trousers: 'they then got straws and tied our members just like theirs'. They also made the contact team shave their heads, and the women painted their bodies with red urucum dye. Carvalho said that he had never met Indians like these Parakanã. 'They make contact, converse, and then vanish.'

This part of the tribe lived dangerously close to the new highway, so that 'on three occasions these Indians made incursions onto the highway construction front, but there was no aggression since the road workers became accustomed to them.' The labourers proudly told the author that 'they made no hostile or even defensive move – despite the removal of a large quantity of clothes, hammocks, suitcases, knives and shorts.'

Finally, in June 1971, the Parakanã invited João Carvalho and seven of his men to visit their village where 'as a demonstration of friendship, the Parakanã gave him their weapons . . . [Back at the expedition's camp] they fraternized, in a true party with dancing and typical songs, all of which clearly signifies their desire for peace and their complete confidence.'

The tribe's confidence was tragically misplaced. Immediately after the various contacts, the Parakanã caught influenza and also suffered from malaria, dysentery, and conjunctivitis. Forty or fifty adults and children died, out of a group of only 130 people. The Parakanã were consumed with grief. It was a horrible repeat of the disastrous contacts by the SPI in the 1950s. João Carvalho used such medicines as he had, but he complained of great difficulties. Up to a hundred people lived in the spacious main hut, with their fires constantly lit, amid dogs and other animals, with little hygiene and a plague of flies. The Indians were also, uncharacteristically, suspicious of Western medicine, which they feared might be causing the fatal diseases. Once they overcame this reluctance they wanted treatment at all times, preferably by large injections of serum into veins, and even for relatives who had died, in the hope that they might be revived. Additionally, a doctor from Belém, Antonio Madeiros, found a 'pattern of promiscuity' between the Indians and Funai's agents, when he visited the village in November 1971: thirty-five Indian women and two Funai men had venereal diseases, children had been born blind, and six others had recently died of dysentery. (The two Funai men found to have gonorrhoea were sacked in May 1972.) When the survivors were hit by another influenza epidemic, doctors were rushed to the village, but again with inadequate medical supplies. The attraction campaign had been hideously bungled. The Parakanã were relatively isolated 'until the moment when the Transamazonica burst upon them like an inferno. Over two hundred Indians died during that terrible period'.

Funai moved this wretched group three times, allegedly so that they could be more accessible to medical attention. They were finally located on a creek called Lontra ('Otter'), a mere sixteen kilometres (ten miles) from the Transamazonica. When I saw them there in 1972, they were reduced to some eighty people, still naked and with their heads shaved in the traditional manner. They were in a state of shock from the traumas of contact and deaths. We found that 'the village was bereft of artefacts; very few bows and arrows were to be seen, although those that remained were of a quality that suggested a once-thriving artistry. It seemed that the tribe's store of artefacts had already been exchanged for such things as guns and ammunition and that their culture was being disrupted with shattering speed, leaving the Parakanã bewildered.'

When Expedito Arnaud saw this group in 1975, it was still undergoing change. Its ninety-two people occupied three large, traditional huts – fine rectangular buildings with pitched roofs – and they had another for ceremonial uses. They continued to live among their dogs and other animals and shared food and drink with them, but they were more hygienic about defecating outside the houses. The Parakanã now wore clothing, often only one garment which was washed only occasionally. The women used razor blades to shave hair, and they had taken to consuming salt, sugar, and coffee. The men now hunted with guns rather than bows and arrows; they fished with hooks and line as well as bows and arrows; and they of course used metal axes and machetes in their forest clearing. Such manufactured goods came via Funai or from selling artefacts or Brazil nuts. 'Craft techniques in basketry, ceramics, wooden artefacts, weaving in cotton, and house building continued not only to be practised by the adults but also taught to the children. The division of labour between the sexes remained unaltered, as did the routine of daily work,' with the men out hunting all day and the women gathering forest produce and firewood or staying in the huts to make food and other necessities. These practices were shattered when in April 1979 '95 per cent of the Parakanã of Lontra village were attacked by a violent epidemic of flu resulting from contacts.'

Other Parakanã avoided contact. Funai's teams of sertanistas almost met one nomadic group of sixty Indians in 1972, but they retreated into the forests. There were divisions among the Parakanã, just as there had been among the Kayapó to their south, in the confused period before they decided to accommodate with the invaders. Different leaders reacted differently to the unprecedented threats and opportunities. Funai was under urgent orders to contact the fragments of this tribe. So during subsequent years it sent out 'penetration fronts', which one anthropologist defined as 'a team that pushes through the forest, following vestiges of tribal groups until it gets close to their *tapiri* shelters or villages, and then forces a contact'. (This aggressive policy of a 'penetration front' differed from a more passive 'attraction front' where the contact team established itself near the Indians' territory and waited for them to choose when to undergo the trauma of a face-to-face meeting.) More Indians were contacted in 1976. One small band moved into the forests of the Bacajá river, but clashed with the Xikrin Kayapó and suffered six dead and nine captives. Further divisions in the following years ended with contacts in January and November 1983 and March 1984. Another group of Parakanã had a series of battles with the Araweté near the Xingu, with deaths in both tribes. Mineral prospectors and fur hunters were also penetrating their forests, which lay to the south of the Lontra Parakanã. The sertanista in charge of the operation, Sydney Possuelo, was frustrated by lack of funds; but he finally contacted seventy of these Parakanã in 1983, and the last band of thirty-two were met in March 1984. The various contacts during these thirteen years were made over a vast area of forest, hundreds of kilometres apart from one another. This shows how mobile – and how frightened and unsettled – tribes could be. It also demonstrates the tenacity of Funai's attraction teams in searching through such great tracts of tropical forest.

The Parakanã suffered terribly during the years of their encounters with frontier society. The team who made the contact on the Bacajá in 1976 was in poor health, so that those Indians were immediately infected with malaria and influenza and eleven out of forty died. That group was moved first to the Anapu river opposite Altamira on the Xingu, then bussed back along the Transamazonica to a Funai reserve called Pucuruí in what the anthropologist Antonio Magalhães called 'an affront to their right of self-determination'. Once at the new location, its agent housed them in wattle-and-daub shacks instead of their large traditional malocas, forbade their customary burials inside the houses, and replaced their ceremonial area with a football field.

Worse was to come. In addition to the Transamazonica highway, two further gigantic projects encroached on the Parakanã territory: first the floodwaters rising behind the huge Tucuruí hydroelectric dam on the Tocantins; and then the development of the world's largest iron-ore mine at the Serra dos Carajás, near where Funai contacted the final groups of Parakanã in the 1980s. The Tucuruí dam was a 'Pharaonic enterprise' that was hoped to generate eight million kilowatts of electricity, partly to refine bauxite from a mine on the Trombetas river into aluminium. The trouble was that the Amazon basin is very flat. The Tucuruí dam was built over rapids on the lower Tocantins; but because the river is not enclosed by hills, the dam was planned to flood an expanse of 2,160 square kilometres (834 square miles). This artificial lake would drown almost all the 237 square kilometre (91 square mile) Pucuruí reserve. The official plan for the dam did not even mention the flooding of Indian lands. Funai accepted the project without protest. It even profited from its Indians' misfortune, by authorizing the construction of a large sawmill on the Pucuruí reserve – which destroyed the forest to within a kilometre of the recently transferred native village. 'This fact caused the most serious distress to the Indians, who withdrew from the area' and tried to return to the richer forests far away on the Anapu. The Parakanã on the Lontra stream, who had been contacted in 1970, were also forced to move by the rising floodwaters.

A journalist in 1977 wrote a moving piece about the plight of the Parakanã relocated to Pucuruí. He told of the disastrous contacts by poorly prepared Funai teams, the frequent moves after contact, and now the imminent flooding. 'They have had their culture completely destroyed, maintain not one of their traditions, saw many of their people die, lost their hunting grounds, and have not a single field from which to gather manioc to make farinha, nor yams, maize or urucum [annatto for red dye].' Funai responded to the resulting outcry by appointing Antonio Magalhães to organize a 'Parakanã Project' for the Indians' well-being in a new reserve. When nothing happened about Magalhães' proposals, a group of concerned Brazilian anthropologists in 1980 called a meeting with the electricity company Eletronorte and demanded recognition of the Indians' constitutional right to their lands and compensation if they were moved. On the medical front, there were vaccination campaigns of BCG and against polio, measles, and tetanus. However malaria raged uncontrolled, since the villages were so near the Transamazonica highway. This disease killed several people and so weakened others that they succumbed to an intestinal bacillus.

There was a rumour of gold inside the tribe's territory in 1981, with some hundred prospectors invading it. Then, no sooner had the Indians left their lands that would be on the banks of the new dam reservoir, than a local Funai official released these for occupation by 600 settlers. So, when President Figueiredo formally inaugurated the gigantic Tucuruí dam in November 1984, angry Parakanã were threatening to expel by force the colonists who had invaded their traditional territory. In 1985 Funai finally got a new Parakanã indigenous area declared, covering 317,000 hectares (1,220 square miles), but it was well to the west of the Tocantins and the lake behind Tucuruí. The bewildered Parakanã had had to move repeatedly since contact. Mércio Gomes summed it up: 'The Parakanã saw their lands invaded by landless squatters, loggers, a logging company called Capemi, and the contractors who built the dam . . . It was a useless and wearisome experience for the Parakanã and a corrupt and demoraliz-ing one for Brazil and its government.'

The forests on the east bank of the lower Xingu were home to another Tupi-speaking tribe, the Asuriní. These gentle people suffered from aggressive neighbours. In the distant past they fought the Juruna, before these migrated up the Xingu into what became the Villas Boas' park. (The name Asuriní means 'Very Red' in Juruna, because the Asuriní love to paint their entire bodies in either red or black designs.) Then they fled from Gorotire and Xikrin Kayapó. At one time in the 1950s, the Asuriní tried to escape by crossing the Xingu. They made a 300 metre (1,000 foot) liana bridge, from rock to rock across the river's thunderous rapids; but they were surprised by a motor launch full of seringueiros, who opened fire on them with rifles. In the 1960s the Asuriní were on the Bacajá river, which joins the Xingu downstream and opposite Altamira; but the threat of the warlike Xikrin Kayapó from the south-east forced them to move to the Ipiaçava, a smaller tributary that joins the Xingu opposite the mouth of the Iriri. In those years there were fleeting encounters with rubber-tappers or feline-skin hunters. The Asuriní were tempted to steal goods from the colonists' huts; but two who were caught were killed, decapitated, and horribly mutilated, and left for the vultures. Two more moves brought them to the Ipixuna, a tributary further up the Xingu, where they lived for ten to fifteen years.

Funai's sertanista who contacted the Asuriní was the thirty-year-old Antonio Cotrim Soares, a dedicated idealist in the Indian service. Cotrim told the author how he made the contact. He left the Kararaô post near Altamira in September 1970 with a tiny team of only one woodsman, a pilot, and two Indians. They had a very tough eighteen-day struggle up sixty rapids on the Ipixuna before finally sighting an Indian trail. The weary men followed this for fifteen days, often lost and eating nothing but palm-hearts, some game, and three vitamin pills a day. They saw an abandoned camp, then continued in heavy rain for a further four days until they came to the edge of an Asuriní village and heard Indians talking. Cotrim decided that they were too debilitated and bedraggled to attempt a contact. Also, one of his men seemed to have a cold; and one of his Indians had a pierced lower lip and might have been mistaken for a Xikrin enemy. So Cotrim turned back. However, resting on the trail back to their boat, the small team suddenly found itself surrounded by twelve Asuriní warriors. It proved to be a friendly meeting, so Cotrim returned in February 1971. After ascending the Ipixuna, he paused for five days of hunting to ensure that any diseases among his men would manifest themselves. The team again hid at the edge of the Asuriní clearing. A woman and child approached. Cotrim darted out of the forest, touched the woman and gave her a machete, then grabbed the startled infant and danced around with it, partly to show that he was unarmed. He told me that he wanted to take the tribe by surprise, so that it could not plan any hostile move. His method was totally different to the huge teams of Chico Meirelles (with whom Cotrim had once served, among the Kayapó on the Baú). Cotrim's tactics worked, and the amiable Asuriní accepted contact with the whites. After years of retreating from frontiersmen, the tribe had decided to seek accommodation. This was partly in order to obtain trade goods, but more importantly to seek protection from other Indian enemies.

When Regina Müller studied the Asuriní a few years later, she found that these Tupi-speakers had many customs reminiscent of the first Tupinamba encountered by Europeans on the Atlantic coast in the sixteenth century. Shamanism was very important, particularly in medical cures. Shamans smoked extremely long cheroots – half their body height long – of a cultivated tobacco rolled inside barkcloth tubes, and they puffed the aromatic smoke over their patients amid ritual dances and incantations. Dr Müller herself underwent this treatment, to cure a painful boil. Friends within the tribe formally asked the shaman to help her; he performed the elaborate procedures; and 'the shaman sucked the boil in such a gentle manner that I scarcely felt the suction; I immediately felt relief and the pain disappeared.' The anthropologist observed many ceremonies and learned the tribe's rich mythology.

One of the Asurini's artistic skills is in making pottery: large cooking pans and lovely water vessels with geometric patterns on a shiny yellow glaze. They carve elegant stools from a single piece of wood. Their communal huts are long, barrel-vaulted structures of woven thatch, which look just like houses shown in sixteenth-century woodcuts. But much of their creativity goes into body paint and tattooing, with torsos and limbs covered in patterns of black genipap dye, and the lower faces of both sexes often adorned with a beard-like mat of black paint. Both sexes of Asurini cut their hair in a bowl above the ears, part it in the middle and fix it to their foreheads with shiny beeswax. Unlike most other tribes, who pluck body hair, the Asurini do not mind some facial hair on men or pubic hair.

One of the first observers of Brazilian Indians, in the 1550s, noted that they loved people to be joyful and liberal and hated those who were taciturn, melancholy, or stingy. The descendants of those Tupi, the present-day Asurini and Araweté, share that attitude. Constantly in good spirits, they are baffled by white men's changes of mood and occasional surliness. The Austrian ethnologist Anton Lukesch saw the Asurini in May 1971 and was enchanted by 'the exceptional warmth, gentleness, and hospitality' of this people – far more than any tribe he had met during twenty years of work in Amazonia. The Asurini 'offered us food, with almost exaggerated insistence: jabuti [land tortoise], mutum [curassow, or wild turkey] and tender jacu [guan, another game bird], macaxeira [sweet manioc], maize, and beiju [manioc bread]' – for the hard-working Asurini were fine farmers and hunters. A team from the Aborigines Protection Society (including the author) visited the tribe in the following year and we were equally delighted by these people who were 'fatter, more cheerful and relaxed than any other Indians we saw'.

Despite their remoteness, the admirable Asurini suffered many of the familiar problems after contact. There were the usual new necessities. By 1976, Müller reported that 'bows and arrows were replaced by guns, whose ammunition represents a fundamental manufactured item [necessary] for obtaining meat. Axes and machetes, used in felling forest for planting, are now essential tools for farming; and fishing now depends on hooks and nylon line . . . The Asurini also use clothing, soap, kerosene, batteries, etc.'. They sold handicrafts through Funai in order to buy these new wants, but the resulting income was insufficient.

A blow came in 1976, with a violent attack by the Asurini's Tupi-speaking kindred the Araweté, who were themselves harassed by the Parakanã. This battle was so sudden and fierce that the Asurini had to abandon all their possessions and the food growing in their clearings. It was a traumatic episode for them – worse than contact with the whites. They fled to the banks of the Xingu, destitute and vulnerable to the diseases of riverine settlers – malaria, influenza, and, later, tuberculosis. There were further deaths and despair. Thus, the tribe's population fell by a third during its first decade of contact, to a mere fifty-three people. Recontacted by Funai, the Asuriní were moved back up the Ipixuna and, after surviving a further attack, in 1977 built two villages beside an Indian post called Koatinemo.

In 1980, Berta Ribeiro found the Asuriní 'destructured, sick, desolate and possessed of a strong feeling of defeat'. A serious impediment was the tribe's tradition of abortions. The Asuriní never wanted many children and if any of the omens surrounding a birth were bad, a father might violently abort his pregnant wife or kill the infant. Then, when offspring were desired, women who had suffered such miscarriages often proved infertile. In 1972 the Aborigines Protection Society team was struck by the almost total lack of children in a society of healthy adults. Berta Ribeiro wrote that in the first seven years after contact the Asuriní's death rate was 20 per cent but its birth rate continued to be almost non-existent. She said that 'they want no more children, they know that they are finished'. But Regina Müller watched them pull back from the brink. By the mid-1980s she found the Asuriní recovering from social disintegration and the threat of extinction. They were saved by their fruitful farming, hunting, and fishing; the emergence of new leaders; the intensification of ritual and religious activities, with a revival of traditional ceremonies; and the protection of their own indigenous area.

A year after he had contacted the Asuriní, Antonio Cotrim resigned in disgust from Funai. After the Asuriní, he had gone on to contact the Jandeavi, another group threatened by the advancing Transamazonica. A missionary was allowed to visit this tribe and brought a flu epidemic. Cotrim appealed for urgent medical help, but it took seven weeks for this to arrive. By that time sixteen of the seventy-six members of the group, 21 per cent, were dead. Also, the infection of the Parakanã with venereal diseases was not an isolated case: it was symptomatic of brutal attitudes to newly contacted Indians along the new roads.

In a well-publicized press conference in May 1972, the brilliant young sertanista said that he was tired of being 'a grave-digger of Indians' whom he was dedicated to help. He felt 'an enormous sense of remorse' when contacting a new tribe. 'What we are really doing is a crime. When I enter into contact with Indians I know that I am forcing a community to take the first step on a road that will lead them to hunger, sickness,

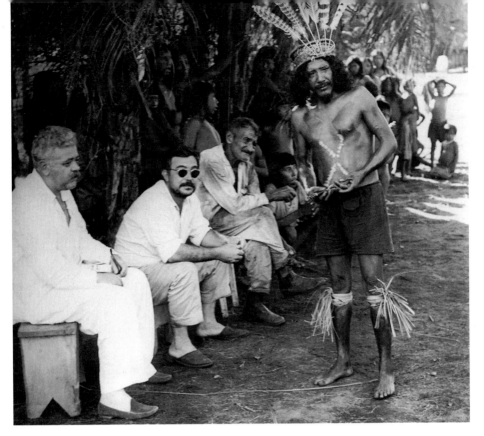

19. Noel Nutels, the charismatic doctor who first treated the Xingu Indians and later led the Indian Protection Service, Cláudio Villas Boas, and the Kayabi leader Prepori. (*Orlando Villas Boas*)

20. The Villas Boas brothers Orlando and Cláudio on one of the many river journeys that made them outstanding explorers as well as Indianists. (*Orlando Villas Boas*)

21. Funai's agent João Moreira discusses problems of encroaching ranchers with Canela (Ramkókamekra), Maranhão.

22. A Gavião mother. This Timbira people suffered from clashes with settlers on the lower Tocantins and was later displaced by the Tucuruí dam.

23. The chief of the Canela's Ponto village and his wife.

24. *Above, left.* António Cotrim, an able sertanista who contacted Asurini and Gavião, but resigned in disgust over Funai's broken promises to Indians.

25. *Above.* The great sertanista Sydney Possuelo examines an arrow of the feared Arara, at contact near the Transamazonica highway, 1980. (*Sydney Possuelo*)

26. *Left.* The tireless anthropologist Curt Nimuendajú was with a tribe every year between 1905 and 1945.

27. Salesian missionaries organized wedding ceremonies for young Tukano as soon as they left boarding schools in the theocratic realm on the Upper Rio Negro.

28. Xavante girls learn sewing at the Salesians' São Marcos mission.

29. Salesian education was rigidly disciplined and often irrelevant to Indian needs and culture. Iauareté mission on the upper Uaupés.

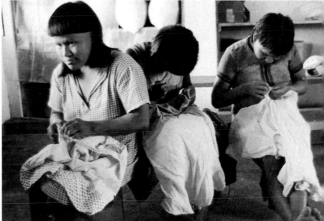

30. A Desana grating manioc, the staple of peoples of the Upper Rio Negro.

31. The Parakanã were decimated by disease after contact in 1971.

32. A Parakanã with trussed jaboti tortoises.

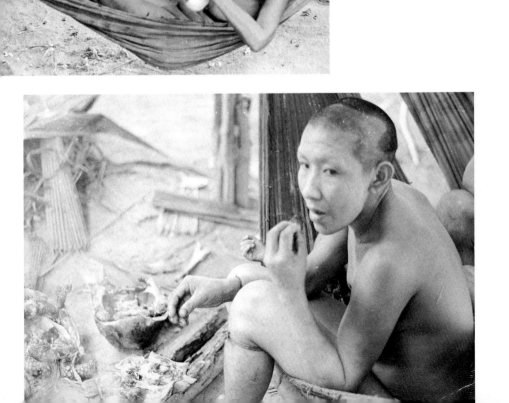

33. The author with a girl from the amiable Asurini, soon after contact, 1971.

34. An Asurini couple. At first deeply demoralized by accommodation with Brazilian society, the Asurini have since regained their self-esteem.

35. Salesian missionaries introduced Indians to the market economy. Xavante baskets and shoppers in the mission store, Sangradouro, Mato Grosso.

36. Funai's Fritz Tolksdorf controversially relocated newly contacted Nambiquara from their forests on the Galera river, 1972.

37. *Left*. Squatters invade the edge of Suruí territory in Rondonia in the 1980s.

38. *Below, left*. The BR-364 road ran dangerously close to the newly contacted Suruí. A bewildered warrior, with bow and a capivara-tooth knife hanging down his back, investigates a pickup truck.

39. *Below*. A Suruí, shortly after first contact by Apoena Meirelles, offers cauim manioc beer.

disintegration, quite often to slavery, the loss of their traditions, and in the end death in complete misery that will come all too soon.' But the dilemma was that contact by well-meaning people like him was preferable to leaving them to the mercy of aggressors. Cotrim also objected to Funai's slavish connivance in the road-building programme. The Indian Foundation was a department of the Ministry of the Interior, whose mission was to open up the Brazilian frontier, so that there was a glaring conflict of interest. Property companies were making huge profits from land along the penetration highway. Cotrim expostulated: 'I do not intend to contribute to enrichment of economic groups at the cost of the extinction of primitive cultures'. But Cotrim's resignation did nothing to slow the construction of the unnecessary Transamazonica.

As the Transamazonica pushed westwards from Altamira, into the magnificent forests between the Xingu and Tapajós, it was entering the lands of an elusive people known as Arara ('Macaw'). There had been fleeting contacts with these delicate-featured, pale-skinned Carib-speakers ever since the mid-nineteenth century. The boastful French explorer Henri Coudreau predicted in the 1890s that the advance of 'civilization' would soon mean the destruction of the Arara, whose memory would survive only in a few place names. Darcy Ribeiro in 1957 listed them as extinct. Coudreau and Ribeiro were wrong. Although some Arara had accepted accommodation with settlers in the 1940s and tragically succumbed to 'catarrh', or influenza, the majority stubbornly refused contact. There was an attack on them by police from Altamira; and the Indians harassed turtle-hunters and other intruders. In 1964 an adventurer called Afonso Alves da Cruz saw broad trails and impressive swidden (forest-clearing) plantations of people on the Penetecaua river, whom he estimated to number 300. Both Orlando Villas Boas in 1967 and then Chico Meirelles attempted in vain to contact the tribe.

The few rubber-tappers or jaguar-skin hunters who ventured into these forests were attacked by Indians and some were killed. The Arara gained a reputation for ferocity. They had to defend themselves against aggressive neighbours such as the Kayapó and Juruna. The Kayapó were particularly brutal: not content with raiding for women and a few human trophies, they apparently wanted to exterminate the Arara completely with genocidal surprise attacks on villages. By contrast, Arara relations with Brazilian frontiersmen were confused – varying between friendly contacts and hostility. In 1969 a group of skin-hunters or *gateiros* shot up an Arara village, murdering twelve people, and left a present of poisoned food. A former gateiro described his ilk as 'shameless toughs who respect nothing. They kill everything, whether animals or Indians: they kill for the sake of killing.'

Funai made occasional, unsystematic attempts to contact the Arara during the 1970s. The 'attraction teams' were desperate to 'pacify' this people before the arrival of the Transamazonica and its settlers. But they alarmed the Indians with their persistence in locating trails and villages, their skills and cunning. And they made the fatal mistake of using long-haired Kayapó as trackers. In Arara mythology, the Kayapó were the incarnation of malevolent spirits who had destroyed the primordial order of the cosmos and were sent to earth as the tribe's persecutors. Whites now came to be identified with the Kayapó. Chief Tojtxi, leader of the Arara resistance, later recalled that anxious period, how he had seen his first white men and became convinced that they wanted to kill his people. He told the Arara that they must fight back. Tojtxi remembered the roar of earth-moving machinery shattering the silence of the forest. 'The whites saw our footprints and followed us. We wanted to know why they kept following us. We went further and further away. The whites came to our village and we fled, leaving our plantations, our *caxiri* [manioc drink], and everything. The whites left presents.'

The Arara are fine swidden farmers, so that when Incra started awarding plots to colonists along the new Transamazonica the most sought-after sites were Indian clearings – even though such occupation was blatantly illegal under the Constitution. One settler from Paraná admitted: 'When I reached here [Kilometre 80 west of Altamira] in '72 I managed to get this scrap of roça and settle here. All these papayas, bananas, and manioc were [planted] by the Indians who had fled from here.' The route of the highway passed only a few hundred metres from a large abandoned Arara village; and in 1974 a tract of almost 400,000 hectares (1,500 square miles) of indigenous land south of the road was sold by Incra to a property company. The east–west highway was a monstrous scar across the Arara's forests on the Iriri–Tapajós watershed. It formed an iron curtain dividing this people and disrupted their intricate system of exchanges, trading, and intermarriage between communities.

The Arara in May 1976 killed three workers of a government geological survey and in 1977 a Transamazonica settler. In September 1977 a Funai employee was seriously hurt. In July 1979 two sertanistas and a woodsman were gravely wounded: they fled in a hail of Arara arrows and two were evacuated by helicopter with arrows protruding from them. The Arara now mutilated the bodies of dead white men and removed heads and bones as trophies, just as they did to the few Kayapó they captured.

One of Funai's most experienced sertanistas, Sydney Possuelo, decided to take personal charge of the contact operation. At this time, he was aged forty and had already had malaria twenty-eight times during his fifteen years of fieldwork. Tall and lean, handsome with a full black beard and receding hairline, Possuelo was intensely concerned about the ethics of contacting tribes and the rights of indigenous peoples. After careful study of aerial photography and all reports of contacts with the Arara, in 1980 he got Funai to 'interdict' (reserve, pending further investigation) the area south of the Transamazonica between kilometres 80 and 160 west of Altamira – even though some of this had already been awarded as settlers' plots. A monitoring post was established, to try to exclude squatters, trappers, or other adventurers. There was also interdiction of another Arara territory north of the road, even though this had also illegally been granted to a property enterprise.

Possuelo decided to stop expeditions to seek the Arara, and to adopt a passive strategy. He built a camp of two stout houses, with a watch-tower protected against arrows, powerful security lights, and tapiri shelters for presents. Funai's Indians shouted friendly messages into the forests – but often in the wrong language. The tribe responded by placing liana barriers on their trails, smashing a saucepan, and retreating into the forest. Then a few presents were taken, and Indians kept the attraction post under constant observation. At first light on 12 July 1980, when the Funai men were sitting down for breakfast, arrows started to fly in through cracks in the walls. The men sheltered behind their upturned table, but two were wounded. Someone managed to start the generator and the Arara fled when the lights came on. It was assumed that the attack had been provoked by a forest-clearance operation only a few kilometres from the post – the Arara could scarcely be expected to understand the different intentions of the two groups of their 'civilizado' enemies.

The post continued, with some additional fortification, and so did the presents. As always, this strategy gradually succeeded. The Indians could not resist the manufactured blades and other useful items, and they became convinced that it was *they* who were taming the hostile whites. Presents seduced them as inevitably as a matador's red rag confuses a bull. It was found that bricks of *rapadura* brown sugar and flutes made by a Waiwái Indian were the most appreciated – the men in the post could hear Arara in the forest testing their new musical instruments. The next breakthrough came in mid-September, when the Arara left presents in return for those they had taken – a land tortoise, five festive headdresses of babaçu palm leaves, and bamboos that were taken to mean a request for more flutes. A young Arara later told the anthropologist Márnio

Teixeira Pinto that his people often watched Possuelo's team. 'The most powerful image he kept from that time was of the "white" men stopping an immense earthmover with some shouts and hand signals. It was such power of the "white" men, and above all the many material goods they left in the tapiris . . . that most impressed the Indians.' Such generosity (and the absence of Kayapó trackers) led to a new concept of whites in Arara thinking, and a more benign place for them in the mythology of creation.

The attraction team then became more active, penetrating forests north of the road, finding trails blocked by Indians warnings, some plantations still being used, and a massive but abandoned hut twenty-three metres (seventy-five feet) long. Sydney Possuelo led a tough expedition for 120 kilometres (75 miles) southwards into dense forests near the lower Iriri, hoping to locate another group of the elusive Arara. His men found a village and plantation, but no Indians. Back on the Transamazonica, Possuelo sought to educate settlers to respect the Arara, just as he continued to pursue contact with the tribe. Another positive event happened in late October, when the Arara took the usual presents from the tapiri and left two bamboo sections full of honey. The delighted sertanistas returned to their camp, played flutes on the veranda, and were answered by music from the forest. But there was still no face-to-face contact.

Finally in February 1981, after taking presents on four consecutive days, a group of Arara appeared at the post. They brought gifts (a tortoise, roast peccary, and honey) and remained for almost an hour. The emissaries consisted of two men, two youths, and a child. One man was Tojtxi, the warrior-chief who had led the long campaign of resistance. 'The atmosphere was festive . . . The meeting took place amid many smiles and much talk which, although incomprehensible, resembled a long conversation among old friends.' The men looked almost Western, with hair cut short, pale skins devoid of hair or paint, and no ornament whatever apart from modest necklaces of nuts. They promised to return, bringing their women and children. Other meetings ensued. At one of them an aged Indian made a speech that lasted for ninety minutes. Although the Funai team could understand almost nothing of what he said, a Txikão interpreter felt that his heartfelt message was: 'My people have been moving for a long time, running, running. Many people, on all sides. We have nowhere else to go.' It was the end of defiance, isolation, and innocence for those Arara. They then helped the whites to contact a northern group in 1983, and another group that had fled south-westwards to distant forests in 1987.

The Arara were contacted by a Funai 'attraction front', which enjoyed extra funding and could afford to be generous with tools and manufactured goods. But after a time, the Arara indigenous area became a standard Funai post, and the flow of presents dried up. It was later explained to the Arara that the whites were threatening to inundate their land with hydroelectric dams. So this people again had to revise its favourable impression of non-Indians and their place in mythology. Teixeira Pinto analysed how the tribe sought to interpret the history of the first two decades after contact and the bewildering changes in behaviour by the whites.

The Arara were granted two long strips of land near the lower Iriri, most of it some fifteen kilometres (nine miles) south of the Transamazonica, but nothing north of the road. The tribe faced two serious threats: from settlers and loggers. The problem of Incra's award of lands along the highway would not go away. The controversial President of Funai, Romero Jucá, in 1988 conceded those lands in the northern part of what should have been the Arara reserve to colonization, since they were already occupied by 2,000 settlers. This abandonment of Indians living north of the road was unconstitutional. Lawyers of the Pro-Indian Commission (CPI) tackled the delicate problem of removing settlers (who had wrongly been granted title deeds) from the main Arara reserves to the south. Incra and Funai had neither the funds for compensation nor alternative lands to offer to such evicted people. Boundary markers of the demarcated reserve were shot full of bullet holes by angry frontiersmen. Chief Tojtxi in 1992 told Fiona Watson of Survival of his people's despair. 'All these people who are living in our territory, our Arara land, they have to be removed. We are very worried because our land is being finished off. It is really being invaded . . . What do they want in Indian land? There is nothing for them in our land, because this is Indian land.' However, the dispute continued through the 1990s, with contradictory rulings by a local judge, intervention for the Indians by the Procurator of the Republic, and attempts by local Funai agents and Catholic clergy to protect the reduced reserves. In May 1995, 600 families staged an organized invasion of the registered Arara indigenous area that had to be repelled by the police.

The principal reason why settlers wanted Arara forests was that they are full of hardwood trees, notably mahogany. Illegal logging within indigenous land reached alarming proportions by the mid-1990s, with the timber men returning as fast as Funai and the police tried to stop them. The chief culprit was the large logging company Bannach, which flagrantly cut a road south across the western Arara indigenous area and built a large sawmill near the Iriri river in the midst of the tribe's territory. Bannach started operations in this region in 1988. It was not restrained until May 1995 when a federal judge condemned its plunder and spoliation; but the timber giant fought back, with lawyers and compliant local politicians. The British film-maker George Monbiot made a powerful documentary, in which he actually showed mahogany trees being felled clandestinely within the Arara reserve, and the illegal logs (which he had marked) passing all the supposed checks to reach the British furniture market. It was known that the felling and removal of one mahogany tree caused the destruction of an average of twenty-seven other rainforest trees. The Arara could not understand the frenzy for mahogany, but knew that the loggers were well aware that their activities were illegal. The Indians were angry about the rape of their homeland. Chief Tojtxi explained why the Arara love their forests, the place where they were born and had always lived. 'We only hunt: that's what we do. We eat a lot of animals from the forest. We eat monkeys, mutum [curassow], deer, tapir, tortoise, armadillo. Things from the forest are best, and nothing is wasted. The forest is very good for us . . . We are suffering. We are surrounded. Where will we hunt?'

12. Rondônia: Frontier Frenzy

By the 1960s the territory that is now the State of Rondônia had changed little since Cândido Rondon drove his telegraph line through at the beginning of the century and then accompanied President Theodore Roosevelt down the river named after him, or since Claude Lévi-Strauss was enchanted by the Nambiquara in 1937. During the 1940s the region was ignored by colonists, and prospectors had not discovered that it contained mineral deposits. Rondon's telegraph line still ran across savannahs and through forests – a few decades later, this author was able to see its abandoned poles and heavy ceramic insulators. Over the years, there were sporadic attacks by Indians living in the forests north of the line. A few settlers were killed on isolated farms or rubber posts. Reprisal expeditions often ensued, in the familiar pattern of the Indian frontier.

The SPI established some posts in the region. The anthropologist Betty Mindlin read the reports from these poor outposts and tried 'to imagine what life was like [on these] during the forties, fifties and sixties. Functionaries isolated in the forest tried to supplement their meagre budgeted resources with commercial activities such as selling Brazil nuts, *poaia* (rice powder) and rubber, making little farm clearings with the help of the Indians, hunting and fishing, building a base house and sometimes precarious infirmaries and schools, raising cattle and complaining about the penury in which they lived, and preoccupied about distributing presents that were always insufficient, such as fish-hooks, axes, knives, machetes and food to any Indians who came.' Some SPI agents had grandiose dreams of building model villages or schools, a museum (although there were no visitors), even 'an avenue' and a club. 'They of course protested against invasions, killings and sale of alcohol to the Indians, and they fought for medical attention. But the impression that remains is of small farmers in mediocre business activity, very little interested in the dense tribal universe that surrounded them.'

At the western edge of Rondônia, a short distance upriver from the frontier town of Guajará-Mirim, lie the forests of a people that Rondon named Pakaá Nova, after a river of that name. They call themselves Wari or Oro-Wari, meaning 'we' or 'people', but Rondon's misnomer has persisted. These warlike Indians occasionally clashed with railway workers or rubber-gatherers. So in 1939 an assistant inspector of the SPI, Francisco (Chico) Meirelles, was sent to try to contact this tribe. The first attraction of the Wari lasted for three years. In June 1942 Meirelles reported that he had reached a place where the Indians were building a new maloca. His team was surrounded by Indians during a moonlit night. 'Hostilities broke out at 4.30 a.m. when they tried to shoot us with arrows at short range in a savage crescendo. They have been seeking us for a long time; but we suspected this and had prepared a good shelter . . . We did not fire a single shot nor even let off the rockets we had brought with us. During the attack we shouted to the Indians "Ane, ane" which means "friend" and is a favourite word of theirs. When we withdrew, after daybreak, I left in the tapiri shelter all their arrows, many presents, and the clothing, bandages, cotton and other things stained with the blood' of two Karipuna Indians who had been wounded in the attack. It was later claimed that, during the contact, 'eleven SPI workers were killed and many others shot by arrows but managed to survive. However, Meirelles' men never retaliated for the attacks. Nor were they deterred by the Indians' constant refusals to gather presents they left, nor the threats shouted from the depths of the forest, nor the frequent attacks and hostilities to which they were subjected. Their reward came when Meirelles exchanged tools for arrows, and the Pakaá Nova took him to visit their village.'

The tribe proved to speak a rare language called Txapakura, which related them to the once-formidable Tora of the middle Madeira and to indigenous people living to the south-west in Bolivia. It was suspected that they were cannibalistic, in that they ate the flesh of dead relatives. For a decade the Wari were left alone, apart from occasional forays into their forests by rubber- and Brazil-nut extractors and mineral prospectors.

In 1947 an army lieutenant disappeared in the forests east of Guajará-Mirim and the Wari were thought to have abducted him; they might also have killed a Benedictine missionary in 1950. In the early 1950s another SPI official, Alfredo José da Silva, established an attraction hut on the Ouro Preto stream on the north bank of the Mamoré-Guaporé. The Austrian anthropologist Etta Becker-Donner was with the SPI team and recalled how the Wari were attracted by the presents left for them. 'They came by night at first, then gradually by day. At first they shot their arrows defiantly, but later they removed their points and embellished them with decorative featherwork. Finally we were able to approach closer to them; they accepted small presents and exchanged them for their own. But they would not yet allow us to visit their village.'

Three years later, in 1955, the seringueiro Manussakis sent gunmen up the Ouro Preto to destroy villages: they brought back an ear as proof of their success. In 1956 the Canadian missionary Abraham Koop of the adventist New Tribes Mission reached the Wari with Inspector Alberico Pereira of the SPI. They built a hut on the Ocaia tributary of the Rio Negro in the tribe's territory, but were eventually driven off by the Indians' arrows. Both confirmed that this tribe did eat human meat – as had been done by the Tupinamba and other nations of the Atlantic seaboard first encountered by European explorers in the sixteenth century. Local people had long been convinced that the Wari removed legs and arms from frontiersmen they killed in order to eat their flesh; but the SPI initially denied the rumour that the Wari were anthropophagous.

In 1961 the Governor of Rondônia wanted to make another attempt to 'pacify' the elusive tribe. The SPI had no funds for this, so the Governor financed it from the Amazon development agency and the local bishopric. He enlisted an ex-SPI sertanista called José Fernando da Cruz, who pushed up the Negro tributary of the Pakaanovas – the river after which the tribe was named. Cruz called his venture 'Mafra' after the Governor, Lieutenant Colonel Alvarenga Mafra. After several months, his expedition was attacked by what they thought were Wari but were in fact unrelated Indians. The publicity-seeker Cruz went on to meet a group of Wari and photographed them eating the body of a girl who had died of dysentery, and his pictures caused a sensation in the press of Rio de Janeiro.

It was subsequently learned that such ritual partaking of dead relatives was an important element of this tribe's funerary mourning. There was much lamentation over a death. An elder relative then supervised the cutting-up and roasting of the dead person. Runners were sent to alert other villages, which came to pay their respects. The meat was eaten, in small pieces and delicately, but only after it was partly rotten so that there would be no pleasure in consuming it. The bones were ground up, burned, and buried; and the soul could then complete its destiny unencumbered by the body that lived on in the surviving Indians.

Atrocities against the Wari did not cease. In that same year 1961 there was news of a massacre of a camp on the banks of the Ocaia stream where the Canadian missionary had located his base. But a greater slaughter was caused by Cruz's careless introduction of alien diseases.

This attraction had become a major media story. So another expedition in January 1962 contained the Director of the entire SPI, Lieutenant

Colonel Moacyr Ribeiro Coelho, and (contrary to SPI regulations) two Protestant missionaries. After a punishing journey hacking through dense vegetation of flooded igapó forest, it reached Cruz's furthest attraction post. This was occupied by a few peaceful Indian families, but the Director of the SPI was appalled by their condition. The Indians contacted in the previous year were 'all thin, squalid, starving, and sick'. The Director wept in dismay at seeing them thus, famished and ill. 'But he did not want to remain for more than one night, for fear of witnessing the necrophagy that the Indians were going to perform [on their dead relatives].' Colonel Coelho said that he had been 'greeted by a theatrical spectacle replete with misery, abandon, and sickness – tragic consequences of the improvidence and ineptitude of those who ordered, organized, and led the so-called Mafra Expedition.'

Director Coelho praised the New Tribes Mission for giving invaluable help to the desperate Wari. A later observer agreed that without the Protestant missionaries' money, boats, supplies, and dedicated nursing, the tribe would not have survived the contact diseases – for the SPI was, as usual, woefully unprepared for such follow-up work. A Catholic missionary, Father Roberto Arruda, fallaciously told the Wari that they would catch diseases if they persisted in their funerary rituals. The sertanista Gilberto Gama said that after they had eaten an old man 'influenza invaded the village and caused deaths. The Pakaá Nova asked for medicines. Father Arruda took this opportunity to repeat to them that they would die if they continued to devour their dead. This time his warning was received with more respect. Eleven Indians perished, which convinced them that the missionary was right. And they requested Christian burial. It was victory.'

Despite this 'victory' post-contact diseases took a terrible toll. Some Wari were so weakened that they did not have strength for burials: they abandoned their beloved dead to vultures and jaguars. Others continued to eat the deceased in secret, although they were punished by the SPI or missionaries if caught. In 1968 a later head of the Indian service, José de Queiros Campos, condemned the way in which the Wari had been contacted and 'later criminally abandoned to their fate' without adequate medical cover. 'The Pakaá Nova of Rondônia are now hungry, sick, and marginalized.'

East of the Wari (Pakaá Nova) lived one of the last major uncontacted tribes in Brazil. This was a semi-nomadic people called Uru-Eu-Wau-Wau (spelled in various ways, including Uruéu-au-au), Tupi-Kawahib speakers related to the Parintintin contacted by Curt Nimuendajú in the 1920s and to groups (wrongly) known as Arara further north. Before contact, these Uru-Eu-Wau-Wau – then known to rubber-tappers as Black-Mouths because they tattooed and dyed the skin around their mouths with black genipap – were often confused with the Wari, although the two tribes spoke different languages and had distinct customs.

During the Second World War, with Malayan rubber plantations in Japanese hands, there was an emergency revival of rubber-tapping in Amazonia. Hundreds of seringueiros were brought from north-east Brazil and known as 'Rubber Soldiers'. This led to a cycle of violence on tributaries of the Madeira in what is now western Rondônia. For decades there were vicious attacks on the region's Indians by rubber men, and revenge killings of isolated seringueiros.

A rubber boss called João Chaves boasted that in 1945 'in an encounter with Indians he massacred with rifle shots 118' Black-Mouths (probably Uru-Eu-Wau-Wau) on the upper Jamari river. This Chaves also had 600 Indians whom he had contacted (with help from the Parintintin) and whom the SPI described as slaves who gathered rubber latex for him. Forty of these Tupi-speaking people, led by two chiefs, were brought to Porto Velho and given presents by the SPI. But they were decimated by influenza when assembled near the Samuel waterfall during the return journey. Their Paramount Chief Tabarerana died, and the distraught Indians tried to carry his body back across the Samuel falls.

At this time, in 1947, the army officer Lieutenant Fernando Gomes de Oliveira disappeared near the source of the Jamari while surveying for what became the BR-364 road. As we have seen, the Wari were suspected of his death, but it was probably done by the Uru-Eu-Wau-Wau. Some colonists even speculated that 'Indians had kidnapped Lieutenant Fernando to purify their race'. Marshal Rondon organized a major search for the missing officer, along the banks of the river and using a plane. One search party, led by the notorious Chaves and containing the Salesian José Francisco Pucci, was guided by the 'Black-Mouths' back to the maloca of the dead Chief Tabarerana. The dwelling was a fine open-sided structure measuring 40 by 50 metres (130 by 165 feet); but its inhabitants were prostrate with flu – the Salesian father baptized over sixty of them as they died. A neighbour of Chaves called Rocha decided to exploit this tragedy. He sent an expedition to capture 'Black-Mouths', to be slave-labour in his rubber operation. The Salesian Father Vitor Hugo praised this action: 'Flu prevented them from opening roças and they thus lacked sustenance. They were dying of starvation . . . Mr Rocha was, however, able to save some of those lives. He clothed all those naked Indians and invited them to his property at a place called União. In despair from their sufferings, the Black-Mouths accepted, even though they thus lost some of their secular freedom. But it was for their good.' A decade later in 1958, this same Father Hugo reported that the wretched Indians were 'reduced to an insignificant minimum, just twenty-five!' These slave labourers lived in two sheds and were controlled by Parintintin overseers.

Isolated rubber-workers and settlers continued to be killed by arrows, and huts or rubber stores were sometimes burned. As usual, there were murderous reprisals. In 1952 Francisco Meirelles reported that fifteen armed rubber-tappers exterminated a village of 'Oroin' (a Wari word meaning 'Those who are painted'). This was at a place where the SPI had already left presents. The raiders murdered twenty men, women, and children. Meirelles reported that 'it is known that they gouged eyes from the Indian children and then left them abandoned in the forest. Such barbarities make new pacification work difficult, since those Indians are increasingly rancorous.' Meirelles commented that it was the fourth such massacre in two years, but that 'the criminals remain immune'. A decade later, there was an even more barbarous massacre, at a place called Teteripe creek. Funai later gathered from witnesses that there were thirty-one dead Indians from this group of fifty-two Oroin. There were said to have been horrible scenes, such as 'children who fled were killed by machetes, many thrown into the air and impaled on knife points' and pregnant mothers cut open.

Fighting between seringueiros and Indians continued throughout the 1950s. Another notorious rubber boss known as Alfredão ('Big Alfred') admitted that he led a raid that killed six Indians and led off women prisoners chained to one another. Two women and a boy soon died of influenza; but one woman survived and became Alfredão's wife Maria. Alfredão believed that he was protected by forest spirits: this was known to the Uru-Eu-Wau-Wau, which was why they did not attack him.

The adventurers Gilberto Gama and Fernando da Cruz made their 1961 unauthorized attraction expedition into the heartland of the Wari – which was also the hills into which the Uru-Eu-Wau-Wau had retreated. 'For eight months, hunger and malaria caused them great sacrifices; but courage overcame all in that unknown world.' After months of searching in vain in the forests, one of the expedition's boats suddenly heard the hiss of an arrow and an Indian shout from the forest. 'The [acculturated Wari] Indian Tiam and [another man] dived into the water as a rain of arrows hit their canoe. It was an Indian attack, unexpected and violent. José Fernando da Cruz shouted: "All naked! Quickly! All get naked!" . . . Dozens of men immediately undressed to show the savages that they were similar [to them].' Perhaps alarmed by this display, the Indians disappeared into the forest and the (reclothed) expeditioners pursued them, guided by the Tupari Indian Saul. After some hours, they came across a wounded warrior who had fallen and dislocated his ankle. Reassured by his pursuers, the young man guided the team to his village. There was a friendly meeting with his group, who were later found to be Oroin speaking a remote dialect of the Wari's Txapakura language.

A strongman emerged among the seringueiros: Manuel Lucino da Silva, 'a tall, strong Potiguar who would stop at nothing to make his fortune', an illiterate and self-made man who built up a private rubber empire. In Guajará-Mirim, Lucino became respected as an example of a tenacious migrant who had made good. He had cordial relations with the local SPI officials, and persuaded them to authorize an attempt to contact the elusive Indians who often clashed with his seringueiros. The team left in May 1963, guided by Valdemar Cabixi, who had been with Fernando da Cruz in the previous year, and containing seven Wari who had recently been contacted and worked for Lucino. (Valdemar Cabixi was a Wari whose parents were sole survivors of a massacre on a stream called Cabixi and who had grown up in SPI posts knowing nothing about his tribe's culture.) The expedition moved up the Negro tributary of the Guaporé. After two weeks Lucino's men captured a child who tried to climb a tree, then two women who sought to escape into the forest. The women led the explorers to their camp where, after some apprehension, the Indians fed the intruders and invited them to sleep in their hut. Everything was peaceful and cordial. The new group were Oroin, of a clan known as Jabuti. Cabixi invited his hosts to accompany him back to the rubber seringal, and ten accepted. The atmosphere started to sour, particularly because the Wari on the expedition tried to dominate the Oroin and even to steal domestic fowl, hammocks, and goods from their maloca. During the march to the seringal, the tension degenerated into a bloody fight that left the acculturated Wari dead or seriously wounded. The injured were taken to Guajará-Mirim by boat.

The boss Lucino was furious and vowed vengeance: the annihilation of the Jabuti maloca. In July 1963 he himself led the reprisal expedition, which contained one of the wounded Wari called Tremendoi and the guide Cabixi. When the attackers reached the Oroin village, some of these were in their hut, others fishing with timbó poison. Cabixi fired the first shot, and there was then a fusillade. 'Many Oroin fled, some wounded. At least three wounded women and four children survived. One woman had her arm broken by a shot, a girl had gunshot in her back and breast, another pellets in her buttocks.' Tremendoi shot the man whom he thought had killed his friends. He then 'went crazy and set fire to the great hut. An old woman ran out of it, and he grabbed her by the hair and killed her. He also gave a coup de grâce shot to kill a wounded man.' There were references to a child killed by Lucino, who snatched it from its mother's neck. Nine Indians were murdered and others wounded. After the main massacre, Lucino worried that survivors might tell the SPI about it. 'He ordered the three women and four children to form a line, seated on the ground. Cabixi [and others set off, but] they heard many shots.'

Despite such brutality and the subsequent killing of members of the expedition who might have confessed, rumours of this massacre – one of the worst in the second half of the twentieth century – reached SPI headquarters in Brasília and its Director Dr Noel Nutels. There was an inquiry against Lucino. But he intimidated Cabixi and other witnesses into silence and was neither convicted nor punished. Mauro Leonel wrote that the case against Lucino 'gradually withered, pursued without competence or conviction by the protective organs the SPI and Funai, developing into farce through the law of inertia, thanks to the indifference and connivance of the police and judicial authorities in a region beyond the law.' His victims fared worse. By 1970 Cícero Cavalcanti of Funai wrote that 'the small group of Oroin was struck by influenza and malaria and is reduced to representatives living together on São Luís seringal, the property of Manuel Lucino on the upper Pakaanovas river.' However, the crime was not forgotten by pro-Indian activists. They got the case reopened in 1985, when one of Lucino's business colleagues argued in his defence that he was a pioneer who had fifty-three descendants and 'gave employment' to some 200 seringueiros. Brazilian justice moves slowly. In 1991 Lucino was finally expelled from his fazenda within Indian territory, where he and his overseers had been terrorizing the surviving Oroin for many decades. Then, in May 1994, a jury finally condemned the eighty-three-year-old Manuel Lucino da Silva to fifteen years in prison. He was the first person in Brazil to be convicted of genocide against Indians.

Soon after Lucino's massacre of the Oroin in 1963, there were atrocities against 'Black-Mouths', to the north of them on this lawless frontier. In 1966 a seringueiro told the SPI that he had seen fourteen abandoned Indian shelters near the river Muqui. Some huts were burned, and there were spent cartridges on the ground and trees scarred by bullets. Another rubber man called Ze Milton sent out many extermination raids, which would leave presents for the Indians, hide, and shoot them when they came to collect the gifts. In 1972, on the upper Machadinho, a rubber-tapper's wife was shot in the eye and two of her children killed by arrows, made by a tribe that was not the recently contacted Suruí – Apoena

Meirelles was sure that it was the Uru-Eu-Wau-Wau. He argued, in the Indians' defence, that they might have approached the seringueiro's hut in search of food and shot their arrows only when the wife fired a shotgun at them. Sporadic skirmishes continued throughout that decade; but Meirelles, father and son, wanted to leave the tribe in peace for as along as possible.

Rondônia's isolation ended abruptly in 1967–68, when army engineers pushed the BR-364 road north-westwards to Porto Velho on the Madeira. Francisco Meirelles was sent to attract the Suruí tribe, who lived dangerously near the road's route. Meirelles was now ageing and had always had a lame leg from a riding accident, so he entrusted most of the contact routine to his son Apoena. (This handsome young man was named after the Xavante chief who had accepted contact with Chico Meirelles in 1946. Meirelles' wife died when Apoena was an infant, so the boy was reared by a Xavante foster-mother and he loved the tribe, who trained him to be an expert woodsman.) The father-and-son team undertook the Suruí contact only when convinced of its urgency. It was a classic and delicate 'wooing' campaign.

For nine months presents were left at a place frequented by Indians, until the Suruí finally decided that it was in their interest to have a peaceful meeting with the whites. This occurred on 21 June 1969 near the Sete de Setembro, a small headwater of the Roosevelt–Aripuanã. One day Apoena was placing presents in a shelter, looked up, and, to his surprise, saw some fifty Indians armed with bows and arrows approaching him. He handed their chief two machetes and was given fish in return. 'They were fairly apprehensive, and the one who handed him the fish was trembling.' At the next face-to-face encounter, Apoena appeared naked to show that he was friendly and had no weapons. The Indians later recalled how frightened they had been, but they could not resist the presents. Apoena's team 'were the first strangers who had not come as slaughterers. The ambiguity of the outcome became apparent when the Indians later reflected on the transition. One Suruí said that Apoena was a very good friend who stopped his people from continuing to kill the tribe. He brought machetes, axes, pans, guns, mirrors – all objects that the Indians did not have and desired. But the points of the suspended machetes also carried disease and death. The Indians grew ill when they visited their new friends, and very many died.'

After various subsequent contacts, it was learned that there were five tribes speaking the Mondé dialect of Tupi in the forested hills north of the road. The Cinta Larga lived to the east between the Juruena and

Roosevelt; the Suruí west of the Roosevelt; to the north of them the Gavião ('Hawks'), who had been contacted in the late 1940s; the Zoró or Cabeça-Seca ('Dry Heads'), a pale-skinned people with delicate features who were not contacted until 1977; and the Aruá west of the Zoró. These tribes were also related to the warlike Parintintin (Tupi-Kawahib), who lived north of them on another river flowing into the Madeira and who had been contacted in a hail of arrows by Curt Nimuendajú in 1922.

These tribes are similar in many ways, but they often fiercely fought one another, and they can scarcely understand their different versions of the Mondé Tupi language. Suruí is a name given to the north-eastern group by Chico Meirelles, and the name has stuck; but the Suruí refer to themselves as Paiter, meaning 'We' or 'Real people'. Suruí men wore belts of black bark-cloth some ten centimetres (four inches) wide around their stomachs, straw penis-guards, and rows of black-nut necklaces; the women wore nothing apart from occasional body paint. The Cinta Larga ('Broad Belt') are so called because their men also wore a wide girdle of black bark, but no other clothing apart from a penis-sheath held by a cord. Dr Jean Chiappino, a French medical doctor and linguist, reckoned that the Suruí numbered 400–500 in 1972 (of whom he personally met 250 in two main villages and several nomadic groups), but that there had been many more a decade earlier before the onslaught of diseases. Chiappino also guessed 400 or 500 for the Cinta Larga.

Dr Chiappino was appalled by Funai's handling of these tribes after contact. The doctor wrote angry protests to Funai's management, but in vain. He then published a devastating account of neglect so serious that he felt that it amounted to genocide. The Suruís' condition 'was disastrous one year after their first contact with whites – a contact which took place too rapidly and without the benefit of any medical assistance.' First, Apoena Meirelles organized a helicopter mission to a village stricken by measles. To Chiappino's dismay, this did not apply serious preventive medicine. 'Hastily put together and brutal in form, it was a total failure. All that it did was to fly over and visit one Suruí village, quickly abandoned by its inhabitants at the arrival of such a machine.' The outcome was not the saving of Indian lives, but merely an anodyne article in the *National Geographic* magazine about how well Brazil was protecting her newly contacted 'Broad-Belt Indians'. Dr Chiappino found that the so-called pharmacy at the Indian post closest to the Suruí was devoid of any medicine. At his insistence, another medical mission was organized. But this was just another 'propaganda number' that did no more than inject intra-muscular Eucalyptine and a series of tetanus injections that were irrelevant to the epidemics threatening the Suruí. It was a rushed job, with no notes about who was vaccinated, and no observation of the results. So the Suruí were unprotected against alien diseases whose lethal impact had been known for centuries.

With the inevitability of Greek tragedy, a terrible epidemic struck all age groups. Dr Jean Chiappino observed how 'death occurred within two months after the appearance of a hoarse cough, which filled the forest in the evenings and which we learned to be the warning symptom signifying contamination. This was soon followed by a pussy expectoration which was very difficult to cough up, and which exhausted the patient. Associated with this syndrome was a persistent fever.' This bronchial pneumonia rapidly carried off children and old people in terminal cachexia. 'Family and social groups were distressed, disoriented and destroyed by the scope of this epidemic.' It was later learned that this was a rare disease called blastomicosis. Local medical teams had no idea how to prevent or treat this difficult scourge.

As a result of Funai's friendship with American Protestants, a couple from the Summer Institute of Linguistics was allowed to join the contact team. Missionaries were not supposed to be with Indians at this delicate initial stage. However, Willem and Carolyn Bontkes proved to be intelligent and reasonably tactful missionaries, who helped the Indians. The Bontkes counted 363 Suruí in 1971, but reported tragically that within three years 193 of these had died, mostly from influenza and measles. That was a loss of over half the population, a catastrophe that would have caused unimaginable trauma to any community anywhere in the world. Dr Chiappino could not find a single responsible or competent doctor in Funai's health department. None was vaccinating the newly contacted tribe, and Chiappino's offer to do so was ignored. The criminally mismanaged contact with the Suruí and Cinta Larga was grotesquely similar to the efforts of the disgraced SPI, which had been disbanded three years previously. A decade later, Betty Mindlin found that the Indians 'often speak about that period of sadness, comparable to a great massacre, to a war. Each person is desolate as he or she enumerates dead relatives: various brothers and sisters, father, mother, children, husband, wives.'

Alongside their appalling demographic losses, the Suruí had to undergo the intense changes of contact with Brazilian society. Theirs had been the usual SPI/Funai attraction campaign, in which they were seduced by quantities of presents. This flow of free goods ceased abruptly as soon as the last Indian was contacted and they had all laid down their arms. Funai's 'attraction front' then became an Indian post, manned by staff who were more concerned with their own wages, their children's education, and eventual return to the comfort of city life, than with their strange and ungrateful charges. Carmen Junqueira watched how the Suruí and nearby Cinta Larga were impoverished by this transition. 'In contrast to the indigenous vivacity and cultural richness, our national culture . . . exposes its suffocating face . . . The former quality of life, sustained by a balance between limited needs and relative abundance of resources, is broken. The community has to experience a situation of poverty. Regular work, which is more intensive in the new system of production, cannot begin to satisfy the many new needs that accumulate. Among these are dreams inspired by the mystique of "the new", which bear no relation to their usefulness.'

The tribe's social structure was disrupted. Elders often had to cede power to younger men who were better able to negotiate with outsiders. By visiting towns, learning some Portuguese, and experiencing the dynamism of freewheeling frontier society, young Indians inevitably distanced themselves from the older pre-contact generation. Women remained tied to their domestic roles, while men had stimulating experiences outside the village; and new tools such as machetes, axes, and guns tended to ease the workload of men more than women.

Although everyone knew that the two imperatives for a hitherto-isolated tribe were health and land, the territories of the Suruí and Cinta Larga were just as seriously threatened as was their medical survival. The new road from Cuiabá to Porto Velho passed only a few hours' walk from a Suruí village. Indians wandered onto the extraordinary clearing that sliced through their land, and fraternized with passing traffic. I saw naked Suruí women begging food from bus passengers, and a young warrior trying out the driver's seat of a van. Although overtly good-natured, such meetings were inevitably patronizing and must have been deeply unsettling for the Indians – as well as posing an obvious health risk. Thirty years after contact, Junqueira saw that 'for the Indians the result is always the same: loss of lands, sickness, misery, and death'.

More seriously, the BR-364 highway brought a stream of mineral prospectors and colonists into Rondônia. The 1963 'Massacre at Parallel 11' was done by adventurers seeking gold and diamonds. During the 1960s mining companies discovered substantial tin deposits in this Territory. Prospectors turned to this cassiterite tin dioxide: by the end of that decade fifty heavy trucks a day were bringing the ore to Porto Velho. When the Cinta Larga were contacted in 1968, their presumed territory was interdicted; and the Indian park of Aripuanã was created within this area in June of the following year. However, the decree that established this park carefully reserved its mineral deposits for Funai to exploit. In April 1970 the government outlawed individual prospecting in Rondônia, leaving the field clear for it to sell licences to large mining companies. These provided jobs for some 1,500 of the wildcat garimpeiros, but a further 2,000 were told to stop prospecting and either leave the Territory or turn to farming.

Other immigrants poured in, attracted by reports that the new road ran through patches of rich 'purple-earth' soil, and enticed by the military government's colonization schemes, which offered title deeds to land and some tools, seed, advice, and credit to each settler family. A myth arose that social betterment and land ownership were within the grasp of all the destitute and unemployed of Brazil, if they could only reach this frontier. There was soon a string of towns along the highway, each stimulated by a different colonization scheme: Ouro Preto ('Black Gold') in 1970, Ji-Paraná (near the Suruí) and Sidney Girão in 1973, Paulo de Assis Ribeiro in 1974 and Burareiro and Marechal Dutra in 1976. By 1971, Jean Chiappino reported that 3,000 colonists had just come to the town of Cacoal and that the Gleba Itaporanga land company was employing 1,000 settlers at Espigão do Oeste ('Western Ridge') in the Suruí's forests beside the Ji-Paraná river. The Aborigines Protection Society's fact-finding mission next year was appalled to discover (only by comparing maps) that the boundaries of the Indian reserve had been redrawn to accommodate this São Paulo colonization company. 'The ceding of this huge slice of excellent land to outside colonizers . . . appeared to be as bad as the worst example of the practice that reached scandalous proportions in the last days of the SPI.' Settlers' shanty huts were crowded along a stream at the edge of Indian territory.

The Itaporanga colonization company was the most flamboyant of all these immigration schemes. This company was launched in 1968 – the year in which army engineers pushed the dirt highway from Vilhena in central Rondônia to Porto Velho – by four brothers from São Paulo called Melhorança. They arrived in Rondônia with thirty-six family members and headed by the chubby eldest brother, Nilo, a charismatic orator who projected himself as a spiritualist and who attracted settlers with his vision of a fraternity of poor pioneers struggling against the wilderness, the authorities, and the Indians. The Melhoranças moved along the new BR-364 to Pimenta Bueno ('Good Pepper'), then cut a road for thirty-five kilometres (twenty-two miles) north, and claimed an expanse of 1.4 million hectares (5,400 square miles) of forest – an area half the size of Belgium. They said that they had acquired an old rubber concession; but their land-grab had no more legality than the hundreds of plots they sold (often on credit) to their poor settlers. The Melhoranças had the good sense to treat the Suruí, whose land they had brazenly invaded, tolerably well. They gave the Indians small gifts, fascinated them with rides in their vehicles, and traded knives and goods for their food or for their labour in clearing forest. But they also introduced alcohol, disease, and permanent occupation and destruction of the forests on which the tribe depended for its hunting and well-being.

By good fortune for the colonization companies, some of the watershed in central Rondônia lies on terra roxa (purple volcanic soils that seemed more fertile than others in Amazonia) and in the early 1980s a huge area of equally promising thick, loamy topsoil was also discovered. So, in the decade of the 1970s, Rondônia's population grew by more than four times to over 490,000. In the six years between 1977 and 1983, 271,000 immigrants arrived – with some 70,000 in 1980 alone. By that time, the journalist Jonathan Kandell wrote that the 'BR-364 has sparked a land rush into Rondônia unmatched in speed and ferocity by any rural migration since the settling of the nineteenth-century American West. Nowhere else in the world are people moving into virgin territories on the scale witnessed in Rondônia.' Like Kandell, I saw big trucks ploughing down the red dust or mud of the highway, with families living in the back, their furniture and possessions piled high around them. Many of these were industrious farmers from southern Brazil, whose smallholdings were engulfed by agribusiness of huge soya-bean and coffee plantations. Others came from the city slums or the drought-stricken north-east – as President Médici had intended for the failing Transamazonica. Jonathan Kandell watched the flood of colonists 'joined by armies of labourers deployed by real-estate speculators and big ranchers to raze the jungles. And in their wake have come the hired gunmen, con artists and other criminals who flourish in the inevitable disputes over possession of land. By the time the government realized the scope of this migration, Rondônia had become the scene of the most violent, confused and widespread struggles over land anywhere in Brazil. The land wars have pitted white man against aboriginal Indian, peasant against large property owner, legal settler against squatter and private developer against government land agent.' It all started with the giant land grab by the Melhorança clan – whose surname happens to mean 'Improvement'. The government encouraged and tried to harness this wave of internal migration. In 1970 it created a national agency for colonization and agrarian reform known by its acronym Incra.

In December 1971, 200 Indians overran the cluster of huts of Funai's Roosevelt post. They killed Possidônio Bastos, a former journalist now working for Funai, the telegraph operator Acrísio Lima, and an Arara Indian woman called Maria. The attack may have been the work of Cinta

Larga, angered by Funai's heavy-handed attempts to reconcile them with the Suruí. But the Brazilian press had no doubt that this tragedy was provoked by the property company that had illegally planted hundreds of families of poor settlers within indigenous territory. Apoena Meirelles complained that Funai had done nothing to expel the invaders. The young sertanista said that 'in less than four years, the lands of the Cinta Larga and the Suruí have been divested. Epidemics have left their mark, and the tribes have already begun the first steps down the long road to misery, hunger, and the prostitution of their women ... I would rather die fighting alongside the Indians in defence of their lands and their right to live, than see them tomorrow reduced to being beggars on their own lands.' The land-colonization company was the effective winner. Apoena was transferred to another assignment.

Meanwhile, the simmering dispute between the colonization agency Incra and the freebooting Melhoranças had come to a head. Incra brought a legal action, and the court ruled that Itaporanga's scheme at Espigão do Oeste was illegal – not least because it was well within the belt of land on either side of a national highway that belonged to the state. The 700 settler families, inspired by the messianic Nilo Melhorança, refused to move. They were well armed, with lookouts along their approach road. Incra's surveyors were stripped of their instruments and sent packing. Then the colonists went too far, blowing up a federal government bridge on the road to Espigão. So in 1976 heavily armed police, supported by helicopters, moved in. They arrested Nilo Melhorança and impounded a mass of documents that revealed how large the enterprise had been.

An Incra lawyer told Jonathan Kandell: 'We had to tell the settlers that they were victims of a land hoax of gigantic proportions.' These poor people had paid or borrowed money for their spurious title deeds, worked hard to clear and plant their land, and sided with their leader against the distant federal authority that seemed determined to evict them. Melhorança 'was strong, confident, convincing. He opened up a wilderness for people who had always been losers, and he even gave them a sense of religion.' It took four years to unscramble the mess. Melhorança served a term in prison and never recovered his business. Many smaller settlers were allowed to remain; larger ones had their holdings reduced to 100 hectares (247 acres); later arrivals were set adrift, to earn a living by casual labour. But it never occurred to anyone to return the land to its original owners: the Suruí Indians. Kandell met a few Suruí on the highway in 1981. 'These supposedly warlike Indians were dressed in tatters, fatigued by either disease or hunger and wearing smiles that seemed to plead for mercy. I felt a deep sense of shame.'

Matters came to a head in 1976. There was a serious clash between the Suruí and the settlers, with people killed and huts sacked. The Minister of the Interior went to the scene and said that he would get the reserve demarcated, which was done, and expel the invaders, which was not done. There were still 300 families of settlers within the Aripuanã park, a reserve designated for the Cinta Larga, Suruí, and neighbouring Tupi-speaking tribes. By the late 1970s, Betty Mindlin found that 'the proximity of the settlers is alarming: their first houses are three kilometres [under two miles] from Sete de Setembro post (and at a slightly greater distance from the other village). From the roça where the women collect food and comment on the presence of the spirits of their dead, you can hear the chainsaws of their neighbours felling the forest.' In 1979 Chief Itabira of the Suruí went to Porto Velho to protest to Apoena Meirelles, who was then the head of that region of Funai, and to the Governor of Rondônia. The colonists were felling forest and burning large areas, so that the Indians could hardly hunt, and they were fishing with explosives in the reserve's rivers. Itabira said that the Suruí women were particularly angry because the whites had been cutting down babaçu palms, which contained their favourite *gongo* larvae, and also the reeds used for thatching. He declared: 'The colonists brought sicknesses and malaria. My people are hungry and have nothing left to hunt. They are saying that they will no longer obey Itabira, because I always say to be patient and wait for Apoena [to do something]'. Apoena, in turn, said that he could not understand why the government had not evicted the intruders. 'It is up to the government to take a decision that is provided by law . . . I feel that the resolution of the Suruí problem is a point of honour for me: if there is no solution, there is no reason for my continuing in Funai . . . I can see no sense in continuing to work for something in which I do not believe.'

North of the Suruí, further down the Roosevelt river, are the forests of the Zoró – enemies of the Suruí even though they speak the same Mondé dialect of Tupi and are culturally similar. By 1977 there was concern that the Zoró might be struck by the measles or influenza that had decimated neighbouring tribes or see their land invaded by settlers. So in November of that year, Apoena Meirelles led a contact expedition that included Indians from four tribes likely to speak the Zoró language. It went smoothly: knives, metal pots, mirrors, and other goods exerted their usual magic. These presents were left in a tapiri shelter until a brave Indian came to take them. Apoena asked the President of Funai to interdict the Zoró area; which was done rapidly by April 1978. A vaccination campaign was initiated, even though eighty Zoró had already caught flu from nearby ranchers; but the inoculation was interrupted when the Suruí chose to attack their Zoró enemies.

The first Funai agents left by Apoena among the Zoró were disastrous, bullying the Indians and abusing their women. So most of the tribe fled westwards in 1979 to take refuge with the related Gavião and Arara in Lourdes reserve. While there, many Zoró were converted by missionaries of the New Tribes Mission, so that when they returned home in 1981 (to a far better Funai manager called Natalício) they had 'acquired a sense of shame because they are what they are and from their nudity.' Another strong influence was a huge ranch, Fazenda Castanhal, that was already established to the north-west with 19,000 head of cattle, extensive crops, an orange orchard, houses containing eighty farm-workers, a full complement of food-processing equipment, a shop, and two airstrips. The Zoró often visited Castanhal and were fascinated by it. 'They do not in any sense perceive the fazendas as a threat to their lands or cultural integrity. On the contrary, many of them would like to be able to work in them and have asked to do so. The workers' clothes and houses are already a powerful influence for the Indians, as well as a desire to possess what the settlers possess, from radios to watches and their language . . . Chief Paiô had his hair cut at Fazenda Castanhal, in a symbolic gesture of acceptance of its world.'

Relations with Funai staff were good, but the agency's main concern was to get the Indians working to produce an agricultural surplus. Every morning forty-five men and boys trooped off to their fields, wearing shorts, straw hats, and rubber boots, and carrying machetes, to work for eight hours growing rice, maize, and other vegetables. Their reward was a weekly issue of trade goods – soap, batteries, clothes, powder and shot, oil, salt, and store food. By 1983 the anthropologist Roberto Gambini reported sadly that 'the general impression is of galloping cultural impoverishment. Clothing diminishes and worsens the image of the Indians, often making them look like peasants or beggars. Nakedness seems to be synonymous with a past that is starting to shame them. The Zoró no longer want to be Zoró: they want to be something else, but they do not know what.' Intrigued by everything to do with whites, the Zoró rapidly converted to the missionaries' Protestantism. They abandoned all traditional ceremonies, decorations, and ritual. All that replaced these were Christian services, 'long, drawn-out, monotonous, and dead. What can it possibly mean to these people to go on repeating the narrative of Genesis or to say that "Jesus Christ is the way"?'

The situation had been even worse at the Igarapé Lourdes reserve, the seat of the New Tribes missionaries. This area contained over 300 Gavião ('Hawks', who knew themselves as Digüt) and Karo Arara, but it was invaded by some 350 squatters. These Indians had had their first contacts with rubber-gatherers, then with the SPI in the 1960s. But the greatest influence came from six New Tribes missionaries of different nationalities who for seventeen years converted the tribes to their Baptist sect. 'They brought medicines against diseases unknown to the shamans, they taught reading in Gavião, they sold industrialized goods, and they had a plane and an excellent radio. [The Gavião] soon became a model "new tribe" . . . Once a community with its own culture, they now awoke and went to sleep threatened by "sin".' The missionaries forbade profound and trivial aspects of the Indians' former way of life – festivals, polygamy, courtship, fermented manioc chicha, and personal ornaments. A distinguished old shaman, who knew hundreds of plant uses, was branded as a victim of Satan and forbidden entry to the chapel. Instead, younger men were raised as chiefs and pastors who led the services and hymn-singing.

There was then a surprising reaction. The austere missionaries went too far in prohibiting celebrations, even of Funai's 'Day of the Indian'. The mesmerizing shaman Alamah and a young chief organized a defiant festivity that lasted far into the night. The revolt grew, a majority of Indians happily returned to traditional customs, and by 1980 they demanded the departure of the missionaries. Apoena Meirelles ordered this in late 1981, and when the missionaries refused, the police removed them. A limited return to traditional customs, handicrafts, and spiritualism followed, although the Gavião and Arara continued to resemble frontier settlers in dress, farming, and accommodation.

Having rid themselves of missionaries, the Gavião needed to recover their lands from invading settlers. Funai sought to achieve this by judicial means, but some of Rondônia's judges were slow to uphold indigenous rights. So in September 1984 the Gavião took the initiative. Armed with bows and arrows, they confiscated Funai's radio, announced their exasperation, and demanded Apoena's presence. They then seized sixteen settlers as hostages. These were well treated in the village for a month but not released until there was a firm promise of expulsion of all the invaders. Finally, with Apoena Meirelles as intermediary, backed by a legal judgement and the presence of twenty-five policemen, most of the colonists departed. They left behind areas devastated by predatory logging.

In 1981 Funai also obtained a judicial order expelling squatters from the Suruí's Sete de Setembro reserve. Most left, but thirty-five stubborn families had to be forcibly evicted, for resettlement on other plots. Armed police prevented clashes between the colonists and Funai officials. The young Suruí warrior Tabira declared that settlers who had been there for some years could stay and would be protected, but that no more could come. So when two new whites invaded the reserve on 1 October, they were killed by the Indians.

Mineral prospectors flagrantly invaded the Aripuanã park during these years. Some were expelled by Funai, but they returned in force to other streams in this vast and largely unexplored area. A hundred of them and a company called Ancon Mining worked a garimpo (mine) called Ouro Preto on the Guariba tributary of the Roosevelt and at one ironically called Rondon on the rio Branco. Some men molested Cinta Larga women and a young girl was raped, so that by 1983 the situation was very tense. Funai's director of the park tried to order the garimpeiros to leave. Carmen Junqueira and Mauro Leonel were appalled by the quantity of alcohol and guns at the miners' camp. 'Indians from a village a few kilometres from the garimpo are naturally curious to observe activities at the mine-working and the goods that arrive there. But they are rightly revolted by the presence of the disrespectful invaders and by the harm and diseases they have disseminated in the area.' Unless the garimpo were closed, there was great danger that the Indians would attempt a confrontation, 'in an action that would certainly be suicidal'. The magazine *Porantim* reported that a massacre of Cinta Larga did in fact occur, on the Guariba in April 1982, with twelve Indians killed by prospectors. But there was no confirmation by any eyewitness. Funai did finally get police help to remove this mining camp.

Having the highway and its colonists so close to their reserve meant rapid acculturation for the Suruí. Although they resented the invasion of their forests, the Indians were impressed by the way in which the settlers worked hard at their farming, lived in separate houses without much communal life, and seemed to enjoy plenty of manufactured goods. The Indians naturally wanted to have the same possessions as the regional inhabitants, but this required money. Earning money led to a change in tribal routine. The Suruí, and to a lesser extent the Cinta Larga, had to survive the dilemmas of being at the junction of two worlds.

Adaptable and resilient, the Suruí overcame their demographic catastrophe and built back their numbers by having many children. Carmen Junqueira was amazed by how quickly the Suruí investigated and came to understand national Brazilian society. They moved from exchanging presents at first contact to trading in a market economy. They changed from hunter-gathering to an understanding of writing, law, and ownership of land. It was an extraordinary feat. By 1985 Junqueira wrote that 'anyone who saw them last year visiting the National Congress [in Brasília], speaking fluent Portuguese, and demanding their rights, could never have supposed that they were immersed in the tribal world less than a decade ago. But they had decided with determination to decipher our world.'

A young chief told Betty Mindlin of his utopian vision, which contrasted with the political awareness described by Carmen Junqueira. He hoped to send half his people to the forests to the north, far from the road and the intrusive settlers. 'There the Suruí would live as before: without clothing, in large clean malocas, with spacious plazas for their discussions and dances, using many ornaments and feathers, eating game and fruits from the forest, making large farm clearings, and holding many festivals. Far from the towns, they would not catch flu or other diseases: they would die only of old age. In a few years there would be many of them.' The problem was manufactured goods, for which the Suruí had developed an appetite. The chief imagined half the tribe remaining near the road and the Funai post. There they could obtain the desired tools and would then trade them with their kinsmen living in the forest paradise.

In June 1985 the Suruí held an assembly that demanded the removal of the Director of the Aripuanã Indian park, whom they accused of trying to divide them and of being corrupt. They wanted a road between their two villages, which would help in an emergency. They condemned 'the lack of medical assistance and the absence of medicines to fight the diseases that are ending our lives . . . [and also] the presence of a veritable industry of invasions of our people's land, as well as that of the other indigenous peoples of Rondônia.'

South-west of the Suruí and Zoró lived the remnant of the Wari – the Pakaá Nova contacted in the 1960s and then decimated by diseases. These people had an experience with Protestant missionaries similar to that of the Zoró. Fundamentalist New Tribes missionaries were (wrongly) present at the first contacts with the Wari, and they then managed to save some Indians from epidemics. Medicine was the main weapon of conversion. The Mission's leader Henry Loewen said that, after the initial contact, 'the SPI men pulled back a number of times and left the work entirely to the missionaries. These kept at it until the naked tribesmen yielded to their friendship.' Then came a terrible period of deaths from epidemics. 'The missionaries stayed with the dying Indians applying medicines as best they were able to.' At first the Wari were allowed to continue their practice of roasting and ritual eating of dead relatives.

A missionary called Royal started holding services in 1961, initially under a tarpaulin, and he learned the complicated Wari language. Conversion to

Christianity did not come until 1968, but it was then very rapid: all the tribe decided to practise the new faith. By 1970 the missionaries could boast that 'the Indians have portions of God's Word in their tongue. Many follow biblical teachings and live a meaningful life. They are well dressed by now and are at peace with all. They work at gathering rubber, Brazil nuts and other jungle products . . . Most of the men speak Portuguese by now. They are well on the way to permanent integration.' All Wari (apart from a few in an old Catholic station) became *crentes*, Protestant 'believers'. 'They appeared to have lost interest in polygamous marriages and extra-marital relations, inter-tribal fights with clubs ceased, as did festivities at which guests drank until they lost consciousness, and the practice of funerary or warlike cannibalism.' One old man later recalled that 'club fights ended, rage ended. There were no Wari with rage, we were all crentes.' Much about Protestant teaching appealed to the Wari. They liked standing up and confessing sins such as adultery or robbery, of which they had always disapproved. They also appreciated the concept of brotherly love, for consanguinity was important to the Wari, but they had formerly achieved consanguinity with all people only in the afterlife. Once converted, they held great banquets – without drinking or dancing, of course – at which hunters divided up their catch, and everyone sang religious songs about peace and friendship.

The anthropologist Mauro Leonel was appalled by what he saw, in 1984. The missionaries used their limited knowledge of the Wari language to dominate the group politically and culturally. They concentrated on young Indians, from whom they chose future pastors. Shamans were opposed and converts rewarded. Most tribal customs, rituals, beliefs, and even indigenous names were prohibited as sinful. The missionaries prevented their congregation from obtaining money or even learning arithmetic, so that all outside goods could be obtained only through the men of God – who were also the only outsiders who could reward Indians for labour. The foreign missionaries opposed Funai officials, apart from the many of these who converted to Protestantism, and they forbade Catholics to enter their villages. (The Catholics, who controlled one Wari community at Sagarana, were equally violent in fighting Protestants.) Leonel felt that 'Funai's tolerance of such a situation is unacceptable . . . Allowing missionaries to live there without authorization is a flagrant violation of legislation that obliges it to defend the Indians' right to their own culture.' Denise Meirelles was struck by the difference in the morale of Indians without missionaries and those who were controlled and browbeaten by them. She was shocked that the missionary schools taught reading only of texts concerned with their fundamentalist cult.

In fact, the Wari never fully believed in a God. They could not understand talk about 'our father' creating all things for, as one missionary admitted, 'the central question for the Wari is humanity, not divinity'. Nor would they accept the concept of salvation through Christ: to them Christianity meant only virtuous living. They never abandoned beliefs about the spirit world or visions of the afterlife by the very ill or dreamers. So the Wari abandoned Christianity. They did so almost as abruptly and finally as they had embraced it.

When Aparecida Vilaça of the National Museum was with the Wari in 1986 few were still crentes, and by 1993 there were only six out of four hundred. Curiously, they did not dislike their decade of Protestantism. 'Far from saying that they were unhappy when Christian and not cannibal, the Wari had nostalgic memories of those collective feasts, the absence of club fights and marital infidelity, and for the music that spoke of the way of life they wanted to live – in peace and love. They were then crentes, and they liked it.' One man told Vilaça that he used to pray to God for good hunting and got plenty, whereas after ceasing to be Christian his catches were disappointing. So why did the Wari reject Christianity? Vilaça thought that it was because they had never really abandoned old beliefs. Also, Funai started to become a better source of outside goods than the missionaries, and its anthropologists were non-crentes who encouraged a return to traditional tribal values.

Rondônia's other great indigenous nation, the Nambiquara (or Nambik-wara), had been in contact for far longer than the Cinta Larga and other Tupi-speaking groups. Although less sophisticated than the Tupi, many Nambiquara lived and roamed on the relatively open plateau along which Rondon had built his telegraph line and which was the route of the BR-364 and its hordes of settlers. The Nambiquara had few tools and were sometimes nomadic: as Lévi-Strauss had noted, the women carried most of a family's meagre possessions in long open-weave baskets. They wore no clothes and slept on the ground in the ashes of their fires. Nambiquara men were fine hunters, immensely skilled in finding, stalking, and killing all types of game, from birds and monkeys to alligators and snakes. They hunted with bows and arrows, but changed to guns after contact. A man's weapon is the symbol of his masculinity, and he is judged by his ability and luck. The French anthropologist Pierre Clastres was thrilled by the beauty of a hunt. 'The Indians are so agile, so skilled, their gestures so precise and efficient – this was total mastery of the body.' For them, 'hunting is always an adventure, sometimes a risky one, but constantly inspiring ... Tracking animals in the forest, proving that you are more clever than they are, approaching within arrow's range without revealing your presence, hearing the hum of the arrow in the air and then the dull thud as it strikes an animal – all these things are joys that have been experienced countless times, and yet they remain as fresh and exciting as they were on the first hunt. The [Indians] do not grow weary of hunting. Nothing else is asked of them, and they love it more than anything else.' The women tended vegetable gardens or gathered edible grubs and insects.

The Nambiquara were not a cohesive tribe. They lived scattered in small communities, some of which had been in touch with frontier society since Rondon's day while others were still completely uncontacted by the late 1960s. David Price, an anthropologist from Chicago and then Cornell universities, did his doctoral research on the Nambiquara of the Sararé valley between 1967 and 1970, then returned and worked for Funai from 1974 to 1976, trying to establish programmes of health care, education, agriculture, and trading for these Indians; and in 1980 was employed by the World Bank, which was contemplating a major loan to help Brazil develop Rondônia by rerouting the BR-364 (through Nambiquara territory) and paving the highway. Price's book *Before the Bulldozer* is a masterful account of one anthropologist's insight into a tribal people and his struggles to help them. The book gave the most penetrating study I know of Funai, with its staff ranging from dedicated and admirable agents and nurses in the field, to devious schemers and yes-men at headquarters in Brasília.

When he first reached the Nambiquara, Price found tuberculosis raging among them: he helped Funai organize a vaccination campaign. The tribe had previously suffered from the worldwide influenza epidemic of 1918–19, and from measles in 1946. So this people was already reduced to a mere 600, from estimates of up to 20,000 at the start of the twentieth century, and 2,000–3,000 in 1938. The survivors were fragmented. As Price explained, 'The Nambiquara have always been independent individualists; the largest group they feel they belong to is the village – which, traditionally, seldom contained more than thirty or forty people. The Nambiquara are a "tribe" only because the Brazilians say they are; even the word "Nambiquara" is the Brazilians' name for them. Among themselves, they are just "people".' There was no paramount chief, and no mechanism for the entire tribe to unite to defend its lands and rights.

Despite Rondon's great affection for these people, he never created any reserve for them. Finally, in 1968, a large expanse of arid savannah scrubland was set aside, but the decree that fixed the reserve was done with no regard to the advice of local Funai people about where the Indians actually lived. Almost none was within the area. Fritz Tolksdorf, a German immigrant to Brazil and former Lutheran missionary, was given the task of relocating Nambiquara groups into their new territory. In 1972 the Aborigines Protection Society team saw some Indians who had been contacted in rich forests of the Galera tributary of the upper Guaporé, then moved onto the sandy plateau of this reserve. Protestant missionaries reported that the Galera Nambiquara had been content and flourishing in their homeland. But a land-colonization company in 1966 used the missionaries' trail to 'develop' those forests for thirty settler families. Funai reported that 'for some time the landowners have been trying to convince the missionary to move the village ... [They] think that the best solution is to move the Galera to another village to the west.' Instead of protecting its charges, Funai agreed to this disgraceful and illegal relocation. Subjected to the trauma of 'attraction' and snatched from their comfortable forest homes, they were clearly bewildered and wretched in this open habitat. 'When the Chief and many others returned to the ancestral grounds to bury a dead girl, they had been deeply distressed to find farmers already cutting down their forest homelands.' Their land of origin on the Galera contains sacred caves which were found to contain ancient carvings, some of which represent female genitalia and gave rise to the notion that this was once the home of Amazons. The idealistic *sertanista* Antonio Cotrim was involved in moving the Galera Nambiquara and was helpless when they were struck by malaria and influenza in their unhealthy new home. These poor people realized that they could not possibly survive there. So, 'utterly abandoned, they sought to return to their former villages. Almost 30 per cent of the tribe died during this return. It was a tragic march, with Indians dropping by the roadside.' Cotrim resigned from Funai in disgust.

In 1973 Fritz Tolksdorf moved another village from the fertile Guaporé valley up to the arid reserve. He then appreciated that the relocations were not working, so got Funai to interdict 3,000 square kilometres (1,160 square miles) of forests between the Galera and Sararé rivers. ('Interdiction' meant that the land should not be settled or its forests felled until Funai had decided whether to seek reserved status for it.) Once again the chosen area contained no villages, although Nambiquara did hunt over it. Price overcame his misgivings and in January 1985 airlifted two groups of newly contacted forest people into the interdicted area. This proved to be a 'dreadful mistake': the new arrivals fought other Nambiquara, some died of malaria, and they all trekked back to their homes.

During his years with Funai, David Price tried to help the Nambiquara in various ways – but without imposing social engineering on them. One problem was to find a source of protein when their hunting grounds were being destroyed or their game killed by settlers. Missionaries and Indian agents had tried to introduce pigs, poultry, or cattle, but the Nambiquara had no wish to be pastoralists. They either hunted animals or kept a menagerie as pets; they would not raise animals to be eaten. Nor could they come to terms with unfamiliar farmyard stock, which they regarded as distasteful. And, as inveterate hunters, they were not prepared for the herdsman's routine of watching and protecting domestic animals. If there was a rumour of passing peccary, all the men dashed off to hunt them. Price had no easy answer to this problem. However, he was able to help the Indians to sell their necklaces, bows, and other handicrafts without being swindled.

David Price instituted a successful health-care programme for his group of Nambiquara. By 1976 most had been vaccinated against measles and tuberculosis, intestinal parasites had been treated and malaria checked. And, with help from the SIL linguists Menno and Barbara Kroeker, a literacy programme was started in the Indians' own language. By 1980 most could read and write in Nambiquara, and some progressed to literacy in Portuguese. Arithmetic was also taught, since this seemed even more important for a people struggling to survive at the edge of frontier society.

Price also chose and helped to train three excellent Funai agents, who devoted their careers to helping the tribe; and his Nambiquara Project sought to involve Indians at every stage of planning. The best recruit was Sílbene de Almeida, tall, thin, and full of energy. 'He had a boisterous, self-deprecating manner that nobody could find offensive; he was tolerated by ranch supervisors, and a friend and protector to Indians and peasants.' When David Price returned to the area in 1980, he found that Sílbene had created an Indian post built at Manáirissu (near a remote village of the Hahaindesú Nambiquara, on the Guaporé side of the watershed). The admirable Sílbene had not awaited Funai's authorization, which might never have come, but paid for the materials with his own money and personally erected the buildings and an infirmary. Price 'was repeatedly assured [by the Wasusu Nambiquara] that Sílbene was good . . . He took care of all the villages, curing small health problems himself and taking the more serious cases to Vilhena. They said he had explained how they could grow cash crops to buy anything they needed; he and one of the villagers named Etreca had made a garden that year and expected to produce manioc for sale, and the following year they planned to plant rice. Sílbene told them that if they wanted beef, they need not kill cattle, because they could trade their crops for it.' Another recruit, Marcelo dos Santos, worked with the Negaroté group of Nambiquara for twenty years, and in the late 1980s he helped them form a successful support association called Awaru.

Sílbene left Funai after twenty years, but later returned to visit his old Nambiquara friends. He received an emotional welcome. He was delighted by the young Indians, playing football, eager to learn everything, full of warmth and tenderness like their parents. But Sílbene was dismayed by the abject poverty. The Nambiquara had hardly any cooking apparatus, clothes, guns, or fish-hooks; but they were happy. His host told how he sold his timber, but had no idea how to measure it or count money, so that his timber-merchant was probably cheating him. The Nambiquara had bought some heavy furniture – a double bed, table, and chairs – but 'it looked out of context, alien to the fire and ashes on the ground, bits of plastic, corn husks, a dog and old pans. Nobody used it: they all sat on the ground. Very sad. By contrast was the chatter and happiness of the youngsters, the beauty of Namur's wife Yolanda, and the animation for their school and teacher Tereco.' Sílbene's delight in the Nambiquara's cheerful resilience in near-destitution was the same as Lévi-Strauss's sixty years previously.

Fifty kilometres (thirty-one miles) south of Sílbene's Hahaindesú lived the Aladndesú Nambiquara, the last remnants of several small groups. Almost all the people were young adults, since the old or young had generally succumbed to a terrible series of epidemics and malnutrition. David Price said that the rate of childbirth was very high, but few infants survived. Another dedicated Brazilian was working with the Aladndesú: the nurse Lia Aurora, who had been there for a decade. 'She had developed a deep love for the Nambiquara, and worked selflessly for them, often when there was little to work with – for funding, and even paychecks, were meagre and often delayed.' In 1986 her Indians were suffering from a painful kidney ailment, possibly induced by a nearby ranch's spraying of the Vietnam War defoliant Tordon, and from the testicular disease orchitis, which left some men impotent. Another pathetic nearby group, the Waikisú, were living in a shack made of scraps of building material and stored their water in Tordon cans – they could not read the warning on these that the contents had been highly toxic.

Some forty acculturated Nambiquara at Camararé were browbeaten by the Protestant missionary Dudley Kinsman of the South American Indian Mission. Kinsman was 'a missionary of the old school: limited, intolerant and almost fanatical in his religious fervour'. He helped the Indians in their commerce. But he forbade them to hold initiation or other ceremonies, to pierce men's lips or nose septums (Nambiquara men like to push an eagle feather horizontally through this nose hole), dance, sing in their own language, play their flutes, smoke, or wear their bracelets or neck-laces. Indians who disobeyed were severely punished. All were forced to attend a conical wigwam-style church of corrugated iron, beside which the missionaries had a large house that contrasted with the natives' wretched huts. A Red Cross team noted that all traditional activities had been terminated and artefacts destroyed. When Funai's regional inspector Hélio Jorge Bucker visited Camararé to check on David Price's denuncia-tion of Kinsman's conduct, the missionary told his Indians that Bucker was under the power of the Devil. So this group of missionaries was expelled, in 1970 after eight years at Camararé. By contrast, the SIL were allowed to remain, since they were considered less aggressive and were doing useful work on the Nambiquara language.

The Red Cross investigators found that the Mamaindê remnant of Nambiquara at Fifano (near the highway, fifty kilometres (thirty-one miles) east of Vilhena) were in a 'really desperate situation' and seemed doomed. These Indians had lost their land to a developer. They could hardly grow a few vegetables, and all their game was gone. Robin Hanbury-Tenison wrote in 1971 that 'epidemics are frequent and without the assistance of the young English SIL couple, whose resources are very limited, it is likely that this group would have become extinct.' When I was there the following year, the missionaries had left but there was no assistance from Funai – which seemed to have washed its hands of these fragments of semi-acculturated Nambiquara. A small schoolhouse was empty and forlorn, and the Indians' five huts were makeshift affairs of thatch, boards, and corrugated iron.

In 1973 Fritz Tolksdorf moved the Mamaindê into the large but infertile Nambiquara reserve; but within a few years almost all had returned to their traditional homelands. They built two villages in forests near the source of the Pardo tributary of the Guaporé, south of Vilhena. In the 1980s the Mamaindê struggled to get their land protected. They were helped by another effective Funai worker called Marcelo dos Santos, and eventually succeeded, with a small territory adjacent to that of the Negaroté Nambiquara on the upper Piolho river. Marcelo told Price that property owners were clearing the Negaroté land as fast as they could, in order to demonstrate their possession of it before Funai demarcated its boundaries. (Demarcation is a later stage of establishing an Indian reserve. The perimeter, often hundreds of kilometres, is surveyed; crews of woodsmen clear a swathe through the forest, swamp, or cerrado; and boundary markers are planted. It can be laborious, slow, and expensive work.)

The 1970 Red Cross team was also shocked by the poverty and lack of hygiene of another Nambiquara sub-tribe at Serra Azul. 'In spite of nine years' contact with the Summer Institute of Linguistics, they are still living in utmost misery. Medical care given by the missionaries is rather scanty because they have no adequate training and only a very small quantity of medicaments.' Hanbury-Tenison was, however, impressed by the barter system that the missionary had established, so that the Indians could trade their considerable output of necklaces, nose flutes, earrings, etc. for such new needs as soap, cooking pots, and knives.

In late 1981, Funai announced three reserves for the Nambiquara of the Guaporé valley forests. There was an outcry from local businessmen and state politicians, one of whom denounced the 'outrage' of 135 native people having almost 2,000,000 hectares (7,700 square miles) of land – he had added the poor land of the original Nambiquara reserve to the new areas. Funai replied that it was not removing land from any business, but 'merely returning to an indigenous group the areas that belong to it.' But Funai still hesitated, suspending the new reserves until anthropologists could 'restudy the area in dispute'.

The Jê-speaking Rikbaktsa were a warrior nation of formidable canoers, woodsmen, and fighters. They once controlled a rich area between the Aripuanã and the Juruena and Arinos headwaters of the Tapajós, in north-west Mato Grosso. The Rikbaktsa used to fight the Cinta Larga to their west, the Kayabi north-east of them, and the Irantxe to their south. When rubber-tappers started to penetrate the area in the 1940s and 1950s, there were clashes in which the bellicose Rikbaktsa held their own.

Some seringueiros were recruited in the jails of Cuiabá and these desperadoes resorted to murderous ambushes and even biological warfare. Professor Rinaldo Arruda wrote that in the 1950s the Rikbaktsa 'suffered many deaths, principally caused by poisoned sugar, infected clothing, and armed attacks. However, they were excellent warriors, and they managed to organize simultaneous attacks at far-distant locations, thus containing the advance of the seringueiros and impeding their establishment in the region.' The accusation of genocidal gifts of contaminated food and clothing kept occurring in this part of Brazil at that time – it was one of the reasons for the Villas Boas' decisions to rescue the Kayabi (in 1952, 1955, and 1966) and then the Tapayuna in 1968–69. There is now no way of proving whether such terrible crimes were committed. But it was not far from where seringueiros massacred the Cinta Larga at 'Parallel 11' in 1963, an atrocity that came to light only because one of its perpetrators confessed to the Jesuit Father Schmidt.

The only help came from the Jesuit Missão Anchieta, which was also assisting the Kayabi at that time. Between 1956 and 1962, Father João Evangelista Dornstauder undertook a series of expeditions to locate and 'pacify' the Rikbaktsa. The contacts were made by his Kayabi Indians, and they were financed by rubber men who were frightened of the warlike 'Canoers'. Some forty villages were discovered, scattered over almost 50,000 square kilometres (19,300 square miles) of forests.

The Anchieta Mission – and the SPI – were medically unprepared. This was another case of tragically mismanaged contact. Rinaldo Arruda commented that 'peace proved more murderous than war', for epidemics raged among the pacified Rikbaktsa. Three-quarters of some 1,280 survivors of the fighting against seringueiros – over 950 people – perished from disease. Virtually every Indian who was taken to the Santa Rosa mission died, and in 1961 the few who remained were transferred westwards to a post on a tributary of the Juruena called Escondido ('Hidden').

The Jesuits also misjudged the location of the Rikbaktsa reserve. They got Funai to protect an area for the tribe in a stretch of forest between the Juruena and Sangue rivers, whereas the majority of these people lived downriver in the Japuíra, a triangle of forests between the Juruena and Arinos, and in the Escondido between the Aripuanã and Juruena. A tin-mining company called Silex, farmers moving into the Japuíra, and the difficulty of attending to isolated groups all combined to spur the Jesuits into contacting remote Rikbaktsa, who were then moved first to Escondido, then upriver to the Japuíra, and then on to their inappropriate reserve.

Rival missionaries further disoriented the shattered Rikbaktsa. The Catholic Jesuits had most Indians living near their Santa Rosa post on the Arinos, but maintained two other stations on the Juruena. In 1960 their work was confused by the arrival of Protestant Lutherans helped by the sertanista Fritz Tolksdorf. The Lutheran mission was on the Escondido tributary of the Juruena, over 200 kilometres (125 miles) downriver (north) of the Jesuits. And in 1962 the fundamentalist Summer Institute of Linguistics started work, first at the Lutheran mission and later near the Jesuits' Santa Rosa.

The Anchieta Mission caused further disruption by removing Rikbaktsa children to a boarding school at Rondon's former telegraph post of Utiariti. This was a severe place whose purpose was frankly acculturative – to suppress ethnic identity and transform the children into docile civilizados who would work in the local economy. The young Rikbaktsa were mixed with children from other tribes (Paresi, Kayabi, Nambiquara) and encouraged to see themselves as Indians devoid of tribal identity.

They learned settler farming techniques and, of course, the Christian religion. One anthropologist considered how wretched the Indian children must have been. 'It is not difficult to imagine how the little boarders felt: far from their homes and parents [whom they saw only twice a year], effectively orphans . . . walled in by a rigorous disciplinary regime, obliged to talk a strange language, and to obey rules of behaviour and time-tables that were totally alien to everything with which they were familiar.' All tribal distinctions, in ornament, haircuts, custom, or language, were suppressed, and any sign of rebelliousness was punished. One Rikbaktsa later recalled that 'two or three boys could not mix together – that meant certain punishment.' And Christian teaching, coupled with preoccupation about sexuality, was of course intensive. The Jesuits maintained the school at Utiariti from 1945 to 1970. Some of its pupils had good memories of its teaching, particularly in carpentry, farming, and mechanics for the boys and sewing and tending children for the girls; others saw these as irrelevant. The experience could be disorienting. 'When they returned to their aldeias, young men from the boarding school, full of aspirations to belong to the "civilized" world, did not succeed in incorporating themselves into tribal life. Some came to form a separate village, others attempted to live as settlers or even to work in the towns.'

One of the Catholic missions, Barranco Vermelho ('Red Bank'), created in 1965, became a model of intensive acculturation. It had two lines of buildings on either side of an airstrip – one for the Jesuit fathers and sisters, the school, and the church, the other a tidy row of Indian huts. The weekly regime was five days of agricultural work, Saturdays for hunting and fishing, and Sundays for worship. Father Edgard Schmidt commented that 'the elderly find it difficult to adjust to this programme. The human ballast for it will come from boys and girls recruited in Utiariti. We have over sixty Rikbaktsa children there. A good part of these are reaching marriageable age, and these new couples will form the basis for the acculturation post.'

13. The Triumph of Activism

When Funai replaced the disgraced Indian Protection Service in 1968 it promised brighter prospects for the surviving Indians. Most of the law authorizing Funai was sensible, at times idealistic. Its mission was to apply Indian policy based on five principles: a) Respect for the persons of Indians and of their tribal institutions and communities; b) The guarantee of permanent possession of lands they inhabit and exclusive enjoyment of natural resources and utilities that exist on them; c) Conservation of 'physical and cultural equilibrium' of Indians in their contacts with the national society; and medical assistance, promotion of the Indian cause in the media, and exercising police powers in indigenous areas 'for the protection of the Indians'. d) More controversially, it was assumed that Indians would achieve spontaneous acculturation; but this dubious goal was tempered by a wish that 'their socio-economic evolution should be fulfilled without violent change'. To this end, Funai was bidden to 'promote basic education appropriate to the Indians, with a view to their progressive integration into national society'. It was also told to conserve and improve the 'Indian patrimony', even though this had led to most of the corruption and exploitation in the old SPI.

Funai's first President was a journalist, José de Queiros Campos. He sought – in vain – to rebut the international press outcry that had caused the disastrous collapse of the old SPI. He protested that during the previous five years fewer than twenty Indians had been murdered (none by SPI officials), whereas tribal warriors had killed about the same number of settlers and missionaries (including the nine people of Father Calleri's attempt to contact the Waimiri Atroari). This was hardly the 'genocide' of some headlines.

Campos also wanted to revive the morale and competence of 'over 500 functionaries inherited from the SPI, with little training for their mission, many of whom were chosen on [left-wing] political criteria'. Over a hundred agents had been named in the Figueiredo report, but only for 'subordination, dilapidation of resources, and neglect of Indians by those responsible for them', and these had been suitably punished. In fact, few lost their jobs and none was imprisoned. Queiros Campos built up Funai's research department and recruited a few anthropologists; but he had a staff of thirty in his personal Directorate. He starved Funai's welfare department, so that its head, Álvaro Villas Boas, resigned, accusing the new agency of 'excessive centralization of administration and of transport'.

There was an unfortunate attempt to train a few warriors as native guards, known as GRINs, to police certain tribal reserves. The recruits were dressed in green-and-yellow military uniforms and given basic training at a police academy. But this new force violated traditional lines of tribal authority: Indians treated its ridiculously dressed guards with contempt; and after a few years they were disbanded. Another failure was a grandiose attempt to build an Indian hospital in the Karajá reserve on Bananal Island in the Araguaia. When the Aborigines Protection Society's team saw this in 1972, they were appalled by its lack of staff, medicine, and patients. All but a handful of Indians kept well clear of this charnel-house, and its doctor could not use the 'operating theatre' because of rain and debris falling from the ceiling. Campos himself was forced to resign in 1970, when his sister was accused of milking the hospital's funds.

For the next four years Funai's President was General Oscar Jeronymo Bandeira de Mello, a retired military man with a background in intelligence. Short, wiry, and energetic, Bandeira de Mello deluded himself that Funai could be run with the central control and efficiency of a military unit. He liked to reel off statistics about numbers of 'flying medical teams', 'model pharmacies', vaccinations, resident nurses, teachers, and schools, and he told the author that over half Funai's reserves had been demarcated with markers at kilometre intervals around their perimeters. Most of this was, of course, fantasy. Orlando Villas Boas commented about the General's staff changes: 'Funai keeps having these grandiose reorganizations, as if it were some large and successful outfit. It is all done just to shuffle the generals around and to provide jobs for the boys.' Most of Funai's regions were run by retired military officers, some of whom had scarcely ever seen an Indian.

There were more sinister aspects to Bandeira de Mello's period in office. His stated intention was to integrate Indians rapidly. This appealed to the high-profile Minister of the Interior, José da Costa Cavalcante, to whom Funai answered even though its mission conflicted with the ministry's aim of opening Brazil to development. Bandeira de Mello's administration coincided with the tough authoritarian government of President (General) Garrastazú Médici, so he consolidated Funai's policy of integration under the slogans 'national security and development'. Funai made no protest whatever about the Programme for National Integration (PIN) that in 1970 drove the Transamazonica and other highways across Indian territories with a view to their colonization. On the contrary, the Indian foundation signed an agreement with the Amazon development agency SUDAM, to send teams to make rapid contact with and 'pacify' thirty isolated tribes that lived in the path of the bulldozers.

Despite the repressive military government that ruled Brazil from 1964 to 1986, there was a glorious burst of activity by pro-Indian NGOs (non-government organizations) during the 1970s and 1980s. On 14 June 1971 over eighty academics and scientists sent an open letter headed 'Indians and the Occupation of Amazonia' to the Brazilian Association for the Advancement of Science. This and a report in the following year criticized Funai for perpetuating many of the faults of the disgraced SPI. The scientists warned of the serious threats posed by the Transamazonica and the rest of the Programme for National Integration, and deplored Funai's supine attitude. At that time, anthropologists were curiously silent.

Funai's President General Bandeira de Mello was interested in money, so he revived the renda indígena, the 'Indian yield' of income from extractive and farming activities on tribal reserves. This was supposed to prepare indigenous people for 'economic emancipation'; but its other aim was to improve Funai's trading accounts. The General claimed that Funai took only 10 per cent of the renda indígena: the rest was theoretically divided between 'continuing the project' and 'returned to the benefit of the Indian group that produced it'. However, herds of cattle on Bananal Island or at São Marcos ranch in Roraima belonged exclusively to Funai. The Indian foundation decided how profits should 'benefit' a tribe, and its President was adamant that there should be no 'paternalism'. Indians were 'given nothing free after contact', they were paid for their labour, but they had to buy meat and other goods. Also, whenever there was a conflict of interest between Indians and developers, the General tended to side with the latter – as in the cases of the Tembé in Pará, Nambiquara of the Guaporé valley in Mato Grosso and Rondônia, or the Kayapó at the northern end of the Xingu park. He authorized some dubious 'negative certificates' – declarations that an area was devoid of Indians and therefore ripe for development – and when he retired in March 1974 he went to work for a tin-mining company.

It was, however, during Bandeira de Mello's administration that indigenous affairs were regularized with a code of conduct. On 19 December 1973 President Médici signed Law 6,001, known as the Indian Statute. Most of this was surprisingly enlightened. Work on the Statute had started in early 1970, by a good jurist but one who knew nothing of Indian needs. The Indians' constitutional right to the land on which they lived or hunted was confirmed. Land is fundamental. One definition of Indians is 'people who possess a common territory, generally isolated or semi-isolated, whose autonomous ownership and exploitation is a sine qua non condition for their survival as an ethnic group.' Land not only provides the basis for farming, hunting, fishing, and gathering. It means far more than that: it is the very foundation of ethnic identity, the location of sacred and mythical sites, of ancient villages and ancestral cemeteries. The Statute also repeated the right of each tribe to live collectively, subject to its own traditions. Indians continued to be exempt from Brazilian law and free from religious or civil coercion to change. Funai was ordered to complete the demarcation of all indigenous reserves within five years (something that it conspicuously failed to accomplish).

However, despite its liberal and modernizing tone, there were danger signals in the new Indian Statute. It encouraged Funai to increase the yield from Indian lands, and even to introduce private business for this purpose. Article 9 empowered individual Indians to petition to leave tribal jurisdiction and become ordinary citizens subject to civil law (but almost none did). Article 20 allowed the government to 'intervene' in Indian areas in the name of 'national security' or for 'public works that are in the national interest' such as mines, roads, or dams, or to exploit mineral wealth of importance to 'national security and development' from the subsoil of Indian reserves. This distinguished 'possession of land' from 'property'. Tribes might possess lands; but their exploitation must either revert to the indigenous community, or swell Funai's income (to be spent however Funai chose), or go to the national interest in the case of mines, roads, or dams. Article 33 even said that land might not be entered into a state's property register collectively by a tribe, but only in small plots by detribalized individuals. Thus, Brazil admitted collective possession but not collective property by indigenous communities.

Another flaw in the Indian Statute was that it placed all indigenous peoples under the tutelage of Funai. The federal Foundation thus became the legal guardian of some 200,000 people. But, whereas the legal guardian of an individual could be removed by a court if incompetent, Funai was outside judicial control. The lawyer Dalmo de Abreu Dallari noted that Funai's statutes make it 'function in close and constant relationship with the Ministry of the Interior. All the personnel in its departments of management and control are appointed by the President of the Republic. Thus, the exercise of its tutelage is inevitably conditioned by the Indianist policy of the federal executive power.' Should that policy be anti-Indian, the native people were effectively defenceless.

When he introduced the Statute, President Médici admitted that its 'cardinal objectives . . . are precisely the rapid and healthy integration of Indians into civilization.' Anyone aware of Brazilian history would know that there had often been attempts at 'rapid integration' and that they had invariably failed. 'Healthy integration' (whatever that meant) was a delusion; and the only 'civilization' offered to Indians was to be marginalized at the bottom of the tough world of frontier society.

Catholic missionaries and bishops issued a powerful pamphlet against the Indian Statute – partly because they were peeved at having their missions remain under Funai's nominal control. They condemned government policies that favoured business concerns and 'national development' over the interests of Indians.

Funai suffered the same pendulum swings as its SPI predecessor. 'Good' presidents and 'bad' presidents succeeded one another in the revolving-door atmosphere of Brazilian administrations, where senior officials are sacked and reshuffled with bewildering speed. The mid-1970s witnessed what the anthropologist Alcida Ramos called 'a period of relative respite for the Indians'. The five-year administration of retired-General Ismarth Araújo de Oliveira saw a marked increase in demarcations of Indian reserves – a crucial and expensive stage in the legal protection of land. He sought to foster 'community development projects' in tribes, and brought anthropologists, Indianists, and missionaries together in Funai. However, General Ismarth's boss was the Minister of the Interior, Rangel Reis, who announced a 'policy of accelerated integration'. When this led towards a dangerous attempt to 'emancipate' Indians (removing their legal protection and casting them adrift in frontier society), General Ismarth publicly opposed the move and had to resign. His successor, an engineer who had previously run the national highways department, 'proved surprisingly inclined to defend the Indians'; but he also resigned in protest after only seven months. Funai then fell into the hands of Colonel João Nobre da Veiga, who proved to be the worst of all the heads of that beleaguered Foundation.

The most exciting and significant development of the 1970s was a transformation in the attitude of the Catholic Church. Queiros Campos sought to harmonize its relations with the missionary organizations. He started by declaring that Funai would 'no longer permit catechism pure and simple, nor religious conversion as a process of acculturation'. He deplored the disgraceful competition between Catholic and Protestant missionaries in the conversion of some tribes. 'When Indians are the objects of missionary ambition, they become perplexed and end by abandoning their ancestral beliefs without absorbing any other. Such abusive practices, aggravated by a terrorising doctrine of sin, provoke

emotional instability and an identity crisis among the Indians.' But Queiros Campos renewed the Summer Institute of Linguistics' licence in 1969,
and he invited Father Calleri of the Consolata Mission to try to contact
the Waimiri Atroari. He also called the first symposium between Funai
and the religious missions. The aim was to enlist missionaries as Funai's
adjuncts, provided that they did not proselytize too aggressively. Dr
Wilbur Pickering of the SIL had the audacity to challenge Funai's tutelage
of the Indians, on the grounds that the Universal Declaration of Human
Rights gave tribes and individuals the right to change their religion. He
was disabused: freedom for Indians meant freedom from 'imposed change'
– which included religious conversion. So the SIL and other missionary
organizations all agreed to act as Funai's agents where appropriate.

The Catholic Church in Brazil was undergoing fundamental change.
The Vatican II Council of 1965 had told the Church to side with the
poor and underprivileged throughout the world. In Brazil, this meant
the poor in urban shanty towns, landless peasants – and indigenous
peoples. Missionaries were told to 'discover the seeds of faith hidden
there, with joy and respect'. This sounds innocuous, but it was a far cry
from the traditional missionary determination to obliterate indigenous
beliefs. These revolutionary new ideas were summarized in an influential book, *Diretório Indígena* ('*Indian Directorate*'), by the Jesuit Father
Adalberto Holanda Pereira.

Two years later, the National Conference of Brazilian Bishops (CNBB)
reorganized its missionary secretariat. In February 1968 it held the first
Indigenist Pastoral Meeting, to start formulating new policy towards
Indians. This gathering included many priests who were to become leaders
of the reforming 'liberation theology' in indigenous affairs: the Jesuit
Antonio Iasi, Egydio Schwade, the Salesians Ângelo Venturelli and José
Vicente César, and the pro-Church anthropologists Egon Schaden and
Protásio Frikel (a former Franciscan). Some of the resulting research into
tribes, populations, missionary activity, and social conditions of Indians
appeared in August 1969 in a report called *Os nossos índios* ('*Our
Indians*').

Thus inspired, and stung by the condemnation of severe old-style
missionaries in the Barbados Declaration of the radical World Council of
Churches, the CNBB in 1972 issued revolutionary new guidelines for
missionaries dealing with Indians. Henceforth, such priests must receive
anthropological training before going into the field. They must respect
native cultures. Far from being ridiculed or suppressed, indigenous beliefs
should be respected and every manifestation of spirituality should be
encouraged. 'Evangelism does not in any sense require the destruction of

cultures, but rather their perfectionment – this accords with Christ's phrase: "I came not to destroy, but to improve" . . . Announce the Gospel, but consider the [indigenous] group not as pagans but as devout. Consider this primitive religion as an expression of the presence of God among them, "the seeds of the Word".' Missionaries should, of course, practise their faith. But conversion of indigenous people must come only at *their* volition, because they were impressed by what they observed and not because it had been imposed on them. Catechism was to be subtle and subdued.

The Catholic Church went on to found a missionary council, CIMI (Conselho Indigenista Missionário), which was to become one of the major protectors of Brazilian Indians. Relations with Funai were good in the early 1970s. There was another seminar between the Foundation and the missionary orders, both Catholic and Protestant, in November 1973. A few months later, Funai's moderate President General Ismarth de Oliveira Araújo went up the Rio Negro with Father César, the President of CIMI, and the two were full of praise for the way in which the Salesians were educating and acculturating Indians. So missionaries were disappointed when the Indian Statute insisted that they could work with Indians only as agents of the government service.

The harmony deteriorated irreparably during 1975. Many Funai staff members wanted to return to Rondon's ideal of a lay service that kept missionaries at arm's length, as the Villas Boas brothers always did in the Xingu. CIMI also became increasingly militant, and scathingly critical of Funai's shortcomings. One spokesman called the Minister of the Interior, Rangel Reis, a 'lightweight' and Funai 'funereal' because so many of its charges died. CIMI's first two Presidents resigned because they could not tolerate its radicalism.

The Church's new policies culminated in a first Indigenist Pastoral National Assembly, which included some Indian leaders. Held at Goiânia in 1975, this Assembly established six principles for missionaries, in the new spirit of liberation theology. First came land, without which tribes rapidly starve and lose their cohesion. Missionaries must support at all levels the indigenous peoples' right to recover and guarantee the ownership of their land. Tribal culture was equally important: 'Recognize, respect, and openly support the right of all indigenous peoples to live according to their customs. In particular, animate groups who are disintegrating in order to revitalize their culture.' A massive policy change was to empower Indians to be self-sufficient, to determine their own destinies. Wherever possible, political and other powers should be devolved to the Indians. The religious mission was not forgotten. But indigenist pastoral work was to be liberationist, seeking to help the oppressed and marginalized. To achieve this, missionaries were to incarnate Christ's humble ways, 'to live with the indigenous peoples; investigate, discover, esteem, and adopt their culture; and espouse their cause with all the consequences, overcoming ethnocentric and colonialist attitudes to the extent of being accepted as one of them.'

Lastly, missionaries were to wage a campaign of awareness of the cause and problems confronting the Indians. 'The task of consciousness-raising applies at different levels: among the Indians themselves, the surrounding population, the Church, and national and international public opinion.' The words of the Cabixi Daniel Matenho were quoted with approval. He asked friends of the Indians to make everyone aware of 'our struggle, our true struggle for emancipation . . . But it will [ultimately] be done by us, by us Indians ourselves'. Courses were organized to teach missionaries public relations, alongside training in indigenism and basic anthropology, linguistics and missionary practice.

The Indigenist Missionary Council, CIMI, was not wholly disinterested. It became an official arm of the influential National Conference of Brazilian Bishops (CNBB). One of its purposes was to resist Funai's attempts to reduce missionary influence over Indians. The anthropologist Cláudia Menezes argued that CIMI 'arose as the expression of an ecclesiastical sector preoccupied with the preservation of [control of] indigenous lands and patrimony.' But CIMI did much good. It gained a permanent secretariat in 1976 and later devolved its operations to regional offices in each part of Brazil. It published a Bulletin and the crusading bimonthly newspaper *Porantim*; it organized assemblies and conferences, particularly of Indian leaders; it helped to form an excellent research organization, CEDI, that published the best and most thorough studies of Indians; and it trained missionaries to change to the new pro-Indian liberationist methods. For the final quarter of the twentieth century, CIMI was a potent force for Indian rights. 'It not only revealed a new face of the Catholic Church in its work among Indians – apologizing for [the Church's] complicity in the colonial enterprise – it also established a vigorous channel for denunciation at a time of press censorship.' It took courage to oppose Brazil's military rulers, but the Catholic Church had the stature to do so.

By the late 1970s, 'there was a veritable effervescence of the Indian question. The situation of calamity and violence endured by the Indians obliged us [in CIMI] to amplify our efforts.' The radical missionary-Indian organization entered new regions of Brazil and 'flung itself wholeheartedly into the defence of the Indians, denouncing land invasions and other injustices against Indian groups, helping to organize assemblies of Indian chiefs and representatives, offering courses in linguistics and indigenist work to missionaries in the field . . . and generally trying to stimulate awareness of the Indians' predicament . . . amongst Brazilian society.' Greg Urban, the American anthropologist who worked with the Kaingang, wrote that 'it is difficult to overestimate the role that Catholic missionaries and the Catholic Church itself have played . . . Catholic missionaries fought in the front lines, so to speak, for liberalization and for Indian rights. Some of them actually died in this cause.' Mércio Gomes praised CIMI for 'its seminal and most complete document, written at the end of 1973, *Y-juca pirama*, a Tupi expression meaning "The Indian, the one who must die"'. This booklet proclaimed a new concept of Indians, it combined anthropology with liberation theology, and it politicized pastoral action. The Jesuit Father Paulo Suess, one of the founders of CIMI, articulated the theories behind its new approach to missionary work in a series of important (albeit somewhat opaque) papers and books.

It is worth noting that the radicals of CIMI did not represent the entire Catholic Church in Brazil. Many bishops remained conservative and traditionalist. They condemned their liberation-theology colleagues as Communists. The Salesian missionaries of the Upper Rio Negro clung to their seminary-like establishments and cradle-to-grave control of their charges' moral and spiritual welfare. When the activists of CIMI's Manaus office in 1978 started to publish the sometimes outrageous newspaper *Porantim* (which Greg Urban described as required reading for anyone interested in Brazilian Indians) the Salesians further up the Negro river would not even allow it into their mission buildings.

The 1970s also witnessed a flowering of non-religious activists. CIMI itself paid tribute to their importance. 'We [missionaries] participated in a veritable multiplication of groups, organisms, publications, associations, conferences, and symposia' in all parts of Brazil. Concern about Indians ceased to be the preserve of professionals: anthropologists, missionaries, and sertanistas. 'Representatives of diverse classes – from lawyers and scientists to students and workers – came to voice their opinions on the situation of the indigenous peoples.' The debate burst out of closed offices of government departments 'to the universities, the media, conferences, city suburbs, and workers' meetings.' The oppressed Indians were identified with the underprivileged masses in Brazilian society. In its move to the political left, CIMI espoused '700,000 threatened squatters . . . and ten million families without land' as well as Indians – even though in practice the two groups often clashed, when poor squatters or prospectors tried to invade tribal lands.

Some anthropologists felt that they must emerge from their academic ivory towers and become politically active. In 1974 a group of them addressed a polemic, 'The politics of genocide against the Indians of Brazil', to an international Congress of Americanists. This document started by quoting the Minister of the Interior, ex-General Maurício Rangel Reis, who promised: 'We will assume a policy of integrating the indigenous population into Brazilian society in the shortest possible time . . . We believe that the notion of preserving indigenous people within their natural habitat is a very nice ideal, but is unrealistic.' The Brazilian anthropologists condemned their country for violating Convention 107 of the International Labour Organization, to which Brazil was a signatory. This forbade the use of force or coercion to integrate tribal peoples or their displacement from their lands without their consent. The letter also argued that Brazil *had* committed genocide against its Indians, since the United Nations' definition of genocide included submitting a group 'to conditions of existence which forcibly produce their total or partial physical destruction'.

By the end of the twentieth century, there were some thirty pro-Indian NGOs and very many more run by Indians themselves. The oldest was Dr Roberto Baruzzi's Escola Paulista de Medicina, the São Paulo medical hospital that had been delivering health care to the Indians of the Xingu and other areas since 1965. CIMI itself was founded in 1972 and its research affiliate CEDI shortly after; and the Protestants started the less vigorous evangelical missionary work-group GTME in 1979. Lay sympathizers launched a national association to support Indians (ANAI) in different states – in Porto Alegre (Rio Grande do Sul) in 1977, Bahia in 1979, and with chapters in most large cities. ANAI consisted mostly of lawyers and anthropologists who could give practical legal help. There were also pro-Indian commissions (CPI) in Acre, São Paulo, and other states. These CPIs opted for lobbying government and media, using expert panels of jurists, medical doctors, or anthropologists to prepare their campaigns. CPIs were centres of Indian work that carried out development aid projects in indigenous areas. Greg Urban pointed out that this proliferation of support groups was necessary, because the 'Indian problem' in Brazil was 'a multi-faceted reality that varies from region to region, according to the degree and kind of contact with Brazilian national society.' This was why CIMI, ANAI, and CPI had to have branches in different states, and each devised regional strategies to help local Indians.

Lobbies developed to support individual tribes. The first and most famous of these was the CCPY to help the Yanomami, created in 1978 by the photographer-turned-activist Cláudia Andujar and interested anthropologists. This was followed by Awaru for the Nambiquara, MAREWA for the Waimiri Atroari (founded in 1983 by Egydio Schwade, later secretary of CIMI), GAIPA for the Pataxó of Bahia, and very many others.

These non-government action groups sometimes grew from venerable academic societies such as the Association of Brazilian Anthropologists. They drew inspiration and encouragement from international NGOs, particularly Survival International in Britain and other countries; Cultural Survival, the Anthropology Resource Center and others in the United States; and IWGIA (International Work Group for Indigenous Affairs) in Denmark. But they were genuinely Brazilian, launched and run by Brazilians. This was important, since Brazil is a great nation that does not welcome outside interference. The Brazilian government would have been quick to reject foreign intervention and to brand it as covert colonialism. Being pro-Indian became a youthful cause in the radical 1970s, a worthy crusade that was also environmentally sustainable – and an acceptable way of expressing opposition to Brazil's military government.

More exciting than the efforts of sympathizers in Brazil and abroad was the political awakening of the Indians themselves. Here again, CIMI was a catalyst. It organized the first assembly of Indian leaders in April 1974, and by the end of 1976 it had held six such meetings in different parts of Brazil. There were fifteen assemblies in that decade, and forty-two during the first five years of the 1980s. The Church provided hospitality, usually in an ecclesiastical building, and travel, with individual missionaries accompanying contingents of their congregations. These assemblies became larger annual events, national rather than local, with indigenous leaders congregating from all parts of the country. Although there were religious overtones, the emphasis was to empower the Indians themselves. After a while, it was they who invited delegates, organized the meetings, and prepared agendas. Topics for discussion always included local issues, and the assemblies were often opened and closed with traditional dances or stimulated with tribal beverages. Indians did almost all the talking.

The regional gatherings tapped the power and eloquence of indigenous oratory, for every community has regular, often daily, discussion of its affairs. At one assembly, in Sergipe on the Atlantic seaboard, the Indianist Sydney Possuelo dared to suggest how the meeting should be conducted. He proposed that it hear the problems of each tribe in turn, and begged delegates not to repeat answers one after the other or to make rambling speeches. But Possuelo's attempt to impose discipline was in vain. 'The meeting followed its normal course, as the Indians wanted.' Because there are many indigenous languages, assemblies were usually held in Portuguese. This inhibited some less acculturated leaders, who 'do not say what they think or want to say, but only what they can within linguistic and cultural limitations. Their messages are thus often distorted by being conceived in one culture and expressed in another.' But the theme that emerged was abundantly clear: anger over past wrongs and determination to fight for justice.

Critics of the assemblies said that they consisted mainly of each speaker introducing himself, followed by a list of his tribe's problems, and some generalities about indigenous unity. Speeches were often unconnected monologues. But such criticism was superficial and ethnocentric. It missed the point that simply airing problems was beneficial; and practical solutions or strategies often did emerge. Delegates honed their political skills. Above all, the assemblies introduced indigenous leaders to one another. They learned that they were not fighting in isolation and could present a united front.

As they evolved and became more frequent, the indigenous assemblies changed from being gatherings of 'indigenous leaders' to 'indigenous peoples'. Delegates tended to be younger men who spoke better Portuguese than traditional chiefs. Such spokesmen had often had a Brazilian education, lived outside their aldeias, and made a career of indigenous politics. Some learned the rhetoric of left-wing activism and the class struggle. Radical missionaries encouraged this. Father Paulo Suess, who wrote polemics about indigenism, declared that 'two different types of alliance are needed for the defence of indigenous people's lands and achievement of their self-determination. First, the ethnic alliance, the union of all the indigenous peoples themselves . . . Second, a class alliance of other segments of national society whose survival is equally threatened.' A typical speech, by a Miranha delegate to an Assembly in 1981, declared that 'not all whites are guilty of the massacres and deaths of Indians. It is the big landowners and capitalists: they are the guilty ones.'

This confusion of the Indians' cause with the 'class struggle' and Cold War politics was a mistake. It caused a reaction by Brazil's right-wing government. One Minister of the Interior, Maurício Rangel Reis, declared in 1976 that he wanted to accelerate Indians' integration into Brazilian society and ordered an end to teaching in indigenous languages – something that actually happened only in some mission schools, since Funai's teachers could not speak tribal dialects. The Minister felt that it was 'a waste of time and money' to teach anything other than Portuguese. He also wanted to expel all missionaries. This was not because their preaching might undermine tribal beliefs. It was for the opposite reason: because they were 'dreamers' whose work with Indians was 'backward and feudalistic' and therefore slowed integration. In fact it was because the Minister feared left-wing ecclesiastics as opponents of Brazil's military rulers, and he was stung by CIMI's personal attacks on him.

Such talk aroused an irate response from Indianists such as the Jesuit Antonio Iasi or Funai's Apoena Meirelles. It even angered Vicente, Cardinal Sherer, a senior ecclesiastical conservative and government supporter. Cardinal Sherer declared that 'the long and tortuous history of Indians in our country has been one of pain, tears, and revolting injustice. God save us from the destructive power that exists among decision-makers of this nation.' Minister Rangel Reis met the Cardinal. There was also internal debate within the government. So the Minister climbed down. He decided that the Church and government wanted 'the same things for Indians' and that a dialogue with missionaries would be productive.

The feud between Funai and CIMI grew increasingly acrimonious. In June 1975 the normally moderate General Ismarth forbade Fathers Iasi and Schwade from visiting Indians anywhere in Brazil. Funai insisted 'that *it* alone held responsibility for the Indians and could speak for them'. So police acting for Funai broke up both the sixth Indigenous Assembly in Roraima in January 1977 (at which Bishop Tomás Balduino and Father Egydio Schwade were present), and the seventh assembly in Amapá later that year 'on the grounds that no permission for it had been secured from Funai and that it was therefore illegal'.

Unable to do much about Catholic missionaries, the government vented its fury on foreign anthropologists. Early in 1976, research permits for three excellent field-workers were revoked, on the spurious pretext that they were studying tribes close to Brazil's boundaries: the American David Price who was with the Nambiquara in western Mato Grosso (he later returned under different auspices), and the Britons Kenneth Taylor, a champion of the Yanomami (who later continued his work, for the University of Brasília), and Peter Silverwood-Cope among the nomadic Makú in forests near the Colombian border (who was shattered by the expulsion and never recovered). The distinguished anthropologist Júlio César Melatti deplored these expulsions, since the three foreigners alone had performed years of 'field work with the groups concerned and therefore have the authority to speak out about what should be done for them'. Melatti felt that the move was to stop General Ismarth's liberalization of Funai by giving anthropologists more say in its policies. Each of the three ousted foreigners had also crossed swords with vested interests such as miners or Salesian missionaries.

In September 1977 Father Antonio Iasi issued a long report on the situation of Indians that violently criticized Funai. He condemned the Foundation's vacillating policies and called for its abolition. He also attacked the Summer Institute of Linguistics for being too subservient to the government and for religious teaching that harmed Indians. *Porantim* declared that 'Minister Rangel Reis is today without a shadow of doubt the Public Enemy Number One of the Brazilian Indians'. Funai fought back. It reported, generally unfavourably, on the work of fifty-three religious missions active in indigenous areas. As a result, the President of Funai in October 1977 refused to renew SIL's agreement and asked it to remove all its missionary linguists. Not everyone was happy with CIMI's constant attacks on Funai. Two of the Council's early leaders resigned because of its radicalism. Orlando Villas Boas said: 'I don't believe in this policy, which gets no practical results.' He felt that CIMI was all rhetoric and no action. 'Funai is tired of calling on bodies like CIMI for concrete work, to which they do not respond.' Even the Indians themselves, at one assembly, asked CIMI and Funai to stop squabbling and unite to assist them.

The vigorous new pro-Indian NGOs soon had an obvious villain and serious threats to combat. The villain was Colonel João Nobre da Veiga, President of Funai from 1979 to 1981. David Price (the expelled anthropologist sent back by the World Bank to comment on the Polonoroeste's impact on the Nambiquara) described the Colonel as 'a bull of a man – loud, ignorant and rude'. When appointed, he admitted that he had no experience of Indians; but this did not matter since running Funai was merely a management job. By common consent the worst President in Funai's chequered history, Nobre da Veiga 'issued outright anti-Indian statements, and his allegiance to economic groups interested in Indian resources was unconcealed'. When thirty-nine Indianists and anthropologists sent a letter to the Minister of the Interior complaining about Funai's policies, he fired all those who were on Funai's staff. The Indian Foundation was thus bereft of any expertise. Instead, Nobre da Veiga hired incompetent or ultra-right military advisers, and he banned any outside observers from Indian territories. Alcida Ramos recalled his administration as 'a period of terror for Indians and for whites involved in Indian problems'. Price, who had previously worked for Funai, wrote an angry open letter concluding that the Foundation's inefficiency and corruption were a deliberate attempt to destroy the Indians. 'In short, Brazil's real Indian policy is one of genocide through institutionalized neglect.'

There were three threats to the Indians in official policy. Each sounded innocuous, even desirable. But the pro-Indian activists rapidly spotted the flaws in these policies; and they mounted fierce, sustained, and ultimately

successful attacks on each in turn. The first was an Emancipation Proclamation. In January 1975 Minister Rangel Reis announced a plan to alter
the Indian Statute to permit the 'emancipation' of entire indigenous
communities. Tribes 'in an advanced state of acculturation' would be
freed from Funai's tutelage and led to economic self-sufficiency. During
the ensuing three years, anthropologists, the Villas Boas brothers, missionaries, activists, and Indian leaders all protested that the beguiling term
'emancipation' was a euphemism for headlong integration. The trouble
was that emancipation could be *imposed* on those deemed to have lost
their ethnic identity. Such Indians would be cast adrift in frontier society.
Emancipation meant the abandonment of communal traditions, dispersal
of reserve territories, and disintegration of tribal societies. Opponents of
emancipation cited the well-intentioned but ultimately disastrous Dawes
Act in the United States in 1887, which had 'freed' Indians from their
communities and divided reserves into smallholdings. The result was that
speculators were easily able to buy land or resources from individual
Indians. Ninety million acres (365,000 square kilometres) of US Indian
lands (out of a total of 140 million acres (565,000 square kilometres))
passed into non-Indian ownership; and the cohesion and identity of many
tribes were destroyed for ever.

The debate raged, with the Minister claiming that the Terena people
wanted emancipation, and that Funai's policies would have failed if no
Indian group left its care to enter Brazilian society. Condemnation came
from the chiefs of nine native nations at the first National Assembly of
Brazilian Indians in April 1977 and from many individual tribes (the
Gavião expressed their views in a tape-recorded message to Brasília), as
well as from countless meetings of anthropologists, missionaries, and the
new NGOs, media round-tables, and publications. The Xavante spokesman Mário Juruna told General Ismarth of Funai that 'our people will
disappear, become caboclo peasants'; and the Jesuit Father Iasi realized
that 'those who appear interested in the illusory emancipation of Indians
are more preoccupied with the emancipation of those Indians' *lands*.' The
young leader Marcos Terena wrote: 'I see Funai taking the entire indigenous nation towards the abyss of integration, which would certainly be a
form of *dis*integration for indigenous society . . . "Emancipating" Indians
means taking what is most important for the survival of our people,
namely our land.' He spoke eloquently about the paramount importance
of habitat. 'We respect land as a sacred being, trying not to harm it nor
destroy it, but if possible to conserve it intact, worshipping its rivers, its
forests, its animals, because it transmits the greatest benefit we can
possess: life itself.'

A slightly modified emancipation declaration was submitted to President Ernesto Geisel for his signature. But the campaigners won. In December 1978 it was abruptly announced that 'for strategic reasons' the President had decided not to approve the emancipation of indigenous groups.

No sooner had the emancipation threat been averted than a new danger appeared. This was *estadualização*, devolution to states – a move to devolve Indian affairs away from federal control in Brasília to the separate states of the Brazilian federative republic. Once again, it sounded good. Critics of the SPI and Funai had often deplored its excessive expenditure 'on the asphalt' of the federal capital instead of in the Indian posts and reserves. But it is a constant of Brazilian Indian history that attitudes harden with proximity to the settlement frontier. The central government tends to be more idealistic and liberal than the frontiersmen. Also, state governments can be influenced by local business lobbies who covet Indian land and resources. State legislators usually sided with settlers, prospectors, and speculators, who had votes, against Indians who did not. The activist support groups immediately saw danger and swung into action. By 1980 they had won another victory, with the shelving of *estadualização*.

The third threat was a weird concept devised by one of Nobre da Veiga's worst military cronies. Air Force Colonel Ivan Zanoni Hausen was put in charge of Funai's department of community planning, and it was he who had sacked all the qualified anthropologists and replaced them by a few people who had done some undergraduate courses in the subject. David Price described the colonel as 'an imposing figure . . . large and muscular, he looked like (and was in fact) an ex-boxer. A man of about forty-five or fifty, he had short hair and a large, drooping moustache.' Price heard a rumour that Zanoni had been a torturer and liquidator of subversives during the worst period of the military government.

Colonel Zanoni's dangerous idea was 'Criteria of Indianness'. He got some (totally unqualified) Funai staff to list sixty attributes that would show whether someone was a 'true Indian' or, if not, was ripe for integration. The list included such absurdities as 'a primitive mentality', 'the mongol-spot birthmark', or 'showing social marginalization'. Anyone deemed to have less than half these criteria was to be considered a non-Indian and outside Funai's protection. There were obvious analogies to the bogus physical anthropology of Nazi Germany or apartheid in South Africa. 'In response, outraged Indians, missionaries, anthropologists, lawyers and journalists bombarded Funai in the press, in public gatherings, and in professional meetings, with accusations of racism.' In one such attack, CIMI's Bulletin fulminated: 'Through the massive presence of colonels within Funai, this guardian department has become a barracks of blind and dry obedience . . . Funai would have us believe that Indians under its protection live better than other marginalized workers or peasants. But [under Zanoni's proposed criteria] the "privilege" of being protected by Funai would be earned by the "good behaviour" of Indians.'

Zanoni's criteria of Indianness were both illegal and unrealistic, and they were dropped. Colonel Zanoni had dismissed the Indian Statute as 'a book of poetry to feed the fantasies of eggheads'. But the eggheads won. The Statute had defined an Indian as 'anyone of pre-Columbian origin who considers himself to be Indian and who is considered as such by others' and this definition continued in force. Also, the Statute *did* provide for individual Indians to move from tribal to national society – if they were well trained for the transition and, above all, if they themselves requested the change. But none had chosen to do so.

The Church suffered martyrs during these turbulent years. The first was a French Dominican, Father François (Francisco) Jentel, who had worked with the Gavião and then for ten years with the Tapirapé on a tributary of the Araguaia opposite Bananal Island. This was the tribe that had enchanted Peter Fleming with its innocent cheerfulness. The Tapirapé had survived terrible depopulation from disease, and were reduced to under a hundred people by 1950. Since then their numbers had grown, thanks partly to care by the Dominican priests and nuns. Loss of land then became their overriding concern. In 1954 a property company obtained a concession for a great tract that included not only Tapirapé and Karajá villages, but even the SPI's post. Settlers and the 'Tapiraguaia Ranch' occupied Indian land, and there were protests to Brasília by CIMI and by the Tapirapé themselves. In 1967 the property company 'donated' 9,000 hectares (22,240 acres) of the reserve territory to the SPI on behalf of the Indians. But it was land liable to flooding, and the tribe refused to accept this bogus 'gift' of the worst part of their homeland.

In 1973 armed police arrested Father Jentel in the Tapirapé village. In addition to his work among the Indians, where he lived simply and was much loved, Jentel had been active among landless peasants of the Araguaia valley. For this 'he had been branded as a "subversive" and "agitator", and [in May 1973] was condemned to ten years' jail by a military tribunal.' Pardoned after serving a year's imprisonment, Father Jentel was expelled from Brazil in 1975 and died soon afterwards in France.

Frustrated by Funai's failure to demarcate their territory, the Tapirapé took matters into their own hands. The Assembly of Indian Chiefs of 1977 was held in the Tapirapé village, and this encouraged the tribespeople to intensify their protests to Brasília. They themselves worked for months (with a surveyor) to complete the demarcation trail around their perimeter. It was no use. The ranch continued to graze thousands of head of cattle within the Indian reserve. There were more meetings, at which Funai ordered the Tapirapé to cede the pasture-lands to the ranch and not to evict the settlers. In January 1981 the normally gentle Tapirapé decided that they must fight, first by killing cattle, and if that failed, a white man. They declared: 'We have no alternative! Now we must kill a *tori* [white man] or Funai will do nothing. Funai settles matters only when there is a disturbance. Now, either a white dies or we all die; but this land issue must finally be resolved.' The Indians, armed with arrows and clubs, killed seven animals. Funai's local director hurried over from Bananal and made conciliatory noises; and four Tapirapé leaders were taken to Brasília for a meeting with Funai's president, the hardline Colonel Nobre da Veiga, and his henchman, Colonel Zanoni. The chiefs reported that 'Funai had spoken very forcefully to them. Funai wants them to accept a proposal [of a large extension of 'seasonally flooded' swamp land in return for ceding the 750 hectares (1,850 acres) occupied by the ranch] . . . If the Tapirapé fought or attacked the ranch, Funai would send police into the area. Should any Indian die [as a result], Funai would do nothing.' The Indians tried to refuse; the Dominican nuns angrily rejected an accusation that they had incited the tribe to resist; and many armed police were sent to defend the ranch. So Funai's unfavourable definition of the Tapirapé reserve prevailed: it was finally fixed and demarcated in the reduced dimensions in 1983.

There were other violent struggles for land and tragic martyrdoms of priests during the late 1970s. The Salesian mission of Meruri, north-east of Cuiabá in Mato Grosso, had been home of the Bororo since time immemorial; and Xavante had fled to the adjacent mission of São Marcos when driven from their territory north of the rio das Mortes in the 1960s. The lands of Meruri/São Marcos were under constant pressure from surrounding fazendeiros. The head missionary at Meruri was a young German, Father Rudolph (Rodolfo) Lukenbein, a priest who sought to introduce the new liberation theology. 'Meruri and many other missions admitted the consequences of past errors. With great liberality and humility, the missionaries abandoned ideological strictures, discovered radical faith, and criticized themselves.' Father Rodolfo started by completely changing the education of Bororo children – adapting it to Indian needs, teaching in Bororo, ending boarding-school separation of children from parents, and 'favouring the cultural values of the tribe'.

These changes coincided with a struggle to defend the reserve's land against claims and threats from settlers, large ranches, and elements of the state government. (Mato Grosso's Secretary of Justice called Indians 'lazy imbeciles with too much land'.) Funai even sought to enlarge the indigenous area. Squatters were expelled, bars along the BR-70 that crossed the reserve were closed, and in 1976 Meruri's demarcation was about to begin. But surrounding farmers objected strenuously to losing what they regarded as their land, on which they had developed farms. The dispute reached a climax. On 15 July a caravan of cars with sixty-two men and women, many armed, invaded the village. There were angry exchanges. The settlers accused one missionary of being a robber; to which a Bororo woman answered: 'It's *you* who are a robber, coming here to live on our land!' Father Rodolfo tried to calm matters, assuring the settlers that they would get grants of land elsewhere. Everything seemed resolved and the colonists started to leave; but one João Mineiro continued his abuse; he jostled Father Rodolfo; Indians sought to protect the missionary. A gun was fired, and four other farmers then shot at the priest. 'The Bororo Simão Cristino, who went to help Father Rodolfo, was also mortally wounded. Five shots made Rodolfo fall into the arms of his Bororo. [There were] a few moments of agony, with Rodolfo prostrate on the ground, shirtless, his work-trousers stained with oil, in the midst of the mission patio.' The missionary died and several Indians were seriously wounded. The killers were tried two years later, but acquitted because they had been 'protecting their patrimony'. But the demarcation of the enlarged Indian reserve did take place.

Less than three months later, on 12 October 1976, the fifty-nine-year-old Brazilian Jesuit Father João Bosco Burnier was in the police headquarters of a town called Ribeirão Bonito in northern Mato Grosso, to intercede for two poor settler women who had been arrested and tortured. He told the policemen to uphold the law, but one of them struck him and killed him with a shot in the head. Father João Bosco was coordinator for CIMI in the state. Much of his career had been in poor frontier parishes; but he worked with – and learned the languages of – the Bakairi and Paresi tribes, and he introduced indigenous elements into the mass in their villages. He agonized about the damage being done by catechism, which inevitably led to cultural change and ethnic friction. 'The general situation of the [Bakairi] Indians is one of penury, a mentality of constantly having to beg for aid, either from Funai or from the [Jesuit] Anchieta Mission.'

The sea-change in the Church's attitudes helped to introduce a new era of militancy and activism by the Indians themselves. The Barbados Declaration of 1971 concluded that 'Indians must organize and lead their own liberation movement; otherwise it ceases to be liberating'. Such indigenous self-help gathered momentum throughout the decade of the 1970s. It was nurtured by CIMI's assemblies of tribal leaders. When Funai was at its worst, in 1980, the leaders of Indian tribes held the thirteenth of their by now regular assemblies, at Campo Grande in south Mato Grosso, and created their own umbrella organization: the Union of Indigenous Nations, known as UNI or UNIND. A Guarani leader, João Carvalho, later declared: 'We know that a root is being born in the depths of the earth that no one can tear out, so that Indians will always have the strength of the unity that links Indian to Indian.'

The formation of UNI – a union of Indians by Indians – was a landmark, the culmination of a decade of indigenous assemblies. By now, the chiefs and delegates were skilled at organizing conferences, setting agendas, and presenting their cause through eloquent debate and effective lobbying. Anthropologists and the pro-Indian NGOs welcomed the new Union, but the government was unhappy. President Figueiredo forbade Funai from giving any assistance to the new organization. 'The presidential decision is based on a report by the SNI [secret service] according to which it is seriously inconvenient for the indigenous nations to group themselves in a single organism supported by persons inclined to incite Indians against the government.' CIMI released a leaked document that advised a rapid revision of the Indian Statute, to accelerate 'emancipation'. This and other measures might curb 'the growing organization of the indigenous peoples and UNI, an independent organ created by the Indians themselves.'

The anthropologist and activist Alcida Ramos asked: 'Why did Brazilian Indians take so long to organize themselves?' One answer lay in the size of Brazil and problems of transport and communications. The Indians were fragmented into a myriad of small societies each with its own language and customs. Ironically, the new roads that had caused so much harm to many tribes made it easier for delegates to reach the new assemblies: the cheap buses that brought settlers along the dusty new highways also transported Indians back to the cities. Failures in official tutelage also played a part. 'The government, first through the SPI and later through Funai, has been an inadequate guardian – both by omission and by its harmful actions.' This may even have been deliberate. 'Lack of access to education, as well as economic, administrative, and political obstacles to intercommunication are the norm. Keeping the Indians ignorant is one way of retaining control over them.'

The new UNI soon elected as its president the dynamic twenty-seven-year-old Marcos Terena, a student of business administration at the University of Brasília. He had gone to a Protestant school among non-

Indian children and had encountered racial prejudice. 'I was a "bugre", which in my region is a cruel pejorative for a stupid, ignorant Indian, like some irrational animal.' But Marcos Terena became proud of his ethnic identity. 'My origin is different, my home and customs are different, my language is different, and even my face is different . . . But when I see the poverty, unemployment and misery of the urban poor [in Brazilian cities] I ask myself what is meant by "civilization". What does "integration" mean? Where is the nation of my fathers going?'

The government attempted a clumsy counter-attack on UNI's new president, by ordering Marcos Terena and other indigenous university students back to their tribal villages on the grounds that they were wards of Funai; but pro-Indian lawyers reversed this by invoking the young men's human rights. Despite such provocation, UNI was remarkably moderate. In October 1981 the Minister of the Interior, Mário Andreazza, met Marcos Terena and other indigenous leaders. The young President of UNI assured the Minister that his Union would not play party politics. 'Our intention has always been cordiality, to present our problems man-to-man and legally. We respect the authorities; but they must also respect indigenous communities, within the principles of human rights.'

In those early days of indigenous consciousness, the Indians produced a shrewd, ebullient political leader. Mário Dzururá – always known as Juruna – was the chief of the Xavante village of Namunkurá within the Salesian mission of São Marcos. He was sixteen before he saw his first white man; but he then taught himself 'civilizado' ways by working on ranches. He travelled around the country, with remarkable drive, energy, and curiosity to learn. Helped by Darcy Ribeiro and his own political instincts, this forceful, corpulent chief rapidly became a national celebrity. Mário Juruna's irreverent and witty comments on official hypocrisy caught the imagination of the Brazilian media. He was syndicated in sixty newspapers and appeared frequently on television. He became famous as the 'Indian with the tape-recorder' who recorded white men's false promises. CEDI noted that 'Funai responded to his rise as a politician with a barrage of leaks about his private life and his "integration" into the customs of the whites . . . However, this attempt at "emancipation through defamation" did not dampen the chief's spirit. During 1981 he enriched his battery of telling phrases, always full of humour and making fun of official indigenist policy.' One distinguished journalist wrote that Juruna 'has an incredible personal magnetism . . . Even silent he has more force than all the Brazilian Academy of Letters talking. All Indians respect him, and Indian women are ravished by him.'

Funai tried in vain to argue that Mário Juruna could not speak for

Indians as a whole or even for his Xavante tribe, but only for his village. When the Russell Tribunal on Human Rights invited him to its meeting in the Netherlands, Funai removed his passport and denied him permission to travel. But lawyers from the Pro-Indian Commission (CPI) intervened with a writ that enabled him to go, and he eventually presided over the Tribunal. He wrote that the President of Funai, Colonel Nobre da Veiga, had not wanted him 'to tell the world what harm he is doing to the Indians ... That colonel doesn't like Indians. So why does he go to work at Funai – just to get rich? He shouts at Indians, doesn't listen properly, gets angry. What's he doing? Nothing. He just takes Indian lands, censures any friends of the Indians, and fights anyone who wants to help us.'

The combative Mário Juruna stood for election for the PDT (Democratic Workers' Party) in the State of Rio de Janeiro in the 1982 federal election. Since this was almost the only state with no tribal Indians, he was promoted as the representative of all oppressed people. Juruna won with a majority of over 30,000. The new deputy lost no time in publicizing his cause, by such photo-opportunities as placing a feather headdress on the President of the Federal Chamber on the 'Day of the Indian'. But he surprised his critics, who were accustomed to his flamboyant speeches, by his hard work and pragmatism as a legislator. He soon pushed through two measures: a Permanent Parliamentary Commission for Indians, which had to be consulted on all legislation affecting indigenous matters; and a change to Funai's statute to create a governing council composed of people nominated by indigenous communities. These important innovations raised the Indian cause in national consciousness. Juruna declared that 'the Brazilian government has never allowed Indians to be represented by anyone but a white man, because they say that Indians need guardians ... But we do not need guardians: we are responsible human beings. I am not just here [in Congress] for entertainment value. I am here to work, to defend my people and to struggle for them.'

Mário Juruna was a good deputy, representing his constituents and meeting government ministers; but he was also an unofficial spokesman for all Indians, with visits to tribes engaged in struggles in all parts of Brazil. Ligia Simonian wrote that the achievements of Deputy Juruna in his first year of office 'amazed the nation ... The hope of the Brazilian Indians, he deserved the votes of his electors in Rio de Janeiro.' In 1984, Mário Juruna addressed a United Nations Working Group on Indigenous Populations in Geneva. According to one observer, the Xavante deputy 'stole the show with the European press and television'. He described the terrible depopulation of Brazil's native peoples and noted that 'in the past twenty years Indian lands have been reduced by more than half. Gatherings and meetings are being started among indigenous leaders in Brazil, and these congresses are gradually increasing the resistance of indigenous peoples.' A self-taught orator, Juruna was in demand as a speaker to every type of audience, and he exuded sincerity, generosity, and concern for the oppressed.

Mário Juruna enjoyed telling audiences how his election had shocked conservative Brazilians 'who do not like to see a representative from a conquered ethnic group voting alongside the conquerors'. He was right. Such a charismatic figure attracted enmity, and the right-wing media soon found his weaknesses. Mário Juruna was accused of financial peccadilloes, unpaid debts, abusing his position to bully people, an arrogant manner, and a turbulent private life. He made the political mistake of standing in the 1986 democratic election as a candidate of the PDS (Social-Democratic Party), which was the creation of the military regime that had ruled Brazil since 1964. So the Xavante deputy was heavily defeated. He found work as an adviser to Funai, but his prestige and influence were gone. However, he had already made a crucial contribution as the first – and for twenty years the only – Indian elected to the federal legislature. He threw away all his tapes; but his famous tape-recorder became an exhibit in the Museum of the Indian in Rio de Janeiro.

The cause that inspired these indigenous NGOs and the cement that held them together was invariably land and the resources on that land. It is almost impossible to exaggerate the emotional, spiritual, and economic importance of land to indigenous communities. Land was the burial place of their ancestors, the root of their legends and beliefs, the source of their livelihood (hunting, fishing, farming, and extraction of every form of natural product), the cradle of their communal cohesion, and their protection from outside threats. Without land, a tribe collapses and disperses.

Before contact, land had been used as freely as air or water. This was why it took some tribes time to grasp the concept of ownership based on legislation, written title-deeds, and marked boundaries. By the time an indigenous community understood these arcane legal processes, it was often too late: the territory had been fraudulently sold, allocated to settlers or extractive businesses, violated by roads or dams, or invaded by squatters. However, once Indians learned the principles of land ownership, they quickly discovered how to mobilize public opinion and influence legislative and legal processes. When Mário Juruna achieved the permanent parliamentary commission to defend Indian rights, its document of creation opened with the words: 'The usurpation of indigenous lands has been the cause of a movement that is taking shape and organizing itself'. Most of the speeches at assemblies of Indian leaders concerned land. The indigenous movement then became unstoppable, and it steadily won victories in local struggles over land rights.

The birth of a national indigenous union was not easy. There was turbulence among its leaders. Funds for UNI's headquarters in Brasília ran out, and it cost too much to keep bringing Indian leaders to meetings or for the Union's organizers to travel constantly around Brazil. When CIMI had arranged assemblies of indigenous leaders during the 1970s, these tended to be from missionized tribes. But by the end of 1984 David Maybury-Lewis wrote: 'It seems that CIMI is cool toward an Indian movement that is too independent of its control, as is Mário Juruna himself, while Funai would prefer there to be no Indian movement at all.' The root problem was that Brazil's tribes were too diverse, too small, too remote from one another, at varying stages of acculturation, and confronting such different threats. They therefore needed strong regional organizations more than one national one.

By the mid-1990s Indian populations were increasing strongly, but there were still only some 250,000 indigenous people. They were dispersed in 200 tribes speaking 170 different dialects (most derived from the language 'trunks' Tupi, Jê, Aruak, Carib, and Panoan, but were often mutually incomprehensible). So the indigenous movement fragmented into local pressure groups, which were generally highly effective. Their leaders could assemble without travelling great distances, they found common cause, and they could put pressure on state administrations as well as the distant federal government. So although UNI disintegrated after a few years, it lived on in strong regional affiliates, such as UNI (Sul) for the tribes of southern Brazil.

The all-important issue of land was threatened by a decree in February 1983 that gave every interested branch of government a say in deciding which territories should be reserved for Indians. An Inter-ministerial Working Group was created, with members from the Ministries of Interior, Agriculture, and Agrarian Reform, and the military's powerful National Security Council. Before an indigenous area could be ratified, Funai had to put a proposal and an anthropologist's evaluation to this Working Group – which was always known as the Grupão ('Big Group'). The potential conflicts of interest within the Grupão were obvious, and it was seen as a bid by the military to strengthen their position before the now-inevitable return of Brazil to democratic rule. (The attitude of the armed forces towards Indians was ambivalent. At the operational level, many officers came into contact with Indians and liked them. They were aware of Rondon's army background and were proud to continue his tradition of protection and assistance, particularly through the air force's supply flights. But higher echelons had often never seen tribal people. They worried that the existence of ethnic enclaves might weaken national security.) An evaluation of the Grupão after its first two years showed that it had not rejected any claims outright, but it had greatly slowed down the legislative process. Of fifty reserves submitted to it, only one was fully registered and fourteen had passed the first stage of presidential delimitation.

In November 1983 came a draft decree authorizing mining companies and gold prospectors to operate under licence on Indian lands. There was an outcry, from NGOs, from Indians – many of whom were now living in cheap hotels around Brasília and were well aware of their political nuisance-value – and from activists who had been readmitted to Funai. The President of Funai resigned in September 1984 rather than put this mining decree into operation, and it was surprisingly withdrawn next year. However, Brazil's new civilian President, José Sarney, in practice authorized several such mining concessions.

The short-lived central Union of Indigenous Nations (UNI) was important at a critical time in Brazilian history – when the nation in 1985 emerged from two decades of military government and decided its future direction. Carlos Alberto (Beto) Ricardo, of the research centre CEDI, concluded that 'UNI effectively fulfilled the role of being a reference point of Indianness during the [return to democracy] and up to the process of devising a new Federal Constitution (1986–88). To achieve this, it made use of a mass of non-Indian alliances that included, among others, various non-government support organizations, CIMI itself, parliamentarians from various political parties, and professional associations such as [those of the geologists and anthropologists]. The "Indian scene" that was formed in Brasília at that time included representatives of roughly half the country's indigenous peoples, empowered by the support they received from their non-Indian allies.'

The 'New Republic' under President Sarney was disappointingly indifferent to Indians. Many of Sarney's actions went against indigenous rights, particularly concerning land and mineral prospecting. So the Indians' supporters mobilized a massive lobbying effort when a Constituent Assembly started work on a new Constitution in February 1987. Marlene Ossami called this campaign 'the moment of greatest effervescence of the indigenous movement'.

In the discussions and drafting of the Constitution, indigenous affairs came under the Committee of Social Order, one of eight main committees and twenty-four subcommittees. At first the debates in this Committee went well, stressing 'the importance of [Indians'] ethnic and cultural identities' even though they must remain under government tutelage. Brasília was full of vociferous lobbies, each clamouring for recognition in the Constitution. Some of these mounted threats to the Indian cause. 'The first thrust against Indians came with the move to assimilate them into Brazilian society rather than treat them as a separate group, which would deprive them of protection and special status. This was roundly defeated in the Committee of Social Order, where overwhelming support was given to maintaining the pluri-ethnic character of Brazilian society.'

A far more serious threat came from the mining lobby. The first draft of the Constitution, in August 1987, gave the government the right to mine on Indian land through state-owned companies (this had appeared in the 1983 decree). Private mining companies and unions of garimpeiros mounted a 'fierce and vicious' campaign to extend this. They won concessions in other constituent committees, and they orchestrated a media onslaught on indigenous rights. The influential conservative *Estado de São Paulo* newspaper ran a series of seven articles against the indigenous movement and CIMI in particular. The first piece was headed 'Conspiracy against Brazil', another trumpeted that 'CIMI proposes the division of Brazil'. The propaganda claimed that the Catholic Church, spearheaded by CIMI, had since 1971 mounted a plot 'whose objective is to make the Brazilian state accept the concept of restricted sovereignty over indigenous territories, besides agreeing that the mineral riches of Amazonia and other regions inhabited by Indians should not be exploited'. It harked back to the notions that other nations coveted Brazilian Amazonia and that multinational companies conspired to thwart Brazilian exports or capture its natural resources. It even condemned 'European and Anglo-Saxon' neo-colonialists for 'patronizing' Latin Americans. The accusations were so extreme that the Church tried to sue the newspaper for libel. A Parliamentary Committee of Inquiry was set up to examine the charges; and it rapidly rejected them as ludicrous and fraudulent. But this evil campaign persuaded Deputy Barnardo Cabral, who had the task of coordinating all the strands into one text, to make some prejudicial changes. The conditions that must be met before the government could permit mining on Indian land were watered down. Ideas about 'Indianness' were revived, with the suggestion that more acculturated Indians should cease to enjoy full rights of legal immunity and land protection. The coordinator even tampered with the fundamental right of Indians to permanent possession of land they had always occupied. The campaign also caused Funai to expel summarily nine foreign missionaries, particularly those working among the Yanomami.

The indigenist movement intensified its activities. Hundreds of Indian leaders descended on Brasília, with the Kayapó at their head. The Gorotire and Xingu Kayapó had the necessary funds from their gold-mining licences, they lived relatively close to the federal capital, they had a warrior tradition, and they had a natural flair for political agitation and public relations. So there was a succession of rallies and meetings – often with Indians stripped to the waist and adorned with body-paint, necklaces, and headdresses to ensure maximum media exposure. Meanwhile, supporters issued an avalanche of pamphlets and posters. Their lawyers (such as Carlos Frederico Marés of the campaign 'Indigenous Peoples in the Constituent Assembly', Carlos (Beto) Ricardo of CEDI, and Júlio Gaiger of CIMI) and anthropologists (including Manuela Carneiro da Cunha of the University of São Paulo and Mércio Gomes of Rio de Janeiro) negotiated every clause of the sections dealing with Indians. Amazingly, Funai did not bother to participate in these discussions and negotiations, doubtless because it was run by Romero Jucá, an economist who put business interests above those of the Indians. Mércio Gomes wrote that President José Sarney deliberately appointed Jucá head of Funai in order to shatter the indigenist movement, suborn individual tribes to seek profit rather than collective gains, paralyse the process of land demarcation, and turn public opinion against the Indians. But the indigenous cause did have many supporters among politicians, even if these did not include the civilian President Sarney. In short, 'the Indians and their allies were present in Congress, submitting claims, discussing proposals, applying pressure upon congressmen and mobilizing public opinion in favour of indigenous rights'.

The final text of the Constitution dealt with indigenous matters in eight separate titles and paragraphs and an important chapter called 'About Indians'. When the final votes came, in June 1988, most of the offending changes had been omitted. 'After a meeting lasting almost eight hours, the leaders of the political parties agreed on the chapter "About Indians". Representatives of thirty-five indigenous nations, who had been concentrated in the National Congress throughout the day, paid homage to the Constituent Assembly with a dance, when they learned that the leaders had agreed to drop article 271, which excluded "acculturated" Indians from all rights laid down in the text of the Constitution.'

The pro-Indian campaign achieved far more than merely rectifying damaging changes, or even reiterating rights enshrined in earlier

Constitutions. It introduced two radical new concepts. One was the omission of the idea of 'assimilation', because that implied that Indians were a transient social class ultimately doomed to disappear. The Constitution acknowledged the right of Indians to remain different. They were guaranteed due respect for their way of life – social order, customs, languages, and beliefs. Cultural diversity was guaranteed. The second innovation was to recognize that Indians' rights to their lands were *original*, antedating the establishment of the state of Brazil itself. Article 231 of the Constitution defined indigenous lands as those 'traditionally occupied by Indians . . . on which they live, . . . those used for productive activities and those indispensable to the preservation of the environmental resources necessary for their wellbeing and their physical and cultural reproduction'. This Article also prohibited, under legal penalty, the occupation or degradation of any Indian lands or reserves. The authorities were also ordered to complete the delimitation of all Indian territories by the end of 1993. This important clause was to be the bedrock that helped Indians in their struggles for land throughout the 1990s. The only setback was that the article did not recognize tribes' *collective* ownership of land. This was discussed but rejected. Mércio Gomes, who spoke in favour of this innovation, wrote that it would have guaranteed inalienable land to any group who defined itself as Indian. 'Furthermore, present-day Indian lands could have passed directly into the hands and responsibility of the Indians themselves, without the [Brazilian] Union as intermediary.' So indigenous territories were protected, but continued to be owned by the government's agency Funai.

Article 232 defined the status of Indians within Brazil. Drafted by anthropologists, jurists, and Indians, it was 'in the finest spirit of Brazilian indigenism. It reiterates the rights of Indians over the lands they inhabit and the exclusive use of their goods and resources. It places the services of the Public Attorney's office at their disposal and grants them the right, individually or collectively, to bring suit against whomever offends them, including the federal government. In short, the Constitution raises them to the status of citizens with full rights, without removing from them the security of state protection.' William Balée hailed the 1988 Constitution as 'perhaps the most environmentally sound and humane legal document concerning [indigenous] peoples within the borders of a world nation'.

In 1992 President Fernando Collor welcomed over a hundred heads of government to the 'Earth Summit' (UNCED or the United Nations Conference on Environment and Development) in Rio de Janeiro. It was no accident that this great gathering coincided with the five hundredth anniversary of Columbus's 'discovery' of the Americas. Nor was it surprising that the indigenous peoples did not share any euphoria about such a celebration. Many tribes, headed by the Kayapó, made their disapproval known. I attended the Earth Summit and saw indigenous spokesmen dominating sessions of the Forum that accompanied the UN conference, visited malocas erected by groups who had travelled to Rio de Janeiro, and watched colourful events staged by peoples to reinforce their political messages. Ailton Krenak, the handsome young leader of UNI, said that in his opinion Indians had nothing to celebrate in the first arrival of Europeans. It was up to the whites 'to assess their relations with the peoples of this land during those five centuries. If they concluded that they had erred, they should commemorate the five hundred years with a gesture of goodwill and reconciliation.' One response to this challenge was the creation of a commission, an exhibition, and public debates in São Paulo to honour the cultural achievements (and the depopulation and sufferings) of Brazil's original inhabitants.

More importantly, there was to be a revision of the Indian Statute of 1973. A new Statute of Indigenous Societies started to progress through Congress in 1992–94 with help from the many pro-Indian activists. CIMI in 1995 created Capoib, a new central council to speak for all Brazilian indigenist organizations and hoped-for successor to UNI. Focused NGOs continued to develop all over the country. By the end of the century, CEDI's successor ISA (Social-Environmental Institute) recorded 130 associations organized by Indians on behalf of their local communities; and the anthropologist Luis Donizete Grupioni published a directory of 200 such entities. Many of these were action groups for single tribes (such as the Yanomami, Waimiri Atroari, Ticuna, Sateré-Mawé, Suruí, Kayapó, Xerente, Timbira, and many others) or those living along a single river or in a distinct area.

Mércio Gomes commented that it became clear that Indians did not need intermediaries or spokesmen when dealing with the authorities or the public. 'The physical presence of Indian leaders and their understanding and acceptance of certain issues have become a sine qua non of any agreement' brokered by Funai. Their exotic manners and appearance, forceful expression in often-halting Portuguese, and unique attitudes 'have come to be perceived as the accoutrements of a different but real people, of political beings integrated in their own cultures if not completely in ours. In the minds of average Brazilians the Indians have become real thinking persons.'

14. Jê on the Warpath

The Jê-speaking tribes of the central Brazilian plateau are born warriors. They tend to be tough and lean, expert club-wielders and archers, and physically fit from log races and outrunning game on their campo cerrado. Unlike many other indigenous groups, they were uninterested in alcohol or hallucinogens, although their shamans used elaborate trance-states, chanting and dancing in their medical rituals. Before contact, the societies of groups like the Kayapó and Xavante revolved around their men's huts and a culture of warfare, raiding, and feuds.

These Jê-speakers also happen to live at the eastern edge of the mass of the Amazon rainforests, near the forest–savannah boundary, and thus on the most active colonization frontier in twentieth-century Brazil. The nation's new capital, Brasília, was created in the 1950s to be closer to that frontier; and the most successful new highways were the Belém–Brasília and the BR-364 Cuiabá–Porto Velho, which ran along the plateaux on the eastern and southern edges of the Amazon forests. So the Jê were both vulnerable to settler invasion, but also relatively close to the new seat of power at Brasília.

As we have seen, when the Xavante were 'pacified' in the 1940s and 1950s, they were disgracefully cheated of their homelands north of the rio das Mortes. Instead of the single large territory that was proposed for them and that was their right under the Constitution, the Xavante were dispersed in an archipelago of reserve fragments, and some of their aldeias were destroyed and absorbed into large cattle ranches. One group of Xavante – decimated by disease and persecuted by colonists – fled across the rio das Mortes and took refuge in the Salesian missions of São Marcos and Sangradouro ('Outlet') alongside their former Bororo enemies.

The gigantic 696,000 hectare (2,700 square mile) Suiá-Missu ranch was created with government subsidy on Xavante territory. One of its labourers recalled how they had spent three years felling forest to try to make pastures. They ensured that the Indians would not oppose this rape of their territory by a steady diet of presents, 'of salt, meat, sweets, brown sugar, clothing, red cloth, and coarse blankets. We could not afford good things.' For a time the ranch had 263 Xavante living in the midst of the cattle, as curiosities whom the fazendeiro showed off to his guests. As the Suiá-Missu ranch developed, the Xavante would raid its rice and maize fields. 'Then, entering into contact with the whites, they came to live at their expense. They no longer stole, they begged. They received a steer every day.' But in 1966 these people were abruptly evicted, with the connivance of the SPI, and airlifted by the air force to São Marcos mission; tragically, many died in a measles epidemic soon after arrival, and the survivors eventually dispersed to other Xavante reserves. Humbler settlers poured in to other areas once occupied by this great warrior nation, with help from the colonization agency Incra. In the decade before 1975, the population of the local authority Barra do Garças increased ten-fold to 150,000.

In the years prior to contact, the Xavante had been confused and divided, unsure about how to react to the threats to their existence. In the 1970s this uncertainty started to change. Cláudia Menezes wrote that 'the Xavante, reduced to islands of land, saw the encirclement of their areas closing ever tighter . . . They launched an offensive whose objective was the guarantee of the lands on which they used to live and the recovery of part of their lost territories.' Having survived the first shock of contact, these people were learning the ways of their opponents. It was no accident that the first Indian to be elected to the national Congress was the Xavante Mário Juruna. By 1972 all the Xavante groups were united, for the first time in many generations. Headlines in national newspapers warned that 'three thousand Xavante' were ready for war, and one reporter reminded his readers: 'The Xavante Indians possess a latent vocation for fighting'. Armed with their traditional clubs, but also with guns and revolvers, the warriors of the wretchedly poor village of Areões moved against anyone occupying what they regarded as their land. The injustices of twenty years led to settlers' 'huts burned, tools and guns "confiscated", as well as direct threats of death and total devastation of the properties of farmers and ranchers.' Trucks on a new road being driven from Xavantina north-westwards to Cachimbo were stopped and some-times sacked.

There was constant pressure on the land of the relatively small São Marcos mission south of the rio das Mortes. When the Aborigines Protection Society's team visited the mission-reserve in 1972, the Xavante begged it to do something; and the Indians kept appealing to Funai. Finally, in 1975, the government did enlarge São Marcos, awarded the areas surrounding the Salesian mission to Funai, and evicted settlers with compensation.

Funai in 1969 tried to ease tension at the western edge of Xavante territory by creating a small reserve called Couto de Magalhães on a headwater of the Xingu; but this did little to satisfy the Indians' situation. In 1970 the westernmost group of Xavante, on the Batovi headwater to the Xingu, rebelled against American missionaries who were interfering with their 'sinful' customs and charging for presents in money or prospected diamonds. The Xavante were about to kill the missionaries, but their Chief Cevemecê went to Brasília to complain to Funai. The agency's solution was to remove the offending missionaries – but then permit others to take their places.

Further improvement came in 1976, with the creation of a 51,000 hectare (200 square mile) reserve nearby on the Culuene river, but the Xavante were still unhappy. They wanted the return of their beloved circular village Parabubure, situated near a delightful lake outside the new territory. They had been forced to flee two decades earlier by a massacre by gunmen hired by an American-owned fazenda.

Chief Celestino Tsererob of the Xavante in Sangradouro made an impassioned hour-long speech in Jê to an Assembly of Indigenous Chiefs. He translated his message into broken Portuguese: 'In April [1979], after the rains, I am going back to Parabubure, the village of my grandfather and father. I, too, was born in Parabubure. The Americans killed Xavante, burned houses, and sent measles, and then many Xavante died . . . There the Americans bulldozed our Xavante cemetery and made it the seat of their farm. Now I am returning, back to Parabubure to make a new village near the cemetery of my grandfather. The fazenda ends, and Parabubure is once more!' The warrior Tsererob led many of his people on a long exodus from São Marcos/Sangradouro to a temporary village in Couto de Magalhães reserve.

Efforts to regain the lost land by legal means dragged on intolerably. So the Xavante decided on direct action. They drove their tractors and farm vehicles to surround the buildings of the 140,000 hectare (540 square mile) Xavantina fazenda, which were located on top of their cemetery. Armed Xavante made it known that they would attack at dawn on 2 December 1979. They issued an ultimatum to the farm workers (who were numerous and well armed): 'We Xavante do not want to kill anyone, we are only ordering you to leave. But if the fazenda's personnel will not leave, there will be fighting.' The Xavante had instinctively learned about public relations: they prepared for battle in black and red body-paint, and they encouraged journalists to photograph them. The President of Funai, Colonel João Carlos Nobre da Veiga, understood force and the power of the media. He rushed through a long-delayed decree that joined up the two reserves near the Culuene and added the entire Xavantina ranch. He himself hurried to Couto de Magalhães to hand the decree document to the Xavante leaders on the eve of their attack. The new Indian Area of Parabubure was 226,555 hectares (875 square miles) of campo savannah and low forests between the Culuene and Couto de Magalhães headwaters of the Xingu. The Xavante rapidly recreated their lovely Parabubure village.

The northernmost Xavante reserve, Pimentel Barbosa far down the rio das Mortes, was also heavily invaded by farmers, many of whom had title deeds, and by squatters. Pimentel Barbosa had been enlarged in March 1979 to rectify a massive and deliberate 'error' by Funai cartographers. But the Indians then discovered further fraud when surveyors came to fix the enlarged boundaries.

The Xavante decided that their only hope was to deploy warriors against the invaders of Pimentel Barbosa. Chief Zacarias explained: 'We will not leave until [the settlers] pack their bags. What we want is for them to leave our land.' Funai's local director, Odenir Pinto de Oliveira, and the future Congressman Chief Mário Juruna arrived to persuade them to desist, partly because the farmers were armed and had appealed for police protection. So Chief Uarodi of Pimentel Barbosa, the son of the old Paramount Chief Apoena, took his case to Brasília on a series of visits. He was encouraged by Odenir Pinto de Oliveira, who was born to a sertanista in a Xavante village and whom Chief Warinatse Abhodi of São Marcos described as 'our brother, our chief and our friend'. Odenir publicly blamed Colonel Nobre da Veiga for the injustice and prevarication at Pimentel Barbosa; so the Indians twice had to save him from police arrest for inciting them to rebel.

The protests culminated in May 1980, when thirty-one tribal leaders went to the capital and met Colonel Nobre da Veiga in his office, wearing Western clothes but (for the benefit of press photographers) armed with clubs and bows and arrows. It was an angry meeting, with police surrounding the ministry building. At the end, the chiefs named twelve Funai officials as 'enemies of our people': most of these were military men, and they included Colonels Nobre da Veiga and Ivan Zanoni. On 12 August 1980 the Xavante regained the 28,262 hectares (109 square miles) that had been excluded by corrupt surveyors when they demarcated the land in the previous year's decree. Congressman Mário Juruna blamed a lady lawyer for the fraud and, a year later, was angry that 'she stole but has not gone to jail . . . There she is, as happy as can be, more important than ever, working at the Ministry of the Interior.' Also, Nobre da Veiga broke a promise to negotiate through Odenir Pinto de Oliveira: he and two other pro-Xavante agents were fired, followed later in 1980 by a purge of thirty of Funai's anthropologists, doctors, and teachers.

The Xavante did not desist. In June 1983 fourteen of them occupied the office of the next President of Funai, the more amenable Colonel Paulo Moreira Leal. The press published a picture of them, neatly dressed and sitting all over the office's white sofas and armchairs. They demanded the dismissal of Colonel Zanoni and his military colleagues. They bundled the ex-boxer Zanoni into his car and told him: 'Now, you go home. Keep very calm, but you have no business here. Go and look after your family.' The various colonels were duly removed.

The Xavante victories in reversing injustices were impressive. They were achieved by a shrewd combination of threats of violence, intimidation of invaders, manipulation of the media, and political action in Brasília with the help of well-wishers. Apart from Odenir Pinto de Oliveira, Funai gave little assistance – it often seemed more aligned to the forces planning and financing regional development than to its indigenous charges.

The struggles brought repercussions within Xavante society. Chiefs who excelled in these conflicts rose in stature. These knew Portuguese and became familiar with Brazilian politics, and they were often younger men. The politically active leaders succeeded because they combined with chiefs from other Xavante groups and because they could operate beyond their village limits. Also, in response to enforced contraction from widespread hunting and semi-nomadism to more settled agriculture, the Xavante split into a greater number of smaller villages. This meant that they occupied their reserves more evenly and could repel intruders more effectively. Aracy Lopes da Silva noted that 'Xavante successes show that a society equipped for warfare is better at confronting external domination'.

When I visited São Marcos and Sangradouro in 1972 with the team from the Aborigines Protection Society, we were impressed by the Xavantes' enthusiasm for plantation-farming of rice and beans. The Salesian missionaries had introduced the Indians to agricultural machinery and mechanized food-processing, and Xavante men were paid for their communal labour in addition to having plots to farm for their own families. Funai took note. Its public-relations department liked to issue pictures of handsome Xavante driving tractors or operating machinery, dressed in boxer shorts and with their long hair flying behind them. In the late 1970s, when the reserves were being legalized, settlers expelled, and relations between Funai and the missions improved, the government agency tried to grow upland rice on a large scale and to raise some cattle on these reserves. Funai invested heavily, with a modern rice-dryer at São

Marcos, tractors, trucks, tools, sacks, and storage equipment. The land and the work crews were divided by age groups. The labour was collective, so it did not disrupt the communal nature of tribal society – apart from rewarding the young men's age group, which did the most work, with the most produce. Nancy Flowers, who was with the Xavante at that time, noted that 'although they have adopted upland rice as their staple, largely for commercial reasons, maize continues to have great ceremonial importance for them.' They carefully separated different colours of maize, since these strains had symbolic significance.

Large-scale mechanized rice projects were also introduced to other Xavante reserves. Laura Graham described the Indians' eagerness to grow rice at Pimentel Barbosa and their pride in tractors and trucks at Parabubure. They felt that this farming would satisfy their material needs. They also saw the investment in such agriculture as their victory, won by pressure on the authorities and successful lobbying. Funai was also enthusiastic. It hoped that sale of the rice would make the Indians self-sufficient and even produce a surplus for its version of the discredited renda indígena. The scheme seemed modern, a productive use of Indian land and labour, and it consolidated political control over this belligerent and awkward people. Funai's leaders were worried by Xavante successes with the media, and hoped that this injection of capital would make them speak better of their protective agency.

This project was grandly named the Plan for the Development of the Xavante Nation. Unfortunately, it did not bring all the hoped-for benefits. The introduction of new working patterns and salaries for some workers and cowhands gradually affected the tribe's traditional economy. These cut across social hierarchies. Nutrition and health were also affected. Monoculture of rice often required deforestation, and this curtailed hunting and changed diet. Most importantly, the rice projects and the confinement in relatively small reserves led to fragmentation. Xavante population rose steadily, thanks to a booming birth rate and better health care, but the number of villages rose far faster. In 1980 there were sixteen Xavante villages; by 1985 there were thirty-five; by 1987, fifty; and by 1992, almost seventy. The need for machinery and its maintenance, and fuel, made the Indians more dependent on Funai.

The rice-growing enterprise was not a sustainable success. Natural vegetation on the Xavantes' plains is sparse, because the savannah is on weak, sandy soil and subject to long dry seasons. Aracy Lopes da Silva explained that 'large-scale mechanized agriculture on cerrado soils is very difficult if not impossible'. By the mid-1980s, 'when the dire consequences of the project were obvious – in terms of the social, economic and political condition of the Xavante – Funai started to distance itself from the affair'. During these decades, the Xavante were increasingly inserted into national society, despite their stubborn battles to regain at least part of their lost territories. Lopes da Silva admired the Indians' resilience: 'They sought to retain their autonomy, freedom and dignity. They showed great capacity for response, and simultaneously reordered their society to preserve tribal structure. However, the latter is [by the 1990s] showing signs of exhaustion after the economic interference of the Plano Xavante.'

One Xavante territory remained to be recovered: the gigantic Suiá-Missu ranch. On the low watershed of the Serra do Roncador ('Snorer Hills') between the Araguaia and upper Xingu, the fazenda ran almost from the lands of the Tapirapé in the north to the rio das Mortes some 300 kilometres (190 miles) to the south. It was an area of transition between campo cerrado and lofty rainforest. This immense ranch attracted millions of dollars of government subsidies but, after changing hands several times, it failed. It eventually passed into the reluctant ownership of the Italian government's petroleum giant ENI. The Italians at first invested heavily in a doomed attempt to raise cattle on this weak, dry savannah; but they eventually sold or abandoned most of the ranch.

The Xavante yearned to regain all this land, since it was full of ancient village and cemetery sites. It was rightfully theirs under the Constitution. They knew it as Maraiwatsede, meaning 'Pretty Forest'. Part of it was recovered at the south of Pimentel Barbosa, and that became home to 1,000 Xavante (of a total of some 8,000 for the entire nation). Mariano Mampieri of a foreign-aid NGO in Italy and Iara Ferraz of the Brazilian CTI (Centre of Indigenous Work) helped Funai negotiate with ENI and its subsidiary AGIP for the restoration of the remainder of Suiá-Missu to its original owners. The Italian oil men had lost interest in the costly and controversial ranch, so ENI's President gave it back to its original owners, in a grand gesture at the Earth Summit in Rio de Janeiro in 1992.

Local farmers thought otherwise. A group that called itself 'Settlers of the Suiá' moved in to seize the ranch's machinery and 32,000 head of cattle. Incited by local politicians, they 'vehemently declared that they don't want Indians as neighbours'. They then proceeded to fell and burn the area's low forests as rapidly as possible. The Xavante chief Paridzané went to Rome to meet Italian deputies, press, and activists; but the matter was thwarted by a corruption scandal involving the President of ENI who had made the declaration about restoring the ranch. After almost two years of legal wrangling and pressure from the Italians, Funai and its parent Ministry of Justice seemed to have regained most of the disputed land. It was theoretically returned to the Xavante in a decree in October 1993, demarcated in 1994, and registered in August 2000. Funai set up a technical commission to guarantee the return of Xavante from other reserves to their homeland in Maraiwatsede. But 3,000 squatter families refused to leave, and in December 2000 their lawyer wrangled another delay by demanding one more anthropological report on the validity of the Xavantes' prior occupation.

It had taken the Xavante half a century to recover most of the territory stolen from them after contact. Over 6,000 Xavante now occupy sixty villages – but only within their six non-adjacent reserves. They have achieved this by a shrewd mixture of political pressure, judicial wrangling with help from legal friends, some support from Funai, intimidation through their bellicose reputation and their extra-judicial status as legal minors, and adept use of the media. They won their campaigns with no bloodshed.

The Jê-speaking Kayapó were less subtle and more violent than the Xavante who lived to the south and south-east of them. In 1971, as part of the 'PIN' Programme for National Integration, the government announced a road from the frontier towns of Barra do Garças and Xavantina towards Cachimbo on the new north–south Cuiabá–Santarém road that had invaded the land of the Panará. The new BR-80 road was to start northwards across Xavante territory, alongside the Areões and Pimentel Barbosa reserves, and then swing north-westwards. This route meant that it cut across the northern part of the Xingu Indian park. The author was in the Xingu at the time and I saw that there was no consultation whatever with the Villas Boas brothers. I flew out with a disconsolate Cláudio, who went to Brasília and São Paulo in a forlorn protest against the violation of unquestioned Indian land. Not only was the road planned to cross the protected Xingu area, but the presidential decree also removed all the forests north of the road from the jurisdiction of the park – an area of over 8,200 square kilometres (3,170 square miles). A comparable area was added to the south of the park; but this was campo savannah and low woods, in contrast to the mature rainforests of the excised northern quarter; and the southern addition contained some ranches but no Indians, whereas the amputated forests were home to various Kayapó groups. Far from protesting at this mutilation of Brazil's finest Indian area, the President of Funai, General Bandeira de Mello, declared that 'the National park of the Xingu cannot impede the country's progress'.

The Kayapó who migrated westwards across the Xingu in the first half of the twentieth century are collectively known as Menkragnoti. As we have seen, they fragmented and occasionally reunited, and often moved their villages during the turbulent years before and after contact in the 1950s. The southernmost group, who came within the Xingu park, are the Mentuktire (known as Txukahamãe when contacted by the Villas Boas). Some of these lived on the Jarina river, which happened to be north of the BR-80 crossing and was therefore removed from the park.

The Villas Boas went in 1971 to ask all Mentuktire to move south into the park, but most refused – unable to grasp the magnitude of the threat to their forested homelands. The only group to accept the invitation was that of Raoni, the extrovert and feckless teenager whom Adrian Cowell had known in the 1950s, now matured into a forceful chief. Raoni's people built a village called Porori (later renamed Kretire) on the site of a former Juruna village twenty kilometres (twelve miles) south of the road and therefore within the Xingu park. Megaron Mentuktire gave his version of events during these years: 'My people moved again, but the village was already divided. My uncle Raoni came to live south of the BR-80 with part of my people, but my uncle Krumare and Kremoro [after a brief stay at Porori] returned to live on the Jarina river, near Kapoto and the Agropexim fazenda. From 1971 to 1975 the park officials did not help my people. In 1975 about seventy-four people caught measles from outside contact on the road and brought it in to Jarina. Measles killed many people.'

There were endless requests to Funai to try to recover lands north of the road and to demarcate the old village of Kapoto; but Funai was powerless to countermand a decree by President Médici. Megaron argued passionately that 'Kapoto is our true village and our true land. It is white men who come to our land. It is white men who invade our land. We have been living in that land for a long time . . . The whites took almost all the land from the Indians; do they now want to take what is left to us?'

All the Mentuktire, within and outside the park, were outraged by the road that sliced across their forests and amputated their sanctuary. Traffic along it soon brought an influenza epidemic. So in 1976 ninety-one warriors from six villages (including some non-Kayapó) united to show their anger: they sank a ferry raft and ransacked some trucks and cars trying to use the new road. Two labourers of the Agropexim fazenda in the amputated area were killed later that year. The Indians felt menaced by Piaraçu, a new hamlet that was springing up near the river crossing: four residents of this roadside halt were killed in 1974; and by 1979 men from Kretire village had expelled its last people. But the Mentuktire could do nothing about São José do Xingu, forty kilometres (twenty-five miles) east of the crossing. Despite its sonorous name, São José was a nasty frontier shanty-town known locally as Bang-Bang because of its many brothels.

Their belligerence gradually won concessions for these Kayapó. In May 1976 a Funai edict created a reserve called Jarina for one group of Mentuktire living north of the road. The Jarina reserve was a swathe forty kilometres (twenty-five miles) wide west of the Xingu as far north as the Von Martius rapids. It gave protection to some 200 Indians, most of them in a village under chiefs Kremoro and Krumare near the mouth of the Jarina.

The eastern or right bank of the Xingu north of the road was still unprotected, and it was here that tensions degenerated into open conflict. A ranch called São Luiz was advancing towards the river, its men felling forest ever closer to the Xingu. In June 1980, Raoni warned the fazendeiro to desist and leave; but in August an Indian saw that woodsmen were back, clearing land only five kilometres (three miles) from the river. When Raoni was informed, he enlisted Suyá, Kayabi, and Juruna allies to help the Mentuktire expel the invaders. In the words of Megaron, his uncle Raoni told his men 'to hit the farm workers so that they would not return. But the warriors hit the workers too hard.' Bedjai, whose father had been killed by whites, wielded his club in a frenzy of revenge. 'Because of this, and because the workers were very badly hurt, the warriors decided to kill the wounded workers, and that's how they died.' As reported by a labourer who escaped, Indians suddenly appeared in their clearing and ordered them to leave; five did so; the warriors told the remaining twelve 'to strip and kneel, then bludgeoned ten of them to death. Another was killed by an arrow when he tried to escape. Only one of the labourers managed to get away, running through the forest until he reached a fazenda twelve hours later.' This killing of poor farm workers was a wretched mistake, a reversion to the Kayapó's warlike past when they thought nothing of taking lives. However, despite local grief and anger, there were no recriminations against the Indians because of their constitutional immunity.

A leader of the ranchers complained that twenty of them had moved into the vacant area and invested heavily in it, attracted by 'negative certificates' issued by Funai to say that the forests were empty of Indians. Orlando Villas Boas denounced Funai's irresponsible action. He declared that when he first entered the area twenty years previously there were uncontacted Indians on both banks. 'All that stretch of land [north of] the BR-80 was always considered as an area of perambulation for Indians moving in search of better hunting grounds.' The fazendeiros were therefore illegal invaders, and the Indians had every right to defend their lands. The Indians wanted a reserve forty kilometres (twenty-five miles) wide on the right bank of the Xingu from the BR-80 road for some eighty kilometres (fifty miles) to the Von Martius rapids. This was opposite the Jarina reserve, which had similar dimensions on the left (west) bank. These were roughly the areas removed from the Xingu park in 1971. But some Kayapó were prepared to settle for a fifteen-kilometre (nine-mile) strip, which would at least protect the river and its fishing.

The months dragged by. There were further meetings, including one in November 1980 with Colonel Ivan Zanoni in the Xingu, and petitions. But by 1984 the Mentuktire had still not obtained protection of the east bank of the Xingu below the road. In February 1984 Raoni went to Brasília to demand action from the new President of Funai, Otávio Ferreira Lima, who promised to address a meeting of all the interested parties at Kretire village, but failed to attend. Chief Megaron met farmers at São José do Xingu to assure them that the Indians' quarrel was with Funai, not them. Both sides admitted that they were frightened of the other. A typical settler attitude was that 'Indians and peccary are the same thing. If either comes onto my land, I don't think twice – I kill them'. And whenever the Indians left the Xingu park, by road or air, they witnessed the devastation right up to its edge: 'a desert of ashes and calcinated tree trunks . . . where nothing moves except an occasional herd of cattle in search of scattered tufts of grass . . . "If we lose our land," says Raoni, "then the whites will destroy the whole forest. Where will we go to hunt tapir, ant-bears [coati], or jaguar? What will we eat? There will be no game left."'

The frustrated Indians decided to act, but in a dramatic and bloodless way that would achieve the greatest publicity. In March 1984 they embarked on what became known as 'the War of the Xingu'. They started by seizing the big metal pontoon raft that ferried traffic across the Xingu, then demanded the dismissal of Ferreira Lima as well as the recovery of the disputed land. At the end of March they raised the stakes by kidnapping the non-Indian Director of the Xingu park, Cláudio Romero, when he went to Kretire to negotiate. Romero and other white hostages were treated well, fed with large quantities of fish and monkeys, and 'entered into the life of the village' by fishing and bathing with the Indians. The ferry raft was occupied for weeks, with trucks paralysed on the BR-80 and police unsure what to do about the Indians. Newspapers carried dramatic pictures of a hundred muscular warriors on the raft, wearing black war paint and boxer shorts and brandishing their clubs and bows – an intimidating sight. There were also pictures of tough Kayapó women wielding machetes 'as proof that they were also ready to fight'. Other Xingu tribes lent their support. Ipó Kayabi recalled that 'our war lasted for almost two months. It was hard, but it was great to see all the Xingu tribes fighting together, all united. Everyone helped: the Suyá, the Kayabi, the Txukahamãe (Mebengokre Mentuktire), the Txikão, and the Kren-akrore (Panará).'

The Indians gradually won their public-relations war. The press was generally sympathetic, and lay and ecclesiastical organizations clamoured for Funai and the government to give the Mentuktire what they wanted. On 14 April two senior Funai officials and the sertanista Sydney Possuelo went to parlay at the guard post where the road enters the park; but they too were seized, threatened, and held as hostages.

The Mentuktire chiefs Raoni, Kremoro, and Krumare joined the Xavante Congressman Mário Juruna in negotiations with the Minister of the Interior, Mário Andreazza. On 16 April 1984, Funai interdicted (closed, pending stronger protective legislation) a fifteen-kilometre (nine-mile) strip on the right bank of the Xingu – it was claimed that a forty-kilometre-wide reserve would be too expensive because the twenty incumbent ranchers would have to be compensated. The Indians threatened to send armed warriors to demarcate the reserve as they defined it; the settlers said that they had mined the land with explosives. Raoni and the other chiefs were inflexible. They often wore headdresses, lip-discs, and genipap warpaint for meetings with the Minister, for maximum publicity impact. They gained the sacking of Otávio Ferreira Lima from the presidency of Funai. They then released their hostages after three weeks' captivity, and freed the ferry on condition that Indians would in future control the Xingu crossing. On 3 May 1984 the Minister signed an agreement giving the Mentuktire the fifteen-kilometre strip, as well as the rich and sacred area called Kapoto, north of the Jarina reserve and west of the Von Martius rapids. In a famous televised gesture during the signing ceremony, Raoni pulled the ear of the embarrassed but smiling Minister, to show that he needed better judgement.

A few days later, the new President of Funai appointed Raoni's nephew Megaron as the new Director of the Xingu park. He had been a crucial negotiator in ending 'the War of the Xingu'. In a sense, this was vindication of the policy of the Villas Boas, who had ceased to run the Xingu in 1977, in grooming indigenous leaders to manage their communities and decide their destinies. A newspaper headline called it 'the greatest victory achieved by the Indians'. The released hostages were heavily bearded, tired, and ill, and their lives had been threatened during captivity. But they applauded the Indians for being so steadfast, for remaining united, and for their effective campaign. Cláudio Romero was happy to hand over the running of the park to Megaron and declared that 'the important thing is to celebrate their conquest', while Possuelo rejoiced that 'for the first time the Indians have won without having to kill'.

In October work started on the demarcation of the new reserve areas. Megaron, the new Director of the Xingu, recalled that they had struggled for these lands for thirteen years, ever since the BR-80 truncated the park. 'We nearly lost the Kapoto, our best land, our sacred land. These things need not have happened, had the whites from the outset respected and demarcated our lands. From now onwards we want the fazendeiros to honour our boundaries and we will respect their farms.'

Life continued tranquilly within the main Xingu park, under the white directors who succeeded the Villas Boas and now under Megaron and successive Indian directors. In 1981 the tribes cooperated to produce a newsletter. An article signed by various leaders was a lament for vanishing traditions.

> In the old days, we Indians used to perform rituals at all times. But the rituals are gradually disappearing, because the whites have arrived . . . There's an end to all the rituals, languages, and food because people stop making gardens. The Indians also stop making ornaments and all the things that they need to live: baskets, sifters for manioc and corn flour, manioc graters, clay pots, drills for fire, mats . . . and tipitis to squeeze [poison out of] manioc dough to make flour, canoes, paddles, basketry fish-traps, houses, hammocks, and gourd dippers. They don't poison fish with timbó, hunt, use herbal medicines, make poisoned arrows, bark blankets, necklaces of monkey teeth, large painted baskets with fringes to carry hammocks, or tattoo themselves and apply body paint of [red] anatto and [black] genipap, or practise shamanism and witchcraft, and other things as well . . . Why is it important not to lose our customs? Because if we cease being Indians, we are neither white nor Indian. [This would lead to miscegenation] and if this happens, we will lose our land.

Because the Indians were running their own affairs, they were better able to confront the dilemma between modernization and tradition, to fulfil the Villas Boas' hope that they change only at a speed that *they themselves* wanted.

Further down the Xingu, 350 kilometres (220 miles) north-east of Kapoto and some 700 kilometres (440 miles) north of the Xavante, was the big Gorotire village, a heartland of the warlike northern Kayapó. Although the Gorotire had a large reserve dating from the 1940s, it was still not properly demarcated forty years later. Surrounding farms threatened to encroach on Indian territory. In June 1980 the Gorotire learned that 600 labourers were felling woods near one of their boundaries; and in August an Indian patrol heard that 1,800 men had been recruited to clear forest where the Cumaru fazenda joined the eastern edge of their reserve.

The Gorotire went on the warpath. Painted in black warpaint, they invaded the nearby Espadilha ranch. One warrior later said that 'we just wanted to shave the hair of the men who were hostile to us and said that they did not like Indians.' But the farm manager pointed a shotgun at them, his daughter Lúcia wounded two Indians with a knife, and another Kayapó was hit by an axe handle. 'This provoked a massacre. Lúcia was killed, and even two children who tried to run off into the forest did not escape. Twenty bodies were smashed by club blows and also hit by several gunshots. After the Indians returned to their village, they spent the entire dawn in celebratory dances and then washed off their warpaint in the waters of the Fresco river.' They then purged themselves in ceremonies in the men's hut in the centre of the village. 'Chief Kanhok, who led the Gorotire group in the Espadilha massacre, declared: "We are very sad. Indians do not want to kill anyone; we only want them not to destroy our forests. But the white man attacked Indians and cut an Indian."' The massacre happened very fast and was not premeditated. It was a new experience for the younger Gorotire warriors – for there had been no fighting by these Kayapó for twenty years. Not surprisingly, it heightened tension, with armed fazendeiros threatening to shoot any Indian who strayed onto their land, and the Gorotire mounting patrols to protect their perimeter.

The Kayapó were now changing rapidly, increasingly aware of Western values and political systems, possessing plenty of guns and manufactured goods, but maintaining their own cultural heritage. A majority of Kayapó professed Christianity, with the various villages divided roughly between Catholics, Protestant *crentes*, and adherents to tribal beliefs (known to missionaries as 'indifferents'). The American anthropologist Terence Turner saw that the Gorotire resented the presence of rival missionaries and a Funai agent in the midst of their main village. Thirty years of dependence on such alien agencies bred 'despair, heightened by disease and severe demographic decline.' The Gorotire village was relatively large, with ninety houses on a sandy plateau. Half the village was planned by Funai, with tidy houses along a broad avenue between the Fresco river and the men's house. The other half was the traditional circle of huts, at the foot of the surrounding hills.

A powerful new force now entered the region, one that brought both wealth and ultimately environmental damage to the Kayapó. In the 1970s the world's largest iron-ore deposit had been developed at Carajás, some 150 kilometres (93 miles) north-east of the main Kayapó reserve and close to the land of the Xikrin Kayapó. Then in 1979 a farmer stumbled across gold in the mud of Serra Pelada ('Bald Hill') between Carajás and the frontier town of Marabá on the Tocantins. Serra Pelada yielded nugget after nugget of gold. Tens of thousands of prospectors poured in and excavated a huge crater in their antlike frenzy. These garimpeiros created a wild mining community that was for a time beyond government or police control. In 1980 another rumour of gold took the gold-rush southwards into the Kayapó part of Brazil. Twenty thousand adventurers moved into the region; in July the Kayapó evicted 200 garimpeiros; thousands invaded other farms; and to calm the situation the government opened a garimpo called Goiaba for anyone to pan. The police tried to expel prospectors from Cumaru fazenda; but by mid-1981 it was established as the headquarters of the region's mining operations. The garimpeiros' crude methods were environmentally disastrous. Jets of water from diesel-powered pumps thrashed the gold-bearing earth into muddy ponds. The resulting slush was pumped into sluices, where the gold ore was separated. Torrents of effluent poured into the river, a noxious mixture of mud, sewage, and diesel fuel. Abandoned craters were breeding grounds for mosquitoes, and the garimpeiros were riddled with malaria. The once-sparkling Fresco was grossly polluted by the Cumaru mine, upstream of the Indian village. The Kayapó could no longer bathe or fish in its filthy water, and they had to pipe drinking water from a stream two kilometres away.

The Kayapó are resilient and resourceful. They came to terms with the gold rush on their territory and used it to their advantage. By 1982 they were in an extraordinary state of transition. They readily adopted hooks and lines for fishing and guns for hunting. But they also continued to use traditional timbó poison for fishing, and men still went on long hunting expeditions to bring back dozens of living land tortoises carried in high racks that towered above each returning warrior. The Gorotire started to extract levies from gold prospectors inside their reserve, and they used the income fairly shrewdly. At first they chartered planes to bring in manufactured goods – boxes of rice and beans, soap, ammunition, and clothing – which the chiefs distributed around the village houses. They then acquired more sophisticated goods, such as metal boats with outboard motors and butane gas cookers, and they brought in brick, cement, and corrugated iron as well as the builders to turn them into houses.

The village of Kikretum, which split off from Gorotire in 1976 following a dispute, drove a harder bargain with its garimpeiros than the larger village had done; so the chiefs of Gorotire raised the cost of their licences. The Indians then began their own prospecting at 'Garimpo Kayapó', but they employed four outside miners to work it for them. Funai donated ore-washing equipment, and the Gorotire chiefs opened bank accounts in nearby cities as well as a credit line at the miners' big store in Cumaru just east of the reserve. David Cleary, in a history of Brazil's extraordinary gold rush, admired the Indians' sophistication. 'The Kayapó showed commendable restraint in the circumstances. They did not kill a single garimpeiro.'

While she was with them in 1982, the British-born anthropologist Vanessa Lea attended a Protestant service. She was appalled to hear the preacher tell his congregation that heaven awaited those who believed in God, but hell fires would burn the rest. This contrasted with the Indians' vision of an afterlife for all, where men sleep by day and hunt at night. Despite Christian worship by some Gorotire, the tribe lavished most of the previous year's mining income on a magnificent *Bemp* naming-ceremony, at which boys and girls were initiated into tribal ways amid days and nights of dancing and festivity. Much of the food consumed at this feast was bought at the miners' depot; but, in accordance with Kayapó custom, there was no alcoholic drink.

Dr Lea also heard chiefs vow to end the internecine feuds that had always divided the bellicose Kayapó. This was an important and radical change, a milestone in tribal history. One elder declared that all Kayapó were now brothers. As such, they must cease to fight one another but should combat whites who were threatening their land.

Terence Turner noted how men's clothing was a bellwether of changing attitudes during the years of accommodation to white society. Shorts were the first item of clothing to be universally adopted by the Gorotire and Kapot (Kayapó) – although traditional penis-sheaths and body paint might still be used underneath. Next came shirts and T-shirts, which tended to be worn only when outside visitors were present. Men cut their hair short in the Brazilian manner. Then came a reaction, with new self-assurance and pride. Chiefs and other men reverted to wearing long hair flowing over their shoulders. By the late 1980s Kayapó who visited cities (which they did frequently, being relatively close to Brasília) often had bare chests with necklaces and (if a television camera crew were present) body paint and feather ornaments.

An agreement in 1981 between Funai and the Ministry of Finance awarded the Kayapó a meagre 0.1 per cent of the sale price of all gold mined at the garimpos called Tarzan and Maria Bonita ('Pretty Mary'), where 6,000 prospectors had poured into the Gorotire reserve area. From 1981 to 1984 the SNI (secret service), the Ministry of Mines, the Ministry of Finance, and the police tightly controlled both this Cumaru gold-prospecting area and the Serra Pelada to the north. 'Discipline was perfect . . . The only discontents were the Gorotire Indians and the company that owned nearby invaded property . . . Then in April 1984, for unknown reasons, the SNI decided to withdraw from command of the "Operation Garimpo" . . . which had been their pride.'

This was a difficult period of transition for the Kayapó. At Kikretum village at the north of the Kayapó area, the Indians had 'total control of the garimpo, levying fees for every suction [of gold-bearing mud], establishing a trading post, and even charging for planes landing on the airstrip'. But the higher income led to problems of 'accelerated acculturation'. Funai's local agent warned that 'the younger men do not want to know about agriculture, fishing or hunting. They should realize that the mineral activity is finite. They need to invest what they are receiving in some lasting activity.' Unscrupulous traders and bush-pilots were cheating Kikretum's gullible Chief Tutu Pombo and his people. This village was also threatened by the large Tucumã colonization project nearby. Meanwhile, the Kuben-Kran-Kégn village to the north-west suffered invasions by loggers seeking valuable mahogany trees – there was a near-tragedy when a group of Kayapó warriors occupied the offending sawmill. Equally seriously, the State of Pará planned a colonization project called Trairão on land that was shown to be on a cemetery of the Kayapó of Kuben-Kran-Kégn.

The Kayapó now produced an able spokesman: Paulinho Paiakan from Kuben-Kran-Kégn village. The tribe was exasperated by the smallness of its royalties, by delays in payment, continued invasions by prospectors, pollution of the Fresco river, and Funai's failure to demarcate the reserve. So, on 1 April 1985, 200 armed Kayapó invaded the airstrip of Maria Bonita garimpo and prevented planes from landing. It was a bold move, since there were hundreds of tough and gold-hungry prospectors there; but the police had removed the invaders' weapons, so that they could not retaliate. Some Indians were said to have wanted to repeat the killings of settlers at Fazenda Espadilha four years earlier. Paiakan restrained the hotheads, but maintained the non-violent protest. The Indians showed their customary flair for public relations: the press and television carried dramatic pictures of club-wielding warriors, wearing nothing but warpaint, boxer shorts, and headdresses, glowering across a muddy water-logged mine-working at rows of lean miners, and another of a line of angry Kayapó surrounding a grounded plane.

There was a negotiation between the leader of the Cumaru miners and the President of Funai, Nelson Marabuto. 'Under the decisive stares of Indians painted in red and black and armed with clubs, shotguns and bows and arrows, Marabuto did not hesitate: "It is the Indians who decide." [The Kayapó] thus came to assume total control of the garimpo. With the protection of eight armed federal policemen, they demanded the departure of all prospectors – who offered no resistance since they had been prevented from bearing arms.' The Ministry of Finance, which controlled mining activities, agreed with Funai to 'deactivate' the three garimpos inside the Kayapó area, and the air force helped to evacuate the prospectors. Hundreds of suction pumps, mini-dredgers, and mills were left behind, and the Indians later demanded heavy compensation for releasing this equipment.

Paulinho Paiakan was chosen to speak for all the villages because he was 'an authentic Kayapó leader, who conveyed the protests of the older Indians to the mediator at Cumaru and managed to keep his people calm whenever they attempted a more violent reaction'. After that success, Paiakan went to Brasília for discussions with government officials and miners' representatives. He threatened that, without massive concessions, he could hardly prevent a general revolt of the entire Kayapó nation. This won a fifty-fold increase in royalties to 5 per cent, the Indians' right to expel all garimpeiros if they wanted, and a definite promise of demarcation of the vast reserve within six months. The garimpos were reopened.

The American anthropologist Darrell Posey, who had worked with the Kayapó since the 1970s, felt that they had no alternative to this accommodation with the miners. The total population of these Kayapó was 900, from which they could muster 300 warriors. How could they repel 4,000 desperate and determined garimpeiros, who returned as fast as they were expelled? The government offered no positive protection. 'So the Kayapó were forced to put up with gold mining, and it was very controversial because the old people didn't want it and still don't want it. It brought them a lot of diseases, a lot of pollution, and questionable goods.' It created more problems than it resolved, not least in the way that it enriched a few chiefs who had difficulty in distributing the new wealth to the rest of the community.

But these Indians did manage to make the most of their strange situation. 'During the following years, a model for relations between the Gorotire and the garimpo was gradually established. This was peculiar to the Kayapó. The involvement of the community's men was . . . rigorously organized in a system of relays by the oldest chiefs and their adult sons – but while they continued to pursue their [traditional] activities of swidden agriculture, hunting and festivals.' By 1990 three garimpos were permitted inside the reserve. These had their own township, which was also the seat of the tribe's 'Operation Gorotire Gold' with an office and dormitory. The Indians did not themselves perform prospecting work: they monitored it and controlled the export of gold. 'Tokran, son of a chief called Kanhonk, selects teams of some eight warriors who are sent from the village to the base at Maria Bonita for periods of a month. At the end of this they receive wages, do personal shopping at the town of Redenção, and return to their homes . . . At checkpoints at places of entry to the area, the warriors' task is to inspect all who enter or leave. This is done with a fine-tooth comb, with miners remaining naked during the inspections to avoid concealment of gold. At times they make raids to find guns or drink. The entry of women is prohibited.' Every prospector had to weigh his gold in the Kayapó counting-house, obtain an official export permit, and pay a 12 per cent tax to the tribe. Royalty payments were made at weekly meetings, which also served to resolve tensions or grievances by either side. The garimpeiros also bought their supplies from stores run by Indians – a reversal of the usual trading exploitation of natives by outsiders. Clandestine prospecting was also tightly controlled. There were five guard posts around the perimeter of the huge Kayapó reserve, young bachelors did monthly tours of duty on frontier patrols, and the tribe's plane made regular flights to spot intruders.

The Kayapó learned to cope with their new wealth. Indians eventually ran everything in Gorotire village, including the management of Funai's post and the radio station. Their leaders had bank accounts in the town of Redenção and the city of Belém; the village bought a house in Redenção to accommodate Indians shopping or doing business there; and they owned a plane with a salaried pilot. Gorotire chiefs went to the town every Tuesday to shop for the tribe (by pickup truck in the dry season or plane in the rainy months). They bought everything, from clothing, tools, and batteries to frozen chickens, watermelons, and basic foods. The Gorotire operated twelve vehicles, outboard motors for their boats, and a generator – all maintained by Indians and one Brazilian mechanic. Indian nurses ran the medical dispensary.

The Indians made imaginative use of camcorders and videos to film and record their traditional ceremonies. One chief told Terence Turner that this was 'so that our children will see them and not forget'. In March

1986, 600 Indians of Gorotire village watched a three-hour video film shot by the thirty-year-old Paiakan: it showed the Minister of the Interior promising Raoni (of the Mentuktire Kayapó) the fulfilment of various Indian demands including the sacking of Apoena Meirelles as President of Funai. Thus, the Gorotire systematically changed from dependence on outside technology to its exploitation for their own ends. 'They converted [these appliances] into fundamentals of the community's autonomy.' They saw ownership of these manufactured gadgets as a way of eliminating any cultural inequality between them and Brazilians. Chiefs also used their income to visit other Kayapó groups, former enemies with whom they now developed cultural affinities.

Even religion became more indigenous, with an Indian conducting Protestant services on Sundays but making no effort to convert other members of the tribe. Thus the number of Gorotire *crentes* halved in two decades, and Turner wrote in 1993 that 'the Gorotire seem to be further than ever from conversion to Christianity'. There was a corresponding revival in shamanism. Western medicine had finally halted the ravages of imported diseases; so that the Indians could return to shamanistic healing, smoking out illness with tobacco and deploying their rich pharmacopoeia of forest plants. However, the Kayapó's ancient circular villages, whose moieties symbolized the cosmos, gave way to rectilinear layouts. This coincided with a new vision of the universe in which Brazilians were admitted to be fully human and social beings, and the Kayapó 'ceased to be the exclusive paradigm of humanity'.

All this was part of the general revival of indigenous consciousness of the latter part of the twentieth century. Terence Turner was impressed by 'how many tribal peoples of Amazonia have succeeded, against all expectations, in maintaining their social, cultural and ethnic identities. Many native communities have offered effective resistance against aggression by the national society. They increased their populations, and demonstrated a surprising capacity to incorporate and to dominate aspects of national culture – from the Portuguese language to medicine and telecommunications – without thereby "losing their culture".'

There was a price to pay for this rapid change. The Kayapó saw some of their land stripped bare and irredeemably churned up and their rivers polluted by unbridled mining operations. Bishop Erwin Krautler, President of CIMI, was worried that the sudden influx of wealth 'is creating a strong dependency on the money, culture, and consumer goods of the whites.' But Kroy, the Gorotire in charge of taxing miners at Maria Bonita garimpo, was not unduly concerned. 'We lose some things but we gain others, and in general our life has improved. Today, we have refrigerators, television, and good clothes; but the penalty is to have our rivers polluted with mercury.'

Kroy was perhaps unduly complacent. In addition to gouging riverbeds and devastating surrounding vegetation, miners used massive quantities of mercury. They found that mercury amalgamated with gold dust and could easily be separated from gravel and slurry. The mercury was then burned off and the gold remained. But mercury is non-degradable and highly toxic. It was estimated that Amazonian garimpeiros used 140 tons a year: most was released into the atmosphere, but a fifth entered the rivers whence it passed to human beings from drinking water or fish. A medical team in 1994 found that Kayapó babies were born with dangerously high levels of mercury, absorbed in the womb and from their mothers' milk.

Gold was not the only source of wealth and environmental degradation. The Kayapó of Kikretum village at the north of the main reserve, and the Xikrin to the north-east of it, both allowed loggers to ravage their forests by removing quantities of mahogany. Since mahogany trees are widely dispersed in the forests, their extraction caused terrible devastation. In 1984 Funai negotiated a licence to sell 8,000 cubic metres (282,528 cubic feet) of mahogany for a payment equivalent to $140,000: the Xikrin were initially to receive none of this, but they learned about it and got the royalty money. The Xikrin then negotiated a disastrous contract with the Bannach timber company. Lux Vidal wrote that 'the Xikrin of Cateté exploit timber; but they themselves are exploited by the timber-loggers'. In 1988 alone, the Kayapó sold some 70,000 cubic metres (2,472,000 cubic feet) of timber and the Xikrin reserve sold 8,000 cubic metres (390 cubic feet). However, Darrell Posey defended the Kayapó's granting of licences to cut mahogany. This was partly because, unable to count much beyond ten, they could not grasp what was meant by felling 10,000 trees. But it was also because they wanted revenue to finance roads to their villages. 'They did want contact . . . This idea that native peoples hung around and were always in some stagnant state before they were contacted by white people is just not true. They like change, they like things that are new, they want to see what's going on . . . They're no different from us in that sense.'

Socially, some tribal elders had their authority undermined by the community's collective dealings with the Brazilians. An elite of a few chiefs and 'young technocrats' gained power by controlling tribal finances and the investment of the new wealth. One such was 'Colonel' Tutu Pombo, chief of the northern village of Kikretum, an ebullient, Western-ized leader who amassed a personal fortune from logging and mining concessions. Tutu Pombo's life epitomized the violent changes that were buffeting his people. Born in 1932, he was soon orphaned (either from disease or white men's bullets) and was brought up by settlers. He worked as a teenager in Brazil-nut gathering, and was captured in 1947 in a Kuben-Kran-Kégn raid that killed his white companions. He fled back to the frontier and helped both Pedro da Silva in his contact of the Kuben-Kran-Kégn and Chico Meirelles of the Menkragnoti. The SPI rewarded him for these services with a chief's title. In 1969 'Chief' Pombo told the Funai agent about a clandestine airstrip built by prospectors; these lured Pombo into an ambush and pistol-whipped him with rifle butts; and the Kayapó immediately organized a reprisal that killed three garimpeiros. But Tutu Pombo lost a power struggle for supremacy of the Gorotire, and in 1976 led his followers down the Fresco to found Kikretum village near the site of the old Nova Olinda.

Massive deposits of gold and reserves of mahogany were discovered near Kikretum, and Tutu Pombo exploited them with gusto. The period from 1982 to 1992 was

> ten years of veritable frenzy in Kikretum village, with Pombo as the pivot in the super-accelerated process of contact and shock with Brazilian society. On one side was a mass of mining prospectors, daring loggers, many traders, doctors, and owners of private clinics. On the other side, some 350 Kayapó who had little contact with the whites, immersed in a sea of consumer goods that was as unexpected as it was novel. This was the milieu in which Colonel Tutu Pombo flourished . . . [but at a price to his people]. In 1992 six children died for lack of resources – the Indians could not pay for medical treatment – and the community went hungry. As if this were not enough, the Fresco river was soon totally polluted, with a high level of mercury poisoning, and parts of the forest were devastated by the tractors of various timber companies who continued to pillage that region.

For all his Western trappings – designer dark glasses, gold watch, baseball cap, and private plane inscribed 'Kayapó Indigenous Nation Dudjutukty' – Pombo kept his long hair flowing and was a forceful champion of the Kayapó. So when he died of a stroke on the way home from the UN's Earth Summit in Rio de Janeiro in 1992, he was mourned by his people.

The forceful Kayapó now took their cause to the outside world. When in 1985 Brazil emerged from two decades of military rule, the Kayapó were at the forefront of efforts to gain benefits for Indians in the new democratic constitution. A steady stream of Kayapó spokesmen went on lobbying missions to Brasília, and deputies of the Constituent Assembly visited Gorotire village in a plane chartered by the tribe to be told about its problems. Poropot Kayapó was photographed in Brasília fixing a feather headdress onto the bald head of the Assembly's venerable leader, Ulysses Guimarães.

All seemed to be going well until 1988, when a formidable new threat confronted the Kayapó. There was a proposal to build a string of hydro-electric dams on the lower Xingu river, to harness the rapids where the river drops off the geologically ancient Central Brazilian Shield towards the main Amazon river. By flooding vast areas of forest in this flat region, it was hoped to produce as much energy as was generated by the gigantic Tucuruí dam on the Tocantins.

In January 1988 Funai gave permission for Darrell Posey to take Chiefs Paulinho Paiakan and Kube-I to an environmental symposium at the University of Florida. The three then went to Washington, to persuade the World Bank not to finance the disastrous Xingu dams, and to appear before the Human-Rights Alliance of Congress. Paiakan's dignity and determination and his forceful oratory (translated by Posey) impressed the Americans, so that funding for the proposed dams was denied. Back in Brazil, the National Security Council was furious at this setback to the government's cherished dam project. In March 1988 the three travellers were arraigned under an old 'Foreigners' Law' that forbade non-Brazilians from damaging the national interest. Paiakan and Darrell Posey appeared before a federal judge in August; but the judge refused to hear Kube-I because, wearing only shorts and body paint, he was incorrectly dressed. Indian sympathizers and the media gleefully exploited the 'racism' of the judge's dress ruling, and above all the absurdity of two indigenous chiefs being charged as 'foreigners' in the land of their ancestors. Four hundred Kayapó warriors in headdresses and body paint paraded in front of the Forum in Belém, and Paiakan was present at a press conference organized by CEDI in São Paulo. When the State of Pará asked the anthropologist Heraldo Maués of its Federal University to give an expert opinion he refused to do so, saying: 'I cannot possibly understand how two Brazilian Indians and an American anthropologist can be tried under the Foreigners' Law for a fundamental scientific opinion that they may have stated in the United States.' The case was dismissed by the federal Supreme Tribunal in February 1989.

Paiakan made a triumphant visit to London, Milan, and Rome to mobilize opposition to the Xingu dams. He was sponsored by the tribal-rights organization Survival International and the skin-care chain the Body Shop. This large business felt that it could help the Kayapó by using their palm-nut oil for hair conditioner – this was proclaimed as a better (albeit infinitely smaller) source of income than gold-mining or logging concessions. The Body Shop derived the greatest possible publicity from its Kayapó friends, with huge pictures of the handsome Chief Pykaty-Re (Pukatire) making a thumbs-up sign in the windows of its branches in forty-six countries. When he learned about this, the Chief was angry about the way in which his image had been exploited.

In December 1987 the British pop star Sting (former lead singer of the group Police, now solo) started a world tour with a concert for 200,000 people in Rio de Janeiro's gigantic Maracanã football stadium. It was noted that his audience was as large as the entire indigenous population of Brazilian Amazonia. Indian sympathizers took Sting to the Xingu, and the rock star was appalled by the desolation as he approached the sanctuary. For three hours his plane flew over 'a land mutilated by progress. The great forest had been hacked down . . . In its place lay a desolation of dust and ashes, the ghosts of giant forest trees . . . Now there was only the scorched earth and the raw wounds of mines and landing strips. Suddenly the wasteland ended in a giant wall of trees . . . Sting and [his partner] Trudie Styler stared in amazement at the stark contrast between the dead planet they had just flown over and the virgin beauty of the rain forest.' The visitors were naturally enchanted by the beauty of the Xingu and the romance of its Indians. They particularly liked the forceful Chief Raoni of the Mentuktire, now a tall and dignified man 'with shoulder-length hair, ceremonial beads, a lip-disc and Levi's'. So, at another huge concert in São Paulo in October 1988, Sting defied the Foreigners' Law by making an impassioned appeal for the rights of indigenous peoples.

Back in England, Sting founded the Rainforest Foundation, determined to help the Indians by doing more than singing for their environmentally fashionable cause. He and Raoni met Brazil's civilian President José Sarney in February 1989 and won a promise to create and demarcate a Menkragnoti reserve. This was a massive victory. It created a huge Indian area, adding almost 5,000,000 hectares (19,300 square miles) of forests and rivers between the Xingu and Iriri. This gave the Kayapó nation a triangular territory as extensive as the Xingu park itself, larger than many member states of the United Nations. As the *International Herald Tribune* writer Juan de Onis noted, the Menkragnoti reserve was 'the missing link for a "Kayapó corridor" between Mato Grosso and Pará that would create a natural barrier to forest destruction . . . in a critical zone that is surrounded by cattle ranchers, colonization projects, mining camps and lumber mills.' The joining of the Kayapó and Xingu lands formed an immense 133,240 square kilometre (51,430 square mile) triangle of protected land – an area larger than England – in the geographical centre of Brazil.

Sting made Raoni Honorary President of his Rainforest Foundation and in 1989 took him on a highly successful fundraising journey to sixteen countries in five continents. The highlights were a televised meeting with President François Mitterrand of France, at which Raoni said, in a mixture of French and Portuguese, 'Help us to protect our lands,' and an audience with Pope John Paul II. The resulting picture of a Brazilian Indian standing between the Pope and a glamorous pop idol gave Brazilians a new image of their indigenous people, in sharp contrast to poverty-stricken tribals at the margin of frontier society.

Sting donated the proceeds of this promotional visit and his own concerts to the Rainforest Foundation, so that it could give $1.3 million to help Funai demarcate the great new Menkragnoti Indian Area. There were three years of legal action before the new reserve was ready. This demarcation was an elaborate operation, involving scores of workmen, a plane, two helicopters, boats, and trucks. Five tons of sensitive surveying equipment, global-positioning systems, and satellite imagery were taken into the field to map the reserve's coordinates. It took three teams three months in late 1992 to cut a perimeter swathe and fix boundary markers. The teams were based at the villages of Kapot, Kubenkokre, and Pukanu, each supervised by Kayapó or Xavante Indians. Survival International was unhappy about this large sum being devoted to demarcation work that was the responsibility of Funai, rather than to other indigenous aid, and to the fact that it all went to the richest indigenous people in Brazil. But Funai might have balked at the expenditure and would certainly have delayed. The demarcation did ensure the rapid ratification of the Menkragnoti area that completed the massive corridor of indigenous lands in the heart of Brazil.

The proposal to build six hydroelectric dams along the Xingu and Iriri had not disappeared. The Brazilian authorities were still seeking funding for them, despite the success of Posey and the Kayapó chiefs in getting the World Bank to refuse finance and the subsequent fiasco of the attempt to prosecute them. Paiakan and CEDI organized a protest meeting at the Gorotire village in November 1988. This decided to hold a great rally at Altamira on the Xingu, to coincide with the Kayapó's big *baridjumoko* maize festival there, and because Altamira was close to the first proposed dam alongside the Kararaô Kayapó reserve. Letters were sent to tribal leaders and indigenous sympathizers inviting them to the gathering on 24 February 1989. Sixteen chiefs, including Ropni (Raoni) and Kremoro from the Xingu Mentuktire and Tutu Pombo from Kikretum, signed these invitations. They asked for the recipient's 'presence and advice, which are very important to us Kayapó and to the Arara, Asuriní, Parakanã, Araweté, Kararaô, Juruna, Xipáia, Kuruáia, and Xikrin of Bacajá who will also be present.' In desperation, the power company Eletronorte took forty Kayapó to visit the gigantic Tucuruí dam on the Tocantins. It was a public-relations disaster. The Indians were unimpressed by one of the world's largest hydroelectric projects. They utterly rejected the engineers' reasons for damming the Xingu, and demanded instead to know what the company proposed to do about the Parakanã and Gavião lands it had already flooded from Tucuruí.

The Altamira meeting was brilliantly organized. The attendance of men from every Kayapó village was guaranteed because the maize festival is an annual gathering, equivalent to a great collective hunt. Paiakan flew in on 20 February to a hero's welcome of the traditional Kayapó weeping ritual, and a media frenzy of 121 reporters. On the following day, 5,000 local people paraded *in favour* of the Kararaô dam, because they wanted the jobs in building it and the subsequent energy royalties. But all the press attention went to the protest meeting. This included representatives of twenty-four tribes as well as 300 Brazilian and foreign ecologists, politicians, trade unionists, and human-rights and indigenous activists.

One televised highlight occurred when Eletronorte's chief engineer was trying to justify the dams. Paiakan's cousin Tuira strode up to the platform and brandished a machete in an elegant sweep that ended with a tap on the hapless businessman's face. With devastating logic, she told him: 'You are a liar. We don't need electricity. Electricity won't give us food. We need the rivers to flow freely – our future depends on them. We need our forests to hunt and gather in. We do not want your dam.' The engineer spoke of further studies and of economic benefits from the dams. The Indians would have none of it. They pointed out that Eletronorte had neglected to consult *them*, that other hydroelectric dams had failed, and that Altamira itself was a wretched place where 'conditions are terrible and the people live miserable lives. Is this what you are offering us? Is this progress?' Thousands of years of adaptation had taught the indigenous people how to live there successfully. 'Don't talk to us about relieving our "poverty". We are not poor: we are the richest people in Brazil. We are not wretched. We are Indians.' The great gathering, the largest such event in Brazilian history, lasted for five days and ended with two hours of ceremonial dancing by the Kayapó.

The Altamira meeting issued a moving environmental declaration.

The indigenous nations of the Xingu, together with relatives from many parts of Brazil and the world, affirm that we must respect our mother nature. We urge that the forests and rivers, which are our brothers, should not be destroyed. We decided that we do not want the construction of dams on the Xingu or on other Amazonian rivers, because they threaten indigenous nations and other riverine settlers. For a long time, white men have assaulted our thinking and the spirit of our ancestors. This must now stop. Our territories are sacred sites of our people and the dwelling-place of our creator: they must not be violated.

The Altamira gathering achieved its objective. The proposed dams on the Xingu were not financed or built – although they resurfaced thirteen years later in a plan to build the world's third-largest hydroelectric plant, at Belo Monte near Altamira, with resulting flooding of immense areas of forest and indigenous land.

There were also positive moves during these years for non-Kayapó tribes whose lands had been violated by the Transamazonica highway. The Parakanã, Asuriní, Araweté, and Arara gained contiguous reserves totalling over 2.5 million hectares (some 10,000 square miles) south of the Transamazonica on either side of Altamira. This large area abutted, to the south and south-east, against 1,663,000 hectares (6,420 square miles) of two Kayapó reserves, of the Xikrin of Bacajá and the Kararaô.

Paiakan continued to be an influential indigenous leader, awarded international medals, appointed as an adviser to the President of Funai, and lauded by the *Washington Post* as 'a man who would save the world'. However, the important Brazilian newsmagazine *Veja* took an anti-environmental stance and ridiculed Paiakan as the leader of a mercantilist and acculturated people. So *Veja* could hardly believe its luck when, on 31 May 1992 on the eve of UNCED, an eighteen-year-old girl, Sílvia Letícia Ferreira, accused Paiakan of raping her. Without awaiting details of this complicated case, *Veja* published a cover picture of Paiakan emblazoned: 'THE SAVAGE. The chief who is the symbol of ecological purity tortures and rapes a white student, and immediately flees back to his tribe'. Long before any trial, the Globo television company distorted an interview with Paiakan to make it appear that he admitted committing the rape after heavy drinking and that his wife Irekran had caught them in flagrante and beaten the girl to punish her. Before even hearing Paiakan's side of the story, the Body Shop issued a statement deploring the conduct of the man they had entertained and, some would say, exploited.

The case proved to be a legal minefield, and it seemed to drag on interminably. At first it was unclear whether Paiakan could be tried under ordinary Brazilian law: it was finally decided that he was sufficiently detribalized to do so, but that his wife Irekran still enjoyed legal immunity as an Indian. The testimony of the only independent witness was full of inconsistencies; the medical examination of Sílvia Letícia showed only that she had been beaten (by Irekran) but probably not raped. Local witnesses told how they used to frequent Paiakan's house and that he was of good character. In November 1994, a judge cleared the Kayapó chief because 'there is insufficient evidence, either material or from witnesses, that Paiakan raped the student'. But the Pará state prosecutor did not give up. Years later, in December 1998, Paulinho Paiakan was sentenced to six years' imprisonment for the rape. Paiakan's villagers of A'ukre mobilized to defend their leader. The sentence was later commuted to banishment from his tribe, and appeals to superior federal tribunals in 1999 failed to reverse this decision. Sympathizers pointed out that whites who raped or murdered Indians never seemed to be convicted. For instance, soldiers accused of gang-raping Tukano women on the Upper Rio Negro, at the time of Paiakan's alleged crime, were cleared because their commanding officer said that the Indian women had 'provoked' his men. Paiakan's rape case effectively ended his brilliant career as a spokesman for his people.

The Xikrin, whose territory lies to the north-east of the main block of Kayapó reserves, became steadily more commercially savvy. They asked technicians from CEDI/ISA to help them and Funai devise a 'Xikrin Project' for the sustainable exploitation of their resources, particularly Brazil nuts and mahogany. Collecting Brazil nuts has always had strong social significance for the Xikrin, both the core community on the Cateté and those who had moved to the Bacajá. A revival in this profitable activity led to a reaffirmation of tribal consciousness. 'It involved their leaving the sedentary life of the village, organizing themselves for work (in groups according either to parentage or age), gathering the raw material, hunting and fishing in inaccessible corners – which meant regaining contact with their rivers, rapids, and waterfalls and rediscovering their territory and traditional trails, even within areas owned by the [Carajás mining giant] Companhia Vale do Rio Doce and the Aquiri/Tapirapé national forest – and thus transmitting knowledge to the younger and most inexperienced. This is extremely important to the Xikrin.' After this Project had functioned successfully for about a decade, the Xikrin asked for help in improving the management, processing, and marketing of their nuts. Consultants were brought in to devise a 'vertical' structure for the Brazil-nut trade. Their research included taking Indians to see the extractive reserve named after Chico Mendes in Acre, and some of its rubber-tappers went to help train Xikrin. There were setbacks, including the death of a key expert. But in 1997 the Xikrin themselves mobilized their entire community in a massive effort to gather and transport the harvest (including clearing the Cateté river so that they could use boats) and its sale, after hard bargaining, in the city of Marabá. This collective effort continues, subject to fluctuations in the size of the crop and its market value. Meanwhile, Funai helped the Bacajá Xikrin to collect, process (with new machetes to split the tough nut cases), transport, and sell their crop in Altamira.

A similar project to improve sustainable logging of mahogany by the Indians themselves had a rockier history, thanks in part to suspicion of ISA's motives by Funai. When Funai's President failed to respond to repeated appeals by the Xikrin, they took direct action – in typical Kayapó fashion. In 1998, 'after strong political mobilization, which culminated in the blockade of the road between Parauapebas and the Carajás mine, the Xikrin gained the formal and written support of the President of Funai.' In October 2000, suitably ornamented and club-wielding Xikrin men and women performed a ceremonial dance around a truck loaded with mahogany logs. This became a new 'Timber Festival', to celebrate the tribe's gaining control of the entire logging process. A civil action against illegal invasions by timber companies was successful. A forest-management plan and Timber Exploitation Project were devised, and in 1995 the Cateté Xikrin formed a Bep-Nói Association (after the *Bep* men's naming ceremony) to protect their culture. However, tensions continue. Every summer, the Xikrin are besieged by mahogany-loggers trying to negotiate licences. A new road takes trucks loaded with timber from the Cateté village to the frontier town of Tucumã (between the Xikrin and Kayapó indigenous areas). The anthropologist Isabelle Vidal Giannini observed severe damage to the forest, but found that 'discussing the subject with the Indians is difficult, since they are clearly aware of the risks to the forest and game animals but remain seduced by the profits.' Mahogany dealers pay partly in food and supplies, but also in cash that is thought to be monopolized by a few men. Funai and the police failed to expose or put a stop to this traffic.

By the end of the century, the Kayapó had generally ceased internecine feuding and they presented a formidable united front. Many of their leaders proved to be natural politicians and media personalities on a national and international stage. They continued their headline-grabbing actions, exploiting their immunity as 'legal minors'. In 1995 the Xavante invaded the office of President Márcio Santilli of Funai (a former pro-

Indian activist), complaining of his bad management and thus hastening his resignation. They did the same in June 1999 to another President, ex-Senator Márcio Lacerda, who escaped in a taxi and later resigned. In April 2000, Megaron (who had been director of the Xingu park) criticized Funai's President Carlos Marés and the NGO ISA (with which Marés had fought very effectively for indigenous rights) for not doing enough to 'defend Indian traditions or demarcate lands'. This was one of several reasons for Marés's resignation; but he was replaced by a less-sympathetic president.

In that same month the Kayapó of Baú reserve kidnapped sixteen tourists who were fishing in their waters, to protest about Funai's failure to demarcate their heavily invaded reserve. This was another publicity coup, which harmed no one but achieved a promise of immediate action. In May 2000, Chief Raoni was in France again, meeting President Chirac and gaining massive television exposure, to attract funding for an institute for ecological development of the Xingu. Thus, in a series of victories, the Kayapó won legal titles to great tracts of their homelands, often got their preferred candidates in charge of Funai, and some even coped successfully with sudden wealth from mining or forestry.

In some respects the Jê-speaking Kayapó and Xavante nations had started the twentieth century less sophisticated than Tupi-speakers. Despite the brilliance of their ornaments, their elaborate beliefs, and their environmental lore, the Kayapó had been less skilled as farmers, potters, basket- and hammock-makers, boatmen, fishermen, or even hunters. But they ended the century at the forefront of indigenous activism. This was the result of their warlike traditions, their innate toughness, their moral resilience, and their indifference to alcohol and hallucinogens. It was also achieved by the political skills of leaders such as Raoni, Megaron, Mário Juruna, and the unfortunate Paiakan.

These warrior tribes became almost too aggressive in flexing their political muscles. At the end of the century, there was some backlash against them. The 8,000 Xavante 'have become famous for their mania for launching invasions of Funai's headquarters and threatening its officials.' They forced the resignation of the lawyer Júlio Gaiger as President of Funai in 1997, connived with his successor Sulivan Silvestre to oust officials who tried to stand up to their demands, and argued with the pro-Indian politician Márcio Lacerda when he was President in 1998. Such spectacular stunts annoyed other tribes, who accused the Xavante of gaining advantages for themselves. Another President whom they disliked, the distinguished anthropologist Roque Laraia, resigned in 2000 after only a month in office because 'it is impossible to administer Funai with the

Xavante in their present mood'. Laraia felt that the majority of Indians were deprived of assistance because one tribe was monopolizing the Foundation's management time and resources. The Kayapó then demanded an indigenous area known as Badjônkôre, claiming that it was their traditional territory. Even the pro-Indian ISA research institute regarded this as too greedy. The Kayapó already had over 10 million hectares (38,600 square miles) for fewer than 6,000 people; they had not been seen in Badjônkôre in recent decades; and the suspicion was that, having sold the mahogany on their homelands, they wanted access to more of these lucrative hardwoods.

15. Brazilian Guiana

The tribes in the forests between Roraima and the Atlantic seaboard survived into the twentieth century relatively unmolested. There was serious depopulation from disease and slavery near the main Amazon during the colonial era, but the forests and black-water rivers north of the lower Amazon do not contain *Hevea brasiliensis* trees, so they escaped the ravages of the rubber boom. The rivers that flow south from the geologically ancient Guiana Shield (which is Brazil's northern frontier) are relatively short, so that they tumble down waterfalls and rapids that proved to be an effective barrier to riverine exploration. Remote from the rest of the country and with few open savannahs, the roadless region known as Brazilian Guiana had nothing to attract settlers. As late as 1983, a map by the authoritative research institute CEDI still marked many areas as 'occupied by isolated Indians'.

In 1914–15 William Curtis Farabee of the University of Pennsylvania's museum led a remarkable expedition across this difficult terrain and along some of its rapid-infested rivers. He had exciting but cordial encounters with various Carib-speaking tribes. For almost five months his team was among Indians who had never seen a white man, or clothing, guns, or matches. After five arduous weeks of travel from Boa Vista, Farabee's expedition reached the southernmost Waiwái village, and found that these people were famous among surrounding tribes for the quality of their manioc graters, and for their hunting dogs which were carefully trained, exercised daily, lodged on platforms high above the ground, and pampered more than animals among any other Indians. Both commodities were traded from tribe to tribe, over great distances. When the expedition arrived, the Waiwái were entertaining Parikotó visitors from far to the east, with elaborate dances. 'The women catch hands and dance around a small circle, singing to the rhythm of the dance. The men, decorated with palm leaves, dance around the women in a larger circle.' The dancers were plied with drink, and entertained by the antics of 'clowns' in peculiar dress. The visitors were delighted by the hospitality they received, and by the beauty of the Waiwái warriors' body paint and long hair (seventy centimetres (twenty-eight inches) long) held in handsomely decorated hair tubes.

These southern Waiwái were decimated by an influenza epidemic in the 1920s and many of the survivors migrated northwards to the upper Essequibo in British Guiana. Apart from this, little had changed in the region when another American expedition in 1938 crossed the Acaraí Hills from British Guiana into Brazil, or when the British botanist Nicholas Guppy made the same journey with Waiwái and Wapixana Indians in 1953. Guppy's team built a huge bark canoe, and managed to reach the Mawayena group of Parikotó on a headwater of the Mapuera. This tribe was thrilled to meet white men, of whom it had heard only dimly. Guppy was charmed by the warmth of the Indians' welcome. The visitors shook hands with every member of the tribe, even feather-ornamented infants, and were then served a drink of crushed yams in large glazed earthenware bowls. They marvelled at the tenderness shown to a menagerie of pets in the village – from chubby capybara rodents to parakeets – by people who were ruthless hunters.

The isolation of tribes on the upper Mapuera and Nhamundá rivers in Brazil changed abruptly during the 1950s, with the advent of aggressive Protestant missionaries from British Guiana. When Nicholas Guppy flew into Gunn's Strip on the Essequibo at the south of that colony, he saw amid the handsome Waiwái 'another astoundingly clad group – the missionaries, two men and one wife, in vivid jitterbug shirts'. This was Claude Leavitt of the Unevangelized Fields Mission. He was frighteningly frank about his violent proselytizing. The Indians' souls '"are in danger, and we must save their souls for Christ . . . There is a terrible lot of sin here, unbelievable. Why, at times the Indians . . . get drunk and – ugh! – they are quite disgusting. They do things that are too terrible to talk about. Do you know that sometimes they may go off with a woman who is not even their own wife? We intend to stamp out all drinking and dancing, and we have already managed to stop a good deal of smoking."' A Jesuit who visited the mission was surprised when his cigarette was smashed from his lips with the remark: 'You have brought the devil to our village!' He later learned that the prohibition on tobacco was because Waiwái shamans used it in their healing ceremonies.

The missionaries tried to change Waiwái farming and eating habits. They wanted them to plant vegetables in favour in the West – tomatoes, onions, lettuce, etc. – to raise chickens and pigs, and to stop fermenting manioc into 'sinful' cauim beer. All these attempts failed. The Indians disliked unfamiliar vegetables, and all those planted by the missionaries themselves were promptly eaten by insects. The Waiwái liked rearing chickens and pigs, but only as beloved domestic pets that it would be abhorrent and cannibalistic to eat.

The missionary Claude Leavitt openly admitted to Guppy that it was the Waiwái and other tribes inside Brazil that really interested them. They had established a mission called Kanashen (meaning 'God Loves You') close to the frontier. They sent converted Waiwái south to '"act as seeds, spreading the Word . . . We are trying to get the Brazilian Indians to leave their villages and come and settle over here. We are offering them beads, knives, mirrors – everything they love."' Native preachers warned their Carib brethren that 'the world will end in an enormous conflagration, but they could show the way to salvation and a better life'. The campaign was very successful. In only three years, the missionaries at Kanashen swelled their native congregation from about 80 to 250, by attracting Indians north from the Mapuera river.

One Waiwái village called Yakayaka resisted the Christian message, because its shaman Ewká was too sure of his tribe's beliefs. Danish anthropologists in the early 1960s explored the Waiwái's rich spirituality, based on the notion of the soul (*ekati*) and the spirits of human beings, their ancestors, and animals. At death, a person's ekati changes and moves into upper levels of the cosmos alongside his ancestors – a clear belief in the afterlife. The tribe had a rich mythology of origin legends and supernatural beings, and its shamans played an important role in organizing rituals and collective farming and other activities, healing, and transmitting knowledge of medicinal plants and the natural world.

The Protestant missionaries Neill and Robert Hawkins realized that the conversion of the shaman Ewká was critical. Although a young man of only eighteen, he was a natural leader who had great spiritual and political influence in his village. He had achieved an impressive number of cures, and he never used his shamanistic powers to bewitch his opponents. The Americans learned that Ewká was identified as possessing the spirit of a peccary, which he was forbidden to eat. So they challenged him to eat the meat of this forest pig, and guaranteed that Jesus his Saviour would protect him from any harm if he did so. When he survived, Ewká was forced to admit that Jesus was the more powerful spirit. At the same time, the missionaries used their Western medicine to save a sick girl whom Ewká had failed to cure. The shaman was having serious doubts about his powers, and this coincided with deaths (in a canoe accident and from disease) of other shamans. Ewká therefore underwent a Pauline conversion to Christianity. In 1956 he migrated with his village to the Protestant mission; and his prestige was such that many others followed. Once at Kanashen, Ewká was impressed by the Protestants' condemnation of alcoholic drink. So he organized a festival using only soft drinks and told his people: 'We are going to have a period of games, and let us see who can run fastest, jump highest, shoot arrows better.' Not surprisingly, the sober Waiwái excelled in these sports.

The conversion of tribal leaders was not the missionaries' only weapon. They also relied on the power of medicine to convince the Waiwái of their spiritual powers. This tribe had been seriously depopulated in the nineteenth century, by inter-tribal massacres and then by diseases such as malaria. When Guppy was there in 1952, he saw the Waiwái afflicted by new epidemics: influenza, various forms of pneumonia, and even venereal diseases transmitted from savannah tribes. The missionaries at Kanashen told him how hard they were working to treat these new scourges. When a woman died of pneumonia, the pastors told the English botanist: '"It is most worrying that she should have died, just when the Indians are beginning to come across and live round the mission. They will think that an evil spirit has killed her. It may seriously interfere with our work."' But the mission in British Guiana grew steadily, by attracting Indians from other Carib-speaking groups within Brazil, and by eradicating infanticide whereby the Waiwái used to kill any infants whose omens were bad. Kanashen had a population of 450 by 1970.

Alarmed by this exodus, the Brazilian authorities in 1962–63 organized 'Operation Mapuera', a tripartite enterprise of air force, Catholic missionaries, and Indians, to try to recover some of 'our Indians'. This was led by the genial and energetic Air Force Colonel João Camarão. He loved and admired Indians and often had them staying with him in Belém. But he was also impressed by the apparently disinterested dedication of foreign missionaries. So he achieved little on the Mapuera, beyond establishing friendly relations between the Brazilian air force and the Protestants at Kanashen. The missionary Irene Benson recalled translating for the Brazilian officer while he tried to persuade Ewká to return to the Mapuera and also to help contact isolated Indians.

Kanashen finally succumbed to politics. The British colony achieved independence as Guyana in 1968, and its first Prime Minister, Cheddi Jagan, was a socialist who disliked the fundamentalist American missionaries in the south of his country. So in 1971 the aggressive Protestants were expelled.

The Christianized Waiwái dispersed, with many returning to their former villages in Brazil or Suriname. Ewká took his people back to the Mapuera river, in1974; his brother Yakutá and another indigenous pastor organized a move by fifteen families to the Anauá river north of the

Waimiri Atroari territory in Roraima. The expelled missionaries also went to Brazil, some to join the Waiwái Baptist mission in Roraima, others to an Evangelical mission on the Mapuera. The Indians who returned to Brazil said that they did so because of the poor soil and forests in Guyana, the high cost of goods in the new republic, and Guyanese abuse of their women. But they remained ardent Protestants.

There were further contacts with isolated Indians during the decades of the missionaries' charm offensive. Ethnographers identified five further villages of Parikotó in the forests of the upper Nhamundá, and there were sporadic encounters between these and Brazil-nut collectors and timber men. The German Franciscan missionary Protásio Frikel (who was attached to the famous Goeldi Museum in Belém do Pará) contacted a group of eighty handsome Hixkaryana on the Mapuera in the early 1950s. The Summer Institute of Linguistics also entered the region. In 1968 these missionary-linguists gathered the Hixkaryana into a village called Cassauá on the Nhamundá, where they flourished in numbers thanks to the SIL's medical and health programmes and to its Indians' efforts to attract other groups. Funai opened a base at Cassauá in 1971; and six years later the SIL's linguist-missionaries departed, when their Institute's licence to operate in Brazil expired.

Among the many contacts with isolated Indian groups, one was remarkable, because it was undertaken entirely by Indians. In 1981, the Protestant Ewká on his own initiative cut a long trail for about 300 kilometres (190 miles) from his Waiwái's new village, Yxamná, on the Mapuera north towards the old Kanashen mission in Guyana. This picada crossed the Jatapuzinho river as well as a new highway, the Perimetral Norte ('Northern Perimeter') that the Brazilian government was trying to cut, west–east from Roraima towards Amapá parallel to the country's northern frontier. In the forest near Guyana, Ewká's people met an isolated group that called itself Karafawyana. The Waiwái themselves launched an 'attraction campaign', inviting tribal leaders back to Yxamná village and showering them with presents. One part of the Karafawyana succumbed and was integrated into the Waiwái; the other part of the new tribe chose to remain independent and isolated. In the following year, 1982, Funai sent a sertanista on another expedition to contact further Indians; but the effort was mainly by Waiwái from the Mapuera, led by Ewká, and from Kashimin village in Roraima led by his brother Yakutá. The Christian Indians continued to send out contact expeditions almost every year in the later decades of the twentieth century. When a Brazilian anthropologist asked them why they did it, they replied: 'We believe that those

Indians must be sick and suffering greatly.' They recalled the epidemics that had devastated them during the years before their missionary conversion.

The successes of the Protestant missionary effort profoundly changed the Waiwái and other Carib-speaking tribes. This was sledgehammer acculturation. Communal huts – conical thatched structures of sophisticated architecture – were replaced by family houses, and this diminished both the unity of the group and the influence of its chiefs. Villages were laid out on a new pattern, without a central hut. The system of hereditary chiefs and shamans was replaced by rule by native pastors, keen crentes who had been educated by the missionaries. Ewká was a prime example of such a leader. These pastors in turn appointed councils of ten or twelve converts, who met every Sunday to discuss tribal affairs. 'This group sanctions norms of conduct and imposes punishments on transgressors – from cleaning the village, to the suspension of hunting or collective fishing activities.' A large temple was built in the heart of the village, roofed in traditional thatch and alongside the missionaries' houses. There are now three services a week, one of them only for women. 'In addition to prayers, the [fourteen] pastors give advice on good behaviour (for instance, condemnation of adultery), information about events that complement their worship (such as a meeting with representatives of Funai) and they allocate collective work each week (for example, clearing the landing strip) . . . The mission has [in 1995] already translated the New Testament into Waiwái and is in the final phase of translating the Old Testament. Almost all Indians possess a Bible.' Indians trained by the MEVA evangelical organization taught in the school, under the direction of the missionary Irene Benson, and manned the well-stocked medical dispensary. As with many tribes whose land and health were reasonably secure, the Waiwái were short of money for their basic needs. So young men travelled far afield, to the big cities in Guyana and along the Amazon, to try to sell their artefacts or earn money as casual labourers. At the start of the new millennium there was a plan to build a hydroelectric dam, Porteira on the Mapuera, which the Waiwái welcomed as it might bring jobs and its waters would drown rapids that blocked movement along their river.

Communal agriculture and other work were further undermined by a system of paying individuals for labour and by the dispersal of families. Because the mission villages (Yxamná on the Mapuera, the SIL's Cassauá on the Nhamundá, and Kashimin on the Anauá) were permanent, they depended on new technology to feed their people. Outboard motors meant that clearings could be further afield and hunting or fishing expeditions went for longer distances; chainsaws and metal axes made forest clearance easier; and guns, fish-hooks, and nylon line facilitated hunting and fishing. Tobacco, fermented caxiri drinks, and traditional rituals and dances were all prohibited.

Above all, the spiritual beliefs of these tribes were completely reversed. Shamans were mocked and discredited, along with their legends, knowledge of indigenous medicine, and relations with the animal spirit world. Instead, the Baptist converts studied the Bible, substituted Christian worship for their own ceremonies, prayed before every meal, and themselves conducted Sunday services. All aspects of marriage were changed, including the ending of matrilocal residence for a newly wed couple, occasional polygamy, sexual 'promiscuity', and too-easy 'divorce' – even though most of these customs were far less permissive than mores in contemporary American society. The infanticide of twins or of other infants considered of bad omen, naming ceremonies, puberty rites, and initiations were all stopped.

The missionaries were astute enough not to change all tribal customs, so that huts continued to be of thatch even if their layout and size were different, everyday clothing was a slightly more 'modest' version of the previous small aprons but not necessarily full Western dress, and much farming and hunting continued to be collective. The output of traditional handicrafts increased; as did the population, helped by better medicine and a high birth rate. So these communities are generally contented, just as the more successful Jesuit missions had been in the colonial era. The spiritual leaders ran their villages with the zeal of converts, and most Indians willingly accepted the pious regimentation imposed on them. But this was at the cost of their cultural heritage and identity.

For their part, the Waiwái tried to make the most of the missionary onslaught. They developed a network to trade the coveted manufactured goods that they received from the whites with neighbouring tribes. Such barter was an elaborate ritual, unhurried and conducted according to rules of conduct, and it was seen more as a gesture of friendship than profit-driven commerce. These trade goods – everything from metal cutting blades, cooking equipment, hammocks, and clothes, to batteries for torches and ammunition for their few shotguns – were compensation for the strangeness of the missionaries. 'Coming from the edge of their world, the whites transmitted chaotic energies, both natural and subhuman, powerful and superhuman, dangerous and anti-social.' The Waiwái sought to control these contradictory forces. 'The manipulation of manufactured goods, as a substitute for the white men, was one way of overcoming their powers and resisting the Indians' own economic and social subordination.'

Having occasionally ventured into towns, the Waiwái were shocked by the whites' drinking and licentiousness (they regarded the large populations of whites as the result of their being oversexed and unable to control their appetites). They felt that missionaries and Funai officials lived lives of luxury because of their (relatively few) possessions, and were amazed that they were not more generous in sharing these with them. They also disapproved of the whites' hasty and unfriendly manner of trading. To the Waiwái, Western goods were far more than utilitarian possessions. In a sense they represented the whites themselves, and all the misfortunes that came with contact. Thus, by owning and trading many goods, the Waiwái turned the tables on the dominant society.

Air Force Colonel João Camarão formed a good impression of the Protestant missionaries of the Worldwide Evangelization Crusade (formerly Unevangelized Fields Mission): 'This is a well-organized group, with competent men.' The Catholic Salesians had persuaded the army to expel the New Tribes Mission from the Upper Rio Negro, on the grounds that they were foreigners too near a sensitive border region. But when the Catholics asked the air force to do the same to the Crusade, Camarão refused, because all religions were equal under the Brazilian Constitution. This officer told the author that the SPI and Funai were ineffectual and almost absent from his command sector north of the Amazon. Although aware of the shortcomings of some missionaries, he felt that they alone had the selfless dedication that was needed for tutelage of Indians. He particularly admired foreign missionaries, many of whom were Protestant. 'When dealing with Indians, the work of the missionaries is very specific, very serious, whether it is Catholic or Protestant.' Colonel Camarão could also be critical of missionaries. He told me that he once instructed his pilots to dump an obnoxious group with Indians *inside Venezuela* – it was only when these people made a map that they found the rivers running northwards, because they had been deposited across the watershed frontier.

Colonel Camarão also had a powerful impact on the Tiriyó, a Carib-speaking tribe living to the east of the Waiwái and Parikotó, on either side of the border between Brazil and Suriname. When he took up his command in 1957, Colonel Camarão visited the Munduruku of the Tapajós-Cururu in central Brazil and was most impressed by the work of the German Franciscans, who had been with that once-warlike tribe since 1911. Camarão soon offered his transport planes (Dakotas and Catalinas) to take Munduruku rubber to market in Belém, and this was greatly appreciated. From this experience 'emerged the idea of "trinômios" [triumvirates]: points on the frontier where Indians would congregate around missionaries supported by the presence of FAB [the air force], which was responsible for emergencies'. The Colonel read how Rondon had travelled up the Paru river in 1928 and been welcomed by the Tiriyó, so he decided that this tribe should have one of the first trinômios. He heard that the Franciscan Protásio Frikel was an anthropologist who had led an expedition up a nearby river; so in 1959 he invited Frikel to leave the Munduruku mission and replicate it among the Tiriyó. The Franciscan Provincial was persuaded to sanction this new mission at the northern edge of Brazil.

There are extensive natural savannahs in part of the Tiriyó territory, near the Tumucumaque Hills that form the watershed-frontier between Brazil and Dutch Guiana (Suriname); so it was relatively easy to send an expedition upriver to make an airstrip for the air force's transport planes. The handsome, amiable Tiriyó welcomed the missionaries and airmen, just as they had welcome the handful of outsiders who visited them during the previous decades. Their only bad contact had come from mineral explorers from Suriname, who entered the region in the 1950s looking for bauxite. Protásio Frikel said that those disorganized incursions introduced 'a series of illnesses, particularly gonorrhoea and a malignant furunculosis [boils] that decimated the indigenous malocas. Apart from other cases, we learned of two villages on the upper Tapanani that were practically extinguished, with only two or three survivors. Twenty-five people died at the aldeia at the foot of the Awarari, shortly before our arrival [in 1960].' The number of Tiriyó was halved by these pernicious and uncontrolled invaders.

The Franciscan mission flourished, thanks to the all-important logistical support of the air force. The Tiriyó seemed to like the Franciscans, who have always been one of the more relaxed and down-to-earth of the Catholic missionary orders. The brown-robed friars gave medical and material help, but without violent proselytizing. By 1970 Frikel listed the equipment of the mission on the Paru de Oeste river as:

> a mechanical workshop, sawmill, tile-kiln, two Unimog vehicles, one tractor for agriculture, a dredge, a generator (being installed), a well-equipped pharmacy, a small bakery, an array of twelve sewing machines (where Indian women and girls learn simple dressmaking), a little grange for raising chickens, turkeys, ducks, and pigs, a kitchen garden, electric light, piped water (with a stand-pipe for the village population), a rice husker, a creamer for making butter, a small cold-room, two refrigerators, roça clearings that serve the entire mission (for both missionaries and Indians), a manioc flour house, a small corral of cattle, another rather larger one for water buffaloes (thirty-five head), and a start in raising horses, goats, and sheep.

There were roads, bridges, a thatched chapel, and a small school. The friars and nuns lived in thatched huts like those of the Indians. Frikel admitted that some people felt that the mission was too mechanized. But the Indians reacted very favourably to all the development. 'We cannot but admire the Tiriyó's capacity for adaptation to the new conditions they encountered. Far from shunning or rejecting all this machinery, once they saw how it worked, they became enthusiastic and truly interested in it.' They rapidly learned to handle vehicles, chainsaws, and other machines. Frikel was amazed by the 'capacity for adaptation and assimilation by the Tiriyó who, in one decade [of the 1960s], jumped centuries of our civilization'.

A positive aspect of the Franciscan's Tiriyós Mission was its excellent health care. The Aborigines Protection Society team in 1972 described the pharmacy as easily the best they saw anywhere in Brazil. There had been a severe measles epidemic in the previous year, but although sixty Indians caught the disease none died. In later years, this medical programme greatly reduced infant mortality, so that the number of Tiriyó living around the mission almost doubled, from 200 to 380, during the 1980s.

The Franciscans were tolerant about most aspects of Tiriyó life. Men and women continued to wear only a small apron of bright red material, some body paint, and if they felt inclined a cascade of bead necklaces for both sexes and a diadem of macaw feathers on the men's upper arms. Both sexes wore their lustrous black hair in a fringe across their foreheads, but hanging down their necks in a splendid mane. However, if an individual wished to adopt Western dress or haircut, that was tolerated; and most gradually did. One serious loss to the Indians was a decline in shamanism. By 1982 Dominique Gallois found that shamans were no longer active and 'as a result, they do not transmit to the young their knowledge of the uses of medicinal plants and the categories of spirits that they prescribed in their cures. The impoverishment of Tiriyó religious philosophy, destruction of shamanism, and loss of many mythological traditions were accompanied by other modifications in the Indian mentality, under the influence of the "missionary front".'

For a while, the relatively easy-going Franciscans in Brazil lost out to the tougher, more puritanical Protestant missionaries in Suriname. The Tiriyó moved freely between the two countries and two missions. They could not understand why the Catholics permitted festivals, dances, mild drinking, and other practices that the Worldwide Evangelization Crusade condemned as evil. So the Indians deduced that 'the Franciscans, who at that time abstained from intensive catechism, could not be masters of all the secrets of religion, and that the Protestants knew more than they and, therefore, deserved more credit.' In 1972 Frikel deplored the damage done by the religious divide. It was causing dissension, uncertainty, and even unnatural migrations. He told the author that the conflict between Catholics and Protestants was a disgrace for the Indians, who could not understand the different languages (Portuguese, Dutch, and French) nor the nuances between branches of Christianity. 'The missions have put an end to the era of tribal festivals. I don't think these will return. The Indians have a physical future, but not a cultural one.' Frikel was right. The Catholics gradually intensified their religious effort, so that by the late 1970s there were two well-attended masses every day, one in Portuguese and one in Carib, with much of the officiating done by Indian deacons. By 1980 the only dance performed in traditional feather ornaments, beads, and body paint was at Christmas. This was accompanied by buffalo meat and *sakura* manioc beer, but 'the content of this "festival" has nothing to do with traditional rituals ... Children and adolescents know no traditions other than Christmas, baptism, and marriage.' All Tiriyó now regard themselves as Christian.

Another result of Franciscan tutelage was a concentration of the native population around the new mission centres. The Tiriyó used to live in small extended-family units, of some thirty people guided by an elder. The idea behind Colonel Camarão's tripartite governance was that Indians should congregate near the mission and air force airstrip, and the Tiriyó did just that, drawn by the obvious lure of the mission's medical and farming equipment, domestic animals, church, and football field. One problem caused by this concentration was impoverishment of land around the mission. By switching from shifting subsistence farming to large-scale sedentary agriculture, the Indians had to learn about fertilizers and mechanized ploughing. However, the Franciscan fathers encouraged rotation of crops in forest clearings, so that the Indians did not denude the forests by opening too many roças. The missionaries also trained Indians in mechanical skills and paid them for such work. This was to prepare them for a possible future alongside frontier settlers.

In the late 1980s there was a move by some Indians to disperse back to their former small village sites. The Franciscans tolerated this, claiming that the earlier concentration around their mission had been necessary to combat the lure of the Protestants in Suriname: now that the Brazilian Tiriyó seemed solidly Catholic, they could revert to smaller units. In the event, many Indians, particularly younger men, have tended to drift back to the large mission.

The homeland of the Tiriyó and related Carib-speaking Kaxuyana and

Wayana Apalaí was protected in July 1968 as the Tumucumaque Indian park. At the beginning of the twenty-first century this immense area (2,700,000 hectares: 10,420 square miles) remained inviolate. Its terrain is mostly savannah, with some forests and rivers. There have been threats: in 1972 army engineers were surveying the route of the BR-163, a south–north road from Santarém on the Amazon to Suriname, but it was mercifully never built; a decade later the west–east Perimetral Norte (Northern Perimeter) BR-210 highway approached but was not completed across Tiriyó territory. There have been few incursions by prospectors up the difficult northern tributaries of the Amazon, and to date there is no threat from an approaching settlement frontier. Access is still only by plane, and the FAB controls this for the benefit of the Indians. Thus, 'the area inhabited by the Tiriyó constitutes one of the last internal frontiers not impacted by economic interests of [Brazilian] national society.' And, although their way of life has changed irrevocably, the Tiriyó have benefited from this isolation and in some ways from the care of the Franciscan missionaries supported by the air force. In 2002 they were further protected by the creation of a huge Tumucumaque national park to the east of their reserve.

To the south of the Tiriyó, the related Wayana Apalaí were receiving similarly benevolent – but equally transforming – tutelage from the Summer Institute of Linguistics. Edward and Sally Koehn of the SIL spent fifteen years from 1962 to 1977 among these Indians, translating the New Testament into the Apalaí dialect of Carib. When the agreement between Funai and the foreign missions expired the Koehns departed, but 'without leaving any resentment among the Apalaí and Wayana who, on the contrary, remembered them with high esteem.' The SIL's effort was concentrated on education, with bilingual schools in the indigenous language and Portuguese. By the 1990s, much of the teaching was done by Indians. Of course, one motive for this effort was religious conversion, delivered first by Protestants from the missions in Suriname, and then by converts among the Apalaí and Wayana. There were services on three days of the week, coupled with Bible-study classes and discussions.

The SIL defined another objective of this efficient and intensive teaching as 'a bridge by which the Indians may and should empower themselves, enhance their self-esteem, and emancipate themselves. This will make it possible for them to be integrated into the national life and educational system.' The Koehns wanted to prepare their Indians to be 'educated members contributing to national society'. It was a similar objective to that of the Catholic missionaries to the north. Assimilation of Indians to become 'useful citizens' of Brazil has been a mantra of governments ever since the Portuguese colonial era; but it has almost never succeeded to the benefit of the indigenous people.

The SIL missionaries were sufficiently intelligent to leave most customs of the Wayana Apalaí intact. In the 1980s both sexes still performed their traditional roles. 'The principal tasks of women are: planting, harvesting, and conservation of roça farm-clearings, gathering firewood, preparing and cooking food, brewing fermented drinks, spinning cotton, weaving hammocks and slings for carrying infants, ceramics, beadwork, and educating young children. Men have the following duties: preparing land for planting (opening undergrowth, felling trees, burning and clearing brushwood), hunting, fishing, building houses and canoes, making bows and arrows, basketwork, and creating feather and other ornaments. Gathering wild food and fishing with timbó fish-poison are mixed activities. Building meeting houses and *tukussipan* festivals are collective work by the men.' Both sexes wore no clothing other than red aprons hanging from belts in front and behind for men, and girdle-like miniskirts for women. They were very active in making magnificent feather ornaments, for their own use and for sale through Funai shops. Some of these are huge baroque diadems of macaw feathers topped by festoons of white egret feathers. Anthropologists found that the Wayana Apalaí still observed elaborate ceremonial in their cooking, with ritual and symbolism surrounding the cooking processes, and with many dishes peculiar to one or other sex. For them, 'true' food is meat and fish, as opposed to manioc, vegetable, and fruit dishes.

The anthropologist Lúcia van Velthem gained an insight into Wayana attitudes to non-Indians by the (generally pejorative) words they used for them. Outsiders' skin-colours were either *tikorokem* (whitened) – resembling sick Indians or those undergoing ritual seclusion – or 'blackened' as were Wayana exposed to prolonged sun-tanning. Bearded men were 'like *Chirapates* apes', hairy ones 'like *coatá* monkeys', and fair ones 'like howler monkeys'. There were similar variations in describing whites' clothing (particularly military uniforms) and distinguishing different intruders – mineral prospectors, loggers, missionaries, or Funai staff.

The SIL sought to 'preach by example', hoping to inspire the Wayana to imitate the wholesome way of life of missionary families and to identify their Protestant religion with the many desirable manufactured goods that they introduced. This strategy was not entirely effective. The Wayana retained different words for 'things' made by outsiders and 'mine' for those crafted by the Indians themselves – which were more highly valued. Such distinctions applied even to such useful objects as aluminium cooking pans, used by every Wayana woman, and less utilitarian but more

beautiful indigenous pots. By studying Indian names, aesthetic appreci-
ation, and symbolic value for each manufactured item, Lúcia van Velthem
'was able to demonstrate and understand the process by which such goods
were "domesticated" and became "captive objects".' This was because
outsiders were still, in a sense, enemies, so that their goods were absorbed
with the rituals that had once applied to captives of inter-tribal wars.

In 1973, during the frenzy of road-building that produced the Transamazonica and other penetration roads, there was a plan to cut a highway
through the forests north of the Amazon. A western stretch of this
Perimetral Norte (Northern Perimeter) sliced into the edge of Yanomami
territory. Meanwhile, the eastern end was started from the city of Macapá
near the mouth of the Amazon. After some 370 kilometres (230 miles)
the road-gangs started seeing signs of Indians. Funai was summoned, and
its sertanistas made contact with the Amapari group of Wayampi (also
spelled Waiãmpi or Waiãpi). This Tupi-speaking people had for several
centuries had intermittent dealings with Brazilian society. Originally
settled near the lower Xingu, they found conditions there increasingly
intolerable, particularly after the collapse of the Cabanagem rebellion in
1839, so they crossed the Amazon river and moved up its northern Jari
tributary. The Wayampi shrewdly retreated far upriver to the headwaters
of the Jari, so that they escaped involvement in the billionaire Daniel
Ludwig's grandiose Jari Project near its mouth in the 1960s and '70s. But
the Northern Perimeter road did push for thirty kilometres (nineteen
miles) into their lush forests before it was abandoned as unnecessary in
1976. This is a land of magnificent tall Hyleian forests. Its hilly terrain is
well watered by fast-flowing rivers, but these are broken by waterfalls and
rapids – natural barriers that protect the region from colonization.
    The Wayampi practise an intense ceremonial calendar. Their lives are
enriched by great rituals such as the maize feast during the rains, the
honey feast, and fish dances, all joyous but solemn gatherings involving
much dancing, singing, and music from different types of flute. Huge
quantities of mildly intoxicating caxiri are drunk at these communal
celebrations. Numbering about 150 at the time of contact (or, rather,
recontact), the Wayampi had adopted the dress of the Carib-speaking
Tiriyó: nothing but crimson aprons hanging front and back from belts, a
profusion of feather and bead ornaments, and hair flowing long over the
shoulders of both sexes.
    During the first half of the twentieth century, the Wayampi had
intermittent contact with whites – mostly bad, with aggressions by the
few skin-hunters or prospectors who penetrated the upper Jari. They also

developed a desire for metal tools. So when Funai established a post in 1973, the Wayampi rapidly realized that these were friendly compared to earlier intruders. 'There were few of them, but they possessed impressive equipment: canoes with outboard motors, chainsaws, firearms, and box after box of the goods that had previously been obtained with difficulty from settlers or other indigenous groups.' So many Wayampi moved from their villages to be close to the Funai post on the unfinished Northern Perimeter road. Then, in the early 1980s, Protestant missionaries arrived – the Summer Institute of Linguistics in Taitetuwa village and New Tribes Mission in Ytuwasu. These also encouraged the abandonment of distant, scattered aldeias and the concentration of the tribe into sedentary communities.

The Wayampi produced a natural leader, Chief Waiwai (who has nothing to do with the Carib-speaking tribe of the same name). This chief was one of a new generation of tribal leaders who learned how to fight for their people in the Brazilian media and political system. Handsome, with an intense determination, Waiwai had a hint of black moustache (rare for an Indian) and wore his hair full in the manner of a Renaissance prince. His fine oratory, his honour and candour, and his passion made Waiwai a spokesman for his Wayampi people and for Indians in general. He confronted politicians in Brasília, visited other tribes, starred in documentary films, and addressed meetings in the United States. Everywhere he went, Waiwai's presence commanded respect.

A Scottish anthropologist, Alan Campbell, wrote one of the most perceptive books about Brazilian Indians in honour of this charismatic leader. *Getting to Know Waiwai* described Campbell's two years' living with the Wayampi soon after their contact in 1973 and his return to them fifteen years later. He saw that 'Waiwai's consuming concern was with the survival of Wayampi people. True, he didn't have phrases like "our culture, our way of life", or "our heritage, our traditions" to justify what his vision was. But he didn't need words like that. For him, the question was whether his people were to get through or die. His struggle was a fierce vocation and nothing distracted him from it. I found that severe passion admirable.'

Alan Campbell lived and hunted with the Wayampi, learned their language, studied their customs with sympathy, shared their sprees getting drunk on caxiri manioc beer, and dressed like them in nothing more than a small red apron. He developed a profound admiration for their way of life. He observed the Wayampi as a scientific anthropologist would, but his time with them became far more than that. 'We're living with people, talking, laughing, getting alarmed, mourning, helping, sulking, misunderstanding, cheering up again, and so on . . . a human engagement, and not a scientific experiment.' He watched the first changes, the forces that were gradually overwhelming the Indians. He saw their cultural certainties and material self-sufficiency eroded by the need for powder and shot for their hunting guns (which Funai gave them to replace effective bows and arrows), batteries for torches and tape recorders, and 'outsiders' medicines for the diseases the outsiders brought'.

As an academic anthropologist teaching at Edinburgh University, Alan Campbell was well aware of the modern caution about romanticizing Indians. It is now considered wrong or naive to think of tribes living in 'a unique, timeless society, with no history; living for centuries in the forest with their bows and arrows, and gardens, and free estates in a kind of suspended animation; and who were suddenly overwhelmed by out-side forces, culturally eviscerated, and left marginalized and washed up on the edges of the dominant society.' The correct modern view is that indigenous people have always adapted to change, which is why many of them can handle contact and modernization without losing all their ethnicity. Campbell accepted some of this new thinking. But he also argued passionately that it would be disastrous to forget that the 'pris-tine' Indian way of life had evolved into a highly effective system. Look-ing back at his two years with the newly contacted Wayampi, he could find few blemishes on their harmonious and happy existence. At that time, they were 'monolingual, isolated, vulnerable [to outside forces], though managing quite well with their antiquated technology.' It was almost impossible for an anthropologist to appreciate what the memory of that pre-contact world means to modern Wayampi. Campbell realized that he was one of a dwindling band of outsiders who experienced the mystery of that life, and who could therefore write 'with great sadness about what is being lost. When we see what's happening we cannot just jauntily say: "Oh well; let the great world spin forever down the ringing grooves of change. Nothing to worry about. Their ethnicity will survive albeit in a different form." That would be unforgivable – a terrible betrayal.' Campbell did not believe that everyone carries a personal eth-nicity 'like a kind of human phlogiston', and that this would automati-cally survive acculturation. The challenge to sympathizers was to allow tribes to change at their own pace and volition. But Campbell's sadness was fully justified.

The Wayampi were buffeted and contested between Funai and the missionaries, just as crassly as their neighbours were. Alan Campbell was able to observe the two organizations at work, almost from an Indian perspective; and he came to despise both groups of aliens. Funai sent a teacher, nurse, and the husband of one of these to care for the newly contacted tribe. These were hopelessly unqualified, and yet they 'were sent off into the woods to make decisions about the future of an entire culture. Suppose we thought of the Lord God Almighty as having the temperament of an excitable teenager and the administrative vision of a school janitor. That's what the Indians were landed with.' The health care and sporadic 'education' administered by the trio were worse than useless. Funai's presence with the Wayampi, at the extremely delicate time after their contact, was one of bogus authority, by agents of an incompetent institution, who were socially and morally ignorant. 'It was horrible to see chiefs like Waiwai and Renato, men who would [later] face up to the Brazilians with the stern cultural dignity of an entire Indian people, being shouted at and ordered about by a pompous half-wit invested with power by virtue of being a minor official in a decadent organization.' It was equally shocking to see skilled mothers, many of whom had lost children to alien diseases, 'being treated like silly schoolgirls, their anxieties and pleas brushed aside as if they were just minor nuisances. It was horrible to see people whose lives were informed by the decency of an integral culture being treated as if they were all in need of the kind of special care that might be offered the feeble-minded or the mildly delinquent. How did those petty officials dare think they could deal with Wayampi people in that way?'

Funai's teacher gave the children an occasional class when she felt like it. She hoped to teach them to read and write in Portuguese. This pathetic effort contrasted with the efficiency of the Summer Institute of Linguistics, whose agents operated in another community three days' walk away. They followed a disciplined timetable, worked hard, and taught Indians of all ages. Alan Campbell was dismayed by the incompetence of Funai's efforts, but even more by the frightening expertise of the SIL's literacy classes. The anthropologist appreciated that literacy was far more than just another skill: it was the basis of cognitive processes that shaped people's entire outlook. But it was unnecessary. The Wayampi soon learned passable Portuguese without literacy, because they were superb hunters with the ability to mimic animal sounds. The missionary teacher, an amiable young man but a religious fanatic, 'had them in the grip of his presbyterian discipline, enticing them, with the lure of the reading-and-writing magic, into the dark tabernacle of The Book.'

Campbell found it despicable of these missionaries to target vulnerable tribes and 'think it's some kind of achievement to gain control of their minds, hearts, and spirits, and their souls too.' It was hard to forgive the hypocrisy of the missionaries. They brought health care, and they believed that their teaching was preparing the Indians for integration into Brazilian society – which, they argued, was what the Indians themselves wanted. They claimed to respect native societies and not to interfere or judge. Yet their entire effort revolved around the Bible, which they were determined to translate in its entirety into Wayampi, and which they curiously believed to hold the answer to every aspect of tribal life. Another British anthropologist, Stephen Hugh-Jones, reported that 'a Summer Institute of Linguistics worker once said that the most important thing that he'd done was to convince the people who thought that humanity was fundamentally good, that in fact it was fundamentally bad'. Their real objective was to 'enthral their subjects into their theologies of damnation, destroying en route delicate ways of thinking, ways of being, ways of acting, ways that are beyond their comprehension and compassion, all the time saying that they are doing good.'

The tragic irony in all this was that the Wayampi *wanted* education. Their leader Kumai in 1983 begged for a school, so that the Indians themselves would learn how to be their own nurses, teachers, and administrators. But the only efficient education they received came at the price of violent missionary proselytizing, by the amiable but fanatical couple Silas and Edna Lima of the New Tribes Mission and their SIL colleagues. The Funai agent, João Evangelista Carvalho, accepted the Limas without a moment's hesitation. The missionaries, as always, also brought better medical care than the government agency, and the Wayampi appreciated the way in which there was always at least one missionary present in one of their villages, in case of emergency. But Edna Lima's description of their 'preaching the Gospel to the Wayampi' spoke of Indians 'manifesting hope in Christ' while she and her husband were 'very gratified to have the privilege of harvesting these fruits'. When the Wayampi accepted the New Tribes missionaries, they were suffering terribly from diseases and were terrified of extinction. The strangers had plenty of resources, and they were willing to live with the Indians to help with education, health, and commercial transactions. They presented themselves as good people, bringing the 'good news' of Christianity. But at least one Wayampi community felt that the price for these 'benefits' was too high – for the NTM's stated objective is conversion of primitive peoples to Protestantism as a step towards their integration into national society. Chief Kumai of Aramirã village said, 'I know that missionaries are good, but I do not want the mission – no way!' Kumai saw what the 'good missionaries' did to destroy the culture and self-esteem of Ytuwasu village, so he repeatedly refused to admit them to his.

Dominique Gallois observed how Wayampi pronouncements and

attitudes to whites changed during the first decades after contact. At the outset, they feared that they were too few and were going to expire, with their land gone, game exhausted, and environment ruined. They were defiant, stressing their fighting prowess and how whites should not despise them as inferior. Wayampi chiefs had a long list of goods they wanted from the outsiders, but 'we are not your relatives; we did not wish to intermingle with you. We want to remain as before, when there were only Wayampi.' They were proud of their knowledge – and conservation – of the plants and animals of their forests.

The passion of Chief Waiwai, helped by the better elements in Funai and by Brazilian and foreign volunteers, did at least achieve a protected homeland for the Wayampi. In May 1985 their land was designated as a 543,000 hectare (2,100 square mile) reserve, containing 289 people. Exasperated by official delays, the Wayampi themselves organized its demarcation. They were helped by the department of geodesy and cartography of Pernambuco University and by Funai's department of lands, so that they used the latest surveying equipment and satellite imagery to augment their intimate knowledge of their territory. The Wayampi also built villages at strategic points to secure the reserve's perimeter.

Wayampi self-help was even more impressive in dealing with gold prospecting. Garimpeiros started to enter the tribe's land sporadically during the 1980s. The Wayampi response was not only to expel the invaders themselves, with threats but no bloodshed, but also to learn how to find and extract the precious metal. They themselves had no use for gold, but they had learned that it could be the answer to their needs for imported goods. They began by occupying the workings of the prospectors they expelled, but then went on to seek and discover new deposits. Dominique Gallois wrote that in the 1990s 'over a third of Wayampi family groups now dedicate themselves to panning alluvial gold, in a seasonal rhythm and at family level with each unit producing an average of seven grams of gold a week. Prospecting is just one of their extractive activities, totally integrated into their cycle of traditional subsistence.' They did not alter their dress – barefoot and naked apart from red aprons – to work the pressure hoses, separating pans, and wooden sluices that they themselves built. They did this without using toxic mercury to separate the mineral. The Wayampi were helped in these mining operations by the NGO Centre for Indigenous Work (CTI), which provided a mineral engineer and advice about transporting and selling the gold, and some working capital came from European aid agencies.

The 550 Wayampi (seventy-eight families) now continue their traditional farming and gathering of the fruits of the forest: Brazil nuts, copaíba oil, bananas, pupunha (peach-palm), and açaí-palm fruit. But they run into the perennial problem with such produce: prices paid in city markets often do not cover even the cost of transport. They also make feather ornaments of baroque fantasy and other handicrafts for export sale. Young chiefs, Waiwai, Kumai, and Kumare, led the community in these efforts to enter the market economy without losing any tribal identity or damaging their natural environment. It was not easy. The CTI provided training and commercial advice in making the difficult transition from subsidized extractivism to larger-scale but sustainable production. They had to help the Indians choose products (in addition to gold) that would be successful, to guide them into some collective work above family level, to persuade them to invest some of the profit in capital improvements rather than immediate spending, and to manage their enterprises with more care about cash-flow and cost-control. The Wayampi were eager learners, and their experiences with gold prospecting had taught them business rudiments.

Part of the tribe's development depended on better education, so the CTI engaged the anthropologist Marinha Kahn to train Indian teachers and to devise a curriculum – in Wayampi Tupi, of course – that was relevant to the tribe's heritage, habitat, and relations with Brazilian society. The Wayampi also promoted their own health projects. It all amounted to one of the best self-help initiatives by any Brazilian tribe. And it was achieved without missionaries. In fact the Indians now attribute most of their problems (from loss of land to ill-health) to Funai and the missions. They deplore how these agents 'encouraged them to abandon their most distant villages and congregate in settlements near the posts, alleging that they would receive better assistance – which in practice never materialized. So now [at the start of the new century] those who remain around the post do so largely because of the school. Life in these villages is seen as a sacrifice, done in the hope that in the near future, thanks to the school, they will be better able to control interventions by the whites.' In the decades after contact, the Wayampi learned to distinguish between different types of non-Indians – those who lived near or far away, hostile garimpeiros and skin-hunters or 'friendly' officials from missionary sects, Funai or government road-builders and military. But a leader called Semente declared: 'I do not like *karai-ko* [whites], none of them, not even when they are friendly. They are all harmful to us.'

Wayampi success in mining aroused hostility. Prospectors continued to try to invade the reserve. Expelled garimpeiros orchestrated rumours that Funai's agent and Dominique Gallois of the CTI were running a private gold-mining operation that exploited underpaid Indian labour. A federal deputy challenged the tribe's ownership of its territory and accused the Indians of stealing the gold they had panned. He also tried to get the New Tribes Mission reinstated – it had been evicted by Funai in 1991, then readmitted, then expelled again in 1996 at CTI's instigation after twelve years' work converting and helping the tribe. There was an attempted boycott of indigenous gold by local bullion traders. The campaign of vilification gathered such momentum that in late 1993 Wayampi leaders and Gallois had to refute them in the press and the state assembly.

In 1994 the tribe formed its own Council, called Apina after a legendary group of warriors. Two years later, an enlarged 607,000 hectare (2,300 square mile) Wayampi reserve was fully demarcated and registered, an achievement celebrated with a great party in Aramirã village. It was by then home to 525 people. In that same year 1996 Apina and the CTI launched a project to reclaim land and riverbeds that had been contaminated by gold-prospecting. The project gained support from the Ministry of the Environment. Apina's President, Chief Kasiripinã, declared to government officials:

It was we Wayampi, all our chiefs, who discussed and created the project. We know that you, the authorities, are our friends, but you do not understand our project so I must explain it to you. The project is to cleanse pollution of our land, but it is more than that. It is also to extract gold, to maintain our way of life . . . White men just talk about garimpo, garimpo, garimpo! It's not that! Whites say that Indians are going to turn into prospectors. We are not going to become garimpeiros. Garimpeiros destroy the land. Would white men care for Indians' lands? No . . . So we Indians need to learn to work alone, without needing money from the whites. That is what we want.

The garimpeiros of Amapá contrived to be bitterly opposed to the Wayampi mining their own gold. There was an unholy alliance of Funai's local staff and its department of the 'Indigenous Patrimony' in Brasília with the miners and politicians of Amapá. They instigated judicial and police inquiries. But in April 1999 a judge ruled in favour of the CTI's disinterested work. Pro-Indian activists hailed this judicial victory as a defeat for the 'protective corporatism' of Funai, which wanted to stop the Wayampi from developing their own business project. However, local interests did not cede easily and they continued the campaign of vilification against CTI sympathizers. The tribe was divided. A faction of Protestants who had been converted by the evicted New Tribes Mission joined the accusations against Dominique Gallois. These were vigorously refuted by the Wayampi Council Apina.

In May 1989, Brazilian television showed a contact with a new tribe, a Tupi-speaking people living on forested creeks to the south-west of the Tiriyós' Tumucumaque park. The finding of a relatively large tribe – 133 people in four villages – in the late twentieth century, only 300 kilometres (190 miles) north of the city of Santarém, caused a sensation. The newly contacted people lived on the upper Cuminapanema river, which joins the Curuá and flows into the Amazon opposite the mouth of the Tapajós. The television programme showed Paul Nagell, a missionary of the New Tribes Mission, wearing a checked shirt and flanked by two smiling, naked, and very fit Indians. The new group called itself Zo'é, and its most obvious identification was a broad wooden labret (measuring up to 15–20 centimetres long by 2.5 wide; 6–8 by 1 inches) suspended from the men's lower lips. Their only other clothing or adornment was a small straw penis sheath.

There was immediate conflict between Funai and the American missionaries, both about who had first contacted the Zo'é, and more importantly about who should be responsible for them. Funai had become aware of the existence of these Indians in the early 1970s and even planned an attraction post to contact them. In 1982, the New Tribes Mission saw the Zo'é villages from the air, and two Brazilian missionaries made a lightning contact. 'The missionaries walked for twenty days through the forest to meet the Indians. They were accompanied by an Apalaí interpreter, but he could achieve no verbal understanding with the Indians. Since the Indians were "rather agitated", the missionaries affirm that they did nothing more than give some presents and immediately withdraw.' There was a lull of a few years, during which the New Tribes Mission located villages from the air and threw presents down to them. In 1985 missionaries cut a long trail upriver, built a base called Esperança (Hope), and opened an airstrip. Contact with the frightened tribe occurred on 5 November 1987. Some Zo'é appeared on the hill behind the station, followed by other families, until a hundred people were gathered. 'It was a moment of great tension. The missionaries communicated by sign language and kept their distance, but signalled that they were offering presents. The Indians responded by offering arrows whose points had been broken. One of them, trembling, approached the missionaries to grab a machete, immediately returning to the group, which then decided to approach.' Others came on the following days and stayed for a while. Funai forbade the New Tribes Mission to establish a post within a village of these newly contacted people. So the missionaries (five adults with five children) moved cautiously. They maintained the Esperança base, three days' walk from a Zo'é village, but visits to tribal villages were made only every few months and were brief. This strategy succeeded, when in 1989 and 1990 various indigenous families moved to be near the mission. The missionaries' plan was first to learn the Zo'é version of the Tupi language, then transcribe it, so that the New Testament could be translated into it. Paul Nagell explained that, once the Indians understood something of Western culture, they could work to pay for the goods they wanted. 'This would avoid paternalism that would make them dependent.' In a television broadcast, he admitted that his Mission's ultimate objective was to dominate the Zo'é spiritually, enter into their lives, and 'teach them the word of God, thus giving the group on the Cuminapanema the same opportunity as all other Brazilians have.'

Funai learned that the new group's health was deteriorating, so, in 1989 and subsequent years, the fine sertanista Sydney Possuelo took teams to administer a full range of vaccinations. There was friction between the government Indianists, disinterested but few in number and poorly equipped, and the well-entrenched, lavishly financed, and aggressive missionaries. The Funai men were angry with the missionaries for their failure to inoculate the Indians – and there were an unacceptable number of deaths from pulmonary diseases during the years of contact.

The Indians, meanwhile, introduced white men into their tribal mythology. The intruders were seen as friendly (unlike some hostile neighbouring tribes) and the providers of desired goods. But they were disagreeably *noisy*, with their outboard motors, planes, and helicopters, and the chainsaws used by the missionaries to clear their base. The anthropologist Dominique Gallois was intrigued to observe the Zo'é who visited the mission and a Funai base. They were eager to obtain trade goods (tools, clothes, batteries, and appliances), but also to gather information, and they even evolved an 'anthropology' of the personnel of the bases which they exploited to obtain the desired objects.

There was a profound difference in the approach of the two groups in contact with the Zo'é. 'Only the fundamentalist missions believe that they are capable of cultural engineering by which "positive aspects" are reformatted to eliminate "negative aspects". Nowadays, the work realized by Funai teams in remote areas seeks to reinforce the autonomy of isolated indigenous peoples. This goal can be obtained only by giving such groups opportunities to opt for determined forms of coexistence. They can thus affirm themselves as the authors of their own future.' In October 1991 Funai assumed control of the area and asked the missionaries to leave.

Dominique Gallois showed a video film of the newly contacted Zo'é to the Wayampi, who live some 300 kilometres (190 miles) to the east and who share a variant of the Tupi language. The two groups also have some common cultural heritage, even though the Wayampi have been in intermittent contact for two centuries and under the tutelage of Funai since 1973. When they saw the video, the Wayampi leaders asked to meet their brethren. Gallois organized a visit by six men in December 1992, and it was a great success. The Zo'é asked the other Indians to bring them canes for making arrows and curassow feathers for headdresses, and they wanted to hear the Wayampi chants. They were also interested in signs of acculturation by the Wayampi – some clothing such as shorts and caps, and different haircuts. 'For the Wayampi, the encounter represented a voyage in time, in two directions. It was a return to the past, for the Zo'é are people who retain intact the knowledge and practices of the ancients. But it was a past leading to a future, because of all that they were bringing to the isolated people.' In the event, the meeting highlighted the cultural politics of traditional versus new. 'The Wayampi appreciated the traditional. They alerted the Zo'é to the perils of new technologies, which threatened them both physically and culturally, for these might obliterate their ancient customs. The Zo'é were of course more interested in acquiring the new, with all the novelties that the Wayampi could bring them.'

Soon after contact, diseases reduced the Zo'é to 133 individuals, but they ended the century at 152. Their beautiful forested hills and streams remain isolated, so that they are not threatened by invasion. But their indigenous area is only 'interdicted', still awaiting demarcation and eventual registration.

The land between the mouth of the Amazon river and French Guyana is the State (former Territory) of Amapá. With a seaboard on the Atlantic Ocean and relatively close to the Amazon waterway and the city of Belém do Pará, most of Amapá was long ago denuded of Indians, by the ravages of slavers and imported diseases. It is only in the extreme north of the state that some tribes have survived in a triangle between the Oiapoque river, which marks the boundary between Brazil and the French possession, and the Uaçá river, which joins the Oiapoque as it flows into the Atlantic. The northern part of what is now Amapá was contested between the two nations, but awarded to Brazil in an arbitration in 1900. This is a flat land of mangroves, low forest, and swamps, *várzea* seasonally flooded from heavy rains during almost half the year and, inland, savannah with gallery forest along the rivers. There are plenty of fish, alligators, turtles, and aquatic birds – and also clouds of biting insects: blackflies, mosquitoes, and ticks. The Indians make the most of their diverse ecosystems. They glide along the rivers and channels between their islands in dugout canoes that often have round thatched shelters amidships.

It took some time for the indigenous peoples of this territory to change their allegiance from the French creoles to the Brazilians, partly because they recalled brutal slaving raids by Portuguese Brazilians in past centuries. Three language groups coexist in what was eventually to become the Uaçá reserve: Tupi-speaking Karipuna to the north, Aruak-speaking Palikur in the middle, and Carib-speaking Galibi to the south. The Galibi were once the most formidable tribe of this region, with several thousand people in villages deep into the interior of Guyane Française and Suriname. One group of Galibi migrated south into Brazil and coexisted alongside the two other tribes. When the ubiquitous Curt Nimuendajú was there in the early 1920s, he found that most Brazilians considered Indians as despicable beasts. The Palikur were insulted by common Brazilians and abused by soldiers and officials. 'The authorities exercised their functions with considerable arrogance. They wrongly accused the Indians of speaking Patois rather than Portuguese, and imposed exaggerated prices on goods – but when they preferred to trade on the French side they were called smugglers. The Palikur therefore preferred to maintain relations with the amiable and peaceful Creoles, who were more accustomed to principles of equality and who called them "Muché and Madame" – although they, too, cheated them in commercial transactions just as flagrantly as anyone else did.' The Karipuna reached this region only in the late nineteenth century: they were refugees from the island of Marajó in the mouth of the Amazon, having fled after the collapse of the great Cabanagem rebellion in 1839.

In the 1930s the SPI attempted short-lived schools for these tribes. The Service then sent one of Rondon's officers, Major Thomaz Reis, to see whether these Indians could be used as unofficial frontier guards. He found that, although the Karipuna were clothed and settled in villages, they were too unacculturated and ingenuous to be enlisted in this way; the Galibi were orderly and peaceful and seemed satisfied with their way of life; while the Palikur were 'in a very retarded state of education, with primitive habits, using much urucum but few clothes, and had not abandoned their arrows'. The Palikur were frightened of Brazilians, particularly those in uniform, and they clung to French names. So Major Reis did not recommend using any of these men as guards, and he sensibly condemned an attempt to assemble them all in a single nucleus – none of the estuarine islands could support many people, and the tribes had different interests and a history of mutual hostility.

During the SPI's phases of vigour in the 1940s and 1950s it tried to motivate these Indians, so that their SPI post might be self-sufficient and they would become those elusive but sought-after 'useful citizens' of Brazil. However, attempts to modernize fishing and farming, to introduce water buffaloes and cattle, and to extract Brazil-wood dye all foundered from lack of funds, native indifference, and administrative incompetence. Plantations of manioc and rice were ravaged by a large population of wild rats, which had arrived in European ships; and piranhas chewed through fibre fishing nets. For a time, the SPI agent had his Indians catching alligators, for their skins; but indiscriminate fishing soon wiped out the populations of these reptiles. The Indians never grew to like cattle meat or milk, and the introduced animals always lacked pasture. They were reduced to fewer than a hundred in 1950 by two successive flood seasons. A workshop to make furniture from lianas, another to polish rice, and commercial fish-drying all failed for different market reasons. Single men were sent off to the forests for long periods to gather andiroba nuts, which contain a valuable oil; but with no processing machinery the profit from cargoes of nuts sent to Belém was 'infinitesimal'. 'New SPI projects, a tile pottery and a sawmill, had an ephemeral existence.' However, the Indians did make just enough to buy some mosquito nets, guns, ammunition, and metal tools. Expedito Arnaud of the Goeldi Museum in Belém worked for the SPI among these tribes in the 1950s, and returned as an anthropologist during the next two decades. So he observed the commercial failures, and the inadequacy of SPI staff starved of money and forced to try to live off their charges' profits. 'The business activities did not achieve their desired objectives, for lack of better studies of the environment, tribal peculiarities, market conditions, and an absence of resources in both quantity and quality.' The SPI agent Djalma Sfair, who was there from 1951 to 1967, did try to introduce schools, dig wells, and disburse basic health care.

Of the three tribal groups, the Aruak Palikur best resisted these half-baked enterprises and shunned 'official paternalism'. The rivers of northern Amapá were invaded by gold prospectors; and the swarm of itinerant traders who supplied these garimpeiros wanted to buy the Indians' manioc and fish. The Palikur rebelled against the SPI's attempted monopoly of this trade. They were incited by an Indian who kept his French name Paul Émile Labonté (also known as 'Sans-sous') and whom an SPI official in 1948 called 'the prototype of an undesirable native'. In the 1950s there was another movement to shake off official interference, led by a chief called Camille Narcise. During the next decade, although the SPI post had virtually collapsed, many Indians of all three tribes drifted across to the French side of the Oiapoque, seeking casual labour on farms and fishing and, for the elderly, social security. Despite all these upheavals and minimal health care, the populations of the tribes increased: from a total of 693 in 1931 to 1,162 in 1965. Expedito Arnaud noted that the groups preserved relative autonomy and the possession of their ancestral lands, 'probably thanks to the low density of regional [settler] population . . . Despite suffering socio-cultural modifications caused by external contacts, the loss of their original languages (in the case of the Galibi and Karipuna), and the actions of the SPI . . . they still keep their tribal identities very much alive.' These included shamanism, which was an important element in tribes that, although nominally Catholic, received little ecclesiastical attention.

It was almost inevitable that Protestant missionaries would target these tribes, which were largely left to their own devices by the government Indian service and the Catholic Church. Harold and Diana Green of the Summer Institute of Linguistics moved into a Palikur village in 1965 to start studying its language. They left for a while two years later, and their place was occupied by the American Pentecostalist Pastor Glen Johnson. His was an ascetic sect that shunned alcohol, tobacco, and other 'sinful' pleasures, but believed in miraculous cures based on the gift of tongues that the Holy Spirit instilled in the apostles at the Pentecost. At its services, amid hymn-singing, the congregation raised its arms in rapture as it received divine inspiration.

Johnson could speak no Portuguese or tribal language, but he got a soldier who was a Pentecostalist to interpret for him. He was fortunate to find himself in the village of one of the few Palikur who could speak Portuguese and this man, Paulo Orlando (Watay), became an ardent Protestant and the agent of his group's conversion. Paulo Orlando had had some schooling, in Belém and at the SPI's school for the Karipuna, and had tried unsuccessfully to be appointed as a chief by the SPI. Paulo Orlando later recalled that 'when the missionary Glen Johnson came back for the fifth time, he gave me permission also to tell the others about Christ, and I started to understand something. Three days passed. Many people decided to accept Jesus. He [the missionary] said: "In this way you are going to receive many benefits for your people, in this place that is so forgotten by men, but Jesus does not forget you." He prayed, blessed me, and promised to undertake the task. Then the Pastor said . . . : "This people was chosen, it was found by God and now He is going to do much:

the head [of Funai] is going to come, with teachers, a nurse, and all the rest. You are going to live in unity and to found a new village."' Once again, a tribe's destiny was shaped by one determined leader. By 1978 Funai's agent among the Palikur reported that the missionary-chief Paulo Orlando was 'endowed with a gift of oratory, a brilliant intelligence, and sufficient determination . . . to form a community of crentes where they would all be true brothers. As a start, he sought to abolish all obstacles to "peace", such as polygamy, alcoholic drink, festivals, the use of tobacco, etc. All "idols" of sin were broken, burned, and forgotten – namely, all instruments linked to vice, such as jars of caxiri, artefacts used in the Turé ceremony, etc.' There were religious services throughout Saturdays and on Sunday evenings, with prayers and hymns interspersed with readings from the Bible. All the tribe's beliefs were eradicated, and even shamans and faith-healers converted to Pentecostalism. The Palikur became clean-living, artificially good to one another, and obedient to authority; and Indians of all ages sought schooling in order to be able to read the Bible. Their new religion taught a work ethic, so that production from their collective farming increased markedly.

The Greens of the SIL returned, and were seen by Funai as a restraining influence on the excesses of Pentecostalism. They tried in vain to remove a sign proclaiming that the village's new church was the 'House of Prayer of the Assembly of God'. The new creed totally dominated this group of Palikur. Afonso Yoyo, one of the most passionate crentes, explained why he had converted from Catholicism: 'The priest explained almost nothing: he just said that we should be with God, but he did not make the doctrine penetrate our hearts. Now I pray, sing, and weep because I am happy. Since I love myself, I love all other people, even those I do not know.'

By the late 1970s there was confusion in the Pentecostal theocracy at Ukumenê village. Preachers from other Protestant sects, including the Greens from the SIL, told the Indians that their creed was wrong. At one time the Indians themselves interpreted passages in the Bible to mean that the earth would provide for them, so that they ceased work and were threatened with starvation. The most damaging blow came when the chief pastor, Paulo Orlando, fell in love with his wife's young niece. For two years Orlando left, taking many Indians with him to form a new village where he permitted drinking, dancing, and other forbidden pleasures. The congregation of believers shrank, although it continued under Pastor Moisés Yapahá; but in 1980 Paulo Orlando returned, to resume control of the village and its church. The Catholics also mounted a counter-attack. The nearby Karipuna and Galibi had remained Catholic, and their church sent a delegation headed by a bishop and skilled missionaries to try to win back the Palikur.

An enlightened missionary, the Italian Father Nello Ruffaldi, had started to work among the Karipuna in 1971. Alongside his religious work, Father Nello was active in community projects. One of his initiatives was a 'Filter Campaign', whereby any family that dug a latrine was given a water filter: the result was a reduction in the intestinal worms that plagued these people. In 1978 Ruffaldi wrote an account of his first seven years: how he had arrived to find the Indian areas constantly invaded by traders and prospectors, who plied them with alcohol and robbed them in trading transactions; how he was welcomed by every tribe, including the Protestant Palikur; and how he maintained no house in most villages, but slung his hammock in any Indian hut. The Catholic Church had been present in the region since time immemorial, but it had often been inactive: the tribes themselves had built and maintained a few of their own churches. Father Nello described his efforts to improve the Indians' health and literacy and to help them establish successful trading cooperatives. When he found that the tribes kept a tradition of communal life and society, he claimed that he sought to enhance their self-respect. But he tried to do this through religious conversion, with masses, prayer, and teaching of the word of God. The missionary proudly said that: 'I saw this people revive and become more confident human beings, as they ceased to deny their Indianness, as they discovered that the Gospel is to unite and not oppose them, and as they gained pride in themselves and lived according to that Gospel.'

Father Ruffaldi in 1976 helped to organize the first local indigenous assembly, held at the Galibi village Kumarumã. The tribal leaders were unanimous in resisting invasions of their territory – by settlers on land, by poachers up the rivers, and by a new road, the BR-156 Macapá–Oiapoque, that would cut across the headwaters of the Uaçá and its tributaries. The chiefs wrote to the President of Funai demanding the demarcation of a reserve for all their peoples and protesting about the evil influences that the road would bring. It was a hard struggle. A local press campaign sought to incite local settlers against the Indians, and in 1980 the Procurator of the Republic publicly called for the expulsion of the foreigner Father Nello because he was a bad influence in inciting the indigenous peoples. But the campaign for land resulted in a victory for the Indian cause: the Uaçá reserve for the three tribes, planned in 1977 and fully demarcated by 1983. The reserve *was* traversed by the new road at its south-western corner and western edge; but its boundaries were otherwise those requested by the Indians – sufficiently far inland to inhibit access to the rivers by prospectors and alligator poachers. The reserve's 434,660 hectares (1,680 square miles) contain over 2,600 people – a tripling of population in recent decades.

The tribal assemblies started in 1976 developed into important annual events. Representatives were invited from nearby tribes, such as the Wayampi, Wayana Apalaí, Tiriyó, and peoples of French Guyana. The assemblies last for three days and include intertribal competitions in archery, canoe racing, and football. 'On the final day, everyone joins in a traditional Turé festival, organized by the host tribe. Each people demonstrates its peculiar traditions in the songs, style of dancing, and ornaments of the Turé. But the tone that dominates the Assembly's discussions is normally a united exposition of complaints about problems common to all the peoples represented. The indigenous organizers seek to avoid thorny questions relating to internal disputes. What prevails is a clear confrontation of the "authorities" who are present.' The latter defend their positions and give politicians' promises; but action does finally result from repeated demands. By the late 1980s, the assemblies were considered sufficiently important to attract the Governor of Amapá, local military commanders, senior officials from Funai, missionary organizations, non-government organizations, and the media. They tackled issues of land demarcation, threats by roads and other invaders (not just to the Uaçá reserve, but also to other Indian lands), lack of understanding of Indians by school teachers, health, and emigration by people to French Guyana.

The assembly of 1995 closed, as usual, with the Turé celebration, many speeches by native orators, plenty of caxiri beer, presentation of trophies to sporting victors, and a big dance to lambada and other Brazilian music. But there was an innovation: 'a religious celebration on ecumenical lines, presided over by pastors of the Assembly of God active among the Palikur, missionaries of the New Tribes Mission of Brazil, and by Father Nello Ruffaldi'. This ecumenical service was symptomatic of recent development. The indigenous peoples of Amapá had gained physical survival, some material prosperity, and political awareness from the missionaries; but they were divided between the sects of Christianity; and they had lost forever most of their tribal culture.

By the end of the century, the situation of the Amapá Indians had improved somewhat. The economy is still based on subsistence farming and fishing (fish, alligators, and turtles). Manioc flour is still the main export, and the Indians can easily navigate to the Oiapoque and then along the coast to sell their manioc, dried fish, canoes, and handicrafts in French Guyana. Funai has finally succeeded in introducing plantations of rice, sugar cane, and maize, and the missionaries have installed trading shops that do not cheat the Indians. Primary schooling and health care are better, thanks to Funai, the state education system, and of course the missionaries – the Baptists of the SIL, the New Tribes Mission, Palikur Pentecostalists, and Catholics particularly among the Galibi and Karipuna.

16. Panará

In 1950 the Villas Boas brothers crash-landed a plane on the low Cachimbo ('Pipe') Hills, between the Xingu and Tapajós rivers, some 300 kilometres (190 miles) north-west of Diauarum. They had just finished cutting the trail across to the Tapajós and had made contact with the Kayabi tribe. A reconnaissance flight across the Cachimbo Hills went wrong. Flying through cloud, they were suddenly confronted by a jagged bald outcrop. The pilot just managed to lift the plane's nose above the rock, but its tail struck. This crash caused the nose to dive and there, miraculously, was a patch of clear open campo amid the surrounding forest. 'What we did not know was that our "guardian angel" was there beside us, laughing.' The pilot managed to land and the three brothers scrambled out unscathed from tumbled boxes of cargo. They later decided to land another plane on the hard, sandy savannah; and during 1951 the air force (FAB) built an airstrip with a few stone houses alongside it. Cachimbo always remained an air force base, manned by a handful of airmen and serving as a weather station in this very remote part of central Brazil.

Ten years later in 1961, I myself flew in to Cachimbo in an air force Dakota. My friend from Oxford days, Richard Mason, wanted to lead the first expedition down the unexplored Iriri river, which rises in the Cachimbo Hills and flows northwards for some 1,100 kilometres (almost 700 miles) before joining the lower Xingu. We recruited Kit Lambert, the son of a distinguished composer and later famous as a pop-music impresario, as the expedition's cameraman. Once in Brazil, our plan was well received. FAB offered all help, because it was exasperated by its pilots getting lost over that part of Brazil. The national mapping agency, IBGE, sent three of its best surveyors since, in those days before satellites, this region had had no aerial photography and was unmapped and unexplored. We were given permission to name any features we discovered. I went to consult Orlando Villas Boas and found him looking out of place in the SPI offices in a new green-glassed ministry block in the half-built capital city, Brasília. He assured me that no Indians had been seen near Cachimbo itself; but halfway down the Iriri we would pass through the territory of the Menkragnoti Kayapó, so should take care and try to sleep on islands. Orlando even offered to lead our expedition, if we could postpone it to the following year. This was not possible, so we hired five woodsmen in Cuiabá and our eleven-man team flew to Cachimbo with all our supplies and equipment.

The Iriri River Expedition went well. For five months we cut a picada trail north-eastwards from Cachimbo towards the supposed source of the Iriri. We soon moved out of the campo and cerrado, off the low plateau into beautiful tall rainforest. Each day three men took turns as the cutting party. One of us led, taking a compass bearing to the next tree, then pushing and slashing forward to it while the other two opened a small trail behind. This was often exhausting, thirsty work in the dry terra-firme forest. Although we frequently stopped to sharpen our machetes with a file, by the end of the day our weary arms took several swipes to sever a sapling or creeper that would have fallen with a smart ping in the morning. While the main trail advanced steadily, the other men carried heavy loads up from Cachimbo airstrip. This was arduous, boring work. Camps were moved every few weeks, always to the bank of a small stream, with a circle of hammocks slung in deep shade far below the forest canopy. There was plenty of game in this uninhabited forest. So we sometimes had fresh meat – game birds, peccary, tapir, even jaguar – to supplement our carefully rationed daily dish of black beans, rice, and manioc. But after some months we were thin, pale from seeing direct sunlight only when back at Cachimbo, and covered in scratches and insect bites. The surveying work went well. With radio time signals and a theodolite, we were able to take accurate star fixes – sometimes having to fell a tree to see the stars we needed. But although we knew our coordinates, the lie of the land emerged only gradually from a network of exploratory trails. There was the excitement of breaking through a screen of vegetation to be the first non-Indians to see a lovely river, flowing gently and reflecting the green foliage and dappled sunlight. Each man was allowed to name one new discovery, but we wasted this by using names of current girlfriends – so the map we submitted to the IBGE was covered in variations of Maria.

We set our woodsmen to work making two dugout canoes, each of which took the five men a week with their axes and adzes. These were beautiful craft, fashioned by the illiterate men entirely with biblical finger and hand measurements. Meanwhile the rest of us continued to carry stores forward, including a rubber inflatable boat, an outboard motor, and petrol. Further explorations convinced us that the river on which the

canoes were built curved south-*westwards* towards the Tapajós and was
therefore not the one we were seeking. So weeks were wasted making
fresh canoes on a similar river we had discovered a few kilometres to the
east, which was clearly the Iriri.

By the end of September, we were almost ready for the descent and
surveying traverse of the unknown river. Then tragedy struck. Richard
Mason's body was found, lying on the main supply trail a few kilometres from our camp. He was carrying a load (mostly sugar) up from
Cachimbo and had walked into an Indian ambush. He had been hit by
eight arrows, and his skull and thigh were smashed by club blows. Some
forty arrows and seventeen heavy clubs were arranged around the body.
Richard had been an inspiring and charismatic leader, always optimistic,
cheerful, and working harder than any other member; and he was also a
close friend. The attack was a complete surprise, since we had seen no
signs of Indians during those months in the now-familiar forest; and the
ambush could have caught any one of us. The shattered and frightened
remainder of the expedition hurried back to Cachimbo. After a few days,
the famous sertanista Francisco Meirelles flew in. He sent the SPI's
Hilmar Kluck and Bepunu Kayabi back with us to verify that Richard
had been killed by an Indian attack and try to ascertain which tribe had
done it. The air force sent a squad of jungle troops and a medical team;
these embalmed the body and wrapped it in canvas; we carried Richard
back, slung beneath a pole; and his body was flown to Rio de Janeiro for
burial in the British cemetery. Our expedition was carrying machetes as
presents for Indians we might encounter. I decided to leave a pile of
these at the site of the ambush, in the hope that the assailants might be
less aggressive towards the next stranger they met. We felt that Richard
could have convinced them of his good intentions, had he been given a
chance. But the ambush had clearly been instantaneous. Richard Mason
was the last Englishman ever to be killed by an unknown tribe.

The Kayabi had told the Villas Boas about their fear of a warlike tribe
of big men with powerful voices who lived to the north-east of them.
Various Kayapó groups (who lived to the east) confirmed that they often
moved their villages for fear of attack by a fierce tribe in that region. They
called the unknown people the Kren Akróre ('Men with Heads Cut
Round') because of their pudding-bowl haircuts; but it was later learned
that that tribe referred to itself as Panará. A rumour spread that the
fearsome strangers were giants: a boy called Mengire, captured by the
Mentuktire Kayapó, grew into a man 2.06 metres (6 feet 9 inches) tall.
There was a famous photograph of Orlando Villas Boas measuring this
giant, but coming up only to his shoulder.

An unfortunate encounter in June 1967 caused a setback in relations with the unknown tribe. A group of Indians appeared at the edge of the Cachimbo airstrip. They came with some women and children, apparently seeking presents – particularly metal cutting tools. The few men on the base saw ten Indians with bows and clubs, and a further horde seemed to be waiting among the trees behind. The regular weekly flight by a C-47 cargo plane happened to be approaching Cachimbo. When the base radioed its pilot that there were Indians at the airstrip, he assumed that it was an attack: he twice buzzed the strip at low level, sending frightened Panará fleeing into the forest; and he then radioed for urgent reinforcements. The air force overreacted hysterically. Four planeloads of heavily armed troops were flown in and established trenches and machine-gun nests around Cachimbo. One plane tragically became lost and crashed: a massive search-and-rescue operation involving thirty-four planes and helicopters finally found the wreckage and five survivors of the plane's complement of thirty. As Orlando Villas Boas said at the time, the tribesmen had obviously come peacefully or they would not have filed onto the open airstrip with their women. 'Shout "Indian" and the whole world goes crazy. The civilizados shoot. They fly aeroplanes all over the jungle. A brigadier is photographed crouched behind a machine gun.' The Indians concluded that the whites were extremely ferocious and dangerous.

At the end of 1967 there was a further disaster for the Panará. The Menkragnoti Kayapó, who lived near the middle Iriri many days' walk to the north, had been enemies of the Panará for many decades. After their contact by Francisco Meirelles in the previous decade, they had obtained guns and ammunition from him and from a missionary. They decided to use these to settle old scores. 'The Menkragnoti party surrounded [a Panará] village before dawn and attacked by firing guns into the houses. The [Panará] were taken totally unaware . . . Resistance was brief in the face of the gunfire, with most of the inhabitants fleeing into the forest.' Adrian Cowell later got twenty black-painted Menkragnoti to re-enact their murderous onslaught. They charged out of the forest, screaming and firing into the air, onto a mock village. Cowell concluded that 'it was obvious that many [Panará] must have been shot down in their huts, and that only one of two would have had time to fire back with their bows. It must have been sheer butchery.' But the attackers were very proud of their victory. One young warrior recalled how they had shot an Indian on the trail who was weaving buriti palms. ' "Then we were onto them, coming down on them in the houses. I shot and missed, hitting only a gourd. The enemy ran after me. I dodged an arrow I saw coming –

twisting and falling aside. So I knocked the enemy down with a shot. He sat there and my older brother, Kayti, shot him right down. Ha! Kren Akróre, I just killed one of you!"' Ayo shouted his recollection: '"I killed this enemy and beat him. There was one that I shot with his child, and he fell so."' Kanga said that it was revenge for the Panará having killed his and other young men's parents. '"My uncle and I took our guns and shot two of them dead. *Be!* There they lie. And there one tried to hide in the grass. *Be!* I got my gun and killed him."' Other Kayapó retold different killings, including the clubbing of women captives because they resisted and bit too much. Twenty-six Panará may have been killed in the 1968 slaughter. One Panará woman later told of the horror. '"Everyone died, my father, my uncles; and I was crying, yes. There, the Kayapó killed my uncle Tausinko. There they killed Pengsura, who was a boy. They killed Sungkrekyan . . . They killed my husband and nephew, they killed my eldest brother, Peyati, my son Yosuri, my brother Kyotisura . . . The Kayapó massacred these people. For this I am angry: I remain angry and I do not forget."'

Later in 1968, Cláudio Villas Boas started trying to make contact with the supposedly gigantic tribe. On one flight he located round plantations of banana trees in the midst of the unending expanse of forest, with a burned village nearby. On another flight they found an inhabited village, alongside amazing gardens in organized geometric patterns. Rows of trees outlined graceful circles of crops or bisected them in neat grids – it was symmetry never seen in any other Amazon tribe, and all done by blunt stone axes. By contrast with the sophisticated plantations, the village's huts were small and shabby. But its men showed their defiance by shooting arrow after arrow up at the circling plane. During the ensuing months, further flights located more villages, all roughly a hundred kilometres (sixty miles) south of Cachimbo, close to a tributary of the Tapajós called Peixoto de Azevedo. Then the Villas Boas recruited an expedition from among their Xingu Indians – mostly Kayabi, led by the astute and charismatic Prepori (who had taken part of his tribe to the Xingu sanctuary, with Cláudio Villas Boas, in 1952), and Juruna. The expedition moved from Diauarum up the Manitsauá river, cut an exhausting 150 kilometre (90 mile) trail westwards, cleared airstrips near the Panará's river, awaited air drops, and built dugout canoes to navigate on the narrow and tortuous Peixoto de Azevedo. It was hard work that took many months.

There was a fleeting glimpse of Indians on a river sandbank, lines of presents suspended on trails, and brave entries into recently abandoned villages. Cowell described one such incursion, which could have been met with a barrage of arrows. 'Orlando's bare belly led the way, forming the spearhead of what must have looked a very odd procession. In his hand he swung an aluminium pot like a thurible, [the Menkragnoti chief] Kretire came next waving a mirror, and Cláudio made benedictions with his saucepan, as if we were some religious order about to exorcise the devil.' On another occasion, the Villas Boas recalled the forest opening before them in a clearing. 'It was a village. The Indians, seeing our approach, abandoned everything and departed so hurriedly that they left bows and arrows, clubs and stone axes.' Near the village were two parallel paths that had evidently been used by teams running a log race; and littered among the huts were massively heavy logs, stripped of their bark, which had been used by the teams of men in such races.

During the weeks of waiting between sightings, the expeditioners pondered the morality of what they were doing. They knew that contact with the Panará was becoming inevitable, so that it had to be made by skilled and well-intentioned professionals like them. But Cláudio insisted that there must be no attempt to coerce the tribe: it must come to accept contact of its own volition. So the expedition was eventually abandoned, during the rains of 1969. Adrian Cowell made a prize-winning television documentary and book, *The Tribe that Hides from Man*, about it. But when the approximation team returned to its camp a few months later, it found that everything left in it had been smashed by clubs.

In 1970 President Médici launched his National Integration Programme to open Amazonia with a grid of penetration roads. One of these was the BR-163 Cuiabá–Santarém. Army engineers pushed this highway northwards, parallel to the Teles Pires headwater of the Tapajós, and by 1972 they were approaching the Peixoto de Azevedo river and the forests of the Panará. There were over 2,000 men, 210 earth-moving machines, and 350 trucks on this massive construction effort. Meanwhile the diagonal BR-80 road was to be driven north-westwards from Xavantina across the northern part of the Xingu Indian park, to join the Cuiabá–Santarém near Cachimbo. It became increasingly imperative to contact the Panará before the arrival of the road-builders and the settlers who moved in their wake. So the Villas Boas resumed their attempted approximation.

In January 1972 Cláudio led an expedition of twenty-six Indians southwards from Cachimbo. As he explained, 'We went not so much to pacify the Kren Akróre [Panará] as to prevent their being victims of a clash with the road workers . . . Rain was the greatest obstacle we had to overcome. The trail progressed slowly.' They cut their trail with only machetes and axes, and moved their camps forward every few weeks – just as we had done on the Iriri Expedition eleven years earlier. Cláudio and Orlando paid tribute to their Kayabi during this and other demoralizing expeditions. 'There is nothing to compare to the spirit of these Indians. They are always ready for whatever is to be done or whatever happens. They do not lose heart, and nothing blunts their good humour and cheerfulness . . . Cold rains, exhaustion, unexpected but inevitable falls, painful hornet stings, hunger and thirst resulting from setbacks and dry stretches [of forest] – in short, everything is cause for gaiety and laughter.' Even the veteran Cláudio complained of the heavy rains, high streams, flooded trails, and slippery mud.

There were increasing signs of Indian presence. In May a worker from the nearby road-builders was shot by arrows, possibly because he had disobeyed orders and fired at Indians. At one burned village, the Villas Boas found a stone axe and bows and arrows that they assumed were meant as presents. The Panará eagerly collected any gifts left for them. Some of these were wrapped in plastic, with pictures of the brothers embracing Indians with round haircuts similar to those of the Panará. But, just as a contact seemed near, the anxious tribe burned another village – but again left presents in its midst. In mid-October a group of fifty Panará appeared on the bank of the Peixoto de Azevedo, shouting and gesticulating while they removed presents. No one could understand what they were saying – was it thanks for the presents, or asking to be left alone, or saying that they planned to leave? And they refused any face-to-face contact.

Cláudio concluded that 'the logical thing for a sertanista to do is to await their return. We cannot force them. Our weapon now is patience.' Orlando echoed this. He insisted that contact with Indians is achieved by patience and resignation. 'Haste achieves nothing, and it can lead to death.' But the great Indianist was frustrated and depressed by what they were attempting. 'In reality, we never achieve our true objectives. All pacified Indians gradually lose their characteristics, their authenticity, and have their culture corrupted by the whites. Once pacified, they cease to be free, to perpetuate their culture. They will gradually lose their customs and abandon their arts. For, even if they remain in their habitat, they will suffer constant pressure from the civilizados.'

It was later learned from the Indians that they were deeply confused by the behaviour of the strangers. In the Panará language 'stranger' and 'enemy' were the same word, so that in a sense this small bellicose nation was at war with the rest of humanity. The hostile reception they received at Cachimbo and Cláudio's flights over their village both occurred just before the Menkragnoti's murderous attack. This convinced them that planes were their enemies. Their northernmost village, Sonkanasan (the one from which the hunting party that killed Richard Mason had come), was burned by the Menkragnoti. Most of its inhabitants took refuge further south in a village called Sonsenasan; but when the Villas Boas flew over it, dropping presents and having arrows shot back at them, it was also burned and abandoned. These exoduses put great pressure on the garden plantations of the remaining five or six villages.

Panará society is governed by frequent debate among the men of each village. This pure democracy tended to divide the Indians into dualistic debating factions. Understandably, there was desperate discussion about how to react to the outside forces that were closing in on the tribe. Did the peaceful behaviour of Cláudio's expedition – which was, of course, constantly watched – and the coveted presents mean that these strangers/enemies were not 'wild' or hostile? On the whole, it was younger men who wanted to have friendly contact with the strangers, while the elders insisted that they were dangerous and untrustworthy and should be killed. A robust Panará warrior, Teseya, later described the anxious debates. '"Many whites have come! The whites have come! What will happen to us? Will they be hostile?" Then I [Teseya] said: "They hung up machetes, so they are not hostile." The old men advised us not to mix with the white men, to leave them alone or they would kill us. They had come to kill us. Those who were not afraid said that the white men had not come to kill us.'

The conciliatory view of the younger warriors prevailed, and the Villas Boas' patience was rewarded on 4 February 1973. A group of twenty or thirty Panará suddenly appeared among the trees across the river from the Villas Boas camp, at a place where presents were frequently left for them. The brothers took a canoe and crossed the river with some Kayabi. Cláudio removed his shoes, waded ashore holding a knife, and talked to the Indians in the various native languages he knew. With him was Dr Belfort de Matos, one of the team of medical doctors from the São Paulo medical school who gave years of voluntary care to the Xingu Indians. Cláudio tried to hand the knife to an Indian, but they indicated that he should leave it on a tree trunk. So 'this enigmatic man went forward, with dark glasses covering his eyes, dishevelled, with a greying beard hanging from his chin, his fragile body covered in torn clothes. And the lords of the forest, both fearful and happy, went towards the tree trunk.' But Cláudio withdrew the knife. Finally a young man advanced and, despite the tension, accepted the offering from the white hand. 'It was contact, at last.' Teseya later described the decisive moment from the Indian point of view. 'We told Hawkene to pick up the machete and he did so. Hawkene approached Cláudio, and Cláudio embraced him and said: "I am not hostile. Do not be afraid of me." Our men said, "We will all come." Hawkene was a small man, and he remained there quietly.'

In another version of the contact, Cláudio sat and pretended to have a painful foot. The Indians were curious about his injury and crowded around to see what was wrong. 'Cláudio rose with difficulty, helped by the Kren Akróre [Panará] and . . . he embraced them and was embraced for a long time.' Orlando said that the expeditioners joked with the Indians. 'We laughed, even guffawed, tapped them on the backs, everything that people do instinctively when they want to show friendship. We could understand nothing that they said, and vice-versa.' The meeting ended with an aged Indian making a long speech, after which they withdrew gradually and vanished into the forest.

In April 1973 the Villas Boas withdrew, exhausted by months of effort in the rain-soaked forests. They were replaced by Apoena Meirelles, wiry, energetic, with a thin black beard and moustache and a mane of curly black hair. There were more exchanges of presents, more fleeting encounters. Once a canoe-load of expeditioners came upon three Panará, who immediately started to fit long arrows to their bows. The genial German photographer Jesco von Puttkamer was there and recalled that they tried to make as much noise as possible, as a sure sign that they were not hostile. So they sang, laughed, and shouted, and Jesco tried to play Viennese waltzes on his accordion. His fingers were trembling so much that he hit wrong notes. But the Panará lowered their bows and allowed the strangers to step slowly onto the river bank. There were more women and children watching from the forest. It was a dangerous moment, and the Indians were naturally tense. But they accepted an invitation to return to the camp in the canoe, and spent a few hours there, conversing in sign language and taking food.

Then came a visit to the attraction camp by a large group of Panará, followed next day by an invitation to visit a village. Apoena, four Xavante, and the portly camera-festooned Puttkamer marched for some thirty-eight kilometres (twenty-four miles) through the forest. They finally passed through neat plantations to a rough circle of huts covered in banana leaves. They were given an elaborate reception. A shaman blew ceremonial breath onto them (perhaps to purge any alien diseases), warriors chanted prayer-like greetings, and there was a traditional weeping welcome. Women painted Apoena's and Jesco's faces. In the evening, they ate bananas and manioc cakes wrapped in banana leaves, cooked on fire-heated stones. The Panará looked undernourished, because road-builders and sertanistas had interrupted their usual farming and hunting, and the abandonment of some villages had swelled others with refugees. Most

Indians had skin infections and some were too stricken by malarial fevers to walk. The visitors were able to give some simple medicines. After eating, the feared Panará sang for their guests, in the light of campfires, smiling beatifically. Every line of their chants ended in the shout 'Ahow!'. The warriors then danced, and throughout the night they watched the visitors, occasionally pounding the ground with heavy war clubs; so no one slept. All these contacts confirmed that the Panará were not giants: the one very tall man captured by the Mentuktire was evidently an aberration, and he died quite young. Their villages belied the elegance of the nearby plantations. They consisted only of a rough circle of seven or eight huts of very primitive construction, roofed with interwoven broken branches covered in banana leaves. The Indians slept on the same leaves, near small fires, and they had no household utensils.

When anthropologists studied the Panará, they were surprised to discover that they were Jê-speaking Kayapó – but the last surviving remnant of the *southern* Kayapó, who had once dominated the plateau east of the Araguaia from southern Mato Grosso to Goiás, but were thought to have been extinguished in the eighteenth and nineteenth centuries. Although their version of Jê was incomprehensible to the northern Kayapó, they retained many traditions such as the log race, bellicosity, preferring to fight with war clubs, sleeping on ground mats or leaves rather than hammocks, dislike of alcohol, tobacco, and hallucinogens, and unfamiliarity with canoes and ceramics.

The BR-163 was opened to traffic in December 1973. The Panará then suffered a crushing succession of disasters, as if the gods were determined to destroy them. Some Indians drifted towards the road, readily accepting trinkets from passing motorists. They loved brown sugar and ate too much in the army engineers' camps; indeed they stopped planting altogether and lived off food handouts from construction workers. Apoena Meirelles left in September 1973 and was succeeded by Antonio Campinas; but Campinas was soon removed because he was accused of having homosexual relations with Indians. Other Funai operatives were found to be sleeping with Panará women, to the dismay of their men. The army was said to be keeping Indians as curiosities in its camps and bribing the tribe to admit gold- and diamond-prospectors to its rivers. The military engineers built a huge camp with many houses only four kilometres (two and a half miles) from the Peixoto de Azevedo river. 'They didn't give a damn about the Indians – their camp could easily have been further north.'

All this promiscuous contact led to the inevitable diseases. There had been some inoculation of the indigenous people after contact but, yet again, not enough medical preparation. Fiorello Parise, the next leader of the attraction campaign, reported that 'they went to the road and caught colds. I removed the ill ones to their villages, but many died. They were like skeletons . . . When we followed their trails, there were only burials.' Another Funai official said that many went to die in the forest, of pneumonia or malaria. He recalled that he himself had pulled some corpses out of the river, into which Indians had jumped to try to alleviate their fevers. The anthropologist Stephan Schwartzman heard about these terrible times from the Indians themselves. Akè, a short, barrel-chested, and forceful man, was a boy at the time, but he remembered twenty years later that 'when the whites came, the Panará all died. Coughing, catarrh, and chest pains killed virtually everybody . . . My mother died then, there in Yopuyupaw village. My brother and my mother died, there in the new houses. The others left, and everyone died on the road . . . They were too weak to bury the dead . . . They all rotted on the ground. Vultures ate them all, on the ground, since they had not been buried.' This failure to bury the dead was almost unknown, and a sign of how frightened and weakened the tribe had become. The tall, handsome Teseya Panará later told Schwartzman: 'Then my grandfather Sewakri died. On arrival [at the new village] my mother died, from fear of the white men . . . Then our people started to get ill, ill. Everyone was lying there, prostrate. The others went into the forest, one here, another there. One died, died, died, everyone was ill. "What is happening to us? Perhaps the white man is to blame," they said. Everyone died there.' In desperation, they returned to an old village; but the situation did not improve. 'We slept in the forest. Children, adults, all were dying . . . People died from every family. "What will happen to us?"' Some survivors congregated at Topayurõ village, and the less devastated gathered honey and bananas. But the deaths continued.

The two anthropologists who first studied the Panará pieced together the locations and movements of their villages in the period before contact. From this, Richard Heelas estimated the population had been 425 to 525 people in seven villages, whereas Stephan Schwartzman reckoned 700 to 750. Schwartzman also deduced, from his many interviews, that one of the worst epidemics had struck the Panará *before* the moment of contact with Cláudio Villas Boas. The catastrophic depopulation was exacerbated by other factors: abandonment of villages from fear of diseases and planes, without taking seeds to plant elsewhere; ritual executions of shamans suspected of having brought the epidemics; and even debilitation from the extreme mourning required of survivors of dead relatives. Thus, over sixty people died violently, immediately after contact. Schwartzman appreciated that 'It is difficult to imagine the degree of social disorganization that accompanied the arrival of the road, the contacting expedition, and the sudden deaths of so many people.' By the end of 1973 the Panará were reduced to about 110 people, a year later to 82. Twenty years later, Schwartzman got Teseya and three old women to list the names, clans and approximate ages of all the people who perished between 1973 and 1975. It was a chilling roll, of 176 Indians of all ages and both sexes.

Funai tried to react to the catastrophe. There was a campaign of inoculation and attempts to give medical treatment, but this assistance was confused, fragmented, and inadequate. The task was almost impossible, because only parts of the Panará had been contacted and others were fleeing into the depths of their forests or seeking the lure of the new road. The denunciation of homosexual misconduct by Antonio Campinas, the new leader of the Panará attraction, appeared in the press in March 1973. Suddenly, the fierce and proud 'giants' of the previous year's stories were portrayed and photographed as sickly, starving, and dirty Indians, begging from traffic on the new road, and degraded by civilization's diseases, alcohol, tobacco, and sexual interference. (The Panará later vigorously denied that they had accepted alcohol, tobacco, or prostitution; but such emotive words added to the impact of the press reports.) At that same time, Funai obtained a decree 'interdicting' (which means secluding an area prior to possible reserve status) 400,000 hectares (1,500 square miles); but the designated area was in the wrong place – it omitted five Panará villages and even the Funai post. The anthropologist Valéria Parise reported that 'a great sadness and melancholy is evident among these Indians. They live in a state of expectancy, with artificial behaviour, continually having to adapt to the ways of the camp and decisions of the [Funai] sertanista.' In June 1974 her husband, Funai's local agent Fiorello Parise, moved some Panará survivors to a new village called Inkonakoko, fifty kilometres (thirty miles) from the road.

When the Panará were first contacted, there was a suggestion that they should be moved eastwards into the forests of the Xingu Indian park. In January 1972 Orlando dismissed this idea as crazy, since the Panará were devoted to their ancient homelands, and the Xingu contained alien tribes including their bitter enemies the Mentuktire (Txukahamãe). At that time, he demanded a large reserve for the tribe they were trying to contact; and such a reserve had been in the initial proposal for the Xingu park, twenty years previously. But by 1974 the situation of the Panará was deteriorating so fast and so catastrophically that the Villas Boas and others changed their minds. They started to argue that the tribe must be moved or face extinction. A well-meaning new President of Funai, General Ismarth Araújo de Oliveira, sent Fiorello Parise to see whether the tribe could remain in its lands. This was what he wanted. But, in his instructions, he told Parise: 'If you find no way for them to survive and you cannot get them away from the road, I shall start the transfer plan'. Cláudio Villas Boas now felt that a rescue operation was 'the only way to prevent these Indians from disappearing . . . Even if a large reserve were demarcated for them, it would not be a satisfactory solution' since they were too nomadic. Settlers were already starting to investigate the edges of Panará land, which was rumoured to be rich in gold and diamonds. Parise's report on the health and social disintegration of the tribe was devastating. So the President of Funai decided that he must act immediately. He personally removed the interdiction on the 400,000 hectares earmarked for the Panará. And he ordered Villas Boas: 'Orlando, transfer them!'

The decision to evict the tribe, for its salvation, was controversial. Fiorello Parise argued against the move, as did Father Antonio Iasi of the nearby Jesuit Anchieta Mission. They said that the transfer would benefit only the colonization and mining companies that were greedily eyeing the forests of the Peixoto de Azevedo. In the event, such fears were justified. Funai awarded the formerly interdicted area to the government's colonization department, Incra. Ranchers, settlers, and prospectors poured in; a decree of June 1979 formally nullified the Indian reserve; and the beautiful forests of this part of Brazil were destroyed for ever and their rivers polluted. Twenty-three towns eventually sprang up along the BR-163, including Matupá on the site of a Panará village. All this was technically illegal under the Constitution and the Statute of the Indian, which guaranteed a tribe the land on which it had always lived and hunted. Parise argued that the Panará were already coming to understand that the road brought disease, and were losing their fascination with this sinister invader. He later said that: 'For me, the move was a disaster . . . You cannot take a people and transport them from one place to another' like cattle. The migration would later be seen as 'ethnic cleansing'. But in the crisis atmosphere of 1974 it was felt that any delay could be fatal – there would soon be no Indians left, either to rescue or to leave in their habitat. The fate of the Panará had in fact been decided a few years earlier – when the government ordered the building of the Cuiabá–Santarém highway that passed through their land.

Cláudio Villas Boas took Kreton and another Panará chief to see the Xingu, and they were impressed by the friendly reception given them by the tribes around Posto Leonardo. They also liked the hens and other domestic animals they saw there. Back on the Peixoto de Azevedo, there was a hasty consultation with the tribal elders. Orlando Villas Boas called this a 'plebiscite' and said that everyone agreed to move eastwards to the sanctuary of the Xingu park. But some Funai officials later doubted whether the Panará realized that they would be migrating for ever – they left all their meagre possessions behind and had not even harvested beloved peanuts, which perform a central role in tribal custom and were ripe for picking.

The exodus took place on 1 January 1975. All the Panará were transported in three forty-minute flights of a C-47 (the workhorse transport plane of the Brazilian air force) with the tribe's four clans each travelling together. After a night of welcoming celebrations at Diauarum, the Panará were taken to a clearing on the edge of the Xingu, where the Kayabi had prepared two huts and a small plantation of corn for them. The leaders were embraced by Raoni, chief of the Mentuktire (Txukaha-mãe), and Chief Prepori of the Kayabi – both tribes that had been enemies of the Panará. Journalists reported that the Panará seemed as relaxed as seasoned travellers during the flight, that they enjoyed the banquet of roast peccary, papaya, and bananas, that their Chief Sokriti was pleased with a headdress given him by Raoni, and that the Indians were smiling when they first saw the clearing prepared for them. But one Panará later told Stephan Schwartzman that some people were crying from fear during the flight, even though they appreciated that they had to go to escape the diseases and fevers killing them in their homelands. And Sokriti said: 'We thought we were going to meet relatives. I was trembling with fear in the plane and clung to the seat.' Another journalist felt that the handshakes with avowed enemies were 'a violent humiliation' for Sokriti.

On arrival at Diauarum, the Panará were given thorough medical examinations and further inoculations by a team from the São Paulo teaching hospital. These doctors were led by the gentle and indomitable Roberto Baruzzi, a specialist in preventive medicine who took teams of volunteers every year to tend to the health of the Xingu Indians. Professor Baruzzi devoted his life to the well-being of the Indians, just as much as the Villas Boas did. The medical team found that the seventy-nine Panará were in generally satisfactory health, although most were underweight and some were anaemic. All suffered from hookworm, all had evidence of malaria in their blood, and almost half had chronically enlarged spleens. During the tribe's first eighteen months in the Xingu, it suffered a further eleven deaths, from influenza and pneumonia but above all from 'frequent, severe attacks of malaria'. The doctors concluded that 'the group that entered the [Xingu] national park had been decimated beyond the most pessimistic calculations. They were profoundly socially disorganized and there was not the necessary cohesion among them to resist the hostile forces of the new environment. A growing apathy affected their already weakened state of health.'

The move into the Xingu was not a success. The Panará had never seen a large river, could not use canoes, and disliked the huts and clearing prepared for them by the Kayabi. The garden of maize ran out in a few weeks. But the greatest problem was that the forests of the upper Xingu were lower and drier, weak in the game and forest fruits that had abounded in the verdant valley of the Peixoto de Azevedo. The tribe was soon moved downriver to the Mentuktire village of Kretire. This almost destroyed them. They were arbitrarily divided among the huts of their erstwhile enemies, who were now far tougher, numerous, self-confident, and prosperous than the emaciated remnant of the once-feared warriors. It became clear that Chief Raoni wanted to absorb them altogether, particularly since his tribe had an excess of young men whereas there were more unattached women among the newcomers.

Luckily, a newly arrived head of the Xingu park, Olimpio Serra, convinced Cláudio Villas Boas that his latest move had been a disastrous mistake; so he transferred the Panará, yet again, in October 1975. Some women and children remained with the Mentuktire. The remainder now resided in a circle of four huts near the former Suyá village not far from Diauarum. This was a semblance of their traditional village layout; they were learning to fish with boats and hooks; they planted gardens and hunted. Cláudio gave them presents of clothing and even guns and ammunition – distributed by night so that others would not be jealous, and with strict instructions that the firearms were for hunting and not for use against other Indians. So their morale improved. From a nadir in 1976, their health and population also recovered. Professor Baruzzi and his medical team continued to give regular checks and treatment to each Panará throughout the final quarter of the century. Thus the Indians enjoyed better medical attention than almost anyone in South America, and they ultimately prospered physically as a result. From the low point of 69 people, the Panará increased to 84 by 1980 and 95 by 1982 – all from births since the move to the Suyá village.

Such was their renaissance that in May 1983 the Panará decided to move to a new village far to the north down the Xingu river. This move, 'contemplated and discussed long before by the Panará, was regarded by them as a matter of their survival, and they have shown every intention of continuing as an autonomous group'. Now that the Panará were more accustomed to the ways of Xingu hunting and fishing, they became better providers for their families. Thus, some Panará men succeeded in recovering women who had settled among the Mentuktire or Kayabi. Akè Panará told Stephan Schwartzman that in 1983 the Panará had 'searched and searched, and downriver seemed good. I went to look. We left once more, down the Xingu river. But in that place more people died.' In 1989 the tribe made a further move, to a location far up the Manitsauá-Missu tributary, at the western edge of the Xingu park towards their former homelands. In Akè's words: 'From there, we left again, to come here [to the Manitsauá-Missu]. Here . . . no one has died, we have plantations, and we are not dying.' However, all was not well. When the film-maker Brian Moser interviewed Akè in 1991, the tough chief complained: 'I do not enjoy being here on the Xingu. It is wretched being in a place you don't like . . . On the Peixoto we had good land, we had fruit trees, much game to hunt – there was plenty. I have great nostalgia to be back in such a rich place. I greatly miss the Peixoto, my land, where I was born.' To Schwartzman, Akè listed the riches he missed. 'There on the Peixoto there are many fruits – açaí [a palm with fruit rich in vitamins], papaya, cupuaçu [the delicious fruit of a tree related to the chocolate-making cacao], cashews, pupunha [the fruit of the spiny peach palm *Guilielma speciosa*] – many kinds of honey, abundant peccary, much fish, much game, plenty of mutum [curassow or wild turkey]. But it has all ceased . . . On my river there were plenty of Brazil nuts: we used to eat them during hunts, when we were hungry returning to our village.'

Akè was a born leader, who could switch from being jovially charming to angrily forceful to get results. He appealed for help to Olimpio Serra, who had in 1975 succeeded the Villas Boas as their chosen successor in running the Xingu park; and Serra turned to the research centre CEDI to obtain satellite images of the devastation of the Panará forests on the Peixoto de Azevedo. Akè also enlisted the help of Stephan Schwartzman and of lawyers of the NDI. (Schwartzman was the Panará's closest friend, having lived with them for fourteen years; he went on to work for the influential Environmental Defense Fund in Washington. The NDI was the Nucleus for Indigenous Rights, a dynamic pro-Indian NGO in Brasília led by Márcio Santilli, a future President of Funai.) At the end of 1991 these well-wishers took Akè and two other tribal leaders by buses up the BR-163 to Matupá, a bustling frontier town on the site of a former Panará village. They then walked into the Peixoto de Azevedo, for the first time since their exodus sixteen years earlier. They were confronted by desolation. Vast stretches of the former paradise were barren mud, the forests gone and the rivers gouged and polluted. The Indians gazed in horror at the effects of two decades of uncontrolled deforestation, aggressive but largely futile cattle ranching, and profligate mineral prospecting. Brian

Moser filmed Akè, wielding a club, angrily confronting garimpeiros who had destroyed the beautiful forests of his boyhood. The team then hired a plane to overfly the area. This saw that six of the tribe's eight villages were obliterated by ranches; but it noted that the forests north of Cachimbo were still intact. Cachimbo itself had expanded in 1979 into a large but secret air force base, strictly off-limits and rumoured to be the site of atomic-weapons testing.

In 1992 Panará leaders and Stephan Schwartzman returned, on an eighty-kilometre (fifty-mile) expedition into the surviving forests, to try to locate Sonkanasan, the village of Richard Mason's ambushers and the one destroyed by the Mentuktire attack. On another journey in 1993 they met ranchers, who had opened an airstrip on the Iriri and were surveying the forests with a view to claiming them. So the lawyers and surveyors had to act fast. They drew up plans for a large reserve on the upper Iriri and Ipiranga rivers; obtained the support of Sydney Possuelo, the experienced and sympathetic President of Funai; and in August 1994 launched a legal action against the government of Brazil claiming the permanent possession of this land – under Article 231 of the Constitution – as well as its demarcation. Lawyers from ISA even demanded monetary compensation for the sufferings of the Panará people.

Akè and others had already hired a plane to take them to Kubenkokre, the village of their former Menkragnoti enemies on the middle Iriri, from whence they moved up the river and started to build a new village. They named it Nacypotire, meaning 'Iriri river'. The anthropologist Ana Gita de Oliveira helped the tribe to repossess its land, defending it in a tense confrontation with armed gunmen from a nearby town and ranches. In November 1994 there was a three-day meeting at the Panará village back on the Manitsauá-Missu, to discuss whether the tribe should leave the sanctuary of the Xingu and attempt to return to a corner of its former territory. Chief Raoni of the Mentuktire was there, with his nephew Megaron who was now the Director of the Xingu park, and so was Mairawe, the Kayabi chief now in charge of Diauarum post. A few of the younger Panará wanted to remain in the Xingu, but most of the eloquent speeches were in favour of a new life on the Iriri. Other tribes who had been transferred into the Xingu – the Kayabi, Txikão, and Tapayuna – spoke of their own nostalgia for former lands. In December 1994 Funai issued an interdiction order, to keep intruders out of the would-be reserve, and asked the Minister of Justice to confirm its protected status. This was finally done on 1 November 1996, with the Panará given permanent possession of a 495,000 hectare (1,900 square mile) reserve.

The Panará gradually moved back to the Iriri during 1995 and 1996.

The return from their unhappy twenty-one-year diaspora was completed in nine flights in a light plane capable of landing on the new village's small airstrip. Nacypotire village is in a beautiful location, on a bluff above a curve of the Iriri. The river's waters are dappled dark green from the reflection of the tall trees and creepers towering above it. Inland, the Panará created the geometrical plantations of peanuts, bananas, and other crops for which they are famous. Paths lead down the steep riverbank to three bathing places: one upriver for the children to play for hours on end in the sandy shallows; another for adult Indians to take their frequent baths; and a third, downriver, for visitors. The village started as a small circle of traditional thatched huts, but in 1998 the Panará started to enlarge this circle by facing some huts in the opposite direction and building handsome new ones around a larger perimeter. In the centre is the men's hut and a dusty football pitch. There is constant activity, with both sexes making headdresses and other ornaments (for themselves and for sale), women using pedal sewing machines to make pretty dresses or working on piles of peanuts and other foods. The men provide game and fish from regular hunting and fishing expeditions – nowadays making good use of guns, fish-hooks and line, and canoes with outboard motors. They wear shorts and T-shirts proclaiming exotic advertisements or slogans. Most have Brazilian haircuts rather than their traditional pudding-bowl crowns. One hut even has a solar panel rigged to a car battery that powers a tape-recorder, on which the Panará can play Brazilian music or their preference: a recording of themselves singing.

Despite the changes in clothing and some possessions, all traditional customs of the Panará are still practised in the normal way. There is in fact a marked increase in the frequency of festivals and rituals. Panará morale has soared with the return to their own territory, where they are in charge of their own affairs. André Villas Boas (the leading anthropologist in the Xingu park, a distant relative of the famous brothers) realized that there the Panará had been an insignificant minority, dealing with Funai and other whites through more powerful tribes. 'When they moved, it was their turn to manage relations with the outside world, with Funai, ISA, loggers, and farmers'.

The grass airstrip is immediately alongside the village, and beyond it are buildings for Funai's administrator, with a small workshop, a dispensary for Professor Baruzzi and his doctors to give regular health checks, wells, latrines for outsiders, and a new school hut. Thanks to medical treatment and improved diet and morale, there are plenty of children: the tribe's population passed 200 at the start of the twenty-first century. The Panará have been shrewd about choosing elements of outside society that are of most benefit to them. Their large reserve supplies their food needs, but they have difficulty in earning money to buy manufactured necessities such as ammunition and petrol.

Lawyers from the Centre of Indigenous Work (CTI) launched an audacious claim for compensation for the tragically mismanaged contact of the Panará. In a landmark judgement, unprecedented in Brazilian history, Judge Novély Vilanova in October 1997 found in their favour. Although the judge accepted that the government agents had been well intentioned in contacting the tribe and later moving it into the Xingu park, they were guilty of certain 'acts and omissions . . . and had failed to adopt vigorous provisions to protect the community'. He ordered damages paid to the family of every Indian who died in the terrible two years 1973–75, with the amounts based on actuarial calculations of each victim's life expectancy. Judge Vilanova also awarded a substantial payment to the tribe as a whole, as 'moral damages' for its sufferings and cultural disruption.

Bountiful rainforests will never return to the former homeland of the Panará on the Peixoto de Azevedo river. After its spoliation by prospectors and ranchers, the area was found to be ideal for commercial growing of soya beans. The 'Advance Brazil' programme, to develop Amazonia at the end of the twentieth century, financed massive agribusiness and the asphalting of the Cuiabá–Santarém highway, the road that stabbed into Panará territory. Experience from Rondônia showed that paving roads, so that they are not impassable from mud in the rainy season, brings an avalanche of migrants and trucking. Soya from the Peixoto plantations will be transported to the main Amazon river at Santarém. And forests on either side of the road will be obliterated, just as wantonly as those beside the BR-364 were in Rondônia in the 1980s.

This author visited the Panará soon after their return to Nacypotire. They had been told that I was on the expedition they had ambushed back in 1961, so they were slightly apprehensive that I would be angry or vengeful. To my amazement, these people who had suffered such catastrophes recalled every detail of their killing of Richard Mason so many years earlier. They confirmed what we had originally guessed: that a long-range hunting party had come across our main trail – pounded during five months of porterage and quite unlike an Indian path, which is almost invisible to Western eyes – and had laid an ambush. That hunting party went from Sonkanasan village, but none of its members was still alive. However, I talked to the gentle giant Teseya, a man of my age who had been a young warrior in another village at the time. Teseya was lying in his hammock late one afternoon, and his account was translated for me by Elizabeth Ewart, a young British anthropologist who had lived with the Panará for several years and was completing a doctorate about their vision of the outside world. Teseya said that the Indians waiting in ambush had heard the swish, swish of Richard's jeans as he approached – this was a novel sound for people who had no experience of clothing. Seeing that he was alone, they killed him. That had always been the Panará way.

Teseya also said that, when the warriors returned, the village elders were angry about the killing for fear that it would bring reprisals. While we were talking, an old lady interrupted. This was Yopó, widow of Chief Sokriti, who had died earlier that year. She said that we should have asked her late husband, since he had been one of the ambush party. Yopó recalled many items found on Richard's body, all of which were unfamiliar to the Panará at that time. She even said that there was something shiny that the men tried to smash with their clubs. I then remembered that we had found Richard's shiny metal cigarette lighter lying, dented, near the body. I asked Yopó whether her husband had recovered the machetes we left there when we removed the corpse. She certainly *did* remember those machetes: they had had a tremendous impact on the tribe, which had no metal cutting tools. Yopó ran into her hut and returned with a rusty machete. 'They were good machetes, long ones, very long! The old men were angry that *they* had not got these machetes. They struck them against logs to try to break them; but they could not.' She slammed the machete against a block of wood for dramatic effect. Teseya later put his arm around my shoulders and said that it had all happened a long time ago – a time when the Panará were at war with all other tribes, when they had the same word for 'stranger' and for 'enemy'. 'At that time we did not know that there were good white men and bad white men.' He then named the good white men who had helped them recover some of their forests. 'You are a good white man: you can come back and visit us whenever you want.'

17. Struggles for Land: the South

It is often said that the prerequisites for Indians' survival are land and health. Tribal health gradually improved during the final quarter of the twentieth century. Almost every tribe had suffered catastrophic population decline from epidemics of alien diseases; but the few who survived tended to transmit genetic immunity to those lethal afflictions. Funai's campaigns of preventive medicine were often inadequate and disorganized, but they did help to spread some protection of Brazil's indigenous peoples. One breakthrough was a vaccine against measles, one of the worst killers of Indians, which was gradually administered during the 1970s. Some fine doctors dedicated themselves to the cause, notably the Villas Boas' charismatic friends Noel Nutels and Roberto Baruzzi. Professor Baruzzi of the São Paulo Medical School's department of preventive medicine took teams of volunteer doctors to examine and treat every Indian in the Xingu during the last third of the twentieth century, and for a time he was in charge of medical treatment of all Brazilian Indians. The team from São Paulo then started courses to teach the Indians to do their own preventive medicine and to carry norms of sanitation and healthy living back to their villages. There were doctors, dentists, and nurses scattered among Funai's many posts, unsung heroes and heroines who were often deeply frustrated by failures of support and supply. The missionaries also played an important medical role. If indigenous people were to turn from shamanism to Christianity, they had to be convinced that the Western medicine delivered by missionaries was more effective than their own herbal remedies and faith healing. Mission villages therefore had trained nurses, and pharmacies that were better stocked and equipped than those of the government posts.

Tribes who overcame the traumas of contact and depopulation regained self-respect, which in turn led to a rise in the birth rate. In 1953 the distinguished anthropologists Darcy Ribeiro and Eduardo Galvão guessed 150,000 as the population of Brazil's tribal Indians. (In a fit of pessimism four years later, Ribeiro lowered this to 100,000.) In separate documents in 1972, Funai gave 150,000 and 180,000. Indigenous peoples had by then passed their nadir, with almost every tribe increasing in numbers during the final four decades of the century. Such recovery was of course relative, since tribes had fallen almost to the point of extinction; and the national population also increased massively during this period.

Land was a greater problem. In 1987 CEDI and the National Museum published an excellent survey of 518 indigenous territories that were by then home to 213,000 Indians. The report's authors strongly criticized Funai for its slowness in legalizing indigenous lands. The Indian Statute of 1973 had given Funai five years to demarcate *all* Indian reserves. In the event, fifteen years later, over half the areas were 'in the delicate situation of being merely identified by Funai, which amounts to a veritable "administrative limbo" regarding the guarantee of their rights'. Funai was equally remiss about protecting areas that were 'identified' or 'delimited'. A third of these was affected by 'non-Indian prospecting, research, and extraction by mining companies, implantation of hydroelectric dams, or passage of roads.' There was no firm data on invasion by farming, ranching, or extractive activities, but every indication 'makes us believe that this phenomenon is almost generalized.'

It was these last threats that caused most of the conflicts in the heavily populated parts of southern and eastern Brazil. We have seen how tribe after tribe had to resist invasion of its territory – Nambiquara, Suruí, Tapirapé, Bororo, and many others. The danger was often greatest with tribes that had been in contact for centuries, because these had small reserves, in more open farmlands where property was valuable, long since surrounded by settlers, and in developed parts of Brazil near the Atlantic seaboard and far from the Amazon forests.

The Kaingang and Xokleng of Brazil's southernmost states suffered acute pressure on their reserves. These were the tribes that had been persecuted by professional Indian-hunters during the nineteenth century, and were then 'pacified' in some of the SPI's earliest successes. By the 1970s they were largely acculturated: farming and occasionally hunting, just like the surrounding caboclos of the rolling farmlands of this temperate part of Brazil. They were among the most sophisticated Indians and they were emboldened by the oratory of the NGOs and at CIMI's assemblies held in their area.

Although relatively small, some of the southern reserves still contained stands of Paraná pines (*Araucaria brasiliensis*), a magnificent endemic tree that was coveted by the timber trade and therefore threatened with extinction. This made indigenous lands vulnerable. On 12 May 1949 an unscrupulous Governor of Paraná, Moysés Lupion, had signed an agreement with the Federal Ministry of Agriculture (the ministry that controlled the SPI at that time) to remove great swathes of Indian land – so that he and his cronies could acquire it for 'development' and 'colonization'. The scale of reductions was astounding: Paraná's six reserves lost three-quarters of the areas they had been granted at the beginning of the twentieth century. The transfer of some 132,000 hectares (500 square miles) from federal to state control without authorization by the Senate violated three laws or articles of the Constitution. The lands were then awarded to so-called colonization agencies; and many soon passed into the hands of property companies.

The situation was just as bad in Brazil's southernmost state, Rio Grande do Sul. A federal inquiry in 1961 found massive irregularities. 'The forested reserves of Nonoái, Guarita, and other posts had been ruined by irregular and uneconomic concessions to timber firms.' SPI agents were easily persuaded to make such awards. One timber company got a licence to fell 13,558 pine trees at the Cacique Doble post. It proceeded to cut down *all* the reserve's trees, but its quota was not fulfilled; so the SPI gave it permission to acquire the balance from posts in Santa Catarina State; in the end it took 150,000 trees – eleven times the original licence. The historian of Brazilian Indians Carlos Moreira Neto wrote, in despair: 'As a result the area over which the exuberant pine forest of the Cacique Doble Indian post formerly extended is now covered only by a spontaneous growth of low [weedy] vegetation' that brought erosion.

There was equal devastation at Nonoái and Guarita. Originally some 35,000 hectares (135 square miles), Nonoái reserve had been reduced by over half to 14,910 hectares (58 square miles), when a temporary state government in 1941 designated some 20,000 hectares (77 square miles) as a 'forest reserve'. Nonoái then had its boundaries further reduced by invasions by 1,300 families of settlers, encouraged by left-wing politicians during the government of João Goulart, 1961–64. Goulart's brother-in-law Leonel Brizola was the populist Governor of Rio Grande do Sul, and his officials openly sided with squatters who had votes against unenfranchised indigenous peoples. Many of the scandals revealed in the 1967 Figueiredo inquiry that put an end to the SPI related to financial irregularities in southern Brazil. Even after corrupt officials of the SPI were removed, Funai was 'cautious and dilatory – which tends to strengthen the status quo.' The parliamentary commission was appalled by what it found. At Guarita post, Kaingang families were 'camped in a pigsty, under bridges or in open forest, for lack of resources to house them'. Others were described as living like favela shanty-town dwellers, in the midst of their former forests and plains. There was an acute shortage of land, so that Indians had to migrate from one reserve to another. Atrocities against

Indians included a man at Nonoái being stoned to death over land – the stones used in the murder and a photograph of it were shown to the Commission.

In July 1969 a further 200 colonist families occupied another large part of Nonoái, even taking land that the Indians had cleared to plant wheat and evicting some native people from their homes. Thus, 'Nonoái is a native reserve occupied by white colonists, where the Kaingang are steadily becoming more impoverished and powerless.' The loss of farmland and of pine forests that had supplied so much food 'reduced the Indians of Nonoái to a starvation diet', with all age groups undernourished and three or four people a month dying of neglect. One woman eloquently explained what this meant to the Kaingang: 'Today my people see their land invaded, their forests destroyed, their animals slaughtered, and their hearts lacerated by this brutal weapon that is civilization. For the whites and so-called civilizados this may seem like romanticism. But not for our people – for us it is our life.'

In 1970 there were 1,400 Kaingang and Guarani living in Guarita reserve, but two-thirds of its 23,000 hectares (57,000 acres) had been leased to white settlers by Funai. A local journalist charged that during the past five months ninety-one Indians, including seventeen children, had died through the negligence of their post's chief, retired Lieutenant Herminio dos Santos. There were grisly stories of this agent leaving a man with a burst appendix dying in agony, and 'himself deciding to examine a sick woman, saying that "he knew about such things". He prescribed some medicine and charged 5 cruzeiros [$1] for the consultation.' A doctor said that most deaths resulted from poor food – children were fed only manioc flour, which is rich in calories but devoid of protein – and bad hygiene, with scabies, worms, and flu almost endemic. The state delegate Plínio Dutra wrote to President Médici: 'Today in Rio Grande do Sul Indians are wretched smallholders. White invaders occupy their fertile lands and the banks of fishing rivers and are destroying forests rich in game. They are, in short, doing everything necessary to condemn the Indians to death.'

Conditions were equally desperate in the neighbouring state, Santa Catarina. Funai's regional inspector blamed ignorant politicians for inciting land invasions, particularly at a reserve near Xanxerê. Here the Xokleng 'suffer every sort of privation, living in miserable huts that would not even serve as pig-pens.' Funai continued to extract large quantities of timber from Xapecó post south of Xanxerê. But when in 1976 an epidemic of whooping cough killed thirteen people there, the chief complained bitterly that none of these profits returned to the Indians: 'Our brothers continue to die for lack of medical assistance'. Three hundred Kaingang once lived east of Xapecó, in the Toldo (Tented Camp) of Chief Chimbangue. After the Second World War, property companies reached this part of western Santa Catarina and gradually sold off the lands of Toldo Chimbangue. The Kaingang were forced into a triangle where the Irani river joins the upper Uruguay. A local newspaper reported that these Indians 'have been victims of constant threats and physical violence from white colonizers, who occupied their areas by force' from the 1950s onwards. These evictions were done 'by force of the guns of hired *jagunços* [gun-men], or by the presence of the judiciary and police who were constantly manipulated by property companies or businessmen acquiring their deeds'. Some of the SPI's agents in southern Brazil behaved like feudal masters, forcing their Indians to work in collective labour from which they took most of the profit. The Kaingang at Toldo Chimbangue were a wretched remnant of a once-proud nation, in debt-bondage to a boss who took half their farm produce to pay for grossly inflated or illusory debts. By 1970 a mere seventy of them clung stubbornly to their ancient lands.

By the end of the '70s the situation had deteriorated, with settlers intimidating the surviving Kaingang. Huts were burned, and armed colonists brazenly invaded Indian land to start clearing it for farming. In April 1980 three Indians were shot and wounded by farmers of the Schmidt family while shopping in a nearby town: as usual there were no convictions – for lack of witnesses among the many people present. Funai did not help. Its team visited Chimbangue in December 1981, but simply tried to persuade the Kaingang to abandon their land and move into Xapecó. This group's aged chief died, and it elected the forceful Clemente Xeyuyâ (Fortes do Nascimento) as its leader. Chief Clemente sought to recover their lost territory by peaceful means. In June 1982 he led a delegation to Funai's regional headquarters in Curitiba and delivered a desperate letter addressed to the President of Funai: 'We need our land, to raise our children and for older people to live more at ease, not subject to a boss who exploits what is ours. We also need Funai's help in guaranteeing that settlers will expel no more Indians and will stop their violence, until the time when our land question is finally resolved.' Funai's agent promised action; but nothing happened. Chief Clemente tried again, with a delegation to Florianópolis in April 1983. The local branch of the Organization of Brazilian Lawyers said that 'there is no doubt whatever that the Chimbangue land belongs to the Indians'; President Moreira Leal of Funai agreed; but other lawyers, including the Procurator of the Republic, felt that the written evidence submitted by the Indians was inadequate. In despair, this poverty-stricken, beleaguered but defiant group wrote to the President of Brazil in July 1984: 'We cannot believe that the highest government of Brazil would sanction a crime such as the theft of our lands that belonged to our ancestors. This is where the fathers of our grandfathers were born and raised and where they are buried in our cemetery.' If nothing were done, the Kaingang would try to acquire guns and 'act by brute force'.

Carlos Moreira described the climate of racism in Brazil's deep south. 'To the contempt and oppression that habitually characterize the attitude of colonists towards the Kaingang, the latter respond with a deep-seated and lasting hatred. This at times explodes in spasmodic reprisals, which are almost always frustrated and incomplete because of [the Indians'] awareness of their own inferiority and worthlessness in a world of white men'. In September 1976 Vitor de Paula, a Kaingang from Nonoái, killed one of the invaders. He explained why: 'Seven years ago they killed my uncle, and two years ago they cut all my trees and also killed my brother. On the 18th of last month I went to the bodega in the evening and encountered my cousin lying dead – and it was the intruders who had also murdered him. At that I resolved . . . today I will die or kill.' He came across five colonists; machetes and knives were drawn; and he killed one Vilibaldo Kunzler. 'I did it because we live here, robbed by them and dying, and no one does anything about it . . . These squatters live here, harassing us for our land, hitting Indians, deceiving them, flogging and killing them and taking what they have, taking our houses.' There were by then seven times as many settlers within the territory as there were Indians.

Some 9,000 hectares (22,200 acres) were removed unconstitutionally from Mangueirinha Indian post in southern Paraná. The expropriated land changed hands several times, and in 1961 was bought by the powerful F. Slaviero e Filhos timber company. The purchaser violently expelled the Kaingang and Guarani from their ancient homeland, burned their houses, destroyed their farms, and killed their livestock, and then started felling the state's largest surviving forest of Paraná pine trees. Ten years later, in 1973, Funai brought an action to recover the land from Slaviero. The lawsuit was initially successful but, after five years of legal wrangling, was reversed on appeal by the company. The case dragged on into the 1990s, with trees removed throughout these decades, 'leaving a trail of irrecoverable losses to the Indians' forests and lives'.

At Rio das Cobras ('Snake River') post, on the upper Iguaçu river in southern Paraná, Funai's agent Leonardo Machado was in league with the timber company that was systematically raping the reserve, felling pine trees by day and night. Machado tried to involve the Indians in his fraud by bribing some leaders, but in December 1977 other chiefs went to Curitiba, where the President of Funai, General Ismarth de Araújo Oliveira, happened to be visiting. The General hurried to Rio das Cobras and sacked Machado. But the exasperation turned to desperation. A Kaingang woman wrote an eloquent plea to the head of Funai: 'Our tiny reserves, all that remain of [our former vast dominions] are being usurped by anarchic and destructive white people, disguised as farmers but with the spirit of vandals . . . Today, my people see their lands invaded, their forest destroyed, their animals exterminated and their hearts lacerated by this brutal weapon called civilization. To the white and so-called civilized people, this may seem like romanticism, but for our people it is not. For us it is a way of life, it is our reason to live, and therefore reason enough to die'.

An invading settler burned an Indian's house, and this was the spark that ignited the Indians' latent fury. They rebelled. On 16 February 1978 Chief Valdomiro of Rio das Cobras led 780 Kaingang and 400 Guarani to take up arms and expel some 2,000 colonists who had been settled in their land. According to a Funai report, 94 per cent of the reserve was occupied by non-Indians, much of it by a few families with large holdings. There was some shooting but no fatalities. Funai and the police negotiated a ninety-day truce for the removal of all intruders from the reserve. This victory was a turning-point, the start of recovery of land by Indians all over southern Brazil.

After this success at Rio das Cobras, the 'rebellion' spread southwards to Nonoái in Rio Grande do Sul, where the Kaingang were devastated by the loss of forests on which they had depended for game, fish, pine nuts, and other food. Chief Xangrê and his family were briefly arrested for trouble-making. His wife Hodfei recalled how she and her eighteen-month-old baby were thrown into a jail 'where we were in the midst of shit, blood, and bugs. They hurt me and abused me even though I was three months pregnant with Xangrê's child.' Candetê, another Kaingang from Nonoái, felt that the continual violence suffered by his people had to be answered by violence. 'To get white men off Indians' land, Indians have to risk their lives.' Chief Xangrê declared: 'I believe that the problem is so serious that we must plan and *act*, for no one else will do so. The whites won't. We ourselves must do it!'

In May 1978 Nonoái's Indians started by burning seven small schools for the settlers' children. Then, armed with guns, machetes, clubs, and bows and arrows, they went to each colonist's house and told the occupants to pack and clear out. Funai and 150 police restored order, disarming the Kaingang but giving the colonists a month to leave. Xangrê, who led the revolt at Nonoái, was worried that the settlers would return once the Indians were disarmed. 'Should they attempt to repossess their homes, he was determined to use incendiary arrows to set fire to their houses, cars, and furniture'; but they did not dare to return. Then at Xapecó post in Santa Catarina, across the Iguaçu river from Rio das Cobras, Funai got the invading settlers to sign a document agreeing to leave by July 1978.

These evictions were notable Indian victories. But for the expelled settlers they were a human tragedy: poor families were abruptly ousted from homes in which their younger children had been born. After temporary housing in refugee camps or wandering the streets of local cities, most were taken for resettlement in Mato Grosso. The Kaingang of Nonoái followed up their success by commandeering tractors, pickup trucks, and other machinery that Funai had been using for its own farming. Their Chief Pagungue (also called Mário Farias) 'claimed that this equipment had been bought with the fruit of the exploitation of [his people's] territory, and therefore belonged to the community.'

The Kaingang of Mangueirinha now produced a charismatic young leader, Ângelo Kretã. Intense and handsome, with a black moustache and tousled hair, Kretã looked every inch a Seventies radical. As a child he had witnessed the removal of Mangueirinha's araucaria pine forests. He then left his reserve, partly to escape a crazy SPI agent, a retired army lieutenant who liked to don his uniform and make the Indians do obeisance to a plaster statue of the Virgin Mary. Kretã's exile introduced him to other Indian activists, and taught him how Brazilian politics worked. Back at Mangueirinha, he was soon chosen as chief by its 680 Kaingang and Guarani, as his father and ancestors had been; and he went on to be elected to the council of the local authority for a political party – the first Indian in southern Brazil to be so elected. Soft-spoken, lucid, and persuasive, Kretã was destined to be a leader among Brazilian Indians. Although his Kaingang had largely abandoned their language (a variant of Jê) and many tribal customs, Kretã felt that the group could still have a strong identity, based on land, its produce, and self-determination. There was no need for cultural revivalism to reverse the tide of acculturation: 'We no longer perform any of our old rituals, and will not seek to recreate them artificially'. But the reinvigorated Kaingang still lived communally and regarded themselves as Indians. So they determined to fight for their rights by political action.

Funai's effort to recover the pine forests of Mangueirinha from Slaviero was not disinterested. In 1976 the Foundation's notorious DGPI, the department managing the Indian patrimony, established its own sawmill.

By 1979 it had felled 10,000 trees, three-quarters of the total on the reserve. 'The scars on the landscape produced by this activity were immediately visible wherever one went, and the Indians repeatedly complained of the loss of forest cover in the area, not only with regard to the shade and visual delight it afforded, but also in terms of the important resources of game, pine nuts, and *erva-mate* [gauchos' herbal tea] which had been lost.' Funai's DGPI was supposed to reinvest some of its profit to the benefit of the indigenous community, but it failed to do so. 'The only "benefits" accruing from the sawmill were to be seen in the dismal rows of clapboard houses built to resettle the Indians in a pattern reminiscent of a company town or concentration camp, each painted a regulation blue and fenced off from its neighbours by barbed wire.' Chief Kretã opposed this desecration, as well as the drain on tribal manpower by men being employed (for derisory wages) in the sawmill.

Protests to Brasília from all quarters in 1979 led Funai's well-intentioned President Adhemar Ribeiro da Silva to abolish the 'cancerous' DGPI; but he was forced to resign after only six months, and he was replaced as President by the obnoxious Colonel Nobre da Veiga. The situation in Paraná deteriorated rapidly. Having won the court action, Slaviero enforced its ownership with hired gunmen; but the Indians resisted, encouraged by the local office of CIMI and the lawyers of ANAI. The thirty-eight-year-old Chief Kretã was at the forefront of the struggle, by now recognized as the leader of all the 9,000 Kaingang of southern Brazil. He had played a fundamental role in the rebellions at Rio das Cobras and Nonoái. On 23 December 1979, Kretã told a pro-Indian rally of over 1,000 sympathizers in Curitiba that his people would reoccupy their forest. 'You cannot talk of an "invasion" of an area that always belonged to the Indians and from which they were expelled. We are simply going to reoccupy it.'

Kretã was harassed by the police when he sought to enlist their help, and he received death threats. On 22 January 1980, he was driving with three policemen in his car, when a Volkswagen full of Slaviero gunmen pulled out and stopped abruptly, causing the Kaingang to swerve into the path of an oncoming heavy truck. Kretã died in hospital a few days later. This was probably an assassination; but it was later whitewashed as no more than a tragic accident. The charismatic Indian leader had a large funeral with moving addresses by sympathizers from all over Brazil; but his death was a crippling loss to the indigenous movement.

Kretã's people did regain the disputed area of Mangueirinha in August that year, and the recovery of lost lands continued steadily during the 1980s and 1990s. At Nonoái the Kaingang and Guarani finally reoccupied most of the 20,000 hectares that had been removed in 1941 and turned into the so-called Nonoái forest reserve. This was one of the largest surviving stands of araucaria pines in all Brazil, and therefore very valuable: the Indians had to overcome violent opposition by business and political forces to get it back. The anthropologist Ligia Simonian felt that the Kaingang struggle was inspired by the negotiations surrounding the Constitution of 1988, after Brazil had returned to democratic rule, and by the indigenous resistance to celebrations in 1992 of Columbus' discovery of the Americas. In 1993 the Kaingang of Inhacorá won back 1,750 hectares (4,300 acres) that the left-wing Governor Leonel Brizola had seized in the late 1960s and transferred to the agricultural department of Rio Grande do Sul. In these two cases the Indians put pressure on Funai to take legal action to recover stolen lands. They had to overcome official lethargy and incompetence, and judicial delays and complications. But in the end they, Funai, and the soundness of the Brazilian legal system won the day. There were similar small gains at four other reserves in Rio Grande do Sul. As Simonian explained, this struggle was in the broader context of 'exasperation by the Indians at anti-indigenous actions by the Brazilian government and society'.

Similar struggles for land preoccupied acculturated tribes in the long-colonized south of Mato Grosso. The Kadiwéu are the only survivors of one of the great fighting nations of South America. In the eighteenth century their ancestors adopted horses, became expert riders, and for a time defeated and terrorized Portuguese and Spanish colonists along the Paraguay river. By the nineteenth century this proud people had made peace with the Brazilians. When Paraguay invaded Mato Grosso in the War of the Triple Alliance, at the time of General Rondon's birth in the 1860s, the Kadiwéu (or Caduveo) gave valuable support to the beleaguered Brazilians. Their reward was the confirmation of a large territory in the verdant Bodoquena Hills by the Emperor Dom Pedro II.

The Kadiwéu survived with their beloved horses. When the future doyen of French anthropologists, Claude Lévi-Strauss, visited them in 1935 he was at first dismayed to find the extent to which they had been acculturated, then intrigued to see that they were maintaining, even reviving, many ancient customs. At the outset of the SPI, there had been an attempt to congregate the Kadiwéu into villages and to modernize them, with 'a smithy for ironwork, a sawmill, a school, and a chemist's shop'. They were given tools, clothing, and blankets. Then, as the SPI declined, it abandoned its efforts with this tribe and left it to its own devices. 'From their ephemeral experience of civilization, the Indians had retained only Brazilian clothes, axes, knives, and sewing-needles. Apart from this, it had been a failure. Houses had been built for them, but they lived outside. An effort had been made to settle them in villages, but they continued as nomads. They had demolished their beds to burn them, and slept on the ground.' To Lévi-Strauss' delight, some Kadiwéu women continued to adorn their faces with elaborate tattoos in asymmetrical arabesques, and both sexes made pottery, carved figurines, and toys for their children. They preferred to live in barrel-vaulted thatch shelters, open at both ends, than in the government's wooden houses. 'The inhabitants are grouped around a fire that burns day and night. The men generally wear a ragged shirt and an old pair of trousers; the women a cotton dress next to their skin, or sometimes a simple blanket rolled under their armpits; the children are completely naked. All wear . . . broad straw hats, which constitute their only industry and source of income . . . Only one room is occupied. At any hour they eat yams, which they roast under cinders and grab with long bamboo tongs. They also sleep here, on a thin layer of ferns or on mats of maize straw, with each person's feet stretched towards the fire. In the middle of the night, the few remaining embers and the wall of badly jointed trunks provide feeble defence against the freezing cold at an altitude of a thousand metres [3,300 feet].'

A decade later, Kalervo Oberg formed a poorer impression of the Kadiwéu. To him, these descendants of proud warriors suffered from the ending of warfare and their superiority from possessing vassals such as the Terena. The Terena had multiplied and prospered, whereas the Kadiwéu were 'an impoverished and demoralized people . . . reduced to itinerant labourers, hunters, and indifferent agriculturalists'. Oberg admired the SPI, whose managers marketed the Indians' cow hides or employed them in daily labour around the post, and in return supplied their few manufactured wants. In return, the Kadiwéu seemed feckless, preferring long hunting trips to labouring for the SPI, and killing their cattle for the feasts they loved to give. Thus, there were frequent quarrels with their SPI agents. 'Managers seldom remain at this post more than a few months. Some managers left in fear of their lives.'

The rolling grasslands, hills, and woods of the Kadiwéu were too tempting for nearby cattle-ranchers, whose land was seasonally flooded by the world's largest swamp area, the Pantanal. In February 1957 twenty of them organized an invasion of the reserve by 15,000 head of cattle. Two years later, a state deputy tried to claim that much of the large reserve given by the Emperor was *devoluta* – legally unoccupied and ripe for colonization. The Indian Service's lawyers got the case referred to the federal Supreme Court, which found entirely in favour of the Indians. But the SPI kept the land for its own 'indigenous patrimony' – to earn rent for the Service rather than for use by the Kadiwéu themselves.

When this author was with the Kadiwéu a quarter-century later, their Funai agent was little more than a policeman who rode around the huge reserve on his horse, controlling 400 ranchers to whom Funai had leased the tribe's estate. The old SPI post Nalique was now a Funai ranch with 2,000 head of cattle. The agent said that he wanted to help the tribe but had no resources. Everything was left to Protestant missionaries who had arrived in Bodoquena in 1968: German and English couples did all the teaching, traded for the Indians, and above all worked incessantly to cure them of measles, tuberculosis, and malaria. I found the 450 Kadiwéu to be clean, open, and manly people, excellent horsemen who worked hard when given an incentive. Their living conditions, in open-ended barrel-vaulted huts, were just as described by Lévi-Strauss. They were dignified in a melancholy way, as befitted descendants of the aristocratic Guaikurú. But they seemed content, in their beautiful valley ringed by steep wooded hills in which there was still good hunting of peccary and tapir.

North of the Kadiwéu live the Terena, once servants of the proud Guaikurú-Kadiwéu horsemen warriors, but now better attuned to life in the interior of twentieth-century Brazil. They were the populous, industrious people whom Rondon had helped to gain possession of a remnant of their land. Docile and eager to learn Western ways, the Terena presented a perfect field of endeavour for missionaries. So the tribe had a long but often difficult and divisive history of missionary activity. Dale Kietzman of the Summer Institute of Linguistics started working among them in the 1950s, and his doctoral thesis was a study of their contacts with Christianity.

The Terena were nominally Catholic throughout the nineteenth century. Protestantism reached them in 1913 through the Inland South America Missionary Union, with the greatest number of converts being made at a village called Bananal ('Banana grove'). There was a conflict with the SPI's agent in 1920, which led to the banishment of the missionaries; but they returned in 1925 as the South American Indian Mission. A leading Protestant convert was Chief Marcolino Wollily. He was jailed and stripped of office in 1933, because he led his village in a protest against Brazilian ranchers penetrating its territory and the SPI who abetted them. The SPI agent attempted to rule by a triumvirate with Catholics and Protestants, 'but this system did not work and a year later Marcolino was reinstated as chief of the Indians'. Kietzman felt that 'they acquired from this incident a greater self-respect and a better sense of their own problems than is true of other Terena villages.' In 1946, under new pressure, Wollily took his family and followers to found a Protestant village called União.

Dale Kietzman commented: 'The opposition of the Protestant faction to the Catholic Terena at Bananal can be understood as representing primarily the opposition of the Terena to Brazilians in general.' Darcy Ribeiro also noted the political attraction of the minority Protestant religion. 'To the Terena, conversion to Protestantism is to oppose the whites, all Catholics, and at the same time to negate the regional image of Indians as lazy and drunkards.' Roberto Cardoso de Oliveira saw the tribe's split between Catholics and Protestants as relatively unimportant from a religious point of view. Although Protestant Terena abstained from drinking, smoking, and dancing, such behaviour was common to many other Indians. 'Thus we do not find two really distinct modes of conduct generated by the activity of the missions. Everyone, to a greater or lesser degree, attends shamanistic practices and appears at both the religious and profane festivals that mark the life of the community.' An Indian group's decision to convert to Protestantism was often mildly political. It irritated the SPI agent, who tended to be Catholic and who found the Redentorist fathers more relaxed about their religion. Also, 'the Protestant missionaries are more active, more aggressive in their action on the reserves, even using loudspeakers to propagate the Gospel, with music and perorations. All this is combined with a fairly efficient organization, bringing the "believers" to more intensive group life, through various weekly acts of worship and the training of Indians to perform proselytizing.' The tranquil routine of the post was disturbed. The Protestants represented a coherent force that could oppose the SPI's tutelage and authority. Despite all the missionary activity, Kietzman commented that 'a good bit of shamanism has persisted and has not been replaced by missionary teachings'.

There were other forces of acculturation for the Terena, notably the attractions of the nearby towns of Miranda and Aquidauana, and military service for young men. But Cardoso de Oliveira paid tribute to the SPI for, unwittingly, giving these Indians a sense of separate identity simply by segregating them in protected areas. The Terena's reserves are not large by Brazilian standards, but they were enough for each family to have a small farm and to graze some animals. The author found that most families had ten to fifteen head of cattle, and one man at Ipegue village had 300. Parts of the tribe that did not enjoy SPI protection virtually disappeared. In 1960, Cardoso de Oliveira noted that 'the Indians find in [the SPI's] tenuous "protection" a sufficiently strong attraction to cause them to seek out the posts and to settle there. This they do even though they receive no assistance of an economic, sanitary or educational nature.'

However, Terena groups owe their survival to the Service's protection of Indian lands, 'for without such protection many of them would be greatly decimated.'

The Terena were diligent farmers on their small plots of land. They had nothing to compare to the vast Bodoquena reserve of their former symbiotic partners, the Kadiwéu. And yet, the ownership of so much prime land was to cause the Kadiwéu decades of strife. In 1981 students doing voluntary service for the Projeto Rondon (Brazil's equivalent to the American Peace Corps) inspected the 400,000 hectare (1,500 square mile) Kadiwéu reserve and were horrified to find that the Indians were reduced to a fraction of it. According to the Pro-Indian Commission, the reserve 'is almost totally occupied by 98 tenant farmers and 10,000 squatters'. The ranchers paid derisory rents, and the squatters were planting a full range of crops, from rice and black beans to coffee and soya. As always, tribal morale depended on land. The volunteers claimed that 'Funai assumed a paternalistic character and forced the Indians to lose their true identities', and Funai staff were heavily involved in leasing land to ranchers. This was confirmed by a federal deputy who feared that the Kadiwéu were 'losing their identity and rapidly moving toward extinction'.

The Indians of this region started to react. They held their first assembly in Campo Grande in 1980, at which Deputy Mário Juruna declared: 'The whites must respect Indians, the Government must demarcate our lands, and no fazendeiro may invade Indian lands or touch their families. For Indians are not objects whom everyone can seize and put wherever they like. Indians are not dolls: they are men and human beings, and the original owners of the lands of Brazil.' Emboldened by such rhetoric, the Kadiwéu rediscovered their warlike spirit. In April 1982 a group of fifty Indians, armed with revolvers and shotguns, started to ransack and burn squatters' houses; and in November they demanded that Funai remove 119 tenant ranchers from their lands or 'they will be expelled by force'.

Funai did start to cancel a number of leases and sent teams accompanied by police to evict some of the estimated 18,000 people who had invaded the reserve. When Funai tried to install an Indian family in the Tarumã fazenda in March 1983, there was a shoot-out in which two ranchers were killed and Indians were wounded. Despite this, the evictions continued, with 174 families removed during ten days' work in April. The ranchers (some of whom had been farming on Kadiwéu land for half a century) fought back with legal actions and enlisted the state colonization agency, while the squatters sought help from local politicians. The indigenous leader Paulino Bagodarquis accused the state's Secretary of Justice of paying poor favela-dwellers of Campo Grande to invade the reserve 'and he is then going to buy the invaders' land and keep our reserve. The [socialist PMDB politicians] promised during the political campaign to take our lands, and they new seem to want to do just that.' Both sides examined past property records and legislation. The case went as far as the Supreme Court, which rejected all the settlers' claims and ordered their removal.

Funai in 1982 got the army's geographical service to help demarcate the huge reserve, a task that took two years because of the lack of roads into the area, the difficult terrain – much of it hilly or wooded, and sloping westwards towards the Pantanal swamps – and obstruction by the many non-Indian farmers. President Figueiredo formally ratified this measurement in a decree on 24 April 1984. The ranchers then mounted a protest, because the army's demarcation of the Emperor Pedro II's donation had massively *increased* the reserve, to 538,535 hectares (2,079 square miles), which included 165,000 hectares (640 square miles) for which forty fazendeiros held title deeds issued by the state. The state's colonization agency Terrasul claimed that the demarcation was arbitrary, but the President of Funai insisted that it was immutable.

There were more armed conflicts between Indians and farmers. In September 1984 Kadiwéu warriors confiscated the property of two invaders in illegal colonies and gave 404 other families ninety days in which to leave. A scandal erupted within Funai that same month. The agency's procurator (legal officer) accused its past President Jurandy Fonseca and others of a massive fraud, in which they secretly sold to eighty-four fazendeiros renewals of their five-year leases on lands totalling almost 300,000 hectares (1,160 square miles) – or half the Kadiwéu reserve. The accusation was particularly astonishing because Jurandy Fonseca, a lawyer and Funai veteran, was considered a radical champion of the indigenous cause – he had installed Megaron as director of the Xingu park and Marcos Terena as his own *chef de cabinet*, and was sacked after only five months in office because he refused to agree to a decree authorizing mining in Indian lands. Funai's next President, Nélson Marabuto, cancelled the fraudulent lease extensions. By the end of the year, the Kadiwéu had occupied a further fifteen ranches, and the President of Funai wanted all lessees to leave the reserve – even though they included some of the richest families of the State of Mato Grosso do Sul.

The Kadiwéu were by now organized in a Commission of the Indians of the Bodoquena reserve. This noted that their territory was divided into forty fazendas, half of which were leased out and the other half in indigenous control. The Kadiwéu Commission demanded an end to all future leases, and it wanted schools, teachers, medical staff, and tractor drivers for some 600 native people living dispersed over 538,500 hectares. 'The Commission's great preoccupation concerns the education of their young, because the future trend is native occupation of the entire reserve.' As in other parts of Brazil, the Indigenous Communities of Mato Grosso do Sul were wonderfully united for the first time in their history. In January 1985 the Kadiwéu were joined by Guarani, Terena, and Kaiowá in lobbying in Brasília, but also in rituals to prepare bows and arrows 'to declare war on the whites'.

In 1985 the land-settlement agency Incra made a survey of 400 squatter families, and managed to find some former railway land on which to try to resettle them. Matters dragged on. At the end of June the exasperated Indians invaded the Santo Onofre ranch. They seized the fazendeiro Honorivaldo Alves, who had 20,000 head of cattle on nine ranches, and some of his men, and threatened to burn his Cessna plane. But they soon released their hostages in return for an undertaking (brokered by the head of Funai) that the rancher would definitely quit, leaving most of his cattle to the Indians. The Kadiwéu now had forceful leaders, Martinho and Ambrósio da Silva, and in July 1985 these led 150 Indians to the state capital, Campo Grande, where they met the Governor, the President of Funai, Deputy Mário Juruna, and even a delegation of fazendeiros. During these months, Incra was steadily removing dozens of squatter families from the Kadiwéu reserve – a sad business, often a human tragedy for the poor farmers. A stubborn few were reluctant to leave, but in December the last families were finally relocated to Nioaque, north of Bodoquena, with funds from Incra to build access roads, schools, and hospitals, and to help the farmers clear their new land.

Meanwhile the indigenous leaders had persuaded Funai to get the reserve transferred from ownership by the Brazilian state to the Kadiwéu nation. Then in August they signed an agreement with the ranchers. The eighty-four 'fraudulent' leases were cancelled; but in their place the indigenous community awarded 153 grazing contracts. In the new arrangement, each animal being grazed on Kadiwéu land had six hectares, for which the tenant farmers paid rent directly to the tribal community, and an Indian resided in the ranch buildings. The grazing fees were well below market rates, but they represented a notable victory for the Kadiwéu. In five years of struggle, this proud nation had recovered all its magnificent ancient territories, and it replaced Funai as the recipient of their ranching rentals.

Both sides claimed to be delighted with the agreement of August 1985, but it was not easy to implement. There were problems over distribution of the tribe's new wealth. Funai built a school and infirmary at Bodoquena, but could not find teachers and nurses to man them. The Kadiwéu in 1988 tried their own alternative education, aided by the NGO Centre of Indigenous Work. Jaime Siqueira watched 'the school start to function, with four Kadiwéu monitors and teaching-material devised by the Indians themselves, but adequate to their specific cultural universe.' Some parents welcomed this training, but others felt that it was not sufficiently rigorous for their children to learn reading and writing in Portuguese. So Funai tried bringing in two Terena women teachers, but lack of resources and management led to the failure of this school. The tribe did not want Protestant missionaries (of the United Evangelical Mission and the Summer Institute of Linguistics) to renew their residence in the aldeia; but these obtained Funai's permission to do so. The American Peter ('Pedro') Carlson of the SIL 'claims to be doing research on the Kadiwéu language and to be involved in the activities of the school's indigenous monitors, together with his wife who also gives some medical assistance', but his main effort continued to be religious conversion.

There were also political problems. Chief Ambrósio da Silva was discredited on suspicion of having stolen hundreds of head of cattle left by an evicted rancher and because he spent too much time living in a nearby town; and the much-respected leader João Principe died of a snake bite in 1986. A succession of chiefs who followed him failed to gain authority, some because they were too strongly identified with the Protestant missions or Funai. This people therefore created Acirk, an association of indigenous communities of the Kadiwéu reserve, with Jõao Principe's son Ambrósio as its president. There were difficulties in collection and distribution of the new grazing rents, which were paid weekly. Some Indian families had ranches to lease out while others did not, so that this income was not handled communally, although the richer indigenous families did give support to the poorer. Another difficulty came from widespread invasions of remoter parts of the reserve, by illegal loggers extracting mahogany and other hardwoods, and by trappers taking thousands of alligator skins from the ponds of the Pantanal. There were too few Kadiwéu to police their borders, although one group of armed Indians did drive off surveyors and farmers attempting to fix clandestine markers within their territory.

Once their land was secured, the Kadiwéu had to confront the delicate balance between their tribal heritage and Brazilian society that surrounded them. 'For many years, the principal question for the Kadiwéu concerned their survival in both ethnic and material terms. Today [1995] they are preoccupied with the sustainability of their traditional way of social life, which is intimately linked to the environment of the Chaco and the cerrado of South Mato Grosso. They have to make careful use of their natural resources [in this fragile ecosystem], seeking to balance an ecological equilibrium with the well-being of the community.' The Kadiwéu had a dedicated supporter in Alain Moreau, a local lawyer and later a trained anthropologist. As early as 1978, he had presented Funai with a proposal for a partnership between Indians and ranchers. By 1993 he helped the Kadiwéu's association Acirk submit a new version of this partnership for funding by the World Bank. This grant was made, with Moreau himself and the sympathetic Austrian anthropologist Georg Grünberg as its assessors. It was intended to enable the Indians to gain control of all the ranches and cattle, to improve their business management, to branch into other forms of farming and animal husbandry, and to maintain the reserve's ecological equilibrium – even reintroducing native fauna: rheas, peccary, capybara, and alligators.

The Kadiwéu entered the new century with their beautiful rolling plains securely protected, their population gradually increasing, and a modest revival of tribal culture. Households of family units are the norm, and there is considerable intermarriage with the Terena – who had once been willing slaves of the dominant Kadiwéu. In the largest village, Bodoquena, some thousand people live in 110 houses. But only two families claim to be 'pure' Kadiwéu, as descendants of the former masters, and these enjoy privileged status in ceremonies.

Thanks to the Emperor Pedro II, to the SPI and Funai, to many well-wishers, and above all to their own efforts, the Kadiwéu are masters of a fine territory. Other nearby tribes are less fortunate. The Guató are a quiet, shy people who live on their canoes and seasonal islands, deep in the labyrinth of channels, marshes and mudflats of the Pantanal. They are of course brilliant boatmen and skilled fishermen and artisans. Darcy Ribeiro wrote in 1957 that the once-numerous Guató had become extinct; and this was confirmed in a government decree in the 1970s.

To everyone's surprise, in 1977 a few Guató families were 'rediscovered' by a Salesian missionary sister, living on an isolated island. It was found that there were perhaps 400 of these macro-Jê-speaking people, scattered in the vast wetland of the Pantanal and in towns near the Paraguay river. A Guató leader, Severo Ferreira, revealed his joy when he learned that the indigenous nations of Mato Grosso do Sul were united and 'being one family we are disposed to assist one another'. His group had lost ownership of its island home, and he begged Funai to help the Guató recover it. 'How we suffer, by having no place where we may plant and live in tranquillity, so that when night falls we may lie down and sleep knowing that when dawn breaks we will have a place just for us! We could be secure in the knowledge that all that we see is ours and no one is going to expel us.' There was a proposal to make the sacred island where most Guató live into a reserve for them, but this was vetoed by the army because it lies on the frontier with Bolivia. The military promised to protect the Guató and their island, but would not surrender the 'strategically important' land to Funai or to the Indians themselves.

Another people whom Darcy Ribeiro recorded as extinct in 1957 were the Ofaié-Xavante, who lived near the Paraná river in the south-east of Mato Grosso do Sul. At the end of the nineteenth century, these Ofaié-Xavante had numbered 2,000. But Ribeiro was wrong about their extinction, for a few had survived.

Expelled from a farm in their homeland in 1978, this remnant was exiled to Bodoquena near the Kadiwéu. They lived there for a decade. Back in a temporary camp beside the great Paraná river, twenty-seven Ofaié-Xavante worked as freelance labourers on one ranch and a dozen others were scattered among other farms. The destitute survivors were united under Chief Xehitâ-ha (Ataíde Francisco Rodrigues), who in 1988 wrote a moving appeal to Funai: 'We Ofaié-Xavante . . . urgently need a solution to the problem we have been confronting for over twenty years. We are also Indians and we have a right to a piece of land for our survival.' They begged for a small territory to which they had historical title, for education for their children, a resting-place for the tribal elders, and food and medicine. 'Until [some land] is granted, we Ofaié-Xavante are suffering every form of misery, hunger, illness, etc.'. Funai acted to save an estimated seventy-one Indians from extinction. The Foundation bought a fazenda, and in May 1992 the Minister of Justice signed an order to Funai (which was then under his ministry) to create a reserve of 1,907 hectares (4,712 acres) for the tribe. This was not a final victory. The Ofaié-Xavante still had to get their land demarcated. Then, only a year after the award, the São Paulo electricity company CESP revealed that its new Porto Primavera hydroelectric dam on the Paraná would form a gigantic lake, 250 kilometres long and 8 wide (155 by 5 miles), which would flood half the tribe's small reserve. An outcry by environmentalists and indigenous organizations forced the electricity giant to move the Ofaié-Xavante to a new 484 hectare (1,196 acre) reserve and to build a medical dispensary, school, communal buildings, and artesian wells for them.

*

There are many pockets of Guarani in southern Brazil, close to the frontier with Paraguay, where Guarani is an official language and the name of the currency. The thousands of scattered Guarani form one of Brazil's largest native peoples. They live in small communities throughout the nation's southern states. Highly acculturated, these Guarani are descendants of a great nation that had readily converted to Christianity and lived for 150 years in the seventeenth and eighteenth centuries in the Spanish Jesuits' famous Paraguayan 'reductions'. Most now live in rural poverty surrounded by farms and ranches.

One group of Guarani, the Kaiowá at Dourados in the southern tip of Mato Grosso, had a difficult history of adaptation to frontier society. Curt Nimuendajú (whose honorific surname was bestowed on him by another Guarani group) said that the Kaiowá migrated to Dourados at the end of the nineteenth century. Then, soon after its creation in 1910, the SPI moved some Terena from their homes near Corumbá to Dourados, and the prolific and industrious Terena prospered far more than their Kaiowá neighbours. The American James Watson studied an isolated group of Kaiowá in 1950 and found that it seemed to be adapting well to acculturation. At that time, the SPI's presence was minimal. The only education was sporadic teaching by the agent's wife – some basic reading and arithmetic, and allegiance to the Brazilian flag. 'The level of teaching is low, unprofessional and little adapted to Kaiowá needs.' Local settlers treated these Indians with amused contempt and often cheated or threatened them. More shockingly, Watson found that the SPI's own encarregados shared such frontier attitudes more than 'the high-minded idealism of the SPI's creed'. Egon Schaden was with the Kaiowá at that time and formed a gloomier view. He saw the tribe being weakened by tuberculosis and alcohol and felt that it had 'no notion of reciprocal relations' with the whites. A feeling of inferiority made these and other groups of Guarani turn to mysticism – which in turn alienated them from Brazilian society and religion.

Protestant missionaries were establishing a strong presence among the Kaiowá, but the Indians used the mission more for training in farming techniques and for medical help than for spiritual conversion. They had switched to metal tools for farm labour, and made most of their own Western clothing. Vestiges of tribal customs, ornament, and domestic belongings were gradually disappearing. The main agent of change was contact with surrounding farmers, through casual labour by Kaiowá men and barter of agricultural produce and artefacts such as hammocks or winnowing baskets. These contacts led to more individual than collective work, single-family houses instead of communal long-houses, and chiefs appointed by the SPI.

When this author visited Dourados two decades later, it was a sleepy place but with an air of unease, almost menace. The Kaiowá lived scattered amid woods, fields, and streams and the reserve was criss-crossed by dirt roads. Most houses were thatch shelters, open-sided or with wattle-and-daub walls, but some were brightly painted wooden bunga-lows. There were plenty of domestic farm animals, and emaciated dogs and cats. The 3,500 hectare (8,650 acre) reserve housed almost 1,500 Kaiowá and Guarani, and 500 Terena. Both communities were good farmers, producing record harvests of grain. Medical treatment was quite good, with a hospital maintained by a Brazilian Presbyterian mission (in which ten beds were paid for by Funai) and daily visits by a doctor of Japanese origin. The Kaiowá complained to me about their encarregado, who gave them no tools or basic necessities but who sold the reserve's timber to Paraguayans. The agent in turn blamed the Indians for going into nearby towns where they mixed with the lowest strata of society. The result was drunkenness from cachaça rum, fights, wife-beating, and petty pilfering. I was struck by the attitude of the agent's wife, who spoke to the Indians in the sharp, condescending but tolerant manner of a colonial memsahib, but imagined herself to be loved by her husband's charges.

There were other tensions in this reserve. One was caused by lack of land for a fast-growing population. Another came from conflict between the indigenous communities. Although a minority in Dourados, the Terena were visibly more successful than the Guarani in selling their produce and were considered as some of the state's most enterprising farmers. The Terena adopted white lifestyles, language, and politics, whereas the Kaiowá made a conscious effort to preserve some of their culture, to remain Indians. The Kaiowá tenaciously clung to their Tupi-Guarani mother-tongue, and they evolved their own devout religious ceremonies led by *rezadors* (prayer-leaders). A third problem arose from Funai's policy of promoting its pliant favourites as *capitão* (captain), thus undermining traditional Guarani caciques. Some powerful captains devel-oped private police forces, which continue to this day to dominate the larger reserves, Dourados, Amambaí, and Caarapó.

The Kaiowá-Guarani produced one of Brazil's most charismatic indig-enous leaders, Marçal de Souza or Tupã-I. This Kaiowá started by working as a nurse for Funai, but his oratorical skills made him a natural leader of his community and then of the regional indigenous assemblies. Lean, intense, and passionate, Marçal became the finest advocate of indigenous rights. He spoke at the United Nations in defence of all the world's minorities. When Pope John Paul II visited Brazil in 1980, Marçal was chosen to welcome him in Manaus on behalf of the Indians of Brazil. In his speech he told the Pontiff that hired gunmen were killing Indians like animals.

Back in the overcrowded Dourados reserve, the orator Marçal Tupã-I had to confront inter-tribal rivalries. An aggressive Terena called Ramão Machado emerged as the chief of his community. The Indians of Dourados were deeply divided about who should lead them, with some Kaiowá supporting Ramão Machado and some of his own Terena fearing his dictatorial style. An election in April 1983 degenerated into a pitched battle among 500 Indians. The Machado faction was accused of vote-rigging and political chicanery, of beating Indians, forcing them to work for him, and stealing their produce.

For five years, Marçal Tupã-I strove to get the land of the Kaiowá of Pirakuá village demarcated. Then in November 1983 an employee of the nearby Serra Brava fazenda offered him a bribe if he could persuade his Kaiowá to leave their aldeia. When he refused, he was warned that he would regret this. By the end of the month, Marçal was gone, shot while he slept next to his wife on the veranda of his house. No one was ever convicted of his murder. Suspicion naturally fell on the fazendeiro's henchmen, so that Marçal Tupã-I was another martyr of the indigenous cause murdered in a dispute with a landowner. But some of his Guarani relatives were convinced that he had been killed by supporters of his Terena rival Ramão Machado.

In 1982 the press started to report a terrible affliction among the Kaiowá: teenaged boys and girls were committing suicide with alarming frequency. They killed themselves either by hanging from trees or roof beams, or by drinking poison. Marçal Tupã-I called these tragedies 'a sad and macabre reality' and blamed them on his community's sufferings: 'We are a nation subjugated by powerful forces, a nation that is slowly dying and unable to find its way . . . our lands are invaded, our lands are taken, our territories are diminished, and we do not have the means for survival'.

Marçal also blamed his rivals – 'mestizos, Paraguayans, and Terena, who constitute a veritable police armed with truncheons and revolvers'. This was a reference to Ramão Machado's so-called Indian Council. But that petty tyrant survived an attempt to oust him. Two years after Marçal's murder, Machado was said to 'exercise a dominating role, exploiting the labour force and seizing Guarani plots of land through intimidation and frequent use of force by a veritable organized militia.'

He was accused of murders of various opponents. He had about a hundred armed men to enforce 'security' on the reserve, and the distant Funai office in Campo Grande turned a blind eye to his oppressive regime.

The number of suicides increased. 'Suicides had always occurred among the Kaiowá. Before the end of the 1970s there were at most two cases a year. From 1980 onwards, this number grew: in 1985 for example five cases were reported; in 1986 six cases . . . Most suicides occur among young people aged between twelve and twenty; cases are rare among the over-forties.' Fourteen were recorded in the year 1990.

Funai tried to explain this terrible phenomenon. Perhaps it was because the tribe's conditions of survival were so precarious. Its population was increasing alarmingly: from some 2,000 in 1970, to 5,000 in 1990, and 9,000 by 1996. It was difficult to feed so many people on the reserve's small cultivable areas. Chief Irênio lamented the lack of hunting: 'Today there are no more game birds, we have to raise chickens; there are no more tapirs, we have to keep cows'. Hundreds of Indians had to find work as casual labourers on neighbouring farms. Conditions there were wretched, working ten-hour days cutting sugar cane for a cachaça distillery or harvesting soya beans. Men laboured in blazing heat during two months of uninterrupted work, for about a dollar a day, and slept with their women and children under shelters of plastic sheeting. The growing town of Dourados was immediately alongside the reserve. Some Indian women and children tried to beg in the town's streets, others turned to prostitution.

In 1990 Senator Severo Gomes drew attention to the terrible number of suicides: 'What is happening is virtual genocide'. He blamed the deaths on the tribe's many afflictions, which seemed to grow in proportion to the quantity of organizations supposedly helping them – Funai, CIMI, and the many missionary cults. In the following year *Newsweek* magazine published a chilling picture of a Kaiowá girl's suicide. She was hanging from the rafters of a hut, looking like any Western teenager, smartly dressed in clean shirt, jeans, and trainers. The magazine reported that the rash of suicides had 'taken off' with fifty-one in the past nineteen months, and the victims had an average age of only seventeen. The root problems seemed to be overcrowding, lack of farming land, and poverty. There were also spiritual causes. *Newsweek* said that 'the Guarani-Kaiowá's culture, based on a mystical religion deeply linked to their homelands, is unraveling. Confounded by the suicides, tribal elders blame sorcerers and evil spirits. They have summoned witch doctors or *pajés*, and have held dancing and chanting rituals to banish the spirits. But these days few of the tribespeople know the ritual dances, and the reserve no longer has its own pajé.' A shaman was imported from the Guarani in Paraguay. The government's reaction was to send a counselling team with a doctor, to forbid Indian women to leave the reserve to find work, and to try to stop the import of alcohol since cachaça was thought to have emboldened many suicides. 'But', the journalist concluded, 'so far the government has put off the one measure that could clearly ease the strain – enlarging the size of the Guarani-Kaiowá reserve. The tribe cannot find stability without more land, or fewer people.' This was a reversal of the usual problem – overpopulation rather than demographic decline.

Suicide was a tragedy peculiar to the Kaiowá and it grew steadily worse, reaching an appalling fifty-six in the year 1995. Some Indians shot themselves, others drank poison, but most hanged themselves from trees or rafters. The research institute ISA published a heart-rending list of every suicide during a five-year period, with the names, ages (mostly young), and place and method of death of each. The tragedy had not abated by the end of the century. In September 1999 five young Kaiowá in the squalid enclave Panambizinho attempted collective suicide, by drinking a lethal mixture of insecticide and rum, and four of them died. This brought the number of suicides during the previous fifteen years to the terrible total of 320.

ISA's Rubem de Almeida tried to discover the causes of this suicide pact. Encirclement by aggressive white society was one obvious factor. In the early days of the SPI, the Guarani-Kaiowá had been herded into eight small reserves in order to 'cleanse' their rich lands for development by agribusiness. Their territory was systematically converted into commercial farms of sugar cane and soya or cattle ranches. The flora and fauna of the Guarani's traditional habitat were destroyed. Contact with whites was crushing the sensitive Kaiowá. 'Missionaries, fundamentalist sects, fazendeiros, the proximity of urban centres, compulsory work that at times degenerates almost into slavery, forced transfers from their traditional lands, degradation of ecosystems, and other afflictions could certainly provoke reactions . . . that could bring the Indians to terminate their lives.' Almeida also blamed official indigenous policy, which sought to settle these people into aldeias so that they would 'integrate into national society'. There was no mercy for any Guarani who resisted this 'assimilation' and preferred to live in extended families, often isolated deep in their surviving forests. All Kaiowá and Ñandeva Guarani groups living in a large fertile quadrilateral of land were resettled – often forcibly – into the reserves of Caarapó, Amambaí, and particularly Dourados.

The anthropologist José Meihy, who knew these people well, noted the terrible conditions in the reserve – where by the 1990s, 8,000 people were crammed into too small an area almost in the suburbs of the town of Dourados. There was serious inter-tribal friction. The Kaiowá and Guarani got on well with one another, both 'desperately seeking to reconstitute their culture (language, moral principles, food, and folklore). But the Terena try to maintain as "white" a lifestyle as possible'. They look different, choose different schooling, and try to make money as eagerly as any settler. 'Installed within the reserve, they assume the role of colonizers.'

Proselytizing missionaries had not helped. The Evangelical Mission had been active among the Kaiowá since 1928 and the Methodists for many decades, as well as the Catholics and other Protestant cults. In the late 1970s a missionary in Ramada village 'committed the sacrilege of grabbing the *mbaraka*, a sacred Guarani instrument, from the hand of a pajé (shaman) and "in the name of God" threw it into the fire.' Such denigration of the beliefs of the highly spiritual Guarani was counterproductive: despite the intense efforts of the missionaries, many Indians preserved their traditional religion. A psychologist in 1990 blamed the spiritual insecurity caused by five missionary sects working in the area: Pentecostalists, the Bethel Evangelical Church, Tabernacle of Jesus, God is Love, and God is Truth.

Rubem de Almeida admitted that the epidemic of suicides among the Kaiowá could not be fully explained by despair resulting from their many afflictions. The problem was more complex. Other Guarani groups in Paraguay and Brazil had land pressures as acute as those of the Kaiowá or lived in equally abject poverty, but they did not resort to suicide. There was no history of suicide among the Guarani during the preceding four centuries of contact with white society. Kaiowá who took their own lives showed none of the usual symptoms of depression, apathy, loss of self-respect, rebelliousness, or anger. So the phenomenon seemed to be a spiritual movement, among a people who value mythical and supernatural forces far above material advantages. Teachings about the after-life by Christian missionaries or Guarani shamans may have had a bearing – in colonial times, other Guarani had followed messianic prophets who promised 'a land without evils'. There were other theories. A local Funai agent thought that young Kaiowá killed themselves 'as a reaction to the alcoholism of their parents'.

In addition to the obvious afflictions – weakening of culture, economic exploitation, competing Churches, alcoholism, and unemployment – José Meihy noted that most young suicides chose a death by hanging or poisoning that involved their throats and caused no bloodshed or bodily damage. The throat is important to the Kaiowá, for whom the voice represents spirituality. Adolescent Indians whose voices were breaking may have feared transition from childhood to the harsh world of poor adults. Whatever the reason, the suicides 'are a cry by the Kaiowá to be heard: we whites must listen and stop destroying them'. The tragic loss of so many young lives has never been fully understood, by anthropologists, psychiatrists, or the tribe's own elders.

The Kaiowá and other groups of Guarani ended the twentieth century in a wretched state. The anthropologist-activist Márcio Santilli was angry that there was no conviction of the criminals who in 1983 murdered Marçal Tupã-I. 'The Guarani, Brazil's largest indigenous nation with a population of over twenty thousand Indians, are dispersed in a scattering of diminutive plots – probably the smallest in the country . . . The lack of lands has led to the overpopulation of small areas, where the different communities find themselves prevented from occupying their own territories.' Santilli blamed the local judiciary for ruling after ruling in favour of the farmers who had taken Guarani land. The international organization Survival battled for Guarani rights, which helped the Kaiowá of the small communities of Jaguapiré and Jarará in 1996 to win legal actions for their lands. But in 1997 other Kaiowá of Sucuriy and of Panambazinho were fighting against brutal eviction from their tiny enclaves. A Kaiowá leader told Fiona Watson of Survival: 'Our land is very small, with nowhere to plant our corn and beans. All of this land has been ours for hundreds of years, but now it is all destroyed. There is no hunting and no trees. We are suffering . . . Everyone, the colonists, state and federal deputies, and the mayor are all against us. Our survival will be very difficult.' Another shaman agreed that his people's despair was because 'our religion and our way of life are under attack. We do not have enough land to continue our old ways in the correct manner.'

The Guarani struggle for land continues unabated. Their growing numbers are crammed into pockets of land, remnants of the eighteenth-century Jesuit *reductions* and long since occupied or surrounded by farms and ranches. One group of Kaiowá, led by Chief Marcos Veron, sought to reoccupy its traditional village Takuará near Juti in Mato Grosso do Sul, a place now known as Brasília do Sul fazenda. Four years of litigation in the late 1990s went against them and led to their judicial expulsion. They took refuge for a time in the Caarapó Guarani reserve, but then had to migrate and camp in abject squalor on the edge of a highway. These desperate Kaiowá sought to return to reclaim Brasília do Sul farm. In January 2003 Marcos Veron was brutally murdered – one more victim of the struggles for land.

18. Manaus to Roraima

The city of Manaus, at the junction of the main Amazon and its greatest tributary, the Negro, lies at the very heart of the world's largest river system and greatest expanse of tropical rainforests. Manaus had flourished in wild extravagance at the height of the rubber boom. It boasted the continent's first electric trams, a floating dock built by British engineers, the famous Teatro Amazonas opera house, public buildings imported stone by stone, and rubber millionaires who sent their laundry to Europe, watered their horses on champagne, and lit their chandeliers with the oil from hundreds of thousands of freshwater turtle eggs. All that ostentation vanished abruptly with the crash of the Amazon rubber monopoly after 1912. Trading houses went bankrupt, the opportunists departed, and Manaus decayed.

The Brazilian government wanted to rescue this city in the middle of nowhere that had lost its raison d'être. Its curious solution proved remarkably effective. In 1967 the city of Manaus was declared a *Zona Franca* (free port), to which Brazilians could fly to buy tax-free imported goods and where manufacturers enjoyed generous tax concessions. The Manaus free-trade zone SUFRAMA was a surprising success, in attracting business and settlers to the city far up the Amazon. It brought duty-free shoppers from the rest of Brazil (as long as the country had ludicrously high tariff barriers) and it also helped Manaus become the country's manufacturing centre for 'white' kitchen goods, motorcycles, and other appliances. As a result Manaus grew explosively, from some 150,000 people in 1965, to 600,000 a decade later, and 1,100,000 by the end of the century. It has always contained roughly half the population of the huge state of Amazonas.

This regeneration was a disaster for the Waimiri Atroari, a pair of related tribes who have the misfortune to live only 250 kilometres (160 miles) due north of Manaus. Of all tribes in Brazil, the Waimiri Atroari resisted colonial invasion longest and with most determination. They fought off incursions into their lands along the Jauaperi and Alalaú tributaries of the Rio Negro throughout the eighteenth and nineteenth centuries. At times they even counter-attacked with raids that spread terror among settlements on the middle Negro. They survived repeated attempts to exterminate or 'pacify' them. So they effectively blocked overland communications between Manaus and the cattle-ranching plains of Roraima far to the north.

The Waimiri Atroari paid a high price for their independence. There was a series of massacres by official military expeditions in the 1870s. In 1905 they expelled a seringueiro who had killed an Indian, and the Governor of Amazonas sent a force to 'clean up' the Jauaperi river. The troops, led by Militia Captain Júlio Catingueira, behaved barbarously, attacking villages, burning huts sometimes with occupants inside, leaving 283 corpses of unburied Indians, and bringing eighteen men and one woman back to Manaus. These wretched captives were housed in a harsh police barracks, but whenever possible they would go to the bank of the Negro to gaze at its broad waters in profound melancholy. When the last of them died, in a hospital, a doctor reported that he had raised his head with difficulty, shed a single tear, and intoned a chant of his ancestors. 'It was a litany that seemed to evoke his nostalgia for the forests or perhaps the memory of the spirits of his dead relatives.'

Despite terrible provocation, the Waimiri Atroari were surprisingly friendly to visitors who did not threaten them. They had good relations with a naturalist-ethnographer, João Rodrigues Barbosa, in the 1880s. They welcomed an Austrian called Richard Payer, who visited them twice at the start of the twentieth century, and also two of Rondon's best officers, Captain Alípio Bandeira and Colonel Bento Lemos. There followed a half-century of calm after the rubber boom collapsed and Manaus was in decline. These proud tribes maintained their traditional way of life and independence.

In 1942 the SPI official Humberto Brighia tried to make a contact, establishing a post called Barbosa Rodrigues on the Camananaú river. But something went wrong, and Brighia and five colleagues and members of his family were killed. Two years later, as part of the war effort, the US Army sent its 4th Photo-Charting Squadron to make an aerial reconnaissance of this region, to see whether a land route could be opened to Brazil's rubber and mineral resources. Some of the surveyors went up the Alalaú river; and on 5 October 1944 the Waimiri Atroari killed Lieutenant Walter Williamson, Sergeant Baitz, and their Brazilian guides and companions. The SPI reopened its attraction post, but although its men got on well with the local Waimiri, all twelve of them were massacred by a different group of Atroari, in 1946. A chief called Cândido later said that his wife had deplored that killing: she wept and wept, because the SPI boss had been a good man.

A quarter-century later, the military government was determined to defend Amazonia against 'foreign envy' and exploit its resources, to open Brazil's frontiers to settlement, and to unite the vast country. A road between Manaus and Boa Vista (the capital of the northern territory of Roraima) seemed imperative. Tragically, this link would have to slice through the territory of the Waimiri Atroari, since the land to the west and east was considered too swampy.

Gilberto Pinto de Figueiredo Costa, one of Funai's most experienced and altruistic sertanistas, was told to try to contact the Carib-speaking Waimiri Atroari. In June 1968, Pinto began by dropping trade goods from a plane; then, in July, he landed by helicopter in a village and exchanged presents; and in August he went up the river by boat and met a lone Indian in a canoe. This Waimiri asked whether the five strangers were friendly, then paddled over to the Funai boat and 'after examining the whites in silence, he formulated an invitation to accompany him to his maloca, where his wife was'. Reporting this to the regional office of Funai, Pinto praised the Indian's admirable courage in showing no sign of fear as he approached the intruders. The maloca proved to be a magnificent conical structure, like a thatched circus tent, 50 metres (165 feet) in diameter and with segmented divisions for twenty-two families.

In October 1968, Gilberto Pinto was moved elsewhere and Funai invited a thirty-four-year-old Italian missionary, Father Giovanni (João) Calleri, to continue the attempted contact. Father Calleri, of the Consolata Order, had good experience of making contact with the Yanomami on the Catrimani, and was considered a relatively moderate proselytizer. He established an attraction post and wooed the Waimiri Atroari with the usual presents. The missionary entered a maloca on 21 October, with the Indians helping to unload his canoes and erect a hut. But he seemed baffled by their changes of mood. In one radio message he noted that 'they use subtle techniques to show themselves furious and threatening'. The missionary's attitude was apparently too aggressive. In another message to Manaus, he said that he had firmly resisted the Indians' attempt to take all his 'merchandise' because 'Indians are well aware that this is our right, as superior beings'. He also reportedly entered malocas uninvited. He waved a shotgun at an Indian to move him out of his hammock. 'He did not heed hints that he should leave. Despite his good intentions he was an intruder.'

Calleri's insensitivity, coupled with inability to speak the tribe's Carib language, and his undue haste, had a tragic consequence: on 30 October 1968 he and his eight companions, including two nuns, were killed. There were other theories for the Calleri massacre, however. One was that the missionary was trying to persuade the Indians to move from homes on the upper Uatumã (at the south-east of their territory) to the Alalaú further north. Gilberto Pinto told the author that the presence of the nuns may have been a mistake, since the Indians were short of women – but they killed the nuns rather than abduct them. A more sinister theory was that the tribe was reacting to ill-treatment by an expedition of Protestant missionaries of the Worldwide Evangelization Crusade, who had just moved through the territory guided by Carib-speaking Waiwái Indians. Conspiracy theorists believed that the missionaries were in league with American mining interests, whose surveyors were said to have been exploring the region.

In the following year, 1969, there was a massacre of Atroari – just as serious as that of the Consolata missionaries but not a reprisal for it. A boatload of hunters and fishermen saw Indians on the bank of the Jauaperi, in the northern part of the tribe's territory, halted their boat in the middle of the river, and lured two canoeloads of Atroari to them with offers of food. The Indians 'paddled towards the motorboat, calling "Jacunum mare" which means "good white men"', but when they were a few feet away the murderers grabbed shotguns and massacred all eight of them. The bodies fell into the water, and were later concealed by the killers. A few days later, the same hunters caught two Atroari, whom they knew by name, and shot them. Funai sent Gilberto Pinto to investigate reports of these atrocities and he managed to get a young man to confess. But the most guilty man, Francisco Gomes Damasceno, was released 'for lack of evidence'.

The whites' wooing campaign was intensified but, with the massacres by both sides, the Waimiri Atroari were understandably divided about how to react. However, when Gilberto Pinto approached them again in October 1969, this time up the Camanaú from the Rio Negro, he was welcomed. The Paramount Chief Maruaga and chiefs later called Cândido, Mina, and Raimundo came to Funai's attraction post with their men, and there was a joyful meeting, exchange of presents, and an invitation to visit the tribe's malocas. Chief Maruaga was aged about sixty, and 1.80 metres (almost six feet) tall; he spoke little but with great authority and he had united the warring Waimiri and Atroari. Pinto behaved with tact, not visiting the village until invited and even then not entering any hut. He showed the Indians how to plant corn, sugar cane, and watermelons in a clearing they had prepared for this purpose. He also played a tape-recording of Chief Cândido, to which 'Maruaga listened with great attention, at first remaining serious but then laughing delightedly'. When Pinto was given fish and manioc for his return journey he

immediately withdrew. At a second peaceful parlay, in January 1971, he
had to start preparing the tribe for the onslaught of a road being hacked
towards their forests, and took some officers of the 6th Battalion of Army
Engineers, whose chainsaw gangs and earthmovers were pushing the
BR-174 highway north from Manaus. By the end of the year, Funai's
publicity bulletin reported confidently that 'contacts became increasingly
frequent, with the Indians peacefully accepting the presence of surveyors
and forest-clearance teams of the military engineers'.

Gilberto Pinto was an admirable sertanista: gentle but self-assured,
disinterested in his love of the Indians, kindly, and very experienced –
having worked in the Manaus region of the SPI and Funai since the 1940s.
He told me that he was pleased by the progress of his contact mission,
although he clearly disliked having to 'soften up' the Indians for the
highway through their land. A reserve was decreed for the Waimiri
Atroari in June 1971, but it was far smaller than the original proposal.
Pinto told me that he did not know who had reduced it, by omitting tribal
lands north of a curve in the Alalaú and forests rich in Brazil-nut trees
south of the Uatumã. Pinto's friendship with the charismatic Paramount
Chief Maruaga strengthened during the next three years. The sertanista
also sought to control the behaviour of the army engineers, but he could
not disguise the way in which the monstrous gash of the highway would
violate the tribe's fiercely defended independence.

The road workers brought the inevitable diseases. There was a wave of
Indian deaths in the early 1970s. A preventive-medicine campaign was
tragically mismanaged, with Multivac vaccine mistakenly given in doses
that were far too strong and past their use-by date, so there were mass
deaths after the vaccination teams left, with fifteen dying at Camanaú
post alone. The Waimiri Atroari understandably concluded that the whites
were firing poison or sorcery into them, and they attacked Funai posts in
revenge.

Atrocities against the Indians continued. In mid-1974 the entire Atroari
village of Kramna Mudí on the lower Alalaú was gunned down while
preparing a festival, with forty-six dead. This massacre went almost
unrecorded – unlike the murder of the Cinta Larga a decade earlier that
was the worst crime in Figueiredo's inquiry into the SPI. None of the
gunmen confessed. The murders came to light only a few years later,
when the Indians listed the name of every one of the victims to Egydio
and Doroti Schwade.

Not surprisingly, the tribe retaliated with killings of isolated construction workers and Funai agents. In December 1974, Gilberto Pinto was at
his post on the Abonari when twenty-seven Indians emerged from the

forest, seeking to trade for tools and medicine. They were clearly angry
about the village massacre, deaths from epidemics, and the destruction by
the road gangs. A planeload of presents arrived, but the Indians 'remained
dissatisfied and agitated. Early next morning [29 December 1974], a
fierce war cry brought Pinto Figueiredo rushing out of the camp. As
he approached an Indian leader [known as] Comprido ['Tall and thin' in
Portuguese] he was fatally struck in the chest by two arrows.' Gilberto
Pinto died instantly. Three other Funai men were also killed before the
warriors disappeared into the forest.

Orlando Villas Boas said that he was sure that the attack was done by
a single Indian – and it is true that Pinto had warned that Comprido was
the main opponent to white invasion. A young chief later said that
Comprido had done it because he blamed Pinto for the lethal epidemics:
'Comprido wanted to kill Gilberto since, as he said "After that fat man
came, many people died".' Orlando deeply regretted the tragedy, for Pinto
was 'a truly exceptional Indianist'. The anthropologist Roque Laraia
stressed that 'the Waimiri Atroari are not a band of savage murderers . . .
These Indians are interested only in safeguarding their lands . . . Their
revolt is not against Funai's employees, but against the road-building
machines that are invading their territory.' Father José Vicente César,
President of the Catholic missionary Indian council CIMI, blamed Funai
for not having forced the government to route the highway to the west of
the tribe's lands. Whatever the reason, Gilberto Pinto was the last senior
sertanista ever to be killed by Indians. The attack on him was the final
battle in the Waimiri Atroari's long struggle for independence.

Other commentators were less understanding of the Indians. The
commanders of the military engineers were furious at the tribe's delaying
their highway. One of them, Colonel Arruda, even made the wild
suggestion that the Waimiri Atroari should be banished from their territory and moved into the Xingu park, 1,500 kilometres (950 miles) to the
south-east. Someone issued a violent leaflet called *Operation Atroari*, with
a drawing of an Indian clubbing a construction worker, next to the
Brazilian flag, and warning that: 'The true enemy could be beside you.
Repudiate, imprison, and kill him!' The Federal Police opened an absurd
investigation against the Indians who had killed Pinto. But the most
amazing outburst came from Sebastião Firmo Amâncio, the sertanista
appointed by Funai to continue Pinto's attraction campaign. In a press
interview, Amâncio declared that he had had enough of Funai's 'war
without weapons'. The traditional policy of wooing tribes with presents
had failed. The time had come to give the Waimiri Atroari 'a demonstration of the force of our civilization' by terrifying them with dynamite,

grenades, tear gas, and bursts from sub-machine guns. This armoury would be stored in a fort that he planned to build on the Abonari, a stockade like those of the American Wild West. The Indians would go into hiding, and the highway could be driven through their land. 'I am going to use an iron fist against them. Their chiefs will be punished and if possible deported far from their lands and people. Thus, they will learn that it is not right to massacre civilizados.' The embarrassed President of Funai repudiated his official's remarks; Amâncio was moved to the Yanomami; and Apoena Meirelles was brought from Rondônia to lead the 'pacification' of the 'intransigent' Waimiri Atroari. Apoena employed his father Francisco's technique of using large teams, and no less than four Funai posts were planted along the new road where it traversed the Indian reserve.

The BR-174 highway from Manaus to Boa Vista was formally opened in April 1977. It had taken seven years to cut 624 kilometres (388 miles) through the Amazon forest. Opening a swathe 70 metres (230 feet) wide involved felling 4,400 hectares (10,900 acres) of primary rainforest. The army engineers employed 565 soldiers and 704 casual labourers, many of whom were acculturated Indians from Roraima; but four soldiers and twenty-eight civilians died from accidents during the difficult construction. It was a rough highway with steep gradients, dusty in the dry season and covered in a treacherous veneer of slippery red mud in the rains; and it crossed three large rivers on metal barges, hundreds of streams on wooden bridges, and many swamps on causeways. I drove along this BR-174 several times in the late 1980s. Traffic was still quite light, with only two buses a day doing the long journey. But settlers had already cleared all the forest on either side of the road. The exception was the 120 kilometres (75 miles) where the highway traversed the Waimiri Atroari reserve. Only here was the road flanked by protected forest.

The loss of almost half its adults from disease and massacres threatened the survival of precious tribal lore. The British botanist William Milliken and Brazilian colleagues published a study of the amazing range of Waimiri Atroari ethnobotany. This showed that they had uses for over 300 plants. In a 1 hectare (2.5 acre) patch of forest, the Indians were utilizing four-fifths of 214 tree and liana species. This knowledge extended beyond the tall *terra-firme* forest, to seasonally flooded igapó and dense dry caatinga. The botanists concluded that the tribe was 'heavily dependent upon the forest for every aspect of their physical, cultural and spiritual lives. In order to retain an adequate supply of the plants which they need (many of which are present in very low densities on account of the diversity of the flora), and of the animals which they hunt, extensive tracts of forest are clearly required.' The tribe's spiritual heritage was further threatened by the Carib-speaking Waiwái, who had become ardent Protestants and sought to convert their indigenous neighbours. But the Waimiri Atroari resisted the imposition of any external religion or customs that they themselves did not choose.

The BR-174 was only the first threat to the territory, independence, and survival of this proud tribe. Its fate was sealed by two further catastrophes: major mining interest in its land, and flooding from a hydroelectric dam. As early as 1973 Eletronorte, the energy company that supplied Manaus, commissioned a survey of hydroelectric potential of rivers north of the fast-growing city. This concluded that it might be possible to dam the Uatumã river at a place called Balbina, 146 kilometres (91 miles) to the north-east. But Balbina was not a suitable site for such a project. The lake above the dam would have to be unacceptably vast, because there were no surrounding hills; Balbina was only a few metres above sea level; the soil was porous; and the generator's turbines would be clogged by waterlogged vegetation from the dammed lake. The official estimate was that the dam would flood 165,000 hectares (some 650 square miles); but it was known that it could cover 400,000 hectares (1,500 square miles) – an area larger than the lakes behind Brazil's two biggest dams, Itaipú and Tucuruí, and greater than many nation-states in the Caribbean. This gigantic reservoir would drown a large part of the Waimiri Atroari reserve, the south-eastern sector on the Abonari river where both Calleri and Pinto had been killed. Even the dam itself was on land that had traditionally been hunted over by the Indians. Funai in 1981 commissioned a report by the anthropologist Ângela Baptista, but when she argued that work should cease until far more was known about the tribe's movements, she was removed and her report suppressed. The Balbina dam would be by far the most expensive in Brazil to build, and yet it would generate only 250 megawatts – a thirtieth of the electric output of Tucuruí. The environmental impact would also be terrible. But the giant project went ahead despite all the opposition, financed by the French government and the World Bank. The head of Brazil's environmental agency roundly condemned Balbina: 'This hydroelectric dam is the greatest stupidity in the Brazilian energy programme. It is absurd. It is unjustifiable. And it must be the last: Brazil cannot indulge in repeating a disaster like this.'

The dismal predictions proved correct. Balbina was officially opened in October 1987, and its reservoir 'transformed some 2,340 square kilometres (903 square miles) of the traditional territory of the Waimiri Atroari into a cemetery of trees under a lake of fetid waters ... Almost a third of the total population of the Waimiri Atroari was dislocated from its immemorial territories in the valleys of the Santo Antonio do Abonari, Taquari, and their tributaries.' It cost $700 million, but its generator could not function properly because of 'technical errors', silting, and lack of water power. There was even a wild plan to divert the Alalaú river, via a twenty-five kilometre (sixteen mile) canal through the forest, to fill the Balbina reservoir; but this was stopped by the environment agency Ibama.

There was a third threat to the beleaguered Waimiri Atroari. Not only was their land on the route of the Manaus–Boa Vista highway and in the catchment of the Balbina dam's reservoir, it was also found to contain minerals. Government surveys in the 1970s, partly using the Radambrasil side-looking aerial radar, found huge cassiterite tin deposits on the upper Uatumã. The giant Paranapanema mining company obtained advance access to these reports and registered claims in the names of subsidiary companies. In 1979 Funai objected that 80 per cent of these claims lay within the north-eastern part of Waimiri Atroari territory; but Paranapanema protested; and there was a suspicious change of attitude inside Funai. A report in August 1980 said that an aerial survey found 'no presence' of Indians in that area, and this was corroborated by Funai's local head, Giuseppe Cravero, who claimed that he had 'no knowledge of the existence of Indians in this sector of the reserve, nor that this region was one traversed by Indians.' Cravero later admitted that he had made this claim, not because the tribe did not hunt and collect in that area, but because it was a 'zone whose natural [mineral] resources they do not use'. Meanwhile, cartographic companies removed almost 530,000 hectares (2,000 square miles) from the Waimiri Atroari reserve by the simple expedient of renaming the headwaters of the Uatumã, so that the river's main stream appeared to be seventy-five kilometres (forty-seven miles) west of its true course – which happened to be designated as the reserve's boundary in this valuable area. At this time, 1980, Funai was controlled by Colonel João Nobre da Veiga. He had no qualms about recommending to the President of Brazil a revision (reduction) of the reserve, and this was duly done by a decree in November 1981. No environmental-impact assessment, as required by Brazilian mining law, was ever filed. In the following year, Paranapanema was given permission to build a seventy-eight kilometre (forty-eight mile) spur road off the BR-174, across Indian land, to its Pitinga cassiterite mine. It was later authorized to flood more native forests for its own small hydroelectric dam.

There was growing non-governmental resistance. An opposition Senator, Evandro Carreira, condemned the 'pure robbery' of lands that the Waimiri Atroari 'had since time immemorial inhabited and defended as their own, drawing from it sustenance for their people.' In 1983 the missionary teacher Egydio Schwade, the Bishop of Itacoatiara on the Amazon, and the sertanista Porfírio Carvalho launched MAREWA, a movement to support Waimiri Atroari resistance. It became a David fighting the Goliath of electricity-generating and tin-mining companies.

The British anthropologist Stephen Baines described a strange and sinister development within Funai's Waimiri Atroari attraction front. This team became dominated by detribalized Indians from the Amazon and Rio Negro. These workers wanted to gain control over the tribe's leadership, its trade in handicrafts, and its women. So they depicted themselves as true Indians and schemed to oust 'whites' from any authority in these posts. This included Baines because they feared his exposure of their activities. 'They used the rhetoric of the Indian-rights movement to conceal their manipulations of ethnic identities and their domination of the Waimiri Atroari.' They elevated young men such as brothers called Dalmo and Dario to be chiefs, because these shared their love of Western trappings (radios, watches, suitcases, brick houses, and visits to hotels and brothels in Manaus) and despised and shunned tribal ceremonies. Chief Dalmo became the main prop for their power-play, so they praised him as more 'intelligent', 'educated', or 'advanced' than other members of his nation.

The main psychological weapon of these aggressive pseudo-Indians was to persuade the Waimiri Atroari that it was 'whites' (and not these Indians working for Funai) who brought lethal diseases and that the infection was deliberate, done by sorcery and firing poison through injections. Chief Djacir told Baines that 'the whites killed us. Poison. The white men fired sorcery at us.' And Chief Mauro at Abonari echoed this: 'At night, in the darkness, spirits of whites. The whites killed us. Illness, poison, aches in the body.' When Baines tried to question the nefarious politics of Funai's pseudo-Indians, embarrassed Waimiri Atroari answered: 'Funai knows best'. The same anger over 'white spirits' who fired lethal poison into Indians occurred in shamanic incantations, even though 'modern' chiefs like Dalmo were violently opposed to any revival of shamanism.

Influenced by the modernists, the Waimiri Atroari became quite acculturated. Some people adopted Western clothing, the men abandoning the narrow waist band of araceous aerial roots from which they supported their penises, and the women the *tanga*, a small cup of paxiy seeds (*Socratea exorrhiza*) that covered their pudenda and was held by a string of bromeliad fibres. Apart from these small garments they had worn no ornament, beyond some body paint and simple feathered head-bands during festivals. A decade after they laid down their arms, the Waimiri

Atroari also left most of their handsome circular malocas to congregate in ten small settlements. Some of these were in locations chosen by Funai or the power company Eletronorte, often on *terra preta* ('black earth') sites where the soil was enriched and blackened by centuries of human occupation.

The forces of big business moved to consolidate their position. Before long, Porfírio Carvalho was indicted by the military police for releasing a classified document to the press; and in 1985 Funai abruptly banished Schwade from his school among the Indians. These activists had got young Atroari leaders, Viana Uomé and Mário Paroé, to write to the President of Brazil and ministers to complain about the concessions to Paranapanema's Taboca subsidiary: 'Until today, ever since President Figueiredo let Taboca go there, it has been stealing our cassiterite just for itself. To date we have gained nothing, neither compensation, nor demarcation: the Funai team is still helping Taboca, and we get no aid. Taboca goes on mining our riches and deforesting our land, but nothing was agreed with us.' Stephen Baines angrily wrote that 'Paranapanema has made nearly $60 million in profits from the mining of cassiterite on land which it has stolen from the Waimiri Atroari Indians, leaving in its place nothing but social upheaval and ecological degradation.' If it was allowed to extend its operations into other parts of the reserve – through fraudulent agreements with tribal leaders – 'it would be the end of a people whose traditional territory would then be entirely overrun by mining activities'. Funai's complicity with big business was disgraceful. Within a few months of writing this, Baines was vilified in the press – partly with an amazing accusation that he was acting for Asian tin-mining interests – and he was also expelled from the tribal area.

By 1985, Pitinga was described as the world's largest open-cast tin mine, with reserves of 291,000 tons of ore. The mining company became all-powerful, keeping rival companies and small prospectors out of the reserve, building schools and other amenities for the Indians, and supporting the impoverished Funai with 'a doctor, nurse, dentist, medicines, hospital, laboratory, infirmary, food supplies, lifts by car and plane, technical assistance, building materials, automobile parts, bulk transport, electrical materials, petrol and lubricants'. Not surprisingly, Funai officials told the Indians to help the company, and the Waimiri Atroari came to depend on company stores. An Indian who claimed that as a child he had survived a massacre of Waimiri Atroari on the Alalaú and then been educated in Rio de Janeiro was brought back to be 'chief' of this tribe that knew nothing of him. He and other leaders were bribed with such luxuries as brick houses, mattresses, and refrigerated processed food. In return, they formed a delegation to Brasília to speak up for the mining company, and signed a concession for it to extend its ranching and other activities into the reserve.

In 1987 a retaining dam burst and 700,000 cubic metres (920,000 cubic yards) of mine waste poured into a tributary of the Alalaú, turning the river yellow with pollution. This catastrophe affected the drinking water of three villages, caused immediate medical problems, and killed the fish on which the Indians depended. But it did not prevent the civilian government of President Sarney from issuing, in May 1989, a 'concession to wash tin minerals in a place called Alalaú'. In the following year, the Indians had to block the access road across their land, to try to get payment of compensation awarded to them and in a vain attempt to have the road closed. And in April 1993 another retaining dam burst, spilling further mineral contents of washing lakes into the Alalaú.

The huge influx of construction workers, settlers, mine-workers and passing traffic brought malaria, which reached epidemic proportions in this part of Brazil, as well as the gamut of other imported diseases. Many Indians died from a measles epidemic in 1981. Stephen Baines watched twenty-one Indians die at Posto Terraplanagem, which he blamed on the inefficiency of the 'community assistance project' and the policy of herding people into the new post. The tribe's population fell disastrously. Father Calleri had guessed in 1968 that there were 3,000 Waimiri Atroari; a few years later Gilberto Pinto reckoned between 600 and 1,000; Funai in 1980 thought that there were 800; but by 1983 Baines found the population reduced to only 332. That was the nadir. A strong birth rate, coupled with better medical care, brought this number up to 450 by 1990 and it was still rising strongly at the end of the century. But it is a young population. Disease wiped out many elders who could have transmitted tribal knowledge.

Waimiri Atroari who lived near the road and the Funai posts were rapidly acculturated. Those in remote villages on rivers to the south-west of the reserve were less exposed; and there is still an uncontacted group known as Piriutiti or Piridipi in the forests east of the mine. The tribe is coming to terms with its violent initiation to the modern world through the three major projects that descended upon them. It receives compensation from two of the invading companies: Paranapanema pays 0.38 per cent of the value of the cassiterite extracted from the Pitinga mine, and Eletronorte pays a fee for the land drowned by the Balbina dam. Eletronorte set up a Waimiri Atroari Programme, administered by its employees and Funai's. This has done good work, particularly in health care and primary schooling, but it has also introduced cattle and other imported foods. All this activity left the tribe divided and often unsure about its traditions and roots. Some of the aid is inappropriate, such as suffocatingly hot houses of brick and corrugated iron, or the cattle which the Indians do not understand or appreciate.

Fiona Watson of Survival International visited three villages in 1992 and reported that 'materially the Waimiri Atroari are probably better off than most Indians in Brazil . . . However, the relationship between Funai and the Indians is extremely paternalistic – whatever the Indians demand, such as transport for fishing or food, they get. Consequently they are very reliant on Funai whom, as they have no other yardstick, they believe is wonderful.' By now the young Funai agents administering this aid were well-meaning, but they spoke almost no Carib and, with no anthropological training, they were uninterested in maintaining any tribal customs. Despite this, some cultural traits are maintained by the Wamiri Atroari themselves: hammocks of liana fibre, beautiful basketwork, some hunting with bows and arrows, and initiation of boys by an ordeal of biting fire-ants. A few Indians returned to live in the forest, which others now fear as a hostile environment. Watson was optimistic that this tribe, with its long history of resistance, would have the inner strength and pride to nurture its cultural traditions.

The reason why the BR-174 was cut through the forests of the Waimiri Atroari – at such a high environmental, social, and engineering cost – was to link Roraima by land to the rest of Brazil. There is a vast natural savannah, campo, stretching for hundreds of kilometres around the low hills of the geologically ancient Guiana Shield (which form the watershed and are therefore the northernmost frontier of Brazil). The open plain extends across the boundary hills into Venezuela, where it is called the Gran Sabana (Great Savannah), and eastwards into Guyana where it is known as the Rupununi. It is a beautiful land. The prairies extend to the horizons, undulating gently, sometimes peppered with curatella and other hardy little campo trees or lines of graceful buriti palms (*Mauritia flexuosa*) along watercourses, the grasses broken only by pink termite mounds. Sometimes a distant table mountain is visible – Tepequém, the Parima Hills, or Roraima itself. Above, the blue firmament is filled with piles of the clouds that add such grandeur and movement to all Amazonian scenery.

The first Europeans to see these broad grasslands appreciated their potential for cattle. A few cows and bulls were taken up the rivers Negro and Branco in the late eighteenth century. The cattle roamed almost wild and multiplied. By 1913 there were thought to be 200,000 head, and by

1930 over 300,000; the cattle were then devastated by a disease that drove the cows mad, and the herd was reduced by two-thirds. It has recovered gradually ever since, and Roraima retains a ranching economy to the present day.

The tribes that lived on the open plains of Roraima were very exposed to European interference. The two main nations – Aruak-speaking Wapixana and Carib-speaking Makuxi – had endured slaving in the eighteenth century and the inevitable decimation from disease. There was then international rivalry over them, first between Portuguese, Spaniards, and Dutch; then, when Britain acquired Guyana from the Dutch during the Napoleonic Wars, between the British and Brazilians. But travellers described both tribes as handsome, hospitable, and good-natured.

By the beginning of the twentieth century, the Wapixana and Makuxi were considerably acculturated, and the men of both tribes had become skilled cowboys. The Wapixana were originally the more numerous; but they had the misfortune of occupying some of the best cattle land not far from the capital town, Boa Vista. The German anthropologist Theodor Koch-Grünberg explained that 'friendly and submissive by nature, the Wapixana have always been exposed to [European] influence, mainly because they live very close to the main rivers Branco and Uraricoera. As a result of their prolonged relations with the white and mestizo population . . . they lost much of their own character and some are considerably morally corrupted. They work as cowhands and boatmen. Many speak Portuguese.' The Italian Count Ermanno Stradelli, who lived for many years in this part of Brazil, found the Wapixana greatly reduced in numbers and often driven from their lands to remote locations further from the rivers. 'Hard-working and docile, they voluntarily lend themselves to work for the whites.' Wapixana women were famous for making fine cotton hammocks and the best manioc flour for Boa Vista's market.

The French explorer Henri Coudreau had in the 1890s contrasted the fate of the compliant Wapixana with that of the more independent Makuxi. 'It is curious to note that tribes who become acculturated fastest also disappear quickest. Such are the Wapixana, who became civilized faster than the Makuxi. Many of them speak Portuguese. By contrast, the Makuxi are far more rebellious against civilized discipline. They are reluctant to teach their language to the whites; and they are insolent and insubordinate. Conclusion: the Wapixana *were* the most important tribe of the rio Branco a century ago, but they now number scarcely a thousand. The Makuxi, on the other hand, are far more numerous today than a century ago . . . : you can count three or four thousand of them.'

Sadly for the Makuxi, their 'insolence and insubordination' could not protect them against disease and natural calamity. In 1910, thousands died in a violent epidemic of measles. This was followed in 1911–12 by a terrible drought from which more people died of starvation. These plains Indians could not draw on the riches of surrounding forests, but depended on plantations for food. A Belgian missionary wrote that 'it did not rain for eight months and all the plants were annihilated. The savannahs looked as though they had been burned, and a large part of the cattle died.' A third scourge struck the Makuxi in November 1912. The missionary Dom Adalbert reported that 'a great epidemic of fever has been raging in this region. The Indians died en masse. The population of the area that comes under our mission has been decimated, if not annihilated.' This virulent malaria – presumably the falciparum strain – inflamed spleens and livers and caused anaemia and 'a form of dropsy'. It raged throughout that decade, and prostrated Indians and settlers alike.

Roraima's few hundred colonists, the ranchers who owned the herds that roamed across its unfenced prairies, were interested in the plains Indians for only two reasons: land and labour. The beef barons evolved a 'godfather' system, each acting as a kindly, paternalistic boss who protected 'his' Indians. He advanced them goods on credit to subject them to classic debt-bondage. He became godfather to their children and took some into his own household, theoretically for education but in practice as unpaid domestic servants. A Brazilian commentator in 1949 deplored 'the inhuman exploitation of the labour of Makuxi children, boys and girls, by the majority of inhabitants of the Territory.' The Oxford anthropologist Peter Rivière found this system still current in 1967, and he noted extreme discrimination by foster families against Indian children they were rearing in their homes. These unfortunates were made to do all manual chores, but lived and ate apart from the family's own children.

'When fostered Indian boys grew to manhood, they became cowhands. Any heavy labour is done by the poor Indians, without any remuneration or assistance'. Edson Diniz called the system 'disguised slavery'; but the Indians tolerated it. They received no pay beyond a few animals and some land on which to graze them. The British anthropologist Iris Myers, who studied the Makuxi in both British Guiana and Brazil in the 1940s, noted that 'this training has such deeply modifying effects on the Indian psyche that many of the individuals so brought up are more akin to the simple Brazilian ranchers of the region than to their own folk, speaking Portuguese much better than their own tongue and preferring the civilized way of life to that of the "maloca".' Myers also noted that the acculturation was a two-way process: the Indians taught settlers how to survive on those hot plains only a few degrees north of the equator. They also introduced them to the dubious practice of annual burning of grasses, theoretically to produce a new growth in the ashes of the old and to kill ticks and snakes that molest the cattle. But these great conflagrations seriously weaken the soil, and they occasionally rage out of control and destroy adjacent forests. In later years, government agronomists tried to persuade farmers to stop the burning; but in vain.

Land was the Indians' great problem, throughout the twentieth century. They themselves had no tradition of land ownership. The handful of settlers in nineteenth-century Rio Branco (Roraima) started by regarding any of its plains as suitable grazing for their cattle: and towards the end of the century some claimed almost limitless expanses of prairie as their private ranches. Such men completely ignored any native land rights. If Indians tried to maintain small villages or farms within a fazenda, they would be evicted by armed gangs of cowhands and their plantations destroyed. The Wapixana were particularly hounded in this way. But the territory was vast and very thinly inhabited, so that most Makuxi could continue to live unmolested, as did the related Carib-speaking Taurepang (Pemon) on the foothills of Mount Roraima, and a few hundred feared Ingarikó in forests to the north of them. (The name Roraima means 'Blue-green Mountain (or Tree)' in Carib.)

In 1927 General Cândido Rondon, now in his sixties, was sent on an inspection of Brazil's northern frontiers. When he was in Roraima, he met various Makuxi and Wapixana chiefs, all of whom welcomed him as the champion of Brazil's Indians. Some complained of ill-treatment by fazendeiros; and the latter accused the Indians of killing or stealing their cattle; but Rondon was able to warn the ranchers to behave correctly.

The greatest concern for the Brazilian authorities was that their Indians were being attracted to emigrate to adjacent countries. When Rondon was on the Tacutu – the small river that marks the boundary between Brazil and Guyana – Chief Manuel Barreto of the Makuxi complained that abuse by the local sheriff was forcing his people to seek greater freedom in the nearby British colony. Rondon commented on the different approaches by the two regimes. The English 'seek to attract all the Indians of the region to their territory; but [the Brazilians] persecute their compatriots and force them into exile . . . It is interesting to note that in Brazil these Indians have a reputation of being thieves; but when they cross into Guiana they are well received by the English, who consider them good men.' Another Brazilian General, Lima Figueiredo, found that there was no improvement in the 1940s. British missionaries had attracted both Makuxi and Wapixana. 'There has been formidable emigration and, unless there is government action, it will be total. The affectionate manner of the Guiana priests contrasts with the crude brutality of the Amazonian fazendeiros and authorities. Civilizados seeking riches invade the lands from which the Indians support their families: they trample on them and humiliate their families.' This general praised the Makuxi, Taurepang, and Wapixana as strong, docile, intelligent, and totally civilized people. The drift towards British Guiana was confirmed by Iris Myers, who saw it as 'the habitual Indian reaction of flight from any difficult or complicated situation.' The Makuxi preferred the laissez-faire approach in the British colony; although when they adopted European attitudes these tended to be Brazilian.

Myers noted how seriously Makuxi numbers had declined by her day, down to a total of 1,800. Malaria was the biggest killer; 'respiratory diseases, chiefly bronco-pneumonia, also take a large toll'; and infant mortality exceeded 50 per cent in some villages. This decline in numbers exacerbated a malaise among the Makuxi, a disorientation so serious that it affected some Indians' will to live. Now it was the Makuxi who found it difficult to come to terms with technological change, whereas the neighbouring Wapixana seemed to be increasing and prospering. 'Life is becoming increasingly a difficult and irksome business to the Makuxi, saddened by their awareness of what is happening to them, and by their frequently expressed sense of being a doomed people, continually restricted in their activities by the decrease in their numbers.' Myers noticed many examples of the Makuxi's confusion. Their adoption of Western tools – from hoes to cooking pans – meant the abandonment of many traditional crafts. All now wore shabby European clothes in favour of handsome body ornaments. Even once-prized hunting dogs were no longer trained to fetch game. Instead, 'the Makuxi dog is usually now a mangy thieving cur, whose staple diet is human and animal excrement, and against whose depredations a continual war must be waged.' The tribe's shamans retained much of their extensive knowledge of medicinal plants, hallucinogens, and powerful curare poison – but used these alongside imported medicines.

Cattle made the most profound change in the tribe's way of life, and the Makuxi were by now well adapted to the animals: both sexes were skilled at milking and corral work, and all the men could round up cattle, slaughter it, and make salt beef. Petty thieving and some cattle-rustling were commonplace, among a people who had once been scrupulously honest. Cultural change greatly diminished the practice of traditional ceremonies and dances. Younger men and women turned from 'old-fashioned' tribal music to the latest Brazilian sambas and dance rhythms. Myers noticed that 'the Makuxi reaction to the disintegration and despair following on the rapid and alarming decrease in numbers . . . seems to have been an Epicurean one. The "paiwarri" spree [a traditional ceremony] has become almost continual, in a very degenerated form.' People consumed all their manioc in making intoxicating paracarí, and danced incessantly. 'The mania has become so strong that many individuals seem to live only for pleasure, and the excessive drinking and fatigue caused by hunger on these occasions help to swell the death rate.' These dances were the Makuxi's form of milleniarism, their release from the anxieties of cultural change.

The Indians of Roraima were relatively unmolested during the first half of the twentieth century. A missionary effort by Belgian Benedictines collapsed, first from a clash between the clergy and Freemason cattle barons, then from financial wrongdoing by their abbot. Some missionary work continued among one group of Makuxi on the Surumú, provided by nuns from Bavaria. By 1940 the Benedictines were writing that 'the good Indians are docile and receptive to the civilizing action of the missionaries. You could even say that they show themselves to be extremely open to religious catechism.' This teaching was highly conservative, consisting largely of cards about the Sacred Heart of Jesus in all the native dialects. Meanwhile, British Protestant and Catholic missionaries were active on their side of the frontier. The one who most alarmed the Brazilians was the Jesuit Father Cuthbert Cary-Elwes, who established his mission of Saint Ignatius among the Makuxi right on the Tacutu frontier river, and was there from 1909 to 1923. The Indians responded to his teaching; but he did not operate inside Brazil as Rondon and others suspected. A Brazilian boundary surveyor in 1940 counted 1,400 Makuxi living along the Maú river, mostly on the British side. He noted that 'the religious conversion is skilfully done; but the religious objective that justifies it gives way to ambitions of colonial conquest.'

The spiritual atmosphere changed in 1948, with the arrival in Boa Vista of six missionaries of the Italian Consolata Order, led by Dom Giuseppe Napote. During the second half of the twentieth century, the Consolata fathers ran the diocese of Roraima and all its missionary works. They were of the new breed of Catholic priests – relaxed, politically radical, and more concerned with the welfare of their Indians than with their conversion to Christianity. Consolata fathers normally wore jeans and check shirts rather than cassocks, and there were none of the seminary-like boarding schools or effigy-laden churches of the Salesians on the nearby Rio Negro.

During these decades, the Indian Protection Service had almost no presence in Rio Branco (Roraima). It had been awarded a large government-owned cattle ranch called São Marcos, in the 'V' where the Tacutu and Uraricoera rivers join to form the rio Branco. São Marcos was always a commercial concern, a working ranch, and the main purpose of its Makuxi and other tribal Indians was to act as cowhands tending the fazenda's cattle. It was one of many places where the Indian patrimony had been ransacked: when the SPI took over São Marcos, a rancher had ruthlessly plundered its herd, which was down to 3,500 head of cattle, but by 1921 a visitor was impressed to find 8,000 animals of good quality, and the Makuxi well housed with their children receiving primary schooling. The SPI's report of 1923 was proud of its training of Indians as smiths, carpenters, and masons: for the Makuxi 'constitute the mass of labourers and cattle-hands of the entire Upper Rio Branco region'. General Rondon in 1927 was equally impressed by the work of his SPI on São Marcos. There were more schools for Indian children, a sanatorium on the Cotingo river two days' ride from the ranch village, and an outpost called Limão on the upper Surumú. But this burst of activity was short-lived: São Marcos suffered during the lean years of the SPI in the 1930s. Another visitor in 1944 reported that the fazenda was 'in utter decay, which is accentuated daily by its abandonment: no advanced techniques of cattle or horse breeding have been introduced.' After further vicissitudes, the São Marcos fazenda was named in the 1967 Figueiredo parliamentary inquiry into corruption in the old SPI.

The anthropologist Edson Diniz described the Makuxi and Wapixana at that time, scratching a living in hamlets and primitive farms scattered amid Roraima's sprawling cattle ranches. 'The economic situation of the Makuxi is dire. Since they produce no surplus for sale, they sacrifice their subsistence and have the lowest standard of living. Of their agricultural produce, they mostly sell manioc flour; but the yield from this sort of produce is not enough for their subsistence. Some also raise a few cattle, but in such small numbers that they are not worth mentioning.' They had almost ceased to make their former handsome utensils. To eke out a living, the Makuxi were hiring themselves out for every form of manual labour, from cattle ranching to prospecting in Roraima's rivers. As always, the main cause of inter-ethnic friction was over land. Settlers had many devious ways of acquiring Indian land: one was by introducing a corral and then creating a ranch around it; another was to buy a title from a detribalized Indian who had drifted into a town. Even when the Indians were persuaded to retreat to the remoter parts of Roraima, the cattle men eventually followed. 'Disorientated, and possessing no title deed, [the Indians] were at the mercy of the civilizados who considered their lands as "unoccupied" from a legal point of view . . . In this clash of interests, it is obvious that the minor society always emerged as the loser. Its members were also harassed by means of the police. The fazendeiros controlled the police, the prisons, and the threat of punishments – such as a hand-thrashing or the "seal" of branding with a hot iron.'

Then attitudes started to change. The docile and downtrodden Indians of the Roraima plains gradually became more militant. This new identity was partly the product of the emergence of politically active chiefs, *tuxauas*, in each Makuxi and Wapixana maloca. When Rondon visited the region he was welcomed by a tuxaua in each community, and he encouraged this system. From 1950 to 1972 the maloca of Raposa on the Cotingo became pre-eminent in Makuxi politics, because it was led by Chief Gabriel Viriato Raposo, who was considered paramount tuxaua of all the Makuxi. When Tuxaua Gabriel died, his cousin Odalício succeeded him; but the missionary fathers and Funai elevated Gabriel's brother Abel. This Makuxi was presented in Brasília as a model indigenous leader, taken to Rome for the Holy Year 1975, and given posts such as inspector of the region's schools; but he was never as popular or influential among the Indians as his cousin had been.

The main catalyst in making Roraima's Indians more radical was the religious missions. The Italian Consolata missionaries were active among the Yanomami and in Boa Vista itself, but they had three missions among the Makuxi and Taurepang (Pemon) to the north-east. The Baptist Church MEVA (Missão Evangélica da Amazônia) flourished in twelve villages of the savannah tribes, where the converted Indians saw themselves as Protestant crentes. There was obviously no love lost between Catholics and Protestants, but the two branches of Christianity sometimes cooperated when it came to organizing indigenous meetings or protests.

Fundamentalist Seventh-Day Adventists came from Venezuela and Guyana in the 1960s and now completely dominate three Taurepang villages in the northernmost tip of Roraima. 'Their devotion to the Adventist religion makes direct interaction between the Taurepang and representatives of regional society virtually impossible. Their villages have become an inward-looking universe.' Indians strictly observe a prohibition on commercial activity on Saturdays, and never venture onto roads or into nearby towns on that day of the week. 'The ritual life of the aldeias is visibly marked by church activities. In addition to a long worship on Saturdays, there are others throughout the week, on Sunday, Thursday, and Friday evenings.' In these services, there is always a sermon preached in their Carib language, and the Indians value those who proclaim 'the good word' with most passion. Most Taurepang are literate, possess a Bible and hymn-book, and scrupulously attend services; and yet their faith retains elements of pre-conversion mythology and cosmology.

From the mid-1970s, the tuxauas of all Makuxi malocas started to meet annually. The Church provided the food, funds, and transport for these reunions, which were of crucial importance in asserting tribal identity. Towards the end of that decade 'the character of the [annual] meetings [of tuxauas] started to change, from being simple tribal gatherings promoted by the Church, to events whose tone was increasingly political and militant . . . That of January 1985 distinguished itself by an attitude and language typical of [Brazil's] modern indigenous movement.' That meeting, at the mission of Surumú, was a tremendous gathering of 150 people: representatives of six indigenous peoples, Brazilian and foreign NGOs, anthropologists, Funai, and the missionaries who organized the event.

As always, loss of homelands was the main grievance of the Makuxi. Their problem was particularly acute because they lived on open grasslands that had for decades been cattle country, and ranchers were convinced that they had title deed to most of these plains. Between 1982 and 1984 Funai finally decreed and demarcated over twenty small reserves for the Makuxi, Wapixana, Ingarikó, and Taurepang. In a third of these, the once mutually antagonistic Carib- and Aruak-speaking tribes coexisted peacefully. But they were small islands of land hemmed in by immense ranches.

The gentle Wapixana were some of the most acculturated Indians in Brazil. For many decades they had supplied cowhands and domestic servants for the ranchers that occupied most of Roraima's open plains. The Wapixana suffered from occupying some of the state's best lands, in the Serra da Lua ('Moon Hills') south-east of the capital, Boa Vista, and the Taiano region to the north-west. The Secchis, a couple who wrote a fine study of the Wapixana in the 1980s, noted that 'it is common to meet many Indians in Wapixana malocas who behave exactly like cattle-ranchers . . . Their interests, preoccupations, desires, dreams, and topics of conversation all exactly reproduce the world of cattle men, among whom they have lived for over a century'. Some Indians raised modest herds. Fine farmers, the Wapixana also tried to survive by selling surplus crops (maize, beans, bananas, pineapples, and citrus fruits) but they were at the mercy of low and fluctuating prices. Funai provided an occasional truck to transport produce to Boa Vista market, but it did not take Indians back, so that they frequently spent their earnings on drink and consumer goods, or they were robbed and made their way home empty-handed. Funai also demarcated the tribe's pockets of land – albeit belatedly and after years of complaints, invasions, and conflicts – and gave meagre medical assistance. The city exerts a strong attraction for the Wapixana, many of whom left tribal society for the shanty-towns around Boa Vista and found work on ranches, as garimpeiro prospectors, or recently as loggers. Wapixana traditions and language survive precariously in malocas towards the Guyana frontier; but closer to Boa Vista they have given way to the Portuguese language, Western clothes, Catholicism, football, and Brazilian dances. These Indians remain dignified but some, uncharacteristically, seek to deny their ethnic roots. So the Wapixana may be seen as an example of assimilation into Brazilian society, which has been the aspiration of a few politicians, missionaries, and founders of the Indian Protection Service.

The big issue for Roraima's savannah tribes became the ownership of a huge area in the north-east of their territory: the Lavrado (literally 'Tilled Land', the plains between the Cotingo-Surumú and Maú (Ireng) rivers. This beautiful region is known after its two main reserves, Raposa (the base of Tuxaua Raposo) and Serra do Sol ('Sun Hills'). Stretching north to Mount Roraima and bounded to the east by the Guyana frontier, this savannah is the heartland of the Makuxi and, north of them, the related Taurepang. Long ago in 1917 a state law had conceded in Rio Branco (Roraima) 'all lands currently owned by wild or semi-civilized Indians, as owners in perpetuity by right of primary occupation'. This decree specifically mentioned the lands along the Cotingo and Surumú rivers and the adjacent hills – the region still in dispute at the end of the century – but it excluded and exempted any ranches already granted to or farmed by settlers. By the 1980s, the Cotingo valley had forty Makuxi villages; but it also had ninety-two ranches with over 150,000 head of cattle occupying as much land as the Indian malocas. The Makuxi finally started to react to the invasions – by a steady stream of protests to Funai, by killing cattle or pigs that occupied native land, and by demanding demarcation of their reserve territories. Almost all the tuxauas pressed for a single great Indian area, adjacent to the São Marcos ranch and extending all the way to Guyana and Venezuela. They did not want an 'archipelago' of reserve fragments.

Funai initially sided with the state government and the ranchers, and tried to persuade the Indians to accept such a solution. The struggle continued for years and there were ugly incidents. In 1982 the police and a fazendeiro arrested some Makuxi on the upper Cotingo and forced them to dismantle a corral. In the following year, a fazendeiro set fire to the house of an Indian of Mundubim maloca for 'invading' his ranch. The local delegacy of Funai was accused of 'barbaric treachery' when it forced two Indians to sign away a vast tract of land to this same rancher. Tuxauas of villages of the upper Cotingo and Maú sent a protest to the President of Funai about the local bureau's support of thirty-two ranchers who were invading their land. 'We request, on behalf of the communities we represent – over 3,500 persons – and of other communities in the hills and Lavrado, *a single area*. We have been deceived many times with promises that it would be demarcated . . . but nothing has been done. Our patience is now coming to an end.' But the oppression and intimidation continued, with local politicians complaining that far too much of Roraima belonged to the Indians, and redneck sheriffs arresting Makuxi and Wapixana on flimsy charges, or evicting native people and destroying their corrals or farm plots. It was reminiscent of the American Deep South in the bad days of the mid-twentieth century.

19. Yanomami

The Yanomami are the largest indigenous nation to survive isolated and unacculturated into the mid-twentieth century. Since then, they have changed less than most native peoples. They owe this survival to the remoteness of their territory, in deeply forested hills of the far north of Brazil and south of Venezuela. To penetrate their beautiful homeland, travellers had to surmount countless rapids on distant headwaters of the Orinoco or of the Amazon's Negro and Branco tributaries. The Yanomami's pristine condition and numbers are not the only reasons why anthropologists and all other observers are fascinated by them. This vibrant nation differs in many respects from other Brazilian Indians, from whom they have been isolated for millennia in both language and customs. The Yanomami speak distinct languages. Their babies are born with a 'mongol spot' birthmark at the base of the spine – a sure sign of their central-Asian origins.

Yanomami society is based on some 320 *yano* (also called *shabono*), communal roundhouses widely scattered in their undulating forests. A yano is an architectural masterpiece, of two patterns: either a mighty conical thatch on a great framework of pillars and beams that soars above the tree canopy like a proud circus tent; or the same thatched circle open in the middle, so that the families live in a sheltered arc that looks in towards the round central yard. Diameters of these dwellings range from 15 to 23 metres (48 to 75 feet). There are no windows, so that the interior has a cathedral-like gloom lit only by light filtering through the thatch or from family fires. The outer perimeter is fortified by a wall of logs.

A yano houses between thirty and two hundred people, with each family unit's hammocks, hearth, and possessions in a segment of the perimeter. The Yanomami prefer to marry within their community, but they are in contact with surrounding villages a few hours' or days' walk away on a network of trails. These yano meet one another for ceremonies, barter, or occasional intermarriage, but there are also feuds and skirmishes between villages or raids to seize the most desirable commodity – women.

Each yano is surrounded by forest clearings planted with bananas (their favourite food), manioc, yams and sweet potatoes, protein-rich pupunha (peach-palms, *Bactris gasipaes*), sugar cane, maize, taro, and a profusion of other useful plants and trees. Beyond these gardens is an expanse of forest, perhaps 700 square kilometres (270 square miles) per village, to supply its hunting and gathering needs. Many botanists have marvelled at Yanomami knowledge and uses of forest plants – notably Richard Schultes on hallucinogens, Ghillean Prance on edible fungi, Anthony Anderson on palms, and recently the French and British anthropologist-botanists Bruce Albert and William Milliken on medicinal plants. Such studies show that the Yanomami know and use a vast array of species – for instance, some 200 plants with medical uses – and they incorporate them into a rich mythology. This ethnobotany is made more copious by the diversity of habitats in the Yanomami's extensive homeland.

There is debate about the extent to which the pre-contact Yanomami relied on hunting and gathering rather than gardens for subsistence. Before obtaining metal blades they had only a limited number of stone axes, and it was difficult for them to clear roças in the forest. The anthropologist Brian Ferguson has shown experimentally that steel axes are up to ten times more efficient than stone ones. The Yanomami also rely on trekking to hunt and gather. They 'are superb at living off nature, and frequently opt to do so for weeks or even months at a time'. But when compelled to live without gardens they suffer hunger, for the 'Yanomami are able to survive as pure hunter-gatherers, but with difficulty.' Various authors have worked out the kaleidoscope of treks by the Yanomami during the decades before contact – hunting expeditions of short and long duration, splits within communities and visits to neighbouring yanos, raids or flights from enemies, and migrations to different habitats.

The artificial separation of the Yanomami into the two modern countries Brazil and Venezuela results from the Treaty of Madrid of 1750, whose negotiators chose the watershed between the Amazon and Orinoco rivers as the frontier between the Portuguese and Spanish empires in South America. At that time this boundary was totally unexplored. It remained so until recent times, because of its remoteness, forbidding hilly rainforests, rapid-infested rivers, and the warlike reputation of the Yano-mami. This nation occupies a great quadrilateral of forests, roughly 550 kilometres (340 miles) from east to west and 300 kilometres (185 miles) from north to south; and it divides into subgroups with slightly different languages within this vast area.

There were fleeting glimpses of different groups of Yanomami, who were then known as Waika, during the two centuries after the Treaty of

Madrid. The first contacts were by a group of brilliant Portuguese explorers who surveyed some of these new frontiers in the 1780s. Alexander von Humboldt heard about them when he went up the Orinoco in 1800. Robert Schomburgk in 1838-9 was the first European to travel up the Uraricoera river in Roraima and across the northern part of Yanomami territory to the Orinoco. Another great German anthropologist, Theodor Koch-Grünberg, repeated Schomburgk's epic journey in 1911-12. All these explorers were of course guided, paddled, and fed by Indians, notably by the Yekuana (Maiongong), who know every rock and channel in the labyrinth of rapids and waterfalls.

In December 1911 Koch-Grünberg had a first encounter with two malocas of Xirianá, a subgroup of Yanomami. The Indians trembled at first, but then relaxed and started trading. They had typical Yanomami attributes: muscular men with round haircuts and penis sheaths, and pretty women naked apart from red aprons. Unlike other tribes, neither sex pluck their scant body hair. The women wear palm spines projecting from three holes below their mouths like the whiskers of jaguars and a pencil-thin piece of wood through the septums of their noses. They love painting their skin with waving lines or blocks of dye, and both sexes wear ornaments of flashy sprays of feathers or flowers. Superb hunters, the Yanomami wield powerful bows. Their very long arrows have an armoury of detachable points for different types of game: some tipped in curare poison, others with barbs from monkey or curassow bones, or spear-shaped with serrated edges. They use simple hammocks of tree fibres, and a wide inventory of domestic tools and appliances.

Yanomami shamanism, ceremonial, and mythology are as rich and complex as those of any other indigenous people. Both sexes love chewing tobacco (*Nicotiana tabacum*), with a sausage-shaped wad constantly puffing out their lower lips; and the men frequently inhale powerful brown *epená* or *yakuana* snuffs, derived from red bark resins of varieties of *Virola* trees or from seeds of the *Anadenanthera* legume which are the source of *yopo* hallucinogens. A shaman blows this snuff up men's nostrils through a long bamboo tube. Many botanists and anthropologists have experimented with Yanomami hallucinogens. Like them, this author has had blasts of snuff blown up his nose. I experienced the resulting sensation of mental and visual clarity: the inhaler of epená thinks that he can solve any problem, and the pillars and furnishing of the yano stand out from the gloom with deceptive sharpness. Richard Schultes, the Harvard botanist who founded the discipline of ethnobotany, noted that in addition to taking these drugs formally in their ceremonies the Yanomami – unlike any other Indians – use them casually and recreationally. Schultes' pupil

Wade Davis wrote that 'in every house hung a large bamboo tube of snuff and . . . any man was free to dip into the stash if he felt the urge. It was not uncommon to see an individual high on *epená*, dancing and singing alone while the rest of the village went about the daily round'.

Yanomami isolation was not seriously breached until the 1950s. In 1919 the British-American explorer Dr Alexander Hamilton Rice went far up the Orinoco in Venezuela but had a bloody battle with a strong group of Yanomami. On a later expedition he briefly met some friendly but, to him, miserable eastern members of this nation. In September 1931 many Indians made a 'spirited attack' on 'civilized settlements' on the Araçá tributary of the Demini, during which the Yanomami captured two women and a child but lost seven men to seringueiros' guns. Despite this, Desmond Holdridge of the Brooklyn Museum went up these rivers in 1932. His team visited a Yanomami maloca on the upper Demini and, after initial suspicion, was hospitably received. During the 1940s the Indians launched raids on balata latex collectors and fishermen on the rivers flowing from the Yanomami Hills into the Middle Rio Negro. Seringueiros were killed and some of their women and children abducted. Salesian missionaries reported that frightened caboclos completely abandoned the area, and would not land on the north bank of this part of the Negro.

Then, in 1957, a canoeload of Yanomami containing a woman called Napaúma, her husband, and four children appeared near a Salesian mission. This woman was also called Helena Valero, a mission-educated caboclo girl who had been seized from the Dimiti river, at the western edge of Yanomami territory, in the mid-1930s, when she was eleven. Helena–Napaúma had lived for some twenty years with her Indian captors, but still remembered Portuguese. The Italian medical-anthropologist Ettore Biocca interviewed her and published her amazing story, told dispassionately and in great detail. It is a fine ethnographic record of Yanomami life in the mid-twentieth century.

Helena Valero described merciless raids by the Karawetari group of Yanomami against the weaker Kohoroshiwetari. Men and infants were killed without compassion and the frightened women rounded up for a ten-day trek through the forest. She told of repeated skirmishes, abductions of women, and constant fear of attack; periods of hunger and privation; but also happiness and plenty, with good fishing expeditions, gathering, and farming, and the pleasures of epená snuff. There were times when Napaúma–Helena feared for her life, from jealous women, from her lack of family to protect her, and once when a warrior thought that she had insulted him and she had to flee and hide in a forest cave for days, hungry and wounded by his arrows. At most other times she experienced friendship, generosity, and compassion, and the serenity of life in a yano. Helena was junior wife to chiefs of four successive groups, and she told Biocca about the fathers of her four children – one of whom was killed in inter-tribal fighting. Finally, she and her taciturn fourth husband took her children and fled from possible massacre by another yano back to 'civilization' – which she later disliked because its selfishness contrasted with the communal harmony of the villages she had left.

Helena was healthy during most of her time with the Yanomami, but she experienced one terrible epidemic that almost killed her first child. She described the shamanistic rituals to try to draw the sickness out of its victims, the grief, and the funerary rites for the dead. A chief understood the cause of his people's distress. He said to her: 'Last night I dreamed of very many white men, all clothed and with cloaks over them; when they shook the hoods, smoke emerged and that smoke entered into us. When the whites undress they leave the illness in their clothes. We die because of . . . the whites. White men cause illnesses; if the whites had never existed, diseases would never have existed either.' When the epidemic struck them, the Yanomami instinctively scattered, with each family living in a hut apart from the rest.

As late as 1949 the French ethnographer Alfred Métraux wrote that the Yanomami 'are regarded as fearsome savages'. Then the American Napoleon Chagnon, one of the first anthropologists to study the Yanomami, called them 'the fierce people' on the basis of their feuds and raids. Chagnon's book about Yanomami aggression became a standard text, outselling any other academic anthropology book about Amazonian Indians. Other anthropologists strongly dispute his thesis. They point out that Chagnon mistranslated the Yanomami ideal of *waiteri* as 'fierce', whereas it really means a subtle combination of valour, generosity, and good humour. Even one of Chagnon's own students, Kenneth Good, called his use of this epithet as 'the biggest misnomer in the history of anthropology'. Those who have lived with the Yanomami know that their fights may result in bashed heads and some seizure of women, but rarely in deaths. This nation is no more bellicose than many other Amazonian peoples – and infinitely less murderous than modern Western societies. In all their contacts with anthropologists, medical teams, missionaries, SPI/ Funai agents, and adventurers, there was never any act of aggression against a well-intentioned outsider. The Yanomami were invariably friendly and hospitable to these many visitors. The French anthropologist Bruce Albert described encounters from the Indian point of view. 'The expeditionaries, following their "pacification manual", swamp the Indians with presents with febrile zeal. The Yanomami run off precipitously to give these, as fast as they receive them, to their children hidden in the forest, keeping only metal tools and cotton clothing.' The Yanomami were naturally suspicious when whites tried to disarm them, not least because their bows were their main hunting weapons. They also feared white menace if strangers entered a yano unexpectedly.

One legend about the arrival of the first whites said that, long ago, a very young married couple were in an isolation hut for the girl's first menstruation. The husband broke the seclusion to help his brother-in-law in a chest-pounding duel with another warrior. 'Suddenly the sky turned dark and a tidal wave surged up from the foot of a nearby hill. A wall of water swept through the forest', drowning many. Some who tried to escape were eaten by animals, and their blood mixed with the floodwaters to create the Catrimani river (or other rivers, in variants of the myth). Remori, the spiritual hero of the Yanomami, moulded the foam from the bloody torrent into human figures. Remori brought his creations to life and taught them to fly, as he himself could. 'When these figures began to speak they uttered the language of the white people, and that is how Remori brought white people into the world . . . It was he who gave the white people radios, machetes, pots and pans, and told them to return to the Yanomami lands carrying these objects as gifts . . . Ever since this time, white people created by Remori have continued to visit the Yano-mami, the people from whom they were created.'

There is no doubt that the Yanomami's peaceful attitude to white men was because these had long been seen as the source of metal tools. In the 1950s and '60s there was increasing trade with Brazilian settlers on the lower rivers, with the Indians providing food or doing occasional labour in exchange for coveted goods. They were also curious to learn more about the newcomers. The Canadian missionary John Peters was there at that time and saw that the two societies had much in common. 'Both groups hunted, fished, and felled trees to grow gardens with their staples of bananas and manioc . . . The Brazilians possessed few consumer goods. For travel, they walked and canoed, just as the Yanomami did.' But such contacts could breed misunderstanding and hostility. 'The Yanomami found it hard to stand the greed, arrogant authoritarianism, and detestable manners of [frontiersmen] intruders. The "whites" were irritated by difficulty in mobilizing Indians to work for them, by their constant demands for manufactured goods, and their refusal to put women at their disposal.' Indians regarded settlers as strangers and therefore potential enemies. So some warriors wanted to kill them with their long arrows;

but the elders restrained them because the strangers could retaliate with guns.

Some Indians migrated to the banks of the Orinoco or other rivers in order to obtain tools. When missionaries built airstrips in the Parima Hills, Yanomami left forest homes to move close to the missions even though these were on impoverished savannahs. Once they had obtained plenty of steel axes, the Yanomami could develop larger sedentary villages surrounded by forest gardens. But this in turn could lead to depletion of game – particularly when they also acquired shotguns and cartridges. Once settled, the Yanomami would spend about half their time farming near their villages, a third of the year on hunting treks, and some time visiting old garden clearings.

Brian Ferguson was convinced that Yanomami intertribal fighting was to improve access to Western goods. Wars were fought both over the distribution of such goods and to drive rival groups away from obtaining them. Such tools were so important that they shaped political relationships. Although wars were 'ostensibly fought over revenge, sorcery, women, or prestige', their true cause was tools. Other anthropologists disagree, arguing that these 'ostensible' motives – particularly feuds and capture of women – continued to be the true cause of raiding.

The Yanomami are just as hospitable as they can be warlike. One of their greatest festivals, the *reaho*, is held to welcome visitors from other malocas. For weeks beforehand, most of the men make long hunting expeditions to distant forests. 'The grilled game-meat is brought into the hut and placed on a great platform near its centre. Soon afterwards, shortly before the arrival of the guests, it is common to see a hundred or more bunches of long bananas hanging from the rafters to ripen and be eaten by hosts and guests. On the platform there are also hundreds of kilos of game, to be offered to the guests when they arrive and leave.' The invited group pause near the maloca, to adorn themselves with body paint and feather ornaments. 'The guests enter, dancing ritually around the centre of the hut in front of the hosts. First come the young men and girls, then the adults, and finally married women with their babies and baskets full of their belongings. After the ritual entry, each guest is shown a place to sling his hammock. When this is done, all partake of prepared drink (a brew of bananas, yams, peach-palm, etc. depending on the season). Guests and hosts challenge one another for who can drink the most of this *mingau* – but it is never allowed to ferment. The festival lasts between five and eight days, and during these days and nights there are a great many rituals and activities: dances, challenges with the men striking one another's chests, shamanistic ceremonies, trading of goods, exchange of information, conversations and parlays, promises of marriage, etc. On the morning of the final day of the festival, the men take hallucinogenic *yakuana* to reaffirm the alliance between them and to communicate with the spirits of their ancestors.' The guests leave laden with food; and they will soon repay the hospitality with their own reaho ceremony.

The first outsiders to settle permanently among the Yanomami were all missionaries. The earliest were the Catholic Salesians. Strongly entrenched along the Rio Negro since the start of the twentieth century, these missionaries in the 1960s had increasing contact with Yanomami on the rivers flowing south into the middle Negro. They developed two large missions for these Indians: Maturacá on the upper Cauaburi in the west; and Marauiá on the river of that name, which joins the Negro near the old Salesian mission of Santa Isabel. These missions were founded by Father Antonio Gois, 'tall and powerfully built, with the black flowing beard of a biblical patriarch. He wore canvas sneakers and a plain white cassock, under which he sometimes carried a revolver.' His attraction technique was based on leaving presents, but then departing swiftly while Indian curiosity was still high. He told a young American traveller, Fred Salazar: 'You don't contact them. They contact you . . . Never show you are afraid . . . undecided . . . or ill. When they know you are a strong and courageous person, they will respect you and believe what you tell them. At the same time you must show generosity: give them food, clothing, tools, medicine . . . In return they attend mass, send their children to the mission school, and settle around the mission to learn to live like Christians . . . [If they don't cooperate] I stop giving them gifts . . . Eventually they learn to value the rewards of a civilised life.' Salazar wryly compared this approach to that of drug-pushers who hung around American high schools trying to get the children addicted. However, although the rectangular huts of these missions had all the apparatus for religious conversion, the Araraibo Yanomami nearby continued to live unmolested in their open round yanos. The Salesians were far less conservative and aggressive with them than they were with the more-acculturated Baré and other tribes of the main Rio Negro.

The other Catholics to settle among the Yanomami were the Consolata Order from Turin, who also ran the bishopric of Roraima's capital Boa Vista and were very active among the Makuxi and other plains tribes. These were some of the most attractive missionaries anywhere in Brazil. They established a mission in 1965 on the Catrimani river, at the southeastern edge of Yanomami territory. When I visited Catrimani with the team from the Aborigines Protection Society, we were most impressed by the tact, consideration, and sympathy of Father Giovanni Baptista Saffirio – who later obtained a doctorate in Yanomami anthropology. 'We detected no evidence of any religious indoctrination, and on the contrary found a deep respect for Yanomami culture. Ornaments, medallions and all other features so evident [in old Salesian missions] were conspicuously absent.' Instead, there was excellent health provision and preventive medicine, a sensitive attempt to trade coveted goods with the Indians in return for token work, and care taken to avoid having imported boxes and pots compete with indigenous ware (as was done by the Villas Boas on the Xingu).

Protestant missionaries also approached the Yanomami from the east. In November 1958, Neill Hawkins and John Peters of the Unevangelized Fields Mission (later called MEVA – Missão Evangélica da Amazônia) were guided by their Waiwái converts up the Mucajaí river and encountered a yano of Xilixana Yanomami. These Indians had obtained a few cutting tools by trading with Brazilian settlers downriver, but they were desperate for more. So, as Peters wrote, 'the villagers were delighted with the presence of the outsiders with their steel goods and beads. A small, permanent mission station with an airfield was established near the site.' During the following years, these Yanomami took the American and Canadian missionaries on long journeys to meet other groups of Yanomami, on the Uraricoera, Apiaú, Ajarani, and Parima rivers. Such visits between yanos were important for the Indians. They broke their isolation and facilitated intermarriage; and all the groups were eager to obtain the missionaries' trade goods.

In 1963, other UFM missionaries settled in the Yanomami heartland of Surucucu, 120 kilometres (75 miles) north of Toototobi. Surucucu is in a beautiful location, a grassy valley at an altitude of 850 metres (2,800 feet) amid forested hills. The nearest indigenous hut was on a hillside forty-five minutes' walk from the mission houses and airstrip. Here also, a missionary couple, Robert and Gay Cable, and others were having little success in converting the Yanomami, apart from persuading the men to wear polka-dot red aprons instead of penis-cords. They also sought to introduce a work ethic by trading manufactured goods (for labour, artefacts, or food) rather than giving them: 'We don't want to turn them into beggars.' Stealing was a problem, among people who had a tradition of generosity with all their belongings. Surucucu was also in the heart of the Yanomami Hills, with 50 Indians resident near the mission and a further 3,000 within a few days' walk; so the missionaries had a problem in supplying so many people with all their needs. The mission had an efficient dispensary and an excellent health programme. Robert Cable explained that 'at first the

Indians were suspicious of medicine, but now they come for miles to get it.'

The anthropologists Alcida Ramos and Kenneth Taylor studied relations between the Protestant missionaries and another group of Yanomami, the Sanumá, in the north. They found that the presence of these rich strangers, with their plenteous supply of tools and medicines, had altered tribal society from within. The mission's medical care (and teachings against birth control) were increasing the population; villages were larger and more sedentary thanks to steel tools for felling forest gardens; and game around these villages was disappearing because of a supply of shotguns.

Despite their coveted tools, the arrival of the first white men was a traumatic experience. Davi Kopenawa, who later became the Yanomami's most eloquent champion, recalled the first such visit to his yano on the Toototobi when he was an infant. 'When I saw them, I cried from fear . . . I thought that they were cannibal spirits who had come to devour us. And I found them very ugly, drained of colour and hairy.' There was a fear that the strangers had come to seize children, so Davi's mother hid him under a pile of baskets and told him to make no sound.

John Peters, a Canadian then with the Unevangelized Fields Mission who later became a distinguished academic sociologist, knew that the Indians valued missionaries most as 'healers and traders'. So medical work absorbed much of the visitors' time – to such an extent that some collapsed from exhaustion and had to leave to recuperate. The mission also maintained a store full of desirable goods, and the Yanomami eagerly attended the weekly 'trade days'. They were obliged to earn goods by simple labour or selling produce, and this was seen as a practical lesson in market economics. In the isolated world of missions in the Parima Hills, the strangers knew that their simple everyday utensils and their information about the outside world were of intense interest to the Indians. But Peters admitted that these human services supplemented the main motive, which was conversion to Protestant Christianity. 'The religious goal of the missionaries was to found a self-sustaining Xilixana [Yanomami] church with a lifestyle based on an evangelical interpretation of the Bible. The missionaries translated portions of it into Ninam. Being baptized was the symbol of commitment to this way of life. Elements of traditional Yanomami culture explicitly rejected by the missionaries were the practice of shamanistic rituals, the use of hallucinogenic drugs, and infanticide.' Such puritanical teaching had only limited appeal. Only a tenth of the Indian community accepted baptism, and some of these later lapsed. The Protestants did not proselytize too violently (despite trying to suppress shamanism, unlike the more enlightened Catholics), so that the majority of Yanomami at their missions retained their traditional way of life.

Good medical treatment was essential, since the Yanomami were as vulnerable to introduced diseases as every other indigenous community in Brazilian history. Measles has always been a major killer, so that the discovery of a vaccine against it was hailed as a potential salvation for isolated peoples. James Neel, a doctor and geneticist who had worked with the US Atomic Energy Commission, in 1968 conducted a major campaign of vaccination among the Venezuelan Yanomami. Neel used the powerful new vaccine called 'Edmondston B', which has since been branded as inappropriate and dangerous to a people with no inherited experience of the disease.

In 2000, a year after Neel's death, the investigator Patrick Tierney accused him of deliberately using the strong vaccine and even ordering his colleagues to provide no medical assistance to dying Indians since they 'were there only to observe and record the epidemic, and that they must stick to their roles as scientists'. Tierney claimed that Neel was conducting a crazed pseudo-eugenic experiment in which only 'genetically superior males' would survive and improve the stock by breeding with the remaining females. Everyone who had known Neel came to his defence, citing his published works and field notes to show that these terrible accusations were unfounded. The Yanomami of the upper Orinoco were in fact stricken by a powerful measles epidemic just as the Americans arrived among them. The disease spread rapidly, through the Yanomami's love of visiting one another. Neel and his colleagues worked hard to save lives. He wrote that 'in villages stricken by measles, our efforts to collaborate with the missionaries with medical care, nursing instructions, and provision of antibiotics did not permit a prolonged stay in any one village.'

Measles also struck the Yanomami in Brazil. At Toototobi and Mucajaí missions the lethal disease was apparently brought from Manaus by a missionary's daughter. It spread to the Apiaú river area in 1967–68, and the Ninam Yanomami there suffered a hundred deaths. Dr Neel therefore sent 1,000 ampoules of vaccine from Venezuela to the Brazilian authorities. The average death rate among those Yanomami struck by measles who were treated with Western medicine was 8.8 per cent. This was an appalling figure; but it was comparable to fatalities reported by Dr Noel Nutels for *treated* patients in the measles epidemic on the Xingu in 1954, where the death rate for *untreated* Indians had been 27 per cent. By 1975 there were only thirty Yanomami on the lower Apiaú, which represented a loss of over three-quarters in eight years.

Tierney's sensationalist book was aimed more at Napoleon Chagnon than at James Neel. The controversial Chagnon helped collect blood and other samples for the medical team. But in his research he prided himself on becoming 'sly, aggressive and intimidating' in order to smash the Yanomami's taboo about revealing their own names or particularly those of dead ancestors. He made flying visits to over forty malocas, but his macho behaviour and devious tactics broke many rules of orthodox anthropology. This, the huge success of his book, and his obsession with Yanomami 'fierceness' incurred the wrath of Chagnon's peers.

In 1972 the Aborigines Protection Society team found the atmosphere at the Protestant Toototobi mission very different to that at Catrimani. Toototobi is on a headwater of the Demini in the heart of the Yanomami's Parima Hills. The Canadians Keith and Myrtle Wardlaw of the evangelical New Tribes Mission started proselytizing there in 1963. They told me frankly that 'our principal purpose in being here is to bring the gospel of Jesus Christ . . . We meet every Sunday. We have to teach them to read as a necessary step towards learning Christianity'. The conversion was going badly. Most of the sixty-five people in the adjacent yano, and forty more in four other malocas with which the mission was in contact, were cheerfully practising their traditional culture. Only one man had, briefly, 'made a profession of faith in Jesus Christ': a dejected elder called Plinio, who wore a mustard-coloured Playboy Club shirt to distinguish him from his handsome naked and painted kindred. The Wardlaws explained that 'the biggest problem is that [the Yanomami] are satisfied with their culture. There is no desire to improve. They are not interested in becoming acculturated or learning to read. Their main interest is getting things, yet there is no incentive to "get ahead" in their culture. They won't accumulate: if someone comes and asks them for something, they have to give it.' To their credit, these ardent missionaries admitted that they had made mistakes by 'plunging in too fast'. After nine years at Toototobi, they had long since abandoned any attempt to introduce clothing. They had also developed a profound respect for Yanomami beliefs, since 'they have definite contact with the spirits' and had shown the strangers how to communicate with them. In a sense, the Yanomami had converted the Christians, rather than the reverse.

Alongside the medical threats, the Yanomami were increasingly exposed to invasion of their lands. They had lost their reputation for ferocity. There were rumours of mineral wealth in their hills, and the colonization frontiers in both Brazil and Venezuela were approaching this remote region. In 1968 the newly formed Funai took a first step by declaring much of the Catrimani river area to be Indian territory. In

December of that year Alcida Ramos and Kenneth Taylor made a far bolder proposal: the creation of a Yanomami Indian park. It would be on the lines of the 22,000 square kilometre (8,500 square mile) Xingu Indian park created in 1961 – and of a comparably vast area. Ramos and Taylor argued that this huge reserve would work, for three reasons: there were no non-Indian frontier settlers in Yanomami territory; there was a large indigenous population with its culture intact; and the environment was still undamaged, so that it was capable of supporting the Indians and deserved conservation in its own right. But there was no time to be lost, for each of the three justifications was threatened. This was the start of what was to become the longest and most passionate campaign for indigenous land rights in Brazilian history. In the following year, 1969, these anthropologists provided supporting data about the Yanomami; the Bishop of Roraima (a Consolata missionary) endorsed the request; and a draft law was submitted to the President of Brazil by Funai's parent Ministry of the Interior. But nothing happened: President Costa e Silva never signed the decree to create the Yanomami park.

The first malign invader of Brazilian Yanomami territory appeared at this time. In 1973 the government tried to extend its network of penetration highways into these forests – even though such roads elsewhere were already failing. The idea was to build a 'Northern Perimeter' road running east–west north of the Amazon, roughly parallel to the Transamazonica south of the mighty river. Such a route looked good on planners' maps, but it had no justification since it joined no towns or settlements and did not reach land suitable for ranching or colonization. The western arm of this BR-210 ploughed through forests westwards from Caracaraí on the rio Branco towards the Catrimani mission. It thus violated the south-eastern corner of Yanomami territory. Hundreds of labourers were brought in by the road-construction company. In order to avoid conflict, these workers were told to give Indians all that they wanted, and not to try to recruit them or obtain food from them. But there was no plan whatever for protecting the indigenous people's health or culture.

The unnecessary highway brought three scourges to the Yawarib Yanomami living in that south-eastern region: destruction of forests and game, cultural shock from the influx of settlers, and above all diseases carried by the construction workers. By the end of 1973 the road had hit two villages with devastating impact. Arapishi suffered 364 dead, and Castanheira 208. The once numerous Yanomami of the Ajarani river were reduced to a remnant of 63 people. Alcida Ramos watched angrily how 'after losing many of their relatives, they also lost their land to Brazilian colonists. Now, consumed by alcohol, they live as a favor on the "properties" of these new settlers. Epidemics prove once again to be efficient instruments for creating empty lands for white occupation.'

Funai opened two 'attraction posts', at Kilometre 49 (later moved to Kilometre 211), and at a checkpoint near the Ajarani river at Kilometre 120 on the roadworks. By 1975 Ramos found that these posts were without medicines, trade goods, or food, and that almost a quarter of the Indians living near Kilometre 49 had already died of influenza. The lay missionary Carlo Zacquini wrote, in despair: 'In the vicinity of the stretch of the BR-210 that cut the area, more than twenty malocas vanished, leaving a legacy of perhaps a thousand deaths. A few survivors exist by the roadside. The splendour that characterized their authentic society has disappeared in a few years, bringing them to absolute physical and cultural decadence, reduced to begging. At Kilometre 145 of the Northern Perimeter road indigenous groups were struck by countless epidemics of influenza, pharyngitis, and measles.' In the three years after the arrival of the labourers, almost 2,000 Yanomami caught alien diseases, compared with 36 during a comparable period beforehand. 'Some groups living within sixty kilometres of this area were reduced by half.' The Consolata missionaries attended over 18,000 cases of illness during those three years. In May 1977 they told Funai that everyone in their village had gone down with measles caught from road workers, but medical efforts had prevented any deaths; however, in a second outbreak of this disease a terrible sixty-eight people had just died. Diseases also raged among more isolated communities, particularly since they could not reach such medical care as was available. In 1977 half the population of the upper Catrimani river succumbed to measles. Professor Orlando Sampaio Silva reported in 1978 that there was also tuberculosis and venereal diseases resulting from the prostitution of Indian women. And Ramos found that 'malaria, which has been endemic in the area for a long time, has taken on epidemic proportions' thanks to deforestation, pools of water along the road works that bred mosquitoes, and the many infected men among the labourers.

The situation was equally desperate in the western part of Yanomami territory. In 1978 over a hundred deaths, from malaria and famine, were reported on the Maiá tributary of the Cauaburi. A Salesian missionary went to investigate and 'saw a desolate picture: bodies abandoned around the maloca and on the trails, men and women too weak even to flee from that place of death. Hunger had struck them so hard that they could scarcely stand. Those who survived that march of moribunds were admitted to the hospital at São Gabriel da Cachoeira.'

Bruce Albert learned that the Yanomami associated the arrival of white men and their manufactured goods with the lethal epidemics. They naturally sought an explanation for the diseases, and reasoned that they may have come from the oily smell in crates of metal tools. One man told Albert: 'The whites say to us "Come here, compadre" and we breathe in this smell. It is in fact the vapour of metal tools . . . The smoke gets into us. This odiforous metal smoke that was shut into the boxes of machetes . . . once released, makes us die. We had fever. Our living skin started to peel. It was terrifying. The elders asked: "What have we done for them to make us die?"' Some men made themselves vomit after getting tools, and they scrubbed and soaked the metal in streams to cleanse it.

As time went by, Albert noticed a new mythology. It became clear that whites from missions and non-government organizations were well-intentioned and doing their utmost to help, so the Yanomami changed their theories about epidemics. They saw that all strangers, whether friendly or hostile, could bring diseases. So they reasoned that these scourges were spread by evil spirits, which haunted the white men's lands and possessions just as they did the Yanomami's forests. They even gave names to the four main classes of evil spirits, the spreaders of measles, malaria, diarrhoea, and coughing. These malevolent deities used the fumes from outboard motors, vehicles, planes, and trade goods to help attack and devour their victims.

Another serious threat to the Yanomami came in 1975 when the Radam aerial survey of Brazilian Amazonia located radioactive minerals alongside the Surucucu mission. The Minister for Mines immediately declared the area open to mineral survey, even though it was in the heart of an Indian homeland. The Scottish anthropologist Kenneth Taylor wrote that 'what had been a more-or-less closed area under the control of the air force [and Protestant missionaries] was blown wide open by this discovery'. The Governor of Roraima enthusiastically declared that the Surucucu Hills contained great 'wealth waiting to be mined . . . : not only uranium, but gold and diamonds and who knew what else besides.' The Governor also felt that 'an area such as that cannot afford the luxury of half-a-dozen Indian villages holding up development'. (The Governor was guessing about the mineral deposits, but he knew full well that there were far more Yanomami there. Survey flights by Funai later located seventy-four yanos around Surucucu.)

Six prospectors immediately flew in to these isolated hills and dis-covered deposits of cassiterite, a mineral that produces tin. By the end of 1975, 200 unauthorized garimpeiros were panning for cassiterite in streams around Surucucu; by January 1976 clandestine flights had brought in over 500 miners. The President of Funai said that he could not evict the invaders since this hill, in the geographical centre of Yanomami territory, was not officially restricted or reserved as Indian land. Kenneth Taylor reported the many landings by unauthorized planes. He flew a helicopter around Surucucu and mapped forty-five malocas close to the mission; and he persuaded both the Governor of Roraima and the President of Funai that the area was unquestionably 'a region inhabited by forest Indians'. But just as the police and Funai personnel were about to evict the miners in February 1976, their unregistered company claimed that it had received permission from the Ministry of Mines and Energy to operate at Surucucu. Armed with Taylor's data, Funai's lawyer went to Roraima to fight for the miners' removal. A judge agreed with their arguments, but he refused to evict the prospectors, on compassionate grounds.

At first, the miners got on well with the Indians. They were often starving, so relied on trade with the Yanomami to obtain bananas and other food. Such barter involved guns and ammunition, and these firearms were sometimes used in inter-tribal skirmishes. Then in mid-1976 a few Indians raided garimpeiro camps to take tools, clothes, hammocks, and guns. There was a fight, with seriously wounded on both sides. American missionaries protested about 'the murder of Indians who insisted on remaining in the region of the prospecting garimpo'. The prospectors were finally ordered out, and were evacuated in September 1976.

At this time, there were also threats to award colonization contracts in stretches of land at the eastern edges of Yanomami territory, particularly on the Mucajaí river and near the Catrimani mission. The plan was to clear-fell forests in an attempt to create cattle ranches and farms – even though it was well known that such clearance was doomed to fail because soils beneath tropical forests were too weak.

Meanwhile, the campaign to protect Yanomami land continued. The Roraima missionaries pursued the matter with proposals and petitions during the early 1970s. Kenneth Taylor in March 1975 submitted to Funai a recommendation for one large reserve and two smaller ones that would embrace the Yanomami in Roraima and in Amazonas north of the Rio Negro as far west as the Pico da Neblina. This area was an impressive 6,448,200 hectares (24,890 square miles) and its indigenous population was estimated at 8,400 people. General Ismarth of Funai asked for detailed studies of every Indian yano and hunting area – an impossible task; but Taylor did his best and in May 1976 presented Funai with a 'proposal for the correct and appropriate demarcation' of Yanomami lands. Funai also asked Taylor to establish a 'Yanoama Project' to bring medical and other aid to the Indians. Enthusiastic workers started to implement this, both along the new Perimetral road and at the missions.

This promising start was abruptly aborted. The French expert Bruce Albert recently discovered a letter to the President of Funai from the powerful General Demócrito in June 1977. The General repeated Chagnon's flawed observation that the 'fierce' Yanomami lived in small groups constantly at war with one another. He then wrote eugenic absurdity about rampant incest 'which is causing, over centuries, the physical and intellectual atrophism of the indigenous group'. Funai's response was to kill the Yanoama Project. Taylor's permit to work in a 'national security area' near the Venezuelan border was not renewed, and some aid workers and missionaries were denied support and expelled. The military always loved Chagnon's notion of Yanomami belligerence. General Demócrito used it to argue against a single large park. He preferred 'islands' of Indian territory surrounded by settlement, that would keep the yanos from attacking one another.

Cláudia Andujar, an acclaimed photographer of Indians, spent 1978 working as a voluntary nurse among the Yanomami. She became steeped in Yanomami culture, learned their intricate Yanomam language, and meticulously catalogued every artefact of their material culture. Alex Shoumatoff saw Cláudia Andujar at Catrimani at this time. She was 'fathoming their complex belief in witchcraft and myth, which took hours of patient recording from the storytellers, transcribing, then translating; and ultimately learning to convey or suggest this other world through her own medium, photography . . . Cláudia showed me some of her extraordinary portraits. They had been taken with a combination of time exposure and flash: lucid Indian faces frozen against a backdrop of swirling smoke.' She became so horrified by the scenes of suffering along the road that she joined Bruce Albert and the missionary Carlo Zacquini to create an NGO to fight for Yanomami land rights. They called it CCPY, the Campaign for the Creation of the Yanomami Park. Henceforth, the struggle was between the CCPY and its supporters and the many 'villains' who coveted Yanomami land and resources. The CCPY became an outstanding example of a Brazilian-born campaigning organization – tenacious, skilful, combative, pragmatic, and ultimately successful.

During the rainy season of 1977 Funai undertook a rapid aerial survey of Yanomami lands in Brazil. This accurately located over 160 malocas, but it totally omitted some areas. On the strength of this survey, Funai joined the opponents of the Yanomami park proposal. It declared that the Indians lived in an archipelago of twenty-one unconnected fragments of land. The President of Funai defined these twenty-one areas in four Decrees issued between December 1977 and July 1978. Kenneth Taylor immediately identified thirty-eight yanos that he knew to lie outside any of the fragments. He noted that Funai had belatedly declared Surucucu hill to be an Indian area (thereby ensuring that the agency would receive a commission on cassiterite mined there) but had failed to provide nearly enough land for the many Yanomami living in that region. Funai's twenty-one areas totalled 2,228,270 hectares (8,601 square miles), little more than a third of the park proposal.

The new CCPY published a powerful justification for a *continuous* Yanomami park that should be far larger than the twenty-one 'islands'. One cogent argument was that studies showed that each yano needed the plant and animal resources within a radius of 15 kilometres (9.3 miles), an area of 707 square kilometres (273 square miles). This might seem too much land for one small community; but non-Indians would be quite incapable of sustainable survival in these forests. The Yanomami needed to migrate constantly, both in long-distance moves of villages and shorter hunting trips or visits to former gardens. 'Every patch of forest is used, has a name, is intimately known and impressed upon the memory of the group'. The Yanomami would perish if 'confined to minute islands of ecologically exhausted forest' surrounded by colonists. A further consideration was that an intricate network of trails connected yanos to one another. Yanomami society depended 'on constant ceremonial and political exchanges between villages' along these trails. In a later report to the Attorney-General of Brazil, Alcida Ramos stressed the importance of such communications. 'Radiating from each village, these trails compose an elaborate network of paths that link the villages to new and old fields, to hunting grounds, to gathering and fishing sites, to summer camps, and to neighbouring as well as distant villages.' Every stretch of trail was the stuff of Yanomami legend, the scene of a hunting or fighting exploit, the location of resources or of encounters with the spirit world. Ramos also told how these people understood and valued streams, for fishing, but also for the many signs on their muddy banks of animals, crabs and molluscs, and even of approaching enemies. She described these waterways as 'veins and capillaries that irrigate [Yanomami communities] not only with water but also with memory and cultural meaning'.

The CCPY also advanced medical arguments. Pockets of land would hugely increase potential infection of Indians from surrounding colonists. Epidemics of tuberculosis, malaria, measles, and onchocerciasis (African river blindness) would be inevitable. Medical treatment and vaccination campaigns would be far more difficult. The archipelago of islands would undermine Yanomami society through contact with the ubiquitous settlement and mining frontiers. There were also legal arguments: the constitutional rights of the many indigenous communities living *outside* the new areas would be violated.

The campaigners redoubled their efforts to prevent Funai's suggested areas becoming fixed as the Yanomami's only reserves. In June 1979 Cláudia Andujar and Carlos Moreira Neto made another proposal for a homogeneous Yanomami park. All NGOs in Brazil and abroad, missionaries and anthropologists supported this plan, which was unanimously approved by the government's Indigenist Council. The Minister of the Interior, Mário Andreazza, started by promising that a park would be created; but in May 1980 he was reported as saying that it was 'on hold'; and he later suggested a 'national reserve' that would cater for environmental, forestry, mining, and Indian interests. These retreats were because the opposition was also active. The President of Funai, the aggressive Colonel Nobre da Veiga, had visited the Yanomami in February 1980 and proposed that any park for them should be reduced from the CCPY's 6.4 million hectares to some 4 million (25,000 to 15,500 square miles). He wanted to 'liberate' from Indian control the valley of the Couto de Magalhães (a southern headwater of the Mucajaí) precisely because it was thought to be rich in gold.

A deputy from Roraima, Hélio Campos, claimed that a Yanomami park would be a step towards dismembering Brazil, with 'a type of tribal socialism' undermining the nation's security. He drafted a bill proposing that Indians should be *deported* from a 150 kilometre (93 mile) swathe of land along Brazil's borders and relocated deeper inside the country. This preposterous bill would have involved massive ethnic cleansing, since the Yanomami and many other tribes live near the remote watershed frontiers. Deputy Campos was already on record as saying that 'the donation of excessive lands to the Indians' retarded their 'integration into civilization', and that indigenous people should be emancipated from Funai's tutelage. His friend, Air Force Brigadier Ottomar de Souza Pinto, the appointed Governor of Roraima Territory, was equally determined to have Yanomami lands made available for 'development' by his local business cronies. All three – Nobre da Veiga, Campos, and Souza – were former military officers who had served in the powerful National Security Council. The Campos bill was defeated, but Governor Souza Pinto in October 1980 authorized illegal flights by prospectors into the Couto de Magalhães gold fields. Funai got the police to remove some of them; but several hundred were still there, with five clandestine airstrips, two years later. The campaigning charity Survival commented that, with the transformation of Funai itself into 'a centralized intelligence outfit and a series of ineffectual and corrupt local bureaucracies, the offensive against Brazil's Indians by venal interests flying the banners of "development" and "national security" has returned with a vengeance'.

The struggle continued. There was a new government proposal for seven separate Indian reserves within a forest park. This was immediately opposed by the CCPY, CNBB (Conference of Brazilian Bishops), and CPI (Pro-Indian Commission), all of which repeatedly protested to the Minister of the Interior. Many NGOs orchestrated letter-writing campaigns. When President Figueiredo was on a state visit to France in February 1981 he was handed a petition with thousands of signatures, including those of two Nobel prizewinners; the American Anthropological Association and Survival International wrote to the Human Rights Commission of the Organization of American States; the American Association for the Advancement of Science passed a resolution; and the Geneva-based International League for Human Rights sent a request to the Brazilian government. The Brazilian Association of Anthropology, the UN Commission on Human Rights, the Fourth Russell Tribunal on the Rights of the Indians of the Americas meeting in Rotterdam in November 1980, the President of Italy (inspired by a campaign organized by Survival) in 1984, the great anthropologist Claude Lévi-Strauss and the Académie française in the following year all urged immediate action for a continuous park. Funai finally became an active proponent under a new president, Paulo Moreira Leal.

These and many other pleas and protests yielded a partial victory. On 9 March 1982 the government interdicted an area of some 7.7 million hectares (30,000 square miles). Cláudia Andujar's CCPY hailed this as 'the first significant initiative' after its ten years of campaigning. But it warned of 'the strength of the political and economic forces that are firmly opposed to this initiative and will continue to undermine the project'. Interdiction of the area was only a first step, a notice that it would probably receive further protection. Also, Minister Andreazza declared that he was not sure whether Yanomami land would eventually be a park, one reserve or several reserves.

The prospectors who were allowed to fly into the Yanomami Hills at the end of 1980 brought the almost-inevitable scourge: a terrible epidemic of measles and whooping cough raged among the Indians in mid-1981. Funai launched Operation Yanomami to try to treat the victims, but one of its doctors reported that twenty-seven Indians had died in his area and that supplies of vaccine were hopelessly inadequate. The CCPY gave direct medical help to the Indians, in addition to its political campaigning. Concerned NGOs sent a desperate plea for help to the International Red

Cross: 'We are facing a catastrophic scene. The epidemics have reached the regions of Palimiu, Surucucu, Couto de Magalhães, Mucajaí and recently Ajarani – areas in which over five thousand Indians live. What makes this tragedy unacceptable is the fact that it could have been avoided. Despite repeated warnings and requests to the organizations responsible for the Indians and reports by Funai itself, essential preventive measures were never taken. The disease arrived before the vaccines. This is the fifth outbreak of measles since 1968, the date of the first proposal for a Yanomami park. It has resulted in 139 deaths.' Funai and others sent medical teams who worked valiantly; but the epidemic increased before they could control it.

There was a wretched setback to the medical campaign when in December 1982 Dr Rubens Belluzo Brando was killed in a helicopter crash at Surucucu. I was once on an expedition with Dr Rubens, a saintly, black-bearded charmer. The press described him as 'a man who left no equals in his idealism, his knowledge and his pioneering work in bringing health to indigenous tribes.' Dr Rubens was from the famous preventive-medicine team of the São Paulo Medical School and had worked with Indians in São Paulo state, then for four years in the Xingu, followed by a survey of the health of the Xavante, before joining the CCPY's Yanomami vaccination programme.

Up to the mid-1980s, most Yanomami were unaware of the threats to their homeland or of sympathizers' efforts on their behalf. A few now started to grasp the issues and campaign for themselves. Several hundred prospectors had invaded the north-eastern parts of Yanomami territory, on the Uraricaá and Mucajaí rivers. At the end of 1984 some Yanomami wrote to enlist the help of Deputy Mário Juruna: 'During the past two years garimpeiros have been invading our Yanomami lands, removing our gold, bringing diseases, desiring and taking our women, and stealing from our gardens . . . Our lands are not demarcated, and we Yanomami Indians want demarcation immediately. Otherwise all our lands will soon be invaded by garimpeiros and ranchers . . . We only want to live peacefully with our wives and children. If the garimpeiros do not leave our lands, we are going to give them one more warning; and if they don't leave, we will fight.'

The threat from mining now extended to some of the 13,500 Yanomami living across the watershed in southern Venezuela. From 1911 onwards, the Venezuelan authorities had entrusted care of their Yanomami to the Salesian missionaries who, like their counterparts in Brazil, were conservative and authoritarian until the 1970s but then changed radically with the move to liberation theology following the Vatican II

Council and the Medellín Conference of 1968. A proposal to create a Biosphere reserve for the Venezuelan Yanomami and their pristine habitat was first made in 1979. This ran into opposition from frontier development and colonization interests, although the pressure was less than in Brazil since Venezuela has a far smaller population and great oil wealth. In 1984 the developers seemed to have won, with a concession to mine cassiterite near a source of the Orinoco. This was deep in the heart of Yanomami territory, not far west of Surucucu and in an area of largely uncontacted Indians. In later years, Brazilian garimpeiros often moved across the unmarked forest frontier, to prospect in Venezuelan rivers.

Rumours persisted that Surucucu was a mountain of mineral riches, and this was confirmed by the release of data from the Radam aerial-radar project. Large mining companies sought to obtain concessions to extract its cassiterite and possibly gold. Cláudia Andujar wrote that 'in 1984 there was a veritable offensive in the National Congress to open Surucucu to mining operations' led by two deputies who, ironically, were members of the parliamentary Indian Commission. But another deputy, Márcio Santilli, proposed that the minerals of Surucucu be set aside in a national reserve, because 'the survival of the Yanomami population and its incalculable culture are riches of far greater value [to Brazil] than any that might be obtained from mining'.

Meanwhile, the prospectors of Roraima formed themselves into an Association under a leader called José Altino Machado. José Altino (as he was known) was a formidable populist, who had emerged as a leader of the garimpeiros operating in the Gorotire Kayapó reserve. Tall, with weather-beaten good looks, a tidy black beard, simple and smart clothing, and regulation green aviator glasses, José Altino performed equally well at press conferences, in front of television cameras, demolishing naive conservationists in debates, and inspiring rallies of prospectors. He depicted himself as a miner, a true Amazonian free spirit, a 'little man' opposed to interference from distant federal authorities. He said that 'the Church lives in dreams, the military in ideology, but we in reality'. In fact, José Altino was an experienced bush pilot who had made a small fortune as the owner and manager of garimpos.

In 1984 a presidential decree permitted large companies to mine on Indian land, if this was deemed to be in the national interest. José Altino decided on a pre-emptive move, to try to generate a gold rush into Yanomami lands before the big companies could obtain licences. So, on 14 February 1985 he hired five planes to land on a disused airstrip near the Venezuelan border. He took sixty-seven prospectors (the vanguard of a threatened 3,000 invaders) and they rapidly hacked to the Surucucu

Hills, started clearing a camp and airstrip, and confirmed that the earth was full of minerals. For once, the authorities reacted promptly. Within a week, air force planes with Funai officials and armed police removed the trespassers, confiscated their weapons, and briefly arrested José Altino.

A genie had been released by the miners' raid. Cláudia Andujar wrote that Roraima was abuzz with the fantasies that Surucucu was a gold mine so rich that it would pay off Brazil's foreign debt and make millionaires of Roraima's garimpeiros, air-taxi operators, and citizens, and that the American missionaries were really miners conniving with Funai to export this fabled wealth. The anti-Indian deputies claimed that the proposal for a Yanomami park was a foreign plot to create an autonomous Indian land that other nations could exploit. Deputy João Batista Fagundes declared: 'I intend to diminish the immense expanse of territory that is blocked for any form of economic activity.'

The 'immense territory' was being expanded. When the government in 1982 approved the concept of a Yanomami territory, it appointed a working group to make a thorough survey of Indian settlements for a new inter-ministerial committee. This working group, composed of Funai and CCPY experts, reported on the exact locations of 149 Yanomami yanos or shabonos and three Yekuana (Maiongong) villages. It proposed a continuous park for these indigenous peoples with an area of 9,419,108 hectares (36,358 square miles) – a 22 per cent increase on the 7.7 million hectare reserve envisaged in 1982. This new proposal was submitted by Funai to the inter-ministerial committee in January 1985, and was issued as a draft law by a senator in December 1985. There was a wave of opposition. The central square of Roraima's capital, Boa Vista, which contains a heroic statue of a gold-washing prospector, was filled with rallies of garimpeiros and fazendeiros. Fiery speeches denounced missionaries, Funai, the CCPY, and rapacious foreigners. The Governor of Roraima admitted that Indians had an inalienable right to their land, 'but you cannot deny the rights of the 200,000 inhabitants of Roraima . . . The people of Roraima also have an inalienable right to run their own affairs.' He condemned the park proposal as 'an attempt to internationalize parcels of Amazonia'.

Very few Yanomami could speak Portuguese, and none understood the weird concept of a written law or of legal ownership of land. The pro-Indian campaigners needed an indigenous spokesman, someone who could represent his people and speak for them as eloquently as Mário Juruna did for the Xavante, Raoni for the Mentuktire, or Paulinho Paiakan for the Kayapó. Such a leader emerged, providentially, in the form of Davi Kopenawa (which means 'Angry Hornet'), a young shaman living near the Toototobi mission on the upper Demini. Born in 1956 in the isolated Watoriki yano on the upper Toototobi, Davi's people were contacted and he was taught Portuguese by Protestant New Tribes missionaries. Most of his family were killed by imported diseases in the 1960s. The orphaned Davi was then employed for ten years by Funai, as an interpreter for medical teams. He became head of a Funai post at the point where the Perimetral Norte was intended to cross the Demini. The CCPY saw the potential of this burly, round-faced man, who spoke with quiet authority and became passionately aware of the forces threatening his people. Davi rejected any Christian conversion and trained to be a shaman, believing strongly in his people's creed. He and others were taken by Funai and CCPY to a school to learn about Brazilian society and property law, but the Indian Agency then tried to confine Davi to his village. He complained that 'Funai wants to keep me hidden. It wants to keep me quiet, not to protest, not to talk to others, not to speak to white supporters . . . But I am not willing to sit still and keep quiet while my people are dying. I need to go out into the world . . . to cry out, to protest what is happening.' In another interview, he condemned white men for deceiving the Yanomami with their presents and false friendship. Their diseases negated any good intentions. 'The whites are treacherous. They have many machines and goods, but they have no knowledge' of the spirit world or their origins.

In March 1986 Davi Kopenawa convened the first Yanomami Indigenous Assembly at his Demini post near his yano Watoriki ('Hill of Winds'), a lovely open-style circular hut beneath a granite outcrop as spectacular as one of Rio de Janeiro's sugarloafs. A hundred Brazilian Yanomami from fourteen groups attended, and they had invited their supporter Senator Severo Gomes, a representative of the Minister of Justice, Ailton Krenak of UNI (the Union of Indigenous Nations), two effective Funai agents, Raimundo Nonato from the Boa Vista office and Francisco Bezerra from Surucucu, and of course supporters from the CCPY. Cláudia Anduja took a charming group photograph of this historic occasion, with the Yanomami men standing with their bows and arrows, decorated with some body paint and fluffy feathers stuck across their foreheads, and the foreground filled with seated women and children. The Assembly called for a stop to invasions, the demarcation of Yanomami territory, and systematic medical treatment. Many chiefs had been unaware of the seriousness of the threats they faced, but 'those who did not know learned, and those who did know realized that they themselves must seek solutions to their problems.'

Davi Kopenawa took his cause to Brasília. In 1988 the United Nations Environment Program gave him its prestigious Global 500 Award. In the following year, Survival asked him to collect a major international award on its behalf. I chaired a public meeting in London at which Davi and Cláudia Andujar described their terrible problems. Speaking Yanomami, Davi told about garimpeiro invasions and Indian deaths from disease, how some Brazilian authorities regarded Indians as animals or felt that they had too much land. 'But we are people, just like you: people with blood and mouths to speak. I am a Yanomami who struggles, who suffers many dangers to confront [our opponents] . . . to win the land for my people to live in'. He showed how important the forest was to its inhabitants, its spiritual meaning for them, and their harmony with this environment. He contrasted the freedom of Yanomami life in the forests with that of urban dwellers in their high-rise 'pigsties', and I later learned that he hated the noise and human coldness of London. He pleaded for help for his cause.

By 1986 Brazil had emerged from two decades of military government, and a Constituent Assembly was drawing up a new constitution. The civilian President José Sarney announced that he would support the 9.4 million hectare Yanomami park. But he then surprised the nation by approving a bizarre plan devised by his military and security services that directly threatened the Yanomami and other tribes. This was the Calha Norte ('Northern Gutter or Headwaters') Programme. The plan was to protect Brazil's northern frontiers with a series of garrisons and a 150 kilometre (93 mile) swathe of militarized land for thousands of kilometres from Colombia to the Atlantic Ocean. The Calha Norte was patently absurd. The frontier follows the watershed between the Amazon and the Orinoco and other Guianan rivers, and it had never been disputed since its designation in 1750. Brazil has friendly relations with its northern neighbours, who are all too weak to threaten South America's largest nation. The proponents of this unnecessary plan tried to justify it by saying that it would protect Brazil from drug traffickers and subversives – as though such undesirables would hack through some of the toughest terrain on earth rather than travel by conventional transport. It was also argued that the Calha Norte would 'develop' the frontier zone. This overlooked the fact that none but Indians could sustain themselves in or penetrate those forested hills where there were no roads and almost no navigable rivers. Another argument was that tribes such as the Yanomami wanted to create an independent state at the expense of Brazil and Venezuela – an idea that Berta Ribeiro dismissed as sophistry, since this indigenous people had no plan or capability.

Nevertheless, barracks buildings were constructed and airstrips enlarged at some Salesian missions on the Upper Rio Negro and at Surucucu in the Yanomami heartland, and there were plans for more such outposts in

Indian reserves in Pará and Amapá. This grandiose scheme ignored failures such as the Perimetral Norte highway, which had been abandoned because it led nowhere and was now called 'a monument to the megalomania of the military government, devoured by the jungle'.

There were angry protests about the ridiculous Calha Norte programme. CIMI condemned it as 'the final solution' to destroy Indians, and deduced that it was intended to open places like Surucucu to mining, or was 'a means for the armed forces to participate in development and stay in politics'. The military, unable to answer their Brazilian critics, turned against foreigners and the vociferous Catholic Church. Funai joined the xenophobia and in August 1987, 'pressured by corrupt authorities of Roraima, exploiting a wave of calumnies and denunciations in the Roraima and national press against . . . the Church's actions in favour of Indians, in an arbitrary and irresponsible police action, expelled the [Italian] team from Catrimani mission'. This was a serious setback, for the Consolata missionaries at Catrimani had for twenty-three years been magnificent protectors of Yanomami health, land, and society. They were some of the most dedicated champions of Indians in Brazil. Protestant missionaries and their valuable air-transport and medical services were also banished, as were the Brazilian health-workers of the CCPY.

The situation of the Yanomami now deteriorated catastrophically. Just when the twenty-year campaign for their homeland seemed to be succeeding, the historical pendulum swung against this indigenous nation. The motive power was gold. The rumour that the Yanomami's Parima Hills were full of gold became a conviction. 'Gold' was a siren call to garimpeiros and adventurers from all parts of Brazil. They were emboldened by the view that the Calha Norte was intended to open the frontier to 'development' – namely its mineral riches to their prospecting. So the sleepy and remote Territory of Roraima was engulfed by a gold-rush of Klondike proportions. There was some basis to this stampede, for these hills on the southern edge of the geologically ancient Guiana Shield *do* contain gold, diamonds (whose mother lode has never been found), cassiterite, and radioactive minerals such as molybdenum, tantalite, and columbite. The adventurers could reach Roraima easily, for the BR-174 Manaus–Boa Vista had been built in the previous decade – this was the road that destroyed the isolation of the Waimiri Atroari. They were soon pouring in at an average of 200 a day. Roraima's population had gradually increased to about 100,000 by the mid-1980s; but it grew to 215,000 during the four years of the gold boom. The Territory's farm labourers hurried off to try their luck in the garimpos, so that local food production fell by a third at a time when demand for produce multiplied. The city of

Boa Vista was an agreeable tree-lined place, laid out by a town-planner in the 1940s. It suddenly mushroomed to 50,000 people, many living in shanty towns. I was in Boa Vista at that time, so witnessed the crazy transformation. Most shops put up 'We Buy Gold' signs, and the traders now had their counters covered in round film boxes or medicine phials full of gold dust, with loaded revolvers alongside. Bars and brothels did a roaring trade, as did stores selling prospectors' tools and camping equipment. But the biggest profits went to air-taxi operators: Boa Vista airport became the busiest in all South America, with planes taking off every few minutes, minimal air-traffic control, and a fearful rate of accidents.

Tragically for the Yanomami, the minerals sought by the adventurers lay deep inside their territory. Some prospectors penetrated those forests by river – missionaries on the Mucajaí watched in horror as boatloads moved upriver. 'While the traffic was irregular, the missionaries estimated that about twenty miners and their equipment passed each day during the height of the gold rush from 1987 to 1989. The miners stopped at [Yanomami] villages in the vicinity of the river and wanted the villagers to provide food, labor, sex, and so on. The miners needed extra help to move their boats upriver through the rapids or to portage around them.'

The garimpeiros were not naturally anti-Indian. At first, apprehensive of warriors' arrows, the miners were generous with manufactured goods. The Yanomami responded by trading with these strangers, although they had difficulty in knowing how to treat them since they were so different either to missionaries who had lived there for years or to well-intentioned visitors. The French anthropologist and activist Bruce Albert wrote that 'in their eyes the work of the gold miners seems enigmatic and irrelevant. With irony, condescendingly, they call them "earth-eaters" and compare them to a band of peccary [wild hogs] snuffling in the mud. Later, the number of garimpeiros increases substantially and their initial generosity [to Indians] is no longer necessary.' As the number of prospectors grew, the Yanomami no longer presented a threat and became a nuisance with their importunate demands. 'The gold miners got irritated and tried to shoo them away with false promises of future presents and with impatience or aggressive behavior.' So the flow of free goods dried up. 'By now the Indians have begun to feel a rapid deterioration in their health and diet.' All the noise drove off game, and garimpeiros competed with Indians to shoot what was left.

To get at the minerals, prospectors deployed high-velocity pumps and jets to blast river beds into muddy wastelands. The English writer Denni-son Berwick watched 'torrents of mud flushed out with high-pressure hoses to be pumped through machines where the gold, in fine powder form, is caught. Waste pours into streams and rivers and fills stagnant pools where mosquitoes thrive. Gold and impurities are separated by rinsing them in water with mercury and burning off the mercury to reveal the precious yellow droplets.' The highly toxic mercury was washed into the rivers as effluent that poisoned fish and drinking water. Hardly surprisingly, Japanese researchers found high rates of mercury contamination in samples of Yanomami hair. Abandoned garimpos were full of stagnant pools, perfect breeding grounds for anopheles mosquitoes, which transmit the malaria with which the miners were riddled. 'The rivers are polluted, the game has disappeared, and many people begin to die because of the constant epidemics of malaria, influenza and so on, so that the economic and social life of the communities becomes destructured.' Indians who had become dependent on the garimpeiros' goods and food, and who regarded these as compensation for the new afflictions, were now deprived of the flow of presents. Carlos Alberto (Beto) Ricardo of CEDI lamented that 'the garimpeiros brought only the evils of white society to the Indians, and none of its achievements'.

This was an explosive situation, and it degenerated into violence. In 1987 there was a clash on the Mucajaí river, when garimpeiros tried to take over a claim that the Indians themselves were working. Four Yanomami and one prospector were killed in the skirmish, and there was a half-hearted attempt to remove miners from that area. It was estimated that in the first four years of the gold rush, thirty Indians and twenty miners were killed in fighting; but very many more Yanomami died of disease and malnutrition.

In May 1988 seven senators (including Severo Gomes, Jarbas Passarinho, and the future President, Fernando Henrique Cardoso) wrote to President Sarney that the Yanomami were suffering genocide of unprecedented proportions. At the end of that year senior officials from the Ministry of Justice visited Roraima and, as their Minister told the President, witnessed 'air-traffic violations, illegal mining activity, environmental degradation, abuses of constitutional rights, . . . absence of government authorities, violation of human rights, and denunciations of corruption'. The only way to curb uncontrolled mineral prospecting was for the civil aviation authority to apply its rules of air-traffic control, the environment agency Ibama to enforce its protective measures, Funai to deploy enough staff to protect the Yanomami, the finance ministry to send tax inspectors, and the government to station police at points of entry. None of these difficult measures was adopted, because the political will was lacking. There seemed to be tacit agreement to let the gold-rush become irreversible.

The Association of Gold Miners of Boa Vista issued a defiant thousand-signature proclamation saying: 'We are not afraid of the police or of Funai. We are not going to abandon the region. We have political guarantees that the army and the air force will not intervene. We have the support of the business class of Roraima that we will not be removed from the gold-mining areas.' By 1989 there were thought to be 45,000 garimpeiros in Roraima. At their head was the sinister and charismatic José Altino Machado, the man who had led the brief invasion of Surucucu five years previously, and had then spread rumours of gold as part of his agenda for expansion. He had recently won the support of a new Governor of Roraima, Romero Jucá – a former president of Funai, who now championed the garimpeiros and argued that the Yanomami should be corralled in reserves to liberate mining areas. The American film-maker Geoffrey O'Connor knew José Altino quite well and marvelled at 'how brilliantly he had manipulated both the press and the government to create a smoke screen around those forty-five thousand miners out there in the forest, an army of peons toiling away in the shadow of sad King Midas'. Dennison Berwick admitted that he was impressed by José Altino's 'physical power and his style as a speaker. He was a true demagogue, thirsty for the challenge of a hostile audience, well practised with statistics . . . and charming to sweeten people to his views.' But Berwick regarded the garimpeiro leader not just as someone who did wicked deeds, but as a truly evil man.

Although a few miners entered by river, most used light planes. Clandestine airstrips were cleared in forests in many parts of the interdicted Indian reserve, but the main mecca for the garimpeiros was a landing-ground called Paapiú that army engineers had enlarged as part of the Calha Norte programme. It was some kilometres from the small garrison at Surucucu, but conveniently alongside a lucrative garimpo – and a Yanomami yano. Senator Severo Gomes led a human-rights delegation to Paapiú in June 1989 and was appalled by what he witnessed. He was convinced that the improvement of this airstrip, its location beside a mine, and the uncontrolled invasion by garimpeiros coinciding with the banning of missionaries and health-workers were all part of a deliberate plan to destroy the Yanomami in the name of national development. The journalist Memélia Moreira called it 'the strategy of Yanomami genocide' so that 'sectors of the army, prospecting entrepreneurs and the governor of Roraima' could get their hands on these mineral-rich hills.

Senator Gomes wrote that 'Paapiú looks like a scenario from the Vietnam War. A plane lands or takes off every five minutes. Helicopters roar against the rainforest backdrop – three hundred grams of gold for an hour's flight. The wealth that leaves here is difficult to estimate as it follows secret frontier trails, leaving behind death of nature and men. Funai's post has been abandoned. Medicines and disposable syringes are piled chaotically, mixed with empty beer cans. The medical ledger is ruffled by the wind. The radio transmitter has vanished, no one knows where. The Indians have been abandoned to the garimpeiros . . . Disease, malnutrition, infant mortality. Malaria did not exist here, but it now scourges a large part of the population. Chicken-pox scars the faces of those who survive, marks of a time when there was no treatment. Beside the runway, fifty metres from where planes prepare for takeoff, is the Yanomami maloca, once surrounded by flights of birds and butterflies. The noise is infernal: it is impossible to converse inside the hut. After sundown the planes are silent. "Then," said one old Indian, "we have a far worse noise: children crying all night long."' One photograph showed a disoriented youth, with the wall of his yano decorated with centrefolds from *Playboy* magazine. The anthropologist Alcida Ramos, who had fought for the Yanomami since the 1960s, described the 'pandemonium of frenetic machines and airplanes spitting out noises of hell and exhalations of plague . . . where red hosepipes, coiled like cobras in the mud, serve as seats for prostitutes and Indians, where guns, alcohol and short tempers combine in Hobbesian scenes and a climate of apocalypse.' Such were the airstrips where many Yanomami had their first encounter with white men, in 'the most resounding cultural mismatch'.

Whether deliberately or not, the authorities all felt that the gold rush was unstoppable. Roraima's few hundred policemen had their hands full with the violence in Boa Vista itself – where murders in gunfights outnumbered deaths from venereal diseases or malaria. The police chief said that he could not possibly remove the estimated 45,000 prospectors from their forest airstrips and garimpos. Funai abandoned its posts and even its preventive-medicine teams. The army felt that it was not their duty. The journalist Jan Rocha, who eloquently reported the tragedy in Roraima, was with a group of demoralized Funai staff in 1989. They told her: 'We feel impotent, dreadful. The Indians have become dependent on the garimpeiros. Their game has fled, fishing is ruined. The garimpeiros have brought in alcohol – the Indians are transformed by it. They've become just cheap labour for the prospectors, and they've been turned against us.' Funai's staff were frustrated by lack of resources (they had to reach their Indians as passengers on prospectors' planes), inadequate medical back-up, and bureaucratic meddling from Brasília. They said that although some Yanomami liked the garimpeiros because of the goods they brought, others were shot dead by the tough adventurers. 'Nobody ever gets arrested for killing Indians.' The police were reluctant to investigate crimes deep in the forest; and if they ever did so, the Indians had long since cremated the victims in their traditional funerary ceremonies. Rocha was told that there were places where the Indians were so confused that they abandoned their crops and stopped planting. Many were reduced to begging at mining camps where there was dreadful diet, crime, drugs, and squalor.

Jan Rocha went to see Funai's only doctor for all Roraima, in the dilapidated 'Indian House' outside Boa Vista. This Dr José Pereira 'spoke with quiet despair about what was happening to the Yanomami. "They were a healthy people living sustainably, happy and always smiling. They had worms, a bit of flu, a few cases of malaria. Now we're overwhelmed. Between forty and a hundred cases a month of malaria . . . and drink problems, and TB, and venereal diseases"'. Indians evacuated for medical treatment were the chronically ill: they had their first sight of Western society and a bustling city in this pitiful condition. Later that year, another doctor told Rocha that there were 200 Yanomami in the makeshift Indian hospital. It was a shocking sight. 'Dying mothers lie in the same hammocks as their delirious children in the throes of malarial attacks. Sickly mothers have swollen breasts due to the deaths of their breast-feeding babies. Nearly all the Indians are suffering from acute malaria with profound anaemia and undernourishment.'

Dennison Berwick watched Davi Kopenawa record a message to other Yanomami. He warned his compatriots: 'Don't allow the garimpeiros to enter. The whites only speak lies to you. They give many things to cheat you.' Davi's own forests were full of prospectors, polluting the rivers and destroying the fish and game. 'The Yanomami become perplexed when the white men come. They're sick all the time and catch a lot of malaria. Epidemics of great poison come.' Davi was anguished because of this, and because some of his people ceased hunting and farming. So he urged the people of the Marauiá to keep prospectors out or order them to leave – but they must do it peacefully. 'If you use arrows, it will be bad . . . you will be killed. This is what other Yanomami did at the headwaters of this river, and they are dead.' He also begged those Yanomami to maintain their traditions and to respect the spirits of nature. 'The white men want to come, giving money and presents; and they want us to become whites. Tell them we don't want to become whites.'

Berwick later visited those western Yanomami on the Marauiá. He noted that the Salesian mission among them had made no converts in twenty years: it concentrated on trying to give medical help, and this was done with tact. He watched the two cultures grappling to save the life of a man known as Geraldo who was dying, probably of tuberculosis. 'A dozen shamans adorned with parrot, macaw and other feathers and red body paint took *pariká* [epená snuff] and battled to save their relative's soul. They attacked his house three times, chanting, beating the ground with their black clubs and shrieking to drive out the spirit eating the man's soul. The strongest shaman tried to suck the monster from the sickly body ... Late in the afternoon, an Italian nurse from the mission and her husband were allowed to try to feed Geraldo with a drip-bottle, but his veins were too sunken to take the needle.' All efforts failed. 'The man died – eaten by an evil spirit or weakened by tuberculosis. Men and women wailed and danced, brandishing the man's few possessions: machete, plastic bowl, feather ornaments, a small torch ... Five men fetched wood from the gardens to make a pyre in the shabono. The man and his possessions were burned two hours later in a crescendo of crying and wailing. The man's brother howled and sobbed beside the smoke and flames engulfing the pyre. This catharsis of love and grief marks Geraldo's journey to the world of the dead above the sky.' There was similar lamentation for every dead Yanomami.

Davi Kopenawa told Bruce Albert why the Yanomami associated the diseases that were killing them with the gold sought so feverishly by the garimpeiros. In tribal legend, the creator spirit Omamé had gone deep into the forest to bury the *xawara* – the Yanomami word for lethal disease – deep in the ground. Omamé said that if the xawara came to the surface, all the Yanomami would die from it. Xawara was also the word for gold, for the minerals that the strangers dug up from the ground. So there was a third reinterpretation of the causal link between white men's fumes and their epidemics. The shaman Davi feared the smoke emitted by mercury fires with which garimpeiros rendered their gold: he was convinced that it was full of xawara, the evil spirit of disease. 'If the garimpeiros continue to operate in our forests, if they do not return to their homes, the Yanomami will die, they will truly come to an end.' The xawara had a voracious appetite for human flesh. So gold was cannibal. Davi told Albert to warn white men that they also risked death from these evil spirits, which were multiplying fearfully, and from the revenge of shamans who had died in the epidemics and would cause the heavens to crush humanity. 'The epidemic-smoke threatens the entire world. Winds carry it into heaven. Once there, heat gradually burns it and it disintegrates. The entire world is then wounded as if burned, like a plastic bag melting in the heat.'

The first president after Brazil's return to civilian government, José Sarney, was no friend to Indians. First, he introduced the Calha Norte programme. Then, to appease the garimpeiros, Funai in September 1988 reverted to a somewhat enlarged version of the nefarious proposal of an archipelago of nineteen pockets of Indian land. In total, these territories amounted to 2,435,215 hectares (9,400 square miles), which was a fraction of the area needed for the tribe's sustainable survival. Bruce Albert condemned this as 'a politically insidious plan for the progressive reduction of the indigenous territory, intended to make possible the exploitation of its natural resources on a grand scale'. The Yanomami would gradually be confined into their enclaves through 'a project for economic acculturation and imposed fixed settlement'. The archipelago was confirmed by presidential decree in February 1989. The plan cleverly located the nineteen Indian reserves within three huge environmental areas: the national forest of Roraima in the north, national forest of Amazonas in the centre, and the existing national park of Pico da Neblina in the west. Such environmental protected areas looked good to the outside world. But 'national forests' have little meaningful protection in Brazil and could, in time, be released for timber, mining, or colonization projects. This was exactly what happened a year later. In July 1989 an inter-ministerial commission chaired by the Minister of Mines and Energy, and including Funai, announced that prospecting activities would be permitted in the national forests that now embraced Yanomami territory. Early in 1990 three 'prospecting zones' were designated within the environmental areas; but the garimpeiros were not prepared to restrict their activities to these concessions.

Despite the apparent finality of the presidential confirmation of the Indian areas and the surrounding national forests, campaigners continued the struggle. Davi Kopenawa met President Sarney. The influential General Bayma Denys said that it was 'impossible' to remove the garimpeiros, although the President later promised to do so. The miners' associations issued a proclamation saying that their business was 'a source of wealth and progress' that 'served Brazil by occupying its frontiers'. Closure would cause chaos in Roraima. They brazenly claimed that theirs was 'a tax-paying activity' that would 'respect the Indians, their culture and environment, and preserve the harmony of salutary cohabitation between men'. This 'harmony' was tragically belied when four Yanomami were killed in a skirmish at Paapiú in August 1987; Paulo Yanomami in September reported to the Procurator-General that many Indians had been murdered; in August 1989 two Indians were killed when they tried to stop garimpeiros entering the Surucucu reserve; and in November five Yanomami were killed and three miners wounded in a battle between guns and bows and

arrows. The four Yanomami victims at Paapiú were abducted and murdered in reprisal for the killing of a prospector in a drunken brawl; their
remains were cut into pieces and left near the airstrip to intimidate others.

In October 1989 there were two contradictory developments. A judge
granted the Federal Public Minister 'threshold authorization to interdict'
the original 9 million hectare area of 'immemorial possession' by the
Yanomami and to remove garimpeiros from it – this despite the presidential decree parcelling it into an archipelago. Meanwhile, the environment
agency Ibama started to examine its new forest reserves to see what
'sustainable' activities could be permitted within them. In January 1990,
surveys by Funai and the police located eighty-two clandestine airstrips
inside Yanomami territory, 200 rafts pumping the beds of the Mucajaí
and Uraricoera rivers alone, dozens of garimpo mines in the forests with
up to 500 tarpaulin-covered shelters in each, and '15,000 garimpeiros
occupying the villages of Paapiú, Mucajaí, and Uaicás'.

President Sarney vacillated, first ordering the miners' removal, then
acceding to their clamorous protests and suggesting that they congregate
in four prospecting areas within Yanomami territory. Campaigners redoubled their efforts. A group of important Brazilian activists, who called
themselves 'Citizens' Action', issued a devastating report of the horrors
they had witnessed around the mining camps. CIMI wrote to Sarney:
'Many Yanomami have died as a result of the miners' invasion, which
your government never impeded ... This is genocide, Mr President.'
Survival in London launched a Yanomami Campaign in which the Prince
of Wales described the prospectors' illegal invasion as a 'dreadful pattern
of collective genocide'; Prince Charles repeated this powerful accusation
in speeches and at a meeting with Brazil's newly elected President
Fernando Collor, and there were protests in countries in many parts of
the world and from the United Nations' Working Group for Indigenous
Populations.

In March 1990 President Collor, wearing a jungle-camouflage uniform,
visited a Yanomami yano and a garrison of the Calha Norte, flew over
'decommissioned garimpos' and ordered the dynamiting of 110 clandestine airstrips. The Brazilian press exposed all this as a public-relations
exercise to gain credibility with the World Bank and other foreign
financiers. The dynamiting of airstrips proceeded at a leisurely pace, and
was condemned by CCPY and others as a sham 'pyrotechnic show' since
the garimpeiros easily repaired the damage and reoccupied their bases.
By the end of the year, the police ended their 'Operation Free Forest/
Yanomami' after blowing up only fifty-six airstrips – these included the
largest, those of Altino Machado and on the Couto de Magalhães, but

sixty others were undamaged. There were more shootings of Indians by miners. Bruce Albert reported a serious outbreak of malaria among the Yanomami of the Demini headwaters, a hitherto uncontaminated area that had been invaded by garimpeiros apparently moving away from the police actions in Roraima.

A Brazilian reporter described the surreal scene on the Surucucu plateau at this time as 'perhaps the most agonizing human landscape on the planet. Indians and prospectors wander in bands around airstrips either abandoned or operated clandestinely by mining bosses disputing what is left of the former garimpeiro opulence.' He watched an old Dakota taking off with almost four tons of cassiterite. 'Indians watch it all dumb-struck, and walk across the airstrip in confusion. Some help the garimpeiros load the plane in return for scraps of rice and manioc, others hide in the shadows of crashed helicopters or planes. The Romochethere maloca is the capital of grief on this plateau. In January of this year [1990] almost 150 Indians were living there. Last week, there were just over fifty. What was formerly an imposing yano of woven thatch has been transformed into a circular camp covered in the remains of garimpeiros' tarpaulins. Indians dressed in dirty shorts and shirts look like ragged beggars. Their chief wears a tight swimsuit with a comb in its waist. The shaman, who should be frightening off evil spirits, is ill in his hammock surrounded by his sick and undernourished children . . . Almost half the Indians have acute pulmonary infections. The "noble savage" has been reduced to a shanty-dweller in the midst of his forest.' This report also noted that in the past two years cases of malaria had increased by 60 per cent, of respiratory infections by 45 per cent, and of anaemia by 75 per cent.

In October 1990 a new head of Funai formally asked that the archipelago of Indian areas be replaced by a single park. Fortunately, President Collor wanted to project himself as a dynamic young leader concerned with the environment. To prepare for the United Nations Conference on Environment and Development (UNCED), in April 1991 he formally revoked Sarney's decrees creating the nineteen small Yanomami reserves. The pro-Indian Minister of Justice, Jarbas Passarinho, interdicted the large Yanomami area and forbade non-Indians from entering it. For health purposes, the vast region was divided up between Funai, the Ministry of Health, missions, and NGOs – including the CCPY, which became responsible for medical treatment of 1,000 Yanomami.

Triumph came on 15 November 1991, when President Collor announced that the Yanomami would finally get their full, contiguous, and inalienable 9.4 million hectare (36,300 square mile) park, and that its

3,071 kilometre (1,908 mile) perimeter would be demarcated. At the televised ceremony, the President was flanked by his very 'green' Environment Secretary, José Lutzenberger, and the admirable new President of Funai, the sertanista Sydney Possuelo; but the Minister of the Army kept his head bowed, and other opposing ministers boycotted the occasion. Praise poured in from all over the world. There was dismay and angry protest by Roraima's politicians; several generals condemned the park as madness; opponents in Congress demanded its repeal; and opposition politicians promised to abolish it. But the twenty-three-year campaign for a Yanomami park seemed to be triumphantly won, with a full definition of that nation's homeland in Brazil. Minister Passarinho explained why he had championed the park: 'I tried to save a people . . . at a moment when its contact with our illusory white so-called civilization brought only epidemics, diseases of all types, prostitution, undernourishment, and death.'

Meanwhile, there were political manoeuvres among the half of the Yanomami population who live on the Venezuelan side of the watershed. When the controversial anthropologist Napoleon Chagnon tried to return to the Yanomami in the 1980s, he was barred by hostile Venezuelan colleagues. In 1988 he published another paper about Yanomami blood-revenge and warfare; it was roundly condemned by the Association of Brazilian Anthropologists because it was widely cited by the tribe's opponents. It 'nearly destroyed the chances of the Brazilian Yanomami having their territory properly demarcated'. In 1990 Chagnon was back, with a scheme to make a 'Biosphere Reserve of the Upper Orinoco–Casiquiare'. At 8.3 million hectares (32,000 square miles), this reserve would have embraced most of the 13,500 Yanomami in Venezuela. But it was exposed and condemned as a cover for tin-mining operations by some dubious associates of the flamboyant anthropologist.

The 1992 UNCED 'Earth Summit' in Rio de Janeiro was a resounding success. Many indigenous groups, particularly the publicity-aware Kayapó, set up camps and performed eloquently at the Earth Forum that ran alongside the more formal UN conference. President Collor basked in environmentalists' acclaim, particularly for having decreed the Yanomami park. It was a pity for the Indians that he was accused of massive corruption in the following year, and resigned before being impeached. The Yanomami park survived intact into the next century, but there were constant setbacks. A serious anomaly was that the four environmental reserves (two national forests, a state park, and a federal national park) that overlapped the park remained on the map. In theory, mining and logging could be permitted in these areas. They reduced land in total

Yanomami control by three-quarters. However, during the first decade after the 1991 decree, no extractive licences were issued in the environmental zones within the park.

At the time of Collor's disgrace, Davi Kopenawa was Brazil's representative at the UN's International Year of the World's Indigenous Peoples, and he warned of the massive threat to his people from renewed prospecting. The press noted that 'in the past three years, some 1,500 [Brazilian Yanomami] have died, almost fifteen per cent of their population'; and everyone knew that this tragic mortality was from diseases brought by the miners. Many garimpeiros were still active inside Indian land and the efforts to remove them seemed half-hearted. Some operated from within Venezuela, and there were cross-border tensions because of them. Those who were expelled from the park in Brazil left an estimated 600 tons of refuse (an average of three tons in each of their 160 abandoned airstrips) – everything from ruined campsites to broken machinery, pumps, and even crashed planes, all of which filled with water and became mosquito breeding-grounds. They also left shattered forests, polluted rivers, and many disoriented or sick Indians. In February 1993 there was a revival of 'Operation Free Forest' with Funai, the air force, army, and police combining to rid Yanomami lands of 4,000 garimpeiros in the eastern part in the state of Roraima and 3,000 in Amazonas. A more effective agent for their removal was a slackening of gold fever: many left voluntarily, believing that there was now less chance of striking gold. By July, it was reckoned that 4,000 miners had left (roughly half of their own accord) and that only 400 remained. However, Davi Kopenawa warned that the situation remained tense.

As if to confirm his fears, in August 1993 word emerged from the Yanomami heartland of a massacre of Indians by garimpeiros. The Haximú yano near the source of the Demini had been brutally attacked, with many Indians gunned down and their great huts burned. The first report of the atrocity came from Sister Alessia, a French nun working for the government health service at the nearby village of Xidéia. Her handwritten note said that Yanomami from Haximú had fled to her village with news of the murder of at least fourteen men, women, and children. She said that the chief told her that the garimpeiros had attacked on a day when fortunately most people were away. 'I believe that it is true because they are terrified.'

Details of what had happened slowly emerged. The French anthropologist Bruce Albert, who speaks perfect Yanomami, and Davi Kopenawa were able to interview survivors and heard their chilling accounts. Some Yanomami had made friends with Brazilian garimpeiros on the Taboca source of the Orinoco (and thus technically within Venezuela). They thought that they had been promised a rifle; but when this was not given, they had taken a radio, pans, and other goods from an empty camp. The angry miners vowed to punish the Indians if they continued to pester them. So when six young men went to ask for presents, the garimpeiros sent them on to another camp with a note saying, cryptically, 'Make the most of these suckers'. The second group of miners were playing dominoes: they gave nothing to the six Yanomami, but decided instead to kill them. This was done by a curious invitation to hunt tapir together. As the party filed into the forest, four of the youths were suddenly shot at point-blank range and in cold blood. As he was murdered, one young Indian covered his face and said the only words of Portuguese he knew: 'Garimpeiro friend.' Only two escaped, wounded, by running into the trees and diving into a stream. The people of Haximú recovered the bodies of the dead, for the ritual cremation that is an essential element of their funerals. In late July, they returned to make a revenge attack on the prospectors' camp. In tropical rain, they encountered only two men around a cooking fire; one was killed by gunshot and then quartered and shot with arrows, and the other escaped, wounded.

The enraged miners organized a major reprisal attack, with men recruited from various camps and guns and ammunition supplied by their bosses. They were determined to kill the eighty-five inhabitants of Haximú's two yanos. Luckily, these Yanomami feared such revenge and had left, partly to accept an invitation to a celebration by another group. So their empty yanos were riddled with gunfire and burned. Most Yanomami had pressed ahead to the other village, but they left their slower-moving women, children, and old men in an abandoned garden clearing – confident that in warfare among the 'fierce' Yanomami women were never killed. The garimpeiros found this roça and surrounded it for an attack. It was midday, so 'children were playing, women cutting firewood, and the rest lying in hammocks'. Fortunately, many women were off gathering fruit. 'One garimpeiro fired a shot and all the rest followed, opening close fire as they advanced on their victims.' A few Indians escaped into the vegetation, some of them wounded by gunshot. 'From their hiding-place the fugitives continued to hear cries drowned by the roar of the firing. After long minutes, the garimpeiros stopped shooting and entered the shelters to finish killing any who were still alive. They killed with machete cuts not only the wounded but also the few who had not yet been hit; they then mutilated or quartered all the bodies riddled with bullets and shot. In all twelve people died: one old man and two old women, a young woman from Homoxi who was visiting, three adolescent girls, one infant girl aged one and another three-year-old, and three boys between six and eight.' The murderers ran back to their garimpo, walked for three days to an airstrip, threatened to kill any other miner who betrayed them, flew back to Boa Vista, and then dispersed through Brazil. The distraught Indians cremated their dead and destroyed their belongings, in the traditional ritual. (Rapid cremation makes sense, for any dead creature in a tropical forest is immediately consumed by decomposition, bacteria, fungi, insects, and animals.) They then fled for weeks through dense forest, convinced that the miners would want vengeance on warriors rather than mere women and children. Sixty-nine survivors finally took refuge at Makos maloca on a headwater of the Toototobi-Demini. They performed full funerary ceremonies for the dead, and keep their ashes and pulverized bones in gourds within baskets.

When Sister Alessia's note about the Haximú massacre reached Funai in Boa Vista and thence Brasília, the Minister of Justice told the world about the terrible crime. The Brazilian media made it front-page news; the efficient publicity service of the CCPY swung into action; soon the American and world press were reporting the squalid murders deep in Yanomami forests. Police, Funai agents, television camera crews, newsmen, and local and national politicians hurried to the remote area. The journalist Jan Rocha watched as 'reporters whose normal beat was the political jungle of Brasília suddenly found themselves in the rainforest, hot and sweaty, still dressed in their city clothes. As the Minister [of Justice] climbed out of the helicopter he was startled to find himself surrounded by seven Yanomami warriors in black warpaint, chanting war-cries and shaking bows, arrows and clubs at him. One of them was Davi Kopenawa, one of the very few Yanomami who speaks Portuguese and the only one to have travelled widely outside his territory. He explained that they were preparing for war against the garimpeiros, not against the Minister.' Davi had already made an impassioned statement to the world, that the killing of his people must stop, the miners be removed, and the criminals brought to justice – which included the businessmen and politicians behind the prospecting operations. All the investigators wanted gory details, an accurate body count, interviews with survivors, and above all pictures of corpses. Little was available, for the people of Haximú had cremated their dead and themselves fled; so the only 'evidence' was the bullet-scarred ashes of the two burned huts. There were wildly fluctuating estimates of the dead, which included a group of Roraima politicians suggesting that there had been none – that it was all a conspiracy by international forces who coveted the region's wealth. The confusion was heightened when it was discovered that Haximú was technically inside Venezuela, so that all the Brazilians had violated international law. Nevertheless, many Brazilian embassies were picketed, Survival organized a protest at the United Nations, and condemnations poured in from concerned organizations. The President of Brazil took emergency measures, including the creation of a new Ministry of the Amazon.

In November 1993 a parliamentary commission concluded that there had been 'a crime of genocide committed by Brazilian garimpeiros on Venezuelan territory'. They used the powerful term 'genocide' because the miners had tried to wipe out an entire community rather than murdering known individuals; and Brazil was a signatory to the international convention on genocide. The identities of the guilty garimpeiros gradually emerged through patient detective work: the prosecutor was soon able to name the garimpeiro leader João Neto and his accomplices, and he had witnesses from among other prospectors who deplored the massacre. But, as always, the law was slow to indict criminals who attacked Indians. This case was complicated by being joint between Brazilian and Venezuelan judiciaries. A murder verdict was difficult without bodies, and Yanomami custom forbade interference with the ashes of their dead. By June 1995 the *New York Times* was still complaining about the delay; and human-rights organizations joined the condemnation in the following year. Finally, in December 1996, a federal judge sentenced five garimpeiros, in absentia, to long prison sentences for their cruel and premeditated murders of defenceless men, women, and children. João Neto was arrested in Boa Vista and he and one other are in jail; but the others have vanished into the shadowy world of the wildcat prospectors. An appeal against the convictions was unanimously rejected by the Supreme Tribunal in September 2000. The atrocity in distant forests, which might so easily have gone unrecorded, at least resulted in a ruling that the collective killing of tribal people is genocide. The Procurator General's regional official hailed this decision as a paradigm, 'a highly important precedent. By accepting that genocide is a crime against a tribe the tribunal not only respects the indigenous group as such, but also in practice sows a seed of hope that crimes committed against Indians will not remain unpunished.'

Despite the confirmation of their vast park in 1991, and the removal of many garimpeiros, the Yanomami continued to be under pressure. Throughout the 1990s there were reports of prospectors flooding back into the gold fields – Survival said that hundreds returned in 1992, and five years later 6,000 were reported to have invaded the area. Davi Kopenawa was back at his Demini post, completing his initiation as a shaman, when a group of garimpeiros arrived to dig a pit alongside the village. The seam of gold soon ran out, but the miners left an epidemic of influenza. Davi declared that 'the gold- and diamond-hunters threaten us with guns and illness. They are killing my people, and they keep coming into our lands even though the government promised to keep them out.' He repeated his warning that digging up gold was exhuming xawara, the evil spirit of pestilence that would strike Yanomami and white men alike.

When a human-rights commission was allowed into the area in 1995, it accused the state government of Roraima of contributing to the Indians' misery by weak and vacillating action against invading garimpeiros. The Yanomami were suffering 'a situation of permanent danger and continuing deterioration of their habitat.' And in the following year 280 Yanomami leaders from twenty-seven malocas held an assembly that begged the new President, Fernando Henrique Cardoso, 'We do not want garimpeiros on our land because they are very bad. They pollute our rivers and creeks, they make holes in the ground looking for gold. The fish die, the game die. All the Yanomami are dying because the garimpeiros bring diseases that kill us: malaria and influenza. This is why we don't want garimpeiros or other whites – ranchers, politicians, loggers, soldiers, or fishermen.' Despite this plea, Funai's operation to monitor Yanomami lands ceased in March 1996 from lack of funds, and incursions by prospectors immediately accelerated. It was not until the end of 1997 that pressure by the CCPY, Survival, and others achieved a resumption of the removal operation; and some 2,000 miners were expelled.

The other continuing threat to the Yanomami is medical, exacerbated by the presence of poor and often sickly garimpeiros. Health teams did their utmost, working long hours, with meagre food, as volunteers or on minimal pay. They had to overcome inadequate medical supplies, hazardous communications (a number died in air crashes), Indian incomprehension about taking remedies, and respect for tribal taboos or shamanic practices that often contradicted Western medicine. A dedicated Funai nurse admitted that 'To survive, the Indians need much more help. What we are doing is little.' Claudinei Alves, a young New Tribes missionary who gave up a career as a brilliant footballer to devote his life to the Indians, worked late into the night testing blood samples for malaria and found that 60 per cent of the Yanomami at Toototobi were infected with that debilitating disease. Claudinei felt that 'what matters is that they accept the idea of the existence of the Lord'; but his colleague Brian Wardlaw was more restrained in proselytizing – there were very few converts after thirty years of missionary presence. Wardlaw was more concerned to teach Indians about a market economy since 'Civilization is beating at their doors, so they must learn how to protect themselves'. Dr

Marcos Pellegrini, who worked for CCPY within the government's Yanomami Sanitary District, estimated that in the five years to 1991 there had
been a staggering 1,500 deaths among some 10,000 Yanomami in Brazil.
'Malaria was the great villain', with prevalence among these Indians seven
times worse than in the rest of Roraima. 'In some areas, the Yanomami
have been so incapacitated that they could not perform subsistence
activities, so that malnutrition heightens the lethality of infectious diseases.' Even when matters improved somewhat with better medical
treatment, there were still 199 deaths from malaria among the western
Yanomami in 1993 – a total twice that of the huge city of Rio de Janeiro.
Infant mortality (some of it deliberate for spiritual reasons) was many
times the national average, and Indians also suffered from calazar (visceral
leishmaniasis), influenza, and tuberculosis, all introduced by infected
garimpeiros. In 1994, malaria still accounted for 30 per cent of Yanomami
deaths.

Another fine doctor, Deise Alves Francisco, described how health teams
and Indians gradually learned to work together. 'We observe [them
cooperating] in mobilizing for collective activities like vaccination, taking
blood samples for malaria and the mass-treatment of worms, and in the
number of requests for [us to make] medical visits to malocas or for
medicines for their communities.' Indians also helped build airstrips for
emergency evacuations. This cooperation was partly because the health
teams always worked *with* shamans, and were tactful in persuading Indians
to learn Western medical practices. However, all this heroic medical
attention alleviated but did not stop an appalling level of disease among
the once-healthy Yanomami. Throughout the 1990s the death rate was
2.4 times the national average, with an appalling 1,211 Yanomami in
Brazil dying in the seven years between 1991 and 1998. Malaria accounted
for 23 per cent of these fatalities, with some 4,300 cases in 1997 alone;
respiratory infections caused 13 per cent of deaths. Although the Yanomami birth rate was high, their infant mortality continued to be far worse
than among other Brazilians. The situation deteriorated in 1998, when
government austerity measures slashed funds for Indian health care; but
there was a dramatic improvement in deaths from malaria when in 2000
the Yanomami health budget was entrusted to an independent organization called Urihi – the Yanomami word for 'our land'. So the population
increased. In 1980 there were thought to be 16,500 Yanomami, with
more than half living in Brazil and the remainder in Venezuela; but by
the end of the twentieth century their numbers had increased by roughly
a quarter in each country.

Roraima was swept by raging forest fires during the dry season of

February–March 1998. The conflagration was caused by ranchers burning their grasslands during a drought-stricken El Niño year. A sixth of the territory of the large State of Roraima burned uncontrollably. Hardest hit were the savannah Indians, Makuxi and Wapixana; but some eastern Yanomami communities were also threatened with destruction. The journalist Gabriella Gamini flew over the malocas of Ajarani and Alto Mucajaí and saw them 'surrounded by a cemetery of fallen, burnt trees'. Three yanos were reduced to ashes, and the loss of forests deprived these Indians of their game and food. Then the fires were miraculously extinguished by unexpected rains, for which Davi and some Kayapó shamans claimed some credit.

After four turbulent decades, the Yanomami entered the new millennium with their culture largely intact. Some groups might still have been uncontacted in both Brazil and Venezuela; others had had little contact with the outside world; and very few have converted to Christianity. A high birth rate had counteracted the ravages of imported diseases. Above all, Yanomami lands in both Brazil and Venezuela were protected to their full extent. Cláudia Andujar's CCPY deserved credit for this great achievement, helped by missionary organizations and many other national and international supporters. Another important development was in education. A formidable team, including Davi Yanomami and the dedicated French anthropologist Bruce Albert, devised a curriculum that respects Yanomami language and culture but also teaches responses to contact with white society. By 2000 all thirty-one schools among the eastern Yanomami in Roraima taught in the tribal language, whereas those in the state of Amazonas to the west still used Portuguese.

The Indians themselves are now playing an increasing role in their own defence, first through Davi Kopenawa, then in assemblies with other chiefs. These culminated in August 1997 in an unprecedented gathering of eighty indigenous leaders, representing 35,000 people from both forest and savannah tribes of the three nations Brazil, Venezuela, and Guyana. This international assembly demanded demarcation of all indigenous lands and full control of education, health, natural resources, and communications by the tribes themselves, with government subsidy where necessary. This was amplified in a programme for human rights launched by President Cardoso in December 1997, which invited indigenous peoples to participate in decisions regarding their own rights.

But the Indians and their sympathizers must remain vigilant. The highway from Manaus to Boa Vista and on to Venezuela has now been paved, so that settlers are pouring into Brazil's northernmost state. Roads now push from Roraima to the Caribbean through Venezuela and Guyana. The government of Roraima is promoting inward migration to its 'millions of hectares of fertile land'; and the mineral riches of the Yanomami's Parima Hills remain a magnet for prospectors and mining companies. Roraima has the highest rate of colonization of any state in Brazil. The military also remain a threat. Some strategists cling to the discredited Calha Norte programme of garrisons along the nation's northern borders. In early 2001 Deputy Marcos Rolim, President of the Commission on Human Rights, visited the Yanomami and was appalled to find barracks still being constructed deep inside their territory. Davi Kopenawa told the deputy that the military claimed that they were there to defend the Yanomami against intruders. 'But they are single men whose wives remain in Boa Vista. They come here, and they start interfering with Indian women. They want to sleep with them, and give them such things as food, rice, manioc. They use our women. Now these are ill from sexually transmitted diseases, gonorrhoea, syphilis.' Deputy Rolim concluded that 'in addition to the specific problem of sexual abuses and the grave risks . . . of sexually transmitted diseases, military units are deforesting in order to obtain additional firewood, they throw their refuse into streams that supply the Indians, and they induce the Indians to relations of dependency.' In that same year, the Minister of Defence said that the Yanomami park had been an 'error' committed by President Collor to impress foreigners and that it should be 'corrected'.

Jan Rocha concluded her book on the Haximú massacre by noting that 'unwittingly and often reluctantly, the Yanomami have played an important role in both Brazilian politics and in the wider world's perception of the indigenous peoples of the Americas'. As the largest pristine nation, the Yanomami have provoked more legislation than any other tribe, and they caused Brazil to be vilified in international tribunals. Their afflictions – deaths from disease, invasion by unscrupulous miners, and constant threats to their land and culture – have been extensively reported by the media. 'Few indigenous groups have captured the imagination of the world quite so powerfully as the Yanomami. There is perhaps a feeling that, because of their direct link with the world of the rainforest, because they are themselves a link with the past, they must not be destroyed.'

20. The Far West

At the end of the twentieth century the largest indigenous nations in Brazil were the highly acculturated Guarani in the extreme south, and the Ticuna (Tikuna or Tukuna) on the Solimões river close to the frontier with Peru and Colombia. All nineteenth-century travellers on the main Amazon had visited the Ticuna. They marvelled at their elaborate shamanistic masks – in which heads of exotic, fanciful, and even comic animals or demons tower above wearers who are enveloped in sheaths of bark-cloth. The Ticuna were also famous for their girls' great puberty ceremonies, at which each maiden emerged from months of seclusion and had her hair plucked in handfuls to the sound of a drum and rattle.

The populous and docile Ticuna had moved down to the Amazon's floodplains in the late eighteenth century, after their enemies the once-powerful Omagua and Yurimagua were extinguished by disease and slavery or driven upriver into Peru. Because they moved into this vacuum after slavery had been outlawed, the Ticuna survived the worst colonial oppression and were the only tribe still living on the main river in the nineteenth century. Although not technically enslaved, Ticuna were pressed into service as paddlers before the advent of steam navigation, and during the rubber boom these gentle Indians were violently conscripted by Brazilian rubber bosses and Peruvian caucho collectors.

The first person to study the Ticuna in depth was the tireless Curt Nimuendajú. The meticulous German-Brazilian anthropologist visited them in 1929, then spent many months there in 1941 and 1942, and was with them when he died in 1945. He started to learn the 'isolated' Ticuna language, one of the most difficult in Brazil, in which some words have five tones. For Nimuendajú, the Ticuna were notably 'tame and peaceful, even submissive. I never heard of their reacting violently against the numerous abuses by civilizados.' Their main defence was to retreat to the headwaters of streams or to hide on islands in the várzea floodplain, a watery labyrinth when the Amazon rises and inundates tens of thousands of square kilometres of forests during each rainy season. 'They are amiable and hospitable, but always respectful and modest in the extreme. They never importuned me with requests. Their honesty is notable: I experienced it on various occasions . . . I never noticed laxity in the behaviour of girls and women, who are noted for their conjugal fidelity.' The Ticuna's only vice was drink. They loved alcohol brewed from manioc, macaxera (sweet manioc), or maize; and, 'when drunk, they became insolent and dangerous, frequently wounding one another in fights that break out when they are intoxicated.'

With their long history of contact, and their natural modesty, Ticuna men and women were always fully clothed in Western dress. Nimuendajú noticed that their habitations changed because of mosquito-nets acquired from the whites. They stopped building large thatched malocas that were closed against insects, and adopted small platform houses with minimal walls. When this author visited the Ticuna in the 1970s, most lived in these open houses on stilts, with little privacy and very few belongings on their broad log floors.

In 1942 the SPI bought the Umariaçu ranch near the frontier post of Tabatinga and established Posto Ticunas. Although it was very remote from the Service's head office in Rio de Janeiro and typically under-resourced, the presence of this post mitigated the excesses of the rubber men. Some Ticuna worked directly for seringueiros, while others tapped trees themselves but clashed with the bosses when they tried to sell rubber that they had smoked. Roberto Cardoso de Oliveira was there in the late 1950s and noted that the post 'made indiscriminate use of force impossible or at least more difficult, because those guilty of it could be denounced to the SPI and punished by law. However, the emergence of federal protection of Indians was not enough to end the entrenched system of exploitation of indigenous labour.' Even when rubber-gathering diminished and the Ticuna could return to their traditional production of manioc flour and dried fish, they were exploited in the usual debt-bondage. They were paid too little for their produce, and overcharged for goods 'such as meat offal, salt, fat, sugar, tools like machetes, and above all cachaça rum'. So the Ticuna were pathetically grateful for the SPI's presence. 'The Indians find in this tenuous "protection" a sufficiently strong attraction to cause them to seek out the post and to settle there. This they do even without receiving any assistance of an economic, sanitary or educational nature.' To qualify for SPI tutelage, the Ticuna emphasized their Indianness. Even in the few instances of inter-marriage with outsiders, children chose to remain with their mothers in order to obtain the post's meagre benefits. Thus, paradoxically, the Ticunas post 'exercises a counter-assimilation effect – in contradiction to the integrationalist objectives of the SPI.' As was often the case, the good behaviour of the SPI came down to an individual, Manuel Pereira Lima, who ran their post in the mid-1940s. The Ticuna called him Manuelão ('Big Manuel') and loved him partly because he was the first to trade their manioc flour for manufactured goods at a fair price, he built a road to help get produce to market, he championed them against settlers trying to invade their most fertile lands, and he encouraged them to reoccupy lost fazendas.

By the 1960s, the Ticuna were divided roughly between 'Indians of the river' and 'Indians of the creeks'. The former lived in relative freedom on the banks of the main Amazon–Solimões. They survived as 'totally bilingual casual labourers in regional enterprises, small and precarious dealers in artefacts, and to a lesser extent [by selling] the produce of their subsistence farming'. They were far more acculturated than those on the creeks, still dominated by rubber men who took almost all the profit from their latex, food, and animal skins.

Relations between Indians and 'bosses' varied. Nimuendajú saw some rubber men who interfered in tribal life, trying to arrange marriages for the benefit of their enterprises, and one who even attempted to forbid customs such as the girls' puberty rite. Others were far more benign. At the São Jerónimo trading depot, the owner's family mixed with Indians in the greatest harmony. However, the Aborigines Protection Society's team in 1972 saw the boss of the riverside village of Belém claiming that he owned half of what was clearly an ancient Indian site, grossly overcharging the Ticuna for 'trade goods, trinkets, and patent medicines', and his portly son molesting girls over whom he claimed a droit de seigneur. This boss, Jordão Aires de Almeida, and his son had been arrested for using Indians as virtual slaves and punishing those who tried to escape with chains and shackles – but they had immediately been released on good behaviour. A police investigator reported seeing two islands full of skeletal Indians suffering from leprosy, others being used as forced labourers, and one called Verissimo who had been punished by beatings and 'spent seven days without eating or drinking, chained by his hands and feet . . . wearing only a pair of trousers, forced to relieve himself on foot and badly bitten by mosquitoes'.

At that time Funai's presence was still small: such medical and educational help as the Ticuna received came from Capuchin Franciscan or Protestant Baptist missionaries and from military vaccination teams. The Ticuna gained by being near a frontier. The garrison at Tabatinga was reinforced and modernized in the 1960s, and it helped protect and release the Indians from subjection to the rubber bosses. At an operational level, the Brazilian armed forces – particularly air force pilots – liked Indians and often assisted them with transport and moral support.

So the gentle Ticuna survived and multiplied, despite many abuses of their land and liberty. In 1957 Darcy Ribeiro guessed that there were up to 1,500 of them, and this was still the SPI's estimate a decade later. But an SIL missionary who knew the Ticuna well 'suggested a total population which may reach above 10,000' divided between Brazil and Peru; and Cardoso de Oliveira confirmed this larger figure of 5,000 in Brazil. No one really knew how many Indians lived 'on the creeks' away from the Solimões. By the early 1980s, the tribe was estimated at 15,000. The first serious survey, by CEDI in 1987, recorded almost 18,000 in twelve Indian Areas in Brazil.

The Ticuna gradually realized that they must improve their conditions, particularly in land tenure and liberation from oppressive bosses. Their first – desperate – move was to follow visionary preachers who offered a promised land. Nimuendajú recorded instances of messianism during the 1940s. This was an embodiment of traditional Ticuna narrative and myth, a reaction to the difficult transition to coexistence with frontier society. Baptist missionaries, who worked among the Ticuna from the late 1950s, used these ancient millennarist legends to further their proselytizing.

A more serious messiah was a Brazilian who called himself José da Cruz. In the late 1960s he founded an Order or Brotherhood of the Cross among Tupi-speaking peoples of the Amazon upriver in Peru. Cruz warned that the destruction of the world was imminent, that Jesus Christ had told him of the power of the Cross, that those who followed his movement would be the only survivors of the coming apocalypse, and that it would herald a new world of peace and plenty. He predicted 'a Day of Judgement in 1975, when all places that did not have his crosses would be flooded and subjected to seventy hours of darkness'. Followers of the new Order dressed in white gowns, lived soberly without alcohol or dancing, and eschewed the 'prostituted' ways of the outside world. There was veneration of the cross, with services at which Christian hymns were sung and the Bible studied.

Despite its Christian trappings, the puritanical cult of the Cross taught a return to indigenous values, to the Tupian peoples' search for a terrestrial paradise free from the sordid reality of the colonization frontier. In the new order, there would be brotherly equality between Indians and whites. Paradoxically and deviously, some rubber bosses used the movement to regain part of their former control. They welcomed José da Cruz, built churches for him alongside their depot-stores, and played an important role in the Brotherhood. In masses and processions of the Brotherhood of the Holy Cross, 'the rubber men acquired great moral and religious importance, thus establishing a new form of legitimacy for their dominance'. These bosses, Funai agents, and the 'captains' or chiefs appointed by them, all liked the way in which the movement persuaded Indians to abandon their cherished drinking – and the ceremonial dances and shamanism with which it was associated. In the past, the Ticuna were full of alcohol when they performed collective labour or *uajuri*; now only lemonade was consumed.

In 1972 I watched Cruz's flotilla of canoes sweep into the village of Belém. The Ticuna had prepared an open church, with a large cross surrounded by a palisade, an altar decorated with inspirational messages and plastic flowers, and many benches for a huge congregation swollen by isolated Indians from up-country. José da Cruz and his wife and followers looked like any other middle-aged Brazilian caboclos, but his preaching was electrifying. Catholic missionaries watched in dismay as he inspired the Ticuna with fear and hope. He then sailed off downstream, his boats laden with produce that the faithful had brought as offerings. The movement had a powerful impact on this people. A decade later, the radical missionary paper *Porantim* deplored the way in which the Ticuna 'are losing almost all their traditions as a result of adherence to the messianic Holy Cross movement'. The puritanical Brotherhood forbade music, dancing, listening to the radio, playing football, smoking, drinking, wearing long hair, or even attending girls' puberty celebrations. When the mystic José da Cruz died, in June 1982 aged about seventy, there was consternation among the estimated 80 per cent of Ticuna who followed his teachings. Thereafter, the movement gradually lost influence, although there were still Ticuna communities faithful to it in the 1990s.

The 1970s was a time of change in Indian affairs. The Programme of National Integration, that launched the harmful Transamazonica and other penetration roads, also gave Funai added resources. The Indian foundation enjoyed a few years of better management. More importantly, this was the time when Catholic missionaries radically changed their attitudes to conversion of Indians: they founded CIMI, the newspaper *Porantim*, and the first indigenous assemblies. In 1974 the liberationist missionary Egydio Schwade submitted a proposal to Funai for a Ticuna reserve at Belém on the Solimões; and this was discussed at a 'Seminary' meeting between Funai and the missionaries in Manaus in April 1975.

Every tribe needed a champion, and for the Ticuna it was João Pacheco de Oliveira, an anthropologist from the National Museum in Rio de Janeiro. This slim, quiet, determined man with a trim black beard worked tirelessly for his adopted people while also producing an impressive corpus of anthropological books. To help this large, and largely forgotten, tribe, Oliveira devised 'the Vendavel Pilot Project'. This was intended to give the Indians control of their destinies. It accepted that a process of assimilation was in progress, but sought to disrupt Ticuna society as little as possible. The Project caused Funai to establish a post in Vendavel, a village on the Solimões in the heart of Ticuna territory. A tough rubber man controlled all the trading of these villagers and hence their very existence. This boss had to be outmanoeuvred and stripped of his power. The Project's personnel showed that they had abandoned the old SPI practice of working through an appointed chief. They were also impartial and conciliatory in an internal dispute between followers of Fernando da Cruz and traditionalist Catholics. Oliveira felt that all the objectives of the Vendavel Project were gradually achieved. It ushered in a new attitude by Funai, one of protection without intervention and of steadily passing responsibility to the Indians themselves.

Not surprisingly, it was at Vendavel village that the Ticuna started to mobilize in defence of their lands. In late 1980, chiefs held their first meeting to confront this and other problems. Although numerous, the Ticuna had none of the advantages of other tribes who were battling for land rights at that time. They had no reputation for warfare that could intimidate invaders. They had been in contact for centuries and dressed as soberly as other riverbank settlers, so they had none of the glamour that attracted television cameras and photojournalists. Their concerns were not sufficiently dramatic to gain international attention, like those of the Yanomami. Isolated on their distant river, they could not board buses to Brasília to invade Funai's headquarters or lobby Congressmen. And they did not have the public-relations flair of the Xavante or Kayapó, nor a spokesman who could mix with world leaders. So the Ticuna had to campaign doggedly through Funai and other official channels. Their main weapons were their intelligence, discipline, unity, and education (initially from missionaries, then from their own teachers). For many Ticuna, their self-assurance was enhanced by the Brotherhood of the Cross. They developed a parliament called CGTT (General Council of the Ticuna Tribe) and battled for designation and demarcation of their tribal lands.

By the 1980s, a variety of business enterprises were threatening the Ticuna. Commercial fishing was robbing the Indians of their staple food, with trawlers from Manaus denuding the Solimões of its abundant stocks – and to this day, such large-scale fishing remains a major issue for small settlers all along the river. These refrigerated fishing boats did not respect tribal waters, their owners slung nets across streams full of migrating fish, and they even trawled inside Ticuna lagoons. At a smaller scale, commercial fisheries seduced individual Ticuna into debt bondage, by supplying them with boats, outboards, nets, and fuel and then making them repay the loan by selling their catch at depressed prices. This, in turn, forced the Ticuna to fish in remote creeks and breeding lagoons, so that their stock was further depleted. Loggers were extracting timber from easily accessible tributaries, particularly the Javari, so that the once-decaying port of Benjamin Constant enjoyed a minor boom. Large petroleum companies were exploring these rivers in the hope of striking oil on the scale of Ecuadorian or Peruvian Amazonia. And ranchers found that they could breed water buffalo successfully on the seasonally flooded Amazon várzea, so that they invaded riverside farmlands.

The Ticuna campaign started to have an effect. Leaders of parliamentary opposition parties demanded that Funai start demarcating the tribe's territory. Five Congressmen wrote in December 1981: 'The infiltration of whites into Ticuna land has accelerated during the past three years. Indigenous communities are being displaced. There is an attempt to change the area's character by settling non-Indian families there, granting bank credit to install cattle pasture and plantations of permanent crops.'

The Ticuna now stepped up their non-violent campaign. They organized an enormous assembly of 1,140 delegates led by thirty-one chiefs. 'It was at this meeting that, for the first time, a proposal emerged for the delimitation of their lands, resulting entirely from claims and discussions by the Indians themselves. A map was drawn up with the participation of all the chiefs present at the assembly.' They launched a news-sheet called *Magüta* (meaning the Ticuna people), which they wrote, illustrated, and published unassisted. The first issue declared that 'this is the start of the task of fighting for the demarcation of Ticuna land. From now on, every Ticuna must be involved in the problems of our people.'

A delegation of chiefs was sent to Brasília and, luckily, met the sympathetic President of Funai Colonel Paulo Moreira Leal, who succeeded the notorious Colonel Nobre da Veiga at the end of 1981. Funai acted impressively. Its Solimões office was now run by Omar Landi, who favoured Indian assemblies and self-help – unlike his predecessor, who had tried to stop them. A team was sent to translate the Ticuna demands into legislation and also to map tribal areas. Under the overall direction of João Pacheco de Oliveira, surveyors and Indianists worked from 1982 to 1984 with the anthropologist Maria Auxiliadora Cruz de Sá Leão. This was a punishing task, in difficult roadless, densely forested, and partly flooded terrain. There were frequent clashes with large landowners, squatters, and Indians complaining that the boundaries did not exactly represent their lands. The Funai team generally agreed with the Indians' definition of their seven territories. In September 1984 Funai set up a study group containing these and other anthropologists, missionaries, and the sertanista André Villas Bôas, and these formally endorsed the seven areas. In the usual way, the matter dragged on for year after year. The Ticuna held regular assemblies: that of 1983 chose Pedro Inácio Pinheiro as paramount tribal leader. Delegations went to meet Funai officials in Brasília and Manaus, and they gained the support of the Order of Brazilian Lawyers. There were decrees about Ticuna land, and promises to demarcate it – although successive Presidents of Funai complained about the high cost of this exercise. The sophisticated Ticuna were aware of the importance of education as well as land; but their teachers – almost all Indian men and women – had to keep protesting about months of failure to pay their meagre wages.

Conflicts multiplied between Indians and those who invaded their territories for timber, fish, or settlement. One of the most determined aggressors was one Quintino Mafra, who settled alone among the Ticuna and then gradually induced white rubber-tappers and loggers in his employ to build houses on Indian land. Mafra was held responsible for the shooting of Indians near Vendavel in 1980. There were continuous conflicts between Indians and the Mafra clan, with animals killed by both sides. In February 1984, 150 Ticuna from Vendavel broke into the store of one of the Mafras, ransacked it, and threw the contents into the river. 'There was no robbery and no one was hurt, nor did the Indians take anything for themselves. Next day, all the families who were invading the Indian reserve gathered up their belongings and abandoned the place in their motor boats.'

The General Council of the Ticuna Tribe patiently pursued its cause, non-violently and through proper channels. One of its assemblies named the eleven worst invaders of indigenous land. At another meeting, in Tabatinga in August 1984, it tried to regulate fishing areas and methods by non-Indians within its waters. But after one incident when illegal fishing degenerated into violence, a Ticuna report concluded that 'Funai and the Federal police support [the intruders] because Funai and the police live off robbery and are the biggest crooks of all.' When Indian leaders went to local towns to protest, they were often violently abused. A police chief shouted at a Ticuna leader that if he argued he would be thrown into jail, and he told Chief Pedro Inácio that he had no indigenous rights because 'here on the Amazon there are no more Indians, for Indians kill people, eat people, and go about naked'.

A boat full of Ticuna stopped overnight at Benjamin Constant on the way back from a tribal assembly, in February 1985. A police patrol met three celebrating Indians in the street and, when they resisted unfair arrest, violently beat them with truncheons. The three were seriously wounded; but in the ensuing melee, other Ticuna overpowered and hurt some police. So when the Indians took their wounded to hospital next day, three policemen were waiting for them. From ambush behind parked vehicles, these emptied their revolvers on the procession, wounding eight Indians (one with a punctured lung, who miraculously did not die) and also beating up Funai agents who tried to protect their charges. When senior Funai officials went to investigate, they found 'a climate of hatred against the Indians and Funai staff'. Bands of citizens roamed the streets ostentatiously armed with guns, at the instigation of the local police chief. The police report of the incident was outrageously distorted – in their version, the aggressors were heavily armed, drunken Indians and 'non-Indian agitators' who attacked innocent policemen.

The Ticuna patiently continued the struggle for their land. Five village leaders went to Brasília in March 1986 and, with some difficulty, had meetings with government officials. On 15 April, President Sarney signed demarcation decrees for four of the smaller reserves. But he omitted by far the largest, most densely populated and important areas, known as Évare I and II. Évare is a stream from which the Ticunas' legendary creator Yoi fished the Magüta people, who became the Ticuna. Évare I covered the forest and várzea; Évare II was a smaller area to the east, on the right bank of the Solimões. One problem was that most of this lay within a 150 kilometre (93 mile) wide zone that the security service wanted to reserve along Brazil's northern frontiers as part of the Calha Norte programme. The government offered various concessions, such as reducing the width of the security zone and placing the Ticunas' sacred sites in the care of the Historical Patrimony; but the tribal leaders, dignified and determined, would have none of this. Back on the Solimões, their stand was endorsed by another great assembly, attended by fifty-one Ticuna chiefs and by representatives of the many organizations who now supported the Indian cause – the indigenous union UNI, Funai, the Brazilian Lawyers, CIMI, and local missionaries, and the anthropologists who devoted themselves to the Ticuna. This was another instance of strength through unity: the Ticuna were no longer isolated and easily victimized.

Tribal pride was bolstered by the launch of a school textbook in the tribal language. The jubilant leader Pedro Gabriel declared that 'this book was made according to our culture, in our language, and it is the greatest benefit we have. It was our victory, which we won by our own efforts –

the efforts of the Ticuna people – and this raises us up to a higher level, in view of all and above all.' For this acculturated society that had been in contact with frontier society for three centuries, education was all-important. Outsiders helped Indian school-teachers prepare bilingual texts in the difficult Ticuna language – for the great majority of this people could not speak Portuguese. Teachers were a respected element of tribal society: they formed a strong trade union and resolved to go on working even when their pay was seriously in arrears. They developed a curriculum that was attuned to Ticuna history and geography; they had their own teacher-training; they made videos about tribal culture; and they recorded it in a small museum, in a corrugated-iron-roofed wooden house in Benjamin Constant. In the 1990s, Ticuna educationalists developed greater environmental awareness and community participation. There was also a very sensible move towards fish-farming. Fish is the favourite food of the Ticuna and an important source of income for them. When the first Europeans sailed down the Solimões in 1542, they marvelled at the massive rearing of turtles by the Omagua – the Ticunas' predecessors in the area. So it is logical and timely for modern Indians to farm fish in the Amazon, which contains a fifth of all the riverine fresh water that flows into the world's oceans.

Then there was a tragic setback. On 28 March 1988, Ticuna from four villages had assembled in São Leopoldo near Benjamin Constant, to get the authorities to resolve who had killed an ox. While they were lunching in a house on Capacete creek, some Indian girls ran in to warn that armed civilizados were approaching. There were twenty men 'armed with 20-bore shotguns, rifles, a revolver, and a machine gun.' One Ticuna recalled that he ran to the door, raised his hands, and asked for peace. He said that the Indians had not come to attack the caboclos, only to settle differences with them and obtain justice. 'Then a civilizado answered: "Now the time has come. Every one of you Ticuna is going to die, and none will escape." Then a youth of fifteen started shooting my friends beside me. One man was hit and fell backwards. I was appalled, and jumped on top of the oldest civilizado when the shooting started.' When the carnage was over, fourteen Ticuna lay dead and twenty-three wounded. The murdered Indians included women and four boys aged between nine and twelve. Everyone assumed who was behind this massacre: Oscar Castelo Branco, a leathery timber man who owned a plot near São Leopoldo. For the past ten years, Castelo Branco had settled nine families of his woodsmen on Indian land, encouraging them to build houses, cut trees, hunt, and fish inside a disputed area. The Ticuna had complained to Funai and the police about these violations but nothing was done, partly because Castelo Branco's brother was mayor of Benjamin Constant.

There was a massive outcry about the Ticuna Massacre (also known as the Massacre of São Leopoldo or Capacete Creek). It was one of the worst atrocities against Indians in modern Brazil. There was extensive media coverage at home and abroad; six Ticuna leaders went to Brasília for meetings with ministers and parliamentarians; the tribe published a moving booklet of testimonies by survivors and the bereaved; and Survival International issued an urgent-action bulletin and staged a mass protest. But the brazen, unrepentant killers posed for a photograph, and this was published with the caption 'The group of gunmen who ambushed the Ticuna on Capacete creek'. Eleven men were arrested – dirt-poor squatters and fishermen who were soon released on bail because their families starved while they were incarcerated. As always, the case dragged on for years. The Nucleus for Indigenous Rights (an NGO of pro-Indian lawyers) wanted the trial moved to Manaus, since any jury in Benjamin Constant would be too anti-Indian; and Amnesty International protested about the delays. Successive Ticuna assemblies complained bitterly about the lack of justice. This was all in vain. By the end of the century, twelve years after the massacre, not one murderer had been convicted; although in 2000 the trial was finally moved to the state capital, Manaus.

Deeply saddened but not disheartened, the Ticuna pressed on with their campaign for land recognition. By the early 1990s, the absurdity of the Calha Norte and the security council's frontier zone was widely recognized. So in October 1991 President Fernando Collor, encouraged by his pro-Indian Minister of Justice, Jarbas Passarinho, and the sertanista President of Funai, Sydney Possuelo (the same team who had decreed the Yanomami park), declared that 'the Indian areas Évare I and Évare II were permanent possessions of the Ticuna' and initiated their demarcation. There was powerful opposition from the anti-environmental Governor of Amazonas, Gilberto Mestrinho, and from local politicians. Funai baulked at the cost of demarcating the large Évare reserves, but the Ticuna obtained funds from an Austrian aid agency. So, on 5 January 1996, the President of Brazil ratified the two large territories. It was the end of a twenty-year struggle, another great victory for indigenous activism and tenacity helped by a band of dedicated anthropologists and sympathizers. The Ticuna nation entered the new millennium as Brazil's second-largest tribe, with 26,000 of its total population of 35,000 in that country. (The other Ticuna live upriver in Peru and Colombia; and Brazil's largest indigenous nation is the Guarani, scattered in the southernmost states.)

*

The Javari river joins the Solimões–Amazon at Benjamin Constant and forms the frontier between Brazil and Peru. These forested rivers are very remote from the capital cities of both countries, reached only by boat or plane, and largely forgotten. With the collapse of the rubber boom in about 1915, the surviving Indians of the Javari enjoyed a respite disturbed only by activities of loggers and a handful of riverine settlements. Some tribes were partially acculturated after decades of contact with – and often oppression by – the seringueiro frontier; others were hardly disturbed, hunting, gathering, and occasionally migrating in seemingly endless forests; still others remained uncontacted at the end of the twentieth century.

The Peruvian side of the middle Javari is home to some 500 Matsé – formerly known, wrongly, as Mayoruna. A large tribe in Peru, some Matsés migrated eastwards into Brazil during the rubber period in search of an area rich in game and free from murderous civilizados. In 1964 isolated groups of them were located by planes of the Summer Institute of Linguistics, whose largest base in South America was not far away on the Ucayali in Peru. The planes threw down presents of metal tools and cooking pots, but at first the suspicious Indians used sticks to push these into the river so that they did not touch them. However, the Matsé eventually succumbed to the presents; and they were contacted by missionaries who then studied their Panoan language.

Some Matsé took to logging on a commercial scale. Funai opened a small post called Lobo, and its head helped the Indians sell their timber and rubber in Benjamin Constant. 'With the money obtained, the chief of the post acquired the merchandise that the Matsé already felt was necessary for their way of life, such as soap, kerosene, clothing, needles and sewing thread, pans, shotguns, cartridges, machetes, axes, etc.'. The anthropologist Terri Valle de Aquino, who became a leading champion of Indians throughout this part of Brazil, saw 119 magnificent trunks of *cedro* (*Cedrela meliceae*, a member of the mahogany family) ready to float down the river in 1980; and the Indians also logged commercial softwoods such as andiroba (*Carapa guaianensis*), jacareuba (*Calophyllum brasiliense*), and aucuba. Medical assistance on this remote frontier was sporadic. But in 1978 the São Paulo Medical School, which did such admirable work on the Xingu, sent a team to help Funai vaccinate these Indians against measles and other diseases.

Near the sources of the Javari and of its tributaries the Curuçá, Arrojo, and Ituí lives a cluster of tribes known collectively as Marubo. Gentle and amiable people, the Marubo are skilled artisans in pottery and basketry and build elegant pyramidical houses of woven thatch whose four flat sides rise to a tall apex. Both sexes wear body paint in geometric patterns and distinctive garlands of white beads looped between their nose septums and ears.

The first recent contacts with well-intentioned outsiders were in 1960 with Protestant missionaries of the New Tribes Mission and translators of the Summer Institute of Linguistics. Although bent on translating the New Testament into Marubo in order to convert these Indians to Christianity, the missionaries did their best to help the tribes medically and with some education to equip them to resist external pressures. Relations between Indians and missionaries were benign. The strangers were friendly, learned to speak excellent Marubo, and brought coveted manufactured goods, without imposing their cult too aggressively. By 1967 the SIL historian Dale Kietzman described the Marubo as 'the most isolated of Panoan tribes in contact with civilization, it has maintained the largest population group with over 400 individuals in a single location.' Henry Loewen, head of the NTM in Brazil, confirmed that the Marubo maintained many customs, including their magnificent long houses. 'An industrious people', they traded animal skins and timber 'for hardware and clothes . . . Most of the Indian braves sell from twelve to up to fifty logs per year' and were paid reasonably for them.

During the 1970s, the missionaries treated successive epidemics of measles, meningitis, influenza, and tuberculosis. (The anthropologist Júlio César Melatti found that the Indians had strung hundreds of empty medicine phials as decoration on their great thatched maloca.) The Marubo population grew steadily, although the groups on the Ituí became alienated from those on the Curuçá. Both communities were active rubber-tappers. Two of their chiefs, Zé Barbosa on the upper Curuçá and Alfredo on the Ituí, acted as dealers for this rubber, timber, and export artefacts, but the Indians also relied on regatões, itinerant traders who had plied Amazonian rivers since colonial days. Funai entered this area only in 1974 with the creation of the Curuçá post. But when the government agency tried to close the headwaters of these rivers to non-Indians, some Marubo protested because they enjoyed selling rubber and timber to itinerant brokers. 'All the traders have total freedom of action regarding prices charged for merchandise, the value of rubber, and percentage deducted for carriage, without any control or monitoring by the protective agency'. Both groups of Marubo decided that they wanted an airstrip, so that small missionary planes could make emergency evacuations or take their chiefs to attend indigenous assemblies. So, when Funai delayed, they took the matter into their own hands and used their relatively few tools to clear the forests.

*

There were exciting contacts with new indigenous groups in the great unexplored area south of Benjamin Constant, along the Ituí and adjacent rivers in the very heart of the Amazon rainforests. Sightings of unknown Indians became increasingly frequent during the 1960s, so Funai established an Ituí Attraction Front. In December 1976 a strange Indian appeared on the bank of the river and 'with a stick imitated cutting grass with a machete . . . and then made the motions of felling a tree with an axe.' An old man, woman, and youth joined this Indian and 'after an hour of dialogue [in sign language and imitating words] they indicated that the Funai people should leave, but promised with signs that they themselves would return.' At the next encounter, six Indians appeared on a path of the attraction team and asked for axes, machetes, a dog, and scissors. Once again metal cutting tools were the catalyst of contact, just as they had been ever since Cabral's first landing in Brazil in 1500. Funai's Pedro Coelho tape-recorded the new Indians, and Matsé interpreters identified their language as a distant relative of their own Panoan. It was later learned that this tribe was called Matís. The men wore nothing but a penis string and distinctive facial ornaments of black wooden bars projecting upwards on either side of their noses, feline-like whiskers tattooed on either side of their mouths, often small bristles of bamboo needles in their lower lips and noses, curving mollusc shells below their nostrils, and large round molluscs on their ear lobes like the golden ear-discs of Inca nobility. Matís men were lean and tough, understandably wary but not hostile.

Groups of Matís visited the attraction post sporadically throughout 1977. The post often had nothing to give them apart from food and some animals: hens, and dogs that particularly pleased them. In one conversation through Panoan-speaking Matsé interpreters, a young man asked whether the Funai people had come to kill them, but these 'answered "no": they wanted friendship and to defend them against other *nawa* [white men] who always attacked them.' It was gradually learned that the various groups visiting the Funai post were hostile to one another – one maloca had been burned – and that some had caught potentially lethal colds from the Brazilians. Dogs and puppies (which the Matís called *uapá*) were the most coveted presents, more even than machetes: they loved having them as pets.

The Funai team behaved with restraint, receiving visits from groups of Indians – sometimes as many as eighty people – but never trying to visit a village until invited. At one meeting an Indian woman called Tupân started singing. She was answered by songs from a Marubo, and 'thus three hours were spent in singing and smiling on both sides'. The first visit to a Matís village was finally made by the anthropologist Delvair

Montagner Melatti in 1978. Their huts proved to be long, narrow rectangular structures, with sloping eaves of woven cacao leaves and family partitions along either side of a central passage. The Matís were typically skilled hunters, using both bows and arrows and accurate blowguns, good fishermen, and farmers in forest clearings.

As they came to know the Funai team, the Matís revealed that their greatest preoccupation was the entry of white men up their rivers to collect turtle eggs or timber. They feared murderous attacks by these intruders and begged Funai to keep them out. But the most serious threat, as always, was from introduced diseases. Once again, the authorities had made a contact with insufficient medical preparation or back-up. The Matís were struck by terrible epidemics of influenza that killed a third of one entire group. A young French anthropologist, Philippe Erikson, witnessed this unforgivable bungling. 'There were various epidemics introduced by, among others, the Funai team, which was incapable of combating them. The last months of 1981 were particularly tragic, costing the lives of some fifty Matís. The traumatized survivors abandoned their habitats that were dispersed in the forest, and congregated around the Funai post on the banks of the Ituí river in order to obtain medicines . . . [They suffered] demographic and psychological shock from this absurd, banal, and unnecessarily murderous contact.' A Brazilian medical student sent to try to help found the majority stricken by pneumonia and in 'appalling condition'. The sudden deaths of so many people naturally shattered tribal society. 'Through its brutality, the experience of contact destructured the Matís' population and pattern of territorial occupation, which caused serious modifications to their systems of governance and daily life. Their social organization was also seriously affected, for the depopulation obliged various widows to violate traditional rules of marriage to find a new partner. Finally, the abundance of manufactured goods (salt, cartridges, soap, etc.) and the new necessities resulting from them imposed a new pattern of economic behaviour.' The only slight consolation was that they did not succumb to alcoholism or debt bondage.

Erikson found that Matís shamans and powerful men possessed a trait called *sho*. This force could be either positive, a source of bravery and hunting skill, or sinister, for instance in transmitting poison or infection. (The Matís associate the lethal imported diseases with white men, but do not blame them or seek revenge.) The sho is also either 'bitter', more masculine and potentially dangerous, or 'sweet', feminine and protective. Whites have plenty of bitter sho that gives them some of their powers and relative immunity to disease. Some Indians felt that whites benefited from consuming salt, pepper, and sugar. The bewildered and grief-stricken

Matís who survived the influenza catastrophe naturally sought new definitions of sho.

Philippe Erikson observed the reactions of Maké, one of the Matís most nostalgic for the past and affected by contact. 'Although he must have been under forty, Maké behaved just like a *darasibo*, an elder. Since all the old men had perished in the epidemics, he had apparently decided to take their place: he hunted little but worked in the roça clearing, he sang often, made blowguns, and gained respect as a specialist in ritual. A traditionalist psychologically aged by contact, Maké suffered – even physically – from its effects, coughing almost every night and cursing the *nawa* [whites].' Maké was disgusted to see his people gradually abandon their distinctive body ornaments. But he became uncertain about his sho, ceased hunting although he had been a fine hunter, and 'although this man visibly embodied ancient values, he felt obliged to renounce the most important of them.' For the few Matís elders, coexistence with the whites meant abandonment of their sho.

Adolescents now felt less urge to acquire sho, and there was debate about whether to continue tattooing young people at puberty, to continue living in large communal huts or in Funai-type thatched houses on stilts, or to adopt some Western clothing. In the first years after contact, the Matís earned money by selling their fine blowguns (potent symbols of a man's sho) to Funai or other visitors – and they delighted in demonstrating the accuracy of these weapons to camera crews. In the late 1980s they switched to logging hardwoods as their main source of cash. However, 'some years after contact, the Matís found themselves in an impasse: they had no desire whatever to become whites, but on the other hand they felt it impossible to maintain the practices most important to them as symbols of their identity.' Visitors to the Matís received a warm welcome and saw the Indians as cheerful and relaxed; but the tribe continued to fear whites. Although manufactured goods were desired and used, they were stored in special shelters alongside communal huts – never inside them. Smoke frightened the Matís, so that they had to overcome suspicion of cigarettes and even matches. 'Smoke causes coughing, and a cough, principally that transmitted by whites, continues to be seen as a precursor of death.'

When Philippe Erikson returned to the Matís in the mid-1990s, he found that their population had doubled, to some 240. The increase was all organic, so that young people he had known a decade earlier were now parents. 'Thus a new generation of adults did not know the period before contact, and they confront very different issues to their predecessors.' They now take the presence of Funai and neighbouring Marubo for granted. The trauma of disease mortality is part of oral history. They all

40. Upper Xingu women grappling with clothing, even though it required imported cloth, thread, and needles. The Villas Boas tried to exclude only goods that competed with tribal specialities.

41. Mentuktire mother, Jarina river, Xingu. These Kayapó loved to adorn their children with glass beads.

42. Tapayuna, after relocation to Diauarum, Xingu, in 1968–69. These people were called 'Wooden Beaks' because of their lip-discs.

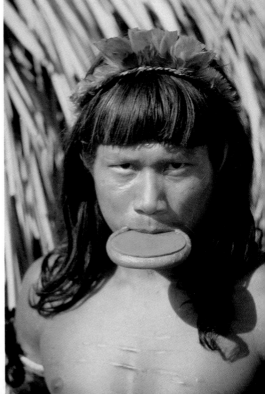

43. Aritana Yawalipiti as a young man. Groomed by the Villas Boas, Aritana became Paramount Chief of the upper Xingu tribes.

44. Upper Xingu warriors.

45. The Quarup funerary ceremony in honour of Cláudio Villas Boas, 1998: shamans chant around a decorated tree trunk that symbolizes the dead man.

46. A class for Xavante boys, on São Marcos mission, Mato Grosso.

47. Salesian missionaries taught Xavante to use agricultural machinery, but a scheme for large-scale rice farming was a failure.

48. Xavante warriors pride themselves on their martial bearing.

49. Tiriyó. Tumucumaque, Brazilian Guiana.

50. Sorrowing Yanomami hold baskets containing the ashes of relatives killed in the Haximú massacre of 1993.
(*Cláudia Andujar*)

51. Yanomami archers use powerful bows and very long arrows with different heads for each type of game.

52. Yanomami communal huts either rise to a great conical roof or have the middle open as a round patio

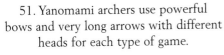

53. A Yanomami mother's decoration is feathers in her ear lobes and gummed onto her forehead, body paint, and palm spines around her mouth like feline whiskers.

54. A Kamayurá man prepares for wrestling.

55. All tribes of the upper Xingu love *huka-huka* wrestling, performed almost daily in each village and in inter-tribal contests.

56. Xikrin Kayapó mothers and children soon after contact. Most wear black genipap body-paint and the children's crowns are shaved.

57. Bororo warriors wore magnificent headdresses with feather visors and mother-of-pearl labrets.

58. Nambiquara women carry all their belongings in basket hods.

59. Nambiquara eke out a living by making necklaces to sell on the highway that traverses their land.

60. Panará children playing in the Iriri river below their village. They were delighted to return to part of their forests in 1996, after twenty-two years of exile on the Xingu.

wear clothing, some receive schooling, and a few speak the Marubo dialect of Panoan or even Portuguese. Some leaders have left the malocas to attend meetings of the Javari Valley Indigenous Council, or have seen distant cities. Protestant missionaries appear in the two villages, and preach in Marubo 'when Funai's back is turned'. Young Matís are learning political rhetoric, and seek a tribal identity – with the name Deshan Mikitbo rather than Matís – and an aggressive return to traditional values.

North of the Matís, in the forests between the lower Ituí and Itaquaí, there were other unknown Indians. It was extraordinary that these people should have remained isolated, living little more than a hundred kilometres (sixty miles) south of Benjamin Constant and the main Solimões (Amazon) river. There had been a major battle with them in 1928, at which over forty Indians were killed by seringueiro guns. During the ensuing decades, there were sporadic encounters, some friendly but others violent. Log-cutters were sometimes killed, or had their houses destroyed or children captured by the mysterious Indians. In the early 1970s Funai tried to make contact, but abandoned its attraction post after two of its men and the wife of one were killed in separate incidents.

Further west, between the lower Ituí and Javari, woodsmen told of another isolated group of Marubo that they called Maya. So in April 1977 Sydney Possuelo took a boatload of three Indians (Marubo, Kulina, and Matsé) and an assistant on a twenty-seven-hour boat journey up the Itaquaí (Itacoaí) and its Quixito tributary. It was a tough expedition, for the stream was blocked with flooded vegetation, and the team then hacked through sixteen kilometres (ten miles) of dense forest to an abandoned loggers' camp. There was a call from the forest and a naked Indian appeared, followed by some women and children. Although the expedition's interpreters could not make themselves understood, friendly contact was established by sign language. The loggers had told Possuelo that these Indians seemed to love buttons, so the team had taken quantities of these. Sure enough, the Indians 'showed themselves content with axes and machetes, but their greatest pleasure came when they received boxes of multicoloured buttons'. The team also had to part with buttons from their clothing. At this first contact, it was not known how these people used buttons, for they were entirely naked apart from a necklace of black nuts that one woman wore festooned beneath her breasts. The men seemed to hunt only with long blowguns, of consummate manufacture, and darts with a variety of poisons. The Funai men persuaded the log-cutters to leave the area, and then felt that there was no need for further contact with this self-sufficient group.

As contacts increased with these and other small tribes during the 1970s, Funai staff started to worry about protection of their forests. In 1972 there was a proposal for a reserve embracing all known groups; but this plan was forgotten. In 1981 the anthropologists Júlio César Melatti and his wife Delvair (whose doctoral thesis was a fine study of Marubo shamanism) and others gathered all that was known about the region's tribes in a volume published by CEDI. Funai asked three work-groups to survey different areas, one led by Terri Valle de Aquino, another by Delvair Montagner Melatti, and the third by Marco Antônio do Espírito Santo. They jointly proposed one vast national Indian park of the Javari Valley. Covering some 6 million hectares (23,200 square miles), this would embrace the entire river systems of the Curuçá, Ituí, and Itaquaí and their many tributaries and extend as far east as the upper Jutaí. It lay at the very heart of Amazonia, the world's greatest mass of tropical rainforests. No one can grasp the magnificence and magnitude of these forests until they have gone for weeks up their meandering white-water rivers, cut into the edges of their mighty vegetation, or at least flown for hours on end over a carpet of tree canopies stretching to the horizon in every direction. So if it were achieved, the Javari Indian park would also be an environmental sanctuary of global importance.

There were of course serious threats. An area this large contained almost 300 rubber and logging concessions and claims, as well as plans for a perimeter road near the Brazilian–Peruvian frontier. The colonization agency Incra also wanted to grant settlement plots – although it admitted that there was little demand for them in these remote and roadless forests. In 1983 a private speculator tried to settle a hundred families of seringueiros in Matsé territory on the upper Javari. Delvair Melatti reported that on the Ituí–Curuçá river basins 'Funai daily watches the dilapidation of indigenous areas, year after year, and maintains peaceful relations with their exploiters, on the pretext of its deficient infrastructure and paltry annual budgets'.

The next problem came from the state petroleum monopoly Petrobrás, which wanted to prospect for oil and natural gas near these rivers. Geophysicists working for Petrobrás and the French oil giant Elf-Aquitaine moved into the remote headwaters of the Ituí. They operated in secrecy until late 1984 when their activities were exposed by CIMI's radical journal *Porantim* and by Survival International in London. Oil exploration is a messy business, involving camps and airstrips for the engineers, tall derricks and drilling platforms, and worst of all seismic tests with subterranean explosions of dynamite. The large scale of the operations gradually emerged, with large teams of workers and test 'lines' running for hundreds of kilometres through the forest, supplied by airstrips and trails. All this was done in the final years of military government, with Funai's secret approval, in forests inhabited by uncontacted tribes. Not surprisingly, there were clashes. A worker was wounded by arrows on the Jandiatuba river in November 1983; another near the Itaquaí in March 1984. On 4 September of that year, a group of fifty Indians from an unknown tribe thought to be Korubo approached a Petrobrás camp on the Itaquaí. A Funai sertanista and a geophysicist 'attended to their signals, transmitted by gestures and much shouting; but it ended with their being dragged into the forest' and clubbed to death. This tragedy – combined with a lack of significant gas discoveries – caused the oil-men to promise to evacuate the sensitive region.

The campaign for a Javari Indian park moved slowly. The President of Funai interdicted the huge area in April 1985, but more information was needed about the tribes living there. So in 1985 Funai combined with CIMI, the Catholic prelacies of the Solimões, and Incra to make an ethnographic survey. The authors, Silvio Cavuscens and Lino João Neves, submitted a massive report in 1986. 'It was certainly a difficult task, because of the enormous distances to be travelled by boat (with a central motor) and by launch (canoe with an outboard) for a total of 650 hours of voyages, and also because of the hardships in reaching the headwaters of the rivers where the most distant malocas are located.' They showed that the region was still being heavily invaded, and named the loggers, seringueiros, traders, and settlers operating on each river. They had seen frequent traces of three or four different uncontacted groups on the upper Itaquaí and Jandiatuba. These people occasionally attacked log-cutters and their huts: as a result, the timber-men went to work heavily armed and may well have shot at Indians.

Although the Javari park was interdicted – meaning that it was closed to non-Indians pending demarcation as a protected reserve – nothing happened. Delvair Melatti, working as an anthropologist for Funai, wrote a damning report about its shortcomings. 'The park is a fantasy project and Funai is an entity seeking a purpose. The only realities are clandestine logging and attacks by wood-cutters against tribes who are deprived of contact with Funai.' Chronic lack of funds and of resolve meant that Funai's regional headquarters in a town south of Benjamin Constant was decrepit, with empty medicine shelves, broken radios and outboard motors, and boats sinking at their moorings instead of supplying the posts upriver. By the late 1980s, timber extraction was rampant, with up to 1,000 loggers extracting perhaps 10,000 trees a year. Melatti wrote: 'The timber-men are the park's greatest predators because of the immense "roadways" they open in the forest to roll logs down to creeks or rivers. We saw many loggers' roadways all along the Ituí, increasingly close to one another . . . It was common to encounter logs being assembled ready to be rafted downriver. The Coari tributary of the Ituí is the loggers' "gold mine" from which they removed thousands of softwoods'. This area had already been denuded of mahogany and other hardwoods, but these valuable trees were still abundant at the southern part of the Javari park – in forests inhabited by twelve tribes, four of whom were uncontacted.

Conflicts multiplied between Indians and intruders. Atrocities went unrecorded. One deliberate massacre of isolated Korubo occurred in September 1990, when fifteen loggers caught four Indians in a barrage of firing and killed three of them. Church authorities got the police to investigate, but the case was referred to a judge in the loggers' town, so that – as always – there were no convictions. In the following year, two log-cutters were clubbed to death on the Coari, and others were killed elsewhere. There was the usual cycle of reprisals: in 1993 a Marubo Indian said that a group of loggers tried to get him to guide them to a Korubo village so that they could destroy it; and there was a report that one Flávio Perez had attacked a maloca of bow-wielding Korubo on the São José creek and 'killed all the adults, men and women, leaving only the children'. In 1995 a civil servant was clubbed to death when fishing on the Quixito, near the northern limit of the park; it was rumoured that a reprisal raid by woodsmen killed ten Indians of the Maya group contacted by Sydney Possuelo eighteen years previously.

Both sides started political action. In December 1990 missionaries and Funai organized the first Encounter of the region's indigenous peoples, attended by Marubo, Matsé, Kulina, and Kanamari. This was not an easy undertaking, since the Marubo and Matsé were traditionally bitter enemies, and travel along the rivers was precarious. The meeting complained about Funai's failure to provide medical care, education, or protection of land rights. It established an Indian Council of the Javari Valley (Civaja). But this Council could never achieve the political and public-relations successes of similar organizations for the Yanomami or Kayapó, since its three or four thousand Indians were from such diverse tribes that ranged from largely acculturated to isolated. They also lived in remote forests devoid of roads and with few airstrips, and thus beyond the range of journalists and camera crews. In 1992 the new Council held its first Assembly, with eighteen chiefs meeting at Funai's Curuçá post; in 1994 the more sophisticated Marubo met to press their particular grievances; and in 1995 there was a second Javari Assembly at an aldeia on the upper Ituí. Civaja succeeded because it had a clear objective: the creation of the Javari indigenous territory. Sílvio Cavuscens, the sociologist who battled alongside the Indians from 1984 onwards, wrote: 'Although driven by young leaders, principally from the Marubo people, the traditional chiefs encouraged Civaja's work by participating, speaking and discussing problems in its assemblies. Among such leaders, Tuxauá João, the paramount Marubo chief, never ceased to believe in this movement and sought to stimulate, protect and guide Civaja's management.' Civaja also tried to improve education and to seek economic alternatives – including an agreement between Indians and riverine settlers for 'sustainable' logging in the indigenous area.

Funai wanted to start demarcating the Javari park in 1992. This was an almost impossible mission in many hundreds of kilometres of often unexplored forests; but Funai could at least control the riverine entry points and it asked the police to prevent loggers from entering the area. The timber men protested vociferously, at mass rallies in the towns near the park. They accused Funai of hypocrisy with no moral right to deny them entry, since it encouraged tribes in its tutelage to cut timber and helped them market it. Grievances multiplied when the supply of timber to the sawmills diminished, leading to unemployment. During the dry season of 1994–95, the environment agency Ibama got army detachments to confiscate hundreds of logs being floated down from the Indian Area. There was an immediate outcry from poor loggers deprived of their year's work; rallies of hundreds of timber workers; vilification of Indians, NGOs, missionaries, and Funai; and political action in the Amazonas state legislature. No one was ever convicted for the illegal logging or theft of millions of dollars' worth of wood from an indigenous area. Instead, 21,000 cubic metres (740,000 cubic feet) of confiscated timber 'disappeared' and was clearly recovered by the traders. Logging resumed unabated.

There was another thorough survey of some 4,000 Indians (acculturated and uncontacted) thought to live in the Javari basin. The indigenous cause seemed to have triumphed in December 1998 when President Cardoso signed a decree for the demarcation of the entire Javari Valley reserve. It was even larger than the area interdicted thirteen years previously – a gigantic 8,338,000 hectares (over 32,000 square miles). Funds for the demarcation came from a 'Pilot Plan for the Amazon' (PPTAL) financed by the G7 group of rich nations. Civaja wrote to thank Survival and other supporters for this 'present for which we never dared hope . . . for [we were] oppressed, massacred people who starved because our land had been invaded and we could not get enough food for our children'.

*

In 1995 Funai reported fifty-eight boats on the mahogany-rich rivers of the isolated Korubo. So Sydney Possuelo decided that he must attempt a contact with the 'club-wielding' Korubo (as opposed to another group further south who preferred bows and arrows). This experienced and committed sertanista felt that the group's isolation was now seriously threatened, by loggers who would shoot Indians at sight or mount murderous raids on their malocas. A large sign was erected at the mouth of the Ituí warning trespassers not to enter that Indian area. Funai built a floating 'vigilance post' at the place where the Itaquaí joins the Ituí, to try to enforce this exclusion.

Possuelo's contact expedition lasted throughout the second half of 1995, with two forays deep into the forest. Traces of Indian trails and abandoned villages were found, including a camouflaged ambush site presumably intended for an attack on the attraction team.

On 15 October 1995 food and presents were taken by the Korubo, who must have been very close by. Matís Indians on the Funai team shouted into the wall of vegetation that they were friendly. Amazingly, there was an answer. Going towards it, the team saw four men and a woman bravely standing on a fallen tree, with their bows set aside, naked and painted. Both sides were frightened. For the Indians there was the trauma of face-to-face contact; and for Possuelo's team the knowledge that these Korubo were warriors who had killed forty whites during the previous thirty years. But the meeting was friendly. The Korubo took clothing (particularly caps and hats), pots, and food. They rubbed crushed leaves onto the team's faces, apparently to pacify them, and then invited them to dance. They also felt the men's genitals and the one woman's breasts to confirm that they were ordinary people, and they were fascinated by Possuelo's bushy black beard. The peaceful contact with this small group of twenty people lasted for five days.

Possuelo was now worried for two reasons: that clandestine loggers would pour back into forests if they thought that the feared Korubo were now at peace; and that the newly contacted Indians would succumb to alien diseases. The French anthropologist Philippe Erikson shared this fear and condemned the attraction team for inadequate medical preparations. It was also learned that there had been acute tensions among the Korubo, so that the small group contacted by Possuelo had had to flee across the Ituí river – into the territory of potential enemies who have yet to be contacted by whites. Funai maintained its isolated floating vigilance post for a few years, deterring invaders despite efforts by the loggers to have the post removed. There was a tragic misunderstanding in September 1997 when the Indians killed the sertanista Sobral Magalhães, after months of apparently friendly contacts. By 2000 the feared epidemics and loggers' invasions had not happened, and relations between the Korubo and Matís working for Funai have gradually improved. Erikson described the situation as 'increasingly serene'. True to Funai's new policy, Possuelo left this group isolated and essentially uncontacted.

Because *Hevea brasiliensis* rubber trees grow most abundantly in the state of Acre, this region had been the mecca and nucleus of the Amazon rubber boom. The Acre river is a headwater of the Purus, a great southern tributary of the Amazon that, with its neighbour the Juruá, had been heavily invaded by seringueiros. The Indians of Acre and other sources of the Purus and Juruá had been battered during the rubber era: either exploited in debt-bondage by rubber men, or killed by their bullets and diseases, or forced to flee deeper into the forests to escape them. There was a lull during the 1920s and 1930s; but Brazilian rubber-tapping revived during the Second World War, and after it a few wild-rubber-tappers continued to find a market for their produce.

In the late 1960s, the last of the rubber bosses were still tyrannizing families of detribalized Indians on their rubber concessions or *seringals*. They even continued to organize massacres of uncontacted groups in the south-western forests near the Peruvian border. Terri Valle de Aquino complained that the plight of the Indians had been totally ignored until the mid-1970s – the time when cattle ranchers started to acquire half the state's land. There was a conspiracy of silence about these 'non-people'. 'Why recall that Acre's Indians had had their lands violently expropriated, were massacred in raids by the bullets of "yellow-bellied" rifles and by virulent diseases, and then transformed into a grossly overworked and enslaved labour force by the rubber colonels?' Browbeaten, uneducated, and with no medical care, the shattered remnants of these tribes were among the poorest of Brazil's landless peasantry.

Because Acre is far from Funai's headquarters in Brasília it was largely ignored by the government agency. Protestant missionaries of the New Tribes Mission and Summer Institute of Linguistics therefore moved into the vacuum. They became active in this region from the 1960s onwards. In 1970 the head of the New Tribes Mission reported that the Kulina 'are an abused people: everywhere they live, the "land-owners" exploit them as much as they can', and 'the national dwellers of the Iaco river abuse [its Yaminawa] extensively. When they work for pay they receive very little, and at times their pay is liquor'. Although these New Tribes missionaries provided some medical care and education, Terri Valle de Aquino wrote that they were 'entirely preoccupied with religious proselytizing. They were accused of dividing communities between "believers" and "non-believers"; of lacking respect for cultural traditions, inculcating the idea that the Indians' rituals, songs and dances are "things of the devil", and of allying themselves with [the tribes'] former and current bosses.'

Funai appeared late on the scene. After making a survey of Acre's tribes, in 1976 it opened an office in the state capital Rio Branco and posts at two places of tension between Indians and settlers: Boca do Acre (in the state of Amazonas just north of Acre) and Fronteira near the source of the Iaco river. In the following year, Funai teams identified fourteen indigenous areas in the state – the majority among headwaters of the Juruá to the west. During the ensuing quarter century, these and other tribal areas progressed gradually – often painfully slowly – along the legal process from preliminary identification, to interdiction, demarcation, and full legal registration. Since most Indian areas had been invaded or usurped, they had to be cleared of non-Indians, who were supposed to be compensated. Hardly surprisingly, this return to Indian (or Funai's) ownership involved frequent conflicts. In 1979–80 the Apurinã of Boca do Acre had violent clashes with farmers and squatters; an Indian shot and killed the leader of a farmers' trade union; soldiers intervened in what was described as a 'state of war'; and the tribe begged Funai to send an anthropologist they trusted, Ezequias Heringer, to help them define their territory.

The struggles for land were made possible by three developments in the late 1970s: visits by Indian leaders to the city of Rio Branco, where they met one another, formed regular assemblies, and lobbied collectively for their rights; the arrival of CIMI; and the creation of an Acre branch of the Pro-Indian Commission (CPI). The latter was led by Terri Valle de Aquino, the local-born anthropologist who devoted his life to the region's Indians, a passionate and stubborn campaigner who clashed in turn with Protestant and Catholic missionaries, Funai, and other authorities.

A typical example of oppression occurred on the Jordão river, a headwater of the Juruá in south-west Acre. This remote river, reachable only by days of boat travel, was home to some 240 Kaxinawá who lived in thirty-eight huts and were totally in thrall to six seringals. These subsistence farmers worked for their bosses to 'pay off' fraudulent or inflated debts for renting rubber-tapping trails or the purchase of basic necessities. They would open trails, supply food and fish to the depot, or take rafts laden with rubber downriver. They owned no land and received no help from any agency. They referred to this period, which lasted until the mid-1970s, as their 'captivity'.

Fortunately for these Jordão-river Kaxinawá, one seringal, called Fortaleza, was bequeathed by its boss's widow, a black woman, to the Indians who worked it. They were then led by Sueiro Sales Cerqueira, the son of another boss and an Indian woman but who regarded himself as indigenous. During the captivity period, this one seringal represented liberty. On it, 'the Kaxinawá performed festivals and rituals of their rich cultural heritage. There they also enjoyed freedom to plant their roças on dry land and on the floodplain, to hunt with dogs, and to fish with *oaca* poison . . . all forbidden on neighbouring seringals'. This inspired other Indians to struggle against their captivity.

In 1977 Funai started to identify Indian lands throughout Acre and included much of the Jordão valley as such, despite political pressure from its rubber bosses. A crusading newspaper called O *Varadouro* ('The *Channel*') took up the cause of helping the Jordão-river Kaxinawá create their own cooperative. They had a champion in Terri Valle de Aquino. Between 1978 and 1980, the Indians' leaders – including the shrewd and experienced manager Sueiro Sales Cerqueira – gradually escaped the commercial monopoly of the old system, and persuaded the now-impoverished white seringueiros to leave. This was not easy. Business and banking interests in the nearest town refused markets or finance, and the police confiscated the Indians' rubber because their land was not yet demarcated by Funai.

Terri Valle de Aquino realized that the key to liberation from rubber bosses was financial. Many of Acre's Indians were hard-working and skilled seringueiros, quite capable of managing their own affairs if they could only obtain bank credit. So in April 1979 he took Kaxinawá leaders to Brasília and São Paulo to tell about their 'captivity' and the attempt to suppress their fledgeling cooperative. This worked. The CPI and CIMI arranged finance for the Indians' rubber, and Funai helped to obtain greater funding from Oxfam and other foreign charities. By 1980 Funai had defined most of the state's indigenous areas and was hiring companies to demarcate some of them. So in 1982 Terri (as he was always known) could write that 'the 800 Kaxinawá of the Jordão river expelled all the bosses and bogus lessors from the six seringals established within their reserve. The 250 Kaxinawá of the Humaitá river already control for themselves the three rubber stands that exist there. [One] Apurinã community has just organized its harvests of rubber and Brazil nuts independently of its former bosses. Through their cooperative, [another group of] Apurinã also permanently occupy the Brazil-nut groves and rubber trails of Seringal Aripuanã.' But there was still much to be done. The 4,000 Indians of western Acre 'are [still] living totally subjugated by their old rubber-trade bosses'.

In the 1970s another group of Kaxinawá settled on the banks of the upper Purus, near Funai's Fronteira post. By working for rubber men, a Kaxinawá called Pancho Lopes saved enough to buy, in 1979, a run-down rubber station called Recreio. Indigenous families gathered round, and Pancho created a self-help village of Indians free from debt-bondage. In August 1984 a meeting of Kulina and Kaxinawá of the upper Purus was so exasperated by Funai's prevarication and unfulfilled promise to demarcate their reserve that tribal leaders decided to take direct action. The community amassed manioc, tools, and all necessary provisions and then sent eighty men to open its own perimeter trail. After a month of hard work, the two cutting teams met and waved their machetes in triumph. Chief Pancho invited Funai to send surveyors to inspect the demarcation trail and fix markers. He told his people that they could now hunt, fish, farm, tap rubber, and raise their children in tranquillity. He boasted: 'When Indians undertake something we are serious, and we do it ourselves. We were born in the forest, so we understand the forest and we know how to work. Now we are going to secure our area [in cooperation with the Kulina].' In 1985 Pancho persuaded a further sixty people to join his community, bringing its population to two hundred; and in 1989 he founded another aldeia a few hours' journey upriver.

In December 1984 President Figueiredo signed a decree for the Indian Area of the Jordão river. But when Funai delayed the reserve's demarcation, these Kaxinawá took matters into their own hands. Men from each seringal moved into the forests to open trails and cut a perimeter along the watersheds. They themselves carried their surveying equipment, hunted, and built shelters, while their women gathered firewood and fed them in their forest camps. During these years, their rubber production increased impressively. The new independence brought stability and security, so that the population also multiplied (partly from immigration by Indians from other oppressed rubber areas) from 383 in 1975, to 774 in 1983, and 1,085 in 1992. Funai hired a company to confirm the accuracy of the demarcation.

By the late 1970s, a newspaper described Acre as 'a state in agony', with huge tracts being sold to large and small ranchers and land-speculators. Funai issued 'negative certificates' that resulted in the banishment of one group of Kaxinawá, so that their land could be deforested by the Companhia Novo Oeste. Another example of exploitation occurred when a consortium of big companies from southern Brazil bought a large area on the upper Gregório river. Local Iauanawá and Katukina Indians 'denounced in the press that they were being truly enslaved by [the company]. For, in addition to being obliged by its managers to pay rent for rubber trails within their indigenous areas, they were forced to hand over all their rubber production and to buy merchandise only through this company's depot.' In 1982 these Indians, with help from NGOs and Funai, expelled the company's manager and recovered control of their seringal.

Acre's independent (and non-Indian) rubber-tappers became world-famous during the 1980s, when their struggle to protect their forests against cattle ranchers developed into an environmental cause célèbre. Rarely has an environmental issue seemed so clear-cut between good and evil. The seringueiros' tapping was environmentally sustainable and they wanted to protect rainforests. Against them were ranchers determined to clear-fell tropical trees to plant desiccated grasslands, to replace the opulent biological diversity of Amazonia with a single imported and inappropriate species: cattle. The rubber-tappers were poor caboclos striving to feed their families, whereas the ranchers represented ruthless big business.

The seringueiros produced a charismatic leader, Chico Mendes, in whose homeland, the valley of the Xapuri near the Bolivian border, 10,000 hectares (25,000 acres) of forest were being felled each year. The independent rubber-tappers formed a Union of Rural Workers, and developed a tactic called *empate* (stalemate) in which labourers and their families formed a human wall in the path of bulldozers or chainsaw gangs. In June 1980, Mendes' mentor Wilson Pinheiro – the founder of the union and architect of the empate system – was murdered by hired gunmen. During the ensuing years, the seringueiros organized forty-five empates. Hundreds of protesters were arrested, some were tortured, and leaders were killed. Only fifteen empates worked: but they were increasingly successful in slowing and almost stopping destruction of the *Hevea*-rich forests.

The BR-364, the highway that had brought ruin to Rondônia's Indians and environment, continued to Acre and then westwards towards Peru. In 1985 the Interamerican Development Bank (BID) helped to finance the paving of this highway from Porto Velho westwards to Acre's capital, Rio Branco. The BID was aware how severely the World Bank had been criticized for its disastrous financing of the paving of this same road through Rondônia. Similar dire consequences happened with frightening speed. Rio Branco's population mushroomed to 250,000, swollen by landless peasants evicted from ranches and immigrants from other parts of Brazil. The lure of this new El Dorado shifted from the soil beneath rainforests (for conversion to cattle ranches) to the wood in their trees. By 1988 Rio Branco municipality had *forty* sawmills, and trucks rolled in constantly with mahogany and other hardwood trunks.

The BID salved its conscience with a plan called PMACI to protect the environment and Indians affected by its controversial paved highway. This awarded Funai funds to demarcate more reserves. So in January 1986 a delegation from nine tribes went to Brasília to beg the Minister of Justice to accelerate the work. They declared: 'Mr Minister, we are a group of indigenous leaders from the most distant region of the country who have come here to claim our rights. We always struggle together for our peoples, so we are requesting the demarcation not only of our communities' lands but of *all* the indigenous areas in our region.' They proposed that the new funds be used to compensate whites expelled from Indian lands, and then to finance the Indians themselves in demarcating their own reserves. Another plan sought capital to help indigenous rubber-tappers to establish their own cooperatives. As always, progress was slow. Successive indigenist assemblies petitioned Funai for action. It eventually identified eighteen smallish Indian areas in Acre, totalling almost 1.5 million hectares (6,000 square miles).

Chico Mendes was portly, with tousled black hair and moustache. He was energetic, eloquent, and charming, and exuded quiet authority. He became an international celebrity thanks partly to an NGO headed by an attractive campaigner named Maria Helena (Mary) Allegretti, and the American anthropologist Stephan Schwartzman. Mendes everywhere received awards and accolades – but also repeated death threats. He was given police protection. But on the night of 22 December 1988, Chico Mendes opened his kitchen door to take a shower in his garden bathhouse. He was shot dead by assassins. There was a massive outcry at the murder of this champion of rainforests and poor rubber-tappers. Everyone was certain that the gunmen were the sons or workers of a minor land-speculator, rancher, and logger called Darli Alves; but the murder trial dragged on in the usual contorted manner. Innumerable articles, a dozen books, television programmes, and a feature movie were produced about the tragedy. Chico Mendes' most enduring legacy was that the forests around Xapuri were protected as Brazil's first 'extractive reserve' – a national park in which sustainable rubber-tapping was permitted – and this was named after the martyr.

Chico Mendes had sought to overcome the traditional hostility between Indians and poor seringueiros. Both groups had been exploited by similar bosses. Mendes wrote, just before his death: 'Our proposals are now not just ours alone, they are put forward by Indians and rubber-tappers together. Our fight is the fight of all the peoples of the forest.' Despite such fine words and the creation of an Alliance of Forest Peoples, the struggle of Acre's seringueiros and murder of Chico Mendes had little direct impact on the state's Indians – although the tribes would have suffered severely had the loggers and ranchers won.

Having started a local branch of the CPI, Terri Valle de Aquino then cooperated with missionaries to mobilize the state's indigenous peoples into their own pressure groups. Tribal leaders met regularly to demand demarcation of their reserves as well as better education (by Indian teachers) and health care. They still had to identify and demarcate many indigenous areas. Constant protests by Indian leaders finally led Funai after 1985 to establish working groups to redefine some reserves and interdict five new ones. An Indigenous Assembly of Acre and South Amazonas in 1988 decided to create a branch of UNI (Union of Indigenous Nations), and this UNI-Norte became the Indians' main political force, working with sympathizers in CPI-Acre, CIMI, and the Lutheran Church. UNI saw its role as health care and politicizing Indians, both long-term objectives. In 1991 Terri's Kaxinawá of the Jordão and those of the Envira and other rivers formed their own seringueiros' associations.

Meanwhile, Pancho Lopes's Kaxinawá on the upper Purus pressed ahead with the reconquest of their region, persuading whites to depart. 'This occurred in a climate of tension, resentment, and fear, but without bloodshed. Missionaries from CIMI, other members of the Catholic Church, and Lutheran pastors played an important role in these reclamations of land' and the presence of Funai's post gave governmental legitimacy. But the Kaxinawá themselves engineered the victory. The result was the 263,000 hectare (1,000 square mile) indigenous area of the Upper Purus, fully demarcated and registered in 1996.

The British anthropologist Cecilia McCallum studied this group and found that, although there were instances of good relations with the whites – some godparentage, visits, games of football, or trading – the two communities generally lived separate lives based on a long tradition of hostility. The Indians could not forget decades of virtual slave-labour, followed by innumerable acts of ill-treatment, scorn, insults, and stinginess. They loved telling stories of their past, particularly of movement – migrations of villages, or journeys across settlers' ranches to the seat of power in Rio Branco. Confirmation of their reserve gave them confidence, so that recent narratives tell of Indians bravely expelling armed white hunters from their forests, or demanding police protection.

McCallum witnessed an example of new pride. The Kaxinawá of Recreio in 1990 decided to commemorate the eleventh anniversary of its foundation with a festival. This included a football match against whites from another seringal, popular lambada dances, *and* the revival of the

damiain, a long-abandoned ceremony in which costumed dancers honoured mythological spirits. The damiain started with masked men enacting
the negotiation whereby Pancho Lopes purchased Recreio from a grotesque white man with big ears, bushy eyebrows, a horrible beard, and a
cigarette hanging from his lips. There were then rituals in honour of
spirits, notably the Incas who, in Kaxinawá mythology, were primordial
strangers, both beneficial and frightening, who dwelled in the land of the
dead and were creators who had introduced many customs, objects, and
techniques. (The Inca empire, crushed by Pizarro's conquistadores in
1532, had had contact with forest tribes to the west of Brazilian Acre.)
Formidable hunters and farmers, these mythical Incas were desired by
Kaxinawá women, but feared because they killed and ate human beings.
The closest modern relatives of these Inca spirits are the nawa, white men
and non-Indians. These also bring desired goods but, unlike the Incas, do
not impart knowledge and 'are authoritarian and miserly, many are ugly,
and few are worthy to be called txai, an honorific bestowed on friends
and potential relatives which gives the status of Incas of excellence.' The
title Txai was awarded to Terri Valle de Aquino, and he adopted it with
pride.

Another champion of the Kaxinawá was a former Funai agent called
Antonio Batista Macedo. The son of a poor seringueiro, Macedo was
brought up near the Tarauacá (another headwater of the Juruá, just east
of the Jordão), so he knew the life of debt-bondage, and he learned the
Kaxinawá language and customs from Indians on the seringal. He became
the only member of his family who could read, learned basic mechanics
during his military service in western Acre, and then joined Funai on its
Apuriná post. He later said: 'I quickly realized that instead of being an
organization to help the Indians . . . it monopolized their rights.' During
the late 1970s, Macedo established one of the first indigenous cooperatives. He then protested that the reserve being delimited for this group
omitted much of its traditional land. His fight to get it enlarged brought
him up against military and landed interests. 'In 1980 I went to Brasília
with nine Indians to plead for the rights of the Apuriná and was fired [by
Funai] for insubordination.' Macedo met Chico Mendes, was enthralled
by his charisma, and spent the decade rousing the rubber-tappers of the
upper Juruá to defy their bosses, refuse to pay rent, organize cooperatives,
and oppose forest-clearance; so he was branded as a communist agitator
and suffered brief imprisonment, beating, and threats. Macedo also helped
the Poianawá and Kaxinawá.

When the American journalist Alex Shoumatoff met Antonio Macedo in 1989, he was 'a young-looking thirty-seven-year-old, with curly, dirty-blond hair, a fleshy sensual mouth, and blue eyes behind round, metal-rimmed glasses'. The Indians adored him and adopted 'our Macedo' as their Txai or blood-brother, as they also did for Terri. Macedo fought for and won the 'Extractive Reserve of the Upper Juruá' (on the model of the one named after Chico Mendes) for the Kaxinawá living on the Parauacá and Tejo headwaters of the Juruá in western Acre.

In the period 1985–87 Funai used PMACI funds to demarcate eight Indian Areas and started to define the areas and legal status of three others. But in the late 1980s, during the administration of the civilian President José Sarney, indigenous activity in Acre was paralysed by interference from the National Security Council, the same department that was seeking to impose the Calha Norte programme north of the Amazon. So it was not until 1991–93 that seven of these reserves were confirmed by presidential decrees of the pro-Indian President Collor and his successor. The others were gradually demarcated in subsequent years, and three new areas were identified.

As always, creating indigenous areas was complicated and laborious work, involving surveys by Funai work groups, negotiations to decide exactly where the territories lay, eviction and occasional compensation of intruders, and demarcation in often difficult and remote terrain. The Interamerican Development Bank's funds through PMACI were not great, but they were generally well used. In the early 1990s its efforts 'were primarily directed towards aid programmes in education and health, as well as to support local non-governmental organizations that were giving political and technical help to the Indian movement . . . and the seringueiros'.

The Jordão-river Kaxinawá realized that they must have education in Brazilian business methods, so they persuaded two volunteer teachers to join them. Sian, the young president of their association and a grandson of Sales Cerqueira, explained that: 'One problem we had to confront at the outset of our Cooperative was that no one could read and write, to organize the accounts, or note the output of the rubber-tappers or the merchandise they consumed'. Soon, teaching was done by the Indians themselves. 'We thus continue our struggle, organizing our people within our area, acting in both the production and sale of our rubber, and in the education and health of our community. In this way, we guarantee our land, our survival and our freedom.' Such was their self-confidence, that these Kaxinawá in 1993 purchased two rubber seringals to extend their area into the neighbouring Tarauacá valley; and they renamed the Jordão river 'Yuraiá', meaning 'River of our Body'. In that same year, Sian Kaxinawá won an international prize for a series of moving television documentaries that he had directed.

By the end of the twentieth century, all the indigenous areas in Acre were either fully registered or well on the way to such legal status. Because the region's tribes had been so shattered in the rubber boom, because their campaign for land rights started relatively late, and because some of this plateau was suitable for cattle, their reserves were fragmented and small by Brazilian standards. Indian lands account for about 10 per cent of Acre and there is a roughly equal area of environmental areas – national parks, national forests (which enjoy little protection), and the new extractive reserves. But large cattle-ranches and rubber enterprises still own over half the state.

Racial prejudice continues against Acre's Indians. In 1996 drunken police killed a young Indian because he was embracing a mission-worker's daughter on a sandbank; next year, two Kaxinawá rubber-tappers were tortured by police in Feijó, apparently on the orders of seringueiros; other Kaxinawá sought official protection after violence between them and settlers near Humaitá; and in May 2000 a Manchineri (Maxineri) man was murdered by machete blows in Sena Madureira, after being taunted that 'an Indian's place is in the jungle'.

Surprisingly, there are still uncontacted tribes in the forested hills between Acre and Peru. During the 1980s and 1990s, Ashaninka Kampa migrated from Peru to escape cruel cauchero latex bosses and then the ruthless Sendero Luminoso ('Shining Path') guerrillas. These Kampa and other tribes were employed by rubber bosses in the dirty work of pursuing isolated tribes, and suffered revenge attacks from their arrows. 'There have been frequent conflicts, involving innumerable cases of death among on one side the "isolated Indians" and on the other Kaxinawá, Ashaninka, Kulina, Manchineri, and rubber-tappers of Acre.' In June 1998 the great sertanista Sydney Possuelo sighted a large village of an unknown tribe. He said that 'their [twelve to fifteen] huts are hidden below thick vegetation, and we just happened be flying at an angle that made it possible to spot them'. It was unprecedented for Indians to build their huts *beneath* the forest canopy: this group must have appreciated that planes could contain their enemies. The tribe is in forested hills, close to the Peruvian frontier near the source of the Humaitá river. Possuelo decided not to attempt a contact, because the group is already within a Kaxinawá protected area and is under no immediate threat. In that same year, other isolated Indians were seen on the upper Envira river; and in 1999, 300 naked, painted warriors armed with bows and arrows suddenly appeared near the Funai base on the Iaco. 'They peacefully watched the flight of the [frightened] contact team. They stole nothing, but killed the dogs and domestic animals.' The experienced Indianist in charge of the contact group, José Carlos Meirelles, thinks that they are a nomadic group known as Masko, most of whom are on the Peruvian side of the border. Still other uncontacted Indians live in the Xinane reserve, on the right bank of the Envira.

Further down the Juruá and Purus, in the area known as Southern Amazonas, the situation is somewhat better for the Indians. The forests here are denser and unsuitable for ranching, and there are no roads to attract settlers. The problem for these tribes is timber. As on the rivers of the Javari basin to the west, logging has accelerated alarmingly on the middle Juruá and Purus. The environmental agency Ibama awarded many logging licences, but illegal felling of trees was also rampant in these vast and unpoliced forests. By the mid-1990s, some 680,000 cubic metres (24 million cubic feet) of timber a year were being extracted from the rivers of Amazonas. Woodsmen felled mahogany, gigantic sumaúma (kapoks) that tower above the forest canopy, and many other species. They cut the trees during the dry season and then floated them downstream in their thousands when the rivers rose during the rains. Funai was aware of clandestine logging in almost every indigenous reserve, but was powerless to prevent it. In June 1995 Funai's contact team on the Purus caught one of the richest traders of the town of Lábrea with great quantities of copaíba oil and meat and skins from protected forest animals, all illegally taken from an indigenous area that contained an isolated tribe. However, the poacher was released after only one day in prison because of 'political pressure'.

As in the Javari, the loggers brought disease, so that malaria became almost endemic. Measles killed thirty-five of the remote Deni tribe in 1992 alone, and two years later a CIMI nurse reported that this group suffered so terribly from malaria and tuberculosis that it could not farm its forest roças. Some Indians died from cholera that swept down the Amazon from Peru in 1992. There was also leishmaniasis, transmitted by sand flies, and an outbreak of hepatitis among the Apurinã.

The 915 Kulina of the middle Juruá had a reserve of 770,300 hectares (2,970 square miles) interdicted in 1987; but there were delays in demarcating it. So an agreement was signed between Funai, the Acre branch of UNI, and the Kulina, for the tribe to undertake its own demarcation. This was a difficult task, for the boundary trails could be cut only during the dry months when the Indians also had to make their farm clearings. To be valid the perimeter trail had to be 6 metres (20 feet) wide with clearings of 100 by 100 metres (327 by 327 feet) at any angles, so the Indians had to be trained in surveying techniques. Nevertheless, the Kulina worked with enthusiasm, and gradually cut the 580 kilometres (360 miles) of perimeter throughout the 1990s.

Funai's agent among the Kanamari and Kulina in the late 1980s was interested only in his own commercial enterprises, so that it was left to Catholic and Lutheran missionaries to 'care for indigenous rights' and give these Indians 'an understanding of Brazilian society and the Portuguese language, as an instrument for their relations with the national society and state.' With such help, these tribes gradually gained their land rights. By the end of the century, some 1,500 Apuriná had a cluster of small-ish territories near the middle Purus fully registered. A great swathe of forests running east–west between the Purus and Juruá, measuring some 1,840,000 hectares (7,100 square miles) and home to some 1,400 Kanamari, Deni, and Zuruaha, was either demarcated or being registered with help from the G7 and other aid donors. North of this, 400 Katukina of the Biá river near the lower Jutaí had an area of 1,180,000 hectares (4,550 square miles) confirmed.

21. Rondônia: the Last Major Contact

In western Rondônia in 1979 the English film-maker Adrian Cowell met a shattered settler, Chico Prestes, whose two sons had just been attacked in a stream near his cabin. 'The two were lying there stuck with arrows. Shot down in the shallows, with arrows sticking out of them in every direction.' One of these boys died soon after, from arrow and machete wounds; the other, critically injured, recalled how he had looked round from his fishing 'and there behind us, it was black with Indians, 25 to 30 all with bows drawn'. The tribe also abducted a six-year-old called Fábio. His distraught father chased after him in vain, and launched fruitless search expeditions during the ensuing years.

The experienced seringueiro Alfredão told Cowell that the killing of the boys was certainly an act of revenge by the Uru-Eu-Wau-Wau. These were the uncontacted 'black-mouths' who lived near the Wari, on a plateau between the BR-364 road and the Guaporé-Mamoré river. Alfredão guessed that the Indians had tracked back to someone (probably a professional ocelot-skin hunter called Atanasio) who had stayed with Prestes before penetrating their forests and shooting at them. The frontier town of Ariquemes was full of stories of Indian cruelty and cunning, and there was talk of a reprisal raid to 'cleanse' the forest of natives. CIMI reported that 'between 1977 and 1979 all the inhabitants of an Indian village were decimated by a group commanded by the gunman João dos Santos, nicknamed Sapecado ['Red-haired Animal'], and a certain Azulão ['Big Blue'] on the orders of fazendeiros.' But this was another uncorroborated and unpunished massacre.

It was rumoured that the Uru-Eu-Wau-Wau were led by a bald man, who may have been of white origin since Indians do not go bald. The more fanciful military men wondered whether this might be connected with Che Guevara, whose guerrilla band had operated across the Guaporé in Bolivia. So Funai decided that the time had come to make the contact. Apoena Meirelles took a thirty-man expedition in a flotilla of aluminium boats up the Jamari river south from Ariquemes. It was a tough journey with 'much battling against rapids and other adversities'. The team made a camp and airstrip on the Alta Lídia plateau.

In June 1980 Meirelles managed to land a plane on open savannah in the heart of the Uru-Eu-Wau-Wau territory, 300 kilometres (185 miles) south of the state capital, Porto Velho. Adrian Cowell was there, and he described the ancient cliffs, windswept grasses bisected by bands of riverine forest, and sacred caves of this plateau as a place of 'the sort of unexpected beauty which inspires legend'. The expedition started to leave the usual gifts wherever they saw signs of Indian movement. Cowell recalled that 'all the trails on the tableland were clanking with pots, machetes and knives blowing against each other in the mountain wind, calling to the Indians. It was here that the initial attacks, the passing of the first present, the long process of contact and adaptation, would take place.' Apoena Meirelles wondered what effect this would have. 'Massacred by seringueiros, harassed by prospectors, steamrollered by government expeditions, what will the Uru-Eu-Wau-Wau make of people who walk around hanging up presents?'

The attraction effort continued for two years, at this outpost called Comandante Ary on the Alta Lídia plateau. It was led by João 'Baiano' Maia and the sertanista José 'Zébel' Sanatana. An Indian hunting camp was found, of eleven tapiri shelters beneath the canopies of tall trees. At other times the Funai men would follow Indian trails through the forest to sunlit plantations of manioc, sweet potato, fruit trees, and other useful plants, and into villages that were temporarily unoccupied because nearby streams were low in the dry season. It was later learned that the Uru-Eu-Wau-Wau had stopped building great thatched malocas, because these were too vulnerable to attack. Instead they became 'true gypsies', using the guerrilla tactic of constant movement and temporary bivouacs. For many months, the Uru-Eu-Wau-Wau ignored or broke the presents left for them. 'The Indians remained hidden in the thickets, shouting veritable discourses.'

The settlement frontier was never far away, advancing from all directions in a noose around the tribe's homeland. It responded with more killings and woundings of colonists and seringueiros. In October 1980 the state government of Rondônia started to drive a road from Ouro Preto on the BR-364 down towards the Guaporé river, straight into Uru-Eu-Wau-Wau territory. Funai men followed the road for a hundred kilometres (sixty miles) and watched in horror as its yellow bulldozers toppled tall but shallow-rooted forest trees.

Then came the first attack, up at Comandante Ary attraction post. A Suruí called Maoira was bathing in the river near the attraction camp. As he raised his soapy body above the stream bank, he saw a dozen Indians creeping towards him. He ran back, zigzagging between a fusillade of arrows – whose heads were carved in ugly barbs coated with anti-coagulant poison. The leader of the attacking Indians was clearly bald. During the ensuing days there were frequent sightings of Uru-Eu-Wau-Wau, sometimes prowling near the camp at night, or firing arrows and letting out frightening guttural roars at the Suruí. Presents were refused. There were lulls during the next months when the Indians presumably went hunting, interspersed with bouts of aggression. The apprehensive men in the camp were ordered to go about their daily routine, vigilant and obviously armed, to continue to leave presents, but of course never to shoot back.

30 December 1980 was a bright day, and most of the expeditioners were at the airstrip awaiting a plane. Three Uru-Eu-Wau-Wau crawled up and peered into one of the camp's houses. They did not see the young cameraman Vicente Rios; but when he looked out through a crack he was only inches from a naked Indian with drawn bow. Rios crept out and raced for the next hut, in which Adrian Cowell was lying in his hammock; but he slipped and fell into a pool of mud, as three arrows flashed over him and thudded deep into the wooden hut. Cowell appeared at his door, brandishing a revolver, just as the three Uru-Eu-Wau-Wau were drawing their bows to kill the prostrate Rios. Everyone froze. Then two Suruí armed with shotguns came pounding round another hut and the assailants fled, 'leaping with huge kangaroo bounds over the logs that lay between us and the forest'.

The Funai team was changed. Its new leader reasoned that the Uru-Eu-Wau-Wau (who were watching constantly) would expect a revenge attack from anyone at whom they had fired. But their response was different. In January 1981, the Indians suddenly took all the presents suspended on their various trails. And on 10 March came a moment of truth for the Uru-Eu-Wau-Wau. Some of them shouted from the savannah, and Baiano Maia walked towards them, waving presents. The Suruí Ibaroba removed his clothes to show that he was an Indian. The Uru-Eu-Wau-Wau leader advanced, with a machete in one hand and holding up five fingers of the other. Baiano Maia realized that the chief wanted five more bush knives, so he went to fetch them. Maia and Ibaroba walked forward. 'The leader backed away. He was big, and painted in red and black. So the Suruí stopped and I went on. The leader watched me until I stopped with the machetes held out. Then he came forward – alone. He took the first machete from my hand, and then another – without a tremor.' It was all over in five minutes; but it was the end of this people's defiant isolation.

When Apoena Meirelles heard about his team's 'success' he admitted to a pang of remorse because the Indians lost some of their freedom every time they accepted a present.

A group of twenty-five Indians (including six women and three children) reappeared a week after that first contact, and asked for more presents. The leader was remarkably self-assured, but he and his men were constantly on guard against white treachery. A second group came a week later, under the leadership of the bald Indian Djaí – whom the Brazilians always knew as Careca ('Bald'). With his domed bald brow, his greying whiskers, his tanned pink skin, and his dignified demeanour, the naked Careca looked like a European company chairman. It was obvious that he had some white ancestry, and he may have been a seringueiro's child kidnapped many years previously; but he spoke no word of Portuguese. Using a camera hidden in the wall of a hut, Jesco von Puttkamer took a remarkable photograph of Baiano Maia handing a machete to an apprehensive 'Careca' Djaí, who was holding his bow and sheaf of arrows and accompanied by a naked girl.

Funai intensified its efforts, with four attraction posts on the edges of the tribe's territory. The situation continued to be tense. Desperately poor colonists were trying to scratch a living along the new road, and there were attacks on them, with settlers killed by Indian arrows and their meagre huts ransacked. Meanwhile, more Uru-Eu-Wau-Wau appeared at Funai's post to receive presents; and in August 1981 they brought gifts in return – necklaces, arrows, bows, and a club. The attraction was unhurried and uneven. After one misunderstanding, warriors shot three arrows at Baiano Maia while he was brushing his teeth, almost killing him. One arrow pierced his lung. When the nurse Marina pulled the arrow out, blood spurted an arm's length; she stanched the wound, and Maia was airlifted to hospital. In August 1983 fifty Uru-Eu-Wau-Wau stayed for five nights at the camp, but their first invitation to visit their village came much later.

Mauro Leonel has unravelled how the Uru-Eu-Wau-Wau reacted during these tense months. He learned that there had been anxious debate between the tribal leaders before they had accepted contact. The group led by Canindé (whose mother and sister had been kidnapped by the rubber-tapper Alfredão) was opposed to any accommodation with the hated whites. The bald Djaí also disliked the invaders: he complained that 'they respect nothing, not even tapir barriers or fishing places'. But Djaí gradually tired of the constant fighting, and he insisted that the Funai men were different to other civilizados. He had noted that they practised Rondon's instruction 'Die if you must, but never kill' and that they were generous with coveted presents. So Djaí's group started to live at the camp.

Months after that first contact, a lookout saw the approach of Canindé's people. Djaí went out to meet him. The two chiefs stood side by side, holding their bows and arrows, with heads bowed, delivering ritual chants. The bald Djaí was by now dressed in a red T-shirt and sports trousers. Canindé wore a necklace of peccary teeth, a broad girdle of brown nuts, some black genipap paint – and had a revolver bullet in his arm, a relic of his many battles with white invaders. In their chanting, Djaí repeated the virtues of the Funai team, 'The strangers are *catú* [good]'; while Canindé's counterpoint was 'Let me kill. Let me kill.' When this ritual was over, the new arrivals danced with the attraction team and received presents. It was also learned that the kidnapped settler's child, Fábio Prestes, had not survived: the Indians had soon killed him, because he cried too much.

The contact team did not try to impose themselves on the Indians. They never visited a village uninvited. But white men's afflictions *did* spread to uncontacted parts of the tribe. With dreadful inevitability, the Uru-Eu-Wau-Wau started to contract alien diseases. By 1985 it was known that at least eight Indians had died of measles, and most of those who visited the post had serious pneumonia. In the following year, Funai nurses were allowed to visit two of their remote villages, to treat people dying of respiratory disease, malaria, and snake-bite. The tribe continued to defend its territory tenaciously. Its warriors killed settlers, prospectors, loggers, and mining surveyors. When the American author Loren Mc-Intyre was taken in 1987 on an eleven-hour march through the forest to visit Djaí's village, he saw beautiful Indians, naked and unadorned, in a verdant Garden of Eden of tall trees and rushing streams. He witnessed the bald chief and his warriors performing a circular victory dance, re-enacting their killing of a seringueiro. But he also found that this group were starting to visit a tin mine called Bom Futuro, where thousands of prospectors were sluicing the forest floor. At this lawless place Indians received better presents than Funai's – and they learned Portuguese swear words.

By the end of that decade, the three villages with which Funai was in closest contact were reduced to a hundred people – less than a third of their estimated population of 350 a few years earlier. At the end of 1990, the anthropologist Ligia Simonian lamented that the survivors of one group were 'all very enfeebled by malaria, pneumonia, dehydration, and, principally, lack of adequate medical attention and the absence of any policy of preventive medicine.' Only one infant had survived its first year of life. 'Chief Djaí also suffered a sad fate. Twice taken to Porto Velho with pneumonia, twice sent back to his area, he died at the beginning of 1989. It was he who had made contact possible. At first he did this with his own group or clan; then he persuaded the rest of the need to make Funai their ally against invaders of all types, in the permanent state of war in which they lived.' In the later 1980s there were contacts with other groups of Uru-Eu-Wau-Wau, including those of chiefs Manguetá, the deeply suspicious Canindé, and Mondaua; but Funai men tactfully did not go to their villages. By 1988 some 350 Indians had visited the attraction post, out of an estimated total of 1,000 or more.

The other fundamental of Indian survival – land – was protected as erratically as the tribe's health. The territorial question seemed resolved with decrees of 9 July and 21 September 1985 that confirmed the Uru-Eu-Wau-Wau as the occupiers of a reserve that embraced the former Pakaá Nova Indian park, with a total area of 1,832,300 hectares (7,070 square miles). Indian sympathizers made it known that this great expanse had soils too weak to support settlers, even though it was close to the rampant colonization frontier along the now-paved BR-364 highway. The beautiful cliffs at the heart of the reserve were the source of many of Rondônia's rivers, and therefore a watershed of great environmental importance. When there was delay in demarcating the reserve, the World Bank got action by threatening to withhold a tranche of its loan.

There were powerful contrary pressures. Word spread that the reserve was full of tin, gold, diamonds, amethysts, and other minerals and had plenty of valuable hardwood trees. Uru-Eu-Wau-Wau warriors were constantly having to kill or frighten off mining prospectors and loggers. They could not eliminate politicians or civil servants as easily. Romero Jucá, one of Funai's worst presidents, in 1987 signed two fraudulent contracts with timber companies, granting them huge quantities of ipê (*Caesalpinia echinata* Brazil wood, and *Bignonia*), mahogany, angelim (*Hymenolobium*), and other valuable trees. Since it was illegal to sell timber from indigenous lands, Jucá claimed that this was a 'contra deal' whereby the wood was traded for access roads to Funai posts and other constructions; but these works were never built.

The colonization department Incra proceeded with projects that encroached on Uru-Eu-Wau-Wau land without even bothering to consult Funai or obtain 'negative certificates' that an area was free of Indians. Mauro Leonel commented that 'Incra behaved as if it did not belong to the same government as Funai, and vice-versa'. Another family called Prestes was attacked while clearing a plot awarded by Incra. Its deaths caused a temporary halt, but Incra soon resumed awarding concessions on every side of the interdicted reserve. Much of the land north of the reserve was owned by subsidiaries of the Arantes family of São Paulo, whose 'economic group was a sort of hydra in this business world'. Its Burareiro colonization scheme invaded the Uru-Eu-Wau-Wau from the north.

By the mid-1980s there was a strong anti-Indian lobby among politicians of the mushrooming State of Rondônia. The Governor appointed by the New Republic that succeeded two decades of military rule fought for a reduction in Indian lands. There was constant talk of 'redefining the indigenous polygon', of 'liberating' land for the 'natural and spontaneous expansion of the colonization process', and of filling the 'demographic vacuum' of the Uru-Eu-Wau-Wau reserve. Leonel noted that 'of all intrusions, the most fatal to the Indians are always roads because they make possible every sort of invasion, from public works to private initiatives'. First came the paving of the BR-364 artery, opened in September 1984. This led to the immediate and headlong growth of cities like Ariquemes, Ouro Preto, and Jaru, many of which were on the sites of Indian malocas. Lateral and feeder roads were then opened on every side of the indigenous reserve. The road-building crews frequently encountered Indian trails or campsites, proof that they were invading what should have been a protected area. 'As far as the Uru-Eu-Wau-Wau are concerned, it is flagrant how the construction of roads near their lands led to an increase in conflicts. Coincidentally, there was an intensification of "attraction" and "pacification" expeditions – which was particularly disastrous for their health.' The worst roads were the BR-429 that ran southwestwards from the BR-364 to the Guaporé river, skirting the eastern and southern edges of the reserve, and the BR-421 that opened a northern area to loggers and mineral companies.

In 1971 the Bennesbys, one of the wealthiest families of Guajará-Mirim, bought São Tomé, a former rubber seringal on the Cautarinho river, well within the south-western part of Uru-Eu-Wau-Wau territory. It had been the scene of constant conflicts between Indians and seringueiros during the previous fifty years. The Bennesbys had excellent contacts at every political level. One brother, Congressman Moisés, obtained a breakfast meeting with President José Sarney and persuaded him that the Uru-Eu-Wau-Wau Indian area was 'invading' the land he was developing for logging, mineral prospecting, and colonization. In January 1990, just before the end of his term of office, President Sarney signed a decree that annulled the demarcation of the reserve; he then asked Funai to reduce the tribe's land by 200,000 hectares (772 square miles) – the area to its north-east that was thought to contain a huge cassiterite deposit and was closest to the colonization roads, and a southern section rich in rubber trees. Funai obliged, with an inquiry by a self-styled sociologist on its staff that proposed new borders for the reserve. Brazilian and foreign activists had to mount a ferocious campaign to persuade the next President, Fernando Collor, to restore the integrity of the Indian area and the environmental park within it.

The pressure of invasions of the protected area continued unabated. Because the tribe occupied hills and a plateau, power companies built hydroelectric dams on several rivers draining from this watershed. In the early 1990s there were regular expulsions of garimpeiro prospectors. Major operators had also been active in Rondônia since the 1960s. Four of Brazil's largest mining companies, led by Paranapanema (who had desecrated Waimiri Atroari territory with the world's largest open-cast tin mine), extracted half of Brazil's total of the tin-oxide cassiterite from what was once Uru-Eu-Wau-Wau land.

The Uru-Eu-Wau-Wau fought back. Young Indians told Fiona Watson of Survival International about their resistance. One called Purei admitted, 'I have killed three white people – miners. They invaded and we went after them . . . We told them to go off and they went, and we followed them. There were three prospectors in front, and my brother and I shot them with arrows. Two died and we left them there and later went back to collect their bones. We use [anti-coagulant] poison on our arrows so that animals and people bleed a lot.' Purei also told how his brother died of snake bite. The Indians asked a farmer (whose settlement was within their lands) to help evacuate him; when he refused, 'another brother went back and killed four people on the farm, and the dog too, with arrows.' Another, Piaka, said that there were about a hundred garimpeiros within the reserve. 'I thought: what do they want? I decided to kill them. I returned to the maloca and then went back to kill them. I killed two of them. The other miners fled and never returned . . . After I killed the miners, I myself killed a rubber-tapper . . . We don't accept loggers here. They give us nothing – they just take, and take, and take.' The Indians found the back-breaking work of prospectors and loggers incomprehensible; but they knew that life had been better before their arrival – there had been more game to hunt, and people did not die of influenza and malaria. An old widow called Murika recalled the devastation: 'My father was shot by a white man. I had two brothers and five sisters. They were all killed by white people or died from illnesses. My husband was killed by a jaguar . . . Before we knew the whites, it was better. Now all the game is gone.' By the end of the century, the tribe was down to about a hundred people, and the majority of its children were still dying in infancy.

By the mid-1990s logging was rampant in Rondônia. The NGO Aparai calculated that in 1991, 1.5 million cubic metres (53 million cubic feet) of hardwoods (especially mahogany and cerejeira (*Eugenia involucrata*)) were cut in the state; and the quantity accelerated in later years. World demand for these fine woods seemed insatiable, so there were huge profits to be made. Local politicians were involved – and it was suspected that drug money from nearby Bolivia was being laundered through this trade. It was almost impossible to police the remote Uru-Eu-Wau-Wau area. In 1994 an inspection team confiscated one company's eight heavy trucks, two tractors, various chainsaws, guns, and a great quantity of cut timber. It found that, in three months, 'the ecological disaster that these criminals committed against the state of Rondônia . . . totalled some 150,000 cubic metres [5.3 million cubic feet] of fine wood [particularly cerejeira, mahogany, and cedro (*Cedrela meliceae*)].' Also in 1994, Friar Antonio Marchi of CIMI carried out an inspection of the vast reserve, and found loggers and settlers still invading many parts of it.

Another valuable asset being taken from the Uru-Eu-Wau-Wau was the intellectual property right over the anti-coagulant that they use on their arrowheads. The Indians knew that a viscous yellow resin squeezed from the bark of the *tike-úba* tree (*Cariniana domestica*) could be processed into a poison that causes intense haemorrhaging. Animals or people hit by arrows coated in this resin bleed to death. Jesco von Puttkamer sent samples to the German Hoechst company in 1986, and its scientists were 'very excited' by the way the drug prevented blood coagulation and heart palpitations. The American pharmaceuticals Merck and Monsanto sent teams to Brazil to pursue this potential medicine; various botanical gardens did research on it; but the tribe received no reward.

In 1989 Betty Mindlin wrote a survey of the Suruí (Paiter) after twenty years of contact. Demographically, they were recovering from the loss of half their people in the epidemics of the early 1970s: a vigorous birth rate had brought them back to a population of 470. 'The daily life of the Suruí has altered greatly in recent years. Their villages are today scattered amid plots of coffee planted by invading settlers who were expelled in 1981, and they contain ever fewer traditional thatched huts. Their diet is less varied, less rich in game and fish, more similar to that of the settlers using purchased commercial produce.' This change to commercial food brought a problem that confronts almost every tribe: a need for money.

The Suruí had also lost half their lands. However, the various reserves in Rondônia were gradually protected, at least on paper, and demarcated thanks to the efforts of Betty Mindlin, Carmen Junqueira, Mauro Leonel, and other determined anthropologists in the 1980s. The Suruí reserve was joined to the Cinta Larga Aripuanã park and then augmented in a series of contiguous protected areas (for other groups of Cinta Larga, Zoró, and Gavião) that eventually totalled over 3 million hectares (some 11,700 square miles). Mindlin paid tribute to the efforts of the Indians themselves. She told me that 'indigenous resistance was fundamental, for the claims to be met. There were innumerable episodes of armed struggle – with deaths of Indians and invaders – seizure by Indians of vehicles, timber and machinery, delegations and expeditions to Brasília, protests, etc. The Indians learned much in that period: they organized themselves, and ended by knowing how our society functions.' They were trained and encouraged by her and other supporters, who were equally tireless in writing reports, articles, books and polemics, lecturing, lobbying, broadcasting and participating in countless conferences in Brazil and abroad.

Venal Funai officials encouraged the Suruí to 'dilapidate their resources' by selling timber. The President of Funai, Romero Jucá, and his local manager Nilson Moreira were both accused in 1988 of shady deals to admit commercial loggers to indigenous areas in Rondônia and western Mato Grosso. This was one of the more disgraceful episodes in Funai's chequered history. The Procurator-General of Brazil denounced the two for corruption and embezzlement; CEDI published a damning list of timber concessions granted during Jucá's term of office; yet in May 1988 he left the Indian foundation to be Governor of Roraima – where he did no good for the Yanomami – and he was later elected to the Senate. Romero Jucá was a young economist, with a thick black moustache, tousled hair, and an engaging, fast-talking manner. He appeared sympathetic to the Indians, who crowded into Funai's headquarters. But Mércio Gomes felt that Jucá had been deliberately appointed by his friend President Sarney 'with the task of shattering the indigenist movement, diverting the Indians' struggles from collective interests toward personal gains, paralyzing the process of land demarcation ... and finally of weakening public interest in the Indian cause ... He made internal changes in the Indian agency, hired a considerable number of staff who had never seen Indians, and fired several anthropologists and indigenists who condemned his actions and denounced his deals with loggers and gold prospectors.'

Invasions by timber companies, mineral prospectors, and squatters continued to be the great problem for all these Tupi-speaking tribes throughout the 1990s. On 4 March 1991 the Cinta Larga of the Serra Morena reserve had an altercation with a group of timber cutters and ended by killing a family of five. There was much tension when the victims' heads were exposed in the local town, Juína. These same Indians had their rivers seriously polluted by garimpeiros prospecting nearby. The more cunning loggers bribed tribal leaders with presents of televisions, videos, and satellite dishes. In 1993 illegal extraction of mahogany from the Roosevelt Indian Area alone was 25,000 cubic metres (880,000 cubic feet). The police caught a gang flagrantly removing huge quantities of timber from the reserve. But these criminals had suborned the Indians. So fifty Suruí and Cinta Larga invaded the police station of Espigão do Oeste, not to protest at the rape of their forests, but to demand the release of their thirteen logger 'friends'.

The timber men moved on to the Zoró reserve north of there, and the effect was dramatic and generally disastrous. The Zoró had been envious of the trucks and other goods owned by the Suruí and Cinta Larga after they had admitted loggers, so they wanted the same. Young Zoró who worked with the *madeireiros* left their traditional houses for small sheds of plastic, stopped planting roças, and adopted a poor diet of convenience foods. 'There is a tremendous daily traffic of quantities of trucks; and diseases, principally diarrhoea and flu, have become uncontrollable. There is no traditional leadership [in the timber village] . . . The Zoró territory is totally criss-crossed by roads, clearings, and trails opened for the extraction of timber.'

The anthropologist João Dal Poz watched in despair as timber companies sacked the forests of these indigenous peoples, almost with impunity. 'There were no management plans or measures of environmental control. But the loggers never lacked authorizations and permits to transport, sell across state boundaries, and even export boards and logs of mahogany, cerejeira, angelim, ipê and other hardwoods that they had criminally extracted. Since [Funai's notorious permits] in 1987 neglect, connivance, corruption, and extortion have come to dominate local branches of government agencies. Their managers and staff have been suborned to the predatory interests of the timber men. Throughout these years neither Funai, nor [the environment agency] Ibama, nor the revenue authority took any effective action to prevent the corruption of indigenous leaders, environmental damage, nor the plunder of the public patrimony. The results could not be more tragic, in every sense. Alcoholism, drugs, prostitution, malnutrition, and social disruption are undermining the community life and cultural traditions of the indigenous peoples. If urgent steps are not taken, environmental degradation will destroy 3.5 million hectares [13,510 square miles] of Amazon forests.'

With so much money at stake, the timber business became increasingly criminalized. The Cinta Larga used Carlito, the young son of Chief Mário Parakida of Taquaral village, as their principal negotiator in timber deals.

He was a hard bargainer, and of course knew everyone involved in illegal logging. He denounced some of the guilty men to the Public Minister (the official champion of indigenous rights) – although according to Dal Poz all mahogany had gone from indigenous areas, and cerejeira and ipê trees were becoming rare. Carlito's father Parakida was on a communal hunt and came across loggers' chainsaws and a skid tractor. They promptly burned the equipment, provoking fury and death-threats by the loggers. So on the night of 19 December 2001, the twenty-eight-year-old Carlito Kaban Cinta Larga was murdered, shot in the head in a contract killing as he left his pickup truck to enter his people's house in Aripuanã – a remote frontier town far down the Aripuanã river.

Three months later, in the adjacent Roosevelt indigenous territory, César Cinta Larga disappeared from his village. His body was later found floating in the river with one hand amputated. He had apparently been tortured and murdered in connection with the lawless Roosevelt diamond garimpo on the river of that name – the former River of Doubt that Rondon and Teddy Roosevelt had explored some ninety years previously. The Cinta Larga complained that they had lost control of the wildcat prospectors in their land, so Funai briefly closed the Roosevelt garimpo. Beto Ricardo of ISA commented bitterly that the government had yielded to commercial interests when it demarcated indigenous lands in this region during the 1990s. 'It abandoned the Indians to their fate, oppressed by a predatory frontier that has produced a veritable social and environmental disaster during the past thirty years. In this case, the government has failed to guarantee the integrity of demarcated lands. It casts the Indians in the path of crime, from loggers, drug traffickers, and mineral prospectors.' The expelled prospectors were back a few weeks later, after a gunfight that left dead and wounded. The police response surprised everybody. They briefly arrested four Cinta Larga chiefs on charges of murder, favouring illegal prospecting and environmental degradation. These chiefs had tried to negotiate a licence with the (unstoppable) garimpeiros; but then sought their removal when the situation deteriorated. Another Indian was named on the indictment: César Cinta Larga, the man whose murder was being investigated. This criminality came four decades after the nearby 'Massacre of Parallel 11' of the then uncontacted Cinta Larga, the atrocity that helped finish the SPI.

In 1980 the Brazilian government decided to accelerate the development of Rondônia and of Acre beyond it. It launched an ambitious plan called Polonoroeste ('North-Western Pole' or Axis). The first concern was to improve access, by paving the BR-364 to convert it into an all-weather highway so that trucks and buses could pour into Rondônia every day of the year instead of floundering in a mire of pink mud or clouds of dust. The eastern (Mato Grosso) end of the road was also to be straightened with a 400 kilometre (250 mile) 'variant' loop south into the forests of the Guaporé – the homelands of the less-acculturated Nambiquara.

It was hoped that a quarter of the Polonoroeste's cost would be met by a $256 million loan from the World Bank. The Bank engaged experts such as David Price to advise on the Plan's environmental and social impact. But Price's dealings with the Bank's hierarchy and with the sinister managers of Funai (which was then under Nobre da Veiga, the worst President in its history) convinced him that his involvement was a sham, mere window-dressing to 'provide a paper justification for funding a project whose support was a foregone conclusion'. Critical reports were suppressed, and recommendations – that the Indians be given reserves where they actually lived, that those reserves be demarcated and enforced, and that Funai was too corrupt and mismanaged to be trusted to advise on or implement indigenous safeguards – were ignored.

Brazilian and international non-government organizations mounted a concerted campaign, particularly against the 'variant' route of the highway. But it was in vain. In December 1981 the World Bank loan went ahead. Price thought that the Bank hoped to make a profit from the loan; but its experts' estimates of the plan's benefits were arbitrarily inflated – apparently to show that the region could help Brazil's balance of payments and its ability to repay other gigantic foreign debts.

The Bank made a condition that part of its funding be devoted to the welfare and survival of indigenous peoples affected by the regional development. Betty Mindlin was asked in 1982 to monitor this critically important issue, for Rondônia contained many Indian groups, some still uncontacted, and was being inundated by unbridled immigration. Working for her University of São Paulo's institute of economic research, Mindlin assembled a team of fifteen people – lawyers, doctors, and above all anthropologists. Fortunately for Rondônia's indigenous people, these were not aloof academics who continued to take notes as the last Indian expired, but active and committed experts who did not hesitate to penetrate difficult terrain or to champion these victims of the 'economic miracle'. From 1983 onwards Carmen Junqueira, Mauro Leonel, Roberto Gambini, and Betty Mindlin issued a series of brilliant reports on the tribes of central and western Rondônia.

By mid-1984 Mindlin was convinced that the Polonoroeste Programme was doing little for the survival of indigenous people affected by the regional boom. Its one achievement was the demarcation of some

Nambiquara reserves. But there had been no attempt to stop the Juína hydroelectric dam project on the Aripuanã river, to remove prospectors from the Aripuanã indigenous park or squatters from Lourdes reserve, or to demarcate the lands of the recently contacted Salumã and Zoró. She wrote that the newly designated State of Rondônia 'is suffering pressure from both sides of unbridled capitalism: a deluge of those coming in search of lands, and occupation by opportunistic businesses.' She listed sixteen indigenous areas that needed demarcation and twelve from which invaders should be removed.

Also in 1984 José Lutzenberger (a future Secretary of the Environment of Brazil) declared to an American Congressional committee that the Polonoroeste was proving to be an environmental and social disaster. It was a cruel deception for the tens of thousands of migrants evicted from large farms in southern Brazil. 'It transfers them from rich soils in a subtropical climate, which can regenerate relatively quickly, to poor tropical soil where deforestation does permanent damage.' The Plan also led to the felling of forests that had been occupied and sustainably exploited by Indians, rubber-tappers, and caboclo woodsmen. 'The Indians are being pitilessly destroyed culturally, if not physically. And yet there is so much that we could learn from them ... The loss of these cultures is just as irreversible as the loss of a species ... An indigenous culture is the result of thousands of years of living in harmony with the ecosystem.'

Lutzenberger's concerns were echoed in a letter to the President of the World Bank in October 1984 from representatives of over thirty leading environmental and indigenous NGOs from Brazil and many other countries. They castigated the Bank for its criminal failure to predict the environmental and social impacts of Polonoroeste. The Bank's loan had 'so far contributed to uncontrolled migration, accelerated deforestation, conversion of land to unsustainable cattle ranching, land speculation, and increased encroachment on Indian land areas.' The letter also said that, in relation to Indians, the World Bank had made the mistake of trusting Funai to monitor their protection, and had failed to check on Funai's fulfilment of its undertakings. Hardly any reserves had been demarcated, squatters continued to occupy indigenous lands, and in the case of the Lourdes reserve there had been armed confrontations between Indians and settlers. The tension was exacerbated because many ranchers were from the military or had powerful connections, 'making resolution of the situation even more difficult for such an institutionally weak agency as Funai, a division of the pro-development Ministry of the Interior'.

The sustained protests by Brazilian, British, and American organizations did bear some fruit. The World Bank was rattled by angry denunciations that it had financed an environmental disaster. It appointed the German anthropologist Maritta Koch-Weser – who knew Brazil but had never studied its Indians – as its watchdog for indigenous peoples. Koch-Weser was struck by the powerful reports from Betty Mindlin's team. She wrote to the Brazilian government that if it did not take action about demarcations of Indian lands and removal of their invaders, the next tranche of the Bank's loan would be withheld. Nothing happened. So for three months in 1985 the World Bank delayed payment, and this had the desired effect. The paving of the BR-364 was completed at this time, so that settlers and adventurers poured into Rondônia; but at least the lands of its original inhabitants started to be fully protected.

David Price returned to his Nambiquara in south-eastern Rondônia and western Mato Grosso in 1986. He was shattered to find that entire areas, like the Sararé valley, had been deforested. Dead leaves hanging from trees showed that defoliants had been sprayed from the air – and Nambiquara were still using abandoned Tordon canisters as water vessels. Land speculators had even sold cerrado brush country, on which they planted a layer of pasture. 'Unwary buyers found that after the first year nothing would grow, not even grass, and the land became desert.' Price concluded, sadly, that 'Polonoroeste is turning out to be a calamity of enormous proportions. Poor people are flocking to the region . . . They struggle to clear the land, only to find that it will not produce annual crops. They wind up with nothing for all their hard work, and they displace the native population, leaving the land deforested and useless.' Adrian Cowell filmed the appalling and senseless destruction, from which almost nobody gained, in his prize-winning television series 'The Decade of Destruction'. Having watched poor migrants struggle to scratch a living from Rondônia's poor soil, and fail bitterly, Cowell gradually realized that the boom was driven by artificial property investments. 'The speculation frontier seemed like a giant, spinning top, gyrating in ever-wider circles, devouring all the land from Paraná to Rondônia. How good the soil was, what the land grew, were almost irrelevant, so long as it served as collateral for pieces of paper acceptable on the land market [and that] justified a tax discount or government subsidy.'

The predictable diseases struck the Nambiquara. A shaman told Fiona Watson: 'My father said that before the whites [came] we had hardly any illnesses. In 1984 my father died of a lung infection. At the time of [building the 'deviant' road] everyone got flu and measles and everyone died. When I got measles, I went into the forest and slept and slept until it passed over.' He had then returned to his village, when medicine arrived. Under pressure from Brazilian NGOs and the World Bank, Funai had established a mobile health unit to care for the Nambiquara. Marcelo dos Santos said that 'rivers of money' were poured into this health programme, but a lavish clinic in Vilhena did little to help the Indians. It had 'four nurses, a doctor, a medical technician, a cook, a chambermaid, a doorman, a chauffeur, and *two patients!*'

Also from external pressure, the archipelago of small and separated Nambiquara reserves south of the BR-364 was joined together into a narrow band, on the Guaporé flank of the Paresi Plateau of western Mato Grosso. This was in addition to the large but infertile Nambiquara indigenous area, created in 1968 on scrubland north of the road, and a reserve west of Vilhena in Rondônia. These territories were also demarcated – a crucial stage in their legal confirmation – thanks to pressure from the Bank. And the Nambiquara population started to increase again: by 1987 it was almost 850 living in six reserves totalling nearly 1.6 million hectares (6,100 square miles), with other Indians outside the protected areas.

By the 1990s immigration into Rondônia declined, because the poverty of the soil became obvious. Sadly for the Nambiquara, another threat emerged. José Nambiquara told Fiona Watson that 'the whites came in and started to cut down [our forest] with chain saws. In 1986 they started to rob our wood in the indigenous area ... [The asphalted BR-364] passed through our land and the forest is finished ... For me the BR is not good, because it passed through our reserve. It goes right through the Wasusu, where the spirits of our ancestors live in the caves. We never got any compensation for the BR ... These people rob our wood. People in other countries think it's bought, but it is stolen. There is no mahogany left in white areas – there's only mahogany left in indigenous areas.' Marcelo dos Santos and Cristina Alves, who had both worked valiantly for these Indians for many years, finally organized the individualistic and disjointed Nambiquara into a pressure group called Awaru, funded from Germany. The gentle Nambiquara then started to defend their territories. The Negaroté Nambiquara told Watson: 'We always go armed now. We warn them: If you shoot, we will shoot too.'

The Indians still adored hunting, and they were distressed that hungry settlers were shooting their game. Chief Jodo of the Negaroté exclaimed: 'The whites come in and hunt our game too, so now there's nothing left to hunt. Rear pigs and chickens? I want none of that! I want to hunt, to hunt armadillo, paca [spotted cavy rodent] and mutum [curassow or wild turkey]. I eat from the forest. The forest has everything – jacu, jacutinga [game birds], cateté [peccary], cutia and paca [rodents] . . . To look for meat to hunt, we walk all day. We have meat in the forest – tapir, which is good fat meat, deer, monkey, cuatá [*Ateles* spider-monkey], coati [racoon-like honey bear] and pitiú [tortoise]. We eat a lot of monkey – it's delicious! We eat everything.'

Illegal logging is as great a threat in Sararé, the southernmost Nambiquara reserve in Mato Grosso. It is relatively small; it abuts the BR-174, the old road between Cuiabá and Vila Bela (Mato Grosso City); and is near an area that has long been farmed and settled. So Sararé is seriously invaded by loggers and garimpeiros. There was a massive gold rush there in 1996. A local journalist reported five separate garimpos for 8,000 prospectors, with tented towns providing hardware shops, chemists, brothels, and even bingo halls. In November 1996 these miners launched a surprise attack on the Kithaulu Nambiquara, in which eighty Indians of all ages were savagely beaten, robbed, and even tortured; but none of the aggressors was identified or punished. Funai got the police to expel thousands of invaders from the reserve, but some were back within a few months.

After years of delays, pro-Indian lawyers have finally obtained some justice. In 1998 one of the most flagrant and persistent loggers of mahogany and other trees, Sebastião Bronski Afonso, was finally sentenced to three years in jail and a fine. Bronski had many previous convictions, and he was exploiting the Nambiquara as cheap labour for his logging. But the export price of mahogany remains high, so it is unlikely that he will serve his full punishment or that it will deter others. The police operation did not stop tension in Sararé: in May 2000 an Indian was shot dead in a confrontation with loggers. Two years later, another judge sentenced a logger with the exotic name Anilton Antonio Pompermayer to reimburse the Hahaintesu Nambiquara for huge quantities of mahogany and other hardwoods he had stolen fourteen years previously in 1988. Pompermeyer was also made to pay for the cost of reforestation.

The Wari (Pakaá Nova) of western Rondônia have settled down to a peaceful existence as farmers, on seven Funai posts and Sagarana fazenda run by the Catholic diocese. They sell tons of manioc flour in the market in Guajará-Mirim, as well as maize, black beans, and bananas, and they raise chickens and ducks. New Tribes missionaries are still active in most villages, giving primary teaching and dispensing basic health care with help from indigenous monitors. Tuberculosis and malaria are the main disease problems. But with a high birth rate the Wari population is increasing faster than the national average, rising to 1,650 by the mid-1990s and almost 2,000 at the end of the century.

In September 1995 there was great excitement in Brazilian and world media with the discovery of unknown and uncontacted Indians. Over the years there had been many sightings of an indigenous presence and glimpses of Indians by loggers, in the forests leading down towards the Guaporé. In 1990 one isolated group had penetrated the biological reserve of the Guaporé (sixty kilometres (forty miles) south of the south-eastern edge of the Uru-Eu-Wau-Wau area), apparently migrating from homelands that had been heavily invaded and devastated by settlers. These elusive people were remarkable for having seeded roads being cut into the forests with sharp stakes capable of puncturing tyres. And they left behind immensely long bows of pupunha (peach-palm) wood, which measured three metres (ten feet) and took superhuman strength or great dexterity to draw, and which fired even longer arrows.

Deforestation by colonists advanced rapidly towards this region, so that Funai urgently wanted to contact the isolated groups in order to protect them. The first face-to-face contact was made by Funai's blond-bearded young sertanista Marcelo dos Santos. He had spent 'ten long years searching, assembling evidence, mounting hypotheses, and dribbling around obstacles of loggers, land-speculators and ranchers who were advancing upon the forests of south-eastern Rondônia'. Santos's team pored over satellite images, and finally located tiny patches of secondary forest. This led them on another arduous expedition through the humid vegetation, finding and losing Indian tracks, to a small maloca and eventual contact.

The new Indians were a nuclear family of a few adults and children, but with a rich culture – small huts thatched in açaí palm fronds, roças with a range of vegetable crops, household gourds, manioc raspers, very long bows and arrows, even rubber balls for 'head-ball' games, and flutes. The photographer Vincent Carelli filmed these people's beautiful body ornaments: halo-like coronets of straw and macaw feathers on a cotton base, elegant necklaces and pectorals of seeds, shells, peccary teeth, and even scraps of plastic from objects taken from settlers. One man wore shorts that he had acquired from such a raid – which led nearby fazendeiros to claim that the 'isolated' Indians were just a plant by Funai in order to interdict the area. The contacted group proved to be Kanoê-speakers, almost the last survivors of a tribe and language-group that was thought to have been extinct. They told a harrowing tale of a visit by two black and two white men, who had lived in the village for a time, had children by its women, and then suddenly left taking their male children. The group was so disconsolate that it had tried to commit mass suicide by drinking poison. It had also been frightened by hearing chainsaws and trees crashing, seeing the edges of settlers' clearings, and having four of its men killed by gunfire. After some persuasion, these Kanoê led the Funai team to another tiny cluster of Indians, whom they called Akuntsu and who were totally different to them in customs and language. Funai immediately got the area declared indigenous territory.

Matters improved for the Rikbaktsa, who lived on the Juruena and Arinos to the north-east of the Nambiquara and Kanoê. With the profound change in the Catholic Church in the 1970s, missionaries became far gentler about proselytizing. Jesuits of the Anchieta Mission, with Father Antonio Iasi at their head, were the most radical reformers in CIMI. The Utiariti boarding school was closed in 1970. The regimented mission station Barranco Vermelho was decommissioned and its nuns withdrawn in 1978. The new emphasis was on a return to traditional culture. Indians were given greater control of their own affairs and destinies, and in 1985 the Rikbaktsa themselves took charge of marketing the rubber they had collected. Even children who had been educated in Utiariti college returned to their villages and relearned their native language. Instead of congregating the Rikbaktsa into 'model' missions, they were encouraged to continue living in extended nuclear families scattered throughout their forests. This revival of a sustainable way of life led to a healthy growth of population. By the 1970s there were some 520 Rikbaktsa in seven larger villages along the Juruena and thirteen smaller settlements in the interior. But the majority were still outside protected indigenous areas.

A settler called Luis Tavares established a farm called São Marcos at the abandoned mission in the Japuíra, which was now designated as a forest reserve. But the Rikbaktsa continued to fish and hunt in this part of their homeland. Encouraged by the Anchieta Mission, the tribe kept begging Funai to get the area designated as indigenous land. In 1984 they wrote another formal request to the Indian Foundation, but they also started visible occupation of the Japuíra – with farm clearings and their own rubber-tapping trails. A government Working Group went to the area to report on the validity of Indian claims. Then in May 1985 forty exasperated Rikbaktsa occupied the São Marcos fazenda, peacefully removing its eight workers and all Mr Tavares' belongings to a settlement an hour's journey down the Juruena. Meanwhile, Funai had refused a 'negative certificate' (declaring the area to be free of Indians) to a colonization company that wished to sell off and settle the Escondido forests. All seemed to be going well. But the dislocated farmer and the other business interests reacted forcefully through complaints, lawyers, and lobbying. They accused missionaries, Funai, and anthropologists of inciting the Indians. Pressure was brought to bear on Funai from the state Governor of Mato Grosso and from President Sarney; and in June Apoena Meirelles, as Funai's local superintendent, asked the police to remove the Indians 'peacefully'. In July the Working Group reported that the Rikbak-tsa had lived in the area since time immemorial.

The Indians occupying São Marcos found that the overseers they had removed had been very violent, keeping frightened caboclos in slave labour, murdering some and forcing others to flee for their lives into the forests. Rinaldo Arruda watched Rikbaktsa families return amid great joy and excitement – but maintaining constant vigilance. 'They started to clear forest and prepare roças. They built huts, rough at first but to be improved later . . . I saw them all there, that July: families concentrated in that retreat, rebuilding their village.' They carefully tended the farm's orchard, rice crop, and cattle. They prepared new fields and caught plenty of game and fish. 'At night around the fire they were melting jatobá resin to coat arrowheads. Moonlight bathed the scene. There was a cauldron of Brazil-nut and maize porridge, with shredded trumpeter meat. Fish and monkey. Plenty. Stories of battles with seringueiros, of hunting, fishing, roças. There was happiness, jokes and above all much laughter and high spirits . . . Tension from the threats was diminished by contact with their roots.'

Funai's envoy Célio Horst went to Japuíra and seemed to promise the Indians that their claims would soon be satisfied. But Horst was suborned by the fazendeiros. His report to the Mato Grosso authorities was full of wild accusations, that the Rikbaktsa were being incited to destabilize the state government, that Father Balduíno had threatened him with a .44, that he was held captive, and that the Indians plotted to kill him. On 27 July, Célio Horst returned to Japuíra with ten policemen and five gunslingers – including the fazenda's murderous overseer Bráz – but they failed to persuade the Indians to leave São Marcos.

Apoena Meirelles and the President of Funai were unsure what to do; but the state government unleashed 'Operation Juruena'. The Rikbaktsa had acted as extras in a film about the 1963 massacre of the Cinta Larga, and they could scarcely believe it when they were subjected to a similar scenario. 'First came the planes, two of them circling the fazenda. Then they heard the motors of boats descending the river. There was one big one with some thirty soldiers, and two smaller ones full of police. In all there were forty-seven soldiers, armed for a war with rifles, machine guns, bombs, and bayonets, commanded by Lieutenant Altair Magalhães, a specialist in anti-guerrilla jungle combat.' Chiefs Rafael and Arlindo, unarmed, greeted the soldiers when they jumped from the boats. But the Indian leaders were immediately flung to the ground, spreadeagled and tied, with revolvers to their heads and automatics in their backs. Other soldiers poured petrol onto the dry grass and lit a violent brush fire, for this was the end of the dry season. Some Indians fled through the flames, but armed police held thirty of them for eighteen hours in the farmhouse. Father Balduíno happened to arrive in a boat with an Indian family, and was promptly arrested, shackled, and taken downriver through some of the worst rapids on the Juruena – had the boat capsized his chains would have drowned him. He was then moved to Cuiabá, under arrest; but released after three days when there was no case against him. Next day, two planes flew into Japuíra with more soldiers, Célio Horst, and the evicted fazendeiro Tavares. The Rikbaktsa were disarmed and forced to walk back through the forest for forty kilometres (twenty-five miles) to their reserve, with no boat, bows and arrows, hammocks, or utensils. The fazendeiro gave a big party in the nearest town to thank the victors of Operation Juruena, and Horst handed out as souvenirs the 44 bows, 551 arrows, and 15 ancient shotguns he had taken from the Indians.

There was an immediate outcry, from personalities, organizations, and the local and national media. For Brazil had returned to democratic rule and had outgrown histrionic, reactionary manoeuvres like Operation Juruena. A delegation of twelve dignified Rikbaktsa leaders went to Brasília to protest. Funai stopped dithering and wrote to the Governor of Mato Grosso condemning the illegal fazendas, and sympathetic anthropologists made expert reports on the validity of the Indian claims. But back in Japuíra, Luis Tavares strengthened his position. He built a new road to the Juruena opposite his farm, imported 500 more cattle and new sawmills, and hired eighty additional labourers. The dispute was now judicial, with the familiar pendulum swings during the ensuing years. The Rikbaktsa delegation remained in Brasília for four months, maintaining daily pressure that seemed to triumph when in December 1985 President Sarney signed a decree creating the Rikbaktsa Japuíra indigenous area. But Tavares countered with a ruling from a superior tribunal guaranteeing his continued occupation. The Indians were allowed to return in October 1986, but not to the north-western part of the reserve where the farms lay. Survey teams were repeatedly frustrated in attempts to demarcate the reserve, and in 1987 the fazendeiro hired a dubious anthropologist to make a report in his favour. However, the demarcation was completed in September 1988, with two teams of Rikbaktsa guiding the surveyors through their forests. The tribe returned and built villages in its former territory around São Marcos. They were optimistic and delighted to return to the good hunting and fishing of this homeland. The last cattle ranches were finally removed in 1992.

The Escondido area, 150 kilometres (90 miles) downriver to the north, was not so fortunate. Its status remained ill-defined, despite being identified as the home and hunting-ground of Rikbaktsa and Apiaká. The Cotriguaçu colonization company had a title deed to 1.6 million hectares (almost 6,200 square miles) that included these indigenous areas. There was also thought to be gold in those rivers. An Apiaká was killed, probably by prospectors from a mining operation forty-five minutes by fast boat from their reserve. 'This Juruena garimpo contains a population of some 5,000 garimpeiros and 2,000 prostitutes, and is a hotbed of a culture of extreme violence.' The colonization company claimed that it had bought its vast area from the State of Mato Grosso at public auction in 1974. It removed signs defining the indigenous area, created a town, and sold innumerable plots – even in forests that had been defined as Indian in 1985. The company claimed that the Rikbaktsa did not live in the Escondido, but were trying to invade its property. For its part, the tribe pursued a campaign for complete protection of the area and, when this failed to achieve results, in 1992 occupied farms and clearings there. The requisite government-appointed Work Group examined the area in 1992–93, there was an acrimonious meeting between the two sides in Cuiabá, and Funai in 1994 issued a decree outlining an Escondido reserve of almost 170,000 hectares (660 square miles) which was far smaller than the area delimited in 1985. The reserve was fully registered in 1998 and is home to 40 Rikbaktsa, while a further 700 live in the Japuíra and Erikpatsa territories.

22. Struggles for Land: the North-East

There were ugly incidents all along the Atlantic seaboard of eastern and north-eastern Brazil during the final quarter of the twentieth century. The disputes were always over land, and they affected pockets of tribes that had long since been surrounded and almost engulfed by settlement. These Indians are highly acculturated – farming in much the same way as surrounding colonists, loving football, and dressing in the standard trousers, shirts, baseball caps, and dresses of the Brazilian interior. The anthropologist João Pacheco de Oliveira commented that 'Of the twenty-three indigenous peoples of the north-east only one (the Fulniô) possesses its own language. All the rest express themselves only in Portuguese. There is a high incidence of marriages with non-Indians or with Indians of other tribes . . . It is very difficult to find customs peculiar to a group – family patterns, houses, economic or religious practices. On the contrary, they are constantly intermeshed with cultural manifestations typical of the rural population.' The same could be said for other 'eastern' tribes, of southern Bahia and Espírito Santo states.

In the early days of the SPI, three posts in eastern Brazil were manned by Rondon's dedicated officers; but they saw their mission as integration of Indians into national society. The survivors of the eastern tribes seemed well on the way to total assimilation, so that they scarcely needed government tutelage. SPI posts were created in 1921 for Botocudo Krenak in Minas Gerais, in 1924 for the Fulniô in southern Pernambuco, and in 1932 for the Potiguara at the coastal Baía da Traição ('Bay of Treason'). These were the only north-eastern tribes deemed to be sufficiently 'Indian' to merit SPI protection. A radical parish priest, Father Alfredo Dâmaso, helped persuade Rondon to open these posts and, despite the Service's anti-clerical stance, he praised the SPI's efficiency, usefulness, and humanity. Father Dâmaso was the mouthpiece of 'the complaints and cries for help of 500 wretched [Fulniô] . . . defenceless victims of all the villainies of backwoods potentates'. Only one more Indian post was created in the 1930s. That was the era of the *renda indígena*, when the SPI sought to generate income from its charges and their lands: so north-eastern Indians were expected to labour for the upkeep of their posts, and in some areas the SPI derived income by leasing lands to non-Indians. Matters improved during the 'golden age' of the Service under Gama Malcher in the 1950s. For eighteen years until 1960, the 4th Regional Inspectorate, based in Recife, was run by the efficient and sympathetic Raimundo Dantas Carneiro. Eight more posts were opened during that period, so that semi-acculturated groups (such as the Atikum in the Serra da Umã, the Pankararu, Kiriri at Mirandela, Tuxá near Rodelas, and the Truká on an island in the São Francisco) started to have their indigenous roots acknowledged. Leasings were tightened up, with rent-defaulters expelled and attention paid to securing and demarcating the boundaries of reserves.

There was a powerful reaction towards the end of the twentieth century. Almost all these north-eastern tribes are now seeking to rediscover their indigenous heritage. They choose to remain as collective tribal communities rather than disperse into the surrounding society. Pacheco de Oliveira called this process 'ethno-genesis'. It is helped by three factors. One is pressure on land, which forces Indians to mobilize collectively and fight for their rights. Another is encouragement from sympathizers – Funai (and before it the SPI), CIMI, and missionaries, and NGOs with Pacheco de Oliveira himself at their head. The third is self-interest: people want the special status and legal protection of being Indian.

One threatened tribe is the Tupiniquim (meaning 'Neighbouring Tupi') of the Atlantic coastal state of Espírito Santo. These people had been in contact with Europeans since the first arrivals in the sixteenth century. They were awarded a substantial territory in colonial times, and this was confirmed by the Emperor Dom Pedro II when he visited their village Nova Almeida in 1860. This was a region of virgin Atlantic forest, in which indigenous families lived and hunted, scattered among the trees or in single-family villages that gradually merged into larger communities. However, from the 1940s onwards wanton commercial logging destroyed these endemic forests. The Tupiniquim worked for the timber company Cofavi, felling trees and making charcoal. This people successively lost 40,000 hectares (150 square miles) of its patrimony. Squatters arrived, and the forest around the village of Pau Brasil ('Brazil-wood') was turned into common pasture-land.

In 1967 the Aracruz Florestal company bought the disputed land and planted huge quantities of imported eucalyptus trees, for use in a new factory producing cellulose to bleach paper. Eucalyptus plantations destroyed all game and required the eviction of Indians. There were ugly scenes of violence and racial abuse. Eleven villages ceased to exist. The exiled Tupiniquim provided cheap labour for the cellulose operation. In 1979 the Indians themselves sought to demarcate the 8,500 hectares (21,000 acres) remaining to them; but Funai subsequently reduced even this by more than half. One chief complained that 'when Aracruz came to plant its eucalyptus trees here, it took land away from many Tupiniquim. One day we would have a field well stocked with crops, and the next we would wake up to find the whole thing stripped bare by bulldozers.'

The inhabitants of a village near the cellulose factory 'suffered continual harassment and intimidation from the Aracruz guards, who threatened to burn down their houses. The area all around this village is totally devastated, and the air is seriously polluted.' Industrial effluents poisoned the rivers. Then in 1981 the poverty-stricken Tupiniquim were bullied into accepting the loss of most of their land and the impoverishment of the remainder from eucalyptus, all for a derisory compensation. The deal was brokered by the aggressive President of Funai, Colonel Nobre da Veiga, who personally distributed pay-outs of some $150 per family with the words: 'Aracruz and the government have helped you. Now go and work on your land – if there's any agitation you'll go to jail.'

By 1993 the Tupiniquim were reduced to three villages engulfed by endless plantations of eucalyptus. Some of its land is sandy and impoverished and, with hunting ended, there was serious undernourishment. The tribe was still fighting for the return of 13,274 hectares (32,800 acres) lost in the 1980 demarcation. A product of the decades of struggle for land was the emergence of chiefs and community councils – previously the only Tupiniquim leaders had been the masters of their traditional Drum Dance and 'Congo' bands. These chiefs held a press conference, there were meetings of all the state's deputies, intervention by the Federal Chamber's commission on minorities and environment, and help from Funai's anthropologists; but Aracruz Cellulose refused to yield a hectare of its eucalyptus woods. The company finally agreed, in April 1998, to pay an inflation-linked rental for a twenty-year licence to plant eucalyptus trees on Indian land. This helped to finance new initiatives for health, hygiene (septic tanks, lavatories), and education (primary schools and adult education). But by the end of the following year, the Tupiniquim already regretted this agreement. Five hundred of them – men, women and children – protested at the gates of the cellulose factory, claiming that they had 'made a truce with the company at a time when we were suffering great pressure'. One chief vowed to 'resume the struggle for the remainder of the 13,274 hectares'.

Some 1,800 Pataxó Indians now occupy the balmy coast of Porto Seguro in southern Bahia, where the first Portuguese navigators landed in 1500. The Pataxó are the last survivors of a cluster of Jê-speaking peoples who lived on forested rivers that flow into this part of the Atlantic seaboard. They were known collectively as Botocudo ('Lip-disc Wearers'), but most had succumbed and disappeared during four centuries of sporadic immigration and missionary efforts.

Another remnant of this indigenous nation lives some 200 kilometres (120 miles) to the north-west and is known as Pataxó Hã-Hã-Hãe. The SPI in 1926 awarded the Pataxó Hã-Hã-Hãe an inalienable reserve of 36,000 hectares (140 square miles), which was demarcated in 1937 as the Caramuru-Paraguassu Indian post. This was during the fascist-sympathizing Vargas government, and it coincided with a scare that Communist insurgents were active in the area. So the Indians were promptly expelled by the police on the pretext that they were in league with the supposed subversives. The SPI then harmed the Indians in three ways: it agreed with the State of Bahia to reduce the size of the reserve; it allowed farmers to lease much of this land, often for growing cacao (chocolate) trees; and it relocated remnants of other tribes into the truncated and impoverished area. The SPI eventually abandoned its post altogether.

Chief Tururim started the process of recovery from poverty and near-disintegration of the Pataxó Hã-Hã-Hãe. In 1972 he sold a few arrows to buy a bus ticket to the state capital and begged for old clothes and other aid for his desperately poor people. A further blow came in 1976, when the state government forcibly dispersed these remaining Pataxó and sold the land to the fazendeiros who had been farming it. The Pataxó Hã-Hã-Hãe were described in 1979 as 'the most detribalized and wretched of indigenous nations. Expelled from the area they occupied . . . they now perambulate in the southern part of the State [of Bahia]' and many were homeless and destitute, reduced to begging.

The Pataxó Hã-Hã-Hãe are now recovering from the verge of extinction. Families gradually drifted back to their ancestral lands and built peasant houses and subsistence farms, since they were by now assimilated into local Brazilian society. Some intermarried with settlers, and all forgot their language. But the remainder kept a stubborn pride in their Indian status and heritage, and they were determined to recover their territory. The Pataxó Hã-Hã-Hãe's precarious situation was complicated by an invasion of a hundred squatters and by political pressures in the election year 1982. Funai suggested that the tribe surrender almost 30,000 hectares (120 square miles) of the old SPI reserves and settle for 6,500 hectares (25 square miles); but the Indians refused. During the election campaign, part of the tribe was 'temporarily relocated' to sheds on a small fazenda devoid of farmland or drinking water; but others refused to move. These Pataxó were hemmed into a 'concentration camp' and denied access to their lands for traditional 'hunting, fishing, and collecting shellfish and crustaceans in mangroves near their living area'. Inter-tribal tensions ran high and Chief Edísio was killed by another Pataxó. 'After this tragedy, one group . . . of Indians in August 1983 reoccupied a fazenda on another part of the reserve. Surrounded by the police, who were in turn surrounded by farmers on a war footing, without food or support from Funai, the Indians were removed at dawn one Sunday and relocated on Fazenda São Lucas.'

At least the Pataxó Hã-Hã-Hãe were no longer struggling in isolation. The press published pictures of pathetic Indian refugees in inadequate shelters, and Deputy Mário Juruna, his new parliamentary commission for Indians, and the many new pro-Indian organizations swung into action. This tribe's fight for its lands was the big issue for campaigners in 1982–3. CEDI commented that 'the resistance of the Pataxó Hã-Hã-Hãe in southern Bahia and the attempts to expel them from their lands' became 'the highest-profile case during the year in the press, from the coverage obtained and the way in which it really aroused public opinion.' But, despite these efforts, a federal judge decided that the Indians could remain only on the 1,080 hectare (2,670 acre) São Lucas fazenda – a tiny fraction of their land and a place without adequate water.

Two years later in 1985, little had changed. For once, the campaign by supporters failed, because the fazendeiros were firmly entrenched on the disputed land which they had bought from the SPI and farmed for several decades. One Pataxó described the desperate conditions on the farm: 'We have many children on the reserve, living threatened by gunmen hired by the fazendeiros. We do not have good drinking water, for the farmers have guards who stop us crossing their land to seek river water, and we have no food. In short, they are gradually killing us.' There were sixty sick children, suffering from pneumonia, dehydration, and hunger. Delegations of Indians went to Brasília, seeking help from successive presidents of Funai. In November, 140 Pataxó Hã-Hã-Hãe occupied four small farms alongside São Lucas. But they were soon violently ejected by police, who riddled one farmhouse with machine guns, fired tear gas, assaulted Indian women, wounded many men, and almost killed Chief Naílton Munis. There were strong protests, particularly by a team from the local CIMI office; and Apoena Meirelles (now, briefly, President of Funai) vowed to make the restitution of Pataxó lands his department's top priority. Funai bought another small farm for some of the Indians. But the conflict continued, with a dozen Indians and settlers killed during these turbulent years, one Indian lynched, and others imprisoned and beaten by the police when they ventured into a nearby town.

The legal actions to recover the original tribal territory dragged on for over a decade, well into the 1990s. The Pataxó Hã-Hã-Hãe formed their own pressure group. In September 1991 they wrote to President Fernando Collor that they were fed up with broken promises. 'We were given a father without arms or legs – namely Funai. We do not know whether its intention is to help us or kill us gradually ... Funai long ago lost all powers of decision-making, dependent as it is on four ministries and a secretariat.'

Sixteen hundred Indians continued to live precariously on the 1,080-hectare São Lucas fazenda. They were struck by cholera in 1992. In December 1993, 800 Pataxó Hã-Hã-Hãe seized three further farms, all within their original territory – as they had done seven years earlier; but they were again evicted in a night raid by armed police. In desperation, they tried hijacking trucks taking timber from their lands, and they briefly held two senior Funai officials hostage. Appeals to successive Ministers of Justice were in vain. Tactics that had succeeded so well for the Xavante and Kayapó in the interior did not work for acculturated Indians hemmed into reserves on the Atlantic coast. The seemingly insoluble problem had its origins in the defunct SPI's leasing out most of the 36,000 hectare (140 square mile) Paraguassu-Caramuru reserve, which the government of Bahia subsequently sold to the farmers. These entrenched fazendeiros refused to leave; and no one could find the substantial sums needed to buy them out.

There seemed no end to the miseries of the Pataxó Hã-Hã-Hãe. In April 1997 one leader called Galdino attended a meeting about land rights in Funai's offices in Brasília. On his return, he was sleeping at a bus station when five 'middle-class youths' threw alcohol and set fire to him in an act of gratuitous racist savagery. Galdino died in hospital next day. The young killers confessed, but were initially acquitted because it was a 'prank that had gone wrong' and they were 'of good character'. However, the case was so monstrous that the Indians and their friends did not let it drop: there were public petitions and a press campaign; in November 2001 the murderers were each sentenced to fourteen years' imprisonment; but they were rapidly paroled.

The related Pataxó live on the Atlantic coast near the town of Porto

Seguro, south-east of the Pataxó Hã-Hã-Hãe. These southern Pataxó have their own territorial problems. These were exacerbated in the 1970s by a 'false agreement' that Funai made with the national forestry department, whereby most of the tribal territory was designated as the Monte Pascoal national park and Indians were forced to leave.

In April 1999 the chiefs of these 1,600 Pataxó were still protesting that they were reduced to only 8,000 hectares (20,000 acres) of weak and sandy territory. Even this was heavily invaded and none had been demarcated, and most of their community was without health care or education. Funai found funds to evict and resettle 300 squatters from the Santa Cruz part of the reserve. In June, exasperated by the lack of further progress, 200 Indians put on warpaint and, brandishing clubs, threatened 95 families who had for years been occupying another fazenda. Two months later, 300 Pataxó symbolically reoccupied the rolling forests of the Monte Pascoal national park and camped within it. They had documents to prove that it had been Indian land since 1805, so that their move was 'moral and legitimate'. They then hosted a great gathering of 112 indigenous leaders from all parts of the country. These declared that the Pataxó recovery of Monte Pascoal was 'the best possible present for all the Indians of Brazil' – because of the symbolism of Paschal Mount as the place first 'discovered' by Portuguese navigators at Easter 1500. Of course, the act of occupation was only a first step towards legal ownership.

The new millennium started with high tension. Two policemen were killed in November 1999; settlers' school buses were stoned as they crossed land claimed by the Indians; and an anti-Indian police chief replaced a more conciliatory one. The Pataxó Chief Gerson complained in December that 'our people are cooped up there by over 200 police: they are too frightened even to venture into the town.' Then Chief Gerson himself was arrested, while returning from a civil-rights meeting in Salvador, threatened with death in revenge for the dead policemen, and released a week later only after a rally by hundreds of his Indians and a writ of habeas corpus. There was another great assembly of both Pataxó peoples and their sympathizers, in April 2002. Perhaps surprisingly, 'local white communities tend to support the Indians, largely thanks to a campaign instituted by the Catholic Church which is fairly influential in the area'. Nevertheless, fazendeiros whose farms were reoccupied by Pataxó were seeking recovery through the courts, and some resorted to hiring gunmen.

Other tribes in the State of Bahia were reduced to extreme poverty by lack of land. The American anthropologist William Hohenthal found, in

1950–51, that these 'surviving groups have been subjected to acculturative influences for so many generations that, superficially at least, they are culturally indistinct from local neo-Brazilian peoples'. He was amazed that they managed to retain some vestiges of tribal identity. 'They are generally suspicious of the neo-Brazilians, and the commonest accusation is that . . . the "Brancos" seek to rob the Indians of their patrimony, seduce their women, and pervert or destroy their culture.' Twenty years later, Paulo Amorim painted a gloomy picture of poverty-stricken groups whose lands were far too small and impoverished to sustain them either physically or spiritually. Of Funai's protected tribes in Bahia, 'the Fulniô and Pankararu dispose respectively of 12,568 and 8,100 hectares [31,056 and 20,015 acres] for 1,805 and 2,511 inhabitants. As for the other groups, their lands are flagrantly insufficient in relation to their populations: the Xukuru (1,318 Indians) find themselves dispersed in the midst of the regional population with a few individuals possessing private properties of no more than a hectare or half a hectare; the Kiriri and Xokó of Porto Real do Colégio possess 50 hectares [124 acres] for 338 people; the Xukuru-Kariri, 404 Indians, inhabit a 400 hectare [988 acre] reserve; finally the Tuxá on the São Francisco river (357 individuals) use two parcels of land that add up to 240 hectares [593 acres].'

The north-east, the 'bulge' of Brazil into the Atlantic Ocean, has always been a land of extremes. In the early years of Portuguese colonization, this was the economic powerhouse of Brazil because sugar cane grows abundantly in its equatorial climate and sugar was highly prized in Europe. But cutting and milling sugar is labour-intensive, so that the north-east's tribes suffered the full impact of colonial domination and oppression. As Indians succumbed to imported diseases or escaped from slavery, African slaves were imported in considerable numbers. There was heavy fighting in the mid-seventeenth century when the Dutch tried to seize this part of Brazil. More recently, the region has been one of acute social disparity, with a few territorial magnates and a large underclass of desperately poor caboclos – rural peasantry, generally of a racial mix of Indian, black, and white. The surviving Indians have sometimes sided with the peasantry who surround them; at other times the two almost-indistinguishable groups have competed for the sparse available resources. The poverty of north-easterners has been exacerbated by climate. Severe droughts can turn the interior into near-desert, a dust-bowl where leathery cowhands drive their emaciated cattle between water-holes. It was drought that compelled thousands of caboclos from Ceará to seek survival in the Amazon rubber boom; and another severe drought in 1971 inspired the

Programme for National Integration that drove penetration roads into the rainforests.

The Kiriri are a north-eastern tribe struggling to recover lost indigenous identity. They live in Bahia, 225 kilometres (140 miles) north of the state capital, Salvador. Their first defined territory had been a Jesuit mission, demarcated in 1700 as an octagon measuring the then-regulation 'one square league' (12,320 hectares; 30,442 acres). The Jesuits were expelled in 1760, but in the nineteenth century the Emperor Dom Pedro II confirmed this land grant. The Kiriri were drawn into the desperate Canudos revolt of 1896 by backwoodsmen in this northern part of Bahia. The rebels were distressed by the Republic that in 1889 ended the rule of their beloved Emperor and introduced a republic dominated by wealthy landowners. Under a charismatic leader known as Antonio Conselheiro, the Canudos Rebellion became a messianic crusade, a heretical search for a promised land. The Canudos defeated successive punitive expeditions with ferocious bravery, before finally being overwhelmed and destroyed. Their redoubt was razed and most of them, including many Kiriri, were massacred. Shattered Kiriri survivors became subjected to local settlers, abandoned most of their Indian culture, were driven onto barren land, and sought release in alcohol.

In the 1940s the SPI became aware of the Kiriri land problem, but did nothing until a warm-hearted priest, Father Galvão, wrote to urge Marshal Rondon to take action. The dispersed Kiriri were inspired by a leader called Josias, 'a man of good moral formation, honest and deserving of his people's great admiration'. They started to organize themselves and took a census that showed over 800 people in this group. The SPI opened a token post, but it did little more than hand out some tools. The Kiriri were still known as 'drunken and lazy Indians' and in 1957 Darcy Ribeiro concluded that this was 'an extinct linguistic family . . . whose survivors are a highly mestizo group who have forgotten their language and preserve nothing of their culture'.

The tribe's rehabilitation came from an improbable quarter: the Bahai, a sect of Persian origin that preached cultural diversity based on pseudo-science. American Bahai missionaries put a stop to alcoholism and thievery, and persuaded the local authorities to build a school and other buildings – which was more than Funai or the Catholic Church had done.

A Bahai convert called Lázaro Gonzaga was elected chief of these Kiriri in 1972 and, despite the strangeness of his cult, he saw the need to revive indigenous activities – ceremonials and communal work. He led a hundred

Kiriri north to their Tuxá relatives, at Rodelas on the São Francisco. The visit was ostensibly to play football, but in reality it was to relearn the *toré* ritual that had become the defining symbol of Indianness throughout the north-east. Lázaro explained that 'the toré is something Indian, so we are proving to the whites that we do have different customs and are therefore Indians.' Back in the 1930s an enlightened regional head of the SPI had 'instituted the performance of the toré as a basic criterion of recognition of indigenous heritage. It then became an obligatory expression of Indianness throughout the north-east.' The toré is performed on Saturday nights on an open space beside an enclosure containing a sacred *jurema*, a mimosa plant that yields hallucinogenic resin. The ceremony starts with smoke from burning jurema gum relayed to the crowd of celebrants through large conical pipes, and they inhale it throughout a night of serpentine processions, chanting, and dances. Shamans direct the proceedings, which include purification rites and a climax with the appearance of enchanted spirits.

The Kiriri struggle to assert their identity and recover their 'square league' of land lasted for two decades. It started in 1979, with the clearing of a communal farmland, and another milestone was Funai's declaration of the Indian Area in 1981. In November 1982 the Indians occupied Picos, the most important fazenda within their territory and a symbol of settlers' power. The press published pictures of Kiriri men and women starting to clear a field on this fertile ranch. Farmers who had titles to the land threatened to expel the Indians, who claimed more ancient constitutional rights and were trying to continue their territory's demarcation. Armed police had to be called in; but these tended to side with the farmers. In May 1984 the Kiriri were accused of killing and eating over sixty head of cattle; a Funai team found that, although a few animals had been killed, this was because they were destroying Indians' plantations. The confrontation came to a head on a Saturday afternoon in July 1984, with 'a massacre of the Kiriri village by farmers and their employees, armed with guns, revolvers and machetes. They made a surprise attack, allowing no reaction by the Indians. They then beat a retreat, leaving a toll of three dead and some fifty wounded.' One of the murdered men was a beloved leader, José ('Zezito') dos Santos. The atrocity provoked an outcry from Funai, ecclesiastical and non-government organizations. Although the influence of the Bahai faith waned, its disciple Lázaro continued to be a forceful leader, despite opposition by factions of his tribe.

There was another attempt to start demarcation in 1987, and in 1990 the Kiriri reserve was registered in full. But the tension continued throughout the 1990s with violent threats by farmers, blockade of a road by

Indians, invasion of the reserve, and burning of its houses by hundreds of armed squatters, Kiriri delegations to Salvador and Brasília, Indian occupation of the Funai agent's house, and prevention of work on a road that crossed their land. Sheila Brasileiro concluded that 'by such strategies, the Kiriri gradually occupied significant portions of the indigenous area, displacing some of their most powerful enemies – fazendeiros who were well connected in regional circles'. In 1995 Funai removed and compensated 176 bitter residents of the village of Mirandela, and during the next three years they similarly expelled seven more squatter settlements. The Kiriri now hope to consolidate their gains by rebuilding their impoverished economy. 'Their successive repossessions, amply reported in the press and in indigenist circles – state, Church, non-government supporters, Indian assemblies – brought prestige and political visibility to the Kiriri. They were hailed as an example to be emulated by other indigenous peoples of the north-east.'

The Pankararé, who live further north in the State of Bahia near the São Francisco river, had since the seventeenth century suffered the familiar loss of territory and oppression. In the nineteenth century, they were evicted from lands on which the Jesuits had settled them. They took refuge on a stretch of fertile land deeper in the interior, but were then threatened on it. In 1957 Darcy Ribeiro described them as mestizos who had completely lost their language and any trace of their original culture. Pressure on this tribe intensified during the 1970s. The problem was exacerbated because Indians and surrounding peasantry are 'almost indistinguishable genetically, all having typical characteristics of backwoodsmen. However, roughly a quarter of this [district's] population is some 1,200 Pankararé who preserve and practice Indian traditions. Because of this they suffer systematic persecution from the majority.' People of Indian descent tried to revive their ethnicity, in order to obtain the slight privileges and protection that went with indigenous status; and this was resented by their equally poor non-Indian neighbours. The Pankararé tried building a ritual house, but this was destroyed and they were prohibited from reviving their traditional ceremonies. There was an attempt to tax them as non-Indians. They sought to assert their culture by inviting the related Pankararu to teach them the toré dance, despite attempts by armed police to stop them.

The Pankararé champion and Paramount Chief was Ângelo Pereira Xavier. With the help of the anthropologist Pedro Agostinho and the local office of Funai, Chief Ângelo signed what the press called 'a form of non-aggression pact' with local civic and military authorities. But surrounding farmers and land-speculators were jealous and angry. On 26 December 1979 the Pankararé chief was ambushed and killed by the shotgun of a hired gunman. Although Chief Ângelo's son gave precise testimony of the murder and the press openly named the assassin, he was never brought to justice. In 1984, exasperated by Funai's delays in demarcating their reserve, the Pankararé themselves undertook this. Meanwhile, Quitéria, the new Chief of the 4,500 Pankararu, made a desperate appeal to Funai to help his wretched people 'before they all die of hunger' from drought and malnutrition bred of poverty. One group of Pankararu migrated south to eke out a livelihood in the Real Parque slum of the city of São Paulo.

Other tribes suffered violence as they tried to assert ancient land claims and to revive their precarious Indian identities. The Funai agent with the Atikum, a numerous but impoverished people living in the dusty scrublands of the Pernambuco interior, was too diligent in opposing gangs stealing timber from his tribe's unregistered reserve. In May 1984 the Funai officer and his daughter were murdered, by gunshot and machete blows; and later that year the main Indian witness of the crime was ambushed and shot dead.

Some 4,000 Atikum live in sixteen villages, on 10,000 hectares (24,700 acres) of the bone-dry Umã Hills. They are descendants of roaming bands of Indians who were hunted down in early colonial times, and then found refuge in a Jesuit mission around a water-hole in the Pernambuco badlands. These people were uncharacteristically welcoming to fugitive blacks seeking refuge from slavery, and there was much intermarriage so that they became known as 'the blacks of the Umã Hills'. Their campaign for 'ethno-genesis' started in 1946 when they asked for SPI protection. The SPI Inspector Tubal Vianna reported that 'although intermingled with civilizados, [the Atikum] retain customs and religious festivals with all the rituals of their ancestors. They are orderly, affable, hard-working and not corrupted by alcohol.' In a recent study of Atikum renaissance, Rodrigo Grünewald admitted that 'they were in fact a peasant population who were almost identical to the regional inhabitants, for their social and economic organization, and their cultural values were almost the same. However, the caboclos of the [Umã] Hills retained a memory of being descended from "wild" Indians.' Grünewald then showed how 'this population achieved recognition as an indigenous group, despite being blacks in appearance, referring to themselves as caboclos [rather than Indians], and being identified by others as caboclos or blacks'. The SPI inspector wanted to know whether they practised the toré, so they asked the Tuxá for help in relearning this defining ritual. This led in 1949 to an SPI post and reserve. Since then, the Atikum have regained pride in their Indian ancestry, even if it was done initially to gain protection by the SPI/Funai – there has never been a government agency to protect blacks. Indigenous status has been crucial in defending the reserve against claims and inroads by surrounding farmers.

The troubles of the Atikum are now compounded because this remote area is perfect for growing marijuana. Some of the farmers trying to invade their land were therefore violent drug-traffickers. The Atikum chief Abdon Leonardo dared to alert the police. As a result, in December 1990 Chief Abdon and his brother were murdered by shotgun fire while driving in a Funai pickup truck. The press named the Cirilo brothers, sons of a local farmer, as the assassins; but, as always, no one was convicted of the crime. The next chief decided to try to coexist with the drug-growers who occupied parts of the reserve. But he complained of chronic neglect by Funai. Its vehicle, which should be used in emergencies, was broken. 'Our farming is also insufficient, because tools are old and seven kilos of promised seeds never arrived. The post's medical dispensary is known as "ornamental" because its cupboards and shelves are empty. The indigenous schools have ceased for lack of teaching materials and resources. Children suffer from worms and constant diarrhoea.' No agricultural adviser had visited for five years. The new Chief of the Atikum predicted that 'if it rains we will have a crop; but if not we face certain starvation.'

At the mouth of the São Francisco river, some 200 Xokó-Kiriri had always lived on the island of São Pedro and the Caiçara ('Palisade') on the mainland of the State of Sergipe. Over the centuries, this tribe had lost most of its traditions, language, and social customs. It was difficult to distinguish the Xokó from surrounding caboclos in their farming, clothing, or housing, but the tribe clung to its communal identity; and in the late 1980s Funai started to recognize such groups as legitimate Indians entitled to protection under the Brazilian Constitution.

The Xokó's conflict was with the powerful Brito family, which claimed ownership of these lands. Starving and landless, the Indians in 1978 reoccupied São Pedro island, but found that its buildings had been ruined. The Britos hired gunmen to evict them. The Xokó had a determined chief, José Apolônio, who wrote with pride that 'We remained firm in our struggle.' The government of Sergipe awarded the island to the Indians, indemnifying the Britos for its loss. But the Britos' cattle continued to enter native lands and destroy their farming. José Apolônio admitted that 'we had a little snake that we had been rearing with much affection, and we decided to release it to kill the whites' cattle that were destroying our roças. The [result] was nothing but dead cattle.' The Britos sued for compensation for their animals killed by snake bite. In June 1984 an agreement was signed, whereby the Island of São Pedro was formally acquired by Funai and given to the Xokó. But the Indians still wanted to recover 'our beloved Caiçara', which was by now controlled by one Jorge Pacheco 'who has a revolver, a rifle and other guns to shoot at us Xokó'. In 1985 this Pacheco threatened that if the Xokó tried to reoccupy the Caiçara he had bought two machine guns with which to mow them down. The tribe enlisted the help of Funai's local agent, who in turn alerted the police. Two years later, some 300 Xokó men, armed with bows and arrows and shotguns, made a dawn raid to occupy the Caiçara ranches. Their leader declared that they would leave only as dead men, because the lands belonged to their ancestors. The farmers' gunmen in fact offered no resistance; but they summoned armed police, who violently expelled the angry Indians on the night of 1 September 1987.

In the new climate of Brazilian politics, the Xokó were supported by other tribes (Kiriri and Pataxó), by the local bishop, by Funai's legal department, and of course by their regional NGOs – the Xocó leader Apolônio was the active head of the north-east branch of UNI (Union of Indigenous Nations). Brazilian law triumphed. A federal procurator removed the case from a local judge who was considered too biased in favour of the fazendeiros, and by March 1988 the Minister of Justice found in favour of the Xokó and authorized Funai to demarcate Caiçara for them. The Xokó acted with political savvy: they democratically elected a succession of chiefs who vigorously pressed their case. In April 1989 forty-seven of them invaded Funai's local offices and refused to leave until the farmers still occupying the Caiçara were expelled – but with compensation for them confirmed. In December 1991 President Fernando Collor signed a decree that awarded both the Island of São Pedro and the nearby Caiçara to the tribe. But the tension continued, with shoot-outs between farmers and Indians. It was not until May 1993 that the Brito and Pacheco fazendeiros were finally compensated and left, and the Xokó reoccupied their beloved Caiçara. It was a great victory, after fifteen years of 'unequal struggle, [in which] we Xokó people learned some lessons – lessons that have helped our community to grow and develop ourselves'. The victors celebrated by holding a big party for all their indigenous and non-Indian supporters. They unanimously elected Apolônio Xokó as their chief. He started campaigns of literacy and education, and secured loans to improve farming and buy breeding cattle.

*

Far up the São Francisco river, the remnant of the Tuxá tribe underwent a slightly different ordeal. This tribe had almost merged with the peasant community of the sleepy town of Rodelas during the nineteenth century. But when Rodelas was drowned by the Itaparica hydroelectric dam in the 1970s, the town and its Indians were relocated nearby. Part of the Tuxá has migrated to the west and is trying to survive by traditional farming, but this is a struggle in the dry interior of northern Bahia. In 1993 eighty-five Tuxá occupied the head office of the electricity company in the state capital Salvador, in a desperate bid to obtain long-promised irrigation pumps. Nothing happened, so the Tuxá tried another occupation in 1997; then legal action against both Funai and the electricity company; and in 1999 the Federal Public Ministry (which has a duty to support Indians) launched another legal action for land to be purchased to resettle 150 Tuxá families near their flooded homelands.

Over 4,500 Xukuru live in seventeen villages in the Ororubá Hills of the dry interior of Pernambuco. Heavily acculturated, the Xukuru subsist as poor caboclo peasant-farmers, and they have forgotten their native language. But these people passionately wish to retain their Indianness, to dance their toré ritual with shamans wearing conical straw hoods called *shenunpre*. Some white observers invited to watch a toré were struck by the fervour and conviction with which it was performed. 'The Indians dance and sing with their entire bodies, all their souls and every sense.'

Until the late 1980s, only a handful of Xukuru had even a scrap of land. 'Most have for decades practised subsistence farming, paying rent to fazendeiros for land of which they themselves were the traditional owners.' Despite its aridity, Xukuru territory was threatened by a large farming–livestock ranch backed by the regional development agency. In February 1989 six Xukuru chiefs wrote a moving letter to Funai: 'Our community wants the authorities to take steps to disarm the fazendeiros, who say that they are prepared to confront us. We do not wish to take land from anyone, but we want Funai to demarcate our area, which is the oldest in Pernambuco but [legally] the most ill-defined. We are frightened. We no longer feel safe to walk alone but are obliged to go in groups, even for recreation . . . We beg the authorities to care for us Indians, because we have no land for planting. We are true men only when we have broad beans, manioc beiju, and maize to eat. We are dying of hunger, and demand action from the authorities.' Funai did finally identify a 26,980 hectare (104 square mile) Xukuru reserve in March 1989, and it was demarcated in 1991. But almost all of it had been occupied for decades by non-Indians, and nothing was done to evict or resettle them.

The main author of the 1989 letter was Chief Francisco de Assis, known as Chicão ('Big Frank'), and he emerged as the forceful leader of his people. Chief Chicão was a controversial figure: various Indians complained that he intimidated and even tortured them to join his band of heavily armed henchmen. The chief clashed with Funai over the years, but was backed by radical elements in CIMI.

Xukuru leaders complained bitterly that the entire reserve was parcelled up among 960 squatters, thirty-one of whom were large fazendeiros and the rest small farmers. The Indians effectively occupied only 4,300 hectares (10,630 acres) – less than a sixth of their reserve – on which they grew their own food, and bananas, guavas, and tomatoes for sale. So in November 1990 the Xukuru resorted to direct action, by occupying a woodland that was sacred to them. Attempts at mediation, between the Indians and farmers who had long been settled in their land, failed.

Exasperated by Funai's delays, Chicão's band determined to start taking over farms. At dawn on 22 March 1992, the Chief led 500 Xukuru 'bearing bows and arrows and agricultural tools as a means of defence' to occupy the largest invading fazenda. This 1,200 hectare (2,970 acre) farm belonged to a tough local politician, but it lay within the delimited indigenous area. In September of that year José Everaldo, the son of the Xukuru shaman, was shot dead by a shotgun and revolver bullets as he crossed the farm of one Egivaldo Farias. The police did absolutely nothing, doubtless because the Chief of Police of nearby Pesqueira had land in the reserve. Egivaldo fled, and Indians found his farmhouse full of incriminating evidence, including spent cartridges and a hit-list of Indians; so the farm was burned. Then in April 1995 a young lawyer called Geraldo Rolim, who regularly defended Indians, was ambushed and shot by four men. Angry settlers obstructed and shot at the car trying to take Rolim to hospital, and he died before receiving treatment. Despite this second murder, the Xukuru continued to reoccupy and regain successive fazendas. And, an industrious people, they added coffee and bee-keeping to their range of farming.

Chief Chicão pursued the struggle to clear his tribe's demarcated land, by political pressure, agitation, and direct confrontation. He was elected President of the Association of Indigenous Peoples of the North-East; and he received death threats. In 1997 the Xukuru reserve was about to be legally registered, but this was stopped by Decree 1,775. This legislation invited claimants to contest recent indigenous areas. It was the brainchild of the Minister of Justice, Nelson Jobim, but may have been engineered by Cardoso's Vice-President Marco Maciel whose relatives were said to have interests in the Xukuru area. Under this Decree, 271 claims were launched within the reserve – more than against any other tribe in Brazil. The Xukuru indigenous area was withdrawn at the last minute from a group of reserves about to registered by Presidential signature. There were accusations and counter-accusations between Indians and local politicians (many of whom were farmers claiming land) and the air was thick with the menace of violence.

On 20 May 1998 the dynamic Chief Chicão was murdered, by four shots as he emerged from his house. It was an assassination similar to that of Chico Mendes, at the other end of Brazil a decade earlier. The press named a man with a long criminal record called Jurandir Gomes as the killer but – yet again – the police felt that they had 'insufficient evidence' to convict him. Thousands of Indians from every north-eastern tribe attended the Chief's funeral, at which a Catholic choir was asked to yield to shamanic chanting so that Chicão could be buried as a true Indian. Chief Chicão was hailed 'as an example of courage and struggle in defence of the indigenous peoples of [Brazil's] East and north-east', and a prize was created in his name. The century ended with the Xukuru still fighting for their land. Their new leaders, Chicão's widow and sons, had to ask for police protection against continued threats.

Another group of Xukuru, known as Xukuru Kariri, live in Alagoas some 130 kilometres south of their compatriots in Pernambuco. This group of some 460 people was also dominated by a forceful and controversial chief, Manoel Celestino da Silva. Partly because of him, the tribe was split by internal dissension that led to a wave of crimes and killings in the early 1990s. Chief Celestino, in turn, complained of an influx of missionaries: 'We are losing our cultural identity to the Catholic Church, the Candomblé [a cult of African origin], the Universal Church and the [Adventist] Assembly of God. The worst is that none of these religions preaches unity among our brothers, or still less defends the preservation of our cultural values.' In 1988 Funai directives registered two Xukuru Kariri reserves totalling 13,020 hectares (32,172 acres) – a return to the 'square league' of Jesuit missions in colonial times – and the required expert working-group was established to substantiate the claim of 'immemorial occupation'. There was the usual ugly cycle: judicial findings (in favour of the Indians in August 1992), police invasions of Indian homes (January 1994), protests by farmers and squatters facing eviction, and death threats against Indians and CIMI activists. In September 1994 Chief Celestino led 350 of his people to occupy two fazendas and expelled their farmers. He justified this move because the farmers had been felling forests near the sources of rivers, which seemed to cause drought. Despite this, Celestino was removed as chief because he was thought to be too close to other fazendeiros in the reserve. In November he was visiting a pro-farmer lawyer in the nearby town, when his rival Chief Luzanel Ricardo came to seize him, and in the melee Luzanel was shot dead by revolvers of Celestino's nephews. The land disputes and internal feuds raged in the final years of the twentieth century. When Celestino's uncle, a venerable shaman, was buried in 1998, there was a shoot-out between the former Chief and his rival gang at the graveside.

Further north, the Potiguara of the coast of Paraíba State waged a dispute with a powerful company, in a campaign similar to that of the Tupiniquim against Aracruz. The Potiguara, who had fought great battles against the Portuguese in the sixteenth century, now struggled to defend the 57,000 hectare (220 square mile) Monte-Mor reserve, which the Emperor Dom Pedro had granted them in 1868. This land is mostly dusty scrub. But, unfortunately for the Indians, it abuts on the Atlantic coast at the evocatively named Baía da Traição (Bay of Treason) and its beautiful beaches have considerable tourism potential.

Inspired by the new indigenist assemblies, the Indians themselves spent eleven months in 1981–82 demarcating their land, often discovering old imperial boundary markers. They decided to surrender lands that were heavily occupied by settlers, and in fact demarcated only 34,320 hectares (132 square miles) – two-thirds of the original donation. However, when they went to Brasília in 1982 to get this confirmed, Funai had to bow to local pressures, not least from the town of Baía da Traição within the reserve area, and therefore reduced this to 20,000 hectares (77 square miles). A national election was imminent and Mário Andreazza, the Minister of the Interior (whose department then controlled Funai), had his electoral redoubt in the area. So the liberal President of Funai, Colonel Paulo Moreira Leal, was sacked and replaced by an economist from the Ministry, Otávio Ferreira Lima, and he broke off negotiations with the Potiguara. In 1983 Chief Severino Fernandes was imprisoned for six months because his people had toppled an electricity line being erected on their lands; and his aide Tiuré was then beaten by the police, framed for possession of a marijuana cigarette, and imprisoned as an agitator. In December 1983 a presidential decree confirmed the truncated Potiguara reserve of some 20,000 hectares for 800 families; but 1,000 Indians who lived in the additional 14,000 hectares also claimed by the tribe vowed to continue the struggle.

The Potiguara came up against the Rio Tinto textile company, belonging to the Lundgren family who owned one of Brazil's largest chain-store groups. This wealthy conglomerate wanted to plant sugar cane on Potiguara land, to make *álcool* petroleum substitute (which was subsidized by the government as the answer to imported oil). The tribe was split. A small faction followed a false chief who ceded a large area to Rio Tinto. The local anthropologist Frans Moonen wrote that 'the majority are being turned into cheap labourers working for the cane planters. The Potiguara reserve has become an immense sugar cane plantation, in which space for traditional farming is starting to be scarce.' Forests and mangroves had been destroyed. Moonen felt that the tribe's only hope lay in political cohesion, the removal of Funai-appointed chiefs who had sold out to the cane-growers, and the creation of a militant Potiguara Council. The struggle continued until the end of the century. In 1995 the 6,200 people in sixteen Potiguara villages started an 'uprising' to expel the cane-growers and the Lundgren interests. However, for many Indians the back-breaking labour in cane fields, often amid the pollution of seasonal fires or toxic herbicides, is preferable to the poverty of unemployment. The tribe's cause was helped by the election in 1995 of the Potiguara Nanci Cassiano Soares as mayor of the town of Baía da Traição – Brazil's first elected Indian mayoress – and she was succeeded in 1998 by another Potiguara mayor. But the millennium ended with exasperated Indians making their own demarcation, and a number of claims were launched against them under Decree 1,775.

Far to the north-west, another tribal remnant of some 2,250 Tremembé have two reserves on the coast of Ceará. Their original language is unknown so that present-day Tremembé speak only Portuguese, and their ethnic roots are tenuous. Although there were plenty of Indians in Ceará in colonial times, in recent years this state was considered by anthropologists and Funai to be devoid of indigenous peoples. This changed in the late 1980s, when the archdiocese of the state capital Fortaleza sent teams to discover Indians. They found many poor people intermingled with regional settlers, who were aware of being Indian and retained some customs, including their own *torém* dance (not to be confused with the toré ceremony of tribes in Pernambuco and Bahia). Carlos Guilherme do Valle described the evolution of this people's subsequent ethnic renaissance. 'The political figure of a chief was a discovery of the 1980s. Apart from the torém dance, the Tremembé had few other tactics of social or political mobilization. There were individual protests against occupation of the land, but these were isolated attitudes.' The majority of this remnant did not perform the dance nor assert their Indian descent, so that there were near-violent decisions about who belonged to which community. The minority of Tremembé who practised the torém and felt themselves to be Indian had to be circumspect, for fear of antagonizing their regional and tribal neighbours. The tensions are familiar ones: conflicting claims to land, and an attempt by Indians to assert their ethnicity in order to enjoy Funai's protection.

The national press published powerful articles about the extreme misery of Ceará's last Indians, eking out an existence in shacks on river sandbanks. Catholic missionaries then started to stimulate Tremembé Indianness, encouraging dances and the manufacture of Indian-style artefacts. Funai helped later, and there were moves to link three separate Tremembé enclaves under a single chief. It was a subtle process. At first sight the Tremembé are identical to other local people, in language, dress, and way of life. 'Their ethnicity depends on a conjunction of diacritic signs and traits, cultural elements, social attitudes, insignia, ethnic symbols and types of discourse – all of which condense and can be perpetuated.' No one of these is sufficient to define ethnicity; but combined, they do. Perhaps the main criterion is the way that family units live, occupy land, farm, and sometimes combine in communal labour. The tribe's campaign is helped by the creation of a Tremembé Council known as Cita; and this is represented at an Indigenous Assembly of tribes of Ceará that has met annually since 1994. The fifty delegates at one Assembly sent a letter to Funai saying: 'We are Indians, but we are not accredited nor recognized as such. If we are not recognized, our land cannot be free and demarcated.'

Tremembé land disputes are now being fought in the courts. Funai in 1993 organized an anthropological inquiry that found that the tribe had occupied its land since time immemorial, so this was defined as an indigenous area of 4,900 hectares (12,110 acres). There was a setback in September 1996 when a judge ruled that their claim and the Funai report were inadequate. The Indians issued an impassioned protest: 'How can the lady judge say that this land is not traditionally occupied by us, the Tremembé Indians? We have never ceased to live here, and if some families left, they did so only from subjection, because they were expelled and intimidated and could not endure the suffering.' They recalled that their parents and ancestors had always told them that the land was theirs. The large Ducoco agricultural company claimed the area and started selling it in lots; poor squatters moved in; and there was ecological destruction of natural resources. The Public Ministry in 1997 contested the judge's ruling; and in March 1999 a judicial tribunal overturned the adverse decision and permitted the demarcation of Tremembé land to proceed – subject to yet another report proving their immemorial occupation.

*

In the 1970s the acculturated and law-abiding Guajajara in Maranhão were in trouble again. With a population of 540, their village of Canabrava was large for a Tupi-speaking tribe in that part of Brazil. So there was tension between those in Canabrava and settlers at the revived Franciscan mission of Alto Alegre – the place that their grandfathers had destroyed at the beginning of the century and which the Italian Capuchins had later reoccupied. Some Guajajara wanted to recover their well-watered lands at Alto Alegre and the nearby colony of São Pedro dos Cacetes.

The tribe's difficulties were exacerbated in 1975 by a quarrel between Funai's regional chief, Colonel Armando Perfetti, who sided with the friars and settlers, and Funai's local manager, Porfírio Carvalho, who demanded the withdrawal of all colonists from what he insisted was Indian land. When the Guajajara tried to enforce this expulsion and destroyed rice crops planted on their land, their chief of the post of Canabrava was murdered by squatters, in September 1976. No one was convicted of this killing. Instead in 1977 the police visited the area, looking for illegal marijuana plantations, and tortured two Guajajara called Celestino Lopes and Djalma. CIMI devoted an entire issue of its Bulletin to these tortures and an accusation that it was actually Funai's Colonel Perfetti who was trafficking in marijuana.

Funai went ahead and demarcated Canabrava, with an area of 131,868 hectares (509 square miles) – but with the old convent and the colony of São Pedro in its midst. A Franciscan team in 1979 reported that 'in our view there is no true conflict between [the Guajajara] and local populations. However, there is an attempt to incite such a dispute, which comes from above and is perhaps being nourished by political and business interests.' A detachment of police was sent to the area to keep the peace between Indians and settlers. But it was now the farmers and squatters who complained of violent harassment. The legal wrangles between Franciscans and Funai grew increasingly acrimonious. Then, in March 1980, a quarrel between some Guajajara and farmers led to the death of one of the latter. The angry fazendeiros returned with a police escort. Two elderly Indians, Mateus and Moacir, were led off to Fazenda Xopé and 'a session of beating ensued. The two Indians were killed by machete blows, shots and kicks. Their bodies were then dragged to a river where they were later found.' Despite this atrocity, a few Indian leaders did not give up. They pressed their case with politicians, many of whom sided with the vote-bearing settlers; but surprisingly the Guajajara gained public support. They cut power lines, which led to dramatic blackouts; they kidnapped bus passengers traversing their land; and they even briefly held policemen who entered their village to search for marijuana. So in 1981, the year after the murders, the Guajajara 'won a victory that they had been seeking for over a century: the settlement of Alto Alegre ... embedded in the midst of their 130,000 hectare reserve, was [to be] abandoned by the 183 families who were brought there eighty-six years ago by Capuchin missionaries.' This apparent success resulted from a decision by a federal judge, who ordered that the expelled farmers be compensated by Funai. But the settlers refused to leave.

So the dispute continued. In 1985 the State of Maranhão made São Pedro dos Cacetes a *município*, in clear violation of the federal Constitution which forbade this within an indigenous area; the Indians appealed; and in March 1991 they won legal cancellation of the state's action. Violence resumed, with attacks, tortures, and even murders of Indians near São Pedro. The federal authorities reacted with a (leisurely) inquiry, the formal registration of Funai's 1977 demarcation, closure of a new electricity supply to the inhabitants of São Pedro, and an order that the State of Maranhão must evict them.

In 1992 the settlers seized seven Indians as hostages until they obtained a better judgement. In May of that year some police entered Sabonete aldeia on the pretext of searching for marijuana; they abused Guajajara women and children, and were disarmed and beaten by Indian men. The murder of the son of a chief of Canabrava by gunmen led to further escalation. In October the exasperated and angry Guajajara blocked the BR-226 highway which crossed their reserve and took several hundred hostages. These prisoners were released on 10 November after the various authorities signed an agreement promising to transfer the town of São Pedro out of the reserve. The German anthropologist Peter Schröder commented that 'it is disturbing to note that a threat of violence was the immediate cause for the Guajajara obtaining this victory, after so many past attempts to resolve the conflict through negotiations and peaceful protests.' It took many months to find other land for São Pedro's 2,400 inhabitants and to release their compensation funds. The settlers were finally evicted for ever in 1995. São Pedro de Cacetes was a humble place, just a line of single-storey houses on either side of a broad dirt road, but it was the largest settlement ever removed from an indigenous area in Brazil. When the bitter inhabitants left they demolished everything, using trucks with steel cables to pull down the walls and roofs of their school, church, and houses, poisoned an artesian well, and tried to topple the water tower. But Funai's indigenist Porfírio Carvalho, who had helped the Guajajara in every move of their long struggle, commented: 'What matters is that the Indians have got their lands back'.

Meanwhile, other Guajajara at Araribóia were under pressure from timber companies to grant licences to take trees from their reserve. The well-educated Guajajara made what they considered a robust agreement and obtained substantial income. When Funai tried to intervene in these dubious logging deals, the exasperated tribe in 1987 took some of the agency's staff hostage until they allowed trading with outsiders to continue. There were material benefits for the village, and some leaders could even afford to buy houses in nearby towns. But, inevitably, the bonanza was finite. Mércio Gomes watched in dismay as 'ten years later most of that land's hardwoods had been cut down, and the Indians were no better off than before the process started.'

The Tembé, the western branch of Tenetehara living in the State of Pará, suffered far greater loss of land, depopulation, and invasion than their Guajajara cousins in Maranhão. Land conflicts had been simmering in this region for many decades, but came to a head in the 1970s when a company called Cidapar acquired a huge concession that cut across the Tembé reserve and included the farms of hundreds of small settlers. The struggle became very violent. Cidapar employed squads of armed guards and enjoyed police support, so people were killed on both sides, houses burned, and cattle destroyed. Cidapar collapsed in 1980, but its assets and claims were pursued by the Denasa Bank and other large companies, and there were complicated legal actions throughout the 1980s.

In 1982 twenty pro-Indian organizations in Belém signed a motion 'to support the Tembé in their struggle to reclaim and defend their land'. They accused Funai of forcing eighty Indian families to accept plots of 200 hectares (494 acres) or lose their land altogether. 'The area supposedly reserved for the Tembé is partly occupied by squatters with the rest, over 300,000 hectares [1,200 square miles], placed at the disposal of large companies and ranchers who have been after it for years: Denasa, Mejer, Grupiá, Itaú, Swift, etc.' Politicians had encouraged squatters to invade the reserve, and they facilitated this by building a road across it. The squatters were also championed by a 'Robin Hood' figure called Quirino da Silva, whose band of former squatters fought the company *pistoleiros*, and whom the police hunted everywhere during 1984 and finally caught and killed in January 1985. The beleaguered squatters felt that they had common cause with the Indians against big ranches.

For their part the Tembé were divided. Some younger leaders feared that the invasions could only intensify, so that their own hope of survival was to move to the security of the Gurupi indigenous area. Others, particularly those intermarried with whites, wanted to remain in the traditional tribal areas on the upper Guamá, despite the external pressures.

The Tembé produced an able leader, Raimundo Tembé, 'through whom they have a representative of their own tribe who is familiar with the authorities and who forcefully pursues their interests.' Some Tembé remained in the 280,000 hectare (1,100 square mile) Alto Rio Guamá reserve, alongside Indians from four other ethnic groups. The situation worsened in 1993 (the year in which Funai registered the reserve) with the creation of a town called Nova Esperança Piriá partly within it. This further split the Tembé, with twelve villages remaining on the Guamá and fifteen near the Gurupi. However, Chief Clemente of the Guamá Tembé felt that his people were doing well, even though few could still speak their Tupi language or knew how to hunt or fish. 'In 1945 we were only forty on the Guamá side, but now we are 1,100.' He had forbidden intermarriage with whites or blacks. 'To survive, we have to put an end to mixing.' Invasions were widespread: in the year 1996 alone there were thirty-two arrests for illegal logging and fifteen for mineral prospecting. In that year, a group of Tembé sacked a store and killed animals in the town of Livramento inside their reserve. The settlers retaliated by enlisting hundreds of supporters from other towns and seizing seventy-seven Indians and four Funai officials. The frightened hostages were held in a crowded shed for two days until the Governor of Pará promised to hear the settlers' grievances. These protested: 'We are not vagabonds, we are workers.' By the end of the century, Funai admitted that 60 per cent of this reserve was invaded by settlers, only some of whom had accepted compensation and moved elsewhere. The reserve contained some 5,000 Indians from the Tembé and other tribes; but it was also home to 7,000 squatters.

In 1969 the BR-316 highway was built to link Maranhão to Belém in Pará. This route between the two state capitals cut through the eastern edge of the territory of the Kaapor. This forest people had resisted for many decades, were contacted by the SPI in the 1930s, and then studied by Darcy Ribeiro and Francis Huxley. The American anthropologist William Balée now watched in horror as 'white settlements soon arose in the dust of abandoned Kaapor villages along the new road. Many trees have been cut down on both sides of the highway, and the land once covered by these trees is now under pasturage. The consequences for the Kaapor living near the BR-316 have been fourfold: more epidemics, loss of people, disappearance of game animals, birds, and fish, and cultural decline.' The Funai agent organized roads within the reserve, to help the Indians enter the regional economy through intensive agriculture. Balée concluded in 1979 that 'the immediate future looks bleak for the Kaäpor'.

A government colonization scheme brought settlers into the Turiaçu valley, where the non-Indian population doubled during the 1970s. The Kaapor were forced to abandon ancient settlements in the Paruá river basin, which was completely deforested by settlers by 1985. They took refuge in the 530,524 hectare (2,048 square mile) Alto Turiaçu indigenous reserve, which was demarcated and registered in 1982. There is an abrupt ecological boundary at the northern edge of this sanctuary, where 'the forest legacy of the Kaapor meets in an uneasy truce with the open pastures and monoculture rice swiddens of the newly arrived settlers'. During the 1990s, 'as much as a third of the reserve has been illegally deforested and converted to towns, rice fields, and cattle pastures by landless peasants, cattle ranchers, loggers, and local politicians'.

The Kaapor are a conservative and resilient people. Their population fell from over 1,000 in the 1940s to a nadir of fewer than 500 in the mid-1970s, from measles, respiratory diseases, and lack of medical attention. Many still die from tuberculosis, but they have acquired immunity to other lethal diseases and they get better health care. So the Kaapor are increasing by 3 per cent a year, to 700 or more by the end of the century. Traditions in their twelve villages remain strong, as do family and blood relationships, so that Kaapor very rarely marry outside their tribe. They also continue *coivara* farming, in which small forest gaps are burned but not cleared: manioc and other crops are planted among the dry trees and foliage. They cultivate some fifty other domesticated plants, for everything from food and medicine to fibres and weapons. Hunting and fishing are also important sources of food. Very few Kaapor speak Portuguese, and they have no desire to mingle with surrounding farmers and ranchers.

Various companies claimed that they owned parts of the Alto Turiaçu reserve, and they mounted a massive and determined campaign to invade this land. By 1991 some 1,100 families of settlers and several large ranches occupied a swathe of 46 by 15 kilometres (28.5 by 9 miles) within the protected area. The Kaapor, Timbira, and Tembé tried every form of non-violent action. They confronted the colonists and tried to persuade them to leave. 'The denunciations by the Indians became frequent and generalized, culminating in the peaceful occupation of the Legislative Assembly of the State of Pará in order to attract the attention of public opinion and politicians, and to force the authorities to take energetic and immediate measures against the invaders.' A legal action found in favour of the Indians, but there was no improvement.

In September 1993 the Kaapor had to revert to their warrior heritage. A pair of hunters ran into a group of invading squatters who disarmed the two Indians, held them captive for a day, and warned them that the land no longer belonged to them. Kaapor chiefs held an emergency meeting and decided to take direct action. They went round all villages and assembled an impressive force of several hundred warriors. They ordered their Funai agent not to radio to his superiors, but invited him to accompany one contingent of 150 armed men. Emerging from their forest, 'the group's vision of the total devastation of their lands aroused the greatest indignation. Scarcely a kilometre from one aldeia, we encountered fresh trails, plots marked out, stumps of felled trees, etc. The group of Indians was commanded by chiefs who adopted the following strategy: the houses of the invaders were surrounded, the inhabitants overpowered, and then everything was destroyed. In this group, the Indians destroyed 80 houses and captured 119 guns such as shotguns, revolvers, and a Beretta pistol. Six chainsaws and a theodolite used in measuring plots were also taken.' The Indians moved fast through the forests they knew well, so that they rapidly surprised, overpowered, and destroyed each invading dwelling. The greatest tension occurred at a settlement called Nicodemos, where there were some fifty houses and 400 heavily armed men who seemed ready to fight. The Funai agent feared that the Indians, who outnumbered the invaders, 'would attack with total force and spare no one'. So he bravely emerged from the forest and advanced, alone and unarmed, towards the settlers. Their leader agreed to leave at once; but two hired gunmen tried to foment resistance. The settlers were given a day in which to gather their belongings and depart, which they did. But the two gunmen – who were known to the Indians for past aggressions – rashly returned. They were surrounded by angry warriors; and in a confused melee one called Davi was shot dead and the other escaped. This bold action preserved the reserve from a determined attempt to invade and dismember it.

In March of that same year, Kaapor warriors had joined Guajajara and Timbira (Krikatí and Canela) in a blockade of the Carajás railway across their lands. They were demanding action by the mining company CVRD (Companhia Vale do Rio Doce) to demarcate Awá-Guajá and Krikatí reserves – tasks that it was committed to do under the terms of its 1982 World Bank loan. The two-day blockade was very effective, in stopping both the export of iron ore and the movement of fuel and farm produce. The state police were about to move against the Indians when CVRD caved in and promised Funai to fulfil its obligations. So, thanks to their own robust actions, the Kaapor enter the new millennium with their culture, language, morale, and reserved land in good condition – even though CVRD has not yet fully honoured its commitments.

*

In 1957 Darcy Ribeiro listed the Krikatí as an extinct group of Timbira. He was right to call them Timbira, Jê-speakers closely related to the Canela, Krahó, and Apinayé, but his epitaph of 'extinct' was premature. There are now some 600 Krikatí, but they live dangerously close to the town of Montes Altos in south-west Maranhão.

The Krikatí were the last Timbira group to have their land protected. This should have happened in the 1970s, but it was prevented by local farmers, politicians, and lawyers. Instead, owing to the negligence of Funai's Maranhão office, these interests obtained licences to occupy and demarcate lands that had always been Indian. This was a flagrant violation of the Constitution. Funai finally resisted and, after acrimonious negotiations, there was a judicial hearing in 1991. One hundred and twenty farmers and land-speculators had rushed to claim title to parts of the tribal land prior to this hearing. But a federal judge engaged an expert anthropologist and eventually threw out every single bid on the grounds that each had 'neither a name, nor location, nor adjacent boundaries, nor a defined area'. So the Krikatí achieved a 146,000 hectare (560 square mile) reserve – in theory but not in practice. The anthropologist Maria Elisa Ladeira commented bitterly that it was 'a devastated area . . . They will have to wait for the generous forces of nature to restore their forests, game for hunting, and fish. [These resources] will sustain future generations of their people, who are endowed with a profound knowledge of and respect for their environment and a sophisticated and complex society, rather than a few privileged families [of land-grabbers].'

The unsuccessful settlers appealed against the 1991 ruling, and many refused to leave. So the Krikatí were desperate to get their reserve demarcated. When Funai failed to do this, the Indians took action. In June 1993 they piled a mass of firewood around the pylon of a power line that ran across their land, and threatened to set fire to it if their land were not demarcated immediately. Toppling the pylon would have cut electricity power lines from the Tucuruí hydroelectric generators to large parts of north-east Brazil. It was another example of clever public relations: the press carried pictures of sixty Krikatí warriors posing on the unlit bonfire. And it achieved immediate results. Funai and the army promised to complete the demarcation within two weeks. However, local politicians and farmers forced the military to stop their surveying; there were threats of bloodshed from both sides; two Funai health workers were seized and held hostage by farmers, and the Krikatí retaliated by taking four farm workers. Mércio Gomes reported that 'by late 1996 the situation had become extremely tense, and the Krikatí were about to enter into open conflict with the ranchers and their henchmen.' In February 1997 the exasperated Indians finally set fire to their bonfires and toppled two pylons. This caused blackouts in most cities of Maranhão, including the capital, São Luís. There were further negotiations between Funai and the state authorities. The World Bank exerted pressure, since its loan to CVRD for the Carajás railway carried a requirement that indigenous lands be demarcated. The decisive factor was solidarity. Demarcation of the 146,000 hectares finally took place in March 1998, with the surveyors protected by 'a group of courageous indigenists and the Krikatí, with help from some 160 Indians from other areas . . . much to the chagrin of ranchers and recent land-invaders'.

The Gavião or Parketeyê, who had been settled at Mãe Maria on the right bank of the Tocantins in the 1960s and 1970s, suffered from three major projects: flooding from the Tucuruí hydroelectric dam, power lines traversing their territory, and after 1980 the railway to extract ore from the Carajás iron mine.

In 1983, $1 million compensation was paid for the railway violation, thanks to the tribe's bargaining skills and help from indigenist supporters. The mining company Vale do Rio Doce made the most of the grant that it was obliged to pay: its advertising boasted of the company's 'social responsibility to Amazon Indians'. But Mércio Gomes felt that the tribe had paid too high a price. He argued that the Carajás project was even more damaging than the Transamazonica highway had been to Indians along its route. 'The railroad attracted new investments in agriculture and ranching, pig-iron mills, and the use of vegetal charcoal, all of which has brought more land conflicts, distorted economic expectations, [and caused] dissatisfaction, increases in land prices, and uncontrolled development of rural areas . . . The Indians are pushed into a world of continuous and unpredictable change, where money buys everything from trinkets to prostitution.'

It was difficult for the Gavião to cope with the sudden influx of wealth. For a time the Indians lived off interest from the grant, but with low inflation during the 1990s they started to consume the capital. They became reluctant to perform the hard labour of gathering and selling Brazil nuts when there was so much easy money from the railway compensation. When this dried up, the Gavião felt that they must receive equivalent aid from Funai, since the Brazilian state had forced them to congregate in a small reserve surrounded by colonists and had introduced them to new needs. Funai was unable to answer these dubious arguments. The Gavião 'pushed their demands as hard as they could . . . and the exacerbation of misunderstandings between the Indians and Funai was another sinister consequence of the economic projects and ... their compensations.'

High up the tributaries of three main rivers of Maranhão – the Gurupi, Turiaçu, and Pindaré – live one of Brazil's remaining groups of nomadic hunter-gatherers: the Awá ('People'), known to other Indians and Brazilians as Guajá. The Awá-Guajá's dense and hilly forests, roughly between the lands of the Kaapor and Guajajara, remained inviolate until the second half of the twentieth century. These forests are ecologically unique, survivors of a precious habitat known as pre-Amazonian. But in recent decades farmers displaced from southern Brazil and land speculators started to move into this pristine region – which is only 250 kilometres (155 miles) south-west of the state capital, São Luís.

The Tupi-speaking Awá-Guajá may once have been agriculturalists, living on the lower Tocantins. In the late nineteenth century they retreated from that wild colonial frontier, from attempts to enslave them, and from contact with other tribes. But they had to abandon sedentary farming and now live in small, highly mobile bands of from one to seven families. Their livelihood depends entirely on hunting and gathering within the forests. Mércio Gomes, who has studied the Awá-Guajá for many years, admires this adaptation. 'Cultural flexibility and group nimbleness constitute the very essence and raison d'être of a nomadic way of life. However, this nomadism should not be interpreted as a disorderly and random pattern of population movements over a boundless territory.' The Awá-Guajá know exactly what they are doing. Their migrations are based on 'commonly shared and in some cases minutely detailed knowledge of the seasons for every forest product'. Furthermore, each group roams within its own large area.

From 1913 onwards there were fleeting sightings of Awá-Guajá and mentions of them by SPI officials, by Curt Nimuendajú, and by others. In 1948 some Awá-Guajá attacked a settler woman washing clothes by a stream; a revenge expedition was mounted, and this boasted that it had killed many Indians. Most Awá-Guajá now move within the Gurupi forest reserve, which was decreed in 1961; others were in hills called Serra da Desordem because of their disordered topography.

There were further massacres in the early 1970s by road gangs building the BR-222 road from Santa Inés south-westwards to Imperatriz on the Tocantins. Funai reacted by sending an attraction team led by Valéria Parisi, which in March 1973 made contact with a group of thirteen people on the upper Turiaçu. These Awá-Guajá cut their hair short in a bowl shape, and had no ornaments. Men wore only penis-strings and thick bracelets to protect their left wrists from searing when shooting bows; and women had skirts of tucum palm fibre, slings to carry their babies, and baskets for the group's few possessions. There were no huts, just rough lean-to shelters of palm or banana fronds. The Awá-Guajá lived very simply, as true hunter-gatherers, following fixed routes in their constant migrations, and their favourite food was babaçu coconuts.

Women carried many of the group's few belongings, and had two sticks to rub together for making fire at each camp. Some Awá-Guajá are a matriarchal society, with old women as chiefs even after contact with Brazilian society. One characteristic is fondness for pets – monkeys, coatimundi 'honey-bears', baby anteaters. These furry creatures twine themselves around women's bodies and necks and looked to the journalist Christina Lamb 'like bizarre fashion accessories'. This intimacy comes from the women's practice of breast-feeding baby monkeys and other animals. Monkeys are considered sacred by the Awá-Guajá, so girls from puberty onwards constantly suckle and share their hammocks with either small animals or their own infants.

Funai founded a Guajá post and another 'attraction front'. There were more killings of Indians by settlers. But the tools given to the first group of Awá-Guajá attracted others, so that by 1976 five or six groups totalling ninety-one people were in contact with Funai's post. There was then the too-familiar and disgraceful post-contact neglect. 'With Funai's more intensive presence, but with no permanent medical team, these Awá-Guajá started dying of influenza/pneumonia, malaria, and other diseases. A precipitous vaccination campaign even caused [more dead] because it provoked the flight of the Indians far from the post, and the deaths of a dozen of them. The number [in permanent contact] fell to twenty-five people by January 1980.' Since then, these Awá-Guajá in the Turiaçu indigenous area have increased slightly in numbers; but other hidden groups are known to have died of disease deep in their forests.

In October 1978 Funai's expert woodsman Sydney Possuelo took two Awá-Guajá from the post to contact more of the elusive nomads. Possuelo's thirty-seven-day expedition paddled along 390 kilometres (240 miles) of streams and rapids and cut a punishing 194 kilometres (120 miles) of forest trails. They finally found traces of Awá-Guajá and sighted a group of eleven men, women, and children resting in the forest. Because Possuelo was heavily bearded and obviously white, he had arranged that any contact should be made by his Awá-Guajá running into the midst of their compatriots. 'But at the decisive moment they looked at one another and desisted. I tried to push them, but got nowhere. They were scared. In order not to lose this opportunity, I took them by the arms and we advanced into the midst [of the Awá-Guajá] shouting words that I had learned from my brief sojourn with these Indians, like "Friends", "We are friends", "We will do no harm". This surprise caused some confusion among them. The women fled with their children and I was surrounded by three Awá-Guajá.' There was great tension on both sides. But, as always, an understanding was reached thanks to presents – the Awá-Guajá had a few much-used metal tools that they had managed to steal, and they were desperate for more. In 1980 another group of twenty-eight Awá-Guajá appeared at a farm being cleared near the Pindaré. This pathetic band was suffering from influenza and starvation because the babaçu on which they depended for food had been felled, so a quarter of them died of disease. Funai moved the survivors to a new Awá indigenous post in the Caru reserve; but more died from lack of medical treatment.

In 1988 a solitary Indian was discovered at Barreiras in the state of Bahia. This man was later learned to be called Karapiru, an Awá-Guajá who in 1978 had survived an attack by farmers near Amarante in Maranhão – 600 kilometres (370 miles) to the north of where he was found. His family had been killed or dispersed, so Karapiru survived alone for ten years, sleeping in tree-tops, hiding from Brazilian farmers, and occasionally killing farm animals for food. He found a machete, which helped him get honey. 'I spent a long time in the forest, hungry and being chased by ranchers. I was always running away, on my own. I had no family to help me, to talk to. So I want deeper and deeper into the forest.' Farmers complained about dead pigs and donkeys and, in October 1988, one of them tracked and caught the solitary nomad. He was trembling with fear and suspected a trap. But he was taken in by the caboclo family, who eventually notified Pedro Agostinho and other anthropologists from Bahia University. The fugitive was taken to Brasília, where the press made a big story about his discovery. But Funai still did not know his tribe. He stayed with Sydney Possuelo, who brought a Tupi-speaking interpreter to try to learn more about him. This young interpreter happened to be an Awá-Guajá and he was astounded when he heard the man's name: it was the same as his lost father's. So the young man asked Karapiru to lift his shirt and, when he saw the shotgun pellets in his back, he knew that he had rediscovered his own father. To Possuelo it was a stroke of destiny. Karapiru was eventually returned to his people, where he is now remarried and has a new family.

Once again, an anthropologist and a missionary took up the cause of a defenceless tribe. The anthropologist was the distinguished Mércio Gomes, later director of the Institute of Anthropological Research in Rio de Janeiro. In 1985, with support from Funai and the CVRD mining giant that owned Carajás, Gomes proposed a continuous homeland of 276,000 hectares (1,100 square miles) that would join Funai's Turiaçu and Caru reserves and would cover most of the Tiracambu Hills. This should be 'exclusively for [Awá]-Guajá groups who live in scattered areas distant from one another, areas that are being transformed into "islands" by the massive presence of settlements, farms and expansion fronts'.

Two years later Father Cláudio Zannoni, of CIMI's Maranhão office, launched a passionate appeal for recognition and demarcation of this indigenous area before it could be converted to eucalyptus plantations to fuel the pig-iron smelters. The campaign started fairly well. In May 1988 an Interministerial Order declared the area as 'of indigenous occupation' – but it reduced it to 147,500 hectares (570 square miles), which was only half the size of Gomes's proposal. The remainder of the land was designated as the Gurupi biological reserve, because it contains unique endemic pre-Amazonian flora and fauna.

A mere four months later, in September 1988, the government of President José Sarney – who came from Maranhão and disliked Indians – yielded to pressure from timber companies, farmers, and land-speculators and drastically dismembered the Awá indigenous area. In 'an arbitrary and unconstitutional act' he reduced the protected territory to 62,000 hectares (240 square miles), with an absurd corridor of forest joining the two previous reserves. CIMI named the main culprits as a farming-industrial company from São Paulo, a man from Paragominas in Pará who claimed to own much of the area and started selling it off in plots, and above all logging companies, particularly from Paragominas, which is infamous for the quantity of its sawmills. 'Deforestation is increasing at a vertiginous rate . . . of 15 per cent a year . . . The loggers are active in the indigenous area and biological reserve, removing enormous quantities of timber with absolutely no control by the competent authorities. This criminal omission by the government has created a veritable frenzy to remove the region's wood.'

The activists had to start again. The Public Ministry (the newly created government watchdog with a mandate to protect Indian interests) immediately challenged the second Portaria of September 1988 as uncon-stitutional, and obtained a favourable response from the Procurator-General. Funai sent teams into the area to reassess and remeasure indigenous land; CIMI relaunched its campaign 'Land for the Guajá'; Survival issued an urgent-action bulletin; and an 'Association of Friends of the Guajá People' was founded in a nearby town.

By 1990 the situation of the Awá-Guajá – 'the last nomads' – remained dangerous. 'Most of their historic territory, the Gurupi Forest reserve, is occupied by thousands of squatters, invaded by hundreds of landowners (with farms of from 1500 to 4500 hectares [3,700 to 11,100 acres]) and by agro-industrial enterprises (Cacique, União, Varig, Sunil [and others]) that are installed illegally and with impunity, lacerated by the Carajás railway, divided into plots by Getat [the legal-aid agency for small farmers], and with an appeal pending for the remainder to be the site of projects planned by the Greater Carajás Programme (pig-iron, charcoal, cattle ranching). The Guajá are abandoned to their fate.' Although the biological reserve of the Gurupi had been created to protect a unique and vulnerable ancient forest, it was not policed in any way. So by 1991 'deforestation has reached alarming proportions. Some 40 per cent of the area has been cleared. Even slopes at an angle of 45 degrees and the banks of rivers and streams are not being respected' – despite the prohibition on logging in this reserve. 'The Guajá are on the brink of extinction, for their habitat is already badly degraded and there is interference everywhere by non-Indians.' The three indigenous areas, Awá, Turiaçu, and Pindaré, were each threatened by invasions by settlers and loggers, and by bogus claims of property speculators.

Funai's team reported in 1992 that part of the Guajá forests had been irredeemably destroyed, but it recommended that Sarney's 1988 decree be revoked and the territory increased to 118,000 hectares (455 square miles). Sydney Possuelo, now President of Funai, promptly endorsed this, and on 17 July 1992 the Minister of Justice declared the area to be of permanent possession by the Indians and ready for demarcation. A decade earlier, the World Bank had insisted that the mining company CVRD pay for such demarcation when it financed the railway; but nothing had happened. The sertanista Fiorello Parisi, head of the Friends of the Guajá, said that they urgently needed a solution of their land problem, as well as health and vigilance. 'Otherwise, we shall watch the death-throes of a people who possess characteristics that are unique on this planet.'

Survival in London issued another urgent-action bulletin in 1993 to try to speed demarcation. But seven years later, in July 2000, it had to issue yet another appeal to the Brazilian authorities to complete the registration. Survival denounced the critical situation to the United Nations Commission on Human Rights, protested to the Brazilians again in May 2002, and its Fiona Watson helped to make a film about these threatened nomads to influence the environmental summit in Johannesburg at the end of the year. Mércio Gomes was sure that the delays were deliberate. One reason was that CVRD (now privatized) held a concession to a large bauxite deposit on the tribe's Tiracambu Hills. Another was that the medium-sized ranchers and timber companies who invaded the Gurupi

Forest reserve were politically influential. Fiona Watson of Survival blamed the European Union and the World Bank for helping to finance CVRD in 1982 but failing to require that part of its revenues be used to demarcate the lands of 'the most threatened indigenous society in the Amazon today'. The anthropologist Louis Carlos Forline criticized Funai for downgrading the Awá-Guajá from 'isolated' to ordinary status (which meant less aid), for being authoritarian and paternalistic, favouring men over women (in a society where the sexes were roughly equal), distorting social order by promoting and rewarding young leaders, and for not standing up to CVRD.

So the new century started with much of the Awá-Guajá's forests irredeemably destroyed. There are some 250 members of the tribe in Funai's three posts. They are content to survive as hunter-gatherers, uninterested in the agency's attempts to introduce them to agriculture or bee-keeping. A visitor to the Pindaré post in 2000 was distressed to see many Indians 'seriously ill with malaria and tuberculosis, under siege from settlers, ranchers and loggers ushered in by a mining project,' and with their isolation violated by the thunderous roar of a mile-long train carrying ore along the nearby Carajás railway.

There are undoubtedly still uncontacted nomadic groups in the forests – once thought to total as many as 150 hunter-gatherers, but only about 30 according to Louis Forline. It would be preferable to leave them alone. But they must be contacted for their own good, since there are estimated to be 276 properties illegally planted within Awá-Guajá territory, and workers from these ranches could kill Indians they encounter. A young Awá called To'o told Watson of his despair. 'The ranchers and settlers are all over the place, and we are being pushed and pushed and pushed. Now we are at the limit. We are prepared to fight back if demarcation doesn't happen. But we are weak because there are so few of us – there is no way that we can match the whites.'

When the solitary Indian Karapiru was found in northern Bahia, it was at first assumed that he was an Avá-Canoeiro. For a time in the early nineteenth century, a tribe known as Canoeiros ('Canoers') had dominated the upper Tocantins, wiping out farms and settlements on its colonization frontier. They fought with great bravery, ferocity, dash, and cunning, and they terrified their opponents. They then disappeared. Some were killed in savage reprisal attacks that sought to exterminate the Canoeiros, but the rest were either wiped out by disease or hid in the mesopotamia of streams and wetlands between the Tocantins and Araguaia.

During the twentieth century there were sporadic sightings of Indians, or their traces, in the wild scrubland between the states of Bahia and northern Goiás (now the State of Tocantins). This dry hill country, covered in low woods or dense thorny maquis and full of cliffs and caves, is perfect guerrilla terrain. Although it is only 200 kilometres (120 miles) north of the new capital, Brasília, there is little to attract people to this forbidding region. The Serra Negra hills therefore became a refuge of the last remnants of Canoeiro, who call themselves Avá. They had long ago abandoned the rivers and lived by gathering, hunting, and foraging in the high county. The Avá-Canoeiro occasionally took the tempting livestock or vegetables of the few farmers who were trying to settle in these hills. Their punishment in 1962 was a genocidal reprisal raid by fazendeiros. The whites surprised a village of Avá-Canoeiro while it was celebrating the festival for planting manioc. Iawi, a boy who escaped the massacre, recalled that terrible day when 'suddenly came lots of white men with guns. There was much shooting and smoke and everyone was dead: my mother, father, men, women, and children . . . I cried a lot.' There were only four survivors, including the boy, and one man who was later killed by a jaguar. The others hid in caves, too terrified to light fires at night, and subsisting from what they could collect or hunt in that barren environment.

In the 1980s construction crews and earth-moving machinery broke the silence of this craggy country to build the Serra da Mesa hydroelectric dam, to generate power for Brasília. The waters that rose in the dammed reservoir drowned Avá foraging grounds. So after twenty years on the run, which included Iawi and a young woman called Tuia marrying and having two children, the tiny band of Avá in 1983 gave up the struggle. They appeared in a settler's garden, and he took pity on the emaciated Indians and told Funai. The film-maker Adrian Cowell made a heart-rending documentary about the contact with these six people and their story of survival. The hills around the dam are now an indigenous area of 38,000 hectares (150 square miles) for the Avá-Canoeiro, who live in a brick house, which they prefer to a thatched hut prepared for them by Funai. Sydney Possuelo, now head of Funai's department of isolated Indians, has made several fruitless expeditions to try to locate other bands of Avá. He sought to marry the daughters of Iawi and Tuia to boys from a dozen Avá who live far to the west, among the Karajá on Bananal Island in the Araguaia. This other remnant had been found in 1973, starving in a marsh near the Tocantins, having been shot up by gunmen from the Camagua ranch. But Possuelo's match-making did not succeed.

23. Rio Negro, Rio Branco

Far away in the north-west corner of Brazil, the tribes of the Upper Rio Negro entered the final decades of the twentieth century battered by centuries of enslavement, oppression during the rubber boom, and intense missionizing by Catholic Salesians and, in the north, by Protestants. The Salesians of the Rio Negro were slow to adopt the 'liberation theology' promulgated after Vatican II. For a time they opposed CIMI, refusing to allow its crusading magazine *Porantim* into their missions, and they considered the most radical priests as subversives or even Communists.

Some 10,000 Indians lived in the Upper Rio Negro, divided roughly into three groups: Aruak-speaking Baré and Hohodene and others collectively known as Baniwa on the Içana, Xié, and Negro in the north; Tukano-speaking Tukano, Desana, Cubeo, Wanana (Kotiria), and others on the rivers Uaupés, Papuri, and Tiquié in the centre; and Aruak-speaking Tariana and nomadic groups known as Makú in the forests to the south. All these tribes live on rivers that flow from Colombia towards the Upper Rio Negro, and for most of them Tukano was the common language adopted by the Salesians. On the Rio Negro itself, Baré, Dow, and others speak Portuguese or the lingua geral ('General Language') based on Tupi-Guarani that the Jesuits imposed before their expulsion in the eighteenth century.

Gentle, regimented, and law-abiding, these tribes lacked the fighting spirit of the Jê-speaking peoples or the glamour of the less-acculturated Yanomami to the east of them. They needed political leaders to clamour for their land and redress of their grievances. One such was a young Tukano, Doethiro (or Álvaro Sampaio) from the Uaupés, who in November 1980 was taken to the 'Russell Tribunal on the Rights of Indians of the Americas' in Rotterdam. He accused the Salesians of taking Tukano girls from their villages to work for nuns in the booming city of Manaus. During the past two years some seventy girls had been removed for such domestic service, working eight-hour days for derisory pay. 'At the weekends they start to frequent cabarets, learn to drink cachaça rum, and end by being prostituted. They prefer to work in night clubs because the pay from the nuns is so low; but when they return to their villages they no longer want to eat what we eat. They no longer respect our customs, and their parents are saddened.' Some Indian girls also became domestic servants in Manaus households, so there was an outcry about missionaries organizing a 'maid trade'. The Salesians vehemently denied the accusation: their bishop said that many of some 150 Indian women in Manaus were happily married there. The President of Funai, the notorious Colonel Nobre da Veiga, went to inspect the Salesian establishments in the Upper Rio Negro and was delighted by what he saw. He reported that the missionaries did marvellous and disinterested work in defending the tribes. He imagined that if there was prostitution of Indian girls, it was because they were free to leave their villages whenever they chose, so that it was impossible to control them. But the Russell Tribunal also heard that the Salesians were practising ethnocide, the deliberate destruction of native cultures. One Salesian Father confirmed that his colleagues punished Indians who failed to talk Portuguese or who practised their own rituals.

The perceptive American anthropologist Janet Chernela felt that the furore over the 'maid trade' was an exaggeration by urban intellectuals in Manaus. But it was symptomatic of a crumbling of the missions' paternalistic monopoly of 'key resources and labour in the outlying areas, hindering the emergence of free markets in labor, commodities or land'. She was amazed to find that in the Upper Rio Negro 'the mission system had remained relatively intact' until the late twentieth century. This was because it suited the government to delegate such control of a remote frontier region. 'The missions continued to serve the national governments by organizing Indians into productive units, instilling national identities, claiming and cultivating lands, and providing a permanent Brazilian presence in an otherwise underpopulated and potentially disputed region.'

The denunciations at the Russell Tribunal stung some missionaries into wanting change. But they were frustrated by the arrival of the conservative Bishop Miguel Alagna to run the Rio Negro prelacy. He was convinced that the Indians 'want our faith ... We do not consider ourselves as destroyers of their culture, but through Jesus Christ we are sowers of hope.' So Salesian missionaries in north-west Brazil were slow to discard their soutanes, religious icons, and cradle-to-grave management of their charges. Bishop Alagna noted that he had only twenty priests and forty-five nuns for the region's 22,000 Indians. There were 2,000 children in Salesian primary schools, and 936 who chose to continue their studies in the six regimented secondary schools. The Bishop declared that 'the boarding schools should continue'. He claimed that Christianity was not imposed – but children learned about Brazilian society and realized that 'witchcraft was wrong'. *Time* magazine described Alagna as 'a strongman . . . undisputed lord of . . . the Salesians' placid principality resembling an 18th-century Jesuit compound . . . Though the Salesians deny it, critics say Dom Miguel meddled in tribal politics to advance pro-mission Indians, threatened excommunication for those who disobeyed, and even controlled access to the military planes that until lately provided the only transportation in and out of the area. A fervent anti-Communist and admirer of the military, Dom Miguel belongs to the minority of Brazil's bishops who oppose left-wing liberation theology.' The frail bishop finally retired aged seventy-five and returned to Sicily, in 1987.

Of course, most of these gentle Indians welcomed paternalistic Salesian rule. They liked the pious priests and nuns, were grateful for the security and social services they provided, and were committed Catholics. Many had known no other way of life. A catalyst for change was financial – the cutting of federal-government subsidy for Salesian schools. Between 1979 and 1987 the five boarding schools for Indian children were closed. Bishop Alagna's successor, Dom Valter Ivan Azevedo, revitalized Salesian activity, but with the emphasis on health and education rather than religious conversion or social control.

Political change was also underway. The indigenous peoples started to organize themselves, and there was soon a separate association for each river or area as well as assemblies for the entire region. As usual, land became the burning issue. The Tukano leader Henrique Castro said that during the 1970s he was encouraged by General Ismarth of Funai to draw a map of all indigenous claims. He cooperated with tribes from Iauareté, Taraquá, and the Içana to define the entire region. Castro recalled another general saying to him: '"You are asking for a lot of land: this piece is very large for you people." Then I said: "The Statute [of the Indian] says that we indigenous people can ask for land where we fish, where we hunt, where our ancestors lived: we may mark land as far as that. So how can this be [too big]?" And he was silent.' But repeated promises to act on these maps were always broken. Two Tukano, Carlos Machado and Gabriel dos Santos Gentil, went to Brasília in 1981 to demand that Funai honour its promise to demarcate twenty Indian areas. 'We have been deceived since 1970' when plans of these areas were first sent to Brasília. 'Many tears have been shed by Indians [over the centuries] . . . It is our intention to change the course of history and struggle for the creation of an indigenous territory'.

In 1975 the British anthropologist Peter Silverwood-Cope, working for Funai, recommended an indigenous territory of the Upper Rio Negro. His proposal did not succeed. Four years later, Funai did designate three

Salesian parishes of the upper Uaupés as 'of indigenous occupation'. In December 1981 the French anthropologist Dominique Buchillet (then with the University of Brasília) redrew these plans to create one enormous, continuous indigenous area for the region; and tribal leaders presented this to Funai. The 'Indigenous Territory of the Upper Rio Negro' would embrace all lands between Colombia and the Rio Negro, as far south as the Curicuriari river. It measured 7,650,000 hectares (29,500 square miles) and became known as 'the Dog's Head' because its shape resembled the profile of a barking dog. This demand was audacious. The aspirations of all the region's indigenous peoples were combined in a single gigantic territory.

The Dog's Head proposal faced fierce opposition. The first threat, in 1982, was for the Tukano mission of Iauareté (at a waterfall on the Uaupés that marks the frontier with Colombia) to be designated as a local-government *município*. The Tukano protested, fearing that this would undermine tribal culture in their heartland. In the following year there was a threat to define the Upper Rio Negro region as a Federal Territory. Benedito Machado, Paramount Chief of the Tukano, led six leaders of different tribes to Manaus to try to prevent this. They reminded the Governor of Amazonas how disastrous for the Indians the Territories (later States) of Roraima, Rondônia, and Acre had been. This limited campaign was successful. But the military warned the Indians that they could not hope for a large homeland since they inhabited a frontier region.

In 1983 there was concern that Colombian drug traffickers were active in these forests of north-western Brazil. But Gabriel Gentil, now a leader of a new Tribal Council of the Tukano Indians, protested that his people had always chewed small quantities of *epadu* (one of the 240 varieties of coca) in their shamanistic rituals. 'We Indians certainly do plant coca, but not as a vice, not to be addicts or traffickers like the whites. Planting coca signifies our life. From it we receive our intelligence and memories enriched by our cultural traditions.' Chewing coca leaves is a fundamental practice of all Andean Indians. But chewed coca provides less stimulus than drinking coffee, and it is rich in vitamins and calcium. Coca leaves become a dangerous addictive drug only after an elaborate laboratory process to distil them into cocaine. Despite this, the federal police made raids to destroy large coca plantations on the Solimões and Upper Rio Negro.

A far more potent drug now threatened these Indians. Gold fever struck the region. The Tukano activists Gabriel Gentil and Álvaro Sampaio wrote that in November 1983 'garimpeiros invaded the Uaupés river and discovered gold. They encouraged the Indians to follow the same road, which is destabilizing our traditional political structure ... Our nations are unprepared to receive this type of civilization, for [the gold] is in an exclusively indigenous area ... [Of the first four garimpos] the largest is in the Traíra Hills, where there are 2,000 men and it is reckoned that in a few months we will have 6,000. This is a very sad situation, because our families are becoming increasingly dependent on the whites. Only women and children remain in the villages. Prospecting is a hard life, with no food nor any form of security.' Boatloads of adventurers poured up the Uaupés. 'The worst is that these boats bring white garimpeiros who have not the slightest education but are tough and show much savagery when they converse with Indians.' Many Tukano wanted to mine the gold themselves, so they enlisted guards and tried to police their indigenous areas; but they had no hope of fending off quantities of heavily armed and ruthless prospectors.

Optimists imagined that Traíra might contain a gold deposit to rival South Africa's Rand, so that Brazil needed a modern mining enterprise to extract it. A concession for the Traíra area was therefore granted to Paranapanema, the mining company that already dominated the territory of the Waimiri Atroari Indians north of Manaus. The big company flew in heavy machinery to explore caves on a tributary of the Castanho – although this was in the midst of Indian territory, the government had always reserved subsoil (mineral) rights in such areas, and Tukano lands were not properly protected. During 1985 Paranapanema used police and military force to remove wildcat garimpeiros, who kept returning to this jungle El Dorado. The prospectors, led by lean and black-bearded desperadoes, vowed to leave only under extreme duress. The anthropologist Robin Wright was concerned about the Indians. 'In the midst of all this are the Tukano, increasingly more united and sophisticated in their dealings and negotiations with the government and the company, but increasingly disillusioned that Funai, the agency supposed to protect them, has neither the capacity nor the inclination to act in their favour.'

Many garimpeiros expelled from Traíra found their way to a gold strike discovered by the Tukano themselves near Pari-Cachoeira, another indigenous concentration on the upper Tiquié tributary of the Uaupés. Indian leaders repeatedly asked the prospectors to leave their territory, but the intruders were defiant and scornful. They flaunted their guns and shot at tins while they conversed, and when a chief sent them a letter 'it was not even opened, merely used for target practice'. The Salesian missionary at Pari-Cachoeira wrote that the prospectors were adventurers who despised anyone weaker then them, mocked indigenous culture, and introduced disease, cachaça rum, robbery, abuse of Indian women, and all the other vices of so-called civilization.

The two sides were on collision course. On 26 October 1985 some ninety Indians went to the garimpeiros' camp to demand that they leave, but found only eight armed men present. The parlay degenerated into a hand-to-hand struggle between Domingos Tukano and a miner called Moreira. In the confusion another prospector fired a shotgun; Moreira ran off and drew a revolver, but he was shot dead by an Indian shotgun; and the Tukano managed to seize other guns. 'It was all very rapid. The result: three dead garimpeiros, who were buried there and their belongings burned; and no Indian wounded.' These Indians are not naturally violent, so it was readily accepted that they had acted in self-defence. There was then a rumour of a revenge massacre of Tukano with many dead, but this mercifully proved false. The 'battle' against the garimpeiros rapidly entered Tukano legend. The anthropologist Berta Ribeiro found it alongside origin myths, in an illustrated history of their people by Luiz and Feliciano Lana from a village on the Tiquié. This same history also depicted in great detail an ugly episode that occurred in the following year 1986. 'On the [totally false] allegation that the Indians were smuggling gold to Colombia in exchange for guns, tools, and food, that they were paying no taxes, that the area belonged to Paranapanema and that it was infiltrated by Colombian guerrillas, a detachment of thirty soldiers mounted a repressive operation. Guns were taken, machinery destroyed, shelters cut down with chainsaws and burned, and 120 Indians, men, women, and children, were expelled.'

The Tukano Cláudio Barreto had learned how to interpret maps, and he used satellite images in 1987 to discover another mineral-rich grotto on the Castanho that became known as the 'Garimpo Tukano'. In the following year the Desana Antonio Lana found a third gold-bearing grotto that became the 'Garimpo Desana'. The Indians tended to prefer Paranapanema to individual 'peasant-prospectors', since the company made expansive promises to demarcate their land and bring them various material benefits. So on 12 April 1987 the Tukano of the Tiquié signed agreements with the mining company.

Further north there was another mining empire, among the Baniwa of the Içana. A flamboyant, burly entrepreneur from south Brazil called Elton Rohnelt and his company Gold Amazon explored for gold within indigenous territory. Rohnelt personally commanded a 'foreign legion' of a hundred footsoldiers wearing green shirts marked 'Amazonia Our Fatherland', and a flotilla of two planes, two large boats, and fifteen launches. Gold Amazon later operated alongside Paranapanema at Traíra and Pari-Cachoeira, freely used military airstrips and government boats, and tried to seduce the Indians away from allegiance to either the Salesians or Funai.

The next force to invade the Upper Rio Negro was the Calha Norte Programme launched by President Sarney's military advisers in 1987. The National Security Council (CSN) chose the mission at Pari-Cachoeira as a perfect laboratory for its experiment in military-style indigenous policy on a northern frontier. Dominique Buchillet explained that this seemed justified because 'since 1971 the Tukano leaders had mobilized themselves to obtain legal recognition of their territory; they had frequently reaffirmed a wish to establish direct dialogue with the government and to participate in all decisions that might affect their destiny; and, finally, they desired economic independence.' The first that the Tukano heard of the CSN and Calha Norte was when Funai's plan to bring the Traíra Hills goldfield into the Tiquié indigenous area was abruptly cancelled because this was a frontier area 'of national security'. Tribal leaders went to Brasília and met the powerful General Bayma Denys of the CSN. He proposed 'Indigenous Colonies' in which each Indian family would receive a title deed to its own land, and he offered many inducements in demarcation of territory, education, health care, transport, and public works. Military personnel arrived to start building their Calha Norte installations in the following year.

The Indians' response was to hold a great 'Assembly of Indigenous Organizations of the Upper Rio Negro', with 300 delegates meeting in a covered stadium in São Gabriel da Cachoeira in April 1987. The National Security Council helped to finance this gathering, in order to persuade it to welcome the new regime. Some leaders were suspicious of the Indigenous Colonies – which seemed to be a return to the 'Emancipation' decree so violently rejected earlier in that decade. They also questioned a proposal to have their indigenous areas surrounded by national forests, since it was well known that logging and mineral prospecting was often permitted in such forests. Even more ominously, there were to be non-indigenous colonies alongside the indigenous ones, to create a 'mosaic' with the national forests. The sceptics were unhappy about the massive militarization of their region, and they doubted whether the promised benefits would ever materialize. However, it was explained that there would be no fixed boundaries between Indian and forest areas, and that the Indians themselves might exploit forest resources. So the Assembly was divided. The leaders from the Tiquié 'finally accepted this proposition which, although it fragmented their territory, guaranteed them (after eighteen years) a prospect of ... land registration and autonomous economic development.' It was this vision of future freedom, in addition to the promised aid projects, that swayed the delegates.

Álvaro Tukano (the man who had denounced the Salesians to the Russell Tribunal) wanted mineral wealth for his people. 'We think it is a good idea to negotiate the riches of which we are masters, so that we may develop our own economic projects.' But Dominique Buchillet, after carefully analysing the negotiations, concluded that 'these measures, stemming from the supposed "social vocation" of the CSN, serve only . . . to mask their true objectives . . . We maintain that their intention is the forced integration of the Indians through the expropriation of the greater part of their territories, masquerading as the creation of pseudo-reserves for environmental conservation, their confinement in lands reduced to a minimum, and their economic acculturation.' Buchillet also felt that the military were seeking to supplant the missionaries as the dominant power in the Upper Rio Negro. There was a clear split between Indians who wanted to cooperate with government plans for the region and those loyal to the missionaries or to CIMI.

The Assembly in 1987 created Foirn (Federação das Organizações Indígenas do Rio Negro), an umbrella organization of all indigenous peoples of the Rio Negro. This Federation was holding one of its regular General Assemblies in March 1990 when there was 'an explosive coup by President José Sarney against the indigenous peoples of that region: decrees to ratify the physical demarcation of eleven indigenous areas and nine national forests'. Government officials present at the Assembly were as stunned by this move as were the delegates. The decrees granted the Indian communities an 'archipelago' of unconnected reserves, no larger than the Indigenous Colonies of the Calha Norte programme, and surrounded by poorly protected national forests that were 'corridors for invasion' by outsiders bent on extracting timber and mineral resources. It was ominously similar to what Sarney was proposing for the nearby Yanomami.

Prompted by Indian protests, the Public Ministry (which had a duty to protect Indians, under the 1988 Constitution) immediately challenged the presidential decrees and launched a legal action against the Union of Brazil, Funai, and the environmental agency Ibama. It wanted the cancellation of the decrees and a return to the 'Dog's Head' proposal for a single indigenous area of the Upper Rio Negro, now of 8,150,000 hectares (31,500 square miles), instead of fragmented reserves totalling 2,600,000 hectares surrounded by national forests of some 5,500,000 hectares (10,000 and 21,200 square miles). The Ministry asked Dominique Buchillet and another

Funai anthropologist to make a survey of all Indians in the region, and their report in mid-1992 confirmed that all the tribes had occupied their lands since time immemorial. A new President, Fernando Collor de Mello, proved to be far more pro-Indian than Sarney had been. Collor made Sydney Possuelo President of Funai, and the demarcation of indigenous lands was immediately simplified and accelerated.

There were other developments in the early 1990s. The mining company Paranapanema pulled out of its concessions, because its explorations had discovered too few minerals. Most garimpeiros had also left. The ill-conceived Calha Norte programme was also wound down, with most of its promises to the Indian communities unfulfilled. By June 1994 the anthropologist Jorge Pozzobon wrote that the Indians had been deceived by both the mining company and the military. 'All this had proved to be not just ineffective, but pernicious. Paranapanema divided the Indians into factions, favouring some to the detriment of others. The Calha Norte remained nothing more than paper promises, but it caused the suspension of Funai's precarious medical assistance in favour of a fictitious new structure. Perhaps it was necessary [for the Indians] to undergo this calvary to reach their present political consciousness.'

Another group of Indians became active at this time: the highly acculturated Baré and other tribes of the Middle Rio Negro. These peoples had been in full contact with slavers, colonial administrators, missionaries, and traders for almost three centuries. They were in many ways indistinguishable from non-Indian caboclos – peasant workers, woodsmen, and fishermen of Amazonia.

The Indians of the middle and lower Negro started to organize themselves in 1988. They appealed to the Procurator-General of Brazil, whose Public Ministry cared for indigenous interests, and in 1990–91 he sent another team to make an anthropological survey of the new areas requested by these Indians. Márcio Meira, the anthropologist in charge, explained: 'for this investigation, I started by using historical, cultural, and ecological information, and also undertook a detailed population census in order to identify the tribes existing in the region as well as the location and names of their settlements, communities and areas used either for economic activity or of symbolical or mythological significance. From my field observations and the relevant literature, from available historical or archaeological sources, as well as from the indigenous mythology and oral tradition, the immemorial occupation of that territory by peoples of the Tukano, Aruak, and Makú linguistic families is incontestable.' Meira identified sixty-six groups or campsites containing some 2,250 people; but he knew that there were others deep in the forests.

Meira's findings were presented to a senior official of the Public Ministry at the Indians' regional Assembly, at São Gabriel da Cachoeira in 1992. This was a very formal affair, at which chiefs from the more distant communities 'could express all the dramas they had been keeping in their bosoms, through a profusion of speeches. Some protested against the oppressions they had suffered (from garimpeiros, mining companies, or regatão traders); or they objected to not being considered as Indians, and reaffirmed their ethnic identity, particularly through their language.' The gathering involved much indigenous ceremonial, with the *dabacuri* celebration (an exchange of goods, such as food or handicrafts, between groups), traditional singing and dancing to different types of flute, drinking of fermented caxiri, and elaborate ritual about the discourses. But the national anthem was sung, flags of Brazil and the state of Amazonas were raised, military spokesmen played a prominent role (and advised the Indians not to enlist the help of 'foreigners'), and there was an elaborate welcome for government representatives. Speeches were in both native languages and in Portuguese. The paramount indigenous leader of the region, the Baré Braz de Oliveira França, declared: 'We are the original peoples – Baré, Tukano, Desana, not just "Indians"! . . . We are not asking to preserve our traditions and to honour our origins in order to return to past times. We . . . have the ability to develop our people within our own organization and [through] our creativity.' The delegates decided to form an Association of Indians of the Lower Rio Negro.

The forests west of the middle Negro are home to bands of nomadic Makú. As we saw in the chapter on missionaries, these Indians are dramatically different to the sedentary and acculturated peoples along the main rivers. There is a curious symbiotic relationship between the two types, with the more sophisticated river peoples looking down on the Makú but respecting their hunting skills and culture. During the 1970s, the Salesian missionaries made crass attempts to settle the Makú in fixed and accessible locations. 'In the case of the Makú, who used to live isolated in the forest, the mission took them to the riverbanks, which resulted in tremendous distortion of their way of life, apart from causing the deaths of many of them.' The anthropologists Peter Silverwood-Cope and Howard Reid demonstrated the folly of these relocations, and Dominique Buchillet condemned them as ethnocide.

Funai in 1990–91 sent a team of anthropologist-explorers to locate wandering bands of Makú in their endless, trackless forests. It was arduous work in unexplored terrain. The product was a proposal that a great swathe of land between the Curicuriari and Marié tributaries of the Negro be joined to the 'Dog's Head' territorial claim on the upper river. It was felt that more data was needed to substantiate this additional proposal, so in 1994 the requisite Working Group was sent, with a further three anthropologists, to make a census of all Indians of the Middle Rio Negro. Their research added two more potential protected areas for Makú groups that they had tracked down in their forest camps: on the Apaporís to the west, and along the Tea far down the south bank of the middle Negro.

Despite President Sarney's bombshell of the archipelago embedded in national forests, the tribes of the upper river had not abandoned the dream of a single great protected homeland. The legal action brought by the Public Ministry slowly made its way through the judicial system. Then in 1992 President Collor decreed a new system for defining indigenous reserves that required the approval of the interested tribes. Funai's anthropologists used this as an argument for scrapping Sarney's fourteen indigenous areas surrounded by national forests and reverting to a single homogenous territory for the region's 13,000 inhabitants. Sydney Possuelo, as President of Funai, publicly approved this proposal, and leaders of the Upper Rio Negro federation went to Brasília to enlist the help of their supporter the Procurator-General of the Republic. They pointed out that the military had reneged on most of its promises under the Calha Norte Programme, and that it was never made clear to them that the 'national forests' were open to exploitation by non-Indians. Unusually, the environment agency Ibama lent its support, on condition that its national forests would continue *within* (not alongside or surrounding) the continuous indigenous area. In 1993 the next, interim, President, Itamar Franco, was formally advised to approve the 'Dog's Head' because it was correct 'on socio-cultural, ecological, and economic criteria'.

After further inquiries and reports, in October 1995 President Cardoso's Minister of Justice went to the Rio Negro and confirmed that the continuous territory corresponded to the four norms for indigenous reserves in the 1988 Constitution: 'areas of permanent habitation, areas destined for productive activities, areas to preserve natural resources, and areas needed for the physical and cultural survival of the indigenous people'. It was abundantly shown that the tribes of the area had adapted over centuries to sustainable use of their region. The Upper Rio Negro is environmentally weak. Its blackwater rivers (stained by tannin from vegetation on the geologically ancient and eroded Guiana Shield) and low forests are impoverished in nutrients, and much of the woodland is seasonally flooded igapó. Most of its soils are extremely acidic, clayey and sandy, leached of nutrients and therefore unsuitable for agriculture. Even if all the cultivable areas were used, they could support only 2.2 people per square kilometre (5.7 per square mile). The tribes therefore needed the entire area, and it could not support other settlers. The Tukano and neighbouring peoples have evolved an economy based on fish and manioc, with a hierarchy corresponding to proximity to rich fishing sites. Berta Ribeiro listed the remarkable range of plants, fish, and animals used by these peoples.

There was some protest from local authorities and state politicians, particularly on the Middle Rio Negro. But the pro-Indian arguments prevailed. In June 1996 President Cardoso confirmed all the requested indigenous areas: the vast 'Dog's Head' of the Upper Rio Negro; two areas on either side of the Middle Rio Negro; and the Makú forests of Apaporís and Tea. A year of demarcation ensued, with Indians fully involved at every stage of the work by twenty-one teams – everything from scouting through forests, to opening trails and helicopter pads, sophisticated surveying using the latest laser technology, and planting bronze markers. Having the demarcation done by the Indians themselves and ISA halved the cost of the demarcation, from $1.5 million to $700,000. It was not necessary to cut a demarcation trail around all the thousands of kilometres surrounding this immense area, since most of its boundaries are national frontiers or major rivers, and since 'satellite reception points' were fixed at strategic locations so that the area could be defined and monitored by remote sensing. Even so, Beto Ricardo of ISA described it as 'an unprecedented situation, given the vast area, the locality, the ethnic diversity, the number and distribution of communities, and the distances and difficulties of access'.

In April 1998, the President of the Rio Negro indigenous federation, Foirn, was handed the final registration documents by the Minister of Justice, and he raised them in triumph to a great assembly of his peoples' leaders. There was a joyful celebration of this successful outcome of thirty years of patient struggle. The total area of these five contiguous areas is 10,865,800 hectares (41,940 square miles) for 16,100 Indians of eighteen ethnic groups. It was another major triumph for the Indians, after a dignified campaign that mirrored that of the Yanomami in many respects – but without the international attention, and by gentle peoples who had none of the glamour of their ethnically homogeneous neighbours.

Having gained control of the entire region (subject to the tutelage of Funai), the peoples of the Rio Negro now have to confront bewildering challenges. They are still adjusting from a century of strict Salesian control and catechism. The missionaries remain there and many Indians are Catholic, but the Salesians are now more concerned with empowering the

Indians than converting them. Buchillet and other anthropologists encouraged 'cultural recuperation': they recorded each tribe's rich mythology and promoted indigenous teachers. In the early 1990s, the Desana of the São José tributary of the Tiquié built the first great maloca for half a century. Although not used as a communal dwelling, it is a symbolic museum and cultural centre. However, languages other than Tukano are dying out, and even that is giving way to Portuguese or the Tupi-based lingua geral.

Fiona Watson of Survival described the situation in the Rio Negro as extremely complex. There are tensions within tribes and between the great diversity of ethnic groups. Tribal leaders reacted differently to the military, the missionaries, mining interests, Funai, and the NGOs, so that some chiefs were accused of enriching themselves at the expense of their communities, while others were considered too compliant to the Salesians, or too politically subversive. Although the land has triumphantly been secured, there is always the threat of garimpeiros and loggers invading remote parts of this immense territory. Education and health remain serious issues. As in most parts of Brazil, money for basic necessities is also a perennial problem. Even sophisticated Indians of the Middle Rio Negro have great difficulty in getting their produce – manioc flour and other vegetables and fruit – to market and selling it without being cheated. There is limited demand for beautifully made handicrafts such as baskets, hammocks, manioc graters, or tribal ornaments. A new commercial activity that invades reserves is 'ornamental fishing', of 20 million live specimens a year for the world's aquaria, particularly cardinals (*Paracheirodon axelrodi*). A positive development is fish-farming, by the Indians themselves (of aracu and other delicious species) – environmentalists argue that fish, not cattle, are the logical source of protein for Amazonia. But for the foreseeable future, the hard-working indigenous peoples of the Upper and Middle Rio Negro must struggle to enjoy the prosperity of other parts of Brazil.

The last great indigenous area still in dispute at the start of the twenty-first century is the Makuxi and Ingarikó heartland of Raposa/Serra do Sol. The once-compliant Makuxi lost almost all the plains of Roraima to cattle ranchers during the nineteenth and twentieth centuries. This made them all the more determined to keep the savannahs and forested low hills that rise towards Mount Roraima in the north-east of the state of that name. Raposa/Serra do Sol divides into three regions, all of which are essentially open grasslands studded with gnarled cerrado trees, stands of buriti palms, or glades of low woodland. The western third of this territory is the huge cattle ranch of São Marcos, which has been Indian territory since the early days of the SPI. The 'lavrado' east of there is a seasonally flooded plateau covered in pasture suitable for humped cattle, but not for other farming. To the north, the foothills of the Guiana Hills have streams thought to contain gold and diamonds, so that they attracted prospectors expelled from the Yanomami park.

The conflict and campaigning over these choice plains has a long history, and it intensified as cattle-men and prospectors continued to invade. The Makuxi responded by becoming more organized and militant, because this is their ancestral homeland. Catholic missionaries arranged regular meetings of *tuxauas*, Makuxi chiefs; and their speeches show them to be gentle, reasonable men who had been pushed too far. Some admitted that part of the blame lay with their ancestors, who had been duped into selling land. Others worried about the damage brought by a new settlers' town that was too close to their malocas: drunkenness, brawls, and marriages of Indian girls with settlers. In 1977, 1979, 1984, and 1988, Funai sent teams into the area to assess the validity of Indian occupation. These led to identification in 1993 of an area of 1,678,800 hectares (6,480 square miles) as established indigenous territory.

The situation in Raposa/Serra do Sol was very tense because, unlike forested indigenous areas elsewhere in Brazil, this is open cattle country that had already attracted many colonists and ranchers. The Diocese of Boa Vista published a wretched chronology of outrages against Indians, in every month between 1978 and 1983. Such aggressions grew worse, often with the police siding with colonist farmers against Indians and their missionary priests. Ugly incidents continued in the early 1990s: threats, beatings, murders, arbitrary arrests, and deaths from alleged 'alcoholism' of Indians in custody. The identity of one *pistoleiro* (hired gun) who had killed two Indians was well known; but he escaped arrest. There was also constant pressure on land, with cattle invading malocas and trampling crops, evictions, and burning or destruction of houses, farms, and even churches. On 17 May 1994, the Makuxi Bento Sampaio of Napoleão maloca was murdered and his wife raped by an employee of the local rancher. In January 1995 fifty police and seven soldiers expelled 400 Makuxi of all ages from their community Carapuru II: livestock was destroyed and twelve men were seriously beaten. The Makuxi Euclides Pereira wrote in 1996 that 'the violence practised against the [Indians] of Roraima is notable for the institutional support of government organs. This permits criminal practices to be perpetrated with impunity and perpetuated . . . Alongside the invasion and non-demarcation of lands, and the destruction of their natural resources, the native communities' greatest problem is the institutionalized violence that supports such violations – by death threats, illegal imprisonments, destruction of property, corporal abuse, and even murder of individuals from indigenous communities, all committed by the civil and military police ... During the past eight years, twelve Makuxi were murdered by non-Indians within this indigenous area [of Raposa/Serra do Sol]'.

The situation was exacerbated by rumours of diamonds and gold in rivers in the Indian territory, which attracted an invasion by 1,000 determined garimpeiros. In March 1994 hundreds of Indians blockaded the roads to the gold workings, to prevent supplies reaching the prospectors and to draw attention to their plight. But armed police dispersed the protesters and used bulldozers to destroy their blockades. There was then a threat to flood part of the Cotingo valley for a hydroelectric dam. The Makuxi in 1995 occupied the construction site of this dam, which had not yet received planning approval. All this coincided with the paving of the BR-174 highway from Manaus to Boa Vista and then on to the Caribbean through Venezuela and also on a rough new road through Guyana. Brazil's northernmost state, Roraima, already swollen by the huge gold rush of the late 1980s, became the country's new El Dorado with the most massive influx of internal migrants.

A greater blow came in 1996 when the Brazilian government passed Decree 1,775, which allowed commercial interests to contest recent indigenous reserves and file claims for alleged rights or interests within them. The ranchers active in Raposa/Serra do Sol immediately petitioned under this Decree. Nelson Jobim, the Minister of Justice, visited the Makuxi malocas and seemed to support the Indians' position. In December 1996 he issued a long 'Despatch 80' that rejected every rancher's claim. But Jobim then went on to propose a massive reduction to the reserve, by the removal of land to the south and the validation of five garimpeiros' hamlets that he described as 'consolidated centres of population'. The Makuxi homeland seemed about to be divided into small reserves and reduced by a fifth (300,000 hectares; 1,160 square miles).

In the changed political climate of Brazil, such legal setbacks and physical oppression did not go unnoticed. Márcio Santilli, ISA's expert on this case and a future president of Funai, exposed several errors of fact in the Minister's Despatch, and warned that it would invite invasion of Makuxi land and set a dangerous precedent for reductions of indigenous territories elsewhere. Other activists, headed by the Diocese of Boa Vista, the Indigenous Council of Roraima, national pro-Indian lobbies, and international non-government organizations such as Survival International in London and the American Human Rights Watch, mounted a powerful campaign for justice for these people. Makuxi representatives were brought to various European countries on a lobbying tour, and there were orchestrated letter-writing campaigns and petitions to the Brazilian authorities. President Fernando Henrique Cardoso was petitioned when he visited Italy and England. The national (but not the local) media helped. This long effort apparently triumphed, when on 11 December 1998 the Minister of Justice signed a decree by which the plains and hills of Raposa/Serra do Sol should form a single Indian reserve. This was the full territory, stretching to the frontiers of Guyana and Venezuela, and embracing the basin of the Surumu–Cotingo river. There was jubilation among the supporters of the Makuxi. The Indigenous Council of Roraima wrote 'to thank all who supported us during all the years of struggle to achieve the demarcation of the Raposa/Serra do Sol indigenous territory, which is a great victory.'

The ranchers did not give up easily. They claimed that there were 300 fazendas and four small towns within the disputed area. The Governor of Roraima complained bitterly that the decision impeded the state's progress, since most of its territory was now in Indian hands. He said that 45 per cent of his state would now belong to Indians, with 15 per cent reserved for environmental and military uses or too hilly for farming, and only 40 per cent remaining for colonization. 'It is absurd, an insult to the people of Roraima and most of its indigenous leaders . . . This state cannot grow if there is no space for agricultural development.' He declared on television that there would be a bloodbath if President Cardoso ratified the Raposa/Serra do Sol reserve in full.

The settlers mounted a furious public relations campaign, with posters accusing Funai in Roraima as being run by foreign NGOs, or denouncing 'the apartheid they want to impose on Roraima'. One of their leaders was the local Senator Romero Jucá – a former president of Funai, but no friend of Indians. There was also physical violence. In early 1999 two more Makuxi of Maturucá maloca were killed (or 'committed suicide') and there were murder attempts on the Makuxi leader Paulo José de Souza and the missionary Egon Heck. So in May 1999, Survival issued another urgent-action bulletin, called *Violence in Raposa-Serra do Sol*. But the pendulum was swinging against the Makuxi and other tribes. A presidential meeting, attended by legal and military officials, favoured Jobim's proposed reduction, and Funai acquiesced. There was a further setback in July 1999 when the federal Superior Tribunal of Justice upheld the State of Roraima's action against the demarcation of Raposa/Serra do

Sol Indian Territory and ruled that non-Indians with title deeds should be permitted to remain within it; but in December 2002 another court overturned this injunction.

Meanwhile, the military pressed ahead with installations in the midst of reserve areas. One army barracks was erected in the heart of the Makuxi village Uiramutã. In July 2001 the Indigenous Council of Roraima (CIR) protested that, far from bringing promised medical and other aid, the soldiers' attitudes threatened tribal society and they molested women. Later that year, troops suddenly launched a massive 'training exercise' into the Makuxi's São Marcos reserve, using fifteen battle tanks and other vehicles, without prior warning to Funai or the indigenous organization.

By mid-2000, ISA reported that 'the elite of Roraima seems to have gone completely mad' in its efforts to stop President Cardoso signing the decree to demarcate the indigenous area. A group of priests and Indians was ambushed and their truck pushed into a river; armed police harassed Indians inside the reserve in an attempt to arrest their leader Jerónimo Pereira da Silva; and the state Governor threatened to close 138 schools within Raposa/Serra do Sol if its demarcation went ahead as proposed by Funai. There were impassioned speeches in Congress, some returning to the hysterical xenophobia of an Anglo-Saxon environmental plot to keep Brazilian Amazonia uninhabited. The Governor bribed some Indians by giving their villages electricity, so that they would form associations *opposed* to the single large reserve. These breakaway groups countered the Diocese, Funai, and their own Indigenous Council of Roraima and, surprisingly, advocated less land for Indians and more for settlers.

When President Cardoso visited this northern region in 2001, he was greeted by hoardings that proclaimed: 'Mr President! Unjust demarcations threaten peace in Roraima. Amazonia is the patrimony of Brazilians.' The Indians managed to expel some fazendeiros during the following year. But a huge rice farm was established near Surumú and the two settlers' towns of Pacaraima and Uiramutã grew unabated. In 2003 the energetic left-wing President Luiz Inácio Lula da Silva took office. Some Roraima politicians switched to President Lula's Workers' Party and sought to enlist his support for the ranchers against the Indians. Despite this, it is still likely that Raposa/Serra do Sol will be ratified as indigenous territory for some 12,000 Makuxi, Wapixana, Taurepang, and Ingarikó who have always lived there. If so, it will be the last great indigenous area in Brazil.

24. Present and Future

Amazingly, in the twenty-first century, there is evidence of over forty totally uncontacted groups in Brazil. Amazon rainforests continue to be destroyed at a terrible rate, but they still contain roughly half the world total of this ecosystem. These forests are therefore almost the only place on earth where indigenous people can survive in isolation from the rest of mankind. Many of these small tribes live in remote fastnesses of demarcated reserves, such as in the huge Javari Valley park (which has seventeen such groups), on the deeply forested frontiers between south-western Acre and Peru, among the Awá-Guajá of Maranhão, in forests of the upper Guaporé, in parts of Brazilian Guiana, and surprisingly even near the geographical centre of Brazil.

Sydney Possuelo, the bearded, dynamic sertanista who heads Funai's isolated peoples department, has a good idea where these groups live. With thirty years' experience of contacts on countless arduous expeditions, Possuelo is one of the world's greatest active explorers. But he is an idealist who keeps the locations of isolated peoples strictly secret. He has no intention of trying to contact them until some threat makes this imperative. And he wants no publicity-seeking adventurers trying to do so. Small isolated groups have no immunity to introduced diseases so are acutely vulnerable and risk extinction. Most have probably had fleeting glimpses of frontier society or other Indians, but they have decided to shun further contact. Despite Possuelo's intuitions about and fragmentary evidence of isolated peoples, 'no one knows for sure who they are, where they are, how many they are, and what languages they speak'.

The year 2000, the start of the new millennium, was also the 500th anniversary of the first Europeans landing on the coast of Brazil. The government decided to commemorate this Cinquecentennial with a ceremony at Porto Seguro and Monte Pascoal ('Paschal Mount') where the Portuguese flotilla had arrived at Easter 1500. The Presidents of Brazil and Portugal were to sail from Salvador da Bahia in a replica of the original caravel (complete with modern engines and air-conditioned cabins) and there was to be a Discovery theme-park on this coast of southern Bahia. To the wry delight of the media, things did not go according to plan. The caravel repeatedly failed to start; the theme park was soon abandoned; the Minister of Tourism and the President of Funai resigned; and the two heads of state had to be protected by riot police from a peaceful demonstration by indigenous peoples and landless Brazilians.

The trouble was that those who planned the extravaganza failed to appreciate that Indians deplored the arrival of Europeans. Its fifth centenary was no cause for celebration. To them, the landing was their nemesis, the start of the conquest that was to annihilate their populations, rob them of most of their land, and shatter their cultures. So CIMI and the other pro-Indian NGOs orchestrated a great rally of indigenous leaders. Over 3,000 Indians converged on Porto Seguro from all parts of Brazil, some travelling for thousands of kilometres from the borders of Peru and Colombia.

Monte Pascoal also happens to lie in the homeland of the Pataxó – it is the territory that they had been struggling for many years to recover, and in 1999 they had symbolically invaded and reoccupied the national park surrounding the hill. So a great conference was organized at the Pataxó village Coroa Vermelha ('Red Crown') in Monte Pascoal national park. Indigenous delegates discussed policy for the coming century, and regional groupings confronted local issues. But when a delegation went to present a petition to President Fernando Henrique Cardoso, the crowd of Indians was greeted by hundreds of police firing tear gas and rubber bullets. There was angry recrimination about this abuse of human rights, the illegal prevention of peaceful protest and movement, and the detention of CIMI activists including two bishops. The President of Funai, Carlos Frederico Marés, resigned because 'I cannot remain in a government that commits physical aggression against the organized Indian movement. The confrontation was an act of violence comparable to the military repression of the 1960s . . . Whatever one says in favour of the Brazilian Indians would be inadequate. For the nation's debt to them is immense.'

A balance sheet of Brazil's indigenous peoples at the end of the twentieth century is remarkably positive. The Indians will survive physically. Their populations have grown steadily since a nadir of near-extinction in the mid-twentieth century. Having fallen to little more than 100,000 in the 1950s they have more than tripled to some 350,000 and are generally rising fast. The reasons for this dramatic increase are partly medical, in better preventive medicine and health care. Although malaria is rampant, other lethal diseases – measles, tuberculosis, pneumonia, cholera, and smallpox – are now preventable or curable and epidemics of them are rarer than they were. Some Indians have acquired antigens to give inherited immunity to Western diseases. The improvement also has a social explanation: security of land tenure and cultural revival have produced a strong birth rate and improved life-expectancy. There are now as many indigenous peoples as when Rondon founded the SPI in 1910 – although they are of course a fraction of the 3.5 million or more who occupied Brazil in 1500, and they represent only 0.2 per cent of Brazil's national population of 165 million. Mércio Gomes commented that 'the demographic growth of [indigenous] peoples is the most positive historical event that has happened in Brazilian inter-ethnic relations. It is perhaps an augury for new times.'

There are 218 tribal groups ('ethnies' in some modern parlance). These prefer to refer to themselves as indigenous peoples. They are defined as regarding themselves as Indian, living communally on ancient lands, and retaining at least a vestige of their traditions. They vary hugely in degree of adaptation to national society. The Indians of southern and eastern Brazil are survivors of centuries of cohabitation: some are almost assimilated into the surrounding society in language and customs, but cling to a few traditions. Elsewhere, tribes have been contacted only recently; others have changed significantly since their first accommodation with frontier society. And, as stated, there are still uncontacted isolated peoples.

Tribes are very small, with a third of those who remain having fewer than 200 people. Fifty indigenous peoples number over 2,000. Of these, the ten that exceed 5,000 are, in ascending order: Sateré-Mawé (on the middle Amazon), Potiguara (east coast), Xavante (centre), Yanomami (north-west), Guajajara (Maranhão), Kaingang, Terena (south), Makuxi (centre-north), and the two largest – Ticuna (west Solimões) and Guarani (south) who each have some 30,000 people. To these should be added twice this number, over 700,000 people, who regard themselves as Indian but do not live in a tribal community.

The other success story of the past half-century concerns land. In 1987 CEDI published the population, legal status, and area of each indigenous territory. The situation had improved greatly during the previous twenty years. However, at that time a third of tribal areas were known to exist but had no defined boundaries or legislative protection. The remaining two-thirds – 351 entities with some 203,000 inhabitants, occupying almost 74.5 million hectares (287,600 square miles) – were at different stages of the process towards full legal title. Few had reached the final stage of full registration. Jõao Pacheco de Oliveira noted that Funai had conspicuously failed to meet the Indian Statute's target to demarcate all Indian lands by 1978. (Funai later failed to do the work by 1993, as ordered in the Constitution of 1988.) Oliveira commented that the majority of undemarcated land was in the Amazon basin. He suspected that this was deliberate, because Amazonia was 'the region in which the economic frontier is advancing, overriding or colliding with older expansion frontiers'. There was, however, a simpler explanation for that failure. Demarcation of the gigantic reserves in the remote, wild terrain of the Amazon rainforests was far more difficult and expensive than of those in open farmlands of eastern Brazil.

By the end of the century, the situation had greatly improved. A remarkable 11 per cent of the land-mass of Brazil is now reserved for Indians. The 587 indigenous areas total almost 105 million hectares (405,000 square miles) – an area greater than France, Germany, and Benelux combined. This is 40 per cent better than the situation in 1987. Of this immense area, over 3 million hectares (3 per cent) is still at the earliest stage of merely being identified, but this involves 136 smallish territories. A further 24 territories covering 2,471,530 hectares (2.4 per cent) have been identified and approved by Funai but can still be legally challenged. 67 territories covering almost 14.2 million hectares (13.5 per cent) have had their boundaries 'declared' by the Minister of Justice (Funai's minister). The great majority, 360 reserves totalling over 85 million hectares (81 per cent), have been either demarcated, homologated by presidential decree, or finally registered in the land registry. In 1999 a Pilot Program to Conserve Brazilian Rainforest was launched by various European aid agencies, the G7 group of rich nations, and the World Bank. Its indigenous peoples component (PPTAL) is devoting large sums to help Funai complete the expensive and exhausting task of demarcating the remaining indigenous areas.

Although many peoples have secured only a fraction of their ancient territories – particularly those in southern and eastern Brazil – a series of very large indigenous parks or areas has been won. Of the ten over 2 million hectares (7,700 square miles) in area, the pioneer was the Xingu indigenous park (1961), extended northwards to join the Kayapó (1991) and Baú (1991) reserves by the creation of the Menkragnoti indigenous area (1993). Others were: Tumucumaque (1968), Aripuanã and adjacent reserves (1988–1991), Waimiri Atroari (1989), Vale do Javari (1985/1998), Uru-Eu-Wau-Wau and Pakaá Nova in Rondônia (1991), Yanomami (1992), and Alto Rio Negro (1993). The only major area still in contention is the Makuxi's Raposa/Serra do Sol.

It is often asked why so few Indians control so much land. The introduction to CEDI's 1987 survey effectively countered this complaint. It showed that most surviving tribes are in local authorities where human habitation is very thin, so that Indians do not occupy a greater share than their colonist neighbours. And, even if tribes were given all the land earmarked for them, there would still be plenty left for rural settlement programmes. The majority of Brazilians prefer to live in cities, and very few could survive in the habitats where Indians hunt and subsistence-farm. So it is pointless to contrast the populations of tropical forests with those of urban shanty-towns. Most indigenous areas are in Amazonian rainforests or cerrado, land whose soils are too weak to support Western agriculture. Only small indigenous groups have learned to survive sustainably in this difficult environment, which would be useless for even the most resilient urban poor. They need large domains for hunting, fishing, collecting, and migration.

Playing the demographic numbers-game is a futile exercise. It is not the Indians' fault that their populations are so small. This is the result of decimation by alien diseases and centuries of oppression, and because tribes restrain population growth so that they will not outgrow surrounding natural resources. They should not be penalized for this laudable practice, at a time when the world's population is increasing explosively.

Indian hunter-gatherers are also excellent custodians of their environment – unless they are drawn into a market economy and seduced into commercial logging, mineral-prospecting, or hunting animals to extinction. The millions of hectares of indigenous reserves thus serve to protect endangered tropical biodiversity. Far more Amazon rainforests would have been destroyed had there not been tribal reserves within them. From the air, the Xingu park now stands out as an immense rectangle of verdant vegetation framed by the dismal brown of arid ranch-lands. The Xingu forests are as starkly outlined as an urban park in its built environment.

Today's protected indigenous areas are the product of decades of determined struggle. Tribe after tribe has had to fight for its rights, using a combination of direct action, occasional violence, political lobbying, media manipulation, and legal muscle. Success has come from the Indians themselves, who have buried old feuds and combined to fight for their rights. At the start of the twenty-first century, ISA listed no fewer than 125 associations of Indians, and there are many more small local pressure groups. Indigenous leaders are experienced orators. Many have shown a remarkable flair for public relations and (although not enfranchised) for political manoeuvring.

The indigenous assemblies are encouraged and supported by an equally remarkable contingent of thirty-three non-government organizations, a tireless band of missionaries, anthropologists, well-wishers, journalists, doctors, and lawyers, both in Brazil and abroad. Fortunately for the

Indians, their cause caught the imagination of young Brazilians, and during the two decades of military government it was a legitimate means of expressing disapproval. Typical of these many campaigners was Ana Valéria Araújo, featured by *Time* as an environmental 'leader for the new millennium'. Ana Valéria was praised as 'a key strategist and litigator in two organizations – the Nucleus for Indigenous Rights (NDI) and Social-Environmental Institute (ISA) – . . . who is very courageous in advocating the Indian cause in remote and dangerous corners of Brazil.'

The much-maligned Funai tried to fulfil its mission of protecting Indians and their lands. It did this despite having a bewildering succession of presidents (twenty-seven during its first thirty-three years, from 1967 to 2000), with constant shifts in policy and fortunes. Territorial successes also depended on a robust rule of law in Brazil. Each federal constitution has enshrined indigenous rights. Funai now comes under the Ministry of Justice, and the 1988 Constitution gave the Public Ministry and the Procurator-General a duty to care for indigenous rights. Thus, although judicial processes have been convoluted and painfully slow, and although few oppressors or killers of Indians have been convicted, the courts generally upheld indigenous claims against the powerful forces arrayed against them.

There is no cause for complacency. Although most battles for land rights have been won, a few are still in contention. Even when a reserve is legally registered, it is often scarcely possible to police it. Developed countries have great difficulty in excluding drugs, smuggled goods, or illegal immigrants: it is equally hard for Brazil to control the thinly inhabited rivers and forests of its reserves, immense in area, often unex-plored, and in some of the planet's most challenging terrain. Funai and the NGOs admit, helplessly, that 85 per cent of indigenous areas are invaded by loggers, prospectors, or squatters. Although demarcation and registration are essential, they alone do not guarantee an area. In 1989 Funai created an environmental department, now known as Codema. It reckons that '150 indigenous areas are affected by railways or roads, 28 areas are disturbed by mineral exploitation, and 54 are impacted by extraction of forest resources, in addition to 120 that suffer or could in the near future suffer from interference by works of the electricity sector.'

The Indian Statute and successive constitutions have always reserved *subsoil* mineral rights (as opposed to surface prospecting) on indigenous lands to the state. In 1999 Senator Romero Jucá (the controversial President of Funai in the late 1980s) and other Roraima legislators drafted a bill to open Indian lands fully to mining concessions. The bill proposed a fund from mineral income, to pay for education and health care for

Indians. Márcio Santilli of ISA surprisingly supported this legislation, since in the Constitution (in which he had fought for indigenous rights) subsoil rights did not belong to the Indians; but Santilli wanted all income from this source to go to the tribes themselves. Another ISA activist and President of Funai, Frederico Marés, declared that it was impossible to reconcile mining with the preservation of some tribes' cultures.

CEDI and its successor ISA combined with the geologists' associations to monitor research concessions awarded by the Ministry of Mines. In 1988 they published a detailed list of 2,245 such titles on 77 indigenous areas; and a decade later the number of exploration awards had tripled and affected 126 areas. For geological reasons these concessions are all on the ancient Central Brazilian and Guiana Shields, to the north and south of the main Amazon river and its great forests. So the most heavily affected tribes are Kayapó and other Jê-speakers and those in Rondônia, Roraima, and Brazilian Guiana. Most concessions were for gold exploration and half went to the largest mining companies such as Vale do Rio Doce, Silvana, and Itamaracá. By the end of the century, no major mine resulted from these concessions – if the huge tin mines alongside the Waimiri Atroari and various Rondônia tribes, and the Carajás iron-ore mine near the Xikrin are excepted. However, the threat of another gold- or diamond-rush by wildcat garimpeiros is ever present, particularly in the territory of the Yanomami or of the Cinta Larga and Suruí in Rondônia.

Another curious problem is overlap between environmental reserves or national forests and indigenous lands. This duplication is particularly acute in the Yanomami park, where a staggering 6.9 million hectares (27,000 square miles) overlap with four national or state parks, and also in the nearby Upper and Middle Rio Negro indigenous areas, where twelve national forests occupy 4.2 million hectares (16,000 square miles). There are smaller overlaps in indigenous areas in many other parts of Brazil. So far, this has not proved a problem since no extractive concessions have been awarded in these environmental reserves, and indigenous people have not been prevented from hunting in them – which is, of course, their constitutional right. Legislation is being drafted to overcome the dual use of these overlapping areas, possibly by creating a new category called Indigenous Reserve of Natural Resources which would seek to preserve the interests of both Indians and the environment.

Modern indigenous policy seeks to empower tribes to manage their own affairs. But it is not easy to exercise such self-determination responsibly. Entrepreneurs offer royalties or coveted possessions (everything from brick houses to refrigerators and televisions) for the resources on indigenous lands. Some tribal leaders or entire peoples make short-term gains by selling timber or mineral concessions. This is understandable, given the urgent need for cash by isolated tribal people who cannot profitably get their produce to market; but it can be environmentally disastrous and unsustainable. There is no easy answer to such 'corruption' of Indians or their leaders. These people are only human, their cultures are being swamped by dependence on imported goods, and the urge to sell resources to get the cash for such needs is often overwhelming. As Mércio Gomes commented, 'some think it ridiculous when an Indian wears jeans and flaunts a wristwatch and dark glasses' – but this is only imitating nearby frontier society. 'It is rather tempting to enjoy the allurements of civilization without making any great effort, by simply living off the royalties from minerals [or timber] found on one's lands.' Gomes suggested that indigenous territories could be considered as *strategic reserves* whose resources would be left untouched for a number of years. But this goes against market forces, and it negates giving tribes true control over their own affairs. A more optimistic view comes from the Macuxi Euclides Pereira (former President of Coiab, a coordinating body of indigenous organizations, in Manaus) who feels that most tribes are too sensible and responsible to sell out in this way. Coiab has therefore created 'sustainable models' to stop Indians trading their natural resources profligately with outsiders.

The destruction of Amazon forests and their precious biodiversity continues at a furious pace. The worst predators are now loggers, although deforestation to try to create farms or ranches is still a threat in some regions. Indigenous areas are therefore increasingly essential for environmental conservation. The Cardoso government proclaimed a policy called 'Advance Brazil' to develop Amazonia. This was almost a return to the grandiose Programme for National Integration (PIN) of 1970, that launched the Transamazonica and other penetration roads that did so much damage to indigenous peoples. This new plan involves paving four roads that had invaded Indian lands – including the Cuiabá–Santarém that destroyed Panará territory, the Transamazonica that damaged the Parakanã, Asuriní, Arara, and others, and the Manaus–Boa Vista that was so bitterly opposed by the Waimiri Atroari. Xavante living along the Mortes river are also objecting to a projected *hidrovia* canal system to make the Mortes–Araguaia–Tocantins rivers a waterway with locks bypassing their rapids. The main beneficiaries of this expensive hidrovia would be commercial growers of soya beans, which has become Mato Grosso's main export crop – but vast fields of soya are displacing small farmers and threatening tribes such as the semi-isolated Enawenê-Nawê. 'Advance Brazil' also involves more hydroelectric dams, power lines, mines, and, of course, immigration of settlers who pour in to regions served by paved highways. The programme was roundly condemned by Orlando Villas Boas, Sydney Possuelo, and respected environmentalists in Brazil and abroad.

One of the greatest successes is the pioneer, the Xingu national park. The anthropologists Darcy Ribeiro and Eduardo Galvão and the Villas Boas brothers devised the concept of a huge reserve that would combine protection of indigenous peoples and of nature. The idea was mooted in 1952 and passed into law in 1961, but no one imagined that it would still be flourishing half a century later. There are two reasons for the success. One is the Indians themselves. The upper Xingu region was unique in having a dozen tribes of different languages living in harmony, and these have maintained and strengthened that alliance; while downriver warrior tribes that were once bitter enemies ended their feuds, united, and have produced some of the most forceful advocates of Indian rights in Brazilian national politics. The other reason is the foresight of the Villas Boas who, having guaranteed the land, realized that the Indians needed a degree of protection (from some imported goods, from the tougher elements of frontier society, alcohol, and missionaries) in order to change at the speed and in the manner that they themselves chose. The brothers then devoted their lives to staying in the Xingu to make this revolutionary policy work.

Positive indicators are everywhere in the Xingu. Its Indians have tripled in numbers, to 3,600. Part of this increase is from tribes who have found sanctuary in the park (Kayabi, Tapayuna, Txikão), but most of the growth is natural. Peace and stability have brought a booming birth rate and greater life expectancy. And the Xinguanos enjoy excellent medical care. For almost forty years, volunteer doctors and dentists from the São Paulo Medical School (EPM) have gone to the Xingu to administer preventive medicine. Every Indian man, woman, and child has a complete medical record. I recently visited many villages with Professor Roberto Baruzzi, who has led this campaign since its inception, and saw how well he knows every individual man and woman and the affection in which they hold him. I also watched a positive new experiment: young men and women from each village are given intensive training as paramedics and in preventive skills. Dr Douglas Rodrigues of the EPM runs these courses, in which serious study is done in an Indian idiom. The Xingu Indians are not just surviving numerically; they are in perfect health, bursting with vitality, with magnificent physiques from a balanced diet, plenty of wrestling and other exercise, and no alcohol, hallucinogens, or smoking.

Reporters from *Veja* magazine were amazed by the Xingu park at the

turn of the millennium. They praised it as 'a treasure protected by Indians
. . . the guardians of the environment . . . If the present [increase in life
expectancy] continues, the day will soon come when the Xingu Indians
will be living longer and, without doubt, better than their neighbours in
the heart of the country. Thanks to the wisdom of some indigenous and
white leaders, the Xingu is today a rare harmonious accommodation
between disparate cultures.' The journalists paid tribute to the resident
'tribe of whites, composed of social scientists, doctors, teachers, nurses,
biologists, and agronomists from all parts of Brazil. A large measure of the
ingenious social and cultural engineering that keeps the Xingu park
functioning harmoniously is due to the work of these specialists . . . They
do not grow beards, but wear their hair long or braided. Lean, fed on
boiled fish with manioc beiju, peanut porridge, and fruit, they talk quietly,
go to bed early, and have only one topic of conversation: Indians.' Their
leader is André Villas-Boas, Director of ISA, a distant relative of the
brothers of the same name. Villas-Boas has worked with Indians since the
late 1970s, with the Xavante, Ticuna of the Solimões, and latterly in the
Xingu where, among other tasks, he is using satellite remote-sensing to
map the environmental pressures on the region. Others who have lived
for decades among the Indians are the dentist Eduardo Biral and his wife
Estela, a dedicated nurse. Both have been honoured by formal adoption
into the Mentuktire Kayapó.

The greatest tribute to the Villas Boas brothers is the way in which
Xingu Indians combine modern Brazilian usage with tribal heritage. Their
villages are unchanged – the same circle of mighty thatched communal
dwellings – as is their diet, predominantly of fish. There are still regular
ceremonies, dances, huka-huka wrestling matches, and moitará bartering
sessions. The reporters from *Veja* visited the village of the Suyá, the once-
fierce tribe that was rescued by Cláudio Villas Boas from possible extinction. 'Today they are almost 300 proud survivors. Even the Suyá language,
which was dying, is being reinvigorated. The heart of their territory, Rikó
village, is a happy place where festivals and work are intermingled. At
three in the morning the silence of night in the forest is broken, suddenly,
by the dull beating of drums. The Kahrankasaka festival is starting . . . It
is just for men. With rattles on their legs and ankles, they sing and dance
in a circle until daybreak, in homage to the rain that makes the water,
that makes the river, that shelters the fish, that feed mankind. The sun,
light, day and night, trees, jaguars and pacas, tapirs and bees are all
honoured . . . The women have their own festivals, of which the main
one is Yamurekumã . . . in which they turn the tables on their men with
token beatings.'

Cláudio Villas Boas died in 1998 and, a few months later, the upper-Xingu Indians decided to hold a great Kuarup funerary ceremony in his honour. Delegations from every tribe came to the village of the Kamayurá, who had prepared mountains of fish, manioc, and rice for their guests. I attended this most moving ceremony. The last surviving brother, Orlando, arrived with his wife Marina and two sons to an emotional welcome. Every elderly man and woman embraced Orlando, who was covered in their red urucum dye and on the verge of tears. There were two days of ritual dancing, flute-playing, wrestling, and mock charges by contingents of muscular warriors in dazzling body paint and feather ornaments. A brightly decorated tree trunk represented the soul of the dead Cláudio. Throughout a moonlit night pairs of shamans, men and women, sang gentle dirges and kept a fire burning in front of this totem. It was a beautiful and fitting tribute to the dedicated Indianist. Aritana, once a handsome young man groomed for leadership by the Villas Boas who had saved his small Yawalapiti tribe, is now the dignified Paramount Chief of the Xinguanos. He wished Orlando long life, but promised to hold a Kuarup in his honour provided that he would be buried in the Xingu. Orlando in turn urged the Indians to preserve the integrity of their lands and way of life. Orlando Villas Boas died, of disease, four years later in 2002.

Just as remarkable as such survivals of tribal traditions are the changes in Xingu society. When not wearing body paint, Indians are smartly dressed in shorts, designer T-shirts, and sandals for the men and brightly coloured dresses for women. I watched the televised final of a football World Cup with the Kayabi at Diauarum, and admired the quality of the Brazilian national football strip that they wore for the occasion. When the Aborigines Protection Society team visited the Xingu in 1972, it was impressed that this was the only place where it saw Indians in charge of operations and the maintenance of the post's basic equipment. This is now the norm. There are computers and other appliances powered from solar panels, generators, or batteries. Movement between villages is often by bicycle or vehicle, many canoes have outboard motors, and Indians manage the airstrips and their radios. Children learn reading and writing, Portuguese, maths, and the geography and history of their region. But their parents also train them to be expert fishermen, hunters, subsistence farmers, and woodsmen. They are taught to protect the environment of their luxuriant forests and rivers, more than ever a paradise in the midst of the degradation that surrounds it. For many years, Funai's Director of the Xingu park has always been an Indian; the upper Xingu tribes have a paramount chief in Aritana; and all fourteen ethnic peoples combine politically in ATIX, the Association of Xingu Indigenous Land.

There are a few introduced problems. Salt and sugar in the diet have brought some arterial hypertension, diabetes, and cardiac diseases; and young men visiting towns outside the park occasionally return with venereal disease and even a case of Aids. However, Professor Baruzzi told me that the greatest killer of young Indians is deaths during traditional but violent initiation rites. There is a serious lack of cash for the relatively few manufactured necessities. Government subsidies have been reduced, so that villages are struggling to develop export crops such as honey or candied dried bananas. So far, the Xingu tribes have been too sensible to succumb to temptation to sell their timber or mineral resources. The most serious threat is environmental. Because the park's creators failed in their bid to have it embrace the entire river basin, all the headwaters and tributaries of the Xingu rise outside the protected area. Settlement on all sides of the park has been intense, with new towns and roads everywhere, and deforestation of a third of the entire Xingu basin. This removal of forest cover has heightened erosion, and effluents from agricultural chemicals and some mineral prospecting are polluting rivers feeding the Xingu. In 1999, therefore, ISA and other organizations launched a campaign called 'SOS Xingu River'. The Indians welcomed this initiative, pointing out that 'We are doing our part [environmentally] and we would like the whites to do theirs.'

To mark the start of the new millennium, ISA commissioned an independent survey of attitudes towards Indians. The findings were amazingly favourable, beyond the greatest hopes of sympathizers, a revelation to the media, and a reversal of hostile prejudices or gloomy predictions of earlier decades. For instance, 78 per cent of Brazilians regarded Indians as naturally good people whose failings had been learned from whites. An amazing 88 per cent believed that indigenous people conserve the environment and live in harmony with it, while even more felt that they had a right to continue living in their forests in their customary manner. Public opinion in this survey overwhelmingly regarded Indians as hardworking in their manner and violent only when provoked by white invasions or aggression. The anthropologist Beto Ricardo of ISA, while overjoyed by this poll, was almost embarrassed by its return to the philosophers' ideal of the noble savage. 'Perhaps people's vision is over-romantic. But the most valuable aspect for the Indians is in its symbolic capital.' An example of this 'capital' came in the answer to the tendentious question whether it was right for 0.2 per cent of Brazil's population to control 11 per cent of its land-mass. An extraordinary 68 per cent of respondents agreed that it *was* right, and half of these felt that the protected area should be greater because Indians are such good custodians!

Politically, the situation of Brazil's Indians is quite good. Some of the most favourable aspects of Article 232 of the 1988 Constitution have not yet become statutory law. The Cardoso government caused alarm in indigenist circles with Decree 1,775 in January 1996. This invited states, local authorities, or individuals to challenge indigenous areas demarcated during the previous five years. They could advance claims to such land, point out alleged mistakes in boundaries, and sue for indemnification. Hundreds of petitions were filed, particularly against the Makuxi reserve of Raposa/Serra do Sol, the Yanomami park, the beleaguered Kaiowá Guarani, and some ancient pockets of land along the Atlantic seaboard, and there was even a rush of bogus occupants of the Krikatí reserve in Maranhão. This was countered by a vociferous campaign by NGOs. One described Decree 1,775 as 'a huge step backward which will likely lead to the violation of the rights of indigenous peoples', another said that 'President Cardoso has declared open season on Indian lands'. NGOs called on international agencies to withhold funds to Brazil until the 'iniquitous' decree was rescinded. In the event, the fears proved unfounded. No claims were successful. It could be argued that Decree 1,775 served as a safety valve – a challenge to interested parties to come forward, or for ever hold their peace.

The most serious legal problem is that Indian law is still governed by the 1973 Statute of the Indian. In 1992 the National Assembly appointed a Special Committee of five deputies to update this statute. Drawing on advice from Funai, CIMI, and the pro-Indian lawyers' of the Nucleus for Indigenous Rights (NDI), these deputies drafted a new Statute of Indigenous Societies. This was intended to bring the fine sentiments of the 1988 Constitution into law. It sought to empower tribes to manage all their own affairs – land, education, economy, health, transport, local policing – but collectively and with continuing government subsidy. Sadly, this radical but logical legislation bogged down in the political process of reviews and committees. It was still paralysed at the start of the new millennium.

The large Indigenous Conference that coincided with the ill-starred Discovery Celebration at Porto Seguro in April 2000 called for the new Statute to be approved forthwith. It also issued a manifesto called *The Next 500* that outlines directions for indigenous rights during the coming centuries. This manifesto wanted tribes to control their land, as defined in the Constitution. All aspects of local government should be devolved to local indigenous assemblies. This is not the discredited 'emancipation' proposed in the early 1980s, because land and resources would still be owned collectively and inalienably. Indians would still enjoy privileged status within Brazilian law – an issue that caused indigenous leaders to don warpaint and carry weapons when they repeatedly interrupted the debate in Congress in May 2000. They insisted that a clause in the draft Statute that would remove legal immunity from 'acculturated' individuals should be struck off. Another step forward came in June 2002, when (after a decade of legislative delays) Brazil formally adopted Convention 169 of the UN's International Labour Organisation. This directive gives indigenous peoples the right to their land and its natural resources, and requires that they may live and develop in a different manner, according to their own customs, and without suffering discrimination.

Other legal issues involve intellectual property right (IPR) and copyright of Indian images and artistic expression. Pro-Indian lawyers are seeking to ensure that ethnobotanical knowledge cannot be pirated – as was attempted by an American firm that 'patented' the medical properties of ayahuasca, the hallucinogenic plant used since time immemorial by tribes of the upper Amazon. Other lawyers are trying to protect collective rights in tribal creations such as body-paint, dance, or rituals. Darrell Posey, the anthropologist with the Kayapó, was a driving force in these campaigns until his death in 2001.

Perhaps surprisingly, the 2000 Conference wanted Funai to continue, but answering directly to the President of the Republic and with its president elected by the Indians from all regions of Brazil. Others feel that Funai's raison d'être has ceased. Indigenous education and health have both been removed from it and assigned to their respective ministries. Many tribes no longer need the presence of a Funai agent – and it is as difficult as ever to recruit and retain dedicated staff for the thankless job of encarregado on an isolated Indian post. So land-protection is Funai's chief remaining purpose, even though most territorial struggles have been won. Funai entered the new millennium with 3,350 staff and fifty regional offices, to care for 215 tribes. This rather bloated workforce makes it an obvious target for closure or slimming down under government austerity programmes. At the end of 1999 Funai itself engaged a management consultancy of the University of Brasília to consider its future. This proposed that the Foundation might become little more than an executive agency to oversee indigenous policy, with more 'autonomy and flexibility' but of course a much-reduced staff and budget. This and other ideas were put to the Indians' own organizations for their comment. The process had come full circle since Rondon founded the SPI ninety years before.

As we have seen, Indians generally enjoy a good press, they have achieved much through astute lobbying, and the ISA public-opinion survey showed that they are highly regarded by the general public; but their small numbers mean that they carry little electoral clout. Since Mário Juruna's feat of election as a federal deputy in 1983–86, the only Indian to enter the national legislature was António Ferreira da Silva (an Aruak-speaking Apurinã from the middle Purus river in Acre and western Amazonas), who became a senator in 2003. They have had more success in local government. Eighty Indian men and women stood for local office in the 1996 elections. In 2000, 350 stood and 75 were elected, one as mayor, three as deputy mayors, and the rest as councillors, and they came from the larger, more sophisticated tribes such as Kaingang, Ticuna, Terena, and Potiguara.

Indian leaders may now have less authority than they did in recent decades. The headline-grabbing antics of the Jê, that were so successful during the 1980s and '90s, have lost their novelty value. Indian affairs are not isolated from Brazilian politics. They depend on a liberal or socialist tendency, in opposition to the free-enterprise drive to exploit the supposed wealth of the interior at the expense of the environment or indigenous peoples. However, the recent survey shows how favourably Brazilian public opinion regards Indians, and the impressive indigenous assemblies and supporting NGOs are all in place and ready for action. The ambitious political objectives therefore seem attainable – particularly if it can be shown that devolved tribal self-government complements rather than conflicts with Brazilian nationalism.

Physical, territorial, legal, and political survival thus seem assured. Will ethnic identity also withstand powerful pressures for change? It is important to appreciate that when Indians complain, it is not because they are poverty-stricken wretches who want land to improve their standard of living. It is about land as the basis of society and identity. Having been humiliated and oppressed for centuries, they want their way of life to be recognized as a valid alternative that should coexist alongside that of the rest of Brazil. This is in no sense a threat to Brazilian nationhood or security, as some military analysts have argued.

Cultural survival is more complex and unpredictable than land rights, health, or legislation. Every group reacts differently to the challenges of contact with Brazilian national society. As we have seen abundantly, each indigenous nation presents a unique case history. Tribes enter the twenty-first century in a bewildering variety of circumstances, ranging from five centuries of contact and virtual assimilation to isolation as hunter-gatherers. There are wide differences of geography, terrain, circumstances of contact, proximity to roads or towns, involvement of missionaries, and availability of resources that attract commercial predators. Social factors within each tribe are equally varied and imponderable. The rate and nature of change depend on the strength of established customs and how these happen to relate to the unforeseen new challenges. There are immense pressures inside tribal society, not least in hierarchies based on age or gender. As intelligent human beings who engage in lively democratic discussion, Indians seek to make the right choices. But their reactions and decisions inevitably differ greatly.

The only generalization that can be made is that most Indians want to preserve their way of life and cultural heritage. This is shown repeatedly in speeches at assemblies of indigenous leaders. With encouragement from anthropologists, supporters, and some missionaries, there has been a powerful revival of pride in indianism. Some tribes, like the Ticuna, have built their own museum and publish their own newspaper, others video-record ceremonial and ensure that future generations continue to practise rituals and learn hunting and survival skills. The Yanomami leader Davi Kopenawa pleads passionately for continuation of his people's natural environment. 'We want our forest to remain, for ever. We want to live in it, in good health, and for the *xaripe* spirits, the game animals, and the fish to continue to live in it. We grow only the plants that feed us; we do not want factories or holes in the ground or dirty rivers. We want the forest to remain silent, the skies to continue to be clear, and the night to be truly dark so that we can see the stars.'

Education is emerging as a major issue in indigenous affairs, but it must be appropriate to each tribe. Anthropologists who fought for land rights are therefore turning their energies to helping groups they know well to devise curricula. Betty Mindlin despairs about the loss of artistic, literary, and musical creativity. 'The vast realms of indigenous imagination are debased, despised, and ignored among us.' This intellectual massacre 'is a spiritual tragedy, as if lost souls were being robbed by missionaries, loggers, miners, the degradation of urban life, and an incompetent government.' Mindlin has done much to record and publish legends of tribes of Rondônia. But prevention of such 'ethnocide' must begin with education of Indian children to know and value their heritage.

There are thought to be 170 native tongues or dialects in Brazil, most of which are a variant of one of the main indigenous language 'trunks' – Tupi, Jê, Aruak, Carib, and Panoan. Some, however, are unique or 'linguistically isolated'. There is now a strong movement for teaching a tribe's children in its own language and cultural idiom, preferably by teachers from the indigenous community itself, as well as bilingual education in Portuguese. The Ticuna have been at the forefront of this trend: as a large and sophisticated nation they have a cadre of impressive teachers who are held in high esteem in the tribe. In Acre, the educationalist Nietta Monte set up courses to train indigenous teachers; and she helped Betty Mindlin start instruction among tribes in nearby Rondônia. Luís Donisete Grupioni joined Monte in devising guidelines for indigenous schools, which the Ministry of Education issued in 1998; and an impressive committee (but containing few Indians) was established to monitor and improve this curriculum. A university in Mato Grosso gives specialized training to indigenous teachers. In 2000 another university in that state launched a five-year degree course for Indians, who could specialize in either natural sciences, social sciences, or language. The 200 places on the course were immediately taken by students from thirty-five tribes.

There is no knowing how long ethnic cultures can flourish naturally. Some anthropologists subscribe to the pessimistic view that acculturation is inevitable. Brazilian Indians are victims of 'social Darwinism' whereby they are doomed to evolution into the powerful and dynamic society that has occupied their land. This theory is regarded as regrettable but realistic. With increased mobility within Brazil, and with radio (and often television) available in Indian villages, the forces of Western culture are overwhelming. Indigenous societies would succumb to global uniformity.

Mércio Gomes realizes that 'the cultural integrity of Indian ethnies is threatened by the craving for consumption, a fatal attraction of modern society.' With some tribes, that understandable craving can easily be satisfied by selling non-renewable resources. The imported goods thus bring both cultural and environmental destruction. Another anthropologist who worries and wonders about the future is Eduardo Viveiros de Castro. He also appreciates the importance of material goods. 'The challenge or enigma confronting the Indians is whether it is possible to utilize the technological power of the whites – namely their pragmatism and their culture – without being poisoned by their absurd violence, their grotesque worship of material possessions, their intolerable arrogance, in short their domineering manner and their entire way of life.' Davi Yanomami warns about the moral cost of these goods. 'The lands of the whites are contaminated, covered in poisonous xawara fumes that extend far up into the bosom of heaven ... The whites never think about things that shamans know ... They continue to think endlessly about their possessions, as if these were their lovers.'

If this theory of inevitable change is correct, beautiful, ancient, and intricate cultures will be maintained only artificially as curiosities for tourists, researchers, or politically correct enthusiasts. But there is a more optimistic view: that the indigenous heritages are sufficiently robust to coexist alongside the national society. Brazil would be a multicultural nation in which Indians are partners with a high degree of self-determination, not inferiors to be patronized or exploited. Tribes would change in ways and at a speed to suit *them*, not ones imposed upon them – in the philosophy evolved by the Villas Boas and enlightened anthropologists of the mid-twentieth century. This is the hope of the Indians themselves and of many Brazilians. Given the physical, political, and legal successes of recent years, there seems no reason why this goal cannot be achieved.

Bibliography

ABBREVIATIONS

ACONTECEU: *Povos Indígenas no Brasil. Aconteceu* (Centro Ecumênico de Documentação e Informação (CEDI/ISA), São Paulo, 1981–) = PIB, see below.

AI: *América Indigena* (Instituto Indigenista Interamericano, Mexico).

ARC: *ARC Bulletin* (Anthropology Resource Center, Boston, 1979–).

ASBA: Herman Lent, ed., *Atas do Simpósio sôbre a Biota Amazônica* (2 vols., Conselho Nacional de Pesquisas, Rio de Janeiro, 1967), 2 *Antropologia*.

BMN: *Boletim do Museu Nacional*, nova série *Antropologia* (Rio de Janeiro, 1944–).

BMPEG: *Boletim do Museu Paraense Emílio Goeldi* n.s. *Antropologia* (Belém do Pará, 1957–).

Boletim do CIMI: Conselho Indígenista Missionário, Brasília, Sep. 1972–Dec. 1981.

BSPI: *Boletim* (Serviço de Proteção aos Índios, Ministério da Agricultura, Rio de Janeiro, 1941–45); *Boletim Interno* (Rio de Janeiro, 1st series, 1957–62; 2nd series, 1965–66).

CNPI: Conselho Nacional de Proteção aos Índios, Rio de Janeiro.

ES: Eduardo Galvão, *Encontro de Sociedades: índios e brancos no Brasil* (Editora Paz e Terra, Rio de Janeiro, 1979).

ESP: *O Estado de São Paulo*, one of Brazil's leading newspapers.

HIB: Manuela Carneiro da Cunha, ed., *História dos Índios no Brasil* (Editora Schwarcz, São Paulo, 1992).

HSAI: Julian H. Steward, ed., *Handbook of South American Indians*, Smithsonian Institution, Bureau of American Ethnology, Bulletin **143**, 6 vols (Washington, DC, 1946–63): **1**, *The Marginal Tribes*: **3**, *The Tropical Forest Tribes*.

IEN: Expedito Arnaud, ed., *O Índio e a Expansão Nacional* (Edições CEJUP, Belém, 1989).

IWGIA: International Work Group for Indigenous Affairs.

JSAP: *Journal de la Société des Américanistes de Paris*, n.s. (Paris, 1903–).

Parabolicas (newsletter of ISA (Instituto Socioambiental) São Paulo, Nov. 1994–).

PIB: *Povos Indígenas no Brasil* (also known as *Aconteceu Especial*), an excellent series of summaries of press reports on Indians and indigenous organizations, with attendant essays, published by CEDI (renamed Instituto Socioambiental [ISA] in 1994) in São Paulo. The first three volumes of *Aconteceu Especial* were *Trabalhadores 78* and two *Trabalhadores 79*; *PIB 1980* was *Aconteceu Especial* 6, *PIB 1981* was 7, *PIB/1982* was *Especial* 12, *PIB/83* was 14, *PIB/1984* was 15, *PIB-85/86* was 17, *PIB 1987/88/89/90* was 18; *PIB 1991/1995*, *PIB 1996–2000* and *PIB 1996/2000* were published by ISA. Confusingly, CEDI used the same general title *Povos Indígenas no Brasil* for its equally excellent series of regional surveys of Indians, of which only three of eighteen planned volumes were published: 3, *Amapá/Norte do Pará*; 5, *Javari*; 8, *Sudeste do Pará (Tocantins)*, in 1981–83.

Porantim (bi-monthly newspaper of CIMI-Norte; Manaus, later from CIMI Brasília, May 1978–).

RA: *Revista de Antropologia* (São Paulo, 1953–).

RAI: *(Revista de) Atualidade Indígena* (Fundação Nacional do Índio, Brasília, 1977–1981) (there was an earlier periodical called *Atualidade Indígena* published by the SPI from 1940–1958).

RIHGB: *Revista do Instituto Histórico e Geográfico Brasileiro* (Rio de Janeiro, 1839–).

RMP: *Revista do Museu Paulista* (São Paulo, 2nd series, 1947–).

SIN: *Survival International News* (Survival International, London, 1st series, 1972–74, issues 6–12 in 1974–75 known as *News from Survival International*; 2nd series, 1983–86; 3rd series called *Survival Newsletter*, 1988–).

SIR: *Survival International Review* (Survival International, London, 1976–82).

SPI: Serviço de Proteção aos Índios.

TD: Robin M. Wright, ed., *Transformando os Deuses. Os múltiplos sentidos da conversão entre os povos indígenas no Brasil* (Editora da Unicamp, Campinas, 1999).

TICN: Paulo Suess, ed., *Textos Indigenistas. Curt Nimuendajú* (Edições Loyola, São Paulo, 1982).

Urihi (Bulletin of the CCPY (Comissão pela Criação do Parque Yanomami), two per year, in both Portuguese and English editions, 1985–91).

BOOKS AND PAPERS

AÇÃO PELA CIDADANIA: *Roraima: o aviso da morte* (CCPY/CEDI/CIMI, São Paulo, 1989).

AGOSTINHO DA SILVA, Pedro: 'Geografia e cultura no alto Xingu', *Geografia* **3:12** (Lisbon, 1967), 20–31.

'Informe sobre a situação territorial e demográfica no alto Xingu', in Georg Grünberg, ed., *La Situación del Indígena en América del Sur* (Tierra Nueva, Montevideo, 1972), 355–80; trans. as 'Information Concerning the Territorial and Demographic Situation in the Alto Xingu', in Walter Dostal, ed., *The*

Situation of the Indian in South America (World Council of Churches, Geneva, 1972), 252–83.

Kwarup: mito e ritual no Alto Xingu (EPU and EdUSP, São Paulo, 1974).

AGUIAR, Naval Captain Bráz Dias de: 'Trabalhos da Comissão Brasileira Demarcadora de Limites – Primeira Divisão – nas fronteiras da Venezuela e Guianas Britânica e Neerlandesa, de 1930 a 1940', *IX Congresso Brasileiro de Geografia. Anais* (Rio de Janeiro, 1942).

ÅKERREN, Bo, Sjouke BAKKER, and Rolf HABERSANG: *Report of the ICRC Medical Mission to the Brazilian Amazon Region* (Comité International de la Croix-Rouge, Geneva, 1970).

ALBERT, Bruce: *Temps du sang, temps des cendres: Représentation de la maladie, système rituel et espace politique chez les Yanomami du sud-est (Amazonie Brésilienne)* (Doctoral dissertation, Université de Paris X, Nanterre, 1985).

ed., *Indiens et Développement en Amazonie (Brésil)* (special edition of *Ethnies*, **11–12**, Paris, 1990).

'La fumée du métal. Histoire et représentations du contact chez les Yanomami (Brésil)', *L'Homme*, Paris, **28:106–7**, Aug.–Sep. 1988, 87–119; trans. in *Anuário Antropológico/89*, 1992, 151–89.

'Terras indígenas, política ambiental e geopolítica militar no desenvolvimento de Amazônia: a propósito do caso Yanomami', *Urihi (Boletim da CCPY)* (CEDI/CONAGE, São Paulo) Jan. 1989, 3–36; in Philippe Léna and Adélia Engrácia de Oliveira, eds., *Amazônia: a fronteira agrícola 20 anos depois* (Museu Paraense Emílio Goeldi, Belém, 1991), 37–58; trans. as 'Indian lands, environmental policy and military geopolitics in the development of the Brazilian Amazon', *Development and Change*, **23**, 1992, 34–70.

'Gold miners and Yanomami Indians in the Brazilian Amazon: the Haximu massacre', in Barbara R. Johnston, ed., *Who Pays the Price? The Sociocultural Context of Environmental Crisis* (Island Press, Washington, 1994), 47–55; also in JSAP, **80**, 1994, 250–7.

'L'or cannibale et la chute du ciel. Une critique chamanique et l'économie politique de la nature', *L'Homme*, *126–128*, 1993.

ed., *Research and Ethics: The Yanomami Case* (CCPY, Brasília, 2001).

'O ouro canibal e a queda do céu. Uma crítica xamânica da economia política da natureza (Yanomami)', in Bruce Albert and Alcida Rita Ramos, eds., *Pacificando o Branco. Cosmologias do contato no Norte-Amazônico* (Editora da UNESP (Universidade Estadual Paulista)/IRD (Institut de Recherche pour le Développement)/Imprensa Oficial do Estado, São Paulo, 2002), 239–75.

and Marcus COLCHESTER: 'Recent development in the situation of the Yanomami', in Marcus Colchester, ed., *An End to Laughter? Tribal Peoples and Economic Development* (Survival International, London, 1985), 105–12.

and Davi KOPENAWA, *Yanomami: l'esprit de la forêt* (Fondation Cartier, Paris, 2003).

and Alcida Rita RAMOS, eds.: *Pacificando o Branco. Cosmologias do contato no Norte-Amazônico* (Editora da UNESP (Universidade Estadual Paulista)/IRD (Institut de Recherche pour le Développement)/Imprensa Oficial do Estado, São Paulo, 2002).

and Carlo ZACQUINI: 'Yanomami Indian Park: proposal and justification', in Alcida R. Ramos and Kenneth I. Taylor, eds., *The Yanoama in Brazil 1979* (ARC/IWGIA/SI document 37, Copenhagen, 1979), 99–170.

ALBISETTI, César and Ângelo Jayme VENTURELLI: *Enciclopédia Bororo*, 2 vols. (Museu Regional Dom Bosco, Campo Grande MT, 1962).

ALLEN, Elizabeth: 'Brazil: Indians and the new Constitution', *Third-World Quarterly*, 11:4, Oct. 1989, 148–65.

ALMEIDA JÚNIOR, José Maria Gonçalves de: *Carajás: desafio político, ecologia e desenvolvimento* (Brasiliense and CNPq., São Paulo and Brasília, 1986).

AMARANTE, Elizabeth Aracy Rondon and Verónica NIZZOLI, eds.: *Precisamos um Chão: depoiamentos indígenas* (Edições Loyola, São Paulo, 1981).

AMODIO, Emanuele and Vicente PIRA: 'História dos povos indígenas de Roraima – Makuxi – Ingaricó – Taurepang e Wapixana', *Boletim* (Arquivo Indigenista da Diocese de Roraima, Boa Vista), 10, Mar. 1985.

'Povos indígenas do Nordeste de Roraima', *Boletim* (Arquivo Indigenista da Diocese de Roraima, Boa Vista), 11, Feb. 1986.

AMORIM, Paulo Marcos: 'Índios camponeses: os Potiguara da Baía da Traição', RMP, 19, 1970–71, 7–95.

ANDUJAR, Cláudia: *Yanomami* (DBA, Curitiba, 1998).

AQUINO, Terri Valle de: *Kaxinawá: de seringueiro caboclo a peão acreano* (Empresa Gráfica Acreana, Rio Branco, 1982).

and Marcelo Manuel Piedrafita IGLESIAS: *Kaxinawá do Rio Jordão: história, território, economia e desenvolvimento sustentado* (Comissão Pró-Índio do Acre, Rio Branco, Acre, 1994).

ARNAUD, Expedito: 'Breve informação sobre os índios Asuriní e Parakanân, rio Tocantins, Pará', BMPEG, 11, Jul. 1961, 1–22.

'Os índios Galibi do rio Oiapoque – Tradição e mudança', BMPEG, 30, 27 Jan. 1966; IEN, 19–86.

'Grupos Tupi do Tocantins', ASBA.

'Os índios Oyampik e Emerilon (rio Oiapoque) – Referências sobre o passado e o presente', BMPEG, 47, 2 Feb. 1971; IEN, 129–58.

'A ação indigenista no Sul do Pará (1940–1970)', BMPEG, 49:6, Oct. 1971, 1–25; IEN, 159–84.

'A extinção dos índios Kararaô (Kayapó) – Baixo Xingu, Pará', BMPEG, 53, 26 Jun. 1974; IEN, 185–202.

'Os índios Mundurukú e o Serviço de Proteção aos Índios', BMPEG, 54, 1974, 1–60; IEN, 203–62.

'Os Gaviões de oeste – pacificação e integração', *Publicações Avulsas, Museu Paraense Emílio Goeldi*, Belém, **28**, 1975, 1–85.

'Mudanças entre grupos indígenas Tupí da região do Tocantins-Xingu (Bacia Amazônica)', BMPEG, **84**, 15 Apr. 1983, 1–50; IEN, 315–64.

'Curt Nimuendajú: aspectos de sua vida e de sua obra', RMP, **29**, 1983/84, 55–72.

'O comportamento dos índios Gaviões de Oeste face à sociedade nacional', BMPEG, **85**, 1984, 5–66; IEN, 365–426.

Os *Índios Palikúr do Rio Urucauá. Tradição tribal e protestantismo*, Publicações Avulsas **39**, MPEG, Belém, 1984.

'A ocupação indígena no Alto Xingu (Mato Grosso)', *Boletim de Pesquisa da CEDEAM*, **6:10** (Universidade do Amazonas, Manaus, Jan.–Jun. 1987), 125–59.

ed., O *Índio e a Expansão Nacional* (Edições CEJUP, Belém, 1989) = IEN.

and Ana Rita ALVES: 'A extinção dos índios Kararaô (Kayapó) – baixo Xingu, Pará', BMPEG, **53**, 1974.

ARNT, Ricardo, Lúcio Flávio PINTO, and Raimundo PINTO: *Panará. A volta dos índios gigantes* (Instituto Socioambiental (ISA), São Paulo, 1998).

ARRUTI, José Maurício: 'Morte e vida no nordeste indígena', *Estudos Históricos*, **8:15**, 1995, 57–94.

ASSELIN, Victor: *Grilagem, Corrupção e Violência em Terras de Carajás* (Editora Vozes, Petrópolis, 1982).

AZEVEDO, Soares de: *Pelo Rio Mar* (C. Mendes, Rio de Janeiro, 1933).

BADET, Charles: *Rondon, Charmeur d'Indiens* (Nouvelles Éditions Latines, Paris, 1951).

BAINES, Stephen Grant: *Relatório sobre a conclusão da etapa III de pesquisa de campo do Projeto Etnográfico Waimiri/Atroari* (University of Brasília, 25 Feb. 1985).

'*É a Funai que sabe': a frente de atração Waimiri-Atroari* (Doctoral dissertation, Universidade de Brasília, 1988; MPEG, Belém, 1991).

'The Waimiri-Atroari and the Paranapanema company', *Critique of Anthropology* (SAGE, London etc., **11:2**, 1991, 143–53); also in *Ethnies*, Survival International France, Paris, **11–12**.

'Comprido: a morte de um líder Waimiri-Atroari', BMPEG, **6:2**, 1991, 145–60.

A Política Governamental e os Waimiri-Atroari: administrações indigenistas, mineração de estanho e a construção da "autodeterminação" indígena dirigida (Universidade de Brasília, Série Antropologia **126**, 1992).

O *Território dos Waimiri-Atroari e o Indigenismo Empresarial* (Universidade de Brasília, Série Antropologia **138**, 1993).

Censuras e Memorias da Pacificação Waimiri-Atroari (Universidade de Brasília, Série Antropologia **148**, 1993).

Government Indigenist Policy and the Waimiri-Atroari Indians (Universidade de Brasília, Série Antropologia **152**, 1993).

Epidemics, the Waimiri-Atroari Indians and the Politics of Demography (Universidade de Brasília, Série Antropologia, **162**, 1994).

A Usina Hidrelétrica de Balbina e o Deslocamento Compulsório dos Waimiri-Atroari (Universidade de Brasília, Série Antropologia **166**, 1994).

'O xamanismo como história: censuras e memórias da pacificação Waimiri-Atroari', in Bruce Albert and Alcida Ramos, eds., *Pacificando o Branco. Cosmologias do contato no Norte-Amazônico* (Editora da UNESP (Universidade Estadual Paulista)/IRD (Institut de Recherche pour le Développement)/Imprensa Oficial do Estado, São Paulo, 2002), 311–45.

BALDUS, Herbert: *Ensaios de Etnologia Brasileira* (Companhia Editôra Nacional, São Paulo, 1937).

Tapirapé: Tribo tupi no Brasil central (São Paulo, 1970); originally in *Revista do Arquivo Municipal*, **96–127**, São Paulo, 1944–49.

'Tribos da bacia do Araguaia e o Serviço de Proteção aos Índios', RMP, **2**, 1948, 137–68.

'Os Oti', RMP, **8**, 1954, 79–92.

'Cândido Mariano da Silva Rondon, 1865–1958', RMP, **10**, 1956/58, 283–93.

Bibliografia Crítica da Etnologia Brasileira, 2 vols., **1** (Comissão do IV Centenário da Cidade de São Paulo, São Paulo, 1954), ed. Hans Becher, *Völkerkundliche Abhandlungen* **3** (Liechtenstein, 1970); **2** (Kommissionsverlag Müstermanns-Druck, Hanover, 1968).

Bibliografia Comentada de Etnologia Brasileira, 1943–1950 (Série Bibliográfica de Estudos Brasileiros, **1**, Rio de Janeiro, 1954).

'Métodos e resultados da ação indigenista no Brasil', RA, **10:1–2**, 1962, 27–42; trans. in *Actas y Memorias, XXXV Congreso Internacional de Americanistas* (Mexico, 1964); and in Egon Schaden, ed., *Homem, Cultura e Sociedade no Brasil* (Editora Vozes, Petrópolis, 1972), 209–28.

BALÉE, William: 'Indigenous history and Amazonian biodiversity', in H. K. Steen and R. P. Tucker, eds., *Changing Tropical Forests: Historical Perspectives on Today's Challenges in Central and South America* (Forest History Series, Durham, NC, 1992), 185–97.

'People of the fallow: a historical ecology of foraging in lowland South America', in Kent H. Redford and Christine J. Padoch, eds., *Conservation of Neotropical Forests: Working from Traditional Resource Use* (Columbia University Press, New York, 1992), 35–57.

'Indigenous transformation of Amazonian forests: an example from Maranhão, Brazil', *L'Homme*, Paris, **33:2–4**, 1993, 231–54.

Footprints in the Forest: Ka'apor Ethnobotany – The Historical Ecology of Plant Utilization by an Amazonian People (Columbia University Press, New York, 1994).

ed., *Advances in Historical Ecology* (Columbia University Press, New York, 1998).

BANDEIRA, Alípio: *Antiguidade e Atualidade Indígenas* (Tipografia do Jornal de Commercio, Rio de Janeiro, 1919).

A Mystificação Salesiana (Litho Typo Fluminense, Rio de Janeiro, 1923).

A Cruz Indígena (Livraria do Globo, Pôrto Alegre, 1926).

Jauapery (Manaus, 1926).

BANNER, Horace: *The Three Freds: Martyred Pioneers for Christ in Brazil* (Marshall, Morgan and Scott, London, n.d.).

'Mitos dos índios Kayapó', RA, **5:1**, Jun. 1957, 37–66; also in Egon Schaden, ed., *Homem, Cultura e Sociedade no Brasil* (Editora Vozes, Petrópolis, 1972), 90–132.

'O índio Kayapó em seu acampamento', BMPEG, **13**, 1961.

Long Climb on the Xingu (Unevangelized Fields Mission, Green and Co., London, 1963).

The Three Freds and After (Graham and Heslip, Belfast, 1975).

BARROS, Edir Pina de: 'Os Bakairi: economia e cosmologia', RA, **37**, 1994, 257–308.

BARROS PRADO, Eduardo: *Yo vi el Amazonas*, trans. Amilcar A. Botelho de Magalhães as *Eu ví o Amazonas* (Imprensa Nacional, Rio de Janeiro, 1952).

BARUZZI, Roberto G.: 'Escola Paulista de Medicina: 16 anos atendendo os índios', RAI, **21**, Jul.–Aug. 1981, 62–6.

et al.: 'The Kren-Akorore: a recently contacted indigenous tribe', *Health and Disease in Tribal Societies* (Ciba Foundation Symposium, **49**, Aug. 1977, Elsevier North-Holland).

BASSO, Ellen Becker: *The Kalapalo Indians of Central Brazil* (Holt, Rinehart & Winston, New York, 1973).

In Favor of Deceit (University of Arizona Press, Tucson, 1987).

The Last Cannibals: a South American Oral History (University of Texas Press, Austin, 1995).

BASTOS, Rafael José De Menezes: *Exegeses Yawalapity e Kamayurá da Criação do Parque Indígena do Xingu e a Invenção da Saga dos Irmãos Villas Boas* (ANPOCS, Campos de Jordão, 1986).

'Indagação sobre os Kamayurá, o Alto-Xingu e outros nomes e coisas: uma etnologia da sociedade Xinguara', *Anuário Antropologico* (Tempo Brasileiro, Rio de Janeiro), **94**, 1995, 227–69.

BELTRÃO, Luiz: *O Índio, um Mito Brasileiro* (Editora Vozes, Petrópolis, 1977).

BERWICK, Dennison: *Amazon* (Hutchinson, London, 1990).

Savages. The Life and Killing of the Yanomami (Hutchinson, London, 1992).

BIOCCA, Ettore: *Estudos Etnobiológicos sôbre os Índios da Região do Alto Rio Negro* (Archivos de Biologia, São Paulo, Sep.–Oct. 1944).

'A penetração branca e a difusão da tuberculose entre os índios do Rio Negro', RMP, **14**, 1963, 203–12.

Yanoáma (Leonardo da Vinci Editrice, Bari, 1965); trans. Dennis Rhodes as *Yanoáma. The Story of a Woman Abducted by Brazilian Indians* (George Allen and Unwin, London, 1969).

Viaggi tra gli Indi Alto Rio Negro-Alto Orinoco (4 vols., Consiglio Nazionale delle Ricerche, Rome, 1966).

BISILLIAT, Maureen: *Xingu, Território Tribal* (Cultura, São Paulo, 1979).

Guerreiros sem Espada. Experiências revistas dos irmãos Villas Bôas (Impresa das Artes, São Paulo, 1995).

BLOMBERG, Rolf: *Chavante. An Expedition to the Tribes of the Mato Grosso*, trans. Reginald Spink (Allen and Unwin, London, 1960).

BODARD, Lucien: *Le Massacre des Indiens* (Éditions Gallimard, Paris, 1969); trans. as *Green Hell* (Outerbridge & Dientsfrey, New York, 1971).

BOGGIANI, Guido: *Os Caduveo*, trans. Amadeu Amaral Júnior (Biblioteca Histórica Brasileira 14, Livraria Martins Editôra, São Paulo, 1945).

BOURNE, Richard: *Assault on the Amazon* (Victor Gollancz, London, 1978).

BRASIL, Governo do: *Brasil Indígena* (Presidência da República, Brasília, 1992).

BROOKS, Edwin, René FUERST, John HEMMING, and Francis HUXLEY: *Tribes of the Amazon Basin in Brazil, 1972*, Aborigines Protection Society (Charles Knight & Co., London, 1973).

BRUZZI, Alcionilio Alves da Silva: *A Civilização Indígena do Uaupés* (Linografia Editora, São Paulo, 1962; LAS, Rome, 1977).

As Tribos do Uaupés e a Civilização Brasileira. O método civilizador salesiano (No publisher, 1979).

BUCHILLET, Dominique: 'Chronique du Groupe d'Information sur les Amerindiens: le Brésil, droits constitutionnels et demarcation des terres au Brésil', JSAP, **79**, 1993, 225–31.

'Droits indigènes, militarisation et violence contre les indigènes au Brésil', JSAP, **80**, 1994, 243–50.

'Contas de vidro, enfeites de branco e potes de malária' (Universidade de Brasília, Série Antropologia, **187**, 1995); also in Bruce Albert and Alcida Ramos, eds., *Pacificando o Branco. Cosmologias do contato no Norte-Amazônico* (Editora da UNESP (Universidade Estadual Paulista)/IRD (Institut de Recherche pour le Développement)/ Imprensa Oficial do Estado, São Paulo, 2002), 112–42.

CABRAL, Ana Suely Câmara and Ruth Maria Fonini MONTSERRAT, eds.: *Por uma Educação Indígena Diferenciada* (Centro Nacional de Referência, Brasília, 1987).

CAIUBY NOVAES, Sylvia: *Mulheres, Homens e Heróis – Dinâmica e permanência através do cotidiano da vida Bororo* (FFLCH, Universidade de São Paulo, 1986).

'Esclaves du démon ou serviteurs de Dieu: les Bororos et la Mission Salesienne au Brésil', *Recherches Amerindiens au Québec* (Société de Recherches Amerindiens au Québec, Montréal), **21:4**, 1991–92, 37–52.

Jogo de Espelhos – *imagens da representação de si através dos outros* (EdUSP, São Paulo, 1993).

'A épica salvacionista e as artimanhas de resistência – As Missões Salesianas e os Bororo de Mato Grosso', TD, 343–62.

CAMPBELL, Alan Tormaid: *Getting to Know Waiwai. An Amazonian Ethnography* (Routledge, London and New York, 1995).

CAMPOS, José de Queiros: 'Informe de la delegación del Brasil ante el VI Congreso Indigenista Interamericano', AI, **28:4**, Oct. 1968, 1076–83.

CARNEIRO, Robert L.: 'Slash and Burn Cultivation among the Kuikuro and its Implications for the Cultural Development in the Amazon Basin', in Daniel Gross, ed., *Peoples and Cultures of Native South America* (Doubleday, New York, 1961), 98–123.

'Tree felling with stone ax: an experiment carried out among the Yanomamo Indians of southern Venezuela', in C. Kramer, ed., *Ethnoarchaeology* (Columbia University Press, New York, 1979), 21–58.

CARNEIRO DA CUNHA, Manuela M.: 'Logique du mythe et de l'action: le mouvement messianique Canela de 1963', *L'Homme*, Paris, **13:4**, 1973, 5–37.

Os Mortos e os Outros (Hucitec, São Paulo, 1978).

Os Direitos do Índio: Ensaios e documentos (Editora Brasiliense, São Paulo, 1987).

ed., *História dos Índios no Brasil* (Companhia das Letras, São Paulo, 1992) = HIB.

'O futuro da questão indígena', *Estudos Avançados* (Universidade de São Paulo), **8:20**, Jan.–Apr. 1994, 12–36.

CARON, Père Raymond: *Curé d'Indiens* (Union Générale d'Éditions, Paris, 1971).

CARVALHO, João Evangelista: 'A pacificação dos Parakanã', *Carta* (Gabinete Senador Darcy Ribeiro, Brasília), 9, 1993, 213–39.

CARVALHO, José C. M., Pedro E. de LIMA, and Eduardo GALVÃO: *Observações Zoológicas e Antropológicas na Região dos Formadores do Xingu* (Imprensa Nacional, Rio de Janeiro, 1949).

CARVALHO, José Porfírio F. de: *Waimiri/Atroari – a história que ainda não foi contada* (Published by the author, Brasília, 1982).

CARVALHO, Wilson de: *Flashes da Amazônia* (São Paulo, 1964).

CASALDÁLIGA, Dom Pedro: *Uma Igreja da Amazônia em Conflito com o Latifúndio e a Marginalização Social* (Diocese de São Félix, Mato Grosso, 1972).

CASPAR, Franz: *Tupari. Unter Indios im Urwald Brasiliens* (Friedr. Vieweg & Sohn, Braunschweig, 1952); trans. Eric Northcott as *Tupari* (G. Bell and Sons, London, 1956).

'A aculturação da tribo Tupari', RA, **5:2**, Dec. 1957, 145–71 (trans. by Egon Schaden of a paper in *Kölner Zeitschrift für Soziologie und Sozialpsychologie*, **9:2**, Köln, 1957).

CASTELO BRANCO, José Moreira Brandão: 'O gentio acreano', RIHGB, **207**, Apr.–Jun. 1950, 3–77.

CAUFIELD, Catherine: *In the Rainforest* (William Heinemann, London, 1985).

CAVALCANTI, Cícero: '12 anos convivendo com os Kaiapó', RAI, **21**, Jul.–Aug. 1981, 18–23.

CAVALCANTI, José Bezerra: *Exposição apresentada ao Sr. D. Pedro de Toledo, Ministro da Agricultura, Indústria e Comércio* (Rio de Janeiro, 1912).

CAVUSCENS, SILVIO: 'A situação dos povos indígenas do Vale do Javari', *PIB 1991/1995*, 333–42.

and Lino João de O. NEVES: *Povos Indígenas do Vale do Javari, Campanha Javari* (CIMI, Manaus, 1986).

CHAGNON, Napoleon A.: *Yanomamö, the Fierce People* (Holt, Rinehart & Winston, New York, 1968) and subsequent editions; revised as *Yanomamo: the Last Days of Eden* (Harcourt Brace Jovanovich, San Diego, 1992, Fort Worth, 1997).

Studying the Yanomamö (Holt, Rinehart & Winston, New York, 1974).

'Yanomamo, the True People', *National Geographic*, **150:2**, Aug. 1976, 210–23.

CHAPELLE, Richard: *Os Índios Cintas-Largas* (Itatiaia, Belo Horizonte, 1982).

CHERNELA, Janet Marion: 'Why one culture stays put: a case of resistance to change in authority and economic structure in an indigenous community in the northwest Amazon', in John Hemming, ed., *Change in the Amazon Basin*, **2**, *The Frontier After a Decade of Colonization* (Manchester University Press, Manchester, 1985), 228–36.

'Righting history in the northwest Amazon: myth, structure, and history in an Arapaço narrative', in Jonathan D. Hill, ed., *Rethinking History and Myth. Indigenous South American Perspectives on the Past* (University of Illinois Press, Urbana, 1988).

The Wanano Indians of the Brazilian Amazon: a Sense of Space (University of Texas Press, Austin, 1993).

'Missionary activity and Indian labor in the Upper Rio Negro of Brazil, 1680–1980: a historical-ecological approach', in William Balée, ed., *Advances in Historical Ecology* (Columbia University Press, New York, 1998), 313–33.

CHIARA, Vilma: 'Le processus d'extermination des indiens du Brésil', *Les Temps Modernes*, **270**, Paris, 1968, 1070–9.

CLEARY, David: *Anatomy of the Amazon Gold Rush* (Macmillan, Basingstoke; University of Iowa Press, Iowa City, 1990).

CNBB-CIMI: *A verdadeira conspiração contra os povos indígenas, a igreja e o Brasil* (Conselho Indigenista Missionário, Brasília, 1987).

COELHO, Vera Penteado, ed.: *Karl von den Steinen: um século de antropologia no Xingu* (EdUSP/Fapesp, Universidade de São Paulo, 1993).

COHEN, Marleine: 'O caminho de volta: a saga dos gigantes Panará', *PIB 1991/1995*, 601–13.

COIMBRA, C.: 'A participação das organizações religiosas na Amazônia', in Artur César Ferreira Reis, ed., *Problemática da Amazônia* (Livraria Edições Casa Estudante, Rio de Janeiro, 1969), 261–76.

COLBACCHINI, Antonio: *I Bororos Orientali 'Orarimugudoge' del Matto Grosso, Brasile* (Turin, 1925); trans., with additions by Cesar Albisetti, as *Os Bororo Orientais Orarimogodógue do planalto oriental de Mato Grosso* (Companhia Editôra Nacional, São Paulo, 1942).

COLBY, Gerard and Charlotte DENNETT: *Thy Will be Done. The Conquest of the Amazon: Nelson Rockefeller and Evangelism in the Age of Oil* (HarperCollins Publishers, New York, 1995).

COMISSÃO PRÓ-ÍNDIO: *A Questão da Emancipação* (Cadernos da Comissão Pró-Índio, 1, Global Editora, São Paulo, 1979).

CORRÊA FILHO, Virgílio: 'Rondon', RIHGB, **266**, Jan.–Mar. 1965, 155–8.

COUTINHO, Edilberto: *Rondon e a Integração da Amazônia* (Arquimedes Edições, São Paulo, 1968).

Rondon, o Civilizador da Última Fronteira (Olivé Editora, Rio de Janeiro, 1969).

COWELL, Adrian: *The Heart of the Forest* (Victor Gollancz, London, 1960).

'Legendary Brothers of the Amazon', *Observer Magazine*, 20 Jun. 1971, 12–25.

The Tribe that Hides from Man (Bodley Head, London, 1973; Pimlico, London, 1995).

The Decade of Destruction (Headway, Hodder & Stoughton, London, 1990).

CROCKER, William: 'The Canela since Nimuendajú. A preliminary report on cultural change', *Anthropological Quarterly* **34:2** (Catholic University of America, Washington, DC, Apr. 1961), 69–84.

'The Canela messianic movement: an introduction', ASBA, 69–84.

and Jean CROCKER, eds.: *The Canela: Bonding through Kinship, Ritual, and Sex* (Harcourt Brace College Publishers, Fort Worth, 1994).

CRULS, GASTÃO: *A Amazônia que eu Vi* (Livraria José Olympio Editôra, Rio de Janeiro, 1930).

Hiléia Amazônica: aspectos de flora, fauna, arqueologia e etnologia indígena (Rio de Janeiro, 1958).

CRUMLEY, CAROLE, ed.: *Historical Ecology: Cultural Knowledge and Changing Landscapes* (School of American Research Press, Santa Fé, 1994).

CUNHA, Ayres Câmara: *Entre os Índios do Xingu. A verdadeira história de Diacuí* (Livraria Exposição do Livro, São Paulo, 1960).

DALLARI, Dalmo de Abreu, Manuela CARNEIRO DA CUNHA, and Lux VIDAL, eds.: *A Questão da Terra Indígena* (Cadernos da Comissão Pró-Índio, 2, Global Editora, São Paulo, 1981).

D'ANGELIS, Wilmar da Rocha: *Toldo Chimbangue. História e luta Kaingang em Santa Catarina* (CIMI-Regional Sul, Xanxerê, SC, 1984).

'Os Kaingang: terra e autonomia política – condições para acesso à cidadania', *Terra*

Indígena (CIMI Centro de Estudos Indígenas, Araraquara), **8:59**, Apr.–Jun. 1991, 45–56.

DAVIS, Shelton: 'Custer is Alive and Well in Brazil', *Indian Historian*, Winter 1973.
Victims of the Miracle. Development and the Indians of Brazil (Cambridge University Press, Cambridge and New York, 1977).

DINIZ, Edson Soares: 'Os Kayapó-Gorotire: aspectos sócioculturais do momento atual', BMPEG, **18**, 1962.
'Convívio interétnico e aglutinação intergrupal', RMP, **14**, 1963, 213–20.
'O perfil de uma situação interétnica: os Makuxí e os regionais do Roraima', BMPEG, **31**, Apr. 1966, 1–31.
'Os Makuxí e os Wapitxâna: índios integrados ou alienados?', ASBA, 93–100.
Os Índios Makuxi de Roraima – sua instalação na sociedade nacional (Editora Faculdade de Filosofia, Ciências e Letras de Marília, São Paulo, 1972).

DOLE, Gertrude E.: 'Ownership and exchange among the Kuikuro Indians of Mato Grosso', RMP, **10**, 1958, 125–33.

DOMVILLE-FIFE, Charles W.: *Among Wild Tribes of the Amazons* (Seeley, Service & Co., London, 1924).

DORIA, Carlos Alberto and Carlos Alberto RICARDO: 'Populations indigènes du Brésil: Perspectives de survie dans la région dite Amazonie Légale', *Bulletin de la Société Suisse des Américanistes*, **36**, Geneva, 1972, 19–35.

DOSTAL, Walter, ed.: *The Situation of the Indian in South America* (World Council of Churches, Geneva, 1972); contains his 'The Indians and the occupation of Amazonia', 338–42, 'Declaration of Barbados for the Liberation of the Indians', 376–81, and 'The indigenous groups of Brazil', 434–42.

DREYFUS, Simone: *Les Kayapo du Nord, état de Para, Brésil: contribution à l'étude des indiens Gé* (La Haye: Mouton, Paris, 1963).

DUARTE FILHO, Otto Carlos Bandeira: *Rondon, o Bandeirante do Século XX* (Livraria Valverde, Rio de Janeiro, 1945).

DURHAM, Eunice Ribeiro: 'O lugar do índio', in Lux Vidal, ed., *O Índio e a Cidadania* (Brasiliense, São Paulo, 1983).

DUTRA, Carlos Alberto dos Santos: *Ofaié: morte e vida de um povo* (CIMI-MS, Brasilândia, MS, 1994).

DUVAL RICE, F. John: 'A pacificação e identificação das afinidades linguisticas da tribu Urubú dos estados de Pará e Maranhão, 1928–1929', JSAP, **22**, 1930.

DYOTT, George Miller: 'The Search for Colonel Fawcett', *Geographical Journal*, London, **72**, 1928, 443–8 and **74**, 1929, 513–40.
Man Hunting in the Jungle. The Search for Colonel Fawcett (Edward Arnold & Co., London, 1930).

EARLY, John D., and John F. PETERS: *The Population Dynamics of the Mucajaí Yanomami* (Academic Press, New York, 1990).

The Xilixana Yanomami of the Amazon. History, social structure and population dynamics (University Press of Florida, Gainesville, Fla., 2000).

FABRÉ, D G: *Beyond the River of the Dead*, trans. from Spanish by Eric L. Randall (The Travel Book Club, London, 1963).

FARABEE, William Curtis: 'The Amazon Expedition of the University Museum', *The Museum Journal*, University of Pennsylvania, Philadelphia, **7**:4, Oct.–Dec. 1916, 210ff. and **8**:2, Apr.–Jun. 1917, 61–82, and **8**:4, Sep.–Oct. 1917, 126–44.

'A pioneer in Amazonia: the narrative of a journey from Manaus to Georgetown', *The Bulletin of The Geographical Society of Philadelphia*, **15**, Jan.–Oct. 1917, 57–103.

The Central Arawaks (University of Pennsylvania Museum, Anthropological Publications 9, Philadelphia, 1918).

'The Apalai', *The Museum Journal*, University of Pennsylvania, Philadelphia, **10**:3, Jun.–Aug. 1919, 102–16.

The Central Caribs (University of Pennsylvania Museum, Anthropological Publications 10, Philadelphia, 1924).

FARIA, Gustavo de, ed.: *A Verdade sobre o Índio Brasileiro* (Guavira Editores, Rio de Janeiro, 1981).

FAULHABER, Priscila: 'A territorialidade Miranha nos rios Japurá e Solimões e a fronteira Brasil-Colombia', BMPEG, **12**:2, 1996, 249–303.

'A reinvensão da identidade indígena no médio Solimões e no Japurá', *Anuário Antropológico*, Rio de Janeiro, **96**, 1997, 83–102.

O *Lago dos Espelhos: etnografia do saber sobre a fronteira em Tefé/Amazonas* (Museu Paranaense Emílio Goeldi, Belém, 1998).

FAUSTO, Carlos: *Inimigos Fiéis: história, guerra e xamanismo na Amazônia* (EdUSP, São Paulo, 2001).

FAWCETT, Lieutenant Colonel Percy Harrison, edited by Brian Fawcett: *Exploration Fawcett* (Hutchinson, London, 1953; called *Lost Trails, Lost Cities* in the New York edition (Funk & Wagnalls, 1953)).

FERGUSON, R. Brian: 'Blood of the Leviathan: Western contact and warfare in Amazonia', *American Ethnologist*, **17**, 1990, 237–57.

'A savage encounter. Western contact and the Yanomami war complex', in R. Brian Ferguson and Neil L. Whitehead, eds., *War in the Tribal Zone* (School of American Research Press, Santa Fé, N. Mex., 1992), 199–227.

Yanomami Warfare: A Political History (School of American Research Press, Santa Fé, N. Mex., 1995).

'Whatever happened to the stone age? Steel tools and Yanomami historical ecology', in William Balée, ed., *Advances in Historical Ecology* (Columbia University Press, New York, 1998), 287–312.

and NEIL L. WHITEHEAD, eds.: *War in the Tribal Zone: Expanding States and Indigenous Warfare* (School of American Research Press, Santa Fé, N. Mex., 1992).

FERRARI, Alfonso Trujillo: *Os Kariri: o crepúsculo de um povo sem história* (Publicações Avulsas da Revista Sociologia, São Paulo, 1957).

FERRAZ, Iara and Mariano MAMPIERI: 'Suiá-Missu: um mito refeito', *Carta* (Gabinete do Senador Darcy Ribeiro, Brasília), **9**, 1993, 75–84; and *PIB 1991/ 1995*, 675–8.

FERREIRA, Jorge: 'Kuarup', O *Cruzeiro*, **29:15**, Rio de Janeiro, 26 Jan. 1957, 58–71.

FERRI, Patricia: *Achados ou Perdidos? A imigração indígena em Boa Vista* (MLAL, Goiânia, 1990).

FIGUEIREDO, José de Lima: *Índios do Brasil* (Companhia Editora Nacional, São Paulo, Rio de Janeiro, etc., 1939).

FISHER, William H.: 'Megadevelopment, environmentalism, and resistance: the institutional context of Kayapó indigenous politics in central Brazil', *Human Organization* (Society for Applied Anthropology, Boston), **53:3**, 1994, 220–32.

FLEMING, Peter: *Brazilian Adventure* (Jonathan Cape, London, 1933).

FOIRN-ISA: Aloísio Cabalzar ed., *Povos Indígenas do Alto e Médio Rio Negro* (Federação das Organizações Indígenas do Rio Negro/Instituto Socioambiental, São Gabriel da Cachoeira/São Paulo, 1998).

FRANCHETTO, Bruna: *Laudo Antropológico: A ocupação indígena da região dos formadores e do alto curso do rio Xingu* (Mimeo, Museu Nacional/Univ. Fed. do Rio de Janeiro, Rio de Janeiro, 1987).

'"O aparecimento dos caraíba". Para uma história kuikuro e alto-xinguana', HIB, 339–56.

and Michael HECKENBERGER, eds.: *Os Povos do Alto Xingu: história e cultura* (Editora da Universidade Federal do Rio de Janeiro, 2001).

FREIRE, Carlos Augusto da Rocha: *Saudades do Brasil, ou as lutas pela criação do Parque Indígena do Xingu* (Museu Nacional/Univ. Fed. do Rio de Janeiro, Rio de Janeiro, 1987).

Indigenismo e antropologia: o Conselho Nacional de Proteção aos Indios na gestão Rondon (1939–1955) (Master's dissertation, Museu Nacional, Rio de Janeiro, 1990).

FRIKEL, Protásio Gunther: *Os Kaxúyana. Notas etno-históricas* (Publicações Avulsas do Museu Goeldi, **14**, Belém, 1970).

Os Tiriyó. Seu sistema adaptativo, BMPEG, **9**, 1960 (Kommisionsverlag Münstermann-Druck, Hannover, 1973).

'Notas sôbre a situação atual dos índios Xikrin do Rio Caeteté', RMP, **14**, 1963, 145–58.

Dez Anos de Aculturação Tiriyó, 1960–1970 (Publicações Avulsas do Museu Goeldi, **16**, Belém, 1971).

'Migração, guerra e sobrevivência Suiá', RA, **17:20**, 1972.

with Roberto CORTEZ: *Elementos Demográficos do Alto Paru do Oeste, Tumucumaque Brasileiro: índios Ewarhoyana, Kaxuyana e Tiriyó* (Publicações Avulsas do Museu Goeldi, **19**, Belém, 1972).

FUNAI (Fundação Nacional do Índio): *Supysáua, o Índio Brasileiro* (Editora Vecchi, Rio de Janeiro, 1972).

O que é a Funai (Editôra Gráfica, Brasília, 1972).

Situação das Terras Indígenas do Brasil: Dados Estimativos (Brasília, 1984).

Situação das Terras Indígenas do Brasil (Brasília, 1998).

FURTADO, Lourdes Gonçalves: 'Alguns aspectos do processo de mudança na região do nordeste paraense', BMPEG, **1**, Jun. 1984, 67–123.

GAGLIARDI, José Mauro: *O Indígena e a República* (Editôra Hucitec, São Paulo, 1989).

GALEY, John: 'Industrialist in the wilderness: Henry Ford's Amazon venture', *Journal of Inter-American Studies*, **21:2**, May 1979, 264–89.

GALLOIS, Dominique Tilkin: 'Índios e brancos na mitologia Waiãpi: da separação dos povos à recuperação das ferramentas', RMP, **30**, 1985, 43–60.

Migração, Guerra e Comércio: os Waiãpi na Guiana (FELCH/USP, Antropologia **15**, São Paulo, 1986).

'De arredio a isolado: perspectivas de autonomia para os povos indígenas recém-contactados', in Luís Donisete Benzi Grupioni, ed., *Índios no Brasil* (3rd edn, Global Editora e Distribuidora Ltda., São Paulo, 1998), 121–34.

and Luís Donisete GRUPIONI: 'O índio na Missão Novas Tribos', TD, 77–129.

GALVÃO, Eduardo, and Mário SIMÕES: 'Noticia sobre os índios txikão, alto Xingu', BMPEG, **24**, 1965, 1–24.

'Mudança e sobrevivência no Alto Xingu – Brasil Central', RA, **14**, 1966, 37–52; also in Egon Schaden, ed., *Homem, Cultura e Sociedade no Brasil* (Editora Vozes, Petrópolis, 1972), 183–208.

GALVÃO, Eduardo Eneas: 'Apontamentos sobre os índios Kamaiurá', *Publicações Avulsas do Museu Nacional*, **5** (Rio de Janeiro, 1949), 31–48; ES, 17–55.

'Cultura e sistema de parentesco das tribos do alto rio Xingu', BMN, **14**, 1953, 1–56; ES, 73–119.

'Aculturação indígena no Rio Negro', BMPEG, **7**, 1959; ES, 135–92.

'Áreas culturais indígenas do Brasil, 1900–1959', BMPEG, **8**, 1960, 1–41; ES, 193–228; trans. as 'Indigenous culture areas of Brazil, 1900–1959', in Janice H. Hopper, ed., *Indians of Brazil in the Twentieth Century* (Institute for Cross-Cultural Research, Washington, DC, 1967), 169–205.

'Encontro de sociedades tribal e nacional no Rio Negro, Amazonas', *XXXV*

Congreso Internacional de Americanistas. Actas y Memorias, **3** 329–40, Mexico, 1962; (Governo do Estado do Amazonas, Manaus, 1966); ES, 257–72.

'Indians and Whites in the Brazilian Amazon', *Zeitschrift für Ethnologie,* **95:2** (Braunschweig, 1970), 220–30; ES, 273–90.

Encontro de Sociedades: índios e brancos no Brasil (Editora Paz e Terra, Rio de Janeiro, 1979) = ES.

GARFIELD, Seth: *'Civilized' but discontented: the Xavante Indians and government policy in Brazil* (Doctoral dissertation, Yale University, New Haven, 1996).

'"The roots of a plant that today is Brazil": Indians and the nation-state under the Brazilian Estado Novo', *Journal of Latin American Studies,* **29**, 1997, 747–68.

GHEERBRANT, Alain: *L'Expédition Orénoque-Amazone, 1948–1950* (Gallimard, Paris, 1953); trans. as *Journey to the Far Amazon* (Simon and Schuster, New York, 1954).

GIACCIARIA, Bartolomeu and Adalberto HEIDE: *Auwê Uptabi – Uomine veri – Vita Xavante* (Società Editrice Internazionale, Turin, 1971); trans. as *Xavante, A'uwê uptabi, povo autêntico* (Editôra Salesiana Mooca, São Paulo, 1972).

GIACONE, Fr. Antônio: *Os Tucanos e Outras Tribos do Rio Uaupés* (Imprensa Oficial do Estado de São Paulo, São Paulo, 1949).

Trentacinque Anni fra le Tribù del Rio Uaupés (Amazzonia – Brasile) (Rome, 1976).

GOMES, Mércio Pereira: 'Porque índios brigam com posseiros: o caso dos índios Guajajara', in Dalmo de Abreu Dallari, Manuela Carneiro da Cunha and Lux Vidal, eds., *A Questão da Terra Indígena* (Cadernos da Comissão Pró-Índio, **2**, Global Editora, São Paulo, 1981), 51–6.

Os Índios e o Brasil (Editora Vozes, São Paulo, 1988); trans. John Moon as *The Indians and Brazil* (University of Florida Press, Gainesville, Fla., 2000).

'O futuro dos índios', *Carta* (Gabinete do Senador Darcy Ribeiro, Brasília), **9**, 1993, 61–74.

O Índio na História – o povo Tenetehara em busca da liberdade (Editora Vozes, Petrópolis, RJ, 2002).

GOODLAND, Robert J. A. and Howard S. IRWIN: *Amazon Jungle: Green Hell to Red Desert?* (Elsevier Scientific Publishing Company, Amsterdam, 1975).

GRAHAM, Laura R.: *Performing Dreams: Discourses of Immortality Among the Xavante of Central Brazil* (University of Texas Press, Austin, 1995).

GRAZIANO FILHO, Romeo: 'History of the invasion of Yanomami lands by miners, 1975–1989', *Urihi* (Bulletin of the CCPY), **11**, Dec. 1990.

GREGOR, Thomas: 'Exposure and seclusion: a study of institutionalized isolation among the Mehinacu Indians of Brazil', *Ethnology,* **9:3**, Pittsburgh, Jul. 1970, 234–50.

Mehinaku: The Drama of Daily Life in a Brazilian Indian Village (University of Chicago Press, Chicago and London, 1977).

GROSS, Daniel R., ed.: *Peoples and Cultures of Native South America* (The Natural History Press, New York, 1973).

GRUBB, Kenneth: *The Lowland Indians of Amazonia* (World Dominion Press, London, 1927).

Amazon and Andes (Methuen, London, 1930).

From Pacific to Atlantic: South American Studies (Methuen, London, 1933).

GRÜNBERG, Georg: 'Urgent research in north-west Mato Grosso', *Bulletin of the International Committee on Urgent Anthropological and Ethnological Research*, 8 (Vienna, 1966), 143–52.

ed., *La Situación del Indígena en América del Sur* (Biblioteca Científica Terra Nueva, Montevideo, 1972); see also Walter Dostal, ed., *The Situation of the Indian in South America* (World Council of Churches, Geneva, 1972).

GRUPIONI, Luís Donisete Benzi, ed.: *Índios no Brasil* (Município de São Paulo, São Paulo, 1992).

'Indian organizations and pro-Indian groups in Brazil: views of the quincentenary', in Leslie Bary et al., eds., *Rediscovering America 1492–1992: National, Cultural and Disciplinary Boundaries Re-examined* (Louisiana State University, Baton Rouge, 1992), 100–110.

Coleções e Expedições Vigiadas. Os etnólogos no Conselho de Fiscalização das Expedições Artísticas e Científicas no Brasil (Editora Hucitec, São Paulo, 1998).

GUPPY, Nicholas: *Wai-Wai. Through the Forests North of the Amazon* (John Murray, London, 1958).

GUSMÃO, Clovis de: *Rondon* (Livraria José Olympio Editôra, Rio de Janeiro, 1942).

HAMES, Raymond B.: 'The settlement pattern of a Yanomamö population bloc: a behavioral ecological explanation', in Raymond B. Hames and William T. Vickers, eds., *Adaptive Responses of Native Amazonians* (Academic Press, New York, 1983), 393–427.

HANBURY-TENISON, Robin: *Report of a Visit to the Indians of Brazil, on behalf of the Primitive Peoples' Fund/Survival International, January–March 1971* (Primitive Peoples' Fund/Survival International, London, 1971).

A Question of Survival for the Indians of Brazil (Angus and Robertson, London, 1973).

and Bruce ALBERT, *Aborigines of the Amazon Rainforest. The Yanomami* (Time-Life Books, Amsterdam, 1982).

HARRIS, Marvin: 'A cultural materialist theory of band and village warfare: the Yanomamo test', in R. Brian Ferguson, ed., *Warfare, Culture and Environment* (Academic Press, Orlando, Fla., 1984), 111–40.

HAY, Alexander Rattray: *Saints and Savages: Brazil's Indian Problem* (Hodder and Stoughton, London, 1920).

HECHT, Susanna and Alexander COCKBURN: *The Fate of the Forest: Developers, Destroyers and Defenders of the Amazon* (Verso, London and New York, 1989).

HEELAS, Richard: *The Social Organization of the Panara, a Gê Tribe of Central Brazil* (Doctoral thesis, University of Oxford, 1979).

'An historical outline of the Panará (Kreen-Akarore) tribe of central Brazil', SIR, **3:2(22)**, Spring 1978, 25–7.

HEMMING, John: 'Tragedy in the jungle', *Sunday Times*, 18 and 25 Feb. 1962.

Red Gold. The Conquest of the Brazilian Indians (Macmillan, London, 1978; revised edition, Papermac, London, 1995).

Amazon Frontier. The Destruction of the Brazilian Indians (Macmillan, London, 1985; revised edition, Papermac, London, 1995).

ed., *Change in the Amazon Basin*, 2 vols: 1 *Man's Impact on Forests and Rivers*; 2 *The Frontier After a Decade of Colonisation* (Manchester University Press, Manchester, 1985).

Roraima: Brazil's Northernmost Frontier (Institute of Latin American Studies, University of London, 1990).

HENRY, Jules: *Jungle People. A Kaingang Tribe of the Highlands of Brazil* (Vintage Books, New York, 1941).

HILL, Jonathan D., ed.: *Rethinking History and Myth: Indigenous South American Perspectives on the Past* (University of Illinois Press, Urbana, 1988).

and Robin WRIGHT: 'Time, narrative and ritual: historical interpretations from an Amazonian society', in Jonathan Hill, ed., *Rethinking History*, 78–105.

HOHENTHAL, William D.: 'As tribos indígenas do médio e baixo São Francisco', RMP, **12**, 1960, 37–71; and 'The General Characteristics of Indian Cultures in the Rio São Francisco Valley', ibid., 73–86.

HOPPER, Janice H., ed.: *Indians of Brazil in the Twentieth Century* (Institute for Cross-Cultural Research, Washington, DC, 1967).

HORTA BARBOZA, Luis Bueno: *O Serviço de Proteção aos Índios e a História da Colonização do Brasil* (Rio de Janeiro, 1919).

Pelo Índio e Pela sua Protecção Official (Departamento de Imprensa Nacional, Rio de Janeiro, 1923).

'Relatório dos trabalhos realizados pela Inspetoria do Serviço de Proteção aos Índios e Localização de Trabalhadores Nacionais em S. Paulo, durante o ano de 1916', RMP, **8**, 1954, 59–77.

HUGH-JONES, Stephen: 'The gun and the bow: myths of white men and Indians', *L'Homme*, Paris, **106–7**, 1988, 138–55.

'Yesterday's luxuries, tomorrow's necessities: business and barter in northwest Amazonia', in C. Humphrey and S. Hugh-Jones, eds., *Barter. Exchange and Value* (Cambridge University Press, Cambridge, 1992), 42–74.

HUXLEY, Francis: *Affable Savages. An Anthropologist among the Urubu Indians of Brazil* (The Viking Press, New York, 1957).

HVALKOF, Søren and Peter AABY, eds.: *Is God an American? An Anthropological*

Perspective on the Missionary Work of the Summer Institute of Linguistics (IWGIA and Survival International, Copenhagen and London, 1981).

IRELAND, Emilienne: 'Cerebral Savage: the Whiteman as Symbol of Cleverness and Savagery in Waurá Myth', in Jonathan D. Hill, ed., *Rethinking History and Myth* (University of Illinois Press, Urbana, 1988), 157–73.

JACKSON, Jean E.: *The Fish People. Linguistics, Exogamy and Tukanoan Identity in Northwest Amazonia* (Cambridge University Press, Cambridge, 1983).

JOBIM, Danton: *O Problema do Índio e a Acusação de Genocídio* (Conselho de Defesa dos Direitos da Pessoa Humana, Ministério da Justiça, Brasília, 1970).

JUNQUEIRA DE BARROS LIMA, Carmen: *The Brazilian Indigenous Problem and Policy: the Example of the Xingu National Park* (IWGIA [International Work Group for Indigenous Affairs], **13**, Copenhagen, 1973).

Os Índios de Ipavu. Um estudo sobre a vida do grupo Kamaiurá (Editora Ática, São Paulo, 1975).

and Edgar de Assis CARVALHO, eds.: *Antropologia e Indigenismo na América Latina* (Editora Cortez, São Paulo, 1981).

and Betty MINDLIN: *The Aripuanã Park and the Polonoroeste Programme* (IWGIA [International Work Group for Indigenous Affairs], **59**, Copenhagen, 1987).

—, Mauro LEONEL, and Betty MINDLIN: *Environment, Poverty and Indians* (Novib, Henk van Andellezing, Amsterdam, 1992).

KAHN, Marina: 'Levantamento preliminar das organizações religiosas em áreas indígenas', TD, 19–75.

KANDELL, Jonathan: *Passage Through El Dorado* (Allison & Busby, London, 1984).

KIETZMAN, Dale Walter: 'Indians and culture areas of twentieth-century Brazil', in Janice H. Hopper, ed., *Indians of Brazil in the Twentieth Century* (Institute for Cross-Cultural Research, Washington, DC, 1967), 1–67.

Indian Survival in Brazil (Doctoral dissertation, University of Southern California, 1972).

KOCH-GRÜNBERG, Theodor: 'Die Indianerstämme am oberen Rio Negro und Yapurá', *Zeitschrift für Ethnologie*, **38**, Berlin, 1906, 166–205.

Zwei Jahre unter den Indianern. Reisen in Nordwest-Brasilien 1903/1905, 2 vols (E. Wasmuth, Berlin, 1909–10).

Vom Roroima zum Orinoco. Ergebnisse einer Reise in Nordbrasilien und Venezuela in den Jahren 1911–1913, 5 vols (Berlin and Stuttgart, 1916, 1917, 1923, and 1928).

KRAUSE, Fritz: 'Die Waurá-Indianer des Schingú-quellgebietes, zentral-Brasiliens', *Mitteilungsblatt der Gesellschaft für Völkerkunde* 7 (Leipzig, 1936), 14–33.

Forschungsaufgaben im Schingu-Quellgebiet, Zentralbrasilien', *Tagungsberichte der Gesellschaft für Völkerkunde* (Leipzig, 1937), 160–72.

KRUSE, Albert: 'Erzälung der Tapajoz-Mundurukú', *Anthropos*, **44** (Freiburg, Switzerland, 1946–49), 314–30 and 614–56.

LAMBERT, Paul: *Fraternelle Amazonie* (Paris, 1964).

LARAIA, Roque de Barros: 'A friccão interétnica no médio Tocantins', *América Latina*, **8:2**, Apr.–Jun., 1965, 66–76.

'Integração e utopia', *Revista de Cultura Vozes* (Petrópolis), **70:3**, Apr. 1976.

and Roberto da MATTA: *Índios e Castanheiros: a emprêsa estrativa e os índios do médio Tocantins* (Difusão Européia do Livro, São Paulo, 1967).

LAS CASAS, Roberto Décio de: 'Índios e brasileiros no vale do rio Tapajós', BMPEG, **23**, Oct. 1964, 1–31.

LEA, Vanessa Rosemary: *Parque Indígena do Xingu. Laudo Antropológico* (Universidade de Campinas, São Paulo, 1997).

ed., *Área Indígena Kapoto: Laudo Antropológico* (Universidade de Campinas, São Paulo, 1997).

'Brazil's Kayapo Indians Beset by a Golden Curse', *National Geographic*, **165:5**, Washington, May 1984, 674–94.

LEACOCK, Seth: 'Economic Life of the Maué Indians', BMPEG, **19**, Apr. 1964, 1–30.

LELONG, Maurice Hyacinthe: *Les Indiens qui Meurent* (Paris, 1952).

LEONEL JÚNIOR, Mauro de Mello: 'Estradas, índios e ambiente na Amazônia: do Brasil Central ao Oceano Pacífico', *São Paulo em Perspectiva* (Seade, São Paulo), **6:1/2**, 1992, 134–67; also IWGIA, Copenhagen, 1991.

'Onde se esconder?' *Carta* (Gabinete Senador Darcy Ribeiro, Brasília), **9**, 1993, 107–12.

Etnodicéia Uruéu-au-au (EdUSP [Editora da Universidade de São Paulo] IAMA [Instituto de Antropologia e Meio Ambiente], São Paulo, 1995).

LÉVI-STRAUSS, Claude: *Tristes Tropiques* (Librairie Plon, Paris, 1955); trans. John Russell as *A World on the Wane* (London, 1961); trans. John and Doreen Weightman as *Tristes Tropiques* (Jonathan Cape, London, 1973).

LEWIS, Norman: 'Genocide. From fire and sword to arsenic and bullets – civilisation has sent six million Indians to extinction', *Sunday Times Magazine*, 23 Feb. 1969, 34–59.

The Missionaries (Secker & Warburg, London, 1988).

LIMA, Antônio Carlos de Souza: *A Expedição Roncador-Xingu* (Museu Nacional/ Univ. Fed. do Rio de Janeiro, Rio de Janeiro, 1981).

'Sobre indigenismo, autoritarismo e nacionalidade: Considerações sobre a constituição do discurso e da práctica da proteção fraternal no Brasil', in João Pacheco de Oliveira Filho, ed., *Sociedades indígenas e indigenismo no Brasil* (Editôra Marco Zero, Rio de Janeiro, 1987), 149–204; trans. as 'On indigenism and nationality in Brazil', in Greg Urban and J. Scherzers, eds., *Nation-States and Indians in Latin America* (University of Texas Press, Austin, 1991), 236–58.

'O governo dos índios sob a gestão do SPI', HIB, 155–72.

Um Grande Cerco de Paz: poder tutelar, indianidade e formação do estado no Brasil (Editora Vozes, Petrópolis, 1995).

LIMA, Edilene Coffaci de: 'Katukina, Yawanawa e Marubo: desencontros míticos e encontros históricos', *Cadernos de Campo* (Universidade de São Paulo), **4:4**, 1994, 1–20.

LIMA, Pedro E. de: 'Distribuição dos grupos indígenas do Alto Xingu', *Proceedings of the XXXI Congress of Americanists*, 1 159–70, 1955.

LISBÔA, Thomaz de Aquino, SJ (JAÚKA): *Entre os Índios Münkü* (Edições Loyola, São Paulo, 1978).

Os Enauenê-Nauê. Premeiros contatos (Edições Loyola, São Paulo, 1985).

LIZOT, Jacques: *The Yanomami in the Face of Ethnocide* (IWGIA [International Work Group for Indigenous Affairs], Copenhagen, 1976).

Le Cercle des Feux (Éditions du Seuil, Paris, 1976).

'Population, resources, and warfare among the Yanomami', *Man* (London), **12**, 1977, 497–571.

Les Yanomami Centraux (Cahiers de l'Homme, Éditions de l'Ehess, Paris, 1984).

Tales of Yanomami Daily Life in the Venezuelan Forest (Cambridge University Press, Cambridge, 1985).

LONGAREZZI, Andréa Maturano: 'Os Kayabi', *Terra Indígena* (CIMI, Centro de Estudos Indígenas, Araraquara), **10:69**, Oct.–Dec. 1993, 40–50.

LOPES, Daniel, Isolda MACIEL DA SILVEIRA, and Roberto CORTEZ, eds.: 'O processo de ocupação humana na Amazônia: considerações e perspectivas', BMPEG, **9:1**, Jul. 1994, 3–54.

LOPES DE SOUZA, Marshal Boanerges: *Do Rio Negro ao Orenoco. A terra – o homem* (Ministério da Agricultura, CNPI, Rio de Janeiro, 1959).

LUNA, Luis: *Resistência do Índio à Dominação do Brasil* (Editôra Leitura, Rio de Janeiro, 1964).

MacCREAGH, Gordon: *White Waters and Black* (The Century Co., New York and London, 1926).

McEWAN, Colin, Cristiana BARRETO, and Eduardo NEVES, eds.: *Unknown Amazon* (The British Museum Press, London, 2001).

MacMILLAN, Gordon J.: *At the End of the Rainbow? Gold, Land and People in the Brazilian Amazon* (Earthscan Publications, London, and Columbia University Press, New York, 1995).

MAGALHÃES, Amilcar A. Botelho de: *Relatório apresentado ao Sr. Coronel Cândido Mariano da Silva Rondon, Chefe da Commissão Brasileira* (Expedição Scientifica Roosevelt-Rondon, annexo no. 5, Rio de Janeiro, 1916).

Pelos sertões do Brasil (Rio de Janeiro, 1928; 2nd. edn., Brasiliana, 5th ser. **195**, São Paulo and Rio de Janeiro, 1941).

Impressões da Commissão Rondon (4th edn., Livraria do Globo, Pôrto Alegre, RS, 1929).

Rondon – Uma Relíquia da Pátria (Editóra Guaíra, Curitiba–São Paulo–Rio de Janeiro, 1942).

'O problema da civilização dos índios do Brasil', *América Indígena*, **3:2**, Apr. 1943, 153–60.

A Obra Ciclópica do General Rondon (Biblioteca do Exército, Rio de Janeiro, 1956).

MAGALHÃES, Antonio Carlos: 'Os Parakanã – o destino de uma nação indígena', in Dalmo de Abreu DALLARI, Manuela CARNEIRO DA CUNHA, and Lux VIDAL, eds., *A Questão da Terra Indígena* (Global Editora, São Paulo, 1981), 83–96.

MAGALHÃES, Basílio de: *Em Defesa dos Brasilíndios* (Conselho Nacional de Proteção aos Índios, separata of Pubn. **101**, Rio de Janeiro, 1946).

MALCHER, José Maria da Gama: Preface to Mário SIMÕES, ed., *SPI – 1953* (Rio de Janeiro, 1954), 1–117.

Índios: grau de integração na comunidade nacional, grupo linguístico, localização (Conselho Nacional de Proteção aos Indios, n.s. **1**, Rio de Janeiro, 1964).

MARÉS DE SOUZA FILHO, Carlos Frederico: 'O direito envergonhado: o direito e os índios no Brasil', in Luís Donisete Benzi Grupioni, ed., *Índios no Brasil* (Município de São Paulo, São Paulo, 1992), 153–80.

MAREWA (Movimento de Apoio à Resistência Waimiri/Atroari): *Resistência Waimiri/Atroari* (Itacoatiara, 1983).

Balbina, Ameaça e Destruição na Amazônia (Manaus, 1987).

MARTINS, Edilson: *Nossos Índios, Nossos Mortos* (Codecri, Rio de Janeiro, 1978).

MARTINS, José de Souza: *Não há Terra para Plantar Neste Verão* (Editora Vozes, Petrópolis, 1986).

MATTA, Roberto da: 'Notas sôbre o contato e a extinção dos índios Gaviões do médio Rio Tocantins', RMP, **14**, 1963, 182–202.

Um Mundo Dividido: a estrutura social dos índios Apinayé (Editora Vozes, Petrópolis, 1976).

MAYBURY-LEWIS, David: *The Savage and the Innocent* (Evans Brothers, London, 1965).

Akwê-Shavante Society (Clarendon Press, Oxford, 1967).

ed., *Dialectical Societies: The Gê and Bororo of Central Brazil* (Harvard University Press, Cambridge, Mass., 1979).

'For reasons of state: paradoxes of Indigenist policy in Brazil', in David Maybury-Lewis, ed., *The Politics of Ethnicity: Indigenous Peoples in Latin American Society* (Harvard University, Cambridge, Mass., and London, 2002), 329–46.

and Jason W. CLAY: *In the Path of Polonoroeste* (Cultural Survival, Oct. 1981).

MEDINA, Cremilda, ed.: *O Primeiro Habitante* (ECA-Universidade de São Paulo, 1992).

MEGGERS, Betty: *Amazonia: Man and Culture in a Counterfeit Paradise* (Aldine Atherton, Chicago, 1971).

MEIHY, José Carlos Sebe Bom: *Canto de Morte Kaiowá: história oral de vida* (Edições Loyola, São Paulo, 1991).

'Suicídio Kaiowá', *Carta* (Gabinete do Senador Darcy Ribeiro, Brasília), **9**, 1993, 53–9.

MEIRELLES, Francisco: 'Meireles fala sobre os Kayapó: seus primeiros e últimos contatos com elementos civilizados', BSPI, **56**, Jul.–Aug. 1962, 3–16.

MELATTI, Julio César: *Índios e Criadores. A situação dos Krahó na área pastoril do Tocantins* (Instituto de Ciências Sociais, Universidade Federal do Rio de Janeiro, 1967).

(as Julio Cezar): *Índios do Brasil* (Coordenada Editôra de Brasília, Brasília, 1970).

O Messianismo Krahó (Editora Herder and EdUSP, São Paulo, 1972).

MENEZES, Cláudia: 'Os Xavante e o movimento de fronteira no leste matogrossense', RA, **25**, 1982, 63–87.

'Missionários e guerreiros: o apostolado salesiano entre os Xavante', TD, 309–42.

MENEZES, Maria Lúcia Pires: 'Parque Indígena do Xingu: as relações entre geopolítica e indigenismo', in Adélia Engrácia de Oliveira and Philippe Léna, eds., *Amazônia: a fronteira agrícola 20 anos depois* (Museu Paraense Emílio Goeldi, Belém, 1991), 83–100.

Parque Indígena do Xingu: a construção de um território estatal (Editora da Unicamp, Campinas/Imprensa Oficial do Estado, São Paulo, 1999).

MENGET, Patrick: *Au Nom des Autres. Classification des relations sociales chez les Txikão du Haut-Xingu (Brésil)* (Doctoral thesis, École Pratique des Hautes Études, Université de Paris X, Nanterre, 1976).

'Entre memória e história', in Adauto NOVAES, ed., *A Outra Margem do Ocidente* (Companhia das Letras, São Paulo, 1999), 153–65.

MÉTRAUX, Alfred: 'Disparition des Indiens dans le Brésil Central', *Akten des XXXIV. Internationalen Amerikanistenkongresses* (Vienna, 1962) and *Bulletin of the International Committee for Urgent Anthropological and Ethnological Research*, **5**, 1962, 126–31.

MIGLIAZZA, Ernest C.: *The Integration of the Indigenous Peoples of the Territory of Roraima, Brazil* (IWGIA [International Work Group for Indigenous Affairs] Document **32**, Copenhagen, 1978).

MILLER, Leo E.: *In the Wilds of South America* (T. Fisher Unwin, London, 1919).

MILLIKEN, William and Bruce ALBERT: *Yanomami, A Forest People* (Royal Botanic Gardens, Kew, 1999).

MILLIKEN, William, Robert P. MILLER, Sharon R. POLLARD, and Elisa V.

WANDELLI: *Ethnobotany of the Waimiri Atroari Indians of Brazil* (Royal Botanic Gardens, Kew, 1992).

MINDLIN, Betty: *Nós Paiter. Os Suruí de Rondônia* (Editora Vozes, Petrópolis, 1985).

'Le projet Polonoroeste et les Indiens', *Ethnies* (Survival International France, Paris), **5:11–12**, Spring 1990, 87–96.

Tuparis e Tapurás (EdUSP – Brasiliense, São Paulo), 1993.

'O aprendiz de origens e novidades', *Estudos Avançados* (Universidade de São Paulo, Instituto de Estudos Avançados), **8:20**, Jan.–Apr. 1994, 233–53.

Moqueca de Maridos: Mitos Eróticos (Editora Rosa de Tempos, Rio de Janeiro, 1998).

MISSÕES DOMINICANAS: *Gorotirés. Prelazia de Conceição do Araguaia* (Missões Dominicanas, Rio de Janeiro, 1936).

MONBIOT, George: *Amazon Watershed* (Michael Joseph, London, 1991).

MONGIANO, Dom Aldo, ed.: *Índios e Brancos em Roraima* (Centro de Informação, Diocese de Roraima, Boa Vista, 1990).

MOREIRA NETO, Carlos de Araújo: 'Relatório sôbre a situação atual dos índios Kayapó', RA, **7:1–2**, 1959, 49–64.

'A cultura pastoral do Pau d'Arco', BMPEG, **10**, 1960.

'Constante histórica do "indigenato" no Brasil', ASBA, 175–85.

'Alguns dados para a história recente dos índios Kaingang', in Georg Grünberg, ed., *La Situación del Indígena en América del Sur* (Biblioteca Científica, Montevideo, 1972), 381–419; trans. as 'Some data concerning the recent history of the Kaingang Indians', in Walter Dostal, ed., *The Situation of the Indian in South America* (World Council of Churches, Geneva, 1972), 284–333.

MÜLLER, Regina Aparecida Polo: 'Os últimos Tupi da Amazônia', RAI, **21**, Jul.–Aug. 1981, 28–41.

Os Asurini do Xingu: história e arte (Editora da Unicamp, Campinas, 1990).

MULLER, Sophie: *Beyond Civilization* (New Tribes Mission, Browngold Publications, Chico, CA, 1952).

MURPHY, Robert Francis: 'Intergroup Hostility and Social Cohesion', *American Anthropologist*, **59:6**, 1957, 1018–1035.

Headhunter's Heritage: social and economic change among the Mundurucú Indians (University of California Press, Berkeley and Los Angeles, 1960).

MURPHY, Robert F. and Buell Quain: *The Trumaí Indians of Central Brazil*, American Ethnological Society, monograph **24** (University of Washington, Seattle, 1955); (J. J. Augustin Publisher, New York, 1955).

MYERS, Iris: 'The Makushi of British Guiana – A Study in Culture-Contact', *Timehri* (Journal of The Royal Agricultural and Commercial Society of British Guiana), **26**, 66–77 and **27**, 16–38, Georgetown, 1945–46.

'The Makushi of the Guiana–Brazilian Frontier in 1949: A Study of Culture

Contact' (ed. Audrey Butt Colson), *Antropologica*, Fundación La Salle, Caracas, 80, 1993, 3–99.

NIMUENDAJÚ, Curt (Unkel): 'Das Ende des Otí-Stammes', *Deutsche Zeitung* (São Paulo, 1910); trans. in Herbert Baldus, 'Os otí', RMP, 8, 1954, 83–8; TICN, 33–40; 'O fim da tribo Oti', *Carta* (Gabinete Senador Darcy Ribeiro, Brasília), 9, 1993, 205–12.

'Carta sobre a pacificação dos coroados', Letter to Dr Hugo Gensch, Blumenau, 14 Apr. 1912, trans. Dagmar Schneider, in TICN, 41–5.

'Die Sagen von der Eschaffung und Vernichtung der Welt als Grundlagen der Religion der Apapocu'va-Guarani', *Zeitschrift für Ethnologie*, 46, 1914, 284–403; trans. as *As Lendas da Criação e Destuição do Mundo como Fundamentos da Religião dos Apapocúva-Guarani* (Hucitec/EdUSP, São Paulo, 1987).

'Os índios Parintintin do rio Madeira', JSAP, 16, 1924, 201–78.

'As tribus do Alto Madeira', JSAP, 17, 1925, 137–72.

'Os índios tukuna' (Belém, 10 Dec. 1929), *Boletim do Museu do Índio. Antropologia*, 7, 1977, 20–68; TICN, 192–208; trans. William D. Hohenthal as *The Tukuna* (University of California Press, Berkeley and Los Angeles, 1952).

Mapa Etno-histórico do Brasil e Regiões Adjacentes (Belém, 1934); republished as *Mapa Etno-histórico de Curt Nimuendajú* (IBGE [Instituto Brasileiro de Geografia e Estatística], Rio de Janeiro, 1987).

'The social structure of the Ramkókamekra (Canella)', *American Anthropologist*, 40, 1938, 51–74.

The Šerente, trans. Robert H. Lowie (The Southwest Museum, Los Angeles, 1942).

The Eastern Timbira, trans. Robert H. Lowie (University of California Press, Berkeley and Los Angeles, 1946).

'Expedição armada contra os índios!', *O Globo* (Rio de Janeiro, 24 Jan. 1946); TICN, 244–6.

'Tribes of the Lower and Middle Xingu', HSAI, 3, 1948, 213–43.

'Reconhecimento dos rios Içana, Ayarí e Uaupés. Relatório apresentado ao Serviço de Proteção aos Índios do Amazonas e Acre, 1927', JSAP, 39, 1950, 125–82.

'Os Górotire. Relatório apresentado ao Serviço de Proteção aos Índios, em 12 de abril de 1940', RMP, 6, 1952, 427–53; TICN, 219–43.

'Apontamentos sobre os Guaraní', RMP, 8, 1954, 9–57.

Trans. from German by Robert H. Lowie as *The Apinayé* (The Catholic University of America, Anthropological Series 8, Washington, DC, 1939); (Anthropological Publications, Oosterhout, The Netherlands, 1967); *Os Apinayé*, BMPEG, 12, 1956 (and, as a book, Museu Paraense Emílio Goeldi, Belém, 1983).

'Indios machacari' (Belém, 22 May 1939), RA, 6:1, 1958, 53–61; TICN, 209–218.

Etnografia e indigenismo, sobre os Kaingang, os Ofaié-Xavante e os índios do Pará (Editora da Universidade Estadual de Campinas, SP, 1993).

NOVAES, Adauto, ed.: *A Outra Margem do Ocidente (Brasil 500 anos: experiência e destino)* (Companhia das Letras, São Paulo, 1999).

NOVAES, Washington: 'O índio e a modernidade', in Luís Donisete Benzi Grupioni, ed., *Índios no Brasil* (Município de São Paulo, São Paulo, 1992), 181–92.

NUTELS, Noel: 'Medical problems of newly contacted Indian groups', in Pan-American Health Organization, *Biomedical Challenges Presented by the American Indian* (Washington, DC, 1968).

OBERG, Kalervo: *The Terena and the Caduveo of Southern Mato Grosso, Brazil*, Institute of Social Anthropology, 9 (Smithsonian Institution, Washington, DC, 1949).

Indian Tribes of Northern Mato Grosso, Brazil, Institute of Social Anthropology, 15 (Smithsonian Institution, Washington, DC, 1953).

O'CONNOR, Geoffrey: *Amazon Journal. Dispatches from a Vanishing Frontier* (Plume, New York, 1997 and Penguin, London, 1998).

OLIVEIRA, Adélia Engrácia de: 'Os índios Jurúna e sua cultura nos dias atuais', BMPEG, *Antropologia*, 35:17, 1968, 1–35.

'Os índios Jurúna do Alto Xingu', *Dédalo*, 6:11–12, Museu de Arqueologia e Etnologia, Universidade de São Paulo, Jun.–Dec. 1970, 2–292.

'Depoiamentos Baniwa sobre as relações entre índios e "civilizados" no rio Negro', BMPEG, 72, 1979, 1–31.

OLIVEIRA, Ana Gita de: O *Mundo Transformado. Um estudo da cultura de fronteira no Alto Rio Negro* (Museu Paraense Emílio Goeldi, Belém, PA, 1995).

OLIVEIRA, Roberto Cardoso de: 'Relatório de uma investigação sôbre terras em Mato Grosso', in Mário F. Simões, ed., *SPI – 1954* (Rio de Janeiro, 1955), 173–84; also in Vanessa Lea, *Parque Indígena do Xingu. Laudo Antropológico* (Universidade de Campinas, São Paulo, 1997), 173–83.

'Preliminares de uma pesquisa sôbre a assimilação dos Terêna', RA, 5:2, Dec. 1957, 173–88.

'Aspectos demográficos e ecológicas de uma communidade Terêna', BMN, 18, Sep. 1958, 1–17.

'A situação atual dos Tapirapé', BMPEG, 3, Jul. 1959, 1–11.

O *Processo de Assimilação dos Terêna* (Museu Nacional, Rio de Janeiro, 1960).

'The role of Indian posts in the process of assimilation: two case studies', AI, 20:2, Apr. 1960, 89–95.

'Estudo de áreas de fricção interétnica no Brasil', *América Latina*, 5:3 (Centro Latino-Americano de Pesquisas em Ciências Sociais, Rio de Janeiro, Jul.–Sep. 1962), 85–90.

'Aculturação e fricção interétnica no Brasil', *América Latina*, 6:3, 1964, 17–32.

O *Índio e o Mundo dos Brancos: a situação dos Tukúna do alto Solimões* (Difusão Européia do Livro, São Paulo, 1964).

'Áreas de friccão interétnica na Amazônia', ASBA, 187–94.

Urbanização e Tribalismo: a integração dos índios Terena numa sociedade de classes (Zahar Editores, Rio de Janeiro, 1968).

A Sociologia do Brasil Indígena (Tempo Brasileiro, Rio de Janeiro, 1972).

Do Índio ao Bugre: o processo de assimilação dos Terena (Francisco Alves, Rio de Janeiro, 1974).

'Indigenous peoples and sociocultural change in the Amazon', in Charles Wagley, ed., *Man in the Amazon* (University of Florida, Gainesville, Fla., 1974), 111–35.

'Movimentos indígenas e indigenismo no Brasil', *América Indígena*, **41:3**, Mexico, Jul./Sep. 1981, 339–405.

A Crise do Indigenismo (Editora da Unicamp, Campinas, 1988).

OLIVEIRA FILHO, João Pacheco de: ed., *Sociedades Indígenas e Indigenismo no Brasil* (Editora Marco Zero, Rio de Janeiro, 1987), which contains his 'O Projeto Tükuna: uma experiência de ação indigenista', 205–40.

'*O Nosso Governo*'; *os Ticuna e o regime tutelar* (Marco Zero, Rio de Janeiro, 1988).

ed., *Projeto Calha Norte: militares, índios e fronteiras* (Universidade Federal do Rio de Janeiro/Museu Nacional, Rio de Janeiro, 1990).

'Frontier society and the new indigenism: nature and origins of the Calha Norte Project', in David Goodman and Anthony Hall, eds., *The Future of Amazonia: Destruction or Sustainable Development?* (St Martin's Press, New York, 1990), 155–76.

ed., *Indigenismo e Territorialização. Poderes, rotinas e saberes coloniais no Brasil contemporâneo* (Contra Capa Livraria, Rio de Janeiro, 1998).

ed., *A Viagem da Volta. Etnicidade, política e reelaboração cultural no Nordeste indígena* (Contra Capa Livraria, Rio de Janeiro, 1999).

O'REILLY, Donald F: *Rondon. Biography of a Brazilian republican army commander* (Doctoral thesis, New York University, 1969).

OSSAMI, Marlene Castro: *O Papel das Assembléias de Líderes na Organização dos Povos Indígenas do Brasil* (Série Antropologia, 1, Universidade Cat. de Goiás, Goiânia, Aug. 1993).

PASSARINHO, Jarbas: 'Terras dos Yanomamis', *Carta* (Gabinete Senador Darcy Ribeiro, Brasília), **4:9**, 1993, 244–53.

PEREIRA, Fr. Adalberto Holanda: 'A pacificação dos Tapayúna (Beiço de Pau) até março de 1968', RA, **15/16**, 1968, 216–27.

PEREIRA, Manuel Nunes: *Curt Nimuendajú: síntese de uma vida e de uma obra* (Belém, 1946).

PETERS, John: *Life among the Yanomami* (Broadview Press, Peterborough, Ont., 1998).

PIKE, Kenneth and Ruth M. BREND, eds.: *The Summer Institute of Linguistics: Its Work and Contributions* (Mouton, The Hague, 1977).

PINTO, Estevão: *Os Índios do Nordeste*, 2 vols. Brasiliana, **44**, **45** (Companhia Editora Nacional, São Paulo, 1935, 1938).

Etnologia Brasileira: Fulniô, os últimos Tapuias (Companhia Editôra Nacional, São Paulo, 1956).

Os Indígenas do Nordeste (Companhia Editôra Nacional, São Paulo, 1956).

PORRO, Antonio: 'Social organization and political power in the Amazonian flood-plain: the ethnohistorical sources', in Anna C. Roosevelt, ed., *Amazonian Indians from Prehistory to the Present* (University of Arizona Press, Tucson, 1994), 79–94.

POSEY, Darrell Addison: 'Pyka-Tô-Ti: Kayapó mostra aldeia de origem', RAI, **3:15**, Mar.–Apr. 1979, 48–57.

'Cisão dos Kayapó não impede crescimento populacional', RAI, **3:16**, May–Jun. 1979, 52–8.

'Indigenous ecological knowledge and development in the Amazon', in Emilio Moran, ed., *The Dilemma of Amazonian Development* (Westview Press, Boulder, Colorado, 1983), 225–57.

'Native and indigenous guidelines for new Amazonian development strategies: understanding biological diversity through ethnoecology', in John Hemming, ed., *Change in the Amazon Basin*, 1, *Man's Impact on Forests and Rivers* (Manchester University Press, Manchester, 1985), 156–81.

'Diachronic ecotones and anthropogenic landscapes in Amazonia: contesting the consciousness of conservation', in William Balée, ed., *Advances in Historical Ecology* (Columbia University Press, New York, 1998), 104–18.

and William BALÉE, eds.: *Resource Management in Amazonia: Indigenous and Folk Strategies* (New York Botanical Garden, The Bronx, New York, 1989).

POULTNEY, Samuel Victor: *Battle for the Big-Lips* (London, 1966).

PRANCE, Ghillean T.: 'The increased importance of ethnobotany and underex-ploited plants in a changing Amazon', in John Hemming, ed., *Change in the Amazon Basin*, 1, *Man's Impact on Forests and Rivers* (Manchester University Press, Manchester, 1985), 129–36.

PRESLAND, Anna: 'Reconquest. An account of the contemporary fight for survival of the Amerindian peoples of Brazil', SIR, **4:1(25)**, Spring 1979, 14–40; **7:3–4(41/42)**, Autumn/Winter 1982.

PRICE, David: *In the Path of the Polonoroeste: Endangered Peoples of Western Brazil* (Cultural Survival, Cambridge Mass., 1981); also in *Porantim*, 4, Mar. 1982.

Before the Bulldozer: the Nambiquara Indians and the World Bank (Seven Locks Press, Cabin John, Md., 1989).

PUTTKAMER, W. Jesco von: 'Brazil protects her Cintas-Largas', *National Geographic*, **140:3**, Sep. 1971, 420–44; trans. in *Funai – Boletim Informativo*, **1:2**, Jan.–Mar. 1972, 28–35.

'Brazil's Beleaguered Indians', *National Geographic*, **146:2**, Feb. 1974.

'Brazil's Kreen-Akarores. Requiem for a Tribe?', *National Geographic*, **147:2**, Feb. 1975, 254–69.

'Brazil's Txukahameis. Good-bye to the Stone Age', *National Geographic*, **147:2**, Feb. 1975, 270–83.

'Man in the Amazon: Stone Age Present Meets Stone Age Past', *National Geographic*, **155:1**, Jan. 1979, 60–83.

RAMOS, Alcida Rita: *Hierarchia e Simbiose. Relações intertribais no Brasil* (Hucitec/ INI, São Paulo, 1980).

'Frontier expansion and Indian peoples in the Brazilian Amazon', in Marianne Schmink and Charles H. Wood, eds., *Frontier Expansion in Amazonia* (University of Florida Press, Gainesville, Fla., 1984), 83–104.

Yanomami: A Homeland Undermined (updated translation of an Expert Report written at the request of the Attorney General's Office, Brasília, 1989).

'Indian voices: contact experienced and expressed', in Jonathan D. Hill, ed., *Rethinking History and Myth: Indigenous South American Perspectives on the Past* (University of Illinois Press, Urbana, 1988), 214–234; trans. as 'Vozes indígenas: o contato vivido e contado', *Anuário Antropológico* (Tempo Brasileiro, Brasília), **187**, 1990, 117–143.

Ethnology, Brazilian Style (Instituto de Ciências Humanas, Universidade de Brasília, 1990).

Os Direitos do Índio no Brasil: na encruzilhada da cidadania (Série Antropologia **116**, Universidade de Brasília, Brasília, 1991).

'A hall of mirrors: the rhetoric of indigenism in Brazil', *Critique of Anthropology* (Sage, London), **11:2**, 1991, 155–69.

Sanumá Memories: Yanomami Ethnography in Times of Crisis (University of Wisconsin Press, Madison, 1995).

'A profecia de um boato, matando por ouro na área Yanomami', *Anuário Antropológico* (Tempo Brasileiro, Rio de Janeiro, 1996).

Indigenism. Ethnic politics in Brazil (University of Wisconsin Press, Madison, 1998).

and Kenneth I. TAYLOR: *The Yanoama in Brazil, 1979* (IWGIA [International Work Group for Indigenous Affairs] Document **37**, Copenhagen, 1979).

—, Marco Antonio LAZARIN, and Gale Goodwin GOMEZ: *Yanomami em Tempo de Ouro: relatório de pesquisa* (Universidade de Brasília, Série Antropologia, **51**, 1985).

REIS, Artur César Ferreira: *Os Índios da Amazônia* (Instituto Nacional de Pesquisas da Amazônia, Pulicações Avulsas **3**, Manaus, 1956).

REVKIN, Andrew: *The Burning Season* (Houghton Mifflin Company, Boston, 1990).

RIBEIRO, Adalberto Mário: 'O Serviço de Proteção aos Indios em 1943', *Revista do Serviço Público*, ano 6, **3:3**, Sep. 1943, 58–81.

RIBEIRO, Berta G.: *Diário do Xingu* (Paz e Terra, São Paulo, 1979).

'A oleira e a tecelã: o papel social da mulher na sociedade Asuriní', RA, **25**, 1982, 25–61.

'Araweté: a índia vestida', RA, **26**, 1983, 1–38.

O *Índio na Cultura Brasileira* (Editora Revan, Rio de Janeiro, 1987).

Amazonia Urgent: Five Centuries of History and Ecology (Editora Itatiaia, Belo Horizonte, 1992).

Os *Índios das Águas Pretas* (Companhia das Letras, EdUSP, São Paulo, 1995).

RIBEIRO, Darcy: 'Brazil's Indian Frontier', *Americas* (Washington, DC), **6**, Mar. 1954.

'Organização administrativa do Serviço de Proteção aos Indios', in Mário Simões, ed., *SPI – 1953* (Rio de Janeiro, 1954), 1–15.

'Convívio e contaminação: efeitos dissociativos da depopulação provocada por epidemias em grupos indígenas', *Sociologia*, **18:1**, 1956, 3–50; also chapter 9 of Os *Índios e a Civilização* (see below).

'Culturas e línguas indígenas do Brasil', *Educação e Ciências Sociais*, **2:6**, Rio de Janeiro, Nov. 1957, 5–102; trans. Janice Hopper as 'Indigenous Cultures and Languages in Brazil', in Janice H. Hopper, ed., *Indians of Brazil in the Twentieth Century* (Institute of Cross-Cultural Research, Washington, DC, 1967), 77–165.

'Uirá vai ao encontro de Maíra', *Anhembi* (São Paulo), **26:76**, Mar. 1957; *Carta* (Gabinete do Senador Darcy Ribeiro, Brasília), **4:9**, 1993, 255–67.

'Cândido Mariano da Silva Rondon', RAI, **6:2**, Dec. 1958, 97–103.

O *Indigenista Rondon* (Ministério da Educação e Cultura, Rio de Janeiro, 1958).

'A obra indigenista de Rondon', AI, **19:2**, Apr. 1959, 85–113.

A Política Indigenista Brasileira (Ministério da Agricultura, Rio de Janeiro, 1962).

'The Social Integration of Indigenous Populations in Brazil', *International Labour Review*, **85:5** (Geneva, May 1962), 459–77.

Os *Índios e a Civilização* (Civilização Brasileira, Rio de Janeiro, 1970 (edition cited); 2nd. edn., Editôra Vozes, Petrópolis, 1977); trans. Betty J. Meggers as *The Civilizational Process* (Smithsonian Institution Publication **4749**, Washington, DC, 1968).

Maíra (Civilização Brasileira, Rio de Janeiro, 1976).

As Américas e a Civilização (2nd edn., Editôra Vozes, Petrópolis, 1977); trans. Linton Lamas Barrett and Marie McDavid Barrett as *The Americas and Civilization* (New York, 1971).

'Um ministro agride os índios', *Boletim do CIMI*, **7:51**, Nov. 1978, 5–17.

Kadiwéu (Editôra Vozes, Petrópolis, 1980).

Uirá vai à Procura de Deus: ensaios de etnologia e indigenismo (Paz e Terra, Rio de Janeiro, 1980).

'A pacificação dos Xokleng', *Carta* (Gabinete Senador Darcy Ribeiro, Brasília), **9**, 1993, 23–51.

Diários Índios: os Urubus-Kaapor (Companhia das Letras, São Paulo, 1996).

RICARDO, Carlos Alberto (Beto), general editor: *Povos Indigenas no Brasil* (CEDI

[Centro Ecumênico de Documentação e Informação], São Paulo, 1983–85): **3**, *Amapá/Norte do Pará*; **5**, *Javari*; **8**, *Sudeste do Pará (Tocantins)*.

'Reports on the Upper Rio Negro (Noroeste Amazônico): 'Jogo duro na Cabeça do Cachorro', *PIB 1987/88/89/90*, 101–6; 'Dos petroglífos aos marcos de bronze', *PIB 1996/2000*, 145–54.

'Quem fala em nome dos índios?' *PIB 1987/88/89/90*, 69–72 and *PIB 1991/1995*, 90–94.

RICARDO, Fany: 'O Conselho Indigenista Missionário (CIMI): Cronologia das transformações recentes da pastoral indigenista Católica no Brasil, 1975–1979', *Cadernos do Instituto Superior de Estudos da Religião*, **10**, 1982.

RIFKIN, Jeffery: 'Ethnography and ethnocide: a case study of the Yanomami', *Dialectical Anthropology* (Elsevier Scientific Publishers, Amsterdam), **19**, 1994, 295–327.

RIVET, Paul and Constant TASTEVIN: 'Les tribus indiennes des bassins du Purus, du Juruá et des régions limitrophes', *La Géographie*, **35:5**, Paris, May 1921, 449–82.

RIVIÈRE, Peter G.: *The Forgotten Frontier: Ranchers of Northern Brazil* (Holt, Rinehart & Winston, New York, 1972).

ROCHA, Jan: *Murder in the Rainforest. The Yanomami, the Gold Miners and the Amazon* (Latin American Bureau/Survival, London, 1999).

RONDON, Cândido Mariano da Silva: *Conferências Realizadas em 1910 no Rio de Janeiro e em São Paulo pelo Tenente-Coronel Cândido Mariano da Silva Rondon* (1st edn., Rio de Janeiro, 1922; 2nd. edn. CNPI [Conselho Nacional de Proteção aos Índios] publication **68**, Rio de Janeiro, 1946); trans. as *Lectures* (Greenwood Press, New York, 1916).

Conferencias . . . de 1915 (Publication **43** of Commissão de Linhas Telegraphicas Estratégicas de Matto-Grosso ao Amazonas; and Imprensa Nacional, Rio de Janeiro, 1946), trans. R. G. Reidy and Ed. Murray (Rio de Janeiro, 1916).

'Problema indígena', *Atualidade Indígena*, **3:1**, Jan. 1943, 23–37.

19 de Abril, o Dia do Índio (speech by General Rondon, 19 Apr. 1945) (Conselho Nacional de Proteção aos Indios, publication **100**, Rio de Janeiro, 1946).

Índios do Brasil (3 vols., Conselho Nacional de Proteção aos Índios, Ministério da Agricultura, Rio de Janeiro, 1946–53): **1**, *Brasil Central, Nordeste e Mato Grosso do Sul*; **2**, *Das Cabeceiras do Rio Xingu, dos Rios Araguáia e Oiapóque*; **3**, *Do Norte do Rio Amazonas*.

'Nuestros hermanos los indios', *Atualidade Indígena*, **15:1**, Jan. 1955, 7–10.

'A expedição científica Roosevelt-Rondon', *Carta* (Gabinete Senador Darcy Ribeiro, Brasília), **9**, 1993, 161–86 (a summary of Rondon's two lectures in 1915).

RONDON, Major Frederico: *Na Rondônia Ocidental* (Companhia Editora Nacional, São Paulo, 1938).

ROOSEVELT, Anna Curtenius, ed.: *Amazonian Indians from Prehistory to the Present: Anthropological Perspectives* (University of Arizona Press, Tucson, 1994).

ROOSEVELT, Theodore: *Through the Brazilian Wilderness* (New York, 1914; John Murray, London, 1922).

ROQUETTE-PINTO, Edgard: *Rondônia* (4th. edn., Brasiliana, São Paulo, 1938).

RUBINGER, Marcos Magalhães, Maria Stella de AMORIM, and Sonia de Almeida MARCATO: *Índios Maxakali: Resistência ou Morte* (Interlivros, Belo Horizonte, 1980).

SAAKE, Fr. Guilherme (Wilhelm), SVD: 'A aculturação dos Bororo do Rio São Lourenço', RA, **1:1**, Jun. 1953, 43–52.

SAFFIRIO, John and Raymond HAMES: 'The forest and the highway', in John Saffirio et al., eds., *The Impact of Contact: Two Yanomamo Case Studies* (Cultural Survival Occasional Paper 11, Cambridge, Mass., 1983), 1–52.

SALAZAR, Fred A.: *The Innocent Assassins* (Robert Hale, London, 1967).

SANTILLI, Juliana, ed.: *Os Direitos Indígenas e a Constituição* (Núcleo de Direitos Indígenas/Sergio Antonio Fabris Editor, Porto Alegre, 1993).

SANTILLI, Paulo: *As Fronteiras da República: História e política entre os Makuxi no vale do Rio Branco* (USP/Fapesp, São Paulo, 1994).

SANTOS, Leinad Ayer O. and Lúcia M. M. de ANDRADE, eds.: *As Hidrelétricas do Xingu e os Povos Indígenas* (Comissão Pró-Índio, São Paulo, 1988).

SANTOS, Silvio Coelho dos: *A Integração do Índio na Sociedade Regional – a função dos Postos Indígenas em Santa Catarina* (Universidade de Santa Catarina, Florianópolis, 1970).

'A situação dos indígenas no Sul do Brasil' in Georg Grünberg, ed., *La Situación del Indígena en América del Sur* (Tierra Nueva, Montevideo, 1972), 421–33; trans. as 'The situation of the Indians of Southern Brazil', in Walter Dostal, ed., *The Situation of the Indian in South America* (World Council of Churches, Geneva, 1972), 334–7.

Indios e Brancos no Sul do Brasil (Edeme, Florianópolis, SC, 1973).

ed., *Os Índios Perante o Direito* (Universidade Federal de Santa Catarina, Florianópolis, 1982).

and Paul ASPELIN: *Indian Areas Threatened by Hydroelectric Plants in Brazil* (IWGIA, Copenhagen, 1981).

SAVAGE-LANDOR, A. Henry: *Across Unknown South America* (2 vols., Hodder & Stoughton, London and New York, 1913).

SCHADEN, Egon: 'O estudo do índio brasileiro – ontem e hoje', *Revista de História*, **12**, 1952, 385–401.

Aculturação Indígena: ensaio sôbre fâtores e tendências da mudança cultural de tribos índias em contacto com o mundo dos brancos (Livraria Pioneira Editôra, São Paulo, 1969; RA, **13**, 1965, 1–315).

ed., *Homem, Cultura e Sociedade no Brasil* (Editora Vozes, Petrópolis, 1972).

SCHADEN, Francisco S. G.: 'Xokléng e Kaingáng', RA, **6**, Dec. 1958, 105–12; and in Egon Schaden, ed., *Homem, Cultura e Sociedade no Brasil* (Editora Vozes, Petrópolis, 1972), 79–89.

SCHMIDT, Max: 'Ergebnisse meiner zweijährigen Forschungsreise in Matto Grosso, September 1926 bis August 1928', *Zeitschrift für Ethnologie*, Berlin, **9**, 1929, 85–124.

'Los Kayabis en Matto-Grosso (Brasil)', *Revista de la Sociedad Científica del Paraguay*, **5:6**, 1942.

'Los Bakairí', RMP, **1**, 1947, 11–58.

SCHMINK, Marianne and Charles H. WOOD, eds., *Frontier Expansion in Amazonia* (University of Florida Press, Gainesville, Fla., 1984).

eds., *Contested Frontiers in Amazonia* (Columbia University Press, New York, 1992).

SCHULTZ, Harald: 'Informações etnográficas sôbre os índios Suyá, 1960', RMP, **13**, 1961/62, 315–32.

'Hombu'. Indian Life in the Brazilian Jungle (Macmillan, New York, and Colibris Editôra Ltda., Amsterdam and Rio de Janeiro, 1962).

'Brazil's Big-Lipped Indians', *National Geographic*, **121:1**, Jan. 1962, 118–33.

'Brazil's Waurá Indians', *National Geographic*, **129:1**, Jan. 1966, 130–52.

and Vilma CHIARA: 'Informações sôbre os índios do alto Purus', RMP, **9**, 1955.

SCHWADE, Egydio and Doroti: *As Terras Waimiri-Atroari no Ciclo de Minério* (Mimeo, Presidente Figueiredo, 21 Apr. 1985).

SCHWARTZMAN, Stephan: *The Panará of the Xingu National Park: the Transformation of a Society* (Doctoral dissertation, University of Chicago, 1988).

Os Panará do Peixoto de Azevedo e Cabeceiras do Iriri: história, contato e transferência ao Parque do Xingu (Environmental Defense Fund, Washington, DC, 1992).

'The Panará: indigenous territory and environmental protection in the Amazon', in Greg Dicum, ed., *Local Heritage in the Changing Tropics: Innovative Strategies for Natural Resource Management and Control* (Yale School of Forestry and Environmental Studies, New Haven, Connecticut, 1995).

'Panará: a saga dos índios gigantes', *Ciência Hoje*, **20:119**, Apr. 1996, 26–35.

SEEGER, Anthony: *Os Índios e Nós. Estudos sobre sociedades tribais brasileiras* (Editora Campus, Rio de Janeiro, 1980).

Nature and Society in Central Brazil: the Suyá Indians of Mato Grosso (Harvard University Press, Cambridge, Mass., 1981).

Why Suyá Sing (Cambridge University Press, Cambridge, 1987).

SEITZ, Georg: *Hinter dem Grünen Unterhang* (F. A. Brockhaus, Wiesbaden, 1960); trans. Arnold J. Pomerans as *People of the Rain-Forests* (William Heinemann, London, 1963).

SHOUMATOFF, Alex: *The Rivers Amazon* (William Heinemann, London, 1979).

The World is Burning. Murder in the Rain Forest (Little, Brown and Company, Boston, 1990).

SICK, Helmut: *Tukani* (Verlag Paul Perey, Hamburg and Berlin, 1957); trans. R. H. Stevens as *Tukani* (Burke Publishing Co., London, 1959).

SILVA, Fernando Altenfelder: 'Mudança cultural dos Terêna', RMP, **3**, 1949, 271–379.

SILVERWOOD-COPE, Peter: *Os Makú. Povo caçador do noroeste da Amazônia* (Editora da Universidade de Brasília, Brasília, 1990).

SIMÕES, Mário: ed., *S.P.I. – 1954* (Serviço de Proteção aos Índios, Rio de Janeiro, 1955).

'Os "Txikão" e outras tribos marginais do Alto Xingu', RMP, **14**, 1963, 76–104.

SMITH, Nigel J. H.: *Rainforest Corridors: The Transamazon Colonization Scheme* (University of California Press, Berkeley and London, 1982).

SMOLE, William J.: *The Yanoama Indians. A Cultural Geography* (University of Texas Press, Austin, 1976).

SNETHLAGE, Heinrich: 'Unter nordostbrasilianischen Indianern', *Zeitschrift für Ethnologie*, **62**, 1931, 111–205.

SOUZA, Marcio, José Ribamar BESSA, Mário JURUNA, MEGARON, and Marcos TERENA: *Os Índios Vão à Luta* (Editora Marco Zero, Rio de Janeiro, 1981).

SPONSEL, Leslie Elmer, ed.: *Indigenous People and the Future of Amazonia: An Ecological Anthropology of an Endangered World* (University of Arizona Press, Tucson, 1995).

'The master thief: gold mining and mercury contamination in the Amazon', in Barbara Rose Johnston, ed., *Life and Death Matters: Human Rights and the Environment at the End of the Millennium* (Alta Mira – Sage, Walnut Creek, Calif., 1997), 99–127.

'Yanomami: an arena of conflict and aggression in the Amazon', *Aggressive Behavior*, **24**, 1998, 97–122.

STAUFFER, David Hall: *The Origin and Establishment of Brazil's Indian Service: 1889–1910* (Doctoral dissertation, University of Texas, Austin, 1955).

STOLL, David: *Fishers of Men or Founders of Empires? The Wycliffe Bible Translators in Latin America* (Zed Press, London, 1982).

SUESS, Paulo: *Em Defesa dos Povos Indígenas. Documentos e legislação* (Edições Loyola, São Paulo, 1980).

SUMMER INSTITUTE OF LINGUISTICS: *SIL in Brazil: Annual Report for 1975* (SIL, Brasília, 1976).

SURVIVAL: *Disinherited. Indians in Brazil* (Survival, London, 2000).

TASTEVIN, Constant: 'Le fleuve Juruá', *La Géographie*, **33**, Paris, 1920.

'Le fleuve Murú. Croyances et moeurs Kachinauá', *La Géographie*, **43**, Paris, 1923/24, 135–44.

'Le Haut Tarauacá', *La Géographie*, **45:1–2**, Paris, Jan.–Feb. 1926.

'Le "Riozinho da Liberdade"', *La Géographie*, **49:3–4**, Paris, Mar.–Apr. 1929, 205–15.

TREECE, David: 'Indigenous peoples in Brazilian Amazonia and the expansion of the economic frontier', in David Goodman and Anthony Hall, eds., *The Future of Amazonia – Destruction or Sustainable Development?* (St Martin's Press, New York, 1990), 264–87.

TURNER, Terence: 'The Brazilian Statute of the Indian', *Bulletin of the American Anthropological Association*, 4:1, Washington, DC, 1971.

'History, myth, and social consciousness among the Kayapó of Central Brazil', and 'Ethno-ethnohistory: myth and history in native South American representations of contact with western society', in Jonathan D. Hill, ed., *Rethinking History and Myth: Indigenous South American Perspectives on the Past* (University of Illinois Press, Urbana, Ill., 1988), 195–213, 235–81.

'Representing, resisting, rethinking. Historical transformations of Kayapó culture and anthropological consciousness', in G. Stocking, ed., *Post-colonial Situations. Essays in the Contextualization of Ethnographic Knowledge* (University of Wisconsin Press, Madison, 1991), 285–313.

'De cosmologia a história: resistência, adaptação e consciência social entre os Kayapó', *Cadernos de Campo* (Universidade de São Paulo), 1:1, 1991, 68–85; also in Eduardo Viveiros de Castro and Manuela Carneiro da Cunha, eds., *Amazônia: Etnologia e História Indígena* (NIHI, Universidade de São Paulo, 1993), 43–66.

ed., *Cosmology, Values, and Inter-Ethnic Contact in South America* (Bennington College, Bennington, Vt., 1993).

'Imagens desafiantes: a apropriação Kayapó do vídeo', RA, **36**, 1993, 81–122.

'Os Mebengokre Kayapó: história e mudança social. De comunidades autônomas para a coexistência interétnica', HIB, 311–38.

'Neo-liberal eco-politics and indigenous peoples: the Kayapó, the "Rainforest Harvest", and The Body Shop', in Greg Dicum, ed., *Local Heritage in the Changing Tropics* (Yale School of Forestry and Environmental Studies, New Haven, 1995), 113–23.

and Davi YANOMAMI: '"I fight because I am alive": an interview with Davi Kopenawa Yanomami', *Cultural Survival Quarterly* (Cultural Survival, Cambridge, Mass.), **15:3**, Aug. 1991, 59–64.

URBAN, Greg: 'Interpretations of inter-cultural contact: the Shokleng and Brazilian national society, 1914–1916', *Ethnohistory*, **32:3**, 1985, 224–44.

'Developments in the situation of Brazilian tribal populations from 1976 to 1982', *Latin American Research Review*, **20:1**, 1985, 7–25.

VASCONCELLOS, Vicente de Paula Teixeira da Fonseca: *Expedição ao Rio Ronuro* (Conselho Nacional de Proteção aos Índios 90, Imprensa Nacional, Rio de Janeiro, 1945).

VERSWIJVER, Gustaaf: 'Os Kayapó: separações e junções dos grupos do norte', RAI, **2:12**, Sep.–Oct. 1978, 9–16.

'Séparations et migrations des Mekrãgnoti, groupe Kayapo du Brésil Central', *Bulletin de la Société Suisse des Américanistes* (Geneva), **42**, 1978, 47–59.

'Les hommes aux bracelets noirs: un rite de passage chez les Indiens Kayapo-Mekrãgnoti du Brésil central', *Naître, Vivre et Mourir* (Musée d'Ethnographie, Neuchâtel), 1981, 95–118.

'The Intertribal relations between the Juruna and the Kayapó Indians (1850–1920)', *Jahrbuch des Museums für Völkerkunde zu Leipzig* (Akademie-Verlag, Berlin), **34**, 1982, 305–15.

The Club-Fighters of the Amazon. Warfare among the Kaiapo Indians of Central Brazil (Rijksuniversiteit Gent, Gent, 1992).

VIDAL, Lux Boelitz: *Morte e Vida de uma Sociedade Indígena Brasileira* (Editôra da Universidade, São Paulo, 1977).

'A questão indígena', in José Maria Gonçalves de Almeida, ed., *Carajás: Desafio político, ecologia e desenvolvimento* (Brasiliense and CNPq, São Paulo and Brasília, 1986), 222–64.

'As terras indígenas no Brasil', in Luís Donisete Benzi Grupioni, ed., *Índios no Brasil* (Município de São Paulo, São Paulo, 1992), 193–204.

VIERTLER, Renate Brigitte: *Os Kamayurá e o Alto Xingu* (Instituto de Estudos Brasileiros, Publicação **10**, USP, São Paulo, 1969).

VILAÇA, Aparecida: 'Cristãos sem fé: alguns aspectos da conversão dos Wari (Pakaa Nova)', TD, 131–54. This paper also appeared in *Mana* (Museu Nacional, Rio de Janeiro), **2**, 1996 and in English in *Ethnos* (Stockholm), **62**, 1997.

VILLAS BÔAS, Orlando and Cláudio: 'Atracão dos índios Txukahamãi', in Mário F. Simões, ed., *S.P.I. – 1954* (Serviço de Proteção aos Índios, Rio de Janeiro, 1955), 79–88.

'Saving Brazil's stone-age tribes from extinction', *National Geographic*, **134**, Sep. 1968, 424–35.

Xingu: os índios, seus mitos (Zahar, Rio de Janeiro, 1970); trans. as *Xingu: the Indians, their Myths*, ed. and trans. Kenneth S. Brecher (Farrar, Straus and Giroux, New York, 1973).

Almanaque do Sertão (Editora Globo, São Paulo, 1997).

Xingu. O velho Káia (conta a história do seu povo) (Editora Kuarup, Porto Alegre, 1984).

Xingu: os contos do Tamoin (Editora Kuarup, Porto Alegre, 1986).

'Memórias de Orlando e Cláudio Villas Boas', *Carta* (Gabinete do Senador Darcy Ribeiro, Brasília), **9**, 1993, 187–203.

A Marcha Para o Oeste. A Epopéia da Expedição Roncador–Xingu (Editôra Globo, São Paulo, 1994).

A Arte dos Pajés: impressões sobre o universo espiritual do índio xinguano (Editora Globo, São Paulo, 2000).

O Xingu dos Villas Bôas (O Estado de São Paulo and Eletronorte, São Paulo, 2002).

VIVEIROS, Esther de: *Rondon Conta sua Vida* (Livraria São José, Rio de Janeiro, 1958).

VIVEIROS DE CASTRO, Eduardo: *Indivíduo e sociedade no alto Xingu: os Yawalipití* (Master's dissertation, Museu Nacional/Universidade Federal do Rio de Janeiro, 1977).

Araweté: os deuses canibais (Jorge Zahar, Rio de Janeiro, 1986); trans. Catherine V. Howard as *From the Enemy's Point of View: Humanity and Divinity in an Amazonian Society* (University of Chicago Press, Chicago, 1992).

Araweté. O povo do Ipixuna (CEDI, São Paulo, 1992).

and Manuela CARNEIRO DA CUNHA, eds.: *Amazônia: etnologia e história indígena* (Núcleo de História Indígena/Fapesp, Universidade de São Paulo, 1993).

WAGLEY, Charles: 'The effects of depopulation upon social organization as illustrated by the Tapirapé Indians', *Transactions of the New York Academy of Sciences*, 2 ser. **3**, 1940, 12–16; trans. in *Sociologia*, **4**, São Paulo, 1942, 407–11.

'Cultural influences on population: a comparison of two Tupí tribes', RMP, **5**, 1951, 95–104; and in Daniel Gross, ed., *Peoples and Cultures of Native South America* (New York, 1973), 143–56.

Amazon Town (Macmillan, New York, 1953).

'Tapirapé social and cultural change, 1940–1953', *Anais do XXXI Congresso Internacional de Americanistas* (Editôra Anhembi, São Paulo, 1955), 99–106.

ed., *Man in the Amazon* (University of Florida Press, Gainesville, Fla., 1974).

Welcome of Tears (Oxford University Press, New York, 1977).

and Eduardo GALVÃO: *The Tenetehara Indians. A Culture in Transition* (Columbia University Press, New York, 1949); trans. as *Os índios Tenetehara: uma cultura em transição* (Ministério da Educação e Cultura, Rio de Janeiro, 1961).

'The Tenetehara' and 'The Tapirapé' in Julian Steward, ed., *Handbook of South American Indians*, **3**, *The Tropical Forest Tribes* (Smithsonian Institution, Washington, 1948), 137–48 and 167–78.

WATSON, James B.: *Cayuá Culture Change: a study in acculturation and methodology*, Memoir **73** (*American Anthropologist*, **54:2**, 1952).

WILLIAMS, Harry: *With Colonel Fawcett in the Amazon Basin* (London, 1960).

WILLIAMS, Suzanne (as 'Anna Presland'): 'Reconquest', SIR, **25**, Spring 1979.

'Land rights and the manipulation of identity: official Indian policy in Brazil', *Journal of Latin American Studies*, London, **15:1**, 1983, 137–61.

WRIGHT, Robin Michael: *The History and Religion of the Baniwa Peoples of the Upper Rio Negro Valley* (Doctoral dissertation, Stanford University, 1981).

'História indígena do noroeste da Amazônia. Hipóteses, questões e perspectivas', in HIB, 253–66.

'A conspiracy against the civilized people', *Religiones Latinoamericanas* (Mexico), **2**, 1991, 43–70; trans. as 'Uma conspiração contra os civilizados: história, política e ideologias dos movimentos milenaristas dos Arawak e Tukano do Noroeste da Amazônia', *Anuário Antropológico* (Tempo Brasileiro, Rio de Janeiro), **89**, 1992, 191–231.

'Pesquisa antropológica e ação em favor dos povos indígenas', *Terra Indígena* (Centro de Estudos Indígenas, Araraquara), **10:67**, Apr.–Jun. 1993, 37–52.

ed., *Transformando os Deuses. Os múltiplos sentidos da conversão entre os povos indígenas no Brasil* (Editora da Unicamp, Campinas, 1999) = TD; includes his 'O tempo de Sophie: história e cosmologia da conversão baniwa', 155–216.

and ISMAELILLO: *Native Peoples in Struggle: Cases from the Fourth Russell Tribunal and Other International Forums* (Anthropology Resource Center and ERIN Publications, New York, 1982).

ZACQUINI, Carlos: 'Os índios de Roraima e a política local. Yanomami', in Dalmo de Abreu Dallari et al., eds., *A Questão da Terra Indígena* (Comissão Pró-Índio, São Paulo, Global Editora, São Paulo, 1981), 97–108.

ZERRIES, Otto: *Waika* (Klaus Renner Verlag, München, 1964).

Mahekodotheri (Klaus Renner Verlag, München, 1974).

Notes and References

1. Rondon

1: persuasion'. Article 2.d., Regulamento do Serviço de Proteção aos Índios, 7 Sep. 1910, in Cândido M. da Silva Rondon, 'Problema indígena', AI, **3:1**, Jan. 1943, 27.

3: heart.' Esther Viveiros, *Rondon Conta sua Vida* (Rio de Janeiro, 1958), 92.

4: frighten them'. Ibid., 67. John Hemming, *Amazon Frontier* (London, 1995), 411. Travelling in this area with some Bororo, ninety years after Rondon, the author saw lines of his telegraph poles and picked up one of their heavy ceramic insulators. The Bororo call themselves Boe – the word Bororo means 'village court'. Their language was originally thought to be 'isolated' – unconnected to other languages – but it is now considered to form part of the Macro-Jê group, although incomprehensible to other Jê-speakers such as the Xavante or Kayapó. The plains Bororo were known as Bororo da Campanha ('open farmland') or Cabaçais ('gourd groves'), while the eastern were formerly called Coroados ('crowned') because of their piled hair.

5: victims.' Ibid., 78–9.

5: unwelcome.' Ibid., 92.

5: starvation.' Ibid., 88–9.

6: intimately.' Ibid., 145–6, 155.

7: piranhas'. Ibid., 172.

7: population'. Report by President Herculano Ferreira Pena, Cuiabá, 1862, in Carlos de Araújo Moreira Neto, *A política indigenista Brasileira durante o século XIX* (doctoral thesis, Rio Claro University, São Paulo, 1971), 151; Annual report by Vice-President Augusto Leverger, Cuiabá, 1863, 13; Hemming, *Amazon Frontier*, 438.

7: cloth.' Hercules Florence, *Esboço da Viagem . . . No Interior do Brasil* (1830), trans. from French by Alfredo d'Escragnolle Taunay, RIHGB, **38:1**, 1875, 425.

8: landowners.' Viveiros, *Rondon Conta*, 179–80.

8: nobility'. Ibid., 180, 182–3.

8: crimes.' Ibid., 203.

9: shame' Cândido Mariano da Silva Rondon, *Conferências Realizadas em 1910 no Rio de Janeiro e em São Paulo* (CNPI Publication **68**, 2nd edition 1946), 88–9.

10: withdrew.' Ibid., 21.

10: happening.' Ibid., 23; José Mauro Gagliardi, *O Indígena e a República* (São Paulo, 1989), 153.

11: fallen on them.' Rondon, *Conferências*, 91.

11: slaughter'. Ibid., 26.

11: rights.' Ibid., 31; Gagliardi, *O Indígena*, 155.

12: reports'. Ibid., 33.

12: medicine'. Ibid., 39.

12: pace.' Ibid., 43.

13: words.' Ibid., 57.

14: months.' Amilcar A. Botelho de Magalhães, *Rondon – Uma Relíquia da Pátria* (Curitiba–São Paulo–Rio de Janeiro, 1942), 16–17.

14: camp.' Edilberto Coutinho, *Rondon e a Integração da Amazônia* (São Paulo, 1968), 31–2, quoting General Amilcar Botelho de Magalhães.

14: melted.' F. McDermott, *The Amazing Amazon* (L. Williams, London, 1933), 109.

15: Rondon. Viveiros, *Rondon Conta*, 92. On Rondon's Positivist beliefs, João Cruz Costa, 'O positivismo na República (notes sôbre a história do positivismo no Brasil)', *Revista da História* (São Paulo), **7**, 1953, 97–110, 289–316, 303–5.

17: exterminate them.' Hermann von Ihering, *The Anthropology of the State of São Paulo* (St Louis, 1904; trans. *Revista do Museu Paulista*, 1907); also his speech to the Instituto Histórico e Geográfico de São Paulo, 20 Oct. 1908, and his article in ESP on the same day.

17: instincts'. Luiz Bueno Horta Barboza, 'Em defesa dos indígenas brasileiros', *Jornal do*

Commércio, Rio de Janeiro, 11 Nov. 1908; Sílvio de Almeida article in ESP, 26 Oct. 1908. The manipulation of anti-German sentiment by Indian sympathizers was expounded in a brilliant thesis by David Hall Stauffer, *The Origin and Establishment of Brazil's Indian Service: 1889–1910* (Austin, Texas, 1955), 66–7, 70, 87, 109. Hemming, *Amazon Frontier*, 474.

17: disappear.' Von Ihering article in ESP, 20 Oct. 1908; Stauffer, *Origin*, 87; Hemming, *Amazon Frontier*, 457.

17: people.' Raymundo Teixeira Mendes to the President of Brazil, published in *Jornal do Commércio*, 11 Nov. 1908; Stauffer, *Origin*, 109.

18: idea.' Statement by Museu Nacional, *Jornal do Comércio*, 6 Dec. 1908 and *Archivos do Museu Nacional*, 15, 256ff; Stauffer, *Origin*, 116.

18: labour.' Leolinda Daltro lecture to the Associação de Proteção aos Selvícolas do Brasil, in her *Da Catechese dos Índios no Brasil* (Typ. da Escola Orsina da Fonseca, Rio de Janeiro, 1920), 623–4; Stauffer, *Origin*, 119–20.

18: intelligence . . .' Rondon telegraph message to Batista de Lacerda, Director of the Museu Nacional, from Posto Barão de Campinas in Mato Grosso, 4 Feb. 1909, in Rondon, 'O exterminio dos índios', *Jornal do Commércio*, 11 Feb. 1909; Stauffer, *Origin*, 149.

18: justice for all.' Teixeira Mendes, *Jornal do Commércio*, 9 Dec. 1909.

18: poverty'. Antonio Carlos Simoens da Silva, 'Proteção aos índios', *Anais do Premeiro Congresso Brasileiro de Geografia*, 9 26 (Rio de Janeiro, 1910); Stauffer, *Origin*, 179.

19: Constitution.' Leolinda Daltro, *Anais do Primeiro Congresso Brasileiro de Geografia* (Rio de Janeiro, 1910), 1 236; Simoens da Silva, 'Protecção aos índios', 9 26; Nelso Coelho de Senna, *Os Índios do Brasil: memória ethnográphica* (Belo Horizonte, 1908); Anon., *A Questão Indígena: appello dirigida à opinião pública do Brasil* (Campinas, 1909); Stauffer, *Origin*, 179–84; Hemming, *Amazon Frontier*, 476–8; Gagliardi, *O Indígena*, 157, 179–80 and on Leolinda Daltro's speech, 129–33.

19: efforts.' Rocha Miranda to Rondon, 2 Mar. 1910, published in *Jornal do Commércio*, 6 Mar. 1910; Stauffer, *Origin*, 225.

20: religion.' Letter from Rondon to Rocha Miranda, Rio de Janeiro, 14 Mar. 1910, in Magal-hães, *Rondon – Uma Relíquia*, 134–9. Viveiros, *Rondon Conta*, 351. The correspondence between Rocha Miranda and Rondon was issued to the press. In a sense it was a political ritual to implement Positivist ideals (Antônio Carlos de Souza Lima, *Um Grande Cerco de Paz* (Petrópolis, 1995), 116).

21: Brazilian'. Mércio Pereira Gomes, *The Indians and Brazil*, Gainesville, Fla., 2000, 78.

21: rustics.' Circular by Minister Rocha Miranda, 5 Mar. 1910, in *Relatório do Ministério da Agricultura*, 1910, II 13; Viveiros, *Rondon Conta*, 351; Stauffer, *Origin*, 234–5; Gagliardi, *O Indígena*, 186–91; Antônio Carlos de Souza Lima, 'O governo dos índios sob a gestão do SPI', in HIB, 156–9; Hemming, *Amazon Frontier*, 480.

21: lodges'. Gagliardi, *O Indígena*, 207.

21: inspiring.' Brasílio Machado debate at Instituto Histórico e Geográfico de São Paulo, June 1910, in *Revista do Instituto . . .*, 15 442; Gagliardi, *O Indígena*, 209.

21: Christians.' Speech by Bishop Armando Bahlman to same meeting; Gagliardi, *O Indígena*, 209.

22: dream'. Ibid., 215. The anthropologists who supported missionaries included Max Schmidt, who had been among the Xingu tribes, Eduard Seler of Berlin, and Franz Heger of Vienna.

22: birth.' Rocha Miranda, *Exposição dos motivos* of Decree 8,072, 20 Jun. 1910; Gagliardi, *O Indígena*, 226–7.

23: circumstances.' Cândido Rondon, 'Discurso', *O País*, 8 Sep. 1910. The pioneer of Indian protection, Leolinda Daltro, was not invited to the ceremony. When she reminded Minister Rocha Miranda of a promise to let her found an Indian colony on the Araguaia, he answered that the new Service was led by Rondon who, as a Positivist, was opposed to having any women in public offices. Daltro saw this as an insult to her sex. 'I then felt the spirit of revolt awaken in me. I realized the necessity for a persistent and tenacious campaign to destroy such terrible prejudice.' This formidable woman turned her energy from defending Indians to launching feminism in Brazil. Leolinda Daltro, *Início do Feminismo no Brasil. Subsídio para a história* (Rio de Janeiro, 1918), 14–15; Gagliardi, *O Indígena*, 235.

2. First Contacts: Kaingang, Xokleng, and Nambiquara

24: methods.' Amilcar A. Botelho de Magalhães, 'O problema da civilização dos índios do Brasil', AI, **3**:2, Apr. 1943, 156.

25: barbaric Indians'. Carta régia of Prince Regent to Governor Antonio José da Franca Horta, Rio de Janeiro, 5 Nov. 1808, in L. Humberto de Oliveira, *Coletânea de Leis, atos e memorias referentes ao indígena brasileiro* (Rio de Janeiro, 1947), 67; John Hemming, *Amazon Frontier* (London, 1995), 113.

25: machine-made.' Franz Keller, *Noções Sobre os Índios da Provincia do Paraná* (1866) in Lêda A. Lovato, 'A contribuição de Franz Keller à etnografia do Paraná', *Boletim do Museu do Indio. Antropologia*, **3**, 12, Rio de Janeiro, Nov. 1974, 15–16.

26: unpunished.' Gustav von Koenigswald, 'Die Coroados im südlichen Brasilien', *Globus*, **94**:2 27, Braunschweig, Jul. 1908. João C. Gomes Ribeiro, *Suum Cuique Tribuere – esboço de um projeto de lei sôbre os índios do Brasil* (Rio de Janeiro, 1912), 8. Pierre Monbeig, *Pionniers et Planteurs de São Paulo* (Paris, 1952), 84–6, 114–16. John Hemming, *Red Gold* (London, 1978; revised edition, London, 1995), 463.

26: massacred.' Clovis de Gusmão, *Rondon: a conquista do deserto brasileiro* (Rio de Janeiro, 1942), 123–4; Amilcar A. Botelho de Magalhães, *Rondon – Uma Relíquia da Pátria* (Curitiba–São Paulo–Rio de Janeiro, 1942), 69; Fausto Ribeiro de Barros, *Padre Claro Monteiro do Amaral (trucidado pelos índios "Caingangs", nos sertões do rio Feio)* (São Paulo, 1950); José Mauro Gagliardi, *O Indígena e a República* (São Paulo, 1989), 64, 97–103.

26: game-hunting.' *Correio da Manhã*, Rio de Janeiro, 16 Oct. 1908.

27: nobody.' Report by bugreiro João Pedro to the Commission of Inquiry into conflicts in the zone of the North-West Railway Company, 1911 (manuscript in the SPI archive), 17–18; Darcy Ribeiro, *Os Índios e a Civilização* (Rio de Janeiro, 1970), 104–6; David Hall Stauffer, *The Origin and Establishment of Brazil's Indian Service: 1889–1910* (Austin, Texas, 1955), 12; Esther de Viveiros, *Rondon Conta sua Vida* (Rio de Janeiro, 1958), 353.

27: encampment.' *Correio da Manhã*, Rio de Janeiro, 16 Oct. 1908.

28: ground.' Curt Nimuendajú, 'O fim da tribu Oti', in TICN, 36.

28: died.' Ibid, 41. The massacre was at Córrego da Lagoa on the Campos Novos in western São Paulo State. Settlers knew the Oti as 'Chavante' although they were Tupi-speakers who had nothing to do with the Chavante or Xavante tribe far to the north-west. They were distantly related to, but distinct from, the Ofaié (also known as Chavante), who lived to the west of the Paraná river and were thought to be extinct until a remnant was found in recent decades.

28: forest' Curt (Unkel) Nimuendajú, 'Carta sobre a pacificação dos Coroados', Letter to Dr Hugo Gensch, Aldeia de Araribá, 14 Apr. 1912, trans. Dagmar Schneider, TICN, 42; Ribeiro, *Os Índios e a Civilização*, 157–8; Magalhães, 'O problema', 156; Cândido Mariano da Silva Rondon, *Índios do Brasil*, **1**, *Brasil Central, Nordeste e Mato Grosso do Sul* (CNPI, Rio de Janeiro, 1953), 335.

29: celebrating.' Viveiros, *Rondon Conta*, 354–5.

29: beads.' Luiz Bueno Horta Barboza, *A Pacificação dos Caingangs Paulistas: hábitos, costumes e instituições dêsses índios* (Lecture in Biblioteca Nacional, Rio de Janeiro, 19 Nov. 1913), 17–19, also published by the Conselho Nacional de Proteção aos Índios, Publication **88**, 1947, 50. Also, Darcy S. Bandeira de Mello, *Entre Índios e Revoluções* (São Paulo, 1982), 24. This book was about the author's father, Manuel Sylvino Bandeira de Mello, who was in charge of the attraction camp with Lieutenants Rabelo and Sobrinho.

29: grateful.' Magalhães, 'O problema', Apr. 1943, 159.

29: cameraderie.' Ibid., 159–60.

30: methods.' SPI Report for 1911, in ibid., 159–60.

30: measles' Luiz Bueno Horta Barboza, 'Relatório dos trabalhos realizados pela Inspetoria do Serviço de Proteção aos Indios e Localização de Trabalhadores Nacionais em S. Paulo durante o ano de 1916', RMP, **8**, 1954, 70–71.

30: night.' Ibid., 72.

31: substituted for them.' Ibid., 73–4. Charles Wagley, *Welcome of Tears* (New York, 1977), 277–80.

31: paddle home. The story about the three chiefs being taken to São Paulo (then a city of only 300,000 people) was told to Darcy Ribeiro by Horta Barboza's son Professor Hildebrando Horta Barboza: Ribeiro, *Os Índios e a Civilização*, 268–9. The son of Manuel Bandeira de Mello, who organized the railway journey, said that the group consisted of men, women, and children, that they lodged in his parents' house for twenty days, were given ice cream and other sweets, and were taken to the cinema and even a prison. Bandeira de Mello, *Entre Índios e Revoluções*, 33–8.

31: had been.' Horta Barboza, 'Relatório dos trabalhos', 70.

32: children died. Ibid., 70–1; also his *O Serviço de Proteção aos Indios e a história da colonização do Brasil* (Rio de Janeiro, 1919), 74–5; Gagliardi, *O Indígena*, 267.

33: oppressors. Dr João Coutinho, President of Santa Catarina, annual address for 1856; José Deeke, *Das Munizip Blumenau und seine Entwicklungsgeschichte* (Blumenau, 1917); José Ferreira da Silva, *Blumenau em Cadernos* (Blumenau, 1967), 104; Silvio Coelho dos Santos, *A Integração do Índio na Sociedade Regional* (Florianópolis, 1969), 32. The Xokleng are also known as Aweikoma, and settlers had previously called them Botocudos or 'wearers of lip-discs'.

34: effects.' Der Urwaldsbote ('Virgin Forest Chronicle'), Blumenau, Nov. 1913.

34: mistrustful'. Report in *Der Urwaldsbote*, 30 Sep. 1914; Basílio de Magalhães, *Em Defesa do Índio e Das Fazendas Nacionais* (Rio de Janeiro, 1925), 78–9; Report in *Blumenau Zeitung*, in Silvio Coelho dos Santos, *Índios e Brancos no Sul do Brasil* (Edeme, Florianópolis, SC, 1973), 144–8, trans. Greg Urban, 'Interpretations of inter-cultural contact: the Shokleng and Brazilian national society, 1914–1916', *Ethnohistory*, **32:3**, 1985, 232.

36: white man".' Ibid., 228–9.

36: continued.' Eduardo Hoerhan, Report of the Plate River Post, 1915, from the SPI archive, given to Greg Urban by Professor Aryon Rodrigues of Campinas Univesity, and quoted by Urban in 'Interpretations', 234. The town of Scharlack was later renamed José Boiteaux. Posto Duque de Caxias, fifty-two kilometres (thirty-two miles) from Ibirama, became a reserve in 1926 when the SPI persuaded the State government to cede some land around it (the State had in 1902 granted land between the Xapecó and Xapecozinho rivers to Chief Vaicrê). Posto Selistre de Campos was created in 1942. The two

Xokleng posts were later renamed Ibirama and Xanxerê.

36: danger'. Hoerhan report, ibid.

37: alcoholic.' Ibid.

37: people died.' Wãnpo's narrative, in ibid., 228.

37: [hunting] horn.' Ibid., 228.

37: medicines.' Ibid., 230.

38: starved.' Ibid., 231.

38: implore him.' Coelho dos Santos, *A Integração do Índio*, 55.

38: everything.' Hoerhan report, in Urban, 235.

39: could for you.' Ribeiro, *Os Índios e a Civilização*, 400; Hugo Gensch, 'Die Erziehung eines Indianerkindes', *Akten, Internationale Amerikanisten-Kongress*, Vienna, 1908.

39: village dogs.' Ribeiro, *Os Índios e a Civilização*, 284–5.

40: degeneration.' Santos, *A Integração do Índio*, 54, 10; Darcy Ribeiro, 'Convívio e contaminação', *Sociologia*, **18:1**, 1956, 32; Jules Henry, *Jungle People* (New York, 1941), xxi; Urban, 'Interpretations', 235. Jules Henry had counted 132 Xokleng in 1932–33. In 1968, Coelho dos Santos said that Duque de Caxias contained 176 Xokleng (plus 11 Kaingang, 33 Guarani, 66 mestizos, and 50 civilizados some of whom were married to Indians, making a total of 336 people on the post). Twenty years later, Ibirama's population had grown to 898 (CEDI, *Terras Indígenas no Brasil*).

40: never kill".' Vicente de Paula T. da F. Vasconcellos, 'O problema da civilização dos índios', *Revista do Serviço Público*, **2:1**, Apr. 1940, 66; Rondon, *Índios do Brasil*, 1 342–3; Santos, *A Integração do Índio*, 42; Gagliardi, *O Indígena*, 272.

41: workers'. José Bezerra Cavalcanti, 'Serviço de Proteção aos Índios e Localização de Trabalhadores Nacionais: Exposição apresentada ao sr. dr. Ministro da Agricultura, Indústria e Comércio', in Dr Pedro de Toledo, Ministro da Agricultura . . ., *Relatório Apresentado ao Presidente da República dos Estados Unidos do Brasil* (Rio de Janeiro, 1912), 148; Antônio Carlos de Souza Lima, *Um Grande Cerco de Paz* (Petrópolis, 1995), 128.

41: coffee.' Carlos de Araújo Moreira Neto, 'Some data concerning the recent history of the Kaingang Indians', in Walter Dostal, ed., *The Situation of the Indian in South America* (Geneva, 1972), 314.

42: defend it.' Bezerra Cavalcanti, 'Serviço de Proteção aos Índios', in Toledo, *Relatório Apresentado ao Presidente da República*; Antônio Carlos de Souza Lima, 'O governo dos índios sob a gestão do SPI', HIB, 159 and *Um Grande Cerco de Paz*, 138–9; Gagliardi, *O Indígena*, 244.

42: satisfied.' Gagliardi, *O Indígena*, 244. The army also recalled personnel from other ministries at this time, not just from the SPI.

43: hinterland' Report in 1917 by Father Antonio Colbacchini (who ran the Salesian mission among the Bororo in the early twentieth century, and wrote a study of their culture) quoted in Sylvia Caiuby Novaes, 'A épica salvacionista e as artimanhas de resistência – as missões salesianas e os Bororo de Mato Grosso', in Robin Wright, ed., *Transformando os Deuses. Os múltiplos sentidos da conversão entre os povos indígenas no Brasil* (Campinas, 1999), 347; and Sylvia Caiuby Novaes, *Jogo de Espelhos* (São Paulo, 1993), 142. Bandeirantes were the explorers/woodsmen/slavers from São Paulo in the seventeenth century.

43: fire to it'. Father Colbacchini, *Boletim Salesiano*, **14:6:2**, Mar.–Apr. 1915, in Caiuby Novaes, 'A épica salvacionista', 345.

43: Catholicism'. Gagliardi, *O Indígena*, 249–50.

44: companion.' Theodore Roosevelt, *Through the Brazilian Wilderness* (New York, 1914; London, 1922), 49. *Scribner's Magazine* published reports of the expedition between April and October 1914; Amilcar A. Botelho de Magalhães described it in his *Impressões da Comissão Rondon* (Pôrto Alegre, RS, 1929); and Rondon recalled it in Viveiros, *Rondon Conta*, 373–419.

45: fatal to them.' Roosevelt, *Brazilian Wilderness*, 184, 186; Viveiros, *Rondon Conta*, 391–2.

46: straight line. Captain Amilcar A. Botelho de Magalhães, *Relatório Apresentado ao Sr. Coronel Cândido Mariano da Silva Rondon, Chefe da Comissão Brasileira* (Rio de Janeiro, 1916), 78–9; Roosevelt, *Brazilian Wilderness*, 208–9.

46: current'. Roosevelt, *Brazilian Wilderness*, 270; Viveiros, *Rondon Conta*, 409–10.

46: friends.' Viveiros, *Rondon Conta*, 410–11; Amilcar Armando Botelho de Magalhães, *A Obra Ciclópica do General Rondon* (Rio de Janeiro, 1956), 12.

46: ceremony itself.' Roosevelt, *Brazilian Wilderness*, 268; Viveiros, *Rondon Conta*, 413.

47: agony.' Roosevelt, *Brazilian Wilderness*, 307; Viveiros, *Rondon Conta*, 418; F. McDermott, *The Amazing Amazon* (L. Williams, London, 1933), 117.

47: importance.' Leo E. Miller, *In the Wilds of South America* (London, 1919), 264; Roosevelt, *Brazilian Wilderness*, 322–3. The expedition brought international recognition to Colonel Rondon: the American Geographical Society in New York gave him its Livingstone Medal and the Société de Géographie Commerciale in Paris awarded him the Médaille Crévaux. Virgílio Corrêa Filho, 'Rondon', RIHGB, **266**, Jan.–Mar. 1965, 157; George K. Cherrie, *Dark Trails: Adventures of a Naturalist* (G. P. Putnam's Sons, London and New York, 1930); John Ure, *Trespassers on the Amazon* (Constable, London, 1986), 91–106.

48: game.' Claude Lévi-Strauss, *Tristes Tropiques* (Paris, 1955), 288. While the anthropologist was at the new Jesuit mission, it was visited by its Superior, a Frenchman who spoke with the exaggerated eloquence of Louis XIV's court. The Hungarian was affected by the isolation of the mission, 'went native', and abused the Superior, who exorcized the devil in him. Claude and Dina Lévi-Strauss made two expeditions to central Brazil, for four months in 1935–36 when they visited the Bororo and Kadiwéu, and he returned for eight months in 1938–39 to work among the Nambiquara. In addition to the great anthropologist's own writings, see Luís Donisete Benzi Grupioni, *Coleções e Expedições Vigiadas. Os etnólogos no Conselho de Fiscalização das Expedições Artísticas e Científicas no Brasil* (São Paulo, 1998), 113–61; Isidoro M. da Silva Alves, 'A expedição Lévi-Strauss ao Brasil Central 50 anos após', in Ubiratan D'Ambrosio, ed., *Anais do II Congresso Latino-Americano de História de Ciência de Tecnologia* (Nova Stella, São Paulo, 1989), 267–70.

49: parts.' Lévi-Strauss, *Tristes Tropiques*, 291.

50: souls. Ibid., 310–11.

50: tenderness. Ibid., 311.

50: dumb.' Kalervo Oberg, *Indian Tribes of Northern Mato Grosso, Brazil* (Washington, DC, 1953), 84–5.

3. Parintintin and Munduruku

53: impotence.' Kenneth Grubb, *Amazon and Andes* (London, 1930), 29–30.

53: thousands.' Ibid., 28.

53: Venezuela.' Ibid.

53: Christians".' Ibid.

54: exception. Ibid., 29–30.

54: constitution.' Ibid., 12.

54: devastation!' Esther de Viveiros, *Rondon Conta sua Vida* (Rio de Janeiro, 1958), 331–2.

54: survive.' Darcy Ribeiro, *Os Índios e a Civilização* (Rio de Janeiro, 1970), 27.

55: power.' Paul Le Cointe, *L'Amazonie brésilienne* (Paris, 1922), 222.

55: arguments.' Ibid., 227.

55: civilization.' Colonel Themístocles Paes de Souza Brazil, *Incolas Selvícolas* (Rio de Janeiro, 1937), 65.

56: failed'. Delvair Montanger Melatti and Julio Cesar Melatti, *Relatório Sobre os Índios Marúbo* (Universidade de Brasília, 1975), 10, 17–18, 23–4; Julio Cesar Melatti, 'Estrutura social Marúbo', *Anuário Antropológico/76* (Rio de Janeiro, 1977, 83–120), 106; Dr João Braulino de Carvalho, 'Breve noticia sobre os indígenas que habitam a fronteira do Brasil com o Peru . . .', *Boletim do Museu Nacional*, **7:3** (Rio de Janeiro, 1931, 225–56), 252; Julio Cesar Melatti, ed., *Povos Indígenas no Brasil*, **5**, *Javari* (São Paulo, 1981), 19–22.

57: camp.' Report by SPI Inspectors, 1911, in Ribeiro, *Os Índios*, 44.

57: possessions.' Another SPI Report, about incidents in Jun. 1913, ibid., 46; John Hemming, *Amazon Frontier* (London, 1995), 294; Gunter Kroemer, *Cuxiura, o Purus dos Indígenas* (São Paulo, 1985), 87.

58: misery.' Report to SPI Inspetoria do Amazonas, 1912, in Ribeiro, *Os Índios e a Civilização*, 46.

58: stores.' Constant Tastevin, 'Le Haut Tarauacá', *La Géographie*, **45:1–2**, Paris, Jan.–Feb. 1926, 54. Tastevin also heard about extermination of Indians, from Chief Teskon, and about Katukina fleeing westwards across the Tarauacá to escape persecution by rubber men: Tastevin, 'Le "Riozinho da Liberdade"', *La Géographie*, **49:3–4**, 1929, 211; and Paul Rivet and Constant Tastevin, 'Les tribus indiennes des bassins du Purus, du Juruá et des régions limitrophes', *La Géographie*, **35:5**, Paris, May 1921, 463.

58: disappearance.' Kenneth Grubb, *The Lowland Indians of Amazonia* (London, 1927), 99; Rivet and Tastevin, 'Les tribus indiennes' (and these same authors' later works on the Panoan and Arawak languages of these tribes); Alfred Métraux, 'Tribes of the Juruá-Purus basins', in Julian Steward, ed., *Handbook of South American Indians*, 3 (Washington, DC, 1948), 657–87.

58: non-existent'. Major José de Lima Figueiredo, *Índios do Brasil* (São Paulo, 1939), 171.

58: Peruvians.' Grubb, *Lowland Indians*, 101.

59: survivor.' Ibid., 100.

59: woods.' Franz Caspar, *Tupari* (London, 1952), 142.

59: strangers.' Ibid., 142–3.

60: alive.' Ibid., 143.

60: forest.' Ibid.

60: knives.' Ibid., 144.

60: died.' Ibid.

60: children, etc.'. Franz Caspar, 'A aculturação da tribo Tuparí', RA, **5:2**, Dec. 1957 (145–71), 149; Emil Heinrich Snethlage, 'Übersicht über die Indianerstamme des Guaporegebietes', *Tagungsbericht des Gesellschaft für Völkerkunde*, **2** (Leipzig, 1936) and his *Atiko: meine Erlebnisse bei den Indianern des Guaporé* (Berlin, 1937).

61: activity.' Caspar, 'A aculturação', 155–6.

61: white men.' Ibid., 159.

61: daughters.' Caspar, *Tupari*, 53.

62: bullets!' Ibid., 57.

63: arrows.' Caspar, 'A aculturação', 150.

63: volumes.' Caspar, *Tupari*, 224. By the end of the century a few Tupari survived among the 407 people from eight tribes in the Rio Guaporé indigenous area.

64: season. Curt Nimuendajú, 'Os índios Parintintin do Rio Madeira', JSAP, **16**, 1924 (201–278), 229–30. Also, Joaquim Gondim, *A pacificação dos Parintintins* (Commissão Rondon, publication 87, Manaus, 1925), 7–8. An English journalist who was on the Madeira in 1922 also gave an admiring account of Nimuendajú's pacification: Charles W. Domville-Fife, *Among Wild Tribes of the Amazons* (London, 1924), 146–52. Herbert Baldus, 'Métodos e resultados da ação indigenista no Brasil', in Egon Schaden, ed., *Homem, Cultura e Sociedade no Brasil* (Petrópolis, 1972), 213–14.

64: people.' Curt Nimuendajú, 'Nimongaraí',

Deutsche Zeitung, **6:3**, São Paulo, 15 Jul. 1910, in Egon Schaden, 'Notas sôbre a vida e a obra de Curt Nimuendajú', *Revista do Instituto de Estudos Brasileiros*, 3 (USP, São Paulo, 1968, 7–19), 18.

65: all this.' Curt Nimuendajú, 'Zur Coroadofrage', *Deutsche Zeitung*, **6:4**, São Paulo, 22 Jul. 1910, 55, in ibid., 15.

65: oppressions.' Nimuendajú in ibid., 16.

65: real people".' Herbert Baldus, 'Curt Nimuendajú', *Boletim Bibliográfico*, Biblioteca Municipal de São Paulo, **2:3**, Jul.–Sep. 1945, (91–9), 93.

65: neighbours.' Herbert Baldus, 'Curt Nimuendajú', *Sociologia*, **8:1**, 1946, 46–52; and in Paulo Suess, ed., *Textos Indigenistas, Curt Nimuendajú* (TICN) (São Paulo, 1982), 27.

65: tribe. Nimuendajú, 'Os índios', 213ff.

68: achieved].' Ibid., 216–17.

68: lands.' Baldus, 'Curt Nimuendajú', *Sociologia*, 29.

68: time'. General Oscar Bandeira de Mello, President of Funai, ESP, 11 Aug. 1970. The Parintintin reserve was 179,640 ha (693 square miles), called Ipixuna after the river of that name to the east of the middle Madeira.

68: workman.' Herbert Smith, *Brazil: the Amazons and the Coast* (New York, 1878), 254; Hemming, *Amazon Frontier*, 278–9, 564.

69: head.' Henri Coudreau, *Voyage au Tapajoz* (Paris, 1897), 144; Hemming, *Amazon Frontier*, 301.

69: Indians'. Raymundo Pereira Brazil, *O Rio Tapajóz* (Belém, 1914), 33.

69: region.' William Curtis Farabee, 'The Amazon Expedition of the University Museum', *The Museum Journal* (University of Pennsylvania, Philadelphia) 8, 1916, 139.

69: anilcatcat (man)".' Wilson de Carvalho, *Flashes da Amazônia* (São Paulo, 1964), 106.

70: past.' Robert F. Murphy, *Headhunter's Heritage* (Berkeley and Los Angeles, 1960), 44. On the growth of the Cururu mission, see: C. von Strömer, 'Die Sprache der Munduruká', *Anthropos* (Vienna, 1932), and 'Unter den Munduruká in Nordbrasilien', *Die Katholischen Missionen*, **65**, 1937, 87–90; Albert Kruse, 'Mundurucú moieties', *Primitive Man*, **7:4**, 1934, 51–7; Donald Horton, 'The Mundurucu', HSAI, **3**, 1948, 272–3; Grubb, *Lowland Indians*, 109; Curt Nimuendajú, 'Rapports entre les Munduruká et les Tupí', *Anthropos*, 33 (Vienna, 1938), 975–6; Roberto Décio de Las Casas, 'Índios e brasileiros no vale do rio Tapajós', 23; Expedito Arnaud, 'Os

índios Munduruká e o Serviço de Proteção aos Índios', BMPEG, **54**, 1974, also in his *O Índio e a Expansão Nacional* (Belém, 1989), 215–16. In 1919 the government of Pará state ceded two areas to the Franciscan mission, one of 10,000 ha, the other of 40 km^2 (25,000 acres and 9,900 acres).

71: scale'. Murphy, *Headhunter's Heritage*, 44–5. In 1943 the head of the SPI Posto Munduruku was ordered to monitor movement to and from the mission, since it was run by Germans and Brazil was then at war with Hitler's Germany. He was also told to check that the missionaries were paying fair prices for Indian rubber. The Franciscans told him that the Indians sold rubber to them because they wanted to, and advised the SPI official to check prices on the Tapajós where the Munduruku received far less for their produce. This was confirmed by Roberto de Las Casas, almost two decades later: he said that the Franciscans were gentler with the Indians than the SPI had been. João Baptista Chuvas, unpublished *Relatório da fiscalização procedida na Missão Franciscana no rio Cururú* (1944) in Arnaud, *O Índio e a Expansão Nacional*, 234–5; Robert and Yolanda Murphy, 'As condições atuais dos Mundurucu', *Publicação do Instituto de Antropologia e Etnologia do Pará*, 8, Belém, 1954, 34–5.

Darcy Ribeiro reckoned 1,000–1,500 Munduruku in 1957: 'Culturas e línguas indígenas do Brasil', *Educação e Ciências Sociais*, **2:6**, Rio de Janeiro, Nov. 1957, 86; so also did Las Casas, 'Índios e brasileiros', 9; Dale Kietzman wrote in 1967 that there were some 1,500, excluding those on the Tapajós: 450 along the Cururu, 700 in the savannah, and 340 living far to the west on the Canumã and Marimari tributaries of the Madeira ('Indians and culture areas of twentieth-century Brazil', in Janice H. Hopper, ed., *Indians of Brazil in the Twentieth Century* (Washington, DC, 1967), 23); in 1972 Friar Ervano told the author that there were some 900 Munduruku on the Cururu, of whom 300 lived alongside the mission; Lúcia Hussak van Velthem estimated a total of 1,400–1,600 a few years later: 'Munduruku, O povo que dominou o Pará antes do branco', RAI, **2:9**, Mar.–Apr. 1978, 40–7. By the end of the century, the tribe's population had tripled to 5,075 in the Munduruku indigenous territory, with others in the adjacent Kayabi reserve, and more far away near the lower Madeira alongside Sateré-Mawé. (The Kayabi are spelled Kayabí in the Museo do Índio's 1998 booklet of tribal names, and both Kaiabi and Kayabí by ISA. The older spelling Caiabi is also frequently used.)

There is an extensive literature about the Ford rubber-plantation experiment, admirably summarized in Warren Dean, *Brazil and the Struggle for Rubber* (Cambridge, 1987), 67–86; also John Galey, 'Industrialist in the wilderness: Henry Ford's Amazon venture', *Journal of Inter-American Studies*, **21**:2, May 1979; Wade Davis, *One River. Explorations and Discoveries in the Amazon Rain Forest* (Simon & Schuster, New York, 1996), 338–41.

72: process.' Murphy, *Headhunter's Heritage*, 155.

72: inland.' Cândido Rondon, Foreword to Major José de Lima Figueiredo, *Índios do Brasil* (São Paulo, Rio de Janeiro, etc., 1939), 20. The expedition that visited the Cururu in 1911 was an exploration of the Juruena led by Captain Manoel da Costa Pinheiro and containing the botanist Frederico Hoehne.

4. The Xingu

74: phenomenon'. Mércio Gomes, *The Indians and Brazil* (Gainesville, Fla., 2000), 137; Eduardo Galvão, 'Áreas culturais indígenas do Brasil, 1900–1959', BMPEG, **8**, 1960, 1–41; ES (193–228), trans. in Janice H. Hopper, ed., *Indians of Brazil in the Twentieth Century* (Washington, DC, 1967), 181, 193–4. There have been studies of every one of the nine upper-Xingu tribes, but three of the best are: Thomas Gregor, *Mehinaku: The Drama of Daily Life in a Brazilian Indian Village* (Chicago and London, 1977), Ellen Basso, *The Kalapalo Indians of Central Brazil* (New York, 1973), and Pedro Agostinho da Silva, *Kwarup: mito e ritual no Alto Xingu* (São Paulo, 1974).

74: social life.' Orlando and Cláudio Villas Bôas, *A Marcha Para o Oeste* (São Paulo, 1994), 261. The sequence of expeditions to the upper Tapajós and Xingu during the decades before Fawcett's attempt was: 1884, Karl von den Steinen's first descent of the Xingu; 1887, Karl von den Steinen and Paul Ehrenreich; 1889, Captain Antonio Lourenço Telles Pires explored the Paranatinga and São Manoel headwaters of Tapajós with the Bakairi, but Telles Pires and many companions drowned and the river was later renamed after him; 1896, Hermann Meyer and Karl Ranke; 1897, Bakairi guided Lieutenant Colonel Paula Castro to the Culiseu on a government-financed bid to seek the legendary Martírios gold mines; 1899, five Americans were killed by the Jê-speaking Suyá, and Meyer returned to the upper Xingu with Theodor Koch-Grünberg; 1900, Colonel Paula Castro again sought the Martírios mines, on an expedition that ended in total disaster; 1901, Max Schmidt; 1913, Commander Fontoura of the Serviço da Defesa da Borracha (Rubber Service). In 1915 Rondon sent Lieutenant Antonio Pyr-

ineus de Souza to map the São Manoel (Teles Pires) and Paranatinga; and in 1920 Captain Ramiro Noronha to map the Xingu's headwaters, when he also founded the Indian post Simões Lopes for the Bakairi. In 1924 Captain Vicente de Paula Vasconcellos, Captain Thomaz Reis and the Swiss Dr Hintermann mapped more Xingu headwaters (Major José de Lima Figueiredo, *Índios do Brasil* (São Paulo, Rio de Janeiro, etc., 1939), 306–10; Cândido Mariano da Silva Rondon, *Índios do Brasil*, **2**, *Das Cabeceiras do Rio Xingu, dos Rios Araguáia e Oiapóque* (CNPI, Rio de Janeiro, 1953), 14–15; Max Schmidt, 'Los Bakairí', RMP, **1**, 1947, 18–19; Eduardo Galvão and Mário F. Simões, 'Mudanças e sobrevivência no alto Xingu – Brasil Central', RA, **14**, 1966, 38).

Note: I prefer the spelling 'Villas Boas'. They themselves occasionally put a circumflex on the o, but I have done this only when directly quoting them or someone else who does it.

74: supplies.' Robert F. Murphy and Buell Quain, *The Trumaí Indians of Central Brazil* American Ethnological Society, monograph **24** (Seattle and New York, 1955), 58.

76: bitter enemies.' Villas Bôas, *Marcha*, 316.

76: embrace.' Murphy and Quain, *The Trumaí*, 91–2. José C. M. Carvalho, Pedro E. de Lima, Eduardo Galvão, *Observações Zoológicas e Antropológicas na Região dos Formadores do Xingu* (Rio de Janeiro, 1949), 44.

76: arrows' Rondon, *Índios do Brasil*, **2** 40. The main guide for this expedition was the Bakairi chief Captain Antonino. He had helped Karl von den Steinen research his books, had guided the ill-fated Colonel Paulo Castro in 1900, and in 1920 was taken to Rio de Janeiro with three Bakairi companions. While there they helped the historian

Capistrano de Abreu, who was studying the Bakairi, and Antonino recorded a legend that was taken back to his people on a gramophone record – the first instance of such a recorded history.

76: attack.' Ibid., 41.

78: coughing.' Bruna Franchetto, 'A celebração da história nos discursos cerimoniais Kuikúro (alto Xingu)' in Eduardo Viveiros de Castro and Manuela Carneiro da Cunha, eds., *Amazônia: etnologia e história indígena* (São Paulo, 1993), 114–15; John Hemming, *Amazon Frontier* (London, 1955), 137–8.

78: savagery.' Brian Fawcett, ed., P. H. Fawcett, *Exploration Fawcett* (London, 1953; published as *Lost Trails, Lost Cities* in the New York edition, 1953), 95, 199–200, 201. Fawcett had previously mentioned stories of 'white Indians with red hair . . . a race with blue eyes . . . and many curious things hidden in the forests of the Amazon basin' ('Explorations in Bolivia', *Geographical Journal*, 35, Jan.–Jun. 1910, 522. This was the text of a lecture on 14 Mar. 1910 to the Royal Geographical Society, which awarded Fawcett its gold medal.) The earlier expeditions to the Xingu are in: Rondon, *Índios do Brasil*, 2 14–15; Ramiro Noronha, *Exploração e Levantamento do Rio Culuene, Principal Formador do Xingu* (1920), Conselho Nacional de Proteção aos Índios, 75, Rio de Janeiro 1952; and Captain Vicente de Paula Teixeira da Fonseca Vasconcellos (who later became Director of the SPI) described his expedition of 1924 in Publication 90 of the Commissão Rondon.

79: tribes one meets.' Fawcett, *Lost Trails*, 17–18; *Exploration Fawcett*, 285. Brian Fawcett gave his father's account of the original finding of the legendary city, in *Exploration Fawcett*, 1–11, and Peter Fleming summarized it in *Brazilian Adventure* (London, 1933), 18–19. Fawcett's story was that a successful mine-owner called Melchor Dias Moreira (Muribeca to the Indians) had a son called Roberio (Rogerio?) Dias who told the King of Portugal in 1610 that he had discovered fabulous silver and gold mines; he plunged back into the interior of Bahia to relocate them, but died in 1622 before revealing what he had found. (There were errors in this version. One was that Fawcett said that Melchor's uncle was Diogo Alvares; but this man (who was known to the Indians as Caramuru and married a chief's daughter called Paraguassu) lived much earlier and died in 1557. Another was that Fawcett named Dom Pedro II as King of Portugal in 1610,

whereas he ruled in the late seventeenth century.) An expedition went to look for the 'Lost Mines of Muribeca' in 1743 and its anonymous report is Ms. 512 in the Biblioteca Nacional in Rio de Janeiro. That expedition consisted of six Portuguese, twelve black slaves, and twenty or thirty Indians. It travelled north from Minas Gerais onto the plateau of western Bahia beyond the São Francisco river. It reported seeing an ancient ruined city and gave detailed descriptions of its buildings and inscriptions. The report reached the then Viceroy of Brazil, but nothing more was heard of its authors.

80: killed.' G. M. Dyott, *Man Hunting in the Jungle. The Search for Colonel Fawcett* (London, 1930), 174; Fleming, *Brazilian Adventure*, 24–5; Robert Churchward, *Wilderness of Fools: an Account of the Adventures in Search of Lieut.-Colonel P. H. Fawcett, DSO* (Routledge, London, 1936), 56; John Ure, *Trespassers on the Amazon* (Constable, London, 1986), 118–19. There were other expeditions on the upper Xingu in the years after Fawcett's disappearance in 1925. Leonard L. Legters (a former missionary among the Comanche Indians in the US, and in Mexico) went in 1926 with three Americans and an SPI agent, during a survey of Amazonia for the Inland South American Missionary Union. In 1927 the German anthropologist Max Schmidt returned to the Xingu Bakairi, twenty-six years after his first visit. Schmidt met Fawcett's Bakairi guide Bernardino, who said that the Englishman had upset these Indians by his aggressive behaviour on the 1920 expedition; but he thought that they probably died in 1925 from the bad climate, lack of game, rapids, and dense forest that had exhausted other earlier expeditions (Max Schmidt, 'Los Bakairí', RMP, 1, 1947, 32). Then came Commander Dyott in 1928.

Three years later a group of American adventurers took a small float plane and cinema equipment to the junction of the Culuene and Culiseu. This expedition included Vincent M. Petrullo, a young anthropologist from the Museum of the University of Pennsylvania, who spent a few days with the Aruak-speaking Yawalipiti. Petrullo also spoke to some Nahukwá and Kalapalo and was convinced that Fawcett's trio had moved safely into and beyond Kalapalo territory (*New York Times*, 3 Apr. 1932; Vincent M. Petrullo, 'Primitive peoples of Matto Grosso: an account of archaeological and ethnological field work at the headwaters of the Paraguay and Xingu Rivers in

Matto Grosso, Brazil, during 1931', *Museum Journal* (University of Pennsylvania), **23**:2, Philadelphia, 1932, 83–180; Eleanor M. King, 'Fieldwork in Brazil. Petrullo's visit to the Yawalipiti', *Expedition* (The University Museum Magazine of Archaeology and Anthropology), University of Pennsylvania, **35**:3, 1993, 34–52.)

A Fawcett-search expedition in 1932 bogged down on the Araguaia and Tapirapé rivers, to the east of the Xingu, but it spawned the first book to make fun of exploration: Peter Fleming's brilliant and iconoclastic *Brazilian Adventure*. Fleming believed that Fawcett's 'whole expedition perished in the summer of 1925, probably at the hands of Indians' (p. 281). In 1933 Colonel Aniceto Botelho found a compass near the Bakairi camp and passed it to an English Protestant missionary, Frederick C. Glass, who in turn sent it to the Secretary of the Royal Geographical Society, who gave it to Mrs Fawcett. She and her son Brian reckoned that it was from the 1920 expedition, as was the metal army-uniform trunk acquired by the Nahukwá. In that same year, Virginio Pessione visited the Culuene river and sent a report back to the RGS via the head of the Salesian missionaries in Mato Grosso. This was from an old Nahukwá woman who had been with the Kuikuro and now lived near the Paranatinga headwater of the São Manoel (Teles Pires). She reported that the three white men were safe but unable to escape from a tribe called Aruvudu, said to live near the Suyá on the Xingu. (Fawcett, *Lost Trails*, 307–8 or *Exploration Fawcett*, 296–7).

The American journalist Albert de Winton went to the Xingu in 1935, determined to bring Fawcett back dead or alive. But he never returned. The Villas Boas brothers later learned the details of Winton's death from those who had killed him. 'Frightened by the appearance of this solitary bearded *civilizado*, the [Kalapalo] Indians did not hesitate for a single second in trying to eliminate him.' They decided to do it without violence, giving Winton sweetened water that had been poisoned by prussic acid from bitter manioc, and then setting him adrift in a canoe on the Culuene. But Winton was healthy and tough and he started to recover from the poison. He met two Kamayurá, Maricá and Avaé, and promised them a Winchester carbine if they would take him to safety. They started down towards the Xingu but, after a few hours, the Kamayurá dragged him ashore and, while he was eating some fish, Maricá smashed the journalist's head with a club. His body was thrown

into the river; his boxes of belongings were left on the bank; and Maricá later traded the carbine with the Waurá for a large manioc-roasting pan. Villas Bôas, *Marcha*, 380–1, and 'As expedições que desapareceram no roteiro de Fawcett', RAI, **2**:7, Brasília, Nov.–Dec. 1977, 49–54.

Other expeditions to the Xingu were not concerned with the fate of Colonel Fawcett. The German anthropologist Fritz Krause worked with the Waurá in 1934, and published a report in the 1936 edition of the *Mitteilungsblatt der Gesellschaft für Völkerkunde* of Leipzig.

From 1926 to 1938 the American Protestants Mr and Mrs Thomas Young had a mission among the Nahukwá and their nurse Marjorie Clarke did fine work during a malaria epidemic there. In 1938 a young American anthropologist, Buell Quain, spent four months with the Trumai on the Culuene near its junction with the Culiseu. He also saw other tribes during three weeks descending the Culiseu from the Young's mission station. (Murphy and Quain, *The Trumaí*.) In the late 1930s a twelve-man Italian-led expedition was wiped out on a small rocky island called Ilha do Massacre, below the Von Martius rapids. Two Bakairi guides were among the dead. In 1953 the Villas Boas brothers saw remains of this tragedy (a rusting radio and collapsible aerial) and were convinced that the Juruna, who were the expedition's paddlers, had done the killing – even though the Juruna tried to blame the Mentuktire Kayapó (Txukarramãe) for it. (Major de Aviação José Leal Neto, 'Levantamento do Rio da Liberdade', in Mário F. Simões, ed., *S.P.I. – 1954* (185–207), 201; Adrian Cowell, *The Heart of the Forest* (London, 1960), 215–16.) In 1944–45 the film-maker Nilo Veloso continued the efforts of the Rondon Commission to record Indians of the Culuene and Culiseu rivers. (Nilo de Oliveira Veloso, 'Expedição Roncador–Xingu', *Revista do Clube Militar*, **20**:80, Rio de Janeiro 1947, 77–86.) When Fernando Altenfelder Silva was with the 250 Bakairi of Simões Lopes in 1947, they all spoke Portuguese and seemed just like surrounding *caboclos*; but they also spoke Bakairi and maintained their tribal identity through dances and belief in the supernatural world. (Fernando Altenfelder Silva, 'O mundo mágico dos bacairis', in Vera Penteado Coelho, ed., *Karl von den Steinen: um século de antropologia no Xingu* (São Paulo, 1993), 347–74).

81: English colonel' The story of Stefan Rattin was told by Brian Fawcett, *Exploration Fawcett*,

293–4; Fleming, *Brazilian Adventure*, 25–7; Churchward, *Wilderness*, 60–1, also his dreadful book *Explorer Lost!* (Thomas Nelson & Sons, Edinburgh, 1957). (Churchward was one of the leaders of Peter Fleming's expedition.) The Swiss Rattin claimed never to have heard about Colonel Fawcett. The staff of a British slaughterhouse in Mato Grosso were so impressed by his story that they clubbed together to pay for his fare to São Paulo, where he was interviewed by the British Consul-General, Arthur Abbott. Rattin said that the old man he met wore four rings (two witnesses recalled that several rings was an affectation of Fawcett's, but his son Brian later denied that his father had worn any) and told him to take a message about his young companions' deaths and his own inability to escape to someone called Paget. (A Major J. B. Paget had helped to finance Fawcett's expedition; Sir Ralph Paget was a former Ambassador to Brazil who had also been a friend of Fawcett's.) Peter Fleming doubted this 'very curious story'. He noted that Rattin was described as a trapper, 'though what he trapped, and where he sold the skins, was never made clear'. Peter Fleming described Rattin's statement as 'a curious document, full of discrepancies and inconsistencies, yet stamped with that rather dream-like inconsequence which is often the hallmark of reality'. General Rondon also questioned Rattin but doubted his story, since the old man's message was too vague for someone of Fawcett's intelligence and the location was too far from the Xingu for the Englishman to have reached it unaided. A later Ambassador to Brazil, Sir John Ure, studied the documents in the consular archive and was impressed that the British Consuls in both São Paulo and Rio de Janeiro believed Rattin, even though the then Ambassador did not. Ure doubted whether these two consuls, trained and sceptical observers, could both have been duped. He wondered whether Colonel Fawcett might have strayed onto a tributary of the São Manoel (Teles Pires) rather than of the Xingu. This seems most unlikely, since Fawcett's team was guided from Simões Lopes post by a Bakairi who knew the easy trail across the savannah to his Xingu cousins. The Swiss never sought any reward for his story. Rattin later tried to relocate the Indian village in order to rescue the Englishman. He rejected Rondon's offer to equip a large expedition, but embarked with two companions on the Arinos, another source of the Juruena–Tapajós to the west of the São Manoel (Teles Pires). They never reappeared. Ure pondered: 'Why should Rattin have invented such a tale: he asked for no fame or fortune, and went back to pursue his quest at the cost of his own life.' Ure, *Trespassers*, 124–7.

Other 'eyewitnesses' of lost Englishmen were: Roger Courteville, who drove across South America by car in August 1927 and saw a white man of 'dull and misanthropic spirit' even further west, in a 'jungle paradise' near the Dúvida (Roosevelt) river; Francis Gow-Smith, an American explorer, was also on the Dúvida in September 1927 but reported that there was no such white man living there; Micael-Angelo Trucchi said that in 1929 he found Fawcett as Chief of the Guida Indians at the junction of the Araguaia and Manso rivers, east of the Xingu; Captain A. H. Morris in 1930 produced a compass and leather pouch stamped PHF, which he said had been given him by the famous north-easterner bandit Lampeão, who refused to reveal their source. Morris speculated that a tribe 'more civilized than its neighbours' had captured Fawcett and regarded a white prisoner as a great prize. An Italian called Realini claimed to have found three skeletons of the Fawcett party; but no one believed him. (Churchward, *Wilderness* 53–6; Ure, *Trespassers*, 126.)

82: to the east.' Cowell, *Heart of the Forest*, 64. Cowell heard this from Orlando Villas Boas in 1958; Orlando also told the same story to this author in later years, and I find it very convincing. The brothers wrote it all in Villas Bôas, *Almanaque do Sertão* (São Paulo, 1997), 104–12.

82: into the water.' Cowell, *Heart of the Forest*, 65.

83: on its bottom."' Orlando Villas Boas, 'As fantásticas histórias do Xingu (VI). Fawcett: Orlando guarda ossada do explorador inglês', RAI, **1:6**, Brasília, Sep.–Oct. 1977 (26–31), 30–1.

83: Xingu.' Opinion by the Director of the SPI to the Council for approving scientific expeditions, 1938, in Luís Donisete Benzi Grupioni, *Coleções e Expedições Vigiadas. Os etnólogos no Conselho de Fiscalização das Expedições Artísticas e Científicas no Brasil* (São Paulo, 1998), 99.

83: recognized in him'. Villas Bôas, *Marcha*, 167, 187. A Brazilian journalist, Edmar Morel, also claimed to have heard this story from Izarari in 1945. The Kalapalo chief told him that his men killed Fawcett's team with arrows because '"White men want to take Kalapalos into country of [feared] Kayapó Indians. Kalapalos not like to go into country of other Indians. White men start to push Kalapalos . . ."'

The American Protestant missionary Leonard L. Legters was on the Xingu in 1926, the year after Fawcett's disappearance, 'accompanied by SPI staff and these all verified the existence of a fair-haired baby, which Mr Legters photographed and about which the Indians maintain a mistrustful reserve' (Opinion by the Director of the SPI, 1938, in Grupioni, *Coleções e Expedições*, 99). Other Protestant missionaries, Emilio Halverson and Thomas Young, who had worked for decades in Mato Grosso, and Martha Moennich, showed the journalist Edmar Morel a picture of the 'white' Kalapalo child. The fanciful missionaries imagined that this mestizo had been fathered by the 'chaste' Jack Fawcett during the few days that he was with the tribe, even though the Indians never mentioned misconduct with women among the Englishmen's misdemeanours. Morel later saw this pale Indian, called Dulipe. But Brian Fawcett assumed that he was an albino. Moennich also gave a version of the three explorers' deaths at the hands of the Kalapalo. (Edmar Morel, *E Fawcett não Voltou* (Emprêsa Gráfica 'O Cruzeiro', Rio de Janeiro, 1950) and articles in the *People*, London, 27 May and 3 Jun. 1951.)

A Brazilian newspaper paid to take Brian Fawcett to confront the Kalapalo, but the journey was a failure. Brian Fawcett thought that Orlando Villas Boas was rehearsing the tribe in what to say to him. When the Brazilian suggested that Colonel Fawcett might have been a tall man with short legs, Fawcett's son retorted that his father was not a dachshund. Brian Fawcett was further unconvinced when an Indian said that the explorer had had as much hair as his son – for the colonel was balding. (The Kalapalo may have referred to a stubbly beard; and Orlando Villas

Boas told me that it was the *freckles* on Brian Fawcett's back that reminded the Indians of his father. He also said that dental work on the skull was of an English type.)

83: payment'. Basso, *The Kalapalo Indians*, 4. The English traveller and film-maker Benedict Allen was given the same denial by the Kalapalo when he visited them briefly in July 1998. Most of their men were at the Kamayurá village (with this author) holding a Kuarup funerary ceremony in honour of Cláudio Villas Boas, who had died earlier that year (*Independent*, 11 Sep. 1999; *Sunday Telegraph*, 19 Sep. 1999).

83: enemy'. Schmidt, 'Los Bakairí', 18–19.

84: explorer. The 1951 tests were done by Professor A. J. E. Cave of St Bartholomew's Hospital Medical College, Miss M. L. Tildesley, MBE, of the Royal College of Surgeons' Museum, Dr J. C. Trevor, a Cambridge anthropologist, and Sir Arthur Keith, FRS (*Report on the human remains from Brazil*, manuscript in the Royal Anthropological Institute, 9 Nov. 1951; Fawcett, *Exploration Fawcett*, 302–3; Ure, *Trespassers*, 120–1.) The finding of the bones was widely reported in the European press in April 1951. The bones were returned to the University of São Paulo, and in 1996 there was an attempt to obtain DNA samples from Fawcett's surviving daughter so that this could be compared with that of the relics: *The Times*, 30 Jan. 1996.

An expedition to 'trace the footsteps' of Fawcett in July 1996, led by the American banker James Lynch and the Brazilian automobile executive René Delmotte, came to grief when the Kalapalo and Kamayurá 'kidnapped' the unauthorized intruders and took their jeeps, boats, and other possessions (*The Times*, 10 Jul. 1996).

5. *Araguaia, Xavante*

85: Buckingham Palace.' Peter Fleming, *Brazilian Adventure* (London, 1933), 244, 14, 30–1, 165.

86: covetous.' Ibid., 205–6.

86: effortlessly. Rayliane de La Falaise, *Caraja . . . Koû!* (Librairie Plon, Paris, 1939), 198.

86: inconspicuous.' Evelyn Waugh, *Ninety-two Days* (Duckworth, London, 1934), 201.

88: race for converts.' Fleming, *Brazilian Adventure*, 205. Herbert Baldus and Charles Wagley recorded the early contacts with the Tapirapé. There were mentions of the tribe in the eight-

eenth and nineteenth centuries, and Couto de Magalhães even had some Tapirapé children in his school at Santa Isabel do Morro in the 1870s (John Hemming, *Amazon Frontier* (London, 1995), 378–9). But the first full contact came in 1911, by a group of Cearense rubber men led by Alfredo Olímpio de Oliveira (reported by Angyone Costa in *Folha do Norte* newspaper, Belém, 29 Jul. 1912, and described by Oliveira as 'Entre os Tapirapés' in *Mensageiro do Santo Rosario* (the newsletter of the Dominican missionaries of

Conceição de Araguaia), Apr. 1934). An SPI Inspector, Dr Francisco Mandacaru, returned several times and spent long periods living with the tribe, who greatly liked him. In 1914 Dominican missionaries, under their bishop Mgr Carrerot and Father Sébastien Thomas, were guided by a Karajá called Valadarão (who later installed himself among the Tapirapé). This contact was followed by brief annual visits and trading by the Dominicans. In 1923, there was a short visit by a Baptist missionary, Benedito Propheta, and in 1930 by Josiah Wilding of the Evangelical Union of South America and an American writer, Elizabeth Steen – the first white female seen by the tribe and, in Wagley's words, 'you can be sure that she was subjected to considerable inspection'. The Scottish missionary Frederick Kegel of the same Evangelical Union of South America first visited the Tapirapé in 1932 and returned for long periods until 1935. Also in 1932, Peter Fleming's group went to Porto São Domingos, at the same time as an American Adventist; and in 1934 there was a film crew from São Paulo. In 1935 Frederick Kegel took the anthropologist Herbert Baldus for a two-month stay. Also in 1935 a couple of French journalists, Dick and Rayliane de La Falaise, with Father Louis Palha, were charmed by the Tapirapé. In 1939–40 the American anthropologist Charles Wagley entered with Valentim Gomes, who in 1947 established the SPI Posto Heloisa Alberto Torres at the mouth of the river. In 1952 Les Petites Sœurs de Jésus (a Franco-Brazilian order of Dominican sisters) opened a permanent mission beside the Tapirapé village and did much to revive the tribe. 1953, a second visit by Charles Wagley. In 1954 Father François Jentel started many years of work among the tribe. At this time, a ludicrous Danish 'explorer' called Jørgen Bisch decided that the Tapirapé were the world's laziest people, and regretted that they were starting to wear clothes: Bisch, *Across the River of Death* (Souvenir Press, London, 1958), 42. Herbert Baldus, *Tapirapé: Tribo Tupí no Brasil Central* (São Paulo, 1970), 46ff.; Charles Wagley, *Welcome of Tears* (New York, 1977), 34–43; Wagley and Eduardo Galvão, 'The Tapirapé', HSAI, **3** (167–92), 167; Wagley and Eduardo Galvão, 'The Tenetehara', HSAI, **3**, 137–48.

88: loved them also.' Wagley, *Welcome of Tears*, 37. In 1935, Frederick Kegel was transferred to another post in north-eastern Brazil, but he died a few years later.

89: died.' Ibid., 42, quoting Leonard Green-

wood, 'Lost 25 Years, Trio Rejoins "Slain" Kin', *Los Angeles Times*, 11 Aug. 1971. Greenwood was told the story by missionaries of the Petites Sœurs de Jésus.

90: debts.' Ibid., 287–8.

90: ceremonials. Ibid., 289.

92: maiden' William Lipkind, 'The Carajá', HSAI, **3** (179–91), 187. Herbert Baldus was with the Karajá in 1935 and 1947 and noticed some changes during those twelve years: *Ensaios de Etnologia Brasileira* (São Paulo, 1937), 291 and 'Akkulturation im Araguaya-Gebiet', *Anthropos* (Freiburg, Switzerland), **41–44**, 1949, 891.

92: Indians.' Fleming, *Brazilian Adventure*, 154–5, 151–2.

92: 1840s. For the census estimates: Francis de Castelnau, *Expédition dans les Parties Centrales de l'Amérique du Sud* . . . (Part I, *Histoire du Voyage*, 6 vols., Paris, 1850–51); Fritz Krause, *In den Wildnissen Brasiliens; Bericht und Ergebnisse der Leipziger Araguaya-Expedition, 1908* (Leipzig, 1911); Sabino de Rimini, *Tra i selvaggi dell'Araguaya* (Rimini, 1925); Lipkind, 'The Carajá', 180. Lipkind's total was 1,510, made up of 795 Karajá proper, 650 of the Javaé subtribe living mainly on southern Bananal Island, and 65 Xambioá. In 1939 the Xambioá were 'nearly extinct', living in two villages downstream of Conceição; whereas in 1845 Castelnau had counted 2,000 Xambioá in four villages. Thus the Xambioá part of the Karajá, which was most exposed to outside influence, suffered a demographic decline of 94 per cent in a century. By the 1950s the Karajá tribe was further reduced. Darcy Ribeiro in 1957 gave only 500–1,000, whereas in 1967 Dale Kietzman reckoned 1,115 for the entire nation. Robin Hanbury-Tenison in 1971 said that there were about 800 Karajá on Bananal (240 of them at Santa Isabel) 'in a thoroughly depressed state' alongside 8,000 settlers. Herbert Baldus, 'Tribos da bacia do Araguaia e o Serviço de Proteção aos Índios', RMP, **2**, 1948; Haroldo Cândido de Oliveira, *Índios e Sertanejos do Araguaia. Diário de viagem* (Edições Melhoramentos, São Paulo, 1949); Maurice Lelong, *Le fleuve des Carajás* (R. Julliard, Paris, 1953); José M. da Gama Malcher, *Índios: grau de integração na comunidade nacional, grupo linguístico, localização* (Rio de Janeiro, 1963), 193; Dale W. Kietzman, 'Indians and culture areas of twentieth-century Brazil', in Janice H. Hopper, ed., *Indians of Brazil in the Twentieth Century* (Washington, DC, 1967) and Darcy Ribeiro, 'Culturas e línguas indígenas do

Brasil', *Educação e Ciências Sociais*, **2**:6, Rio de Janeiro, Nov. 1957, and Hopper, *Indians of Brazil*, 138. Robin Hanbury-Tenison, *Report of a Visit to the Indians of Brazil* (London, 1971), 11; Edwin Brooks et al., *Tribes of the Amazon Basin in Brazil, 1972* (London, 1973), 24–5.

The later President Juscelino Kubitschek visited the Karajá in 1960, and a tourist hotel was built on Bananal and named after him. (When Kubitschek was in disgrace after the military coup of 1964, the hotel renamed itself John Kennedy in order to continue to use tableware marked JK. It later failed and closed.) By the end of the century, there were between 1,500 and 1,900 Karajá, 840 of the Javaé subgroup generally at the southern end of Bananal, and 200 Xambioá: total between 2,540 and 2,940. This people's largest territory remains the Araguaia indigenous park occupying 1,358,500 ha (5,240 square miles) of Bananal. Several other small reserves are in process of registration, and some Karajá live in the Tapirapé indigenous land. Although the Karajá have adopted many characteristics of frontier society, in food, Portuguese language, education, and religion, they still vigorously maintain some traditions and speech. They are still river people, often camping on the sandbanks of the Araguaia and Javaé rivers. But they still suffer from malnutrition, disease (especially tuberculosis), and alcoholism.

92: true fathers.' Darcy Bandeira de Mello, *Entre Índios e Revoluções* (Editora Soma, São Paulo, 1982), 175.

93: were still there. Fleming, *Brazilian Adventure*, 158–9. In a speech, 'José Bonifácio e o problema indígena' (delivered to the Instituto Histórico e Geográfico Brasileiro, Rio de Janeiro, 6 Sep. 1939, in Botelho de Magalhães, *Rondon – Uma Relíquia da Pátria* (Curitiba–São Paulo–Rio de Janeiro, 1942), 60–62), Rondon quoted a letter from Friar José Audrin, Superior of the Dominican mission on the Araguaia, to the director of the SPI in Goiás, 29 Nov. 1931, complaining about the decay of the Karajá post. It was called Posto Redenção Indígena, at Santa Isabel on Bananal, and had flourished from 1927 to 1930 under Rondon's old lieutenants, Alencarliense Fernandes da Costa and Manuel Bandeira de Mello.

93: extinction.' Bandeira de Mello, *Entre Índios*, 176.

93: Karajá.' Kenneth Matthews, *Brazilian Interior* (London, 1956), 236. The efficient Dutch

nurse was called Brendel, and a Swiss anthropologist, Hans Dietschy, was also working among the tribe at that time.

94: torpor.' O *Globo*, Rio de Janeiro, 30 Nov. 1960; BSPI, **46**, Nov.–Dec. 1960. The island of Bananal had just been made the Parque Nacional do Araguaia, but this status did not prevent its thorough invasion by cattle-ranchers.

94: pride.' Hanbury-Tenison, *Report*, 11. Brooks et al., *Tribes of the Amazon Basin*, 24–5.

94: settlements.' Hanbury-Tenison, *Report*, 11.

94: value.' Alcida Ramos, 'Frontier expansion and Indian peoples in the Brazilian Amazon', in Marianne Schmink and Charles H. Wood, eds., *Frontier Expansion in Amazonia* (Gainesville, Fla., 1984), 86.

95: spectacle.' Johann Emanuel Pohl, *Reise im Innern von Brasilien in den Jahren 1817–1821* (2 vols., Vienna, 1832), trans. as *Viagem no Interior do Brasil Empreendida nos Anos de 1817 a 1821* (Instituto Nacional do Livro, São Paulo, 1951), 130. Hemming, *Amazon Frontier*, 71–9.

96: no reply.' Anon., 'Heldische Weltanschauung. Zum Blutzeugnis zweier Salesianer-missionare in den Urwaldern von Mato Grosso', *Die Katolischen Missionen*, **63**:7, Jul. 1935 (173–6), 176. Jean Duroure and Ernest Carletti, *Sur le fleuve de la mort* (Emmanuel Vitte, Paris, 1936), 30; Cândido Mariano da Silva Rondon, 'Apresentação' in Major [José de] Lima Figueirêdo, *Índios do Brasil* (Companhia Editora Nacional, São Paulo, Rio de Janeiro, 1939), 21; David Nasser, 'Enfrentando os Chavantes!', O *Cruzeiro*, 24 Jun. 1944. David Nasser became a popular television presenter; and he acquired a large cattle ranch on what had once been Xavante territory. Herbert Baldus, 'É belicoso o Xavante?', *Revista do Arquivo Municipal*, **142** (São Paulo, 1951), 125–9; Lincoln da Souza, *Os Xavantes e a Civilização* (Serviço Gráfico do Instituto Brasileiro de Geografia e Estatística, Rio de Janeiro, 1953), 22; David Maybury-Lewis, *Akwẽ-Shavante Society* (Oxford, 1967), 3; Bartolomeu Giacciaria and Adalberto Heide, *Xavante, A'uwẽ uptabi, povo autêntico* (São Paulo, 1972), 29; Aracy Lopes da Silva, 'Dois séculos e meio de história Xavante' in HIB (357–78), 367. There had been two brief contacts on the rio das Mortes during the later nineteenth century: by a team sent by Italian missionaries in 1856, which was attacked as it withdrew; and the expedition of one Colonel Tupí Caldas, which was forced to retreat in 1887 (Paul Ehrenreich, 'Die Einteilung und Verbreitung der Völkerstämme Brasiliens nach dem gegenwärtigen Stande unserer Kenntnisse', *Petermanns Mitteilungen aus Justus Perthes*, **37** (Gotha, 1891), 118).

96: struggle.' David Maybury-Lewis, *The Savage and the Innocent* (London, 1965), 204. When this English anthropologist saw the cross in 1958, it was shattered and barely discernible.

97: attackers.' Despatch from Leopoldina, 12 Nov. 1941, quoting the survivor Feliciano Odra, in Cândido Mariano da Silva Rondon, *Índios do Brasil*, **2**, *Das Cabeceiras do Rio Xingu, dos Rios Araguáia e Oiapóque* (CNPI, Rio de Janeiro, 1953), 156. The sad despatch is translated in Edward Weyer, Jr., *Jungle Quest* (Viking, New York, 1955), 41–2. The Paulista adventurers in 1937 organized an expedition called Bandeira Anhanguera (named after a notorious seventeenth-century bandeirante raider). This was a fifteen-man venture, led by the writer and sertanista Hermano Ribeiro da Silva and sponsored by a Paulista radio station. In October 1937 it made a surprise entry into a Xavante village of nineteen huts, was greeted by a hail of arrows (which miraculously wounded no one), and saved by a barrage of fireworks and three thunder-flashes. The frightened Xavante withdrew and the explorers took 'essential ethnographic material' from the huts and left presents in their place, before quitting Xavante territory. Ribeiro da Silva planned a new expedition called Bandeira Piratininga in 1938, but the SPI ordered him to desist: BSPI, **2**, Dec. 1941, 1–2. The Bandeira Anhanguera is described in Bandeira de Mello, *Entre Índios*, 205–41. Souza, *Os Xavantes*, 22; Duroure and Carletti, *Sur le fleuve*, 36; Maybury-Lewis, *Akwê-Shavante Society*, 4–5; Lopes da Silva, 'Dois séculos e meio de história Xavante', 367.

97: hostile.' Maybury-Lewis, *The Savage and the Innocent*, 197.

97: our men.' Amilcar A. Botelho de Magalhães, 'A pacificação dos índios Chavante', AI, **7:4**, Oct. 1947 (333–9), 335.

99: massacres!' Orlando and Cláudio Villas Bôas, *A Marcha Para o Oeste* (São Paulo, 1994), 76–7; *Almanaque do Sertão* (São Paulo, 1997), 209–10. Curiously, the German ornithologist Dr Helmut Sick, who was on this expedition, recalled seeing many signs and warnings of the Xavante but did not mention this attack on the trail-cutting party. He reported that 'although nothing serious happened as far as we were concerned, we nevertheless found the constant threat of ambush or onslaught very oppressive. That we were kept under observation all the time is quite certain.' Helmut Sick, *Tukani* (Hamburg and Berlin, 1957; trans. R. H. Stevens, *Tukani* (London, 1959), 48.

The Roncador–Xingu Expedition was devised by Colonel Flaviano Matos Vanique, the ambitious commander of President Getúlio Vargas's bodyguard. Vanique had fallen out with the President's wife, Dona Darcy, and he was being overtaken in presidential favour by a rival. There were four Villas Boas brothers – Orlando, Cláudio, Leonardo, and Álvaro – but only the first three enlisted on the expedition. Their dates were: Orlando 1914–2002, Cláudio 1916–98, and Leonardo 1918–61. Álvaro (1924–95) was a gentler but equally dedicated man, who later worked for the Indian cause as head of the SPI's São Paulo inspectorate, and was President of Funai for two months in 1985. The author was once on an expedition with Álvaro, and I can confirm that he was also a fine woodsman. The brothers were born in Santa Cruz on the rio Pardo and were brought up in Botucatu in the interior of São Paulo state. The family moved to a house in São Paulo city and, when their father's coffee business faltered, the brothers lodged in a pension. At the time, Orlando was working for Esso, Cláudio in a municipal office, and Leonardo for Nestlé; but they were inspired by books about the Brazilian interior, by Euclides da Cunha and Couto de Magalhães, and by philosophers from Kant to Marx. When they tried to join the Roncador–Xingu Expedition in Aragarças in 1945, Colonel Vanique turned them down as city boys who would only cause trouble – he wanted only illiterate woodsmen; so they got an English engineer called Frederick Lane to hire them. In 1948, when their work on the Xingu was already going very well, they received an order to return from Colonel Vanique; they protested that this would cause the failure of the expedition; and, luckily, President Eurico Dutra ordered Vanique to return to the army. José Marqueiz, 'Memórias dos irmãos Villas Boas', *Visão*, 10 Feb. 1975; Maureen Bisilliat, *Guerreiros sem Espada* (São Paulo, 1995), 22.

99: Council.' Letter from Orlando Villas Bôas to the Royal Geographical Society of London, acknowledging the gold medal awarded jointly to him and Cláudio in 1972, quoted in Anon., 'Os irmãos da selva', *Veja* (Rio de Janeiro, 8 Nov. 1972), 56.

100: in his neck. Raymond Maufrais, *Matto Grosso Adventure* (William Kimber, London, 1955), 190–1. This book was a translation (by Mervyn Savill) of one by Maufrais' father based on his twenty-year-old son's diary of the 1946 expedition. The young Maufrais disappeared on an expedition in French Guiana and his father wrote a moving book about his search for him, translated as *Journey Without Return* (William Kimber, London, 1953). The flight over the Xavante village was reported in David Nasser, 'Enfrentando os Chavantes!', *O Cruzeiro*, 24 Jun. 1944. Nasser also reported that the tribe had that year killed a settler, Antonio Maranhense, and his four relatives. Genil Vasconcelos, a news cameraman, was on the expedition with Meirelles and Maufrais. His account was similar to Maufrais's, except that he said nothing about the man being killed by an arrow (which the Frenchman may have invented), and he noted that when Meirelles advanced shouting 'Coré!', he thought that it meant 'Present!' but it meant something different. Vasconcelos also said that the expedition was guided by Ladislau, a 'fabulous' black who lived on the Mortes with his family and knew the region well. Genil Vasconcelos, 'Meireles, o sertanista sem medo', RAI, **2:13**, Nov.–Dec. 1978 (36–41), 38–9. Chico Meireles spelled his name Meirelles early in life, but later dropped one L. Born in 1908, he joined the army but fell from a horse during training and had to walk with a stick for the rest of his life. He took part in the Revolution of 1930, which brought Vargas to power, but was briefly arrested in 1935. He explained his theories of how to contact tribes in a long interview in *Jornal da Tarde*, 22 Jul. 1970, in which he said that his five-year attraction of the Xavante was the most difficult of the twelve he had done. Meirelles' son Apoena, named after the Xavante chief, was born in an Indian village but his mother died soon after so that the boy was raised by a Xavante woman.

101: unarmed.' Botelho de Magalhães, 'A pacificação', 336. Sylvio da Fonseca, *Frente a Frente com os Xavantes* (Rio de Janeiro, 1948) and 'Meus encontros com o Xavante', *Revista do Arquivo Municipal*, **142** (São Paulo, 1951). Lopes da Silva, 'Dois séculos e meio de história Xavante', 368. She cites a detailed account of the attraction: Diana C. G. Motta, *As frentes de atração: proposta e realidade* (Master's dissertation, História Política Interna, Universidade de Brasília, 1979), 139–55; Oswaldo Martins Ravagnani, *A Experiência Xav-*

ante com o mundo dos brancos (Doctoral thesis, Escola de Sociologia e Política, Universidade de São Paulo, 1977); Cláudia Menezes, 'Os Xavante e o movimento de fronteira no leste matogrossense', RA, **25**, 1982.

101: friendly manner.' Rondon, *Índios do Brasil*, **2**, 163–4. On chief Apewen (Apoena) see: Anon., 'Arodí, filho de Apoena, confirmado na chefia', RAI, **2:11**, Jul.–Aug. 1978, 9–12.

101: signal.' Botelho de Magalhães, 'A pacificação', 336. Lincoln de Souza, *Entre os Xavantes do Roncador* (Ministério de Documentação e Saúde, Rio de Janeiro, 1952). Meirelles begged Minister João Alberto, head of the FBC, to forbid entry into the pacification zone during the delicate period after the contact. This was just in time, for, according to General Botelho de Magalhães, 'as soon as the press of this capital [Rio de Janeiro] received the first note I gave them about the event, a great caravan of reporters, cameramen, and *curiosos* was prepared and had already obtained a plane to fly to São Domingos to see and agitate the Xavante' ('A pacificação', 337). Genil Vasconcelos and half a dozen other cameramen later went to record the contact with the Xavante, and there were pictures and articles about them by José Leal in *O Cruzeiro* in July 1950. There was jubilation in the CNPI when the contact was reported to it. Rondon rose and recited a song in Jê as spoken by the Xerente (cousins of the Xavante) whose central theme was: 'The civilizado's head is handsome . . . but it is full of evil!'

In 1953 there was an incident on the Culuene headwater of the Xingu, at the western edge of Xavante territory. Four American missionaries and twenty Brazilians were moving down the Culuene when they met some uncontacted Xavante. The missionaries frightened the Indians by playing an accordion and a saxophone; some of their possessions were taken; and they refused to join in a dance because they had seen some warriors hiding with their clubs and feared attack. So the intruders fled in their boats, and twice came under arrow fire from the river bank. (Tom Young, 'Among savage Chavantes', *Moody Monthly*, Jan. 1954, 38–40.)

102: undergrowth.' Maybury-Lewis, *The Savage and the Innocent*, 168.

102: Venice'. Ibid.

103: São Felix.' Weyer, *Jungle Quest*, 65–6; Ravagnani, *A Experiência Xavante*, 179–85.

103: destruction.' Anon., 'Vida e idéias de

Meirelles', RAI, **3:21**, Jul.–Aug. 1981 (54–9), 57–8; *Jornal da Tarde*, 22 Jul. 1970.

105: Mato Grosso police.' José Maria da Gama Malcher, Preface to Mário Simões, ed., *SPI – 1953* (Rio de Janeiro, 1954), 51.

105: encroachments.' Maybury-Lewis, *Akwê-Shavante Society*, 6. The government had reserved Xavante lands for colonization in 1941, long before the Xavante were contacted (Decree-law 396, 18 Apr. 1941). The land was parcelled out to 'colonists', including a Senator whose lot covered what became the Xavante reserve of Pimentel Barbosa. Gontran da Veiga Jardim, 'Os guerreiros já não cantam mais', *Correio da Manhã*, 23 Sep. 1967.

106: Tapajós river. Giaccaria and Hiede, *A'uwe Uptabi*, 23–6; Maybury-Lewis, *Akwê-Shavante Society*, 18. Aracy Lopes da Silva was told about some of the migrations by Dzuru-rã (a Xavante who later became famous as a politician called Mário Juruna), and she quotes from the thesis of Marta Maria Lopes, who was told about the move to the Paranatinga (then called Posto Simões Lopes, now known as Área Indígena Bakairi) by Odenir Pinto de Oliveira, son of the encarregado Pedro Vani de Oliveira. Lopes da Silva was also told about the latter movement by two Xavante chiefs. Lopes da Silva, 'Dois séculos e meio de história Xavante', 369–70; Marta Maria Lopes, *A resistência do índio ao extermínio: o caso dos Akwe-Xavante, 1967–1980* (Master's dissertation, Universidade do ESP, 1988).

107: wounded.' Maybury-Lewis, *The Savage and the Innocent*, 196. Santa Teresinha, about seventy kilometres (forty-five miles) upriver or south of São Domingos, was the attraction post of the unfortunate priests Sacilotti and Fuchs, killed in 1934. Areões, further south, between Santa Teresinha and Xavantina, was briefly the base of an American Protestant missionary, whom Maybury-Lewis described as 'a heavily built young man with blue eyes and a centre parting to his fair hair. He was wearing shorts and tennis shoes' (ibid., 202). This missionary decided to close his base in 1958 and sold his boat to the Salesians.

107: miserable. Orlando Villas Boas interview, *Folha de Goiás*, 15 Jan. 1961, also in BSPI, **47**, Jan. 1961, 6–7.

108: Indians.' *Jornal da Tarde*, 21 Jul. 1971 (also ESP, 25 Apr. 1969), quoted in Pedro Casaldáliga (Bishop of São Felix), *Uma Igreja da Amazônia em Conflito com o Latifúndio e a Marginalização Social* (Mato Grosso, 1972), 22. The ranch was called Agro-Pecuária Suiá-Missu and was owned by the Omettos' Companhia de Desenvolvimento do Araguaia (CODEARA). Edwin Brooks, René Fuerst, John Hemming and Francis Huxley, *Tribes of the Amazon Basin in Brazil, 1972* (London, 1973), 29; Hanbury-Tenison, *Report of a Visit*, 26, and *A Question of Survival for the Indians of Brazil* (London, 1973), 101–12; Shelton H. Davis, *Victims of the Miracle* (Cambridge, 1977), 119; Cláudia Menezes, 'Os Xavante e o movimento de fronteira . . .', 66; Marta Lopes, *A resistência do índio ao extermínio*, 67–8.

108: intensified. Lopes da Silva, 'Dois séculos e meio de história Xavante', 373.

109: lost territory. The Xavante reserves were: **Pimentel Barbosa**, on the rio das Mortes (329,000 ha, 1,300 square miles) decreed in 1969, demarcated by Funai in the 1970s, and ratified by decree of 20 August 1986; **Areões**, further south on the Mortes (218,500 ha, 840 square miles), decreed 1969, defined and ratified by edict of 19 September 1972; **Parabubure**, between the Couto de Magalhães and Culuene headwaters of the Xingu (225,500 ha, 870 square miles), decreed 21 December 1979, demarcated in 1981; Reserva Indígena **Marechal Rondon** (formerly **Batovi**), on the Culiseu headwater of the Xingu (98,500 ha, 380 square miles), state decree of 4 May 1965, demarcated by Funai 1972; and the two Salesian missions south of the Mortes: **São Marcos**, which adjoins the Bororo post Merure (188,500 ha, 730 square miles), decreed 14 September 1972, boundaries fixed by decree of 5 September 1975; and **Sangradouro**/Volta Grande, further west towards the city of Cuiabá (100,000 ha, 386 square miles), decreed 14 September 1972, demarcated 1973.

6. The Kayapó

111: seasons.' Darrell Posey, 'Native and indigenous guidelines for new Amazonian development strategies: understanding biological diversity through ethnoecology', in John Hemming, ed., *Change in the Amazon Basin*, **1**, *Man's Impact on Forests and Rivers* (Manchester, 1985), 157; Jean

Bamberger, *Environmental and cultural classification: a study of the Northern Cayapó* (Doctoral dissertation, Harvard University, 1967). A classic study of Xikrin Kayapó society is Lux Vidal, *Morte e Vida de uma Sociedade Indígena Brasileira* (São Paulo, 1977) and this author analysed body-painting in 'Pintura e adornos corporais' in Berta and Darcy Ribeiro, eds., *Suma Etnológica Brasileira* (Editora Vozes, Petrópolis, 1986), and 'A pintura corporal e a arte gráfica entre os Kayapó-Xikrin do Cateté', in Lux Vidal, ed., *Grafismo Indígena* (Studio Nobel: FAPESP: EdUSP, São Paulo, 1976). Her daughter Isabelle Vidal Giannini continued the study of Xikrin Kayapó in *Rainforest Exchanges: Industry and Community on an Amazonian Frontier* (2000).

111: populations.' Posey, 'Native and indigenous guidelines', 165. Darrell Posey wrote about Kayapó bee-keeping skills (apiculture) and other insect uses in: RAI, **20:1**, 1981, 36–41; *Journal of Ethnobiology*, **1:1**, 1981, 165–74 and **3:1**, 1983, 63–73; *Florida Entomologist*, **5:4**, 1982, 452–8; *Revista Brasileira de Zoologia*, **1:3**, 1983, 133–44; *Biotropica*, **15:2**, 1983, 154–8; 'Etnoentomologia das tribos indigenas da Amazônia', in Darcy Ribeiro, ed., *Suma Etnológica Brasileira*, **1**, *Etnobiologia* (Vozes/FINEP, Petrópolis/Rio de Janeiro, 1986), 251–72; *Journal of Ethnobiology*, Supplement, *New Directions in Ethnobiology*, 1986; BMPEG, **2:2**, 1986. He also organized a fine exhibition on Kayapó science at the Goeldi Museum in Belém in 1989.

112: landscapes' Darrell A. Posey, 'Diachronic ecotones and anthropogenic landscapes in Amazonia: contesting the consciousness of conservation', in William Balée, ed., *Advances in Historical Ecology* (New York, 1998), 115.

112: (30%).' Anthony B. Anderson and Darrell A. Posey, 'Management of a tropical scrub savannah by the Gorotire Kayapó of Brazil', in D. A. Posey and W. Balée, eds., *Resource Management in Amazonia: Indigenous and Folk Strategies* (New York, 1989), 159. An earlier version of this paper was in BMPEG, *Série Botânica*, **2:1**, 1985, 77–98. Posey published many papers that changed perceptions of Kayapó agricultural and subsistence techniques, including one with Susanna Hecht on their management of soils (in the above volume, 174–88).

113: years.' Gustaaf Verswijver, *The Club-Fighters of the Amazon* (Gent, 1992), 91.

113: periods'. Darrell A. Posey, 'Environmental and social implications of pre- and post-contact

situations on Brazilian Indians. The Kayapó and a new Amazonian synthesis', in Anna Curtenius Roosevelt, ed., *Amazonian Indians from Prehistory to the Present* (Tucson, 1994) (271–86), 274.

114: them there.' Missões Dominicanas, *Gorotirés. Prelazia de Conceição do Araguaia* (Rio de Janeiro, 1936), 31. The first Gorotire raid on the Curuá was in 1918, and in 1934 they routed the Tupi-speaking Kuruáia of that river. In 1928 a Protestant missionary, Ernest J. Woottens, tried to reach the Gorotire on the Fresco to recover the wife of a Christian Kayapó whom they had kidnapped; but although he had a good guide and interpreter, he took no presents and failed. (Missões Dominicanas, *Gorotirés*, 23; Curt Nimuendajú, 'Os Górotire', RMP, **6**, 1952, 429.) The Pau d'Arco group are spelled differently by various authorities: Irã-Amráire (by Curt Nimuendajú, 1952); Irã-ã-mray-re (by Lux Vidal, 1977); Ira-amrãire (by Darrell Posey, 1979); Ira-amrãyre (by Gustaaf Verswijver, 1981); Irã'a mrayre (by Terence Turner, 1992).

114: command.' Nimuendajú, 'Os Górotire', 446, 429. The missionaries' full names were Fred Roberts, Fred Wright, and Fred Dawson. Their fellow missionary Horace Banner wrote a book called *The Three Freds and After* (Belfast, 1975) about them. Verswijver, *Club-Fighters*, 96. Banner published some of his knowledge about the tribe in 'Mitos dos índios Kayapó', RA, **5:1**, Jun. 1957 (also in Egon Schaden, ed., *Homem, Cultura e Sociedade no Brasil* (Petrópolis, 1972)), and 'O índio Kayapó em seu acampamento', BMPEG, **13**, 1961.

114: matches.' Missões Dominicanas, *Gorotirés*, 35.

114: health.' Ibid., 59.

115: baptized.' Ibid., 83.

115: impossible.' Nimuendajú, 'Os Górotire', 429–30.

115: Silva.' Ibid., 430.

116: annoyed with them.' Ibid., 445.

116: singing.' Horace Banner, *Long Climb on the Xingu* (London, 1963), 88.

117: termites.' Banner, 'Mitos dos índios Kayapó', in Schaden, *Homem*, 131–2.

117: returned to him.' Terence Turner, 'History, myth and social consciousness among the Kayapó of Central Brazil', in Jonathan D. Hill, ed., *Rethinking History and Myth: Indigenous South American Perspectives on the Past* (Urbana, Ill., 1988), 200. The legend of Angme kapran derived from Jê-speaking Timbira and other tribes to the east, and it was adopted only by the Xikrin and Pau d'Arco Kayapó: Nimuendajú gathered it from the latter in 1940, and Lux Vidal from the Xikrin (*Morte e Vida*, 265–6). The snake legend was told to Vanessa Lea by Chief Kretire of the Mentuktire. Both legends are also recorded by Johannes Wilbert, *Folk Literature of the Gê Indians* (UCLA Latin American Center, Los Angeles, 1984) 2 257–9.

117: spokesmen'. Nimuendajú, 'Os Górotire', 452.

118: populations' Carlos de Araújo Moreira Neto, 'Relatório sôbre a situação atual dos índios Kayapó', RA, **7:1–2**, 1959, 59.

118: a fire below.' Cícero Cavalcanti, '12 anos convivendo com os Kaiapó', RAI, **21**, Jul.–Aug. 1981, 18. Cavalcanti said that when the Gorotire were ferried across the Fresco to Nova Olinda in 1937, the farmer who transported them counted 1,200 people, with others remaining in the forest. By 1960, Edson Diniz said that there were some 250 Gorotire at P I Gorotire on the Fresco, with 200 Kuben-Kran-Kégn on the Riozinho. (Edson Soares Diniz, 'Convívio interétnico e aglutinação intergrupal', RMP, **14**, 1963, 216.) A decade later, a Red Cross team reported 450 people at P I Gorotire (of whom 25 per cent were Xikrin and 15 per cent were Kuben-Kran-Kégn). Three groups were seeking to influence these Indians: Funai, a Catholic mission, and the Protestant Missão Evangélica do Brasil. The Kuben-Kran-Kégn post, to the west, had some 350 people. Their village was served by three competing agencies (a Catholic mission, the Protestant Unevangelized Fields Mission, and the Indian agency Funai) and it was visited by weekly tourist flights from Brasília. Bo Åkerren et al., *Report of the ICRC Medical Mission to the Brazilian Amazon Region* (Geneva, 1970), 48–50.

Although all authors agree that their name means 'Shaven Heads', there are many variations in spelling this group of Kayapó. Curt Nimuendajú in 1952 spelled it Kuben-Krãkégn; Arlindo Silva, also in 1952, wrote Kuben Kra Kein; Carlos Moreira in 1959 wrote Kubenkrankégn; José Maria da Gama Malcher in 1962 Kuben-Kran-Kein; Edson Diniz in 1963 used Kuben-Krãkegn, whereas Horace Banner in that year wrote Kubenkran-kane; Bo Åkerren's Red Cross Medical Mission in 1970 and the Brooks–Fuerst–Hemming–Huxley team in 1972 both wrote Kubenkranken; Expedito Arnaud in 1971 used Kubén-Kran-Kegn; Darrell Posey in 1979 used Kuben-Krã-

Kêin; Cícero Cavalcanti in 1981 used Kubenkrankein; and Gustaaf Verswijver in various sources wrote Kubenkrãnkêin.

119: recognize them.' Nimuendajú, 'Os Górotire', 436.

119: cabras.' Ibid., 432. Also, Moreira Neto, 'Relatório . . . Kayapó', 54.

119: witchcraft.' Adélia Engrácia de Oliveira, 'Os índios Jurúna e sua cultura nos dias atuais', BMPEG, *Antropologia* **35:17**, 1968; and her 'Os índios Jurúna do Alto Xingu', *Dédalo*, **6:11–12**, São Paulo, 1970, 32–3. In 1928 Commander Dyott's expedition saw a group under Chief Maricowa, at Popori village one day's journey above the rapids. They were friendly, spoke some Portuguese, and traded fish for knives with Dyott's expedition. Although naked and darker-skinned than other tribes he had seen, Dyott liked their 'many ornaments such as necklaces and ligatures about their arms and legs. Red feathers inserted in the lobes of their ears gave them quite a picturesque appearance and set off their jet-black hair to advantage as it fell in a long wave below their shoulders.' G. M. Dyott, *Man Hunting in the Jungle* (London, 1930), 215.

119: Constantino's life.' Nimuendajú, 'Os Górotire', 433.

120: Nova Olinda'. Ibid., 231–2.

120: distance away.' Ibid., 447.

121: others. Ibid.

121: history.' Verswijver, *Club-Fighters*, 94. He spells this tribe Mekrãgnoti; José da Gama Malcher (1964) gives Men-krang-no-ti; Darrell Posey (1979) uses Mekràngôti; Cícero Cavalcanti (1981) spells it Mekrangnotire; Terence Turner (1992) Mekranoti. The name means 'People who paint their heads red [with urucum dye]'. Their southernmost group, within the Xingu Indian park, was frequently referred to as Txukahamãe or Txukarramãe. This is a Juruna word meaning 'People without bows' since it was thought – wrongly – that these Kayapó used only clubs.

122: lands'. Terence Turner, 'Os Mebengokre Kayapó: história e mudança social. De comunidades autônomas para a coexistência interétnica', in HIB, 329. Gustaaf Verswijver lists the Menkragnoti's village moves and fighting campaigns between 1905 and 1958: *Club-Fighters*, 143–4, 274–311. He also dealt with these migrations in 'Séparations et migrations des Mekrãgnoti, groupe Kayapo du Brésil Central', *Bulletin de la Société Suisse des Américanistes* (Geneva), **42**, 1978.

122: ability.' Verswijver, *Club-Fighters*, 126–7.

122: *fight.'* Ibid., 130.

122: *firearms.'* Ibid., 143.

122: *risks.'* Ibid., 144.

123: *hunting.* Roberto Décio de Las Casas, 'Índios e brasileiros no vale do rio Tapajós', BMPEG, **23**, Oct. 1964, 24–5.

124: *ornaments.'* Cícero Cavalcanti, *Jornal do Brasil,* 22 Jul. 1961. The depot that was raided was just outside the town of Pimentel on the Tapajós, upriver from Itaituba.

124: *brought to bear'* Moreira Neto, 'Relatório sôbre a situação atual dos índios Kayapó', 55.

124: *Indians'.* Cavalcanti, *Jornal do Brasil,* 22 Jul. 1961.

124: *Preto, etc.'* Francisco Meirelles, 'Meireles fala sobre os Kaiapó: seus primeiros e últimos contatos com elementos civilizados', BSPI, **56**, Jul.–Aug. 1962, 4. (Meirelles usually spelled his name with two Ls, contrary to modern Portuguese usage.) The Kokraimoro had broken away from the Kuben-Kran-Kégn, and had been the victims of the massacre by the rubber planter Inácio Silva. After the contact in 1957, they were settled on the former rubber plantation of Isaac Benarroch on the right bank of the Iriri. Another group of Kokraimoro, from the Riosinho do Icatã, also on the right bank of the Iriri, suffered heavy depopulation. Both groups were moved to an island in the Xingu near Serra Encontrada, two days upriver from the frontier town of São Felix do Xingu. José M. da Gama Malcher, *Índios: grau de integração na comunidade nacional, grupo linguístico, localização* (Rio de Janeiro, 1964), 170.

125: *ill.'* Moreira Neto, 'Relatório sôbre . . . Kayapó', 52.

125: *Curuá.'* Meirelles, 'Meireles fala', 5.

125: *paths.'* Ibid.

125: *lived here.'* Ibid., 6.

125: *until then'.* Ibid., 8; 'Os Kayapó: separações e junções dos grupos do norte', RAI, **2:12**, Sep.–Oct. 1978, 15.

126: *"attraction".'* Gama Malcher, *Índios: grau de integração . . .,* 169. Verswijver said that many of the diseases were caught through continued contact with settlers at a place on the Curuá wistfully named Bom Futuro ('Good Future'): Verswijver, 'Séparations et migrations des Mekrāgnoti, groupe Kayapo du Brésil Central', 54. The eighty-two Kararaô (contacted in 1965 and 96 per cent extinguished by disease) were mentioned by Antonio Cotrim, *Jornal do Brasil,* 25 May 1972.

126: *[clearings], etc.'* Meirelles, 'Meireles fala', 9.

126: *chief.'* Ibid., 12. Meirelles then radioed for a Catalina flying boat to come, with more guns and ammunition for the delighted Mekragnotire. This group remained quite isolated, after the contact in 1958, because the SPI was short of funds and because it was difficult to get up the shallow and rapid-infested Iriri. In 1962 there was a publicity visit to them by the head of the SPI, Colonel Moacyr Ribeiro Coelho, and television crews, travelling in a Catalina while other elements approached by boat. They found the village on the Baú to be healthy and well supplied with food from its plantations. Its Indians said that the Mekragnotire were still at peace with the whites, apart from one small group under Chief Ature; but there was a vendetta with the Menkragnoti of the Curuá because Atukran, 'famous for seducing women from other tribes', had killed the popular Chief Nrontuiaro of the Kararaô in a quarrel. Some five years later, these Kayapó of the Iriri used their guns to attack and massacre a village of their old enemies, the Panará.

126: *willingly did so.'* Verswijver, *Club-Fighters,* 145.

127: *groups.'* Moreira Neto, 'Relatório sôbre . . . Kayapó', 61.

127: *title deed.'* Ibid., 59.

127: *contamination'.* Ibid., 58.

127: *forest.'* Richard Heelas, *The Social Organization of the Panará, a Gê Tribe of Central Brazil* (Doctoral thesis, University of Oxford, 1979), 10–11.

127: *relatives'* Missões Dominicanas, *Gorotires,* 9 and 58–9.

128: *[Xikrin] tribe.'* 'Peace reigns on the Rio Vermelho', article in *Folha Vespertina,* Belém do Pará, 14 Apr. 1953; José M. da Gama Malcher, Preface to Mário Simões, ed., *SPI – 1953* (Rio de Janeiro, 1954), 27–8.

128: *children.'* Protásio Frikel, 'Notas sôbre a situação atual dos índios Xikrin do Rio Caeteté', RMP, **14**, 1963, 147.

128: *sick.'* Arlindo Silva, 'Homens brancos na aldeia dos Caiapós', O Cruzeiro, 7 Jun. 1952, 22. The migration of the Xikrin to the Bacajá may have occurred earlier, in about 1926, to escape attack by Gorotire Kayapó. One group of Xikrin disliked the new location and returned to the Caeteté in the 1930s.

128: *savages.'* Folha Vespertina, Belém, 14 Apr. 1953.

129: *users.'* Jorge Ferreira article in O Cruzeiro (11 Jul. 1955) quoted in Vidal, *Morte e Vida,*

33–4. The Xikrin warriors at Las Casas were 'pacified' by the SPI encarregado Miguel Araújo; but their enemies, some Gorotire who were already at the post, insisted that they be taken back to the upper Itacaiúnas. There was a dispute between Araújo and Leonardo Villas Boas about this. Hilmar Kluck of the SPI was sent to adjudicate, and decided that Araújo was right, so that he escorted the Xikrin back to Kokorekre. Bemoti is sometimes spelled Bemotire or Bemotiré. The complicated moves of the Xikrin in and out of Las Casas are fully documented by Vidal in Carlos Alberto Ricardo, ed., *Povos Indígenas no Brasil*, 8, *Sudeste do Pará (Tocantins)* (São Paulo, 1985), 128.

129: peaceful'. Vidal, *Morte e Vida*, 34. Hilmar Kluck was with the Xikrin for a year in 1953–54. He reported that, in the latter year, sixty Xikrin from the Bacajá rejoined their eastern relatives on the Cateté. Motikre village is some twenty kilometres (twelve miles) from Pukatingrô village where they have lived since the 1970s. In 1983 they built a second village, Kamkrokro, twenty kilometres to the south on the rio Seco, in a region rich in Brazil-nut trees.

129: known as 204.' Meirelles, 'Meireles fala', 15. The SPI's *Boletim* (35, Dec. 1959) reported this mission and said that Meirelles had brought some Xikrin to the town of Altamira, where they were given presents. Survivors of the flu epidemic fled into the forests, built a village and were contacted in 1961 on the Carapanã (Mosquito) creek (on the right bank of the Bacajá) by another SPI team. They were moved to a former SPI post on the Dois Irmãos ('Two Brothers') creek, which was renamed Francisco Meirelles; in 1965 they were relocated to their present village, Flor do Caucho ('Latex Blossom'). The population of this Bacajá Xikrin group gradually grew, from a high birth rate, to 172 in 1985 and to 362 in 2000.

130: women' Frikel, 'Notas', 154; Friar Raymond Caron, *Os Índios Xikrin do Caeteté* (unpublished, no date) quoted in Expedito Arnaud, 'A ação indigenista no Sul do Pará (1940–1970)', BMPEG, 49:6, Oct. 1971, 11. Bo Åkerren et al., *Report of the ICRC Medical Mission*, 50 gave 120 as the population in 1970; Edwin Brooks et al., *Tribes of the Amazon Basin in Brazil, 1972* (London, 1973) 83; Gustaaf Verswijver, 'Os Kayapó: separações e junções dos grupos do norte', 15; Lux Vidal, *Os Kayapó-Xikrin do Cateté: relatório*, III Encontro da Associação Brasileira de Estudos Populacionais (Vitória, 1982); Lux Vidal, 'Xikrin

do Cateté', in Ricardo, ed., *Povos Indígenas*, 8 (122–49), 125. The diseases that ravaged the Aldeia da Boca were venereal diseases, flu, an unidentified illness that caused twelve deaths in 1963, and 'left-handed hemiplegia', which paralysed the extremities of limbs. Father Caron first visited the Xikrin on the Cateté in 1963, at the same time as Frikel and Fuerst; he returned to live with them in 1966 and stayed there until ill health forced him to leave at the end of 1970; another Dominican was there for a further two years until 1972, since when Funai has looked after this P I Cateté.

130: goods.' Turner, 'Os Mebengokre Kayapó', 328.

131: rivalries.' Ibid., 332. Verswijver, *Club-Fighters*, 121–2. The Belgian anthropologist spells this group Kôkrajmôr and Turner calls them Kokraymoro. They had split from the Menkragnoti on the Iriri in 1949. After the turbulent years of raids and splits, a group of 97 led by Chief Jakuri was contacted by Francisco Meirelles at Lageiro on the upper Iriri in April 1957. In November of that year, one of Meirelles' assistants contacted 137 of Bepnox's group on a tributary of the middle Iriri. The SPI united the two groups and moved them to a site near the Brazilian settlement São Felix on the middle Xingu. This move was too violent: shortage of food and contact diseases caused the deaths of half the village by the end of 1958. The Kokraimoro were moved further from the Brazilian town, to a reserve which they still occupy. After the disastrous post-contact depopulation, and with the addition of some other Kayapó, their numbers have recovered. In 1968 a settlement called São Gonçalo, ninety kilometres (fifty-five miles) from São Felix, was completely sacked by Kayapó and its eight families fled. The attack was blamed on the Xikrin, but being this far west on the Xingu could have been by Gorotire: ESP, 11 Sep. 1968.

132: consciousness.' Darrell Posey, 'Time, space, and the interface of divergent cultures: the Kayapó Indians of Brazil face the future', *Revista Brasileira de Antropologia*, 25, 1982, 89–104. Simone Dreyfus described Kayapó music in her *Les Kayapo du Nord, État de Para, Brésil* (Paris, 1963) and Terence Turner told about the most famous ceremony, the *Bemp* naming-ritual, in his dissertation *Social Structure and Political Organization among the Northern Cayapó* (Harvard, 1965), chapter 4, section 4.

7. The Villas Boas' Xingu

133: aviation.' Orlando Villas Boas communication to Maria Lucia Pires Menezes, 1985, in her *Parque Indígena do Xingu* (Campinas/São Paulo, 1999), 57.

133: penetrate it.' Ayres Câmara Cunha, *Entre os Índios do Xingu* (São Paulo, 1960), 152.

134: friends.' Orlando and Cláudio Villas Bôas, *A Marcha Para o Oeste* (São Paulo, 1994), 152.

134: word.' Ibid., 164–5.

134: gravity.' Ibid., 166.

134: tranquillity'. Ibid., 184–5.

135: edible.' Ibid., 177.

135: critical.' Ibid., 184.

135: situation.' Ibid., 184–5.

135: face.' Ibid., 189.

136: simple.' Ibid., 191.

136: culture.' Orlando Villas Boas, quoted in Maureen Bisilliat, *Guerreiros sem Espada* (São Paulo, 1995), 14.

136: patients.' Villas Bôas, *Marcha*, 207. Pedro de Lima, 'Níveis tensionais dos índios Kalapalo e Kamayurá', *Revista Brasileira de Medicina*, **7:12**, 1950, and his 'Grupos sangüíneos dos índios do Xingu', *Boletim do Museu Nacional, Antropologia*, **2** (Rio de Janeiro, 1950). Dr Noel Nutels was born in the Ukraine in 1914 but brought up in Brazil's north-east after 1922. Educated by Catholic priests, he was always allowed to practise his Jewish faith. After he qualified as a doctor, Nutels planned to work on malaria, but he found that tuberculosis was an equally serious threat in the interior. He was with the Villas Boas from the outset of their Roncador–Xingu Expedition and later created an airborne medical service for the Ministry of Health (SUSA: Serviço das Unidades Sanitárias Aéreas) that gave great help to both Indians and settlers in the interior. He and his team covered 200,000 kilometres (124,000 miles) a year, by every means of transport, to deliver hundreds of thousands of TB vaccinations and attend thousands of medical emergencies. Orlando named his son Noel after this 'extrovert, cheerful, and talkative' charmer. Villas Boas, *Almanaque do Sertão* (São Paulo, 1977), 51–2; Bisilliat, *Guerreiros sem Espada*, 95–6; Noel Nutels, 'Minha vida com os índios', *Manchete*, 1973, 31–6; Gilse Campos, 'Doce memória indígena', *Jornal do Brasil*, 4 Oct. 1972.

136: fear.' Noel Nutels interview, *Jornal do Brasil*, 4 Oct. 1972.

137: "chief".' Bruna Franchetto, ' "O aparecimento dos caraíba". Para uma história kuikuro e alto-xinguana', in Manuela Carneiro da Cunha, ed., *História dos Índios no Brasil* (São Paulo, 1992), 352.

137: women.' Villas Boas, *Marcha*, 211. The Kamayurá are often spelled Kamaiura or Kamaiurá.

137: hosts.' Ibid., 282.

138: hut.' Ibid., 277.

138: Trumai.' Ibid., 352.

138: die".' Ibid., 382.

139: bow.' Ibid., 389; Orlando and Cláudio Villas Boas, 'Viagem pioneira pelo Maritsauá', RAI, **3:15**, Mar.–Apr. 1979, 20–1. In their article in 1979 they spelled the Juruna's name Tamacã, but they later changed this to Tamacu. The anthropologist Adélia Engrácia de Oliveira, who worked with the Juruna between 1965 and 1967, said that this man's name in Juruna was Xaduná. His return to his native tribe ended in tragedy. The Juruna were suspicious of Xaduná (Tamacu) and Tutuná because they had lived for so long among the Kamayurá. When the Juruna village succumbed to disease, the two returnees were clubbed to death because 'they knew witchcraft that the Kamayurá had taught them. They cast spells on the house and everyone fell ill.' Adélia Oliveira also wrote that the splendid warrior who remained on the river bank was Pauaidê, son of Chief Xubé, who had run off into the forest. Dr Oliveira described the encounter from the Juruna side, in 'Os índios Jurúna do Alto Xingu', *Dédalo*, **6:11–12**, São Paulo, 42–3; and 'Os índios Jurúna e sua cultura nos dias atuais', BMPEG, *Antropologia*, **35:17**, 1968, 11. Helmut Sick also described this first encounter with the Juruna in *Tukani* (London, 1959), 128ff. A magnificent photograph of the Juruna Pauaidê, legs and arms wide apart, was published in O *Cruzeiro*, 4 Jun. 1949, under the caption 'A true Tarzan'; Bisilliat, *Guerreiros sem Espada*, 27. The Juruna were sometimes called Boca preta because of the black dye around their mouths and chins.

139: white man.' Villas Boas, *Marcha*, 389.

139: located.' Engineer Frederico Hoepken, 'Utilização das fotografias aéreas nas explorações

Notes and References

713

geográficas', *Revista Brasileira de Geografia*, **12**:3, 1950, 85; Menezes, *Parque Indígena do Xingu*, 60. The air force base at Jacaré, known as Xingu, later became the main control point for aviation and meteorology in this region. The Villas Boas's two centres, Capitão Vasconcellos (Posto Leonardo) and Diauarum, started as FBC bases but evolved into Indian posts through usage.

139: banquet.' Villas Boas, *Marcha*, 430.

140: inside.' Orlando and Cláudio Villas Boas, *Xingu: os índios, seus mitos* (Rio de Janeiro, 1970), 38; and trans. as *Xingu, the Indians, their Myths* (by Kenneth Brecher, London, 1973), 35.

140: brothers.' Villas Boas, *Marcha*, 388; and in their 'Viagem pioneira pelo Maritsauá', 20; Adrian Cowell, *The Heart of the Forest* (London, 1960), 154–5.

140: knees.' Villas Boas, *Xingu, the Indians*, 35. The Suyás' new village was on a small lagoon called Tamuricumá on the Paranajuva, a tributary of the left bank of the Suiá-Missu not far from the modern eastern boundary of the Xingu park.

141: influence.' Vanessa Lea, *Parque Indígena do Xingu* (São Paulo, 1997), 88; Anthony Seeger, *Nature and Society in Central Brazil: the Suyá Indians of Mato Grosso* (Cambridge, Mass., 1981), 75; Protásio Frikel, 'Migração, guerra e sobrevivência Suiá', *RA*, **17**:20, 1972, 109.

141: expelling us.' Villas Boas, *Marcha*, 393.

142: parts. Villas Boas, 'Viagem pioneira pelo Maritsauá', 22. During 1950, the Villas Boas brothers built an airstrip at Cachimbo, on the Peixoto de Azevedo tributary of the Tapajós. Then, in 1957–58, Cláudio explored the Cururu river – home of the Munduruku – and cut a trail from Cachimbo to it. This completed the hundreds of kilometres of picadas, from the rio das Mortes to the Tapajós.

143: river.' Villas Boas, *Marcha*, 487. In earlier years the SPI had in 1938 founded a Posto Indígena called Taunay on the Kuliseu; this was later moved to the Batovi and called P I Culiseu. (The Kuluene and Kuliseu rivers are usually now spelled Culuene and Culiseu, since the letter K is rare in Portuguese.) In 1945 P I Alípio Bandeira was founded on the spit of land between the Culuene and Culiseu. During the first decade after the Villas Boas brothers reached the Xingu, they opened various airstrips: Garapu, Sete de Setembro (on a headwater of the Culuene) and Culuene (upriver of the Tanguro's junction with the Culuene, at 12° 44' S). In 1953 the Villas Boas built Jacaré ('Caiman'), the airstrip that

became the air force's big military base, later called Xingu. In that same year they founded P I Capitão Vasconcellos (after one of Rondon's explorers of the Xingu, who later became head of the SPI) on the Tutuarí stream, and in 1961 this was renamed Posto Leonardo after their dead brother. (Leonardo Villas Boas spent little time in the Xingu. After the initial FBC expedition, he was often employed by the SPI as a sertanista in other parts of Brazil. Like his older brothers, Leonardo frequently suffered malaria. He contracted rheumatism in the forests; and died in 1961 aged forty-three during a heart operation in São Paulo.) In 1954 came P I Txukahamãe downriver (north) near the Von Martius rapids; and in 1958 an attraction post called José Bezerra on the Batovi, to contact the Txikão. Most of these places were short-lived: only Posto Leonardo, Jacaré (Xingu), and Diauarum developed into permanent bases.

143: connived in it.' Bruna Franchetto, *Laudo Antropológico: a ocupação indígena da região dos formadores e do alto curso do rio Xingu* (Rio de Janeiro, 1987) quoted in Lea, *Parque Indígena do Xingu*, 187; Mário Simões, 'Os "Txikão" e outras tribos marginais do alto Xingu', *RMP*, **14**, 1963, 80–1; Georg Grünberg, 'Beiträge zur Ethnographie der Kayabí Zentralbrasiliens', *Archiv für Völkerkunde*, **24** (Vienna, 1970, 21–186) and his 'Urgent research in north-west Mato Grosso', *Bulletin of the International Committee on Urgent Anthropological and Ethnological Research*, **8** (Vienna, 1966); Pedro Agostinho da Silva, 'Informe sobre a situação territorial e demográfica no alto Xingu', in Georg Grünberg, ed., *La Situación del Indígena en América del Sur* (Montevideo, 1972), 365. The two companies in Kayabi territory were ERION (Empresa Rio Nova Ltda.), a rubber company owned by the Spinelli brothers of Cuiabá, and CONOMALI (Companhia Colonizadora Noroeste Matogrossense Ltda.). The latter in 1956 brought settlers from rio Grande do Sul to its Gleba Gaúcha which became the town of Porto dos Gaúchos. Fr. Bartolomé Meliá, SJ, 'Os caiabis não-xinguanos' (in Vera Penteado Coelho, ed., *Karl von den Steinen: um século de antropologia no Xingu* (São Paulo, 1993) (485–509), 497–9.

144: whips.' M. K. Leal Ferreira, *Da origem dos homens à conquista da escrita: um estudo sobre povos indígenas e educação escolar no Brasil* (Master's dissertation, Universidade de São Paulo, 1992), **2**, 32–5. Ferreira recorded these Kayabi memories when she was a nurse at Diauarum in the late 1980s. Lea, *Parque Indígena do Xingu*, 120.

144: Indians there.' Testimony of Canísio (Chief of Capivara village, a short distance downriver from Diauarum) and Mairawé, recorded by M. K. Leal Ferreira, in Lea, *Parque Indígena do Xingu*, 191. Before 1950 there were reckoned to be over 1,000 Kayabi. After the depopulation of the measles epidemics, Father Dornstauder in 1955 counted 341: 148 in five villages (malocas) on the Teles Pires and a few at Posto José Bezerra; 108 at Tatuí (Santa Rosa) and on the Peixes; 45 down the Juruena in P I Kayabi; and 40 already in the Xingu. By 1966 there were only 273 Kayabi: 70 remaining on the Peixes and Teles Pires; 24 at P I Bezerra; and 179 in seven villages in the Xingu. Since then the numbers of those in the Xingu have increased, to 364 people in fourteen malocas by the 1980s, and to 526 in 1992 – by which time they were the largest tribe in the Xingu. In the latter year, there were also 171 in the Reserva Apiaká-Kayabi on the Peixes; 191 alongside other tribes in the Umutina Indian Area west of Cuiabá; and a few Kayabi among the Munduruku in the so-called Cayabi Indian Area in the state of Pará. There were thus some 900 Kayabi in 1992. The community at Tatuí had grown steadily: from 68 in 1968, to 84 in 1977, and 102 in 1980. For a time, the Jesuits took Kayabi children to an Indian boarding school at Utiariti (Rondon's old telegraph post), but the pupils and their parents generally hated this.

Father Dornstauder originally brought the Kayabi to the Anchieta Mission on the Arinos, but later moved them to the lower rio das Peixes, where an Indian reserve was created for them in Decree 63,308 of 8 Oct. 1968; its boundaries were altered by Decree 74,477 of 29 Aug. 1974 and its 47,450 ha (185 square miles) were demarcated in the following year. Part of this land was disputed by a fazendeiro, and the dispute rumbled on throughout the 1980s. Another reserve called Escondido was added further down the Juruena, and a Kayabi Indian Territory beside that of the Munduruku on the Teles Pires. Expedito Arnaud, 'A ocupação indígena no alto Xingu (Mato Grosso)', *Boletim de Pesquisa da CEDEAM*, **6:10**, Manaus, Jan.–Jun. 1987, 137; Meliá, 'Os caiabis', 491.

144: whites' world. Ipepuri (or Prepori) became chief of the Kayabi village south of Diauarum. Chief Prepori became a right hand of the Villas Boas in getting things done in the Xingu;

but he was said to have murdered both Indians and whites who crossed his path or whose possessions he coveted. The anthropologists Georg Grünberg and later Eduardo Galvão lodged with him and his wife Carolina. The author met him in the 1960s and again a decade later, and I agree with Berta Ribeiro who described him and his wife in 1977 as 'very mestizo, seeming more like caboclos than Indians'. Prepori told her that it was *he* who had suggested to Cláudio Villas Boas that: 'We need land for us. They are surveying land everywhere and there will not be enough left over. So Cláudio talked to [President] Jânio [Quadros] and arranged the trick of making the [Xingu] park.' Berta Ribeiro, *Diário do Xingu* (São Paulo, 1979), 100.

145: live better.' Chief Temeoni quoted by Canísio in conversation with Leal Ferreira, in Lea, *Parque Indígena do Xingu*, 191.

145: ancestors.' Canísio and Mairawé talking to Leal Ferreira, in ibid., 191.

146: ranch. Canísio testimony to Leal Ferreira, *Da origem dos homens . . .*, **2**, 78–9.

146: coveted.' Meliá, 'Os caiabis', 506.

146: battle.' Cláudio and Orlando Villas Boas, 'Atração dos índios Txukahamãi', in Mário Simões, ed., *S.P.I. – 1954* (Rio de Janeiro, 1955), 79. The Villas Boas then spelled the tribe Txukahamãi, but they later changed this to Txucarramãe. Aruak-speaking tribes called them Aveoto, which also means 'Men without bows'. In fact, the Mentuktire had by then adopted bows and arrows, although clubs were still their preferred weapons. The Villas Boas wrote in 1954 that 'the tribe's real name was Mekragnoti or Meakregoroti', but in an entry for 1949 in their book *A Marcha Para o Oeste* they wrote 'Menkragnotire or Metotire'. Gustaaf Verswijver calls them Southern Mekrãgnoti ('People with tonsured hair') since they were the southern part of the Kayapó who had crossed the Xingu; but Vanessa Lea wrote that the southernmost group, on the Jarina river, refers to itself as Mebengokre, while the closely related subgroup that settled at P I Capoto calls itself Metuktire ('Black people'). Lea, *Parque Indígena do Xingu*, 65.

147: date.' Villas Boas, 'Atração', 81. Cowell, *The Heart of the Forest*, 177; Verswijver, *Club-Fighters*, 291.

147: canoe.' Cowell, *Heart of the Forest*, 177.

147: water.' Ibid., 177.

147: pierced.' Villas Boas, 'Atração', 82. This group near the Von Martius rapids was the

Mentuktire, rather than the Mebengokre who were contacted further south on the Jarina later that year.

147: impossible' Ibid., 83.

148: dignity. Cowell, *Heart of the Forest*, 179–80.

149: tripe.' Villas Boas, 'Atração', 85.

150: communities.' Villas Boas, *Almanaque do Sertão*, 227; Bisilliat, *Guerreiros sem Espada*, 29. Anon., 'Os irmãos da selva', *Veja*, **218**, 8 Nov. 1972, 52. This article summarized the brothers' expeditions and achievements to date. A similar biographical article was José Marqueiz, 'Memórias dos irmãos Villas Boas. Os 32 anos de Cláudio e Orlando com os índios brasileiros', *Visão*, 10 Feb. 1975.

150: foreheads.' Villas Boas, 'Atração', 85.

150: followed.' Verswijver, *Club-Fighters*, 110.

151: coming.' Cowell, *Heart of the Forest*, 234–5. Verswijver, with characteristic erudition, gives a chronological record of the bewildering splits and moves of these groups, whom he calls Southern Mekrãgnoti: *Club-Fighters*, 291–2. In 1960 Cláudio Villas Boas persuaded this group to move from their village on the Liberdade westwards across the Xingu to a village called Roikore on the Capoto stream between the Jarina and Iriri Novo. But when the Xingu park was created in 1961, Cláudio got them to move again, in order to come within its boundaries: sixty-five people under Chief Kremoro settled at Porori village, on the Xingu near the mouth of the Jarina river. This village grew in 1964, when 120 people moved to it from the north-west; and another group joined in 1967: Lea, *Parque Indígena do Xingu*, 113–14.

151: no one.' Cowell, *Heart of the Forest*, 237.

152: clothes".' Ibid., 183.

152: see."' Ibid., 186.

152: son."' Ibid., 184.

152: high.' Verswijver, *Club-Fighters*, 234.

153: minimum.' Ibid., 234–5. Dennis Werner, *The Making of a Mekranoti Chief* (Doctoral dissertation, City University of New York, 1980), 49–50; Terence Turner, *The Kayapo of Southeastern Pará* (unpublished ms., 1987, cited by Verswijver).

153: syrup'. Villas Boas, *Marcha*, 355.

153: floor.' Cowell, *Heart of the Forest*, 201.

154: swallow.' Ibid., 204.

154: new-born. Villas Boas, *Marcha*, 364. Of the three tribes that were mentioned as disappearing, the surviving Tsuva were absorbed by the Kuikuro, the Naravute by the Kalapalo, and the Custenaú by the Waurá. They also listed five other groups who were remembered only in name.

155: horrible.' Chief Aritana, Introductory speech to a Course for Indigenous Medical Agents, Posto Leonardo, June 1998.

155: villages.' Dr João Leão da Mota, 'A epidemia de sarampo no Xingu', in M. Simões, ed., *S.P.I. – 1954*, 132. E. Galvão and M. Simões wrote that flu killed 25 Kalapalo in 1946 and 12 Kamayurá and Kalapalo in 1950 and that measles killed 114 people in 1954. 'Mudança e sobrevivência no Alto Xingu – Brasil Central', RA, **14**, 1966, 39, 44. Darcy Ribeiro wrote that the measles had been caught by Indians visiting the air force base Jacaré, where they met labourers who were infected. Ribeiro, citing reports by Drs Serôa da Mota and Leão da Mota, as well as by Cláudio Villas Boas, said that 698 Indians fell ill and 108 died: 61 on the FBC bases Jacaré and Kalapalo and 48 at Capitão Vasconcellos and in the Waurá and Kuikuro villages. He also said that mortality was four times as great among untreated Indians as among those under medical care, but 'they were saved not so much from penicillin and streptomycin as from proper regular food'. Darcy Ribeiro, *Os Índios e a Civilização* (Rio de Janeiro, 1970), 279. In 1950, Eduardo Galvão estimated the upper-Xingu tribes' populations as 180 Kalapalo, 110 Kamayurá, 140 Kuikuro, 95 Waurá, and about 20 each for the Trumai, Aweti, and Yawalipiti, total 585 ('Cultura e sistema de parentesco das tribos do alto rio Xingu', in BMN, **14**, 1953, 56; and ES, 78). By 1959 he reckoned that there were about 800 indigenous people in the area ('Áreas culturais indígenas do Brasil, 1900–1959', BMPEG, **8**, 1960, and ES, 216). When he and Simões returned to the upper Xingu in 1963, they found that its tribes' populations had fallen more slowly, from 652 to 623 during the preceding eleven years. Soon after that, the arrival of regular medical attention from Dr Roberto Baruzzi's teams of doctors from the São Paulo medical school (Escola Paulista de Medicina) started to reverse the decline. By 1990, these doctors reported that the traditional Xingu tribes were up to 2,259, plus a further 842 from four tribes introduced into the sanctuary (526 Kayabi, 146 Txikão, 48 Tapayuna, 122 Panará), giving a total indigenous population of 3,101, *PIB 1987/88/89/90*, 467; Lea, *Parque Indígena do Xingu*, 61. Population growth in the Xingu is carefully analysed in Menezes, *Parque Indígena do Xingu*,

259–69. This includes a chart of the various tribes introduced into the park.

155: five.' Cowell, *Heart of the Forest*, 113.

155: reminiscences.' Ellen B. Basso, *The Kalapalo Indians of Central Brazil* (New York, 1973), 5.

157: men. Kenneth Brecher, 'Foreword' to his translation of Orlando and Cláudio Villas Boas, *Xingu. The Indians, their Myths* (New York, 1973), viii; David Nasser, 'Índio quer ser índio', *O Cruzeiro*, 2 Jun. 1971.

158: masses.' Brecher, 'Foreword', viii–ix.

158: object?' Orlando Villas Boas interview, *Veja*, 6 Aug. 1968, 51.

158: mortification.' Cowell, *Heart of the Forest*, 41–2.

159: grocer.' Ibid., 102.

159: between them.' Brecher, 'Foreword', ix.

159: theories.' Adrian Cowell, 'Legendary brothers of the Amazon', *Observer Magazine*, London, 20 Jun. 1971, 21.

159: midnight.' Ibid.

160: journeys.' Ibid.

160: doses.' Noel Nutels interview in *Jornal do Brasil*, 4 Oct. 1972.

161: fear of attack.' Eduardo Galvão, 'Apontamentos sobre os índios Kamaiurá', *Publicações Avulsas do Museu Nacional*, 5 1949, 31–48, and in ES, 35–6.

161: boat. Villas Boas, *Marcha*, 598–9.

162: carefully.' Harald Schultz, 'Informações etnográficas sôbre os índios Suyá, 1960', RMP, *Antropologia*, 13, 1961/62, 315, 320, 328.

162: [Mentuktire].' Villas Boas, *Marcha*, 599.

163: ash.' Ibid., 579–80. Eduardo Galvão and Mário Simões, 'Notícia sobre os índios Txikão, alto Xingu', BMPEG, 24, 1965 (1–23), 3–4. On fear of the Txikão among other tribes: Kalervo Oberg, *Indian Tribes of Northern Mato Grosso*, Smithsonian Institution, Institute of Social Anthropology, Publication 15 (Washington, DC, 1953), 6; Pedro de Lima, 'Níveis tensionais', 6; Arnaud, 'A ocupação indígena', 135. Another version of the name Txikão is that it means 'earthworm' in their language. One of them was holding a worm at first contact and thought that the whites were asking what it was rather than his tribe's name.

163: saved.' Villas Boas, *Marcha*, 582.

164: forest. Ibid., 584–5.

165: peace. Ibid., 587. Galvão and Simões, 'Notícia sobre os índios Txikão', 5–7; Mário Simões, writing in 1963, gave a slightly different version to the Villas Boas in their book published in 1994. Simões said that Cláudio's first attempt at contact was in 1952, whereas the later book said 1956; he then mentioned a Villas Boas expedition in 1955 that went up the Batovi for eighteen days, but failed to make direct contact. SPI officials from P I Culiseu borrowed a plane from an American missionary in 1958 and located the Txikão village near the Batovi; their attempts at contact, from P I José Bezerra, started well, but ran out of funds in 1959. One theory for the delay is that the Villas Boas *wanted* the feared tribe to remain at the south-western edge of the park, in order to defend it against invasions by rubber men or land-grabbers (Menezes, *Parque Indígena do Xingu*, 290). The 'adventurer' who armed the Mehinaku in 1960 was an SPI official who had temporarily replaced the Villas Boas at Capitão Vasconcellos (Leonardo). Simões, 'Os "Txikão" e outras tribos marginais do Alto Xingu', 91–2; Arnaud, 'A ocupação indígena', 135–6; Ribeiro, *Diário do Xingu*, 24–5.

165: club.' Orlando Villas Boas in Gildávio Ribeiro, 'Txikão foi forte e valente, mas hoje é índio raquítico', *Jornal do Brasil*, 12 Nov. 1967.

165: hands. Villas Boas, *Marcha*, 259.

166: glare.' Gildávio Ribeiro, 'Txikão foi forte e valente'. The Txikão were immediately hit by a flu epidemic, but have since recovered.

166: deceased'. Patrick Menget, *Au nom des autres. Classification des relations sociales chez les Txikão du Haut-Xingu (Brésil)*, Doctoral thesis, École Pratique des Hautes Études, Université de Paris X, Nanterre, 1976, 87; Ribeiro, *Diário*, 181–90.

167: group.' Cowell, *Heart of the Forest*, 87.

167: villages.' Villas Boas, *Marcha*, 333.

168: suitcase.' Ibid.

168: man.' Thomas Gregor, *Mehinaku* (Chicago and London, 1977), 237 and his 'Exposure and seclusion: a study of institutionalised isolation among the Mehinacu Indians of Brazil', *Ethnology*, 9:3 (Pittsburgh, Jul. 1970).

170: settlers. Jornal da Tarde, 14 Feb. 1970 gave a full account of early contacts with the Tapayuna. This included a report by the Kayabi Cândido Morimã who worked as a boatman for the original settlers who settled after 1955 at Porto dos Gaúchos, on the Arinos 730 kilometres (455 miles) north of Cuiabá, also Peret's botched contact and press exploitation. The decree about their reserve was signed by President Costa e Silva on 8 Oct. 1968. Peret had made a first peaceful contact and exchange of presents in January 1968, and in February 1969 observed eleven aldeias from the air. His expedition to reach their village set out in April 1969, but a telegram from him in late June reported that there was sickness in their village and hunger from lack of game (ESP, 8 Oct. 1968 and 17 Apr., 22 May, 8 and 20 Jun. 1969). The issue of 22 May 1969 reported the attack on Father Iasi – during which Father Adalberto was wounded in the leg – and his first contact. Fr. Adalberto Holanda Pereira, 'A pacificação dos Tapayúna (Beiço de Pau) até março de 1968', RA, **15/16**, 1968, 216–27.

170: acculturated'. Antônio Carlos de Souza Lima, 'O governo dos índios sob a gestão do SPI', in HIB, 168; Menezes, *Parque Indígena do Xingu*; José Maria da Gama Malcher, Preface to Mário Simões, ed., *SPI – 1953* (Rio de Janeiro, 1954), 98–106 has the letter of 27 Apr. 1952 and its Justification; Lea, *Parque Indígena*, 73–5 and the text of the Ante-Projeto de Lei, 149–59. Mercio Gomes said that the original proposal was written by Darcy Ribeiro and Eduardo Galvão and taken to President Vargas by Marshal Rondon.

171: profiteering.' Malcher, Preface to *SPI – 1953*, 51.

171: park.' Roberto Cardoso de Oliveira, 'Relatório de uma investigação sôbre terras em Mato Grosso' (in Mário Simões, ed., *SPI – 1954* (Rio de Janeiro, 1955) (173–84), 177; also in Lea, *Parque Indígena do Xingu*, 176. Pedro Agostinho reckoned that 6,427,000 ha (24,800 square miles) – 75 per cent of the Xingu region – had been awarded to land speculators: 'Informe sobre a situação atual e demográfica no alto Xingu', in Georg Grünberg, ed., *La Situación del Indígena en América del Sur* (Montevideo, 1972), 355; an article in ESP, 2 Jun. 1977; G. Ferreira Mendes, *O Domínio da União Sobre as Terras Indígenas: o Parque Nacional do Xingu* (Ministério Público Federal, Brasília, 1988), 128; Cynthia Peters, 'Saque contra a União', *Senhor*, **353**, 22 Dec. 1987.

171: firm.' Cardoso de Oliveira, 'Relatório de uma investigação', 178; Lea, *Parque Indígena do Xingu*, 178.

171: surveying.' Orlando Villas Boas, *Diário do Congresso Nacional*, 28 Sep. 1979, 1078; Menezes, *Parque Indígena do Xingu*, 170.

172: visited them.' Basso, *The Kalapalo Indians*, 2–3.

173: gained from it.' Edwin Brooks, René Fuerst, John Hemming, Francis Huxley, *Tribes of the Amazon Basin in Brazil, 1972* (London, 1973), 124. Their report was done for the Aborigines Protection Society (part of the Anti-Slavery Society). Robin Hanbury-Tenison, *Report of a Visit to the Indians of Brazil, on behalf of the Primitive Peoples' Fund/Survival International, January–March 1971* (London, 1971), 9. Bo Åkerren, Sjouke Bakker, Rolf Habersang, *Report of the ICRC Medical Mission to the Brazilian Amazon Region* (Geneva, 1970), 15.

173: serious men'. Interview with Orlando Villas Boas, *Folha de Goiás*, 15 Jan. 1961. On the row between Orlando Villas Boas and Colonel (later General) Guedes, who ran the SPI from 1957 to 1961: Guedes had praised Orlando 'for his exceptional manner, zeal and dedication to work' in the SPI's *Boletim*, **14**, Apr. 1958; but by October 1959 he advocated that the upper-Xingu tribes be 'brought to agricultural labour in order to create an economy of subsistence' – they should be turned into farm workers (*Boletim*, **33**, Oct. 1959). Guedes then said that 'the area [proposed] for the Xingu park seems to me to be too large' for the number of Indians living there, so that 'we believe that Congress will reject the creation of the park' (Guedes interview in *Seminario*, Rio de Janeiro, 7 Nov. 1959); Villas Boas attack on Guedes and his reply: *Boletim*, **47**, Jan. 1961, 6–7.

173: been there.' Interviews with Orlando Villas Boas and Colonel José Luíz Guedes, *Folha de Goiás*, 15 and 19 Jan. 1961, BSPI, **47**, 6, 7. At that time Orlando was working for the FBC.

173: imports'. Bruna Franchetto, '"O aparecimento dos caraíba". Para uma história kuikuro e alto-xinguana', in HIB (Rio de Janeiro, 2001), 352. Antônio Carlos de Souza Lima, 'O governo dos índios', 168–9.

8. Tocantins–Maranhão

176: character. Curt Nimuendajú, *The Šerente* (trans. Robert H. Lowie; Los Angeles, 1942), 8. Nimuendajú also spelled the tribe Šere'nte; David Maybury-Lewis wrote Sherente; modern Brazilian spelling, by Gama Malcher, Melatti, and others is Xerente.

176: *anything.*' Ibid., 83.

176: *wars.*' Ibid., 9.

176: *of them all.*' David Maybury-Lewis, *The Savage and the Innocent* (London, 1965), 32.

177: *conversation.*' Ibid.

177: *settlers.*' Ibid., 37.

178: *tools.*' Ibid., 66, 67.

178: *against them.*' Ibid., 149.

178: *married.*' Ibid., 97.

179: *efforts.*' Curt Nimuendajú, *The Eastern Timbira* (trans. Robert H. Lowie; Berkeley and Los Angeles, 1946), 26.

179: *had been agreed.*' BSPI, **3**, Jan. 1942, **4** and **10**, Sep. 1942, 7; A. A. Botelho de Magalhães, *Rondon – Uma Relíquia da Pátria* (Curitiba–São Paulo–Rio de Janeiro, 1942), 96–9. Magalhães wrote that the initial raid was by thirty-eight men and killed only five Indians, wounding many more; but he referred to 'scenes of similar savagery' in the police investigation, which might account for the higher number of victims. He named the ranchers who led the raid as José Santiago and João Gomes. The 240 km² (93 square mile) reserve lies between the middle Manoel Alves Pequeno and the Vermelho (a tributary of the Manuel Alves Grande) to the northeast. It is now called Terra Indígena Kraólândia and its Funai post is near the town of Itacajá.

179: *Indian groups*'. Julio Cezar Melatti, *Ritos de Uma Tribo Timbira* (Editora Ática, São Paulo, 1978) 25; Melatti, *Índios e Criadores: a situação dos Krahó na área pastoril do Tocantins* (Rio de Janeiro, 1967), 139–44.

179: *dependent on them.*' Darcy Ribeiro, *Os Índios e a Civilização* (Rio de Janeiro, 1970) 366–7; Melatti, *Índios e Criadores*, 132–3.

180: *reserve.*' Bo Åkerren et al., *Report of the ICRC Medical Mission to the Brazilian Amazon Region* (Geneva, 1970), 48.

180: *log racing, etc.*' Nimuendajú, *Eastern Timbira*, 26. Nimuendajú says that the tribe's name means 'hair of the paca rodent' and he spelled it Krahô; in the early 1940s the SPI used Crao; Melatti and others wrote Krahó. Nimuendajú in 1930 found the Krahó in two subdivisions fifty kilometres (thirty miles) apart, both groups on streams of the Manoel Alves Pequeno, an eastern tributary of the Tocantins. Melatti in 1963 counted 620 people in five villages, but eight years later in 1971 noted only 579: Melatti, *Índios e Criadores*, 54ff.; *O Messianismo Krahó* (São Paulo, 1972), 4; *Ritos de Uma Tribo Timbira*, 28. Robin Hanbury-Tenison, also in 1971, heard that their

population was 583. When this author visited the Krahó in 1972, as part of the Aborigines Protection Society team, we found 608 people living on the reserve. (The discrepancies may have been due to the Krahó's love of travel. The tribe's young men have always moved about Brazil, often successfully asking for favours from the old Imperial government and recently from the republic.) There were also some fifty Indians living alongside the reserve and mestizos living in it, and Melatti omitted these from his count. Robin Hanbury-Tenison, *Report of a Visit to the Indians of Brazil, January–March, 1971* (London, 1971), 18; Edwin Brooks, René Fuerst, John Hemming, Francis Huxley, *Tribes of the Amazon Basin in Brazil, 1972* (London, 1973), 93–4.

180: *assistance.*' Julio Cesar Melatti, *Índios do Brasil* (Brasília, 1970), 18.

180: *"cargo cult".*' Manuela Carneiro da Cunha, *Os Mortos e os Outros* (São Paulo, 1978), 5. Harald Schultz and his wife Vilma Chiara studied Krahó mythology at that time, but learned nothing about the messianic movement. Schultz, 'Lendas dos índios Krahó', RMP, **4**, 1950, 49–164; Chiara, 'Folclore Krahó', RMP, **13**, 1961–62, 33–375. Also, Harald Schultz, 'Children of the Sun and Moon', *National Geographic*, Washington, DC, 1959, 340–63.

181: *ancestors.*' Julio Cesar Melatti, 'O movimento messiânico dos Krahô. Redentor chegaria em forma de chuva', RAI, **1:4**, May–Jun. 1977, 14; Melatti, *O Messianismo Krahó*; Melatti, *Índios do Brasil*, 182.

181: *inheritance.* Carneiro da Cunha, *Os Mortos*, 6.

182: *title.*' Curt Nimuendajú, *The Apinayé*, trans. from German by Robert H. Lowie (The Catholic University of America, Anthropological Series 8, Washington, DC, 1939), 11; *Os Apinayé*, BMPEG, **12**, 1956, 9. The tribe had fallen from 4,200 in the early nineteenth century, to 1,800–2,000 in 1860, to some 400 at the turn of the century, and 150 when Heinrich Snethlage was with them in 1926. Nimuendajú found the same number in 1928, but noted a slight increase a decade later. (E. Heinrich Snethlage, 'Unter nordostbrasilianischen Indianern', *Zeitschrift für Ethnologie*, **62**, 1931, 117, 142; also Carlos Estevão de Oliveira, 'Os Apinagé do alto Tocantins', *Boletim do Museu Nacional*, **6:2**, 1930.) Darcy Ribeiro guessed 100–250 in 1957; Dale Kietzman (of the Summer Institute of Linguistics) 210 in 1967. The tribe now has the 142,000 ha (548 square mile) Área Indígena Apinayes, squashed between the Tocantins upstream of Imperatriz and the BR-230 Transamazonica highway. The population had risen to 718 by 1990.

182: influence'. Nimuendajú, *Os Apinayé*, 12.

182: government.' Ibid.

182: guitars'. Ibid.

182: disappeared.' Ibid., 14.

182: amazing.' Ibid., 15.

182: folk' Ibid., 15.

183: scattered . . .' Nimuendajú, *The Eastern Timbira*, 17. He found the Krikatí (previously spelled Caracaty, Caracatigé, etc.) at a village called Canto da Aldeia near the source of the Pindaré.

183: distinct tribe.' Ibid., 17. Some Krikatí did survive, and there is now a tiny Área Indígena Cricati 100 kilometres (62 miles) south-east of Imperatriz.

183: massacre.' Ibid., 30. These Kenkateyé were on the Ribeirão dos Caboclos headwater of the Alpercatas (which flows into the Itapicuru) south of the Canela Indian Area and the town of Barro do Corda. Snethlage, 'Unter nordostbrasilienischen Indianern', 142. The word 'canela' means shinbone or calf, and also cinnamon, in Portuguese. No one knows how the name stuck to a group of eastern Timbira – it may have related to a hill near their main village, called Serra da Canela on early maps, but it is unlikely to have referred to their calves, which were shapely from constant log-racing.

183: occupied.' Sylvio Fróes de Abreu, *Na Terra das Palmeiras* (Rio de Janeiro, 1931), 225–6; Ministério da Agricultura, Serviço de Proteção aos Índios, *Memória sobre as Causas Determinantes da Diminuição das Populações Indígenas do Brasil* (Rio de Janeiro, 1940), 33.

184: Indian name'. Nimuendajú, *The Eastern Timbira*, 33. In 1934 the Canela were forced to abandon Ponto for lack of timber for clearings. But when they moved downriver to other sites, they were struck by first measles then influenza; Nimuendajú persuaded them to reunite in another village; and they have since moved back to Ponto. Nimuendajú counted 298 Canela (Ramkókamekra and others) in Ponto village in 1933, a reduction to 265 in 1935, and increase to almost 300 by 1936. By 1960 William Crocker reported that the Canela had increased to 380 in two villages, Ponto and Porquin, sixty kilometres (nineteen miles) away (Crocker, 'Os índios Canelas de hoje', BMPEG, **2**, Jul. 1958; and 'The

Canela since Nimuendajú', *Anthropological Quarterly*, **34:2** (Washington, DC, Apr. 1961), 71). In 1970 Ponto village was moved and renamed Escalvado, while the reserve was called P I Kanela, with an area of some 90 km² (35 square miles). By 1970 Funai reckoned 431 (of whom 131 were under fifteen) in Escalvado's fifty-three huts, but Crocker counted 486 by 1972 (Brooks et al., *Tribes of the Amazon Basin in Brazil, 1972*, 91). Twenty years later in 1990 they were up to 833.

Other early anthropologists who studied the Canela were: Wilhelm Kissenberth, 'Bei den Canella-Indianern in Zentral-Maranhão', *Baesslers-Archiv*, **2** (Leipzig–Berlin, 1912), 45–54; Thomaz Pompeu Merrimé Sobrinho, *Índios Canellas* (Typ(ografia) Gadleha, Fortaleza, 1930); Sylvio Fróes Abreu who was with the Canela in 1928 and Heinrich Snethlage in 1929, cited above; and William Crocker in the 1950s.

184: cowardly, etc.' Darcy Ribeiro, *Os Índios e a Civilização*, 361–2.

184: practices.' Crocker, 'The Canela since Nimuendajú', 70–1.

185: abandoned.' William Crocker, 'The Canela messianic movement: an introduction', in ASBA, 69; Manuela M. Carneiro da Cunha, 'Logique du mythe et de l'action: le mouvement messianique Canela de 1963', *L'Homme*, **13:4**, 1973.

185: day came'. Crocker, 'The Canela messianic movement', 73.

185: liar.' Ibid., 70.

185: vagrancy.' Carlos Moreira Neto, 'Constante histórica do "indigenato" no Brasil', in ASBA, 183. Carneiro da Cunha, 'Logique du mythe'; Michael F. Brown, 'Beyond resistance. Comparative study of Utopian renewal in Amazonia', in Anna Curtenius Roosevelt, ed., *Amazonian Indians from Prehistory to the Present* (Tucson, 1994) (287–311), 294–6.

186: people.' Francis Huxley, *Affable Savages* (New York, 1957), 29.

186: regime'. Mércio Gomes, 'Porque índios brigam com posseiros: o caso dos índios Guajajara', in Dalmo de Abreu Dallari, Manuela Carneiro da Cunha, and Lux Vidal, eds., *A Questão da Terra Indígena* (Cadernos da Comissão Pró-Índio, **2**, São Paulo, 1981), 54–5.

187: the whites.' Ibid. Catholic missionaries later tried to blame a trader called Raimundo Ferreira de Melo for inciting the Guajajara to commit the massacre, because he resented the way in which the Capuchins were preventing him from exploiting Indians – although some of Ferreira de Melo's own workers were also killed: *Boletim do CIMI*, **8:56**, May–Jun. 1979, 8. Nimuendajú, *The Eastern Timbira*, 33; Sylvio Fróes Abreu, *Na Terra das Palmeiras*, 146–7, 219; Charles Wagley and Eduardo Galvão, *Os Índios Tenetehara* (Rio de Janeiro, 1961), 27; Egon Schaden, *Aculturação Indígena* (São Paulo, 1969), 149; John Hemming, *Amazon Frontier* (London, 1995), 251; Mércio Gomes, *O Índio na História – o povo Tenetehara em busca da liberdade* (Petrópolis, 2002).

The Franciscan house at Alto Alegre was reopened in 1959, to revive Indian catechism and remember the martyrs of 1901. Mosaic portraits of thirteen of these were put in the tympanum over the door of the church in Barra do Corda: four friars, one lay man, seven nuns, and one lay woman – but no Indians. The Guajajara were initially uneasy, fearing revenge by the friars. The mission also attracted settler families from surrounding areas, who drove away many Indians and whose farming invaded indigenous land.

187: survival.' Charles Wagley, 'Cultural influences on population: a comparison of two Tupí tribes', RMP, **5**, 1951, 95–104, and in Daniel Gross, ed., *Peoples and Cultures of Native South America* (New York, 1973), 147; Wagley and Eduardo Galvão, 'The Tenetehara', HSAI, **3** (137–48), 137–8 and *The Tenetehara Indians of Brazil. A Culture in Brazil* (New York, 1949); Schaden, *Aculturação Indígena*, 15–17; Mércio Gomes, 'Porque índios brigam', 53. In 1971, the Guajajara village of Sardinha had some 100 inhabitants, Colônia had 250, and Posto Indígena São Pedro had 150. Wagley argued that 'after more than three hundred years of contact with Luso-Brazilians the Tenetehara in 1945 still numbered some two thousand people – not much less, if at all, than the aboriginal population.' Mércio Gomes disagreed. He reckoned that these people had originally numbered 7,000. With his original population, the three main groups declined during the first half of the twentieth century, as follows: by two-thirds from some 1,500 to 500 near Barra do Corda on the Mearim; in the same numbers and ratio towards the Grajaú; and with a drop from 2,000 to 1,000 in the Pindaré valley.

188: Tenetehara.' Wagley, 'Cultural Influences', RMP 101 and Gross, ed., 153. There was a 'serious uprising' in 1942 at Posto Tenente Manuel Rabelo (now Área Indígena Bacurizinho) near Grajaú, when a Guajajara called Gregório Carvalho

tried to break the SPI's control of tools and trading activities. *Boletim* (Serviço de Proteção aos Índios), 8, Jul. 1942, 5, and **12**, Nov. 1942, 16.

188: refuge.' Martine Droulers and Patrick Maury, 'Colonisation de l'Amazonie Maranhense', *Travaux et Mémoires de l'Institut des Hautes Études de l'Amérique Latine*, **34** (Paris, 1981), 136.

188: protected.' Gomes, 'Porque índios brigam', 53. The protected area near Barra do Corda now contains Indian posts called Canabrava and Guajajara. To the north-west, in headwaters of the Pindaré, is the large *área indígena* called Araribóia. Both it and the Canabrava–Guajajara reserve suffered massive invasions by squatters in the mid-1970s, partly because many small farmers had been displaced by large and well-financed ranching companies.

189: produce.' Report by Regional Inspector of SPI in Pará, in Anon., *Exposição sobre o Serviço de Proteção aos Índios e Localização dos Trabalhadores Nacionais* (Imprensa Nacional, Rio de Janeiro, 1913), 17; Expedito Arnaud, 'O direito indígena e a ocupação territorial: o caso dos índios Tembé do Alto Guamá (Pará)', RMP, **28**, 1981/82, 224. Also Mércio P. Gomes, *The ethnic survival of the Tenetehara Indians of Maranhão, Brazil* (Doctoral dissertation, University of Florida, 1977), 198–200.

189: helmsmen.' Ribeiro, *Os Índios e a Civilização*, 347–8.

189: fifteen men.' Ibid., 348. Early estimates of Tembé population were: 6,000 by Gustavo Dodt in 1873 (*Descripção dos Rios Parnahyba e Gurupy* (Maranhão, 1873), republished by Brasiliana, Companhia Editora Nacional, São Paulo, 1939, 172); and 1,091 in 1920 by H. Jorge Hurley ('Chorographia do Pará e Maranhão, Rio Gurupy', *Revista do Instituto Histórico e Geographico do Pará*, **7**, Belém, 1932) (3–44), 35. Darcy Ribeiro wrote that by the 1960s there were only 120 Tembé and 10 Timbira on the Gurupi river. Where there had been twenty-six villages in 1910, fourteen in 1920, and eleven in 1930, there were only three by Ribeiro's day. Ribeiro: *Os Índios e a Civilização*, 308. William Balée, *The Persistence of Ka'apor Culture* (Doctoral dissertation, Columbia University, New York, 1984), 61, and *Footprints in the Forest* (New York, 1994), 45.

190: ranchers.' Arnaud, 'O direito', 225. Now known as Alto Rio Guamá, this reserve is not far from the large city of Belém and is eighty kilometres (fifty miles) from the busy Belém–Brasília highway, so it is subject to invasions by thousands of rural families and claims to its territory by investors, farms, and colonization promoters.

190: extinguished.' Nello Ruffaldi, Virginia Valadão, and Noêmia Salles, 'Tembé', in Carlos A. Ricardo et al., eds., *Povos Indígenas no Brasil, 8, Sudeste do Pará (Tocantins)* (São Paulo, 1985) (176–209), 183. The Tembé Tenetehara had migrated westwards to the Gurupi and into Pará in the mid-nineteenth century, leaving the Guajajara Tenetehara behind in Maranhão. Early visitors to the Tembé included Gustavo Dodt, who was with them in 1872 and whose *Descripção dos Rios Parnahyba e Gurupy* was translated from German and published in the Brasiliana series in 1939, the ubiquitous Curt Nimuendajú (then called Unkel) who did some of his earliest work in 1913 on Tembé language and mythology, published in the *Zeitschrift für Ethnologie*, **46** and **47**, Berlin 1914 and 1915, and Jorge Hurley, *Nos Sertões do Gurupy* (Officinas Graphicas do Instituto Lauro Sodré, Belém do Pará, 1928).

190: deforested.' Ruffaldi et al., 'Tembé', 184. On the concession of territory to the Companhia Agropecuária do Pará (a probable subsidiary of the American Swift group), a message by General Oscar Bandeira de Melo, President of Funai, of 28 Nov. 1970 is reproduced in Ruffaldi, 199; the resulting legislation is in *Fundação Nacional do Índio. Documentos da 2a. Delegacia Regional* (Belém, 1970–82) in Arnaud, 'O direito', 226; and a protest by leading champions of the Indians appeared as 'Problemas indígenas brasileiros', *Ciência e Cultura*, **24:11** (São Paulo, 1972), 1015–23. Like the Guajajara the Tembé speak Tenetehara, which is a Tupi-related language. There are other Tupi-speaking remnants near the lower Tocantins.

The **Akuáwa Asuriní** live on the Trocará tributary of the lower Tocantins, downriver from the big Tucuruí dam. These Asuriní had clashed with Brazil-nut collectors and railway workers of the Tocantins Railway (which used to link Tucuruí (formerly Alcobaça) with Jacundá before the rapids were drowned by the reservoir behind the dam) in the 1930s and 1940s, with killings on both sides and attempted slaughters by armed posses. These Asuriní were contacted in 1953 by the noted SPI sertanista Telésforo Martins Fontes and then numbered 190. They were rapidly reduced, by fifty deaths from dysentery and influenza and by Chief Kuatinema taking part of the group westwards into the forests towards the Xingu. His departure was partly provoked by bad

SPI agents, one of whom persuaded Indians to work for him in collecting and prostitution. Roque Laraia and Roberto da Matta commented sombrely: 'Contact was disastrous for the Akuáwa Asuriní. Today they are reduced to thirty-four Indians living on the post, ten dispersed among civilizados, and fourteen Indians who are in the forest' (*Índios e Castanheiros* (São Paulo, 1967), 35; Darcy Ribeiro, *Os Índios e a Civilização*, 189). By 1962 the group was reduced to 35 individuals, but it has since climbed to some 150 by the mid-1980s, and 233 by the mid-1990s, thanks to the protection of a 22,000 ha (54,000 acre) reserve (P I Trocará), a high birth rate, and medical assistance. Expedito Arnaud, 'Breve informação sobre os índios Asuriní e Parakanân: rio Tocantins, Pará', BMPEG, **11**, Jul. 1961, and 'Mudanças entre grupos indígenas Tupí da região do Tocantins-Xingu (Bacia Amazônica)', BMPEG, **84**, Apr. 1983, also in IEN 328–38; Laraia and Matta, *Índios e Castanheiros*; Roque de Barros Laraia, 'Akuáwa-Asuriní e Suruí: análise de dois grupos Tupí', *Revista do Instituto de Estudos Brasileiros*, **12**, 1972, 7–30; a series of reports on the Asuriní language to the Summer Institute of Linguistics, Brasília, by Carl Harrison in 1963 and 1980 and by Velda Nicholson in 1975–78; typed reports by Lúcia de Andrade to Funai in 1982 and 1984 and her 'Asuriní do Tocantins' in Ricardo, ed., *Povos*, 8, 1–17.

Some 120 kilometres (75 miles) east of A I Trocará (and 300 kilometres (190 miles) due south of the city of Belém) is the reserve of the **Amanayé**, a small tribe that had probably split from the Tembé. They were known to travellers such as Dodt in the 1870s, when they numbered 600; they killed a missionary, Friar Candido de Heremence, in 1873 and had to flee from reprisals; some lived under a settler director, others fought more pacified Tembé and Turiwara. In 1910 the SPI Inspector Luiz Horta Barboza met an Amanayé group led by a mulatto woman called Damásia, and he reckoned that the whole tribe numbered 300 in four villages; Nimuendajú was with them in 1914 and again in 1943; the American Algot Lange studied them in 1913; and on 21 March 1945 the SPI got a reserve of some 31,000 ha (120 square miles) decreed for them; the SPI sertanista João Carvalho (who did good work with the Kaapor on the Gurupi) was with the Amanayé in the 1950s. By 1976, Arnaud said that these Indians were reduced to ten people on the Ararandeua river, with more on the upper Capim.

They have virtually merged with the local caboclo population. Curt Nimuendajú and Alfred Métraux, 'The Amanayé', HSAI, **3**, *The Tropical Forest Tribes* (Washington, DC, 1948), 199–202; Algot Lange, *The Lower Amazon* (G. P. Putnam's Sons, New York and London, 1914); Expedito Arnaud and Eduardo Galvão, 'Notícia sobre os índios Anambé (Rio Caiari, Pará)', BMPEG, **42**, Sep. 1969, 7; L. P. Paixão and M. A. Moreira, *Relatório Sobre a Tribo Amanayé* (Brasília, 1975); 'Amanayé' in Ricardo, ed., *Povos*, 8, 162–7.

North of the Amanayé, midway between them and Belém, on the upper Moju, is the indigenous area of the **Anambé** (also known as A I Cairari). Once settled on the main Tocantins river, the Anambé moved east to the Moju and Cairari in the 1930s. Expedito Arnaud, then working for the SPI, visited them in 1948. Since that time, their population has suffered, from measles epidemics and from mixing with settlers, so that there are now fewer than sixty, of whom half live outside their reserve. Arnaud and Galvão, 'Notícia sobre os índios Anambé'; Napoleão Figueiredo, 'Os Anambé', in Museu Paraense Emílio Goeldi, *Cultura Indígena* exhibition catalogue, Belém, 1983; Nello Ruffaldi, 'Anambé', in Ricardo, *Povos*, 8, 150–61.

Some hundred kilometres (sixty miles) southeast of Marabá is the small Sororó Indian area, the reserve of the **Suruí do Pará**. (They are known as the Pará Suruí to distinguish them from the better-known Suruí in Rondônia; they refer to themselves as Aikewara (meaning 'we' or 'people'); and the nearby Kayapó refer to them as Mudjetire.) Known to the Dominican missionaries of the diocese of Conceição do Araguaia since the 1920s, these Suruí suffered from clashes with castanheiro Brazil-nut collectors in the ensuing decades: whenever they attempted a peaceful approximation with the strangers entering their lands, they were greeted by gunfire.

Peaceful contact was made in 1951 by Friar Gil Gomes Leitão, using the usual techniques based on presents. Friar Gil's group walked into a village and caught its inhabitants by surprise. At first hostile, the Suruí seemed to recognize Friar Gil's habit and accepted his cries that he was a friend. A chief, 'a handsome Indian, tall, broad-shouldered, young, smiling and sure of himself', was shown how matches worked and accepted a box. The tribe was pleased to have friendly contact with the intruders. For a time, there were intermittent meetings with these Suruí. Then, in

the 1960s, a local man called João Correia gained influence over the group and persuaded them to hunt animal skins for him to sell. Correia sought to change the Suruí into caboclos. Roque Laraia said that 'he even brought twenty-five skin-hunters to the Suruís' lands, who prostituted their women, devastated their plantations, and accelerated the spread of influenza and other diseases, resulting in a lethal epidemic that reduced the group [from over a hundred] to forty individuals.' Friar Gil helped to expel these bad influences and cared for the tribe until 1973.

These Suruí now all speak Portuguese, but they retain their Tupi language and many tribal customs, and they are determined in opposing aggressions by ranchers or squatters who try to invade their remaining lands. The Indian agency Funai interdicted the tribe's land in 1968, demarcated it as the 26,257 ha (101 square mile) Sororó reserve in 1979 and got it decreed in 1983. The Suruí population recovered to over 120 in the 1980s and 185 by the mid-1990s. Friar Anselmo Vilar de Carvalho, 'Vida e costumes dos Mudjetire' and later articles, *Mensageiro do Santo Rosário* (Conceição do Araguaia) Jul., Aug., and Sep. 1959; Roque de Barros Laraia, 'Arranjos poliândricos na sociedade Suruí', RMP, **14**, 1963, 71–5, 'A fricção interétnica no médio Tocantins', *América Latina*, **8:2** (Rio de Janeiro, Apr.–Jun. 1965), 'O homem marginal numa sociedade primitiva', *Revista do Instituto de Ciências Social*, **4:1** (Rio de Janeiro, 1967), 'Akuáwa-Asurini e Suruí: análise de dois grupos Tupi', *Revista do Instituto de Estudos Brasileiros da USP*, **12** (São Paulo, 1972), 7–30; Laraia and Matta, *Índios e Castanheiros*, 29–30; Iara Ferraz, *Plano Integrado de Desenvolvimento Comunitário Gavião-Suruí* (Funai, Brasília, 1975); Renato da Silva Queiroz, 'O depoimento de Tibakou: as experiências da vida de um índio Suruí', *Revista do Instituto de Estudos Brasileiros*, **18** (São Paulo, 1976), 118–28, 'Por falar em Suruí . . .', RA, **23**, 1980, 81–97; Arnaud, 'Mudanças entre os grupos indígenas', also in IEN, 348–52; Renato Queiroz and Iara Ferraz, 'Suruí', in Ricardo, ed., *Povos*, 8, 100–21.

191: barbarities'. Nimuendajú, *The Eastern Timbira*, 20.

192: pin-cushion' Arlindo Silva, 'Índios em pé de guerra', *O Cruzeiro*, Rio de Janeiro, 3 Mar. 1951; *Estado do Pará*, Belém, 29 Jan. 1948. Gama Malcher spent seven years with the Gavião at Montanha post on the lower Tocantins, after its foundation in 1941 (ESP, 24 Jul. 1969). Expedito

Arnaud, 'Os Gaviões de oeste – pacificação e integração', *Publicações Avulsas, Museu Paraense Emílio Goeldi*, **28**, Belém, 1975, 38–9; and 'O comportamento dos índios Gaviões de Oeste face à sociedade nacional', BMPEG, **85**, 1984, also in Arnaud, IEN, 372–3; Iara Ferraz, *Os Parkatêjê das Matas do Tocantins: a epopéia de um líder Timbira* (Universidade de São Paulo, São Paulo, 1983), 31–5; and 'Gavião', in Ricardo, ed., *Povos*, **8**, 58. (Gaviões is the plural of Gavião in Portuguese spelling.)

192: be seen.' Arnaud, 'O comportamento dos índios Gaviões', 10; 'Os Gaviões de oeste', 33.

192: starving.' Ferraz, *Os Parkatêjê*, 35.

193: die!"' Ibid., 40; 'Gavião', 59.

193: forest.' Arnaud, 'O comportamento dos índios Gaviões', 13.

194: Brazilians.' Roberto da Matta, 'Notas sôbre o contato e a extinção dos índios Gaviões do médio Rio Tocantins', RMP, **14**, 1963, 194–5 and 196. Laraia and Matta, *Índios e Castanheiros*, 123.

195: region.' Carlos Moreira, 'Relatório sobre a situação atual dos índios Kayapó', RA, **7:1–2**, 1959, 61.

195: lived there.' Ferraz, 'Gavião', 67.

195: dogs."' Ferraz, *Os Parkatêjê*, 50; 'Gavião', 63. Mãe Maria was ceded to the Gavião by State Decree 4,503 of 28 Dec. 1943, on the initiative of the then regional inspector of the SPI, José Maria da Gama Malcher – who later became one of the Service's best directors. The SPI later obtained additional land to add to the reserve. (Arnaud, 'O comportamento dos índios Gaviões', 19–20.) The road from Marabá to the Belém–Brasília highway was started in 1964 as the PA-70 and is now PA-332. President Costa e Silva in October 1968 signed Decree 65,515 awarding the Gavião land to the south-east of this spur, so that it ran immediately alongside the Indians' village of Trinta.

196: contact.' Antonio Cotrim Soares, *Relatório sobre o contato com os índios Gavião, na região limítrofe do Pará e Maranhão* (ms., Belém, 28 Nov. 1968) in Iara, *Os Parkatêjê*, 64. Numerically, the once powerful Gavião had been reduced to tiny populations at the time of contact. The two groups of Parketeyê in 1962 numbered only 42 and were on the verge of extinction. There were 58 Kuikatêyê or 'Maranhão Gavião' at their contact in 1968; four years later Cotrim said that these were reduced by a third to 38 (*Jornal do Brasil*, 25 May 1972). By 1972 the two parts of

the tribe totalled only 89. But they then started to grow: a decade later there were 159 Gavião, distributed in 35 households and with 82 of them aged under fifteen. By 1995 they had doubled again from a high birth rate and inward migration, to 333 at Mãe Maria. This reserve covers 352,000 ha (1,360 square miles), but it is traversed by a road, railway, and power line.

196: settlers.' ESP, 30 May 1972, in Ferraz, 'Gavião', 64. The land was sold to a company called Companhia Industrial de Desenvolvimento da Amazônia (CIDA) and the proceeds were spent on the cost of moving the Indians to Mãe Maria. The 'Maranhão' Gavião were initially located at a swampy place called Maguari in the interior of Mãe Maria. In 1970 they were moved to a village known as Ladeira Vermelha, a kilometre from the new road.

197: power'. ESP, 15 Aug. 1969. The tense situation was reported in ESP 24, 27, and 30 Jul. and 2, 9, and 15 Aug. 1969, as well as in the *Jornal da Tarde* and other media.

197: laziness.' Antonio Cotrim Soares, *Veja*, 31 May 1972. Cotrim preferred to call the Gavião by their own name, Pacategé (which Iara Ferraz later spelled Parkatêjê), meaning 'Down-river people' to distinguish them from Gavião living further up the Tocantins, to the south-east in Maranhão.

198: Indians'. *Jornal do Brasil*, 3 Dec. 1976, in Alcida R. Ramos, 'Development, integration and the ethnic integrity of Brazilian Indians', in Françoise Barbira-Scazzocchio, ed., *Land, People and Planning in Contemporary Amazonia* (Cambridge University Press, Cambridge, 1980, 222–9), 225.

198: identity'. Ibid., 226. The sacking of Iara Ferraz was reported in *Jornal de Brasília*, 27 Jan. 1977, and the expulsion of the Funai agent in ESP, 3 Aug. 1977. Richard Bourne described the problems and successes of the Gavião when he visited them in 1976, *Assault on the Amazon* (London, 1978), 222–3. Also, Marcus Colchester, 'Amerindian development: the search for a viable means of surplus production in Amazonia', SIR, **7:3–4(41/4)**, Autumn/Winter 1982 (5–15), 9.

199: road.' Raimundo Lopes, *O torrão maranhense* (Jornal do Commércio, Rio de Janeiro, 1916), 184–5, 190, quoted in Balée, *Footprints*, 39. The name Urubu for the Kaapor tribe may have come from its battle cry *'Uruhu ne u!'* (May vultures eat you!). Balée always writes the tribe's name Ka'apor, to emphasize a glottal stop between the two As; Darcy Ribeiro used an accent, Kaápor. Their version of Tupi is incomprehensible to nearby Tupi speakers – the Tembé and Guajajara who speak Tenetehar Tupi and the Awá-Guajá; it is closest to that of the Wayampi (Wayãpi) living 1,000 kilometres (620 miles) to the north on the far side of the Amazon river. Both Kaapor and Wayampi probably migrated away from a homeland between the lower Xingu and Tocantins.

199: eating.' Anon., 'Cruzada Gonçalves Dias: os índios do Gurupy', *Pacotilha da Manhã* (Rio de Janeiro), 8 Jan. 1912, and 'Os índios do Gurupy', *Correio da Tarde* (Rio de Janeiro), 12 Jan. 1912, in Balée, *Footprints*, 39–40.

199: house.' Report by the SPI agent of Posto Indígena Gonçalves Dias, 1918, in Ribeiro, *Os Índios*, 178–9.

200: slaves. The rumour that Jorge Cochrane Amir, a blue-eyed European, was inciting the Kaapor to help a Swedish mining operator called Guilherme Linde seems to have come from the latter's 'fecund imagination'. Anon., 'A pacificação dos índios Urubús', *O Paiz* (Rio de Janeiro), 17 Dec. 1929; Hurley, *Nos Sertões do Gurupy*, 34 and 'Chorographia . . . Rio Gurupy', 32; Balée, *Footprints*, 40–1.

200: Kaapor.' Ruffaldi et al., 'Tembé', 183.

200: tobacco.' Darcy Ribeiro, *Diários Índios: os Urubus-Kaapor* (São Paulo, 1996), 27. This book is the extensive field notes and letters to his anthropologist wife Berta by the twenty-seven-year-old Darcy from his expeditions of 1950 and 1951. Darcy Ribeiro in 1949 met an Englishman called David Blake, a former Protestant missionary who had visited Kaapor villages in 1927 and 1928, then in 1931 with Miguel Silva, in 1932 with his superior Horace Banner (who later worked among the Kayapó), and in 1938 with another missionary, Leslie Goodman, when in nine villages they saw only 169 people. Blake returned to the Gurupi and married an older Tembé woman, which angered his congregation and finished his missionary career. Blake 'went native', trying to gain greater understanding of Indians by living with them; but he was considered crazy and rejected by his fellow missionaries and his family back in England (ibid., 71–5).

200: received'. Report of P I Pedro Dantas for 1928, in Ribeiro, *Os Índios e a Civilização*, 181–2. The SPI had a series of posts in the region. In 1911 a post called **Felipe Camarão** was founded at the junction of the Jararaca and Gurupi. This was active only until 1915; but some hundred

Tembé were living there in the 1940s, and it was abolished only in 1950. In 1927 **Posto Pedro Dantas** was created on Canindé-Assú island where the Kaapor used to cross the Gurupi; it was later renamed **P I Canindé** and still exists. **Posto General Rondon** was also opened in 1928 on the Maracassumé river, but it closed in 1940.

201: murmur.' Report of P I Dantas for 1930, in ibid., 183; Ribeiro, 'Convívio e contaminação', *Sociologia*, **18:1**, 4; Ribeiro, *Diários Índios*, 29–31, 121–2, 252–3. Ribeiro in 1950 wrote that Oropó (as he called him) shot dead two Indians as well as Araújo, and then established a maloca deep in the forest to escape all contact with any whites or Indians who had had contact with them. No one would take Darcy Ribeiro to meet this feared warrior.

201: non-Indians.' Balée, *Footprints*, 41.

202: worn away. Ibid., 42.

202: value.' Ibid.

202: affection'. BSPI, **25**, Dec. 1943, 432. Miguel Silva started work with Pedro Dantas in 1910 and was active with the Kaapor until his retirement in 1948. He died in extreme poverty in a fishing village a few months later.

203: suckled. Ribeiro, *Os Índios e a Civilização*, 277 and 'Atividades científicas da secção de estudos do Serviço de Proteção aos Índios', *Sociologia*, **8:4**, 1951, 375. Estimates of Kaapor population at the time of contact varied widely. John Duval Rice, apparently using SPI material, reckoned that there were 5,000 (F. J. D. Rice, 'A pacificação e identificação das afinidades lingüísticas da tribu Urubú dos Estados do Pará e Maranhão, 1928–1929', JSAP, **22**, 1930, 312). Seven years later, the engineer Pedro de Moura gave roughly 3,000 (Moura, 'O Rio Gurupy', *Boletim do Serviço Geológico e Mineralógico*, **78** (Rio de Janeiro, 1936), 19). Darcy Ribeiro implied 2,000 at the time of contact. William Balée said simply that, whatever the size of their population, the Kaapor were clearly the largest tribe in the Gurupi basin at that time. Carvalho, who had reckoned only 750 in 1949, estimated the tribe's population at 912 in 1954 – possibly because he was aware of more villages than Ribeiro. By 1962 numbers were down by 10 per cent to 822; and by 1975 there was a drop of a further 41 per cent to 488. On population decline, Balée quoted from Carvalho's reports of 1954 and 1962 and from A. C. Mariz, *Relatório sobre os trabalhos na área dos índios Kaapor e Guajá* (1975) in the archive of Funai, Brasília.

203: hurting him. Ribeiro, *Diários Índios*, 108.

203: medicine'. João Carvalho, *Aviso do P.I.A. Pedro Dantas,* Jan.–Dec. 1954, in Relatórios das Inspetorias: Inspetoria Regional 2 (Pará), Museu do Índio, Rio de Janeiro, quoted in Balée, *Footprints,* 44.

204: goats.' Huxley, *Affable Savages,* 36–7. Huxley visited the Urubu–Kaapor with Darcy Ribeiro in 1951 and then returned for six months' fieldwork with them in 1953. His book is a classic of anthropological literature, telling the tribe's customs and myths through conversations and anecdotes of a delightful cast of characters.

205: ornaments.' Ribeiro, *Diários Índios,* 132. Darcy's wife Berta and he wrote a beautiful book on Kaapor feather art: *Arte Plumária dos Índios Kaapor* (Gráfica Seikel, Rio de Janeiro, 1957). Darcy felt guilty at 'plundering' the Kaapor of their ornaments, in exchange for trade goods, knowing that they would 'take years to remake the collection and would have to shoot down thousands of different birds' (ibid., 259). He consoled himself that this 'jewellery' would become prized exhibits in many museums.

205: recovery.' William Balée and Anne Gély, 'Managed forest succession in Amazonia: the Ka'apor case', in D. A. Posey and W. Balée, eds., *Resource Management in Amazonia: Indigenous and Folk Strategies* (New York, 1989) (129–57), 154. William Balée also showed how Indians manipulate apparently pristine forest to suit their needs, in his introduction to this book with Darrell Posey ('The culture of Amazonian forests', pages 1–21);

in 'Indigenous adaptation to Amazonian palm forests' (*Principes,* **32:2**, 1988, 47–54), 'People of the fallow' (in Kent H. Redford and Christine J. Padoch, eds., *Conservation of Neotropical Forests* (Columbia University Press, New York, 1992)) and 'Indigenous transformation of Amazonian forests' (*L'Homme,* **32:2–4**, 1993). Laura Rival has shown similar manipulation by the Waorani in Ecuador ('Domestication as a historical and symbolic process: wild gardens and cultivated forests in the Ecuadorian Amazon' in William Balée, ed., *Advances in Historical Ecology* (Columbia University Press, New York, 1998, 232–150); Brian Ferguson also made such observations among the Yanomami in Venezuela ('Whatever happened to the stone age? Steel tools and Yanomami historical ecology', in the same book edited by Balée, 287–312); and Darrell Posey has published many papers that show the Kayapó adjusting their environment.

206: whites."' Interview with Colonel Vicente de Paula Vasconcellos (Director of the SPI), *Correio da Manhã* (Rio de Janeiro), 22 Jul. 1942; Adalberto Mário Ribeiro, 'O Serviço de Proteção aos Índios', *Revista do Serviço Público,* ano 6, **3:3**, Sep. 1943, 66–7; Ribeiro, *Os Índios e a Civilização,* 385; Ribeiro, 'Uirá vai ao encontro de Maíra', *Anhembi* (São Paulo), **26:76**, Mar. 1957 and in *Carta* (Gabinete do Senador Darcy Ribeiro, Brasília) **4:9**, 1993, 255–67.

206: vigorous'. Ribeiro, *Os Índios e a Civilização,* 385; Ribeiro, 'Uirá vai ao encontro'.

9. The Rise and Fall of the Indian Protection Service

208: its Indians. Major Alípio Bandeira, 'Em defesa do índio' (2 Feb. 1923) in Luiz Bueno Horta Barboza, *Pelo Índio e Pela sua Protecção Official* (Rio de Janeiro, 1923), 65–71. Bandeira was the SPI Inspector for Amazonas, and Horta Barboza was its Director Interino. This book listed all the Service's posts and activities, which included the attractions of the Kaingang, Parintintin, Kayabi on the Arinos, Cabixi on the Sararé (a tributary of the Guaporé in western Mato Grosso), and others (26ff.). Alípio Bandeira continued his campaign in the powerful book *A Cruz Indígena* (Porto Alegre, 1926). On the Decree 5,484 of 27 Jul. 1928, see L. Humberto de Oliveira, *Coletânea de Leis, Atos e Memorias Referentes ao Indígena Brasileiro* (Impr. Nacional, Rio de

Janeiro, 1947), 158; José Mauro Gagliardi, *O Indígena e a República* (São Paulo, 1989), 273; and Antônio Carlos de Souza Lima, 'O governo dos índios sob a gestão do SPI', HIB, 159 and *Um Grande Cerco de Paz* (Petrópolis, 1995), 124.

208: disappearance.' Darcy Ribeiro, *Os Índios e a Civilização* (Rio de Janeiro, 1970), 209.

209: challenge.' Ibid., 211.

209: Service.' Message by Dr José Maria de Paula, Director of the SPI, 19 Apr. 1945, in *19 de Abril, o Dia do Índio* (Conselho Nacional de Proteção aos Índios, publication **100**, Rio de Janeiro, 1946), 89.

209: following year!' Colonel Vasconcellos, in Adalberto Mário Ribeiro, 'O Serviço de Proteção aos Índios em 1943', *Revista do Serviço Público,* ano 6, **3:3**, Rio de Janeiro, Sep. 1943, 69. This was a period of low inflation in Brazil, so that the fluctuations were in real terms.

209: life'. Esther de Viveiros, *Rondon Conta sua Vida* (Rio de Janeiro, 1958), 492. Neill Macaulay, *The Prestes Column; Revolution in Brazil* (New Viewpoints, New York, 1974).

210: benevolence.' Viveiros, *Rondon Conta*, 326.

210: promising.' Ribeiro, 'O Serviço', 69, quoting Colonel Vasconcellos discussing SPI funding in 1943.

210: funds'. BSPI, **28**, Mar. 1944, 64.

210: entrusted to it.' BSPI, **17**, Apr. 1943, 104.

210: Indian posts' Speech by General Rondon, in *19 de Abril*, 52.

211: crisis.' BSPI, **28**, Mar. 1944, 64.

211: their Indians.' J. M. de Paula, *19 de Abril*, 90.

211: frontiers.' Rondon to the Minister of War, quoted in Colonel Vicente de Paula Teixeira da Fonseca Vasconcellos, *Relatório do coronel chefe do SPI . . . ao Ministro da Agricultura e aos membros do CNPI*, Rio de Janeiro, 30 Dec. 1939, in Souza Lima, 'O governo', 165.

211: to theirs.' Legislation transferring the SPI, 1934, in Luiz Beltrão, O *Índio, um Mito Brasileiro* (Petrópolis, 1977), 23; Suzanne Williams, 'Land rights and the manipulation of identity: official Indian policy in Brazil', *Journal of Latin American Studies*, London, **15:1**, 1983, 144.

211: ceremonies.' BSPI, **3**, Jan. 1942, 2.

211: character.' Rondon report to the Minister of War, in Vasconcellos, *Relatório*, in Souza Lima, 'O governo', 165.

212: society'. Regulamento of 6 Apr. 1936, Art. 2, in Oliveira, *Coletânea de Leis*, 149. Souza Lima, 'O governo', 167.

212: education.' Dr José Maria de Paula, head of the SPI's First Section, describing a visit to Posto Duque de Caxias, BSPI, **1**, Nov. 1941, 5.

212: conscience.' Rondon speech in Itamaratí Palace, Rio de Janeiro, 3 Aug. 1938, in Amilcar A. Botelho de Magalhães, *Rondon – Uma Relíquia da Pátria* (Curitiba–São Paulo–Rio de Janeiro, 1942), 58.

213: farming.' Decree-Law 1,736 of 3 Nov. 1939 (creating the Conselho Nacional de Proteção aos Índios (CNPI)), in Oliveira, *Coletânea de Leis*, 172; Souza Lima, 'O governo', 167, citing Carlos Augusto da Rocha Freire, *Indigenismo e Antropologia: o Conselho Nacional de Proteção aos Índios na gestão Rondon (1939–1955)* (Master's dissertation,

Museu Nacional, Rio de Janeiro, 1990); Gagliardi, O *Indígena*, 277. Rondon was President of the new Council and it contained some of his old team of Indian experts: Professor Edgard Roquette-Pinto (author of an admirable book on the anthropology of Rondon's discoveries, *Rondônia*); General Manoel Rabelo (one of the heroes of the SPI's pacification of the Kaingang in the interior of São Paulo), Colonel Vicente de Paula Vasconcellos (who had explored some headwaters of the Juruena in 1915 and of the Xingu in 1924, and who was Director of the SPI from 1939 to 1944), Professor Boaventura Ribeiro da Cunha, Dr Alfeu Domingues, and the formidable Professor Heloisa Alberto Torres of the Museu Nacional.

213: intelligence'. Rondon's speech of 27 Dec. 1939, reported in the *Jornal do Comércio* of 28 Jan. 1940. John Collier, *Los Índios de las Américas* (Fondo de Cultura Economica, Mexico, 1960); Mércio Gomes, *The Indians and Brazil* (Gainesville, Fla., 2000), 121. Some anthropologists influenced the early SPI, such as Curt Nimuendajú, Edgard Roquette-Pinto, Herbert Baldus, and Heloísa Alberto Torres, and foreigners such as Charles Wagley, Buell Quain, Claude Lévi-Strauss, and Alfred Métraux. But it continued to regard all tribal societies as matriarchal, because this was the Positivist view of groups at an early stage of development.

214: take long.' Rondon's speech *Rumo ao Oeste*, 17 Sep. 1940, reproduced in full in O *Radical*, 4 Oct. 1940. Botelho de Magalhães, *Rondon – Uma Relíquia*, 79–80.

214: human beings'. Herbert Baldus, 'A necessidade do trabalho indianista no Brasil', *Revista do Arquivo Municipal*, **57** (São Paulo, May 1939), 140; Egon Schaden, 'O problema indígena', *Revista de História*, **20** (São Paulo, 1960), 455; Gagliardi, O *Indígena*, 180. The college that initiated Brazilian ethnographic studies was the Escola Livre de Sociologia e Política.

214: in the other. In 1939 the young American anthropologist Charles Wagley got a lift on a boat on the Araguaia making preparations for President Vargas's hunting and fishing trip. The presidential safari was postponed until 1940 because of the outbreak of war. The photograph of Vargas with the Karajá baby was widely published in the Brazilian press. It can be seen in Adalberto Ribeiro, 'O Serviço', 79.

214: chauvinism.' Seth Garfield, '"The roots of a plant that today is Brazil": Indians and the nation-state under the Brazilian Estado Novo',

Journal of Latin American Studies, **29**, 1997, 753, 756.

215: people'. General Cândido Rondon, *Rumo ao Oeste* (a speech delivered on 3 September 1940 to the Associação Brasileira da Educação, published in O *Radical*, Rio de Janeiro, 4 Oct. 1940), 21–2, quoted in ibid., 751–2.

215: charity'. Ministério da Agricultura, Serviço de Proteção aos Índios, *Memória sôbre as causas determinantes da diminuição das populações indígenas do Brasil* (IX Congresso Brasileiro de Geografia, Florianópolis, SC (Ministério da Agricultura, Rio de Janeiro), 29 Jul. 1940), in Garfield, 'The roots', 757. The books praising Indians were: Gilberto Freyre, *Casa Grande e Senzala* (3rd edition, 1943; translated as *The Masters and the Slaves*, 1946); Angyone Costa, *Indiologia* (Rio de Janeiro, 1943); Affonso Arinos de Mello Franco, O *Índio Brasileiro e a Revolução Francesa* (Rio de Janeiro, 1937). Tom Skidmore showed how, although the Vargas regime could not perpetrate extreme fascist racism in a country as mixed as Brazil, it did want to integrate Indians into the 'melting-pot' of national society: *Black into White: Race and Nationality in Brazilian Thought* (Duke University Press, Durham, NC, 1993), 64–77.

215: Olympics'. SPI, *Memória*, in Garfield, 'The roots', 757.

215: been in Brazil.' Rondon's speech, *19 de Abril*, 52.

215: Indians'. Letter from Lírio Arlindo do Valle, Tembé, to President Vargas, September 1945, in Garfield, 'The roots', 765.

216: true.' Ribeiro, *Os Índios e a Civilização*, 213.

216: place.' Ibid.

216: action.' Ministério da Agricultura, SPI, *Memória*, 18. Colonel Vasconcellos, the head of the SPI, commented on its continued erratic funding: 'In 1930 we had an award of 3,880 contos [a conto was 1,000 cruzeiros], which was reduced to 1,560 the next year! And so it went lower and lower steadily until 1939. Then in 1940 it rose to 3,450; in 1941 to 4,897 contos; in 1942 8,095 contos.' Adalberto Ribeiro, 'O Serviço', 69. The head of the civil service who influenced President Vargas to change his mind about Indians was Luis Simões Lopes.

216: powers.' BSPI, **17**, Apr. 1943, 104 and **28**, Mar. 1944, 64. The SPI was given a new Regimento in a decree of 16 October 1942, which was modified in decrees of 27 April 1943 and 26 January 1945.

217: Indians.' Darcy Ribeiro, *Os Índios e a Civilização*, 147.

217: asphalt'. J. M. da Gama Malcher, Preface to Mário Simões, ed., *SPI – 1953* (Rio de Janeiro, 1954), 48.

217: powers that be.' Ibid., 43.

217: arrears.' Gama Malcher, *Anuário – SPI/ 1953*, quoted by him in 'Os remanescentes indígenas da Amazônia e sua integração', *Geográfica*, **22:17** (Sociedade Geográfica Brasileira, São Paolo), Sep. 1973 (75–80), 77.

218: agronomist.' Gama Malcher, 'Os remanescentes indígenas', 4.

218: disaster.' Gama Malcher interview, ESP, 5 Nov. 1972, as part of a four-article series 'O Indígena no Brasil'. Darcy Ribeiro's report to UNESCO was partly published as *A Política Indigenista Brasileira* (Rio de Janeiro, 1962) and Charles Wagley and Marvin Harris drew on it for their chapter on the SPI in *Minorities in the New World* (Columbia University Press, New York, 1958), 20–47.

218: prejudice' Carlos de Araújo Moreira Neto, 'A política indigenista brasileira', *Carta* (Gabinete do Senador Darcy Ribeiro), 9, 1993, 146. Carlos Moreira was for many years a brilliant Director of the Museu do Índio.

218: Brazil.' Gomes, *The Indians and Brazil*, 125; Lima, *Um Grande Cerco de Paz*, 20.

218: anything better.' Gama Malcher, 'Os remanescentes indígenas', 77.

219: disappeared' Ribeiro, 'Indigenous cultures and languages of Brazil', in Janice H. Hopper, ed., *Indians of Brazil in the Twentieth Century* (Washington, DC, 1967), 91. Ribeiro's sources for this important survey were Curt Nimuendajú's erudite *Mapa etno-histórico*, the archives of the SPI of which Ribeiro was a senior official, and numerous books and papers by anthropologists. Nimuendajú handed manuscripts of his ethno-historical map, which showed the locations and languages of every tribe mentioned in Brazilian history, to the National Museum in Rio de Janeiro in 1944 (and another copy to the Goeldi Museum in Belém, Pará). The map, and the erudite bibliography and notes that accompany it, were published after his death, first by FIBGE (Fundação Instituto Brasileiro de Geografia e Estatística) and Funai (Rio de Janeiro, 1981) and again by the IBGE (Rio de Janeiro, 1987).

219: misery.' Ribeiro, *Os Índios e a Civilização*, 148.

219: Indians'. Moreira Neto, 'A política indigenista', 147.

219: *environment.'* Gomes, *The Indians and Brazil*, 81.

219: *1000'* Shelton Davis, *Victims of the Miracle* (Cambridge, Mass., and New York, 1977), 6.

220: *omission.'* José de Queiros Campos, 'Informe de la delegación del Brasil ante el VI Congreso Indigenista Interamericano', AI, **28:4**, Oct. 1968, 1077–8.

220: *elements.'* Ibid.

220: *injustices'. Diário de Notícias*, 29 May 1956. The President who sacked Gama Malcher was Café Filho, who wanted to give the job to 'a bosom friend'. Gama Malcher had joined the SPI in 1940 and worked in its Belém inspectorate (largely with the Gavião) until he became Director-General in 1951. When Funai succeeded the SPI in 1968, he was briefly its Deputy President, until dismissed in 1970 by Queiroz Campos.

220: *should be'.* Ibid.

220: *Indians.'* Ibid.

220: *Brazil'.* Lieutenant Colonel Tasso Villar de Aquino letter to Foreign Ministry, BSPI, **49**, Sep. 1961.

220: *stimulus.'* Lieutenant Colonel Moacyr Ribeiro Coelho report to Minister of Agriculture, 23 Feb. 1962, in BSPI, **52**, Jan.–Feb. 1962. The various Directors of the SPI after its revival were: Colonel Vicente de Paula Teixeira da Fonseca Vasconcellos, 1939–44; José Maria da Paula, 1944–47; José Maria da Gama Malcher, 1951–54; Josino de Assis and others, 1954–57; Colonel (later General) José Luíz Guedes, 1957–61; Lieutenant Colonel Tasso Villar de Aquino, 1961; Lieutenant Colonel (later General) Moacyr Ribeiro Coelho, 1961–63; Dr Noel Nutels, 1963–64; and, following the military coup of 1964, Air Force Major Luis Vinhas Neves, 1965–67.

221: *service.'* J. M. da Gama Malcher, 'Autocrítica e plano de reorganização do CNPI e SPI' (Oct. 1961) in Herbert Baldus, 'Métodos e resultados da ação indigenista no Brasil', RA, **10:1–2**, 1962, 37; Carlos de Araújo Moreira Neto, 'Relatório sôbre a situação atual dos índios Kayapós', RA, **7:1–2**, 1959, 49–64; Silvio Coelho dos Santos, *A Integração do Índio na Sociedade Regional* (Florianópolis, 1969), 71–2; José Mauro Gagliardi, O *Indígena*, 283.

221: *groups.'* Roberto Cardoso de Oliveira, 'O índio na consciência nacional', AI, **26:1**, Jan. 1966 (43–52), 50–1.

221: *Indians'.* Moreira Neto, 'A política indigenista', 148–9. There was one exception to the dismal heads of the SPI in its final years. At the end of 1963 Noel Nutels, the delightful doctor who was a close friend of the Villas Boas brothers, became its director. He tried to revive some of the good work of the Gama Malcher years; but he was ousted after only six months with the military overthrow of the Goulart government in April 1964.

221: *territories.'* Cardoso de Oliveira, 'O índio', 51–2.

222: *Brazil.'* Davis, *Victims of the Miracle*, 10; Darcy Ribeiro, *A Política Indigenista*; Carlos de Araújo Moreira Neto, 'Constante histórica do "indigenato" no Brasil', ASBA, 181–2; Expedito Arnaud, 'O Serviço de Proteção aos Índios: normas e implicações', *MPEG Publicações Avulsas*, **20**, Belém, 1973, 71–88.

222: *myself.'* Curt Nimuendajú to Herbert Baldus, 1939, in Baldus, 'Curt Nimuendajú', *Boletim Bibliográfico*, Biblioteca Municipal de São Paulo, **2:3**, Jul.–Sep. 1945 (91–9), 92; also in TICN, 26. The main fieldwork done by this remarkable anthropologist was: 1905–08, **Guarani** in western São Paulo; 1909–13 various expeditions among the **Kaingang**, **Guarani**, **Xokleng** and other tribes of São Paulo, Santa Catarina, and southern Mato Grosso; 1914–15, **Urubu-Kaapor**, **Tembé**, and **Canela** Timbira of the Gurupi, Maranhão, and eastern Pará; 1915, **Aparaí** of the Paru and Jari rivers, northern Pará; 1916–19, **Juruna**, **Arara**, and **Kayapó** tribes of the Xingu, Iriri, and Curuá; 1921, tribes of the Oiapoque, Amapá; 1921–23, **Parintintin** pacification, and **Mura**, **Pirahã**, and other tribes of the Madeira, for the SPI; 1922–8, excavations on Marajó and Caviana islands and on the Tapajós, Trombetas, Jamundá, Oiapoque, and Tocantins rivers, with Swedish teams from Göteborg Museum; 1927 **Baniwa**, **Tukano**, **Tariana**, and other groups of Upper Rio Negro; 1928–29, **Apinayé**, **Canela**, and other **Timbira**, and **Guajajara** in Maranhão and Goiás, with German museums; 1929, **Ticuna** of the Solimões; 1930–33, **Apinayé**, **Xerente**, **Krahó**, **Canela** of the Tocantins and Maranhão; 1934, **Fulniô** and **Xukuru** of Pernambuco; 1935–37, **Canela**, **Gamella**, **Apinayé**, **Xerente** with the Carnegie Institute and University of California; 1938–39 **Pataxó**, **Maxakali**, and other tribes of Bahia and Espírito Santo with the University of California; 1940, **Gorotire Kayapó** between the Xingu and Araguaia; 1941–42 and 1945 (when he died, disobeying doctor's orders), **Ticuna** of the Solimões for the Goeldi Museum and Museu Nacional. There is much information about Nimuendajú's expeditions in a study of the Council that approved scientific expeditions in Brazil during the early twentieth century: Luís Donisete Benzi Grupioni, *Colecões e Expedições Vigiadas. Os etnólogos no Conselho de Fiscalização das Expedições Artísticas e Científicas no Brasil* (São Paulo, 1998), 163–245. This includes his brief imprisonment, as a suspected Nazi agent, when he was working among the Ticuna on the Solimões in 1942. Sydney Possuelo, a President of Funai and great sertanista, and Terence Turner believe that the Ticuna killed Nimuendajú in a dispute over a woman.

222: dangers' Nimuendajú, 'Zur Coroado-frage', *Deutsche Zeitung*, weekly edition **6:4**, São Paulo, 22 Jul. 1910, 54–5, in Egon Schaden, 'Notas sôbre a vida e a obra de Curt Nimuendajú', *Revista do Instituto de Estudos Brasileiros* (Universidade de São Paulo, **3**, 1968, 7–19), 15.

222: oppressions'. Nimuendajú in Schaden, 'Notas sôbre a vida', 16.

223: thinking.' Jürgen Riester, preface to Curt Nimuendajú, *Los Mitos de Creación y Destrucción del Mundo como Fundamentos de la Religión de los Apapokuva-Guaraní* (Centro Amazónico de Antropología y Aplicación Práctica, Lima, 1978).

223: ethnologists' Darcy Ribeiro, 'Por uma antropologia melhor e mais nossa', *Ensaios insóli-tos* (L. & P. M. Editora, Porto Alegre, 1979), 210; Florestan Fernandes, *A Etnologia e a Sociologia no Brasil* (Ed. Anhembi, São Paulo, 1958), 17; Manuel Nunes Pereira, *Curt Nimuendajú: síntese de uma vida e de uma obra* (Belém, 1946); Thekla Hartmann, 'O enterro de Curt Nimuendajú', RMP, **28**, 1981/82, 187–90; Expedito Arnaud, 'Curt Nimuendajú: aspectos de sua vida e de sua obra', RMP, **29**, 1983/84, 55–72.

223: people".' Baldus, 'Curt Nimuendajú', 93. Nimuendajú enjoyed the company of women in many tribes that he studied. One theory is that he was killed by the Ticuna in an amorous dispute. He was survived by a widow, a humble woman whom he married late in life in Belém. Gama Malcher once told the author that Nimuendajú had said to him that he married the illiterate coloured woman, Dona Jovelina, because 'I spend eight or nine months a year in the forest, and get up at dawn to work on maps. What German or educated woman would marry me?'

224: civilization.' Rondon in *Diário Carioca*, 1949, in 'A última chance dos últimos guerreiros', *Realidade* (São Paulo, Oct. 1971), 207.

224: companions.' Edilberto Coutinho, *Ron-*

don, o Civilizador da Última Fronteira (Rio de Janeiro, 1969), 104.

225: created.' Jornal do Brasil, 7 Jan. 1966. Air Force Major Neves reported that the SPI was caring for some 110,000 Indians in its 126 posts.

225: application.' BSPI, 2 ser. **2**, 15 Aug. 1965.

225: for theirs.' Barão de Antonina, Oficio, 2 Sep. 1843, quoted in BSPI, 2 ser. **3**, 1 Sep. 1965.

226: struggle.' BSPI, 2 ser. **8**, 16 Nov. 1965.

226: creation.' Letter from J. M. da Gama Malcher to Gen. O. J. Bandeira de Mello (a future president of Funai), Petrópolis, 1970, in archive of Editora Abril.

226: exaggeration.' Jáder de Figueiredo Correia testimony, Comissão Parlamentar de Inquérito, *Diário do Congresso Nacional* (Brasília, 28 Apr. 1971), 5; 'A última chance dos últimos guerreiros', *Realidade* (São Paulo, Oct. 1971), 207. Jáder Figueiredo's commission also accused Lieutenant Colonel Moacyr Ribeiro Coelho (director of the SPI under Goulart, from December 1961 to 1963) as equally guilty of serious crimes. During the previous three decades there had been no less than 106 inquiries into irregularities in the SPI, but not one of these resulted in the punishment of a criminal. The most serious such investigation covered the years 1962 and 1963 in three of the SPI's inspectorates: the 1st (Amazonas), 5th (Cuiabá in northern Mato Grosso) and 6th (Campo Grande, in southern Mato Grosso). This inquiry was led by Celso Amaral, who asked the then President João Goulart to sack the Director of the SPI Lieutenant Colonel Ribeiro Coelho; but Goulart refused because Coelho was a friend of his from Rio Grande do Sul.

226: protector".' ESP, 20 Sep. 1967.

226: patrimony'. ESP, 6 Sep. 1963. This Parliamentary Commission of Investigation was established at the insistence of Deputy Edson Garcia, who proposed that the SPI be abolished. The inquiry in 1956 was conducted under a dreadful Director of the SPI, Josino de Assis, a deputy from Rio Grande do Sul who had been tried for embezzlement of municipal funds. His solution was to sack the fine anthropologist Darcy Ribeiro because he had tried to blow the whistle about corruption in the Service (*Correio da Manhã*, 6 Sep. 1956).

226: illiterate.' Jornal da Tarde, 8 Jun. 1966. Professor Paulo Duarte was director of the Institute of Prehistory at the University of São Paulo.

226: affection.' Correio da Manhã, 20 Sep. 1967.

227: *Dachau.*' Procurador Jader Figueiredo press conference, Brasília, 23 Oct. 1967, 'Indígenas perderam 40 milhões', ESP, 24 Oct. 1967. The new National Indian Foundation was the Fundação Nacional do Índio, always known by its acronym Funai.

227: *deserted.*' Norman Lewis, 'Genocide', *Sunday Times Magazine*, 23 Feb. 1969, 53. Lewis wrote that the Cinta Larga were celebrating the Quarup ceremony, but it must have been another ritual as the Quarup (or Kuarup) is the funerary ceremony only of the upper-Xingu tribes. The Junqueira company had been rubber-tappers but, with the fall in value of that commodity, had switched to diamond prospecting.

228: *river.* Ibid., 53, 55.

228: *forest.*' Signed statement by Ramos Bucair, SPI Inspector of Cuiabá, to Parliamentary Commission of Inquiry, *Jornal do Brasil*, 11 Apr. 1968; *Jornal da Tarde*, 15 Mar. 1968; 'A última chance dos últimos guerreiros', *Realidade*, Oct. 1971, 212, and many other press reports.

229: *Cuiabá.*' Jader Figueiredo speech to Câmara dos Deputados, Brasília, *Diário do Congresso Nacional*, 28 Apr. 1971, 6, 9.

229: *area.*' Father Valdemar Veber quoted in Lewis, 'Genocide', 55.

229: *established*'. Ibid. The massacre on Parallel 11 (11° S) was allegedly ordered by Sebastião Palma Arruda (brother of a former Mayor of Cuiabá) and Antonio Mascarenhas Junqueira, principals of Arruda e Junqueira & Cia. Ex-Inspector Helio Jorge Bucker further accused Junqueira of employing the pilot Toschio Lombardi Xatô to bomb the village with dynamite. The powerful company managed to get the Figueiredo Commission's accusation shelved; but the Procurator protested, and the Minister of Justice intervened. The ESP reported on 28 April 1968 that six people were accused of the Cinta Larga massacre. These included Junqueira, Arruda, the pilot, the confessed gunman Ataíde Pereira, and two others. Jáder de Figueiredo Correia testimony before Parliamentary Commission of Inquiry, 19 June 1968, *Diário do Congresso Nacional*, 28 Apr. 1971, 9. Carmen Junqueira, 'Grupo Cinta-Larga de Rondônia e Mato Grosso', in FIPE (Fundação Instituto de Pesquisas Econômicas), *Polonoroeste. Relatório IV, Volume 3 – Parque Indígena do Aripuanã/Zoró/ Gavião* (São Paulo, Mar.–Oct., 1984), 18–19.

229: *area.*' Evidence by Ramos Bucair to Parliamentary Commission, *Jornal do Brasil*, 11 Apr. 1968. The Tapayuna had suffered other attacks:

their villages had been burned by invading Brazilians; on another occasion many died from eating poisoned tapir meat; a crew building the BR-29 road in 1964 shot at them; and when they were contacted by a Funai group in 1968, a reporter suffering from flu infected the tribe and killed over a hundred. Some Tapayuna ran away or were not located, but only forty-one demoralized survivors were airlifted into the Xingu in 1969, to be settled alongside the Suyá near Diauarum. Anthony Seeger, *Nature and Society in Central Brazil: the Suyá Indians of Mato Grosso* (Cambridge, Mass., 1981), 54–5, 112–13; Bruna Franchetto, *Laudo Antropológico: a ocupação indígena da região dos formadores e do alto curso do Rio Xingu* (Rio de Janeiro, 1987), quoted in Vanessa Lea, *Parque Indígena do Xingu* (São Paulo), 114, 118.

230: *government*' Lewis, 'Genocide', 41.

230: *terror.*' Testimony of Major José Luís Leal dos Santos, March 1968, *Jornal do Brasil*, 11 Apr. 1968.

230: *mosquitoes.*' Testimony of Police Captain José da Cunha Barros Filho, who had investigated the Ticuna village of Belém, a few kilometres downriver from Tabatinga. He also recorded complaints by two Indian girls: thirteen-year-old Lita Jacamim that she had been raped by a friend of Jordão Aires de Almeida and forced to have an abortion; and Alaide, who had a baby girl after rape by that same man. Ibid.

230: *more of her.*' Lewis, 'Genocide', 51.

230: *practice.*' Ibid.; *Jornal do Brasil*, 11 Apr. 1968; 'A margem do progresso', ESP, 8 Nov. 1972.

231: *torture.*' Jader de Figueiredo Correia testimony, *Diário do Congresso Nacional*, 28 Apr. 1971, 10.

231: *irregularities.*' *Jornal da Tarde*, 15 Mar. 1968.

231: *authorization.*' Deputy Celso Amaral speech, *Diário do Congresso Nacional*, 28 Apr. 1971, 5.

231: *up there*'. Ibid.

231: *defence.*' Inspector Edú Azambuja, Guanabara Federal Police to the Minister of the Interior, a long, unpublished report (in the author's possession) dated October 1968 giving the findings of the Commission of Inquiry set up by the Minister in 1967, summarizing the evidence and punishment of every one of the indicted SPI officials, 10. References to Flávio de Abreu in the CI are: 1680/83, 4010/16, 4288, and 4257/90, and his lack of defence 6975/92. His dismissal under article 207 of Law 1,711/52 was recommended.

232: Pinto & Cia.' Figueiredo Commission report, 837; Answers by Francisco Meirelles (who now spelled his surname Meireles), Rio de Janeiro, 6 May 1968, in the archive of the Museu do Índio. He said that the lot of the Munduruku improved greatly after he removed a corrupt Inspector, João Batista Chuvas, who had been installed by Gama Malcher; that no Kayapó were hit when they were fired on after removing guns and ammunition from the Arruda, Pinto store; and that the Pakaá Nova (Wari) had been 'terrorizing' railway workers and settlers, which should 'redeem me of any minor faults of a bureaucratic nature in my ever-dynamic management of pacification teams.'

232: lands.' Jader de Figueiredo Correia broadcast, *Jornal do Brasil*, 11 Apr. 1968.

232: service.' Ibid.

232: Rondônia.' Letter from J. M. da Gama Malcher to General O. J. Bandeira de Mello, Petrópolis, 1970, from archive of Editora Abril. Gama Malcher also mentioned José Fernando da Cruz as 'one of the principal accused'. Cruz was made head of the 5th Inspectorate in southern Mato Grosso (Campo Grande) and praised as 'dynamic, talented, and idealistic', in a letter from Moacyr Ribeiro Coelho, Director of the SPI, to ESP, 14 Dec. 1962 (and *Boletim Interno* of Sep.– Dec. 1962). In 1965 Major Neves put Cruz in charge of the lucrative 7th Inspectorate in Curitiba. This Cruz also played a dubious role in the contact of the Pakaá Nova in Rondônia.

233: happen!' Lewis, 'Genocide', 36, 59. The article in the *Sunday Times Magazine* was illustrated by photographs by the acclaimed photographer Donald McCullin, who went inland to visit the Kadiwéu in southern Mato Grosso. Some of the international coverage of the Figueiredo report was in the *Los Angeles Times*, 22 and 29 Mar. 1968, *New York Times*, 21 Mar. 1968, *Washington Post*, 9 Jun. 1968, *Le Monde*, 15 Mar. 1968, *Globe and Mail*, Toronto, 24 May 1969, and many other newspapers and magazines. Books were written about the disgrace of the SPI: Lucien Bodard's exaggerated *Le Massacre des Indiens* (Gallimard, Paris, 1969); A. S. Malkus, *The Amazon: River of Promise* (McGraw-Hill, New York, 1970); Shelton Davis, *Victims of the Miracle*.

233: genocide".' Gama Malcher letter to General O. J. Bandeira de Mello of Funai (of which he was soon to be President), Petrópolis, 1970 (unpublished, in Editora Abril archives).

234: abroad.' Jader de Figueiredo, *Diário do Congresso Nacional*, 28 Apr. 1971, 6.

234: Survival International Survival International was founded in 1967 (originally as The Primitive Peoples' Fund) following a letter to *The Times* by the anthropologists Francis Huxley, Dr Audrey Colson, Nicholas Guppy, and Dr Conrad Gorinsky; and the author and my friend Robin Hanbury-Tenison were active in its formation. Robin Hanbury-Tenison was Survival's President for many years and built it into the leading worldwide organization for tribal rights. The charity shortened its name to Survival in the early 1990s.

10. Missionaries

235: matters.' BSPI, 3, Jan. 1942, 2. The prohibitions about missionaries were from Article 45 of Decree 736 of 6 Apr. 1936.

236: seemed to be.' A. Henry Savage-Landor, *Across Unknown South America* (2 vols., London and New York, 1913), 1, 281; John Hemming, *Amazon Frontier* (London, 1995), 399. The Salesian order was founded in 1859 by St Giovanni Bosco and named after the Swiss St François de Sâles, Bishop of Geneva in the late sixteenth century. The Salesian who established the missions in Mato Grosso was Father Giovanni Balzola.

236: gunpoint.' Letter from Rondon to the

Minister of Agriculture, quoted in *O País*, Rio de Janeiro, Nov. 1912 and in Amilcar A. Botelho de Magalhães, *Rondon – Uma Relíquia da Pátria* (Curitiba–São Paulo–Rio de Janeiro, 1942), 119–20; BSPI, 8, Jul. 1942, 8; Darcy Ribeiro, *Os Índios e a Civilização* (Rio de Janeiro, 1970), 78–9. The anthropological study was: Antonio Colbacchini, *I Bororos Orientali 'Orarimugudoge' del Matto Grosso, Brasile* (Turin, 1925). The four mission villages were all east of Cuiabá: **Sagrada Coração de Jesus** (or **Tachos**) on the Barreiro river; **Imaculada Conceição** (**Merure**) on the Garças headwater of the Araguaia; **Sangradouro** on the river of that name that flows into the Mortes (later occupied by Xavante refugees); and **Palmeiras**. Rondon also reserved areas in the São Lourenço valley: **São João do Jarudori, Colônia Isabel** and **Pobori**.

237: tasks.' Irmhild Wüst, 'The Eastern Bororo from an archaeological perspective', in Anna Curtenius Roosevelt, ed., *Amazonian Indians from Prehistory to the Present* (Tucson, Ariz., 1994), 328. The Salesians César Albisetti and Ângelo Jayme Venturelli predicted the disappearance of **Pobori** (which means 'rapids' in Bororo, and is on the Pogubo tributary of the rio Vermelho) from alcoholism and lack of children: *Enciclopédia Bororo* (2 vols., Campo Grande, Mato Grosso, 1962), **2**, 293. They reckoned that there were about 1,000 eastern Bororo, but that the western part of the tribe was extinct; Frederico Rondon, *Na Rondônia Ocidental* (São Paulo, 1938), 254. The anthropologist Sylvia Caiuby Novaes worked among the Bororo during the final decades of the twentieth century, and was also founder and President of the excellent NGO Centro de Trabalho Indigenista (CTI).

237: tomb.' Guilherme Saake, 'A aculturação dos Bororo do Rio São Lourenço', RA, **1:1**, Jun. 1953, 44.

238: felines].' Caiuby Novaes, *Mulheres, homens e heróis*; also her 'Tranças, cabaças e couros no funeral Bororo', RA, **24**, 1981, and *Jogo de Espelhos*. Apart from Cobacchini's classic study in 1925, another useful work on Bororo thinking is: Christopher J. Crocker, 'My brother the parrot', in Crocker and Sapir, eds., *The Social Use of Metaphor. Essays on the Anthropology of Rhetoric* (University of Pennsylvania Press, Philadelphia, 1977).

238: society.' Caiuby Novaes, *Jogo de Espelhos*, 132–3. She has studied relations between Salesians and Bororo in 'Esclaves du démon ou serviteurs de Dieu: les Bororos et la Mission Salesienne au Brésil', Recherches Amérindens au Québec, **21:4**, 1991–92, and 'A épica salvacionista e as artimanhas da resistência: as missões salesianas e os Bororo de Mato Grosso', in Robin Wright, ed., *Transformando os Deuses* (Campinas, 1999), 343–62. A less critical view is: Enawureu M. Bordignon, *Os Bororos na história do Centro-Oeste Brasileiro, 1716–1986* (Missão Salesiana de Mato Grosso/Cimi-MT, Campo Grande, 1986).

238: holiday.' Herbert Baldus, 'Métodos e resultados da ação indigenista no Brasil', RA, **10:1–2**, 1962, 39.

238: sociology.' Claude Lévi-Strauss, *Tristes Tropiques* (Librairie Plon, Paris, 1955), 225. Lévi-Strauss was at Kejara village on the rio Vermelho, near other independent Bororo villages at Pobori (Tadarimana) and Jarudore, both of which survive to this day. Saake in 1952 was at **Gomes Carneiro** (now known as **Córrego Grande**) which at that time had seventy-six people, with a further ninety at **Presidente Galdino Pimentel** (the former military camp and short-lived Salesian mission **Tereza Cristina**) further up the São Lourenço, and two small villages **Remansa** and **Criação Piebaga** between them.

In the 1970s there were over 450 Bororo: there were 200 in the Salesian mission of **Merure** (or **Meruri**), and Funai had 106 at **Gomes Carneiro**, 32 at **Barbosa de Farias** (formerly **Pobori** and later renamed **Tadarimana**) and 111 at **Perigara**.

By the end of the century there were over 1,000 Bororo, with 572 in the São Lourenço river area south-east of Cuiabá and 452 on headwaters of the Araguaia east of that city. These break down as: 389 at **Meruri** mission and several hundred alongside Xavante at **Sangradouro** mission; and under Funai 320 at **Teresa Cristina** (**Pimentel** reverting to its earlier name, which includes **Córrego Grande** and **Piebaga**); 173 at **Tadarimana**; and 96 at **Perigara** further down the São Lourenço. Apart from the two missions, the Bororo indigenous areas are very small by Brazilian standards, close to towns such as Rondonópolis or Jarudore and often surrounded by farms. Only five are registered as indigenous lands: **Meruri, Sangradouro/Volta Grande, Tadarimana, Perigara**, and **Teresa Cristina** (with legal problems over the latter's status), and there are disputes about most of their boundaries.

The Bororo of Meruri are now welcome at the town of General Carneiro since (unlike the Xavante) they are good payers. They were elected as town councillors in the 1990s. The Bororo love strong cachaça and alcoholism is their greatest health problem, as well as parasitic worms (from poor hygiene) and malaria. The Salesians now adopt a far more liberal attitude, and are active in helping the Bororo with health provision (alongside the government's National Health Foundation) and vernacular education, which is funded by the regional development project Prodeagro and its Tucum Project to train indigenous teachers. This people joined protests about proposed waterways on the Paraguay–Paraná and Araguaia–Tocantins rivers, and about the route of President

Sarney's Ferronorte railway from central Brazil to his state of Maranhão.

238: culture'. Claude Lévi-Strauss, *Tristes Tropiques* (Paris, 1955; trans. John and Doreen Weightman, London, 1973), 224.

239: pseudo-protectors.' BSPI, **11**, Oct. 1942, 31. Edwin Brooks, René Fuerst, John Hemming, Francis Huxley, *Tribes of the Amazon Basin in Brazil* (London, 1973), 29–31.

240: "blancos".' Hamilton Rice, 'Further Explorations in the North-West Amazon Basin', *The Geographical Journal*, **44**:2, Aug. 1914, 162. The psychopath Funes was killed by his own soldiers in 1921. His and other atrocities are reported in Jonathan D. Hill and Robin M. Wright, 'Time, narrative and ritual: historical interpretations from an Amazonian society', in Jonathan D. Hill, ed., *Rethinking History and Myth* (Urbana. Ill., 1988), 95. Garrido angrily rebutted an article in the Manaus newspaper *Jornal de Comércio* that in 1914 accused him of harming Indians; and in 1992 his grandson told the anthropologist Márcio Meira that although Garrido had grown rich and possessed many native women, he had served the people of the Içana and Xié by bringing them trade goods: Meira, *O tempo dos patrões* (Master's thesis, Universidade de Campinas, 1993), 82–3; Robin M. Wright, 'O tempo de Sophie: história e cosmologia da conversão baniwa' (in TD, 165–6), 212; Wright, 'Ialanawinai', 439–40. Adélia de Oliveira in 1971 collected testimonies of Baniwa who fled at that time and later: 'Depoiamentos Baniwa sobre as relações entre índios e "civilizados" no rio Negro', BMPEG, **72**, 1979, 1–31.

241: controls and works.' A. Hamilton Rice, 'Notes of the Rio Negro (Amazonas)', *The Geographical Journal*, **4**, Oct. 1918, 213. Theodor Koch-Grünberg, *Zwei Jahre unter den Indianern. Reisen in Nordwest-Brasilien, 1903/1905* (2 vols, Berlin, 1909–10), **2**, 64, 69, 156.

241: political life.' Hamilton Rice, 'Notes of the Rio Negro', 213.

241: force'. Curt Nimuendajú, 'Reconhecimento dos rios Içana, Ayarí e Uaupés (1927)', JSAP, **39**, 1950, 144, and in TICN, 146. The abuse of Indians by traders and the Brazilian military was reported by the Bishop of Manaus, Dom Frederico Costa, who went up the Negro in 1908, and this led Pope Pius X in 1914 to instruct the Salesian Order of Dom Bosco to take charge of the region. Major (later Marshal) Boanerges Lopes de Sousa, whom Rondon sent to inspect the region in 1928,

confirmed that there was still abuse of Indians (*Do Rio Negro ao Orenoco. A terra – o homem* (CNPI, Rio de Janeiro, 1959)), as did a geographer who was there in 1950 (José Cândido M. Carvalho, *Notas de viagem ao rio Negro* (Publicações Avulsas 9, Museu Nacional, Rio de Janeiro, 1952)). Robin M. Wright, *The History and Religion of the Baniwa Peoples of the Upper Rio Negro Valley* (Doctoral dissertation, Stanford University, 1981), pt. 2, 306–12; Janet M. Chernela, *The Wanano Indians of the Brazilian Amazon: a Sense of Space* (Austin, Tex., 1993), 39–40.

Koch-Grünberg implied that in 1905 the Wanana inhabiting the middle Uaupés numbered 500–600 in ten settlements; Nimuendajú said that by 1927 they had fallen to 218 people, a figure that Janet Chernela found 'surprisingly low' since their numbers were back to 600–800 by 1980. Between the two sections of Wanana are tribes known collectively as Baniwa (which include the Desana) who adopted the language of invading Cubeo tribes.

241: stomach.' Gordon MacCreagh, *White Waters and Black* (New York and London, 1926), 321. MacCreagh's expedition visited various malocas on the Uaupés and Tiquié and was cordially welcomed by the Indians, once he demonstrated his friendship and paid for all services. This contrasted with the hostility experienced by Nimuendajú a few years later.

242: brute.' Nimuendajú, 'Reconhecimento', in TICN, 180.

242: midst' Ibid., 183.

242: inhabitants'. Oswaldo Cruz, *Relatório sôbre as condições médico-sanitárias do Valle do Amazonas* (Ministério da Agricultura, Indústria e Commercio, Typ. do Jornal do Commercio de Rodrigues & C., Rio de Janeiro, 1913); Oswaldo Cruz, Carlos Chagas, and Afrânio Peixoto, *Sobre o Saneamento da Amazônia* (Philippe Daou, Manaus, 1972), 46–119; Dominique Buchillet, 'Contas de vidro, enfeites de branco e "potes da malária"' (in Bruce Albert and Alcida Rita Ramos, eds., *Pacificando o Branco*, São Paulo, 2002 113–44), 117.

242: die!' Prelazia de São Gabriel (Missão Salesiana do Rio Negro, Amazonas), *Usos e costumes dos selvícolas da Amazônia* (Episódios Missionários, Niterói, 1936), 131–2; Buchillet, 'Contas de vidro', 125.

243: dysentery.' Robin Wright, 'Ialanawinai: o branco na história e mito Baniwa' (in Albert and Ramos, eds., *Pacificando o Branco*, 431–67), 457.

244: end to us!' Dom Frederico Costa, *Carta Pastoral de Dom Frederico Costa, Bispo do Amazonas, a seus amados diocesanos* (Fortaleza, 1909), quoted in Aloísio Cabalzar, ed., *Povos Indígenas do Alto e Médio Rio Negro* (São Paulo, 1998), 91.

244: mercantile centres'. Chernela, *The Wanano*, 41; and her 'Missionary activity and Indian labor in the Upper Rio Negro of Brazil, 1680–1980: a historical-ecological approach', in William Balée, ed., *Advances in Historical Ecology* (New York, 1998), 324–5.

244: front wall'. Koch-Grünberg, *Zwei Jahre*, 2 147.

244: human beings.' Fr. Alcionilio Brüzzi Alves da Silva, *As tribos do Uaupés e a civilização brasileira. O método civilizador salesiano* (No publisher, 1979), 21.

244: maloca' Nimuendajú, 'Reconhecimento', 190.

244: gone! Monsignor Pedro Massa, *Missão Salesiana no Amazonas* (Rio de Janeiro, 1928), 192, and his 'Prélature du Rio Negro et du Port-Velho. Après vingt ans d'apostolat', *Bulletin Salésien*, **58**, 236–9, and **60**, 231–5 (Turin, 1936); Darcy Ribeiro, *Os Índios e a Civilização*, 34.

245: have to fall.' Nimuendajú, 'Reconhecimento', 190; Darcy Ribeiro, *Os Índios e a Civilização*, 35.

245: years ago.' A. Hamilton Rice, 'The Rio Negro, the Casiquiare Canal, and the Upper Orinoco, September 1919 – April 1920', *Geographical Journal*, **58**:5, Nov. 1921 (321–44), 325.

246: people.' Chernela, *The Wanano*, 38. By 1946 traditional malocas were to be found only among tribes furthest from the missions.

246: dogma'. Hamilton Rice, 'Notes of the Rio Negro', 213–14.

246: cohabitation.' Ettore Biocca, 'A penetração branca e a difusão da tuberculose entre os índios do Rio Negro', RMP, **14**, 1963, 205.

246: simple acts.' Cabalzar, ed., *Povos Indígenas*, 95; Brooks et al., *Tribes of the Amazon Basin*, 55–6. In 1971 most of the 251 children at the São Gabriel school were mestizo, and a few would continue with further education in Manaus. The author also visited Iauareté on the upper Uaupés, whose large boarding school had 316 Tukano pupils taught by fourteen Salesian fathers and sisters. Iauareté also had twenty-two rural schools in malocas with 436 pupils, and there was an adult-literacy campaign. Seven of the thirty-two teachers in these village schools were Indian girls trained by the Salesians. The

government paid a subsidy of US $116 a year per boarding pupil.

247: scorned. MacCreagh, *White Waters*, 301–2.

247: schools.' Aloísio Cabalzar, 'O templo profanado: missionários salesianos e a transformação da maloca tuyuka' (in TD, 363–96), 369.

247: missionaries. Bráz de Oliveira França, 'Nós não éramos índios' (1999), *PIB 1996/2000*, 40.

247: malocas.' Nimuendajú, 'Reconhecimento', 161; Cabalzar, ed., *Povos Indígenas*, 93. The German-Brazilian anthropologist was shocked by the rudeness of Taraquá's missionary Father Francisco towards him.

248: victims.' Biocca, 'A penetração', 206.

248: eliminate it.' Ibid., 208.

248: civilizados' Ibid.

248: individuality.' Nimuendajú, 'Reconhecimento', 188. The anthropologist ridiculed Monsignor Pedro Massa's *Missão Salesiana no Amazonas* (1928) and *Pelo Rio Mar* (Rio de Janeiro, 1933) for their glaring ethnographic errors. Thirty years later, another Salesian produced a scholarly and accurate study of these tribes: Father Alcionílio Alves da Silva Bruzzi, *A Civilização Indígena do Uaupés* (Linografia Editôra, São Paulo, 1962).

249: contrary. Nimuendajú, 'Reconhecimento', 191.

249: customs.' Gerardo Reichel-Dolmatoff, 'El misionero ante las culturas indígenas', AI, **32**:4, 1972, 1138–49; Alcida Rita Ramos, 'Frontier expansion and Indian peoples in the Brazilian Amazon', in Marianne Schmink and Charles H. Wood, eds., *Frontier Expansion in Amazonia* (Gainesville, Fla., 1984), 95.

249: happens.' P. Van Emst, 'Indians and missionaries on the Rio Tiquié, Brazil–Colombia' (*International Archives of Ethnography*, Leiden, **1**:2, 1966, 145–97), 177, 182, quoted in Cabalzar, 'O templo profanado', 370.

250: goods.' Berta G. Ribeiro, *Os Índios das Águas Pretas* (São Paulo, 1995), 27.

251: diet.' Anon. (but by Peter Silverwood-Cope), 'Maku – in the heart of the forest', SIN, **39**, 1998 (8–11), 10.

251: Hupdu.' Howard Reid, *Some Aspects of Movement, Growth and Change among the Hupdu Maku Indians of Brazil* (Doctoral dissertation, Cambridge, 1979), 185. In the 1970s, Silverwood-Cope reckoned that 300 Bara Makú lived between the Vaupés and Papuri rivers in Colom-

61. *Right*. Zo'é men wear broad wooden labrets. There was press excitement when this tribe was discovered not far north of the Amazon city of Santarém, by Protestant missionaries and then by Sydney Possuelo of Funai (pictured here) in 1989. (*Sydney Possuelo*)

62. Missionaries often deliver the best medical attention to Indians: a Franciscan treating Tiriyó mothers. Tumucumaque near Suriname.

63. Richard Mason and the author carry an inflatable boat along the trail on which Mason was later ambushed and killed by the then unknown Panará, 1961.

64. Defiant Panará fire arrows at Cláudio Villas Boas' aeroplane, during the first overflight of their village in 1968.
(*Orlando Villas Boas*)

65. The moment of contact could be dangerous. An anxious Sokriti Panará indicates to Cláudio Villas Boas where to put his machetes and axe, 1975.
(*Orlando Villas Boas*)

66. Cláudio Villas Boas advances towards the Panará, offering a coveted axe.
(*Orlando Villas Boas*)

67. *Above left.*
The Kaiowá leader
Marçal Tupã-I was a
brilliant orator,
chosen to speak for
all indigenous
people to the Pope
in 1980, but was
murdered in 1983.
(*Marina Helena
Brancher*)

68. *Top right.* The charismatic Kayapó spokesman
Paulinho Paiakan at the 1989 Altamira protest
meeting. His career was later destroyed by a
rape allegation. (*Sue Cunningham*)

69. *Above right.* Jê-speaking Kayapó and Xavante,
wearing necklaces, head-dresses, and some lip-discs,
led the campaign for indigenous rights in the 1988
Constitution. Their banner reads, alongside the
Brazilian flag, 'Now, the decisive struggle for Indians
in the Constituent Assembly.' (*Beto Ricardo*)

70. *Right.* Kadiwéu of southern Mato Grosso were
the first indigenous people to adopt horses. They
struggled for years to recover their Bodoquena
reserve from encroaching ranchers and squatters.

71. First contact with Waimiri-Atroari women and children, 1969. (*Gilberto Pinto*)

72. Nervous Waimiri-Atroari take caps and other clothing from Gilberto Pinto, 1969.(*Gilberto Pinto*)

73. The experienced sertanista Gilberto Pinto, who contacted the Waimiri-Atroari but was killed by them in 1974, with the author.

74. José Altino Machado was the smooth and plausible leader of the gold prospectors who invaded Yanomami land in 1985 and 1989. (*Edson Silva*)

75. The first Yanomami assembly, 1986. Seated in the centre is an indigenous champion, Senator Severo Gomes; behind him to the left is Davi Kopenawa Yanomami; standing at the extreme left is the Indian activist Ailton Krenak. (*Cláudia Andujar*)

76. Yanomami help a Consolata missionary to fumigate their yano hut.

77. A Protestant missionary at Surucucu treats a Yanomami mother.

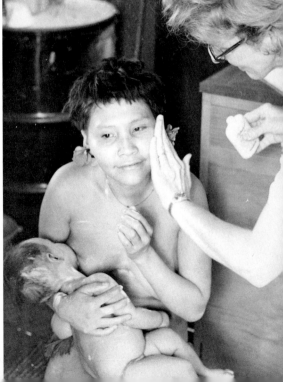

78. The sympathetic Consolata missionary Father João Baptista Saffirio with Yanomami at Catrimani, before the group was devastated by the building of the Northern Perimeter road.

79. The Yanomami are the largest indigenous nation in South America whose culture is largely unchanged.

80. The Yanomami spokesman and shaman Davi Kopenawa. (*Beto Ricardo*)

81. *Above, Left*. The hammocks, hearth, bananas, and dogs of each Yanomami family occupy a segment of the communal yano.

82. *Above, right*. The gentle Ticuna, one of the largest indigenous nations in Brazil, fought a dignified campaign to gain recognition of their territories, on the Amazon river near Peru.

83. Sydney Possuelo, seated, wins the confidence of newly contacted Korubo. Ituí river, western Amazonas, 1996. (*Sydney Possuelo*)

84. The Xavante Mário Juruna, the only Indian to be elected to the Brazilian Congress. (*Julian Burger*)

85. First Contact with the Uru-Eu-Wau-Wau in 1981: the apprehensive bald Chief Djaí accepts presents from João Maia. (*Jesco von Puttkamer*)

86. Nomadic Awá-Guajá hunter-gatherers are constantly on the move in the forests of Maranhão. Sydney Possuelo contacted one group in 1978. (*Sydney Possuelo*)

bia; Reid estimated 1,200 Hup (or Hupdu) Makú between the Tiquié and Papuri in Brazil; while Gerardo Reichel-Dolmatoff claimed a further 1,000 Makú to the north-west in Colombia; and there were Yuhup Makú southwards in the forests of the Curicuriari and Marié tributaries of the middle Rio Negro, and Madeb further south-east on the Tea. Peter Silverwood-Cope, *A Contribution to the Ethnography of the Colombian Maku* (Doctoral dissertation, Cambridge, 1972); Reid, *Some Aspects*, 15.

252: sick and die.' Reid, *Some Aspects*, 15.

253: nutrition.' Ibid.

253: weapons.' Ibid.

253: opportunity.' Ibid., 314. Peter Silverwood-Cope submitted a report to Funai about the Upper Rio Negro: *Plano de desenvolvimento do Alto Rio Negro, 1975–80* (unpublished, Brasília, 1975) and his wife Ana Gita de Oliveira wrote *Pequena contribuição etnográfica sobre a mobilidade Maku* (unpublished, 1976). They collaborated with Alcida Ramos to explain the symbiotic relationship between the Makú and large sedentary tribes: Ramos, Silverwood-Cope, and Oliveira, 'Patrões e clientes: relações intertribais no Alto Rio Negro', in Alcida Ramos, ed., *Hierarquia e Simbiose* (Hucitec, São Paulo, 1980), 135–82.

254: 1976. Dr Silverwood-Cope was deeply depressed by his unwarranted and unexplained expulsion, and died soon afterwards.

255: [vast] area.' Leonard Legters' remark to Cameron Townsend, founder of the Summer Institute of Linguistics, Guatemala, 1933, in James C. and Marti Hefley, *Uncle Cam* (Word Books, Waco, Tex., 1974), 64; Gerard Colby and Charlotte Dennett, *Thy Will be Done* (New York, 1995), 51. Legters also showed Townsend a picture of 'a fine, stalwart, naked Indian' from the Xingu. Legters had a fund-raising arm called the Pioneer Mission Agency.

255: take place.' Colonel Vicente de Paula Vasconcellos to William R. Hunrichs, 13 Nov. 1943, in BSPI, **23**, Oct. 1943, 331–2. Frederick C. Glass, *Through the Heart of Brazil* (South American Evangelical Mission, Liverpool, 1907), 67 about the Bororo, and *Through Brazilian Junglelands with the Book* (Pickering & Inglis, London and Glasgow, c. 1930), 95–103 on the Carijó of the São Francisco valley, and 153–90 about the Karajá. Kenneth Grubb, *Amazon and Andes* (London, 1930) and *From Pacific to Atlantic: South American Studies* (London, 1933).

255: aid' BSPI, **11**, Oct. 1942, 31. The *Regi-*

mento do SPI was Decree 10,652 of 16 Oct. 1942. The Worldwide Evangelization Crusade sent its first 'pioneers' to Pará and Maranhão in 1923 (one missionary died when working among the Guajajara at Sapucaia on the Pindaré in the following year). The Crusade was also active among the Timbira (Canela) and Tembé, and it translated the Gospels into their languages. Various Guajajara villages were converted during the 1920s and '30s, and in 1934 the Urubu-Kaápor 'heard the Gospel for the first time'.

The Unevangelized Fields Mission was founded simultaneously in Britain and Australia in 1931, as a breakaway from the Crusade. It started in the United States in about 1940, and Philadelphia then became the UFM's world headquarters. Highlights of the UFM's work among Brazilian Indians (it was also active among non-Indians) were: 1934, Urubu-Kaápor; 1935, the Three Freds were killed by Kuben-Kran-Kégn Kayapó, and a station opened among the Gavião; 1936–43, work among Kayapó by Horace Banner and others, until missionaries expelled by the SPI; 1944, 'translator missionaries' among Aruak-speaking Wapixana in Rio Branco (Roraima); 1944, permission to reopen work among Indians, first contact with Xikrin Kayapó; 1960, using a new missionary air service, posts opened among more Kayapó (Kokraimoro on the Xingu, Baú on the upper Iriri, and Kuben-Kran-Kégn on the Fresco); 1967, contact with Menkragnoti Kayapó; 1968–69 missionaries briefly expelled from Gorotire Kayapó, but on return translate the Gospel of St Mark into Jê.

256: tendencies.' Wright, 'O tempo de Sophie', 174.

256: evil spirits.' Robin Wright, 'Demons with no heads: NTM and the Baniwa of Brazil', *Bulletin* (Anthropology Resource Center, Boston), **9**, Dec. 1981 (9–13), 9.

256: new faith.' Cabalzar, ed., *Povos Indígenas*, 97.

257: immorality."' David Stoll, 'The adventures of Sophie Muller', ARC, **9**, Dec. 1981, 5.

257: language'. Wright, 'O tempo de Sophie', 176.

257: fanatic'. Father José Schneider talking to Eduardo Galvão in 1954, from the latter's field notes, in ibid., 191.

257: trustworthy.' Henry Roland Loewen, *A summary of Indian work done by Missão Novas Tribos do Brasil in the states of Amazonas and Acre, and the Federal Territory of Rondônia* (typescript,

Brasília, 1970). Between 1962 and 1970, the MNTB had expanded its efforts among tribes of the extreme west of Brazil. In addition to the Marubo of the Ituí tributary of the Javari, in 1967 it started among the Manchineri of the Iaco river in Acre; in 1969 with some Kulina and Kanamari on the Juruá, above and below Eirunepé; and in 1970 with the Yaminawa on the Iaco.

258: hymns.' Eduardo Galvão, 'Aculturação indígena no Rio Negro', BMPEG, **7**, 1959, in ES, 184. Sophie Muller wrote a book about her work: *Beyond Civilization* (New Tribes Mission, Chico, Cal., 1952).

258: heresy.' *Diários Salesianos* (Assunção, Içana, 1961), 62, quoted in Wright, 'O tempo de Sophie', 181.

259: churches.' New Tribes Mission leaflet, quoted in SIR, **6:31(33)**, Spring 1981, 17. This issue of Survival International's *Review* compared the New Tribes Mission and the Summer Institute of Linguistics. The NTM required no educational qualifications from its missionaries, whereas SIL needed a college degree or certificate of linguistics and a period of probation. The NTM was more rigid about Protestant doctrine and on the private lives of its workers (no divorce, preferably no marriage with 'nationals', missionary schooling for their own children, etc.). With some 1,250 missionaries working in sixteen countries, the Florida-based NTM was far smaller than the SIL (or Wycliffe Bible Translators). But the two missions often collaborated, and there was little difference in their wish to convert tribal people to their brand of Christianity.

259: globe.' Report on the SPI by Lieutenant Colonel Moacyr Ribeiro Coelho to the Minister of Agriculture, 23 Feb. 1962, in BSPI, **52**, Jan.–Feb. 1962.

259: languages.' Ibid.

260: exploited by them.' Ibid.

260: nil.' Mauro Leonel, 'Relatório de avaliação das comunidades Oro-Uari, Macurap e Canoé das Áreas Pacaa-Nova, Lage e Sagarana', *Polonoroeste Relatório IV. Vol. 1, Pacaa-Nova* (Fundação Instituto de Pesquisas Econômicas, São Paulo, 1984), 15. Also an article about the New Tribes Mission: Rubem César Fernandes, 'Um exército de anjos: as razões da Missão Novas Tribos', *Religião e Sociedade*, **5**, 1980, 129–65.

260: investigators' Colby and Dennett, *Thy Will*, 66. Cam Townsend launched the Summer Institute of Linguistics during an Inter-American Scientific Congress in Mexico in 1930. Colby and

Dennett's large and well-researched book documents the many links between the SIL and the Baptist organizations funded by John D. Rockefeller, Jr. and his sons. Soon after the Institute's move to Ecuador, the Waorani there in 1945 killed its Nate Saint and four colleagues; Nate's sister Rachel Saint wrote about this tragedy and became America's best-known missionary. Kenneth Pike and Ruth M. Brend, eds., *The Summer Institute of Linguistics: Its Work and Contributions* (The Hague, 1977).

261: critical time.' Earl P. Hanson, *Journey to Manaus* (New York, 1938), quoted in ibid., 105.

261: action.' Felisberto C. de Camargo to Berent Friele, 29 Nov. 1941, in ibid., 133.

261: serious.' J. C. King to Nelson Rockefeller, 17 Jun. 1942, in ibid., 143. Rockefeller planned an Amazon Valley Corporation, to be led by J. C. King (a pharmaceutical company executive); but the idea was vetoed by the Secretary of State, who probably realized that it would arouse Brazilian suspicions. Rockefeller played a part in the coup that in 1945 deposed Getúlio Vargas as President because he was considered too nationalistic and xenophobic. Vargas was re-elected in 1950; but by 1954 American influence made his position untenable and he committed suicide rather than be driven from office again.

262: Indians.' Ibid., 318. Kietzman wrote a paper on the Terena language in the *Revista de Antropologia* of São Paulo, **6**, 1960. The main SIL team, Muriel Perkins and Muriel Ekdahl, worked for some years at Cachoeirinha, an SPI post twenty kilometres (twelve miles) from Miranda, and produced a missionary booklet in Terena in 1968: Alan C. Wares, ed., *Bibliography of the Summer Institute of Linguistics* (2 vols., SIL, Dallas, 1979), **1**, 57, 138. Ethel E. Wallis and Mary A. Bennett, *Two Thousand Tongues to Go* (Hodder & Stoughton, London, 1966), 249.

262: Ecuador.' Colby and Dennett, *Thy Will*, 433. The involvement of the American government, military, and CIA in destabilizing Goulart and in helping the coup that overthrew him is well documented: Phyllis Parker, *Brazil and the Quiet Revolution, 1964* (University of Texas Press, Austin, Tex., and London, 1979); Jan Knippers Black, *United States Penetration of Brazil* (University of Pennsylvania Press, Philadelphia, 1977); Susanna Hecht and Alexander Cockburn, *The Fate of the Forest* (London and New York, 1989), 125–6; Colby and Dennett, *Thy Will*, 440–5. The author's interview with Jim Wilson took place at the SIL's headquarters in Brasília in 1972. The Helio Courier plane given to Darcy Ribeiro's University of Brasília (as cover for its use by the SIL) was donated by such right-wing interests as the Pew Memorial Fund, controlled by J. Howard Pew of the Sun Oil Company, whom Colby and Dennett described as 'profoundly distrustful of everything to the left of Barry Goldwater', including even Nelson Rockefeller. Sun Oil was the second-largest supplier of petroleum to Brazil.

263: Brazilians.' Dale Kietzman, 'Indians and culture areas of twentieth-century Brazil', in Janice H. Hopper, ed., *Indians of Brazil in the Twentieth Century* (Washington, DC, 1967), 14. The SIL missionary's survey appeared alongside important studies by Darcy Ribeiro, Eduardo Galvão, and other luminaries. (Few people knew that the book's editor, Janice Hopper, was the widow of Rex Hopper, a CIA counter-insurgency expert on Latin America, or that the book's publisher, 'The Institute for Cross-Cultural Research', was indirectly funded by that agency.) On page 51, Kietzman published a map of the SIL's thirty-five 'team locations' among Brazilian tribes. His report on the Juruá–Purus region, *Memorandum re: Development in Amazonia and Acre* (29 Oct. 1964), was sent to James Wilson and others, and is in the Townsend Archives in Waxhaw, North Carolina. Colby and Dennett, *Thy Will*, 500–1; and their demonstration of links between Janice Hopper and the CIA is on pages 501–3.

264: live better'. ESP, 11 Jul. 1970.

265: language'. Norman Lewis, *The Missionaries* (London, 1988), 106.

265: level.' William R. Merrifield interview with Jonathan Benthall, Director of the Royal Anthropological Institute, London, in response to two attacks on the SIL – in Søren Hvalkof and Peter Aaby, *Is God an American?* (IWGIA/Survival International, Copenhagen and London, 1982) and Brian Moser's documentary film *War of the Gods* (Granada Television, 1971) – *RAIN (Royal Anthropological Institute News)*, **53**, Dec. 1982, 3. David Stoll, *Fishers of Men or Founders of Empires? The Wycliffe Bible Translators in Latin America* (London, 1982).

265: Protestantism.' Figueiredo report in *Jornal do Brasil*, 10 Oct. 1967, quoted in Norman Lewis, 'Genocide', *Sunday Times Magazine*, 23 Feb. 1969, 44; Colby and Dennett, *Thy Will*, 625.

266: world.' Dominique Tilkin Gallois, 'De arredio a isolado: perspectivas de autonomia para os povos indígenas recém-contactados' (in Luís

Donisete Benzi Grupioni, ed., *Índios no Brasil* (São Paulo, 1992) (121–34), 127). Gallois and Grupioni examined the methods and objectives of the New Tribes Mission in detail in 'O índio na Missão Novas Tribos' (in Wright, ed., *Transformando os Deuses*, 77–129). They drew on such works as H. Dowdy, *Christ's Witchdoctor: from Savage Sorcerer to Jungle Missionary (Unevangelized Fields Mission/UFM)* (Harper & Row, New York, 1963); and Ken Johnston, *The Story of the New Tribes Mission* (NTM, Sanford, Fla., 1985); the training manual Trevor McIlwain and Nancy Everson, eds., *Firm Foundations. Creation to Christ* (9 vols., New Tribes Mission, Sanford, Fla., 1991); and the Mission's journals *Brown Gold* (Sanford, Fla., 1986–) and *Dos Confins da Terra* (Brasília, 1992–). Brazil is the NTM's largest theatre of operations, but it has over 3,000 missionaries active among 172 tribes in twenty-seven countries. Other critical comments include: E. Miller, 'The Christian missionary, agent of secularization', *Anthropological Quarterly*, **43:1**, 1970, 14–22; Fernandes, 'Um exército de anjos'; Robin Wright and S. Swenson, 'The New Tribes Mission in Amazonia', ARC, 9, Special Issue, Boston, 1981; A. Gouveia Mendonça, 'O fundamentalismo protestante', *Contexto Pastoral. Debate*, **5:28**, Sep.–Oct. 1995.

266: Kadiwéu.' Lewis, *The Missionaries*, 106–7.

267: communities.' 'Declaration of Barbados for the Liberation of the Indians', Bridgetown, Barbados, 30 Jan. 1971, in Walter Dostal, ed., *The Situation of the Indian in South America* (World Council of Churches, Geneva, 1972) (376–81), 379.

267: involved'. 'Commandos for Christ', *SI News*, 9, 1985.

267: missionaries were.' Colby and Dennett, *Thy Will*, 684.

267: Protestantism'. 'Declaration of Barbados', in Dostal, ed., *The Situation*, 379; Colby and Dennett, *Thy Will*, 688.

268: "Black Power"' Wade Coggins of the Evangelical Foreign Missions Association, quoted in ibid., 689.

268: statement'. Professor A. R. Tippett of the Fuller Theological Seminary, in ibid., 689.

268: Indians'. Gonzálo Rubio Oribe, of the Inter-American Indian Institute, to the VII Congresso Indigenista Interamericano, Brasília, 1972, in ibid., 698. By the time that Cameron Townsend was granted the sonorous title of Benefactor, he had been removed from active direction of the SIL and elevated to the status of Founder. This was because he was in his late seventies, but more importantly because his views were becoming too liberal and radical for the conservative fundamentalists of the Wycliffe Bible Translators/SIL.

269: security'. Folha de São Paulo, 23 Nov. 1977. The SIL's director, Steven N. Sheldon, vehemently denied any political wrongdoing or prospecting activity, but in vain. SIR, **3:1(21)**, Winter 1978, 28. The SIL's *Bibliografia, 1973–1980* was published in Brasília in 1981, and Father José Vicente César's praise of its work was in his 'Os índios e as missões', *Cristão Hoje (Revista da Div. Teológica)*, **147/8**, 1982, 141–4. The SIL's agreement with Funai expired again in 1992; but its exile was again short-lived.

Towards the end of the century, there was some cooperation between CIMI and OPAN (Operação Anchieta) on the Catholic side and the moderate Protestants of the evangelical GTME (Grupo de Trabalho Missionário Evangélico) and Lutheran IECLB (Igreja Evangélica de Confissão Luterana no Brasil).

270: religions"'. Marina Kahn, 'Levantamento preliminar das organizações religiosas em áreas indígenas' (in TD, 19–75), 22, partly quoting from Rubem Cesar Fernandes, *Missões Protestantes* (Cadernos do Iser, **10**, Rio de Janeiro, no date). Kahn's study of missions at the end of the twentieth century updated CIMI's *Povos Indígenas no Brasil e Presença Missionária* (Brasília, 1985).

11. Generals and Highways

274: civilization'. General Golbery do Couto e Silva, *Geopolítica do Brasil* (Rio de Janeiro, 1981), quoted in Susanna Hecht and Alexander Cockburn, *The Fate of the Forest* (London and New York, 1989), 102. SPVEA stood for Superintendência do Plano de Valorização Económica da Amazônia; SUDAM for Superintendência de Desenvolvimento da Amazônia. The book about Amazonia inciting foreign envy was: Artur César Ferreira Reis, *A Amazônia e a Cobiça Internacional* (Edinova, Rio de Janeiro, 1965). The Manaus free-trade zone (SUFRAMA, established in 1967) was a remarkable success in attracting business and settlers to the city far up the Amazon. It brought duty-free shoppers from the rest of Brazil as long as the country had ludicrously high tariff barriers against imports, and it also helped Manaus become the country's manufacturing centre for 'white' kitchen goods, motorcycles, and other appliances.

274: Transamazonica The correct spelling in Portuguese is Transamazônica, but the highway became well known outside Brazil as the Transamazonica, so this is the spelling I have used in an English-language book.

274: compelling.' Hecht and Cockburn, *The Fate of the Forest*, 109. President Castello Branco took potential investors, generals, and planners up the Amazon in December 1966, on a riverboat called *Rosa da Fonseca*.

276: every way.' R. J. A. Goodland and H. S. Irwin, *Amazon Jungle: Green Hell to Red Desert?* (Amsterdam, 1975), 12. The name Transmiseri-

ana came from F. Morais, R. Gontijo, and R. de O. Campos, *Transamazonica* (Brasiliense, São Paulo, 1970). Plenty of authors were already warning about the weakness of Amazon rainforest soils, notably I. C. Falesi, *Solos da Rodovia Transamazonica* (Instituto de Pesquisas Agropecuárias Norte, Belém, 1972). Among the many books about the construction and impact of the Transamazon highway, three of the best in English are: Richard Bourne, *Assault on the Amazon* (London, 1978); Emilio Moran, *Developing the Amazon* (Indiana University Press, Bloomington, 1981); Nigel J. H. Smith, *Rainforest Corridors. The Transamazon Colonization Scheme* (Berkeley, Cal. and London, 1982).

276: program' Goodland and Irwin, *Amazon Jungle*, 73.

277: Indians.' Ibid., 57; Shelton Davis, *Victims of the Miracle* (Cambridge and New York, 1977), 65. On Funai's estimate of Indians to be encountered: ESP, 22 May 1971.

277: kill!' Letter from Curt Nimuendajú to Harald Schultz, 7 Dec. 1945. Translated by the CNPI, it was published in O *Globo*, 24 Jan. 1946; 'Carta sobre e expedição armada contra os índios Parakanã', TICN, 244.

278: maize' Expedito Arnaud, 'Grupos Tupi do Tocantins', ASBA (57–68), 58, quoting from the Tocantins post's reports; Arnaud, 'Breve informacão sôbre os índios Asurini e Parakanân, rio Tocantins, Pará', BMPEG, **11**, 1961. Roque de Barros Laraia and Roberto da Matta, *Índios e Castanheiros* (São Paulo, 1967), 35.

Lúcia Andrade, who has worked recently with the Asuriní of the Tocantins, says that *they* rather than the Parakanã recall the horrors of the 1953 influenza epidemic. A small group of Asuriní remained with the SPI near the Trocará tributary of the lower Tocantins. Those who fled into the forest reappeared in 1962, but when disease hit them again they migrated, to the Pacajá. Roque Laraia saw a pathetic remnant of thirty-five Asuriní living at Trocará in abject dependence on the government agency. Those on the Pacajá decided to rejoin their kinsmen at Trocará in 1974, thanks to a tape-recorded message of invitation conveyed by Summer Institute of Linguistics operatives called Nicholson and Aberdour. Funai sent a boat to bring them back.

279: agouti.' João Evangelista Carvalho, 'A pacificação dos Parakanã', *Carta*, Gabinete do Senador Darcy Ribeiro, **9** (Brasília, 1993) (213–39), 216.

279: like theirs'. Ibid., 220.

279: vanish.' João Carvalho, unpublished *Diário da frente de atração dos índios Paracanãs*, in Expedito Arnaud, 'Mudanças entre grupos indígenas Tupi da região do Tocantins-Xingu (Bacia Amazônica)', BMPEG, **84**, 15 Apr. 1983, and in Arnaud, ed., *O Índio e a Expansão Nacional* (Belém, 1989), 339–40.

279: accustomed to them.' Anon., 'Frente de atração da Funai em nova missão na Transamazonica', *Boletim Informativo Funai*, **1:1** (Brasília, Oct. 1971) (25–7), 26.

279: shorts.' Edwin Brooks, René Fuerst, John Hemming, Francis Huxley, *Tribes of the Amazon Basin in Brazil, 1972* (London, 1973), 89.

279: confidence.' Anon., 'Frente de atração', 25–6. Colonel Clodomiro Bloise, head of Funai's Pucuruí base, also described these encounters in a series of typewritten reports in the archive of Funai's 2nd Regional Delegacy (Belém).

280: promiscuity' Dr Antonio Madeiros in Report by Valter Sanchez to General Ismarth de Oliveira, President of Funai, *Jornal do Brasil*, 25 May 1972; *Tribuna da Imprensa*, 20 Jun. 1972.

280: period'. Márcio Souza, José Ribamar Bessa, Mário Juruna, Megaron, Marcos Terena, *Os Índios Vão à Luta* (Rio de Janeiro, 1981), 26. This book noted that in 1976 twelve Indians had died of malaria, and in 1977 six died of polio and 'sixteen others were summarily murdered'.

280: bewildered.' Brooks et al., *Tribes of the Amazon*, 89–90; Davis, *Victims of the Miracle*, 67; Anon., 'Transamazonica: Índios no caminho', *Veja* magazine, Rio de Janeiro, 8 Dec 1970; *The Politics of Genocide Against the Indians of Brazil* (document presented to the XLI International Congress of Americanists, Mexico City, 1974; later published in: American Friends of Brazil, *Supysáua: A Documentary Report on the Condition of Indian Peoples in Brazil* (Berkeley, Cal., 1974), 36; Expedito Arnaud, 'Mudanças entre grupos', 340–1, quoting João Carvalho's *Diário da frente de atração*; Antonio Carlos Magalhães and Iberê Sassi, 'Parakanã', CEDI, *Povos Indígenas no Brasil*, **8**, *Sudeste do Pará (Tocantins)* (18–51), 28–9. The medical report by a Dr Pires, a protest by Valter Sanchez of the Pucuruí post to General Ismarth de Oliveira (Funai's man in charge of Transamazonica operations and later its president), and the sacking of the two infected agents were reported in *Jornal do Brasil*, 23 May 1972, and *Miami Herald* on the following day.

280: daily work,' Arnaud, 'Mudanças entre grupos', 341–2.

281: contacts.' Souza et al., *Os Índios Vão à Luta*, 27.

281: contact'. Antonio Carlos Magalhães, 'Os Parakanã – o destino de uma nação indígena', in Dalmo de Abreu Dallari, Manuela Carneiro da Cunha, and Lux Vidal, eds., *A Questão da Terra Indígena* (São Paulo, 1981), 86.

281: self-determination'. Ibid., 88; Arnaud, 'Mudanças entre grupos', 344; Anna Presland, 'Reconquest. An account of the contemporary fight for survival of the Amerindian peoples of Brazil', SIR, **4:1(25)**, Spring 1979, 25. The group contacted in 1976 was near the Anapu river, which the Transamazonica crosses some 120 kilometres (75 miles) east of Altamira; a group contacted in 1977 was between the upper Bacajá and the Xingu, 220 kilometres (135 miles) west of their village on the Lontra; the January 1983 contact was far to the south near the Carajás mine, on the watershed between the upper Itacaiúnas and the São José tributary of the Xingu, 240 kilometres (150 miles) south-west of the Lontra; and the last two groups in 1983–84 were on the Bom Jardim, a small tributary of the Xingu, 270 kilometres (150 miles) south-west of Lontra. These locations are shown on a map on page 25 of *Povos Indígenas do Brasil*, **8**.

The **Araweté**, who fought the Parakanã in 1983, are a Tupi-speaking tribe who moved towards the lower Xingu in the 1950s. They were 'contacted' by Funai's Raimundo Alves in 1976 when they appeared on the banks of the main

Xingu, hungry and diseased (some with their eyes closed from conjunctivitis) and living precariously near the clearings of a settler. They were given the name Araweté, which means nothing in their language – if anything, they refer to themselves as Bide, meaning 'we' or 'people'. It was learned that the Araweté had been aware of white society for many years before the formal contact – their mythology even includes a Shaman of the Whites, and they already possessed a number of metal tools. They had been constantly on the move and often at war with neighbouring tribes, particularly the bellicose Parakanã. Funai decided to move the Araweté on a gruelling seventeen-day march through a hundred kilometres (sixty-two miles) of forest to the upper Ipixuna. A terrible sixty-six people died on this exodus (João Carvalho later found many corpses along the trail) and desperate adults had to kill orphaned children. Only twenty-seven reached their new post, and a further sixty-six arrived two months later. Another group was discovered in 1987 when the Xikrin Kayapó fought and captured some Araweté in forests far to the east – these proved to be survivors of a group led by Chief Iwarawí who had split off in the 1950s and lived a harsh nomadic existence ever since. Numbering some 200 at contact, the entire tribe fell to 120 from the first diseases, but by 1992 recovered to 206 by a strong birth rate. Their 940,900 ha (3,630 square mile) reserve was registered by President Cardoso on 5 Jan. 1996 and in 2000 contained 269 people. In that year eight died from an outbreak of chickenpox, made worse by their continuing to live in collective huts containing forty to fifty in each. But their society and morale had improved greatly since contact and their diet continued to be healthy from hunting and gathering. Eduardo Viveiros de Castro, *Araweté. O povo do Ipixuna* (CEDI, São Paulo, 1992), 22.

282: area' Magalhães, 'Os Parakanã', 90. The logging contract was with Agropecuária Capemi Indústria e Comércia Ltda., part of the Capemi conglomerate. It yielded 13 million cruzeiros to Funai, none of which went directly to the Parakanã. Full details of the concession and its financing by French banks, as well as various violations by the timber-cutters, are in Magalhães and Sassi, 'Parakanã', 39. This paper also contains the text of Decree 91,028 of 5 Mar. 1985 establishing the Área Indígena Parakanã in forests south-west of the Transamazonica (rerouted to escape the flooding), some 130 kilometres (eighty miles) north-

west of the growing city of Marabá, and much detail about invasions by settlers. Also J. Carlos de Assis, 'O escândalo Capemi', in his *Os Mandarins da República* (Paz e Terra, Rio de Janeiro, 1984), 79–99.

Two subgroups of Parakanã were contacted in 1983 and 1984, some 250 kilometres (155 miles) to the south-west. A 980,000 ha (3,780 square mile) reserve called Apyterewa was created for these 250 people in 1992 (off the right bank of the Xingu, south of the indigenous lands of the Araweté of the Ipixuna and the Asuriní in Trincheira/Bacajá). Apyterewa was challenged under Decree 1,775 of 1996, and in 2002 was reduced by a fifth to 773,000 ha (2,980 square miles) because its south-eastern side (towards the Xikrin's Cateté area) was occupied more by settlers and loggers (of Exportadora Perachi company) than by Indians.

282: dye].' Ricardo Carvalho, 'A dramática opção dos Parakanã', *Folha de São Paulo*, 15 Oct. 1978; Presland, 'Reconquest', 25.

283: government.' Mércio Gomes, *Os Índios e o Brasil* (São Paulo, 1988); trans. John Moon, *The Indians and Brazil* (Gainesville, Fla., 2000), 196.

284: disappeared.' Regina Müller, 'Os últimos Tupi da Amazônia', RAI, **21**, Jul.–Aug 1981, 34 (also in *Revista Geográfica Universal*, **71**, 1980) and her Doctoral dissertation: *Os Asuriní do Xingu (de como cinquenta e duas pessoas reproduzem uma sociedade indígena)* (Departamento de Ciências Sociais, Universidade de São Paulo, 1987). On the Asuriní's pre-contact migrations: Curt Nimuendajú described a defeat of the tribe by the Gorotire Kayapó in the 1930s, 'Tribes of the Lower and Middle Xingu', HSAI, **3**, 1948, 225; Darcy Ribeiro, *Os Índios e a Civilização* (Rio de Janeiro, 1970), 264 on the attempted Xingu crossing; Berta G. Ribeiro, 'A oleira e a tecelã: o papel social da mulher na sociedade Asuriní', RA, **25**, 1982, 26–7; Arnaud, 'Mudanças entre grupos', 352–3. On Cotrim's contact: Anon., 'Primeiros contatos com os Assurini do Xingu', *Boletim Informativo Funai*, **2:1**, First quarter, 1972, 42–50, and personal communication by Antonio Cotrim to the author in 1972.

285: manioc bread]' Monsenhor Dr Anton Lukesch, 'Os índios barbudos da Amazônia', *Manchete*, Rio de Janeiro, Jul. 1971, 64, and *Bearded Indians of the Tropical Forest* (Graz Akademisch Druck, Graz, Austria, 1976). The reference to Tupi being cheerful is from Jean de Léry, *Histoire d'un voyage faict en la Terre du Brésil*, autrement dite Amérique (La Rochelle, 1578), in Eduardo Viveiros de Castro, *Araweté: os deuses canibais* (Rio de Janeiro, 1986); trans. Catherine V. Howard, *From the Enemy's Point of View: Humanity and Divinity in an Amazonian Society* (Chicago, 1992), 335.

285: saw'. Brooks et al., *Tribes of the Amazon Basin*, 78.

285: batteries, etc.' Müller, 'Os últimos Tupi', 36–39; Lukesch, *Bearded Indians*, 6; Arnaud, 'Mudanças entre grupos', 352–3.

285: defeat'. Berta Ribeiro, 'A oleira', 27.

286: finished'. Ibid., also quoted in Peter T. White, 'Nature's dwindling treasures, rain forests', *National Geographic*, **163:1**, Jan. 1983, 45.

287: too soon.' Antonio Cotrim, 'O Indígena no Brasil', ESP, 5 Nov. 1972.

287: cultures'. Antonio Cotrim in *Veja* (Rio de Janeiro), 31 May 1972, 20; Davis, *Victims of the Miracle*, 68. He also cites a report about Cotrim's resignation in *Miami Herald*, 24 May 1972, and it had extensive coverage in the Brazilian press.

288: killing.' A former gateiro, in Bita Carneiro, 'O longo, difícil, e perigoso namoro do Brasil civilizado com os arredios índios Araras', AI, **21**, Jul.–Aug. 1981 (6–17), 10; ESP, 29 Aug. 1980.

288: presents.' Tojtxi Arara to Fiona Watson, 27 Jun. 1992, in her manuscript report to Survival International. Sydney Possuelo was born in 1940 and worked with the Villas Boas in the Xingu for five years, before joining Funai in 1972. His countless expeditions (which led to over thirty bouts of malaria) included seven first contacts. These included the Parakanã in Pará in 1973, Maya (Morubo) near the Javari, Amazonas in 1977, Awá-Guajá in Maranhão in 1978, Arara in Pará in 1980–81, and Korubo in the Javari area in 1996. Possuelo was President of Funai in 1992–93, a period that saw the demarcation of as many indigenous territories as in all previous regimes. He then returned to active fieldwork, as head of Funai's Isolated Indians Unit.

288: fled from here.' Seu Honório quoted in Carneiro, 'O longo', 8; *Boletim do CIMI*, **10:70**, Mar. 1981, 39–41; O *Liberal* (Belém), 17 Jul. 1977; 'Anna Presland' (Suzanne Williams), 'Reconquest', SIR, **25**, Spring 1979, 23–4. No one knows who gave the tribe the name Arara, which is not their autodenomination. Curt Nimuendajú said that in 1843 a group of 343 Arara had appeared on the lower Xingu. At the time of contact there were thought to be 120

Arara. Orlando Villas Boas's contact expedition in Oct. 1967 took vast quantities of presents but met no Indians. It entered an aldeia where the tall babaçu-palm-thatched huts were reinforced against settlers' guns. Villas Boas thought, not unreasonably, that the Arara might be Juruna who had migrated from the lower Xingu in colonial times: ESP, 14 Sep., 7 Nov. 1967.

The property company that got the huge tract of Arara land was Contrijuí (Cooperativa Triticola de Ijuí) from Rio Grande do Sul: it hoped to bring 2,000 families of settlers from southern Brazil. Incra sold the huge tract for a derisory US $3.60 a hectare ($1.46 an acre) with twenty-year credit. In practice, all that Contrijuí did was rape the area's forests with two sawmills, and build a sugar mill for its own crop of sugar cane (E. J. Silva Lima, J. L. Fernandes, E. Griner, E. R. Machado and S. Brisolla, 'Projeto Cotrijuí-Norte', *Arquitetura*, **20**, 1978, 48–59; Smith, *Rainforest Corridors*, 90–1).

288: captured. One of the Araras' worst persecutors was a guerrilla leader called Inácio Silva, known as 'Carrasco do Rio Pardo' ('Brown-River Executioner'). Twelve Arara are thought to have died in clashes in 1976, and in that year they killed three surveyors from a mineral-exploration company called CPRM. The Funai operative killed in September 1977 was Milton Lucas, and the sertanistas wounded in 1979 were Afonso Alves, João Carvalho, and António Corró. Another leader of the Arara attraction campaign was Wellington Figueiredo. The main interpreter was the Txikão Karaiwá from the Xingu, since it was thought that he spoke the Arara language. In fact the Txikão language is linguistically 'isolated', and the Arara proved to speak Carib.

290: Indians.' Márnio Teixeira Pinto, 'História e cosmologia de um contato: a atração dos Arara', in Bruce Albert and Alcida Rita Ramos, eds., *Pacificando o Branco* (São Paulo, 2002) (405–29), 415–16.

290: friends.' Carneiro, 'O longo', 15.

290: else to go.' Luiz Cláudio Cunha, 'Os Arara saem da mata', *Veja*, 11 Mar. 1981, 76.

291: land.' Tojtxi to Watson, Survival International, 1992. The main supporters of the Arara in the São Paulo branch of CPI were Maria Lúcia de Andrade and Leinad Santos, and among local clergy Fathers Renato Trevisan of the Xingu Diocese (led by the active Bishop Erwin Krautler) and Tarcisio Feitoso da Silva of Altamira. Their opponents were led by politicians from Altamira and the town of Medicilândia on the Transamazonica. The two Arara reserves are: **Área Indígena Arara**, 274,010 ha (1,058 square miles), delimited in 1978, homologated in December 1991, and registered in the Altamira land registry in 1992 with a short frontage on the Transamazonica, home to some 140 Arara, mostly in a village called Laranjal built by Funai; and **A I Cachoeira Seca do Iriri** ('Dry Rapids of the Iriri') adjacent to the west, 760,000 ha (2,930 square miles), delimited in 1993 with further anthropological studies in 1994 to establish Indian title but not yet confirmed or registered, home to some 50 Arara. A 46,000 ha (180 square mile) area north of the Transamazonica was interdicted in 1983 as **Arara II**, but never confirmed as a reserve and the Indians have had to abandon it. Chief Tojtxi and his brother Akito went to Brasília in 1991 to witness President Collor confirming the Arara indigenous area. Isaac Souza of the Summer Institute of Linguistics first studied the Arara dialect of Carib in the late 1980s – and his presence was the pretext for other Protestant missionaries to influence this people. The study of the Arara language, society, and culture was then pursued by Márnio Teixeira Pinto of the Federal University of Paraná. Many Arara learned Portuguese, and some work for settlers in order to buy goods that Funai used to give them. Association with settlers has led to some alcoholism – previously unheard of. But the Arara are generally tenacious in maintaining their traditions and mythology; and their birth rate is now vigorous.

292: hunt?' Tojtxi to Watson, Survival International. The judicial condemnation of Madereira Bannach Ltda. for its invasion of the western AI Cachoeira Seca do Iriri (whose legal status was less than that of the A I Arara to the east) was pronounced in Brasília on 23 Jun. 1995 (*Porantim*, Sep. 1992; *Pastoral Indigenista*, Xingu Prelacy, 9 Nov. 1992; *O Liberal*, 4 Aug. 1995; *PIB 1991/1995*, 433–5). George Monbiot's television documentary *Your Furniture, Their Lives* was broadcast by the BBC on 11 May 1992 and Survival issued an Urgent-Action Bulletin, *Arara Indians Face Extinction*, in that month.

12. Rondônia: Frontier Frenzy

293: surrounded them.' Betty Mindlin, *Nós Paiter. Os Suruí de Rondônia* (Petrópolis, 1985), 21–2. Mindlin studied some 4,000 pages of documents from posts in the SPI's 9th Regional Inspectorate (Cuiabá) in the Museu do Índio in Rio de Janeiro: listed in ibid., 155–6. The many skirmishes along the telegraph line include: the Rondon–Roosevelt's brushes with Indians, on the Dúvida (Roosevelt) in 1913; an attack, presumably by Cinta Larga, in an attempt to wipe out the expedition of Lieutenant Vicente de Paula Vasconcellos (later Colonel Vasconcellos who ran the SPI) when he was descending the Sangue tributary of the Juruena – he was saved by firing into the air but some expeditioners were wounded (Rondon's 1915 speech, and A. A. Botelho de Magalhães, *Pelos Sertões do Brasil* (1928), 80–5). Rondon then sent Lieutenant Marques de Souza to explore the Ananaz tributary of the Roosevelt, in 1915. When his team was making canoes, it was attacked in a hail of arrows. Marques de Souza fired his gun into the air, then opened his arms and confronted the Indians, shouting, 'Friends, do not shoot me!' but he was hit by two arrows fired from the forest; he dived into the river, bleeding, but drowned. A member of the team hid in the woods and watched the Indians examining the photographic and surveying equipment, which they smashed and threw into the river 'like someone ridding himself of dangerous instruments of torture' (ibid., 464).

In 1916 Captain Nicolau Horta Barboza led an expedition down the Anari tributary of the Machado and Ji-Paraná and was surrounded in a major attack from which his men fled to their boats. Horta Barboza knew that these Indians (who may have been Suruí or neighbouring Gavião or Zoró) had often been harassed by rubber men: 'The seringueiros attack the Indians like any other jungle animal. Some have even shown great surprise to hear us reprove such crimes: to them these seem very legitimate acts.' (Ibid., 164).

There is little data from the ensuing decades, apart from Lévi-Strauss's mention of attacks on telegraph stations. During its renaissance in the 1940s, the SPI opened four posts: Major Amarante (1940), Dr Tanajura and Tenente Lira (1945) and Tenente Marques. In 1948 five Suruí attacked and robbed a seringueiro at the village called Rondônia (now Ji-Paraná).

The Jesuit Father João Dornstauder of the Missão Anchieta tried to contact the Cinta Larga in 1962. Then, after the 1963 massacre on 'Parallel 11' (which was confessed to another Jesuit, Father Edgard Schmidt), there were further killings in most years. These culminated in a battle between prospectors and Cinta Larga, possibly near the present P I Roosevelt, in which ten Indians and one prospector died. In 1965, a year of serious drought when hunting was difficult, Indians sacked stores in the settlement of Vilhena. In 1967 a woman and boy were killed at Riozinho; and Cinta Larga then killed a man and wounded his son. During all these years, there were also many skirmishes with the Wari (Pakaá Nova) who lived on the Mamoré–Guaporé watershed southwest of the telegraph line. These are all listed in ibid., 19–21. The Jesuits named their missionary operation after Father José de Anchieta, a much-loved missionary among tribes of the Atlantic seaboard in the second half of the sixteenth century.

294: blood' Telegram from Francisco Meirelles, Villa Murtinho, 9 Jun. 1942, in BSPI, **7**, Jun. 1942, 2. The Pakaá Nova escaped rubber-tappers by retreating to tributaries of the Pacaás Novos river – hence their name. They are also known by their autodenomination Wari (or Huari, Uómo, or Jaru). Their Txapakura language is also spoken by the Torá and Oroin in Brazil and the Moré (Itenes) in Bolivia.

294: took him to visit their village.' Anon., 'Vida e idéias de Meirelles', RAI, **3:21**, Jul.–Aug. 1981 (54–9), 56. Various killings and attacks were attributed to the Wari during these decades – but some of these were doubtless by unrelated tribes such as the Uru-Eu-Wau-Wau or Suruí who lived in the same region. In 1949 a worker was killed at kilometre 280 on the Madeira–Mamoré Railway; in 1950 Indians attacked Vila Murtinho and killed a workman; and in 1951 a rubber trader complained that Indians had attacked his property, shooting arrows at seringueiros and burning his entire stock. In that same year of 1951, another rubber man at Cacoal complained to Francisco Meirelles about the killing of his son – but this could have been done by Suruí Indians from the north. In 1952 the Wari killed a member of Meirelles' attraction team as well as a latex-gatherer near Guajará-Mirim in reprisal for the massacre they suffered at Ouro Preto. Also in 1952 a prospector complained that one of his men was killed and eaten, as was another in a later attack. Two

years later the *Jornal Alto Madeira* reported that the telegraph station José Bonifácio was attacked by ferocious and anthropophagous Indians, who killed a guard. In 1955 the Wari attacked rubber posts at Mutum-Paraná, Jaci-Paraná, and Ouro Preto: two seringueiros were killed and a girl (who had taken a photo of a man transfixed by thirty-six arrows) was wounded. The Wari in 1957 shot arrows at workmen at João de Deus. The next year, Ribeirão Indian post was attacked, as was another place where the Indians killed a seringueiro and removed his head. The Wari also killed a man near Pimenta Bueno in 1960 and set fire to the José Bonifácio station. There were, of course, reprisal expeditions armed with guns which killed far more Indians; but these were rarely reported. Betty Mindlin, *Nós Paiter*, 19–20.

295: allow us to visit their village.' Etta Becker-Donner, 'Vortrag über die Brasilienexpedition 1956', *Österr. Akademikerbund*, **11**, 1957, in *Gedächtnisausstellung Etta Becker-Donner 1911–1975* (Museum für Völkerkunde, Vienna, 1975), 8; also her 'First report on a field trip to the Guaporé region (Pacaas Novos)', *Anais do XXXI Congresso Internacional de Americanistas*, **1**, São Paulo, 1955, 107–12; and 'Notizen über einige Stämme an den rechten Zuflüssen des Guaporé', *Archiv für Völkerkunde*, **10**, Vienna, 1955, 275–343. The missionary thought to have been devoured by the Indians in 1950 was the Benedictine Father Mauro Wirth from São Paulo.

Darcy Ribeiro guessed, in 1957, that there were between 500 and 1,000 Wari. In 1979 the Bishop of Guajará-Mirim gave a population of 1,090 (148 in Funai's P I Lage, 490 in P I Pakaá-Nova, 87 in P I Ribeirão, 250 in P I Negro-Ocaia and 115 in his diocese's P I Sagarana). He also reported 366 neighbouring Makuráp and Jabuti Indians (*Boletim do CIMI*, **10:71**, Apr.–May 1981, 39).

296: sick'. Report by Lieutenant Colonel Moacyr Ribeiro Coelho to the Minister of Agriculture, 23 Feb. 1962, BSPI, **52**, Jan.–Feb. 1962.

296: relatives].' Bernardino de Carvalho and Henry Ballot, 'Pakaanovas, os antropófagos da Amazônia', *O Cruzeiro*, Rio de Janeiro, 3 Mar. 1962, 58. Also Carvalho's articles in *O Cruzeiro*, 27 Jan., 6–11, and 10 Feb. 1962, 20. The photographs of cannibalism were confirmed at a meeting of distinguished anthropologists, including Orlando Villas Boas and Chico Meirelles, in the *Cruzeiro* offices in Apr. 1962. The SPI had previously sent Dr Leão Gondim to investigate the allegations of cannibalism, and denied this possibility in the *Correio da Manhã*, 27 Apr. 1960. José Maria da Gama Malcher, former head of the SPI, in 1967 joined the accusations against Cruz, who had been tried for stealing cattle from the SPI and for homicide, expelled, but later readmitted. Gama Malcher thought that the fierceness of the Pakaá Nova was exaggerated in order to get funds for their 'pacification'. He called the cannibalism 'Cruzeirofagia', invented to please readers of that magazine (*Tribunal da Imprensa* and ESP, 28 Dec. 1961). On the anthropological significance of the cannibalism: Aparecida Vilaça, 'O canibalismo funerário *Pakaa-Nova*: uma etnografia', in Eduardo Viveiros de Castro and Manuela Carneiro da Cunha, eds., *Amazônia: etnologia e história indígena* (São Paulo, 1993), 285–310. Cruz's Mafra expedition set out from Tanajura Indian post on the left bank of the Pacaás Novos river.

296: Expedition.' Coelho, BSPI.

296: victory.' Gilberto Gama in *Última Hora*, 15 Jan. 1962. Beth Conklin wrote a Doctoral dissertation about this anthropophagy and the tribe's reactions to post-contact diseases: *Images of health, illness and death among the Wari (Pakaás Novos) of Rondônia, Brazil* (University of California at Berkeley, 1989). She showed that the Wari did not eat people who had died of pulmonary disease or whose organs were damaged. So they avoided victims of flu or TB who had pus in their lungs. The favourable remark about the role of New Tribes Missionaries in saving lives was by Aparecida Vilaça of the Museu Nacional, 'Cristãos sem fé: alguns aspectos da conversão dos Wari (Pakaá Nova)', TD, 135. There was an unseemly row between the SPI and the Catholic Bishop of Guajará-Mirim in 1965, with the cleric accusing the SPI of gross neglect of Indians dying of TB, and the head of the Service countering by calling the bishop a land-grabber unlike other missionaries: *Jornal do Brasil*, 11 Apr. 1965.

296: marginalized.' José de Queiros Campos, 'Informé de la delegación del Brasil ante el VI Congreso Indigenista Interamericano [at Pátzcuaro, Mexico, April 1968]', AI, **28**:4, Oct. 1968, 1076. The final contacts of Wari were made at this time: six families on the Ouro Preto and other rivers in 1964; seven people in 1966; and five families who had fled from an SPI post in 1969.

297: 118' João Chaves in *A Noite*, Rio de Janeiro, 14 Sep. 1948; Mauro Leonel, 'Onde se esconder?', *Carta* (Gabinete do Senador Darcy Ribeiro, Brasília, **9**, 1993), 109; Leonel, *Etnodicéia Uruéu-au-au* (São Paulo, 1995), 76. The massacre took place on the watershed between the Preto (a tributary of the Jamari, the river that joins the Madeira at Porto Velho) and the Machadinho, not far north-east of the modern town of Ariquemes on the BR-164. Chaves was briefly arrested, but his case was shelved.

297: for him. The 'slaves' that Chaves kept on his seringal were mentioned in various reports by the local SPI man, Pedro Silva in 1948 (in papers found by Mauro Leonel). The Samuel waterfall is now a hydroelectric dam of that name.

297: race.' Fr. Vitor Hugo, *Desbravadores* (2 vols., Missão Salesiana, Humaitá, 1959), **2**, 235, 240; Leonel, *Etnodicéia*, 79. A decade later, in October 1957, the Bishop of Guajará-Mirim wrote to the newspaper *O Globo* criticizing the SPI for not doing enough to find the missing officer, Lieutenant Fernando Gomes de Oliveira of the 6th Frontier Company. Inspector Benedito Pimentel wrote to the same newspaper refuting the criticism and naming various SPI martyrs thought to have been killed by the Pakaá Nova. Even Orlando Villas Boas was sent by the SPI in a vain attempt to try to find some trace of the officer (BSPI, **8**, Oct. 1957).

298: good.' Hugo, *Desbravadores*, **2**, 245; Leonel, *Etnodicéia*, 91.

298: just twenty-five!' Hugo, *Desbravadores*, **2**, 245; Leonel, *Etnodicéia*, 91.

298: rancorous.' Francisco Meirelles, radio message to SPI's 9th Regional Inspectorate, Porto Velho, 25 Jan. 1952; Leonel, *Etnodicéia*, 103–4.

298: immune' Meirelles, in ibid., 103.

298: knife points' Report of eyewitness accounts of the massacre, gathered by SPI official Dídimo Graciliano de Oliveira, 28 Apr. 1980, in records of 8th Regional Inspectorate, in Leonel, *Etnodicéia*, 111.

298: attack him. 'Alfredão' was Alfredo dos Santos, who had captured his wives on expeditions organized by the Canarana and Santa Cruz seringals in the 1950s. Mário Arruda da Costa, *Relato de uma Expedição de Contato Indigenista* (Universidade Católica de Goiânia, Goiânia, 1980), 85; Leonel, *Etnodicéia*, 99.

298: world.' Carvalho, 'Pakaanovas', *O Cruzeiro*, 27 Jan. 1962, 9.

298: similar [to them].' Bernardino de Carvalho, 'Pakaanovas antropófagos da Amazônia', *O Cruzeiro*, 10 Feb. 1962 (18–21), 20.

299: fortune' Leonel, *Etnodicéia*, 103. Details

of the second massacre, in about 1962, emerged in testimony by Indians at the trial of Manuel Lucino in May 1994 (*Porantim*, Jun. 1994). Two of its leaders, known as Nenem Cardoso and Bronzeado ('Tanned'), were still alive in 1994, but unpunished. The Oroin tribe are also spelled Uruim, Orouin, Oro-Win, etc. Manuel Lucino is also spelled Manoel Lucindo; as a Potiguar or Potiguara, he was an Indian from north-east Brazil.

300: shots.' Ibid., 111. The great French anthropologist Claude Lévi-Strauss wrote, from data gathered by Rondon's expeditions, that the Arua living on the Branco tributary of the Guaporé (presumably Oroin) spoke a Tupian language; the Jabuti were linguistically distinct and seemingly related to Jê; whereas the Huari (Wari or Pakaá Nova) were similar to the Tupari to the east. Lévi-Strauss, 'Tribes of the right bank of the Guaporé River', HSAI, **3**, 1948, 371–2.

300: law'. Leonel, *Etnodicéia*, 113.

300: river'. Report by Cícero Cavalcanti, 9 Jun. 1970, in Museu do Índio, in ibid., 115. It was Cavalcanti, influenced by his superior in the SPI Alberico Soares, who had authorized Lucino's 'contact' expedition in May 1963. The seringeiro Alfredão told the English film-maker Adrian Cowell that after Lucino's attack (Cowell called him Ossada), 'there were bones scattered all around. Maybe fifty bodies or more. They opened fire on them, then burnt the huts and everything in them. Nothing was left but the bones and a pile of . . . fourteen big pots, all shot through with bullet holes.' Adrian Cowell, *The Decade of Destruction* (London, 1990), 103. The final conviction of Lucino, the first under the Genocide Law of 1 August 1956, was made in Guajará-Mirim, 11 May 1994 (*Porantim*, Jun. 1994, 7). Four of the prosecution witnesses were women who had survived the 1963 massacre.

301: trembling.' ESP, 20 Jun. 1969. At that time Funai flights had seen some forty Cinta Larga and Suruí malocas, which was thought to indicate a population of 4,000–6,000. In the previous month, Chico Meirelles had found the decomposing body of a seringueiro with thirteen arrows in it, eight kilometres from the Cuiabá–Porto Velho road and not far from the scene of the 1963 massacre. He had also exchanged presents with a Cinta Larga chief (ESP, 16 May 1969).

301: died.' Mindlin, *Nós Paiter*, 26.

302: cord. Although the Suruí refer to themselves as Paiter, the Cinta Larga have names for all adjacent ethnies but none for themselves. They therefore happily adopted the Portuguese name 'broad belt'. João Dal Poz, 'Os ritos da identidade: um estudo das relações étnicas nos Cinta Larga', in E. Pina de Barros, ed., *Modelos e Processos: ensaios de etnologia indígena* (EduFMT (Editora da Universidade Federal de Mato Grosso), Cuiabá, 1998).

302: assistance.' Jean Chiappino, *The Brazilian Indigenous Problem and Policy: the Aripuanã Park* (Amazind/IWGIA, Copenhagen and Geneva, 1975), 14. An (unreliable) Salesian missionary had guessed that there were 2,000 or 3,000 Indians on the rio Roosevelt in the 1950s: Fr. Victor Hugo, *Os Desbravadores* (Rio de Janeiro, 1959). Willem and Carolyn Bontkes of the Summer Institute of Linguistics counted 170 Suruí in their Sete de Setembro village in 1974 and 173 in 1976 (W. and C. Bontkes, *On Suruí (Tupian) social organization* (ms, Summer Institute of Linguistics, 1974). Betty Mindlin witnessed a growing birth rate in that village, so that its population grew steadily from 181 in late 1979 to 235 by the end of 1982. She also saw the Suruí population at their other village, Linha 14, grow from 91 to 105 during the same three-year period, so that the total in the two villages in 1983 was 303. A decade later ISA reckoned 586 Suruí.

302: machine.' Chiappino, *The Brazilian Indigenous Problem*, 15. Jesco von Puttkamer, who was with Apoena Meirelles, was a charming, slightly eccentric photographer-journalist who wrote a series of beautifully illustrated articles about Brazilian Indians for the *National Geographic* magazine. The one about his visit to the Cinta Larga was 'Brazil Protects her Cintas Largas' (Sep. 1971), translated by Funai in its promotional *Boletim Informativo* of the first quarter of 1972. The great-grandson of the Imperial German Governor of South-West Africa (Namibia), Puttkamer fell foul of the Nazis and moved to Brazil. (Although another Jesco von Puttkamer was a close military aide of Hitler in the 1930s.) After his many expeditions, he created a small museum of Indian studies near Goiânia, where he continued to live until his death in 1998.

303: fever.' Chiappino, *The Brazilian Indigenous Problem*, 16.

303: epidemic.' Ibid.

303: wives.' Mindlin, *Nós Paiter*, 27.

304: usefulness.' Carmen Junqueira, 'A esfinge e os índios', *Carta* (Gabinete do Senador Darcy Ribeiro, Brasília, **4:9**, 1993) (99–106), 101.

304: death'. Ibid., 102.

305: SPI.' Edwin Brooks, René Fuerst, John Hemming, Francis Huxley: *Tribes of the Amazon Basin in Brazil, 1972,* Aborigines Protection Society (London, 1973), 46–7. Shelton Davis quoted this in his *Victims of the Miracle* (Cambridge and New York, 1977), 85. He also detailed the discovery of over 4,000 tonnes of tin deposits by Mineração Ferro-União (FERUSA: a subsidiary of the multinational Billiton International Metals, part of Royal Dutch Shell) – and later mining activity by Cia. Estanífera do Brasil (CESBRA, jointly formed by Compagnie Française d'Entreprises Minières, Métallurgiques et d'Investissements (COFREMMI), part of the Patiño tin empire, and by the Brazilian industrialist Antonio Sanchez Galdeano); Companhia Brasileira de Metalúrgia e Mineração (CBMM, jointly owned by the American Molybdenum Corporation and the Banco União of Rockefeller's ally Walther Moreira Salles); and Companhia Espírito Santo de Mineração (owned by the Patiños and by the American Grace Ore and Mining Company) and NL Industries ('Brazil Becomes Self-Sufficient in Tin', *Christian Science Monitor,* 7 Oct. 1967; 'Rondônia, capital do estanho', *Visão,* 28 Aug. 1972; *Mining Journal,* 25 Feb. 1972; Gerard Colby and Charlotte Dennett, *Thy Will be Done* (New York, 1995), 662.

306: Rondônia.' Jonathan Kandell, *Passage Through El Dorado* (London, 1984), 132.

306: land agent.' Ibid., 130. The new agrarian-reform agency Incra launched or authorized a series of colonization projects: PIC (Projeto Integrado de Colonização) at Ouro Preto in 1970; the projects at Ji-Paraná (Itaporanga), Sidney Girão, Paulo de Assis Ribeiro, and PADs (Projetos de Assentamento Dirigido) at Burareiro and Marechal Dutra in 1976: Mindlin, *Nós Paiter,* 17.

307: lands.' Apoena Meirelles, quoted in Leonard Greenwood, 'Brazil Indian expert ousted over protests', *Los Angeles Times,* 16 Mar. 1972, and in Davis, *Victims of the Miracle,* 84–5. The *Jornal do Brasil,* 17 Dec. 1971, reported that Possidônio Cavalcanti Bastos might have been killed by the Cinta Larga because he had come to them with six Suruí warriors, in too abrupt an attempt to bring the two related but hostile groups together. The bodies of the radio operator Acrísio Lima and of the Arara Indian woman Maria were not found; but the President of Funai ordered that there must be no reprisal expedition or attempt to 'ransom' them (*Manchete,* 18 Dec.

1971). There was a second attack a few weeks later, in which Apoena was wounded in the shoulder. But, despite the danger, fifteen Funai employees continued to work calmly at the post. In December 1971, Apoena took seven Suruí warriors to Porto Velho because they insisted on going to tell the 'great white father' Francisco Meirelles that they were innocent of the killings. While they were gone, other Suruí occupied the post, to ensure their safe return.

There was another contact post called Serra Morena, on the Aripuanã river, forty minutes' flight north of the Roosevelt post. There was a first exchange of presents with the Kabano Pomon group of Cinta Larga there in August 1972. But the attraction team found an abandoned civilizado camp nearby, containing high-velocity cartridge cases: this was thought to have been the scene of an atrocity by the Hungarian Tibor, a notorious gunman employed by the Junqueira company. Loren McIntyre was at Serra Morena five years later and he reported that the Kabano Pomon Cinta Larga were suffering badly from colds and some were dying of pneumonia. McIntyre watched a contact with warriors from the Kabano Iára group of Cinta Larga: fifteen men wearing wide red belts and feather headdresses. 'The warriors strode up the bank with heads erect, eyes darting from side to side but never locking with ours for fear of a hex.' Some of the Indians had scars from bullets or lead slugs under their skins. (McIntyre, 'Brazil's wild frontier', *National Geographic,* **152:5,** Nov. 1977, 705.)

307: religion.' Kandell, *Passage through El Dorado,* 140. The Melhoranças' property company Cia. Colonizadora Itaporanga was often known as the Gleba.

307: shame.' Ibid., 157.

308: forest.' Mindlin, *Nós Paiter,* 24. The two Suruí villages, Sete de Setembro (named after Brazil's National Day, 7 Sep., but which the Indians called in their language 'the place where machetes were suspended') and Linha 14, were ten kilometres apart, and each about fifty kilometres (thirty-one miles) from the growing city of Cacoal. Funai's base for the Aripuanã park was still right on the BR-364 at a place called Riozinho.

308: something].' ESP, 9 Aug. 1979. The Indians were critical of the director of the Aripuanã park, Aymoré Cunha da Silva, for not doing enough to help them. Another report in that newspaper at that time accused Funai operatives of prostituting Suruí women or getting them to live with settlers. The judicial order expelling squatters from Sete de Setembro was made by the Tribunal Federal de Recursos on 1 Feb. 1981. It and the subsequent quarrels between Indians and settlers are reported in *PIB 1981*, 22–3.

308: believe.' ESP, 9 Aug. 1979.

309: nudity.' Roberto Gambini, 'Relatório de visita à frente de atração Zoró' (Nov. 1983) in Roberto Gambini, Carmen Junqueira, Mauro de Mello Leonel, and Betty Mindlin, *Avaliação da situação Zoró – Aripuanã, Karitiana, Karipuna, Gavião, Arara (Karo), Uru-eu-wau-wau e Uru-pa-in* (Report **3:1**, Ministério do Interior – SUDECO, Fundacão Instituto de Pesquisas Econômicas (FIPE), Jun.–Dec. 1983); Betty Mindlin, 'Avaliação do Programa Polonoroeste', *PIB/83* (167–70), 167.

Apoena Meirelles thought that there may have been 800 Zoró in eight villages at contact (*Revista Geográfica Universal*, **38**, Nov. 1977); some 400 were vaccinated in 1978; but by the time of Gambini's visit five years later there were only 200 living at the attraction post.

309: world.' Gambini, 'Relatório'.

309: know what.' Ibid.

309: way"?' Ibid.

310: sin".' Mauro de Mello Leonel, 'Relatório de avaliação da situação dos Gavião (Digüt) – P. I. Lourdes', in Gambini et al., *Avaliação da situação Zoró* (77–117), 90; and a 'Relatório complementar' in their *Relatório IV* of Mar.–Oct. 1984, 86–100.

311: suicidal'. Carmen Junqueira and Mauro Leonel, 'Observações recolhidas no Parque Indígena do Aripuanã' in their *Relatório IV*, 20. The massacre of the Cinta Larga was discovered by pilots and missionaries of the Catholic Missão Anchieta. It was apparently connected with a violent quarrel between the American mining company Ancon, which had been given a concession, and some seventy garimpeiro gold prospectors who were being evicted. CIMI blamed Funai for having failed to demarcate the Aripuanã park. *Jornal do Brasil*, 5 May 1982. Also, Carmen Junqueira, Betty Mindlin, and Abel Lima, 'Terras e conflito no Parque do Aripuanã', in Silvio Coelho dos Santos, ed., *Os Índios Perante o Direito* (Florianópolis, SC, 1982), 111–16; Richard Chapelle, *Os Índios Cintas-Largas* (Belo Horizonte, 1982).

312: our world.' Carmen Junqueira, writing on the jacket of her friend Betty Mindlin's *Nós Paiter*.

As superb hunters, the Suruí could imitate most animal sounds. This mimicry made them natural linguists. Immediately after contact, I saw them calling out their first Portuguese word: 'Positivo', which is the Brazilian radio parlance for 'sim' or yes.

312: many of them.' Mindlin, *Nós Paiter*, 26.

312: Rondônia.' Statement by Suruí meeting, P I Sete de Setembro, 25 Jun. 1985, signed by Chief Itabira and others at the town of Cacoal on 30 Jun., PIB-85/86, 307. Another Director of the Aripuanã park whom they wanted sacked was Francisco de Assis da Silva ('Chicão').

312: able to.' Henry Roland Loewen, *A summary of Indian work done by Missão Novas Tribos do Brasil in the states of Amazonas and Acre, and the Federal Territory of Rondônia* (typescript, 1970).

313: integration.' Ibid. In that same year, 1970, a Red Cross team visited two Pakaá Nova posts (Tenente Lira on the Lajes river, and Pitop village an hour's walk from Dr Tanajura post) and reported favourably on the medical work of the New Tribes Mission. They were equally satisfied by the work of Dr F. A. Bendoraitis of the Catholic Church in Guajara-Mirim at the Pakaá Nova village Sagarana – even though a raging measles epidemic had just killed seven of the village's hundred people, with a further twenty sick patients lying in their hammocks. Bo Åkerren, Sjouke Bakker, Rolf Habersang, *Report of the ICRC Medical Mission to the Brazilian Amazon Region* (Geneva, 1970), 30–3.

313: cannibalism.' Aparecida Vilaça, 'Cristãos sem fé: alguns aspectos da conversão dos Wari (Pakaa Nova)', in TD (131–54), 133.

313: crentes.' Ibid., 137.

313: culture.' Mauro de Mello Leonel Jr., 'Relatório de avaliação das comunidades Oro-Uari, Macurap e Canoé das Áreas Pacaa-Nova, Lage e Sagarana', *Polonoroeste. Relatório IV, Volume 1 – Pacaa-Nova* (FIPE, São Paulo, Mar./Oct. 1984), 18. Funai's anthropologist Ana Maria da Paixão had condemned the behaviour of the New Tribes Mission in an official report in 1975, but nothing was done to expel them. This view was repeated in another Polonoroeste report, by Edgard de Assis Carvalho and Lúcia H. Vitalli Rangel, *Avaliação da Área dos Pacaa-Nova* (FIPE, 1983). Others who criticized the missionaries' destruction of Wari society included: Bernard von Graeve, *Protective Intervention and Interethnic Relations: A Study of Domination on the Brazilian*

Frontier (Doctoral dissertation, University of Toronto, 1976); Omar Landi Santos, *Uma Solução para a Sobrevivência dos Índios do Guaporé* (Campinas, 1980); Rubem César Fernandes, 'Um Exército de Anjos. As razões da Missão Novas Tribos', *Religião e Sociedade*, 1980; Denise Maldi Meirelles, *Populações Indígenas e a Ocupação de Rondônia* (Proedi, Universidade Federal de Mato Grosso, Cuiabá, 1984).

314: divinity.' Vilaça, 'Cristãos sem fé', 149. Also, Vilaça, 'Os Wari', *PIB 1991/1995*, 556–8, and Gilles de Catheau, 'Os Warí: subsistência, saúde e educação', ibid., 559–61.

314: liked it.' Vilaça, 'Cristãos sem fé', 149. Also, Vilaça, 'Os Wari' and Catheau, 'Os Wari', 556–61.

315: anything else.' Pierre Clastres, *Chronique des indiens Guayaki* (Paris, 1972, translated by Paul Auster, *Chronicle of the Guayaki Indians*, Faber & Faber, London, 1998). Although this description of the inspiration of hunting was about the Aché of northern Paraguay, it applies equally to the similar Nambiquara some 500 kilometres (310 miles) north-west of them.

315: "people".' David Price, *Before the Bulldozer* (Cabin John, Md., 1989), 13–14. Price preferred the old spelling Nambiquara because the Portuguese language does not use the letters K and W except for loan words; but the modern usage is to employ these foreign letters when writing tribal names. He caught the Funai agent (and former Lutheran missionary worker) Fritz Tolksdorf and his superior, General Demócrito Soares de Oliveira (director of Funai's Department of Native Resources), doing dubious deals with the big Bamerindus bank, which had bought the Madeirama land development company; and he found that Tolksdorf had been given a four-wheel-drive vehicle by the Amburana ranch, whose land he had certified as clear of Indians: ibid., 20–1, 149.

316: west.' Report by Hélio Bucker of Funai and the American anthropologist David Price to Funai's Cuiabá office, 1969, in Roberto Cardoso de Oliveira, 'Indigenous peoples and sociocultural change in the Amazon', in Charles Wagley, ed., *Man in the Amazon* (Gainesville, Fla., 1974) (111–35), 129. The missionary who in 1962 contacted the Nambiquara on the Galera river was Hilmar Gluck of the South American Indian Mission. He was still with them after their forced move.

The 'Amazon' carvings in the caves were discovered by Jesco von Puttkamer in 1969 (O

Globo, 27 Jan. 1970, 17). They are in the Chapada dos Parecis, at the extreme south of Nambiquara territory, near the source of the Galera tributary of the Guaporé and the settlements Fazenda Guaporé on the BR-364 variant and Posto Uirapuru on the highway's old route. The female carvings showed a Y that seems to represent the pubis, with a deep cut like a vagina, and some had associated penises and even a smaller internal triangle that could have been a womb. The archaeologist Altair Sales Barbosa of the Catholic University of Goiás examined the caves in 1971 ('Women's lib, Amazon style', *Time Magazine*, 27 Dec. 1971, 54) and he returned for a fuller excavation seven years later. The digs at thirteen nearby sites yielded thousands of stone artefacts, 9,000 fragments of pottery, some with geometric incisions, a gold ornament, and charcoal that was dated to 9,000–12,000 BP. (W. Jesco von Puttkamer, 'Man in the Amazon: stone age present meets stone age past', *National Geographic*, 155:1, Jan. 1979, 60–83.) These investigators seemed unaware that the earliest Spanish explorers had heard rumours of Amazons in this region, near the headwaters of the Paraguay river. The German Ulrich Schmidel wrote about an expedition to find them in the early 1540s – at much the same time as Francisco de Orellana was descending the Amazon and naming it after tribes supposedly led by female warriors. Schmidel, *Warhaftige Historie einer wunderbaren Schiffart* (Frankfurt-am-Main, 1567) trans. Luis Dominguez, *The Conquest of the River Plate* (Hakluyt Society, 81, London, 1889); John Hemming, *Red Gold* (London, 1995), 46.

316: homelands.' Brooks et al., *Tribes of the Amazon Basin*, 43. Tolksdorf's full name was Friedrich Paul, but he was always known as Fritz. He was credited with contacting the Rikbaktsa (or Erigpatsa) and living with them as a missionary; he then joined Funai as a sertanista and was active among the Nambiquara for many years.

316: roadside.' Antonio Cotrim Soares in *Veja*, 31 May 1972; 'Development against the Indians', *Brazilian Information Bulletin* (American Friends of Brazil, Berkeley, Cal., Jan. 1973), 10.

317: peasants.' Price, *Before the Bulldozer*, 18.

317: for it.' Ibid., 111–12.

318: Tereco.' Sílbene de Almeida's diary of his return to the Haihai Nambiquara, in Jul. 2000, in the obituary on the ISA Web site *Notícias Socioambientais*, 25 Sep. 2001. Sílbene left Funai to work for the environment agency Ibama. He was murdered at his house near Brasília in September 2001, aged fifty-one. The ISA obituary described him as 'a master of joy and discreet irreverence' and praised his thirty years of inspirational work with Indians.

318: delayed.' Price, *Before the Bulldozer*, 120.

318: fervour'. Report by David Price to Hélio Jorge Bucker of Funai, July 1970, in 'Deus do mêdo e da morte, Deus da Funai', *Jornal da Tarde*, 3 Jul. 1970. When the Aborigines Protection Society's team visited Camararé in August 1972, it found its Indians much cheered by the expulsion of Dudley Kinsman and his colleagues Donald Grump and Harris Gregory. (Kinsman had the Indians call him Parente, which is the Portuguese for 'kinsman' or relative.) The road to Camararé branched off the BR-364 105 kilometres (65 miles) south-east of Vilhena and then ran for 72 kilometres (45 miles) through weak *campo* country to reach the village of fourteen huts and some eighty people. Åkerren et al., *Report of the ICRC Medical Mission*, 26–7; Brooks et al., *Tribes of the Amazon Basin*, 41–2.

319: extinct.' Robin Hanbury-Tenison, *Report of a Visit to the Indians of Brazil* ... (London, 1971), 16; Brooks et al., *Tribes of the Amazon Basin*, 40.

320: medicaments.' Åkerren et al., *Report of the ICRC Medical Mission*, 26. Serra Azul ('Blue Hill') is inside the southern tip of the Nambiquara indigenous area, 140 kilometres (87 miles) south-east of Vilhena.

320: in dispute'. Darcy Alvares da Cunha, Funai's delegate in Mato Grosso, quoted in ESP, 1 Jan. 1982. The new reserves were published in the *Diário Oficial* on 3 Dec. 1981: **Pirineus de Souza**, 30,000 ha (115 square miles), **Sararé**, 68,000 ha (260 square miles), and **Vale do Guaporé**, 243 ha (600 acres). The opposition was started by a rancher, and pursued by a state Desembargador (Chief Justice) and the Governor of Mato Grosso, Frederico Campos. The case dragged on through 1982. A better President of Funai, Air Force Colonel Paulo Moreira Leal, said that the agreement with the World Bank

required that the reserves be created, sent teams to demarcate them, cancelled a fraudulent Negative Certificate that had been issued to the Sorama company (*Diário Oficial*, 16 Apr. 1982), and in May created two new posts: **Paresi** for the tribe of that name, and **Aroeira** for the Nambiquara in Mato Grosso. *PIB 1981*, 20–22; *PIB/1982*, 32–4.

320: region.' Rinaldo S. V. Arruda, 'A luta por Japuíra', *PIB-85/86* (313–21), 313.

321: than war' Ibid.

322: familiar.' Joana A. Fernandes Silva, 'Utiariti – A última tarefa', in TD (399–424), 404. Utiariti was 550 kilometres (342 miles) north-west of Cuiabá at a rapids on the Papagaio headwater of the Juruena. The Federal University of Mato Grosso in Cuiabá published various research papers about Utiariti, in its sixth-monthly reports to the National Research Council CNPq in 1991–92.

322: punishment.' Ibid., 407.

322: towns.' Arruda, 'A luta por Japuíra', 315. The Rikbaktsa were also known to seringueiros as Canoeiros ('canoers') and spelled Erigpactsa (Gama Malcher, 1963) and Aripaktsá (Kietzman, 1967). Their language was 'unclassified' by Kietzman, but is Macro-Jê, meaning that it is loosely connected to other Jê tongues. The Lutheran missionary was Friedrich Richter of the Inland South American Missionary Union, and his base on the Escondido stream was some forty kilometres (twenty-five miles) above the famous Augusto Falls on the Juruena, far downriver or north of the Jesuit mission. An early account of them was: Fritz Tolksdorf, 'Ethnographische Beobachtungen in Zentral Brasilien', *Zeitschrift für Ethnologie*, **81**, 1956, 270–86, and the archives of the Conselho Nacional de Proteção aos Índios contained reports by Tolksdorf and Father Dornstauder.

322: post.' Report by Father Schmidt, in Arruda, 'A luta por Japuíra', 315. The intensive-acculturation mission Barranco Vermelho was on the right bank of the Juruena, near the later Japuíra reserve.

13. The Triumph of Activism

323: society'. Law 5,371 of 5 Dec. 1967, quoted by Funai's first President, José de Queiros Campos, 'Actividades de la Fundação Nacional do Índio del Brasil', AI, **30:2**, Mexico, Apr. 1970 (536–60), 536–7.

323: criteria'. Ibid., 544. Campos was well

aware that the press campaign was intended to discredit the military regime that had seized power in 1964. He therefore accused many incompetent SPI staff of being placemen of 'the defunct Brazilian Labour Party'.

324: transport'. Álvaro Villas Boas, a younger brother of the famous Orlando, Cláudio, and Leonardo, in O *Globo*, 2 Oct. 1968. Álvaro was a gentle man who later ran Funai's operations in the State of São Paulo. The author was with him on an expedition in 1972, and found him idealistic and very competent, but shy of publicity and not sufficiently charismatic to appeal to Indians. He was President of Funai for a few weeks in September and November 1985, but the Indians demanded and got his removal. He died in 1995, aged seventy-one.

324: disbanded. GRIN was the Guarda Rural Indígena; it lasted from 1966 to the mid-1970s. Most of these militarized Indians came from tribes along the Araguaia and Tocantins (Krahó, Xerente, Gavião, and Karajá) or from the north-east. They were trained at the police academy in Belo Horizonte, dressed in green-and-yellow uniforms, armed with revolvers, paid salaries, and supposed to discipline their fellow Indians (ESP, 2 Oct. 1969 and 3 and 9 Jun. 1970; Edwin Brooks, René Fuerst, John Hemming, and Francis Huxley, *Tribes of the Amazon Basin in Brazil, 1972* (London, 1973)). There was also a nasty reformatory for Indians at the Krenak post in Minas Gerais, although resisters from the Krenak tribe itself were exiled to a labour camp at Fazenda Guarani in south Brazil. Queiros Campos's sister was Cecília Campos, accused in May 1969 of irregularities in buying supplies for the hospital on Bananal. Her brother was sacked in June and replaced by General Bandeira de Mello, who had led the intelligence service's investigation against her.

324: boys.' Orlando Villas Boas, personal communication, 1972. During Bandeira de Mello's administration, Funai issued publicity material including a *Boletim Informativo* and booklets called *Funai em números* and *Supysáua: o índio brasileiro*. The statistics pamphlet said that the Foundation cared for 180,000 people on its 140 Indian posts and 15 parks and reserves (the four parks were Xingu, Tumucumaque, Aripuanã, and Araguaia; and the eleven reserves were Waimiri/Atroari, Parakanã, Kararaô, Nhambiquara, Pareci, Irantxe, Erigpactsã, Tapayuna, Apiaká, Kayabi, and Karitiana). There were said to be 115 teachers in 144 schools teaching 15,112 pupils, which would

imply that some teachers taught at more than one school, and gave a teacher–pupil ratio of 1:131. The figures for health care (11,960 treatments, 5,300 dental sessions, 27,718 vaccinations in 1971), 1,537 house starts in southern Brazil alone, and farming of 1,126 ha of wheat, 480 ha of soya, 60 ha of maize, and 60 of beans (2,782, 1,186, and 148 acres) in that same region, are all equally suspect. An earlier booklet of Funai statistics in 1969 was so inaccurate that the distinguished anthropologists Ney Land and Heloisa Torres rejected it, and were sacked from Funai's Research Department by Queiros Campos as a result.

325: contact' Oscar Jeronymo Bandeira de Mello, President of Funai, remarks to Aborigines Protection Society team, Brasília, 4 Aug. 1972 (summarized in Brooks et al., *Tribes of the Amazon Basin*, 15–19); also Bandeira de Mello letter to Edwin Brooks of the APS, Brasília, 20 Nov. 1972. These policies were often repeated in Funai's publicity material and pronouncements, such as those in the previous note.

326: group.' Berta Ribeiro, O *Índio na Cultura Brasileira* (Rio de Janeiro, 1987), 163; João Pacheco de Oliveira, 'Os índios e a questão fundiária', *Tempo e Presença* (CEDI, Rio de Janeiro, 1983). Work on the Indian Statute was started by the jurist Professor Themistocles Cavalcanti at the request of the Minister of the Interior Costa Cavalcanti in February 1970, and the first draft handed to the Minister in June (ESP, 14 Feb., 3 Jun. 1970).

326: power.' Dalmo de Abreu Dallari, 'O índio, sua capacidade jurídica e suas terras', in Comissão Pró-Índio – SP, *A Questão da Emancipação* (Global Editora, São Paulo, 1979) (77–82), 78; Suzanne Williams, 'Land rights and the manipulation of identity: official Indian policy in Brazil', *Journal of Latin American Studies*, London, **15:1**, 1983, 138–9.

327: civilization.' President Médici, 'Explanation of the aims of the Ministers of Interior and Justice' in the Law of the Statute of the Indian, Brasília, 12 Oct. 1970, clause 7 (b). Also, Statute of the Indian, section 1, Principles and Definitions, Article VI (Law 6,001, 19 Dec. 1973).

327: respite for the Indians'. Alcida Rita Ramos, 'Frontier expansion and Indian peoples in the Brazilian Amazon', in Marianne Schmink and Charles H. Wood, eds., *Frontier Expansion in Amazonia* (Gainesville, Fla., 1984), 92. General Ismarth Araújo de Oliveira was President of Funai from March 1974 to March 1979 and had previously been one of its superintendents. Engineer Adhemar Ribeiro da Silva was in office from March to November 1979. During those months, despite his good record in many respects, Ribeiro da Silva granted concessions for mineral prospecting in Waimiri-Atroari lands. His resignation was apparently because of clashes with General Demócrito de Oliveira, who had been Funai's 'strong man' for a decade. His departure was lamented by the anthropologists Manuela Carneiro da Cunha and Carmen Junqueira and the photographer Cláudia Andujar who was fighting for the Yanomami. The three issued a note saying that he had finally modified Funai's policies to become of 'real benefit to the Indians' (ESP, 16 Oct. 1979).

327: defend the Indians' Ramos, 'Frontier expansion', 92.

328: among the Indians.' Queiros Campos, 'Actividades de la Fundación', 546–7. The appointment of missionaries as unpaid agents of Funai was reported in *Comunicado Mensal* (Conferência Nacional dos Bispos do Brasil, Rio de Janeiro, **205–6**, Oct.–Nov. 1969), 63.

329: Word".' *Relatório* of the third 'Encontro Sôbre Pastoral Indígena' organized by CNBB, and Anthropos, Brasília, April 1972. The first such Encontro was in São Paulo in February 1968. The 1972 meeting also established CIMI (Conselho Indigenista Missionário) with the Salesian Fr. Ângelo Venturelli as its first president and Fr. José Vicente César as secretary. New operational methods for missionaries were proposed at a meeting of bishops of Amazonia, at Santarém in May 1972.

In a sense, CIMI evolved from the Anthropos Institute. A priest called Wilhelm Schmidt in 1906 founded *Anthropos*, an international review of ethnology and linguistics with a Catholic bias, then an Anthropos Institute in Vienna in 1932. The Instituto Anthropos Brasileiro de Ethnografia (later Instituto Anthropos do Brasil) became active in São Paulo in 1965 under Fr. César and he moved it to Brasília in 1971.

330: ourselves'. Conclusions of the 'Assembléia Missionária Indigenista', Goiânia, 27 June 1975, in Anon., '1975/79: quatro anos de ação', *Boletim do CIMI*, **8:57**, Jul. 1979 (5–21), 10.

330: patrimony.' Cláudia Menezes, 'Os Xavantes e o movimento de fronteira no leste mato-grossense', RA, **25**, 1982, 85–6. One of CIMI's first efforts was a Draft of what it wanted in the new Indian Statute (*Anteprojeto do Estatuto do Índio*, Cuiabá, Mato Grosso, 12 Aug. 1972); but this was not successful. Fany Ricardo, 'O Conselho Indigenista Missionário (CIMI): cronologia das transformações recentes da pastoral indigenista Católica no Brasil, 1975–1979', *Cadernos do Instituto Superior de Estudos da Religião*, **10**, 1982, 1–25.

330: censorship.' Marlene Castro Ossami, O *Papel das Assembléias de Líderes na Organização dos Povos Indígenas no Brasil* (Goiânia, 1993), 12. The rise of the indigenous movement during the 1970s was also chronicled in M. C. Ortolan Matos, O *processo de criação e consolidação do movimento pan-indígena no Brasil (1970–1980)* (Master's dissertation, Universidade de Brasília, 1997). The CNBB (Conferência Nacional dos Bispos do Brasil) was the Catholic Church's influential governing body. CIMI was based in Brasília and CEDI (ISA) in São Paulo. CEDI stood for Centro Ecumênico de Documentação e Informação – in 1991 it changed its name to ISA, Instituto Socioambiental (Social and Environmental Institute). Ricardo, 'O Conselho'.

330: efforts.' Anon., '1975/79: quatro anos de ação', 18.

331: society.' Suzanne Williams, 'Reconquest', SIR, **25**, Spring 1979, 8.

331: cause.' Greg Urban, 'Developments in the situation of Brazilian tribal populations from 1976 to 1982', *Latin American Research Review*, **20:1**, 1985, 17.

331: must die"'. Mércio Gomes, *Os Índios e o Brasil* (São Paulo, 1988); trans. John Moon, *The Indians and Brazil* (Gainesville, Fla., 2000), 209. The full title of the booklet was *Documento Y-Juca Pirama – o índio: aquele que deve morrer* (CNBB, 1973). Paulo Suess, *Em Defesa dos Povos Indígenas. Documentos e legislação* (São Paulo, 1980) and many long articles in *Boletim do CIMI*.

331: buildings. The name Porantim came from a sacred paddle of the Sataré-Mawé, which was covered with pictures showing the history of the world and a code of laws. That tribe's Chief Honato called 'the Porantim [illustrated paddle] the gospel of our people. It gives us laws. It tells us that we must love our brothers.' (*Folha de São Paulo*, 1 Mar. 1981.)

331: meetings'. Anon., '1975/79: quatro anos de ação', 18.

331: land' Conclusions of the 'Assembléia Missionária Indigenista', Goiânia, 27 Jun. 1975, in Anon., '1975/79: quatro anos de ação', *Boletim do CIMI*, **8:57**, Jul. 1979 (5–21), 6.

332: unrealistic.' The Politics of Genocide *Against the Indians of Brazil,* document presented to the XLI International Congress of Americanists, Mexico City, 1974; later published in American Friends of Brazil, *Supysáua: A Documentary Report on the Condition of Indian Peoples in Brazil* (Berkeley, Cal., 1974), 35–41. The earlier *Os Índios e a ocupação da Amazônia,* São Paulo, 19 May 1971, was handed to the Sociedade Brasileira para o Progresso da Ciência and reported in *O Globo,* 15 Jun. 1971 and elsewhere. In the following year, the 24th Annual Meeting of the SBPC approved a damning report into 'conditions of life and threats to . . . the country's indigenous communities': this was submitted to the Interamerican Indigenist Congress in Brasília in August 1972. Two Brazilian newspapers also published long and sympathetic reports on the critical state of the Indians: Mário Chimanovitch, 'A triste história da integração indígena', several articles in *Jornal do Brasil* during September 1972; and 'O Indígena no Brasil', with articles by Gama Malcher and staff reporters, ESP, 5–9 Nov. 1972. The government tried to fight back with works such as Danton Jobim, O *Problema do Índio e a Acusação de Genocídio* (Conselho de Defesa dos Direitos da Pessoa Humana, Ministério da Justiça, Brasília, 1970).

332: destruction'. United Nations General Assembly, Resolution 96 of 11 Dec. 1946, Article 2, c, in American Friends of Brazil, *Supysáua,* 40.

332: society.' Urban, 'Developments', 8. The acronyms or initials of some early NGOs were as follows: the Protestant GTME was Grupo de Trabalho Missionário Evangélico; ANAI stood for Associação Nacional de Apoio ao Índio; CPI for Comissão Pró-Índio; CTI for Centro de Trabalho Indigenista. CCPY was the Comissão Pró-Yanomami (originally Comissão pela Criação do Parque Yanomami); AWARU was Comissão de Apoio Indigenista ao Povo Nambikwara; MAREWA was Movimento de Apoio à Resistência Waimiri Atroari; GAIPA was Grupo de Apoio ao Índio Pataxó. All the many pro-Indian organizations were listed by Carlos Alberto (Beto) Ricardo in two articles, 'Quem fala em nome dos índios?' in *PIB 1987/88/89/90,* 69–72, and *PIB 1991/1995,* 90–4.

333: wanted.' Roque Laraia, 'Integração e utopia', *Revista de Cultura Vozes,* **70:3**, Apr. 1976, 201; Ossami, O *Papel,* 44.

334: another.' Laraia, 'Integração', 201; Ossami, O *Papel,* 44.

334: threatened.' Fr. Paulo Suess in *Correio Braziliense,* 22 Apr. 1984; Ossami, O *Papel,* 46.

334: guilty ones.' Lino Miranha speech to Assembly at Rio Andirá, December 1981, in ibid., 42.

334: money' Minister Rangel Reis, *Jornal de Brasília,* 28 Dec. 1976; Brazilian Anthropologists, 'The politics of genocide against the Indians of Brazil' (summary of a document presented to the XLI International Congress of Americanists, Mexico City, 1974) in American Friends of Brazil, *Supysáua,* 35.

335: nation.' Cardinal Sherer, Archbishop of Porto Alegre, quoted in Bruce Heller, 'Indians in Brazil are trapped in a government–church feud', *Miami Herald,* 30 Jan. 1977; SIR, **18**, Spring 1977, 21.

335: speak for them'. Editorial, ESP, 18 Jun. 1975; Ricardo, 'O Conselho', 11.

335: illegal'. David Maybury-Lewis, 'Indian & Pro-Indian Organizations in Brazil', *Cultural Survival Quarterly* (Cambridge, Mass.), **8:4**, Dec. 1984 (19–21), 19–20.

335: done for them'. Júlio César Melatti in Fátima Murad article, *Movimento,* 16 Feb. 1976; trans. in SIR, Spring 1976, 26.

336: Indians'. Porantim, **7:51**, Nov. 1978, 5.

336: respond.' Orlando Villas Boas speaking at a meeting of NGOs in Porto Alegre (which created ANAI), O *Liberal,* 1 May 1977; Ricardo, 'O Conselho', 19. Father Iasi himself resigned as Secretary of CIMI in November 1977, because its freedom of independent action was curtailed by the CNBB. This was because the row between the missionary factions had been referred to the Pope, who told them all to calm down and improve relations with the Brazilian government.

336: rude'. David Price, *Before the Bulldozer: the Nambiquara Indians and the World Bank* (Cabin John, Md., 1989), 69.

336: unconcealed'. Ramos, 'Frontier expansion', 92.

336: problems'. Ibid.

336: neglect.' Price, *Before the Bulldozer,* 49.

337: peasants' Mário Juruna, February 1978, in Comissão Pró-Índio, *A Questão da Emancipação* (São Paulo, 1979), 12. This book listed all the meetings and statements by both sides during the four-year debate (pages 9–16) and contained cogent essays by the lawyer Dalmo de Abreu Dallari, anthropologists, and Indians. CIMI published an attack on Minister Rangel Reis by the veteran Darcy Ribeiro (recently allowed back into

Brazil after years of political exile): 'Um ministro agride os índios,' *Boletim do CIMI*, **7:51**, Nov. 1978, 5–17.

337: lands.' Ibid., 12–13; the same argument is in José de Souza Martins, 'A emancipação do índio e a emancipação da terra do índio', ibid., 73–5, and in a useful summary of the debate about 'Who is an Indian?' by Manuela Carneiro da Cunha in SIR, **37/38**, Winter 1981, 5–6 and **39**, Spring 1982, 32; ARC, **5**, Mar. 1981, 7–9. *Time* magazine fell for the seductive government argument that emancipation 'freed' Indians to become 'generals, politicians, even President' (13 Nov. 1978).

337: life itself.' Márcio Souza, José Ribamar Bessa, Mário Juruna, Megaron, Marcos Terena, *Os Índios Vão à Luta* (Rio de Janeiro, 1981), 72.

338: moustache.' Price, *Before the Bulldozer*, 153.

338: racism.' Ramos, 'Frontier expansion', 96.

339: Indians.' *Boletim do CIMI*, **10:70**, Mar. 1981, 5.

339: eggheads'. Price, *Before the Bulldozer*, 144.

339: tribunal.' *Boletim do CIMI*, **8:53**, Jan.–Feb. 1979, 15. Both the orders to arrest Father Jentel and then, after his pardon, to expel him were signed by President Geisel. His conviction was for many years' help to landless peasants of Santa Terezinha, since 1964, to squat on unoccupied land and to form a cooperative; but his protests on behalf of the Tapirapé land dispute did not help his cause. He had reached Brazil in 1954 and worked for a decade with the Gavião and Tapirapé. The Dominican nuns, the Irmãzinhas de Jesus (Little Sisters of Jesus), had been with the Tapirapé since 1952. Funai's behaviour toward the Tapirapé was reported in *Boletim do CIMI*, **4:24**, Nov.–Dec. 1975, 5–8; **5:25**, Jan.–Feb. 1976, 17; and extensively in the article 'Tapirapé: povo ameaçado', **10:73**, Jul.–Aug. 1981, 37–40. In 1976 the nuns had reported that tourist cruise ships were regularly visiting the Tapirapé, to film the Indians and buy their handicrafts even though such exploitation was forbidden by the Indian Statute. Such intrusion disrupted the tribe's normal farming cycle (ESP, 3 Sep. 1976). The land grant to CIVA (Companhia Imobiliária do Vale do Araguaia) in 1954 included even the SPI post Heloísa Torres (Roberto Cardoso de Oliveira, 'A situação atual dos Tapirapé', BMPEG, **3**, Jul. 1959). The settlers and Tapiraguaia ranch moved in in 1966, and the 'donation' of land in Jul. 1967 was 'accepted' on behalf of the Indians

(but not by them) by the local SPI Inspector, Ismael da Silva Leitão. Dom Pedro Casaldáliga, *Uma Igreja da Amazônia em Conflito com o Latifúndio e a Marginalização Social* (São Felix, Mato Grosso, 1972), 23.

340: resolved.' 'Diário de uma revolta', *Boletim do CIMI*, **10:69**, Jan.–Feb. 1981, 9.

340: nothing.' 'Tapirapé: povo ameaçado', *Boletim do CIMI*, **10:73**, Jul.–Aug. 1981, 40. The Brazilian press carried many stories about the Tapirapé during 1981 – actions in support of the tribe by the Bishops of Brazil, a report to a Papal nuncio, the nuns' protests of innocence from having incited the tribe: *PIB 1981*, 34–6. The visit by Funai's new President, Colonel Paulo Moreira Leal, and Marcos Terena (President of the new UNI, Union of Indigenous Nations) was reported in the *Folha de São Paulo*, 6 Dec. 1981. President Figueiredo signed Decree 088,194 on 23 Mar. 1983 confirming the smaller Tapirapé/Karajá Indian Area, demarcated according to Funai's wishes.

340: tribe'. Paulo Suess, 'O santo que deve ser canonizado agora', *Porantim*, **3:18**, 18 May 1980, 9.

341: too much land'. Ibid.

341: on our land!' Ibid.

341: patio.' Ibid. The Minister of Justice and the Interior Minister, Rangel Reis, vowed to bring the guilty to swift justice (*Folha de São Paulo*, 20 Aug. 1976). But only three of the five men who killed Rodolfo Lukenbein and Simão Cristino were tried, two years later in Barra do Garças, and all were acquitted. The accused, who had been full of tearful remorse during the trial, celebrated the verdict with a triumphant party. The many Bororo and Xavante who had been brought to watch the verdict showed no emotion: they were sure that the guilty farmers would never be punished (ESP, 29 Mar. 1979; *Boletim do CIMI.*, **8:55**, Apr. 1979, 38–40). Father Rudolph Lukenbein was born in 1939 to German peasant stock, educated at the Salesians' school at Buxheim, went to Brazil in 1958, and after a decade of study there and in Germany was ordained in 1969. He returned to Meruri next year and spent the rest of his life among the Bororo, as well as serving on the council of CIMI. Fr. Rodolfo was one of the hosts of the Third Assembly of Indigenous Chiefs, held at Meruri in September 1975. This was the first such assembly to be entirely planned by Indians, in this case Bororo, and it undoubtedly strengthened their resolve to stand up for land

rights. The guests included many active missionary priests, including Fr. João Bosco Burnier of the
Missão Anchieta (later killed by a policeman),
Bishop Thomas Balduino, and Fr. Egydio Schwade
(who had been expelled from the Waimiri-
Atroari, and later ran CIMI). The Assembly's
programme included a visit to the nearby Xavante
mission São Marcos, at the invitation of the venerable Chief Apoena, who had made peace with
Chico Meirelles thirty years previously.

341: Mission.' Fr. João Bosco Burnier's introduction to CIMI's missionary training course, *Boletim do CIMI*, **5:33**, Nov. 1976, 28.

342: Indian.' Speech by João Carvalho Guarani, 14th Assembly of Indigenous Leaders, Brasília, Jun. 1980, ARC, **5**, Mar. 1981, 5; *Porantim*,
Oct. 1980, Jan.–Feb. 1981.

342: themselves.' *Jornal do Brasil*, 11 Apr.
1981; *Porantim*, May 1981, 4.

342: control over them.' Ramos, 'Frontier
expansion', 99.

343: going?' Souza et al., *Os Índios Vão*, 64,
67.

343: human rights.' ESP, 27 Oct. 1981.

343: policy.' 'Mário, ex-cacique, Juruna, depu-
tado?', *PIB 1981*, 74; Maybury-Lewis, 'Indian &
Pro-Indian Organizations', 19–21; Darrell Posey
interview in Susanna Hecht and Alexander Cockburn, *The Fate of the Forest: Developers, Destroyers
and Defenders of the Amazon* (London and New
York, 1989), 216. Juruna's name, a corruption of
his Jê name Dzururã, was confusing because he
was a Xavante, whereas the Juruna are a Tupi-
speaking people of the upper Xingu. Juruna's
PDT party was that of the firebrand Leonel Brizola and the anthropologist/politician Darcy
Ribeiro – both of whom were deprived of political
rights after the military coup of 1964. By the time
of his election in 1983, Brazil was about to return
to democratic rule.

343: ravished by him.' Affonso Romano de
Sant'Anna, 'Enterrem meu coração na Serra da
Bodoquena', *Jornal do Brasil*, 4 May 1980.

344: help us.' Souza et al., *Os Índios Vão*, 54.

344: struggle for them.' Mário Juruna speech to
Congress, Day of the Indian, 19 Apr. 1983, SIN,
3, 1983, 3.

344: Janeiro.' Ligia T. L. Simonian, 'A presença de Juruna', *PIB/83*, 15; also Manuela Ligeti
Carneiro da Cunha, 'Ofensivas contra os direitos
indígenas', ibid., 11–13, and innumerable mentions in the Brazilian press. After Mário Juruna
lost his seat in Congress, he worked for some

years as an adviser to Funai but then declined in
both health and prestige. By 2000 he was fifty,
living in poverty, reduced to a wheelchair by
rheumatism and chronic diabetes, and longing to
return to his village Namunkurá in the São Marcos
reserve. He died in Jul. 2002, in hospital in Rio
de Janeiro.

344: television'. Richard Chase Smith, 'Amazonian Indians participate at UN', *Cultural Survival Quarterly*, **8:4**, Dec. 1984, 29.

345: peoples.' Ibid.

345: conquerors.' SIN, **9**, 1985, 9.

346: itself'. *Ato Público Pela Criação de Comis-
são Parlamentar Permanente de Defesa dos Direitos
Indígenas*, Comissão Pró-Índio SP, Universidade
Católica, São Paulo, 14 Apr. 1980.

346: at all.' Maybury-Lewis, 'Indian & Pro-
Indian Organizations', 21. By the mid-1990s the
ten largest indigenous nations were: Guajajara,
Potiguara, Xavante, and Yanomami between
5,000 and 10,000; Terena, Makuxi, and Kaingang
between 10,000 and 20,000; and only the many
groups of Guarani in southern Brazil and the
Ticuna on the Solimões totalling over 20,000.

347: allies.' Carlos Alberto (Beto) Ricardo,
'Quem fala em nome dos índios?', *PIB 1991/1995*
(90–94), 91. (The first part of this excellent summary was in *PIB 1987/88/89/90*, 69–72.) Indian
legislation during the presidency of Fernando
Henrique Cardoso was a start on the Estatuto das
Sociedades Indígenas and Decree 1,775 of 9 Jan.
1996 that accelerated demarcation of Indian lands
but allowed them to be challenged at any stage of
the demarcation process. Capoib stands for Conselho de Articulação dos Povos e Organizações
Indígenas do Brasil. It was founded in 1992 at a
meeting of the Amazon-region umbrella organization Coiab (Coordenação das Organizações Indígenas da Amazônia Brasileira, founded in 1989).

347: movement'. Ossami, *O Papel*, 3.

348: society.' Elizabeth Allen, 'Brazil: Indians
and the new Constitution', *Third-World Quarterly*, **11:4**, Oct. 1989, 153.

348: exploited'. 'A conspiração contra o Brasil',
ESP, 9 Aug. 1987. This accusation was triggered
by a resolution passed by 47,000 Young Austrian
Catholics to influence the Brazilian Constitution.
The article spoke of secret Church archives and
financial reserves for the campaign. Later articles
(11–16 Aug.) had wild allegations about the
Church seeking to protect its 'Tin brothers' in
Malaysia from competition by Brazilian cassiter-
ite, attempts to cripple Brazilian exports, and

deny World Bank loans, and plans for gold mining throughout the Amazon.

349: Yanomami. The missionaries who were either expelled or forbidden to enter indigenous lands included: Egydio Schwade and Doroti Müller Schwade from the Waimiri-Atroari (December 1986); Silvio Cavuscens and Marlete de Oliveira from the Javari valley in January 1987; João Saffirio, Guilherme Damioli, and Sister Florença Lindey (a much-respected nurse) from Yanomami territory in August 1987, and nine others from the north-east, CIMI headquarters, and other places.

349: rights'. ISA Web site 'Indigenous rights in the 1988 Constitution'. These rights were fully analysed by lawyers in a book edited by Juliana Santilli, *Os Direitos Indígenas e a Constituição* (Porto Alegre, 1993); and summarized in the Brazilian Government's pamphlet *Brasil Indígena* (Brasília, 1992).

349: Constitution.' *Jornal de Brasília*, 1 Jun. 1988; *PIB 1987/88/89/90*, 29.

350: reproduction'. Article 231, paragraph 1, Federal Constitution of 1988.

350: intermediary.' Mércio Gomes, *The Indians and Brazil*, 180.

350: protection.' Ibid., 98.

350: nation'. William Balée, 'Language, law,

and land in pre-Amazonian Brazil', *Texas International Law Journal*, **32:1**, Winter 1997, 127.

351: reconciliation.' Laymert Garcia dos Santos, 'Amigos dos índios: os trabalhos da Comissão Índios no Brasil', in Luís Donisete Benzi Grupioni, ed., *Índios no Brasil* (São Paulo, 1998) (29–36), 29. Ailton Krenak was born in 1954 in his Krenak tribe's land in Minas Gerais. Well educated, Ailton worked as a journalist before dedicating himself to the Indian cause, in UNI (of which he became president), in the debates about the 1988 Constitution (when he famously wore a smart white suit but painted his face black with genipap, in mourning for indigenous rights), with Chico Mendes at the Forest Peoples' Alliance, then back with the Krenak working for the Núcleo de Cultura Indígena. An eloquent and much-quoted orator, Ailton Krenak was accused by his enemies of being a phony Indian because he was too handsome and Westernized. In 1990 Ailton Krenak went to Athens to receive the Onassis Prize for Service to Man and Society (The Aristotelis Prize), and a book was published to commemorate this and quote from his speeches: Liz Hosken and Kathy Steranka, eds., *A Tribute to the Forest People of Brazil* (The Gaia Foundation, London, 1990).

351: persons.' Gomes, *The Indians and Brazil*, 224–5.

14. Jê on the Warpath

353: every day.' Report on the Suiá-Missu ranch, *Jornal da Tarde*, 21 Jul. 1971; ESP, 25 Apr. 1969; Pedro Casaldáliga (Bishop of São Felix, Mato Grosso), *Uma Igreja da Amazônia em Conflito com o Latifúndio e a Marginalização Social* (São Félix, Mato Grosso, 1972), 12, 22, 99–100.

353: territories.' Cláudia Menezes, 'Os Xavantes e o movimento de fronteira no leste matogrossense', RA, **25**, 1982, 70; Shelton Davis, *Victims of the Miracle* (Cambridge and New York, 1977), 148; Marta M. Lopes, *A resistência do índio ao extermínio: o caso dos Akwe-Xavante, 1967–1980* (Master's dissertation, Universidade do Estado do São Paulo, 1988), 42 and 67–8; Aracy Lopes da Silva, 'Dois séculos e meio de história Xavante', in HIB (357–78), 372. The Suiá-Missu ranch was originally owned by one Ariosto da Riva, a Brazilian of Italian extraction. He sold it in the late 1960s to a Paulista company called Ometto, which achieved fame by attracting no less than

$30 million in government subsidies for this fazenda during the decade 1966–76. The ranch grew to a massive million hectares, and in 1972 was sold for $5 million to the Liquigás company owned by the Ursini family. Sue Branford and Otto Gluck, *The Last Frontier: Fighting over Land in the Amazon* (Third World Books, London, 1985); Iara Ferraz and Mariano Mampieri, 'Suiá-Missu: um mito refeito', *Carta* (Gabinete do Senador Darcy Ribeiro, Brasília), **9**, 1993, 75–84 and *PIB 1991/1995*, 675–8. Later government programmes that favoured large ranches were PRO-TERRA and then POLAMAZONIA (Programa de Ocupação da Amazônia). The huge local authority of Barra do Garças had three new municipios carved out of it: Canarana (just south of the Xingu park), Água Boa, and Nova Xavantina.

The Secretary-General of CIMI in 1972 reported a tragic epidemic in which a hundred Indians died of tuberculosis and flu on the Salesian missions; but this was vigorously denied by the local Salesian health worker, Sister Ada, who said that they had lost only nine children, from measles (ESP, 17 Aug. 1972; *Jornal do Brasil*, 20 Aug. 1972).

353: ranchers.' Mário Chimanovitch, 'Índios armados exigem demarcação de sua reserva', *Jornal do Brasil*, 13 Aug. 1972.

354: take their places. The creation of new Xavante reserves (on about a tenth of the tribe's true territory) was done by Decree 65,212 of 23 Sep. 1969. The row between the Xavante who had taken refuge at Batovi post and the South American Indian Mission Inc. was reported in ESP, 28 Apr. and 5 May 1970. It led to the resignation of one of Funai's best sertanistas, Hélio Bucker, who was angry that the missionaries were allowed to continue.

354: once more!' Celestino Tsererob speaking at the Tenth Assembléia de Chefes Indígenas at the Tapirapé village in 1977, quoted in A. C. Moura, 'Parabubure, a nova reserva Xavante, nasceu do sangue dos índios massacrados', *Boletim do CIMI*, **9:61**, Jan.–Feb. 1980 (5–11), 5. The original owners of the Xavantina ranch were thought to have been an American–Portuguese consortium. These were said to have hired gunmen in Barra do Garças to massacre Xavante in their hammocks, then supplied poisoned rice, beans, and maize, and finally brought the 1957 measles epidemic through contaminated clothing. The ranch was sold in 1976 to the Amurada Estradas e Projetos SA, a powerful Paraná construction company with links to the state politician Ney Braga. Amurada planted pasture and extensive rice fields at Xavantina. Meanwhile, anthropologists and Indianists put pressure on Funai to recover the lost land, but there were long delays.

354: fighting.' Antonio Carlos Moura, 'A criação da reserva evita o ataque Xavante', ESP, 3 Dec. and 22 Dec. 1979; Menezes, 'Os Xavantes', 71–2. Had the incident degenerated into fighting, the fifty or sixty Xavante would have had a difficult battle against perhaps four hundred armed farm-workers and cowhands. The attack on Xavantina fazenda had been carefully planned by Chief Joãzinho (of São Domingos Savio village) who summoned Chiefs Martinho Celestino and Dario (of Couto Magalhães) and Zacarias (of São José village). São Marcos is about a hundred kilometres (sixty miles) south-east of Parabubure (Culuene/Couto Magalhães) but on the right bank of the Mortes. The São Marcos mission was

the last to be created by the Salesians, during the 1950s, and it was planned to resemble a traditional semicircular Xavante village – unlike the nearby Meruri (created in 1902) and São José on the Sangradouro river (1906) for the Bororo. On 14 September 1972, Decree 71,106 awarded the São Marcos Indian reserve to Funai to administer on behalf of the Xavante, with the Salesian mission in its midst. The reserve was enlarged by Decree 73,233 of 5 September 1975. Changes in Xavante attitudes to Salesian management of São Marcos during four decades after their move there in 1956 were chronicled in Cláudia Menezes, 'Missionários e guerreiros: o apostolado salesiano entre os Xavante', in TD.

355: land.' ESP, 22 Dec. 1979. The Xavantes' conflicts to regain some of their land are described in detail by Marta M. Lopes, *A resistência do índio*, 71–9 and Cláudia Menezes, 'Os Xavantes'. 73–4.

355: friend'. *Correio da Manhã*, Goiânia, 3 May 1980. The chiefs were also accompanied by three parliamentarians, including Gilson de Barros, a state deputy of Mato Grosso. The fraud at Pimentel Barbosa started when four Funai cartographers 'confused' the names of streams called Água Amarela ('Yellow Water') and Água Suja ('Dirty Water') when drafting the 1975 decree, thereby removing over 100,000 ha (390 square miles). The leader of this cartographic scam, Valdênio Lopes, then acquired some of the excluded land and sought to buy the silence of the Indians with presents of a pickup truck, some cattle, and sewing machines (*Correio Braziliense*, 6 May 1980). When that error was being rectified, surveyors from the government mapping agency IBGE altered a demarcation path at the southwest of the reserve, thereby reducing its frontage onto the BR-158 road by ten kilometres (six miles).

355: people' *Jornal de Brasília*, 6 May 1980; ESP, 13 Aug. 1980; *Guardian*, London, 15 Oct. 1980. In their efforts to regain land stolen from them, the Xavante felt sorry for poor settlers who had to be evicted. They tried to insist that these innocent victims (who had been granted title deeds in the disputed area) should be compensated.

355: Interior.' Márcio Souza, José Ribamar Bessa, Mário Juruna, Megaron, Marcos Terena, *Os Índios Vão à Luta* (Rio de Janeiro, 1981), 54. The lawyer was Laia Mattar Rodrigues.

356: family.' *Folha da Tarde*, 24 Jun. 1983. Later that year, twenty-three Xavante returned –

armed with their usual clubs and bows – and demanded a meeting with the new President of Funai, Otávio Lima, about threats to allow mining on Indian lands (*PIB/83*, 198).

356: domination'. Lopes da Silva, 'Dois séculos', 375.

357: importance for them.' Nancy M. Flowers, 'Subsistence strategy, social organization, and warfare in central Brazil in the context of European penetration', in Anna Curtenius Roosevelt, ed., *Amazonian Indians from Prehistory to the Present* (Tucson, 1994) (249–69), 254; Menezes, 'Os Xavantes', 77–82.

357: impossible'. Lopes da Silva, 'Dois séculos', 377. Laura Graham, *Performance Dynamics and Social Dimensions in Xavante Narrative: Hoimanauô Wasusu*, and *The Always Living: Discourse and the Male Life Cycle of the Xavante Indians of Central Brazil* (Master's and Doctoral dissertations, University of Texas at Austin, 1983 and 1990).

When the Suiá-Missu ranch was owned by the Ursini subsidiary Liquigás it was known as Liquifarm Agropecuária Suiá-Missu SA. Its grandiose modernization plans foundered when the entire Ursini empire failed and its remnants passed in 1979–81 to ENI (Ente Nazionale Idrocarburi) and its subsidiary Agip do Brasil. Agip invested heavily to make the ranch succeed. It was pressure by Mariano Mampieri of the Italian NGO Campagna Nord/Sud and Brazilian activists led by the anthropologist Iara Ferraz that achieved the restitution. They described the tortuous process in Ferraz and Mampieri, 'Suiá-Missu'.

358: affair'. Lopes da Silva, 'Dois séculos', 377; Graham, *The Always Living*, 72–5.

358: Xavante.' Lopes da Silva, 'Dois séculos', 378; Marta M. Lopes, *A resistência do índio*, 145.

358: neighbours'. Ferraz and Mampieri, 'Suiá-Missu: um mito refeito', 79. Funai's technical report about demarcating the Suiá-Missu land was dated 3 Aug. 1992, and it established the Área Indígena Maräiwatsede by Proceder 1318/92.

359: progress'. General Oscar Bandeira de Mello, *Visão*, 25 Apr. 1971, 22; Casaldáliga, *Uma Igreja*, 24.

360: killed many people.' Letter by Megaron Txukarramãe, Kretire village, 1 Nov. 1980, SIR, **6:2(34)**, Summer 1981, 75–6. Megaron also described these events and his role in them in Souza et al., *Os Índios Vão*, 59–63; *Porantim*, Jan.–Feb. 1981; ARC, **5**, Mar. 1981, 11. The future head of the Xingu park was born in 1955.

360: left to us?' Letter by Megaron Txukarramãe, 1 Nov. 1980.

361: they died.' Letter from Megaron to the British film-maker Chris Kelly, 5 Sep. 1980, SIR, **5:3–4(31–32)**, Autumn/Winter 1980, 27. Raoni helped Kelly to co-produce an eponymous documentary film about himself (with Jean-Pierre Dutilleux). Its English version was narrated by Marlon Brando and it gained an Oscar nomination. The decree that changed the shape of the Xingu park was 68,909 of 13 Jul. 1971; the creation of P. I. Jarina was Funai Portaria 369/N of 26 May 1976: texts of these two edicts are in Vanessa R. Lea, *Parque Indígena do Xingu. Laudo Antropológico* (Universidade de Campinas, São Paulo, 1997), 161–2. The Mentuktire village south of the road was Porori; it was renamed Kretire in honour of the chief of that name who had died during the move there in 1971.

361: later.' 'Violence in Xingu National Park', *Time*, 8 Sep. 1980; Stuart Wavell, 'Wounded Indians fight for their land', *Guardian*, London, 15 Oct. 1980.

362: hunting grounds.' ESP, 7 Sep. 1980.

362: kill them'. Jean-Pierre Dutilleux, introduced by Norman Lewis, 'The tribe that won't surrender', *Observer Magazine*, London, 25 Jan. 1981, 35.

362: left."' Ibid.

362: village' O Globo, 19 Apr. 1984. The hostages included some good friends of the Indians, such as the dentist Biral and his wife the nurse Estela – an attractive couple who devoted their lives to working with the Xingu Indians and were still treating them at the end of the twentieth century.

363: ready to fight'. O Globo, 31 Mar. 1984. A blow-by-blow account of the events of 1984 is: Vanessa Lea and Mariana Kawall Leal Ferreira, '"A guerra no Xingú": cronologia', in *PIB/1984*, 246–58.

363: (Panará).' Lea, *Parque Indígena*, 121; and her *Área Indígena Kapoto: laudo antropológico* (Universidade de Campinas, São Paulo, 1997), 105–6.

363: hostages. The senior Funai officials were Carlos Grossi and Lamartine Ribeiro de Oliveira. Possuelo, a later President of Funai, was deeply sympathetic to Indians but he had offended the Kayabi, who now stripped the hostages, broke their glasses, and might have harmed them had Megaron not intervened.

363: Indians'. Jornal do Brasil, 4 May 1984.

364: kill'. Marina Wodtke, 'Consenso no Xingu', *Manchete*, 19 May 1984.

364: farms.' *Cidade de Santos*, 30 Oct. 1984, in Lea and Ferreira, '"A guerra no Xingú"', 258.

364: land.' Article signed by Maírawe Kayabi and others, *Memória do Xingú* newsletter, quoted in ARC, **10**, Feb. 1982, 7.

365: like Indians.' José Uté Gorotire, ESP, 7 Sep. 1980.

365: cut an Indian."' *Boletim do CIMI*, **9:66**, Aug.–Sep. 1980, 9–10. Warren Hodge described this attack, and the Mentuktire's killing of the caboclos on the Xingu, in three articles in the *New York Times* (31 Aug., 3 and 6 Oct. 1980) which elicited a letter from Professors Joan Bamberger and Daniel Gross (22 Oct.) complaining about his lurid description of twenty white corpses 'strewn around their jungle encampment amid symbolic red parrot feathers'. *Guardian*, 11 Sep. 1980; SIR, **5:3–4(31–32)**, Autumn/Winter 1980.

365: decline.' Terence Turner, 'De cosmologia a história: resistência, adaptação e consciência social entre os Kayapó', in Eduardo Viveiros de Castro and Manuela Carneiro da Cunha, eds., *Amazônia: etnologia e história indígena* (São Paulo, 1993), 47.

366: frenzy. The world was stunned by photographs of hellish conditions of antlike, near-naked miners clawing at the crater of Serra Pelada, and there were good studies of its gold rush by David Cleary, *Anatomy of the Amazon Gold Rush* (London and Iowa City, 1990), and Gordon MacMillan, *At the End of the Rainbow? Gold, Land and People in the Brazilian Amazon* (Basingstoke and New York, 1995).

367: garimpeiro.' Cleary, *Anatomy of the Amazon Gold Rush*, 186. Also Vanessa Lea, 'Brazil's Kayapo Indians Beset by a Golden Curse', *National Geographic*, **165:5**, Washington, May 1984, 674–94.

368: pride.' The miner's leader João Lanari do Val told his bitter version of events, ESP, 28 Apr. 1995.

368: activity.' Salomão Santos of Funai, quoted in *Interior*, Mar./Jun. 1985, 62.

369: bearing arms.' Ibid., 61–2.

369: reaction'. Ibid. The agreement, 'Ata da Reunião A.I. Kayapó', was signed on 3 May 1985 by the Minister of the Interior, the President of Funai, and Paulinho Paiakan 'for the indigenous community'. Its text is in *PIB-85/86*, 224.

369: goods.' Darrell Posey, interviewed in 1988, in Susanna Hecht and Alexander Cockburn, *The Fate of the Forest: Developers, Destroyers and Defenders of the Amazon* (London and New York, 1989), 217. Darrell Posey was one of the most active anthropologists. His doctoral dissertation at Louisiana State University was on Kayapó knowledge and use of bees, wasps, and other insects. Years spent with the Kayapó taught him much about their extraordinary biological lore. He was also a great champion of Indians, as we shall see in this chapter – which Darrell vetted just before his death. He achieved notable successes over the proposed Xingu dams in 1988, at the Earth Summit in Rio de Janeiro in 1992, and then while a don at Oxford as a fierce protector of indigenous intellectual property rights. He died of cancer in 2001, aged fifty-three.

370: festivals.' Ibid.

370: prohibited.' Carlos Ricardo and the CEDI team, '"Operação Ouro-Gorotire" financia assistência e consumo em estilo Kaiapó', *PIB 1987/ 88/89/90*, 310–11. In 1990 Maria Bonita had some 3,000 miners and 450 pumping systems, Cumaruzinho had 300 men, and there was a third, smaller garimpo called Arara Preta ('Black Macaw'). The Gorotire village was linked by a new forty-three-kilometre (twenty-seven-mile) road to the mining base of Cumaru just outside the reserve, and 128 km (80 miles) to the ironically named town of Redenção ('Redemption') on the north–south BR-158 Marabá–Aragarças road not far west of Conceição on the Araguaia. The tribe got 12 per cent of the value of each miner's gold, plus 1 per cent of the turnover of businesses licensed to buy gold. The Gorotire Pedro Aybi remained at Redenção to bank the income, helped by a small team of salaried non-Indians.

370 and 371: forget' and *autonomy.'* Terence Turner, 'De cosmologia a história', 51; on the use of videos, his 'Imagens desafiantes: a apropriação Kayapó do vídeo', RA, **36**, 1993, 81–122; and on public relations, 'Kayapó on television: an anthropological viewing', *Visual Anthropology Review*, **8:1**, 1992, 107–12. Another analysis of the impact of gold income on the Kayapó is: William Fisher, 'Megadevelopment, environmentalism, and resistance: the institutional context of Kayapó indigenous politics in central Brazil', *Human Organization*, **53:3**, 1994, 220–32; and reports of lavish spending by Indians, for instance in *Jornal do Brasil*, 5 and 12 Jun. and 12 Dec. 1987.

371: Christianity'. Turner, 'De cosmologia a história', 49.

371: *humanity'*. Ibid., 58.

371: *culture".'* Ibid., 43. In 1979–80 three Catholic missionaries made twelve visits to villages in the main Kayapó Indian Area, to re-establish Catholicism, which had been losing out to the Protestants. Fathers Renato Trevisan, Mário Pezzoti, and Zezinho Leoni reported in December 1980 (*Boletim do CIMI*, **10:72**, Jun. 1981, 7–11). At **Gorotire** village they found 537 Indians, of whom 182 were baptized Catholics and the remainder Protestant or 'indifferent'; at **Kokrai-moro**, 180 people of whom 60 were baptized Catholics; **Kikretum**, 160 people, mostly Catholic; **Kuben-Kran-Kégn**, 375 people, 91 baptized Catholics and the rest Protestant or indifferent; **Oukré**, 120 people who had left Kuben-Kran-Kégn, mostly Protestant. The total for the five villages was 1,372, but another eight villages brought the huge Kayapó Indian Area's population to some 3,000. The reserve measured 2,738,850 ha (10,572 square miles).

371: *whites.'* Dom Erwin Krautler in *Veja*, 5 Jul. 1989, 84.

372: *mercury.'* Ibid., 83. The Mercury Project team, headed by Professor Aguinaldo Gonçalves of the University of Brasília, worked in Gorotire and Kikretum villages (*A Crítica*, 9 Nov. 1994; CIMI *Newsletter* **136**, 28 Oct. 1994; Rainforest Foundation *News*, Summer, 1993, 6).

372: *timber-loggers'*. Lux Vidal and Isabelle Giannini, 'Xikrin do Cateté exploram madeira. E são explorados por madeireira', *PIB 1987/88/89/90*, 315. The first timber concession was in February 1984 to a company called SEVAT, for 2,000,000 cruzeiros (about US $140,000) which was about a tenth of its market value. In 1990 the anthropologists Vidal and her daughter Giannini, assisted by Funai, CEDI, the Núcleo de Direitos Indígenas, and the nearby iron-mining Companhia Vale do Rio Doce, got the grossly one-sided contract between the Xikrin community and the Bannach timber company annulled. José Ferreira Campos Júnior, Funai's manager in Marabá, inspected the terrible damage caused to the Xikrin reserve by the extraction of 600 mahogany trees and the miles of roads opened to drag the trees out. Campos did this work at his own expense, and sent the damning report to the federal prosecutor, but little came of it.

372: *sense.'* Posey interview in Hecht and Cockburn, *The Fate of the Forest*, 217.

373: *region.* Father Renato Trevisan, 'Colonel Tutu Pombo: a morte de um líder Kayapó', *PIB*

1991/1995, 420–1. The Menkragnoti Indian Area was finally homologated by President Collor on 19 August 1993 and legally registered in December of that year. The Baú and the Capoto/Jarina Areas had been delimited in 1991.

374: *United States.'* Heraldo Maués, *Diário do Grande ABC*, 6 Nov. 1988; *Correio Braziliense*, 16 Dec. 1988 and 15 Feb. 1989, *PIB 1987/88/89/90*, 326–8.

375: *rain forest.'* Brian Jackman, 'Singing in the Rain Forest', *Sunday Times*, London, 3 Apr. 1988, 36. The man who organized Sting's visit to the Xingu was the Belgian film-maker Jean-Pierre Dutilleux – who was later discredited and sacked from the Rainforest Foundation.

375: *Levi's'*. Ibid., 37.

375: *lumber mills.'* Juan de Onis, 'The Green Cathedral', *The Rainforest Foundation Journal*, London, Sep. 1992, 4. (De Onis also published a book of that name in 1992.) When Sting returned to Brazil after the journey with Raoni, he was criticized by Mário Juruna (who had failed to be re-elected as a deputy) for exploiting the 'purity and innocence of the Indians for publicity purposes (*Veja*, 5 Jul. 1989, 82). The Rainforest Foundation was later attacked in a British television documentary, and by Survival International, for naivety and for allegedly allowing funds to be frittered away or stolen by its staff. The Menkragnoti indigenous area measured 4,915,255 ha (18,973 square miles). It joined the A I Kayapó (3,284,005 ha: 12,676 square miles), A I Baú (1,850,000 ha: 7,141 square miles), and A I Capoto/Jarina (634,915 ha: 2,451 square miles) to the north with the Xingu Indian park (2,642,003 ha: 10,198 square miles) to the south. In 1995 the AI Panará was added to the west of the Menkragnoti reserve.

377: *present.'* Letters signed by Kanhon and other Kayapó chiefs, Gorotire, 2 Nov. 1988, *PIB 1987/88/89/90*, 330; Terence Turner, 'Baridju-moko em Altamira', ibid., 337–8.

377: *dam.'* Nicholas Hildyard, 'Adios Amazonia?', *Ecologist*, London, **19:2**, 1989 (53–62), 53. Eletronorte is the north-eastern division of the government energy company Eletrobrás. It claimed that the Kararaô dam near Altamira (renamed Bel Monte to sound less Indian) would flood 'only' 615 km² (237 square miles), but independent analysts reckoned that it would destroy 1,125 km² (434 square miles). At least the Xingu river dropped 90 metres (295 feet) in the Kararaô rapids; all observers agreed that

760 *Notes and References*

shallower dams upriver would flood far vaster areas.

Most of the affected people would have been Indians. The São Paulo branch of the Comissão Pró-Índio therefore issued an admirable volume about the proposed dams, with expert essays on each of the tribes of the lower and middle Xingu whose land would have been drowned by them: Leinad Ayer O. Santos and Lúcia M. M. de Andrade, eds., *As Hidrelétricas do Xingu e os Povos Indígenas* (São Paulo, 1988). The costs of building the dams and attendant distribution networks would have been astronomical and far outweighed potential benefit to the Brazilian economy. Barbara Cummings also warned about the dire potential of the dams, in *Dam the Rivers, Damn the People* (Earthscan, London, 1990). The Altamira meeting was also summarized by Marcus Colchester in *Geographical Magazine*, London, Jun. 1989, 16–20.

377: progress?' Hildyard, 'Adios Amazonia?', 53.

377: Indians.' Ibid.

378: violated. Indigenous Declaration of Altamira, 24 Feb. 1989, *PIB 1987/88/89/90*, 335. Later that year, the Body Shop donated a Cessna plane to Paiakan's village A'Ukre. This author helped persuade a major international bank not to finance the Xingu dams, by pointing out that the Amazon basin is too flat to have hydroelectric dams without flooding unacceptably vast areas of forest. The Altamira protest achieved massive coverage in the world's media.

378: tribe'. *Veja* cover, 10 Jun. 1992, and three subsequent issues in which Brazil's largest serious weekly news magazine stooped to inventing racist stories about the victim's breast being torn, a blood-bath with cannibal overtones, and attempted strangulation. The *Washington Post's* cover story was in its weekend magazine *Parade* in April. The rape, alleged to have taken place on Sunday 18 May, was first reported in the Belém newspaper *O Liberal* on 5 June. Sílvia Letícia said that she and some friends had been drinking with Paiakan and his wife in their cottage. Paiakan's car took some of the party home, and the rape was said to have occurred on the back seat when it returned. Medical examination showed that the girl's hymen had recently been ruptured, but there was no evidence of sexual violence or attempted murder with a piece of barbed wire – as alleged by the only witness. Paiakan later admitted that they had all been drinking heavily – forty-eight

bottles of beer – and that his wife Irekran had beaten the girl; but he was adamant that he had not raped Sílvia Letícia. Memélia Moreira pointed out that wealthy Kayapó were highly regarded in the mining town of Redenção. She wrote that Paiakan and Letícia had been lovers for some time: the girl had promised to bear the chief a male heir – something that Irekran could no longer do, as she had been irrevocably sterilized by a doctor without her full consent. Irekran's beating of her rival, caught having intercourse with her husband, was correct Kayapó behaviour (Memélia Moreira, 'Estupro e preconceito', *Carta* (Gabinete do Senador Darcy Ribeiro, Brasília), 9, 1993, 133–6). Letícia later married a young farmer, and in 1995 was in trouble for trying to help her husband escape after he had been imprisoned for murder. The press coverage of the case was admirably summarized in *PIB 1991/1995*, 412–17. Márcio Santilli, executive secretary of the Nucleus of Indigenous Rights, commented on the racist media coverage in 'The Cannibals', *The Rainforest Foundation Newsletter*, Sep. 1992.

379: student'. Judge Élder Lisboa Corrêa da Costa, Redenção, 28 Nov. 1994, *Jornal do Brasil* and other papers, 29 Nov. 1994. The judge agreed that Irekran had beaten the student; but as an Indian she was immune for punishment for this. In December 1999 and June 2000 the Supreme Federal Tribunal upheld the sentence by the Pará justices and then refused a writ of habeas corpus to acknowledge Paiakan's Indian status and prevent his being jailed (*O Popular*, 17 Dec. 1999). The Body Shop made its peace with Paiakan, but in 1997 it was accused by him and other Kayapó leaders of exploitation for paying too little for their forest produce – only $70,000 per village per year for four tonnes of oil that had taken weeks to collect and process (*The Times*, London, 7 Jun. 1997). In that same year, Paiakan was sent to Belém by his community to attend a congress and trade fair on logging of tropical timber (*Gazeta Mercantil*, 5 Nov. 1997). He defended the Kayapó right to improve its standard of living by selling timber.

379: Xikrin.' Isabelle Vidal Giannini, 'Para entender o polêmico Projeto de Exploração Madeireira na TI Xikrin do Cateté', *PIB 1996/2000*, 496.

380: Funai.' Ibid., 499.

380: profits.' Isabelle Vidal Giannini, 'Xikrin' entry in ISA Web site, *Indigenous Peoples in Brazil*, May 2001.

381: *demarcate lands'. Jornal do Brasil*, 6 Apr. 2000. The Makuxi joined in the criticism, but other peoples, such as the populous Ticuna of the upper Solimões, NGOs, and Funai's own staff, defended Marés. He was also condemned by the press for having sent a curt fax to dismiss the eighty-six-year-old Orlando Villas Boas from a job as adviser to Funai: it was felt that Brazil's greatest champion of the Indians deserved more respect.

381: *action*. The Baú dispute involved some 600,000 ha (2,320 square miles) to the west of the lower Curuá near a town called Novo Progresso. This land was included in a reserve of 1,850,000 ha (7,140 square miles) awarded when Jarbas Passarinho was Minister of Justice, but it was withdrawn under his successor Nélson Jobim using his controversial new Decree 1,775. The justification was that 512 settler families were growing rice and other crops and raising cattle there, and had vowed to die fighting rather than move. But the presence of these squatters on Indian land was illegal. The fifty Baú Kayapó released their fifteen tourist hostages in August 2000, after receiving a promise that the 770 kilometre (478 mile) perimeter of their *entire* reserve would be demarcated.

381: *officials.' Veja*, 13 May 1998. This comment related to a Xavante exploit, when their leaders Arnaldo and Celestino led warriors on an invasion of Funai's building (aided and abetted by the then President of Funai, Sulivan Silvestre de Oliveira) to demand the sacking of two officials who had vetoed a demand for the purchase of a hundred vehicles for their reserve.

382: *mood'*. Roque de Barros Laraia, May 2000 on resigning after one month as President of Funai, *PIB 1996/2000*, 123.

15. Brazilian Guiana

383: *circle.'* William Curtis Farabee, 'A pioneer in Amazonia: the narrative of a journey from Manaos to Georgetown', *The Bulletin of The Geographical Society of Philadelphia*, 15, Jan.–Oct. 1917, 78; and his *The Central Caribs* (University of Pennsylvania Museum, Anthropological Publications 10, Philadelphia, 1924), 166. This university museum has good unpublished accounts of the Waiwái by John Ogilvie, dated 1942, which confirm that they absorbed the survivors of the Tarumã who had been wiped out by the 1920s flu epidemic. The name Waiwái is from the Aruak-speaking Wapixana and means tapioca.

384: *smoking."'* Nicholas Guppy, *Wai-Wai. Through the Forests North of the Amazon* (London, 1958), 21. Dr Terry and Dr William Holden of the American Museum of Natural History went from British Guiana down the Mapuera, in 1938. A British–Brazilian boundary commission was active on the watershed at that time, led by Captain Bráz Dias de Aguiar on the Brazilian side and Peberdy on the British; but it met no uncontacted Indians. The Danish anthropologists Niels Fock and Jens Yde worked among the Waiwái in the 1950s: Fock, *Waiwai: Religion and Society of an Amazonian Tribe* (Nationalmuseets Skrifter, Etnografisk Raekke, Copenhagen, 8), 1963; Yde, *Material Culture of the Waiwai* (Nationalmuseets Skrifter, Etnografisk Raekke, Copenhagen, 10), 1965. Farabee and Guppy spelled the Parikotó as Parukutu; Nimuendajú Parikotó; and the British boundary commissioners Barokotos. The Gunn's Strip mission's name later became Kanashen. It was founded by the brothers Neill and Robert Hawkins, who had been active in southern British Guiana since 1945.

384: *village!'* Fr Anthony Metcalfe, SJ, *Journal of a Flying Priest* (Rockview and St. Ignatius Mission, Guyana, 1994), 24.

385: *better life'*. M. H. da Penha de Almeida, *Eleição e Delimitação da Área dos P.I.s Nhamundá e Mapuera (AM/PA)*, Funai, Brasília, 1981, in Irene Benson and others, 'Índios do Nhamundá/Mapuera', CEDI, *Povos Indígenas no Brasil*, 3, *Amapá/Norte do Pará* (São Paulo, 1983), 233.

386: *arrows better.'* Ewká in an account of his conversion by the missionary Irene Benson, Ruben Caixeta de Queiroz, 'A saga de Ewká: epidemias e evangelização entre os Waiwai', in TD (255–84), 274.

386: *work."'* Guppy, *Wai-Wai*, 330; Caixeta de Queiroz, 'A saga de Ewká', 268–9; W. Neill Hawkins, *The Winning of a Waiwai Witch Doctor* (Bible Fellowships, Dallas, n.d.); Robert E. Hawkins, *Bob's Diary: Four Months in the Forests of North Brazil* (Radio Revival, Dallas, 1953–4); Fock, *Waiwai*, 242.

386: *Indians*. Colonel Camarão later became

Brigadeiro do Ar, in charge of the air force's operations throughout the Amazon. Since his transport wing was the main means of supply in the region, he had a profound influence on its missionaries and Indians: Wilson de Carvalho, *Flashes da Amazônia* (São Paulo, 1964), 137–40; Edwin Brooks, René Fuerst, John Hemming, Francis Huxley, *Tribes of the Amazon Basin in Brazil, 1972* (London, 1973), 86–8; CEDI, *Povos Indígenas*, **3**, 190–2 for an interview with Camarão in 1982. The Baptist mission was called MEVA (Missão Evangelista da Amazônia), and was related to the evangelical MICEB (Missão Christã Evangélica do Brasil) in Roraima.

388: greatly.' Caixeta de Queiroz, 'A saga', 276.

388: activities.' Sebastião Amâncio Costa, *Relatório: Trabalho de Assessoramento Funai/Eletronorte na Área Nhamundá-Mapuera (23/07/81–16/08/81)*, Funai, Brasília, 1981; Penha de Almeida, *Eleição*, in CEDI, *Povos Indígenas*, 241.

388: Bible.' Caixeta de Queiroz, 'A saga', 265. George Mentore in 1987 gave a total population of 1,137 for the four Waiwái villages (755 on the Mapuera; 54 on the Jatapuzinho; 200 at Kaxmi village on the rio Nova tributary of the Anauá in Roraima; and 137 on the Essequibo in Guyana) (Mentore, 'Wai Wai women: the basis of wealth and power', *Man*, **22:3**, 1987). Catherine Howard, who studied the Kaxmi group in the mid-1980s, gave similar figures: 'A domesticação das mercadorias: estratégias Waiwai', in Bruce Albert and Alcida Rita Ramos, eds., *Pacificando o Branco* (São Paulo, 2002) (25–60), 39. By 1995 Ruben Caixeta had increased this to 2,010, with 1,060 on the Mapuera, 400 on the Jatapuzinho, 50 on the rio Nova, and 500 in Guyana ('A saga', 264).

389: subordination.' Howard, 'A domesticação', 40.

390: Protestant.' Brigadeiro do Ar João Camarão, interview with Dominique Gallois, Lucia van Velthem, and Vincent Carelli, Campinas, 1982, in CEDI, *Povos Indígenas*, 192. For an account of the construction of the air force's airstrip in Tumucumaque, see: Genevieve Hofer, 'Brasil na idade da pedra', *O Cruzeiro*, Rio de Janeiro, 27 Jul. 1963.

391: emergencies'. Camarão interview, CEDI, *Povos Indígenas*, 191.

391: [1960].' Protásio Gunther Frikel, *Dez Anos de Aculturação Tiriyó, 1960–1970* (Publicações Avulsas do Museu Goeldi, **16**, Belém,

1971), 14. The earlier contacts were: Farabee in 1916, who saw Tiriyó in both Brazil and then to the north in Dutch Guiana (Suriname); Rondon's visit in 1928 to the Mapaxó group of Tiriyó (whom he called Pianakotó) and the Rangu group on the Paru de Oeste river (Gastão Cruls, *A Amazônia que eu Vi* (Rio de Janeiro, 1930), 166 ff.): the boundary commission in 1937–38 (Bráz Dias de Aguiar, *Nas fronteiras da Venezuela e Guianas Británica e Neerlandesa*, Rio de Janeiro, 1943, 135); the Dutch official Lodewyjk Schmidt from the north in 1941; brief visits by Brazilian latex-gatherers and garimpeiro prospectors, none of whom found deposits worth extracting; and equally brief visits by Frikel from 1950 onwards.

Darcy Ribeiro in 1957 guessed 2,000–3,000 Tiriyó (of the subgroups Pianokotó, Aramayâna, and Proyâna or Rangu-Piki, while the Okomoyâna and Aramihotó groups were virtually extinct); Dale Kietzman in 1966 reckoned 1,200 Tiriyó in both Brazil and Suriname. By 1980, Lucia Hussak van Velthem of the Goeldi Museum recorded some 500 Tiriyó and related Kaxuyana and Ewarhoyana (of whom 333 lived near the Franciscan mission on the Paru de Oeste, and a further group of 32 Tiriyó recently returned from missions in Suriname who settled on the Aracoepina tributary of the Paru de Leste); also 229 Wayana Apalaí south of Tumucumaque on the Paru and a small group of 23 Apalaí on an island in the Jari. Lucia Hussak van Velthem, 'Um parque indígena com aldeias fora de seus límites: o Parque Tumucumaque', in Dalmo de Abreu Dallari, Manuela Carneiro da Cunha, Lux Vidal, eds., *A Questão da Terra Indígena* (São Paulo, 1981), 109–12. In 1987 CEDI gave 745 as the population of the Tumucumaque park but only 68 in the Wayana Apalaí reserve to the south-east (*Terras Indígenas no Brasil*).

The Kaxuyana are a Carib-speaking tribe that had once lived on the main Amazon but had migrated up the Trombetas and Paru do Oeste to escape the colonization frontier. In the 1920s this was a powerful group of perhaps 500 people. It was then hit by a devastating measles epidemic that slaughtered almost all the adult population and reduced the tribe to some eighty people. This was such a disaster that the panic-stricken survivors could not bury the dead. When Protásio Frikel worked with the Kaxuyana twenty years later in 1953, there were only sixty of them. Other related tribes, such as the Warikyana and

Kahyana, were completely extinguished by disease, notably malaria. In the 1960s, the remaining Kaxuyana decided that their only hope lay with the Franciscan–FAB Tiriyós Mission. They sent emissaries to get to know the Tiriyó, then to the Bishop of Óbidos on the Amazon, and then to FAB; and in February 1968 they were airlifted to Tiriyós. With the mission's fine medical assistance, the group gradually recovered its health and prospered. Protásio Gunther Frikel, *Os Kaxúyana. Notas etno-históricas* (Publicações Avulsas do Museu Goeldi, **14**, Belém, 1970), 44–50.

391: sheep. Frikel, *Dez Anos*, 17–18.

392: interested in it.' Ibid., 18.

392: civilization'. Ibid., 19.

392: "missionary front".' CEDI, *Povos Indígenas*, 198.

393: credit.' Frikel, *Dez Anos*, 77.

393: cultural one.' Brooks et al., *Tribes of the Amazon Basin*, 68.

393: marriage.' CEDI, *Povos Indígenas*, 201.

394: society.' Maria Denise Fajardo Pereira, 'Tiriyó do norte do Pará e sua experiência intercultural', *PIB 1991/1995*, 289. The Tumucumaque park was first designated on 25 July 1961 as a *reserva florestal* (forest reserve), then as a national Indian park by Decree 62,998 of 16 Jul. 1968 (altered by Decree 81,335 of 13 Feb. 1978).

394: system.' Report of SIL's activities, Brasília, April 1974, quoted in Paulo Morgado and Eliane Camargo, 'A escola e a evangelização: dois projetos paralelos entre os Wayana-Aparaí', *PIB 1991/1995*, 293. (The intermarried tribes are also spelled Waiana and Waiano, and Apalaí or Aparaí.) After being evicted in 1977, the Koehns returned for visits during the decade 1982–1992: the quote by them is from a report on SIL's activities from Sep. 1988 to Feb. 1989; they left for good in 1992, when their Institute's agreement with Funai again expired. These tribes gave courteous welcomes to the French explorers Jules Crevaux and then Henri Coudreau in the late nineteenth century (John Hemming, *Amazon Frontier* (London, 1995), 342–5). For a time in the 1920s to 1940s, they were persuaded to work for Brazilian balata-gum gatherers: their payment was in red cloth, which they have worn ever since. They now have a huge territory (1,182,800 ha: 4,570 square miles) to the south of the Tumucumaque park: the Área Indígena Rio Paru do Leste (for the Wayana Apalaí Indians): projected in Parecer 133 of 5 Nov. 1986.

395: men.' Anon., 'Waiana-Apalai. História, contato e sociedade', AI, **22**, Sep. 1982 (5–9), 9. The anthropologist who noticed the ritual surrounding Wayana Apalaí cooking was the Swiss Daniel Schoepf, *La marmite Wayana, cuisine et société d'une tribu d'Amazonie* (Musée d'Ethnographie, Geneva, 1979) and 'Historique et situation actuelle des indiens Wayana-Aparaí du Brésil', *Bulletin Annuel du Musée d'Ethnographie*, **15**, Geneva, 1972, 33–64, summarized in 'No cerimonial das refeições Waiana-Apalai toda uma rica e complexa simbologia', AI, **22**, 1982, 10–12. Lúcia Hussak van Velthem has also studied these and other tribes of the Tumucumaque park: 'Representações gráficas Wayana-Aparaí', BMPEG, **64**, 1976; 'O Parque Indígena de Tumucumaque', BMPEG, **76**, 1–31, Oct. 1980; 'Wayana-Aparaí' in CEDI, *Povos Indígenas no Brasil*, **3**, *Amapá/Norte do Pará*, 138–73 and 'Aparai do Jari', ibid., 174–81. Funai established a Posto Indígena Tumucumaque near the Apalaí village in 1973, but this was never very active.

395: monkeys'. Lúcia Hussak van Velthem, '"Feito por inimigos": os brancos e seus bens nas representações Wayana do contato', in Albert and Ramos, *Pacificando o Branco*, 75–6.

396: "objects".' Ibid.

396: 1960s and '70s. The Jari project was a grandiose experiment devised by one of the richest men in the United States, the reclusive shipping tycoon Daniel K. Ludwig, who had the idea of growing huge plantations of softwoods in the Amazon. In 1965 he bought, for only a dollar an acre, some 3.5–4 million acres (14,000–16,000 km²) of forest (an area rather bigger than the state of Connecticut) on either side of the mouth of the Jari. The idea was to import millions of seedlings of the fast-growing *Gmelina* and other softwoods from Burma and Nigeria. He hoped that there would be no pests and parasites waiting to destroy these new arrivals – in the way that Henry Ford's plantations of *Hevea brasiliensis* rubber trees had been obliterated, not far to the southwest on the Tapajós thirty years previously. Ludwig's plan was to imitate, in reverse, the British removal of Amazon rubber seedlings to Malaya in the 1870s.

The installations of the Jari Project were magnificent and included a paper-pulp mill and a huge floating wood-burning power plant from Japan. Highly qualified foresters and some 30,000 Brazilians got jobs from the enterprise. It had the good luck to stumble across one of the world's largest deposits of kaolin china clay, used in making pottery. But the trees did not grow as projected. Ludwig poured money into the failing project. A press campaign in Brazil grew increasingly suspicious of the foreigner who owned so much of the country, and in 1980 Jari's tax concessions were reduced and the government refused to pay for its massive social services. The disgusted millionaire sold out in 1981, after spending about a billion dollars on the colossal failure. Environmentalists were encouraged by this high-profile disaster, hoping that it would deter others from trying to destroy and replant tropical rain forests.

397: groups.' Dominique Tilkin Gallois, '"Nossas falas duras". Discurso político e auto-representação Waiãpi', in ibid. (205–37), 208.

397: admirable.' Alan Tormaid Campbell, *Getting to Know Waiwai. An Amazonian Ethnography* (London and New York, 1995), 211. Campbell spells the tribe's name Waiapí; Dominique Gallois spells it Waiãpi; it has also been written as Oiapi, Oiampik, and variations of these; but Wayampi is the preferred spelling in Maria Elizabeth Brêa Monteiro and Maria Irene Brasil, *Listagem dos Nomes dos Povos Indígenas no Brasil* (Boletim do Museu do Índio/Funai booklet no. 8, Rio de Janeiro, 1998). Campbell and Gallois jointly wrote the 'Waiãpi' chapter in CEDI, *Povos Indígenas*, 3, 98–137. Campbell taught anthropology at the University of Edinburgh and Gallois at the Universidade de São Paulo.

398: experiment.' Campbell, *Getting to Know Waiwai*, 88.

398: brought'. Ibid.

398: dominant society.' Ibid.

398: technology'. Ibid., 221–2.

398: betrayal.' Ibid.

398: phlogiston' Ibid.

399: landed with.' Ibid., 71.

399: organization.' Ibid.

399: in that way?' Ibid.

399: Book.' Ibid., 164.

399: souls too.' Ibid., 59.

400: fundamentally bad'. Stephen Hugh-Jones interviewed in Brian Moser's film for Granada television, *War of the Gods*, quoted in ibid., 60.

400: doing good.' Ibid., 60. The Área Indígena Waiapí, at the western edge of Amapá, was identified in Funai Parecer 049 of 3 May 1985. The deputy who opposed the Indians was Antonio Feijão, and the state prosecutor of Amapá upheld

his attack; but the Wayampi were defended by the Governor, João Capiberibe. Their forests are watered by the gold-rich Mapari and Nipukú tributaries of the upper Jari.

400: fruits'. Edna Lima, in *Dos Confins da Terra* (internal bulletin of the Missão Novas Tribos do Brasil), 31 Oct. 1995, quoted in Dominique Tilkin Gallois and Luís Donisete Benzi Grupioni, 'O índio na Missão Novas Tribos', in TD, 82.

400: no way!' Ibid., 117.

401: Wayampi.' Gallois, 'Nossas falas duras', 217.

401: subsistence.' Dominique T. Gallois, 'Controle territorial e diversificação do extrativismo na Área Indígena Waiãpi', PIB 1991/1995 (263–71), 264.

402: whites.' Gallois, 'Nossas falas duras', 209. Wayampi population fell to 151 after contact by Funai in 1973, but rose again to 550 during the next three decades.

402: harmful to us.' Ibid., 208.

403: we want. Kasiripinã, President of Apina, in 1998, in Angela Maria Schwengber, 'Waiãpi e CTI: uma parceria ameaçada', *PIB 1996/2000* (387–90), 387. The various projects in land-demarcation, education, health, gold prospecting, pollution control, etc. had been launched since 1990 by Dominique Gallois and the CTI, with support from Brazilian authorities and German and other foreign-aid agencies. The campaign of boycott and defamation was run by Antonio Feijão, head of the Amapá garimpeiros' union and later a federal deputy, and Socorro Pelaes, Mayor of the nearby town of Amapari. For a time, they gained the support of the regional Procurator of the Republic, who initiated a judicial hearing and, in August 1997, a civil action to stop the anti-pollution project and a police inquiry against Gallois. Deputy Feijão maintained his opposition to the Wayampi in the Chamber, courts, and press. Survival in London issued an urgent-action bulletin about it in November 1997, and the State Governor João Capiberibe supported the Indians. This 'paper war' (as the Indians called it) was largely resolved in the Indians' favour by a federal judge on 28 April 1999 (*Últimas Notícias/ISA*, 30 Apr. 1999; *Parabólicas*, **6:50/51**, May–Jun. 1999, 20; Survival success bulletin, *Waiãpi win right to carry out projects*, London, Jul. 2000).

404: withdraw.' Dominique Tilkin Gallois and Luís Donisete Benzi Grupioni, 'A redescoberta dos amáveis selvagens', *PIB 1987/88/89/90*

(209–14), 210. The missionaries who made the lightning contact were Francisco Montoni and Mauricio Nobre do Nascimento.

404: approach.' Ibid., 211.

405: dependent.' Ibid., 211

405: Brazilians have.' Ibid., 211–12.

405: future.' Dominique T. Gallois, 'Tupi do Cuminapanema: eles se chamam Zo'é', *PIB 1991/1995* (280–8), 285.

406: bring them.' Ibid., 287; and Gallois's entry on Zo'é for the ISA Web site, 2000. Their land is the Cuminapanema/Urukuriana indigenous area between the Erepecuru and Curuá rivers, not far north of Oriximiná and Santarém on the main Amazon. Vincent Carelli made a successful film of the Wayampi visit to the Zo'é (Dominique Gallois and Vincent Carelli, 'Vídeo nas aldeias: a experiência Waiãpi', *Cadernos do Campo*, **2**, 1993, 70–83).

407: else did.' Curt Nimuendajú, 'Die Palikur und ihre Nachbarne', *Kungl. Vetenshapa – Och Vitterhets-Samnaelles Handligar*, **31:2**, Gøteborg, 1926 (1–144), 16–17, 100; Expedito Arnaud, *Os Índios Palikúr do Rio Urucauá. Tradição tribal e protestantismo* (Belém, 1984), 17–18. In Nimuendajú's day, the Governor of Pará ceded a 2,000 ha (4,950 acre) territory to the 186 Palikur on his side of the frontier.

407: arrows'. Major Luiz Thomaz Reis, *Diário da inspeção da 2a. turma do vale do Rio Uaçá* (unpublished, Belém, 2a. Inspetoria Regional do SPI, 1939) in Arnaud, *Os Índios Palikúr*, 20; also Arnaud, 'Os índios da região do Uaçá (Oiapoque) e a proteção oficial brasileira', BMPEG, **40**, Jul. 1969, reprinted in Arnaud, *O Índio e a Expansão Nacional* (Belém, 1989) (87–121), 96.

408: existence.' 'A Reserva do Uaçá', in CEDI, *Povos Indígenas*, 3.

408: quality.' Arnaud, *Os Índios Palikúr*, 21; 'Os índios da região do Uaçá', 24.

409: alive.' Arnaud, 'Os índios da região do Uaçá', 29. Nimuendajú in 1926 gave a total of 499 Indians in northern Amapá: 189 Palikur, 150 Karipuna, and 160 Galibi. By 1931 there were 593: 202 Palikur, 193 Tupi-speaking Emerillons (a French name) and Karipuna, and 198 Galibi (Eurico Fernandes, 'Contribuição ao estudo etnográfico do grupo Aruak', *Acta Americana*, **6:3/4**, Mexico, 1948, 200–21; and 'Pariucur-Ienê' in Cândido Mariano da Silva Rondon, *Índios do Brasil*, **2**, *Das Cabeceiras do Rio Xingu, dos Rios Araguáia e Oiapóque* (CNPI, Rio de Janeiro, 1953), 283–92. Major Reis in 1936 gave a total

of 538: 151 Palikur but with 20 families absent, 200 Karipuna and 187 Galibi. In 1943 this had risen to 782: 273 Palikur, 262 Karipuna, and 247 Galibi (Eurico Fernandes, *Relatório apresentado à Diretoria do Serviço de Proteção aos Índios*, in SPI's regional archive in Belém, 1943). Expedito Arnaud in 1967 noted a further increase, to 1,162: 263 Palikur, 439 Karipuna, and 460 Galibi (Arnaud, 'Os índios da região do Uaçá', 94). Dale Kietzman at that time gave higher but vaguer estimates, a total of 1,350–1,450: 450 Palikur, 400 Karipuna, and 500–600 Galibi. By 1982 the population in the Uaçá reserve had almost doubled since 1967, to 2,093 – 672 Karipuna, 561 Palikur and 860 Galibi ('A Reserva do Uaçá', in CEDI, *Povos Indígenas*, 3). At the end of the century, the total population in the Uaçá reserve continued to rise dramatically, to 3,665 (Funai census, 1999).

410: village."' Paulo Orlando speaking in October 1982, in 'Palikur', in CEDI, *Povos Indígenas*, 28–31.

410: ceremony, etc.' Cícero da Cruz, *Relatório do chefe do P. I. Palikur ao Delegado Regional Funai*, 6 May 1978, 5–6; Expedito Arnaud, 'O protestantismo entre os índios Palikúr do Rio Urucauá (Oiapoque, Brasil): notícia preliminar', RA, **23**, Feb. 1980 (99–102), 101; CEDI, 'Palikur', *Povos Indígenas*, 3, 31.

410: know.' Arnaud, *Os Índios Palikúr*, 61.

411: Gospel.' Father Nello Ruffaldi, 'Relatório de uma arbitrariedade', Macapá, 18 May 1978 (*Boletim do CIMI*, **7:47**, Jun. 1978, 35–49), 42. This account described Father Nello's expulsion from the Oiapoque area, by armed police acting on orders from Funai, despite the local Funai agents and the Indians begging him to stay.

411: tributaries. The dispute about the BR-156 road and the attempt to expel Father Nello Ruffaldi were also reported in *Boletim do CIMI*, Nov./Dec. 1980 and in SIR, **6:2**, Summer 1981, 77.

412: present.' Dominique Gallois, 'O rodízio de cobranças nas assembleias indígenas do Oiapoque', *PIB 1987/88/89/90*, **9:68**, 230. The letter from the Oiapoque chiefs to Funai, at the end of their first Assembly at Kumarumã village, 23 Sep. 1976, is in *Boletim do CIMI*, **5:32**, Oct. 1976, 5–10.

412: Ruffaldi'. Antonella Tassinari, 'Homologação das terras e associação indígena: os resultados da crescente organização dos povos do Oiapoque', *PIB 1991/1995*, 299.

16. Panará

414: laughing.' Orlando and Cláudio Villas Bôas, *A Marcha Para o Oeste* (São Paulo, 1994), 494. In an interview in *Opinião*, 25 Mar. 1974, Orlando Villas Boas said that in 1949 Brigadeiro Eduardo Gomes (a presidential candidate) had summoned the head of the Fundação Brasil Central and told him of the urgent need to occupy central Brazil. He had put his finger on the map, at Cachimbo, and said: 'I want an airstrip here.' In that interview, Orlando said that Indians had observed the building of the Cachimbo airstrip in 1950 and that eight villages had later been seen from the air, well to the south of the new base. But he did not tell me this when we met in 1961. After Cachimbo airstrip was built, Cláudio Villas Boas spent two arduous years cutting a picada north-westwards towards the middle Tapajós, until the FBC cut off funds for this venture. Cláudio saw smoke of villages in those forests on the far side of Cachimbo. There had been no further sightings of Indians there throughout the 1950s.

417: machine gun.' Orlando Villas Boas, in Adrian Cowell, *The Tribe that Hides from Man* (London, 1973; edition cited, Pimlico edition, London, 1995), 73; Shelton Davis, *Victims of the Miracle* (Cambridge and New York, 1977), 70. The operation to 'protect' Cachimbo from non-existent attack in 1967 cost over $160,000 and the lives of the twenty-five men killed in the air crash. The killing of Richard Mason in 1961 was extensively reported in the Brazilian and British press, notably in 'Morte no Rio Iriri', *O Cruzeiro*, 30 Sep. 1961 and John Hemming, 'Tragedy in the jungle', *Sunday Times*, 18 and 25 Feb. 1962. In 1966 the SPI announced a large expedition of about a hundred people under Francisco Meirelles to try to contact the Kren Akróre (Panará). The Villas-Boas and Dr Noel Nutels (who had been the last Director of the SPI, from mid-1963 to the military coup of April 1964) all condemned the plan, because the Service was too incompetent and under-resourced and because such contacts should be made only by anthropologists and similar experts rather than by military men. The Villas Boas declared that 'Indians should be pacified only in extreme cases, when they are at war with other tribes or with seringuerios'. *Jornal da Tarde*, 8 Jun. 1966; *Jornal do Brasil*, 29 May 1966.

417: forest.' Richard Heelas, *The Social Organization of the Panara, a Gê Tribe of Central Brazil* (Doctoral dissertation, Oxford University, 1979), 10–11. The massacre was first reported to the SPI/Funai in November 1967 by Richard Roche and Dale Snyder of the Christian Evangelical Mission, who were active at the Menkragnoti post on the Pitiatiá tributary of the Curuá, ESP, 12 Dec. 1967. Gustaaf Verswijver, *The Club-Fighters of the Amazon* (Gent, 1992), 145; Stephan Schwartzman, *The Panará of the Xingu National Park: the Transformation of a Society* (Doctoral dissertation, University of Chicago, 1988), 292. The attack was on the Panará village of Sonkanasan.

418: killed him."' Cowell, *The Tribe that Hides*, 117.

418: forget.' Pèritaw Panará interview in Stephan Schwartzman, *Os Panará do Peixoto de Azevedo e Cabeceiras do Iriri: história, contato e transferência ao Parque do Xingu* (Washington DC, 1992), II.A, 10; and in Ricardo Arnt, Lúcio Flávio Pinto, and Raimundo Pinto, *Panará. A volta dos índios gigantes* (São Paulo, 1998), 84.

419: devil.' Cowell, *The Tribe that Hides*, 166. The expedition was reported by Valdir Zwetsch, 'Kren-Akárore, os índios gigantes da Amazônia', *O Cruzeiro*, 24 Mar. 1971, 54–68.

419: stone axes.' Villas Boas, *Marcha*, 515. At the end of 1969 the Mentuktire Kayapó (Txukahamãe) took all their guns and went from their village Poiriri for another attack on the Panará. When the Villas Boas learned about this raid, the Indians said that they had planned to 'pacify' the elusive Panará. Fortunately for the latter, the Mentuktire returned in mid-January 1970, tired and thin and with no captives or dead warriors to boast about. They had entered three Panará villages but found them all overgrown. There was an ominously large burial mound in one village – possibly a sign that white men's diseases had destroyed the Panará before the Mentuktire guns. Adrian Cowell published an account of this raid from letters by the SIL linguist Micky Stout, who had spent years with the Mentuktire: *The Tribe that Hides*, 260–63.

419: slowly.' Cláudio Villas Boas in ESP, 6 Feb. 1973; Arnt et al., *Panará*, 87. There was excellent reporting of the attraction expedition by

Mário Chimanovitch in the *Jornal do Brasil*, 16 May, 30 May, 3 Jun., 21 Jun., and 26 Jun. 1972; by Estevaldo Dias and Pedro Martinelli in O *Globo*, 13 May, 14 May, 15 Jul., 30 Jul., and 13 Aug. 1972, 'Mais uma vez, os Krain-a-Kore fugiram ao diálogo'; by Luis Salgado Ribeiro in ESP and also O *Cruzeiro*, Carnaval issue, 1972. Other glimpses of Panará were reported in ESP, 24 and 31 Oct. 1972.

420: laughter.' Villas Boas, *Marcha*, 517; ESP, 1 Dec. 1972; Arnt et al., *Panará*, 87–8; R. G. Baruzzi et al., 'The Kren-Akorore: a recently contacted indigenous tribe', *Health and Disease in Tribal Societies* (Ciba Foundation Symposium, **49**, Aug. 1977), 183.

420: patience.' Cláudio Villas Boas interview, ESP, 20 Aug. and 12 Nov. 1972.

420: death.' Jornal do Brasil, 6 Feb. 1973.

420: civilizados.' ESP, 6 Feb. 1973; Arnt et al., *Panará*, 91.

421: kill us.' Teseya Panará talking to Stephan Schwartzman, 1994, in Arnt et al., *Panará*, 104.

421: at last.' Veja, 14 Feb. 1973; Arnt et al., *Panará*, 90.

422: quietly.' Teseya Panará to Stephan Schwartzman, 1994, in ibid., 106.

422: long time.' Jornal do Brasil, 14 Jan. 1974.

422: vice-versa.' Orlando Villas Boas, in Takao Miyagui, 'Kranhakarore, os machões da selva', *Manchete*, 24 Feb. 1973.

423: north.' Odemir Pinto de Oliveira interviewed in Arnt et al., *Panará*, 97. Apoena Meirelles, 'A técnica que atraiu os Kreen-Akarore', RAI, **3:18**, Sep.–Oct. 1979. Apoena's visit to the village was reported by Estevaldo Dias and Pedro Martinelli in O *Globo*, 12 Aug. and 14 Aug. 1973. The Funai official who denounced the homosexual behaviour of Antonio Sousa Campinas was Ezequias Heringer (nicknamed Xará) in a report to Funai in Dec. 1973. He had been appalled when Panará men wanted homosexual relations with him and his companions, thinking that this was usual among white men. However, Campinas was also accused of having sex with Indian women and under-aged girls. Schwartzman, *The Panará of the Xingu National Park*, 307–9.

424: burials.' Fiorello Parisi, who led the final phase of the Panará attraction, *Relatório parcial apresentado ao Il. Sr. Coordenador da Amazônia* (Funai, 1975) in Arnt et al., *Panará*, 96.

424: buried.' Akè Panará to Schwartzman, 29 Oct. 1991, in Os *Panará do Peixoto de Azevedo*, IIB; and in Arnt et al., *Panará*, 92.

424: happen to us?"' Teseya Panará to Schwartzman, 1994, in ibid., 105.

425: people.' Schwartzman, *The Panará of the Xingu National Park*, 301.

425: sertanista.' Report to Funai by Valéria Parisi, 4 Jan. 1974, in Arnt et al., *Panará*, 112.

426: transfer plan'. General Ismarth de Araújo Oliveira's instructions to Fiorello Parisi, late 1973, in an interview by Parisi, Jul. 1992, in Arnt et al., *Panará*, 96. Orlando Villas Boas' denunciation of the transfer as crazy was in ESP, 23 Jan. 1972.

426: solution'. Cláudio Villas Boas interview, *Opinião*, 25 Mar. 1974; Jane Monahan, 'Doomed tribe', *Sunday Times*, 18 Apr. 1974.

426: transfer them!' General Ismarth de Araújo Oliveira in conversation with the film-maker Aurélio Michiles, in the film O *Brasil Grande e os Índios Gigantes* (1995); Arnt et al., *Panará*, 95.

426: another' Parisi, in Arnt et al., *Panará*, 98; Schwartzman, *The Panará of the Xingu National Park*, 312–13. General Ismarth's Ofício removing the interdiction on a possible Panará reserve was no. 058/75, and the Decree nullifying the reserve was no. 83,541 of 4 Jun. 1979.

427: seat.' Sokriti Panará to Stephan Schwartzman, 1991, in Arnt et al., *Panará*, 116; Schwartzman, *The Panará*, 316; Baruzzi et al., 'The Kren-Akorore', 186–8. One favourable contemporary report of the transfer was: Mário Antonio Garofalo, 'Os últimos Kren-Akarores', *Manchete*, 1 Feb. 1975, 4–11. But the Funai official Odenir de Oliveira doubted that the Panará really understood what was happening. Other criticism came from Father Iasi of CIMI, and in Luiz F. Marcopito, 'Amarga renúncia à terra de origem', RAI, **3:19**, Nov.–Dec. 1979. Also: Edilson Martins, *Nossos Índios, Nossos Mortos* (Rio de Janeiro, 1978), 83–8; Luiz Beltrão, O *Índio, um Mito Brasileiro* (Petrópolis, 1977), 97–126. From this time onwards, the Mentuktire chief's name was generally spelled Rauni rather than Raoni, and he himself sometimes signed with a Jê spelling, Ropni.

427: humiliation.' Memélia Moreira interview with Sérgio Leitão of the Núcleo de Direitos Indígenas, Brasília, 1992; Arnt et al., *Panará*, 116.

428: health.' Baruzzi et al., 'The Kren-Akorore', 198; RAI, **4:19**, Nov.–Dec. 1974.

428: group'. Schwartzman, *The Panará*, 320.

429: dying.' Akè conversation with Schwartzman, Os *Panará do Peixoto de Azevedo* (1992), and in Arnt et al., *Panará*, 118.

429: born.' Akè in Brian Moser's film *Before Columbus* (October 1991), in ibid., 119. Another fine film about the return of the Panará was Adrian Cowell's *Return from Extinction*, part of his trilogy *The Last of the Hiding Tribes* (Nomad Films, London, 1998).

429: village.' Akè Panará to Schwartzman, 29 Oct. 1991, *Os Panará do Peixoto de Azevedo*, IV. After running the Xingu park, Olimpio Serra in the 1990s was director of the Fundação Mata Virgem (Rainforest Foundation), the Brazilian non-government organization founded by the pop singer Sting.

431: farmers'. André Villas Bôas quoted in ISA editorial team, 'Os Panará consolidam o retorno', *PIB 1996/2000*, 493.

432: community'. Judgement of Judge Novély Vilanova da Silva Reis in favour of the Action for Reparation of Damages, Brasília, 22 Oct. 1997, in Arnt et al., *Panará*, 125–6. The family of each dead Indian received damages of two *salário mínimo* (the minimum wage, fixed regularly by the government) per month for his full life expectancy, plus 4,000 'minimum wages' as compensation to the tribe as a whole. This unprecedented award was routinely challenged, but upheld by the regional tribunal of Brasília on 14 September 2000 with the compensation fixed at 1 million Reals (about $1 million). The damages were divided equally between the Brazilian Republic and Funai. Funai's Parecer interdicting the area was no. 179 of 14 Dec. 1994; and the confirmation of the reserve was Funai's Portaria 667 signed by the Minister of Justice on 1 Nov. 1996. The perimeter of the forest reserve was demarcated with a cleared strip six metres (nineteen feet six inches) wide cut during 1998 and 1999. The events surrounding the return of the Panará were also given in Stephan Schwartzman, 'Panará: a saga dos índios gigantes', *Ciência Hoje*, **20:119**, Apr. 1996, 26–35; and his 'The Panará: indigenous territory and environmental protection in the Amazon', in Greg Dicum, ed., *Local Heritage in the Changing Tropics: Innovative Strategies for Natural Resource Management and Control* (Yale School of Forestry and Environmental Studies, New Haven, Connecticut, 1995); and Marleine Cohen, 'O caminho de volta: a saga dos gigantes Panará', *PIB 1991/1995*, 601–13. This contains the lawyer Márcio Santilli's findings of the seriousness of the threat to the Panarás' surviving forests from ruthless land-speculators and timber men.

433: want.' Teseya Panará talking to the author, Nacypotire, Jul. 1998. Also my account in *The Times Magazine*, 2 Jan. 1999. In another version, told to Brian Moser, the group that killed Mason came from Yopuyupaw, the Village of the Round Fish. They had gone to gather Brazil-nuts, which abound on the upper Iriri, and to hunt.

17. Struggles for Land: the South

435: rights'. João Pacheco de Oliveira, 'Terras indígenas: uma avaliação preliminar de seu reconhecimento oficial e de outras destinações sobreposta', CEDI/Meseu Nacional, *Terras Indígenas no Brasil* (CEDI, São Paulo, 1987, 7–32), 31.

435: roads.' Ibid.

435: generalized.' Ibid.

436: firms.' Carlos de Araújo Moreira Neto, 'Alguns dados para a história recente dos índios Kaingang', in Georg Grünberg, ed., *La Situación del Indígena en América del Sur* (Montevideo, 1972), 381–419; trans. 'Some data concerning the recent history of the Kaingang Indians', in Walter Dostal, ed., *The Situation of the Indian in South America* (Geneva, 1972), 319. The removal of a total of 131,633 ha (508 square miles) was denounced in a legal finding by Dalmo Esteves de Almeida, 19 May 1951, and the SPI's local inspector complained bitterly about it: Gontram da Veiga Jardim, 'Os guerreiros já não cantam mais', *Correio da Manhã*, 23 Sep. 1967; Carlos Moreira reported the drastic reductions in area of seven Indian posts in Rio Grande do Sul: **Nonoái** from 34,908 ha to 14,910, containing 958 Indians; **Serrinha** from 11,950 to none (in an attempt in 1962 to evict its Kaingang and replace them by colonists, which was ultimately unsuccessful and overturned); **Guarita** from 23,183 to 15,900; **Inhacorá** from 5,859 to 1,060; **Votouro** from 3,104 to 1,440; **Guarani Votouro** from 741 to 280; and **Venterra** from 733 to 533. Thus, these seven posts were reduced by two-thirds, from 80,482 ha to 34,123. (In acres: Nonoái, 86,258 to 36,843; Serrinha, 29,528 to none; Guarita, 57,285 to 39,289; Inhacorá, 14,478 to 2,619; Votouro, 7,670 to 3,558; Guarani, 1,831 to 692;

and Venterra from 1,811 to 1,317.) Totals, 198,871 (or 310 square miles) to 84,318 (or 132 square miles). Moreira did not have area data for **Cacique Doble** or **Ligeiro**. Anon., 'Lupion e as terras dos índios', *Boletim do CIMI*, **8**:56, May–Jun. 1979, 15–19.

436: vegetation' Moreira, 'Some data', 319–20.
436: status quo.' Ibid.
436: house them'. ESP, 20 Oct. 1968. To effect this land-grab, Governor Brizola created a 'land-reform' agency called Instituto Gaucho de Reforma Agrária.
437: powerless.' Moreira, 'Some data', 323.
437: diet' Ibid. Governor Moysés Lupion's rape of Kaingang lands was first described in José Maria da Paula, 'Terra dos índios', *Boletim* (Serviço de Informação Agrícola, Ministério da Agricultura), **1**, 1944.
437: life.' Survival, *Disinherited. Indians in Brazil* (London, 2000), 1.
437: consultation.' Denunciation by the Mayor of Tenente Portela, *Jornal da Tarde*, 28 Jul. 1970. Lieutenant Herminio was later sacked by Funai.
437: death.' Plínio Dutra to President Médicis, ibid.
437: pig-pens.' Report by Lieutenant João Alves Ribas, Chief of Funai's 7th Inspectorate in Porto Alegre, referring to Posto Dr Selistre de Campos in Xanxerê, ESP, 23 Oct. 1968. The appalling treatment of Indians in this part of Brazil had been denounced by student volunteers of the Projeto Rondon, ESP, 20 and 26 Oct. 1968; also ESP, 3, 4, and 8 Jul. 1969 about the parliamentary commission's devastating report; and ESP, 2 Aug. 1970 about Funai's investigation. The situation did not improve: a further 200 families invaded Nonoái in May 1969 and also Guarita, encouraged by the mayor of nearby Planalto. Funai's encarregado Lieutenant Waldemar Rosa was shot at by squatters when he tried to protect his Indians.
437: assistance'. Chief Ianguê, in *O Estado* (Florianópolis), 2 Aug. 1976; *Boletim do CIMI*, **5**:31, Aug.–Sep. 1976, 29.
438: deeds'. Silvio Coelho dos Santos, *A Integração do Índio na Sociedade Regional* (Florianópolis, 1970), 29–30. The SPI had started its Xapecó (or Chapecó) post in 1940; in 1949 its agent Wilmar da Costa moved some Kaingang from Toldo Umbu into Xapecó, but those of Toldo Chimbangue refused to relocate; the SPI's Antonio Selistre de Campos reported in 1950 that they were living in a state of extreme poverty. The main property company was called Coloni-

zadora Luce, Rosa & Cia. The aged Chief Chimbangue had died in about 1915, a time when his people were decimated by a typhus epidemic.
438: resolved.' O *Estado*, 27 May 1982; CIMI-Regional Sul, *Toldo Chimbangue: história e luta Kaingang em Santa Catarina* (Xanxerê, SC, 1984), 85; *Luta Indígena* (CIMI-Regional Sul, Xanxerê), **17**, Aug. 1982, 8.
438: Indians' CIMI-Regional Sul, *Toldo Chimbangue*, 87–8. Ofício 526 of President of Funai to the President of the human-rights commission of the OAB/SC (Santa Catarina branch of the Organization of Brazilian Lawyers), Brasília, 17 May 1983. The finding by the Procurador da República was on 12 July 1983. As proof of their right of occupancy, the Kaingang also sent Funai a list of over 200 Indians born at Toldo Chimbangue, many of whom had been forced to leave. The government colonization agency Incra sided with the settlers, claiming that there were only two 'true Indians' living there – the rest being 'mestizos or caboclos'.
439: cemetery.' Letter from Chief Clemente and others to President Figueiredo, 5 Jul. 1984, ibid., 108. The regional delegate of Funai had promised to visit Toldo Chimbangue with a firm answer on the previous day; but had failed to come.
439: force'. Ibid.
439: white men'. Moreira, 'Some data', 323.
439: houses.' Vitor de Paula, *Boletim do CIMI*, **5**:32, Oct. 1976, 22. The left-wing President João Goulart, who governed Brazil from 1961 to 1964, had his power-base in southern Brazil. He tried to seduce farm labourers at Nonoái and other reserves by encouraging them to invade indigenous lands. Regional SPI officials protested in vain. Had Goulart not been overthrown by the military, he would have introduced 'a strange Agrarian Reform in which Indians figured as scapegoats. Had this "reform" based on violence become reality, what remains of the Brazilian Indians might . . . now be no more than a memory.' Gontram da Veiga, 'Os guerreiros', *Correio da Manhã*, 23 Sep. 1967.
439: lives'. Mércio Gomes, *The Indians and Brazil* (Gainesville, Fla., 2000), 181. The legal action about Mangueirinhas between Funai and Slaviero was reported in ESP, 12 Oct. 1979 and analysed in Cecília M. V. Helm, 'A terra, a usina e os índios de P. I. Mangueirinha', in Silvio Coelho dos Santos, ed., *Os Índios Perante o Direito* (UFSC, Florianópolis, 1982), 129–42. The 8,976 ha

(22,180 acres) in dispute were reckoned to contain 120,000 Araucaria pines and 80,000 hardwood imbuia (Brazilian walnut, *Ocotea porosa*),
worth some $20 million at that time. The plight
of these Kaingang was condemned at the Fourth
Russell Tribunal in Rotterdam in November 1980,
ARC, **6**, May 1981, 9.

440: die'. Kaingang woman's letter to the President of Funai, 1975, in Anna Presland, 'Reconquest', SIR, **25**, Spring 1979, 11–12.

440: child.' Hodfei Kaingang, in Elizabeth
Aracy Rondon Amarante and Verónica Nizzoli,
eds., *Precisamos um Chão: depoiamentos indígenas*
(São Paulo, 1981), 48.

440: do it!' Xangrê Kaingang, in Amarante and
Nizzoli, *Precisamos um Chão*, 20.

441: furniture' O Globo, Rio de Janeiro, 15
May 1978; *Boletim do CIMI*, **7:45**, Mar.–Apr.
1978, 18–22; **7:46**, May 1978, 3; **7:48**, Jul. 1978,
8–9. The timber companies that were removing
trees from rio das Cobras were Marochi and Idol-
ina Piassantini.

441: community.' ESP, 2 Oct. 1979. There
was a stand-off with Funai's agent Allan Kardec,
who refused the Indians money to operate the
machinery. On 14 Aug. 1980 ESP reported that
Chief Pagungue had asked permission to sell
3,000 m³ (106,000 cubic feet) of hardwood that
had been cut by the timber companies and was
now rotting. The Kaingang were still trying to
evict a final settler called Dalastra, who occupied
2,400 ha (5,930 acres) but refused to leave.

441: artificially'. Anon., 'Obituary: Ângelo
Kretã (1941–1980)', SIR, **5:1(29)**, Spring 1980
(34–7), 34.

442: lost.' Ibid., 35.

442: barbed wire.' Ibid.

442: reoccupy it.' 'Ângelo Kretã: vamos ocupar
nossa terra', *Boletim do CIMI*, **9:62**, Mar. 1980,
15. The XI Assembly of Indigenous Chiefs, held
at São Marcos in Mato Grosso, declared its solidarity with the Kaingang and Guarani, but also
sympathized with the poor settlers evicted from
reserves in the southern states.

At this time, there were also problems for the
Xokleng neighbours of the Kaingang, at the
Duque de Caxias (Ibirama) reserve in Santa
Catarina. This 1,415 ha (3,496 acre) reserve had
emerged from the peace between the tribe and
Eduardo Hoerhan in 1914, got a definitive title
from the SPI in 1956, and was fully registered in
the state land registry. First, at the end of 1979
the anthropologist Silvio Coelho dos Santos had

to lead a campaign against a dam that would have
drowned much of the reserve, including the
homes of 600 families and the post itself. The
proposed hydroelectric dam on the Hercilio tributary of the Uruguay river would also have
affected Kaingang living in the Xapecó valley
(ESP, 18 and 21 Oct. 1979). In 1980 there was a
curious upheaval at **Ibirama**. The Xokleng were
divided between two rival Protestant missions,
variants of the Pentecostalist Assembly of God.
The Indians were exasperated by Funai's failure
to pay them compensation for flooding from the
dam and sale of their timber.

One Xokleng faction wanted to do a deal with
the Tomelin timber company, which had promised them payment, food, houses, etc. in return
for their wood. So some Xokleng leaders went
first to the local city to register a declaration about
this deal, and then to Brasília to demand 'emancipation' from Funai – under the terms of the
emancipation decree that was so bitterly
denounced by Indian sympathizers. The leaders'
journey to Brasília and their emancipation move
were all organized by Tomelin's lawyers. It was a
clear case of 'emancipation' intended to defraud
gullible Indians of their assets, and it soon
emerged that those who wanted the deal with the
timber company represented only half the tribe.
One theory was that it was all a plot by Funai's
local delegate José Carlos Alves and Tomelin,
because it was *Funai* who wanted to sell out to
the timber men and be rid of the tribe, 'to pass
the Indians from one badly exercised guardianship
[by Funai] to another, the timber market, which
would really be a cemetery for the Ibirama Indians.' ('Ibirama: emancipação em último caso', *Boletim do CIMI*, **9:67**, Oct.–Nov. 1980, 42; trans. in
SIR, **6:2(34)**, Summer 1981, 77; ESP, 23 May
1981.)

By the 1990s, little had changed. The Xokleng
had still not received compensation for 831 ha
(2,053 acres) flooded by the dam, and the tribe
was still divided between those who gained from
selling wood to the timber companies and those
who did not. All were agreed, however, that Funai
officials were selling timber behind their backs.
The Xokleng of Ibirama were still under Funai's
tutelage, but wanted autonomy as Brazilian citizens, so that they could use hospitals, schools, and
banks outside their reserve.

Other groups were threatened by the world's
largest hydroelectric dam, Itaipú on the Paraná
river, which opened in 1988 and formed a 1,400

km² (540 square mile) lake. Nhandeva Guarani (Xiripá) of the Ocoi river were forcibly relocated to escape the rising waters: *New York Times*, 14 Jan. 1981; *Porantim*, Apr. 1981; ARC, **6**, May 1981, 9–11.

442: indigenous movement. The death of Ângelo Kretã, aged thirty-nine, was widely reported in the Brazilian press. His moving funeral mass – with active missionaries such as the Jesuits Fr. João Evangelista Dornstauder and Fr. Thomaz de Aquino Lisbôa among the officiating priests – was attended by hundreds of Indians and white representatives of Funai, the Church, and NGOs (Estella Sampaio, 'A páscoa de Ângelo Kretã', *Boletim do CIMI*, **9:62**, Mar. 1980, 8–14; ESP, 31 Jan. 1980).

443: society'. Ligia R. L. Simonian, 'A reocupacão das terras indígenas no RS', *PIB 1991/1995* (São Paulo, 1996), 782. The situation of reserves in Rio Grande do Sul in 1987, as recorded in CEDI's *Terras Indígenas no Brasil*, was, in descending order by area: **Guarita**, 23,183 ha (for 3,909 Kaingang and Guarani (Mbya)) – which represented a full recovery of land lost pre-1971; **Nonoái**, still reduced to 14,910 ha for 1,452 Kaingang and Guarani; **Kaingang do Rio da Várzea**, 14,310 ha for 161 Kaingang; **Ligeiro**, 4,920 ha for 910 Kaingang; **Cacique Doble**, 4,508 ha for 419 Kaingang and Guarani; **Inhacorá**, 2,810 ha for 451 Kaingang (well up from the 1971 area, but still very small); **Carreteiro**, 601 ha for 168 Kaingang; **Iraí**, 235 ha for 98 Kaingang; **Guarani Votouro**, still 280 ha for 36 Kaingang and Guarani (Mbya). In addition there was the large **Rodeio Bonito**, with an unknown number of Kaingang, and **Guarani Barra do Ouro**, with 1,026 ha for 100 Guarani (Mbya) and three 'unidentified' posts for Guarani. (In acres: Guarita, 57,285; Nonoái, 36,843; Kaingang do Rio da Várzea, 35,360; Ligeiro, 12,157; Cacique Doble, 11,139; Inhacorá, 6,944; Carreteiro, 1,485; Iraí, 581; Guarani Votouro, 692; Guarani Barra do Ouro, 2,535.)

Nine years later, Simonian reported some improvements: at **Iraí** the Kaingang fought hard against the local authority to confirm, and themselves demarcate, a slightly enlarged 275 ha (680 acre) reserve. Fiona Watson of Survival visited Iraí in 1992 and was appalled by the poverty of its Indians, living in bamboo-and-canvas shelters, with too little land to farm, subject to seasonal flooding, and eking an existence from selling artefacts to a few passing travellers. At **Venterra** in

1993, 212 Kaingang regained parts of their 754 ha (1,863 acre) reserve that had been expropriated by Governor Brizola. At **Caseros** the Kaingang in 1995 recovered from local fazendeiros some more of the 1,004 ha (2,481 acre) reserve they had been awarded in 1911: Indians returned from exile in the large nearby reserve of Cacique Doble. At **Serrinha**, 120 Kaingang in 1993 regained part of the land removed from their 11,950 ha (29,528 acre) reserve in 1941 and by Brizola in 1964; they then went on to try to get the rest, but 'as in the other recovered areas, their conditions of occupation are extremely precarious and the Indians had difficulty in securing support for their struggle' (ibid.). They did, however, succeed. Funai in 1997 and 1999 secured compensation for evicted bona-fide settlers, and Serrinha is now home to 440 Kaingang. **Borboleta** is a large area with ill-defined legal status. Some 3,000 Kaingang and Guarani are struggling to displace hundreds of settlers from its 45,000 ha (111,000 acres or 174 square miles). Having failed to obtain much help from Funai or from the colonization agency Incra to resettle displaced farmers, the Indians turned to the environment agency Ibama to help them create an 'extractive reserve' in reconstituted *mata atlântica* (endangered Atlantic rainforest) of araucaria and other species.

In Santa Catarina in 1987 there were: **Xapecó** (formerly **Xanxerê**), of 15,623 ha for 1,900 Guarani (Mbya) and Kaingang; **Ibirama**, of 14,156 ha for 898 Xokleng and Guarani (Mbya); **Palmas**, of 2,944 ha for 465 Kaingang; and **Toldo Chimbangue**, of 928 ha for 60 Kaingang, as well as two 'unidentified' reserves of **Toldo Imbu** for the Kaingang and **Morro dos Cavalos** for the Guarani (Mbya). (In acres: Xapecó, 38,604; Ibirama, 34,979; Palmas, 7,275; Toldo Chimbangue, 2,293.) The return of half the Toldo Chimbangue (which had been taken from the Kaingang by German and Italian immigrants in the nineteenth century) was the result of a protest march by many Indians and the occupation of the office of the President of Funai by seven Kaingang on 18 March 1985.

In southern Paraná in 1987 the Ñandeva Guarani occupied **Rio das Cobras**, of 19,100 ha for 1,626 of them and some Kaingang; **Mangueirinha**, of 7,400 ha for 1,082 Kaingang and Guarani; **Ava Guarani**, of 232 ha for 134 Guarani; **Rio Areta**, of 390 ha for 48 Guarani, and **Ilha de Cotinga** which was not 'identified'. (In acres: Rio das

Cobras, 47,196; Mangueirinha, 18,285; Ava Guarani, 573; Rio Areta, 964.) There were also many
northern Kaingang and Guarani in northern
Paraná, at **Barão de Antonina, Apucarana, Fax-
inal, Ivaí, Laranjinha, Marrecas, Pinhalzinho,
Ortigueira,** and **Guaira.**

444: ground.' Claude Lévi-Strauss, *Tristes Tropiques* (Paris, 1955), 156.

444: [3,300 feet].' Ibid., 159–60.

444: lives.' Kalervo Oberg, *The Terena and the
Caduveo of Southern Mato Grosso, Brazil* (Washington, 1949), 59. The State of Mato Grosso had
confirmed the Emperor Dom Pedro's donation
(with boundaries of the rivers Niutaca, Nabileque,
and Aquidavão, and the Bodoquena Hills) with a
survey in 1899–1900; this survey was approved
by the state governor in 1903; and it was confirmed by Federal Decree 54 of 1 Apr. 1931.
However, state deputy Rachid Mamed led the
attempted seizure of all but 100,000 ha (386
square miles) by drafting Mato Grosso Assembly
Law 1,077 of 10 Apr. 1958. On the strength of
this, the land agency in Campo Grande 'alienated'
270,000 ha (1,040 square miles) of Kadiwéu land
and awarded ranchers and settlers title deeds to it.
SPI lawyers reacted vigorously. They got the 1958
law vetoed by the governor and then quashed by
the Supreme Federal Tribunal on 30 August
1961. A ruling by a court in Cuiabá declaring the
title deeds null was upheld by the Federal
Supreme Court on 26 October 1972. *Correio da
Manhã,* 8 Nov. 1959; BSPI, **34,** Nov. 1959; Darcy
Ribeiro, *A Política Indigenista Brasileira* (Ministério da Agricultura, Rio de Janeiro, 1962); Gontram da Veiga Jardim, 'Os guerreiros já não
cantam mais', *Correio da Manhã,* 23 Sep. 1967;
ESP, 26 Oct. 1972; *Diário da Serra,* 20 Apr. 1983.

446: villages.' Fernando Altenfelder Silva,
'Mudança cultural dos Terêna', RMP, **3,** 1949,
342, translated in Dale W. Kietzman, *Indian Survival in Brazil* (Doctoral dissertation, University of
Southern California, 1972), 269.

446: in general.' Ibid., 268.

446: drunkards.' Darcy Ribeiro, *Os Índios e a
Civilização* (Rio de Janeiro, 1970), 410.

446: community.' Roberto Cardoso de Oliveira, *O Processo de Assimilação,* 108, in Kietzman,
Indian Survival in Brazil, 269.

446: proselytizing.' Roberto Cardoso de Oliveira, *Do Índio ao Bugre: processo de assimilação dos
Terena* (second edition, Rio de Janeiro, 1976), 97.

446: teachings'. Kietzman, *Indian Survival in
Brazil,* 267.

447: decimated.' Roberto Cardoso de Oliveira,
'The role of Indian Posts in the Process of Assimilation – Two case studies', AI, **20:2,** Apr. 1960,
91. Cardoso de Oliveira did field sudies in the late
1950s in eleven Terena villages: Posto Indígena
Cachoeirinha, 834 people, and the villages of
Passarinho and **Moreira** (109 and 130 people
respectively) twenty kilometres (twelve miles)
away at the edge of Miranda town; **União** village
with 10 families, six kilometres (four miles) south
of Miranda, and P. I. **Lalima** (256 people) fifty
kilometres (thiry-one miles) south of the town.
Near Aquidauana were: P. I. **Taunay** and nearby
Bananal village, 617 people, and the villages of
Ipegue and **Limão Verde** (443 and 246 people
repectively); P. I. **Capitão Vitorino,** twenty kilometres north of Nioac, 195 people; P. I. **Buriti,**
twenty-seven kilometres (seventeen miles) from
Sidrolândia towards the city of Campo Grande,
483 people; and P. I. **Francisco Horta** near Dourados, with thirty families alongside Guarani.
Allowing six people per family, this gives a total
of 3,550 Terena under SPI tutelage. Cardoso de
Oliveira, 'Preliminares de uma pesquisa sôbre a
assimilação dos Terêna', RA, **5:2,** Dec. 1957, 177;
Do Índio ao Bugre, 71–88.

447: squatters'. Commissão Pró-Índio – São
Paulo, *Folha de São Paulo,* 18 Aug. 1981; *PIB
1981,* 62.

447: identities' ESP, 24 Feb. 1981. When Robin
Hanbury-Tenison was in the Kadiwéu reserve in
1971 he also found them 'fine and strong-looking
people', but those at nearby Bodoquena were
depressed and demoralized. Although their woods
contained plenty of game, they were not allowed
shotguns and had lost the art of hunting with
bows and arrows (*Report of a Visit to the Indians of
Brazil* (London, 1971), 11–12). Hanbury-Tenison
reported 425 Kadiwéu in the reserve and 218
people (including Terena) at Bodoquena. Pedro
Tavares in 1975 said that there were 552 Kadiwéu
'in miserable conditions' (SIN, **9,** Jan. 1975). Nelson Rockefeller had in 1956 bought a large stake
in the 417,000 ha (1,600 square mile) Bodoquena
ranch from the Brazilian Ambassador to Washington, Walther Moreira Salles, and this abutted
against the Kadiwéu reserve. Gerard Colby and
Charlotte Dennett, *Thy Will be Done* (New York,
1995), 301; Affonso Romano de Sant'Anna,
'Enterrem meu coração na Serra da Bodoquena',
Jornal do Brasil, Especial, 4 May 1980.

447: extinction'. Deputy Antonio Carlos de
Oliveira, *O Povo,* 8 May 1981.

447: Brazil.' Mário Juruna quoted by Affonso Romano de Sant'Anna, 'Enterrem meu coração'. *447: force'. Folha de São Paulo,* 18 Nov. 1982. The raid by the fifty Indians (said to have been accompanied by masked white men) was in *ESP,* 27 Apr. 1982. The first 'Seminário Sul-Matogrossense de Problemas Indígenas' was held in the University in Campo Grande in 1980. *448: just that.'* The Terena leader Bagodarquis in *Folha de São Paulo,* 28 Jul. 1983. The President of Funai, Air Force Colonel Paulo Moreira Leal, made the same accusation earlier in the year (*PIB/ 83,* 227). Darcy Ribeiro wrote a report for the Supreme Court action, and reproduced this in *Carta* (Gabinete do Senador Darcy Ribeiro, Brasília), **9**, 1991, 268–9; and a book, *Kadiwéu* (Petrópolis, 1980).

449: reserve.' Correio do Estado, 9 Oct. 1984.

449: whites'. O Globo, 20 Jan. 1985; *PIB-85/ 86,* 405.

450: assistance' Jaime Siqueira Jr., 'Kadiwéu: as dificuldades da gestão direta dos arrendamentos', *PIB 1987/88/89/90,* 540.

451: community.' 'Uma alternativa econômica para os Kadiwéu', *PIB 1991/1995,* 760.

451: alligators. Acirk: the Associação das Comunidades Indígenas da Reserva Kadiwéu. Georg Grünberg worked for the Austrian foreign-aid agency IIZ; he had edited the proceedings of the Barbados Declaration of 1971. In population, a Funai census in 1995 showed 1,339 people in the Kadiwéu indigenous territory (with 951 in and around Bodoquena, and 388 in the southern post of São João which contains mostly Terena and Kinikináo). By 1999 this had risen to 1,592 (1,041 in Bodoquena and 551 in São João).

452: expel us.' Interview with Maúba (Severo Ferreira) Guató, *PIB 1987/88/89/90,* 550. The Salesian who rediscovered the reclusive Guató was Sister Ada Cambaroto, thanks to an old Guató lady living in Corumbá. They were then visited by a team from Funai and the local indigenous NGO Cedin (Conselho Estadual de Defesa dos Direitos do Índio). The island of the Guató origin legend is Bela Vista do Norte (Insua to the Guató, also known as Uberaba or Porto Índio), between the Pantanal **national** park (Caracará reserve) and the boundary of Mato Grosso state, about 120 kilometres (seventy-five miles) upriver or north of Corumbá. Mário Ramires, 'Filhos legítimos do Pantanal', *Boletim Informativo Ecossistema. Edição Especial* (Governo de Mato Grosso do Sul, Campo Grande, Jun. 1989); on the

expedition in 1991, *Porantim,* Apr. 1991; *PIB 1991/1995,* 762.

452: illness, etc.'. Letter to Funai from the Ofaié-Xavante Association, Brasilândia (Mato Grosso do Sul), 10 Mar. 1988, *PIB 1987/88/89/ 90,* 551–2; Ataíde Francisco Rodrigues, 'O povo Ofaye', *Terra Indígena* (Centro de Estudos Indígenas, Araraquara), **8:**58, Jan.–Mar. 1991, 29–38; Carlos Alberto dos Santos Dutra, *Ofaié: morte e vida de um povo* (CIMI-MS, Brasilândia, MS, 1994). Across the Paraná river to the east, the Xetá were another small group who also faced extinction and loss of land. Their plight was chronicled in Cecília Maria Vieira Helm, 'Os Xetá: a trajetória de um grupo tupi-guarani em extinção no Paraná', *Anuário Antropológico* (Tempo Brasileiro, Rio de Janeiro), **92**, 1994, 105–12.

453: SPI's creed'. James B. Watson, *Cayuá Culture Change: a study in acculturation and methodology,* Memoir 73 of *American Anthropologist,* **54:**2, Apr. 1952, 59; Egon Schaden, *Aspectos Fundamentais da Cultura Guaraní* (Difusão Européia do Livro, São Paulo, 1954) and *Aculturação Indígena* (São Paulo, 1969), 36–40. The tribe's name has also been spelled Caiuá, Kaiwá, Kayová, etc. Curt Nimuendajú, 'Apontamentos sôbre os Guaraní', RMP, **8**, 1954, 13–59. The present-day Kaiowá Guarani of Southern Mato Grosso are descended from communities that had formed another Jesuit missionary province, Itatín, which was destroyed in 1632 by bandeirante slave-raiders from São Paulo. Other Guarani further south found themselves in Brazil because of the Treaty of Madrid of 1750, which divided South America between the Spanish and Portuguese empires and gave Brazil roughly its present frontiers. The Treaty's negotiators chose the Uruguay river as the frontier in southern Brazil, and this separated seven reluctant missions (reductions) of Guarani from their cousins in Spanish Paraguay. This rupture led to the slaughter of Guarani who refused to accept Portuguese rule, by Spanish and Portuguese troops in 1755 – an atrocity that provoked Voltaire's irony and that formed the background to the movie *The Mission.*

453: relations' Schaden, *Aculturação Indígena,* 37.

455: survival'. Porantim, **21:**219, Oct. 1999, 4.

455: revolvers'. Correio Braziliense, 5 Oct. 1982; *PIB/1982,* 82. On Guarani relations with missionaries, see Gilberto Mazzolene, 'Evangelização e tradições indígenas: o caso Guarani',

Revista Brasileira de Ciências Sociais (Anpocs, São Paulo), **9:26**, Oct. 1994, 66–71.

455: militia.' 'A política indígena no espaço da Funai', *PIB-85/86*, 390. Marçal de Souza had written to the local head of Funai in 1980, three years before his murder, that he had been threatened both by the Paraguayan Rômulo Gamarra, who worked for Líbero Monteiro de Lima, owner of the Serra Brava fazenda, and by fellow Indians over land. Gamarra was briefly arrested but disappeared after his release, and Monteiro de Lima was acquitted by a jury when the case was finally heard in Ponta Porã – in March 1993, almost a decade after the killing. Hundreds of Indians from twenty-two communities and representatives of forty-two indigenous NGOs came to the town for the trial, but were prevented from getting near the court-house by 160 armed police. In his defence, the farmer's lawyer argued that Marçal had been disputing the leadership of the Ñandeva Guarani and ownership of a strip of land with Lázaro Morel, and that his killer was that Guarani Indian. The Brazilian anthropologists' organization, CIMI, and other activists argued that the trial had been flawed, omitting crucial evidence in Guarani, that the seven-person jury was weighted in favour of the farmer, and that Monteiro de Lima's strong motives to kill Marçal were not fully revealed. A local teacher, José Laerte Tetila, published a book in praise of the murdered leader: *Marçal de Souza – Tupã'I – A saga de um Guarani.*

456: over-forties.' 'Suicídios em meio à miséria', *Isto É/Senhor*, 24 Oct. 1990; *PIB 1987/88/89/90*, 548.

456: cows'. 'Suicídios', 24 Oct. 1990; *PIB 1987/88/89/90*, 548.

456: genocide'. 'Suicídios', 24 Oct. 1990; *PIB 1987/88/89/90*, 548. Senator Gomes was the great champion of the indigenous cause in the Senate. He also led a team to investigate the Yanomami situation, but was tragically killed in a plane crash.

457: people.' Tony Emerson, 'A tribe turns to suicide', *Newsweek*, 19 Aug. 1991; Marta Maria Azevedo, 'O suicídio entre os Guarani Kaiowá', *Terra Indígena* (CIMI, Centro de Estudos Indígens, Araraquara), **8:58**, Jan.–Mar. 1991, 6–28; Georg G. Grünberg, 'Por que os Guaranis estão se matando?', *Tempo e Presença* (CEDI, Rio de Janeiro), **13:258**, Jul.–Aug. 1991, 32–7; Anastácio F. Morgado, 'Epidemia de suicídio entre os Guarani-Kaiowá: suas causas e avançando a hipótese do recuo impossível', *Cadernos de Saúde Pública*

(Fiocruz, Rio de Janeiro), **7:4**, Oct.–Dec. 1991, 585–98; José Carlos Sebe Bom Meihy, 'Suicídio Kaiowá', *Carta* (Gabinete Senador Darcy Ribeiro, Brasília), **9**, 1993, 53–9.

457: lives.' Rubem Thomaz de Almeida, 'O caso Guarani: o que dizem os vivos sobre os que se matam?', *PIB 1991/1995*, 725. The individual deaths were listed on pp. 729–31.

458: colonizers.' Meihy, 'Suicídio Kaiowá', 58.

458: fire.' Thomaz de Almeida, 'O caso Guarani', 726. The quadrilateral of rich land of which Guarani had been stripped was between the towns of Rio Brilhante, Caarapó, Ponta Porã, and Bela Vista, a vast area with the city of Dourados in its midst. Maucir Pauletti of CIMI-Mato Grosso do Sul blamed this 'cleansing' as the main reason for Kaiowá misery, in an article in *Porantim*, **21:214**, May 1999, 11.

458: parents'. *Folha de São Paulo*, 12 Feb. 1991.

459: destroying them'. Meihy, 'Suicídio Kaiowá', 59.

459: territories.' Márcio Santilli, 30 March 1993, 'A lei protege os índios e o judiciário, seus assassinos', *PIB 1991/1995*, 738.

459: difficult.' 'Kaiowá fight land-grabs in Brazil', Urgent-Action Bulletin, Survival International, London, Apr. 1997. Simone Dreyfus-Gamelon, 'Les Kaiowá-Guarani du Brésil', *Les Nouvelles de Survival*, Paris, Summer 1997, 9.

459: manner.' 'Government inaction triggers wave of suicides', Urgent-Action Bulletin, Survival International, London, Sep. 1999. In this bulletin, Survival showed that 300 Kaiowá were herded into 60 ha (150 acres) of land at Panambizinho, surrounded by colonists' electric fences that were patrolled by gunmen. Four years earlier, the Minister of Justice had decreed that this reserve must be increased to 1,240 ha (3,060 acres) and some settlers relocated; but nothing had been done. There had been some small successes in the previous year. A campaign orchestrated by Survival and CIMI-MS (Mato Grosso do Sul) had helped Guarani of Jarará, Sucuriy, Potrero Guaçu, and Lima-ry regain lost lands (Survival *Success Bulletin*, Oct. 1998). In October 2002 there was another victory when a federal judge evicted ranchers from lands taken from the Kaiowá in the 1950s. Thus 400 Kaiowá of the Marangatu Hills, who had been crowded into just 9 ha (22 acres), were awarded the original 9,300 ha (23,000 acres) which they had repossessed.

18. Manaus to Roraima

461: relatives.' Alípio Bandeira, Jauapery (Manaus, 1926), 6 and A Cruz Indígena (Pôrto Alegre, 1926), 7; John Hemming, Amazon Frontier (London, 1995 edn.), 334; MAREWA (Movimento de Apoio à Resistência Waimiri/Atroari), Resistência Waimiri/Atroari (Itacoatiara, 1983), 14.

461: twentieth century Payer described his visits in 'Reisen im Jauapiry-Gebiet', Petermanns Mitteilungen, 52, Gotha, 1906, 217–22.

461: good man. The killing of Humberto Brighia is in Darcy Ribeiro, Os Índios e a Civilização (Rio de Janeiro, 1970), 184. The killing of the American military men in 1944 is in the Relatório for 1945 of the Manaus office of the SPI, and in Egydio e Doroti Schwade, As Terras Waimiri-Atroari no Ciclo de Minério (Mimeo, Presidente Figueiredo, 21 Apr. 1985), 1.

462: swampy. A land link between Manaus and Boa Vista had been mooted for over a century. A trail was even opened in 1895 by a large team hired by Sebastião Diniz, a rich rancher from Roraima (then called Rio Branco), in response to a premium offered by the government of Amazonas. It was briefly reopened in 1927–28 by a team of forty-five men working for twenty-one months led by the engineer Luiz Ogden Collins, in response to a grandiose scheme by the American explorer Dr Alexander Hamilton Rice to finance a railway to this remote northern corner of Brazil. But it had to cross 815 kilometres (500 miles) of forest, nine large rivers, and over 700 streams; so no horses or cattle traffic used it and the forest soon closed in again. Avelino Ignácio de Oliveira, Bacia do Rio Branco (Estado do Amazonas) (Serviço Geológico e Mineralógico do Brasil, Boletim 37, Rio de Janeiro, 1929), 28; Emanuele Amodio and Vicente Pira, 'História dos povos indígenas de Roraima – Makuxi – Ingaricó – Taurepang e Wapixana', Boletim (Arquivo Indigenista da Diocese de Roraima, Boa Vista), 10, Mar. 1985, 44; Antônio Ferreira de Souza, Noções da Geografia e História de Roraima (Manaus, 1969), 65; João Mendonça de Souza, A Manaus–Boa Vista (Roteiro Histórico) (Manaus, 1977), 260; John Hemming, Roraima: Brazil's Northernmost Frontier (London, 1990), 12–13.

462: wife was'. Gilberto Pinto, Report to 1st Regional Delegacy of Funai, in Boletim Informativo

Funai, 1:3, 2nd quarter of 1972, 33; ESP, 24 Sep. 1969.

462: threatening'. ESP, 21 Nov. 1968. This gives details of Father Calleri's radio messages between 23 and 30 October 1968, with jubilation over his exchanges of presents, first entries into Waimiri-Atroari villages, and later apprehension because they were said to have killed 'in horrible massacres forty whites and 150 natives of the group we are with'. An experienced woodsman, Álvaro Paulo da Silva, ran away from Calleri's expedition on 27 October because he could see that trouble was brewing. He described the many small insults that had alienated Father Calleri from the Indians – such as entering a hut when a chief tried to stop him, making Indian guides carry loads, pointing at Indians when counting them (which they took to be a sign that they would be killed), refusing to give desired objects (including the clothing of one of the nuns), making Indians go to a waterfall to be photographed, etc.: 'Não há genocídio do dócil nativo', ESP, 9 Nov. 1972, 20.

462: superior beings'. José Porfírio F. de Carvalho, Waimiri/Atroari – a história que ainda não foi contada (Brasília, 1982); William Milliken, Robert P. Miller, Sharon R. Pollard, and Elisa V. Wandelli, Ethnobotany of the Waimiri Atroari Indians of Brazil (Royal Botanic Gardens, Kew, 1992), 7.

462: intruder.' Gilberto Pinto interview, ESP, 19 Apr. 1970. The attraction post was on the Santo Antonio do Abonari (Abonari is a nineteenth-century spelling of Atroari), a headwater of the Uatumã, which flows south-eastwards into the main Amazon. Father Calleri's Consolata Order had in 1948 succeeded the Benedictines as the main missionaries in Roraima.

The 1967 expedition of the Worldwide Evangelization Crusade (known in Brazil as the Cruzada da Evangelização Mundial, and the precursor of the Unevangelized Fields Mission) was led by the American pastor William Hawkins. It went from Lethem in southern Guyana up the Tacutu and down the Alalaú rivers, guided by seventeen Waiwái Indians and supported by a light plane of the missionary aviation service. The Indians traded machetes and other goods with the Waimiri-Atroari; and some of them went on to

Manaus with the missionaries (Gilberto Pinto report to Funai, 3 Mar. 1971). Pastor Hawkins learned about the attraction plans of Father Calleri and of Funai's sertanista Gilberto Pinto, and offered to 'open a third front' should there be 'any unforeseen situation'. José da Gama Malcher, *Jornal do Brasil*, 10 Dec. 1968 and 11 Feb. 1969; ESP, 1 Jun. 1969. The *Jornal do Brasil*'s special reporter Mário de Aratanha said that, back in Georgetown, Guyana, Lawrence Thompson of the expedition had shown a slide of a Waimiri village that they had burned 'in order to avoid leaving traces'. The Catholic missionary-teacher Egydio Schwade suspected that there were 'powerful forces' seeking mineral wealth in the region: when Father Silvano Sabatini of the Consolata Mission started investigating the Calleri massacre, he was warned to desist by someone from Brazilian military intelligence (Egydio e Doroti Schwade, *As Terras Waimiri-Atroari*, 3–4; also Noel Nutels in *Fatos e Fotos*, 22 May 1969). Father Sabatini was a fellow-Consolata missionary who had been head of the Roraima Prelacy's pro-Indian commission at the time of Calleri's death. He refused to accept the official version and spent thirty years investigating the tragedy. Sabatini interviewed the Waimiri-Atroari Xará, an old lady called Coowi, and Valdecir Waiwai, all of whom endorsed his belief in a conspiracy between Protestant missionaries and American mineral explorers. He published his findings in *Massacre* (Edições Loyola/CIMI, Bela Vista, Brasília, 1998); *Porantim*, **20:21**, Dec. 1998, 8.

463: white men"' Jornal da Tarde, 16 Apr. 1970; ESP, 15 Apr. 1970.

463: evidence'. The detailed confession by a young eyewitness, 'Ze' Libanio, described exactly how the Indians were killed and their bodies disposed of. He accused a merchant called Antonio Paulino da Rocha of ordering the first massacre. Funai clamoured for justice, but Gomes Damasceno and his friend Rivaldo were released by Manaus police because there were no bodies.

464: delightedly'. Gilberto Pinto interview, *O Cruzeiro*, 11 Aug. 1970. This article describes his visits to the Atroari in great detail.

464: engineers'. 'Índios que sacrificaram Missão Calleri permitem agora abertura da estrada', *Boletim Informativo Funai*, **1:3**, 1972, 35.

463: proposal. The decree that legalized the Waimiri-Atroari reserve was 68,907/71, *Diário Oficial*, 13 Jul. 1971, but the decreed area omitted 20 per cent of the land occupied by the tribe's villages; and Funai was authorized to reduce it further within two years, if it saw fit.

465: arrows.' 'Death at Abunari Two', *Time*, 20 Jan. 1975; Marvine Howe in the *New York Times*, 6 Jan. 1975; 'A morte do sertanista Gilberto', *Boletim Informativo Funai*, **13**, 1975, 3–9.

465: people died".' Stephen Baines, *Epidemics, the Waimiri-Atroari Indians and the Politics of Demography* (Brasília, 1994), 20. Chief 'Comprido' had lost his father to disease, and he himself later died of it. Westernized tribal leaders later blamed Comprido as the scapegoat for all aggressions against whites; but he was also hailed as a model of indigenous political consciousness (Baines, *'É a Funai que sabe': a frente de atração Waimiri-Atroari* (Doctoral dissertation, Universidade de Brasília, 1988; MPEG, Belém, 1991, 288–90, 299–301). Sebastião Nunes Firmo, who later ran the Waimiri-Atroari attraction team, wrote in 1978 that an Indian called Viana told him that Pinto's killing was the result of jealousy by Chief 'Comprido' of Chief Maruaga because he had become such a close friend of Pinto: 'Divergência de líderes tribais matou Gilberto', RAI, **2:11**, Jul.–Aug. 1978, 13–16. Another version of Pinto's death was that he was shot as he went out to the cook-house to stoke the fire for morning coffee. For a conspiracy theory there is José Carvalho, *Waimiri/Atroari*.

The earlier killing of three Funai workers and burning of their post on the Abonari was reported in *Jornal do Brasil*, 1 Feb. 1973; and by Marvine Howe in the *New York Times*, 2 Feb. 1973; René Fuerst, ed., *Amazind Bulletin*, **1**, Geneva, 1973, 32–3. There were also four attacks on construction camps and Funai posts during the first four months of 1974, which resulted in fifteen deaths. The terrible massacre of the Atroari village called Kram-na-Mudó on the Alalaú was recorded by Egydio and Doroti Schwade, who cared for many of its orphans.

465: Indianist'. Orlando Villas Boas in José Marqueiz, 'Os últimos Kren-Akarores', *Manchete*, 1 Feb. 1975; *News from Survival International*, **10**, Apr. 1975, 19.

465: territory.' ESP and *Jornal do Brasil*, 9 Jan. 1975; Leonard Greenwood in *Los Angeles Times*, 8 Jan. 1975; SIN, **10**, Apr. 1975, 19.

466: civilizados.' Sebastião Amâncio in *O Globo*, 6 Jan. 1975; Leonard Greenwood, 'Brazil's chief Indian scout suspended', *Los Angeles Times*, 8 Jan. 1975; Shelton Davis, *Victims of the Miracle* (Cambridge, 1977), 97–8; William Milliken et al.,

Ethnobotany of the Waimiri Atroari Indians, 8. The leaflet of the Anti-Waimiri–Atroari campaign is reproduced in MAREWA, *Resistência Waimiri/Atroari*, 17. Colonel Arruda, commander of the 6th Engineering and Construction Battalion, had been vice-director of the Serviço Nacional de Informações, the Brazilian secret service. His crazy idea of ethnic cleansing was promptly rejected by General Ismarth de Araújo, President of Funai (*Jornal do Brasil*, 22 Jan. 1975) but there were ugly reports of bombings of Indian villages to facilitate the highway construction: Anna Presland, 'Waimiri-Atroari – the massacres behind the myth', ARC, Dec. 1979, 4–5.

467: required.' Milliken et al., *Ethnobotany of the Waimiri Atroari Indians*, 119; Manoel Lima, 'Os uaimiri-atroari já aceitam o branco', ESP, 28 Apr. 1981. The data on construction of the BR-174 is mostly from José Mendonça de Souza, *A Manaus–Boa Vista (Roteiro Histórico)* and Hemming, *Roraima*, 35–6. A stone memorial was erected to honour those who died 'doing their duty' in constructing the highway; but it named none of the Indians who also died because of the road.

467: choose. The Waiwái, who live mostly in Brazil and partly in southern Guyana, had been converted by the Amazon Evangelical Mission (Missão Evangélica da Amazônia or MEVA) the new name of the Unevangelized Fields Mission.

467: disaster like this.' Roberto Messias Franco, Director of SEMA (Secretaria Especial do Meio Ambiente), *Jornal do Brasil*, 5 Oct. 1987. Some of the campaigns against the dam by MAREWA (Movimento de Apoio à Resistência Waimiri/Atroari) included: Egydio Schwade, *Hidrelétrica de Balbina contra índios e labradores* (Mimeo, on the BR-174, 23 Aug. 1984); *Resistência Waimiri/Atroari*, 19–21; *Balbina, Ameaça e Destruição na Amazônia* (Manaus, 1987). The suppressed report was by Ângela Maria Baptista, *Relatório sobre a área indígena Waimiri-Atroari*, Funai, Brasília, 30 Jul. 1981. President Giscard d'Estaing of France visited Brazil in 1978 and personally offered finance for the Balbina dam, provided that it employed French equipment.

468: tributaries.' Verenilde Santos Pereira and Stephen Grant Baines, 'Funai e Paranapanema tomam conta dos Waimiri-Atroari', *PIB 1987/88/89/90*, 200.

468: Indians.' Giuseppe Cravero, in a report of August 1980 by Funai's DGPI (Departamento Geral do Património Indígena), in Stephen G. Baines, 'The Waimiri-Atroari and the Paranapanema company', *Critique of Anthropology* (London, etc., **11:2**, 1991), 145 (also in *Ethnies*, Survival International France, Paris, **11–12**); *Porantim*, Manaus, Jan.–Feb. 1982 and many later reports. In May 1973 Max White of the US Geological Survey mentioned the Waimiri-Atroari territory as a prime area for mineral exploration: 'Probing the unknown Amazon Basin – a roundup of 21 mineral-exploration programs in Brazil', *Engineering and Mining Journal*, Chicago, May 1973, 72–6; Davis, *Victims of the Miracle*, 89–90; and this potential was confirmed by Radambrasil. The DNPM (Departamento Nacional de Produção Mineral) granted five concessions to Paranapanema's subsidiary Timbo Indústria de Mineração Ltda. in 1979, and these were later transferred for exploitation by its subsidiary Mineração Taboca SA.

468: do not use'. Pereira and Baines, 'Funai e Paranapanema', 200.

469: people.' Gazeta de Notícias, 15 May 1982.

469: Waimiri-Atroari.' Baines, *Epidemics*, 7.

469: body.' Ibid., 10–11. Stephen Baines described the machinations of pseudo-Indians (who were mostly bachelors from acculturated tribes such as the Sateré-Mawé and Munduruku of the middle Amazon and Baré from the middle Negro) in Funai's FAWA (Frente de Atração) in: *É a Funai que Sabe* (Belém, 1991) and 'O xamanismo como história', in Bruce Albert and Alcida Rita Ramos, eds., *Pacificando o Branco* (São Paulo, 2002), 311–45.

470: with us.' Letter to the President of the Republic by Viana Uomé Atroari and Mário Paroé Atroari, 10 Mar. 1986, *PIB-85/86*, 142. In May 1987 the power company Eletronorte took these two young Atroari leaders, with Tomás Temerse Waimiri and Paulo Uiribiá Waimiri, to see the gigantic Tucuruí dam on the Tocantins, so that they might cease to view Balbina as 'the end of the world'. They were deeply depressed by the experience. A few weeks later, Funai started moving Indians out of the villages called Taquari and Tapupunã that would be drowned under Balbina's reservoir (*Diário Popular*, 7 May 1987; *Folha de São Paulo*, 11 May 1987).

470: activities'. Stephen Baines, 'The Waimiri-Atroari and the Paranapanema company', 149; MAREWA, *Resistência Waimiri/Atroari*, 21–2; Egydio and Doroti Schwade, *As Terras Waimiri-Atroari*, 9–10. Funai expelled the Catholic missionary teachers Egydio and Doroti Müller

Schwade from the Atroari village Yamara in January 1987 and gave their work to a Protestant team led by Joseph Hill of the Unevangelized Fields Mission (MEVA) (*A Crítica*, Manaus, 20 Dec. 1986). The anthropologist Márcio Silva and nurse Marise had to leave in early 1988. Baines and his assistant Verenilde Pereira were expelled in August 1989, having worked with the Waimiri-Atroari since 1982. All, of course, supported MAREWA and belonged to the SBPC, the Brazilian society for the advancement of science. Baines continued to teach at the University of Brasília.

470: lubricants'. Funai report of Oct. 1984 quoted in Baines, 'The Waimiri-Atroari and the Paranapanema company', 150. Baines also revealed how Aérofoto Cruzeiro and other mapmakers had renamed the upper Uatumã the Pitinga (which became the name of Paranapanema's cassiterite mine) and given the name Igarapé Santo Antonio do Abonari (the river where Calleri and Pinto had made their first contacts) only to the upper part of that stream, thereby moving the coordinates of its junction with the Uatumã. The Waimiri reserve was originally created by Decree 68,907 of 13 July 1971, to which was added an Interdicted Area (Decree 74,463 of 26 August 1974) and two additional areas (Portaria 511 of 5 July 1978). President João Figueiredo undid much of this, when on 24 November 1981 he reduced 1.8 million ha (7,000 square miles) to 'interdicted' status – this included part of the original reserve, the areas added in 1978, and the interdicted area of 1974. Of course, the vast territory that was released by this manoeuvre was precisely where Paranapanema was already mining. Egydio Schwade denounced various Funai officials (Colonel Cláudio Pagano, director of the DGPI, Hildegard Rick, Ney da Fonseca, and Giuseppe Cravero) for issuing the erroneous *certidão negativa* (certificate declaring an area to have no Indians) that made this massive change possible (*Folha de São Paulo*, 16 Feb. 1982; *O Globo*, 28 Feb. 1982; ESP, 20 Oct. 1982). Survival International issued an 'urgent-action bulletin' about the various threats to the Waimiri-Atroari, on 30 Nov. 1982; also Anna Presland, 'Reconquest', SIR, **4:1(25)**, Spring 1979, 25; **7:3–4(41/42)**, Autumn/Winter 1982, 40–42; *SI Newsletter*, **29**, 1991, 9.

The Pitinga mine was opened in 1979 and by 1985 its 3,500 employees were producing 12,000 tons (12,200 tonnes) of pure tin. It was probably the world's largest open-cast tin mine. The Par-

anapanema company gained government approval by stressing that all this metal would be exported to help Brazil's balance of payments. Its private hydroelectric dam was authorized by presidential decree of 25 February 1986, and was planned to produce 10,000 kilowatts at a cost of $18 million to build (Miriam de Aquino, *O Globo*, 21 Oct. 1985). In 1983 Funai prevented a rival mining concern, Acaraí Indústria e Mineração (part of the big mining company Vale do Rio Doce), from exploring for minerals within the reserve.

471: Alalaú'. Portaria 116/89, 13 May 1989. José Porfírio de Carvalho, 'Waimiri-Atroari: agora, a poluição dos rios', *PIB 1987/88/89/90*, 194–9. This paper gives excellent maps, pictures, and data of the mining operations.

472: wonderful.' Fiona Watson reports to Survival, Nov. 1990 and Jun. 1992, and 'The trauma of contact', *SI Newsletter*, **29**, 1991, 9. She visited the NAWA (Núcleo de Apoio Waimiri Atroari) base, then the villages of Jawara (about forty people, alongside Funai's Terra Planagem post), Xeri (thirty-five people, near Funai's Jundia post), and Munawa (seventy-five people, at the northern edge of the reserve), all of which were along the BR-174 highway. In 1987, the Waimiri Atroari reserve was reconfirmed (by Decree 94,406 of 14 July 1987) with the flooded areas, the tin mine, and the strip along the BR-174 excluded: a total area of some 2,440,000 ha (9,420 square miles). The reserve was delimited thanks to the insistence of the World Bank (one of the funders of the Balbina dam), which had also required the payments to the tribe by Paranapanema and Eletronorte.

The Indians Mário and Viana and Funai's sertanista Estêvão Pinto da Silva in 1988 made contact with an isolated group, with whom they exchanged presents: they called this people Piridipi or Piriutiti. They were thought to live up in the forest canopy, on the upper Branquinho on the border between the states of Roraima and Amazonas (*A Notícia*, 1 Apr. 1988; *PIB 1987/88/89/90*, 204; *A Crítica*, 27 Oct. 1995).

On population, Stephen Grant Baines, *Relatório sobre a conclusão da etapa III de pesquisa de campo do Projeto Etnográfico Waimiri/Atroari* (University of Brasília, 25 Feb. 1985) and *Epidemics*, 27–8; Márcio Fereira da Silva, *Romance de primas e primos: uma etnografia do parentesco Waimiri-Atroari* (Doctoral thesis, Museu Nacional/Univ. Fed. do Rio de Janeiro, 1993). Giuseppe Cravero of the Frente de Atração Waimiri-Atroari (FAWA) in 1977 registered 638 in contact with Funai. Baines made a thorough survey of every village in 1983 and counted only 332. The Programa Waimiri Atroari in 1991 estimated the tribe's population at 505 (*PIB 1987/88/89/90*, 161). It claimed all the credit for this increase, even though medical help was under way before the Programme started in 1987 – see propaganda pieces such as *Jornal do Brasil*, 20 Sep. 1993, or Cherie Hart, 'A Brazilian tribe escapes extinction', *World Development* (UNDP, **4:2**, 1991), special issue *Aiding Remote Peoples*. Porfirio Carvalho in 1994 gave a population of 611 (*PIB 1991/1995*, 201).

473: Portuguese.' Theodor Koch-Grünberg, *Vom Roroima zum Orinoco. Ergebnisse einer Reise in Nordbrasilien und Venezuela in den Jahren 1911–1913* (5 vols., Berlin and Stuttgart, 1916–28), **3**, *Ethnographie*, 3; Hemming, *Roraima*, 14.

473: whites.' Count Ermanno Stradelli, 'Rio Branco. Note di viaggio', *Bolletino della Società Geografica Italiana*, 3 ser., vol. 2, anno 23, no. 26 (Rome, 1889), 264. This northern region was known as Rio Branco until 1962 when its inhabitants voted to change the name to Roraima, after the 2,875 metre (9,436 foot) table-mountain at its northern extremity. The area was separated from the State of Amazonas in 1943, to become a Federal Territory; and it achieved statehood in 1988.

473: of them.' Henri Coudreau, *La France Equinoxiale* (2 vols., Paris, 1886–87), **2**, 400–1; Hemming, *Roraima*, 14–15.

474: cattle died.' Dom Adalbert, OSB, 'Correspondance du Rio Branco', *Bulletin des Œuvres et Missions Bénédictines au Brésil et au Congo*, Abbaye de Saint-André par Lophem, Belgium, **14**, Feb. 1913, 40. The Belgians under Dom Adalbert arrived in Boa Vista in 1909, on behalf of the Benedictine monastery in Rio de Janeiro. The Rio Branco region had had almost no religious activity for half a century, and many cattle barons were Freemasons. The zealous missionaries soon had an armed clash when they opposed the Freemasonry of the most powerful of all the ranchers, and they had to flee from Boa Vista. They established a small mission among the Makuxi on the Surumu river, which impressed Koch-Grünberg in 1911. But disease among their missionaries and other reasons forced them to abandon the enterprise in the following year. The last to leave the Surumu was the English Father Thomas. Count Stradelli saw him: 'deserted, sick and famished, he finally made his way with one companion to another mission station, and the effort to christianize the Indians was abandoned.' (Stradelli, 'Rio Branco', 265). Father Thomas transferred his activity to the lower Uraricoera, north of Boa Vista, where the American explorer/anthropologist William Curtis Farabee saw him in 1914: Farabee, 'A pioneer in Amazonia', *The Bulletin of The Geographical Society of Philadelphia*, **15**, Jan.–Oct. 1917, 3.

474: annihilated.' Adalbert, 'Correspondance du Rio Branco', 40.

474: Territory.' Araújo Cavalcanti, 'À margem do Relatório de Rice. (Ligeiras notas sôbre o aproveitamento do Vale do Rio Branco)', *Anais da Comissão Especial do Plano de Valorização Econômica da Amazônia*, Rio de Janeiro, 1949, **3**, 177.

474: assistance'. Ibid.; Edson Soares Diniz, 'O perfil de uma situação interétnica: os Makuxí e os regionais do Roraima', BMPEG, **31**, Apr. 1966, 20.

474: "maloca".' Iris Myers, 'The Makushi of the Guiana–Brazilian Frontier in 1949: A Study of Culture Contact', *Antropologica* (Fundación La Salle, Caracas), **80**, 1993, 19; also 'The Makushi of British Guiana – A Study in Culture-Contact', *Timehri* (Journal of the Royal Agricultural and Commercial Society of British Guiana, Georgetown), 1945–46, **26** and **27**. Peter Rivière, *The Forgotten Frontier: Ranchers of Northern Brazil* (New York, 1972); Edson Soares Diniz, 'Os Makuxí e os Wapitxâna: índios integrados ou alienados?', ASBA.

475: good men.' Cândido Mariano da Silva Rondon, *Índios do Brasil*, **3**, *Do Norte do Rio Amazonas* (CNPI, Rio de Janeiro, 1953), 9; Esther de Viveiros, *Rondon Conta sua Vida* (Rio de Janeiro, 1958), 516–18. Rondon was in Rio Branco in September and October 1927. As well as reprimanding the sheriff who was persecuting Chief Manuel Barreto's Makuxi on the upper Tacutu, he also persuaded Chief Bruno further downriver to bring his people back from British Guiana. The Makuxi of Chief Jesuíno guided the ageing Rondon in a historic ascent of Mount Roraima on 29 October, helped by Indians from the villages of Barro ('Mud') and Monte Aranha ('Spider Mountain').

476: families.' General Lima Figueiredo, 'Fronteiras Amazônicas', in IBGE (Instituto Brasileiro de Geografia e Estatística), *Amazônia Brasileira* (X Congresso Nacional de Geografia, Rio de

Janeiro, 1944) (186–206), 189–90; Hemming, *Roraima*, 20.

476: *situation.'* Myers, 'The Makushi of the Guiana–Brazilian Frontier', 10.

476: *toll'* Ibid., 11.

476: *numbers.'* Ibid.

476: *waged.'* Ibid., 25.

477: *death rate.'* Ibid., 38.

477: *catechism.'* Benedictine Monks, *O Anuário do Rio Branco* (Boa Vista, c. 1940), republished in *Boletim*, Diocese de Roraima, Boa Vista, 3, Oct. 1982, 16.

After the failure of their first effort in 1909–12, the Benedictines tried again in 1921 under a dynamic German abbot, Dom Pedro Eggerath. He brought the Bavarian nuns, the Sisters of Tutzing, to teach in Rio Branco. But Abbot Eggerath was *too* dynamic. He had the 'unfortunate idea' of launching a 'large-scale company' to trade with the isolated and sleepy backwater of Rio Branco. This collapsed with massive debts, exacerbated by his brother-in-law's absconding with much of the funds, and the Abbot was forced to resign in 1929. He had previously published a book about Roraima and its Indians: *O Vale e os Índios do Rio Branco* (Rio de Janeiro, 1924). The SPI disliked the Benedictines. The 1927 Annual Report of the Manaus inspectorate said that the Prelacy in Boa Vista had a college for girls 'that is nothing more than a house for enslaving minors, who are forced to perform mortifying arduous work for hours on end in the open sun'.

477: *suspected.* Father Cary-Elwes' mission was some thirty-two kilometres (twenty miles) south of the junction of the Tacutu with the Maú (or Ireng) river – just south of Lethem. As well as working with the Makuxi, Father Cary-Elwes made three journeys far up the Tacutu to the Waiwái and Tarumã tribes to the south: Audrey Butt Colson and John Morton, 'Early missionary work among the Taruma and Waiwai of Southern Guiana – The visits of Fr. Cuthbert Cary-Elwes, S.J. in 1919, 1922 & 1923', *Folk* (Danish Ethnographical Association, Copenhagen), 24, 1982, 203–61.

477: *conquest.'* Capitão Bráz Dias de Aguiar, 'Trabalhos da Comissão Brasileira Demarcadora de Límites – Primeira Divisão – nas fronteiras da Venezuela e Guianas Britânica e Neerlandesa, de 1930 a 1940', *IX Congresso Brasileiro de Geografia. Anais* (Rio de Janeiro, 1942), 230. For the arrival of the Consolata missionaries: 'A nova missão da Consolata no rio Branco' (trans. from Italian article in *Missioni Consolata*, Turin, May 1949) in *Boletim* (Diocese de Roraima), 4, Dec. 1982, 23–39.

On the native population of Roraima, Iris Myers in 1944 reckoned only 1,000 Makuxi in Brazil (out of a total of 1,800 for the entire tribe), whereas the Consolata fathers a few years later guessed 2,000, plus 500 related Taurepang (also spelled Taulipang, whom the whites used to call Arekuna; Koch-Grünberg changed this to Taurepang; but another anthropologist later found that Taurepang is a Carib word meaning 'ignorant' or 'savage', so that they became known in Venezuela and Guyana as Pemon). Koch-Grünberg had estimated in 1911 that the Taurepang had once been as numerous as the linguistically related Makuxi, but were reduced by disease to 1,000–1,500 in his day. By the 1950s, Darcy Ribeiro and Dale Kietzman both guessed 1,500–2,000 Makuxi in Brazil, 1,000–1,500 Taurepang, and 1,000–1,500 Wapixana. Twenty years later, Edson Diniz and Ernesto Migliazza each felt that Brazil's Makuxi population had doubled to 3,000 – partly from migration back across the frontier (Edson Soares Diniz, *Os Índios Makuxi de Roraima – sua instalação na sociedade nacional* (São Paulo, 1972); Ernesto Migliazza, *The Integration of the Indigenous Peoples of the Territory of Roraima, Brazil*, IWGIA Doc. 32, Copenhagen, 1978). In 1986 the Consolata lay missionaries Emanuele Amodio and Vicente Pira – who had an intimate knowledge of Roraima's savannah Indians – gave far higher numbers: 12,000 Makuxi, 5,000 Wapixana, 550 Taurepang (Pemon), and 500 Ingarikó (Amodio and Pira, 'História dos povos indígenas de Roraima – Makuxi – Ingaricó – Taurepang e Wapixana', *Boletim*, 10, Boa Vista, Mar. 1985). At the same time, the research organization CEDI and the Museu Nacional said that there were 1,224 Makuxi living on eight official reserves, 2,025 Wapixana also on eight reserves, and 2,056 mixed Makuxi and Wapixana on a further eight reserves (CEDI/Museu Nacional, *Terras Indígenas no Brasil*, São Paulo, 1987); but there were also many Indians outside the reserves, particularly in shanties on the edges of the city of Boa Vista.

478: *region'.* SPI *Relatório* for 1923, in Amodio and Pira, 'História dos povos indígenas', 37; Paulo Santilli, *As Fronteiras da República. História e política entre os Makuxi no vale do rio Branco* (São Paulo, 1994).

478: *introduced.'* Araújo Lima, 'A explotação amazônica', in IBGE, *Amazônia Brasileiro* (207–48), 242. The earlier visitor was Joaquim

Gondim, *Através do Amazonas* (Manaus, 1922), 24; Amodio and Pira, 'História dos povos indígenas', 41–2; Hemming, *Roraima*, 19. The ranch had been plundered by one Sebastião Diniz, who had a lease on it from 1888 to about 1912. São Marcos was vast, stretching for perhaps 8,000 km² (3,000 square miles) north towards the Venezuelan frontier; but Diniz removed most of the 18–20,000 head of cattle that Koch-Grünberg saw there in 1911 as well as carving out a huge ranch called Flechal for himself. When Diniz died, his widow and then the J. G. Araújo trading company that acquired her rights had a protracted legal action against the government about São Marcos and its cattle. The Indian Protection Service was awarded the ranch in 1916, to manage on behalf of the Ministry of Agriculture; but it later became part of the Indian patrimony and remained such throughout the twentieth century, albeit reduced to 653,949 ha (2,524 square miles) when it was demarcated in 1975 and decreed by Funai Portaria 1,856 in 1985. When the author visited São Marcos in 1972 with the Aborigines Protection Society's team, we were quite favourably impressed by the cluster of Makuxi houses at the ranch headquarters, by the plentiful meat that the Indians could purchase cheaply, and by a primary school run by a dedicated teacher – it was the only Funai school (as opposed to many missionary schools) that we saw anywhere in Brazil: Edwin Brooks, René Fuerst, John Hemming, Francis Huxley, *Tribes of the Amazon Basin in Brazil, 1972* (London, 1973), 67. When Funai was created from the ruins of the SPI in 1968, the São Marcos fazenda became a Colônia Agricola, which meant that it was a place where Indians and whites could coexist – in other words, it was ripe for invasion by settlers.

478: mentioning.' Diniz, 'O perfil de uma situacão', 14.

479: hot iron.' Ibid., 22–3.

479: evenings.' Geraldo Andrello, 'Profetas e pregadores: a conversão taurepáng à religião do Sétimo Dia', in TD (285–308), 287. The conversion of this people in Venezuela and British Guiana (where they are known as Pemon) started in the 1920s and 1930s under pastors O. E. Davis and A. W. Cott, and in the 1970s Adventists in Venezuela founded a large school in the village of Maurak, among the 1,500 Pemon who live in that country. Also: Audrey Butt Colson, 'The birth of a religion', *Journal of the Royal Anthropological Institute*, **90:1**, 1960, 66–106, 'Hallelujah among the Patamona Indians', *Antropologica* (Fundación La Salle, Caracas), **28**, 1971, 25–8, and 'Routes of knowledge', *Antropologica* **63–4**, 1985, 103–49; and Geraldo Andrello, *Os Taurepáng: migrações e profetismo no século XX* (Master's dissertation, Unicamp, Campinas, 1993).

480: movement.' Alcida Rita Ramos and Marco Antonio Lazarin, 'Assembléia de tuxáuas do lavrado', *PIB/1984* (78–82), 78.

480: century'. Sandra Secchi and Nelson Secchi, 'A situação atual dos índios Wapixana', *Boletim* (Arquivo Indigenista, Diocese de Roraima, Boa Vista), **5**, Mar. 1983 (7–62), 59; also Emanuele Amodio and Nelson Secchi, 'Os índios Wapixana em Roraima', *Boletim*, **2**, May 1982, 7–24. Amodio and Pira, 'História dos povos indígenas', 1–71. In the 1980s there were thought to be 10,000 Wapixana, divided equally between Brazilian Roraima and the Rupununi in southern Guyana, although there were some twenty smaller malocas in Brazil and only ten larger ones in Guyana.

481: occupation'. Law 941 of State of Amazonas, 1917, in Amodio and Pira, 'História dos povos indígenas', 38.

482: to an end.' Tuxaua Jaci José de Souza and twenty-one other chiefs to the President of Funai, Colonel Moreira Leal, 22 Apr. 1983, *PIB/83*, 46.

19. Yanomami

484: difficulty.' R. Brian Ferguson, 'Whatever happened to the Stone Age? Steel tools and Yanomami historical ecology', in William Balée, ed., *Advances in Historical Ecology* (New York, 1998), 293. The experiment in stone versus steel axes was reported by Robert Carneiro, 'Tree felling with stone ax: an experiment carried out among the Yanomamo Indians of southern Venezuela', in C. Kramer, ed., *Ethnoarchaeology* (New York, 1979), 21–58. Marcus Colchester and others have considered how the Yanomami survived before they had metal blades: Colchester, 'Rethinking stone-age economics: some speculations concerning the pre-Columbian Yanoama economy', *Human Ecology*, **12**, 1984, 291–314. For a detailed description of Yanomami building a yano, see William Milliken and Bruce Albert, 'The construction of a new Yanomami round-house', *Journal of Ethnobiology* **17:2**, 1997, 215–23.

485: waterfalls. The boundary commissioners and surveyors in the 1780s included the remarkable explorers Captain **Ricardo Franco de Almeida Serra**, Dr **Antonio Pires da Silva Pontes**, Dr **Alexandre Rodrigues Ferreira**, Dr **José Simões de Carvalho**, and Colonel **Manoel da Gama Lobo d'Almada** (who contacted Yanomami on the upper Catrimani in 1787). Their explorations were described in John Hemming, 'How Brazil acquired Roraima', *Hispanic-American Historical Review*, **70:2**, May 1990, 295–325. Some of these expeditions penetrated the rivers of the Yanomami (Demini, Catrimani, Uraricoera, etc.) and for a brief moment the Portuguese persuaded a group of Waika (possibly Yanomami) to settle near their Fort São Joaquim on the rio Branco north of modern Boa Vista. When **Robert Schomburgk** went across northern Yanomami territory fifty years later, he found evidence that those Indians had manioc plantations that they visited between treks ('Journey from Fort San Joaquim on the Rio Branco in Brazil to Roraima, and thence by the rivers Parima and Merewari to Esmeralda on the Orinoco, in 1838–9', *Journal of the Royal Geographical Society*, **10**, 1840 (191–247), 221]; John Hemming, *Roraima: Brazil's Northernmost Frontier* (London, 1990), 4. The French explorer **Jean Chaffanjon** sought the source of the Orinoco from the Venezuelan side in 1886 (*L'Orenoque et le Caura*, Paris, 1889). **Theodor Koch-Grünberg** made the first recorded visit to the villages of Xirianá (whom he called Shirishana) in December 1911 (Koch-Grünberg, *Vom Roroima zum Orinoco*, **1** (Berlin, 1917), 172–4). (He also had many contacts with the Yekuana (also called Maiongong, and in Venezuela Maquiritare), who are still the great travellers and traders along these rivers.) In 1922 the trader **Ciro Dantas** got some Makuxi to take him up the Uraricoera as far as an Indian village on the south bank opposite the mouth of the Kujuma. A few years later, the American Dr **Alexander Hamilton Rice** approached from the east with a float-plane, going far up the Uraricoera and its Parima headwater. (Previously, between 1916 and 1920, this explorer had investigated the upper Orinoco and Rio Negro, without seeing any Yanomami: Hamilton Rice, 'The Rio Negro, the Cassiquiare Canal and the Upper Orinoco (September 1916–April 1920)', *The Geographical Journal*, **58**,

1921, 321–44.) On 18 March 1925, about a hundred kilometres (sixty miles) upriver from the western tip of Maracá Island, his Maiongong guides took him up a side creek to a yano of Yanam-speaking Yanomami (a subgroup now known as Malaxi-theli). Although impressed by the 80 foot diameter (24.40 metre) conical hut, Hamilton Rice was appalled by the fifty 'stocky . . . hideous' inhabitants who were kindly and inoffensive, but made a 'repellent and unpleasant' impression with their squalor and diet of little more than bananas ('The Rio Branco, Uraricuera, and Parima', *The Geographical Journal*, **71:2–4**, Feb.–Apr. 1928 (113–43, 209–23, 345–57), 216–17). General **Cândido Rondon's** Serviço de Inspeção de Fronteiras in 1927 went up the Uraricoera as far as the Purumame waterfall at the western tip of Maracá island, whence they turned up the Uraricaá and saw a large village of Xirianá on its Ericó tributary. The Brazilian-Swiss botanist **Georges Salathé** met Karimé Yanomami on the middle Catrimani in 1929–30 ('Les Indiens Karimé', *Revista del Instituto de Etnología de la Universidad Nacional de Tucumán*, **2:2**, 1932); but the Indian group was tragically decimated by disease after Salathé's departure. **Desmond Holdridge** also made a recorded contact with Yanomami of this part of Brazil in 1932: 'Exploration between the Rio Branco and the Serra Parima', *Geographical Review* (American Geographical Society, New York), **23**, 1933, 372–84.

486: daily round'. Wade Davis, *One River: Explorations and Discoveries in the Amazon Rain Forest* (Simon & Schuster, New York, 1996), 475. Richard Schultes experienced Yanomami hallucinogens at Maturacá mission on the middle Rio Negro in 1967. Some of the many authors who studied this phenomenon were listed by William Milliken and Bruce Albert (*Yanomami, A Forest People*, Royal Botanic Gardens, Kew, 1999, 35–6): Georg Seitz, 1960; Otto Zerries, 1964; Ettore Biocca, 1966; Napoleon Chagnon, 1966 onwards; Ghillean Prance ('Notes on the use of plant hallucinogens in Amazonian Brazil', *Economic Botany*, **24**, 1970, 62–8); Charles Brewer-Carias and J. A. Steyermark ('Hallucinogenic snuff drugs of the Yanomamö Caburiwe-Teri in the Cauaburi River, Brazil', *Economic Botany*, **30:1**, 1976, 57–66), and others. For a less academic approach, Sangirardi Jr., *O Índio e as Plantas Alucinógenas* (Editorial Alhambra, Rio de Janeiro, 1983).

487: existed either.' Ettore Biocca, *Yanoáma*

(London, 1969, translated from the Italian of 1965), 213; Georg Seitz, *People of the Rain-Forests* (London, 1963, translated from the German of 1960), 21–2. Helena Valero appeared on a sandbank near the Uaupés mission on 1 January 1957. She later told her remarkable story again in even greater detail in Helena Valero, *Yo soy Napeyoma: relato de una mujer raptada por los indígenas Yanomami* (Fundación La Salle de Ciencias Naturales, Caracas, 1984). Another woman who told about life with the Yanomami (the Itoceri group of the upper Orinoco) was an American-Venezuelan researcher called Florinda Donner: *Shabono* (Delacorte Press, New York, 1982); but most experts doubted the authenticity of her vivid and elegantly written account.

After the expeditions and flights of the Brazilian–Venezuelan boundary commissioners in the 1930s and early 1940s, missionaries, anthropologists, and adventurers made a series of incursions into Yanomami country. These included the Salesian missionaries Fathers **Francesco Bigiarelli** and **Antonio Gois** or **Goyz** (up the Cauaburi, Maturacá, and other western rivers), the Salesian **Luigi (Luís) Cocco** and the Protestant **Barker** from the Orinoco side (Luís Cocco, *Iyëwei-teri: quince años entre los Yanomamos* (Librería Editorial Salesiana, Caracas, 1972)), and the Salesian Father **R. Silvestri** on the Apiaú ('Una spedizione tra gli Indios nelle foreste del Rio Apiaú', *Missione Consolata* (Torino), **55**, 1953; **A. Vinci** was on the northern part of Yanomami territory, *Samatari (Orinoco-Amazzoni)*, Bari, 1956. A Franco-Venezuelan expedition went to the source of the Orinoco in 1957 with the biologist **Pablo Anduze** and the explorer **Jean Grelier** (Grelier, *Aux sources de l'Orénoque*, Paris, 1954; English translation, 1957). The French adventurer **Alain Gheerbrandt** repeated Schomburgk's and Koch-Grünberg's route in reverse, *L'Expédition Orénoque-Amazone*, trans. as *Journey to the Far Amazon* (Simon & Schuster, New York, 1954). The German ethnologists **Meinhard Schuster** ('Die Soziologie der Waika', *Proceedings of the 32nd International Congress of Americanists* (Copenhagen, 1958), 114–22) and **Otto Zerries** (*Waika* (Klaus Renner Verlag, München, 1964), and Zerries and Schuster, *Mahekodotheri* (Klaus Renner Verlag, München, 1974) made early studies. The German adventurer **Georg Seitz** visited Salesian missions on the Cauaburi-Maturacá in 1958; and **Volkmar Vareschi** saw them on the Orinoco (*Orinoco arriba: a través la Venezuela siguiendo a Humboldt*

(Lectura, Caracas, 1959)). The massively bearded medical Professor **Ettore Biocca** led a scientific expedition backed by the Italian national research council, in 1962–3, first up the Cauaburi-Maturacá, then from the Orinoco up the Ocama and Mavaca rivers, staying with western Yanomami groups on both incursions; and it was Biocca who recorded Helena Valero's remarkable story.

Later in the 1960s and 1970s there were many studies of the Yanomami, including those by Napoleon Chagnon, Ernest Migliazza, Edson Soares Diniz, Jacques Lizot, Judith Shapiro, William Smole, Bruce Albert, Alcida Ramos and Kenneth Taylor, John (Giovanni) Saffirio, Marcus Colchester, Hans Becher, Raymond Hames, Marvin Harris, John Early, and John Peters. Chagnon's controversial thesis about Yanomami fierceness – he claimed that one man in four died fighting – was first rebutted by Marvin Harris, who in 1979 argued that Yanomami warfare was in response to protein deficiency. Chagnon repeated his 'fierce' thesis in successive editions of his best-selling book, *Yanomamö, the Fierce People* (New York, 1968), and in 'Life histories: Blood revenge and warfare in a tribal population', *Science*, **239**, 1988, 985–92. The resulting furore was discussed in William Booth, 'Warfare over Yanomamö Indians', *Science*, **243**, 1989, 1138–40; Bruce Albert and Alcida Ramos, 'Yanomami Indians and anthropological ethics', *Science*, **244**, 1989, 632; Peter Monaghan, 'Bitter warfare in anthropology', *The Chronicle of Higher Education*, 1994.

The debate about Chagnon's fierceness theory and his dubious working methods is analysed in Leslie Sponsel, 'Yanomami: An arena of conflict and aggression in the Amazon', *Aggressive Behavior*, **24:2**, 1998, 97–122; Terence Turner, *The Yanomami and the Ethics of Anthropological Practice* (Cornell University Latin American Studies Program Occasional Paper Series, **6**, Ithaca, NY, 2001); Bruce Albert, ed., *The Yanomami Case (Brazilian Contributions to the 'Darkness in El Dorado' Controversy)* (CCPY, Brasília, 2001); *Current Anthropology*, **42:2**, Apr. 2001, 265–76, and **43:1**, Feb. 2002. Newspaper reports on the controversy include: Mark Wallace, *Financial Times*, 14 Jan. 2001; Andrew Brown, *Telegraph Magazine*, 3 Mar. 2001.

487: savages'. Alfred Métraux, 'The Shiriana, Waica and Guaharibo', HSAI, **3** (861–4), 862. The four main languages of the Yanomami are: **Yanomamö**, spoken by 9,000 people on the Mavaca and other headwaters of the Orinoco in

Venezuela and on the rivers flowing into the middle Negro; **Yanomam**, spoken by 5,000 people in the Parima Hills, from Surucucu to Catrimani; **Sanumá**, by about 1,000 people in the extreme north on the Ventuari in Venezuela and the Auaris headwater of the Uraricoera; and **Yanam**, spoken by 400 people at the eastern edges of Yanomami country, on the Uraricaá and Mucajaí (Ernest C. Migliazza, 'Grupos lingüísticos do Território Federal de Roraima', ASBA, 153–74; *Yanomama Grammar and Intelligibility* (Doctoral dissertation, Indiana University, Bloomington, 1972)). Migliazza spent five years studying Yanomami languages, for the Baptist Mid-Missions and the Goeldi Museum of Belém do Pará. The Yanomami language used to be known either as Waikan or Xirianá, but Migliazza explained why each of these terms is unsatisfactory. The umbrella name Yanomami was first applied to all the related tribes and dialects of this region in the 1960s by Biocca, Migliazza, and others. Its use for such diverse groups was queried by Colonel Carlos Alberto Lima Menna Barreto, *A Farça Yanomami* (Biblioteca do Exército Editora, Rio de Janeiro, 1995).

488: clothing.' Bruce Albert, 'La fumée du métal. Histoire et représentations du contact chez les Yanomami (Brésil)', *L'Homme*, **28:106–7**, Aug.–Sep. 1988, 96.

488: unexpectedly. Brazil and Venezuela decided that they must map the largely unexplored boundary between them, which had been defined in 1750 as the Amazon–Orinoco watershed that happened to bisect Yanomami lands. In 1929 the Comissão Brasileira Demarcadora de Límites exchanged presents with the Yanomami on the Cauaburi at the western limit of their territory (without actually seeing any Indians); the boundary commission later had five men seriously wounded by Yanomami arrows at its canoe base on the Demini. But when the Commission's surveyors in 1939 explored the Uraricoera, Uraricaá, and other northern headwaters of the Branco they met no Yanomami apart from twenty Xiriana in the village seen by Rondon's men on the Ericó twelve years earlier. (Naval Captain **Bráz Dias de Aguiar**, 'Trabalhos da Comissão Brasileira Demarcadora de Límites – Primeira Divisão – nas fronteiras da Venezuela e Guianas Britânica e Neerlandesa, de 1930 a 1940', *IX Congresso Brasileiro de Geografia. Anais* (Rio de Janeiro, 1942); and 'Geografia Amazônica: nas fronteiras do norte', *Revista Brasileira de Geografia*, **6:3**, Jul. 1944), 19–40.

Matters changed with the advent of planes. A series of flights by a Mixed Brazilian–Venezuelan Commission in 1943 surveyed the Yanomami heartland in the Parima Hills, and sighted various malocas from the air. According to the historian **Artur Ferreira Reis**, who was on some of these flights, members of this Commission 'brought civilization to the bosom of a great number of malocas' on the Orinoco inside Venezuela. Boundary teams on the rivers had friendly contacts and exchanged presents with Yanomami in Brazil, on the Mapalaú headwater of the Demini in 1941, and at the mouth of the Tootobi and the Parima source of the Uraricuera in 1943. (Artur Cesar Ferreira Reis, 'En las selvas del Demini', *Revista Geográfica Americana*, **20**, 1943, 271–6; Reis and Leônidas de Oliveira, 'As cabeceiras do Orenoco e a fronteira Brasileiro-Venezuelana', *Revista Brasileira de Geografia*, **6**, 1944, 93–105; Bráz Dias de Aguiar, 'Geografia Amazônica', 19–40.

488: created.' Geoffrey O'Connor, *Amazon Journal. Dispatches from a Vanishing Frontier* (New York, 1997), 34–5.

488: Yanomami did.' John D. Early and John F. Peters, *The Xilixana Yanomami of the Amazon* (Gainesville, Fla., 2000), 34.

488: disposal.' Albert, 'La fumée', 99.

489: prestige' Ferguson, 'Whatever happened . . .?', 303; and his 'A savage encounter. Western contact and the Yanomami war complex', in R. Brian Ferguson and Neil L. Whitehead, eds., *War in the Tribal Zone* (Santa Fé, N. Mex., 1992), 199–227; *Yanomami Warfare: A Political History* (Santa Fé, N. Mex., 1995).

490: ancestors.' Equipe da Missão Catrimani (Sister Florença Lindey, Fathers Guilherme Damioli and João Saffirio), *O Crepúsculo do Povo Yanomami: sobrevivência ou genocídio?* (Diocese de Roraima, Boa Vista, 1988), 40–1.

490: civilised life.' Fred A. Salazar, *The Innocent Assassins* (London, 1967), 65–6. Salazar and his friend Arnie Dietrich were twenty-one-year-old adventurers. They admired Father Badelotti, who had intense eyes, a tired face, and a long snow-white beard.

Georg Seitz was also deeply impressed by Father Gois (also spelled Goyz), with whom he travelled. Salazar met Helena Valero at Taraquá (Santa Isabel) mission, but found her looking old and ravaged and reluctant to talk about her time with the Yanomami.

491: absent.' Edwin Brooks, René Fuerst, John Hemming, and Francis Huxley, *Tribes of the Ama-*

zon Basin in Brazil, 1972 (London, 1973), 61–2. Two Italian Consolata missionaries of Boa Vista prelacy, Giovanni Calleri (later killed by the Waimiri-Atroari) and Bindo Meldolesi, established the Catrimani Mission in 1965 on the river of that name.

491: site.' Early and Peters, *The Xilixana Yanomami*, 33. Also in 1958, Robert Hawkins and Rod Lewis of the Unevangelized Fields Mission contacted Palimi-theli Yanomami on the Uraricoera, and Ernest Migliazza of the Baptist Mid-Missions took up residence among the Xiliana on the Uraricaá to the north. Early, Peters and Migliazza later became academics in North American universities, as did the Catholic Saffirio.

492: miles to get it.' Robert Cable, personal communication. Brooks et al., *Tribes of the Amazon Basin*, 64–5. **Surucucu** is close to the Amazon–Orinoco watershed and hence the boundary with Venezuela. The Air Force Brigadier João Camarão had personally landed there in 1961, after fire-bombing a stretch of campo to form an airstrip. The mission was later moved to its present location by helicopter. It was supplied by light planes of the missionary air service Asas do Socorro (Wings of Mercy) and by the air force. In the 1970s, MEVA (Missão Evangélica da Amazônia, the former Unevangelized Fields Mission) founded missions called **Mucajaí** near three yanos on that large river; **Parimiú** on a tributary of the Uraricoera, to replace Surucucu which closed; and **Auaris** on a headwater of the Uraricoera of that name for Maiongong and Sanumá Yanomami. In the early years, Funai's only presence was an occasional boat coming upriver to trade with the Indians. It started operating in this region long after the missionaries, and its posts were generally at the outer edges of Yanomami territory and thus largely ineffectual. The first posts, **Cauaburi** (on that river in the western part of Yanomami territory) and **Ajuricaba** (near the mouth of the Demini), were too far from the Indians and were later abandoned. In the 1970s the agency had **Aliança** post on the Padauari, **Km. 211** on the short-lived Perimetral Norte road (BR-210) south of the Catrimani, **Mapulaú** sub-post which was burned by the Indians because of an epidemic, **Ajarani**, an entry point from the BR-210 road, and **Surucucu** in the mineral-rich hills near the abandoned MEVA mission (Alcida R. Ramos and Kenneth I. Taylor, *The Yanoama in Brazil, 1979* (IWGIA Doc. 37, Copenhagen, 1979), 111–13).

492: hairy.' Davi Kopenawa translated by Bruce Albert, 'Descobrindo os brancos', in Adauto Novaes, *A Outra Margem do Ocidente* (Companhia das Letras, Brasília, 1999); *PIB 1996/2000*, 20.

492: infanticide.' Early and Peters, *The Xilixana Yanomami*, 55, 143; John Peters, *The Effect of Western Material Goods upon the Social Structure of the Family among the Shirishana* (Doctoral dissertation, Western Michigan University, 1973), 200–6.

493: scientists'. Letter by Professors Terence Turner and Leslie Sponsel to Louise Lamphere, President of the American Anthropological Association, *Guardian*, 23 Sep. 2000. The terrible allegations were in Patrick Tierney, *Darkness in El Dorado: How Scientists and Journalists Devastated the Amazon* (W. W. Norton & Co., New York, 2000) and in more muted form in Ferguson, *Yanomami Warfare*, 277–306. The vaccinations are recorded in James V. Neel, W. R. Centerwell, Napoleon A. Chagnon, and H. L. Casey, 'Notes on the effect of measles and measles vaccine in a virgin-soil population of South-American Indians', *American Journal of Epidemiology*, **91**:4, 1970, 418–29; 'Lessons from a "primitive" people', *Science* (American Association for the Advancement of Science), **170**, 1970, 815–22; Neel and Kenneth Weiss, 'The genetic structure of a tribal population, the Yanomami Indians', *Journal of Physical Anthropology*, **42**, 1975, 25–52, also in Daniel Gross, ed., *Peoples and Cultures of Native South America* (New York, 1973), 159–82; Neel, 'Genetic aspects of the ecology of disease in the American Indians', in F. A. Salzano, ed., *The Ongoing Evolution of Latin-American Populations* (Thomas, Springfield, Ill., 1971); 'Health and disease in an unacculturated Amerindian population', in *Health and Disease in Tribal Societies* (Ciba Foundation, Symposium **49**, Elsevier North-Holland, 1977). People who knew James Neel at that time, such as Roberto Baruzzi or Marcus Colchester, feel that he had nothing but the Indians' interests at heart. However, Neel's published papers did admit that he and his colleagues were observing genetic evolution and population control among 'some of the most primitive Indians of South America'.

493: village.' Neel et al., 'Notes on the effect of measles', 421. In this paper, Dr Neel explained exactly how the measles epidemic reached the upper Orinoco and how it spread. He admitted that Edmondston B vaccine did have serious, but not fatal, side-effects when administered without gamma globulin. He also showed that many Yanomami died of pneumonia. In Brazil, there were 12 deaths among 150–200 cases of measles in 1968 at Toototobi, but only 1 death among 135 cases at Mucajaí. Neel had worked in these missions in 1967 and found that at Toototobi almost all Indians had palpable spleens from endemic malaria, whereas hardly any did at Surucucu. This might explain the higher death rate at Toototobi in the following year. Medical considerations of Edmonston B and other measles vaccines and the epidemic that struck the Venezuelan Yanomami in 1968 are thoroughly explored in Maria Stella de Castro Lobo et al., *Report of the Medical Team of the Federal University of Rio de Janeiro on accusations contained in Patrick Tierney's 'Darkness in El Dorado'* (UFRJ, 2001; trans. Catherine V. Howard, Gettysburg College). This generally exonerated Neel from wrongdoing, by the medical standards of the 1960s. The notion that Neel and Chagnon had introduced the measles epidemic (deliberately or unwittingly) was refuted by contemporary witnesses Tom Headland of the SIL and Keith Wardlaw and John Early of the New Tribes Mission, in Thomas N. Headland, 'When did the measles epidemic begin among the Yanomami?', *Anthropology News*, 42:1, Jan. 2001.

494: intimidating.' Napoleon Chagnon, *Yanomamö, the Fierce People*, in Marshall Sahlins' review of Patrick Tierney, *Darkness in El Dorado*, *Washington Post*, 10 Dec. 2000.

494: spirits' Keith Wardlaw, personal communication, August 1972; Brooks et al., *Tribes of the Amazon Basin*, 62–3. During the 1970s, the New Tribes Mission added Marari mission on that river, with three *yanos* nearby. Accounts of life in a Protestant mission were: Margaret Jank, *Culture Shock* (Moody Press, Chicago, 1977); and Evelyn Ina Montgomery, *With the Shiriana in Brazil* (Kendall-Hunt, Dubuque, Ia., 1970).

494: Yanomami Indian park. The 1968 proposal by Ramos and Taylor was a manuscript entitled *Sugestões para a criação de um Parque Indígena no Território dos Índios Yanoama no Norte do Brasil. Relatório.* The draft decree that was never dated or signed was published in *Boletim do CIMI*, 8:58, Aug. 1979, caderno 2, 36–9 and in Ramos and Taylor, *The Yanoama*, 156–62. The Ramos–Taylor proposal of 6 Dec. 1968 was for a very large area in both Roraima and the state of Amazonas; that by the Prelacy of Roraima in mid-1969 was just for the Catrimani region.

496: occupation.' Alcida Ramos, *Sanumá Memories: Yanomami Ethnography in Times of Crisis* (Madison, Wis., 1995), 275. Gordon MacMillan chronicled the colonist settlements along the Perimetral Norte, *At the End of the Rainbow?* (London and New York, 1995), 17–30.

496: half.' Carlos Zaquini, 'Os índios de Roraima e a política local: Yanomami', in Dalmo de Abreu Dallari et al., eds., *A Questão de Terra Indígena* (Comissão Pró-Índio, São Paulo, 1981), 101. The first deaths from disease were reported in ESP, 2 Mar. 1975, and there was another report on 12 Dec. 1975. Catrimani Mission to 1st Regional Delegacy of Funai, 3 May 1977, *Boletim do CIMI*, 8:58, Aug. 1979, caderno 2, 9; Orlando Sampaio Silva, *Os Yanoama – Denominação de um povo sem esperança* (XI Reunião Brasileira de Antropologia, Recife, May 1978), 6–8.

496: proportions' Alcida R. Ramos, 'Yanoama Indians in Northern Brazil threatened by highway', in Ramos and Taylor, *The Yanoama*, 1–41, 16.

496: Cachoeira.' *Boletim do CIMI*, 7:49, Sep. 1978, 4; *Porantim*, 1:4, Aug.–Sep. 1978.

497: die?"' Albert, 'La fumée', 97. Other Yanomami made a similar link between fumes and disease: Jacques Lizot, *El hombre de la pantorilla preñada y otros mitos yanomami* (Fundación La Salle, Caracas, 1975), 35–6; Marcus Colchester, 'Myths and legends of the Sanema', *Antropologica*, Caracas, 56, 1981 (25–127), 67–70.

497: development'. The Governor of Roraima, Colonel Fernando Ramos Pereira, *Jornal de Brasília*, 1 Mar. 1975; ESP, 6 Feb. 1976 on diseases caused by the garimpo, and 2 and 3 Sep. 1976 on the expulsion.

498: Indians'. Kenneth Taylor, 'Development against the Yanoama. The case of mining and agriculture', in Ramos and Taylor, *The Yanoama*, 49; Bol. CIMI, Aug. 1979, 9–10. Taylor had seen Ernest Migliazza's map of 1970, which showed many *yano* near Surucucu, in the Governor's office. Radam was a SLAR (side-looking aerial radar) survey of all Amazonia that located various mineral deposits beneath the forest canopy. The Statute of the Indian allowed for underground mining (but not surface panning) on Indian lands, if the operation were licensed by the government. In June 1975 the Ministry of Mines authorized a large mining company ICOMI (a subsidiary of the two giants Bethlehem Steel and the Brazilian CAEMI) to make a geological survey of Surucucu. Ken Taylor realized that he could not possibly resist, so he got ICOMI to agree to restrict its activities to areas where there were no Indians, to provide scrupulous medical control of its people, and to lend its planes for a vaccination programme for the Indians. Then, in 1978–79, the equally large CVRD (Companhia Vale do Rio Doce, the company mining the gigantic Carajás iron-ore mine) started investigating Surucucu (Taylor, 'Development against the Yanoama', 65–6; *Manchete*, July 1976); but it responsibly pulled out, declaring that the potential damage to indigenous peoples overruled gains from mineral extraction there.

498: garimpo'. ESP, 2 Sep. 1976. The orders to evict the prospectors were Portaria 0422 of the Ministry of the Interior and an unnumbered Decree by the Governor of Roraima, both on 3 Sep. 1976.

498: demarcation' Kenneth I. Taylor, *Projeto Terras Yanoama*, 10 May 1976, p. 6; Bruce Albert, Carlo Zacquini, and Cláudia Andujar, 'Yanomami Indian Park: proposal and justification', in Ramos and Taylor, *The Yanoama*, 114; Equipe da Missão Catrimani, *O Crepúsculo do Povo Yanomami* (Boa Vista, 1988), 65.

Ken Taylor was a Scot who had been brought up partly in Argentina and partly in Denmark, embarked on anthropological study of the Inuit at the University of Wisconsin, but fell in love with the beautiful Alcida Ramos from Rio de Janeiro and switched to her fieldwork among the Yanomami. They studied the northernmost group of Yanomami, the Sanumá on the Auaris (Uauaris) headwater of the Uraricoera – their doctorates at the University of Wisconsin in 1972 were both about this group, and they then married and taught at the University of Brasília.

499: group'. General Demócrito Soares de Oliveira (head of the military Coordenação da Amazônia) to the President of Funai, General Ismarth Araújo de Oliveira, 1 Jun. 1977 (Memo 194/COAMA/77 in Funai's archive).

499: smoke.' Alex Shoumatoff, *The Rivers Amazon* (London, 1979), 182. Cláudia Andujar was a Hungarian-born, Swiss- and American-educated freelance photographer who had moved to Brazil in 1957, became a naturalized Brazilian, and showed her pictures in leading magazines and art exhibitions. Her interest in the Yanomami started in 1972, she was a co-founder of the CCPY in 1978, and fought for this people's territory and health during the next two decades. Roberto Cardoso de Oliveira, 'Indigenous peoples

and sociocultural change in the Amazon', in Charles Wagley, ed., *Man in the Amazon* (University of Florida, Gainesville, Fla., 1974, 126–7.

499: July 1978. The decrees defining the twenty-one areas were listed in Ramos and Taylor, *The Yanoama*, 141.

500: group.' CCPY, 'Yanomami Indian Park: proposal and justification', in Ramos and Taylor, *The Yanoama*, 104. The initials CCPY stand for Comissão pela Criação do Parque Yanomami. The arguments against the twenty-one-areas decrees were well set out in *Boletim do CIMI*, Aug. 1979, 17–21. There were environmental areas overlapping Yanomami lands: the Reserva Florestal do Parima (later renamed Roraima) in the north; the huge Pico da Neblina park to the west, which runs from the Cauaburi to the Marauiá tributaries of the Negro and thus includes a number of Salesian missions; and, later, the state park of Serra do Araçá and the national forest of Amazonas around the Demini and upper Araçá.

500: forest' Ibid.

500: between villages' Ibid.

500: distant villages.' Taylor and Ramos quoted in *Jornal de Brasília*, 1 Oct. 1978, in Ramos and Taylor, *The Yanoama*, 121.

500: meaning'. Alcida Ramos, Report to Attorney General's office, 1989, translated and quoted in Jan Rocha, *Murder in the Rainforest: the Yanomami, the Gold Miners and the Amazon* (Latin American Bureau/Survival, London, 1999), 31.

501: civilization' 'Gold nails in the Yanomami coffin?', SIR, **5:1(29)**, Spring 1980,19; ESP, 2 Sep. 1979; *Observer*, London, 4 May 1980. Deputy Campos' draft bill was Projeto de Lei 2,284 of 1979.

502: vengeance'. 'Gold nails', 20.

502: forest park. The seven-reserves idea was reported in ESP, 15 and 22 Apr. 1981.

502: project'. Announcement by CCPY, *Porantim*, Apr. 1982, SIR, **7:3–4(41/42)**, Autumn 1982. The interdiction decree signed by Minister Andreazza on 9 March was no. 025/82. The CCPY published biennial reports in a bulletin called *Urihi*, and every issue of the *SIR* kept Survival's members informed of progress of the Yanomami campaign, as did the ARC (Anthropology Resource Center) in the US. In *SIR's* autumn 1982 issue, Anthony Henman wrote a depressing account of a meeting between Funai, CCPY, the military, and missionaries (but no Yanomami) held in Boa Vista in September. The Protestant missionaries and Catholic Salesians seemed intent only on being allowed to remain and pursue their attempted conversion by getting the Yanomami dependent on their mission stations; and Funai acquiesced in the omission of the Ajarani and Catrimani areas near the Northern Perimeter road from the interdiction.

503: deaths.' Note to International Red Cross by ABA (Anthropologists), CPI-SP and CCPY, ESP, 28 Jul. 1981.

503: tribes.' ESP, 20 Dec. 1982; *PIB/1982*, 29. Dr Rubens was always known as Brandão (Big Brando), and his memoirs were published posthumously as *Vida e Morte de um Indigenista* (Ícone Editora, São Paulo, 1985). During an earlier measles epidemic, in 1977, Drs Vicente Paraense and Ruth Queiros of Funai's 'flying-doctor team' had also died tragically in an air crash near Catrimani Mission. Funai and the Consolata missionaries worked together on Indian health, during the difficult years 1973–77 when the Perimetral Norte was being built. In 1983 Médecins du Monde joined the CCPY in administering BCG, VAS, DPT, and Sabin vaccines to some 1,700 Indians, transported by the air force; and in 1984 Aesculapius International Medicine joined them and Funai in a further campaign (*O Globo*, 24 Feb. 1984). But the majority of Yanomami were still unprotected.

503: fight.' Cláudia Andujar, 'Garimpeiros e mineradoras diputam Surucucus', *PIB/1984*, 88.

504: operations' Ibid.

504: mining'. Márcio Santilli, Draft Law 4,558, in ibid., 89. The deputies who wanted to open Surucucu to mining were Mozarildo Cavalcanti and João Batista Fagundes. Cavalcanti's machinations included a proposal to redefine Yanomami lands by various departments including the colonization agency Incra and the secret service CSN, an accusation that Médecins du Monde was using Indians as guinea-pigs for experiments with a new malaria drug, and the xenophobic canard about American missionaries being clandestine miners. The early garimpos consisted of some 200 prospectors on the Ericó (a tributary of the Uraricaá, a northern tributary of the Uraricoera, alongside the Santa Rosa garimpo that lay outside Indian territory) and 250 on the Apiaú tributary of the Mucajaí. The big companies seeking mining concessions were Codesaima (the Roraima development company) and Mineração São Lourenço. The hawkish Governor of Amazonas, Gilberto Mestrinho (who had campaigned on the anti-environmental slogan 'a chainsaw for

every voter'), was seeking gold concessions in the Couto de Magalhães Hills (between the Mucajaí and Catrimani rivers) and on the Cauaburi at the south-western end of Yanomami territory. On the Venezuelan side, the 1984 concession was to a small company called Mava C.A. (which also obtained a concession to mine on Yekuana (Makiritare) land on the Mavaca river) owned by a grandson of Venezuela's dictator Juan Vicente Gómez. Bruce Albert and Marcus Colchester, 'Recent developments in the situation of the Yanomami', in Marcus Colchester, ed., *An End to Laughter?* (London, 1985), 105–12; Survival urgent-action bulletin about the Venezuelan situation, Mar. 1984.

504: reality'. 'Fronteira sem lei', *Veja*, 19 Sep. 1990, 78.

505: activity.' *Folha de Boa Vista*, 2 Nov. 1984; *Porantim*, Dec. 1984. Deputy Mozarildo Cavalcanti later admitted that the garimpeiros' invasion of Surucucu had been a political move to confuse the government so that it would release land for mineral exploration.

505: December 1985. The working-group's submission to the inter-ministerial *grupão* ('big group') was in Funai Portaria 1,817/E of 8 Jan. 1985. The Senator was Severo Gomes from São Paulo; proposal was Draft Law 379/85.

505: Amazonia'. Speech by Governor Getúlio Cruz, Boa Vista, 15 Sep. 1985, in Cláudia Andujar and Lúcia Prado, 'Os Yanomami ameaçam a soberania nacional?', *PIB-85/86*, 130.

506: happening.' Davi Kopenawa quoted by Rocha, *Murder in the Rainforest*, 39. Bruce Albert, who is a close friend of Davi, gave his biography in 'O ouro canibal e a queda do céu' (in Albert and Alcida Ramos, eds., *Pacificando o Branco*, São Paulo, 2002 (239–74), 244–5), in which he said that Davi learned his shamanic arts from his godfather Lourival Watorikitheri, the traditional leader and chief shaman of the Watoriki yano.

506: knowledge' Davi Kopenawa, 'Descobrindo os brancos', in Adauto Novaes, ed., *A Outra Margem do Ocidente* (São Paulo, 1999), and *PIB 1996/2000*, 21.

506: problems.' *PIB-85/86*, 132.

507: live in'. Transcript of public meeting for Survival International, London, 5 Dec. 1989. Davi Kopenawa Yanomami collected Survival's 'Right Livelihood Award' (the equivalent to an 'alternative Nobel Prize' for NGOs) from the Swedish authorities.

508: jungle'. 'A morte ronda os índios na floresta', *Veja*, 19 Sep. 1990, 71.

508: politics'. Independent, London, 17 Feb. 1987. This was in the first of a series of excellent articles by Richard House.

508: mission'. Equipe da Missão Yanomami, O *Crepúsculo*, III; *Jornal do Brasil*, 26 Aug. 1987. Father Giovanni Saffirio, leader of the expelled missionaries, took his cause to Europe in 1988; his superior, the Bishop of Roraima, Dom Aldo Mongiano (also a Consolata missionary) was named as a subversive by the National Security Council and also threatened with expulsion. Among other actions, CIMI had issued a tract condemning the Calha Norte: *Calha Norte: segurança ou ameaça?* (Belém/Manaus, Feb. 1987); also Márcio Santilli, 'Projeto Calha Norte: tutela militar e política da fronteira', *Tempo e Presença*, **223**, Sep. 1987. Generals Bayma Denys and José Enaldo Siqueira attempted to justify the plan in *Jornal do Comércio*, Manaus, 15 Jan. 1987. The press published pictures of the new barracks at Surucucu and elsewhere, *Folha de Boa Vista*, 4 Dec. 1987. João Pacheco de Oliveira, ed., *Projeto Calha Norte: militares, índios e fronteiras* (Universidade Federal do Rio de Janeiro/Museu Nacional, Rio de Janeiro, 1990); Elizabeth Allen, *Calha Norte: Military Development in Brazilian Amazonia* (Latin-American Studies, University of Glasgow, 1990); Berta Ribeiro, O *Índio na Cultura Brasileira* (Rio de Janeiro, 1987), 168. The concept of military garrisons along Brazil's northern frontiers lingered on. In February 2001 Deputy Marcos Rolim called for an end of all such military installations on indigenous land, following condemnation of soldiers for infecting Yanomami women with venereal diseases. The Minister of Defence, Geraldo Quintão, hit back by accusing President Collor of incompetence in making the Yanomami park far too large and urged that it be reduced.

509: portage around them.' Early and Peters, *The Xilixana Yanomami*, 35–6.

509: behavior.' Bruce Albert, 'Gold miners and Yanomami Indians in the Brazilian Amazon: the Haximu massacre', in Barbara Rose Johnston, ed., *Who Pays the Price?* (Washington, 1994), 60; Early and Peters, *The Xilixana Yanomami*, 60.

509: diet.' Albert, 'Gold miners', 60; Early and Peters, *The Xilixana Yanomami*, 60.

510: droplets.' Dennison Berwick, 'At death's door', *Sunday Times Magazine*, 9 Sep. 1990.

510: destructured.' Bruce Albert quoted by Rocha, *Murder in the Rainforest*, 56.

510: achievements'. Carlos Alberto Ricardo, *Veja*, 19 Sep. 1990.

510: corruption.' The Minister of Justice, Paulo Brossard de Souza Pinto, to President José Sarney, Brasília, 12 Jan. 1989, in Ação pela Cidadania, *Roraima: o aviso da morte* (CCPY/CEDI/CIMI, São Paulo, 1989), 22. The team that called itself 'Citizens' Action' was led by Senator Severo Gomes and included four federal deputies, the President of the Brazilian Bar Association, Marcos Terena of UNI, and activists such as Beto Ricardo of CEDI, Márcio Santilli of the indigenous law association, Júlio Gaiger of CIMI, and Bishop Luciano Mendes de Almeida of the CNBB. It was in the field in Roraima from 9 to 12 June 1989. The letter from the seven senators was reported in *Jornal de Brasília*, 5 May 1988.

511: areas.' Rocha, *Murder in the Rainforest*, 58.

511: Midas'. O'Connor, *Amazon Journal*, 40.

511: views.' Dennison Berwick, *Savages* (London, 1992), 113.

511: Roraima' Memélia Moreira, 'A estratégia do genocídio Yanomami', *Jornal de Brasília*, 27 Jul. 1989; *PIB 1987/88/89/90*, 162. The gold rush was admirably described by MacMillan, *At the End of the Rainbow?*; also Leslie E. Sponsel, 'The master thief: gold mining and mercury contamination in the Amazon', in Barbara Rose Johnston, ed., *Life and Death Matters: Human Rights and the Environment at the End of the Millennium* (Walnut Creek, Calif., 1997), 99–127. There was ample press coverage of the phenomenon, for instance 'Roraima vive hoje a maior corrida do ouro do país', *Jornal do Brasil*, 27 Nov. 1988; 'A nova febre dourada', *Veja*, 18 Jan. 1989; and in much of the Western media.

512: all night long."' Severo Gomes, 'Paapiú – campo de extermínio', *PIB 1987/88/89/90*, 163; Ação pela Cidadania, *Roraima: o aviso da morte* (CCPY, CEDI, CIMI, São Paulo, 1989), 14–15.

512: mismatch'. Alcida Ramos, quoted in Rocha, *Murder in the Rainforest*, 37.

512: against us.' Jan Rocha, 'Blood runs in rivers of gold', *Guardian*, London, 18 Nov. 1989.

512: Indians.' Ibid.

513: diseases"'. Jan Rocha, 'Gold and greed threaten Brazilian tribe', *Guardian*, 30 Nov. 1989.

513: undernourishment.' Dr Maria Selau, in ibid.

513: whites.' Berwick, *Savages*, 31.

514: sky.' Dennison Berwick, 'At death's door', *Sunday Times Magazine*, 9 Sep. 1990.

514: an end.' 'Xawara: o ouro canibal e a quedo do ceu', Davi Kopenawa interview, translated by Bruce Albert, Brasília, 9 Mar. 1990, *PIB 1987/88/89/90*, 171. The CCPY published a summary of garimpeiro invasions: Romeo Graziano Filho, 'History of the invasion of Yanomami lands by miners, 1975–1989', *Urihi*, 11, Dec. 1990.

514: heat.' Albert, 'O ouro canibal', 252.

515: settlement'. Bruce Albert, 'Terra Yanomami e Florestas Nacionais no projeto Calha Norte: uma expropriação "ecológica"', *PIB 1987/88/89/90*, 167.

515: concessions. Funai announced this plan in August 1988; it was promulgated in Portarias 160, 13 Sep. 1988, and 250, 18 Nov. 1988; and rushed into law by twenty-one presidential Decrees: 97,512–30, 17 Feb. 1989, promulgating the Indian areas, and 97,545–6, 1 Mar. 1989, creating the two new national forests. The national forests and the national park covered 5,781,710 ha (22,317 square miles). The three prospecting zones decreed in Jan.–Feb. 1990 were: Gleba Uraricoera, deep inside Yanomami territory near the headwaters of the river of that name; Gleba Uraricaá Santa Rosa, which encroached only slightly on the north-western corner of the Floresta Nacional de Roraima; and the Gleba Catrimani – Couto Magalhães, which occupied 280,000 ha (1,080 square miles) of Indian land between the rivers of those names and the Lobo d'Almada. All this was known as 'Projeto Meridiano 62' because its eastern edge was 62° W.

515: between men'. Proclamation signed by dozens of mining and business associations, Boa Vista, 5 Oct. 1989, *PIB 1987/88/98/90*, 183.

516: Uaicás'. O *Globo*, 6 Jan. 1990. The survey, done between 19 and 21 December 1989, covered only part of Yanomami land. The decision authorizing the Ministério Público Federal to interdict the 9 million ha was by Judge Novély Vilanova da Silva Reis, Brasília, 20 Oct. 1989. (Eight years later, this same judge made another landmark ruling in favour of Indians, by compensating the Panará for their sufferings after contact.) In August 1990 the Ação pela Cidadania (Citizens' Action) group published a second powerful report called *Yanomami: A todos os Povos da Terra*, which documented Yanomami health during the previous year. Survival's campaign pamphlet that same year was called simply *Yanomami*. It summarized the Yanomami way of life, the history of attempts to create their park,

the garimpeiro threat, and a chronology of Survival's impressive efforts since 1968 on behalf of this nation.

516: President.' Mac Margolis, *The Times*, 11 Jan. 1990.

517: forest.' 'A morte ronda os índios na floresta', *Veja*, 19 Sep. 1990, 77 – this was a thorough, thirteen-page report on the garimpeiro problem. There were many other media reports, including one by John Hemming and another by Patrick Cunningham, *Geographical Magazine*, May and Sep. 1990; Dennison Berwick, *Sunday Times Magazine*, 9 Sep. 1990; and *Time*, 5 Nov. 1990.

518: death.' Speech by Senator Jarbas Passarinho in the Senate, 26 Nov. 1991. Darcy Ribeiro liked this great oration (which reviewed the history of the park project) so much that he reproduced it in full in *Carta* (Gabinete do Senador Darcy Ribeiro, 9, 1993, 241–53), 252. Senator Passarinho was later Minister of Justice and thus responsible for Funai, and he warned about continuing threats to the Yanomami that he had read in O *Globo*, 1 Feb. 2000, and in the *Revista do Clube Militar*, in 'Amazônia, Yanomami e os equívocos', *PIB 1996/2000*, 337–9. Davi Kopenawa was invited to the UN Indigenous Peoples meeting in New York in December 1992 by the UN Center of Human Rights, paid by the Indian Law Resources Center in Washington. The Venezuelan Biosphere Reserve for the Yanomami was threatened when in 1992 the newly created state of Amazonas passed a law dividing it into municipalities (which crossed tribal frontiers), thereby enabling the new local authorities to sell mining concessions on so-called 'common land' of indigenous communities. The CCPY helped its Venezuelan counterparts to fight this iniquitous law, on the grounds that it violated the country's constitution. Their campaign succeeded in 1997 when the Supreme Court of Venezuela quashed the law passed by their Amazonas assembly. Rocha, *Murder in the Rainforest*, 13–14.

518: demarcated'. Associação Brasileira de Antropologia letter to American Anthropological Association, about the damaging effect of Napoleon Chagnon's 'Life histories, blood revenge, and warfare in a tribal population', *Science*, 219, 1988, 985–92, published in *Anthropology Newsletter*, Jan. 1989; also in a Statement by Rubin George Oliven, President of the ABA, 9 Nov. 2000. Lêda Leitão Martins showed, in a reasoned paper, how Chagnon's 'laughable' ideas of fierceness had seriously damaged Yanomami interests in various ways, notably among the Brazilian military and public opinion and by jeopardizing medical and other aid ('The swing of the pendulum: the impact of Chagnon's work in Brazil', *Public Anthropology* (Roundtable Forum: Ethical issues raised by Patrick Tierney's *Darkness in El Dorado*. Round One), 2001).

519: population' Davi Kopenawa, *Update/ CCPY*, **63**, 22 Jan. 1993; *PIB 1991/1995*, 229.

519: breeding-grounds. Nelson Jobim Reis, *A Crítica*, Manaus, 28 Jan. 1993.

519: terrified.' Sister Alessia's letter of 12 Aug. 1993, reproduced in Rocha, *Murder in the Rainforest*, 6–7.

521: eight.' Bruce Albert, 'O massacre dos Yanomami de Haximu' (*PIB 1991/1995*, 203–8), 206. This very thorough account of the massacre was pieced together from Indian accounts and from testimonies at the killers' trials. Rocha, *Murder in the Rainforest*, 2–5.

521: Minister.' Ibid., 11; Brazilian and other media from 19 Aug. 1993 onwards. The journalist Janer Cristaldo spoke sarcastically of 'Yanobluff' and asked whether the Haximú massacre was 'genocide or saucepancide' because the only concrete evidence was pans riddled with bullet holes. This racist cited Chagnon's views of Yanomami fierceness to claim that they 'have not even attained a social contract like that of chimpanzees' (Janer Cristaldo, *Folha de São Paulo*, 24 Apr. and 8 May 1994). The *Folha de São Paulo* did publish rebuttals by people like the anthropologists Bruce Albert and Alcida Ramos and the Procurator of the Republic Aurélio Virgílio Rios, and Chagnon himself was sure that the crime was committed by prospectors ('Killed by kindness?', *Times Literary Supplement*, 11–12, 1993).

522: territory'. Report of External Commission of the Chamber of Deputies, ESP, 23 Nov. 1993. In April 1994 the Venezuelan authorities opened enquiries on the miners' leader José Altino Machado for having orchestrated the massacre; but that wily operator said that when one of the murderers sought his protection he had refused to help.

522: unpunished.' Luciano Mariz Maia, regional Procurador da República, 'Foi genocídio!', *PIB 1996/2000*, 341. Federal Judge Itagiba Catta Preta in Boa Vista, Roraima on 19 December 1996 condemned five prospectors, in absentia, to twenty years in prison for genocide – even though the crime technically took place on Venezuelan soil.

522: keep them out.' Davi Kopenawa in *The Times*, 28 Aug. 1997. The earlier invasion was in SIN, **31**, 1992. After the park was finally confirmed, the CCPY retained its initials, but changed its name to Comissão Pró-Yanomami. In addition to its medical work, the CCPY also launched an educational campaign for some thousand Yanomami in twenty yanos in its care. The curriculum was of course relevant to Yanomami life and was taught in their language. By the new millennium, this programme had grown to seventeen schools catering for some 1,500 children.

523: habitat.' Human Rights Commission of the Organization of American States, Dec. 1995, quoted in Rocha, *Murder in the Rainforest*, 73.

523: fishermen.' Letter to President Cardoso and others by 280 Yanomami leaders, Jan. 1996, ibid.

523: themselves'. Brian Wardlaw in 'O céu pode esperar', *Veja*, 19 Sep. 1990, 83. The quotes by the nurse Maria Aparecida da Silva and Claudinei Alves are from the same issue. Brian Wardlaw was the son of the missionaries whom I met at Tootototbi in 1972. The New Tribes Mission in early 1992 moved this mission to a base called Novo Demini a day's walk away, and most of the ninety people in the maloca went with the missionaries. Thereafter, the CCPY and National Health Foundation (FNS) used Tootototbi as a medical base.

524: diseases.' Marcos A. Pellegrini, 'O lugar dos Yanomami doentes no sistema único de saúde', *PIB 1991/1995*, 211.

524: communities.' Deise Alves Francisco and Cláudio Esteves de Oliveira, 'Projeto de Saúde Yanomami, no Demini, Tootototbi e Balawaú', ibid., 215 (Balawaú was a new health district, among Yanomami who had previously had little contact with outsiders). Jan Rocha gave World Health Organization statistics on disease for 1998, in *Murder in the Rainforest*, 77. Many organizations contributed to the medical care of the Yanomami. The government in 1991 created a Yanomami Health District (DSY or **Distrito de Saúde Yanomami**), and it was divided between different organizations (in descending order): CCPY, which by 2000 tended over half the Brazilian Yanomami in 144 villages through its new NGO **Urihi** (founded in 1997, named after the Yanomami word for forest and earth, hence 'homeland'); the government's Health District and **Funasa** (National Health Foundation); **New Tribes Mission** (MNTB) and **MEVA** evangelists;

Médecins du Monde (the better-known Médecins sans Frontières was active among Roraima's savannah tribes); the Salesians' **Secoya (Amazonas)**; **Funai**; and missionaries of the **Consolata Order** (Diocese of Boa Vista). Funding came from many sources, including the British government's Overseas Development Agency (later DfID) and Survival. The new arrangements rapidly halved mortality and malaria and increased the birth rate: ISA editorial team, 'Novidades na gestão da saúde Yanomami', *PIB 1996/2000*, 342–5, 353–5. By 2000 the total programme involved 243 field workers, including 13 doctors and 24 nurses, in 188 yanos, and costing $6.3 million annually. In 2002 a government proposal to cut Urihi's health budget was reversed and it was actually increased, thanks to NGO pressure.

A census by FUNASA in 2001 reckoned 12,445 Yanomami and 350 Yeknana living in the Yanomami Park in Brazil. But remote-sensing analysis by François-Michel Le Tourneau may have located a score of uncontacted yanos.

525: burnt trees'. Gabriella Gamini, *The Times*, 13 Apr. 1998, and Brazilian press throughout March. The forest fires were caused by Roraima's ranchers annually burning their grasslands, a practice they learned from plains Indians such as the Makuxi and Wapixana, but they were exacerbated by an exceptionally long drought.

525: credit. The two Mentuktire (Txukarramãe) shamans were Kukryti and Myti; they came to Roraima to perform rain dances and, not unreasonably, claimed credit when the miraculous rains fell at the beginning of April. Special aid for Indians damaged by the drought and fires came from Oxfam, Christian Aid, and the European Union (*PIB 1996/2000*, 329–31, 356–8).

525: language The CCPY's bilingual curriculum, called Programa de Educação Intercultural, was introduced in 1995. CCPY runs twelve of the schools, the Diocese of Boa Vista (Consolata) fourteen, and the Protestant missionaries five.

526: dependency.' Deputy Marcos Rolim, Report on his visit to Roraima to investigate military abuse of Indian women, CIMI press release, 22 Feb. 2001. A month later, the CCPY issued a rebuttal to the claim by the Minister of Defence, Geraldo Quintão, that the Yanomami park had been a mistake (CCPY press release, Brasília, 23 Mar. 2001). Ex-Senator Jarbas Passarinho also condemned this in a powerful article in ESP, 27 Mar. 2001.

526: destroyed.' Rocha, *Murder in the Rainforest*, 78.

20. The Far West

528: intoxicated.' Curt Nimuendajú, 'Os índios Tukuna' (Report to the SPI, Belém do Solimões, 10 Dec. 1929, first published in *Boletim do Museu do Índio. Antropologia*, **7**, 1977); TICN, 193–4. Also, Nimuendajú, 'The Tucuna', HSAI, **3**, 713–25; and *The Tukuna* (ed. Robert H. Lowie, trans. William D. Hohenthal, University of California Press, Berkeley, CA, 1952). Harald Schultz described girls' puberty rites in 'Tukuna maidens come of age', *National Geographic*, **116**:5, May 1959.

528: nature.' Roberto Cardoso de Oliveira, 'The role of Indian Posts in the process of assimilation – two case studies', AI, **20**:2, Apr. 1960, 91. João Pacheco de Oliveira found much evidence of Manuel Pereira Lima's good management in the SPI's archive in Manaus: 'O Nosso Governo'; os Ticuna e o regime tutelar (Rio de Janeiro, 1988), 164–6; 'Ação indigenista e utopia milenarista. As múltiples faces de um processo de territorialização entre os Ticuna' (in Bruce Albert and Alcida Rita Ramos, eds., *Pacificando o Branco*, São Paulo, 2002 (277–309), 283–8).

529: SPI.' Cardoso de Oliveira, 'The role of Indian Posts', 91.

529: farming'. Roberto Cardoso de Oliveira, 'Áreas de fricção interétnica na Amazônia', ASBA, 189.

529: medicines' Edwin Brooks, René Fuerst, John Hemming, Francis Huxley, *Tribes of the Amazon Basin in Brazil 1972* (London, 1973), 50–2. The local Catholic school-teacher confirmed the abuse by the Almeidas, and the Aborigines Protection Society team saw the surly son, dressed in a Playboy shirt. The enslavement of Indians had been denounced by a passing Brazilian naval vessel; but the Almeidas were released from arrest by the intervention of their friend the Bishop of São Paulo de Olivença.

529: mosquitoes'. Report by Neves da Costa Vale, who was sent by the local police, ESP, 26 Mar. 1968. The leper colonies were on Armaça and Arariá islands in the Solimões. The slave labour was on the Aires fazenda, alongside Belém. Jordão Aires claimed that the Indians had been brought there recently by a priest called Friar Jeremias. The *Jornal do Brasil* sent a reporter who on 21 April filed a devastating commentary about the misery of the Ticuna and a confession of abuse by Aires.

530: 10,000' Dale W. Kietzman, 'Indians and culture areas of twentieth-century Brazil', in Janice H. Hopper, ed., *Indians of Brazil in the Twentieth Century* (Washington, DC, 1967), 12; Darcy Ribeiro, 'Culturas e linguas indígenas do Brasil' (1957), trans. as 'Indigenous Cultures and Languages in Brazil' in ibid., 154; CEDI/Museu Nacional, *Terras Indígenas no Brasil* (São Paulo, 1987).

530: darkness'. Brooks et al., *Tribes of the Amazon Basin*, 52; Pedrinho A. Guareschi, *A Cruz e o Poder: a Irmandade da Santa Cruz no Alto Solimões* (Vozes, Petrópolis, 1985); Michael F. Brown, 'Beyond resistance: comparative study of Utopian renewal in Amazonia' (in Anna C. Roosevelt, ed., *Amazonian Indians from Prehistory to the Present* (Tucson, Ariz., 1994) (287–311), 296–7. José da Cruz was born José Nogueira in Minas Gerais. His movement in Peru was called the Ordén Cruzada and in Brazil the Irmandade da Santa Cruz (Brotherhood of the Holy Cross). His first great successes were among the Cocama and Ticuna as well as some Yagua in Peru. When he first visited Belém village (ninety kilometres (fifty-six miles) downriver from Tabatinga) in 1971, he stayed for six days. Indians listened to his preaching day and night, in the rain. As a result there was an epidemic of influenza from which twenty died; some refused medicines sent by the Catholics; and the village was so disturbed by the Cruz teaching that the army at Tabatinga had to send the Funai encarregado to restore calm.

For the earlier messianic movement in the 1940s, Nimuendajú, 'Os índios tukuna', trans. William Hohenthal as *The Tukuna* (Berkeley and Los Angeles, 1952), 141; M. V. de Queiroz, 'Cargo cult na Amazônia? Observações sobre o mileniarismo Tukuna', AI, **50:4**, 1963, 43–61; Pacheco de Oliveira, 'Ação indigenista e utopia milenarista', 292–7.

531: dominance'. João Pacheco de Oliveira Filho, 'O Projeto Tükuna: uma experiência de ação indigenista' (1977) in Pacheco de Oliveira, ed., *Sociedades Indígenas e Indigenismo no Brasil* (Rio de Janeiro, 1987), 213. Vendaval village is

below Belém, some hundred kilometres (sixty miles) downstream from Tabatinga, in what became the largest Ticuna reserve, Évare I.

531: movement'. Porantim, 1 and 2, 1982, *PIB/1982*, 14. On the death of José da Cruz, *A Crítica*, Manaus, 15 Jul. 1982.

533: crops.' Note by five deputies, each the leader of an opposition party, *Tribuna da Imprensa*, Brasília, 12 Dec. 1981, *PIB 1981*, 13; 'The Tükuna: mobilization and resistance against invasion', ARC, **10**, Feb. 1982, 11–13. The deputies' note said that there were 'over 20,000 Ticuna', whereas the ARC article had 'more than 15,000'.

533: assembly.' Vera M. N. Paoliello, 'A luta dos Tikuna pela demarcação', *PIB/1982*, 11. The great assembly was at Campo Alegre village, a few kilometres downstream from Vendaval, in December 1981.

534: motor boats.' João Pacheco de Oliveira and Vera Paoliello, 'Invasões, conflitos e mais promessas de demarcação para os Ticuna', *PIB/1984* (117–23), 118. On 10 May 1980, CIMI denounced the shooting of five Ticuna and this was widely reported; but it may have been mistaken.

534: crooks of all.' Letter by Pedro Ramos Gabriel, Uriqui, 25 Jan. 1985, in ibid., 119.

534: naked'. Letter from Chief Pedro Inácio, 5 Feb. 1984, presented to the Order of Brazilian Lawyers in Rio de Janeiro on 11 Apr., in ibid., 118.

535: Funai staff'. Pacheco de Oliveira and Paoliello, 'Invasões', 123; ESP, *Jornal de Brasília*, *O Globo*, *Folha de São Paulo*, 20 Feb. 1985.

535: agitators' Pacheco de Oliveira and Paoliello, 'Invasões', 123; ESP, *Jornal de Brasília*, *O Globo*, *Folha de São Paulo*, 20 Feb. 1985.

536: above all.' Pedro Mendes Gabriel, *PIB-85/86*, 167.

536: machine gun.' Report by Mariano Clemente, Pucüracü, 28 Mar. 1988, *PIB 1987/88/89/90*, 243.

536: started.' Alcides Luciano Araújo, *Magüta*, 3 Apr. 1988, in ibid., 245. As always, CEDI's *Povos Indígenas no Brasil* gave excellent coverage of the massacre, including an analysis of the background: João Pacheco de Oliveira Filho and Antônio Carlos de Souza Lima, 'O massacre de São Leopoldo: mais uma investida contra os Ticuna', ibid., 239–42; also João Pacheco de Oliveira, *Atlas das Terras Ticunas* (Museu Nacional, Rio de Janeiro, 1998), entry for 'São Leopoldo'. *Porantim*,

20:204, Apr. 1998, reported a protest by the Ticuna General Assembly because one of the killers of 1988 had shot another Ticuna in February 1997. *Porantim* said that only six of the fourteen killers had been arrested, but none was yet judged (**21:218**, Sep. 1999). The Ticunas' own *Jornal Magüta* reported on the painfully slow progress of the case during 1999, including a plea by the principal who had ordered the murders, Oscar Castelo Branco, that he be kept in house arrest because of his age.

537: Ticuna Portarias by Minister Jarbas Passarinho, 11 Oct. 1991, followed by Decrees by President Collor 'homologating' (ratifying) three earlier Ticuna reserves, 30 Oct. 1991. Évare I had 546,000 ha (2,100 square miles) and contained some 8,000 Indians in twenty-five aldeias; Évare II was 175,205 ha. (677 square miles). Évare I was a considerable improvement on the 313,125 ha (1,209 square miles) proposed in inter-ministerial Portaria 559 in November 1989, but less than the 596,000 (2,300 square miles) when it was first 'identified' in a Funai parecer in September 1985. Meanwhile, Évare II, across the Solimões river, increased from 165,000 ha in 1985 to 176,205 ha when demarcated in 1995 (640 to 680 square miles). João Pacheco de Oliveira Filho, 'Os caminhos para o Évare: a demarcação Ticuna', *PIB 1991/1995*, 307–9, and *Atlas das Terras Ticunas*, entry for Évare. This *Atlas* was published partly by the tribe's own Magüta organization. It showed a total of 35,000 Ticuna, of whom almost 26,000 lived in Brazil, in 118 aldeias within the fifteen indigenous territories.

538: Mayoruna The artificial name Mayo-runa was derived from the Quechua (Inca) words for river and people.

538: axes, etc.'. Julio Cesar Melatti, ed., *Povos Indígenas no Brasil*, 5, *Javari* (CEDI, São Paulo, 1981), 77. The first SIL translators to live among the Matsé (Mayoruna) were Harriet Fields and Harriet Kneeland (known to the Indians as Luisa and Enriqueta): Judith Vivar A., 'Los Mayoruna: en la frontera Perú-Brasil', *AI*, **26:2**, 1975, 329–47. When Harriet Fields was preparing to leave the SIL's Yarinacocha base in Peru in March 1964 to try to contact the Matsé, there was a clash between this tribe and road-builders at Requeña where the Tapiche joins the Ucayali. The road was being cut to help natural-gas prospectors from a consortium including Standard Oil of New York (Mobil). A hail of Matsé arrows wounded some road workers, and the response

was napalm-bombing and machine-gunning of the forest by Peruvian air force helicopters (Gerard Colby and Charlotte Dennett, *Thy Will be Done* (New York, 1995), 461–7).

539: location.' Kietzman, 'Indians and culture areas', 16.

539: logs per year' Henry R. Loewen, *A summary of Indian work done by Missão Novas Tribos do Brasil in the states of Amazonas and Acre, and the Federal Territory of Rondônia* (typescript, 1970), 3. The missionary who first translated Marubo was Gerald R. Kennell, Jr. of the New Tribes Mission (MNTB), and it was also spoken well by the Dutch missionary John Jahnsma, who spent many years with the tribe, and by his colleague Paul Rich and their wives (Melatti, ed., *PIB*, 5, *Javari*, 37). At the outset, Funai tried to attract some isolated Marubo to its new post. The journalist Paulo Lucena accompanied this attraction team, and was shocked when his friend Vitor Batalha, a teacher, was killed by Indians on 4 Apr. 1976. It was later learned that Batalha died because he had taken two Marubo women as wives, and his killers were the men who had intended to marry these women.

539: agency'. PIB-85/86, 185. On population growth, the missionary John Jahnsma in 1963 counted 323 Marubo; Julio Cesar Melatti in 1975 gave 397 and 462 in 1978; by 1980 Terri Valle de Aquino said that those on the Curuçá had increased by a third; in 1985 *PIB* reported that there were 594 (roughly two-thirds on the Ituí and one third on the Curuçá); in May 1994 a census by the Pastoral Indigenista and the National Health Foundtion (FNS) gave 960 Marubo – so that the tribe tripled in three decades. Pastor Jahnsma of the New Tribes Mission spent some twenty-five years with the tribe and provided much-needed medical attention.

540: attacked them.' Pedro Coelho, *Relatório referente aos primeiros contactos com índios arredios . . .*, Rio Ituí Attraction Post, 21 Dec. 1976, in Melatti, ed., *Povos Indígenas*, 5, *Javari*, 85–6; Anon., 'Uapá: cachorros facilitam atração', RAI, 2:8, Jan.–Feb. 1978, 16–24.

540: both sides'. Ruth Wallace de Garcia Paula, *Relatório de viagem*, PIA Ituí, 1979, 11, in Melatti, *Povos Indígenas*, 5, *Javari*, 87.

541: contact.' Philippe Erikson, 'Reflexos de si, ecos de outrem. Efeitos do contato sobre a auto-representação Matis' (in Albert and Ramos, eds., *Pacificando o Branco* (179–204), 179–80). The deaths were also denounced by Paulo Suess of

CIMI, *Folha de São Paulo*, 30 Jun. 1982 and in Julio Cesar Melatti, 'Os índios esquecidos e ameaçados', *PIB/83*, 84–5. They were revealed to an international audience in Jacques Cousteau and M. Richards, *Jacques Cousteau's Amazon Journey* (H. N. Abrams, New York, 1984) and O. Landi and E. Siqueira, *Coisas do Índio* (Icone, São Paulo, 1985) as well as by Brazilian, Japanese, French, Italian, and British television crews.

541: condition'. Márcia Graundenz (a Projeto Rondon student), *O Dia*, 31 Oct. 1982, in *PIB/1982*, 11.

541: behaviour.' Erikson, 'Reflexos de si', 180.

542: important of them.' Ibid., 183.

542: identity.' Ibid., 185.

542: death.' Ibid., 191.

542: predecessors.' Ibid., 193.

543: turned'. Ibid., 194.

543: buttons'. 'Atração pelos botões', RAI, **2:11**, Jul.–Aug. 1978 (2–8), 6; 'Índios do Rio Quixito', in Melatti, ed., *Povos Indígenas*, **5**, *Javari*, 102–9.

544: budgets'. Delvair Melatti, *Relatório* of the Grupo de Trabalho, 1980, 16, *PIB-85/86*, 181.

545: forest' ESP, 6 Sep. 1984, *PIB/1984*, 134. The dead Funai sertanista was Lindolfo Nobre Filho, aged fifty-two. Nine years previously, in 1975, the Korubo had killed another Funai sertanista, Jaime Pimentel. His friend Valmir de Barros Torres, head of Funai's Tabatinga office for many decades, was accused twenty-five years later by the Ticuna Paulinho Ramos (Canhão) of having ordered a revenge raid that massacred thirty Korubo (O *Globo*, 18 Apr. 2000).

On the gas exploration: Araci Maria Labiak and Lino João Neves, 'A Petrobrás e os arredios do Itacoaí [Itaquaí] e Jandiatuba', *PIB/1984*, 130–2; *Porantim*, Nov. 1984; Survival International urgent-action bulletin, 8 Jan. 1985. Petrobrás had previously explored further west, near the Javari in the territory of the Matsé (Mayoruna) and Marubo; and Elf-Aquitaine had caused much damage to the habitats of the acculturated Munduruku and Sateré-Mawé near the mouth of the Tapajós. Exploration engineers from Elf-Aquitaine brazenly invaded the demarcated Mawé reserve in August 1981 and established a major camp a short walk from the Indians' Ponta Alegra village. Pits were dug and hundreds of dynamite charges blown up in seismic testing. The French were working with government approval (for Brazil was desperate to find domestic petroleum) and Funai's docile consent (this was the Nobre da

Veiga era). But the invasion provoked protest from CIMI, local Funai officials, and international NGOs such as Survival International and the Boston-based Anthropology Resource Center (ARC, **10**, Feb. 1982; SIR, **7:2:40**, Summer 1982). The French anthropologist Simone Dreyfus reported on the ugly situation, and the lawyer Dalmo de Abreu Dallari fought for legal action or compensation. Luckily for the Sateré-Mawé and nearby Munduruku, no oil was found. The engineers withdrew in 1983, leaving hundreds of unexploded dynamite charges; but under pressure from NGOs they were forced to remove their debris and the charges, and compensate the tribe with some $70,000 for each drilling.

The 2,000 Sateré-Mawé live on the Andirá and other rivers just south of the lower Amazon. They had fought in the populist Cabanagem rebellion in the 1830s, and by the 1980s were thoroughly acculturated – indeed many had become God-fearing Protestant converts to the Seventh-Day Adventists, Assembly of God, or Baptists of the New Tribes Mission (MNTB), or to the local Catholic diocese. The Mawé are famous for harvesting the sought-after guarana fruit (*Paullinia cupana*, *Paullinia sorbilis*) whose seeds make a delicious, nutritious, and mildly stimulating drink.

545: located.' Silvio Cavuscens and Lino João de O. Neves, *Povos Indígenas do Vale do Javari, Campanha Javari* (Report to Funai, CIMI, Manaus, 1986), *PIB-85/86*, 181. The 8,338,000 ha (32,185 square mile) Vale do Javari Indian Area was interdicted by Funai Portarias 1,848/E and 1,849/E of 28 March and 8 April 1985.

545: Funai.' Delvair Montagner (Melatti), 'Funai no Javari: afinal, existe ou não existe?', *PIB 1987/88/89/90*, 270. Funai's base was at Atalaia do Norte, a brazen, bustling frontier town on the Ituí at the entrance to the nominally interdicted Javari park.

546: softwoods'. Ibid.

546: children'. PIB 1991/1995, 344. The situation in 1995 was summarized by Silvio Cavuscens of Coiab, 'A situação dos povos indígenas do Vale do Javari', ibid., 333–42.

547: management.' Sílvio Cavuscens, 'A demarcação finalmente chega ao Vale do Javari', *PIB 1996/2000*, 426–7. Although demarcation of the Javari Territory was ordered in a Funai Portaria in 1995, there was a requirement for more anthropological surveys of this huge forested area, to supplement studies done in 1980 and 1985.

The new survey was done, in 1995–6, by a team led by the anthropologist Walter Coutinho. It took two years for his report to reach the international funders, PPTAL, so that the work did not resume until 1999. At that time, the Javari area was known to contain some 2,700 people from the four main tribes (Marubo, Matsés, Matís, and Kanamari) plus some 1,250 from at least seven 'isolated' or uncontacted groups.

547: children'. Survival success bulletin, *Victory for the Indians of the Javari Valley*, Feb. 1999. The decree for the Javari demarcation was signed on 11 Dec. 1998. Survival had felt that the situation in the Javari Indian Area remained so tense that it issued an urgent-action bulletin about it in Nov. 1997.

549: serene'. Philippe Erikson, '"Last contact" pour les Korubo?', *Nouvelles de Survival*, Paris, 25, Winter 1996, 12–13 (trans. in *PIB 1996/2000* (431–3), 433). Possuelo's 1996 contact with the Korubo on the Itaquaí was recorded in real time on a Web site of the National Geographic, by the expedition's French reporter Claudia Baran and photographer Nicolas Reynard (*Isto É*, 28 Sep. 1996; ESP, 17 Oct. 1996; *Globo*, 18 Oct. 1996; Tim Rayment, 'The lost world', *Sunday Times Magazine*, 1997, 46–51).

549: colonels?' Terri Valle de Aquino, *PIB/83*, 156. One of the first meetings in Acre was a Pastoral Indigenous Assembly organized by CIMI in the state capital, Rio Branco, in Aug. 1976, *Boletim do CIMI*, **5:32**, Oct. 1976, 20–1.

549: liquor'. Loewen, *A summary of Indian work done*, 4. The New Tribes Mission had started with the Marubo on the Ituí in 1960, with the Kulina of the Juruá near Eirunepé (Amazonas) in 1969, and with the Manchineri and the Jaminawá on the Iaco in Acre in 1967 and 1970 respectively. In 1985 the MNTB's bases were still with the Manchineri and Jaminawá on the Iaco, with the Kaxinawá on the Envira, and the Katukina and Iauanawá on the Gregório.

550: bosses'. Aquino, *PIB/83*, 157.

551: seringals'. Txai ('Blood-brother') Terri Valle de Aquino and Marcelo Piedrafita Iglesias, *Kaxinawá do Rio Jordão: história, território, economia e desenvolvimento sustentado* (Rio Branco, Acre, 1994), 27. Iglesias wrote his master's thesis on the rise of this rubber-tappers' association, *ASKARJ: O astro luminoso* (Museu Nacional/ PPGAS, Rio de Janeiro, 1993). The Kaxinawá refer to themselves, in Panoan, as Huni Kuin, meaning 'true people'.

551: bosses.' Terri Valle de Aquino, *PIB/1982*, 19. In May 1981 an Apurinã Indian fired a shotgun at point-blank range at the organizer of the Rural Workers' trade union of Boca do Acre and killed him. Small farmers accused Funai of inciting the Indians against them; whereas the Apurinã blamed Funai for neglecting to give them aid or demarcate their land. ESP, 21 May 1981.

552: Kulina].' Chief Pancho from Recreio village, in Rosa Maria Monteiro et al., 'Auto-demarcação Kulina e Kaxinauá', *PIB/1984*, 193. Lutheran pastors and Catholic missionaries from CIMI and OPAN (Operação Anchieta) had cooperated to help these two tribes organize their demarcation. The British charity Oxfam also provided aid funds, and the local press was supportive. On 29 and 31 March 1985 the *Folha do Acre* published seven pages of interviews with tribal leaders, Protestant and Catholic missionaries, and Terri Valle de Aquino, President of the local branch of the Comissão Pró-Índio (also reproduced in *PIB/1984*, 195–206). Terri was angry with the missionaries, particularly Americans of the New Tribes Mission who had called him and the CPI 'communist agitators', and the Catholics and Lutherans who falsely accused him (in *Porantim*, 1984) of gaining economic control of Indians with his self-help programmes. The anthropologist-activist said that missionaries had no right to criticize his CPI when they operated in only two of Acre's seventeen indigenous areas, attempted no economic aid programmes, and did not listen to the indigenous leaders.

552: Jordão river. The first two Presidential decrees for demarcation were: for the Iauanawá and Katuquina (Katukina) of the Gregório river near Tarauacá, on 28 December 1983; and for the Katuquina/Kaxinawá in the districts of Feijó and Envira in Acre and Amazonas, on 29 March 1984.

553: depot.' Terri Valle de Aquino, *PIB/1982*, 20. The decree establishing the A I do Rio Jordão was by President Figueiredo, no. 90.645 of 10 December 1984, and the confirmation was by President Collor, Decree 225 of 29 October 1991. Aid for the cooperative was given by the British Oxfam, Canadian government, and German 'Brot für die Welt'. The local association was ASKARJ, Associação dos Seringueiros Kaxinawá do Rio Jordão. A similar organization for Indians of the Envira river, east of the Jordão, was founded in 1988 as OPIRE (Organização dos Povos Indígenas do Rio Envira).

554: region.' Letter to Minister Costa Couto

from Mário Cordeiro de Lima (Poianáua) and others, Brasília, 22 Jan. 1986, *PIB-85/86*, 277. The environmental-indigenous plan set up by the BID bank was PMACI: Plano de Proteção ao Meio Ambiente e às Comunidades Indígenas.

555: forest.' Chico Mendes, *The Fight for the Forest* (Latin America Bureau, London, 1989), 46.

555: land' Cecilia McCallum, 'Incas e Nawas: produção, transformação e transcendência na história Kaxinawá', in Albert and Ramos, eds., *Pacificando o Branco* (375–401), 381.

556: excellence.' Ibid., 390.

556: rights.' Alex Shoumatoff, *The World is Burning* (Boston, 1990), 301; Alexander Shankland, *Guardian*, 8 Dec. 1989.

556: insubordination.' Shoumatoff, *The World is Burning*, 301.

557: glasses'. Ibid., 302; Shankland, *Guardian*, 8 Dec. 1989.

557: seringueiros'. Marcelo Piedrafita Iglesias and Txai Terri Valle de Aquino, 'Regularização das terras e organização política dos índios no Acre (1975/94)', *PIB 1991/1995* (517–28), 525. This article gave a very detailed record of land tenure and legal status of every reserve in Acre and adjacent Southern Amazonas. It also told the history of the region's indigenous organizations.

When funding from the Interamerican Development Bank's PMACI plan finally ended in the mid-1990s, there was some help from the Swiss foreign-aid agency. The costs were then helped by the Programa Piloto para a Proteção das Florestas Tropicais do Brasil (Pilot Program to Conserve the Brazilian Rain Forest), launched with $250 million in 1990 by the G7 richest nations and also funded by the World Bank and European Community. In 1994 a division of this was created to help indig-

enous peoples: PPTAL (Projeto Integrado de Proteção às Populações e Terras Indígenas da Amazônia Legal) (Protection of Indigenous People and and their Lands in the Amazon Region), with $21 million, mostly from the German development bank KfW. This helped to pay for demarcation of many indigenous territories.

557: freedom.' Sian Kaxinawá (or José Osair Sales), in Valle de Aquino and Iglesias, *Kaxinawá do Rio Jordão*, 41–2. Sian Kaxinawá's four documentaries included the critically praised *The Real People* and he won the Reebok Prize for Human Rights (*A Gazeta do Acre*, 28 Oct. 1993; ESP, 15 Dec. 1993).

558: Acre.' Marcelo Piedrafita Iglesias and Txai Terri Valle de Aquino, 'A hora e a vez dos índios no governo da floresta', *PIB 1996/2000*, 567.

558: spot them'. *The Times*, 10 Jun. 1998.

559: animals.' Iglesias and Aquino, 'A hora', 568, 585–6; *Últimas Notícias/ISA*, 26 Jun. 1998, 26 May 1999, 25 Jan. 2000.

559: pressure'. Report by Rieli Franciscato, head of the Purus River Contact Front, Jul. 1995, *PIB 1991/1995*, 354.

560: state.' Lino João Neves, 'Funai no Juruá: não ajuda e estorva', *PIB 1987/88/89/90*, 288. CIMI organized the first assembly of Purus Indians at Lábrea as early as September 1979, fully reported in *Boletim do CIMI*, **8:60**, Nov.–Dec. 1979. The other Catholic aid agency in this area was Opan (the Jesuit Operação Anchieta), which worked with the Ecumenical Lutheran Church of Brazil (IECLB). Additional funding for the demarcation and registration of reserves in the Juruá–Jutaí–Purus area came from BID's PMACI, and then from the PPTAL project of the G7's Pilot Program.

21. Rondônia: the Last Major Contact

561: bows drawn'. Adrian Cowell, *Decade of Destruction* (London, 1990), 94–5. The surviving boy died later in hospital, and the abducted one had not been found by 1992. Francisco Prestes Rosa was a rubber man who had been given a plot by the development agency Incra in its Projeto Burareiro (Mauro de Mello Leonel, *Etnodicéia Uruéu-au-au* (São Paulo, 1995), 120). A similar attack in 1972 on the family of one Euclides Candido da Costa was reported in the *Jornal do Brasil*, 8 Oct. 1972; ESP, 9–10 Oct.; *Veja*, 18

Oct. Apoena Meirelles listed the various killings of seringueiros during the previous three years.

561: Uru-Eu-Wau-Wau. The tribe's name is pronounced 'Ooroo-Ehoo-Wow-Wow'. It was abbreviated to Wau Wau at that time; later often spelled Uru-Weu-Wau-Wau, Uru-Eu-Uau-Uau, Uruéu-au-au, or Uruéu-Wauwáu, or contracted into one word Urueuwauwáu. It was also known as Urupa or Uru Pa In and Boca Preta (Black Mouth). As was so often the case, this name was given to the tribe by another, the Parintintin. Its pre-contact population was thought to have been between 500 and 1,000.

561: fazendeiros.' ESP, 26 Nov. 1981; Leonel, *Etnodicéia*, 121.

562: adversities'. Ibid., 122.

562: take place.' Cowell, *Decade*, 113.

562: presents?' Ibid., 112.

562: discourses.' Mário Arruda da Costa, *Relato de uma expedição de contato indigenista* (Universidade Católica de Goiânia, Goiânia, 1980), 81; Leonel, *Etnodicéia*, 122. Meirelles's guides were Suruí Indians (whom he had contacted eight years previously) but their Mondé Tupi dialect was too different from the Tupi Kawahib of the Uru-Eu-Wau-Wau for the groups to understand one another. It was later found that the Parintintin and Karipuna spoke the language of the people being contacted.

563: forest'. Cowell, *Decade*, 118. At first, the Funai men reasoned that the Uru-Eu-Wau-Wau aggressions were a response to the road being built into their land – they were not strong enough to attack the road crew's large camp. Funai had been planning to plant a camp in front of the road-builders, to force them to stop. Mauro Leonel lists early reports on the region, by Funai's Benamour Brandão Fontes in 1975 and 1977, and by the Army Captain Luís Alberto Must Berniz, who recommended a post at Alta Lídia in 1976 and 1977: Leonel, *Etnodicéia*, 119–20. Denis Mahar of the World Bank heard about the road into the Uru-Eu-Wau-Wau heartland, which was a violation of the terms of the bank's loan for Polonoroeste. Mahar hurried to Brasília and demanded that the federal government make the state authorities stop the road; which was done.

563: tremor.' Cowell, *Decade*, 120. The ESP reported this meeting on 14 March 1981, and another on 20 April 1982. Other contacts and clashes with the tribe are in *PIB 1981*, 24–4 (including the picture of João Maia Brito handing a present to Chief Djaí 'Careca') and *PIB/1982*, 34. The Alta Lídia camp was renamed Comandante Ary, in honour of a pilot whose plane crashed there. Loren McIntyre, 'The End of Innocence', *National Geographic*, **174:6**, Dec. 1988, 816. Also Mauro Leonel, 'Uru-eu-wau-wau: primeira demarcação de um povo isolado', ESP, 2 Feb. 1985; *PIB-85/86*, 296–7.

564: naked girl. The bald Chief Djaí appears in various photographs by Puttkamer and McIntyre in the *National Geographic* article.

564: much later. The first arrival of thirty-four Indians at the camp was reported in ESP, 8 Aug. 1981, the wounding of Baiano Maia on 11 March 1982, and more friendly contacts on 1 June 1982. Benamour Fontes reported that fifty Indians spent a week at the post, *Jornal de Brasília*, 8 Jul. 1983. Leonel, *Etnodicéia*, 123–4.

564: places'. Leonel, *Etnodicéia*, 124.

565: medicine.' Ligia Simonian, 'Os Uru-Eu-Wau-Wau e os Amundáwa no início dos anos noventa', *PIB 1987/88/89/90*, 423–5. Another anthropologist, Maria Lúcia Cardoso, told Fiona Watson at that time that the situation of this tribe was 'calamitous'.

566: lived.' Mauro Leonel, 'A "desmarcação" das terras Uru-Eu-Wau-Wau', *PIB 1987/88/89/90*, 418–22.

566: vice-versa'. Leonel, *Etnodicéia*, 132. There was a curious confusion between Funai and the forestry department IBDF (later part of the environmental agency Ibama). In June 1978 Funai issued a Portaria interdicting 879,800 ha (3,400 square miles) for the Uru-Eu-Wau-Wau. Shortly afterwards, in September 1979, a Presidential Decree created the **national** park of Pacaás-Novos covering most of the same area and making no mention of its indigenous inhabitants. This **national** park violated the Indians' right to hunt and consume their natural resources, and its management plan even considered a 'tourism sub-programme'. The conflict of interest was partly resolved in an agreement between Funai and IBDF in 1985. Despite the ambiguities, the overlapping indigenous area/national park is a crucially important natural sanctuary in the midst of the environmental destruction that surrounded it. With a combined total of 1,832,300 ha (7,070 square miles) this is one of Brazil's largest areas of environmental protection.

567: business world'. Leonel, *Etnodicéia*, 140. The Prestes plot was in Projeto Burareiro at the north-west of Indian territory, towards Ariquemes.

567: initiatives'. Ibid., 156.

567: health.' Ibid.

567: rubber trees. Sarney's 'illegal' decree was no. 98,894 of 30 January 1990. The Funai sociologist who led the team that recommended reduced boundaries of the reserve was José Augusto Mafra dos Santos – who had just done a similar hatchet job to reassess the reserve of the Arara Indians of northern Rondônia. However, in April 1990 other Funai officials persuaded their own director to reinstate protection of the threatened area. Survival International issued an urgent-action bulletin about it, in January 1991; and President Collor revoked his predecessor's sharp practice. President Collor resigned because of corruption; but his actions over Indians and environmental issues were generally admirable.

568: Uru-Eu-Wau-Wau land. The four big companies mining cassiterite in the north and west of Uru-Eu-Wau-Wau territory were Paranapanema (at Massangana), Brumadinho, leading a consortium of other mining companies, Brascan/BP, and the Best group (Leonel, *Etnodicéia*, 164).

568: gone.' Fiona Watson's report to Survival, Aug. 1992. Invasions of Uru-Eu-Wau-Wau territory continued throughout the 1990s. In July 2001 Funai and Ibama got the police to expel eighty intruders; but these soon returned and were evicted by the Indians themselves.

569: cedro (Cedrela meliceae)].' *Alto Madeira* newspaper, Porto Velho, 18 Nov. 1994; *PIB 1991/1995*, 571: a police sergeant was accused of having helped the loggers in this invasion. In the previous year, some Indians blamed Apoena Meirelles (then in charge of the Porto Velho region of Funai, and previously Funai's President for a few months) for having encouraged the tribe to fell its hardwoods. In 1992 Samuel Cruz, the regional coordinator for Funai, accused Rondônia's Secretary of Agriculture, Nilson Campos, of being the 'number one enemy of the Indians' and promoter of widespread logging, around and within Indian territories. Legal actions against Campos had all aborted, apparently because of his powerful political connections. There were three areas of mineral prospecting in the Indian and environmental reserves: on the headwaters of the Jamari and Jaru rivers, which both flow northwards towards the BR-364 and then into the Madeira and Machado rivers respectively, and on the Pacaás Novos river at the western end of the reserve which flows into the Mamoré. Lígia Terezinha Lopes Simonian, *'This bloodshed must stop': land claims on the Guarita and Uru-Eu-Wau-Wau reservations, Brazil* (Doctoral dissertation, City University of New York, 1993).

An isolated group of 'tall and strong' Indians was sighted in 1989 and again in 1990 near the Rio Branco Indian Area and the adjacent Guaporé biological reserve, south-east of the Uru-Eu-Wau-Wau territory (*Folha de São Paulo*, 19 Aug. 1990). In 1995 two other isolated groups were seen in southern Rondônia: a few Kanoê contacted by Marcelo dos Santos, and seven Indians who may

have been Makuráp (ESP, 27 Sep. and 28 Oct. 1995).

569: reward. The research into the anticoagulant arrow poison is summarized by Ricardo Arnt of ISA, 'Biotecnologia e direitos indígenas – os Uru-eu-wau-wau a *tike-úba* e a Hoechst/Merck', Jun. 1994, *PIB 1991/1995*, 572. Jesco von Puttkamer led expeditions from the Catholic University of Goiânia, to discover more, in 1990 and 1992 (before his own death in 1994): *O Popular*, Goiânia, 18 Dec. 1989 and 14 Jun. 1992, and other press reports.

569: produce.' Betty Mindlin, 'Os Paiter: vinte anos depois', *PIB 1987/88/89/90*, 437. Mindlin approved of the way in which Funai's Apoena Meirelles and Aimoré Cunha da Silva had fought with dedication for the Aripuanã park; but their successor Francisco de Assis da Silva admitted to corrupt involvement with loggers.

570: 11,700 square miles). The six contiguous areas, totalling 3,074,648 ha (11,686 square miles), are: **Aripuanã indigenous park**, 1,258,323 ha, created 1968, reduced 1974, later expanded (for Cinta Larga); **A I Sete de Setembro**, 247,870 ha, demarcated 1983 (Suruí/Paiter); **A I Roosevelt**, 235,055 ha in 1986 (for Cinta Larga and Zoró); **A I Aripuanã** (as opposed to the park of that name), 753,400 ha in 1986 (for other Cinta Larga); **A I Serra Morena**, 148,300 ha, 1984 (Cinta Larga); **A I Zoró**, 431,700 ha, 1985 (Zoró, Cinta Larga, Arara Karo). **A I Igarapé Lourdes** is just to the west of Sete de Setembro but not contiguous, 185,534 ha, 1983 (Gavião-Digut, Arara-Karo, Zoró); and north of the Zoró Area is **A I Piripicura** (for related Tupi-Kawahib). (In square miles: Aripuanã indigenous park, 4,857; A I Sete de Setembro, 958; A I Roosevelt, 907; A I Aripuanã, 2,908; A I Serra Morena, 572; A I Zoró, 1,666; A I Igarapé Lourdes, 716.)

571: prospectors.' Mércio Gomes, *The Indians and Brazil* (Gainsville, Fla., 2000), 203. CEDI's coverage of Romero Jucá's timber concessions was in *PIB 1987/88/89/90*, 43–6. The *Jornal do Brasil* published a series of articles on the timber problem, between 30 Oct. and 20 Nov. 1987.

571: timber.' Maria Inês Saldanha Hargreaves, 'A vida dos Zoró, sócios menores da exploração madeireira', *PIB 1991/1995*, 582–3. By the end of the century, there were still many indigenous lands in Rondônia that were not demarcated. These were mostly those of small tribes, fragments of larger groups that had been decimated by disease or the various invasions. By the 1990s there were only eighteen Diahoi, nine Juma, ten Katawixi, twelve Himarimã, seventeeen Torá, twenty-three Kanoê, and fourteen of the newly contacted Omoré (Gomes, *The Indians and Brazil*, 195).

571: forests.' João Dal Poz (of the Federal University of Mato Grosso) in ISA Internet report on the death of Carlito Cinta Larga, *Notícias Socioambientais*, 5 Jan. 2002.

572: prospectors.' Carlos Alberto Ricardo, Coordinator of ISA, in its Internet report of 4 Mar. 2002, followed by another on 26 April.

573: conclusion'. David Price, *Before the Bulldozer* (Colin John, Md., 1989), 178 and his 'The World Bank vs native peoples: a consultant's view', *The Ecologist*, **15:1/2** (London, 1985), 73–7. Survival International in London published a series of articles about the problem: 'The Nambiquara and the road', SIR, **30**, Summer 1980, 22–6; **31/2**, Winter 1980, 28–9; 'The Nambiquara and the World Bank', **34**, Summer 1981, 30, 69; 'Brazil: Polonoroeste Development Project', **35/36**, Winter 1981, 28–31, and Survival corresponded vigorously with officials and presidents of the Bank. Meanwhile, the Harvard-based Cultural Survival was equally active in the United States. Its director, David Maybury-Lewis, advised David Price in his dealings with the World Bank, and in 1981 it published a powerful and well-documented criticism: Jason W. Clay, *In the Path of Polonoroeste: Endangered Peoples of Western Brazil* (Cultural Survival Occasional Paper **6**, Cambridge, Mass., 1981). There were also regular reports in the ARC. Articles in the general press included: Memélia Moreira, 'Uma estrada no Guaporé ameaça a nação Nambiquara', *Jornal do Brasil Domingo*, 27 Apr. 1980; Catherine Caufield, 'The last of the Nambiquara', *New Scientist* (London, 7 Aug. 1980), 460–2.

574: businesses.' Betty Mindlin, 'Avaliação do Polonoroeste: uma proposta', *PIB/1984*, 221.

574: ecosystem.' José Lutzenberger, 'The World Bank's Polonoroeste Project: A Social and Environmental Catastrophe', *The Ecologist*, **15:1/2**, 1985, 69–72. Lutzenberger's testimony to the 'Subcommittee on Natural Resources, Agricultural Research and Environment' of the House Committee on Science and Technology, Washington, was on 19 September 1984. This Subcommittee's chairman, Rep. James Scheuer, wrote to the Secretary of the Treasury to try to rectify the situation in Rondônia.

574: land areas.' Letter from Bruce M. Rich

of the Natural Resources Defence Council and others to T. Clausen, President of the World Bank, 12 Oct. 1984, *New York Times*, 17 Oct. 1984; Stephan Schwartzman in *Cultural Survival Quarterly* (Cambridge, Mass.), **8:4**, Dec. 1984, 75; *Ecologist*, **15:1/2**, 1985, 78. Survival International's American affiliate, SIUSA, also submitted a statement to the 'Subcommittee on International Development Institutions and Finance' of the House Foreign Affairs Committee on 21 March 1984 regarding the misconduct of the World Bank: text in *SI Annual Review*, **43**, 1983. The uproar about the financing of Polonoroeste was also supported by the powerful Senator Robert W. Kasten, Jr. This senator was chairman of a committee that could determine the amount of the US contribution to the World Bank, so when he objected to the Bank's disregard for environmentalists' concerns, it had to take notice. Bruce Rich commented to Adrian Cowell that nothing concentrates a banker's mind as effectively as being separated from his money.

574: Interior'. Report by Neal A. MacDougall, sent to Rondônia in Jul.–Aug. 1983 by the US branch of Survival International, summarized in *SIUSA News* (New York), **3:1–2**, Spring/Summer 1983. The unhappy situation of the various Indian groups in Mato Grosso–Rondônia was reported in Linda Greenbaum (a pseudonym), 'The Failure to Protect Tribal Peoples – The Polonoroeste Case in Brazil', *Cultural Survival Quarterly* (Cambridge, Mass.), **8:4**, Dec. 1984, 76–7.

575: useless.' Price, *Before the Bulldozer*, 189, 181.

575: subsidy.' Cowell, *Decade*, 127. Cowell was also involved in advising the World Bank in Washington, and he helped activists such as José Lutzenberger, Bruce Rich, and Robert Goodland (an environmentalist within the Bank itself). A later President of the Bank, Barber Conable, admitted in May 1987 that it had 'stumbled' over the loan to Polonoroeste, 'a sobering example of an environmentally sound effort which went wrong'. He cited all the ways in which the development of Rondônia had been a catastrophe; and he tightened the Bank's environmental-impact assessments for any future schemes.

575: passed over.' Shaman Gorduska Nambiquara, Urubu Village of the Negaroté Nambiquara talking to Fiona Watson, Aug. 1992, in her report to Survival International.

576: patients!' Price, *Before the Bulldozer*, 184.

576: protected areas. CEDI in 1987 listed the

following reserves: **Área Indígena Nambiquara**, area 1,011,961 ha, population 204, created 8 Oct. 1968, altered 28 Nov. 1973, demarcated 1985; **A I Vale do Guaporé** (the amalgamation of a string of small reserves for the Mamairisu, Wasusu, Mamainde, Alantesu, Negaroté, and Waikisu Nambiquara), 242,593 ha, pop. 289, decreed 29 Apr. 1985; **Pirineus de Sousa**, a small reserve just east of Vilhena (28,212 ha, pop. 103, proposed 6 Aug. 1984); **Sararé**, at the extreme south of tribal territory in the forests of the Guaporé, for the Manairisu and Sararé groups, 57,420 ha, pop. 51, decreed 29 Apr. 1985; **Tubarão/Latunde**, west of Vilhena in Rondônia, for the Latunde, Sabane, and Aikana groups, 116,613 ha, pop. 117, identified 15 Oct. 1986; **Tirecatinga**, north of the main Paresi reserve, on the Papagaio headwater of the Juruena, 130,575 ha, pop. 80, decreed 28 Dec. 1983 (CEDI/Museu Nacional, *Terras Indígenas no Brasil* (São Paulo, Nov. 1987) map p. 133; also *PIB/83*, 172–4.) (Areas in square miles: Área Indígena Nambiquara, 3,906; A I Vale do Guaporé, 936; Pirineus de Sousa, 109; Sararé, 222; Tubarão/Latunde, 450; Tirecatinga, 504.) According to Marcelo dos Santos, it was Maritta Koch-Weser of the World Bank who pressed for the demarcation of the Nambiquara reserves – although David Price had been suspicious of her commitment to the Indians in the previous decade. Betty Mindlin and Mauro Leonel also praised her.

576: indigenous areas.' Watson, report to Survival, 2 Aug. 1992.

576: shoot too.' Ibid.

577: everything.' Jodo Nambiquara (at Urubu village, Negaroté), quoted in ibid.

577: reforestation. The logger Pompermayer had been caught stealing 1,800 m³ (64,000 cubic feet) of timber from the Hahaintesu Nambiquara in 1988; the police confiscated the wood, machinery, and vehicles; but the logger returned and recovered all the confiscated material. In 1992 lawyers from the NDI (Nucleus for Indigenous Rights, which later merged into ISA) launched an action for compensation of the indigenous community; this was granted in a trial in 1993; but appeals continued until they were finally rejected in March 2002.

578: Rondônia'. Virginia Valadão, 'Os índios ilhados do Igarapé Omerê', *PIB 1991/1995*, 545, and Marcelo dos Santos, 'Índios acossados em Rondônia', ibid. 550–3; reports by Pablo Pereira in ESP, 7 Sep. and 28 Oct. 1995; Patrick Menget,

Les Nouvelles Survival International, 20, Autumn 1995. The finding of the long bows and other evidence, in 1990, was reported by Ricardo Arnt, *Folha de São Paulo*, 19 Aug. 1990. Marcelo dos Santos explained in 1994 that his 'contact front' was seeking six different groups of isolated Indians in Rondônia: on the rivers Cautário, Muqui (probably a group of Uru-Eu-Wau-Wau), Karipuninha, Candeias, and upper Jaci-Paraná, and in the Reserva Biológica do Guaporé. The contact with the Kanoê was made on the Omerê creek, which flows into the middle Guaporé in the district of Corumbiara.

578: settlers. Vincent Carelli was an experienced photographer attached to the NGO Centro de Trabalho Indigenista. His remarkable films were immediately seen on Brazilian television.

580: village.' Rinaldo S. V. Arruda, 'A luta por Japuíra', *PIB-85/86*, 317.

580: roots.' Ibid.

581: combat.' Ibid., 318. The film about the Parallel 11 massacre of the Cinta Larga was called *Avaeté* and made by Zelito Viana in 1984. That atrocity also inspired Christopher Hampton's powerful play *Savages* in the 1970s.

582: violence.' Rinaldo S. V. Arruda, 'Rikbaktsa: retomando o Japuíra', *PIB 1987/88/89/90*, 453. The Indianists and anthropologists who wrote favourable reports were Odenir Pinto de Oliveira, Betty Mindlin, and Mauro Leonel. Célio Horst was promoted in Funai, despite his dubious behaviour in the Japuíra affair, and did good work with the Wayampi north of the Amazon.

The Jesuit mission in the area changed its name from Missão Anchieta to Operação Anchieta (Opan for short). In April 1987 a Spanish-born Jesuit, Father Vicente Cañas, was found apparently murdered by a single knife thrust, at his isolated post among the **Enawenê-Nawê** (formerly called Salumã) on the upper Juruena, some eighty kilometres (fifty miles) south of the Erikpatsa reserve. Father Vicente had reached Brazil in 1968 and worked with the Tapayuna before their transfer to the Xingu, then spent five years with the Paresi, during which time he helped contact the Münkü in 1971.

On 28 July 1974 Father Cañas and his fellow Jesuit Thomaz de Aquino Lisbôa, guided by Tapema and two other Irantxe, entered a camp of unknown Indians by a lagoon off the Juína tributary of the Juruena. A child saw them, women emerged from huts and fled into the forest, and the strangers approached a single, crippled man who was crouched in the midst of the patio. Lisbôa wrote: 'I said loudly "Good afternoon!" . . . We approached and ascertained that he was very emotional, trembling with fear. To dispel the impression of terror, we sat at his feet and placed machetes and axes on the ground. The Indian slowly returned to normal, delighted by the presents. He talked and gesticulated a lot . . . The crippled Indian started to shout, calling his companions who had fled.' (Thomaz de Aquino Lisbôa, *Os Enauenê-Nauê. Primeiros Contatos* (São Paulo, 1985), 19; ESP, 24 Aug. 1974.) During ensuing days, contact was made with more of these amiable, Aruak-speaking people, who became known as Salumã. In a village of six circular huts, more gifts were traded for food, and it was indicated by sign-language that the strangers would return by outboard motor. After 1977 the Spanish-Brazilian Vicente Cañas took up permanent residence with the tribe, who awarded him the name Kiwxi. Father Bartolomé Meliá made an anthropological study of these people, whose rituals were so intense that he called them the 'Benedictines of the forest'. But it was not until 1983 that the tribe revealed that they disliked the name Salumã and called themselves Enawenê-Nawê. During his decade of uninterrupted life with them, Vicente

Kiwxi's 'daily life was that of any member of the aldeia: he participated in rituals, fished, gathered wild honey, made handicrafts and learned this people's language' (*Porantim*, June 1987). At the time of his death he was as weather-beaten and emaciated as an early-Christian hermit. His stabbing was never resolved and no one was accused of his murder.

The Jesuits of Opan fought for the designation of the tribe's territory. There was a tragedy on 4 September 1984 when the tribe killed the surveyor João Batista dos Santos and his assistant, because they were measuring the wrong land; but the correct area was finally awarded to them as a 742,000 hectare (2,860 square mile) territory demarcated in 1996 and fully registered by 1998. The 78 Menkü (Myky) have an adjacent reserve of 47,000 ha (180 square miles). At the time of contact there were some hundred Enawené-Nawé; by the mid-1980s, with good medical treatment and a high birth-rate, there were about 150; and they entered the new millennium at 320. The Indians patrol their own extensive borders. They can write their Aruak-based language but have recently requested schooling in Portuguese and arithmetic, with help from the anturopologist Virgínia Valadão.

22. Struggles for Land: the North-East

583: population.' João Pacheco de Oliveira, 'Fronteiras étnicas e identidades emergentes', *PIB 1991/1995*, 478. On the general plight and reawakening of the tribes of the north-east: José Maurício Arruti, 'Morte e vida no nordeste indígena', *Estudos Históricos*, **8:15**, 1995, 57–94; and João Pacheco de Oliveira, ed., *A Viagem da Volta* (Rio de Janeiro, 1999).

583: potentates'. Father Alfredo Dâmaso, *O Serviço de Proteção aos Índios e a tribu dos Carijós no sertão de Pernambuco* (booklet published in Rio de Janeiro, 1931), in José Maurício Andion Arruti, 'A árvore Pankararu, fluxos e metáforos de emergência étnica no sertão do São Francisco', in Pacheco de Oliveira, ed., *A Viagem da Volta* (229–78), 233; Sidnei Peres, 'Terras indígenas e ação indigenista no Nordeste (1910–67)', in ibid., (41–90), 58–9. The Fulniô (often spelled Fulni-ô) were then known as Carijó. The tribe had a mission called Ipanema in colonial times, but this land was disbanded and sold off in the 1860s.

There are now some 2,800 Fulniô. Their 11,500 ha (28,420 acre) reserve was originally divided into 427 family plots of roughly 30 ha (74 acres) each, but with population growth each family now has no more than 6.5 ha (16 acres), so that they supplement their income by selling handicrafts of pottery, rugs, straw hats and mats, and corn and beans. The reserve includes the town of Águas Belas, some 250 kilometres (155 miles) south-west of Recife in Pernambuco near the Alagoas border. The 800 houses of the Fulniô now look like a suburb of Águas Belas; but for three months each year the tribe migrates to perform secret ceremonies at Ouricuri, a sacred place five kilometres (three miles) from the town (*Jornal do Commércio*, 2 Feb. 1997). One Fulniô, Aluízio Caetano de Sá, spent twelve years compiling a 30,000-word dictionary of his Yatê language, which was approved for publication in 1994 by the Ministry of Education and Culture. He sought to preserve his people's customs and traditions, but he omitted all religious words since he wanted to keep this element of Fulniô culture secret (*Diário de Pernambuco*, 24 Sep. 1992; *PIB 1991/1995*, 482).

585: bulldozers.' Antonil, 'British tobacco giant grinds Indians to pulp: Brazil', SIR, **4:4(28)**, Winter 1979, 10. This article showed that British-American Tobacco (BAT) owned a substantial interest in Aracruz Cellulose (a subsidiary of Aracruz Florestal), which supplied cellulose for BAT's paper-making subsidiary Wiggins Teape. Aracruz was named after a nearby town, as was its predecessor Cofavi (Companhia Ferro e Aço de Vitoria – 'Iron and Steel Company of Vitoria'). In the early twentieth century, the local SPI Inspectors Antonio Estigarríbia and Samuel Lobo visited these Tupi communities on the Doce river, and the botanist Augusto Ruschi noted how their forests were destroyed and Indian families evicted between the 1950s and 1970s.

585: polluted.' Suzanne Williams, 'Land rights and the manipulation of identity: official Indian policy in Brazil', *Journal of Latin American Studies*, **15:1**, 1983, 152; *Porantim*, Jun./Jul. 1981, translated in SIR, **7:1(39)**, Spring 1982, 32–4.

585: jail.' ESP, 6 Jun. 1981; Williams, 'Land rights', 153. In 1983 a pliant Funai anthropologist, Lúcia Elena Soares de Melo, paid a brief visit to the tribe and declared that it had lost every trace of its Indianness. This drew an angry response from the Tupiniquim leaders, who wrote to the President of Funai saying that the anthropologist was blind, that they had been Indians from generation to generation, and that they had fought collectively for the land awarded them by the Emperor Dom Pedro II (*ESP*, 6 May 1983; *Porantim*, May 1983). Later that year, the three remaining Tupiniquim villages (Pau Brasil, Caieiras Velhas, and Comboios) had their land confirmed (homologated) by presidential decrees (*Diário Oficial*, 1 Nov. 1983); they were fully registered in 1995. (The tribe's efforts in 1993 were reported in such media as *Jornal do Commércio* and *Correio Braziliense*, 15 Jul. 1993, *Porantim*, Oct. 1993, *Gazeta Mercantil*, 13 Apr. 1994, *A Gazeta*, 25 Sep. 1994; *PIB 1991/1995*, 715–16.) In 1998 all three indigenous areas were increased in area, to a total of 12,625 ha (32,000 acres). But a Funai work-group led by the young anthropologist Carlos Augusto da Rocha Freire recommended that Caieiras be joined to Pau-Brasil. This was rejected, so the Tupiniquim themselves tried to demarcate this link area. By the end of the

century, the Tupiniquim population had grown to some 1,400, of whom two-thirds lived in Caieiras Velhas, and about 20 per cent of this people were married to non-Indians or 'regionals'.

586: hectares'. Internet page of CIMI-Regional Leste, 27 Dec. 1999.

586: Bahia]' 'A vida precária de 10 mil índios na BA', ESP, 10 Dec. 1979. Chief Tururim's pathetic journey to seek help in 1972 was reported in *Jornal do Brasil*, 28 May 1972. He and his successors were helped by the anthropologist Pedro Agostinho and his students at the University of Bahia.

587: São Lucas.' Manuela Carneiro da Cunha and Eunice Paiva, 'Defendem os Pataxó', *Folha de São Paulo*, 18 Oct. 1983; *PIB/83*, 212. The Caramuru-Paraguassu reserve was established in 1926 by State Law 1,916. The agreement between the SPI and Bahia State in May 1937 was no. 1471. For a time, SPI authorities in North-East Brazil saw the arrangements on this Pataxó Hã-Hã-Hãe reserve as a model for integrating Indians as useful members of national society; but in the 1950s the Service tried to crack down on leaseholders who were defaulting on rents and committing other 'irregularities' (Sidnei Peres, 'Terras indígenas e ação indigenista', 72–8). On the tribe's subsistence and return: Maria Rosário Carvalho, *Os Pataxó de Barra Velha: seu subsistema econômico* (Master's thesis, Universidade Federal da Bahia, 1977); Maria Hilda Baqueiro, *Caminhos de ir e vir e caminhos sem volta: índios, estradas e rios no sul da Bahia* (Master's thesis, Universidade Federal da Bahia, 1982).

587: opinion.' 'Apresentação', *PIB/1982*, 5. This issue carried a picture of the displaced Pataxó Hã-Hã-Hãe on its cover, and six pages of extracts of press mentions during the year 1982 (pages 72–8). Survival International reported the problems of the Pataxó Hã-Hã-Hãe and their attempt to recover Fazenda São Lucas extensively in its *Review* and mounted a campaign that culminated in an urgent-action bulletin in March 1983.

587: killing us.' Osvaldo Trajano Pataxó, *Jornal da Tarde*, 1 Mar. 1985; Aracy Lopes da Silva, 'Resistência: até quando?', *PIB/83*, 210.

588: secretariat.' Letter from 1st Encontro da Nação Pataxó Hã-Hã-Hãe, Eunápolis, Bahia, to President Collor, *A Tarde*, 23 Sep. 1991; *PIB 1991/1995*, 711.

588: imprisonment. The 'bus-stop killers' of Galdino Jesus dos Santos were sentenced by a jury in Brasília (after two days' deliberation, and despite the lady judge's condescending attitude to Indians) on 10 November 2001. One of them was released in 2002 after less than a year in jail and promptly got a job as a trainee dentist in the civil service, apparently because his father was a judge in Brasília. Sydney Possuelo and other activists protested furiously at this disregard for the murder of an Indian.

589: Brazil'. A Tarde, 20 Aug. 1999; José Augusto Laranjeiras Sampaio, 'Pataxó: retomadas na rota do Quinto Centenário', *PIB 1996/2000,* 715–21, 719–20.

589: area'. Rosa Maria de Oliveira Costa (coordinator of Anai (Associação Nacional de Ação Indigenista) in Bahia), news report by ISA, 19 Apr. 2002.

590: peoples'. William D. Hohenthal, Jr., 'As tribos indígenas do médio e baixo São Francisco', and a summary in English, RMP, **12**, 1960, 59.

590: culture.' Ibid., 80.

590: acres].' Paulo Marcos de Amorim, 'Acamponesamento e proletarização das populações indígenas do Nordeste brasileiro', *Boletim do Museu do Índio, Antropologia,* **2**, May 1975, 7.

591: admiration'. Lélia Rosalba, 'O posto indígena de Mirandela', *Revista do Museu do Índio,* **1**, 1976, 52–3; Sheila Brasileiro, 'Povo indígena Kiriri: emergência étnica, conquista territorial e faccionalismo' (in Pacheco de Oliveira, ed., *A Viagem da Volta* (173–96), 180). The heroic but doomed Canudos rebellion of 1896–98 was immortalized in Euclides da Cunha's *Os Sertões* and the equally powerful novel by the Peruvian Mario Vargas Llosa, *La Guerra del Fin del Mundo* (1981, translated as *The War of the End of the World*).

591: culture'. Darcy Ribeiro, 'Culturas e línguas indígenas do Brasil' (1957) translated by Janice Hopper as 'Indigenous Cultures and Languages in Brazil' in Janice H. Hopper, ed., *Indians of Brazil in the Twentieth Century* (Washington, DC, 1967), 138.

592: Indians'. Statement by Chief Lázaro, March 1991, in Brasileiro, 'Povo indígena', 184.

592: north-east.' Arruti, 'A árvore Pankararu', 255. The enlightened SPI Inspector was Raimundo Dantas Carneiro, inspired by the then Director of the Goeldi Museum in Belém, Carlos Estevão de Oliveira, who studied cultural survival among north-eastern tribes.

592: wounded.' *Cidade de Santos,* 16 Jul. 1984, O *Estado do Paraná,* 25 May 1984, in *PIB/ 1984,* 182. There are many remnants of Kiriri in the north-east, since this had once been a powerful tribe. The history and renaissance of the main group in Bahia are well recorded in Maria de Lourdes Bandeira, *Os Kiriri de Mirandela: um grupo indígena integrado* (Universidade Federal da Bahia and Secretaria de Educação e Cultura, Salvador, 1972) and Brasileiro, 'Povo indígena Kiriri'. The 1,300 in the main group are at Mirandela, near Ribeira do Pombal on the main road north from Salvador. (The Jesuits settled the Kiriri (or Cariri) in four mission villages in the eighteenth century. Of these Canabrava is now the town of Ribeira do Pombal, and Saco dos Morcegos ('Sack of Bats') is renamed Mirandela.) Reactions to the massacre came from Funai (whose agents received death threats), the Cardinal Archbishop of Salvador, the NGO ANAI and others; and the police hunted for a former mayor of Ribeira do Pombal as the main suspect. The Kiriris' 12,300 ha (30,390 acre) reserve was finally demarcated and registered in 1990, after farmers with legitimate claims were either allowed to remain or compensated for relocation.

593: north-east.' Brasileiro, 'Povo indígena', 188. The Kiriris' struggles and victories were amply reported in *PIB-85/86,* 257–8; *PIB 1987/ 88/89/90,* 387–8; *PIB 1991/1995,* 490–2; and *PIB 1996/2000,* 548–50.

593: majority.' Pedro Agostinho, quoted in ESP, 27 Dec. 1979.

594: justice. The murder of Chief Ângelo Pereira Xavier was reported in ESP, 27 Dec. 1979, *Boletim do CIMI,* **9:61**, Jan.–Feb. 1980 and elsewhere. His killer was named as the gunman known as 'Antonio de Lino'. The Pankararé live near the towns of Brejo do Burgo and Nova Glória some 500 kilometres (310 miles) north of Salvador da Bahia, while the Pankararu are west of them, across the São Francisco river in the State of Pernambuco.

594: alcohol.' Report on Atikum of Serra Umã by Inspector Tubal Vianna, 1946, in Peres, 'Terras indígenas', 84.

594: Indians.' Rodrigo de Azeredo Grünewald, 'Etnogênese e "regime de índio" na Serra do Umã', in Pacheco de Oliveira, ed., *A Viagem da Volta* (137–72), 169–70. The eighteenth-century mission was Olho d'Agua da Gameleira (now Olho d'Agua do Padre). The hills were called Umã only recently, apparently after a nomadic group that roamed throughout the São Francisco valley, and the name Atikum is also a recent one: some Indians think that it was the name of a chief.

594: blacks'. Ibid.

595: starvation.' Chief Elzionélio, P I Atikum, in *Diário de Pernambuco*, 6 Jan. and 1 May 1992, and *PIB 1991/1995*, 481–2. The earlier murder of Aduvaldo Mota, Funai's agent with the Atikum, was reported in ESP, 16 May 1984. By the end of the century, there were 2,743 Atikum on the 16,290 ha (40,250 acre) reserve, which was demarcated and registered in January 1996.

596: Xokó'. Vice-Chief José Apolônio, 'Os Xokó e a luta pela terra', Ilha de São Pedro, 9 Dec. 1984, in *PIB/1984*, 179 and his article in *Porantim*, May 1985. The Xokó had previously sent a desperate appeal about the Brito situation, signed by their leader Antonio Acacio Santiago, to the Pro-Indian Commission in São Paulo: in Beatriz Góis Dantas and Dalmo de Abreu Dallari, *Terra dos Índios Xocó* (Comissão Pró-Índio, São Paulo, 1980); ARC, **5**, Mar. 1981, 13–14.

596: ourselves'. Chief Apolônio Xokó report to ISA, 9 Sep. 1995, *PIB 1991/1995*, 505; also *PIB 1987/88/89/90*, 385–7. The Área Indígena Caiçara/Ilha de São Pedro was confirmed by Decree 401 of 24 Dec. 1991. On the Tuxá, Elizabeth Nasser, *Sociedade Tuxá* (Master's thesis, Universidade Federal da Bahia, 1975) and a report to Eletrobrás by the Instituto de Pesquisas Antropológicas do Rio de Janeiro, *Quatro Estudos de Caso* (Rio de Janeiro, 1989).

597: sense.' Francisco de Assis Siqueira and others, 'Relatório da viagem ao povo Xukuru', 2–3 May 1998, on the Xukuru Web site.

597: owners.' *Porantim*, **146**, Mar. 1992, 8. In August 1999, 45 Tuxá and other Pernambucan Indians danced in front of the Senate in Brasília, to protest that drug dealers had taken two-thirds of the Tuxá reserve on Assunção island in the São Francisco river in order to grow marijuana and coca for cocaine. The government's anti-drug agency ordered Funai to get rid of them.

597: authorities.' Petition signed by Chief José Pereira de Araújo and others, Pesqueira, 20 Feb. 1989, *PIB 1987/88/89/90*, 384; *Diário de Pernambuco*, 22 Feb. 1989.

597: resettle them. A small Xucuru Indian area had been earmarked by Funai in 1969; but the big 26,980 ha (104 square mile) reserve was identified by Funai in Portaria PP 218 of 14 Mar. 1989. It is some 190 kilometres (118 miles) west of Recife in the municipality of Pesqueira, in the Ororubá (formerly Urubu) Hills.

598: farming. The first Xukuru reoccupation was of the 110 ha farm Pedra d'Agua that contained the sacred woodland on 5 Nov. 1990 (*Por-*

antim **133/4**, Nov./Dec. 1990, 1) and the large 1,200 ha (3,000 acre) ranch occupied on 22 March 1992 was Caípe de Baixo, belonging to councillor Amilton Didier (*Porantim*, **14:146**, Mar. 1992, 8). The company that claimed 2,000 ha of the reserve was Agropecuária Vale do Ipojuca. The Minister of Justice declared the reserve to belong permanently to the Xukuru, Portaria 259, 28 May 1992, and it was duly demarcated despite strong opposition from business interests in Pesqueira. The murder of José Everaldo on 4 August 1992, on the small farm of Egivaldo Farias, was reported in *Porantim*, **14:150**, Sep. 1992, 6, and elsewhere.

599: north-east' *Porantim*, **20:211**, Dec. 1998, 9. The killing of Chief Chicão Xukuru (Francisco de Assis Araújo) was reported in *Jornal do Brasil* and elsewhere, 21 May 1998, and his funeral in *Diário de Pernambuco*, 23 May 1998.

599: Pernambuco. The Xukuru Kariri live around the town of Palmeira dos Índios, just inside the State of Alagoas, 130 kilometres (80 miles) south of Pesqueira and 137 kilometres from the state capital Maceio. Disputes between the Xukuru and Kariri groups living in the same reserve date back at least to the 1970s. Another Kariri group in Alagoas, some 500 Tingui-Kariri survived on a scrap of weak land at Olho d'Agua do Meio ('Middle Water-Hole') near Feira Grande. They complained to the CPI about the lack of privacy surrounding their annual *ouricuri* ritual which had to be performed in the midst of farms: Comissão Pró-Índio de São Paulo, *Tingui-Kariri-Botó*, 1980; ARC, **6**, May 1981, 18–19. Alfonso Trujillo Ferrari, *Os Kariri: o crepúsculo de um povo sem história* (São Paulo, 1957).

599: values.' Manoel Celestino da Silva, in *Gazeta de Alagoas*, 30 Nov. 1991; Silvia Aguiar Carneiro Martins, 'Os caminhos das aldeias Xucuru-Kariri', in Pacheco de Oliveira, ed., *A Viagem da Volta* (197–228), 205–6.

600: nephews. *Porantim*, Nov. 1994; *PIB 1991/1995*, 509.

601: scarce.' Frans Moonen, 'A problemática atual dos Potiguara e alternativas para o seu futuro', *PIB 1987/88/89/90*, 377; and his 'Os Potiguara: índios integrados ou deprivados?' *Revista de Ciências Sociais*, **4:2**, 1973, 131–54. For the origins of the conflict: Paulo Marcos Amorim, 'Índios camponenses: os Potiguara da Baía da Traição', RMP, **19**, 1970–71, 7–95.

601: Decree 1,775. On the election of Nanci Soares, *Folha do Meio Ambiente*, Sep. 1995; her successor as mayor was another Potiguara, Marcos Antonio dos Santos. Decree 1,775, passed by Cardoso's government in 1996, allowed claims by anyone who felt that they had a valid title to indigenous land. Surprisingly, one of the areas where the Minister of Justice admitted such claims was in the Potiguara reserve Monte-Mor – even though the tribe had clearly been living there since before the arrival of the first Portuguese in 1500. This judgement in 1999 led Funai to make another anthropological survey of the area.

601: attitudes.' Carlos Guilherme do Valle, 'Experiência e semântica entre os Tremembé do Ceará', in Pacheco de Oliveira, ed., *A Viagem da Volta* (279–337), 289. Henyo Barretto showed after admirable research how a tribal name 'Tapeba' was fabricated by journalists and missionaries. The word Tapeba in Tupi means 'flat rock' and it is the name of a lake near Caucaia; but there has never been such an ethnic group. It was applied to people of indigenous descent who live around the coastal town of Caucaia, a former Jesuit mission a few kilometres west of Fortaleza. Henyo was amazed when a group of 'Tapeba' told him that they had scarcely heard the name until he came to research into its origins. Henyo Trinidade Barretto Filho, 'Invenção ou renascimento? Genese de uma sociedade indígena contemporânea no Nordeste', in ibid., 91–136; Jussara Vieira Gomes, *Relatório sobre os Índios do Município de Caucaia do Ceará* (Museu do Índio, Rio de Janeiro, 1985).

602: sandbanks. Jornal do Brasil, 7 Apr. 1968, and ESP, 6 Jul. 1969 and 2 May 1982.

602: perpetuated.' Guilherme do Valle, 'Experiência', 302.

602: demarcated.' Assembly of Indigenous People of Ceará, Fortaleza, Jul. 1999, in Sylvia Porto Alegre, 'De ignorados a reconhecidos: a "virada" dos povos indígenas no Ceará', *PIB 1996/ 2000* (539–42), 542.

602: suffering.' Statement by leaders of the Tremembé community of Almofala, 20 Oct. 1996, *PIB 1996/2000,* 556. The adverse ruling was by Federal Judge Germana Moraes, 23 Sep. 1996: she upheld the long-standing title deeds of companies such as Ducoco Agricola SA. This was overturned by a Federal Regional Tribunal on 26 March 1999.

602: occupation. The three Tremembé populations and areas are now: Almofala and Varjota (1,175 people on 4,900 ha (12,110 acres)), and far away, near the town of Itarema, Capim-Açu

or Córrego João Pereira (336 on 3,140 ha (7,760 square miles)). Other indigenous groups in Ceará are the so-called 'Tapeba', and Pitaguari, and Paiaku/Jenipapo-Kanindé, each with its own council.

603: interests.' Report by Friar Osvaldo Coronini, Father Manoel Porfírio de Araújo and others, São Luís, 12 Aug. 1979, *Boletim do CIMI,* **8:56**, May–Jun. 1979, 12. The murder of the Chief of Canabrava was reported in ESP, 15 Sep. 1976. The Province of Maranhão had in 1923 given an area of 164,557 ha (635 square miles) to the Guajajara, and this was demarcated by the SPI in 1936 and 1953. Funai's 1977 demarcation reduced the area by some 33,000 ha (130 square miles) to make way for an Incra colonization scheme.

603: found.' ESP, 11 Mar. 1980.

604: missionaries.' ESP, 10 May 1981; Mércio Gomes, 'Porque índios brigam com posseiros', in Dalmo Dallari et al, eds., *A Questão da Terra Indígena* (CPI, São Paulo, 1981), 51–6. Two years later, in Apr. 1983, Guajajara of the Canabrava reserve sacked the buildings of the Franciscans' convent at Alto Alegre, removing all furniture, doors, and windows. Friar Osvaldo Caronini complained bitterly about the attack; but Funai excused the sacking because the convent was supposed to be empty.

604: protests.' Peter Schröder, 'Cana Brava e São Pedro dos Cacetes: um conflito em extinção', *PIB 1991/1995* (449–52), 451. The land-registry of Canabrava was done by Decree 246 of 29 Oct. 1992. The Indians in 1990 founded an Associação Comunitária Guajajara to fight for their rights, but internal divisions meant that this represented only part of the group.

604: back'. O *Globo,* 17 Mar. 1996; Schröder, 'Cana Brava', 452.

605: started.' Gomes, *The Indians and Brazil,* 277.

605: Swift, etc.' Motion in support of the Tembé Indians, by CIMI and other organizations, Belém, 1981, SIR, **7:1**, Spring 1982, 34. The large ranching companies were introduced via the Pará state land agency Iterpa and by the irregular donation of land to the Companhia Agropecuária do Pará by the President of Funai, General Bandeira de Mello, in November 1970.

606: interests.' Karl Henkel, O *Caso Cidapar e o Conflito da Área Indígena do Alto Rio Guamá como Processos de Ocupação e Desocupação do Espaço Social* (Amazon-Consult, Belém, 1995),

26; Expedito Arnaud, 'O direito indígena e a ocupação territorial: o caso dos índios Tembé', RMP, **28**, 1981–82, 35–49; Lourdes Gonçalves Furtado, 'Alguns aspectos do processo de mudança na região do nordeste paraense', BMPEG, **1**, Jun. 1984.

606: 1,100.' and *mixing.'* Folha de São Paulo, 13 Aug. 2000.

606: workers.' Folha de São Paulo and O Liberal, 31 May 1996; *PIB 1996/2000*, 529.

606: Kaäpor'. William Balée, 'Urubu-Kaäpor: ecological destruction in northern Maranhão', ARC, Dec. 1979, 7; his *Footprints in the Forest* (New York, 1994), 46; and 'Language, law, and land in Pre-Amazonian Brazil', *Texas International Law Journal*, **32:1**, Winter 1997, 123–9. The effect of the road was exacerbated by an aggressive colonization scheme of the Alto Turi launched by the north-east development agency SUDENE at this time. Under this programme, 6,000 colonists were given land title in the upper Turiaçu; and they were joined by almost 60,000 squatters and migrants.

607: politicians'. William Balée, 'Ka'apor' entry in *Indigenous Peoples in Brazil*, ISA Web site, 2001.

607: invaders.' Fr. Cláudio Zannoni, O Estado do Maranhão, 16 Oct. 1991; *PIB 1991/1995*, 458. The main ranching companies threatening the Kaapor were: Iguaí Agropecuaria, Joaquim Monteiro and Agropecuária Vale Turiaçu of the Paulista Galletti brothers (who had bought the claims of Nildo Ferreira da Silva), and Nicodemos Martins Marques.

608: spare no one'. Francisco Potiguara Tomaz, head of Funai's P I Canindé, Report on events of 23 September 1993, *PIB 1991/1995*, 459.

608: dismember it. The gunmen Davi and Raimundo were known to work for the Galletti brothers.

608: commitments. In its original loan from the World Bank between 1983 and 1987, CVRD was required to spend $11 million on protecting all indigenous lands along the corridor of the Carajás railway between the mine and the port of São Luís. This work was called Projeto Ferro Carajás, Apoio às Comunidades Indígenas and it cooperated with the Sistema de Proteção Awá-Guajá. In 1985 Mércio Gomes presented a report called *Programa Awá* to CVRD and Funai, with a proposal for full demarcation of that tribe's lands. But this fine anthropologist worried that CVRD's money was squandered on well-meaning reports

by other anthropologists and on lands of tribes other than the most-threatened: the Guajá-Awá and the Krikatí (*The Indians and Brazil*, 191, 198). The impact of the Carajás railway was summarized in Maria Célia Coelho and Raymundo Cota, eds., *Dez Anos da Estrada de Ferro Carajás* (Universidade Federal do Pará, Belém, 1997).

609: south-west Maranhão. Darcy Ribeiro's mistaken report that the Krikatí were extinct was in his 'Culturas e línguas indígenas do Brasil', trans. Janice Hopper as 'Indigenous Cultures and Languages in Brazil', in Hopper, ed., *Indians of Brazil in the Twentieth Century*, 142.

609: defined area'. Finding of federal judge, São Luís do Maranhão, action 1,875/1981, in *PIB 1991/1995*, 641, and a chronology of the devious judicial process, ibid., 648. Settlers had been occupying Krikatí land since 1979, many with Funai's tacit approval; but speculators poured in after 1989 when they learned that claims might be allowed.

609: land-grabbers].' Maria Elisa Ladeira and Gilberto Azanha, 'Os "Timbira atuais" e a disputa territorial', *PIB 1991/1995*, 641.

610: land-invaders'. Gomes, *The Indians and Brazil*, 188. Gomes cites two reports by José Luiz dos Santos addressed to Funai and the CVRD in Dec. 1984 and Mar. 1985 that helped spur Funai into action.

610: prostitution.' Ibid., 192.

611: compensations.' Ibid., 193.

611: product'. Ibid., 142–3.

612: accessories'. Christina Lamb, 'Amazon Inidians who breastfeed monkeys', *Sunday Telegraph*, 30 Apr. 2000.

612: 1980.' Mércio Pereira Gomes, 'O povo Guajá e as condições reais para a sua sobrevivência', *PIB 1987/88/89/90* (354–60), 356.

613: Awá-Guajá.' Anon., 'Guajá', RAI, **3:15**, Mar./Apr. 1979 (3–12), 5–6. Possuelo's contact was near the source of the Igarapé Presidio, a northern tributary of the Pindaré in the Serra do Piracambu. One early mention of the existence of (Awá-)Guajá was by Curt Nimuendajú when he went up the Gurupi to the Tembé in 1912: 'Sagen der Tembé-Indianer', *Zeitschrift für Ethnologie*, **47**, 1915, 281–301. Father Carlos Ubiali (Carlo Ubbiali in Italian) of the Maranhão branch of CIMI gathered data about the tribe from settlers, in 1980: 'Maranhão: grupo Guajá destinado à destruição', *Boletim do CIMI*, **10:71**, Apr.–May 1981, 9–11.

613: forest.' Survival, *Disinherited. Indians in*

Brazil (London, 2000), 31; *Correio Braziliense*, 8 Nov. 1988; André Toral, 'A saga de Karapiru', *PIB 1987/88/89/90*, 363. In 1990 another solitary Indian was discovered in northern Minas Gerais, and he also proved to be a Guajá.

614: fronts'. Gomes, 'O povo Guajá', 358.

614: wood.' Mércio Gomes et al., *Guajá* (CIMI-Maranhão, São Luis, Dec. 1990), 15–16; Gomes, 'O povo Guajá', 358. In these two texts, Mércio Gomes listed all the known groups of Awá-Guajá, of whom 150 people were by 1989 in demarcated Funai reserves. The guilty parties were: the Empresa Agro-Industrial Alto Turiaçu owned by Carlos Azevedo from São Paulo; the influential Galletti brothers also from São Paulo (who created a huge 12,000 ha (30,000 acre) ranch in the northern part of the Awá A I); the land-speculator António Fala Fina from Paragominas; and Nildo Ferreira da Silva from São Paulo, who organized the small settlers. The Interministerial order that reduced the territory was Portaria 158 of 8 Sep. 1988. Also, fine reports by Walter Rodrigues in O *Estado do Maranhão*, 13 Jun. and 12 Sep. 1988.

615: fate.' CIMI-Maranhão, *Terra para os Guajá* (Appeal leaflet, São Luís, 3 Apr. 1987). This leaflet was probably by Father Cláudio Zannoni, who wrote covering letters begging for the support of NGOs and well-wishers throughout the world. The 1987 leaflet was expanded into a twenty-eight-page booklet largely by Mércio Gomes, *Guajá*.

615: non-Indians.' *Correio Braziliense*, 30 Apr. 1991; *PIB 1991/1995*, 455. Survival's second urgent-action bulletin about the Awá-Guajá, *Nomadic tribe faces extinction*, was issued in November 1991 and its third in May 2002.

615: planet.' Fiorello Parisi, O *Imparcial*, Oct. 1992. Parisi had worked, with distinction, with the Panará and Wayampi, and his wife Valéria

had made an early contact with the Guajá in 1973. The team sent by Funai was led by the anthropologist Maria Auxiliadora Leão and Father Carlo Ubbiali of CIMI. Possuelo approved its report on 16 July 1992, and Portaria 373 of the Minister of Justice (Funai's parent ministry) was issued on 27 July and published in the *Diário Oficial* on the 29th. In 1992 a family of five Awá-Guajá was found near Imperatriz on the Tocantins. They were survivors of a terrible massacre twenty years previously, and had subsisted undetected near an area of intense farming – albeit all bearing scars from their ordeals. In December 1998 a further six Awá-Guajá were contacted, after their four relatives had died of disease.

616: today'. Fiona Watson quoted in Lamb, 'Amazon Indians', *Sunday Telegraph*, 30 Apr. 2000, 31.

616: project' Ibid.

616: whites.' *Awá, Brazil: nomads face extincion*, Survival urgent-action bulletin, May 2002; *Survival 2002: land. life. future* (London, 2002), 6. Louis Carlos Forline, of the Goeldi Museum in Belém, entry 'Guajá', *Encyclopédia de Povos Indígenas*, ISA Web site.

617: a lot.' Christina Lamb, 'Last of the invisible people', *Sunday Telegraph*, 16 Apr. 2000; Survival, *Disinherited*, 54–8. Earlier attempts to contact the Avá-Canoeiro had been made in August 1971 by the sertanista Israel Praxedes Batista near Cavalcanti (Tocantins) – Batista's brutal technique was to light a circle of fire to try to smoke the Indians out of hiding; by Apoena Meirelles and Zé Bel (both of whom later worked on the Uru-Eu-Wau-Wau contact) in 1973; then by Funai's Antenor Vaz when the Serra da Mesa dam was being built. For the early history of the Canoeiros see John Hemming, *Amazon Frontier* (London, 1995), 185–91.

23. Rio Negro, Rio Branco

619: saddened.' Doethiro Tukano (Álvaro Sampaio), *Folha de São Paulo*, 12 Apr. 1981. One denial came from the Vatican's *Bulletin of the Episcopal Conference of Latin America*, which pointed out that Doethiro was mission-educated and that he had publicly defended the Salesians in 1979. But it emerged later in 1981 that the Manaus police were hunting for Álvaro, who was

on the run because he had spoken the truth, *Folha de São Paulo*, 30 Sep. 1981.

619: rituals. The Salesian who admitted the punishments of Indians was Father Eduardo Lagório, O *Globo*, 17 Sep. 1981.

619: region.' Janet Chernela, 'Missionary activity and Indian labor in the Upper Rio Negro of Brazil, 1680–1980: a historical-ecological approach', in William Balée, ed., *Advances in Historical Ecology* (Columbia University Press, New York, 1998), 328, 329.

619: hope.' Bishop Miguel Alagna, ESP, 16 Nov. 1980. This newspaper also published an article by Pedro Zan full of praise of the Salesians, on 14 Dec. 1980.

620: wrong'. ESP, 16 Nov. 1980.

620: theology.' Richard Ostling, 'The Gospel and the gold rush', *Time*, 1 Jun. 1987.

620: silent.' Henrique Castro Tukano interview by Carlos Ricardo of CEDI, Pari Cachoeira, May 1987, *PIB 1987/88/89/90*, 116.

620: territory'. Gabriel dos Santos Gentil (a Tukano from Pari-Cachoeira), interviews in Brasília and Manaus, *A Crítica*, Manaus, 6 Jul. and 1 Oct. 1981; *PIB 1981*, 7. The four Indian areas proposed for 'delimitation' in 1979 (Funai Portarias 546, 547, 548/N) were, from north to south: Alto Içana Aiari, 896,000 ha; Içana/Xié, 480,000 ha; Iauareté, 990,000 ha; Pari-Cachoeira, 1,020,000 ha (in square miles: Alto Içana Aiari, 3,460; Içana/Xié, 1,850; Iauareté, 3,820; Pari-Cachoeira, 3,940).

621: traditions.' Gabriel Gentil, *A Crítica*, 9 Dec. 1983; *Jornal do Brasil*, 29 Dec. 1983.

622: Indians.' Gabriel dos Santos Gentil and Álvaro Fernandes Sampaio, 'Febre de ouro no Alto Rio Negro', *PIB/1984*, 68–9. The gold workings were: Tunuí, between the New Tribes' mission of that name on the Içana and the upper Xié; São Joaquim further up the Içana; Serra dos Porcos near Iauareté on the upper Uaupés; and Serra do Traíra near a stream of that name some twenty kilometres south-west of Iauareté.

After denouncing the Salesians at the Russell Tribunal in Rotterdam, Doethiro (Álvaro Sampaio) decided not to return to his Tukano people on the Uaupés, but lived in Manaus and São Paulo and visited other countries. Alcida Ramos said that 'he has had a very important role in the Brazilian Indian movement as a vehement spokesman for the defence of Indian rights against Funai, missionaries, and most whites. The aggressive tone of his discourse reveals much of his life history' as a rebel against Salesian rule and torn between returning to his people or fighting for their rights in the outside world. Ramos quoted a powerful speech he made to the Rio de Janeiro chapter of the Brazilian Bar Association, 18 November 1981, in which he described a bruising meeting with Funai's President, Colonel Nobre da Veiga. (Alcida Ramos, 'Indian voices: contact experi-

enced and expressed', in Jonathan D. Hill, ed., *Rethinking History and Myth* (Urbana, Ill., 1988), 217–19 and 224.)

622: favour.' Robin M. Wright, 'As guerras do ouro no Alto Rio Negro', *PIB-85/86*, 87. The texts of the agreements between Ucirt (the Union of Indians of Pari-Cachoeira) and Paranapanema were published in full by CEDI, *PIB 1987/88/89/90*, 120. Berta Ribeiro (widow of Darcy) described the Indians finding their own garimpos, *Os Índios das Águas Pretas* (São Paulo, 1995), 100–1.

622: practice'. Father Guerino Sartori, Director of Pari-Cachoeira Mission, letter to the President of Funai, Nov. 1985, *PIB-85/86*, 94.

623: wounded.' Ibid., 95.

623: expelled.' Ribeiro, *Os Índios das Águas Pretas*, 101.

624: independence.' Dominique Buchillet, 'Pari Cachoeira: o laboratório Tukano do projeto Calha Norte', *PIB 1987/88/89/90* (107–15), 107. There were articles about Elton Rohnelt and Gold Amazon Mineração da Amazônia Ltda. in *Veja*, 13 Feb. 1985 and *Porantim*, Oct. 1985. In 1990 Rohnelt's Gold Amazon was a major gold-buyer in Roraima and rented helicopters and planes to ferry garimpeiros to Paapiú in Yanomami territory. Amazingly, Rohnelt later obtained a job dealing with indigenous affairs for the Roraima state government.

625: development.' Buchillet, 'Pari Cachoeira', 110.

625: projects.' Álvaro Tukano, *A Crítica*, 8 Jul. 1987.

625: acculturation.' Buchillet, 'Pari Cachoeira', 115.

625: forests'. *Porantim*, Mar. 1990; *PIB 1987/88/89/90*, 127. The decrees were 99,094–99,104 of 9 Mar. 1990. They complemented decrees 98,437–9 of 23 Nov. 1989 that had ratified three AIs and a national forest at Pari Cachoeira.

626: consciousness.' Jorge Pozzobon, 'Índios por opção', *PIB 1991/1995*, 129. In the late 1970s the breakdown by rivers was: on the Uaupés, 2,633 in fifty-six settlements; on the Papuri, 1,359 in twenty-eight settlements (and there were also some Barasana, although the majority of their 6,098 people lived inside Colombia); on the Içana, at most 2,000 Aruak-speaking Hohodene and other tribes; plus 1,000 at Taracuá mission. Funai's census for 1987 gave 12,664 Indians in the entire region, and the Catholic Church now reckons 14,200, of whom 2,700 on the Içana are

Protestant. Ribeiro, Os *Índios das Águas Pretas*, 21; Conferência Nacional dos Bispos do Brasil, Os *Nossos Índios – situação religiosa e outros dados* (Rio de Janeiro, Aug. 1969); CEDI/Museu Nacional, *Terras Indígenas no Brasil* (São Paulo, 1987).

At the start of the 1990s, by the main tribal groups: 10,000 **Tukano** (of whom 6,330 in Colombia); 3,500 **Desana** (of whom 2,036 in Colombia); 1,800 **Tariana** (205 in Colombia); 1,100 **Tuyuka** (570 in Colombia); 1,600 **Wanana** (1,113 in Colombia); 350 **Bará** (296 in Colombia); 4,500 **Kubeo** (4,238 in Colombia); 1,300 **Pira-tapuya** (400 in Colombia); 120 **Miriti-tapuya**; 300 **Arapaso**; 450 **Karapana** (412 in Colombia); 570 **Makuna** (528 in Colombia); 1,000 **Barasana** (939 in Colombia); 17,000 **Baniwa** and **Kuripako** (of which 6,790 in Colombia and 3,236 in Venezuela); 4,000 **Baré** (1,210 in Venezuela); 900 **Werekena** (409 in Venezuela); and 2,000 **Makú** (786 in Colombia). Total in Brazil: 20,992. These figures come from indigenous censuses by the Federation of Indians of the Upper Rio Negro, 1992, and similar but more accurate censuses from Colombia (1988) and Venezuela (1992). Foirn, Aloísio Cabalzar ed., *Povos Indígenas do Alto e Médio Rio Negro* (São Paulo, 1998), 42–53. The Brazilian census published in 1992 gave 18,526 indigenous people in the Upper Rio Negro, whereas the NGO Foirn gave 16,112, with the largest peoples being Baniwa 3,174, Tukano 2,868, and Baré 2,170. (The discrepancy came from individuals failing to mark the 'ethnic' box on the census form.) *PIB 1991/1995*, 154.

The anthropological report of 1992 was done by Funai's Maria Auxiliadora Cruz de Sá Leão and Dominique Buchillet; the Work Group in 1994 was led by Funai's anthropologist Ana Gita de Oliveira, an expert on the Tariana (and widow of Peter Silverwood-Cope), and contained Jorge Pozzobon of the Museu Goeldi in Belém who worked with the Makú, and Márcio Meira, also from the Goeldi, who studied the Werekena. In these censuses the largest ethnic groups were: 'Baniwa', 3,174; Tukano, 2,868; Baré, 2,170; Tariana, 1,630; Desana, 1,458; Makú, 1,241; total 12,541. ISA in 1996 gave a total of 14,600 for the Alto Rio Negro; 2,860 for the two Médio Rio Negro reserves, Rio Tea and Rio Apaporís; and an estimate of 30,000 for the entire region including Indians living in the town of São Gabriel da Cachoeira. Most of these indigenous nations exist, usually in greater numbers, upriver in Colombia,

where some 27,500 Indians occupy 7,153,400 ha (27,610 square miles): *PIB 1991/1995*, 143, 154. The combined area of the indigenous territories of the Rio Negro at almost 11 million ha (42,500 square miles) is 3.6 times the size of Belgium.

626: incontestable.' Márcio Meira, 'Articulações políticas e identidade étnica no Alto Rio Negro', in Maria Angela D'Incao and Isolda Maciel da Silveira, eds., *A Amazônia e a Crise da Modernização* (Museu Paraense Emílio Goeldi, Belém, 1994) (335–42), 339–40.

627: language.' Márcio Meira, '"Finalmente eles entenderam que nós existimos!"', *PIB 1991/ 1995*, 123. The association of Indians of the Lower Rio Negro was known as ACIBRN.

627: creativity.' Bráz de Oliveira França, in ibid., 125. The proposed indigenous area of the Médio Rio Negro measures 1,827,900 ha (7,060 square miles) and is home to 2,826 Indians from fifteen tribes. The areas added by the 1994 census were: **Rio Apapóris**, of 113,500 ha (438 square miles), for 141 Yuhupde (Hup or Hupdu) Makú; and **Rio Tea**, of 414,300 ha (1,600 square miles), for 259 Nadeb Makú.

627: many of them.' Fátima Murad, *Movimento*, 16 Feb. 1976, trans. in SIR, **14**, Spring 1976, 27.

628: criteria'. Geraldo Andrello, 'Área Indígena Alto Rio Negro renasce das cinzas', *PIB 1991/1995*, 220; the area had previously been recommended when Possuelo was President of Funai, *Diário Oficial da União*, 2 June 1992.

628: people'. Ibid., 121.

629: access'. Beto Ricardo, 'Dos petroglifos aos marcos de bronze', *PIB 1996/2000*, 250. The President of Foirn was the dignified Pedro Garcia Tariano. Within this umbrella organization, there were in 2000 no less than forty-six local groupings of indigenous peoples in the Rio Negro region. The military continued to have a presence along this frontier, but within the indigenous area in a similar manner to Ibama's 'flonas' (national forests). A notable development was that most of the soldiers in these garrisons were now Indians, recruited locally but trained and equipped to full standards of the Brazilian armed forces.

631: churches. Alcida Rita Ramos and Marco Antonio Lazarin, 'Assembléia de Tuxáuas do Lavrado', *PIB/1984*, 78; Emanuele Amodio and Vicente Pira, 'Povos indígenas do Nordeste de Roraima', *Boletim* (Arquivo Indigenista, Diocese de Roraima), **11**, Feb. 1986, 17. Survival issued an urgent-action bulletin in April 1994 about the

Makuxis' blockade of the garimpeiros invading their rivers. Another problem for the Makuxi and Wapixana was drift by thousands of Indians into shanty towns around Boa Vista. Patricia Ferri, *Achados ou Perdidos? A imigração indígena em Boa Vista* (MLAL, Goiânia, 1990).

632: Serra do Sol]'. Euclides Pereira, 'Roraima: um Estado de violência institucionalizada', *PIB 1991/1995*, 166–7; also the article 'AI Raposa/ Serra do Sol: a longa espera dos Makuxi e Ingarikó', ibid., 161–5, and a list of newspaper reports of atrocities and oppression, ibid., 169–84. The previous edition, *PIB 1987/88/89/90*, had a similar nasty compendium in Nádia Farage, 'Terras indígenas no Lavrado: o impasse continua', 147–54, followed by four pages of news items. In 1995 Human Rights Watch/Americas issued a bulletin: *In Brazil: Violence against the Macuxi and Wapixana Indians in Raposa Serra do Sol and Northern Roraima from 1988 to 1994.*

632: 'Despatch 80' Despatch 80 of 20 Dec. 1996 of the Minister of Justice Nelson Jobim (the minister responsible for Funai) was criticized by Márcio Santilli, 'Facada na Raposa', *PIB 1996/ 2000*, 297–303; *New York Times*, 21 Jun. 1996; *Parabólicas*, Aug. 1996. Paulo Santilli published a survey showing that Despatch 80 would exclude various Makuxi villages from the demarcation of Raposa/Serra do Sol, and would remove roughly a fifth of their territory including important hunting and farming land.

633: great victory.' Letter by the Conselho Indigenista de Roraima, in Survival's special bulletin *Jubilation in Raposa-Serra do Sol*, London, Feb. 1999. The jubilation of the Roraima diocese, the NGOs Capoib in Brasília and Coiab in Manaus, and the Indians was reported in *Porantim*, **20:21**, Dec. 1998, 4. On the 'suicides' and threats, *O Globo*, 16 Feb. 1999; on the legal ruling of July 1999, *Porantim*, **21:217**, Aug. 1999, 13.

633: development.' Governor Neudo Campos, *Brasil Norte*, 12 Dec. 1998; *Folha de Boa Vista*, 12, 13 Dec. 1998; *PIB 1996/2000*, 313; *Veja*, 19 Apr. 2000. The military manoeuvre into Boca da Mata village and Surumu post, within T I São Marcos, was in November 2001. In that same month, other army commanders wanted to dismantle the checkpoint that the Waimiri-Atroari were allowed to operate on the BR-174 highway, and also to open the stretch that crossed indigenous land to nocturnal traffic. Roraima politicians also favoured this opening, which was opposed by the Indians because of its disturbance of forest fauna.

634: mad' Parabólicas, **57**, Apr. 2000.

24. Present and Future

635: speak'. Entry 'Isolated Indians', *Enciclopedia. Povos Indígenas no Brasil*, ISA Web site, 2002. In this analysis of uncontacted peoples, there are seven 'isolated in their own lands' (in the indigenous territories of Alto Tarauacá and Xinane in Acre; Hi Merrimã in Amazonas; Massaco, Igarapé Omeré, and Rio Muqui in Rondônia; and Rio Pardo where Amazonas and north-west Mato Grosso meet). The majority are 'in lands already protected'. Many of these are within the Javari Valley park. Others are isolated fragments of peoples already in contact: of the Uru-Eu-Wau-Wau in Rondônia; Asuriní of Koatinemo, Xikrin of Cateté, and even Menkragnoti Kayapó in Pará; people called Akurio (perhaps related to the Tiriyó) in the Tumucumaque park in northernmost Pará; the Piriutiti north-east of the Waimiri-Atroari in Amazonas/Roraima; and some Cinta Larga in Aripuanã with related Arara on the rio Branco north of them. In the forested hills between Acre and Peru are Kampa, Machineri, and others in the Envira, Rio Humaitá, and Mamoadate territories. And there may be uncontacted nomads such as Makú near the rio Tea tributary of the Negro, Awá-Guajá in Maranhão, and Avá-Canoeiro north of Brasília. Then there are fifteen isolated groups, possibly on land that has not been recognized as indigenous. These surprisingly include several Kayapó communities, people upriver of the Tapirapé, a breakaway Apiaká group, the Piripicura off the middle Roosevelt river, Wayampi offshoots (similar to the Zo'é found in the late 1980s), and several peoples in remote parts of Acre and western Amazonas. Funai in 1988 published a provisional list of 86 places where uncontacted tribes were thought to exist (*Levantamento Provisório sobre Grupos Indígenas Isolados em Território Brasileiro*, Brasília, Apr. 1988).

636: immense.' Carlos Frederico Marés, *Veja*, 3 May 2000, 46, 48.

637: times.' Mércio Gomes, 'O futuro dos

índios', *Carta* (Gabinete do Senador Darcy Ribeiro, Brasília), **4:9**, 1993, 73; *The Indians and Brazil* (Gainesville, Fla., 2000), 221–3.

637: community. The 2000 census revealed the 700,000 non-tribal Indians. This was a surprisingly high number – a few may have claimed this status in order to have access to the thirty-four new DSEIs, Special Indigenous Sanitary Districts. A university in Minas Gerais did genetic research on Brazilians' DNA and found that 45 million, roughly a quarter of the nation, possessed some Indian ancestry.

638: frontiers'. João Pacheco de Oliveira, *Indigenismo e Territorialização* (Rio de Janeiro, 1998), 29. Oliveira also wrote an introduction to the 1987 report, CEDI/Museu Nacional, *Terras Indígenas no Brasil*, 7–32. During its fifty-seven-year existence the SPI had demarcated fifty-four areas totalling less than 300,000 ha (1,160 square miles) – because they tended to be small reserves in the settled parts of Brazil. In the decade 1972–82, Funai demarcated sixty-six areas totalling almost 12 million ha (46,000 square miles), mostly under Funai's more liberal President General Ismarth de Araújo, rather than under the harsher Bandeira de Mello or Nobre da Veiga. In the 1987 survey, 107 areas had only been 'identified', which meant that Funai had merely noted their existence, with pre-liminary plans and perhaps 'interdiction' signalling that they should progress towards protected status; 171 reserves totalling over 32 million ha (123,500 square miles) were 'delimited', meaning that their boundaries had been defined in a decree or law; only 32 territories had reached the next stage of being 'ratified', with their boundaries demarcated by survey, a perimeter trail, and permanent markers; and only 41 had achieved the final status of 'regularization', with title deeds inscribed in property registers.

The situation at the start of the twenty-first century is from the 'Indigenous Lands in Brazil' and 'Demarcation' entries in ISA's *Enciclopedia. Povos Indígenas no Brasil* on its Web site, 2002. ISA also published a summary of the amount of indigenous territories demarcated (declared or homologated) in the three administrations during the 1990s. President Fernando Collor (1990–92) had 170 territories totalling some 52 million ha (200,000 square miles); Itamar Franco (1992–94, interim President after Collor's threatened impeachment for corruption), 55 territories, 12.7 million ha (49,000 square miles); Fernando Henrique Cardoso (1995–2002), 249 territories, 73.3

million ha (283,000 square miles). Collor's total included the Yanomami park; but the equally vast Javari Valley territory was not finally homologated until May 2001.

640: Brazil.' Time, 24 May 1999, 90. This special issue on 'Latin American Leaders for the New Millennium' listed Cândido Rondon and Chico Mendes among the past century's environmental leaders.

640: sector.' A *questão ambiental em terra indígena* (Leaflet by Funai's Codema [Coordenação do Meio Ambiental], Brasília, 1999).

641: forests. CEDI's survey of mining concessions was *Empresas de Mineração e Terras Indígenas na Amazônia Legal* (CEDI/CONAGE, São Paulo, 1988) and an update of this was Fany Ricardo, 'O subsolo das Terras Indígenas na Amazônia', *PIB 1996/2000*, 178–81.

641: lands. Márcio Santilli and others discussed the problem of overlapping between indigenous and environmental reserves, in ibid., 169–75.

642: dark glasses' Gomes, *The Indians and Brazil*, 239.

642: lands.' Ibid.

642: in this way. Euclides Macuxi Pereira's statement was in *Folha de São Paulo*, 13 Aug. 2000.

643: abroad. The $40 billion Avança Brasil programme plans the asphalting of the north–south Cuiabá–Santarém (BR-163), Humaitá–Manaus (BR-319, between the Madeira and Purus rivers), Manaus–Boa Vista (BR-174) north towards Venezuela and Guyana, and the Transamazonica (BR-230) for hundreds of kilometres between Marabá and its junction with the Cuiabá–Santarém at Rurópolis. Based on destruction of forests alongside earlier paved highways, this could cause the loss of an appalling 180,000 km² (70,000 square miles) of rainforests and expose others to gigantic fires in El Niño years. An environmental-impact assessment showed that the 'Hidrovia Araguaia–Tocantins' would involve considerable and lasting damage to the rivers being opened to traffic. Opponents of 'Advance Brazil' include the respected Ipam (Instituto de Pesquisa Ambiental da Amazônia), ISA, Smithsonian Tropical Research Institute, and the Woods Hole Research Center. The Ministers of Transport and of the Environment vehemently rejected these criticisms (*Folha de São Paulo*, 26 Mar. 2000; *PIB 1996/2000*, 225–7).

644: cultures.' Silvio Ferraz, 'Missionários sem cruz', *Veja*, 30 Jun. 1999, 140.

644: Indians.' Ibid.

644: beatings.' Silvio Ferraz, 'Os guardiães do verde', *Veja*, 30 Jun. 1999, 133–4.

646: do theirs.' *Parabólicas*, Jun. 1999.

646: capital.' Carlos Alberto (Beto) Ricardo, quoted in *Veja*, 12 Apr. 2000, 120. ISA (Instituto Socioambiental, the successor to CEDI) published the findings of its public-opinion survey as *O que os Brasileiros Pensam dos Índios?* (São Paulo, 2000); *PIB 1996/2000*, 57–61. The survey was conducted by the top polling service IBOPE in 2,000 interviews in Feb. 2000.

647: peoples' and *lands'*, statements by a powerful Coalition in Support of Amazonian Peoples and their Environment (which involved eighty US environmental and human-rights groups, including the National Wildlife Federation, Environmental Defense Fund, and the Sierra Club) and by Glenn Switkes of the International Rivers Network (IRN press release, 1 Feb. 1996); releases by Survival International, 8 and 17 Jan. 1997). Decree 1,775 covered the period since Decree 22 of 2 February 1991, which had required Funai to establish an expert Task Force, under an anthropologist, to evaluate every proposed reserve, after which the area to be demar-cated progressed to the Minister of Justice, homologation by the President of Brazil, and entry on the local authority's SPU property registry.

650: stars.' Davi Kopenawa, translated by Bruce Albert, 'Descobrindo os brancos', in Adauto Novaes, ed., *A Outra Margem do Ocidente, PIB 1996/2000* (18–23), 23; Bruce Albert, 'O ouro canibal e a queda do céu', in Bruce Albert and Alcida Rita Ramos, eds., *Pacificando o Branco* (São Paulo, 2002), 253–4.

650: government.' Betty Mindlin, 'O aprendiz de origens e novidades', *Estudos Avançados*, **8:20**, Jan.–Apr. 1994, 233. The Ministry of Education's national guidelines on Indian education were *Referencial Curricular Nacional para as Escolas Indígenas*, Nov. 1998. The University of Mato Grosso course was announced in *O Globo*, 13 Aug. 2000.

651: society.' Gomes, *The Indians and Brazil*, 242.

651: way of life.' Eduardo Viveiros de Castro, 'Os termos da outra história', *PIB 1996/2000*, 49–54, 52.

651: lovers.' Davi Kopenawa, in 'Descobrindo os brancos', 23.

Index

Illustrations are shown at the end of entries, as are grid references locating places and tribes on the maps at the beginning of this book. Locations of places not shown on a map are in brackets.

DATE DUE
